Octateuch:

The Original Orit

SCRIPTURAL RESEARCH INSTITUTE

Published by Digital Ink Productions, 2024

Copyright

Octateuch: The Original Orit

Second Edition. July 4, 2024

Copyright © 2024 Scriptural Research Institute.

ISBN: 978-1-998288-78-6

The Octateuch was translated into Greek at the Library of Alexandria between 250 and 225 BC.

This English translation was created by the Scriptural Research Institute in 2019 and 2024, primarily from the Codex Vaticanus and Codex Sinaiticus, although most other Septuagint codices, Dead Sea Scroll 4QpapLXXLev[b], and Papyrus Fouad 266 were also used for reference. Additionally, the Leningrad Codex, Aleppo Codex Peshitta, Targums, Dead Sea Scrolls, and Coptic and Armenian Bibles were used for comparative analysis.

The image used for the cover is an artistic reinterpretation of 'Moses and his Ethiopian wife Sephora' by Jacob Jordaens, painted circa 1650.

Table of Contents

TABLE OF CONTENTS

TABLE OF CONTENTS

TABLE OF CONTENTS

TABLE OF CONTENTS

TABLE OF CONTENTS

TABLE OF CONTENTS

TABLE OF CONTENTS

TABLE OF CONTENTS

TABLE OF CONTENTS

Forward

After the death of Alexander the Great in 323 BC, his generals ripped apart his empire, and by 305 BC General Ptolemy had gained control of the Eastern Mediterranean, including Egypt, Judea, Cyprus, Cyrene, and the coastal regions of modern Turkey, including Cilicia, Pamphylia, Lycia, and Caria. He established the dynasty of the Ptolemys that would rule Egypt for the next three centuries until Cleopatra VII Philopator committed suicide in 30 BC. The Ptolemys built one of the great wonders of the ancient world, the Library of Alexandria, which at its height was said to house over 400,000 scrolls. The original collection that was amassed in the first century of the library, was largely Greek works, and translations of Egyptian works, however in the mid-3rd century BC, King Ptolemy II Philadelphus ordered a translation of the ancient Israelite scriptures for the library.

A number of Judahite and Samaritan scholars were assembled, numbering either 70 or 72 depending on the version of the story, and representing every Israelite sect. They created a translation of the ancient Israelite scriptures that was later known as the Septuagint. The original version, published circa 250 BC, only included the Torah, or in Greek terms, the Pentateuch, or five books traditionally credited to Moses, circa 1500 BC: Cosmic Genesis, Exodus, Leviticus, Numbers, and Deuteronomy. According to Jewish tradition, the original Torah was lost when the Babylonians destroyed the Temple of Solomon and was then rewritten by Ezra from memory during the Second Temple period. The life of Ezra is estimated to have been circa 350 BC, which is around the time that scholars generally believe the current form of the Torah was written.

The first of these five books was known as Cosmic Genesis (Γενεσισ Κοσμου) in Greek, however, known as Bereshít (בראשית) in Hebrew, which translates as approximately 'In the beginning' the first few words of the book. The first edition was followed by the second, around 225 BC which added the books of Joshua, Judges, and Ruth, which was later known as the Octateuch. This version of the Septuagint was later carried south into the Kingdom of Kush by the Israelites fleeing Egypt in 200 BC when Judea was in revolt and the Ptolemys' attempted to exterminate the Israelites in Egypt. The Octateuch later became the Torah of the Beta Israel community in Sudan and Ethiopia known as the Orit.

It is generally accepted that there were several versions written in Canaanite or Aramaic before the translation of the Septuagint. Fragments of the books comprising the Orit have been found in four languages among the dead sea scrolls, generally dated to between 200 BC and 600 AD. During this time, the land of Judea passed from the rule of the Ptolemys in Egypt to the rule of the Seleucids in Syria around 200 BC. The Seleucids attempted to Hellenize the Judeans and effectively banned traditional Judaism. This Hellenizing activity led to the Maccabean Revolt in 165 BC, which itself created the independent Hasmonean Kingdom of Judea. This kingdom was violently xenophobic and led by a priestly monarchy that combined both the powers of the state and the church.

The Hasmonean dynasty attempted to conquer all of the territory that had previously been part of the Persian Province of Judea, and either evicted or exterminated the people that were living there, depending on their ethnicity. When the Edomites were conquered they were allowed to mass-convert to Judaism as they were considered the descendants of Esau, however, most other ethnic groups were not welcome. When the army of Hasmonean King John Hyrcanus annexed Samaria in 113 BC, he slaughtered the Samaritan priests and more than half the Samaritan population and enslaved the rest. His army also destroyed the Samaritan Temple on Mount Gerizim and burned all copies of their holy books. The Samaritans continued to be slaves under the Hasmoneans until the Roman General Pompey's armies freed them in 69 BC, and restored the independent state of Samaria, along with several other states that fell under Rome's protection from that time forward.

While the Hasmoneans ruled Judea, they converted the national script from the old Phoenician script, today called Paleo-Hebrew, to the Assyrian 'block script,' today called Hebrew. As a result, almost all surviving texts found from the Hasmonean era and later are written in the Assyrian script, and it is unclear how much the Hasmoneans redacted the scriptures when they transcribed them. The scriptures the Hasmoneans left the world were later used as the basis of the Masoretic Texts, which are used today by Rabbinical Jews, as well as by Catholic and Protestant Christians. The Samaritan Torah is believed to have been restored after General Pompey freed the Samaritans, by redacting a copy of the Hasmonean Torah, which is why there are fewer differences between the Samaritan and Jewish Torahs than the either of them and the Septuagint. A copy of the original Samaritan Torah was translated at the Library of Alexandria as well, referred to as the Samareitikon (Σαμαρειτικον), however, it has not survived to the present. Based on the writings of Origen of Alexandria in the early 3rd century, and other early Christians, the Samareitikon was more similar to the Septuagint's Pentateuch than it was to either the Samaritan or Jewish Torahs in use at the time.

The Samaritans also use a Book of Joshua ben Nun, which includes the contents of both the Jewish books of Joshua and Judges, as well as subsequent Samaritan history up until their virtual extermination by the Byzantine Empire. This earliest version of the Samaritan Joshua is likewise accepted by most historians as being a redaction of the Hasmoneans books of Joshua and Judges that was recombined and redacted in an attempt to restore what the Hasmoneans had destroyed decades earlier.

The differences between the Masoretic and the Octateuch's versions of the Torah are both minor and startling, as the two sets of scriptures contain the same stories, but different Gods. The Masoretic text are mostly about the actions of Yahweh, Yahweh Elohim, Yahweh Sabaoth, or Elohim, while the Octateuch contains the Greek translations of various gods' names that appear to have been redacted by the Hasmoneans. The God of the Torah in the Octateuch is called Lord the god (Κύριοσ ὁ θεὸσ) or simplified to Lord (Κύριοσ), or God (Θεὸσ). These terms are mirrored in the Masoretic text by Yehovah elohim (יְהֹוָה אלהים), Yehovah (יְהֹוָה), and elohim (אלהים), respectively.

One explanation for the difference between the texts is the Christian redaction of the 3rd century AD, when the name Iaô (Ιαω) was removed from the Septuagint, replaced by Lord (Κύριοσ). Fragments of older Septuagint manuscripts still exist that contain the name Yhủh, transliterated into Greek from the Aramaic form Yhủ (𐤉𐤄𐤅^) as Iaô (Ιαω), however, none of the fragments of the Book of Genesis, Exodus, Numbers, or Deuteronomy include the name. The oldest fragments of the Septuagint's Leviticus, from the 1st century BC, known as 4QpapLXXLev^b include the name transliterated into Greek as Iaw (Ιαω), partially surviving in chapter 3 and surviving complete in chapter 4. Perhaps more tellingly though, is the lack of any reference to Lord the god (Κύριοσ ὁ θεὸσ) in Leviticus. If the Greeks translated the books of Genesis, Exodus, Numbers, and Deuteronomy correctly, then the god of four of the Torah's books in the Septuagint was El, whose main title in the Canaanite texts was Adon Elohim (𐤀𐤃𐤍 𐤀𐤋𐤄𐤉𐤌), which translates as 'Father of the gods.'

The Aramaic sections of Masoretic Daniel that were not translated into Hebrew maintain the term adonai ha'elohim (אֲדֹנָי הָאֱלֹהִים), meaning the 'Lord the gods' where the Septuagint has 'Lord the god' (Κυριον τον θεον), however, the Hebrew sections have Yahweh elohim (יְהוָה אֱלֹהִים) where the Septuagint has 'Lord the god,' suggesting the Greek more accurately reflects the Aramaic source texts than the Hebrew translation. According to tractate Sanhedrin (103b) in the Talmud, King Manasseh was blamed for removing the name, however, as his grandson Josiah 'restored' the Torah circa 625 BC, one would expect that he would have restored the name as well, if it had have been in Exodus to begin with. Furthermore, the early Torah appears to have already been translated into Aramaic during the era of Manasseh's father king Hezekiah, suggesting that he removed the name during his religious reforms.

The section of text in Cosmic Genesis dealing with the genealogy of nations appears to have been written in Aramaic, and includes a scribal note that identifies Kalhu as the capital of Assyria, which dates the origin of both versions to sometime before 706 BC. Additionally, the presence of the Ashkenaz in the genealogy of nations places the origin of that section of text to sometime after 715 BC, when the Ashkenaz were first documented by the Assyrians, meaning that the Aramaic translation appears to have been made during the rule of King Hezekiah of Judah.

King Hezekiah is recorded in 4th Kingdoms (Masoretic Kings) as initiating several reforms to the religion of Judah, including destroying the bamahs, where Moses instructed the Israelites to worship, as well as destroying the statue of the serpent that Moses had made, and which Solomon had erected in the temple in Jerusalem, suggesting that it was Hezekiah who removed the name from the text. If so, the name removed would not have been Yhŭ, the god that Hezekiah worshiped, but Shaddai, the god of Masoretic Bereshít, Exodus, and Numbers.

The original god of the Temple of Solomon was Ba'al Shalim (𐤁𐤏𐤋 𐤔𐤋𐤌), the god that Jerusalem and King Solomon were named after. The god Shalim was also recorded in the Ugaritic texts as Šlm (𐎌𐎍𐎎), the god of the setting sun. Later in the early Iron Age, Shalim (𐤔𐤋𐤌) was the Canaanite god of the evening who was married to the virgin goddess Asherah and father of the lunar deity Adoni. The earliest surviving reference to Jerusalem is Úru Šalim[ki] (𒌷𒊮𒆠) in Old Akkadian, meaning 'light of Shalim land' or 'setting sun land,' depending on how the term is translated. The spelling of Jerusalem shifted from 'evening land' to 'city of peace,' over time.

FORWARD

During the Akkadian Empire, the region around Jerusalem was in the borderlands of the Akkadian and Egyptian civilizations, suggesting the Akkadians viewed it as the most western land before the end of their empire. During the subsequent Neo-Sumerian era the name was ^{uru}Úrušalim (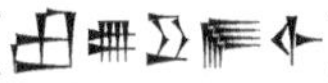), meaning 'city light of Shalim,' indicating that there was a city there. The Egyptian execration texts from the era also spelled the name of the city as Ůrůšalîm () in the Hieratic script, confirming that it was a commonly known name by the Middle Kingdom. In the subsequent Old Babylonian language, the name was ^{uru}Úrušalim^{ki} (), meaning ^{city}light of Shalim^{land}, or ^{city}-sunset^{land}. By the Iron Age, the city was known as ^{uru}Ursaliimma (), meaning the ^{light}city-of-peace in Neo-Assyrian, which continues to be the meaning.

According to the author of 1st Ezra, after he killed King Josiah in 609 BC, Pharaoh Necho II was recorded as restoring the worship of the Lord in Jerusalem. As Necho II is well documented in the ruins of Egypt as a worshiper of the Nubian sun god Amanai (), the South Egyptian sun god Amen (), and North Egyptian sun god Atum (), the Lord whose worship he restored could only be Shalim.

Like Atum, Amen, and Amanai, the Ba'al worshiped at Solomon's Temple was married to a wife referred to as the 'hand of god,' who was worshiped by planting sacred trees. In Egypt and Nubia, the sun god and his wife were also viewed as the parents of the moon god, the Nubian Khasa (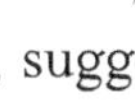), South Egyptian Khonsu (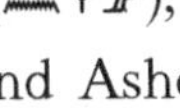), and North Egyptian Îôḥů (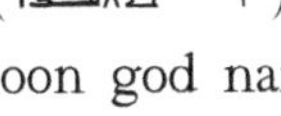), suggesting that the son of Ba'al and Asherah in Jerusalem was a moon god named Yhů, however, this has yet to be proven conclusively. The only archaeologically attested title for the son of Ba'al and Asherah in Jerusalem was Adonay, however, the pottery shards found at Kuntillet Ajrud do confirm that Yhůh was considered the son of Asherah circa 800 BC.

The pottery shards include referenced to Yhůh being worshiped in Samaria and Edom, and depict Yhůh was a calf god, and Asherah as a heifer. This suggests that the statues of heifers worshiped in Samaria at the time, were depictions of Asherah. The kingdom of Edom, and the Levite city of Libnah, in the borderlands of Judah, Edom, and Egypt, had both declared independence from Judah in the 840s BC over a religious dispute, and claimed that the wrong god was being worshiped in Solomon's Temple. Libnah was the city were the later Yahwist priesthood emerged from in the 700s BC, supporting the name of Adony being Yahweh.

Meanwhile, in Edom, the name of their god transitioned from Yhůh to Qůś (𐤒𐤅𐤔) over the following two centuries. Since Yhůh and Qůś are described identically in the literature from the era, most historians accept that the Edomites changed the name of Yhůh to Qůś in the centuries after becoming independent. As the Nubians were dominating Egypt during this era, and had close trade relations with the Edomites, the source of the name Qůś, was likely the Nubian name Khasa, confirming that Yhůh was considered the Judahite moon before the breakup of the united kingdom of Judah and Edom.

The conflict between the worshipers of the sun and moon is well documented during the Neo-Babylonian era, when their worshipers debated which was the supreme god. During the earlier Neo-Assyrian era, the supreme god of Assyria was Anshar (𒀭𒊹) meaning the 'whole sky,' whose Aramaic and Canaanite name appears to have been Šmyn (𐡔𐡌𐡉𐡍) and Šmm (𐤔𐤌𐤌), one of the gods whose worship was banned by King Josiah in Judah, along with the Sun and the Moon. Josiah's banning of the worship of both the sun and moon, along with the 'army/ stars of Shamayim,' indicates that Yhůh was not viewed as being the moon in Judah under Josiah, but another god, apparently outside of the traditional Ba'al-Asherah-Adony trinity of the temple in Jerusalem.

It is unclear how common the name Iaw (Yhů) was in the original Greek translation of Leviticus, however, as the book appears to have been written during the lifetime of King Josiah, whose god was Yhů (Iaw), Iaw would have probably been mentioned exclusively, and therefore the name is copied over from the Masoretic version of Leviticus. The Dead Sea Scrolls support the accuracy of Hebrew translation of Leviticus found in the Masoretic text, as the name Yhůh (𐤉𐤄𐤅𐤄) shows up in the scroll 4QLev[g] and 11QLev[b] where Masoretic Leviticus have Yhůh (יהוה). The Book of Leviticus is also the only book in the Torah that is geographically consistent, referring only to Mount Sinai, and never substituting Horeb, Seir, or Hor, as Exodus, Numbers, Deuteronomy, and the Book of Judges do. This implies that it was not harmonized from a group of older texts like Numbers, but written more or less as it is. There are still archaic elements within it, such as the repeated references to the horns of the altar, however, as archaeology has discovered that Josiah's god Iaw was a calf-god, this does make sense in the context of the era.

The name Yhůh (𐤉𐤄𐤅𐤄 / יהוה) is found in many of the fragments of Exodus, Leviticus, Numbers, and Deuteronomy found among the Dead Sea Scrolls, however, most date to the Hasmonean dynasty or later, and those that are pre-Hasomonean are generally dated to the Maccabean Revolt, between 165 and 140 BC, which created the Hasmonean Dynasty. While the first four books of the Torah were likely organized into their current form during the reforms of King Josiah, circa 625 BC, the fifth book, Deuteronomy, appears to have been a Samaritan book, originally written as an addition to Moses laws in Exodus, likely written sometime before Samaria was conquered by the Assyrians, and later added to the four books used in Judea by the Samaritan priesthood that established itself under Babylonian rule.

The Torah appears to have been redacted by the Hasmonean Dynasty circa 140 BC, in an attempt to forge closer ties with Rome, which was still a distant power across the Mediterranean, outside of Greek domination. As the Maccabean Revolt raged against Greek rule in Judea, between 165 and 140 BC, the Romans were fighting the final, and bloodiest of their wars against the Carthaginians, the ancient Canaanite colony based in modern Tunisia. The Carthaginians were once the great power of the Western Mediterranean, dominating northwest Africa, southern and western Iberia, Sicily, Sardinia, and Corsica.

The Romans had been at almost constant war against Carthage for over a century, beginning with the first Punic war in 264 BC, and in 146 BC finally defeated them, and effectively exterminated the race. Roman records report that they forced the surviving Carthaginian warriors to fight to the death in arenas, while the civilians were sold as slaves to anyone that would buy them. The population of northwest Africa became a slave-race for centuries and was not freed until the rise of Christianity in the 4th century. In 139 BC, seven years after the end of the final Punic war, and the year after the Hasmonean dynasty was established in Judea, the Romans evicted all Jews from the republic because the Jews were attempting to promote the idea that the Roman national god Jupiter (Iovis) was their national god Yahweh Tzevaot (Iaw Sabaoth). This was recorded by Valerius Maximus:

> "Gnaeus Cornelius Hispalus, praetor peregrinus in the year of the consulate of Marcus Popilius Laenas and Lucius Calpurnius, ordered the astrologers by an edict to leave Rome and Italy within ten days, since by a fallacious interpretation of the stars they perturbed fickle and silly minds, thereby making profit out of their lies. The same praetor compelled the Jews, who attempted to infect the Roman custom

with the cult of Jupiter Sabazius, to return to their home."

This Kingdom had a tenuous alliance with the Roman Republic until General Pompey conquered Syria into the Roman Republic in 69 BC. Pompey's goal was to liberate Greek-speaking communities in the Middle East that had fallen under the rule of non-Greeks when the Seleucids Syrian Empire had collapsed, and he carved up Judea, and Edom to the east, placing Greek-speaking cities under the protection of the Roman province of Syria. He also liberated several smaller communities that had been occupied by Judea, granting them self-government, including Ashdod, Yavne, Jaffa, Dora, Marissa, and Samaria.

While the Hasmoneans promoted their god Iaw, much as the Kingdom of Judah did under King Josiah 500 years earlier, the four books of the Torah appear to have long predated Josiah's time. The Greek terms in Cosmic Genesis, Exodus, Numbers, and Deuteronomy are translations of known Canaanite gods, most especially, El, the Canaanite father-god. El translates in Canaanite, Aramaic, and Hebrew as 'God,' and is the primary god worshiped in ancient Canaan in the era Abraham was reported to have passed through the area. El was also the patron god of the Temple of El, built by Jacob near the modern city of Nablus in the Palestinian West Bank, which featured in many of the early Hebrew scriptures before Samaria was conquered by the Assyrian Empire. The word el (אל), meaning 'god,' is used throughout the Masoretic Text, but generally only in relation to other gods, or as a part of a name, such as Israel, or Beth-El, proving El was of primary importance throughout the early era of the Israelite religion, before they adopted Iaw.

There are several specific terms found in both the Masoretic and Septuagint versions of Cosmic Genesis / Bereshít that point specifically to the Canaanite god El being the god of the bronze age Akkadian Cuneiform and early iron age Canaanite versions of Genesis, including the epitaph Olam, meaning 'eternal,' which is used in chapter 21. Olam was an epitaph commonly used for El in Canaan since long before the time of Abraham. Another epitaph used for El in ancient Canaanite material was Elyon, which is used in Genesis chapter 14, which the Greeks translated as God the Highest (Θεω τω υψιστω). Outside of Israelite scriptures, Elyon shows up in the Sefire I Treaty as ål ůålyn (𐤀𐤋 𐤅𐤏𐤋𐤉𐤍), meaning 'God and Highest.' The Sefire Steles are a series of treaties between the Assyrians and the city of Arpad, which date to the 8th century BC. The term Highest God is also found in the religions of neighboring nations, such as the

Greek titan Zagreus, who was described as being the 'highest god' in the epic Alcmeonis, in the 6th century BC.

The terms El Elyovn (אֵל עֶלְיוֹן) found in Bereshít, was probably also the ultimate source of the perplexing word ålhym (אלהים), more commonly rendered in English as Elohim from the accented Hebrew elohim (אֱלֹהִים). Ålhym (𐤀𐤋𐤄𐤉𐤌) is the Aramaic word for 'gods,' and was occasionally translated that way in the Septuagint, such as when referring to the elohim of Egypt. The Hebrew word ålhym (אלהים) translates properly as 'goddesses,' however, it also commonly accepted as a gender neutral term meaning 'deities' due to it's use as the word for 'gods' in the Masoretic text.

The problem with the word elohim is that while it does not mean 'God' in a phonetic sense, it is generally translated that way in the Septuagint, and accepted as meaning 'God' by Jews and Christians. In many sentences where the word is used it is clear from the context that a singular deity is being referenced, meaning that the Hebrew translators saw the Aramaic word as a proper name and simply transliterated it into Hebrew.

The term ålhym (𐤀𐤋𐤄𐤉𐤌), and ålhym (𐤀𐤋𐤄𐤉𐤌), are also direct transcriptions of the Neo-Assyrian cuneiform word elium (𒀭𒇻𒌝), which by the Iron Age meant 'god,' indicating that text had previously been written in cuneiform, and was translated into Aramaic or Phoenician during the iron age. During the bronze age, the word was pronounced as alium (𒀭𒇻𒌝), and referred to a specific god, [deity]An (𒀭) the highest god, and father of the other gods. His Akkadian name was derived from the word elûm (𒂊𒈝), meaning 'higher,' as the term was intended to convey the meaning of 'highest.' He was believed to live in the polar region of the sky, where the modern constellation of Draco is located, making him the highest in the sky, around which all the gods (stars) circled.

During the Old Babylonian and Old Assyrian eras, the gods Marduk and Ashur, the national gods of Babylon and Assyria, replaced the Akkadian Alium as the primary god of the Mesopotamian pantheons, and by the iron age, the word elium had came to mean 'god,' explaining why the Aramaic term ålhym (𐤀𐤋𐤄𐤉𐤌) would have been interpreted as 'god,' by the Greeks. This means that the origin of the first chapters of Cosmic Genesis would have to have been in the Sumerian or Akkadian era, before the emergence of the Old Babylonian empire, and that the form of Cuneiform it was written in before being translated into Aramaic and Canaanite was Old Akkadian.

Nevertheless, Bereshít includes another god known as El Šdy (אל שדי), who is identified as the god of Abraham, Isaac, and Jacob. The term El Šdy was only used 48 times in the Masoretic Text, including 31 times in the book of Job, 6 times in Bereshít, and once in Exodus when Moses' god identified himself as the god of Jacob, who then told Moses his name was Ān (Ων) in the Septuagint's version of the verse. Both the Masoretic and Septuagint's versions of Cosmic Genesis and Masoretic Exodus appear to have been redacted in regards to the identity of El Šdy, as there is no reference to El Šdy in Cosmic Genesis, and there is no reference to Ān in Masoretic Exodus.

Based on the number of Akkadian and Middle Egyptian loanwords in Masoretic Job, it appears the book originated in central or northern Canaan using the Akkadian Cuneiform script before being transliterated into Canaanite using the hieratic script of Egypt during the late Middle Kingdom era. It subsequently appears to have been transcribed back into Akkadian Cuneiform during the early New Kingdom era, before being transcribed into the Phoenician Canaanite script during the early iron age. These transcriptions appear to have generated a number of linguistically unique terms that were subsequently used in southern Canaan, including the relatively obscure ål Šdy.

The Septuagint and Masoretic translations often differ in regards to the name or title Šdy, suggesting that the Aramaic and Canaanite (Judahite or Samaritan) source texts they worked from differed in regards to this word. The term was omitted throughout Cosmic Genesis, suggesting that when the word was first encountered the Greeks did not know how to interpret it, as Cosmic Genesis / Bereshít is the first book of the Torah, the first collection of Israelite texts probably translated at the Library of Alexandria.

It is equally possible that it was the earlier Aramaic translator who had omitted it, however, it was almost certainly in the Canaanite version the translator worked from, as it is used consistently in Masoretic Genesis, and is mentioned again when Moses god's name Ān is introduced in the Septuagint's Exodus.

The cause of the confusion over the term šdy, is likely due to the difference between the meaning of the word in Canaanite versus Aramaic. In Akkadian cuneiform, which was adopted as the written script by many cultures, the term was ^{deity}šēdu (✳⊞), however, it referred to a 'protective spirit' or 'lesser god.' In the later Aramaic language, the word became šydå (𐤍𐤉𐤔𐤏), meaning 'demon' in the classical sense, as a type of muse or nymph. Whereas in Canaanite, šdy (𐤆𐤀𐤅) took on different meaning, generally interpreted as 'powerful' by the Early Classical Era, which is likely where the Greeks ultimately derived the term 'omnipotent' (παντοκράτοροσ), which was used later in the Septuagint where the Masoretic Text generally uses the term šdy.

This alternate interpretation of the šdy (𐤆𐤀𐤅) in Canaanite is likely due to the Egyptian New Kingdom era rule over Canaan, when Shed (𓏏𓂝𓈙𓏏, transliteration: šd), was worshiped in the region. Shed, who was often referred to as 'the savior,' was virtually identical to the earlier Canaanite god Resheph who was largely suppressed after the fall of the Hyksos dynasty.

In the Masoretic Book of Job, Eliphaz referred to humanity as the 'sons of Resheph' (בני-רשף) instead of the 'sons of Adam,' and then uses šdy as the name of a god. This god šdy was explicitly listed alongside the god El in Masoretic Job, whereas in the Septuagint's Job they are not explicitly listed as two separate gods. The Greek translation of Šdy (שדי) in Job is consistent with most of the Septuagint, using a term that translates as 'omnipotent' (παντοκράτοροσ), however, the name El (אל) is generally translated as a word meaning 'strong' (ἰσχυρὸσ). It is likely because the Masoretic Text lists them side by side, as 'god El and god Šdy' (אל-אל ואל-שדי), which the Greek translators did not do, instead routinely dropping the second reference to a god when they were listed together.

The terms 'god Šdy' (אל-שדי) and 'god El' (אל-אל) are repeatedly found in the Masoretic version of Job, and are themselves direct translations of the same terms in Akkadian Cuneiform: ^{deity}šēdu (✳⊞) and ^{deity}An (✳✳). Unfortunately, the Akkadian meaning of the word šēdu was 'demonic,' which is likely the cause of it's redaction. Based on the linguistics of Masoretic Job, the text book existed in a hieratic Canaanite form during the Hyksos Dynasty, and therefore the name Resheph is not out of place, as Resheph was one of the main gods of the Hyksos rulers.

During subsequent the New Kingdom era, Resheph worship was suppressed due to his associated with the earlier Hyksos dynasty. During the early New Kingdom era, holy texts about Resheph would have been updated to Shed (𓏏𓂝𓈙𓏏), which would have been transliterated into Canaanite using the Akkadian Cuneiform script in the late New Kingdom era as ^{deity}šēdu (✳⊞), before being translated into Canaanite using the Phoenician script in the early iron age as šdy (ZΔW), resulting in the confusing 'demonic' (NↃᴧᴜ) god in Aramaic.

In the former Amorite lands of northern Canaan, where Aramaic later became dominant, the Hurrians living under the rule of the Mitanni Empire called him Ablu (⊨◁⊞), generally accepted as a shortened version of aplu ^iluEllil (⊨◁⊞ ✳⊩▦), an epithet of Nergal, the son of the Old Babylonian god Ellil. Like Resheph and Nergal, Ablu was a god of both plague and healing. He was also imported to the Neshite (Hittite) and Trojan civilizations, as the god Apaliunas (⫴⊨◻⊨≪⊨◁⊣◁▬) was mentioned in a peace treaty between the civilizations in 1280 BC. Homer reported in the Illiad that Apollôn (Απολλων) was the god that built the wall of Troy, which confirms that the Greeks did view Apaliunas as Apollo.

In the Illiad, a priest of Apollo called Chryses, referred to Apollo as the 'Lord of Mice' as he was believed to protect from plagues of mice. This suggests that the Pelesets viewed Shaddai as a version of Apaliunas when they captured the box of the covenant in 1st Kingdoms (Masoretic Samuel), as they returned it with golden statues of mice after their cities were plagued by swarms of mice.

While all references to Šdy were striped from Cosmic Genesis at some point, either when the Greeks translated the text from Aramaic, or earlier when the Aramaic translation was made, the term must have originally been in the text, essentially where it is in Bereshít or the later references to it in Exodus and Deuteronomy make no sense, and therefore it is restored in this translation. Moreover, as the term has to either be interpreted as 'demonic god,' from a the Akkadian ^deityšēdu (✳⊟), or 'Resheph,' via the Egyptian Shed (⌐⊏◻⫰), and Resheph is consistent with the rest of the books of the Septuagint, as well as the archaeological record, the name Resheph is used.

The lack of any early mention of Iaw in Genesis, also explains the lack of any names ending in -iah before Beriah, who was born in Egypt. Joseph's marriage to the daughter of the High Priest of Ỉůnů (Greek: Heliopolis, Hebrew: Åůn) after interpreting the Pharaoh's dreams implies that he became the High Priest of Ỉôhů, the lunar god of Heliopolis. The word Ỉôh (⌒) was the Egyptian word for the moon, however, when treated as a god, it was modified to Ỉôhů (⎩⌐⊠⌐⬦), resulting in the two pronunciations of the name Yh (𝉍^) and Yhů (𝉍^) found in Aramaic. The earliest depictions of Yhůh, on pottery shards found at Kuntillet Ajrud, dating to circa 800 BC, depict Yhůh as the calf of Asherah, who was herself the personification of the starry-sky, meaning Yhửh was still considered to be the moon at the time.

The name Ôn is also found in the Septuagint's Book of Hosea, which is mirrored in the Aleppo Codex by the name Åửn (אונ), meaning that this was the god of the Temple of Åửn, near the Temple of El in the region where Shiloh would later be built. In the Book of Micah, the Temple of El is referred to as Jacob's Temple of El, which confirms that the Israelites in the 8th century BC considered the Temple of El at Shiloh to be the Temple of El that Jacob built in Genesis chapter 35. Given that the region was already called the Temple of El when Jacob's grandfather Abraham passed through the area, and he stopped to build an altar to his god, it is plausible that the Temple of Åửn was either already there, or built around the altar he erected, meaning that Åửn would have been Ān (✳), as Abraham's family had come from the lands of Sumeria (southern Iraq) during the era of the Old Babylonian Empire. Ān (✳) was the Mesopotamian version of El (God), the sky-father who created everything. This would explain why the Temple of El was sometimes in the valley at Shiloh, and sometimes at the top of the mountain, as Abraham would have built his altar at the top of a mountain, as described when he attempted to sacrifice Isaac.

Since the 1800s, the majority of Biblical scholars have interpreted the books of Leviticus and Numbers as a later addition to the original laws of Moses found in Exodus, with Deuteronomy being a later addition during the Babylonian era. Cosmic Genesis is either considered to be part of Moses' original work, or a later addition in the Persian era, depending on the scholar. Leviticus and Numbers contain several amendments to Moses' laws in Exodus, as well as establishing the land rights of the various tribes of Israel within historic Canaan, including the assignment of several cities and their environs to the Levitical Priesthood. The most obvious amendment to Moses' laws, is replacing the sacrifice of the firstborn, with the establishment of the Levitical Priesthood. Exodus 13 includes a require-ment that the firstborn Israelites must be slaughtered as a sacrifice to the Lord, however, allowed an animal to be substituted. This law would not have been difficult for a group of nomadic shepherds to follow but would have become progressively more difficult as the Israelites became more urbanized in Canaan.

This seems to have resulted in an increase of child sacrifice which the prophet Jeremiah spoke out against during his lifetime, estimated at between 650 BC and 570 BC. The practice was officially banned by King Josiah around 630 BC when the Levites 'found' the 'original' Torah of Moses during the refurbishing of Solomon's Temple. As this could not have been Moses' original Torah, as Moses had nothing to do with the Temple of Solomon, it was likely when Leviticus and Numbers were added to the Torah. This is likely when the 'authorized version' of Genesis, Exodus, and Numbers were cobbled together from the conflicting Elohist and Yahwist sources, although some groups may have continued to use the older versions of these books, as the Nazarenes had their own Torah in the 1st century BC, which appears to have been the old Elohist Torah.

The substitution of the Levitical Priesthood for the firstborn Israelites was established in Numbers chapter 3. This 'authorized' Torah also removed the Korahites from the Temple of Solomon, adding the Revolt of Korah to the Torah, set long before the Israelites entered Canaan. The Sons of Korah, or Korahites, were a rival priesthood to the Levites that administered the Temple of Solomon from the time of Solomon until Josiah. They are believed to have originally been the priesthood of El Elyon at the Jebusite Temple before David conquered them. Solomon, as David's youngest son, was an unlikely heir, and not the original heir apparent, as his elder brother Adonijah attempted to succeed David by marrying Abishag the Shunamite, David's youngest wife, who was twelve years old at the time. However, Solomon's Jebusite mother Bathsheba and the prophet Nathan conspired to place the fifteen-year-old Solomon on the throne, and then purged the government of non-Jebusites, who appear to have all supported Adonijah. The Sons of Korah were the authors of some of the Psalms, and are documented as existing in Judea as late as the Persian era, although seem to have disappeared by the early Greek era. Some have theorized they may have formed the priest-hood of the Essenes (Nazarenes) in the late-Persian era, as the Essenes had another Torah, and used different holy books from the other Jews, such as the books of Enoch and Jubilees.

Human sacrifice to the Lord is openly discussed in the book of Numbers, indicating that the core texts must have been much older than the time of Josiah. The most obvious statement that the Israelites were sacrificing humans is in chapter 31, immediately after the Israelites slaughtered the Midianites, animals were sacrificed to the Lord, and then humans:

"Of the people, 16,000, and those sacrificed of them to the Lord were 32."

This verse about human sacrifice to the Lord is also found in the Masoretic Text (Leningrad Codex), but not always translated by modern translators, who often skip it entirely, such as the Tanakh (JPS 1985), which simply has:

"and 16,000 human beings."

The Greek terms of God in Deuteronomy returned to the translations of known Canaanite gods, most especially, El, the Canaanite creator-god. The word âl (אל), meaning 'god,' is used throughout the Octateuch, but generally in relation to other gods, or as a part of a name, such as Israel, or Beth-El, proving El was of primary importance throughout the early era of the Israelite religion, before they adopted Iaw. There are a few exceptions in Numbers and Deuteronomy, where the word God (Θεοῦ) in the Octateuch is mirrored by Âl (אֵל) in the Masoretic Text, and in all cases appear to be a proper name. These examples are in Numbers chapter 12 and 16, and the Song of Moses, in Deuteronomy, chapter 32:

Moses cried to the Lord, "El, I beg you, heal her."

They fell on their faces and asked, "El, god of spirits and all flesh, if one man has sinned, will the anger of the Lord be on the whole community?"

You have forsaken the God that fathered you and forgotten El who feeds you.

The name El survives in the Masoretic Text, and could only have been used as a proper name in the time of Moses. In other verses where the word God appears in the Octateuch, the Masoretic text generally has âlhym (אלהים), âlh (אלה), or occasionally Yehvah (יְהוָה), or Lord Yehwih (אֲדֹנָי יְהֹוִה). As the Greeks translated âlhym as gods (θεοὶ), transliterated Yahweh as Iaw (Ιαω), and âlh (אלה) is properly translated as 'goddess,' it is clear that the source texts they used did not have the same terms used in the Masoretic text.

The Song of Moses in chapter 32 describes the Lord as being one of God's messengers, the one who received the Israelites as his portion when God divided the children of Adam among the messengers. In Second Temple era literature, the patron messenger of the Israelites was Gabriel, while the patron messenger of the Persians was Dobiel. There is a story in the Talmud that dates back to the Persian era which explains the rise of the Persian Empire instead of an Israelite Empire. In this story, when the Persians occupied Babylonia, God wanted the Israelites in Babylon to be sacrificed, however, Gabriel took pity on them and let them return to Judea. God punished Gabriel and removed him from office for 21 days, during which Dobiel filled in, and he caused the rise of the Persian Empire.

This belief in the national messengers did not die out when the Second Temple was destroyed, as Dobiel and Samiel were described as the national messengers of the Persians and Romans when the Revelation of Metatron was written, which is broadly dated to between 100 and 1000 AD.

The Octateuch's book of Deuteronomy has what appears to be a reference to Moses praying to Lord Ba'al, king of the gods, in chapter 2, which would imply that he was the Lord of Deuteronomy, while later in chapter 10, the Masoretic version of Deuteronomy has the Lord stating his 'name is Shamayim' (וּשְׁמֵי הַשָּׁמָיִם). Hadad and Shamayim were both Canaanite gods which King Josiah banned during his religious reforms, circa 625 BC. Hadad was more commonly known as Ba'al at the time, however, is called Hadad, his proper name, in modern history books in order to distinguish him from the many other Canaanite gods referred to by the title Lord (Ba'al). The text in which Lord Hadad is possibly identified in the Octateuch is entirely missing in the Masoretic Text, which supports the fact that the Hasmoneans considered it contrary to their religious views. This title of the Lord in the Octateuch was:

lord Lord king of gods (κυριε Κυριε Βασιλευ των θεων)

If this was translated correctly from the Aramaic source text, then the verse read:

lord Ba'al king of the gods (ᒉ^ﬨ𝘓𝘕ﬨ 𝘕Ⅎ𝘓ᒉ 𝘕𝘓ᵛℲ ᒉℲ𝘕)

In the ancient Canaanite Ba'al Cycle, from between 1400 and 1200 BC, Lord Hadad became the king of the gods after defeating Lord Yam and Lord Mot, and gaining the support of the other 70 children of El. It is clear that the Ba'al Cycle was in use among the Judeans during the time of King Josiah, as the prophet Jeremiah quoted it, however, this sentence goes directly against the reforms of Josiah, who explicitly and vehemently banned the worship of Ba'al in 4th Kingdoms (Masoretic Kings) chapter 23:

> The king commanded Hilkiah the high priest, and the priests of the second order, and them that kept the door, to bring out of the temple of the Lord all the vessels that were made for Ba'al, and for Asherah, and all the army of Shamayim, and he burnt them outside of Jerusalem in the fields of Kidron, and took the ashes of them to the Temple of El. He burnt the sacred male prostitutes, who the kings of Judah had appointed, and those burnt incense in the Bamahs and in the cities of Judah, and the places around Jerusalem, and those that burnt incense to Ba'al, Shemesh, Yarikh, the Zodiac, and the power of the armies of Shamayim.

He carried out the Asherah from the Temple of the Lord to the brook Kidron, and burnt it at the brook Kidron, and ground it to powder, and threw its powder on the sepulchers of the sons of the people. He pulled down the Palace of Qetesh that were by the Temple of the Lord, where the women wove tents for the Asherah. He brought up all the priests from the cities of Judah and defiled the Bamahs where the priests burnt incense, from Geba even to Beersheba.

He pulled down the house of the gates that were by the door of the gate of Joshua the ruler of the city, on a man's left hand at the gate of the city. The priests of the Bamahs did not go up to the altar of the Lord in Jerusalem, and they only ate leavened bread among their brothers. He defiled Tafeth which is in the valley of the son of Hinnom, constructed for a man to cause his son or his daughter to pass through the fire to Moloch. He burnt the horses which the king of Judah had given to Shemesh in the entrance of the Temple of the Lord, by the treasury of Nathan the king's eunuch, in the suburbs, and he burnt the Chariot of Shemesh with fire.

The altars that were on the roof of the upper room of Ahaz, which the kings of Judah had made, and the altars which Manasseh had made in the two courts of the Temple of the Lord, the king pulled down and forcibly removed from there and threw their dust into the Brook of Kidron. The king defiled the temple that was near Jerusalem, on the right hand of the mount of Mosthath, which Solomon king of Israel built to Astarte the abomination of the Sidonians, and to Chemosh the abomination of Moab, and to Moloch the abomination of the Ammonites. He broke in pieces the steles, and completely destroyed Asherah, and filled their places with the bones of men. Also the high altar in the Temple of El, which had been built by Jeroboam the son of Nebat, who made Israel sin, even that high altar he tore down, and broke in pieces the stones of it, and reduced it to powder, and burnt Asherah.

Josiah turned aside, and saw the tombs that were there in the city, and sent, and took the bones out of the tombs, and burnt them on the altar, and defiled it, following the word of the Lord which the prophet spoke...

This description of the destruction of the temples of the Canaanite gods makes it clear that neither the Lord's identification as Hadad or Shamayim would have been acceptable under Josiah's rule, which indicates that the Book of Deuteronomy was either not written yet, or was in use among the Samaritans, outside of Judea at the time. The reference to Shamayim found in the Masoretic version of Deuteronomy does not flow in the text and appears to have simply been added by a Shamayim-worshiping scribe, which would indicate it was in use in Samaria under Assyrian rule. Based on the Book of Jonah, the Canaanite god Shamayim was regarded as the local variant of Asshur, the national god of Assyria, who by that time was known as Anshar (⤙✝⥈), meaning 'Whole Sky.' Jonah claimed that he was a prophet of Shamayim, the god of his owner, when he went to Nineveh, which was the only reason the Assyrians would have listened to a runaway slave.

The authorship of Deuteronomy's laws can also be placed outside of Judah by the book's treatment of kedeshah (קְדֵשָׁה) and kadesh (קָדֵשׁ) in chapter 23, which the Greeks translated as healers (τελεσφόροσ) and initiates (τελισκόμενοσ). The kadesh are the sacred male prostitutes that King Josiah executed, however, Deuteronomy's laws simply state that Israelites may not allow their children to become kedeshah and kadesh, implying the practice itself was fine, but only for lesser races. There are a number of Second Temple era texts that stipulate that Israelites may not be prostitutes, yet are accepting of other ethnic groups being prostitutes, which this verse seems to be implying. Deuteronomy's laws certainly do not state "Go forth and slaughter the kedeshah and kadesh," just "don't let your children become kedeshah and kadesh." The two terms, kedeshah and kadesh, are both related to the worship of Qetesh, whose palace in Jerusalem King Josiah destroyed. Qetesh was the title of Asherah, as well as several other goddesses in Canaan and Mesopotamia, and a significant amount of research and debate has gone into the development and history of the cult.

The kadesh were the sacred male prostitutes of the Temple of Qetesh, however, modern scholarship doubts the translation prostitute is accurate, as they did perform sexual acts, but did not get paid, and so the term 'sex-worker' is generally used in academic literature. The cult itself goes back to Sumeria, as the cult of Inanna, which in Sumerian mytho-history originated in the land of Aratta, long before the time of Sumeria. Throughout most of its history, the sex-workers were male, however, the descriptions indicate they were either transvestites or transgender, depending on the local customs regarding castration. The kedeshah, which is sometimes translated as female prostitutes, were in most cases nuns that worked at the palace, and do not appear to have engaged in sexual relations with men, as they were the sacred property of the goddess. This bizarre sex-cult was widespread from the Sumerian era, before 3000 BC, through the Akkadian, Babylonian, Assyrian, Hittite, and Mitanni civilizations. Under Persian rule, the position of eunuchs changed and they began to be hired by the Imperial government to fill bureaucratic positions because it was believed they were less likely to be corrupted by greed, as they had no children to leave their possessions to. This seems to have resulted in the cult having increasing amounts of female prostitutes before it finally died out under Greek rule. Some smaller groups did survive, as documented by the Romans when they conquered Anatolia.

Any of the references to Ba'al, Shamayim, or Qetesh seem out of place in a book used under Josiah's rule, and the fact that all three appear to be present, two mentioned explicitly in the Masoretic texts, and one implied by the Octateuch, indicates that Deuteronomy could not have been in use in Judah at that time. All three of the deities in question were worshiped in Samaria, both before it fell to Assyrians, and under Assyrian rule, and therefore, the Book of Deuteronomy is likely Samaritan in origin. Deuteronomy retells or mentions various stories from the first four books of the Torah, and adds a secondary set of laws, intended to supplement the laws in the book of Exodus. This is the origin of the name 'Deuteronomy' which means 'Second Law.' The retelling of the stories found in Leviticus and Numbers seems to be a parallel tradition, and not simply restating what was already written, implying some version of Deuteronomy may be older than Leviticus and may have even been one of the sources used when Numbers was compiled under Josiah. Many of the terms used in Deuteronomy imply it is older, and likely a collection of laws from the Kingdom of Samaria, however, in chapter 24 the author explicitly states to follow the laws regarding leprosy that the Levites will provide, and to remember what happened to Miriam. This is a clear reference to the books of Leviticus and Numbers, which indicates that Deuteronomy's text was still being added to in the Babylonian era.

Chapters 29 and 30, the Curse of Moses, and the promise of forgiveness certainly appear to have been written after the Assyrians conquered Samaria in 720 BC, as they promise that after the Israelites have been spread through the nations, even to the ends of the earth if they repent, they will be restored to the promised land. This is an odd thing for Moses to have said as the Israelites were preparing to invade Canaan, but, is a great addition to the Torah when the Israelites have been taken as slaves to the far reaches of the Assyrian Empire. It is equally possible that this line was added later, during the Babylonian era, as they took away Judahites as captives, and in either case, it would indicate that Deuteronomy was used by the Samaritan priesthood that became dominant in Babylonian Judea.

The Samaritan priesthood was thrown out of office by Ezra the Scribe circa 350 BC, who is credited in the Talmud as rewriting the Torah from memory, as it had been lost when the Babylonians destroyed Jerusalem, however, the Samar-itan priesthood had to have had a Torah, and Ezra most likely just redacted it to fit the requirements of the priesthood he was creating. Some have theorized that he wrote Deuteronomy, however, that seems unlikely as he would not have been so lenient towards the kedeshah and kadesh, and certainly would not have included the sentences that indicate Hadad and Shamayim were considered the Lord when sections of Deuteronomy were written. It is possible that he added the Curse of Moses, and the promise of forgiveness, however, by his time the Jews were already free to return, and so the promise would have been pointless.

Few books have generated as many debates about geographical features as the books of Exodus and Numbers. They describe in detail a series of wonders that the Lord, the God of the Israelites, performed to cause them to be freed from their slavery in Egypt, and then their trek across the wilderness to a mountain on which God descended and gave them the Torah. The wonders themselves have been the source of much speculation in the past 2500 years, but the trek across the wilderness and the location of the mountain of God are the real issues most commonly debated. Most of the speculation about the geography has been by Christian and Islamic scholars, who have tried to retrace the path the Israelites took out of Egypt in order to find the mountain of God, however, many moun-tains have been found following the places listed along the route, as most of the locations are debated.

Half a dozen mountains have been identified, each with a list of locations along the route that may or may not be the original locations. This doesn't appear to be a new problem, as even then names for the mountain in the Torah and other ancient Israelite texts changes from one paragraph to the next. This mountain is called both Sinai and Horeb throughout the Torah, and then Seir in the book of Judges, which is widely regarded as being the oldest Israelite text that has not been heavily redacted.

Various Jewish and Christian scholars have tried to resolve the issue of the same stories happening on two mountains. In the Middle Ages, the Rabbi Abraham ibn Ezra suggested that there was only one mountain, with two peaks one called Horeb and the other Sinai, while later during the Protestant Reforma-tion John Calvin suggested it was one mountain where the eastern side was named Sinai, while the western side was named Horeb. The question of why Deborah called it Seir has often been ignored by Christians, however, does seem to have influenced the Second-Temple era Jewish view of where the mountain was located.

The 1st century AD Jewish general and historian Josephus implied it was in the southern Abarim mountains, a region the Israelites and Egyptians had historically called Seir. Josephus claimed to take possession of ancient scrolls when the Second Temple was destroyed by the Romans, which is generally considered plausible, from which he drew his information that, among other things, Kadesh Barnea was Petra, and Mount Sinai was in the Roman province of Arabia-Petra. The 1st century AD Christian disciple Paul (Saul) of Tarsus also reported the location of Sinai was in Arabia, meaning the Province of Arabia-Petra. As Paul had been a Pharisee before converting to Christianity and quoted several obscure Jewish texts to support his ideology, such as the Apocalypse of Moses, it is plausible that he had read whatever Josephus was quoting.

The question of the two names of this mountain is further complicated by the fact that the two names are believed to be derived from opposing gods, Horeb, meaning 'burning,' derived from a sun-god, and Sinai, derived from the name Sin, the ancient Semitic moon-god. Biblical scholars in the 1800s and 1900s developed the hypothesis that two names are derived from two Torah traditions, one Solar and one Lunar, which were then united into a single Torah under the rule of King Josiah or earlier. Subsequent theories have suggested the unification of the two Torahs could have taken place later, under the Persian or even Greek rule of Judea, however, it seems unlikely to have happened that late as the Samaritan Torah has virtually identical twin stories about Horeb/Sinai, and the schism between the Jews and Samaritans appears to have happened during the life of Ezra the Scribe, circa 350 BC. Textual analysis shows the name Horeb is generally associated with Moses, while Sinai is more often found in texts about Aaron, which implies that whatever the origin of the story, two versions have developed by the time of Josiah, one focused on Moses' Solar-Snake god, and the other focused on Aaron's Lunar-Calf god. When the two Torahs were harmonized it created several parallel statements and stories, often with different geographical locations.

Josephus' writings shed light on the issue of the mountain's location, by identifying one of the locations along the route, Kadesh Barnea, as Petra, which he claimed was known as Rekem in ancient times. The location of Kadesh Barnea is central to identifying the location of Sinai, as the Israelites went to Kadesh Barnea after leaving Mount Sinai, and both were outside of Edomite territory, which by the 700s BC included the southern Abarim mountains. Nevertheless, Josephus reported that Petra was part of Midian during the Exodus era, meaning the Edomites were still only in the northern Abarim mountains, east of the Dead Sea. Josephus' claims about ancient Petra being named Rekem have been confirmed by archaeology, as has the fact that the region was not Edomite until after 800 BC, meaning it could have been Midianite before that, and also could have been Kadesh Barnea.

As the Greek name Petra simply means 'rock' it has been associated with the location called 'Sela' which means 'rock' in Hebrew since the Roman Era. Jerome translated the 'Sela' from the Book of Isaiah as 'Petra deserti' in his Vulgate translation of the Bible, circa 382 AD. It is not clear if the two locations are the same, as the ruins of Petra are mostly from the later Nabataean capital, built between 300 BC and 106 AD, and then expanded after the Romans annexed it in 106 AD. The Egyptian el-Amarna Letters, written between 1360 and 1332 BC do mention the Shasu of Sôrr, which is translated as the 'nomads of Seir,' implying someone was living in the Seir region of the southern Abarim mountains.

The el-Amarna Letters also mention the Shasu (Nomads) of Rbn (or Lbn), Smôt, Ůrbr, and Pysps, along with the Nomads of Yhů, which are generally accepted as the earliest reference to Yahweh, however, is a toponym, implying a mountain. Some interpret the Nomads of Rbn, as the Tribe of Ruben, however, Smôt, Ůrbr, and Pysps do not match the names of Israelite Tribes. Smt ($+ \text{ツ} +$) was the name of the Canaanite goddess of fate, called Sm (ᛑ—) in the Ugaritic Texts, and later called Ashima in 4th Kingdoms (Masoretic Kings), which stated that Samaritans were worshiping her.

If there was a Mountain of Yhů (Îôhů/Sinai) in Seir, and if it was near Petra (Kadesh Barnea), the likely mountain is Jebel al-Madhbah, which translates as 'The Mountain of the Altar.' The Mountain of the Altar has been associated with Moses since at least the pre-Christian era and includes a Valley of Moses (Wadi Musa) and a Spring of Moses (Ain Musa), connected to the events that happened at Mount Sinai/Horeb/Seir. The mountain's summit is covered in rock-cut ceremonial structures and reached by a rock-cut staircase. There are two giant obelisks, carved out of the rocky surface, near a large rectangular promenade hollowed out so the edges for benches. The site also included large cisterns for collecting rainwater. It is unclear when this complex was carved out of the rock, as the site was later quarried for blue slate, which archaeologists believed once covered the site. This blue slate was likely what was later identified as sapphire in the Octateuch.

Nevertheless, while some scholars have identified the Mountain of the Altar with the Mountain of God, most instead point either to Mount Sinai, at the southern end of the Sinai Peninsula, or one of several other mountains in Egypt, Jordan, or Saudi Arabia as being the holy mountain. This is largely due to how one interprets the route the Israelites took out of Egypt, however, is sometimes shaped by other concerns. In the 1800s, the idea that the holy mountain was an active volcano was proposed, which would then explain much of what happened at Sinai, including the pillars of fire and smoke, and well as the deaths, however, there are no known active volcanoes in the region the Israelites are reported to have traveled through. Nevertheless, the dormant volcano Hala-'l Badr in eastern Saudi Arabia is often suggested. Hala-'l Badr is believed to have been active sometime in the past 10,000 years, and its name does translate as 'Full-moon Volcano,' which could then explain the origin of both the names Sinai and Horeb, however, it is not near the route the Israelites took, and they would have had to march right past Midian to reach it.

As Jethro, Moses' father-in-law came from Midian to visit them while they were traveling, they could not have passed through Midian. Nevertheless, many notable (mostly atheist) scholars have endorsed the Hala-'l Badr theory, as it would explain why the Israelites 'thought they saw God.' While it is a possible explanation for the events at Horeb/Sinai, it does not explain what the fire-messenger that Moses encountered was, which then led the Israelites through the wilderness for 40 years, during which they were generally not in the vicinity of the holy mountain.

Most of the confusion about where the mountain is, is derived from the various interpretations of the route the Israelites took out of Egypt, as well as who the Israelites were while they were in Egypt. Some of this confusion was clearly caused by the translation of the Septuagint at the Library of Alexandria circa 250 BC. The Greek translators used the term Erythraean Sea (ερυθραι θαλασσηι) to translate the Aramaic and Hebrew term ym sŭf (ים סוף) which simply translates as 'Reed Sea' or 'Papyrus Sea.'

The Greeks transliterated the name as the Sea of Siph (θαλάσσησ Σιφ) in the Codex Vaticanus' translation of Judges, confirming that the name Swf was in the

Aramaic text they worked from. Both the Aramaic term sůf (ס‏וף) and Phoeni-cian term sůf (ס‏וף), both meaning papyrus plants were adopted from the Egyp-tian term tjůfî (ꜩwfj), which referred to papyrus, papyrus plants, and papyrus marshes. The Egyptian term continued to be used into the Classical era as the Coptic words čoouf (ϫⲟⲟⲩϥ), conf (ϭⲟⲛϥ), and comf (ϭⲟⲙϥ), all meaning papyrus. Conversely, the Egyptian name of the Red Sea was the Sea of Heh (𓎛), meaning 'very large sea' from the Middle Kingdom era onward, however, believed to have originally been named after the ancient Egyptian frog god Heh (𓁨). As the Greek translation of Erythrean Sea is anachronistic, the translation of Papyrus Sea is imported from the Masoretic text.

The Greek term Erythrean Sea was an adopted Persian term that referred to the Indian Ocean, Persian Gulf, Gulf of Aden, and the Red Sea. No doubt the Greek translators were covering their bases, as they had no idea where the events of the Suf Yam had taken place. This mistranslation has unfortunately been carried into virtually all Christian translations of the Israelite Scriptures as 'Red Sea,' including those made from the Masoretic Text which do not mention the Red Sea. Ironically, this has even been re-imported to Hebrew, where the name for the Red Sea is now Suf Yam, making the ancient Greek mistranslation look correct. Nevertheless, ancient Egyptian records that have been translated in the past couple of centuries clarify the location of the event, and it is not in the Red Sea, which almost all translations and interpretations of the Torah and Bibles report.

The location is identified by the inclusion of the name Ba'al Zephon (Βεελσεπφων) in the Octateuch, and ba'al Tzefon (בַּעַל צְפֹן) in the Masoretic Text. Ba'al Zephon was a Canaanite god, worshiped by the people along the Syrian coast near Mount Zephon (modern Jebel Aqra) in the 2nd millennium BC. These northern Canaanites had established a colony in Egypt, where their main God according to Egyptian records was Ba'al Zephon, who the Egyptians equated with their god Amen (Amun). This colony was in the marshland known today as Lake Bardawil on the north coast of the Sinai Peninsula. Lake Bardawil is a shallow saline lake, estimated to be about 10 feet (3 meters) deep at its deepest, with a surface area of 147,000 acres (59,500 hectares). It is the only known site in Egypt where Ba'al Zephon was worshiped as even the northern motherland of these Canaanites was beyond the reach of the Egyptian Empire.

The region of Lake Bardawil was known throughout Egyptian history as a quagmire, where entire armies had been swallowed by the sea. The Greeks had ancient myths about the place, in which it was known as the Serbonian Bog, or Lake Serbonius, which had a deceptive appearance of looking solid because sand would blow onto it, but was a bog that swallowed people that tried to pass through it. The description is essentially one of a massive lake of quicksand that formed after a sandstorm. The high salinity of the water may have helped slow the rate at which the sand settled, although the phenomenon has not been recorded in the past century and likely points to the specific time when the event happened.

The Greek myths were established during the Greek Dark Age, which was approximately the same time as the Third Intermediate Period (dark age) in Egypt, but later identified as Lake Bardawil when the Greeks ruled Egypt. In the Greek myths, Zeus' ancient enemy, the monster Typhon, lay at the bottom of the Bog. As Typhon was the Greek version of the Egyptian Apophis (Apepi), this Greek myth my help identify the Pharaoh in Exodus as Apepi, one of the last Hyksos Pharaohs, who Egyptologists report died around the time of the Minoan eruption, which they date to circa 1550 BC.

The Minoan eruption was the volcanic explosion of the island of Thera (modern Santorini) in the Aegean Sea, which covered most of the Minoan civilization, based in Crete, with several inches to several feet of ash. It also reigned ash across northern Egypt, which allows Egyptologists to date it to the end of the Hyksos era. Aegean Prehistorians disagree on the dating, placing it around 1650 BC, but, whenever it was, a Pharaoh named Apepi was the king ruling from their capital of Avaris in the Nile Delta, which would later be renamed Pi-Ramesses, and then simplified to Ramesses. They were at war with another Pharaoh's government based in Thebes, in southern Egypt, Ahmose I, whose grandfather Seqenenre Tao, a local governor, had rebelled against the Hyksos, and started an insurrection. The Hyksos appear to have had a significant advantage throughout the war, which spanned about two decades, until the Minoan eruption, when Apepi died, following which Avaris fell to Ahmose I shortly afterward.

Based on the chronology of the Octateuch's books of Exodus, Joshua, and Judges, the year of the exodus from Egypt took place in approximately 1547 BC, which is approximately the same era as the Minoan Eruption according to most

Egyptologists. The Minoan Eruption was the massive volcano eruption on the Greek isle of Santorini, which ejected approximately 60 km^3 (14 miles^3) of debris, which fell across the eastern Mediterranean and covered some parts of northern Egypt in 2 meters (6 feet) in ash. The sky was darkened for weeks and the crops and livestock died in the fields. Southern Egypt was also affected, as reported by the Tempest Stele, a stone tablet erected during the reign of the Theban Pharaoh Ahmose I, who conquered northern Egypt and drove the Hyksos dynasty out of Egypt after a three-year siege of the Hyksos dynasty, the city of Avaris. The Tempest Stele is damaged, however, the surviving text described the flooding in southern Egypt which resulted from the rainstorms:

> [damaged text]...the gods expressed their discontent. The gods of the sky come with a tempest and it darkened the West. The sky was unleashed without [...damaged text...] more than the roar of the crowd [...damaged text...] was powerful [...damaged text...] on the highlands more than the waterfall at the cataract of Elephantine.

> Each house [...damaged text...] each shelter that they reached [...damaged text...] were floating in the water like the barks of papyrus by the royal residence for [...damaged text...] days [...damaged text...] with no one able to light the torch anywhere.

> Then his majesty said 'This surpasses even the power of the great god, and the wills of the divinities!'

> His Majesty descended in his boat, with his council following. The east and the west were silent, as they were naked [...damaged text...] after the power of the god was manifested. Then his Majesty arrived in Thebes [...damaged text...] this statue, and it received what it had desired.

> His majesty set about to strengthen Egypt, and stop the rain around him, and he provided them with silver, gold, copper, oil, clothing, and with all the products they desired, after which his majesty returned to the palace (life, health, strength).

> Then his majesty was informed that the tombs had been flooded, that the sepulchral chambers had been damaged, that the structures of funerary enclosures had been undermined, that the pyramids had collapsed, and all that existed had been annihilated. His Majesty then ordered the repair of the shrines which had collapsed all over the country and the restoration of the...[...damaged text...]

Several scholars have tried to link the wonders (or plagues) of Egypt to the Minoan explosion in the past few decades, however, most seem hampered by the name of the city the Israelites slaves were building, which the book of Exodus records as being Ramesses. This name simply was not used in Egypt as the name of a city until around 800 BC, and therefore has to be viewed as an anachronism, likely a geographical update made during King Josiah's time. Nevertheless, most scholars that try to analyze the Exodus assume the Israelites were working in the city of Pi-Ramesses, which was founded sometime between 1292 and 1250 BC, meaning they try to date the Exodus to after this time. Firstly, this is incorrect because Pi-Ramesses was not called Ramesses until it was revived by Shoshenq I around 930 BC. Secondly, there were already reports of nomads in Canaan that appear to have been the Israelites by the mid-1300s BC, the Shasu (nomads) of Yhǔ and Rbn, implying that the Exodus had already happened.

While most non-religious scholars recognize the Shasu of Yhǔ may have been the early Israelites, few bother looking into the Exodus story anymore, assuming it is historical fiction, likely written between 900 and 600 BC. While they are likely correct, that it was fictionalized somewhat in that era, it appears to have far too many historical tie-ins to the end of the Hyksos era to be entirely fiction. Moreover, there are far too many inconsistencies with the theology of the Josiah-era early-Judaism. The names of the Israelite god being obviously imported from Egypt is itself a strong indicator that the story of Exodus was not new in the era of Josiah. Egypt had been menacing Judea for over 300 years by his time, so why make up a story about a bunch of ancient Israelites that worshiped an Egyptian god?

The conflict between Moses and Aaron's respective statues, Moses' bronze serpent, and Aaron's golden calf, is another example of something no one would have added in the time of Josiah. The conflicting names of the holy mountain, Horeb, Sinai, and Seir are a third example and point to a very old story that had been around for so long that different versions of it were in circulation, yet all reported the God came down on that mountain. These weren't different stories. The Book of the Watchers in the Enochian tradition is somewhat similar, but clearly, a different story, as God did not come down on Enoch's mountain, instead Watchers descended onto it. The Horeb, Sinai, and Sier stories are all essentially the same, except for the name of the mountain.

Using the Septuagint's chronology, the Pharaoh at the beginning of Exodus, whose daughter adopts the infant Moses, was likely Khyan, although if one accepts that Moses was eighty when he returned to Egypt, then it was likely one of Khyan's predecessors. When Moses ran away from Egypt, he could not go into Canaan, as the Hyksos ruled southern Canaan, and so he went to Midian, the Midyan Mountains of northwestern Saudi Arabia. He returned after hearing that the former Pharaoh was dead during the reign of Pharaoh Apepi, who Egyptologists state ruled between approximately 1585 and 1550 BC, although dates vary slightly depending on when the Minoan eruption took place.

The wonders reported in the Octateuch's Exodus, and the plagues reported in the Masoretic Exodus, can, to some degree be linked to the effects of the Minoan explosion, including the fire, hail, and ash falling from the sky, the blisters that broke out on the people, and the darkness that lasted for days. Some of the other wonders do not appear to be related to eruption, such as Aaron turning his wand (Masoretic 'stick') into a snake or the sudden appearance and disappearance of the frogs and locusts. The massive environmental shifts the eruption caused could explain the winds that brought locusts into the land, and blew them away, but not why there were so many.

Additionally, the last wonder/plague does not appear to be related to the eruption, the deaths of all the firstborn. It's possible that the wonders were embellished, however, the concept that the Lord wants all the firstborn sacrificed to him (or a substitute animal for firstborn humans) is embedded deeply within the Torah, and is difficult to dismiss as a later addition. Additionally, the Wisdom of Solomon retells a somewhat different version of these wonder/plagues, in which the Israelites sneaked out of Egypt under cover of the plague of darkness while the messenger of death was slaughtering the firstborn. This is certainly different from the Exodus version of the story in which the Pharaoh kicked them out of Egypt, and then changed his mind and pursued them to the sea where he drowned, although the Pharaoh in Wisdom of Solomon also chased them to the sea when he found out they'd run away. The fact that there were two different versions of the wonder/plagues in the Second-Temple era implies that the story was not as established as many assume, and some of the wonder/plagues may have been added shortly before the Greek translation was made.

The path that the Israelites took on the way out of Egypt is debated to a ridiculous level, given how unimportant it is to the story. Nevertheless, based on the identification of Baal-Zephon at Lake Bardawil, which is on the Sinai Peninsula's northern coast, the following route seems plausible. First, regarding the cities the Israelites were enslaved in, the Septuagint lists Pithom, Ramesses, and Ôn (Ων), while the Leningrad Codex only mentions Pithom and Ramesses.

On (אֹן) was the Hebrew translation of the name of the Egyptian city of Ỉunu (𓉐𓊖) used in the Leningrad Codex's Bereshít, later known as Heliopolis to the Greeks. It was mentioned at the end of Cosmic Genesis as the city where Joseph married the daughter of the high priest, implying he became a priest in Ỉunu. All three of these places were major political or religious sites during the Hyksos era, although, they were major sites in most eras. Ramesses was known as Avaris at the time, the capital of Hyksos-controlled Egypt. Ỉunu was the southern-most Hyksos-controlled city during the era of Apepi, and, like Pithom, was one of Egypt's four major religious centers, the other two being Memphis and Thebes, both under the control of the southern pharaoh. It is unclear why Ỉunu was removed from the Masoretic version, but the Greek translators certainly had no reason to add an ancient Egyptian city to the list, let alone use its ancient Canaanite name.

The ancient Egyptian city of Ỉunu (𓉐𓊖) was commonly called Ỉun (𓉐) in Hieratic, which was adopted into Canaanite and Aramaic as Åun (𐤀𐤅𐤍 / אוּן). It was later renamed Heliopolis in Greek, meaning 'Sun-city,' because most of Egypt's sun-gods had temples there, including Ra, the sun-god that flew the celestial chariot; Atum, the sun-god that created the universe; Aten, the solar-disk who would later become the national god under Akenhaten; and the scarab-beetle god Khepri who rolled the sun into the sky each morning. Heliopolis was the city of the sun gods, and also a moon god named Ỉôhu (𓇋𓂝𓎛𓅱).

Even if one were to accept the idea that the Greeks inserted a transliteration of the Aramaic name of Heliopolis to Exodus when they listed the cities the Israelites were enslaved in, as opposed to a Simon the Zealot dropping it, the city was already mentioned at the end of Cosmic Genesis and Bereshít, which means it already had significance within the overall story. In Cosmic Genesis, after Joseph was freed from slavery for interpreting the Pharaoh's dreams, he was married to the daughter of a high-priest of Heliopolis. This would make him a priest at Heliopolis, and likely place him in line to be a high-priest. The question was which god was he a priest of? Given the options for an interpreter of dreams are a number of sun gods, and a somewhat minor moon god, Ỉôhu seems like the obvious god for him to be the priest of. The earliest depictions of Yhůh, on pottery shards found at Kuntillet Ajrud, dating to circa 800 BC, depict Yhůh as the calf of Asherah, who was herself the personification of the starry-sky, meaning Yhůh was still considered to be the moon at the time.

The meaning of the word Pithom has been debated for at least 2500 years. The Septuagint has variations of Pithôm (Πιθωμ), while the Leningrad Codex has Pitom (פִּיתוֹם), and Dead Sea Scrolls 4QExodᶜ has ptm (פתם). This has generally been assumed to be the town of Per-Atum (𓉐𓏏𓐍), which was the name of two cities located in the Wadi Tumilat at different points in time. The Wadi Tumilat was a seasonal river that ran east from the Nile to the Bitter Lakes in the western Sinai Peninsula, which is the same route Sinuhe took during his flight from Egypt, centuries earlier in the Middle Kingdom era. The ruins of Tel El Maskhuta appear to have been a Hyksos Dynasty city, which bore the name, and is almost certainly the Pithom in question, as it seems to have been abandoned at the end of the Hyksos era, which is the same era the Septuagint places the Exodus. The other Per-Atum was also at the ruins of Tel El Maskhuta, but much later, in the 7ᵗʰ century BC, and appears to have been built by Pharaoh Necho II during his attempt to dig a canal from the Nile through the Wadi Tumilat and Bitter Lakes to the Red Sea. He wasn't the first to attempt this, and during the Middle Kingdom a canal was dug from the Nile through the Wadi Tumilat to the Bitter Lakes, however, it was never connected to the Red Sea.

It is worth noting that while the Hyksos appear to have built the first city called Per-Atum, the Wadi Tumilat was considered sacred to the creator god Atum since pre-dynastic times, and there were likely Temples of Atum (Per-Atum) in the wadi throughout Egyptian history. The wadi, or something in it, was called Pyṯôn (𓉐𓄿𓈖) in the Tale of Sinuhe, which was written centuries earlier in the Middle Kingdom era, and so the name Pithom may be a corruption of Pyṯôn and not Per-Atum. In the Tale of Sinuhe, Pyṯôn was beyond the Egyptian fortifications, and en route to the Kem Wer, the largest of the Bitter Lakes. It is not clear what exactly the term Pyṯôn meant, however, there were two of them, the one in the Wadi Tumilat, and another in southern Egypt. It is known that the kings of Egypt took responsibility for overseeing them, which suggests they were quite expensive to maintain. The only thing known to have been very expensive in the Wadi Tamilat during the Middle Kingdom Era was the canal connecting the Nile to the Kem Wer. This suggests that pyṯôn may have been a Middle Egyptian term for 'canal,' as there was also a major canal in southern Egypt, at Aswan, where the river was altered to allow ships to pass the first cataract of the Nile.

Atum was one of the sun-gods worshiped at Ỉừnừ, but his cult center was at Per-Atum in the Wadi Tumilat. Atum was also very archetypal to the God of Moses. Atum was the creator of the universe, who created the universe in a series of events somewhat similar to the days of creation found at the beginning of Cosmic Genesis. He was not depicted as the sun when he was the creator, but a god that resembled a man, or a serpent, who emerged from the primordial waters, and separated the air, called Shu, from the water, called Tefnut. It is unclear when he became conflated with the sun-gods at Ỉừnừ, but at some point, he became a sun-god, specifically the god of the setting sun.

In the Old Kingdom era, he was believed to lift the ba (spirits and psyche) of the dead to the stars, which does fore-run most of the Christian and Islamic teachings of the spirit and psyche (soul) going up to the sky after the death of the body. This idea was found in some early Israelite and Jewish beliefs, as demonstrated by the Testament of Abraham, but did not become a central belief in Rabbinical Judaism.

The story of Atum does shed light on what Exodus and the retelling of the exodus in Numbers, was about, if one accepts that the Israelites, and Moses, the Egyptian prince that led them, were influenced by the teachings of the cult of Atum, at whose temple they had apparently been enslaved. In addition to being a creator God, Atum was a snake-god, who was so important in the early dynastic era that the Pharaoh's crowns were designed to make them look like snake-headed people. This symbolism is directly linked to the uraeus, the symbol later called the Eye of Ra or Eye of Horus by the Greeks and subsequent civilizations. The uraeus represented a strange story of winged-snakes that came from the sun in uraeus, fiery disks the Egyptians believed were small pieces of the sun, hence the term 'eyes of the sun.' These winged-snakes were found depicted throughout the Hyksos territory, which included southern Canaan, and archaeologists generally accept that they were the original version of the seraphs, the reptilian-messengers of the ancient Israelite religion. Today, seraphs are considered a 'type of angel' in some Christian churches, but, like angels, depicted as Greek gods. This was not how Second Temple or Medieval Jews thought of them, as demonstrated in the Revelation of Metatron.

These uraeuses served as the messengers of Atum, much like the messengers (mal'akh) of the Canaanite religion, and subsequent Israelite and Judaeo-Christian religions, so, the analogy that the seraphs are a form of messenger is not inherently wrong, but the depictions of them as winged-men are a Hellenistic era anachronism. The fact that Moses cast a bronze serpent in the book of Numbers points to his being a worshiper of Atum, as, according to the later Israelite books, this statue was carried to Israel, and placed in the Temple of King Solomon in Jerusalem. King Hezekiah destroyed it around 700 BC when he was trying to get everyone to worship Yahweh, meaning, it was not seen as a statue of Yahweh, nevertheless, it was described in ancient texts as having wings, which has led some scholars to propose it was a Hyksos-era statue of a uraeus.

In Exodus, Moses' brother, the high-priest Aaron cast the statue of a golden calf, which then split the Israelites into two camps, and Moses ordered all those 'on the side of the Lord,' meaning his snake-god Atum, to murder the worshipers of the calf god. There were many bovine gods in Egypt and Canaan, however, almost no recorded cases of a calf god. The two notable exceptions being the Samaritan calf god Yahweh, and the Assyrian calf and sun god Marduk. Generally, the bovine gods were either bulls or heifers, adult cattle, which strongly indicates that Aaron's golden calf, was a statue of Yahweh. The calf god Yahweh was depicted on a piece of pottery dated to 800 BC, found at Kuntillet Ajrud, near Hashem El Tarif in the Sinai Peninsula near the modern Egyptian-Israeli border. The depiction refers to the heifer that is suckling Yahweh as Asherah, the ancient Israelite sky-goddess, implying he was a lunar god, like most of the Semitic bovine gods. This links him back directly to the Egyptian moon-god Îôh, also called Îôhu, who Joseph was most likely the high priest of in Heliopolis.

The twin names of Yh (Yah, Jah) and Yhǔh (Yahweh, Jehovah) appear throughout the Hebrew texts and are difficult to explain. The traditional explanation is that Yh is just short for Yhǔh, but why bother copying a series of very long books, only to abbreviate the name of the God they're about? If the scribes were that lazy, they wouldn't have copied much at all. The twin names do make sense though if one considers them a continuation of the twin names of Îôh, the moon, and Îôhu, the moon god.

The fact that the follower of Moses and Aaron were murdering each other over whether to worship a bronze serpent or a gold calf is anathema to the idea of not carving a statue in the first place, which is what the Lord told Moses. As a result, the questions why these statues were carved is generally ignored by Jews and Christians, and irrelevant to Muslims who can simply dismiss the stories as latter additions to the narrative, however, if one considers what the two statues represent, Atum and Îôḥů, the twin Torah hypothesis begins to make sense. The idea that Horeb and Sinai are named after the sun and the moon in two different versions of the Torah that were circulating before the time of Josiah actually makes sense if the Israelites that were worshiping the sun and moon in that era had different versions of the Torah.

4th Kingdoms also includes a story about King Josiah's people finding the original Torah, which implies he published an authorized version, and also there were other versions in circulation that were not 'original.' This is considered by most scholars the most likely point when the Horeb and Sinai material were merged into a single Torah, creating many repeating stories and statements as the scribes attempted to harmonize the texts. Given that Josiah's god Yahweh combined both the name, and calf image of the Yahwist god, and the sun-god motif of the Baalist god, it appears that he was trying to impose a form of Marduk worship on Judea, likely in an attempt to forge closer ties with the only empire that could help defend his nation against the rising power of Egypt to the south. Ultimately, the Egyptians attacked and he was killed on the battlefield, following which Judea became a puppet-state of the Egyptian Empire.

While most Egyptologists dismiss the entire Exodus narrative as being 1st millennium BC fiction, likely written around the time of Josiah, and historians generally follow their lead, there is far too much that contradicts the theology of Josiah's proto-Judaism to support this conclusion. Meanwhile, Biblical scholars have obsessed over the route out of Egypt, conveniently ignoring the inconvenient Egyptian gods in the texts. 'Surely Moses and Aaron were worshiping the same god, and were absolutely not idolaters.' This runs contrary to what is written.

The Book of Numbers has a longer route, however, what is written there only confirms this route. The first place mentioned in Exodus, immediately after leaving Avaris (Ramesses) was called Socchôth (σοκχωθ) in the Septuagint, implying the name of a city. It is generally translated from the Masoretic Text as Sukkot, however, the Greek translators most likely made a mistake that has subsequently been copied by later translators. The Hebrew word skůt (סכות) simply refers to animal corrals or stables. This is already established in Genesis, and there is no reason to believe that the text wasn't simply stating they went to get their animals from the corrals. The animals were mentioned later, and they could not have kept them in their homes. Traditional interpretations have this as another town in the Nile Delta, although why they'd go to another town is not discussed. Fringe theories have this as a mining settlement in the Sinai Peninsula, which makes no sense in relation to the rest of the route, and there is no mention of a mine in either the books of Exodus or Numbers.

The next place mentioned was 'Othom (Οθομ) on the edge of the wilderness,' in the Octateuch, which again implies a town. This is again an error by the Greek translators that was carried forward into later translations, as the Hebrew term Åtm (אתם), simply means 'fortification.' The sentence is simply reporting they reached the fortification at the edge of the Nile Delta, where the wilderness (desert) began. From this point of they were being led by the pillar of fire and smoke, which some have interpreted as a volcano erupting that they were walking directly towards, however, there simply are no volcanoes within eyesight of the eastern edge of the Nile Delta. The curvature of the Earth makes this interpretation impossible, so whatever the Israelites were following, it couldn't have been a volcano.

The next stop in the Leningrad Codex was pi hchirot (פִּי הַחִירֹת), which was translated as 'the village' in the Septuagint, showing that the Greek translators were not sure about the location, but assumed it was a village. The Hebrew term pi hchirot (פִּי הַחִירֹת) is a combination of the Canaanite p h (𐤁 𐤐), meaning 'mouth of the,' and the Egyptian term hr-t. The ancient Egyptian word transliterated as hr-t meant both watercourse (𓇋𓂋𓏏𓈗) and Nile deposits (𓈊𓈘𓊌) depending on context. The term was generally used in the Nile Delta, where the watercourses moved regularly as sediment built up. This was most likely a reference to the mouth of the Pelusiac branch of the Nile River, the ancient eastern-most branch of the Nile.

The next stop in the Leningrad Codex was pi hchirot (פִּי הַחִירֹת), which was translated as 'the village' in the Octateuch, showing that the Greek translators were not sure about the location, but assumed it was a village. The Hebrew term pi hchirot (פִּי הַחִירֹת) is a combination of the Hebrew term 'mouth of the' (פִּי ה) and the Egyptian term hr-t (𓇋𓂋𓏏), meaning 'watercourse,' meaning they had reached the mouth of the Nile, which empties into the Mediterranean Sea.

This 'mouth of the watercourse' was described as being between Magdôlou (Μαγδωλου) and the sea, across from Beelsepphôn (Βεελσεπφων). Again, these read like names of towns in the Septuagint, however, the Leningrad Codex indicates what they mean. The Hebrew term migdol (מִגְדֹּול) simply means 'tower,' likely a reference to the towers built along the coast to serve as warnings of shallow water. Therefore, the Israelites were following the coast, naturally heading east, which would bring them to Lake Bardawil.

The Hebrew word Bôl Ṣpwn (בעל צפון) shows that the term the Greeks translated as Beelsepphôn (Βεελσεπφων), implying a settlement, as actually Ba'al Zephon, a Canaanite god. This god was only recorded as being worshiped by Canaanites that had settled in Lake Baradwil, the Serbonian Bog of Greek mythology. This means that regardless of the Lord's instructions to not follow the northern road to Canaan, that is what they were doing when the Pharaoh's army caught up with them. The 'Red Sea' incident sounds a lot like the mythology surrounding the Serbonian Bog, beginning with a strong wind that 'blew the sea away' in Exodus.

The Greek story reported that the wind would deposit sand over the water, which would then look like land, but swallow people, and according to Egyptian myths, whole armies that tried to cross it were swallowed. This is a description of quicksand, a massive lake of quicksand with a surface area of 147,000 acres (59,500 hectares). While there is almost certainly no surviving evidence of a bronze age army being swallowed by the Lake Bardawil, as the salt would have dissolved the wood, bone, leather, and bronze, this is what the story in Exodus is about, not something happening in the Red Sea. There are no reports of Ba'al Zephon worshipers in the Red Sea, and there was a major colony at Lake Bardawil.

The fact that the Greek legend of the Serbonian Bog included the story of Typhon, the Greek version of Apophis (Apepi), being at the bottom of it, implies the Pharaoh Apepi, who was named after Apophis, was the Pharaoh whose army tried to catch up to the Israelites, and who ended up drowning in the sea. The Aramaic and Hebrew term suf yam (סוף ים), in no way indicates the modern Red Sea, simply meaning 'Reed Sea,' or 'Papyrus Sea,' either of which would be an accurate description of Lake Bardawil.

If this story did take place in Lake Bardawil, the details were likely somewhat different than the version in Exodus, although similar enough that the later 'authorized version' of Josiah would make sense. If the Israelites were following the northern coast of the Sinai Peninsula towards Canaan, they would have come to Lake Bardawil, and if the wonder/plagues of darkness, ash, and blisters were as a result of the Minoan eruption, then the Lake would have almost certainly have been covered in ash, which would have taken much longer to settle in the highly saline waters than sand. In some regions of northern Egypt, the ash-fall was up to 2 meters deep, which would have likely formed a type of loose cement on top of Lake Bardawil, which, the Israelites could have passed over if they were spread out as expected of a nomadic horde of people mostly traveling on foot, and herding animals. Pharaoh's army, on the other hand, included 600 war-chariots, along with cavalry and infantry, which one would assume were traveling in tight formations. This concentrated weight could have easily broken through the ash layer, shattering it like ice on a river, causing the entire army to be swallowed up, and explaining why the Greeks had a story of a Nile monster (Apophis) being at the bottom of the lake nowhere near the Nile. This story was specifically Greek, and not based on an Egyptian legend, implying the Ba'al Zephon worshiping Canaanites witnessed the event and told the Greeks.

According to the Exodus narrative, the 'princes of Edom and the chiefs of the Moabites' also witnessed the event, and then ran away, presumably back to Edom and Moab, in western and northwestern modern Jordan. These princes and chiefs were not called kings, as Moab and Edom would have been part of the Hyksos' empire, which also explains why they were there. Egyptian armies were advancing from both the Nile and Canaan, trying to trap the Israelites. After the events of the 'Papyrus Sea,' the Israelites suddenly turned back, and headed toward the Nile Delta, and traveled south to the Bitter Lakes, which the Greek translators did understand, both translating the Hebrew word mrh (מרה) as Picria (πικρια), and transliterating it as Merrha (Μερρα). The Bitter Lakes are a group of lakes that are today along the route of the Suez Canal, and in the times of the Ptolemies along the route of the Arsinoe Canal. Aristotle, Strabo, and others claimed that there had been several attempts to dig a canal linking the Bitter Lakes to the Nile, and then to the Gulf of Suez, including attempts by Pharaoh Senusret III in the Middle Kingdom, Pharaoh Necho II circa 600 BC, and Darius the Great when Persia ruled Egypt.

The Bitter Lakes were known by the Egyptian translation of 'Bitter Lakes' since at least the Old Kingdom era, and the Hebrews, Persians, and Greeks all translated the name into their own languages, meaning it is fairly certain that these are the Bitter Waters the Israelites traveled to after leaving the coast. The logical reason for turning back was that the Hyksos armies in Canaan had not been destroyed at Lake Bardawil, and while they had fled in terror, they still existed. Therefore, the Israelites would have turned back, and traveled to the Bitter Lakes to cross the Sinai Peninsula following the dry southern route, which ran from the northern coast of the Gulf of Suez to the northern coast of the Gulf of Aqaba. This route was well established by the Middle Kingdom and was almost certainly the route that Moses would have taken from Egypt to Midian the first time he went there.

The next stop along the route the Israelites took was called Ailim (Αιλιμ) in the Octateuch and Eilim (אֵילִם) in the Masoretic texts. It was most likely an attempt to translate an Egyptian name that has subsequently been lost. Most Christian and Islamic scholars, following Helena August's divine revelation, believe that Mount Sinai is in Southern Sinai, however, this location was chosen by Emperor Constantine's mother when he founded the Imperial Church in the 330s AD. As a result of Christian and Islamic scholars following the 'revelation' of the Emperor's mother, southern Sinai is covered in locations that are linked to Moses and the Exodus in folklore.

The logical route away from Egypt for a band of runaway slaves, would not have been to head south into the heavily garrisoned southern Sinai, where the Egyptians were forcing slaves to work at turquoise mines, but east across the Sinai following the southern road, towards Midian, where Moses had previously lived for decades. In the middle of the Sinai Peninsula is a town today known as An-Nekhel, which lays halfway along the ancient southern road. Archaeological evidence indicates it was used as a watering hole since Pharaonic times. It is postulated to have been a Canaanite town, founded during the Hyksos era, named after the Canaanite goddess Nikkal-wa-Ib, meaning 'Great lady of the Fruitful,' who was the goddess of orchards. If this theory is correct, then there must have been a settlement with orchards in the region, matching to some degree the Exodus' description of a place of wells and trees. It is also believed a garrison was built in the region by the Thebans after they conquered the Hyksos. The settlement was called Du Mafkat, but its exact location is unknown. Nevertheless, there were watering holes in the areas at the time, which would have made it an excellent place to stop along the southern road.

From Elim, they continued on through the Wilderness of Sin en route to the Sinai, although the route in Numbers has them passing the Red Sea before arriving at the Sinai. Continuing east along the southern road, which appears to be the Wilderness of Sin, they would have reached the northern shore of the Gulf of Aqaba, before turning north into the Valley of Arabah, which appears to be the Masoretic Wilderness of Tzin. The Wilderness of Sin (Σιν) is the translation in the Octateuch for both the Masoretic Wilderness of Sin (סִ֔ן) in Exodus and the Wilderness of Tzin (צִ֔ן) in Numbers, which was followed by Jerome in the Latin Vulgate as the Wilderness of Sin. This suggests that the Aramaic version of the Torah did not differentiate between the two. As the book of Numbers was likely organized into its current state during the era of King Josiah's reforms, and it was almost certainly written in the Phoenician script that was in use in Judah at the time, it is likely that it more accurately records the two locations as separate places. In Numbers chapter 33, they are both listed in the long sequence of stops the Israelites made as they traveled from Egypt, confirming that the Hebrew translator, and probably the Phoenician (Paleo-Hebrew) compiler of the original book of Numbers viewed them as separate places.

Conversely, Exodus shows clear signs of having been written in Akkadian cuneiform, which is likely where the pronunciation of Sin is derived, ultimately from the Akkadian spelling of Sīn, which was spelled in Aramaic as Syn (𐤎𐤉𐤍), the direct transliteration of the Hebrew Syn (סין). While the Aramaic spelling would have been standardized by the common spelling of the name of the moon god, there was nothing to standardize the spelling of the toponym in the Phoenician script, resulting in both toponyms being rendered phonetically by the scribes that unified the stories found in Numbers into a book circa 625 BC.

If the Wilderness of Tzin (צִ֔ן) was the southern Arabah Valley, the dry valley between the Gulf of Aqaba and the Dead Sea, it means they were back in the vicinity of Midian, which would explain why Jethro, Moses father-in-law came to visit them. The story of Exodus does include one strange detail that deviates from the rest of the Torah, it identifies Mount Horeb as being at Rephidim (רפידים / Ραφιδιν), a hill or mountain at the edge of the Wilderness of Sin, just before they reached the Gulf of Aqaba (Red Sea). At this mountain, Moses made a spring flow, as there was no water in the region. The Greek translators translated the Aramaic text as 'in Horeb,' which is also how the Hebrew translation could be interpreted, supporting the Aramaic text as being essentially the same as the Hebrew, and reading as bhrb. Unfortunately, the Greek translation does not make sense, as they were not near Mount Horeb at the time. An alternate reading of the Hebrew and Aramaic translations would be 'with a sword,' or 'with a plowshare,' neither of which probably made sense to the Greek translators, and so they opted for Horeb. This appears to be a misunderstanding of the underlying Akkadian cuneiform text, in which the word ḫarbum referred to a specialized heavy plow used to break up hard dry soil, as opposed to a lighter plow which was used to make furrows in fields. The name of this tool was spelled as ḥrb in Aramaic, however, that word also meant any form of plow, sword, or spear. In this case, the Lord was apparently offering Moses a tool to break up the hard soil and allow the water to flow.

Based on their path through the Sinai Peninsula, the mountain in question seems to be Hashem El Tarif, a mountain in the eastern Sinai along the southern road, just before one would reach the Gulf of Aqaba. Hashem El Tarif would have been one of the markers used by people crossing the desert before paved highways and GPS, as it rose above the otherwise flat horizon, and was near the northern coast of the Gulf of Aqaba, meaning they would have reached it as they left the Wilderness of Sin and reached the sea. Hashem El Tarif is certainly close enough to Midian that Moses could have ventured that far while shepherding Jethro's flocks and is far more likely a locality for the original interaction with the fiery-messenger than the mountains in the southern Sinai peninsula, which were occupied by the Egyptians. Additionally, it is plausible he would move his flock that far west, hoping to hear news from Egypt, which is what ultimately happened. Hashem El Tarif is somewhat unusual as it did have a spring near the top of it that once flowed down one side, which could have been the source of the story about Moses opening the spring. Additionally, there is the issue of the Amalekites attacking the Israelites at Rephidim, which makes no sense in the traditional interpretation of everything happening in the southern Sinai Peninsula, as the Amakelites lived in the Negev, directly north of Hashem El Tarif.

From Rephidim, the Israelites moved through the Wilderness of Sinai to Mount Sinai, where God came down and gave them the commandments. If one accepts Josephus' location near Petra, and Deborah's referring to it as Mount Seir in the Book of Judges, then its location is the Mountain of the Altar, Jebel al-Madhbah in southwest Jordan. This site has been associated with the exodus story since pre-Christian times and includes a Valley of Moses (Wadi Musa) and Spring of Moses (Ain Musa) that have been associated with the exodus story since ancient times.

This still leaves the question of who were the Israelites? The earliest mention of them is from the time of Pharaoh Merneptah, circa 1200 BC, where they are implied to be a nomadic people, and listed alongside the towns of Ashkelon, Gezer, and Yenoam, two of which are known to have been in southernmost Canaan. The location of Yenoam is unknown, with possible locations suggested throughout modern Israel and as far north as Syria. Nevertheless, if the Israelites left Egypt around the time of the Minoan eruption they should have been noted, somewhere. The only group tentatively identified as Israelites before the time of Merneptah, is the Shasu of Yhǔ, believed to have been in the Seir Mountains. This identification is debatable, as Shasu is the Egyptian word for nomads, and Yhǔ is a place name.

Several other groups of nomads were listed with the Shasu of Yhǔ, including the Shasu of Sôr, Rbn (or Lbn), Smôt, Ůrbr, and Pysps. These names do indicate the Seir Mountains, and possibly the Tribe of Ruben, and the Canaanite solar-goddess Shapash, however, even this is speculation. They were mentioned in the el-Amarna Letters, dated to between 1360 and 1332 BC, which still leaves a 200-year gap between the Minoan eruption and the first mention of the Shasu of Yhǔ. This gap is less significant than it appears if one considers that after the Hyksos left Egypt, they also disappeared, entirely. According to the 3rd century BC Egyptian historian and priest Manetho, when the Hyksos surrendered Avaris, the Egyptians let 240,000 Hyksos families leave, who returned to Canaan. The Egyptians then occupied Canaan a few decades later, and apparently, there were no Hyksos there. If they didn't record where the Hyksos went, why would they record where a bunch of slaves that ran away from the Hyksos went?

Josephus claimed to have found records in Egypt of Moses, which modern Egyptologists have not found, either because they have not survived, or because he was lying about them. Josephus claimed that the Egyptians did record the flight of Moses, who led a band of lepers out of Egypt, but he did not believe that Moses and those lepers were the ancestors of the Israelites. He believed the ancestors of the Israelites were the Hyksos, and the story about the leper-leader had somehow become mixed up with the story of the Hyksos leaving Egypt. If records about the leper-leader Moses existed, they would have no doubt been destroyed by Christians or Muslims at some point, nevertheless, Egyptologists generally dismiss the claim that they existed.

The fact that the Egyptians called them a band of lepers is irrelevant propaganda, however, Josephus' Hyksos theory has also been refuted by Egyptologists as well as Biblical scholars, as the Hyksos snake-god (Apophis) and a storm-god (Set), is nothing like the Israelite God. While it seems likely the Israelites were in Hyksos-controlled Egypt, they seem more likely the band of runaway slaves that escaped during the Minoan eruption than the deposed Pharaoh. The last

Hyksos Pharaoh, Apepi's heir Khamudi, fought a series of losing wars until the only region of Egypt he held was the fortified city of Avaris. When he surrendered the city, the Hyksos fell back to the fortified city of Sharuhen in the Negev or Gaza Strip, about 3 years after the Minoan eruption. Sharuhen was then conquered by the Egyptians too, and Khamudi retreated north, with evidence that he passed through Jericho and possibly Byblos before disappearing from history. This is not the story found in Exodus. Even if the Hyksos refugees did contribute to the gene-pool that became the later Israelite tribes, the story in Exodus is the story of Moses and his runaway slaves, not the story of the fall of the Hyksos Dynasty.

The Octateuch's book of Joshua also has the first reference to Sabaoth (Σαβαωθ) in chapter 6, as Lord Sabaoth (Κυρίω Σαβαωθ). Lord Sabaoth was the Judahite God during the rule of the Greeks, whom the Greeks equated with Dionysus, and the Romans equated with Bacchus. In Aramaic, the language which was spoken in Judea during the Persian and Greek eras, Ådny Ṣbå (אדני צבא) meant 'lord of desires,' however, when the Hasmonean Dynasty seized control of Judea and made the newly invented 'ancient' Hebrew language official, they changed the meaning of the word to 'military' or 'army,' making the Lord of Desires into the Lord of War.

The Hebrew word transliterated as Sabaoth, which the Greeks and Romans treated as the proper name of the Judean god, is a military term, roughly meaning 'army' or 'military.' As such, the fusion of the Hasmonean god Yahweh with Sabaoth created a militaristic version of Yahweh, a war-god, for a warrior-dynasty. The Hasmoneans may have promoted Yahweh Sabaoth, however, in Joshua, Sabaoth is not called Iaw Sabaoth, but Lord Sabaoth. This cannot be as a result of the Christian redaction of the name Iaô (Ιαω) in the 3rd century, as the Masoretic Text only have Yahweh, not Yahweh Sabaoth. Lord Sabaoth is only mentioned once in Joshua, with all other references to Lord the god, the Lord, or God. He was mentioned when the Israelites were preparing to attack Jericho, however, his Generalissimo (ἀρχιστράτηγοσ) was introduced clumsily at the end of the previous chapter.

> When Joshua was in Jericho, that he looked up with his eyes and saw a man standing before him, and there was a drawn sword in his hand, and Joshua approached and said to him, "Are you with us, or on the side of our enemies?"

> He answered him, "I have now come, the Generalissimo of the army of the

Lord."

Joshua fell on his face to the earth, and said to him, "Lord, what do you command of your servant?"

The Generalissimo of the Lord said to Joshua, "Remove your shoes off your feet, for the place on which you now stand is sacred."

This section of the text does not line up with the text before it or after it. Joshua's people had not attacked Jericho yet, and the Israelites were not in the city. Moreover, if the city was sacred, God should not have destroyed it. This section of text appears to have either been added to the original text, or to be a relic of another, possibly older version of the Jericho story. However it came to be in the book of Joshua, it is in both the Octateuch's and Masoretic version of Joshua, meaning it must have been in the Aramaic version. This Generalissimo of the army of the Lord, appears to be Lord Sabaoth, the 'Lord of War' in Canaanite and Hebrew, mentioned in the next chapter, meaning that he was not God, but a soldier sent by the Lord, or a lord, to Jericho, which was apparently sacred to the lord in question.

This reference to a Lord other than God is consistent with the early Israelite religion before the reforms of King Josiah circa 625 BC when there were many Lords worshiped in Judah. The reforms that took place in Judah under Josiah were both extreme and lasting, as the god Yahweh continues to be the God of Judaism today. Nevertheless, he has not always been the god of the Judahites. The Septuagint's 1st Ezra recounts how after killing King Josiah, the Pharaoh Necho II restored the worship of the 'Lord' in Judah, which could only be a reference to the sun god Amen, which Necho II is recorded as worshiping in Egyptian records, along with the North Egyptian version of Amen known as Atum. The Septuagint's book of Baruch, written by the scribe Baruch in Babylon after Nebuchadnezzar II had destroyed Jerusalem a couple of decades later, describes his god as the sun, meaning that sun worship had been restored in Judah after Josiah's death. Throughout the subsequent Persian and Greek rules of Judea, several gods were reportedly worshiped in Jerusalem, including Ahura Mazda, the Zoroastrian God, and Lord Sabaoth, who seems to have been very different from the militaristic interpretation of the Hasmonean Yahweh of Armies.

The 'Hebrew' language of the Hasmonean Dynasty, was a reformed version of the southern Canaanite dialect spoken in Judea and Edom, written with a specific form of the Aramaic script that the Judeans called 'Assyrian' in the Talmud. While it was a new language in that the Hasmonean Dynasty appear to have been the first government that attempted to standardize it, it was quite similar to both the surviving forms of Ugaritic Canaanite from the Bronze Age, and Phoenician Canaanite from the Iron Age, meaning other than changing the name and script to something that didn't sound or look too Carthaginian, the language was essentially the same as Bronze Age Canaanite. Therefore, the original reference in Joshua to Lord Sabaoth was probably to a military commander, and not a magic genie, like the Aramaic version appears to have read.

The question of who this military commander was, at Jericho, in 1508 BC according to the Septuagint's chronology is generally ignored by those that assume it was God or a supernatural warrior sent by God, however, it is a matter of record that the army of Thutmose I marched through Canaan in the year 1505 BC, using the standard chronology of Egyptian history, and found no one to fight them. According to the archaeological record, the city of Jericho was destroyed sometime shortly before 1500 BC, and not rebuilt until the Iron Age. It is generally accepted that the Egyptian army destroyed the city, although Thutmose I did not report visiting the city himself, and would have mentioned destroying the city. There is no record of an Egyptian military expedition in 1508 BC, however, Egypt was not the only power at the time interested in Canaan, as between 1540 and 1500 BC the Mitanni Empire was rapidly expanding into northern Canaan. It is possible that the Generalissimo was a Mitanni war-chief.

While many scholars have questioned the age of the Book of Joshua, most of the criticism against it seems misdirected at the Hebrew translation, which must date to sometime between 140 and 37 BC. Like the Octateuch's books of Exodus and Job, and the Masoretic book of Exodus, the Octateuch's book of Joshua contains relics of an Akkadian cuneiform version of Joshua that had to predate the Aramaic. At one point when describing the travels of the Israelites after leaving Egypt, the Greek translation uses the term 'the desert the Madbaritidi' (τῇ ἐρήμω τῇ Μαδβαρίτιδι), where the Hebrew translation simply refers to 'the desert' (במדבר). At a later, point the Greek translation uses the term Madbaritis (Μαδβαρῖτισ) as a proper name were the Hebrew translation has 'desert' (מדבר). The first half of both terms found in the Greek translation is clearly the same term the Hebrew translators translated as mdbr (מדבר), meaning desert. In Aramaic, the word was mdbrå (לῐּ), later pronounced as maḏbrā (ܡܕܒܪܐ) in Syriac, the Late-Classical form of Aramaic. The Aramaic term was derived from the Akkadian Cuneiform term madbaru (𒈥𒁁𒊑), also meaning 'desert,' or 'wilderness.'

Conversely, the second half of both words is neither Greek nor Aramaic. It is also not Canaanite or Hebrew. The second half of both words appear to be transliterated Akkadian cuneiform. The second part of Madbaritidi, itidi (ιτιδι), appears to be a Greek transliteration of an Aramaic transliteration of the Akkadian cuneiform term generally transliterated today as itiātu, meaning boundaries, environs, or region. This would make the original text read 'edge of the desert' in Akkadian Cuneiform. The second part of Madbaritis, itis (ἱτισ), appears to be a Greek transliteration of an Aramaic transliteration of the Akkadian cuneiform term generally transliterated today as ita, meaning 'adjacent to,' with a Greek s (σ) at the end, interpreting it as a toponym in the Greek language. This would make the original text read madbaru ita in Akkadian Cuneiform, meaning 'adjacent to the desert.'

As these transliterations must have already been present in the Aramaic version of Joshua, it means the Aramaic version of Joshua was translated from a cuneiform source. A slightly modified form of Akkadian cuneiform was used in Canaan during the Egyptian New Kingdom era, as demonstrated by the Amarna Letters between the Egyptian court and their subjects in Canaan. If the original Book of Joshua was written during or shortly after the life of Joshua, it would have been written in Cuneiform, which these words seem to confirm.

There are other references in Joshua that point to the authorship of Joshua, or at least parts of it, in the Late Bronze Age. Specifically, the treatment of iron. Prior to the Bronze-Age collapse, circa 1200 BC, iron was rare in the Middle East and mainly used for jewelry. This treatment of iron as a valuable metal shows up in Joshua at the Battle of Jericho, when Joshua orders:

> "All the silver, or gold, or brass, or iron, will be holy to the Lord. It will be carried into the treasury of the Lord."

Later, however, iron is treated as a common metal used in chariots, indicating that the Book of Joshua was added to later during the iron age, likely in the centuries before King Josiah's time, when the Israelites were worshiping many gods. The reference to the sun and the moon standing still in the sky would have meant something different to the pre-Josiah Israelites, as Shemesh and Yarikh were gods, but were obeying Joshua. As the author put it:

"The sun and the moon stood still until God executed vengeance on their enemies, and the sun stood still in the middle of the sky. It did not proceed to set until
the end of one day. There was not a day like it either before or after, that god
should listen to man..."

This places the pre-Hasmonean redaction of Joshua before the time of Josiah,
likely when the text was originally translated from cuneiform into Aramaic in
the Kingdom of Samaria. The geographical references cover all of Canaan from
Egypt to Syria, and so it is not easy to place a geographical origin to the text. It
does, however, contradict the books of the Kingdoms, as it has Joshua conquering
Jebus (Jerusalem), and not David. This would point to a Samaritan origin, as the
Samaritans never accepted the city of Jerusalem as having been the capital of
Israel, instead claiming that Shechem, and later the city of Samaria were the
capital. If the text was translated into Aramaic in Samaria, this would have been
between 930 and 720 BC. Nevertheless, some sections of the text must date back
to before the Bronze Age collapse, to explain the value placed on iron.

The longer ending of Joshua is also found in some copies of the Septuagint and
is included in this translation. In it, the Israelites turned away from worshiping
Lord the god and started worshiping Astarte, Athtart, and the gods of the nations
around them, resulting in God withdrawing his protection, and the Israelites
being conquered by the Moabites. These two short verses end the book very
differently from the Masoretic version, in which the Israelites are, presumably,
still worshiping Lord the god, and live happily ever after. The paring of Astarte
and Athtart (Ἀστάρτην καὶ Ασταρωθ) also dates the text to the late Bronze Age,
as, by the early Iron Age, Astarte and Athtart had merged into the goddess
simply called Qetesh, meaning 'holiness.'

The two goddesses mentioned are the wives of El from the Bronze Age
Ugaritic texts: Åṯrt (►►{⊨►►─), later called Asherah (אשרה) by the Israelites; and
Ôṭtrt-ym ({{►─⊨►─ן╫׀ן), later called , later called Ôštrt (⫟⤳⫟ᴡᴏ) by the Phoenicians, Astarte (Ἀστάρτη) by the Greeks, and Ashtoret (עַשְׁתֹּרֶת) by the Israelites.
The Phoenician Ôštrt (⫟⤳⫟ᴡᴏ) was descended from Ôṭtrt-ym ({{►─⊨►─ן╫׀ן), the
sea goddess which also gave rise to Aphrodite, while the Israelite Åšrh (אשרה)
was descended from Åṯrt (►►{⊨►►─), the goddess of the land. In the early
Canaanite mythology, the sea and land appear to have been viewed as the two
wives of El, the bull in the sky. During the Egyptian New Kingdoms era, which
took place at the same time as the events in the books of Joshua and Judges, the
two goddesses merged, along with the Egyptian goddess Hathor, into Qetesh, a

goddess that assumed the 'sky goddess' role of Hathor, which seems to have been how the Israelites viewed her until King Josiah's reforms of circa 625 BC. This merger of Astarte and Asherah clearly dates the authorship of Joshua to the early New Kingdom Era, circa 1500 BC.

The general view of both historians and biblical scholars is that the Book of Joshua holds no historical value, and is simply a book written during the life of Josiah, or during the Babylonian captivity, or even later by Ezra during the Second Temple Era, however, this is based on analysis of the Masoretic version of the book, which is quite different from the Octateuch's version. In Rabbinical history, as a century and a half have been redacted, Joshua's life is dated to the early-1300s BC, instead of the late-1500s BC. This era does not align with anything found in the archaeological record, and therefore the book reads like fiction. Likewise, the Masoretic version is about a god named Yahweh, a name not known to archaeology until around 800 BC, meaning that the Book of Joshua, if the Masoretic version were the original, would have to have been written after that time.

The Octateuch's version is quite different in the details, as the god of the book is Lord the god, almost certainly a translation of the term adonai ha'elohim found in the Aramaic sections of Daniel, and the title of the god El who the ancient Canaanites were worshiping in the 2nd millennium BC. Joshua's invasion of Canaan circa 1508 BC, 42 years after the Minoan Eruption, would also place the Israelites at Jericho at around the time the walls were torn down.

The ruins of Jericho were identified as the mound at Tell es-Sultan in 1869, and this is still generally accepted as ancient Jericho. The city was a major trading center, and heavily fortified city for thousands of years, until circa 1500 BC when the walls were torn down. The exact date when the walls were torn down is unclear, with estimates ranging from 1700 to 1400 BC, however, 1500 BC is the most widely quoted date. In approximately 1504 BC the Egyptian King Thutmose I led an expedition through Canaan and Syria to the Euphrates River, and it is assumed by many historians that he ripped down the walls of Jericho, however, that is not possible. Thutmose recorded that he found no one to fight him in Canaan, and the local peoples submitted to Egyptian power without conflict. Moreover, later the same year he launched his invasion of Nubia, to the south of Egypt, meaning he simply did not have time to secretly lay siege to Jericho. This pacified Canaan ruled by people who were afraid of the Egyptians is consistent with the account in Joshua, however, the Egyptian 'invasion' is not mentioned in Joshua. Given the history between the Israelites and Egyptians, it is not unlikely it would have been omitted, especially if there was no war, and the Israelites surrendered to the Egyptians without a fight.

After 1500 BC the people in Canaan, whoever they were, began fortifying their cities. Thutmose I's heir, Thutmose II, also sent an expedition into Canaan and Syria, and crossed the Euphrates, however, only reported fighting nomads in the Sinai. There are no records of his successor, Queen Hatshepsut invading Canaan. Her heir Thutmose III did send multiple armies through Canaan demanding tribute, however, these campaigns appear to have been mostly peaceful until around 1450 BC, when he marched his army into northern Canaan to invade Syria and occupied all of Canaan in the process. The cities of Kadesh on the Orontes (in modern Syria), and Byblos in modern Lebanon, are mentioned as being major conquests of his campaigns, which laid the foundation for his later attack on the Mitanni Empire in Syria.

After Thutmose's campaign, the region was formally part of the Egyptian Empire for centuries, however, Egyptian records show they generally left the people alone and did not exert much control over the region beyond demanding regular tribute. The Egyptian records show there were many local chieftains during this era, sometimes fighting each other, or a people called the Habiru, which some believe to be an ancient reference to the Hebrews. This era of nominal Egyptian occupation would be the era of the Judges when the Israelites had no king. Obviously, if they did not have a king, they were a subjugated people.

Supporters of the earlier dating for the tearing down of Jericho's walls, generally assume the Hyksos dynasty ripped them down at some point, and as there are few records from the era, it cannot be proven or disproved. Nevertheless, after the walls were ripped down the site was reoccupied briefly, and a small town was present at the ruins until circa 1500 BC, in the dating when the walls were ripped down between 1700 and 1600 BC. In the dating when the walls were ripped down circa 1500, this village existed until circa 1400 BC. In either event, the village was destroyed by someone. If the earlier dating for the walls being torn down is correct, then the walls were already torn down when Joshua's army arrived, and they simply destroyed a small unfortified settlement in the ruins of the ancient city. In that scenario, the story about the walls falling when the Israelites shouted at them was a later fictional element added at some point. However, in either case, whether the Israelites tore down the walls or not, a city or village was destroyed at Jericho circa 1500 BC, according to the archaeological evidence, supporting both the dating of the Minoan eruption in Exodus, and the invasion of Canaan by the Israelites right before the Egyptians occupied the region.

The Israelite invasion of Canaan circa 1508 BC could have been as one-sided as the Book of Joshua depicts it, as the region was divided among many petty 'kings' that emerged from the collapse of the Hyksos Dynasty circa 1540 BC, when their last fortified city, Sharuhen, fell to the armies of Pharaoh Ahmose I. The siege of Sharuhen took the Egyptian army three years, and it was significantly smaller than the ancient fortified city of Jericho, proving Thutmose I could not have leveled Jericho in a few weeks. Between 1540 BC, when Sharuhen fell, and 1450 BC, when Thutmose III formally annexed Canaan into his empire in prelude to his invasion of the Mitanni Empire, the region was in chaos by all accounts, and any resistance the Israelites would have encountered circa 1508 BC would have been minimal and unorganized. The kings they fought would have been in power for less than 40 years, and likely had little control over their dominions.

The Egyptian records report the region was divided among many tribes when they passed through the region in 1504 BC, which, does support the idea that there were 12 autonomous tribes at the time, along with subjugated Hurrians and Canaanites, as described in the Book of Joshua. Some of the names of the tribes are archaeologically attested, such as Dan and Gad, however, most are not, leading to speculation that they may have been later inventions. However, the Egyptians did not have consistent and universal names for countries. For example, the Egyptians called the Mitanni kingdom Naharin, Maryannu, and Mitanni. Naharin is believed to have been adopted from the Akkadian word for 'river,' making it a geographical name. In this case, it appears an Egyptian asked a local what the river was called, and applied the word 'river' to the entire land. This would make sense to an Egyptian, as the Nile was the only river in Egypt.

The name Maryannu is derived from the name of the Indo-Aryan rulers of the Mitanni Empire, known as 'marya' in Mitanni-Aryan, which translates as 'warrior' in Sanskrit. This was the political name of the land, which would have made sense to someone addressing a Pharaoh, as Egypt was his land. The name

Mitanni, or 'me-ta-ni' in ancient Egyptian, appears to be a direct transliteration of the local name, however, was the rarest name they used for the land. Therefore, there is no reason to assume the Israelites were either present in Canaan or absent from Canaan, based on the Egyptian records.

Based on the various references to the Israelites worshiping Ba'al, Asherah, Shamayim, Shemesh, Yarikh, and many other Canaanite gods found in the books of Joshua, Judges, and the books of the Kingdoms, as well as the books of the prophets, it is unlikely the Egyptians would have been able to distinguish them from the Canaanites. Modern archaeologists cannot. Until the era of Josiah, the Israelites appear to have been no different from the Canaanites they supposedly conquered, and most archaeologists doubt there was an invasion. There was the well-documented pillaging of the Habiru, recorded in hundreds of surviving documents from the 2nd millennium BC, by the Canaanites, Egyptians, Akkadians, and Sumerians. These people started out in Sumer and were described as a group of Aramaean nomads that attacked undefended villages and plundered the countryside. Between 1800 and 1200 BC, they lived outside of the major Empires and pillaged the outskirts of Sumer, Akkadia, Babylonia, Assyria, and Canaan.

They were generally described as being murderers and thieves, however, also worked as mercenaries. Based on the Tikunani Prism from around 1550 BC, the majority were Hurrian at the time, although Semitic names were the second most common.

In later centuries Indo-Aryan names appeared among them, likely of Mitanni origin. Many have tried to link the history of the Habiru to the Hebrews, and while the names may be connected, there is no evidence of the Habiru having a common god, tribe, or goal. They operated as 'land pirates' marauding their way across the Middle East. In the Amarna Letters, from circa 1350 BC, the warlord Labaya, the ruler of Shechem, one of Egypt's petty kingdoms, hired Habiru as mercenaries and allowed them to settle in Shechem, meaning that if the Israelites were settled in Shechem by that time, they were not the Habiru. These Habiru settlers did nevertheless contribute to the developing Israelite identity and would have been part of the United Kingdom of Israel if it existed, and the later Kingdom of Samaria. In the Torah, the Israelites were a subset of Hebrews, as Abraham was a Hebrew, however, only the descendants of Jacob were Israelites. It is plausible that the Israelites were a group of Habiru that settled in Egypt under the Hyksos, however, it is equally plausible the name Hebrew was added to the Torah during Josiah's redaction.

The Book of Joshua is itself a continuation of the story found in Numbers and Deuteronomy, themselves both continuations of the story found in Exodus. Specifically, it appears to be a direct continuation of Deuteronomy, which it may have originally been part of, as the closing verses of Deuteronomy and opening verses of Joshua fit together seamlessly.

So Moses the servant of the Lord died in the land of Moab by the word of the Lord. They buried him in Gai near the Temple of Peor, and no one has seen his sepulcher to this day. Moses was a hundred and twenty years old at his death, yet his eyes were not dimmed, nor were his natural powers destroyed. The children of Israel wept for Moses in Araboth of Moab at the Jordan near Jericho for thirty days, and the days of the sad mourning for Moses were completed.

Joshua the son of Nun was filled with the spirit of knowledge, for Moses had laid his hands on him, and the children of Israel listened to him, and they did as the Lord commanded Moses. There did not rise another prophet in Israel like Moses, whom the Lord knew face to face, in all the signs and wonders, which the Lord sent him to work in Egypt against Pharaoh and his servants and all his land, and the great wonders, and the mighty hand which Moses displayed before all Israel.

After the death of Moses, the Lord said to Joshua the son of Nun, the minister of Moses, "Moses my servant is dead. Now then rise, go across the Jordan, you and all these people, into the land which I give them. Every place on which you will step I will give to you, as I told Moses. The wilderness and Anti-Lebanon, as far as the great river, the river Euphrates, and as far as the farthest sea, your coasts will be at the setting of the sun. Not a man will stand against you all the days of your life, and as I was with Moses, so will I also be with you, and I will not fail you, or neglect you. Be strong and act like a man, as you will divide the land among these people, which I swore to give to your fathers. Be strong, therefore, and act like a man, and observe and do as Moses my servant commanded you. You will not turn from them to the right hand or the left, that you may be wise in whatever you may do. The book of this law will not leave out of your mouth, and you will meditate on it day and night, that you may know how to do all the things that are written in it. Then you will prosper, and make your ways prosperous, and then you will be wise. Look! I have commanded you 'Be strong and courageous, do not be cowardly nor fearful, for Lord the god is with you in all places, to wherever you go.'"

Joshua commanded the scribes of the people, "Go into the middle of the camp of the people, and command the people, 'Prepare provisions, for in three days you will go across the Jordan, enter into and take possession of the land, which Lord the god of your fathers gives to you."

Joshua also restates the division of the land of Canaan between the twelve tribes, which is previously covered in Numbers but goes into much more depth, stipulating the exact borders of the tribes. This implies that Joshua may have been one of the sources that the Levites used when they cobbled together Numbers for King Josiah. The fact that Deuteronomy and Joshua fit together so seamlessly, indicates it was likely compiled into its pre-Hasmonean form in the Kingdom of Samaria, where Deuteronomy almost certainly originated. Several factors support the book as pre-Josiah and likely ignored entirely by Josiah's reforms, most especially the references to the sun (Shemesh) and moon (Yarikh) obeying Joshua, or possibly Lord the god, depending on interpretation. After Josiah's reforms, the sun and moon were just the sun and moon, two big lights up in the sky that could not listen to anyone. Before his reforms, they were two of the most powerful gods, Shemesh and Yarikh. Certainly, he would not have allowed the heretical implication that they were hearing and thinking and choosing to obey anyone.

The Book of Joshua has traditionally been very unpopular, both with Jews and Christians, and only 3 copies have been found to date among the Dead Sea Scrolls, compared to 22 for Genesis, 17 for Exodus, 15 for Leviticus, 13 for Numbers, and 33 for Deuteronomy. Even Judges and Ruth were more popular with 4 copies of each discovered among the Dead Sea Scrolls. This unpopularity is generally attributed to the 'heroic' genocidal warfare described, which is the antithesis of Christianity and modern Judaism. Many Christian denominations issue advisories for members reading Joshua, printed directly in their bibles, to 'not take the history seriously,' 'it did not happen,' and to 'focus on the spiritual message.' However, there is little spiritual in the book, other than the first appearance of Lord Sabaoth, who became Yahweh Sabaoth in the Hasmonean redaction.

The Book of Judges does not reference Lord Sabaoth or Yahweh Sabaoth in either the Octateuch or the Masoretic Text, however, the name Yhůh is found throughout the Masoretic version of Judges. The Lord Sabaoth of Joshua is referred to as the generalissimo of the Lord, implying an angelic being of some kind. He appeared at Jericho before Joshua's forces destroyed the city, and is therefore implicated in the destruction of the cities walls, which archaeologists have dated to around 1500 BC, when Joshua's forces invaded Samaria according to the chronology of the Septuagint. In the later book of the prophet Zachariah, Lord Sabaoth (Adon Sabaoth) is the name of a messenger/angel, which appears to be related to the messenger of the lord in the Book of Judges.

The Book of Judges also includes many other gods, which the ancient Israelites are repeatedly accused of worshiping, including Ba'al, Asherah, and the Lords (Baalim) and Ashteroths of the Canaanites. Several of the Canaanite gods are mentioned incidentally, such as the fertility god Lord Lahem, the god of dusk Lord Shalim, the solar-god Lord Shemesh, and the grain-god Dagon. All these gods are part of the old Canaanite religion, in which El (Lord God) and his wife Asherah (commonly called Qetesh) were the parents of the Canaanite gods. The term ba'al translates as lord, however, when used as a name, it generally repre- sented Lord Hadad, the storm god of the Ba'al Cycle literature of the ancient Ugaritic texts in ancient Canaan. The Ugaritic Texts continued to be used well into the era of the ancient kingdoms of Samaria and Judah, as the prophet Jeremiah quoted them circa 630 BC. Additionally, the name of the Egyptian god Aten appears to have been in the Book of Judges before Aten was forgotten as a god. The name appears twice, once in the Song of Deborah, in chapter 5, and later as part of the name of a town in chapter 12:

> "You who move as Aten the sun god at midday, sitting in judgment, and follow- ing the path, and riding the pathway, declare from the noise of disturbers among the drawers of water, and retell the righteous acts of the Lord. Increase righteous acts in Israel, then the people of the Lord will go down to the cities."

> "After him, Abdon the son of Hillel, a Per-Atenite, judged Israel. He had forty sons, and thirty grandsons, that rode on seventy colts, and he judged Israel eight years. Abdon the son of Hillel, the Per-Atenite, died and was buried in Per-Aten in the land of Ephraim in the mountains of Amalek."

In both cases, a word that appears to be a transliteration of Aten survives in the Masoretic Text, although is considered an unknown term, and has been viewed that way for thousands of years. The Book of Judges contains more unknown terms than any other book in the Masoretic Text and the most archaic form of Canaanite other than in the Book of Job. Judges is considered by most biblical scholars to be the oldest book in the Masoretic Text, composed earlier than the surviving versions of the Torah, or Joshua.

Nevertheless, the version in the Masoretic Text still suffers from the damage done by the Hasmonean dynasty and therefore does not align with the recorded history of the Egyptians, Assyrians, or Babylonians, causing many historians to consider it to be a collection of very ancient fictional stories. On the other hand, the Octateuch's version of Exodus, Joshua, and Judges contain a different chronology from the Masoretic Text, covering 460 years from the time of the Exodus, circa 1550 BC, to the era of chaos that started in 1090 BC, and would later end in 1037 BC when Saul became the first king of the independent Kingdom of Israel.

Saul was not the first king of the Israelites, as Abimelech had previously been recognized as King of Israel a couple of centuries earlier. Abimelech's reign had only been for three years and seems to have only controlled the region around Shechem, the city that would later become the capital of Saul's Israel. This earlier attempt at an independent kingdom took place between 1267 and 1264 BC, according to the Octateuch, at the same time that the Egyptian records report that King Ramesses II had lost control over Canaan. The fact that the Egyptians dominated Canaan throughout the era of the Judges is not in doubt; Egyptian, Babylonian, Assyrian, and Nesite records all confirm this, as do the archaeological ruins of Egyptian cities spread through the region. The curious thing is that they are not mentioned in the book of Judges.

There is a reference to what appears to be a transliteration of 'Egypt' found in the Masoretic Text, however, it is for some reason assumed to be a village called 'Egypt' somewhere in Canaan. Like one of the earlier references to Aten, this reference to 'Egypt' is found in the Song of Deborah, in chapter 5:

> "My mighty mind will trample him down. When the hoofs of the horse were entangled, his mighty ones earnestly rushed to curse Southern Egypt. Curse it," said the messenger of the lord.

The place that was cursed in this verse is generally transliterated as Meroz from the Masoretic Text, which is not new, as the Greeks transliterated it as Mêrôz (Μηρωζ) circa 225 BC, and Lucian of Antioch transliterated it as Marôz (Μαρωζ) circa 300 AD.

The question of what Meroz was, has resulted in a great deal of speculation. The commentary in the Talmud (Moed Katan 16a) claims that Meroz is a planet that refused to help the Israelites in their time of trouble, however, the name Meroz does not correlate with the Semitic name of any planet in this star system, and was likely an error based on the misidentification of the Latin name of the planet Mars during the Roman era. In the later school of Merkabâh mysticism, Meroz became a class of angels that lived on the planet Meroz who refused to help the Israelites, instead of the planet itself, meaning in modern terms, Yahweh was cursing a group of extraterrestrials.

Modern scholarship has focused on the idea that there was a village in Israel called Misr, which is the Arabic name for Egypt. This village of Egyptians would then have been the focus of the curse, however, there is no known village called Misr dating to that time period, nor an explanation for the Arabic name. There is a village called Misr in northern modern Israel, however, it appears to have been founded much later.

The connect^mion between Meroz and Misr is generally based on the assumption that Mrôz (מרוז) was a scribal error, a mis-copy of Misr (מצר), however, it is difficult to see how that could have happened. Egypt was known as ^matMuṣru (𒆳𒈬𒊬) in Akkadian, Miṣriâi (𒆳𒈪𒅖𒊑) in Babylonian, Mṣrm (𐎎𐎕𐎗𐎎) in Ugaritic, Mṣryn (𐡌𐡑𐡓𐡍) in Aramaic, Mitzrayim (מִצְרַיִם) in Hebrew, and Miṣr (مِصر) in Arabic. The Myenaean Greeks also used the adopted Semitic name as Misarajo (𐀖𐀭𐀀𐀍). None of the known variants of the Semitic name of Egypt are a close match to Meroz/Maroz, however, the Egyptian name Marēs, is almost phonetically identical.

Mâô-rsî (𓅓𓂝𓏤𓂋𓋴) was an ancient Egyptian name for Southern Egypt, which translates as approximately 'Southern Place.' It continued to be used until the Classical era, when it was spelled as Marēs (Ⲙⲁⲣⲏⲥ) in Coptic, the Classical form of Egyptian. The exact pronunciation of ancient Egyptian names is debated before the development of the Demotic script in the early Iron Age, and therefore it cannot be known how the Egyptians pronounced Marēs during the era of Deborah, however, it is documented in Demotic as being Mâôrs (𓏤/𐍁), supporting the New Kingdom era pronunciation as being very similar to the term used by Deborah.

Nevertheless, the Song of Deborah does not curse a 'village of Meroz,' but 'Meroz' itself, meaning Southern Egypt. Meroz is cursed for not sending troops to help the Israelites during the era when King Jabin of Hazor was dominating the land, which according to the timeline of the Septuagint was a 20 year period between 1334 and 1314 BC. This was the era between the collapse of Egyptian power at the end of the Amarna Period, and the resurgence of Egyptian power under Pharaoh Horemheb. At the time, the capital of the Egyptian Empire was in Thebes, the capital of southern Egypt.

The Amarna Period, as Egyptologists call it, is the era when Pharaoh Amenhotep IV changed his name to Akhenaten, moved the capital of Egypt to a new city he built called Amarna, and instituted a national religion in Egypt today called Atenism. Under his rule, the various temples of the old gods of Egypt were systematically shut down, and a new national priesthood was created focused on the one god that all Egyptians could see every day, the sun, then known as Aten. His reign left the Empire in chaos, and when he died in 1336 BC, the empire rapidly shifted between the Pharaohs Smenkhkare (1335-1334 BC), Neferneferuaten (1334-1332 BC), and Tutankhamen (1334-1325 BC). Pharaoh Tutankhamen was a boy when he assumed the throne, and the real power at the time appears to have Ay, who would later become Pharaoh himself after Tutankhamen's young death left no heirs. Tutankhamen and Ay restored the priesthoods of the old gods, and abandoned Amarna, returning the imperial capital to Thebes. The priesthood of Aten quickly faded away, and Aten disappeared from the list of Egyptian gods, forgotten entirely until Egyptologists rediscovered him in the late 1800s. Ay ruled for just over a decade (1332-1319 BC), and managed to restore some semblance of normality to Upper and Lower Egypt, however, Kush and Canaan remained in chaos until Horemheb (1319-1292 BC) reestablished Egyptian control early in his reign.

This matches what is recorded in the book of Judges, where 80 years of peace under the Judges Ehud and Shamgar ended in 1334 BC when King Jabin of Hazor seized control of Canaan, supported by the Chief-of-the-army Siazara, who lived in the Forge-of-the-Foreigners, and commanded a force of 900 iron chariots. Based on both the Canaanite texts and Egyptian records Jabin was a common Canaanite name, however, Siazara appears to be the Egyptian name Siazårô (◿ 🦅𓏠🦅), meaning 'recognized son of Ra.' This specific name would have denoted a king from either southern Egypt or Nubia, however, Siazara is otherwise unknown from regal records, suggesting he attempted to seize control of the empire after Akhenaten died, however, ultimately failed, and was left out of the regal history of Egypt.

The 900 iron chariots are generally assumed to be an exaggeration, or a flat lie by scholars studying the book of Judges, as no petty Canaanite chieftain could have raised a force of 900 chariots at that time, and iron was generally not in use by armies until much later, after 1200 BC. This is, however, not exactly true. Tutankhamen was buried with an iron dagger in 1325 BC, and that dagger was of very high quality. Modern analysis indicates it may have been meteoric iron, however, it may have simply been made of the iron-nickel residue produced from the gold smelting in southeast Egypt.

Iron smelting was in use across the ancient world by the era of the Amarna Period, including in Anatolia, where the Hattic civilization had been smelting iron since at least 2500 BC, and in Uttar Pradesh, in India, where iron had been smelted since at least 1800 BC, however, in Egypt the high-quality iron-nickel weapons and jewelry found by Egyptologists are believed to have been made from the residue of gold smelting and bronze production. The gold mines of southeast Egypt produced a gold-silver ore with trace amounts of iron and nickel, which the Egyptians may have called djôm (𓈖𓂝𓏏).

Djôm is commonly translated as 'electrum' by Egyptologists, however, was recorded as a metal that the New Kingdom era Egyptians made weapons from, including chariots. The translation of djôm as 'electrum' is not new, the Classical era Greeks didn't know what djôm was either, and translated the word as electon (ἤλεκτρον), the name of a mythical metal that shone like the sun. As the early European Egyptologists knew little about Egyptian mineralogy, they adopted the term as 'electrum,' however, it is unlikely that the Egyptians would have built their weapons out of a soft metal, like gold, or a valuable metal, like gold, and no gold-silver alloy weapons have ever been found, suggesting that djôm was in fact the iron-nickel metal residue left over when the gold and silver was smelted from the gold ore.

The fact that the Egyptian General Siazara was stationed at a place called the Forge-of-the-Foreigners, implies the Egyptians were using something they had conquered from a group of foreigners to build the iron chariots he was reported to have had. The term Forge-of-the-Foreigners, is, unfortunately, not usually translated, but transliterated in most Bibles, and therefore the meaning of the name is lost. This is not a new practice, as the Greeks transliterated the name as Arisôth tôn ethnôn (Αρισωθ των εθνων), meaning: Arisoth of Nations. The Masoretic Text contain charoshet hagGovyim (חֲרֹשֶׁת הַגּוֹיִם), which translates as 'The forge of the gentiles' or 'The forge of the foreigners,' however, this is generally transliterated as Harosheth Hagoyim, or partially translated as Harosheth of the Gentiles.

The Egyptians themselves are known to have produced smelted iron since at least the Old Kingdom era as a by-product of gold and bronze production, however, the quantities were very minimal, and the value of the iron produced was greater than the value of gold until the New Kingdom era.

Iron was used in Egypt in greater quantities during the Hyksos Dynasty, however, an iron industry never became established in Egypt under their rule, indicating they were using one or more forges in Canaan to produce their iron weaponry. One iron smelting site is known from the New Kingdom era, Site 200, in the Timna Valley, in Jordan, however, it is unclear if it was in use during the Hyksos Dynasty. The main reason that iron production was never established in Egypt under the Hyksos, was because the source of iron that would later be used in the Late Period was in the mountains of southern Egypt, near the gold mines, which the Hyksos never gained control over, however, there was likely also another reason.

Even after iron became the primary metal being used across the Middle East and the Mediterranean, between 1200 and 1000 BC, the Egyptians did not widely adopt it, instead, continuing to develop better forms of bronze that could compete with iron. This did not end until the Empire of Kush conquered the Egyptians, and instituted wide-scale iron production between 744 and 656 BC.

By the time the Kushites conquered Egypt, Egypt was centuries behind the metallurgical technology of its neighbors. There is no obvious political or religious reason for Egypt having not adopted iron a thousand years earlier, implying an economic reason, likely an agreement between bronze working guilds that dated back thousands of years to the Old Kingdom or earlier. The Egyptians did not accept change easily, and it appears neither the Hyksos, who conquered them from Canaan nor the Libyans who later conquered them from the Sahara could convince them to implement iron production. Unlike the previous invaders, the Kushites did not depend on their conquest for economic stability as Kush provided all the food and iron they needed to rule their empire. Under the pressure of having to compete with Kushite metallurgists, the Egyptians finally acquiesced, and Egypt finally joined the iron age.

The Forge-of-the-Foreigners referred to in the Judges, was most likely a forge left over from the Hyksos dynasty, somewhere along the Kishion river, in northern Israel. The alliance between the renegade King Jabin and Egyptian General Siazara, which in the Octateuch's chronology seized control of Canaan in

1334 BC, a year when Egypt had three pharaohs: Smenkhkare, Neferneferuaten, and Tutankhamen, implies that Siazara and his army did not accept any of the Pharaohs as legitimate. If Siazara's name was any indicator, he was a Ra worshiper, and as the worship of Ra had been banned by Akenaten, he likely saw the bond between the monarchy and the gods as having been severed, meaning the entire royal family would have been invalidated. This view could only have been validated by meeting Tutankhamen himself, as the boy was the product of generations of inbreeding, and suffered from several hereditary diseases. Even as a child, he could not walk without a cane. His young death, at 18 years of age, has been a matter of wide debate, with historians once having accused Ay of assassinating him. Based on the study of his remains, it appears he died of natural causes related to his genetic diseases.

According to Judges, an Israelite named Barak defeated Siazara and restored peace to Canaan in 1314 BC, when Deborah sang her song that referred to the sun as Aten, implying that the Israelites had remained loyal to the Egyptian monarchy throughout the insurrection of Jabin and Siazara. This would have been five years into the reign of Horemheb, when Egypt restored control over southern Canaan, however, did so without using the Egyptian military. The exact means that Horemheb used has traditionally been a mystery within Egyptology, however, the Book of Judges states it was the Israelites themselves that restored Egyptian control over the region, as Barak became the judge of Israel after defeating Siazara, and the land was peaceful for 40 years, until 1274 BC, which was the same year that Ramesses II marched his army north to attack the Nesite Empire according to Egyptologists.

The synchronizations between the Book of Judges and the records of Egypt are far too many to be overlooked or ignored. As almost all denominations of Christians and Jews agree that King Saul established his kingdom in 1037 BC, and the Septuagint's version of Judges includes 460 years of the land being ruled by Judges, or foreign kings, followed by an era of chaos when there was no king, the latest possible date the Exodus could have taken place was the 1500s BC, which supports the idea that the 10 plagues of Egypt were descriptions of the fallout and effects of the Minoan eruption which Egyptologists date to 1550 BC. According to Joshua, 42 years later the Israelites invaded Samaria, (northern modern Israel and the Palestinian West Bank) under the leadership of Joshua, which would have been 1508 BC. The plan was already laid out in the Book of Joshua to occupy the entire land of Canaan, yet just three years later, when

Joshua was 85 years old, the Israelites stopped their campaign, after having only occupied the cities in Samaria, this would have been in 1505 BC.

The reason they stopped their invasion is not given, however, Egyptian records do explain it, as in the same year, 1505 BC, Pharaoh Thutmose I marched his army through Canaan to reconquer it for the Egyptian Empire. It had previously been under the control of the Hyksos Dynasty whose empire collapsed in the aftermath of the Minoan eruption. In 1550 BC, the Hyksos capital fell to the rival southern dynasty of Pharaoh Ahmose I, and the Hyksos retreated to their fortress of Sharuhen, near modern Gaza in the Palestinian Gaza Strip. This suggests the Hyksos maintained control over Canaan until Sharuhen fell to Ahmose I in 1540 BC. Ahmose I led an invasion of southern Canaan a few years later in an attempt to root out any remaining Hyksos. Egyptologists are not sure when this campaign was, placing it sometime between 1537 and 1527 BC. This campaign is not believed to have reached farther north than Byblos, in modern Lebanon, and did not result in any long-term political control over Canaan. Ahmose I's main goal seems to have been to destroy any remaining Hyksos in the region to ensure they did not try to recapture Egypt.

For decades after the conquest of Avaris, the new 18th Dynasty struggled to control Egypt, with numerous insurrections reported in the Nile Delta and Nubia, and does not appear to have tried to re-exert control over Canaan until Thutmose I's armies occupied the region in 1505 BC. Thutmose I marched his army all the way north to the Euphrates River in Syria, and reported all the peoples of Canaan surrendered to him without conflict, he then returned to Egypt and marched his army south to Nubia to suppress an insurrection there later that year. This means his army was only briefly in Canaan and did not have time to conquer any of the cities there, so either they did surrender without conflict, or, he lied. While the Book of Judges does not mention the Egyptian army passing through, this seems to have been redacted at a later point, as Joshua did stop his campaign in 1505 BC, and did not declare himself king, instead taking the subservient role of judge. Joshua's becoming a judge, means he ruled over a group of people but was under the authority of a king. The people were obviously the Israelites, and the king could only have been Thutmose I. This is an anticlimactic end to the tail of escape from Egypt and was likely redacted during the era of the two kingdoms when Egypt was again a foreign enemy.

According to Judges, Joshua judged the Israelites until he was 110 years old and then died in what would have been 1480 BC, following which Kŭšn Rishatayim ruled the Israelites. While the Hebrew term Kush (כּוּשׁ) referred to the land of Kush, south of Egypt, whose people were known as the Kushi (כּוּשִׁי), Kŭšn (כושן) was a different term, which the Greeks did not recognize, and therefore transliterated it as Chousa (Χουσα). As the term referred to someone who was the king in the rivers of Aram (Syria), the origin of the word was almost certainly Kasium (𒆗𒋗𒁲𒈨), today translated as Kassite. The Kassites were the rulers of Babylonia in the late bronze age from some time in the 1500s BC, until 1155 BC, when they were conquered by the Elamites.

The Hebrew term rishatayim (רִשְׁעָתַיִם) is not proper Hebrew, Canaanite, or Aramaic, however, may be a the ancient Canaanite spelling of the name of king Parshatatar (𒉿𒅈𒐼𒋫𒋫𒅈), king of the Mitanni Empire circa 1485 BC. Parshatatar is recorded as occupying northern Canaan during the reign of Hatsheput by establishing a series of puppet states across the region, and gaining access to the Mediterranean Sea.

In circa 1479 BC, the Egyptian king Thutmose II died, and his former queen Hatsheput seized the throne in the name of his two year old son Thutmose III. Hatsheput was not the mother of Thutmose III, another wife Iset was, whom Hatsheput married after officially changing her sex to male. After changing genders Hatsheput declared himself to be Thutmose III's regent, although later assumed the role of king himself until his death, when Thutmose III inherited the throne. While Hatsheput was a very unpopular king, his rule established the dominant architectural style of the New Kingdom.

The entire concept of a female king was rejected by many, with graffiti mocking King Hatsheput's gender appearing in the archaeological record of the era. Most of Kush appears to have rejected Hatsheput, and rebelled against his rule. After inheriting the throne in circa 1458 BC, Thutmose III attempted to erase Hatsheput's rule from Egyptian records, claiming to have ruled continuously from the death of Thutmose II in circa 1479 BC. While her role as queen of Thutmose II was never erased, the era when Hatsheput ruled Egypt was, and his era as king was not rediscovered until the 1800s.

It is clear that there was a rebellion against King Hatsheput in Syria, backed by the Mitanni, and control of all territory north of Megiddo was lost, as the first thing Thutmose III did after assuming the throne was march north into Canaan, where he fought the battle of Megiddo against the rebelling Syrian kings, and their Mitanni allies. The Battle of Megiddo was the largest battle recorded in Egyptian records up until that time, with both the Egyptians and Canaanite rebels estimated to have fielded around 1,000 chariots and 10,000 infantry. After defeating the Canaanites in the initial battle, the Egyptians plundered 924 chariots and 200 suits of armor. The Canaanite kings fell back to the fortified city of Kadesh, which the Egyptians then besieged for seven months. According to the records at Karnak, when the city surrendered the Egyptians captured 340 Canaanite and Mitanni princes, 2,041 mares, 191 foals, 6 stallions, 924 chariots, 200 suits of armor, 502 bows, 1,929 cattle, and 22,500 sheep.

Between 1458 and 1425 BC, Thutmose III fought a series of campaigns in Canaan, pushing Egyptian control north to the Euphrates River, and then crossed it into the Mitanni empire, where he plundered the country, which apparently had not rebuilt its defenses after the loss at Megiddo. After securing Canaan, Thutmose III marched his army south into Nubia, recapturing territory as far as the fourth cataract, all of which had been lost under the rule of Hatsheput.

It is unclear why the author would have referred to Parshatatar as a Kassite unless it was actually written at the time. The Mitanni rulers are often linked to the Kassites culturally, however, the peoples they ruled were not culturally similar. During the wars of Thutmose III in Canaan, the term Mitanni become common, however, earlier records simply called the land Naharin, meaning 'Rivers,' and called the people Hurrians. While the Hurrians were the primary population of the Mitanni Empire, the rulers were an unrelated group of Indo-Aryans, who spoke a language similar to Sanskrit, and worshiped the Vedic gods. They appear to have seized power over the Hurrians in the Khabur river region in the 1550s BC, from which they expanded in every direction until the Battle of Megiddo.

The Mitanni relationship with the Kassites is unclear, as the Kassites are not viewed as being Indo-Aryans, however, may have been Hurrians. The two cultures were close at the time, and it is plausible that the earliest Mitanni to arrive in the region were viewed as being Kassites by the Canaanites. Nevertheless, by 1457 BC the term would have already been anachronistic, as the term Mitanni would have replaced it, suggesting this verse was written between 1472 and 1457 BC.

In Judges, after the Kassite Parshatatar was deposed, the land was peaceful for 40 years under Judge Othniel, which would have been between 1472 and 1432 BC. This era corresponds to the reign of the Kings Hatsheput (1479-1458 BC) and Thutmose III (1458-1425 BC). Thutmose III fought 17 campaigns in northern Canaan during the era, however, southern Canaan appears to have been peaceful throughout most of the era under the protection of the Egyptian army.

According to Judges, this era of peace in southern Canaan ended in 1432 BC when Eglon the king of Moab conquered the Israelites east of the Jordan River. These Israelites appear to have never been under Egyptian governance, and the war east of the Jordan appears to have been separate from, yet inspired by the general insurrection against Egypt in northern Canaan. This conquest of the eastern Israelites by Eglon the Moabite is referred to at the end of Joshua, right after the death of Joshua, implying the book of Joshua originated with the eastern tribes, who lived in peace between 1480 and 1432 BC. After 18 years of domination by the Moabites, King Eglon was killed by an Israelite named Ehud, which began a period of 80 years of peace, during which Eglon and then Shamgar were the Judges of Israel. This time span would have been 1414 to 1334 BC, ending when the Egyptian monarchical power collapsed at the end of the Amarna period, and King Jabin of Hazor and General Siazara rebelled.

After Jabin and Siazara were defeated the land had another peaceful era of forty years under Judge Barak, who had defeated Siazara. Barak's wife was the prophet Deborah, to whom the Song of Deborah is attributed. The Song of Deborah, which is chapter 5 of Judges, is generally considered by scholars to be the oldest piece of Israelite literature to survive more or less intact to the present. While Barak was the leader who defeated the army of Siazara, it was Jael, the wife of Eber the blacksmith who killed Siazara after taking him to her bed-chamber and then driving a stake through his temple.

The significance of the blacksmiths in Judges is often also overlooked, as the word blacksmith is generally transliterated as Kenite, implying a tribe. This is not a new practice, as the Greeks did the same thing when they translated the Octateuch, transliterating the Hebrew word for blacksmith: keini (קֵינִי) as Cinaeou (Κιναιου). The significance of the metal-smiths, especially iron-smiths, which is what the word keini likely meant in Judges, was lost in the millennium between the age of Deborah, and the age of the Ptolemies, likely because by then metallurgy was universal, including iron-working. These 'Kenites' were so significant at the time, that even Moses appears to have married his daughter to one, named Jobab. This story has been lost, however, the reference to Jobab the 'groom of Moses' has survived in both the Octateuch and Masoretic Text.

The connection between Siazara's army being based at the Forge-of-the-Foreigners, and him being killed by the wife of a blacksmith cannot be ignored. The fact that he was listed as commanding 900 iron war-chariots also cannot be overlooked, as that would have been a major division within the Egyptian army at the time, and likely the entire Egyptian army stationed in Canaan.

After the defeat of Siazara and Jabin, Judges states that the land was peaceful for 40 years under Judge Barak, which would have been between 1314 and 1274 BC. This era of peace ended when the Midianites, Amalekites, and the 'sons of the east' conquered the Israelites in 1274 BC. 1274 BC is also the year that Egyptologists claim that Pharaoh Ramesses II launched his disastrous First Syrian Campaign. The Egyptian army was soundly defeated by the Nesites, allowing nomadic groups like the Amalakites and Midianites to plunder Canaan as described in the Book of Judges. The 'sons of the East' in the Book of Judges are likely none other than the Nesites, commonly misidentified as Hittites, as they came from the region north of the Euphrates, which while being geographic nonsense in the modern mindset, was considered to be the east by the ancient Canaanites, as one had to head north to the Euphrates before heading east into Mesopotamia. It's likely the Israelites did not know where exactly the Nesites were from and assumed it was the east in Mesopotamia, like the Babylonians and Assyrians.

According to Judges, the Midianites ruled Israel for 7 years, between 1274 and 1267 BC, however, it is not clear if these Israelites were east or west of the Jordan, and therefore, they may not have been the Israelites in Egyptian-ruled Canaan. Ramesses II's Second Syrian Campaign, in 1273 BC was equally disastrous, and his army was defeated again, although did make it to the outskirts of Kadesh. His Third Syrian Campaign, in 1271 BC, was focused on reconsolidating Egyptian authority outside of Nesite-controlled areas, and he marched his army from city to city in Canaan demanding tribute. Cities that offered tribute were considered loyal to Egypt, and left alone, while those that refused were sacked. Edom, Seir, Moab, Jerusalem, Jericho, Heshbon, and Damascus are all listed as cities or lands that were visited by the army, although it is not clear which were loyal and which were sacked.

In 1270 and 1267 BC, Ramesses II's armies marched against Kadesh again and managed to drive the Nesites from the region. The Book of Judges claims that the Shechemite leader Abimelech defeated the Midianites and their Amakaite and Nesite (sons of the East) allies in 1267 BC, and became the King of Israel, however, his kingdom appears to have been rejected by most Israelites, and he was described in the Book of Judges as a real bastard, the son of a prostitute. His kingdom only lasted 3 years, until 1264 BC, when the other Israelites under the leadership of Judge Tola overthrew him.

There were 23 peaceful years under Judge Tola, followed by 22 under Judge Jair, which would have been between 1264 and 1219 BC. During this era, King Ramesses was focused on defending Egypt from a naval power called the 'Sea Peoples' by Egyptologists. It is unclear where they were based, however, Sardinia and Greece are the two dominant theories. Ramesses signed a peace treaty with the Nesite King Hattusili III in 1258 BC, and Canaan does appear to have been peaceful throughout the era of Judges Tola and Jair. During that era, Ramesses built a series of forts along the Mediterranean coast of modern Egypt, for the first time in recorded history attempting to protect the desert-routes from the invasions of these Sea Peoples.

This peaceful era in southern Canaan ended abruptly in 1219 BC according to Judges, when the Pelesets and Ammonites seized control of the region. Egyptian records depict this as a time of great unrest, as the war with the Sea Peoples was still going on, and Ramesses II died in 1213 BC, after being Pharaoh for 66 years. In 1208 and 1207 BC, the Sea People launched a major invasion of Egypt, and control of the Nile Delta was briefly lost. Pharaoh Merneptah (1213-1203 BC) appears to have negotiated an agreement with the Sea Peoples in 1207 BC which allowed them to settle in Canaan if they returned the Nile Delta, and the following year, 1206 BC, Canaanite towns and tribes were listed in open revolt against Egyptian authority, with the list of rebels including Gaza, Ashkelon, Yenoam, Israel, and the Arameans. It is unclear what level of authority the Egyptian New Kingdom exerted over Canaan after 1206 BC, however, the Book of Judges reports that Judge Jephthah defeated the Moabites in 1201 BC, and judged the Israelites for 6 years. He was followed by the judges Ibzan, Elon, and Abdon, who judged the Israelites until 1170 BC when the Pelesets seized control of southern Canaan.

This occupation of southern Canaan by the Pelesets, recorded in Judges, is also recorded by the Egyptians, carved into the walls of the mortuary temple of Pharaoh Ramesses III at Medinet Habu. According to the Egyptian records from the era, several groups of Sea Peoples attacked Egypt in waves between 1179 and 1174 BC, including groups known as the Půlåsåtî, Dåîniniů, and Šrhnå. Půlåsåtî (𓂋 𓏏 𓏏 𓏥𓀀𓀀𓀀) is the Egyptian name for the Pelesets, while the Dåîniniů (𓂝𓈖𓏌𓏌𓅱) commonly anglicized as Denyen, are believed to have been the Danoi (Δαναοί) tribe of ancient Greece. The Šrhnå (𓈖𓏏𓄿𓃭𓈖), commonly anglicized as Shardana were the Egyptians' main antagonists of the previous century, generally thought to have been Sardinians.

These attacks during the reign of Ramesses III were the worst Egypt had seen, with allied over land attacks by the Meshwesh (𓈖𓏏𓄿𓂝𓏏𓄿𓃭𓅱) tribes of Libya, and the Sicilians (𓈖𓏌𓏏) who had occupied and fortified the town of Dor on the northern coast of modern Israel a few decades earlier. While Ramesses III's records report that he graciously allowed the Pelesets to live in southern Canaan after he defeated them, it appears that all his forces could do was defend the Nile Delta, and the Pelesets had effectively captured Egypt's northernmost territory.

Based on the records in Judges, the Israelites recognized the authority of the Pelests in 1170 BC, four years after their last battle against Egypt. This appears to have been the end of the New Kingdom's authority in southern Canaan, however, after 40 years of Peleset rule, Samson rose as a Judge of Israel under Peleset rule. He was described as judging Israel for 20 years during the Peleset era, before leading a failed revolt against them and being captured by his favorite prostitute. After Samson's heroic suicide, the Book of Judges indicates that his father Manoah judged Israel for another 20 years, before the era of chaos, when there was no king.

This era of chaos in Canaan would have begun in 1090 BC, shortly before the same thing happened in Egypt in 1077 BC. Egyptologists call this the Third Intermediate Period, as there are few records from the era. In Greece, where civilization collapsed at approximately the same time, it would later be called the Dark Age, which then inspired the name of the Dark Age that followed the collapse of the Roman Empire in Western Europe. During this Dark Age of ancient Canaan, the book of Judges records that there was no king, however, a lot did happen during this era implying it lasted several decades. During this era, the

Danites conquered Laish and renamed it Dan, and the Benjamite genocide took place. The Danites had been described as living on boats until this era, which some modern historians have taken as evidence that they were new arrivals in Canaan, likely related to the Danoi tribe of Greece. This is most likely not correct, as the name Dan appears in many ancient Canaanite texts, and appears to have been common in ancient Canaan.

The Benjaminite genocide was a strange story set in this era as well and likely tied to the downfall of Lord Lahem, the fertility god of ancient Canaan that Beth-lehem was named after. The story involved the Benjaminites in the town of Gibeah attempting to gang-rape a young man who had stopped there for the night. He had been taken in by an old man that lived in the city, and when the men of the city demanded the old man hand over the young man so they could rape him, the old man gave them his daughter and the young man's concubine instead, who were raped to death. When the other Israelite tribes heard of this event, they virtually wiped out the Benjaminites. It is a strange story to have been simply made up and added to the historical narrative of Judges, which up until this dark age had been fairly consistent with Egyptian records of their rule of Canaan, indicating the story was likely based on something that had happened.

The Benjaminite genocide took a number of years and resulted in most of the tribe being destroyed. During the genocide the other tribes vowed to not allow Benjaminites to marry their daughters, however, by the end, the other tribes took pity on them, and allowed their daughters to be abducted by Benjaminites to become their wives. While every aspect of the story is odd, the strangest aspect of the story is the part not found in Judges, but in 1st Kingdoms (Masoretic Samuel), the fact that King Saul was a Benjaminite. As this genocide took place sometime between 1090 and 1037 BC, it is strange that a Benjaminite could have become king in 1037 BC. A lot of this story has been lost in the past 3000 years.

The story of the rape itself appears to have simply been a catalyst for the Benjaminite genocide, as the murder of an entire tribe seems excessive punish-ment for any crime committed by a few members of the tribe. The genocide of Benjamin was likely related to the fall of the Egyptian Empire, as the tribe was the most Egyptianized of the Israelite tribes. Even their name was Egyptian: Pen-Amen (𓉐𓏌𓏤𓇋𓏠𓈖𓀭, Middle Egyptian transliteration pån-jômån), which meant Son of Amen. Amen (𓇋𓏠𓈖𓀭), also transliterated into English as Amun or Amon, was the father god of the Theban triad, and supreme god of Egypt throughout the New Kingdom era, other than during the brief Amarna Period. The Egyptian tale, the Voyage of Wenamen, set during the same era as King Saul, described the journey of a Theban priest of Amen's travels in Canaan, and his shock that everyone in Canaan had lost respect for Amen after the Egyptian Empire had collapsed.

The Book of Judges itself is very old, and the Song of Deborah may be the oldest surviving piece of Israelite literature, as it uses some of the most archaic forms of Canaanite in the Masoretic Text. Within the book of Judges, the spoken dialect was part of the division between the Israelites during the battle between the Gileadites from east of the Jordan, and the Ephraimites from west of the Jordan. The spelling of šblt (שבלת) in the Masoretic Text is not the Hebrew spelling of šybŭlt (שיבולת), but the older Canaanite spelling, recorded as šblt (⟨𐎌𐎁𐎍𐎚—) in Ugaritic Canaanite, and šblt (𐤔𐤁𐤋𐤕) in Phoenician Canaanite.

This older Canaanite spelling developed into the Hebrew spelling during the Persian era, under the influence of Imperial Aramaic. The older Akkadian cuneiform term was šubulta (𒌋𒉺𒌔𒊒𒋫), indicating that the division among the Israelites was already between those speaking Canaanite versus Aramaic. Arameans appeared in Mesopotamian records centuries earlier than the Habirus, and the two cultures were generally described as inhabiting the same regions, although the Arameans were more urban, and the Habirus were more nomadic.

There is evidence that the book was either assembled or redacted in the Kingdom of Samaria, as the book includes the name of the Canaanite sun-god Shemesh, whose worship was later banned in Judah by King Josiah in circa 625 BC. The region of the book also generally corresponds with the territory of the northern kingdom, both the region that had once been under Egyptian authority west of the Jordan and the region east of the Jordan which had generally been independent of Egypt. Conversely, the Aramaic book of Judges which was used as a source text by the Greeks appears to have been translated into Aramaic during the Persian era, as the Greek translation includes Persian loanwords the Greeks would not have used, such as satrap, the title of Persian governors.

Judges is a continuation of the story found in Joshua, but not a seamless one, as Joshua includes the Moabites occupying Samaria after the death of Joshua, which skips past 48 years of history recorded in Judges. This gap in Joshua reflects the fact that none of that 48 years of history affected the eastern Israelites who were outside the sphere of Egypt. This shows that the two books had different origins,

Joshua from the eastern Israelites, and Judges from the western Israelites. The two books were likely united as part of a historical narrative along with Deuteronomy in the Kingdom of Samaria between 930 and 720 BC. As Deuteronomy is a collection of amendments to the laws found in Exodus that generally repeats the amendments and stories of Leviticus and Numbers, it is likely it was composed in Samaria to serve the same function as Leviticus-Numbers would later serve in Judah. Deuteronomy and Joshua flow together seamlessly, implying that Joshua was once a part of Deuteronomy, however, Judges does not flow seamlessly from Joshua and is composed in an older dialect, implying the book was already very old by the time Deuteronomy-Joshua was organized into its pre-Hasmonean state by the Aaronite priesthood of Samaria..

The presence of the name Aten in the Song of Deborah proves that at least Chapter 5 dates back to the time it describes, the late 1300s BC. Only a few fragments of Judges have survived among the Dead Sea Scrolls, and all date to the Hasmonean Dynasty or later, meaning they all date to after the Hasmonean redaction of circa 140 BC. If some of the songs and stories found in the book of Judges were written in the 1300s BC, they could not have been written in the Phoenician script that emerged in the 1100s BC, suggesting an older script was used.

The Ugaritic script was being used in northern Canaan at the time, however, there is no evidence of it being used in southern or central Canaan. At the time, the Egyptian court was corresponding with the governors and judges throughout Canaan using the Akkadian cuneiform script, suggesting that was the script used, however, no clear evidence exists to support any of Judges being written in cuneiform, unlike Exodus and Joshua, which each include Akkadian loanwords. Nevertheless, there are terms related to Egypt that suggest a cuneiform precursor to the Phoenician version of Judges. The presence of the 'unknown' terms Aten and Meroz in the song of Deborah proves it must have been written in some script, and the spelling of the terms prh nôrk (פרה נערך), and prôut (פרעות) in the Aleppo Codex supports this as having been in cuneiform.

Both prh nôrk (פרה נערך) and prôut (פרעות) are also considered 'unknown' terms, resulting in some strange translations. The translators at the Library of Alexandria translated the term as 'Phara the child (or servant)' (Φαρα το παιδαριον), while the Hebrew translates as 'carrying-boy,' or 'cow-servant,' or possibly even 'cow-boy.' Based on the context, this strange sentence appears to be a reference to an Egyptian overseer stationed by Pharaoh among the Tribe of Manasseh.

The Phoenician spelling of 'pharaoh' was prôh (𐤐𐤓𐤏), while the Aramaic spelling was prôun (𐡐𐡓𐡏𐡍), neither of which is an exact match for the transliterated words prh (פרה) and phara (Φαρα), indicating that neither the Paleo-Hebrew nor Aramaic texts included the word 'pharaoh' but a similar sounding word. This indicates that the word, along with the Song of Deborah, was transliterated from another script, likely Akkadian Cuneiform or Egyptian.

The Akkadian Cuneiform spelling of 'pharaoh' was pirôû (𒊩𒀀) during the late Bronze Age, which would have been pronounced the same as the Masoretic word, while the Egyptian spelling was per-ôå (𓉐), which would have been pronounced slightly differently, supporting the Song of Deborah having been written in cuneiform.

Fragments of the book of Ruth have been found among the dead sea scrolls, however, only in the Assyrian script of the Hasmonean Dynasty, and dated to between 140 and 37 BC. Like Judges, the terms used in denoting the gods differ, with the Octateuch using the terms Lord God (Κυριω Θεω) or Lord (Κύριοσ), and the Masoretic text using the names Yhůh (יהוה').

The Masoretic Book of Ruth also includes a reference to the Moabite god Shaddai, who was described as having 'dealt very bitterly' with Naomi when she was in Moab. In the Octateuch, the name was translated as ikanós (ικανοσ), meaning 'capable,' which proves Shaddai was no longer considered the proper name of a god by circa 225 BC when Ruth was translated into Greek. Shaddai was considered a god when the Deir Alla Inscription (KAI 312) was carved between 880 and 770 BC. The Deir Alla Inscription was found during an excavation at Deir 'Alla, Jordan, in 1967 AD, which listed the god Shaddai as one of the gods worshiped by the Prophet Balaam, who was also referred to as a worshiper of Shaddai in the Masoretic version of Numbers. Deir 'Alla is located in the territory of ancient Moab, and the inscription is in the Moabite dialect of Canaanite. It was found engraved into the wall of a building constructed circa 800 BC, confirming that Shaddai was a god in Moab at the time. It is unclear from the archaeological record when Shaddai was first worshiped in Moab, however, if the chronology of the Septuagint's version of Numbers is correct, Shaddai was worshiped in Moab before 1500 BC.

The Octateuch and Masoretic Text have different names for Naomi's husband. He is called Abimelech (Αβιμελεχ) in the Octateuch, but Elimelech (אֱלִימֶלֶךְ) in the Masoretic Text. It is not clear why the Hasmoneans would have changed the name of this minor character, however, it may have been to disassociate King David from the first King of Israel, King Abimelech, who led an insurrection against Egypt and declared himself king in 1267 BC. Other than the name and the fact that both were Ephriamites, the two Abimelechs seem to have nothing in common. King Abimelech was the son of Gideon in the Book of Judges, who was so unpopular the Israelites overthrew him and restored the judges after 3 years, in 1264 BC, following which he was killed.

The book of Ruth appears to be part of a Samaritan story designed to splice the Moabites into the royal genealogy. The Book of Deuteronomy, which was likely edited in Samaria, uses Moabite names of locations along with of Samariatan names, indicating that a Samaritan priesthood was active in Moab before the kingdom fell to the Assyrians.

The Book of Judges refers to King Abimelech as the bastard son of Gideon by a prostitute, which speaks volumes about his memory, however, he was an Ephraimite, as was the Abimelech in the Book of Ruth, indicating that he could not have been viewed that badly a century after his death, when Ruth's father in law would have been born. Ruth, the step-daughter of Abimelech in the Book of Ruth, ultimately became an ancestor of King David, meaning it is possible that some Israelites were connecting the two Abimelechs in the Second Temple era, claiming that David was a descendant of King Abimelech.

The setting of the Ruth is the lands of Judah and Moab in the early-1000s BC, when the Book of Judges claimed there was no king. The last judge under the Pelesets in the books of Judges was Samson's father Manoah, who ruled until 1090 BC when the Peleset Kingdom apparently collapsed. This was just over a decade before the collapse of the Egyptian New Kingdom in 1077 BC, which began the Third Intermediate Period, when Egyptian records became sparse. This collapse of civilization in Canaan and Egypt was mirrored by collapses across the Mediterranean, sparking what the Greeks would later call the Dark Age. This Dark Age is not in doubt, however, is poorly understood due to the sparse records from the era. The story would have taken place around the same era as the Benjaminite genocide in the Book of Judges, which is likely the reason the book of Ruth was placed directly behind the book of Judges in the Octateuch.

It is not clear when the Book of Ruth was written, however, it is not generally considered to date back to the era it is set in. Based on the connection between the Book of Ruth and King David, it seems likely that the book was written no earlier than the era of King David, however, the book is generally dated to the time of Ezra the Scribe circa 350 BC. It is generally interpreted as an attempt to bridge the older books of Joshua and Judges with the newer books of the Kingdoms (Masoretic Samuel and Kings), which are generally accepted as having been compiled during the time of Ezra the scribe.

A number of stories exist to explain the origin of the Beta Israel community, the 'Ethiopian Jews' indigenous to Ethiopia, Eritrea, and Sudan. The recorded story of the origin of the Ethiopian Jews was reported by Eldad ha-Dani in the late 800s AD. Eldad ha-Dani was a dark-skinned Jew from a country south of Kush, modern northern Sudan, who was captured by pagan Ethiopians and ultimately sold on the coast of what might be modern Kenya or Tanzania, to a Jew from the Parthian Empire, who took him back to modern Iran. He later traveled through the Middle East and the Mediterranean Sea. He claimed that he was from a country of Jews, south of Kush, who were the descendants of the tribes of Dan, Gad, Naphtali, and Asher, who had left Israel during the civil war that split the Kingdom into Judea and Samaria. Modern secular scholars doubt there was a united kingdom of Israel, however, if the civil war did happen, it would have happened in 922 BC when Jeroboam I and Rehoboam split the kingdom of Solomon. If true, this would make the Beta Israelites neither Jews, nor Samaritans, but a third branch of the Israelite religions, and older than the others.

The Christian text Kebra Nagast claims that Judaism entered into Ethiopia slightly earlier when the Ethiopian Queen of Sheba traveled to Israel and was impregnated by King Solomon. Her son Menelik I led a group of Jews to Ethiopia when he stole the box of the Covenant. Other than the Ethiopian Orthodox Christians, few consider the Kebra Nagast historically valid. Some members of the Beta Israel community claim the Ethiopian Jews were originally members of the Israelite tribes led by Moses that chose not to enter into Canaan with Joshua, and instead traveled south and settled in the land of Moses' Ethiopian wife, mentioned in Numbers chapters 12. A third story of the origin of the Ethiopian Jews, took place shortly after the Greeks had taken control over Egypt and Judea, when King Ptolemy I resettled Judeans in southern Nubia. This would have taken place between 305 and 282 BC, and later the Jews migrated south for various reasons.

However they ended up in Ethiopia, they have traditionally used a variation of the Octateuch, which they call the Orit. The Octateuch is documented as being the version of the Septuagint that was published around 225 BC. Like the Ethiopian Christian Bible, the Orit appears to have had sections 'updated' from Hebrew and Arabic sources over the past two thousand years. Octateuch: The Original Orit is a 21st century translation aimed at restoring the original Orit.

One of the problems with academic translations of the Octateuch, is the use of unfamiliar names or terms, as the Octateuch was written in Greek, and therefore many names are unrecognizable to modern English readers who are used to Hebrew-derived names. This project uses the more commonly understood Hebrew-derived names instead of their Greek translations, such as Canaan instead of Chanaan, and Melchizedek instead of Melchisedec. Common modern names are also used instead of either Greek or Hebrew terms when geographical locations are known, such as the archaeological name Uruk instead of the Greek Orech, or the Hebrew Erech, and the archaeological term Sumer instead of Shinar or Senar. While this could be argued as not being a correct academic procedure, it does fulfill the goal of making the translation easy to read and understand.

Cosmic Genesis: Chapter 1

In the beginning, God[1] made the skies[2] and land.[3] The land was invisible and unfinished,[4] and darkness[5] covered the abyss,[6] and the air god[7] was above the water.[8]

God said, "Light be born!" and light came. God saw the light was good, and God separated the medium of light and the medium of darkness. God named the light: Day,[9] and the darkness was named: Night.[10] There was evening and there was morning, the first day.

God said, "Let there be a framework in the middle of the water and let it be a division between water and water," and it was so.

God said, "Let there be a framework in the middle of the water and let it be a division between water and water," and it was so. God made the framework, and God divided between the water which is under the framework and the water which is above the framework. God named the framework: Shamayim,[11] and God saw that it was good, and there was evening and there was morning, the second day.

God said, "Let the water that is under the sky be collected into one meeting place, and let the dry land appear," and it was so. The water that was under the sky was collected into its meeting places, and dry land appeared. God named the dry land: Eretz,[12] and the water systems were named: Seas,[13] and God saw that it was good.

God said, "Germinate the land with plants of grass producing seed similar to its kind and according to its species, and the fruit tree producing fruit which has seed in it, according to its species on the land," and it was so.

The land sprouted the plants of grass bearing seed according to their species and according to their likeness, and the fruit trees bearing fruit whose seed is in it, according to its kind on Earth, and God saw that it was good.

There was evening and there was morning, the third day. God said, "Let there be lights in the framework of Shamayim, for shining on Earth, to separate the day and night, and let them be for signs and seasons and days and years. Let them be for light in the framework of Shamayim, to shine on Earth," and it was so.

God made the two great lights, the brighter light to rule the day, and the dimmer light to rule the night along with the stars. God placed them in the framework of Shamayim, to shine on Earth, and to regulate day and night, and to divide between the light and the darkness. God saw that it was good.

There was evening and there was morning, the fourth day. God said, "Export from the waters[14] the living minds[15] of reptiles, and winged creatures flying above the land in the framework of Shamayim," and it was so. God made the great dragon,[16] and every mind of living reptiles, which the waters brought out according to their species, and every creature that flies with wings according to its kind, and God saw that they were good. God blessed them and said, "Increase and multiply and fill the waters in the seas, and let the creatures that fly be multiplied on the land."

There was evening and there was morning, the fifth day. God said, "Let Eretz bring out creatures of living minds according to its kind, quadrupeds and reptiles and wild animals of the land according to their species," and it was so. God made the wild animals of the land according to their species, and the livestock according to their species, and all the reptiles of the land according to their species, and God saw that they were good.

God said, "Let us make man according to our image and likeness, and let them have dominion over the fish of the sea, and over the flying creatures of the sky, and over the livestock and all the land, and over the reptiles that creep on the land."

God made man, in the image of God he made him, male and female he made them. God blessed them, saying, "Increase and multiply. You paid for the land, so conquer it. Have the fish of the seas and flying creatures of the sky, and everything and every living creature of the land."

God said, "Look I have given to you every seed-bearing plant sowing seed which is on all the land, and every tree which has in itself the fruit of seeds that are planted, for you it will be for food, and for all the wild animals of the land, and for all the flying creatures of the sky, and for every reptile creeping on the land, which has in itself the mind of life, including every green plant for food," and it was so.

God saw all the things that had been made, and they were very good. There was evening and there was morning, the sixth day.

Cosmic Genesis: Chapter 1 Notes

1 Papyrus 12: o t̄h̄s (o ⲑ̄ⲥ̄). Translation: the god. This fragment of the Septuagint uses 'gd' (ⲑ̄ⲥ̄) the contracted form of 'god' (ⲑⲉⲟⲥ), common in the era.

• Codex Alexandrinus: o theos (ⲟ ⲑⲉⲟⲥ). Translation: the god.

• Leningrad Codex: elohim (אֱלֹהִים). Translation: gods (Aramaic), goddesses (Hebrew), god (Assyrian), highest (Akkadian)

• DSS 4QGenᵍ: ålhym (א‎לׄהׄיׄםׄ)

• DSS 4QGenᵇ: word damaged, only -m (ם-) survives. Later in chapter 1, the entire word ålhym (א‎לׄהׄיׄםׄ) survives

• Peshitta: ålhå (ܐܠܗܐ). Translation: god

• Targum Onkelos: YY ('‎'). Translation: Yhů

• Fragment Targums: yeyah ('‎'‎). Translation: Yhů

• Targum Jerusalem: yeyah ('‎'‎). Translation: Yhů

The word ålhym also survives in whole or in part in several other Dead Sea Scrolls fragments of Bereshít, including 4QGenᵈ, 4QGenᶠ, and 4QGenʲ from the Hasmonean Dynasty (140 to 37 BC); 1QGen, and 4QGenᵉ from the Herodian Dynasty (37 BC to 6 AD); as well as MurGen from the Wadi Muraba'at, dating to the early Roman era (6 to 135 AD). The word ålhym (𐤀𐤋𐤄𐤉𐤌) has survived in the Canaanite script in Dead Sea Scroll 4QpaleoGen-Exodˡ, which includes fragments of Genesis and Exodus, and is dated to the Hasmonean era (140 to 37 BC). The word in the Masoretic Text is commonly translated as 'God,' but is a plural form of the Aramaic ålhå (ܐܠܗܐ), meaning 'gods,' or a plural form of the Hebrew elah (אֱלָה) meaning 'goddesses.'

The term ålhym (𐤀𐤋𐤄𐤉𐤌), and ålhym (ܐܠܗܝ), are also direct transcriptions of the Neo-Assyrian word elium (𒀭𒈨𒌍), which by the Iron Age meant 'god,' indicating that text had previously been written in cuneiform, and was translated into Aramaic or Phoenician during the iron age. During the bronze age, the Akkadian, Old Babylonian, and Old Assyrian word was Alium (𒀭𒈨𒌍), and referred to a specific god, ᵈᵉⁱᵗʸÅn (𒀭) the highest god, and father of the other gods. His Akkadian name was derived from the word elûm (𒂊𒈠), meaning 'higher,' as the term was intended to convey the meaning of 'highest.' He was believed to live in the polar region of the sky, making him the highest in the sky, around which all the gods (stars) circled.

The term El elyovn (אֵל עֶלְיוֹן), meaning 'highest god,' was translated into Hebrew in Cosmic Genesis: Chapter 14, where the Greeks translated it as theô tô ypsistô (Θεω τω υψιστω), also meaning 'highest god.' El Elyon is known to have been a major god of the

Canaanites, called ål ůålyn (ⵉ⌐ⴷⵏ ⴷⵏ), meaning 'God and Highest' in an Aramaic language Sefire Treaty from circa 750 BC. The Greek translations of Sanchuniathon's bronze age writing that has survived to the present, referred to the primordial creator god of the Canaanites as Elioun (Ελιουν), which appears to be the same god. According to Sanchuniathon, Elioun was the 'highest' (υψιστος) god, who made the sky and the land, and they made the rest of the gods.

During the Old Babylonian and Old Assyrian eras, the gods Marduk and Ashur, the national gods of Babylon and Assyria, replaced the Akkadian An as the primary god of the Mesopotamian pantheons, and by the iron age, the word elium had came to mean 'god,' explaining why the Aramaic term ålhym (ⵉ⌐ⴷⵏⴷⵏ) would have been interpreted as 'god,' by the Greeks. This means that the origin of Cosmic Genesis chapter 1 would have to have been in the Sumerian, Akkadian, or Neo-Sumerian eras, before the emergence of the Old Babylonian empire. The Aramaic language Targums substitute the term yeyah (?֞) for Elohim. Yeyah (?֞) is a Jewish substitute for Yhů (ⵏ⌐ⴷ^) in Aramaic and Yehvah (יהוה) in Hebrew since the Hasmonean dynasty banned the writing of the name by anyone other than their state scribes in the 2nd century BC. This indicates the process of replacing the god(s) in the texts was still ongoing in the early Christian era.

2 Codex Alexandrinus: $\overline{\text{Oynon}}$ (**OȲNON**). Translations: sky, universe, Uranus (the Greek sky-god)

- Leningrad Codex: shamayim (שָׁמַיִם). Translations: skies, Shamayim (the Canaanite sky-god)

- Peshitta: smyå (ܫܡܝܐ). Translation: sky

- Targum Onkelos: shemayya (שְׁמַיָּא). Translation: sky

- Fragment Targums: not mentioned in the verse

- Targum Jerusalem: shemayya (שְׁמַיָּא). Translation: sky

The skies (Shamayim / Uranus) is depicted as the same type of primordial deity in the Septuagint as it was in the Greek myths and called on to witness blessings and curses, implying consciousness. The name Uranus (Ουρανος) was derived from the Neo-Assyrian term ůruanna (𒀭𒂊𒊩𒀫𒀀), meaning 'roof sky stone,' which was also the Greek description of Uranus, as the ceiling above the flat Earth. This term appears to have been absorbed into Greek as the name Uranus during the early iron age, after the collapse of the Mycenaean civilization, as the name has not been documented in Linear-B, the script of the Mycenaeans.

The term in the Masoretic Text, shamayim is the Hebrew word for 'skies,' however, is also the name of the ancient Semitic sky god, spelled as Šamuû (𒂊𒀀𒉌𒈨) in Old

Akkadian, Šmyn (⟨𒀭𒈠𒈾⟩) in Ugaritic, Šmm (𐤔𐤌𐤌) in Canaanite, Smyn (𐩪𐩣𐩺𐩬) in Sabaean, and Šmyn (𐡔𐡌𐡉𐡍) in Aramaic. In Sumerian cosmology, he was [deity]Ān (𒀭𒀭), the god described as creating the sky, which meant the lower sections of the sky that were closer to the ground. In Old Akkadian, the name of Ān was spelled phonetically as Šamuú (𒊓𒈬𒌑𒌝), meaning 'skies,' or spelled phonetically in a modified Sumerian form as Ānu (𒀭𒌝). He continued to be the same god that he had been in the Sumerian mythology, although his son [deity]Enlil (𒀭𒂗𒆤) became more important, arguably the most important god.

In the later Old Babylonian era, the god Šamuú was still the sky, however, Enlil was replaced by [deity]Marduk (𒀭𒀫𒌓), the sun-calf national god of Babylon. To the north in Assyria, Enlil was replaced by Anshur (𒀭𒊹), the national god 'Eternal Sky' of Assyria, and Šamuú virtually disappeared. This indicates that the origin of Cosmic Genesis chapter 1 was probably in the Sumerian or Akkadian eras, before the Old Babylonian Empire.

3 Codex Alexandrinus: gê (γῆ). Translation: land (or earth, country, soil, Ge)

- Leningrad Codex: aretz (אֶרֶץ). Translations: land (or earth, ground, soil, Eretz)

- Peshitta: årôå (ܐܪܥܐ). Translation: land (or earth, ground, soil, bottom)

- Targum Onkelos: ar'a (אַרְעָא). Translation: land (or earth, ground, soil, bottom)

- Fragment Targums: not mentioned in the verse

- Targum Jerusalem: ar'a (אַרְעָא). Translation: land (or earth, ground, soil, bottom)

The Earth (Eretz / Ge) is depicted as the same type of primordial deity in the Septuagint as she was in the Greek myths and called on to witness blessings and curses, implying consciousness. The Greek name Ge (Γη) was derived from the Sumerian logogram Ki (𒆠), meaning 'land' during the Neo-Assyrian era, although the name of the Earth goddess was spelled phonetically as Ašru (𒀸𒊒) at the time, indicating that the adoption was a scientific term at first.

In early Sumerian cosmology, Ān's wife was known as [diety]Urash (𒀭𒅁), the goddess of barley. This term transitioned during the Sumerian civilization into a title of Ān, and Ān's wife was known as Ki (𒆠), meaning 'Earth.' During the Akkadian era, the goddess was known as Arsatu (𒅕𒊍𒌈𒌑𒌓), although the name was still commonly spelled as Ki (𒆠), or shortened to Kitu (𒆠𒌈). In the later Old Babylonian era, Ānu's wife became known as Āntu (𒀭𒌈), while to the north in Assyrian she became Kishar (𒆥), the 'Eternal Earth.' The Akkadian name arsatu (𒅕𒊍𒌈𒌓), meaning Earth or 'land,' is related to various Semitic words meaning 'land,' or the Earth-goddess, or both, including the Babylonian ersetu (𒅕𒊍𒌈𒌓), Ugaritic års (𐎀𐎗𐎕), Sabaean ård (𐩱𐩧𐩳), Canaanite års

(ארק), Aramaic ârq (ארק), Hebrew eretz (אֶרֶץ), Syriac ârôâ (ܐܪܥܐ), Arabic âard (أَرْض), and Somali arli.

4 Codex Alexandrinus: aoratos cae acatasceuastos (ΑΟΡΑΤΟϹΚΑΙ ΑΚΑΤΑϹΚΕΥΑϹΤΟϹ). Translation: invisible (or unseen) and unfinished

- Leningrad Codex: tohu vavohu (תֹהוּ וָבֹהוּ). Translations: emptiness (or nothingness) and void (or emptiness)

- Peshitta: hŭt tŭh ŭbŭh (ܗܘܐ ܬܘܗ ܘܒܘܗ). Translation: unformed and desolate

- Targum Onkelos: tzadeya vereikanya (צַדְיָא וְרֵיקַנְיָא). Translation: unformed and empty

- Fragment Targums: tahaya uvahaya vetzadu min benei enasha vereikanya mikkol be'ir (תְּהָיָא וּבְהָיָא וְצָדוּ מִן בְּנֵי אֱנָשָׁא וְרֵיקַנְיָא מִכָּל בְּעִיר). Translation: delayed in creationand devoid of humans (or sons of mortal / Enosh) and empty of all animals

- Targum Jerusalem: tahayai uvahayai tzadya mibbenei nash vereikanya min kol be'ir (תְּהָיָּא וּבְהָיָא צָדְיָא מִבְּנֵי נַשׁ וְרֵיקַנְיָא מִן כָּל בְּעִיר). Translation: reborn (or rejuvenated, revived, resurrected) and clear devoid of humans (sons of mortal / Nosh) and empty from all animals

The Greek translation assumes the two words are descriptions of the state of the world, however, in Aramaic the structure of the sentence would have read like the Greek: existing invisible and not finished. However, these terms are not the words found in the Masoretic Text, which appears to be a Classical era Hebrew translation. If written in Akkadian cuneiform, the terms found in the Greek translations would have been bapálu (𒅗𒋻𒇻) and šuklulu (�𒁲𒇻). The Akkadian term bapálu, meaning 'unseen' or 'invisible,' became the Aramaic btl (בטל), meaning 'invisible,' or 'invalid,' however, the Hebrew term bātal (בָּטַל) meant 'cease to exist,' and the related term bātēl (בָּטֵל) meant 'void,' the synonym of the term used in the Masoretic text.

The term šuklulu (𒋗𒁲𒇻), meaning 'to complete' or 'to perfect,' became the Aramaic word šql (שקל) meaning to 'finish' or 'remove,' however, the Hebrew term shékel (שֶׁקֶל), referred to a weight and a monetary unit. These two words, Invisible and not Finished, are not references to aspects of the Mesopotamian creation mythologies, but the Egyptian creation mythologies, as Amen (𒄑𓇋), and Atum (𓇌), were the two major creator gods of Egypt, whose names translate as 'Invisible' and 'Completer.' During the Middle Kingdom era, Amen (Invisible) was the creator god of southern Egypt, while Atum (Completer) was the creator god of northern Egypt. During the Second Intermediate Period that followed, both Amen and Atum became associated with the sun, and their creation aspects diminished, suggesting the Egyptian elements were added during the Middle Kingdom or early in the Second Intermediate period, before the Canaanite Dynasty lost control of southern Egypt.

5 Codex Alexandrinus: scotos (**ϹΚΟΤΟϹ**). Translation: gloom (or darkness, shadow)

• Leningrad Codex: choshech (חֹשֶׁךְ). Translations: darkness (in Aramaic, or evil in Hebrew)

  • Peshitta: ḥšůkå (ܚܶܫܽܘܟܳܐ). Translation: darkness

  • Targum Onkelos: chashocha (חֲשׁוֹכָא). Translation: darkness

  • Fragment Targums: not mentioned in the verse

  • Targum Jerusalem: chashocha (חֲשׁוֹכָא). Translation: darkness

The darkness covering the Abyss, is not a reference to Mesopotamian creation mythology, but Egyptian, as Kek (𓎡𓆚) was the embodiment of darkness that accompanied Nun, the Egyptian version of the Abyss, before the world was created. Nun and Kek were two of the best documented members of the Ogdoad, the eight gods who created the world in the Hermopolitian creation mythology.

6 Codex Alexandrinus: epanô tês abyssou (**ΕΠΑΝѠΤΗϹΑΒΥϹϹΟΥ**). Translation: above (or higher, more than) the abyss

  • Leningrad Codex: al-penei tehovm (עַל־פְּנֵי תְהוֹם). Translations: on (or over, around, larger than, greater than) face (or interior) sea (or deep, Tiamat)

  • Peshitta: ôl åpy myå (ܥܰܠ ܐܰܦ̈ܝ ܡܰܝܳܐ). Translation: Translations: on (or over, around, larger than, greater than) face (or interior) water

  • Targum Onkelos: paras al appei tehoma (פְּרַשׂ עַל אַפֵּי תְהוֹמָא). Translation: spread over on (or around, larger than, greater than) face (or interior) sea (or lake)

  • Fragment Targums: not mentioned in the verse

  • Targum Jerusalem: al appei tehoma (עַל אַפֵּי תְהוֹמָא). Translation: on (or around, larger than, greater than) face (or interior) sea (or lake)

The abyss is a common element in most ancient middle-eastern religions. In Egyptian beliefs, the abyss was called Nun (𓇑𓈗), meaning 'sky waters,' and like many of the other religions, this sea was seen as being a cosmic sea, both below the Earth, and above Sky, and reaching off to infinity. The cosmic sea was an early attempt to envision what is now called outer space, assumed to be composed of freshwater. The Sumerian name for the primordial waters was [deity]Nammu (𒀭𒇉), however, they also referred to it as abzu (𒍪𒀊), meaning 'deep water,' and zuab (𒀊𒍪), meaning 'water deep.' The Greek name abyssou may have been derived from the Sumerian term abzu, however, does not appear to have been imported to Greek thought until the early iron age, as the word is not found in the Linear-B script of the Bronze age.

The Akkadians called the Abyss tâmtu (𒀭𒋾), which meant 'lakes,' however, the god that lived in it was replaced with Ia (𒂍), whose name is believed to be derived from the Sumerian words 'praise' (𒂍) and 'water' (𒀀). The transliteration of the word as Ia is modern, and if transliterated in Akkadian, the name would have been Şēriš Muú, meaning 'praise water.' Ea replaced the earlier Sumerian god ^{deity}Enki (𒂗𒆠), whose name translates as 'God Lord Earth.' During the Old Babylonian era, Ea was replaced by ^{deity}Nabu (𒀭𒀝), the sun-calf god's Marduk's son, and the personification of the planet Mercury in Babylonian cosmology. In Old Babylonian cosmology, the deity of the Abyss tâmtu was ^{deity}Timimat (𒀭𒋾𒊩), generally transliterated into English a Tiamat. Both tâmtu and Tiamat are recorded in Ugaritic as thm (𐎚𐎅𐎎) and Thmt (𐎚𐎅𐎎𐎚), indicating they were separate concepts in bronze age Canaan.

In the book of Habakkuk, written around 612 BC, the goddess was referred to as Tehom (תְּהוֹם), presumably in Judahite, the precursor to Classical Hebrew which was written in the Canaanite script. By the era of Habakkuk, the Israelites had been living in Canaan for centuries, and the word yam (יָם) had replaced təhôm as the word meaning seas, however, Bereshít was written at least a thousand years earlier, indicating that the meaning of the word is the Akkadian 'Abyss,' not the seas that would be created later in the chapter.

7 Codex Alexandrinus: pneuma t̄h̄u (ΠΝΕΥΜΑΘΥ). Translation: air (or wind, breath, spirit) god

- Leningrad Codex: ruach elohim (רוּחַ אֱלֹהִים). Translations: wind (or breath, spirit) god (in Assyrian, or gods in Aramaic, or goddesses in Hebrew)

- Peshitta: rûḥh dålḥå (ܪܘܚܐ ܕܐܠܗܐ). Translation: wind (or life, spirit, smell) of god

- Targum Onkelos: rucha min kodam yeyah (רוּחָא מִן קֳדָם יְיָ). Translation: wind (or life, spirit, smell) from in front of Yhů

- Fragment Targums: rachamin min kodam yeyah havat menashva (רַחֲמִין מִן קֳדָם יְיָ הֲוַת מְנַשְׁבָא). Translation: wind (or life, spirit, smell) of mercy (or compassion) from in front of Yhů quickly blew

- Jerusalem Targum: ruach rachamin min kodam yeyah menatva (רוּחַ רַחֲמִין מִן קֳדָם יְיָ מְנַתְבָא). Translation: wind (or life, spirit, smell) of mercy (or compassion) from in front of Yhů blew

In the Masoretic verse, the term ruach elohim (רוּחַ אֱלֹהִים) is used, which is generally translated as 'Spirit of God' by Christians, and 'Breath of God' by Jews. In Aramaic, the term would translate as wind gods, however, the Greeks did not translate Anemoi (Ανεμοι), meaning that they could not have interpreted the name that way in the Classical era.

In the Enuma Elish, the Babylonian creation myth, the supreme god Marduk used the four winds to capture Tiamat, which is similar to this verse. The four winds are well documented in Old Babylonian texts as being the four seasonal winds. The oldest surviving copy of the Enuma Elish was discovered in the ruins of the Library of Ashurbanipal in Nineveh, dating to the Neo-Assyrian era, however, as the text is Babylonian, it is accepted as being a later Neo-Assyrian copy of an Old Babylonian text. It is also theorized by Assyriologists that the Old Babylonian version was a Babylonian version of an older Akkadian text about Ellil creating the world, as Marduk was the national god of Babylon, who took over the rule of Ellil in several Babylonian copies of older texts. In the much older Sumerian creation mythology the cosmic ocean Nammu, gave birth to the sky Ān and land Ki, who were originally united. Then they created Enlil, who separated the Ān from Ki. This is essentially identical to the Myth of Nut and Ra from Egypt, in which the sky Nut and earth Geb were originally united, until Ra separated them. Enlil's name translates as ^{deity}Lord of Líl' (✳▄𒈨), which generally transliterated into English as Enlil, because the concept of líl (𒈨) does not have a simple English translation. The Sumerians did not understand what air was, meaning that the related concepts of breath and wind were also not understood. These invisible forces were considered líl, however, as líl was also what separated the living (breathing) from the dead (not breathing), líl also meant the equivalent of the modern concepts of spirit, phantom, or ghost.

Additionally, as the unseen líl was what separated the 'here' from the 'there,' líl was also a physical concept that would be translated today as emptiness, void, or space (but not outer space, which would have been the cosmic ocean). Both the Hebrew and Greek translations encompass some of these concepts, however, no English term comes close, as English developed after the Classical era when Hero of Alexandria documented the physics of air in his work Pneumatica. In English, 'air,' 'spirit,' and 'space,' have always been separate concepts. During the Akkadian era, the name of Enlil became Ellil (✳𒈨) in Akkadian, meaning 'God of líl,' which meant 'wind god' in Akkadian, which appears to place the origin of Cosmic Genesis chapter 1 in the Akkadian Era. In Old Babylonian era, the Babylonian national god Marduk replaced Ellil as the creator god, and Ellil was demoted to a secondary sky god. During the subsequent Middle Babylonian era, the Assyrian god Ashur replaced entirely Ellil by 1300 BC.

The replacement of Enlil with Marduk and Assur appears to be related to the way the Semitic interpretation the word líl (𒈨) shifted after the decline of the Sumerian language, as it was a near homonym of līla (𒈫𒉌), meaning 'night.' During the Old Babylonian era, the meaning of the concept of líl shifted from 'wind-spirit,' to 'night-demon,' making Ellil the 'god of demons.' This may have influenced the development of Moabite god El Shadyin, also meaning 'god of demons.' El Shadayin is generally accepted as the Moabite counterpart of the Israelite El Shady, however, šdyn (𐤔𐤃𐤉𐤍) specifically meant 'demons,' in Canaanite, while šdy (𐤔𐤃𐤉) only meant 'powerful.'

The Israelite El Shady only became the 'demonic god' after Aramaic became dominant in southern Canaan due to the meaning of šydå (𐡔𐡉𐡃𐡀) in Aramaic. The two gods did probably share a common origin, as Enlíl's (Ellil's) son in Sumerian and Akkadian religion was Nergal, who by the Middle Babylonian era was viewed as the Mesopotamian version of Resheph. By the era that the Aramaic translation of Cosmic Genesis was made, the god Ellil was forgotten, within Canaan, explaining why the name was translated as růhå ålhym (𐡓𐡅𐡇𐡀 𐡀𐡋𐡄𐡉𐡌), meaning 'wind god.' The modern Hebrew translation of Enlil continues to be ådůn hrůh (אדון הרוח), meaning 'Lord of the wind/spirit.'

8 Codex Alexandrinus: ydatos (ΥΔΑΤΟϹ). Translation: water (or rain, freshwater)

• LXX 122: ydatos (υΔΑΤοϲ). Translation: water (or rain, freshwater)

• Leningrad Codex: penei hammayim (פְּנֵי הַמָּיִם). Translation: face (or interior, speak) the waters

• Peshitta: åpy myå (ܐܦ̈ܝ ܡܝܐ). Translations: surface (or face, region) water

• Targum Onkelos: appei mayya (אַפֵּי מַיָּא). Translation: surface (or face, region) water

• Fragment Targums: appei mayya (אַפֵּי מַיָא). Translation: surface (or face, region) water

• Targum Jerusalem: anpei maya (אַנְפֵּי מַיָא). Translation: my face of water

The pairing of Ellil with the 'waters,' which will later create life, indicates that 'waters' or 'face of waters' was being used as a translation for Ia (𒂊𒀀). In Akkadian creation mythology, after Ellil separated the sky from the land, the god Ia created live. Ia's name is derived from the Sumerian words I (𒂊), meaning both 'praise' and 'come from,' and A (𒀀), meaning 'water.' The transliteration of the name as Ia is modern, and if pronounced in Akkadian, the name would have been Șēriš Muú.

9 Papyrus 12 (LXX 912): êmeran (ΗΜΕΡΑΝ). Translation: Hemera (or day).

- Leningrad Codex: yom (יוֹם). Translation: day, daylight

- Peshitta: åymmå (ܐܝܡܡܐ). Translations: daytime

- Targum Onkelos: yemama (יְמָמָא). Translation: daytime

- Fragment Targums: not mentioned in the verse

- Targum Jerusalem: yemama (יְמָמָא). Translation: daytime

The Greek translation used the name Hemera, the name of a goddess that personified the daytime in Greek philosophy. According to the Greek philosopher Hesiod circa 700 BC, she was the daughter of Erebus (Darkness) and Nyx (Night), along with her brother Aether (Brightness), differing somewhat from this interpretation, which has Hemera and Nyx as siblings, or at least counterparts. The generations of these primordial gods were not agreed upon in the Classical era. Around 475 BC, the Greek poet Bacchylides, recorded that Hermera was the daughter of Nyx and Chronus (Time). Her Roman equivalent was Dies (Day), who the Roman mythographer Hyginus circa (10 AD), was the daughter of Chaos and Caligo (Mist), and the sister of Nox (Night), Erebus and Aether. None of the primordial gods of Greece appear to have been worshiped earlier than the iron age as their names do not appear in the bronze age Mycenaean Linear-B script, suggesting that the idea of them was imported from Canaan after the bronze age collapse, circa 1200 BC.

The Masoretic term was not a direct transliteration of the Canaanite word ym (𐤉𐤌), or Aramaic yŭma (ܝܘܡܐ), but a separate classical era pronunciation, similar to the Arabic word yaŭm (يَوْم) and Sabaean word yŭm (𐩺𐩥𐩣), indicating it was a Hasmonean substitution for an older term. The bronze age Ugaritic word ym (𐎊𐎎) was spelled the same as the later Phoenician Canaanite term, confirming the Masoretic and Arabic spelling were a later development in the Classical era. The earlier Old Akkadian phonetically spelling was ūmu (𒌑𒈬) although it was also written with the Sumerian logogram ud (𒌓). The logogram ud (𒌓) was used to denote several related concepts in the earlier Sumerian language. In the form of the word ud (𒌓), it meant day, heat, fever, or summer. In the form of the word zalag (variously written as 𒌓 or 𒍣), meant pure, bright, or shine. In the form of barbar (𒌓𒌓), it meant 'white.' When combined with the dinger it became [deity]Utu (𒀭𒌓), the sun god, however, the sun was created later in the chapter. While Utu was one of the major gods of the Sumerian pantheon, and his Akkadian counterpart Shamash was one of the major gods of the Akkadian pantheon, Night, was not. This section of text seems to be a reference to the Egyptian Myth of Nut and Ra, in which Ra (Day) separated the Nut (Night-sky) from Geb (Earth) creating the world. The Myth of Nut and Ra was popular in the Middle Kingdom. If this verse was inspired by the Myth of Nut and Ra, it must have been before the New Kingdom era, as

Ra had become the supreme god in northern Egypt, and would not have been treated a mere personification of the day be that era.

10 Papyrus 12: nycta (ⲚⲨⲔⲦⲀ). Translation: Nyx (or night)

- Leningrad Codex: layelah (לַיְלָה). Translation: night

- Peshitta: llyâ (ܠܠܝܐ). Translations: night

- Targum Onkelos: leilya (לִילְיָא). Translation: night

- Fragment Targums: not mentioned in the verse

- Targum Jerusalem: leilya (לֵילְיָא). Translation: night

The Greek translation used the accusative singular of the name Nyx, the name of a goddess that personified the night in Greek philosophy. According to the Greek philosopher Hesiod circa 700 BC, she was the daughter of Chaos, along with her brother Erebus (Darkness). Nyx and Erebus were then the parents of Aether (Brightness) and Hemera (Day). None of the primordial gods of Greece appear to have been worshiped earlier than the iron age as their names do not appear in the bronze age Mycenaean Linear-B script, suggesting that the idea of them was imported from Canaan after the bronze age collapse. The word in the Masoretic text, layelah (לַיְלָה), which means 'night' in Hebrew, is essentially the same in all recorded Semitic languages.

It was līlumz (𒆠𒌋𒈨𒍝) in Old Akkadian, līla (𒆠𒌋𒆤) in Ebliate, ll (𒈨𒈨𒈨𒈨) in Ugaritic, ll (𐤋𐤋) in Phoenician, lly (𐩡𐩡𐩺) in Sabaean, lylyâ (𐡋𐡉𐡋𐡉) in Aramaic, and layla (لَيْلَة) in Arabic, Nevertheless, Night did not play a role in the creation mythology of Mesopotamia, suggesting that this verse was adopted from the Myth of Nut and Ra in the Myth of Nut and Ra, Ra (Day) separated the Nut (Night sky) from Geb (Earth) creating the world.

This mirrors the events described in this section of text, however, unlike the rest of the text, does not appear in Mesopotamian creation mythologies. The Sumerian language, the word for night was g̃ig (𒈪𒈪), however, there was no known god named G̃ig, and there is no known mention of g̃ig being part of the Sumerian creation mythology. Conversely, the name Nut, the Egyptian goddess of the night sky, is documented in the bronze age form of Akkadian used in Canaan and Egypt during the New Kingdom era, as Niâ (𒐊𒀸), and later in the early iron age as Nå (𐤍𐤀) in Canaanite, either of which may have influenced the Greek goddess Nyx (Νυξ).

11 Codex Alexandrinus: stereôma ounon (ϹΤЄΡЄѠΜΑ ΟΫΝΟΝ). Translation: framework (or foundation) Uranus (or vaulted sky)

- Leningrad Codex: rakia' shamayim (רְקִיעַ שָׁמָיִם). Translations: framework Shamayim

- Peshitta: rqyôâ šmyå (ܪܩܝܥܐ ܫܡܝܐ). Translation: space (or opening, thickness) sky

- Targum Onkelos: reki'a shemayya (רְקִיעָא שְׁמַיָּא). Translation: space (or opening, thickness) sky

- Targum Jerusalem: reki'a shemayya (רְקִיעָא שְׁמַיָּא). Translation: space (or opening, thickness) sky

The framework or firmament of the skies was a reference to the metal sky above the flat earth in the Babylonian cosmology. The name Uranus (Ουρανος) was derived from the Neo-Assyrian cuneiform term ùruanna (𒀭𒂍𒎙𒄩), meaning 'roof sky stone,' which was also the Greek interpretation of Uranus, as the ceiling above the flat Earth. This term was subsequently absorbed into Greek as the name Uranus during the Greek Dark Age, after the collapse of the Mycenaean civilization, as the name has not been documented in Linear-B, the script of the Mycenaeans. The Hebrew name is essentially the same as the Old Akkadian name Šamuû (𒐊𒌑𒈨), Ugaritic Šmyn (𒍑𒄭𒌋), Canaanite Šmm (𐤔𐤌𐤌), Sabaean Smyn (𐩪𐩣𐩺𐩬), and Aramaic Šmyn (ש‎מין), all meaning 'skies.' As this chapter appears to have originated in cuneiform, the Hebrew name is imported from the Leningrad Codex.

12 Codex Alexandrinus: Gê (ΓΗ). Translation: land (or earth, country, soil, Ge)

- Leningrad Codex: eretz (אֶרֶץ). Translations: Eretz (or land, dirt, country)

- Peshitta: årôâ (ܐܪܥܐ). Translation: land (or soil)

- Targum Onkelos: ar'a (אַרְעָא). Translation: land (or soil)

- Targum Jerusalem: ar'a (אַרְעָא). Translation: land (or soil)

The Greek name Ge (Γη) was probably derived from the Sumerian term Ki (𒆠), meaning 'Earth,' which is not been documented in Linear-B, the script of the Mycenaean era Greeks, and was therefore most likely introduced by Phoenician or Neo-Assyrian traders during the early iron age. The Hebrew name eretz (אֶרֶץ), meaning earth or land, is essentially the same in many Semitic languages, including the Akkadian Arsatu (𒅈𒐼𒌁𒌍), which was also spelled with the Sumerian logogram Ki (𒆠), Ugaritic års (𐎀𐎗𐎕), Canaanite års (𐤀𐤓𐤑), Neo-Babylonian Erṣetum (𒅈𒋼𒌈), Sabaean ård (𐩱𐩧�), and Aramaic årq (ארק). The Egyptian version of was Geb (𓈖𓃀), who was created when Ra (Day) separated him from Nut (Night-sky) in the Myth of Nut and Ra, or by the creator god Shu (Dryness) in the Heliopolite creation mythology. As the

Israelites didn't worship the Greek gods, the name is imported from the Masoretic text.

13 Codex Alexandrinus: Thalassas (ѲⲀⲖⲀⲤⲤⲀⲤ). Translation: seas (or Thalassas)

- Leningrad Codex: yammim (יַמִּים). Translations: seas

- Peshitta: ymmå (ܝܲܡܡܹ̈ܐ). Translation: seas

- Targum Onkelos: yammei (יַמְמֵי). Translation: Yam (or sea)

- Targum Jerusalem: yammei (יַמְמֵי). Translation: Yam (or sea)

The Greek term is the name of a primordial Greek spirit of the sea, and accepted as the Laconian variant of the word 'seas.' In the Attican and Koine dialects, the name was Thalattê (Θαλαττη), which the Hellenistic Babylonian writer Berossus used as the Greek translation of the name Tiamat. Conversely, the Hebrew translation uses the plural form, meaning 'seas.' The Old Akkadian name could only have been tâmtu (𒀀𒈦𒌈), meaning 'lake' or 'sea,' however, during the Old Babylonian era, term became [deity]Tiamat (𒀭𒀀𒈠𒌈). Tiamat was the goddess that replaced Ia in the Abyss, meaning that by the early iron age, when the Canaanite translation was been made, the term would have needed to be replaced with the Canaanite word for 'seas.'

14 Codex Alexandrinus: exagagetô ta ydata erpeta (ⲈⲜⲀⲄⲀⲄⲈⲦⲰⲦⲀⲨⲆⲀⲦⲀ ⲈⲣⲠⲈⲦⲀ). Translation: export from the water reptiles

- LXX 346: exagetô ta ydata erpeta (ἐξαγέτω τὰ ὑδάτα ἑρπετὰ). Translation: lead out of the water reptiles.

- Leningrad Codex: yishretzu hammayim sheretz (יִשְׁרְצוּ הַמַּיִם שֶׁרֶץ). Translations: will swarm the waters swarms

- Peshitta: nrḥšûn myå rḥšå (ܢܪܚܫܘܢ ܡܝܐ ܪܚܫܐ). Translation: will flow from water insects (or reptiles)

- Targum Onkelos: yirchashun mayya rechesh (יְרַחֲשׁוּן מַיָּא רְחֵשׁ). Translation: will crawl from water insects (or reptiles, vermin)

- Targum Jerusalem: yerachashun rekakei moy recheish (יְרַחֲשׁוּן רְקָקֵי מוֹי רְחֵישׁ). Translation: will crawl from swamp water insects (or reptiles, vermin)

15 Codex Alexandrinus: psychôn zôsôn (ⲮⲨⲬⲰⲚⲌⲰⲤⲰⲚ). Translation: minds (or personalities, psyches) living

- Leningrad Codex: nefesh chayyah (נֶפֶשׁ חַיָּה). Translations: minds (or lives, souls, persons) of animals

- Peshitta: npšå ḥytå (ܢܦܫܐ ܚܝܬܐ). Translation: breath (or psyche) living

- Targum Onkelos: nafsha chayta (נַפְשָׁא חַיְתָא). Translation: breath (or psyche) living

- Targum Jerusalem: nafshat biryaita (נַפְשַׁת בְּרְיָיתָא). Translation: breath (or psyche) creatures

This is generally used only in relation to humans and messengers who have a more developed mind. Some Christian, Islamic, and Druze groups take this as a reference to another world before God made Adam. According to the Islamic historian Al-Tabari in the 9th century AD (3rd century AH), this was the time when the Jinn (Genies) rebelled against Allah, and the Hinn fought on the side of the angels under the leadership of Iblis (possibly Satan before his rebellion) against the Jinn.

The Hinn are not described in the Quran, and some view them as the reptiles referenced in Genesis 1. Those that accept the idea of an entire civilization between the 5th and 6th days of creation do not accept the idea of a literal 24 hour day, but an eon of time, which the Hebrew word 'yom' can also be interpreted as.

16 Codex Alexandrinus: cêtê ta megala (ΚΗΤΗΤΑΜΕΓΑΛΑ). Translation: Cetus the Great

- Leningrad Codex: tanninim haggedolim (תַּנִּינִם הַגְּדֹלִים). Translation: crocodiles (or dragons) the great (in Hebrew, or twisted in Aramaic)

- DSS 4QGen^d: tnynym- (-תנינים). Only the first word survives. Translation: dragons.

- DSS 4QGen^b: tnynm hgdlym (תנינם הגדלים). Translation: dragons the great (in Hebrew, or twisted in Aramaic).

- Peshitta: tnynå rûrbå (ܬܢܝܢܐ ܪܘܪܒܐ). Translation: dragon (or sea serpent, monster, serpent, Satan, Draco) lord

- Targum Onkelos: tanninayya ravrevayya (תַּנִּינַיָּא רַבְרְבַיָּא). Translation: dragon (or sea serpent, monster, serpent, Draco) great-master

- Targum Jerusalem: taninaya ravrevaya yat livyatan uvar zugeih demit'attedin leyom nechemata (תַּנִּינַיָּא רַבְרְבַיָּא יַת לִוְיָתָן וּבַר זוּגֵיהּ דְּמִתְעַתְּדִין לְיוֹם נֶחֱמָתָא). Translation: dragon (or sea serpent, monster, serpent, Draco) great-master, he leviathan, and his partner (or wife) which are prepared for the day of consolidation

The Greek term is generally translated as 'whale,' however, the Cetus was a legendary monster in Aethiopia in the legend of Perseus, which was also referenced in the Books of Psalms and Job. In Greek mythology, Cetus was killed by the demi-god Perseus, who, like the seventh sage Lu-Nanna, was part human and part god, suggesting the Greek and

Neo-Akkadian stories had a common origin. Perseus was the legendary founder of the Mycenaean civilization, which would place the origin of the story in the 1600s BC, however, thus far no evidence of the name Perseus has been found in the Liner-B script from the era, and so he is widely believed to have been a fictional character developed later in the iron age.

The translators of the Peshitta and Targums interpreted the term the same as the Greek translators. In the early 2nd century Targum Onkelos, the term was similar to the Greek, indicating that the earlier Aramaic source texts for the Septuagint probably read quite similar. Like the Septuagint's interpretation, Onkelos can be interpreted either as a 'great-master monster,' or as a constellation, however, Onkelos uses the Aramaic name for Draco, instead of the name for Cetus. The 4th century Peshitta reads the same way, however, by the forth century, the term had shifted within Christian Aramaic, and now referred to the Lord Satan, meaning the verse had become about the creation of Satan.

The Canaanite word tannin (──▸──▸ / תַּנִּין / 𐤕𐤍𐤕), and Aramaic word tnynå (ܐܬܢܝܢ / ܬܢܝܢܐ), are both accepted by linguists as being derived from the Akkadian word danninu (𒁭𒅗𒉿𒌋), meaning 'underword.' This suggests the original text was about God creating everything between the sky-waters (υδατα) above the framework (στερεωμα) of the sky (ουρανον), and the underworld (𒁭𒅗𒉿𒌋). The transition of the term danninu in Canaanite from 'underworld' to 'serpent' or 'crocodile,' took place during the Hyksos dynasty, indicating that the original version of Bereshít must have been written during the Egyptian Canaanite Dynasty or earlier.

Cosmic Genesis: Chapter 2

The heavens and Earth were finished, and the whole world of them. God finished on the sixth[1] day the works which he made, and he ceased on the seventh day from all his works which he made. God blessed the seventh day and sanctified it because on it he completed his work, which God started in the beginning.

This is the book of the generations of Shamayim and Eretz, when it took place, in the day in which God made the sky and land, and every plant of the field before it was on land, and all the grass of the field before it sprang up, for God had not rained on the land,[2] and there was not a man to cultivate it. But there rose a fountain out of the land and watered the whole surface of Eretz. God formed the man of the dust of Eretz and breathed on his face the breath of life, and the man became a living mind.

Lord the god planted a paradise[3] to the east, in Eden,[4] and placed there the man that he had formed.

God also made to sprout up out of the land every tree beautiful to see and good for food, and the tree of life in the middle of paradise, and the tree of learning that which is to be known of good and evil. A river proceeded out of Eden to water paradise, where it divided itself into four heads. The name of the one is Pison[5] which winds through the whole land of Euilat,[6] where there is gold. The gold of that land is good, and there is also carbuncle and emerald. The name of the second river is Karun,[7] which winds through all of Khuzestan.[8] The third river is Tigris,[9] this is the one that flows out past the Assyrians. The fourth river is the Euphrates.[10]

Lord the god[11] took the man that he had formed, and placed him in paradise, to cultivate and keep it. Lord the god ordered Adam,[12] "From every tree in paradise you may eat, but from the tree of the knowledge of good and evil, you will not eat, or in whichever day you eat of it, you will die the death."

Lord the god said, "It is not good that the man should be alone, let us make for him a helper according to him."

God formed even more out of Eretz, all the wild animals of the field and all the birds of the sky, and he brought them to Adam, to see what he would call them, and whatever Adam called any living mind, that was the name of it. Adam called names of all the livestock and all the birds of the sky, and all the wild animals of the field, but for Adam, there was not found a helper like himself.

God brought a trance on Adam, and he slept, and he took one of his ribs and filled up the flesh. God built the rib which he took from Adam into a woman, and brought her to Adam. Adam said, "This now is bone out of my bones, and flesh of my flesh. She will be called wife because she was taken out of her husband." Therefore will a man leave his father and his mother and will be cemented to his wife, and the two will be one flesh.

Cosmic Genesis: Chapter 2 Notes

1 Codex Alexandrinus: ectê (ЄКΤΗ). Translation: sixth

• Leningrad Codex: shevi'i (שְׁבִיעִי). Translation: seventh

• Peshitta: šttå (ܫܬܐ). Translation: sixth

• Samaritan Torah: šyšy (ᛘᛦᛘᛦ). Translation: sixth

• Targum Onkelos: shevi'a'ah (שְׁבִיעָאָה). Translation: seventh

• Targum Jerusalem: shevi'a'ah (שְׁבִיעָאָה). Translation: seventh

2 Codex Alexandrinus: ou gar ebrexen o t̄h̄s̄ epi tên gên (ΟΥΓΑΡΕΒΡΕΞΕΝΟΘϹЄΠΙ ΤΗΝΓΗΝ). Translation: not since drenched the god on the land

• Papyrus Oxyrhynchus 1007 (LXX 907): ou gar ebrexen o ZZ epi tên gên (ΟΥΓΑΡ ЄΒΡΕΞΕΝ ZZЄΠΙ ΤΗΝΓΗΝ). Translation: not since drenched Yhůh on the land. LXX 907 is unusual in that it appears to include an attempt to write the Phoenician letters ZZ as a substitute for the word 'God.' At the time, Jews were substituting the equivalent letters in Hebrew for the name of god, in the form of '', however, they rarely used the Phoenician script. It may have been a Greek translation of the Samaritan Torah, known in Greek as the Samareitikon (Σαμαρειτικον), however, is too damaged to be sure.

• LXX 509: ou gar ebrexen cyrios ho theos epi tên gên othos (οουγαρ ϭυρόξόν ο θόϭόϭπι τḷν γḷν οθόϭ). Translation: not since drenched the god on the land the god.

• LXX 17: ou gar ebrexen cyrios ho theos epi tên gên (ουγαρ ϭυρόξόν κυριοϲ ο θόϭ όϭπι τḷν γḷν). Translation: not since drenched lord the god on the land.

• LXX 75: ou gar ebrechen ho theos epi tên gên (ουγαρ ϭυρόχόν ο θόϭ όϭπι τḷν γḷν). Translation: not since rained the god on the land.

• LXX 72: ou gar ebrechen ho theos epi tês gês (ογγαβ βυβϸχϭν ο Θϭος ϭπι τℓς γℓς).
Translation: not since drenched the god on the world.

• Leningrad Codex: ki lo himtir Yehvah elohim al-ha'aretz (כִּי לֹא הִמְטִיר יְהוָה אֱלֹהִים
עַל־הָאָרֶץ). Translation: because not the rain Yehvah elohim on the Earth

• Peshitta: mtl dlå åht mryå ålhå mtrå ôl åyp årôå (ܡܛܠ ܕܠܐ ܐܚܬ ܡܪܝܐ ܐܠܗܐ
ܡܛܪܐ ܥܠ ܐܦܝ ܐܪܥܐ). Translation: roof of everything your master (or lord) god rain
on surface (or region) land

• Targum Onkelos: la achit mitra adonai yeyah al ar'a (לָא אָחִית מִטְרָא יְיָ אֱלֹהִים עַל
אַרְעָא). Translation: not your rain Yhůh elohim (or gods) on land (or region)

• Targum Jerusalem: la imtar adonai yeyah al ar'a (לָא אִמְטַר יְיָ אֱלֹהִים עַל אַרְעָא).
Translation: not your rain Yhůh gods on land (or region)

3 Codex Alexandrinus: paradison (ΠΑΡΑΔΕΙϹΟΝ). Translation: walled garden

• Leningrad Codex: gan (גַּן). Translation: garden

• Peshitta: prdyśå (ܦܪܕܝܣܐ). Translation: paradise, walled garden

• Targum Onkelos: ginta (גִּינְתָא). Translation: garden

• Fragment Targums: ginta (גִנְתָא). Translation: garden

• Targum Jerusalem: ginunita (גִּינוּנִיתָא). Translation: pleasure garden

The Greek word paradise is ultimately derived from the Avestan pairi.daēza (پیرِدَئزَ
وَدئزَ), meaning 'walled enclosure.' It was adopted into Neo-Babylonian as pardēsu
(𒉺𒅕𒌷), Old Persian Cuneiform as paradayadåm (𒊕𒂊𒆠𒐊𒐊𒈨), Aramaic as prdyså
(פרדיסא), and Greek as paradisos (παράδεισος). The Hebrew term gan (גַּן) is a
continuation of the Sumerian word gan (𒃷) which meant 'cultivated field.' The
logogram was also used in Akkadian to mean 'field,' however, the Old Akkadian
pronunciation was eqel (𒂍𒀭), and the later Neo-Assyrian and Neo-Babylonian
pronunciation was eqlum (𒆠𒌋𒌝 / 𒀖𒇻𒌝). The Semitic term is also found in Sabaean as
ḥql (𐩢�𐩡), Aramaic as ḥqlā (נʼגʼ), Arabic as ḥaql (حَقْل), and Ge'ez as häkl (ሐቅል), as well
as the Central Atlas Tamazight akal (ⴰⴽⴰⵍ). The term gan is not generally found in
Afro-Asiatic languages, and the Hebrew word appears to be a legacy of the word
surviving in the Bereshít. While it may have been written in Akkadian cuneiform as
the logogram 𒃷, it could not have been written in Aramaic without being translated
into another tern such as 'field' (נʼגʼ) or 'paradise' (פרדיסא). The existence of the
word in Bereshít suggests that the book originated in the Neo-Sumerian Empire, when
phonetic spelling of Sumerian terms was common in Akkadian cuneiform.

4 Codex Alexandrinus: Edem (ЄΔЄM)

- Leningrad Codex: Eden (עֵדֶן)

- Peshitta: Ôdn (ܐܕܢ)

- Targum Onkelos: Eden (עֵדֶן)

- Fragment Targums: Eden (עֵדֶן)

- Targum Jerusalem: Eden (עֵדֶן)

Most scholars agree this is a transliteration of the Akkadian word edinu (𒂔) meaning 'plain,' itself derived from the Sumerian word edin (𒂔) also meaning 'plain' or 'steppe.' In Sumerian and Akkadian the word referred to the plains of southern Iraq. In the Sumerian creation stories, humans were first made in edin, suggesting this secondary creation narrative in chapter 2 was also part of the text since before the Israelites entered Egypt during the Middle Kingdom era.

5 Codex Alexandrinus: Phisôn (ΦЄΙϹШN)

- LXX 127: Physôn (Φυσων)

- LXX 75: Phêsôn (Φησων)

- LXX 19: Phisôn (Φεισων)

- LXX 246: Phisôn (Φισων)

- Leningrad Codex: Pishon (פִּישׁוֹן)

- Peshitta: Pyšůn (ܦܝܫܘܢ)

- Targum Onkelos: Pishon (פִּישׁוֹן)

- Targum Jerusalem: Pishon (פִּישׁוֹן)

There has been speculation regarding the location of this river for over 2000 years. In the 1st century AD, the Jewish historian Flavius Josephus identified it as the Ganges in India, in his Antiquities of the Jews. The 4th century Cave of Treasures identified it as being the Indus River in Pakistan. In the 11th century AD, the Rabbi Shlomo Yitzchaki (Rashi) identified it as the Nile. It has also variously been identified as the Roini in Georgia, the Aras in the Armenian highlands, and the Amu Darya in Central Asia. Most of these locations have been suggested based on older commentaries from Jewish and Israelite communities spread across the old Persian Empire.

Rashi's theory ultimately derived from Egyptian-Israelite commentary regarding the name Pachnamunis (Παχναμουνίς), a major city in the Sebennytos district of the Nile

Delta, through which one of the major tributaries of the Nile flowed in ancient times. The city was also the capital of Egypt during the 30th Dynasty (380 to 343 BC). The name Pachnamunis seems to have originated in the Libyan 23rd Dynasty of Egypt, between 837 and 728 BC. It is composed of the words Pachn and amun (oᄃol), meaning 'Pachn River' in Libyan languages.

The dominant theory today is that it was a reference to the dried river bed of a major river that once flowed across the Arabian Peninsula from the mountains near Medina to the old Iraqi wetlands, where the Euphrates, Tigris, and Karun Rivers merge. Part of this river still flows seasonally today as the Wadi al-Batin (وادي الباطن) in northeast Saudi Arabia, Kuwait, and Iraq. The Wadi al-Batin is the final section of the much longer Wadi al-Rummah dry river valley that runs across the peninsula, but is today disconnected from the Wadi al-Batin by sand dunes that have covered a section of the former river valley.

When the river still flowed, it was an estimated 1,200 km (750 mi) long, and connected a number of now dried lakes in the interior of the Arabian peninsula. It is unclear when the river last flowed its full length, but some estimates place it at 8000 BC. The wadi that runs out of the mountains near Medina still floods approximately three times a century. In 1838, the wadi overflowed and created a 520 km^2 (200 mile^2) lake that lasted for 2 years. If this name originated in Sumerian, like several other terms in Cosmic Genesis and Bereshít, then the name was probably not a name, but a description of the dried out river bed. In Sumerian, the term pronounced as pí sún (𒈦𒀭𒆠), would mean 'it is destroyed.' This supports the identification of the Pison as being the dried out riverbed of the al-Rummah when the oldest form of the text was written, with the flowing river being a distant memory from an age before the great flood.

6 Codex Alexandrinus: Euilat (ⲉⲩⲉⲓⲗⲁⲧ)

- LXX 707: Euilato (ⲉⲩⲓⲗⲁⲧⲟ)

- LXX 18: Ebitat (ⲉⲩⲓⲧⲁⲧ)

- LXX 121: Euêlat (ⲉⲩⲏⲗⲁⲧ)

- LXX 75: Ebilat (ⲉⲩⲓⲗⲁⲧ)

- LXX 82: Euêlattôn (ⲉⲩⲏⲗⲁⲧⲧⲟⲛ)

- LXX 246: Euilat (ⲉⲩⲓⲗⲁⲧ)

- Leningrad Codex: Chavilah (חֲוִילָה)

- Peshitta: Hůylâ (ܚܘܝܠܐ)

- Targum Onkelos: Chavilah (חֲוִילָה)

Targum Jerusalem: Hindikei (הִינְדְקֵי). Translation: India

According to the author of the Cave of Treasures, attributed to Ephrem the Syrian in the 4th century AD, this was Hend, the ancient name of the Sindh province of Pakistan. Few modern scholars accept this interpretation. Based on the identification of the Pishon River as the Wadi al-Rummah, and the land of Euilat / Chavilah having gold, this would have been the Mahd adh Dhahab (مَهد الذَهب), meaning 'cradle of gold,' near modern Medina, in Saudi Arabia. The region is believed to have still been connected to Sumer via a series of wadis along the Wadi al-Rummah and Wadi al-Batin as late as 3000 BC, and was the site of extensive gold mines at the time. It is still the site of significant gold mines, which appear to have been in constant production since ancient times. The two names in the Hebrew and Greek translations may support this claim, if accepted as beginning in Sumerian, like many of the other terms in this section of text. As the Greek is based on an Aramaic transliteration, and the Hebrew is based on a Canaanite transliteration, the differences can be accounted for by two alternate transliterations from cuneiform.

The Greek transliteration is missing the first sound in the Hebrew transliteration, the ch (ח), which could be accounted for by the original word beginning with a ki (𒆠), meaning 'land' as it could have been interpreted as a repetitive term once translated into another language. Many Akkadian geographical terms included a the term 'land' (𒆠), including ᵈˡᵃⁿᵈSumer' (𒆠𒂗𒄀) and ᵈˡᵃⁿᵈAkkad' (𒆠𒀝). The final sound in the word is also different, however, can be accounted for by different transliterations of the 𒂼 logogram. In Sumerian 𒂼 was pronounced as A, while in Akkadian and later Semitic languages, it was pronounced as ET (or ED). The logogram 𒂼 meant several related concepts involving labor, wages, and military forces. Based on the common Greek and Hebrew spelling of the rest of the word, it appears the Sumerian term would have been ᵏⁱÉuila (𒆠𒂼𒂍𒇧), meaning ᵈˡᵃⁿᵈEstate of the lord of the porter-laborers.' This description of the land supports the idea that the pí sún (𒉿𒋤) river was already reduced to being a series of wadis running from the Cradle of Gold to the wetlands of Sumer.

7 Codex Alexandrinus: Gêôn (ΓΗΩΝ)

- LXX 15: Geôn (Γεων)

- LXX 392: Gêsôn (Γησων)

- LXX 730: Gaeôn (Γαιων)

- LXX 19: Giôn (Γ϶͡ϊοͦν)

- Leningrad Codex: Gichon (גִּיחֹון)

- Peshitta: Gyḥŭn (ܓܝܚܘܢ)

- Targum Onkelos: Gichon (גִּיחֹון)

- Targum Jerusalem: Gichon (גִּיחֹון)

This river's location is debated, as the Greek identification of it flowing through Aethiopia suggests it is the Nile. In modern Sudan (Classical Aethiopia) and Ethiopia (ancient Punt) it has generally been interpreted as the Blue Nile (Abay), which was known as Gʷazzam ('ቦHም) in the earliest records from the region.

The dominant view outside of Northeast Africa, is that it was the Karun River, which flows through Khuzestan province in southwestern Iran. Identifying the Gichon as the Karun is based on the identification of Kush in the Masoretic Text as the Khuz instead of the Kingdom of Kush. If the name Gêôn / Gichon is derived from the Sumerian name, the original name was probably ^idG̃eana (𒀭𒄀𒐼𒈾𒆠), meaning ^riverflowing in rocks,' similar to the Sumerian name for the Tigris: ^idIdigna (𒀭𒄿𒈦𒄘𒁺), meaning ^riverflowing rough,' and the Sumerian name for the Euphrates: ^idBuranun (𒀭𒌓𒉣𒈗), meaning ^riverCopper source.' The Euphrates was the source of the copper for the Sumerian civilization, and the Tigris is a rough fast-flowing river, while the Karun flowed down through the Zargos Mountains into plains of Khuzestan before flowing into the old Sumerian wetlands in Iraq. As the location of 'Kush' is confirmed as being in Khuzestan in the genealogy of nations, the modern name Karun in used as a translation for the Geon.

8 Codex Alexandrinus: gên Aithiopias (ΓΗΝ ΑΙΘΙΟΠΙΑϹ). Translation: land Aethiopia (or Sudan, Kush)

- LXX 392: gên Aithiôpias (γ˞ην Αιθιοοπιλϲ). Translation: land Aethiopia (or Sudan, Kush)

- LXX 319: gên Aithiôpian (γ˞ην Αιθιοοπιλν). Translation: land Aethiopians (or Sudanese, Kushites)

- LXX 75: gên Ethiopias (γ˞ην Εθιοπιλϲ). Translation: land Aethiopia (or Sudan, Kush)

- Leningrad Codex: eretz Kush (אֶרֶץ כּוּשׁ). Translation: land Kush (or Sudan)

- Peshitta: ar'a deChush (ܐܪܥܐ ܕܟܘܫ). Translation: land of Kush (or Sudan)

- Targum Onkelos: ar'a deChush (אַרְעָא דְכוּשׁ). Translation: land of Kush (or Sudan)

- Targum Jerusalem: ar'a deChush (אַרְעָא דְכוּשׁ). Translation: land of Kush (or Sudan)

The Greek term Aethiopia did not refer to the lands of the modern nation of Ethiopia, but the kingdom of Kush in modern Sudan. Aethiopia was also sometimes used for the region of southern India where darker skinned people's lived. The translators of the Septuagint interpreted the name in Cosmic Genesis as referring to the land of Kush, south of Egypt, however, this may have been done for political reasons, as the Ptolemy's had plans to conquer Kush early in their dynasty. Exploratory expeditions were sent, into modern Sudan, and at one point followed the Nile and Black Nile (Atbarah-Tekezé) into the highlands of Punt (northern Eritrea). The majority of the Kushite civilization had been relocated farther south after the Persian invasion, and the Greeks ultimately decided not to attempt the invasion. The dominant theory about what this word means outside of Northeast Africa, is that is refers to Khuzestan province in southwest Iran. The region does not appear to have been known as 'Khuze land,' until the 9th century AD when it became Khuzestan, named after the Khuz people that lived there.

The term Khuz was applied to the dark skinned decedents of the Elamites that originally inhabited the region from at least the Neo-Assyrian era onward. Multiple Classical and Medieval sources suggest or claim that 'Khuze' was the Elamite pronunciation of the Greek Uxi (Ύξι) and Old Persian Uvaja (𐎢𐎺𐎩), both referring to the region later called Khuzestan, however, the earlier Elamite name of Elam before the Persians settled in the region was Haltamti (𒄷𒆷𒁄𒋾), and therefore modern scholars question this claim. The more probable origin of the name Khuz for the dark skinned descendants of the Elamites, was the Neo-Assyrian kusaaa (𒌑𒊬𒈫) and Neo-Babylonian word kuúšu (𒌑𒅖𒌑), which both referred to dark skinned people of any origin. As the term would have been the same in both Aramaic and Hebrew, the Greek translation would have been the first translation to explicitly indicate the land of Aethiopia in modern Sudan. Later in the genealogy of nations, the author of that section of text, who was most likely the original Aramaic translator, uses the name Kush for the name of the people who lived in Sumer, confirming that is was Khuzestan being referred. As års Kůš (ארץ כוש) means 'Khuze land,' the modern name is used.

9 Codex Alexandrinus: Tigris (ΤΙΓΡΙϹ). Translation: Tigris

- LXX 55: Tigris (Τίγρίϲ)

- LXX 319: Tigrês (Τίγρĥϲ)

- LXX 54: Tygris (Τυγρίϲ)

- Leningrad Codex: Chiddekel (חִדֶּקֶל). Translation: Tigris

- Peshitta: Dqlt (ܕܶܩܠܰܬ). Translation: Tigris

- Targum Onkelos: telita'ah Diglat (תְּלִיתָאָה דִּיגְלַת). Translation: royal Tigris

- Targum Jerusalem: Diglat (דִּיגְלַת). Translation: Tigris

Both the Greek and Hebrew names are ultimately derived from the Sumerian name of the Tigris River: [id]Idigna (𒀀𒁁𒄘𒂼𒈾), via the Akkadian Cuneiform name: Idiglat (𒀀𒁁𒄘𒂼𒈾). The Aramaic name was adopted from the Akkadian name as Dyglt (𐡃𐡉𐡂𐡋𐡕), which was adopted by the Persians as Tigrā (𐎫𐎡𐎥𐎼𐎠), which was in turn transliterated into Greek as Tígris (Τιγρις). The Hebrew name appears to be a direct transliteration of the Akkadian name. The reference to the Tigris as 'royal' in the Targum Onkelos, may have use a copy of the Aramaic translation made during the reign of King Hezekiah, when the Tigris river was the most important river in the Neo-Assyrian Empire.

10 Codex Alexandrinus: Euphratês (ΕΥΦΡΑΤΗС). Translation: Euphrates

- LXX 707: Ephratês (ΕϐϼΑΤⱢС)

- LXX 56: Eyphratês houtos o megas potamos (ΕὐϩϼΑΤⱢС ουτος ο μεγας ποταμος).

Translation: Eyphrates other the great river

- Leningrad Codex: Ferat (פְּרָת). Translation: Euphrates

- Peshitta: Prt (ܦܪܬ). Translation: Euphrates

- Targum Onkelos: Ferat (פְּרָת). Translation: Euphrates

- Targum Jerusalem: Ferat (פְּרָת). Translation: Euphrates

Both the Greek and Hebrew names are ultimately descended from the Sumerian name of the Euphrates river: [id]Buranun (𒀀𒁁𒄘𒈨), via the Akkadian name Purattu (𒀀𒁁𒄘𒈨). The Aramaic name was adopted from the Akkadian name as Prt (פרת), which was later adopted into Hebrew as Ferat (פְּרָת). The Akkadian name was also adopted as the Elamite Úipratuiš (𒌑𒅀𒉿𒀉𒋗𒅖), which was adopted into Persian as [h]Ufrātuš (𐎢𐎳𐎼𐎠𐎬𐎢𐏁), and then into Greek as Euphratês (Ευφρατης). The extended text in LXX 56 appear to be a note added by an Egyptian scribe.

11 Codex Alexandrinus: c̄s o t̄hs (ΚϹΟΘϹ). Translation: Lord the god

- Leningrad Codex: Yehvah elohim (יְהֹוָה אֱלֹהִים). Translation: Yehvah elohim

- Peshitta: mryå ålhå (ܡܪܝܐ ܐܠܗܐ). Translation: master (or lord) God

- Targum Onkelos: yeyah elohim (יְיָ אֱלֹהִים). Translation: Yhů elohim

- Fragment Targums: yeyah elhim (יְיָ אֱלֹהִים). Translation: Yhŭ elhim (or gods)

- Targum Jonathan: yeyah elhim (יְיָ אֱלֹהִים). Translation: Yhŭ elhim (or gods)

The Aramaic sections of Masoretic Daniel that were not translated into Hebrew maintain the term adonai ha'elohim (אֲדֹנָי הָאֱלֹהִים), meaning the 'Lord of the gods' where the Septuagint has 'Lord the god' (Κυριον τον θεον). As most books of the Septuagint were translated from Aramaic texts, the Aramaic text almost certainly used the term adonai ha'elohim where the Septuagint has 'Lord the god.' The name Yehvah appears to have been added to most of the books in the Masoretic Text when the texts were translated to Hebrew during the Hasmonean Dynasty of Judea, between 140 and 37 BC.

According to the records from the time, this was to repair the damage King Manasseh had done 600 years earlier when he removed the name Yehvah from the Israelite Texts, however, no evidence has survived from the era of Manasseh or earlier that proves the name was originally in the text, suggesting it was an attempt by the first Hasmonean High-Priest/King Simon the Zealot to create a national Judean religion with a god having a name similar to the god Jove.

The name Yehvah, in the Aramaic form of Yhŭ (וחי^) does appear to have originally been in some of the books of the Septuagint, such as Leviticus, which originated under the rule of King Josiah or later, and Yhŭ was a popular god among Judeans and Israelites under Persian and Greek rule. The translators at the Library of Alexandria transliterated this name as Iaw (Ιαω) in the books it was originally in, however, under the Hasmonean Dynasty it seems to have been added to all the books translated into Hebrew, creating some confusion among early Christians.

There were debates in the early Christian era about which version of the Israelite scriptures to use, the Greek, Hebrew, Samaritan, or Syriac translations, resulting in different versions of the scriptures being used by different churches. Some versions replaced the name Lord with Iaw in the Greek texts, either in the Greek form as Ιαω, or by copying in the Hebrew form of the name Yhŭh (יהוה) or the older Phoenician form of Yhŭh (𐤉𐤄𐤅𐤄), or by mocking the Hebrew with Greek letters as ΠΙΠΙ. This created a great deal of confusion among Christians, and ultimately the books of the Septuagint that had the name Iaw in them were redacted so all the books used the term Lord (Κυριος). Most Christian translations, as well as Jewish translations, have continued to use the term 'Lord' in place of the name Yehvah, due to the prohibition on using any names of God that was introduced during the Hasmonean dynasty.

There are no early surviving copies of the Septuagint's version of Genesis which have the name Iaw (Ιαω / וחי^) in them, like some of the other books of the Septuagint, and therefore it cannot be proven if the name was in the Septuagint's Cosmic Genesis or not, however, the terms used in Cosmic Genesis are consistent with the surviving Aramaic sections of Masoretic Daniel, strongly suggesting the Aramaic source text the Greek translators used, included the term adny hålhyn, and not Yhů hålhyn.

The Biblical Aramaic term Lord of the gods (אֲדֹנָי הָאֱלֹהִים) is a translation of a Sumerian and Akkadian title, applied to Ān by the Sumerians, and Ellil by the Akkadians. The Sumerian title appears to have originally been 'lord of the asterisms,' however, by the Akkadian era Ellil replaced An as the highest god, the one who resided in the polar region of the sky, and Ān moved down into the ecliptic region, specifically as the asterism known in Egypt as Sah, and later known as Orion to the Greeks. Given the description of the creation of man involving wind/spirit being blown into man, it appears this lord of the gods was Ellil.

12 Codex Alexandrinus: Adam (ⲁⲇⲁⲙ)

• Leningrad Codex: ha'adam (הָאָדָם). Translation: the man (or earth, soil, light brown, red)

• Peshitta: lådm (ܠܐܕܡ). Translation: the man

• Targum Onkelos: Adam (אָדָם). Translation: Adam (or man)

• Targum Jerusalem: Adam (אָדָם). Translation: Adam (or man)

Cosmic Genesis: Chapter 3

The two were naked, both Adam and his wife, and neither were exalted. The serpent[1] was the wisest[2] of all the beasts on the land, which the Lord the god[3] made, and the serpent asked the woman, "Has God said, 'Don't eat of every tree in paradise?'"

The woman said to the serpent, "We may eat of the fruit of the trees of paradise, but of the fruit of the tree which is in the middle of paradise, God said, 'You will not eat of it, neither will you touch it, in case you die.'"

The serpent said to the woman, "You will not die the death. For God knew that in whatever day you should eat of it your eyes would be opened, and you would be like the gods,[4] knowing good and evil."

The woman saw that the tree was good for food and that it was pleasant to the eyes to look at and beautiful to contemplate, and she took its fruit and ate, and she gave to her husband also, and they ate. The eyes of both were opened, and they perceived that they were naked, and they sewed fig leaves together and made themselves aprons to go round them. They heard the voice of the Lord the god walking in Paradise in the afternoon, and both Adam and his wife hid from the face of the Lord the god in the middle of the trees of Paradise. Lord the god called Adam and said to him, "Adam, where are you?"

He answered him, "I heard your voice walking in paradise, and I was afraid because I am naked and I was hiding."

The reply was, "Did they tell you that you were naked? Did only one of them eat from the tree? Did you eat?"

Adam answered, "The woman that was given me, she gave me of the tree and I ate."

Lord the god asked the woman, "What did you do?"

The woman answered, "The serpent deceived me and I ate."

Lord the god said to the serpent, "Because you have done this you are cursed more than all livestock and all the animals of the land, on your breast and belly you will go, and you will eat earth all the days of your life. I will put enmity between you and the woman and between your descendants and her descendants, he will keep watch against your head, and you will keep watch against his heel."

To the woman said, "Greatly multiply your regrets and your sighs. In sorrow, you will give birth to children. To your man, you will turn, and he will dominate you."

To Adam he said, "Because you have listened to the voice of your wife, and eaten of the tree which I told you I alone would eat from, cursed is the ground in your labors, in regret will you eat all the days of your life. Thorns and thistles will it bring forth to you, and you will eat the plant of the field. In the sweat of your face will you eat your bread until you return to Eretz out of which you were taken, for dirt you are and to dirt you will return."

Adam called the name of his wife Khawah,[5] that is, the mother of all living.

Lord the god made for Adam and his wife garments of skin and clothed them. God said, "Look, Adam has become as one of us, knowing good and evil, Now if he stretches out his hand, and takes from the tree of life and eats, he will live forever."

So Lord the god sent him out of paradise to cultivate the ground out of which he was taken. He threw out Adam and caused him to live outside paradise, and placed the sphinxes[6] and flaming broadsword that circles to guard the path to the tree of life.[7]

Cosmic Genesis: Chapter 3 Notes

1 Codex Alexandrinus: ophis (ΟΦΙϹ). Translation: snake

• Leningrad Codex: nachash (נָחָשׁ). Translation: snake

• Peshitta: ḥûyå (ܚܘܝܐ). Translation: snake

• Targum Onkelos: chivya (חִוְיָא). Translation: snake (or worm)

• Targum Jerusalem: chivya (חִוְיָא). Translation: snake (or worm)

2 Codex Alexandrinus: phronimôtatos (ΦΡΟΝΙΜШΤΑΤΟϹ). Translation: wisest (or prudentist, most well behaved)

• Cotton Genesis: phronimôteros (ΦΡΟΝΙΜШΤΕΡΟϹ). Translation: sane (or the most 'in one's right mind')

- LXX 56: phronêmôteros (ϕϼονἡμοοτόϼοϲ). Translation: moralist (or with the greatest conscience)

- Leningrad Codex: arum (עָרוּם). Translation: naked

- Peshitta: ôrym (ܥܪܝܡ). Translation: ruggedest (or roughest)

- Targum Onkelos: chakkim (חַכִּים). Translation: wise

- Targum Jerusalem: chakkim (חַכִּים). Translation: wise

This conflicting reference to the snake being the wisest, or most naked creature in the garden, has led to some different translations. It is often assumed that the original reference was the exalted serpent Mušmaḫḫū (𒈲𒈤𒄭) from Sumerian mythology, resulting in some bibles translating the snake in this verse as 'most exalted.' The term arum (עָרוּם) is essentially the same word as the Akkadian erium (𒍪𒌝) and Arabic ôuryān (عُرْيَان). In the case of the Akkadian word, it also meant 'low' and 'poor,' making the Akkadian description of the snake the 'lowest' among the creatures, which does seem to fit the narrative better that 'nakedest' or 'wisest.'

3 Codex Alexandrinus: c̄s o t̄hs (ΚϹΟΘϹ). Translation: lord the god

- Leningrad Codex: Yehvah elohim (יְהוָה אֱלֹהִים). Translation: Yehvah god (in Assyrian, or gods in Aramaic, goddesses in Hebrew)

- Peshitta: mryå ålhym (ܐܠܗܝܡ ܡܪܝܐ). Translation: master (or lord) gods

- Targum Onkelos: yeyah elohim (יְיָ אֱלֹהִים). Translation: Yḥů gods (or god in Neo-Assyrian, goddesses in Hebrew)

- Targum Jerusalem: yeyah elohim (יְיָ אֱלֹהִים). Translation: Yḥů elohim (or god in Assyrian, or gods in Aramaic, goddesses in Hebrew

4 Codex Alexandrinus: theoi (ΘΕΟΙ). Translation: gods

- Leningrad Codex: ålohim (אֱלֹהִים). Translation: godesses (or gods in Aramaic)

- Peshitta: ålhå (ܐܠܗܐ). Translation: God

- Targum Onkelos: keravrevin (כְּרַבְרְבִין). Translation: cherub masters

- Targum Jerusalem: mal'achin ravrevin (מַלְאָכִין רַבְרְבִין). Translation: messenger (or angel) great-masters

5 Codex Alexandrinus: Zôê (ℤѠH). Translations: life (or spirit)

- LXX 400: zôên (ℤ‚∞ℓ‚ᴎ). Translation: alive

- Leningrad Codex: Chavvah (חַוָּה). Translation: farm

- Peshitta: Ḥůå (ܚܘܐ). Translation: life (or Ophiuchus)

- Targum Onkelos: Chavvah (חַוָּה). Translation: life (or Ophiuchus)

- Targum Jerusalem: Chavvah (חַוָּה). Translation: life (or Ophiuchus)

The name Zôê and Chavvah are both direct translations of the name Ḥůh (חוה), meaning 'living.' In other verses the Greeks transliterated the name as Eua (Εὐα), which was translated into Latin as Eve. The Assyrian Christians believe that Eve's real name was Ḥůå (ܚܘܐ), which was corrupted into Eua by the Greeks when they translated the Septuagint. As the Greeks translated the Aramaic name, the Aramaic name is restored as Khawah.

6 Codex Alexandrinus: cheroubin (ⲭⲉⲣⲟⲩⲃⲓⲛ)

- LXX 17: cheroubin (χϐουμϭιᴎ)

- LXX 55: cheroubim (χϐουμϭιμ)

- LXX 75: chaeroubêm (χⲁιϐουμℎμ)

- LXX 664: cherobim (χϐουμμ)

- Leningrad Codex: keruvim (כְּרֻבִים). Translation: cherubs (or griffins, sphinxes)

- Peshitta: krůbå (ܟܪ̈ܘܒܐ). Translation: cherubs (or plow, plowman)

- Targum Onkelos: keruvayya (כְרוּבַיָּא). Translation: cherubs (or plow, plowman)

- Fragments Targums: kerovaya (כְרוֹבַיָא). Translation: cherubs (or plow, plowman)

- Targum Onkelos: keruvaya (כְרוּבַיָא). Translation: cherubs (or plow, plowman)

- Bohairic manuscripts: kheroubin (ⲭⲉⲣⲟⲩⲃⲓⲛ)

- Sahidic manuscripts: kheroubin (ⲭⲉⲣⲟⲩⲃⲓⲛ)

The word 'cherub' (ܟܪܘܒ / כרוב / 𐤊𐤓𐤁 / 𐡊𐡓𐡁) was the West Semitic term for the mythical creature generally called a 'griffin' today. Based in the archaeological record of Canaan, it appears that the concept of the cherub was based on the Egyptian sphinx, as the earliest cherub statues found in Canaan were Egyptian statues of sphinxes. Archaeologists are not sure if the griffins of Anatolia were based on the Canaanite cherub, or the Egyptian sphinxes directly, however, all three mythical beings are closely related in the archaeological record.

In this verse, it seems apparent that the original Akkadian cuneiform text would have read girtablilû (𒄑𒋛𒌍𒁹), as the guardians of the abode of Ān (Heaven) in the Old Babylonian era and earlier were the girtablilû. These creatures are generally called the scorpion-men in modern literature, and were depicted as being scorpion-human chimeras, however, the guardians of Ān were specifically a male and a female girtablilû in the Epic of Gilgamesh. They were replaced early in the Middle Babylonian era by two ancient Sumerian gods.

The term cherub was for some reason reinterpreted as 'baby angels' by Christians, although in the Books of the Kingdoms God was described as riding on cherubs, and it is not clear why any god would ride around on 'baby angels,' therefore the alternate translation of 'sphinxes' is used in this translation, as it is in later books of the Septuagint, as the concept of a Neo-Assyrian karâbu (𒅗𒂖𒀖) would have been anachronistic before the early iron age. In this verse, girtablilû may be a more accurate translation, however, was probably no longer understood in the era when the Israelites left Egypt, as even the Babylonians were no longer commonly using the term.

7 Berlin Genesis: phloginên tên romphaean strephomenên phylassin tên odon tou xylou tês zôês (ΦΛΟΓΙΝΗΝ ΤΗΝ ΡΟΜΦΑΙΑΝ ϹΤΡΕΦΟΜΕΝΗΝ ΦΥΛΑϹϹΕΙΝ ΤΗΝ ΟΔΟΝ ΤΟΥ ΞΥΛΟΥ ΤΗϹ ΖѠΗϹ). Translation: the flaming (or fiery) that circles (or crowns, honors, twists, writhes) broadsword to guard (or protect, defend) the threshold (or road, path) the timber (or wood, log, stick, tree) the life.

• Codex Alexandrinus: phloginên rhomphaean tên strephomenên phylassin tên odon tou xylou tês zôês (ΦΛΟΓΙΝΗΝ ΡΟΜΦΑΙΑΝ ΤΗΝ ϹΤΡΕΦΟΜΕΝΗΝ ΦΥΛΑϹϹΕΙΝ ΤΗΝ ΟΔΟΝ ΤΟΥ ΞΥΛΟΥ ΤΗϹ ΖѠΗϹ). Translation: the flaming (or fiery) broadsword that circles (or crowns, honors, twists, writhes) to guard (or protect, defend) the threshold (or road, path) the timber (or wood, log, stick, tree) the life.

• LXX 55: phloginên rhomphaean meta strephomenên phylassin tên hodon tou xylou tês zôês (φλογἡνην ρομφαφαν μετα στρεφομεινην φυλαγοσσιν την οδον του ξʒλου της ζωης). Translation: the flaming (or fiery) broadsword withcircles (or crowns, honors, twists, writhes) to guard (or protect, defend) the threshold (or road, path) the timber (or wood, log, stick, tree) the life.

• LXX 121: phloginên rhomphaean phylassin tên hodon tou xylou tês zôês (φλογϕνην ρομφαφαν φυλαγοσσιν την οδον του ξʒλου της ζωης). Translation: the flaming (or fiery) broadsword to guard (or protect, defend) the threshold (or road, path) the timber (or wood, log, stick, tree) the life.

• LXX 130: phloginên rhomphaean tên strephomenên phylassin tou xylou tês zôês (ⲫⲗⲟⲅⲫⲛⲗⲛ ⲣⲟⲙⲫⲁⲫⲁⲛ ⲧⲏⲛ ⲥⲧⲣⲟⲫⲟⲙⲅⲛⲗⲛ ⲫⲩⲗⲁⲛⲟⲥⲥⲓⲛ ⲧⲟⲩ ⲝⲫⲗⲟⲩ ⲧⲏⲥ ⲍⲟⲟⲏⲥ). Translation: the flaming (or fiery) broadsword that circles (or crowns, honors, twists, writhes) to guard (or protect, defend) timber (or wood, log, stick, tree) the life.

• Leningrad Codex: lahat hacherev hammithappechet lishmor et-derech etz hachayyim (לְהַט הַחֶרֶב הַמִּתְהַפֶּכֶת לִשְׁמֹר אֶת־דֶּרֶךְ עֵץ הַחַיִּים). Translation: blazing (or enchanted, incandescence, flashing) the sword (or plow, many, a lot, increase) surrounding (or encircling) to guard (defend, protect) the road (or path, way) tree (or wood) the life (or living)

• Peshitta: ůšnnå dḥrbå dmtpkå lmṭr åůrhå dåylnå dḥyå (ܥܠܘܐ ܕܚܪ̈ܒܐ: ܕܡܬܦܟܐ ܠܛܪ ܐܘܪܚܐ ܕܐܝܠܢܐ ܕܚܝܐ).Translation: hated (or fanged, jagged) the desert (or desolate, barren, sword) surrounding protecting (or guarding) way (or path, journey, road) to tree of live (or Eve)

• Targum Onkelos: yat shenan charba demithappecha lemitar yat orach ilan chayyai (יַת שְׁנַן חַרְבָּא דְּמִתְהַפְּכָא לְמִיטַר יַת אוֹרַח אִילָן חַיָּיא). Translation: hated (or fanged, jagged) desert (or desolate, barren, sword) surrounding protecting (or guarding) the way (or path, journey, road) to tree of live (or Eve)

Both the Greek and Hebrew translations read essentially the same, indicating that the Aramaic source text must have read more-or-less identical to the Masoretic version. While the 'fiery sword circling' interpretation is valid in Hebrew, the Aramaic words don't mean exactly the same thing. This appears to be Aramaic translations of names of the guardians of Ān from Middle Babylonian beliefs.

In the Middle Babylonian text *Adapa and the South Wind*, the two guardians were Dumuzid and Ningishzida which appear to be the same two guardians as those listed here. Lht hḥrb hmthpkt (להט החרב המתהפכת) which is generally translated loosely as 'fiery the sword circling' in Hebrew, is Aramaic for 'magnificent cherub that returned from death,' which would be a reference to Dumuzid, the god that returned from the land of the dead each vernal equinox during the Babylonian Akitu festival. The name in the Masoretic text is an Aramaic translation of his title [an]Dağal riåbu-ušum anna (𒀭𒃲𒈨𒈬𒌋𒀭), meaning [deity]vast (𒀭𒃲𒈨) returning (𒈬) dragon (𒌋) from sky-stone (𒀭𒌋).' The word anna (𒀭𒌋), which was the Sumerian word for 'metal,' was a combination of the words an (𒀭), meaning 'god,' 'star,' and 'sky,' and na (𒌋), meaning 'stone.' The word generally meant 'metal,' however, also referred to the metal-sky above the world in Babylonian cosmology, interpreted as the framework of Shamayim in the Septuagint. Therefore, this title of Dumuzid is generally interpreted as describing his return from the land of the dead / sky, each spring.

The other guardian of the entrance to the sky in *Adapa and the South Wind*, was [an]Ningishzida (✳𒀭𒅇𒌓𒍣𒁕), whose name translates as '[deity]Lord (✳𒀭𒅇) to (𒁕) the tree (𒅗) of life (𒌓𒍣),' which is virtually identical to the Masoretic 'guardian the path tree of life' (לשמר את דרך עץ החיים). The oldest surviving fragments of *Adapa and the South Wind*, have been found in El Amarna Egypt, and generally dated to the 1300s BC. The text remained important for centuries, as a copy has been recovered from the Library of Ashurbanipal, dating to the 600s BC. As Cosmic Genesis lists both the 'cherubs' and the two guardians, it suggests that the text originated before Dumuzid and Ningishzida became the guardians of An in the early Middle Babylonian era, and their names were added later, if so, the original version of the text would have probably been written prior to 1595 BC.

Cosmic Genesis: Chapter 4

Adam knew Eve his wife, and she conceived and gave birth to Cain[1] saying, "I have made a man through God."

She later carried his brother Abel.[2] Abel was a shepherd, while Cain was a worker of the ground. It was so, later, that Cain made a sacrifice to the Lord from the fruits of the land. Abel also brought from the firstborn of his sheep and of his lambs, and God looked on Abel and his gifts, but Cain and his sacrifices he did not consider, and Cain was very sad and became depressed. Lord the god said to Cain, "Why have you become very sad? Why have you become depressed? Haven't you sinned if you have brought it rightly, but incorrectly divided it? Be calm. He will submit to you, and you will rule over him."

Cain said to Abel his brother, "Let us go out into the plain," and while they were in the plain Cain attacked Abel his brother and killed him.

Lord the god asked Cain, "Where is Abel your brother?"

He answered, "I don't know, am I my brother's keeper?"

The Lord asked, "What have you done? The voice of your brother's blood cries out to me from Eretz. Now you are cursed on Eretz who has opened her mouth to receive your brother's blood from your hand. When you till the land, it will not continue to give its strength to you. You will be groaning and trembling on the land."

Cain said to the Lord the god, "My crime is too great for me to be forgiven. If you throw me out today from the face of Eretz, then I will be hidden from your presence, and I will be groaning and trembling on the land. Then it will be that anyone that finds me will kill me."

Lord the god said to him, "Not so, anyone who kills Cain will pay seven penalties," and the Lord the god set a mark on Cain that no one that found him might kill him.

Cain left the presence of God and lived in the land of Nod[3] near Eden. Cain knew his wife, and having conceived she carried Enoch.[4] Enoch built a city and he named the city after the name of his son.[5] To Enoch was born Gaidad,[6] and Gaidad fathered Mehujael,[7] and Mehujael fathered Methuselah,[8] and Methuselah fathered Lamech.[9] Lamech for himself had two wives, the name of the one was Adah[10] and the name of the second Zillah.[11] Adah carried Jabal,[12] he was the father of those that live in tents, feeding livestock. The name of his brother was Jubal,[13] he was who invented the lute and harp. Zillah carried Thobel,[14] he was a smith, a manufacturer both of brass and iron, and Thobel's sister was Naamah.[15]

Lamech said to his wives, Adah and Zillah, "Hear my voice, you wives of Lamech, consider my words because I have killed a man to my sadness and a youth to my pain. Because vengeance has been exacted seven times on Cain's behalf, on Lamech's it will be seventy times seven."

Adam knew Eve his wife, and she conceived and carried a son, and called his name Seth,[16] saying, "For God has raised for me another seed instead of Abel, who Cain killed." Seth had a son, and he called his name Enosh,[17] as he had faith to call on the name of the Lord the god.

Cosmic Genesis: Chapter 4 Notes

1 Codex Alexandrinus: Cain (ⲔⲀⲒⲚ)

- Leningrad Codex: Kayin (קַ֫יִן). Translation: craftsman, metalsmiths

- Peshitta: Qån (ܩܐܝܢ)

- Targum Onkelos: Kayin (קַיִן)

- Fragment Targums: Kayin (קַיִן)

- Targum Jerusalem: Kayin (קַיִן)

The story of Cain and Abel is generally accepted in academic studies as being based on the Old Akkadian Debate Between Sheep and Grain, in which the god Ellil created the grain god Ashnan and cattle goddess Lahar who then debate which is the better food for the gods. Tablet 14005 at the University of Pennsylvania Museum of Archaeology and Anthropology is generally viewed as the earliest version of the debate, at only 61 lines long, and in it Ellil did not crate them instead it was the gods Enki and Ia. The tablet is an Old Babylonian copy of an older poem, believed to date to the Sumerian era, however, in either the Akkadian or Neo-Sumerian eras, Ia, the god of the sacred waters, was added to the poem. As Ia is generally viewed as being the replacement of Enki, the surviving version of the poem likely dates to the transitional period between the Sumerian and Akkadian civilizations.

It seems likely that the Ashnan and Lahar story was integrated into the earliest version of Cosmic Genesis near the beginning of the Hyksos dynasty, as the roles of Ashnan and Lahar mirror the roles of Setekh and Heru-ur in Old Egyptian beliefs, as the older brothers of Osiris (pre-Hyksos Seth), with Setekh ultimately killing Heru-ur. Both the brothers in the story have names that appear to have originated in Akkadian cuneiform, however, neither are similar to Ashnan and Lahar, suggesting an Old Akkadian language translation was carried into Egypt. Additionally, as the female Lahar was transitioned to being the male Abel, it supports an Old Akkadian translation, as their would have been no cultural need to change the god's sex either Sumer or Egypt. Cain/Kayin (Καιν / קַיִן) appears to be a transliteration of the Akkadian word qanû (𒈨𒄀𒈨�), meaning 'reeds,' which was also the Ugaritic word qn (𒀀𒈾), meaning 'reed,' or 'cane.' This interpretation has existed since the Second Temple era, as it was included in the Apocalypse of Moses, which while it only survives in Greek, must have originated in a Semitic language or the reference makes no sense.

Abel/ Havel (Αβελ / הֶבֶל) is a transliteration of aplu (𒀀𒉺), pronounced as ablu in Amorite and Hurrian, meaning 'son.' Aplu was a common term applied to the sons of the various father-gods in Mesopotamian religions. In this case, it was likely spelled the older Sumerian and early Akkadian way eduru (𒌉), which was also pronounced as aplu/ablu, however, meant 'heir,' meaning that the reason for Cain's killing of Abel, was because Abel was the chosen heir in the Old Akkadian translation, and Cain was jealous. Kyn (קין) was also the name of the people who Moses forbade the Israelites from killing when they left Egypt, often translated as Kenites, and who he married his daughter to. Joshua also allowed them to leave the cities he besieged before killing everyone else in the cities, however, they disappeared from the Israelite story as soon as Egypt took control of Canaan during Joshua's time, suggesting they were a group of people living under Hyksos rule. Again, this melding of Sumerian and Old Egyptian mythology could only have taken place earlier than the Hyksos dynasty, as during the Hyksos dynasty Setekh replaced Osiris, and by the new Kingdom Heru-ur had been forgotten.

2 Codex Alexandrinus: Abel (ΑΒΕΛ)

- Leningrad Codex: Havel (הֶבֶל). Translation: breath, vapor

- Peshitta: Hbyl (ܗܒܝܠ)

- Targum Onkelos: Havel (הֶבֶל)

- Fragment Targums: Hevel (הֶבֶל)

- Targum Jerusalem: Hevel (הֶבֶל)

The story of Cain and Abel is generally accepted in academic studies as being based on the Old Akkadian Debate Between Sheep and Grain, in which Ellil created the grain god Ashnan and cattle goddess Lahar who then debate which is the better food for the gods.

3 Codex Alexandrinus: Naid (ܢܐܝܕ)

- LXX 120: Aid (ܐܝܕ)

- LXX 500: Gaid (ܓܐܝܕ)

- LXX 72: Naen (ܢܐܝܢ)

- LXX 59: Naena (ܢܐܝܢܐ)

- Leningrad Codex: Novd (נֹוד). Translation: wandering

- Peshitta: Nŭd (ܢܘܕ). Translation: wandering

- Targum Onkelos: be'ar'a galei umittaltal (בְּאַרְעָא גְּלֵי וּמְטַלְטָל). Translation: in land of grass and wandering

- Fragment Targums: ar'a gelei umetaltel (אַרְעָא גְלֵי וּמְטַלְטֶל). Translation: land of grass and wandering

- Targum Jerusalem: ar'a tiltol galuteih (אַרְעָא טִלְטוֹל גָּלוּתֵיהּ). Translation: land of wandering exile

This term was probably a mistranslation of NA ID (𒈾 𒀉), meaning river rocks, suggesting one of the tributaries to the Iraqi wetlands (Eden/edin). There is no precise dating for the genealogy of Cain, unlike the genealogy of Seth. As Seth was listed as born after Cain killed Abel, and Adam was recorded as 205 year old at the time, this would have to predate that. Based on the radiocarbon dating of the flood sediment from the flood or series off floods that engulfed Sumer in approximately 2900 BC, and the Septuagint's dating of the events between the birth of Seth and the flood, Seth should have been born in 4912 BC, and Adam therefore would have been created 230 years earlier, in 5142 BC, meaning Cain's moving to 'Nod,' should have happened during that era. Nevertheless, it is worth noting that the earliest surviving structures in Eridu are estimated to have been built around 5300 BC.

4 Codex Alexandrinus: Enôch (ܐܢܘܟ)

- LXX 15: Enôs (ܐܢܘܣ)

- Leningrad Codex: Chanoch (חֲנֹוךְ)

- Peshitta: Hnŭk (ܚܢܘܟ)

- Targum Onkelos: Chanoch (חֲנֹוךְ)

- Targum Jerusalem: Chanoch (חֲנֹוךְ)

• Bohairic manuscripts: Enôs (Ⲉⲛⲱⲥ)

If read as a series of metaphors regarding temples and cities, wherein 'Enoch's son' Irad was the city of Eridu, Enôch/Chanoch probably started as a reference to the temple of Enki in Eridu, which likely predated the city itself. This temple was known as E-Abzu (𒂍𒀊𒍪) in Akkadian, and E-Engura (𒂍𒇉𒇉) in Neo-Sumerian, however, it's pre-flood Sumerian name is believed to have been Euĝtum (𒂍𒅂𒌓𒋧), which was mentioned in some Emegir Sumerian texts as being the temple of Enki in Uruk. Sumerian had several dialects, however, the main dialect during the post-flood era, was Emegir, meaning 'native tongue,' which was primarily used for business and politics. The other main dialect, was Emesal, the 'fine tongue,' which was generally used in religious songs and the speeches of the goddesses in religious texts.

As the earliest names of many later Sumero-Akkadian gods include the Sumerian title 'Lady' (𒎏), it is generally accepted that most of the early Sumerian deities were goddesses who were later masculinized as the Akkadian culture became dominant. Therefore, Emesal is often viewed as being the older dialect, likely the dominant dialect from the Uruk period when writing was first being developed by the Sumerians. If so, this name 'Enoch' may be derived from the Emesal dialect, as the Emegir name of the Temple of Enki: Euĝtum (𒂍𒅂𒌓𒋧), would have been pronounced as Ekanaĝir (𒂍𒅗𒈾𒄀𒊏) in Emesal. If this is a reference to the founding of the Temple of Enki in Eridu, based on the archaeological evidence, it should have been around 5300 BC.

5 The structure of the sentence in Hebrew does not make it clear if Cain named the city after his son Enoch, or if Enoch named the city after his son Gaidad/Irad. While the Greek text structures the sentence almost the same way, it is clear from context that the Greek translator believed that the city was named after Enoch, however, the Aramaic verse would have read almost exactly the same as the Hebrew, laving the underlying question of the city's name.

Nevertheless, Eridu (𒉌𒀀), was the first city of Sumer according to the Sumerian king lists, and its foundation was a mound of rocks (𒀀 𒄑), in the mouth of the Ephrates River, which flowed into the Iraqi wetlands (Eden/edin) indicating that this was the city being referenced. Additionally, the presence of possible Sumerian kings names in the genealogy of Cain supports this section of text originated as an explanation for the pre-flood Sumerian civilization. Therefore, this translation follows the interpretation that the city was named after Gaidad/Irad/Eridu, and not Enoch.

6 Codex Alexandrinus: Gaidad (ܓܝܕܕ)

- LXX 426 Gaerad (ܓܝܪܕ)

- LXX 422 Caedad (ܟܝܕܕ)

- LXX 414: Gaeddan (ܓܝܕܕܢ)

- Leningrad Codex: Irad (עִירָד)

- Peshitta: Ôydr (ܥܝܕܪ)

- Targum Onkelos: Irad (עִירָד)

- Targum Jerusalem: Irad (עִירָד)

This appears to be a reference to the foundation of Eridu (𒉣𒆠). It is unclear when the settlement became a town, however, settlement in the area is documented as early as 5400 BC. The earliest sections of the Temple of Enki appear to have been built around 5300 BC. Based on the increase in buildings in the region around 4500 BC, it is likely there was a central government of some kind, suggesting that is the era being referenced.

7 Berlin Genesis (LXX 911): Maiêl (ΜΑΙΗΛ)

- Cotton Genesis (LXX D): Mauiêl (ΜΑΟΥΙΑ)

- LXX 509: Maouiêl (Μαουιηλ)

- LXX 15: Maleleêl (Μαλελεηλ)

- LXX 121: Maleleêl (Μαλεηλ)

- LXX 392: Maeouia (Μαιουια)

- LXX 16: Meêl (Μεηλ)

- LXX 120: Maouiaêl (Μαουιαηλ)

- LXX 134: Mauiêl (Μαυιηλ)

- LXX 370: Maliêl (Μαλιηλ)

- LXX 129: Maouêl (Μαουηλ)

- Leningrad Codex: Mechuya'el (מְחוּיָאֵל)

- Peshitta: Mhůâyl (ܡܚܘܐܝܠ)

114

- Targum Onkelos: Mechuya'el (מְחוּיָאֵל)

- Targum Jerusalem: Mechuya'el (מְחוּיָאֵל)

- Bohairic manuscripts: Meouia (Μεογιⲁ)

This may be a transliteration of the name [en]Menluan (𒂗𒃲𒇻𒀭), meaning [lord]Crown-sheep-god, and generally interpreted as something like 'Prince of the sheep of god.' Mechuya'el has no intrinsic meaning in Hebrew, however, the end of the name is el (אֵל), which is a translation of ān (𒀭), as well as the Egyptian nṯr (𒀭), all of which translate as 'god.' Ān (𒀭) and ntrt (𒊹), both also translate as 'goddess.'

Based on the surviving Hebrew translation, this name was probably rendered as mahujyå[ntrt] (𒈨𒄭𒅀𒊹) in Middle Egyptian, meaning Mehit[goddess]. In the Middle Kingdom, Mahujyå was both the name of the north wind, and an ancient Egyptian and Nubian war goddess generally referred to today as Mehit (Egyptian) and Menhit (Nubian). It is also possible that the name was spelled as [ntr]mahujyå (𒀭𒈨𒄭𒅀𒀭), however, this is unlikely as the north wind was not viewed as a god in Egypt. The common modern Egyptological name Mehit is derived from the Old Egyptian pronunciation, however, the pronunciation had shifted to mahujyå by the Middle Kingdom, məhuåså by the New Kingdom, and məheå by the era the Aramaic language genealogy of nations was added to Cosmic Genesis. While the Middle Kingdom pronunciation seems almost identical, a New Kingdom translation of this name is also possible.

In Sumerian pre-flood mytho-history, Lord Menluan, was the king who captured the kingship from Eridu, and carried it to Bad-tibira (𒁁𒉌𒈨𒉌𒆠), the fortress of the smiths. While it is not clear if or when this happened, based on the archaeology, Eridu went into decline around 4000 BC, and was almost abandoned by 3800 BC. This is generally associated with the change of the course of the Euphrates, and the resulting rise of Uruk, not the rise of Bad-tibira. As the city of Uruk appears to have been under the control of the Sethite genealogy, this appears to be a genealogy of a rival bloodline claiming descent from a common ancestor.

8 Codex Alexandrinus: Mathousala (ΜⲀΘΟΥⲤⲀⲖⲀ)

- LXX 121: Mathousaêl (Μⲁθουσⲁⲗλ)

- LXX 16: Mathousaêla (Μⲁθουσⲁⲗλⲁ)

- Leningrad Codex: Metusha'el (מְתוּשָׁאֵל)

- Peshitta: Mtůšyl (ܡܬܘܫܝܠ)

- Targum Onkelos: Metusha'el (מְתוּשָׁאֵל)

- Targum Jerusalem: Metusha'el (מְתוּשָׁאֵל)

The Septuagint refers to this person by the same name as the later Methuselah from the Masoretic Text, suggesting that both names were Methuselah in the Aramaic version, however, the Hebrew translation is different. The Hebrew name may be a transliteration of the name [en]Mengalan (𒀭𒈗𒃲𒀭), meaning [lord]Crown-great-god, and generally interpreted as something like 'Prince of the great god.' Metusha'el has no intrinsic meaning in Hebrew, however, the end of the name is el (אֵל), which is a translation of ān (𒀭), as well as the Egyptian nṯr (𓊹), all of which translate as 'god.' Based on the surviving Hebrew translation, this name was probably rendered as mîtû[ntr]sâh (𓅓𓏏𓏤𓊹𓈗) in Middle Egyptian, meaning 'Likeness of [god]Sah.' Sah was the Old Kingdom's supreme father god of the sky, and therefore, the Egyptian parallel of Ān (𒀭). By the Middle Kingdom he was no longer actively worshiped, however, was known from the ancient texts, and therefore would have made an appropriate reference to the much earlier era of the old kings of Sumer. In Sumerian pre-flood mytho-history, Lord Mengalan, was the king who ruled Bad-tibira, the fortress of the smiths, after Lord Menluan.

9 Codex Alexandrinus: Lamech (ⲗⲁⲙⲉⲭ)

- Leningrad Codex: Lamech (לֶמֶךְ)

- Peshitta: Lmk (ܠܡܟ)

- Targum Onkelos: Lamech (לֶמֶךְ)

- Targum Jerusalem: Lamech (לְמֶךְ)

Like the previous names on this list, Lamech appears to be a reference to the pre-flood kings of Bad-Tibira; in this case the third king Dumuzid (the shepherd). Dumuzid was deified as the god Tammuz, explaining why the name would have been redacted. Additionally, another famous King of Uruk also bore the name, although the existence of the second King Dumuzid (the fisherman) has been questioned by some Assyriologists, who view him as an addition made to the king lists during the Neo-Sumerian era, in order to nationalize Dumuzid/Tammuz.

This redaction would have probably taken place sometime around 2100 BC, when King Utu-hengal established the independent kingdom of Sumer and Akkad, which was then based in Uruk. His seven-year reign is estimated to have been somewhere between 2119 and 2048 BC by various Assyriologists, around the time the texts would have been carried to Harran by Terah. Remku (𓂋𓅓𓂓𓏤) is the Egyptian word for 'fisher,' confirming that this was a reference to Dumuzid, however, also claiming that the earlier Dumuzid was a fisher, and not a shepherd, which is consistent with narrative, in which his son Iôbel/Yaval was the first shepherd. As the Egyptian R sound was interchangeable with the Canaanite L sound, this would have resulted in a transliteration of Lameku (𒇻𒆠𒂊) in cuneiform during the New Kingdom era, which would have subsequently been translated into Lmk (𐤟𐤌𐤋) during the iron age.

10 Codex Alexandrinus: Ada (ⲁⲇⲁ)

- LXX 131: Adda (ⲁⲇⲇⲁ)

- LXX 246: Adad (ⲁⲇⲁⲇ)

- LXX 314: Adada (ⲁⲇⲁⲇⲁ)

- Leningrad Codex: Adah (עָדָ֔ה). Translation: dawn (or ornament)

- Peshitta: Ḥdå (ܚܕܐ). Translation: dawn (or ornament)

- Targum Onkelos: Adah (עָדָה). Translation: dawn (or ornament)

- Targum Jerusalem: Adah (עָדָה). Translation: dawn (or ornament)

- Sahidic manuscripts: Adda (ⲇⲁⲇⲁ)

The two wives of Lemek, which can be read as 'Dawn' and 'Evening,' appear to be a references to ^{deity}Inanna (𒀭𒈹), the wife of Dumuzid (the shepherd), in her form as the planet Venus. Multiple texts dating to the Sumerian era confirm that she was viewed as being the planet Venus, both in the dawn, and in the evening, as the Sumerians were one of the few cultures to realized Venus was both the morning star and the evening star. The movement of Inanna in Inanna's Descent to the Underworld is generally accepted by Assyriologists as a description of Venus' setting after sunset, followed by its rising before the sun seven days later.

11 Codex Alexandrinus: Sella (ⲥⲉⲗⲗⲁ)

- LXX 392: Sela (ⲥⲉⲗⲁ)

- LXX 125: Sala (ⲥⲁⲗⲁ)

- Leningrad Codex: Tzillah (צִלָּ֑ה). Translation: grill (or roast)

- Peshitta: Slå (ܨܠܐ). Translation: descend (or go down, incline)

- Targum Onkelos: Tzillah (צִלָּה). Translation: descend (or go down, incline)

- Targum Jerusalem: Tzilah (צִלָה). Translation: descend (or go down, incline)

The Hebrew word is generally not viewed as reflecting the meaning of the word. In the 11th century AD, Rabbi Shlomo Yitzchaki (Rashi), reported that the original meaning was Tzel (צֵל), meaning 'shadow,' which is generally accepted by Jews, Christians, and non-religious academics. The older Akkadian cuneiform name would have therefore been Ṣillu (𒍑𒆤𒂊), also meaning 'shadow,' however, the original Sumerian term would have been ğissu (𒍑𒆤𒂊), which can mean 'shadow,' 'shade,' 'protection,' darkening,' or 'evening.' The two wives of Lemek, which can be read as 'Dawn' and 'Evening,' appear to be a references to [deity]Inanna (𒀭𒈹), the wife of Dumuzid (the shepherd), in her form as the planet Venus. Multiple texts dating to the Sumerian era confirm that she was viewed as being the planet Venus, both in the dawn, and in the evening, as the Sumerians were one of the few cultures to realized Venus was both the morning star and the evening star. The movement of Inanna in Inanna's Descent to the Underworld is generally accepted by Assyriologists as a description of Venus' setting after sunset, followed by its rising before the sun seven days later.

12 Codex Alexandrinus: Iôbel (ⲓⲱⲃⲉⲗ)

- LXX 509: Iôbêd (ⲓⲟⲟⲩⲏⲗ)

- LXX 15: Iôbêl (ⲓⲟⲟⲩⲏⲗ)

- LXX 120: Iôabel (ⲓⲟⲟⲇⲩⲉⲗ)

- LXX 426: Iôbal (ⲓⲟⲟⲩⲗⲗ)

- LXX 414: Ôbel (ⲱⲩⲉⲗ)

- Leningrad Codex: Yaval (יָבָל)

- Peshitta: Ybl (ܝܒܠ)

- Targum Onkelos: Yaval (יְבָל)

Both this name and the following name Ioubal/Yuval appear to have originated as a transliteration of É-Áblua (𒂍𒀊𒇥), the name of the temple of the moon god Nanna in Urum. While not as old as Eridu, Urum was one of the oldest Sumerian cities, dating back to the Ubaid period, generally dated to 6500-3800 BC. The temple of Nanna is generally accepted as the large 'Painted Temple,' around which the city was built. The name É-Áblua (𒂍𒀊𒇥), translates as approximately 'Temple of cow's and sheep's father,' supporting this being the temple of the 'father of those that live in tents, feeding livestock.' If these names were originally Sumerian, the original text must have also been Sumerian or Neo-Sumerian, indicating a date of earlier than 1900 BC. The reference to the temples instead of the cities built around them also indicates the text probably dates back to earlier than the Akkadian era, earlier than 2334 BC.

13 Codex Alexandrinus: Ioubal (ιογβαλ)

- LXX 75 Ioubad (ιουυλλ)

- LXX 130: Iôbal (ιωουλλ)

- LXX 72: Iobal (ιουλλ)

- Leningrad Codex: Yuval (יוּבָל)

- Peshitta: Yŭbl (ܝܘܒܠ)

- Targum Onkelos: Yuval (יוּבָל)

- Targum Jerusalem: Yaval (יָבָל)

- Sahidic manuscripts: Iôbal (ιωβλλ)

Both this name and the previous name Iôbel/Yaval appear to have originated as a transliteration of É-Áblua (𒂍𒁀𒆪𒈾), the name of the temple of the moon god Nanna in Urum. The temple of Nanna is generally accepted as the large 'Painted Temple,' around which the city of Urum was built. A very similar 'White Temple,' of Nanna was built in Ur in the same era. The name of the 'White Temple,' was É-Kišnuğal (𒂍𒆧𒉻𒃲), the meaning of which is debated, as it has no obvious meaning. Based on the rest of the description of this 'Ioubal,' It is likely that the translator misread the Sumerian name as É-Inuğal (𒂍𒌋𒉻𒃲), meaning 'Temple of stringed instruments that exists,' While not as old as Eridu, Ur was one of the oldest Sumerian cities, dating back to the Ubaid period, generally dated to 6500-3800 BC.

14 Berlin Genesis (LXX 911): Thobel (θοβελ)

- LXX 392: Thôbel (θωουϭλ)

- LXX 426: Thoubal (θουυλλ)

- Leningrad Codex: Tuval Kayin (תּוּבַל קַיִן). Translation: 'You are brought from smiths'

- Peshitta: Tŭbqlyn (ܬܘܒܩܠܝܢ)

- Targum Onkelos: Tuval Kayin (תּוּבַל קַיִן)

- Targum Jerusalem: Tuval Kayin (תּוּבַל קַיִן)

The addition of 'Kayin' (Cain) in the Masoretic Text was likely added to distinguish it from the kingdom, of Tabal (𒋫𒁄), in southern modern Turkey during the Neo-

Assyrian era. Tabal was subjugated by Assyria in 713 BC, suggesting the scribal note was no longer relevant when the Aramaic translation of Cosmic Genesis was made, some time between 715 and 706 BC, and therefore not included in the Aramaic text that the Greeks later translated. Based on this 'Thobel/Tûbal' being described as 'a smith, a manufacturer both of brass and iron,' it seems clear that this was a mistranslation of tibira (𒂍𒈨𒁇𒊩), the Sumerian word for 'smiths. Bad-Tibira^{ki} (𒂦𒂍𒈨𒁇𒊩𒆠) was a major center for metal working in Sumer, and the city where Menluan, Mengalan, and Dumuzid (the shepherd) were king according to the Sumerian king lists. There were several ways that 'tibira' could have been transliterated into Egyptian, however, all of them would have resulted in the R sound being replaced by an L sound when transliterated back into Canaanite.

15 Berlin Genesis: Noemma (ΝΟЄΜΜΑ)

• Codex Alexandrinus: Noema (ΝΟЄΜΑ)

• LXX 121: Noeman (Νοєμᾱν)

• LXX 343: Nosma (Νοσμᾱ)

• LXX 246: Neeman (Νϭϭμᾱν)

• LXX 799: Noemman (Νοϭμμᾱν)

• LXX 53: Noemam (Νοϭμᾱμ)

• Leningrad Codex: Na'amah (נַעֲמָה). Translation: loveliness

• Peshitta: Nômå (ܢܥܡܐ). Translation: ostrich

• Targum Onkelos: Na'amah (נַעֲמָה)

• Targum Jerusalem: Na'amah (נַעֲמָה)

• Sahidic manuscripts: Noemma (Νοєμμα)

Assuming that Thobel/Tuval Kayin was Bar-Tibira, and this is a reference to a sister city, it is almost certainly Umma^{ki} (𒄑𒈣𒆠), a city approximately 30 kilometers north of Bad-tibira. The origin of the N sound at the beginning of the Greek and Hebrew names likely dates back to the original Middle Egyptian translation, as GIŠ (𒄑) was used to spell many disparate words that may have been adopted from other languages, including the word for chariot, spelled logographically as gišgigir (𒄑𒇀), and phonetically as narkabtum (𒈜𒊏𒆏𒌈), and the word for plum, spelled logographically as giškib (𒄑𒉽), and phonetically as šaluruum (𒊭𒇽𒊒𒌝). Umma was one of the Sumerian cities of the Early Dynastic Period (2900-2300 BC), however, it has not been proven to pre-date the

Sumerian flood of 2900 BC.

16 Codex Alexandrinus: Sêth (ϹΗꙹ)

- Leningrad Codex: Shet (שֵׁת). Translation: compensation (or placed, appointed)

- Peshitta: Šyt (ܫܝܬ)

- Targum Onkelos: Shet (שֵׁת)

- Targum Jerusalem: Shet (שֵׁת)

The name is most likely derived from the older Egyptian god Setekh (𓃩𓏏𓊖), which was also transliterated as Sêth (Σηθ) in ancient Greek, and Sêt (ϹΗꙐ) in Coptic, resulting in the other two common English names: Seth and Set. The oldest archaeological reference to Setekh is currently dated to the Amratian culture of pre-dynastic Egypt, generally dated to between 3790 and 3500 BC. Setekh was widely worshiped by Canaanites during the rule of the Hyksos dynasty, which ended around 1550 BC. At the time, he was viewed as the Egyptian version of the Amorite god Rašaap (𒀭𒊏𒊓𒀊), later known as Ršp (𒊏𒉺𒈽) in Ugaritic Canaanite, and Shed (𓈙𓂧𓏤𓃩) in the New Kingdom Egyptian dialect spoken in Canaan. In the Masoretic Book of Job, Eliphaz referred to humanity as the 'sons of Resheph' (בני־רשף) instead of the 'sons of Adam,' and then used Šdy (שדי) as the name of his god, indicating that Shadday was the iron age name of Resheph among the Israelites. The modern academic name of the god is Resheph, based on the later Hebrew word meaning 'plague,' or 'fever.'

In the Eblaite texts, generally dated to the 3rd millennium BC, Rašaap's wife was the Amorite earth goddess Adamma, who continued to be worshiped by Hurrians, and was mentioned as the name of the earth goddess of the Israelites in Masoretic Numbers. Resheph's Babylonian counterpart was the war god Nergal, who was also married to the earth goddess deityEreshkigal (𒀭𒊩𒆠𒃲), and associated with sunset during the Old Babylonian era. This indicates that Resheph was the Amorite version of Baal Shalim, the Canaanite god of the sunset, who was also married to Asherah, a Canaanite goddess of the earth and fertility during the bronze age, whose sacred oak trees were used as important grave markers. If the origin of the name 'Seth' in this verse was a Middle Egyptian translation of an older Akkadian text, it must have taken place before the fall of the Hyksos dynasty, or the name would have been updated to Shed, and then Shadday.

Nergal's father was generally viewed as being Ellil, however, in the Old Babylonian Myth of Nergal and Ereshkigal, he referred to Ia (𒂍𒀀) as his father. Ia was the Old Akkadian replacement of the older Sumerian god Enki, whose name meant 'Earth Lord,' suggesting that the origin of this genealogy was a Sumerian text about Ān (God), Enki (Adam/land), and Nergal (Seth), before being updated during the Hyksos dynasty.

Assuming such a Sumerian text existed, it would have been heretical by the standards of the Neo-Sumerian era onward. Nevertheless, Setekh was nothing like Nergal or Resheph before the Hyksos dynasty, suggesting that Setekh was a Hyksos era replacement of another god. Based on Jacob's dream later in Cosmic Genesis, it was almost certainly Osiris, who also ascended to the sky on a ladder in Egyptian mythology.

During the Hyksos dynasty, the worship of Osiris was suppressed in favor of Setekh/Resheph, explaining why he would have been redacted. The original Middle Egyptian translation of this genealogy, would therefore, have read Atum (creator), Geb (Adam/land), and Osiris, who was then replaced with Setekh (Seth) under Hyksos rule. Like Resheph and Nergal, Osiris was associated with death and rebirth, and prayed to to protect from plague-demons. This translation of Nergal as Osiris could only have happened earlier than the Hyksos dynasty, as the substitution of Setekh could only have happened during the Hyksos dynasty, meaning the latest the Egyptian translation could have been made was the Canaanite (14th) dynasty.

If read as a continuation of the city states of pre-flood Sumer, 'Seth' (Setekh, Resheph, Nergal) would have been a reference to Gudua, the home of Nergal's original temple. The Sumerian name of Nergal had been deityKišunu (✳🔤🔤), meaning 'god of Gudua,' a city in central modern Iraq that was later called Kutha. By the Old Akkadian era, his name had shifted to deityKišurugal (✳🔤🔤), meaning 'god lord of the great city,' a reference to the city of the dead. In Sumerian beliefs, the capital city of the underworld was Ganzir, however, in Akkadian beliefs the name was Kutha, adopted from the Akkadian name of Gudua, where Nergal's original temple had been built. In the Neo-Sumerian era, the era of Abraham and Amar-Sin, an alternate form of name appeared in Ur: deityKišabgal (✳🔤🔤), meaning 'god of all the great water,' which appears to be related to the transition of the 'Earth Lord' Enki, to the 'Sacred Waters' Ia. This suggests that the unstated reason Terah left Ur, was due to religious reforms involving Enki/Ia and Nergal.

The Neo-Sumerian religious reforms involving Nergal appear to have been initiated by King Shulgi of Ur, who rebuilt the temple of Nergal in Kutha. He was the father of Amar-Sin, and ruled for 48 years, confirming that whatever the reason, Terah would have left Ur during his reign if Amarphal/Amrapal was Amar-Sin. See the note regarding Amarphal the King of Sumer for more information. The name later became deityGìrunuggal (✳🔤🔤) during the Old Babylonian era, and then deityUgur (✳🔤) during the Middle Babylonian era, which remained the Cuneiform spelling until the Greco-Roman era. However, the older pronunciation appears to have continued, at some point loosing the GÌR, ending with the Aramaic transliteration of Nrgl (𐎀𐎗𐎂) during the Neo-Assyrian era.

Like the other Sumerian cities mentioned in the pre-flood genealogy, Gudua was a major religious center in pre-flood Sumer. The flooding of the city was extensive, and while the temple reopened, it appears that most of the city was not rebuilt after the great Sumerian flood of 2900 BC. Based on the archaeology done at the site, most of the city remained in ruins until King Shulgi began rebuilding it sometime between 2094 and 1982 BC, explaining how it became to be called the 'city of the dead.' It is not clear when it was founded, but like most ancient Sumerian cities, probably began with the temple.

Based on the Old Babylonian Cuthean Legend of Naram-Sin, which likely originated in Old Akkadian during the reign of the Akkadian king Naram-Sin, Kutha (Gudua) already existed before the time of ^{en}Merkar, the founder of Uruk. While the Cuthean Legend of Naram-Sin is regarded as fiction, it does nevertheless reflect the fact that the Akkadians viewed Kutha as older than Uruk, meaning it also dated to the Ubaid era, like the other Sumerian cities listed in the pre-flood genealogy. The date given in the following chapter, suggests that the temple of ^{deity}Kišunu was founded 205 years before the first king of Eridu ruled in 4707 BC, which would make the founding date approximately 4912 BC. During the era, the region is known to have been occupied, however, no remains of a temple have been found to date.

17 Codex Alexandrinus: Enôs (ⲈⲚⲰⳞ)

- LXX 128: Enôch (Ɛⲛⲱⲭ)

- LXX 130: Enos (ƐⲛⲟⳞ)

- Leningrad Codex: Enosh (אֱנוֹשׁ). Translation: mortal (or human)

- Peshitta: Ånůš (ܐܢܘܫ). Translation: human

- Targum Onkelos: Enosh (אֱנוֹשׁ). Translation: human

- Fragment Targums: Enosh (אֱנוֹשׁ). Translation: human

- Targum Jerusalem: Enosh (אֱנוֹשׁ). Translation: human

The term Ånůš (אנוש) is generally viewed as being the Aramaic word ånůš (𐤀𐤍𐤅𐤔), imported into Hebrew, as it was the common Aramaic word for 'human,' and not generally used in Hebrew, other than sections of the Torah and Tanakh (Christian Old Testament) that are thought to have originated in Aramaic. This may be the work of the editor in the time of Hezekiah, however, it may simply be the relic of the Sumerian term Lugal (𒈗), meaning 'king,' transliterated via its Akkadian pronunciation of Haniš. If so, the text appears to have once stated that the first king, presumably of Eridu, was in power 190 years before there was a Lord of the Land in 4517 BC, which would have been in 4707 BC. According to archaeologists, Eridu was the only recognizable town in Sumer. It is unknown how it was governed, however, if governed like later towns and cities, there would have been either a lugal (king), or an ensi (governor).

Cosmic Genesis: Chapter 5

This is the book of the generation of men in the day in which God made Adam, in the image of God he made him. He made them male and female, and blessed them, and he called their name Adam, in the day in which he made them.

Adam lived two hundred and thirty years and fathered a son in his own form, and in his own image, and he called his name Seth. The days of Adam, which he lived after his fathering Seth, were seven hundred years, and he fathered sons and daughters. All the days of Adam that he lived were nine hundred and thirty years, and he died.

Seth lived two hundred and five years, and then fathered Enos. Seth lived after his fathering Enos, seven hundred and seven years, and he fathered sons and daughters. All the days of Seth were nine hundred and twelve years, and he died.

Enos lived a hundred and ninety years and fathered Kenan.[1] Enos lived after his fathering Kenan, seven hundred and fifteen years, and he fathered sons and daughters. All the days of Enos were nine hundred and five years, and he died.

Kenan lived a hundred and seventy years, and he fathered Mahalalel.[2] Kenan lived after his fathering Mahalalel, seven hundred and forty years, and he fathered sons and daughters. All the days of Kenan were nine hundred and ten years, and he died.

Mahalalel lived a hundred and sixty-five years, and he fathered Jared.[3] Mahalalel lived after his fathering Jared, seven hundred and thirty years, and he fathered sons and daughters. All the days of Mahalalel were eight hundred ninety-five years, and he died.

Jared lived a hundred and sixty-two years and fathered Enoch,[4] and Jared lived after his fathering Enoch, eight hundred years, and he fathered sons and daughters. All the days of Jared were nine hundred and sixty-two years, and he died.

Enoch lived a hundred and sixty-five years and became the father of Methuselah.[5] Enoch was very pleasing to God after his fathering Methuselah for two hundred years, and he fathered sons and daughters. All the days of Enoch were three hundred and sixty-five years. Enoch was very pleasing to God and was not found, because God transformed him. Methuselah lived a hundred and sixty-seven[6] years and fathered Lamech.[7] Methuselah lived after his fathering Lamech eight hundred-two years and fathered sons and daughters. All the days of Methuselah which he lived, were nine hundred and sixty-nine years, and he died.

Lamech lived a hundred and eighty-eight years and fathered a son. He called his name Noah,[8] saying, "This one will cause us to cease from our works, and from the difficulties of our hands, and from Eretz, which the Lord the god has cursed." Lamech lived after his fathering Noah, five hundred and sixty-five years, and fathered sons and daughters. All the days of Lamech were seven hundred and fifty-three years, and he died.

Cosmic Genesis: Chapter 5 Notes

1 Codex Alexandrinus: Cainan (ΚΑΙΝΑΝ)

• Leningrad Codex: Keinan (קֵינָן). Translation: to nest

• Peshitta: Qynn (ܩܝܢ)

• Targum Onkelos: Keinan (קֵינָן)

• Targum Jerusalem: Keinan (קֵינָן)

This name appears to be a transliteration of kinin (𒂗𒆠), meaning 'lord (or lady) of the land,' suggesting an era when there was a single leader of Sumer. The date provided is 170 years before something happen at 4347 BC, making it 4517 BC. During the era, there was only the one city in Sumer according to archaeologists, Eridu, as all other settlements were not much more than villages, and there for there probably was a single 'Lord of Sumer.'

2 Codex Alexandrinus: Maleleêl (ΜΑΛΕΛΕΗΛ)

• LXX 108: Meleleêl (Μϭλϭλϭιλ)

• Leningrad Codex: Mahalal'el (מְהַלַלְאֵל). Translation: glorifying El (or God)

• Peshitta: Mhllâyl (ܡܗܠܠܐܝܠ)

• Targum Onkelos: Mahalal'el (מְהַלַלְאֵל)

• Targum Jerusalem: Mahalal'el (מְהַלַלְאֵל)

This appears to be a translation of ^{en}Menduran (𒂗𒈨𒁺𒊏, meaning approximately ^{dlord}Crowning Ān (or Ilu, deity).' Lord Menduran was the pre-flood king of Sippar according to the Sumerian king lists. Sippar^{ki} (𒌦𒁇𒄿𒆠) was a pre-flood Sumerian city dating back to at least the Uruk Period, generally dated to 4000 to 3100 BC. There is no evidence that the city existed earlier than the Uruk period, however, this verse would seem to be implying that Lord Menduran of Sippar was born 165 years before Uruk was unified in 4182 BC, or at least doing something in Sippar at the time, which would have been in 4347 BC.

Lord Menduran is generally viewed as fictional by Assyriologists, however, appears to have been viewed as import in ancient times, as he is one of only eight pre-flood kings mentioned on the Sumerian king lists. He was the only king of Sippar mentioned in the Sumerian king lists, either before or after the flood, suggesting that something important happened in Sippar in the pre-flood era. According to the Classical Babylonian era scholar Berossus, Ziusudra (Ξίσουθρος) built a library in the Sippar before the flood. No evidence of proto-Cuneiform writing has been found in Sippar, however, proto-Cuneiform writing has been found in Khafajah around 50 kilometers northeast of Sippar, indicating that writing was known in the region before the flood.

The city of Sippar was built around the É-Nunāna^{ki} (𒂍𒉣𒈾𒆠), the temple of Utu the sun god, however, it is unclear when it was built. Tens of thousands of Neo-Babylonian clay tablets were found in ruins of the É-Nunāna, suggesting it was used as a library in the Neo-Babylonian era. If it was used as a library in the Uruk period, all the older tablets must have been removed in ancient times. As Ziusudra was associated with the city of Shuruppak, which was in southern Sumer, near Uruk and Isin, while Sippar and Khafajah were in the north, in modern Baghdad governorate, if there was a library in the region that survived the flood, it was probably built by someone else, and long before they learned there was a flood coming down the river.

3 Codex Alexandrinus: Iared (ιλρελ)

- LXX 509: Iaret (ιλϼϬτ)

- LXX 120: Iareth (ιλϼϬθ)

- Leningrad Codex: Yared (יָרֶד). Translation: todescend

- Peshitta: Yrd (ܝܪܕ)

- Targum Onkelos: Yared (יָרֶד)

- Targum Jerusalem: Yered (יֶרֶד)

- Sahidic manuscripts: Iareth (Ιλρεθ)

Over the centuries, many Rabbis and Biblical scholars have suggested that Iared / Yared (Ιαρεδ / יֶרֶד) and Gaidad / Irad (Γαιδαδ / עִירָד) from the Cainite genealogy were corruptions of the same original name, which would then indicated the city of Eridu was being referenced.

Nevertheless, based on the story, and following reference to what appears to have started as references to the É-Ānki and the É-Ānna in Uruk, the simplest explanation for the origin of the word would be scribal error which altered Uruk to Yared. Uruk was spelled using the letters URU (𒌷) and UNUG (𒀕), in Sumero-Akkadian cuneiform, which could have been misread as URU AD (𒌷𒂊). In Middle Babylonian cuneiform, used during the New Kingdom era, the spelling was still URU UNUG (𒌷𒀕) which still could have been misread as URU AD (𒌷𒂊). If the text had have been transcribed correctly throughout the bronze age, and URU UNUG was transcribed correctly into the Phoenician script as Yrg (𐤉𐤓𐤂), it still could have been easily misread as Yrd (𐤉𐤓𐤃). If this began as a reference to Uruk, being founded 162 years before the Ānu Ziggurat (É-Ānki) was built in 4020 BC, that would place the foundation of Uruk in 4182 BC. Based on the archaeology, the region where Uruk later existed was inhabited since at least 5000 BC, however, in approximately 4200 BC, two smaller Ubaid era settlements merged to from Uruk.

4 Greek: Enôch (ℰℕѠ𝒳)

- LXX 15: Aenôch (ᐱⲓⲛⲱ𝒳)

- Leningrad Codex: Chanoch (חֲנוֹךְ). Translation: dedicated

- Peshitta: Ḥnûk (ܚܢܘܟ)

- Targum Onkelos: Chanoch (חֲנוֹךְ)

- Fragment Targums: Chanoch (חֲנוֹךְ)

- Targum Jerusalem: Chanoch (חֲנוֹךְ)

This is the second reference to an Enôch/Chanoch in the pre-flood genealogy, the first being the son of Cain. See the note regarding Enoch the son of Cain in chapter 4. While this could be another reference to the temple of Enki in Eridu, the settling of this section of text appears to be in Uruk, suggesting this was originally about the E-Anki (𒂍𒀭𒆠), the Temple of An and Ki in Uruk, where Inanna (Venus) was worshiped as the one who could return both from the sky and the underworld. To some degree, this parallel's the later legend of Enoch in the Enochian literature, in which he traveled to the sky (Ān), and never died, becoming trapped in the Earth (Ki), like most mortals do.

Assuming this verse began as a reference to the É-Ānki being built 165 years before the É-Ānna 3855 BC, that would date its foundation to 4020 BC, which is the same era that Assyrologists believe the Ānu Ziggurat was built. The Ānu Ziggurat was a large dirt mound that rose above the rest of the city of Uruk believed to have been built circa 4000 BC. It is generally believed to have originally been dedicated to Ān before Inanna became dominant, and the É-Ānna was built. As writing appears in the archaeological record after Inanna rose to prominence, it cannot be proven that the Ānu Ziggurat was the É-Ānki, however, it is generally accepted by Assyriologists that it was.

5 Greek: Mathousala (ΜΑΘΟΥⳤΑΛΑ)

- LXX 551:Mathousalan (Μαθουσαλλαν)

- Leningrad Codex: Metushalach (מְתוּשֶׁלַח)

- Peshitta: Mtůšlḥ (ܡܬܘܫܠܚ)

- Targum Onkelos: Metushalach (מְתוּשָׁלַח)

- Fragment Targums: Metushelach (מְתוּשָׁלַח)

- Targum Jerusalem: Metushalach (מְתוּשֶׁלַח)

There have been many attempts to decipher the meaning of the Hebrew version of the name. The beginning of the name is 'death' (מת), however, the rest could be interpreted as 'sending' or 'using daggers.' Based on the story of Methusalah, the longest living human, it probably originated in the Middle Babylonian mâtusalàù (𒈗𒋫𒇽𒌦), meaning 'to cheat death.' This translation probably appeared in the New Kingdom era, when the text was translated into Canaanite using Middle Babylonian Cuneiform. Due to the differences between the Egyptian and Canaanite use of the sounds L and R, if it was a transliteration of an Egyptian name, it would have been mtsôrô (𓆓𓊪𓏭𓊨𓏲𓏏), meaning 'death ascended place.' 'Ascended place' is also an accepted translations of the name of the É-Ānna (𒂍𒀭𒈾), the temple of Ianna in Uruk. This temple was near the older Ānu Ziggurat, where [deity]Ān (𒀭𒀭) was worshiped before the rise of the cult of Inanna. This suggests that the original Middle Egyptian translation referred to it as the 'ascended place' of mût (𓅐𓏏), not mt (𓅐𓏏). If so, there must have been an intermediary phonetic translation before the Middle Babylonian translation, possibly in the Hyksos era proto-Sinaitic script, which would have rendered both words as mût (𐤕𐤌).

The É-Ānna was the major religious center of Uruk, both before and after the flood. Based on the archaeological record, Uruk was itself the cultural center of pre-flood Sumer for an estimated 900 years, which Assyriologists refer to as the Uruk period. The period is estimated to have begun around 4000 BC and continued until 3100 BC, during which the Sumerians developed their pictographic proto-Cuneiform script, although the script appears to have mainly been used in Uruk before the Jemdet Nasr period (3100-2900

BC), when it spread to Niru. If this statement was originally about the É-Ānna in Uruk, it appears to be stating that the É-Ānna was built 167 years before Dumuzid (the fisherman), was born in 3688 BC, which would have been 3855 BC. Based on the current archaeological evidence, while Uruk appears to have existed since 5000 BC, the É-Ānna district is believed to have been built between 3800 and 3400 BC, over an older Ubaid era (5500–3900 BC) temple. This suggests that the origin of this 'genealogy' may have started interfring, as records of a priesthood of Ān who relocated to Niru when the É-Ānna was taken over by the priests of Inanna.

6 Berlin Genesis: etê ecaton exêconta epta (ЄΤΗЄΚΑΤΟΝЄϤΗΚΟΝΤΑЄΠΤΑ). Translation: years hundred and sixty-seven (167)

• Codex Alexandrinus: ecaton cae ogdoêconta epta (ЄΚΑΤΟΝΚΑΙΟΓΔΟΗΚΟΝΤΑ ЄΠΤΑ). Translation: hundred and eighty-seven (187)

• Cotton Genesis: hepta cae ogdoêconta cae hecaton etê (ЄΠΤΑΚΑΙΟΓΔΟΗΚΟΝΤΑ ΚΑΙЄΚΑΤΟΝЄΤΗ). Translation: seven andeighty and hundred (187)

• LXX 127: ecaton cae ebdomêconta epta etê (Ϭυⲁⲧⲟⲛ ⲙⲁⲓ Ϭυⲁⲟⲙⲏⲕⲟⲛⲧⲁ Ϭⲡⲧⲁ Ϭⲧⲏ). Translation: hundred and eighty-seven (177)

• LXX 527: hecaton cae hexêconta pente etê (Ϭυⲁⲧⲟⲛ ⲙⲁⲓ Ϭⲍⲡⲙⲟⲛⲧⲁ ⲡϭⲛⲧϭ Ϭⲧⲏ). Translation: hundred and sixty-five (165)

• Leningrad Codex: sheva ushemonim shanah ume'at shanah (שֶׁבַע וּשְׁמֹנִים שָׁנָה וּמְאַת שָׁנָה). Translation: seven and eighty years and hundred (187)

• Peshitta: mââ ûtmnâyn ûšbô šnyn (ܫܢܝܢ ܘܫܒܥ ܘܬܡܢܐܝܢ ܡܐܐ). Translation: hundred and eighty and seven (187)

• Targum Onkelos: me'ah vetamnin usheva shenin (מְאָה וְתַמְנִין וּשְׁבַע שְׁנִין). Translation: century (or one hundred) and eighty and seven (187)

• Targum Jerusalem: me'ah utemanin usheva shenin (מְאָה וּתְמָנִין וּשְׁבַע שְׁנִין). Translation: century (or one hundred) and eighty and seven (187) years

7 Codex Alexandrinus: Lamech (ΛΑΜЄΧ)

• Leningrad Codex: Lamech (לֶמֶךְ)

• Peshitta: Lmk (ܠܡܟ)

• Targum Onkelos: Lamech (לֶמֶךְ)

• Fragment Targums: Lamech (לְמֶךְ)

- Targum Jerusalem: Lamech (לְמֶךְ)

Lamech was previously mentioned in the genealogy of Cain, and based on the generations from Adam to Noah, however, these two Lamechs should not have lived at the same time. As the first Lamech appears to be a reference to Dumuzid (the shepherd), this may be a reference to the second Dumuzid (the fishermen), who is estimated to have lived in the Jamdet Nasr period if he existed.

While he is generally viewed as being a later addition during the Neo-Sumerian era, he was is listed as living in Uruk, and base on the era in this text, if Dumuzid (the fisherman) lived 188 years before the foundation of Niru in 3500 BC, this would mean he was born circa 3688 BC. Based on the archaeological evidence, during the era, Uruk was the dominant Sumerian city. The era is known by Assyriologists as the Uruk period, a period spanning 4000 to 3100 BC. During the era, the pictographic proto-Cuneiform script was developed, however, does note appear to have been used much outside of Uruk until the following Jamdet Nasr period, when it was widely used in Niru.

8 Codex Alexandrinus: Nôe (ⲚⲱⲈ)

- Leningrad Codex: Noach (נֹחַ). Translation: rest

- Peshitta: Nûḥ (ܢܘܚ). Translation: quiet (or calm, rest)

- Targum Onkelos: Noach (נֹחַ). Translation: quiet (or calm, rest)

- Fragment Targums: Nach (נַח)

- Targum Jerusalem: Nach (נַח)

It is generally accepted by academics that the Noah narrative is based on the Sumerian flood survivor stories of Ziusudra, Utnapishtim, and Atra-Hasis. The oldest surviving copy of these stories is found in the Old Babylonian Epic of Ziusudra, which tells a tale similar to the Noah narrative, in which King Ziusudra (𒍣𒋢𒌓𒁺) was warned of an oncoming storm by Enki, the Sumerian precursor to the Akkadian Ea, which is accepted as evidence that it was originally a Sumerian story that had been translated into Old Babylonian. In the story, Ziusurda was told to build a large boat, in which he and others survived the storm and flood that followed, ultimately washing up in Dilmun. Ziusudra, or Zin-Suddu, is recorded as the son of the last king of the city of Shuruppak before the flood in Tablet WB 62 of the Sumerian king lists, the oldest surviving versions of the king lists. The king lists almost all date to the Old Babylonian era, however, Tablet WB 62, also known as the Weld-Blundell prism, has been dated to the earlier Neo-Sumerian era, year 11 of King Sin-Magir of Isin, who is estimated to have reigned sometime around 1800 BC.

There is an older version of the king list from the reign of King Shulgi of Ur, the Neo-Sumerian king of Ur who would have been the king when Terah left Ur in the chronology where Shulgi's son Amar-Sin or Ur was 'King Amarpl of Sumer' who took Terah's nephew Lot captive. The version of the king list from Shulgi's reign is known as the USKL, and does not include the pre-flood kings or the kings of cities other than where Shulgi's ancestors lived.

This indicates that the king lists were massively expanded during the Neo-Sumerian era, but that that expansion does not appear to have begun until after Terah left Ur. If so, the pre-flood records in this section of text would be older than the surviving pre-flood king lists. The earliest surviving reference to Ziusudra, is found in the Sumerian Instructions of Shuruppak, which is dated to circa 2600 BC, however, it is not clear that he was viewed as the flood survivor from the Instructions. The flood deposits that covered Shuruppak, and most of southern Iraq, have been radiocarbon dated to approximately 2900 BC, however, there are debates about whether it was one massive flood, or a series of floods.

During the Old Babylonian era, Neo-Sumerian poems about Bilgamesh were combined and expanded into the Epic of Gilgamesh. In the Epic, Utnapishtim (𒌓𒍣) was the ancient survivor of the flood, whom the gods had granted immortality. The older Neo-Sumerian poems do not mention Utnapishtim, and he is believed to have been an Old Babylonian addition to Gilgamesh, likely based on Ziusudra. Like Ziusudra, Utnapishtim was told of the coming flood by Enki, and built a giant wooden box to survive, known as the Preserver of Life. He took in animals, plants, and various craftsmen to help him rebuild after the flood. Unlike Ziusudra's flood, this one was described as covering all of the land, and Utnapishtim's Preserver of Life ended up at Mount Nisir, theorized to be Pir Omar Gudrun in Iraqi Kurdistan. It is not entirely clear if it was simply built on Mount Nisir, or built elsewhere and washed up on Mount Nisir. If the presence of Enki is taken as a reference to a prophet of Enki, a metaphor, or simply a fictional addition, it is possible that these originated in two separate flood survivor stories.

The oldest surviving copy of the Epic of Atra-Hasis (𒀜𒊏𒄩𒋀) also dates to the Old Babylonian era, to the reign of King Ammi-Saduqa in the 1600s BC. Unlike Ziusudra and Utnapishtim, in the Epic of Atra-Hasis, the Ia was the god who warned Atra-Hasis of the coming flood, although had to do it behind the other gods' backs as they did not want to get involved in Ellil's plan to destroy humanity with a flood. Like Ziusudra, Atra-Hasis builds a large boat, and survives a river flood, ending up in Dilmun, suggesting that Atra-Hasis is an Akkadian or Old Babylonian reworking of Ziusudra. The author of Atra-Hasis also appears to have read Utnapishtim, as when Ellil accuses Ia of interfering, he defends his actions by claiming he 'preserved life,' a reference to Utnapishtim's Preserver of Life.

All of the surviving stories date to after the time that Terah would have left Ur, early in the Neo-Sumerian Empire, however, the presence of Ziusudra in the Instructions of Shuruppak and the Weld-Blundell prism strongly suggest that the original name of the flood survivor hero was Ziusudra (or Zin-Suddu), assuming all the stories share a common origin. The name of Noah may suggest there was more than one survivor epic, as Noah's name appears to be based on the name of Niru ($\triangleright\!\!\Sigma$), the ancient Akkadian name of Jemdet Nasr. Given the northern location, and the similarity to Utnapishtim's story and the final resting place of the giant box, in the mountains north of Sumer, it is plausible that Utnapishtim was the king of Niru. Assuming Noah was originally a reference to the city-state known in Akkadian records as Niru ($\triangleright\!\!\Sigma$), then this is a reference to the last major era of pre-flood Sumerian civilization, the Jemdet Nasr period, generally dated to 3100 to 2900 BC. If this is a reference to Niru being 600 years old when the flood happened, the implication is that the text was reporting that Niru was founded around 3500 BC.

Uruk era seals have been found at the site dated to circa 3350 BC, however, to date, it is not proven there was a city there circa 3500 BC. The era, like the earlier Uruk period, is considered to have been literate, a many tablets have been found with a pictographic script on them known as proto-cuneiform, and therefore, there could have been records of the pre-flood era passed on. As the Egyptian language did not delineate between L and R, the Middle Egyptian translator probably substituted one of the names of the similar sounding Egyptian god of the primordial waters, Nûû ($\text{---}\triangleright\!\!\triangleright$), a Middle Egyptian variant of the name of the god Nu. If the name Noah is based on Nûû, it suggests a Middle Egyptian book of Noah existed sometime before 1550 BC. Moreover, if this stared as the story of Utnapishtim of Niru, some variant must have been carried out of Ur by Terah circa 2075 BC.'

Cosmic Genesis: Chapter 6

Noah was five hundred years old, and he fathered three sons, Shem,[1] Ham,[2] and Japheth.[3] It happened when humans began to be numerous on the land, and daughters were born to them, that the sons of God[4] saw the daughters of humans, that they were beautiful, and took for themselves wives, all whom they chose.

Lord the god said, "My Spirit will certainly not remain among these men forever, because they are flesh, but their days will be a hundred and twenty years."

Now the Gigantes[5] were in the land in those days, and after that, when the sons of God used to go into the daughters of humans, they carried children for them, and those were the ancient Gigantes, the men of infamy. Lord the god, having seen that the wicked actions of men were multiplied in the land and that everyone in his heart was intently brooding over evil continually, then God regretted that he had made man on the land, and he pondered it deeply.

God said, "I will blot out man, whom I have made, from the surface of the Earth, including, men and livestock, and reptiles and flying creatures of the sky, for I have thought that I have made them." But Noah found favor before the Lord the god. These are the generations of Noah. Noah was an honest man. Being perfect in his generation, Noah was very pleasing to God. Noah fathered three sons, Shem, Ham, and Japheth. But Eretz was corrupted before God, and the land was filled with iniquity. Lord the god saw Eretz, and she was corrupted because all flesh had corrupted its way on the land.

Lord the god said to Noah, "The time of every man has come before me because the land has been filled with iniquity by them, and I will destroy them and Eretz. Therefore, make for yourself an box[6] of square timber, you will make the box in nests, and you will pitch it within and without with pitch. You will make the box like this: three hundred cubits[7] will be the length of the box, and fifty cubits will be the breadth, and thirty cubits will be the height of it. You will narrow the box while building it, and in a cubit above you will finish it, and the door of the box you will make out of its side. Make it with lower, second, and third levels. I bring a flood of water onto the land, to destroy all flesh in which has the breath of life under the sky, and whatever things are on the land will die. I will establish my covenant with you, and you will enter into the box with your sons and your wife, and your sons' wives with you. Of all livestock and all reptiles and all wild animals, even of all flesh, you will bring by two, two of all, into the box, that you may feed them with yourself: male and female they will be. Of all winged birds according to their species, and all livestock according to their species, and of all reptiles creeping on the land according to their species, pairs of all will come to you, male and female to be fed by you. And you will take for yourself of all kinds of food that you eat, and you will gather them for yourself, and it will be for you and them to eat."

Noah did all things that the Lord the god commanded him.

Cosmic Genesis: Chapter 6 Notes

1 Codex Alexandrinus: Sêm (ϹΗΜ)

- LXX 319: Sim (Ϲιμ)

- LXX 129: Sêth (Ϲηθ)

- Leningrad Codex: Shem (שֵׁם). Translation: name

- Peshitta: Šym (ܫܝܡ)

- Targum Onkelos: Shem (שֵׁם)

- Targum Jerusalem: Shem (שֵׁם)

2 Codex Alexandrinus: Chaph (ΧΑϕ)

- LXX 31: Cham (Χαμ)

- Leningrad Codex: Cham (חָם). Translation: hot

- Peshitta: Ḥm (ܚܡ)

- Targum Onkelos: Cham (חָם)

- Targum Jerusalem: Cham (חָם)

3 Codex Alxandrinus: Iapheth (ιΑϕεθ)

- Leningrad Codex: Yafet (יֶפֶת)

- Peshitta: Ypt (ܝܦܬ)

- Targum Onkelos: Yafet (יֶפֶת)

Targum Jerusalem: Yafet (יֶפֶת)

Iapheth / Yapet has been considered a Canaanite variant on Iapetus (Ιαπετος) since at least the Classical Era, as recorded by Josephus in the 1st century AD. Iapetus was the Titan who created humans in Greek mythology.

4 Berlin Genesis: huioe tou t͞hu (ΥΙΟΙΤΟΥΘΥ). Translation: sons of the god

- LXX 344: angeloe tou theou (ἀγγέλοι του Θεου). Translation: messengers of the God

- Leningrad Codex: venei-ha'elohim (בְּנֵי־הָאֱלֹהִים). Translation: sons of the elohim

- Peshitta Manuscript 5b1: br ålůhym (ܒ݁ܪ ܐܠܗܝܡ). Translation: sons (or followers, disciples) of gods (or elohim)

- Peshitta Manuscript 7a1: br dynå (ܒ݁ܪ ܕ݁ܝ̈ܢܐ). Translation: sons (or followers, disciples) of the judges (or justice, law, rule, judgment)

- Targum Onkelos: venei ravrevayya (בְּנֵי רַבְרְבַיָּא). Translation: sons (or followers, disciples) of great-leaders

- Targum Jerusalem: venei ravrevayya (בְּנֵי רַבְרְבַיָּא). Translation: sons (or followers, disciples) of great-leaders.

The Greek translators interpreted these beings as either the sons, or messengers of God, while the Masoretic Text calls them the sons of the elohim. They were called ôyryn (𐎓𐎊𐎗𐎐) meaning 'watchers' or 'guardians' in the Books of Enoch, and Grigori (𐎂𐎗𐎊𐎂𐎗𐎊) in the Secrets of Enoch, likely transliterated from the Greek egirô (εγείρω) meaning 'awaken.' Given the similarity of the stories and the connections to Mount Hermon, they were likely based on the older Akkadian Igigi (𒉌𒄀𒄀), a group of lesser gods that rebelled against the ruling ᵃⁿAnuna (𒀭𒀀𒈾).

The name ᵃⁿAnuna translates as 'sons of ᵈᵉⁱᵗʸĀn/sky' in Akkadian, suggesting that term was ᵃⁿAnuna in Cuneiform, and the following mention of the Gigantes were the Igigi who rebelled against them. The ᵃⁿAnuna were a group of ruling gods, conceptually similar to the Olympian gods of Greek mythology. Significant members of this group of gods include Enki, the 'lord of earth,' and Enlil, the 'lord of air/spirit,' and Nergal, the god of the dead. They were also called the ᵃⁿAnunakene (𒀭𒀀𒈾𒆥𒂊), more commonly transliterated into English as Anunnaki, as they were described as being the 'children of An (the sky god) on Ki (the Earth).

The variation found in Peshitta Manuscripts 7a1, from the 7th century, is curious, as the text deviates from both the Septuagint and Masoretic Text. It is possible that 7a1 represents an alternate Aramaic interpretation of ålwhym, in which the term referred to a group of 'judging gods.' If so, this would indicate that the Aramaic word ålwhym also specifically referred to the ᵃⁿAnuna, who were described as the judging gods in the Epic of Gilgamesh, which is itself believed to have originated during the Neo-Sumerian Empire, circa 2100 BC. In the Enûma Eliš, generally dated to the Old Babylonian empire between 1894 and 1595 BC, 900 [an]Anunakene are mentioned, 300 in the sky, and 600 in the underworld, suggesting they originated in a Sumerian of Akkadian star-catalog, which became deified during the Gutian dynasty, or the Neo-Sumerian Empire. If so, then the 'followers of the [an]Anuna,' probably originated in a reference to an astrological religion.

5 Codex Alexandrinus: gigantes (ΓΙΓΛΝΤΕϹ). Translation: Gigantes

• Leningrad Codex: nefilim (גְּפִּ֔לִים). Translation: fallen

• Peshitta: gnbrå (ܓܢܒܪܐ). Translation: strong men (or giants, heroes, Orion)

• Targum Onkelos: gibbarayya (גִּבָּרַיָּא). Translation: husbands (or men)

• Targum Jerusalem: shamchaza'ei ve'uzi'el hinun nefilin min shemaya (שַׁמְחֲזָאֵי וְעוּזִיאֵל הִינוּן נְפִילִין מִן שְׁמַיָּא). Translation: Samyaza and Uziel those fallen (or giants, Orions, guardians) from the sky

While most Christian translations of both the Septuagint and the Masoretic Text translate this word as 'giant,' neither the Greek nor Hebrew terms mean 'giant.' The Hebrew term is accepted as meaning 'fallen,' and, the term is likely related to the Aramaic name for the Orion constellation, Npylyå (ܢܦܝܠܝܐ). The term nefilim (נְפִּלִים) likely originated as a description of the Orionid meteor shower that happens each year, between October 2 and November 7, as the Earth passes through the debris left by Halley's Comet. Peaks of 70 meteors a minute have been recorded, and these meteors fall from the region of the sky where Orion's upstretched arm is located.

The region of the sky where the constellations Orion and Lepus are located was known as the asterism Sah (𓊹𓏏𓇳𓊽) in the religion of the Egyptian Old Kingdom, which represented Sah, the father of the gods. The Sumerian version of Sah was [an]Ān (𒀭𒀭), who was also the father of the gods, and represented by the stars of Orion. The name Greek name Orion (Ὠρίων) is derived from the Babylonian name úru Ān (𒍇𒀭), meaning 'Light of An,' and the asterism was believed to represent the god An. This term was subsequently absorbed into Greek as the name Orion during the Greek Dark Age, after the collapse of the Mycenaean civilization, as the name has not been documented in the Linear-B script. As the Greeks neither translated nor transliterated the term Nephilim, it is unlikely it was in the Aramaic text they translated, suggesting whatever term they found in the text was either conceptually or phonetically similar to the Greek Gigas (Γίγας).

A more detailed version of this story appears in the Books of Enoch, where the term was translated into Ge'ez as ôyryn (ዐይሩን) meaning 'watchers' or 'guardians'. A similar term, egirô (εγείρω) meaning 'awaken,' appears to have been used in the Greek translation of Secrets of Enoch, which was later transliterated into Old Slavonic as Grigori (Ꙃбѱꙃѳбѱ). This indicates the original term was likely something that meant 'watcher' and sounded like Gigas, and given the connections to Mount Hermon, the Orion constellation, and thereby the god An, and his children the ᵃⁿAnuna (𒀭𒉡𒈾), the original term in the Cuneiform text was almost certainly Igigi (𒀭𒅆𒄀𒅆𒄀). The Igigi were described as being a group of lesser gods that rebelled against the rule of the god Anuna, which translates as 'sons of the ᵈᵉⁱᵗʸĀn/sky,' and their name was the homophone of the Akkadian word igigi (𒄿𒄀𒄀) meaning to 'observe and measure.'

6 Codex Alexandrinus: cibôton (ΚΙΒѠΤΟΝ). Translation: box

• Leningrad Codex: tevah (תֵּבָה). Translation: box

• Peshitta: qbwtå (ܩܒܘܬܐ). Translation: container (or cistern, sepulcher)

• Targum Onkelos: tevota (תֵּבוֹתָא). Translation: chest

• Targum Jerusalem: teivota (תֵּיבוֹתָא). Translation: chest

Both the Hebrew and Armenian terms are accepted as being translations of the Aramaic word tybûtå (תיבותא), meaning 'sarcophagus,' 'coffin,' or 'box.' The Greek word cibôton (κιβωτον), meaning 'coffin, or 'box' was also derived from the Aramaic term, and was originally spelled as tibôtos (τιβωτος). The Peshitta uses a term that appears to be a Syrianized version of the Greek cibôton (κιβωτον), while the Targum Onkelos skips the opening consonant, and only renders the second half of the word. The word has been recognized as being derived from the Egyptian word djebat (𓆓𓃀𓏏), meaning 'sarcophagus,' since the classical era, which has resulted in many strange translations. If the word originated in Old Akkadian or Neo-Sumerian, the Egyptian term 'sarcophagus' was probably used as a proper name, and not a description, as the Old Akkadian and Neo-Sumerian flood survivor was described as surviving in a house-barge named the 'preserver of life,' which is approximately what djebat (𓆓𓃀𓏏) means.

7 Codex Alexandrinus: pêcheôn (ΠΗΧΕѠΝ). Translation: cubits

• LXX 319: pêchôn (πηχῶν)

• Leningrad Codex: ammah (אַמָּה). Translation: cubits

• Peshitta: åmyn (ܐܡܝܢ). Translation unclear. It appears to be an Aramaic plural of the Hebrew term for 'cubit.' It is identical to the term used in the Targum Onkelos, suggesting the Peshitta was partially translated from the Onkelos, or that the term was used in an earlier Aramaic translation.

• Targum Onkelos: ammin (אַמִּין). Translation: unclear. It appears to be an Aramaic plural of the Hebrew term for 'cubit.'

• Targum Jerusalem: kolin (קוֹלִין). Translation unclear. The word translates as 'compartments,' 'prisons,' 'light materials,' or 'lenient rulings.' It may be an Aramaic form of the Greek wordcôlon (κωλον), which in this context would translated as 'arm,' as a cubit (πηχεων / אַמָּה) was viewed as being the length of a fore-arm and hand.

The length of the cubit changed between cultures and through time. When the Septuagint was translated into Greek, the Greek cubit was approximately 46 cm (18 inches), while the Judean cubit is believed to have been around 51 cm (21 inches).

Cosmic Genesis: Chapter 7

Lord the god said to Noah, "Enter, you and all your house, into the box, as I have seen that you are righteous in this generation. Of the clean livestock take in sevens, male and female, and of the unclean livestock pairs male and female. Of clean flying creatures of the sky sevens, males and females, and of all unclean flying creatures pairs of male and female, to maintain their descendants on all the land. For after seven days I will bring rain on the land, for forty days and forty nights, and I will blot out every descendant I have made, from the face of all of Eretz."

Noah did all things, whatever the Lord the god commanded him. Noah was six hundred years old when the flood of water was on the land. Then, Noah and his sons and his wife, and his sons' wives with him, went into the box, because of the water of the flood. Of clean flying creatures and unclean flying creatures, and clean livestock and unclean livestock, and of all things that creep on the land, pairs went to Noah into the box, male and female, as God commanded Noah.

It happened after the seven days that the flood of water came over the land. In the six hundredth year of the life of Noah, in the second month, on the twenty-seventh day of the month, on that day all the fountains of the abyss were broken up, and the cataracts of the sky were opened. The rain fell on the land for forty days and forty nights. On that very day, Noah, Shem, Ham, and Japheth, the sons of Noah, and the wife of Noah, and the three wives of his sons, entered into the box. All the wild animals according to their species, and all livestock according to their species, and every reptile moving on the land according to its species, and every flying bird according to its species, went to Noah, and in the box, in pairs, male and female of all flesh in which is the breath of life. They that entered went in male and female of all flesh, as God commanded Noah, and the Lord the god shut the box outside of him.

The flood was on the land forty days and forty nights, and the water surged greatly and lifted the box up, and it was carried up off of the land. The water conquered and flooded greatly over the land, and the box was carried on the water. The water conquered greatly over Eretz, and covered all the high mountains which were under the sky. The water was raised up fifteen cubits high, and it covered all the high mountains. All the flesh died that moved on the land, of flying creatures and livestock, and wild animals, and every reptile moving on the land, and every man. All things which have the breath of life, and whatever was on the dry land died. God blotted out every offspring which was on the face of Eretz, both man and animal, and reptiles, and birds of the sky, and they were blotted out from the land, and Noah was left alone with those in the box. The water was raised above the land for a hundred and fifty days.

Cosmic Genesis: Chapter 8

God remembered Noah, and all the wild animals, and all the livestock, and all the birds, and all the reptiles that crawl, and all that were with him in the box, and God brought a wind on Eretz, and the water stopped. The fountains of the deep were closed up, and the flood-gates of the sky and the rains from the sky were stopped. The water subsided and ran off the land, and after a hundred and fifty days the water was lowered, and the box rested in the seventh month, on the twenty-seventh day of the month, in the mountains of Ararat.[1] The water continued to decrease until the tenth month. In the tenth month, on the first day of the month, the heads of the mountains were seen. It happened after forty days, that Noah opened the window of the box which he had made. He sent out the raven to see if the water had ceased, and it went out and did not return until the water was dried from off the land. He sent the dove after it to see if the water had ceased from off the land. The dove not having found rest for her feet, returned to him into the box, because the water was on all the face of Eretz, and he reached out his hand and took her, and brought her into the box. Having waited another seven days, he again sent forth the dove from the box. The dove returned to him in the evening, and had a leaf of olive, a sprig in her mouth, Noah knew that the water had ceased from off the land. Having waited another seven days, he again sent forth the dove, and she did not return to him again.

It happened in the six hundred and first year of the life of Noah, in the first month, on the first day of the month, the water subsided from off the land, Noah opened the covering of the box which he had made, and he saw that the water had subsided from the face of Eretz. In the second month, the land had dried, on the twenty-seventh day of the month. Lord the god said to Noah, "Come out from the box, you and your wife and your sons, and your sons' wives with you, and all the wild animals, as many as are with you, and all flesh both of birds and animals, and every reptile moving on the land, bring out with you, and increase yourselves and multiply on the land."

Noah came out, and his wife and his sons, and his sons' wives with him. All the wild animals and all the livestock and every bird, and every reptile creeping on the land according to their species came out out of the box. Noah built an altar to God, and took of all clean animals, and all clean birds, and offered a whole burnt offering on the altar. Lord the god smelled a smell of sweetness, and the Lord the god having considered, said, "I will not again curse Eretz because of the actions of men, because the imagination of man is intently bent on evil things from his youth, I will not, therefore, again strike all living flesh as I have done. All the days of Eretz, seed and harvest, cold and heat, summer and spring, will not cease by day or night."

Cosmic Genesis: Chapter 8 Notes

1 Codex Alexandrinus: Ararat (ΑΡΑΡΑΤ)

• Leningrad Codex: Ararat (אֲרָרָט)

• Peshitta: Qrdû (ܩܪܕܘ). Translation: Corduene (or Kurdistan)

• Targum Onkelos: Kardu (קַרְדּוּ). Translation: Corduene (or Kurdistan)

• Targum Jerusalem: tavvrei dekadron shum tavvra chad Kardanya veshum tavvra chad Arminya (טַוְורֵי דְקַדְרוֹן שׁוּם טַוְורָא חַד קַרְדַנְיָא וְשׁוּם טַוְורָא חַד אַרְמִינְיָא). Translation: mountain of Qadron – one indicated a mountain in Corduene (or Kurdistan) and one indicated a mountain in Armenia

• Sahidic manuscripts: Barat (Βαρατ)

The Peshitta and Targum Onkelos use the substitute term Corduene (ܩܪܕܘ / קַרְדּוּ), an ancient reference to Kurdistan, in the region of modern northern Iraq and southeastern Turkey. Corduene was mentioned in Greek sources in the 6th century BC as Gordi (Γορδι), a region in the Persian Empire north of the old Assyrian homeland, but south of Urartu. They were recorded as the Carduchoi (Καρδουχοι), a tribe living north of the Tigris River and in revolt against the Persian Empire circa 400 BC. Between 290 and 278 BC, the Babylonian historian Berossus wrote the Babyloniaca, which reported that the Babylonian flood survivor Xisthros' ship landed in Corduene. In the 1st century AD, the Jewish historian Josephus reported that the box of Noah was still visible in Carron (Καρρον), which is generally accepted as being a reference to Corduene. The Targum Jerusalem includes a scribal note that reports the sources used by the scribe differed, one indicating Cordune, and the other indicating Armenia.

The Hebrew and Greek name is probably older than the Aramaic name, as the Kurds were not recorded in the region until after the fall of the Neo-Assyrian Empire. Ararat is accepted as a Hebrew variation of [kur]Urartu (𒄷𒌲𒊏𒀜𒁺), the name of Armenia during the Neo-Babylonian Empire. Bilingual texts from the Persian empire confirm that [kur]Urartu (𒄷𒌲𒊏𒀜𒁺) and Armina (𒅈𒈪𒄡) were the same country. The presence of the name Ararat in Cosmic Genesis suggests that the early Aramaic text the Greeks translated included the name, however, it does not survive in the Targums or Peshitta.

Cosmic Genesis: Chapter 9

God blessed Noah and his sons, and said to them, "Increase and multiply, and fill the land and have dominion over it. The dread and the fear of you will be in all the wild animals of the land, all the birds of the sky, and all things moving on the land, and all the fish of the sea, I have placed them under your hands. And every reptile which is living will be meat for you, I have given all things to you like the green plants. But flesh with the blood of life you will not eat. For your lifeblood I will require from the hand of all wild animals, and I will require the life of man at the hand of his brother man. He that sheds man's blood, because of that blood will his own be shed, for in the image of God I made man. Increase and multiply, and fill the land, and have dominion over it."

God spoke to Noah, and to his sons with him, saying, "Look I establish my covenant with you, and with your descendants after you, and with every living mind with you, of birds and of animals, and with all the wild animals of the land, all that came out of the box. I will establish my covenant with you and all flesh will not again die by the water of the flood, and there will never again be a flood of water to destroy all the land."

Lord the god said to Noah, "This is the sign of the covenant which I set between me and you, and between every living creature which is with you for perpetual generations. I set my bow in the cloud, and it will be for a sign of the covenant between me and Eretz. It will be when I gather clouds on Eretz, that my bow will be seen in the cloud. I will remember my covenant, which is between me and you, and between every living mind in all flesh, and there will no longer be water for a deluge to blot out all flesh. And my bow will be in the cloud, and I will look to remember the everlasting covenant between me and Eretz, and between every living mind in all flesh, which is on the land."

God said to Noah, "This is the sign of the covenant, which I have made between me and between all flesh, which is on the land."

Now the sons of Noah which came out of the box, were Shem, Ham, and Japheth. Ham was the father of Canaan. These three are the sons of Noah, from these, were men scattered over all the land. Noah began to be a vintner, and he planted a vineyard. He drank of the wine, and was drunk, and was naked in his house. Ham the father of Canaan saw the nakedness of his father, and he went out and told his two brothers outside. Shem and Japheth having taken a garment put it on both their backs and went backward, and covered the nakedness of their father, and their face was turned away, and they didn't see the nakedness of their father. Noah recovered from the wine and knew all that his younger son had done to him. He said, "Cursed be the servant Canaan, a slave will he be to his brothers."

He said, "Blessed be the Lord the god for Shem, Canaan will be his slave. May God make room for Japheth, and let him live in the habitations of Shem, and let Canaan be his servant."

Noah lived after the flood for three hundred and fifty years. All the days of Noah were nine hundred and fifty years, and he died.

Cosmic Genesis: Chapter 10

Now, these are the generations of the sons of Noah, Shem, Ham, Japheth, and sons were born to them after the flood.

The descendants of Japheth were Cimmeria,[1] Magi,[2] Medes,[3] Ion,[4] (Alashiya),[5] Tabal,[6] Mushki,[7] and Troy.[8]

The descendants of Cimmeria were Ashkenaz,[9] Ripat,[10] and Togarmah.[11]

The descendants of Ion were Alashiya, Tartessos,[12] the Cypriots,[13] and the Rhodians.[14] From these, were the islands of the nations divided in their land, each according to his tongue, in their tribes and their nations.

The descendants of Ham were Khuz,[15] Egypt,[16] Put,[17] and Canaan.

The descendants of Khuz were the Sabaeans,[18] Havilah,[19] Shabwat,[20] the Ramanites,[21] and Sabtecha.[22] The descendants of the Ramanites were Sheba,[23] and Dedan.[24]

Khuz fathered Eridu,[25] who became great on the Earth.[26] (He was a strong hunter against Lord the god, and therefore they say, "Like Eridu's Lord Alulim.")[27]

The beginning of his kingdom was Eridu,[28] Uruk,[29] Akkad,[30] and Kish[31] in the land of Sumer.[32] From that land came Ashur,[33] who built Nineveh, and the cities of Rehoboth, Kalhu, and Resen, between Nineveh and Kalhu.[34] (This is the great city.)

Egypt fathered the Lydians,[35] the Upper Egyptians,[36] the Libyans,[37] the Lower Egyptians,[38] the Nubians,[39] the people of the land of Kush[40] (where the Pelesets[41] came from), and the Minoans.[42] Canaan fathered Sidon his firstborn, and the Cypriots,[43] Jebusites, Amorites, Girgashites, Mitanni,[44] Arkites, Sinites, Arvadites, Zemarites, Hamathites, and after these tribes of Canaanites were dispersed. The boundaries of the Canaanites were from Sidon until one approaches Gerar and Gaza, until one comes to Sodom and Gomorrah, Adama and Bet Rabim, as far as Lasha. Those were the sons of Ham, in their tribes according to their tongues, in their countries, and their languages.

To Shem children were also born, the father of all the sons of Eber, the brother of Japheth the elder.

The sons of Shem were Elam,[45] Ashur, Arphaxad, Lud, Aram, (and Cainan).[46]

The sons of Aram were Huz, Hul, Gater, and Mash.

Arphaxad fathered (Cainan, and Cainan fathered)[47] Salah, and Salah fathered Eber. To Eber were born two sons, the name of the one was Peleg, because in his days the land was divided, and the name of his brother Joktan.

Joktan fathered Almodad, Saleth, Hazarmaveth, Jerah, Hadoram, Aibel, Diklah, Eval, Abimael, Sheba, Ophir, Havilah, and Jobab. All these were the sons of Joktan. Their dwelling was from Mesha until one comes to Sephar, a mountain of the east. Those were the sons of Shem in their tribes, according to their tongues, in their countries, and in their nations.

Those are the tribes of the sons of Noah, according to their generations, according to their nations. From them were the islands of the Gentiles scattered over the land after the flood.

Cosmic Genesis: Chapter 10 Notes

1 Codex Alexandrinus: Gamer (ΓΑΜΕϷ)

- LXX 56: Gaber (Γαϭϸ)

- LXX 376: Gomer (Γοµϭϸ)

- LXX 53: Gomor (Γοµοϸ)

- Leningrad Codex: Gomer (גֹּמֶר)

- Peshitta: Gmr (ܓܡܪ)

- Targum Onkelos: Gomer (גּוֹמֶר)

- Fragment Targums: Gomer (גּוֹמֶר)

- Targum Jerusalem: Gomer (גּוֹמֶר)

This term was widely debated for over 1500 years, until the deciphering of Akkadian cuneiform in the past century. In the 1st century, the Jewish historian Josephus claimed the Gomer were the Galatians, which would make them Gauls, as the Galatians were Gauls who emigrated to Anatolia in the 3rd century BC. In the early 3rd century, the Christian theologian Hippolytus of Rome reported that Gomer was the ancient Cappadocian civilization near where the Galatians settled. Near the end of the 4th century, the Christian scholar Jerome claimed that Gomer were the Celts, likely a reinterpretation of Josephus.

Around the same time, the Jewish Bereshít Rabbah was composed, in which Rabbi Samuel ben Ammi claimed Gomer was Germania. After cuneiform was deciphered, and the Assyrian annals were studied, it became clear that Gomer was a reference to the ᵏᵘʳGimirrāya (𒆳𒄀𒈪𒅕𒊏𒀀𒀀), who the Greeks knew as the Cimmerios (Κιμμεριος), and the Armenians knew as the Gamirkô (Գամիրք). The Cimmerians were an ancient Indo-Iranian tribe that lived north of the Black Sea in modern Ukraine and southern Russia. They were driven south out of Europe into Anatolia and settled in the region of Cappadocia.

2 Codex Alexandrinus: Magôg (ΜΑΓωΓ)

- LXX 707: Mgôn (ΜΓοοΝ)

- LXX 246: Magôth (ΜΑΓοοθ)

- LXX 77: Magôn (ΜΑΓοοΝ)

- LXX 53: Machôn (ΜΑΧοοΝ)

- Leningrad Codex: Magog (מָגוֹג)

- Peshitta: Mgůg (ܡܓܘܓ)

- Targum Onkelos: Magog (מָגוֹג)

Fragment Targums: Afrikei veGarmanya (אַפְרִיקֵי וְגַרְמַנְיָא). Translation: Africa and Germany. The Roman province of Africa was roughly the same region as modern Tunisia, which was occupied by the Germanic Vandal tribe in 439, and survived as a North African Germanic state until 554, when Vandal Africa was conquered by the Byzantine empire. The listing of these two regions suggest the list was composed during the era. The identification of Germanic tribes as the Magog was common in the late Classical era, later replaced by the Mongols in the medieval era.

- Targum Jerusalem: Magog (מָגוֹג)

The meaning of Magog has been disputed since the Greco-Roman era, as the term is used in Israelite texts referring to both a tribe and a group of priests or sorcerers. This usage is identical to the use of the term Magos (Μαγος) in Greek literature from the era, which was both the name of a Medo-Persian tribe, and a priestly caste. The Greek term is based the name Mguš (𒈦𒄖𒐊) used in Persian cuneiform during the Achaemenid Empire, however, the earlier Persian spelling in Elamite cuneiform was Makuuka (𒈠𒆪𒌑𒃷). The archaic pronunciation may have been maintained in the Israelite texts in order to avoid seeming rebellious during the Medo-Persian era when the Magi were the official priesthood of the Median and Persian monarchs.

3 Codex Alexandrinus: Madae (ΜΑΔΑΙ)

- LXX 509: Malae (ΜΑΛΑΙ)

- LXX 55: Amada (ΑμΔΔΔ)

- LXX 135: Madaem (ΜΔΔΔΙμ)

- LXX 392: Amadae (ΑμΔΔΔΙ)

- LXX 319: Made (ΜΔΔϬ)

- LXX 129: Mamalae (ΜΔμΔΛΔΙ)

- LXX 56: Madaê (ΜΔΔΔհ)

- LXX 79: Madaea (ΜΔΔΔϬΙΔ)

- LXX 246: Madan (ΜΔΔΔN)

- LXX 77: Madaen (ΜΔΔΔΙN)

- LXX 569: Madim (ΜΔΔΙμ)

- LXX 761:Madiam (ΜΔΔΙΔμ)

- LXX 53: Madam (ΜΔΔΔμ)

- LXX 31: Maedi (ΜΔΙΔΙ)

- LXX 376: Môdae (Μ∞ΔΔΙ)

- Leningrad Codex: Madai (מָדַי). Translation: Medes

- Peshitta: Mdy (ܡܕܝ)

- Targum Onkelos: Madai (מָדַי)

- Fragment Targums: Madai (מָדַי). Translation: Medes

- Targum Jerusalem: Madai (מָדַי). Translation: Medes

- Sahidic manuscripts: Amakha (ⲁⲙⲁⲭⲁ)

4 Codex Alexandrinus: Iôyan (ΙⲰΥΑΝ).

- Cotton Genesis: Iôouam (ΙⲰΟΥΑΜ)

- LXX 15: Iôouan (Ι∞ουΔN)

- LXX 17: Iôuian (ιοουιλν)

- LXX 730: Ayan (ᰠυλν)

- LXX 426: Iouôan (ιουооλν)

- LXX 500: Aynan (ᰠυνλν)

- LXX 75: Iôgan (ιооγλν)

- LXX 413: Uiôuian (Υιοουιλν)

- LXX 71: Iôan (ιооλν)

- LXX 76: Iouan (ιουλν)

- LXX 108: Iôynan (ιοουνλν)

- LXX 527: Ian (ιλν)

- LXX 53: Iôban (ιооυλν)

- LXX 59: Iôian (ιооιλν)

- Leningrad Codex: Yavan (יָוָן)

- Peshitta: Yůn (ܝܘܢ)

- Targum Onkelos: Yavan (יָוָן)

- Fragment Targums: Mikdoneya (מְקְדוֹנְיָא). Translation: Macedonia

- Targum Jerusalem: Yavan (יָוָן)

Bohairic manuscripts: Iôban (Iⲱⲃⲁⲛ)

The Hebrew term is a transliteration of the early Aramaic name Ywn (𐡉𐡅𐡍), and Neo-Assyrian name Iauna (𒅀𒌑𒈾), both meaning 'Ion.' The Neo-Assyrian and Aramaic words are accepted as being transliterations of the archaic Greek Iawôn (Ιαϝων), the name of a Greek patriarch who the Ionian Greek tribes were believed to descend from. Ionian Greeks primarily lived in Ionia, a region of western Anatolia. The term was in common use during the era of the Neo-Assyrian empire for 'Greeks' when pluralized into Yůnyn (𐡉𐡅𐡍𐡍), which was adopted into Late Egyptian as the word Ůynn (𓇋�𓏏𓏥), meaning 'Greek,' which continued to be used in Coptic in the Classical era as Ouainin (Ⲟⲩⲁⲓⲛⲓⲛ) and Ouenin (Ⲟⲩⲉⲓⲛⲓⲛ). As both the Greek and Hebrew transliterations are ultimately derived from a term that has a more commonly spelling in English, the more common name Ion is used.

5 LXX 961: Elisa (ⲉⲗⲉⲓⲥⲁ)

- Codex Alexandrinus: Elisa (ⲉⲗⲓⲥⲁ)

- LXX 15: Lisa (ⲗⲓⲥⲁ)

- LXX 730: Elissa (Ελισσα)

- LXX 120: Elisan (Ελισαν)

- LXX 75: Elisae (Ελισαι)

- LXX 82: Elysa (Ελυσα)

- LXX 107: Elêsa (Ελησα)

- LXX 527: Elca (Ελκα)

- LXX 376: Inesan (ⲓⲛⲥⲟⲁⲛ)

- Leningrad Codex (in the later reference to the son of Yavan): Elishah (אֱלִישָׁה)

- Peshitta (in the later reference to the son of Yavan): Ålyšå (ܐܠܝܫܐ)

- Targum Onkelos (in the later reference to the son of Yavan): Elishah (אֱלִישָׁה)

- Fragment Targums (in the later reference to the son of Yavan): Elishah (אֱלִישָׁה)

- Targum Jerusalem (in the later reference to the son of Yavan): Elishah (אֱלִישָׁה)

Elisa / Elishah is not mentioned in the Masoretic Text, Peshitta, or Targums at this point, only in the following list of the sons of Iôyan / Yŭn. The Kingdom of Alashiya was mentioned in many texts from the late bronze age. Based on chemical analysis of the clay tablets sent from Alashiya to other kingdoms during the bronze age, is believed to have been in southern Cyprus, spanning the region where the cities of Kalavasos (Καλαβασός) and Alassa (Ἄλασσα) are located today. The name of Alassa is probably descended from Alashiya. During the bronze age, the Egyptian court corresponded with the civilization using the Akkadian cuneiform script, in which it was known as Alašiia (𒀀𒆷𒅆𒅀), which is probably the closest to its native pronunciation. The Mycenaean Greeks of the era recorded the name as Arasijo (𐀀𐀨𐀯𐀍), while the Ugaritic Canaanites recorded the name as Ålṭy (𐎀𐎍𐎘𐎊).

6 Codex Alexandrinus: Thobel (Θοβελ)

- LXX 319: Thôbel (Θωυβελ)

- LXX 376: Thoubel (Θουυβελ)

- Leningrad Codex: Tuval (תֻבָל)

- Peshitta: Tûbyl (ܬܘܒܝܠ)

- Targum Onkelos: Tuval (תּוּבָל)

- Fragment Targums: Yetaneya (יְתָנְיָא)

- Targum Jerusalem: Tuval (תּוּבָל)

Tabal was an early iron age kingdom in southeast Anatolia. It was conquered by the Neo-Assyrian Empire in 713 BC, around the time the genealogy of nations was added, after entering into an anti-Assyrian alliance with the Mushki and the city of Carchemish.

7 LXX 961: Mosech (ΜΟϹЄΧ)

- Codex Alexandrinus: Mosoch (ΜΟϹΟΧ)

- LXX 319: Mosôch (Μοσωχ)

- LXX 54: Masôch (Μασωχ)

- LXX 74: Misoch (Μισοχ)

- LXX 106: Masoch (Μασοχ)

- LXX 53: Mesoch (Μεσοχ)

- Leningrad Codex: Meshech (מֶשֶׁךְ)

- Peshitta: Mšk (ܡܫܟ)

- Targum Onkelos: Meshech (מֶשֶׁךְ)

- Fragment Targums: Anasya (אֲנַסְיָא)

- Targum Jerusalem: Meshech (מֶשֶׁךְ)

- Bohairic manuscript: Moskho (Mocxo)

The Muški (𒈨𒅖𒆠) were recorded in Hittite and Assyrian records as invading northeast Anatolia during the bronze age collapse, however, they were repulsed, and initially settled in the region of modern Georgia. Later the tribe divided into two tribes, and one migrated to Cilicia, settling around Tabal. In the era of the Neo-Assyrian Empire, they were recorded in the annals of Urartu as the Muškini (𒈨𒅖𒆠𒈾), while the Greeks later called them the Moschoi (Μοσχοι). Josephus identified the Mosoch as the Moschoi in the 1st century, which is generally accepted today, however, was heavily debated during the Medieval era, with European scholars identifying Mosoch with variety of locations, including France, Britain, and Moscow.

8 LXX 961: Thiras (ⲐⲈⲓⲣⲁⲥ)

• Codex Atheniensis: Thiras (Ⲑⲓⲃⲁⲥ)

• LXX 17: Thêras (Ⲑⳙⲃⲁⲥ)

• LXX 53: Thêras cae Tharsês (Ⲑⳙⲃⲁⲥ ⳗⲁⲓ Ⲑⲁⲃⲟⳙⲥ). Translation: Thera (or Santorini) and Tharsis

• Leningrad Codex: Tiras (תִּירָס)

• Peshitta: Tyrs (ܬܻܝܪܣ)

• Targum Onkelos: Tiras (תִּירָס)

• Fragment Targums: Tarkei (תַּרְקֵי)

• Targum Jerusalem: Tiras (תִּירָס)

The location of Thiras/Tiras has been debated for millennia. In the Second Temple Era Book of Jubilees, the descendants of Tiras had four large lands in the sea, possibly a reference to the Etruscans, who controlled the Tyrrhenian (Etruscan) Sea before the rise of the Carthaginian, Greek, and Roman empires, as the Tyrrhenian Sea is surrounded by Sicily, Sardinia, Corsica, and the Italian peninsula. In the first century AD, Josephus claimed Tiras was the ancestor of the Thracians in the Balkan Peninsula. In the Talmud's Yoma tractate Tiras is identified as the ancestors of the Persians, however, this may simply be a conflation with the early dynastic Persian king Teispes (𐎹𐎡𐏁𐎱𐎡𐏁). In the medieval Jewish Yosippon, Tiras was identified as the ancestor of the Kievan Rus. Since the deciphering of Egyptian hieroglyphs, the dominant theory turned to them being the Tûršå (𓏏�𓈖�), generally anglicized as Teresh, one of the sea peoples who attacked Egypt during the bronze age collapse. The Teresh are often identified with the 'Tyrrhenians,' however, according to Strabo, Tyrrhenian was simply the Greek name of the Etruscans. The Etruscans called themselves the Rassena (𐌀𐌍𐌍𐌄𐌔𐌀𐌓), and the name 'Etruscan' was ultimately derived from the early Greek name for them Tyrsênoe (Τυρσηνοι), essentially meaning 'tower people,' as their cities were built on hills. This means that any identification of the Rassena and Turshå based on the later Greek term Tyrsênoe, is entirely anachronistic.

If any of the sea peoples were the Rassena, they were likely the Ůåshåshå (𓇋𓈖𓈖𓈖), generally anglicized as Weshesh, as the Egyptians had difficulty transliterating foreign words that involved the R sound. Since the deciphering of Akkadian cuneiform, and then the Neshite (Hittite) language in the past century, an alternate interpretation of the Turshå has emerged, as the Neshites referred to their neighbors to the northwest as Taruiša (𒋫𒊒𒄿𒊭). A similar term for the people from the region has been found in Mycenaean Linear-B as Toroja (𐀉𐀬). As this is the same location as the later Greek legends about Troy (Τροία), and the names are clearly similar, Taruiša and Toroja are viewed as alternative ways of writing Troy. Given that the other locations in this list are mostly in Anatolia, the Aegean, or the Black Sea, and Tyrs (תירס) appears to be a transliteration of Taruiša (𒋫𒊒𒄿𒊭), the name Troy is used in this translation.

9 Berlin Genesis: Aschanas (ⲀⲤⲬⲀⲚⲀⲤ)

- LXX 961: Aschenez (ⲀⲤⲬⲈⲚⲈⲌ)

- Codex Alexandrinus: Aschanaz (ⲀⲤⲬⲀⲚⲀⲌ)

- LXX 57: Aschana (Ασχανα)

- LXX 58: Aschanaza (Ασχαναζα)

- LXX 343: Aschanez (Ασχανεζ)

- LXX 426: Aschalez (Ασχαλεζ)

- LXX 72: Chanax (Χαναξ)

- LXX 569: Achanaz (Αχαναζ)

- Leningrad Codex: Ashkanaz (אַשְׁכְּנַז)

- Peshitta: Åšknz (ܐܫܟܢܙ)

- Targum Onkelos: Ashkenaz (אַשְׁכְּנַז)

- Fragment Targums: Asya (אָסְיָא). Translation: Asia

- Targum Jerusalem: Ashkenaz (אַשְׁכְּנַז)

- Bohairic manuscripts: Askhanas (ⲁⲥⲭⲁⲛⲁⲥ)

The earliest records of the Aschanaz date to the Neo-Assyrian era, when the Cimmerians invaded the Urartu, and were repulsed by the Áškuzai (𒅖𒆳𒍪𒀀𒀉), which Armenian historians have accepted as the earliest reference their ancestors arriving in Urartu. As the Armenians were established in the region by the beginning of the Persian era, this interpretation does seem likely, however, the Urartians continued to be the dominant culture until the Neo-Babylonian era. The report regarding the Cimmerian (𒆳𒉺𒀖𒅎𒀀𒄿𒀀) invasion of Urartu was from the reign of Sargon II, and along with other reports show a series of invasionary migrations of the Cimmerians as the Scythians pushed them south through the trans-Caucus into the Armenian Highlands and northern Anatolia. These reports are dated to between 720 and 714 BC, during the early years of Sargon II, which, combined with the subsequent scribal note about Kalhu being the capital city, indicate that the genealogies of nations was likely added between 720 and 705 BC.

10 Cotton Genesis: Eriphath (ⲉⲣⲓ𝜙ⲁⲑ).

- LXX 407: Riphath (ⲣⲓ𝜙ⲁⲑ)

- LXX 15: Eriphat (ⲉ𝜌ⲓ𝜙ⲁⲧ)

- LXX 17: Riphath (ⲣ𝝈ⲓ𝜙ⲁⲑ)

- LXX 58: Riphtha (ⲣⲓ𝜙ⲑⲁ)

- LXX 370: Riphag (ⲣⲓ𝜙ⲁ𝛾)

- LXX 82: Riphat (ⲣⲓ𝜙ⲁⲧ)

- LXX 343: Riphthan (ⲣⲓ𝜙ⲑⲁⲛ)

- LXX 458: Rêphath (ⲣ𝓊𝜙ⲁⲑ)

- Leningrad Codex: Rifat (רִיפַת)

- Peshitta: Dypr (ܪܝܦܬ)

- Targum Onkelos: Rifat (רִיפַת)

- Bohairic manuscripts: Riphat (ⲣⲓⲑⲁⲧ)

11 Codex Alexandrinus: Thergama (ⲑⲉⲣⲅⲁⲙⲁ)

- LXX 407: Thorgama (ⲑⲟ𝛽𝛾ⲁⲙⲁ)

- LXX 426: Thôrgama (ⲑⲱ𝛽𝛾ⲁⲙⲁ)

- LXX 343: Thorgaman (ⲑⲟ𝛽𝛾ⲁⲙⲁⲛ)

- LXX 458: Thogarma (ⲑⲟ𝛾ⲁ𝛽ⲙⲁ)

- LXX 527: Orgomath (ⲟ𝛽𝛾ⲟⲙⲁⲑ)

- Leningrad Codex: Togarmah (תֹגַרְמָה)

- Peshitta: Tůgrmå (ܬܘܓܪܡܐ)

- Targum Onkelos: Togarmah (תוֹגַרְמָה)

- Fragment Targums: Varberi'ah (בְרְבְּרִיאָה). Translation: Algeria (or Eritrea, Bavaria). The term is Greek and was applied to several regions around the periphery of Greek civilization.

  - Targum Jerusalem: Togarma (תוֹגַרְמָא)

12 LXX 961: Tharsis (ΘΑΡϹΕΙϹ)

- Codex Alexandrinus: Tharsis (ΘΑΡϹΙϹ)

- Cotton Genesis (LXX D): Tharsês (ΘΑΡϹΗϹ)

- LXX 426: Tharis (ΘΑΡϬΙϹ)

- Leningrad Codex: Tarshish (תַרְשִׁישׁ)

- Peshitta: Tršyš (ܬܪܫܝܫ)

- Targum Onkelos: Tarshish (תַרְשִׁישׁ)

- Fragment Targums: Alastaresom (אַלְסְטָרְסוֹם). This appears to be a corruption of the Alas and Tarsas (אַלְס וְטַרְסַס) found in the Targum Jerusalem, suggesting that Alas was in additional targums, as the Fragments Targum are generally viewed as older than Jerusalem Targum, and the Jerusalem Targum includes what appears to be quotes from the Fragment Targums.

  - Targum Jerusalem: Alas veTarsas (אַלְס וְטַרְסַס). Translation: Alas and Tarsas

This civilization was also recorded in the Neo-Assyrian records of Esarhaddon as Tarsisi (𒆳𒋻�), where it was used as a metaphor for the most distant known land. It was also recorded as Tršš (𐤅𐤔𐤔𐤕), on the Phoenician language Nora Stone discovered in Sardinia, which is also believed to date to the era. It was later known as Tartêssos (Ταρτησσος) in Greek myths, however, was no longer viewed as being a known land that people sailed to. In the 4th century BC, Aristotle identified Tartêssos as being on the Atlantic coast of Iberia. Around the same time, the Greek geographer and explorer Pytheas reported that the civilization once existed on the Baetis River, the modern Guadalquivir River in southwest Spain. While the location of the civilization has been debated for thousands of years, it is commonly accepted as being the 'Tartessian' culture of southwest Iberia. During the 1900s, extensive remains of a bronze age civilization were discovered by archaeologists working ins southwest Spain and southern Portugal. This civilization existed between approximately 1900 and 700 BC. It controlled extensive mines in southwest Iberia, which produced both metals and gemstones, and it also appears to have traded extensively with both the Phoenicians and Celts. The script used by the Tartessians was similar to the Greek script, which may have been why they were included in this list of nations.

13 Codex Alexandrinus: Cêtioe (ⲕⲏⲧⲓⲟⲓ).

• Cotton Genesis: Cheuothaeim Citioe (ⲭⲉⲩⲟⲑⲁⲓⲉⲓⲙⲕⲓⲧⲓⲟⲓ) Translation: Cheuothaeim Citians

• LXX 135: Chetiim Cyprioe (ⲭⲉⲧⲓⲉⲓⲙ ⲕⲩⲡⲣⲓⲟⲓ). Translation: Chetiim Cypriots

• LXX 57: Cittioe (ⲕⲓⲧⲧⲓⲟⲓ)

• LXX 58: Cheththim cai Citioe (ⲭⲉⲑⲑⲓⲙ ⲕⲁⲓ ⲕⲉⲧⲓⲟⲓ). Translation: Cheththim and Citians

• LXX 343: Chethim (ⲭⲉⲑⲉⲓⲙ)

• LXX 458: Citios (ⲕⲓⲧⲓⲟⲥ)

• LXX 54: Cheththiim (ⲭⲉⲑⲑⲓⲉⲓⲙ)

• LXX 71: Cytioe (ⲕⲩⲧⲓⲟⲓ)

• LXX 107: Cotêoe (ⲕⲟⲧⲗⲟⲓ)

• LXX 106: Cheuothiim (ⲭⲉⲩⲟⲑⲓⲉⲓⲙ)

• LXX 527: Cêstioe (ⲕⲗⲟⲧⲓⲟⲓ)

• LXX 44: Cheuothêiim (ⲭⲉⲩⲟⲑⲗⲓⲉⲓⲙ)

• LXX 376: Citeoe (ⲕⲓⲧⲉⲟⲓ)

• Leningrad Codex: Kittim (כִּתִּים). Translation: Cypriots

• Peshitta: Ktym (ܟܬܝܡ). Translation: Cypriots

• Targum Onkelos: Kittim (כִּתִּים). Translation: Cypriots

• Fragment Targums: not mentioned in the verse

• Targum Jerusalem: Achazya (אֲכַזְיָא)

The various manuscripts of the Septuagint contain a number of variations at this point, some including a Greek transliteration of the Aramaic word Ktym (כת^ל), others including a translation as 'Citians,' and some including both. Only one known Greek manuscript separates them with an 'and' (και), LXX 58 from the 11th century, however, that variation must have been in wide use in Egypt during the medieval era, as it is the variation that was translated into Ge'ez, the classical language of Ethiopia.

Kt (כת) and Kty (כתל) were the Canaanite and Aramaic names of Cyprus during the Neo-Assyrian and Neo-Babylonian era, based on the name of the ancient Cypriot city-state, subsequently known as Cition (Κίτιον) in Greek. The name was recorded as Kåtjåy (𓈎𓏏𓇌𓂢) in Egyptian records from the New Kingdom Era in the late Bronze Age, and appears to have survived the bronze age collapse better than most states. According to Josephus in the 1st century AD, Kytm was originally a place Cyprus, however, the term appears to have come to mean all Greeks, or even all non-Semitic Mediterranean peoples in the Judahite dialect of Canaanite by the seventh century BC, which appears to be the intended usage here. In this verse, as the name 'Citians' is being used to clarify the various transliterations of 'Cyprus' it is treated as a Greek scribal note.

14 Berlin Genesis: Roaeoe (ΡΟΑΙΟΙ). This appears to be a simple scribal error of 'Rhodians' (ΡΟΔΙΟΙ)

- Codex Alexandrinus: Rodioe (ΡΟΔΙΟΙ). Translation: Rhodians.

- LXX 319: Rôdioe (Ροδλιοι). Translation: Rhodians

- Leningrad Codex: Dodanim (דֹּדָנִים)

- Peshitta: Dŭdnym (ܕܘܕܢܝܡ)

- Targum Onkelos: Dodanim (דֹּדָנִים)

- Fragment Targums: Dodanya (דּוֹדָנְיָא)

- Targum Jerusalem: Doredanya (דּוֹרְדָנְיָא)

The Greek translation does not correspond to the Hebrew and Aramaic translations in this verse. The Greek Rodioe referred to people from the island of Rhodes (Ῥόδος), while the Hebrew Dodanim was a plural of Dodona (Δωδώνη). There were two Dodonas in Greece, one in Epirus, and the other in Thessaly near Mount Olympus. Both were oracle sites of Zeus. The difference between the names was almost certainly already in the Aramaic text the Greek translated, as the same deviation is also found in Masoretic book Dibrê Hayyāmîm, which renders the name as Rodanim (רֹודָנִים), mirrored in 1st Paralipomenon by Rodioe (Ροδιοι). The letters representing D and R are almost identical in both Phoenician (𐤀 and 𐤓) and Aramaic (𐡃 and 𐡓), and therefore the error could have originated in either script, however, as the Greek translation uses the name Rhodians in both places, the error was likely made when the genealogy of nations was added to the Torah between 612 and 607 BC.

15 Codex Alexandrinus: Chous (ΧΟΥΣ)

- Leningrad Codex: Kush (כּוּשׁ)

- Peshitta: Kŭš (ܟܘܫ)

- Targum Onkelos: Kush (כּוּשׁ)

- Targum Jerusalem: Kush (כּוּשׁ)

The Septuagint generally uses the name 'Aethiopia' where the Masoretic Text uses 'Kush,' however, as it is interpreted here as the name of a patriarch, as transliterated directly, confirming that the old Aramaic text did use the same name as the Hebrew and Syriac translations. In the context of the genealogy of nations, this 'Kush,' who is the father of the Southern Semites, well as Eridu, can only be interpreted as the Sumerians, who are otherwise conspicuously absent from the genealogy of nations. According to Assyriologists, the Elamites were the ethnolinguistic group most closely related to the Sumerians, and therefore, like the Southern Semites and Elamite, the Sumerians were probably dark skinned, which was called kusaaa (𒂟𒅂𒐖) in Assyrian. This reference to the Sumerians as 'Kush' confirms that the Geon River in Genesis chapter 2 was the Karun River that flows through Khuzestan. For more information on the Geon, seen the note in chapter 2. Therefore, the name Khuz is applied to this 'Kush,' to differentiate it from the Empire of Kush in Africa.

16 Codex Alexandrinus: Mesraen (ⲙⲉⲥⲣⲁⲓⲛ)

- Cotton Genesis (LXX D): Mestraem (ⲙⲉⲥⲧⲣⲁⲓⲙ)

- LXX 15: Mestrem (Μεστρεμ)

- LXX 17: Mesraem (Μεσραεμ)

- LXX 318: Mesraem (Μεσραιμ)

- LXX 319: Mesraêm (Μεσραημ)

- LXX 14: Mesaraem (Μεσαραιμ)

- LXX 25: Messaraem (Μεσσαραιμ)

- LXX 343: Metraem (Μετραιμ)

- LXX 79: Messaraen (Μεσσαραειν)

- LXX 82: Mestrim (Μεστριμ)

- LXX 408: Messaraem (Μεσσαραειμ)

- LXX 54: Mestraem (Μεστραειμ)

- LXX 71: Mesorem (Μεσορεμ)

- LXX 74: Mesrae (Μϵσραι)

- LXX 108: Mesaraem (Μϵσαραϵιμ)

- LXX 376: Misraem (Μισραϵιμ)

- Leningrad Codex: Mitzrayim (מִצְרַיִם). Translation: Egypt (or Egyptians)

- Peshitta: Msrym (ܡܨܪ̈ܝܐ). Translation: Egyptians

- Targum Onkelos: Mitzrayim (מִצְרָיִם). Translation: Egyptians

- Targum Jerusalem: Mitzrayim (מִצְרָיִם). Translation: Egyptians

- Bohairic manuscripts: Nestrem (Ⲛⲉⲥⲧⲣⲉⲙ)

The Canaanite form of the words meaning 'Egypt,' and 'Egyptian,' were both spelled as plural forms of Mṣr, as there were two lands of Egypt, Upper and Lower Egypt. The plural form was used in Ugaritic as Mṣrm (𐎎𐎕𐎗𐎎), Phoenician as Mṣrm (𐤌𐤑𐤓𐤌), Aramaic as Mṣryn (𐡌𐡑𐡓𐡉𐡍), and Hebrew as Mṣrym (מצרים). The origin of the name 'Mṣr' isn't clear, however, it was used as a singular form in Akkadian as Muṣur (𒈬𒍮), and later East Semitic languages as Miesri (𒈪𒅖𒊑), and continues to be a singular form in Arabic as Miṣr (مصر). In the names comprising the genealogy of nations, there are the names of mythical patriarchs, countries, and tribes, and therefore it is not clear if the original list referred 'Egypt,' or 'Egyptians,' or if a mythical patriarch was actually being referred to.

If the Egyptians had a mythical patriarch they all descended from, his name has not survived, however, given the Egyptian's view of their country's early history, when it was ruled by the gods and demigods, a mythical patriarch seems unlikely. It is possible the author was thinking of Menes (𓏠𓈖) the quasi-mythical founder of Egypt.

The Egyptians had legends of Menes, however, to date no clear evidence has been found confirming his existence. It is theorized the legends of Menes may have been based on early dynastic king Narmer, who is known from the archaeological record, but not the king lists, and if so, it is plausible that Muṣur is also a corruption of his name. If so, it probably started as the Sumerians transliterating Nâr-mer (𒊬) as Amar-mu (𒀫𒈬), and the Akkadians reversing the logograms to Mu-amar (𒈬𒀫), as they did with some other names. As the Sumerian AMAR (𒀫) logogram was commonly pronounced as SUR in Akkadian, it would have resulted in the name Mu-ṣur. While the Greeks may have interpreted the name as a literal patriarch, the genealogy of nations appears to be more figurative, attempting to explain which nations descended from which other nations, and so the name 'Egypt' is imported from the Masoretic Text.

17 Codex Alexandrinus: Phoud (ⲫⲟⲩⲇ)

• Cotton Genesis (LXX D): Phouth (ⲫⲟⲩⲑ)

• LXX 319: Phout (ⲫⲟⲩⲧ)

• LXX 57: Choud (ⲭⲟⲩⲇ)

• LXX 120: Phoul (ⲫⲟⲩⲗ)

• LXX 426: Phour (ⲫⲟⲩⲣ)

• LXX 551: Phôoud (ⲫⲱⲟⲩⲇ)

• Leningrad Codex: Fut (פּוּט)

• Peshitta: Pût (ܦܘܛ)

• Targum Onkelos: Fut (פּוּט)

• Targum Jerusalem: Fut (פּוּט)

The Pådu (𒌓𒁀𒀀𒁕) were a Libyan tribe recorded in Egyptian records of the 22nd dynasty, who appear to have lived in Cyrene before the Greeks colonized the region in 631 BC. The annals of Nebuchadnezzar II report that in 567 BC, the Greeks from Putu, called the Putu Iáaman (𒁀𒀀𒈠𒀭) in Neo-Babylonian, were fighting in the Egyptian army. The Canaanites appear to have been trading with the Pådu for centuries before the Greeks established a colony in Cyrene, and so the name Pût (𐤐𐤅𐤈) appears to have been applied to the entire Libyan (Berber) population of northern Africa. When the Persians later conquered Egypt, Cyrene joined the Persian Empire, and they integrated Cyrene as the Satrapy of Putāya (𐎱𐎢𐎬𐎠𐎹).

18 Codex Alexandrinus: Saba (ⲥⲁⲃⲁ)

• LXX 370: Sabatha (ⲥⲁⲃⲁⲑⲁ)

• LXX 77: Saua (ⲥⲁⲩⲁ)

• LXX 761: Saban (ⲥⲁⲃⲁⲛ)

• Leningrad Codex: Seva (סְבָא)

• Peshitta: Šbå (ܣܒܐ)

• Targum Onkelos: Seva (סְבָא)

• Targum Jerusalem: Seva (סְבָא)

This reference, along with the Sabatha / Savtah (Σαβαθα / סַבְתָּה) and Sabacatha / Savtecha (Σαβακαθα / סַבְתְּכָא), appear to be references to Sabaean tribes of southern Arabia. Based on them all being descends of Kush, it appears the other Sabaean tribes were not viewed as being descendants of Saba at the time. Sbâ (ሰባአ), generally anglicized as Saba, was a kingdom in modern western Yemen, based out of its capital of Mryb (𐩣𐩧𐩨). Based on the archaeological evidence, the Sabaeans formed a small kingdom around Mryb circa 1200 BC, and by 800 BC ruled western Yemen.

19 Codex Alexandrinus: Euila (ⲉⲩⲓⲗⲁ)

- Cotton Genesis: Euilat (ⲉⲩⲓⲗⲁⲧ)

- LXX 15: Euilat (Ευϭιλατ)

- LXX 344: Eyila (Ευϭιλα)

- LXX 131: Leuilat (Λϭυιλατ)

- LXX 739: Leeuilat (Λϭϭυιλατ)

- LXX 120: Eyêlat (Ευⳑλατ)

- LXX 128: Leuilat (Λϭυϭιλατ)

- LXX 77: Leuitat (Λϭυιτατ)

- Leningrad Codex: Chavilah (חֲוִילָה)

- Peshitta: Ḥûylâ (ܚܘܝܠܐ)

- Targum Onkelos: Chavilah (חֲוִילָה)

- Targum Jerusalem: Chavilah (חֲוִילָה)

- Bohairic manuscripts: Euilat (Ⲉⲩⲓⲗⲁⲧ)

Based on the geographical description in chapter 2, this appears to be the Cradle of Gold, near modern Medina, in Saudi Arabia. For more information, see the note on Euilat in chapter 2.

20 LXX 961: Sabata (ⲥⲁⲃⲁⲧⲁ)

- Codex Alexandrinus: Sabatha (ⲥⲁⲃⲁⲑⲁ)

- LXX 730: Basa (βασα)

- LXX 319: Sababatha (ⲤⲀⲨⲀⲨⲀⲐⲀ)

- LXX 370: Sabasa (ⲤⲀⲨⲀⲤⲀ)

- LXX 346: Sabbatha (ⲤⲀⲨⲨⲀⲐⲀ)

- LXX 108: Sabathat (ⲤⲀⲨⲀⲐⲀⲧ)

- LXX 551: Sauatha (ⲤⲀⲨⲀⲐⲀ)

- Leningrad Codex: Savtah (סַבְתָּה)

- Peshitta: Sbtā (ܣܒܬܐ)

- Targum Onkelos: Savtah (סַבְתָּה)

- Targum Jerusalem: Sabtā (סַבְתָּ)

This is probably a reference to a kingdom based out of Šbůt (𐩪𐩨𐩩), in central modern Yemen. The root terms Sb (𐩨𐩪) and Šb (𐩦𐩨) were used by most of the tribes of southern Arabia, making identification of the specific land difficult, however, the first century AD guide to the Indian Ocean known as the *Periplus of the Erythraean Sea*, a major trading center named Sabbatha (Σαββαθα) was recorded as being in the interior of modern Yemen. This is the name used in LXX 346, and virtually identical to the spelling in the Codex Alexandrinus and LXX 319, indicating at least some of the classical and medieval scribes viewed this as a reference to Sabbatha (𐩪𐩨𐩩).

Pliny the Elder's Natural History, written at approximately the same time, called the city Sabota (Σαβοτα), and claimed it was the capital city of the Adramitae Sabaean tribes, which is considered to be the origin of the regional name Hadhramaut (حَضْرَمَوْت) for modern eastern Yemen. The ruins of Šbůt, generally anglicized to Shabwat or Shabwa, have been studied by archaeologists in the past century, and were not inhabited by the similarly named Sabaeans to the west, but a different South Semitic people. Sabaean and Hadramitic writing have been found in the remains of the city, but mostly Hadramitic. Based on the archaeological evidence, the city of Shabwat existed from the 1300s BC until the 200s AD.

21 Codex Alexandrinus: Renchma (ⲢⲉⲅⲬⲙⲀ)

- LXX 318: Regma (Ρεγμα)

- LXX 707: Ragma (Ραγμα)

- LXX 730: Recma (Ρεϲμα)

- LXX 400: Resma (Ρόσμᴀ)

- Leningrad Codex: Ra'mah (רַעְמָה)

- Peshitta: Rômå (ܪܥܡܐ)

- Targum Onkelos: Ra'mah (רַעְמָה)

- Targum Jerusalem: Ra'ama (רַעְמָא)

This location is somewhat debated, however, generally accepted as a reference to the Ramanitês (Ραμανίτης) tribe, who Pliny the Elder later recorded in the first century AD, as living in the region of modern UAE. Around the same time, Strabo referred to them as the Rammanites (Ραμμανίτες) in his *Geographica*.

22 LXX 961: Sebecatha (ϹЄΒЄΚᴀΘᴀ)

- Codex Alexandrinus: Sabacatha (ϹᴀΒᴀΚᴀΘᴀ)

- LXX 15: Sebecatha (ϹόuᴅᴋᴅΘᴅ)

- LXX 730: Sacabatha (ϹᴅᴋᴅuᴅΘᴅ)

- LXX 129: Sabaecatha (ϹᴅuᴅᴋᴋᴅΘᴅ)

- LXX 56: Sabecathas (ϹᴅuόᴋᴅΘᴅϹ)

- LXX 79: Sauacatha (ϹᴅuᴅᴋᴅΘᴅ)

- LXX 458: Sararatha (ϹᴅρᴅρᴅΘᴅ)

- LXX 108: Seabacatha (ϹόᴅuᴅᴋᴅΘᴅ)

- LXX 551: Sabatha (ϹᴅuᴅΘᴅ)

- LXX 527: Sacacatha (ϹᴅᴋᴅᴋᴅΘᴅ)

- LXX 53: Sabacathas (ϹᴅuᴅᴋᴅΘᴅϹ)

- LXX 31: Sabathaca (ϹᴅuᴅΘᴅᴋᴅ)

- LXX 122: Catha (Κᴅθᴅ)

- Leningrad Codex: Savtecha (סַבְתְּכָא)

- Peshitta: Sbtkå (ܣܒܬܟܐ)

- Targum Onkelos: Savtecha (סַבְתְּכָא)

- Targum Jerusalem: Savtecha (סַבְתְּכָא)

- Bohairic manuscripts: Sabathaca (Ⲥⲁⲃⲁⲑⲁⲃⲁ)

This may be the same location later recorded as Sachalitês (Σαχαλίτης), in the first century AD guide to the Indian Ocean known as the *Periplus of the Erythraean Sea*. The exact location of Sakhalitês is debated as different Classical era authors placed it either east or west of Suagros, another trading port generally accepted as being in the region of Dhofar, Oman. In Claudius Ptolemaeus' 2nd century *Geography*, it was simply known as Sachlê (Σαχλη), and placed to the east of Suagros, in the bay where islands of Kurya Murya lay, which is also in Dhofar.

23 Codex Alexandrinus: Saba (ⲥⲁⲃⲁ)

- LXX 509: Saban (ⲥⲁⲩⲁⲛ)

- LXX 707: Saba Thauderethader (ⲥⲁⲩⲁ ⲑⲁⲩⲁⲇⲣⲉⲑⲁⲇⲣ)

- LXX 730: Saba Regma (ⲥⲁⲩⲁ ⲣⲉⲅⲙⲁ)

- LXX 79: Sauan (ⲥⲁⲩⲁⲛ)

- LXX 458: Sebae (ⲥⲉⲩⲁⲓ)

- LXX 72: Saba cae Massabaemassada (ⲥⲁⲩⲁ ⲕⲁⲓ ⲙⲁⲥⲥⲁⲩⲁⲉⲙⲁⲥⲥⲁⲇⲁ). Translation: Saba and Massabaemassada

- Leningrad Codex: Sheva (שְׁבָא)

- Peshitta: Šbå (ܫܒܐ)

- Targum Onkelos: Sheva (שְׁבָא)

- Targum Jerusalem: Sheva (שְׁבָא)

This is a reference to the city that the queen who visited Solomon came from, however, it is not clear from the context where it was. Saba, and most of the southern coast of Arabia appears to have been established. The following reference to Dedan, along the incense roads from the southern coast to Canaan, suggests that this Sheba may likewise have been somewhere along the interior roads of Arabia, possibly in the Asir Mountains in the southwest, north of the kingdom of Saba, but south of Dedan.

24 Codex Alexandrinus: Dadan (ⲆⲀⲆⲀⲚ)

- LXX 15: Oydadan (OυⲆⲆⲆⲁⲛ)

- LXX 17: Ioudadan (ιουⲆⲆⲆⲁⲛ)

- LXX 121: Daedan (ⲆⲁιⲆⲆⲁⲛ)

- LXX 135: Ioudas (ιουⲆⲆⲥ)

- LXX 707: Dedan (Ⲇ6ⲆⲆⲁⲛ)

- LXX 18: Daethan (ⲆⲁιθⲆⲁⲛ)

- LXX 134: Ioudiadan (ιουⲆιⲆⲆⲁⲛ)

- LXX 370: Ioudiadam (ιουⲆιⲆⲆⲁμ)

- LXX 82: Idadan (ιⲆⲆⲆⲁⲛ)

- LXX 72: Dethan (Ⲇ6θⲆⲁⲛ)

- LXX 74: Ioudiada (ιουⲆιⲆⲆⲆ)

- LXX 107: Iouddan (ιουⲆⲆⲆⲁⲛ)

- LXX 527: Daddan (ⲆⲆⲆⲆⲁⲛ)

- LXX 53: Daedam (ⲆⲁιⲆⲆⲁμ)

- Leningrad Codex: Dedan (דְּדָן)

- Peshitta: Drn (ܕܪܢ)

- Fragments Targum: Bavel (בָּבֶל)

- Targum Jerusalem: Funetos (פּוּנְטוֹס). Translation: Pontus

- Targum Onkelos: Dedan (דְּדָן)

Dedan was the name of a kingdom in the Hijaz mountains of modern Saudi Arabia during the 7th and 8th centuries BC.

25 Codex Alexandrinus: Nebrôd (ⲚⲈⲂⲣⲱⲆ)

- LXX 509: Nebrôn (Ⲛ6uβϣⲛ)

- LXX 128: Ebrôth (Euβϣθ)

- LXX 75: Nebrôth (Νϭυβωθ)

- LXX 79: Neurôd (Νϭυβωᴧ)

- LXX 376: Ebrôdô (Ευβωᴧω)

- Leningrad Codex: Nimrod (נִמְרֹד)

- Peshitta: Nmrůd (ܢܡܪܘܕ)

- Targum Onkelos: Nimrod (נִמְרֹד)

- Fragment Targums: Nimrod (נִמְרוֹד)

- Targum Jerusalem: Nimrod (נִמְרוֹד)

Based on the description of this 'patriarch,' it has to be a reference to the original Sumerian city of Eridu, which was spelled as Nun^{ki} (𒉣𒆠) in Sumerian. Nun^{ki} can be variously interpreted as 'noble place,' or 'ruling place,' or, more relevantly 'first place.'

The Akkadians pronounced Nin^{ki} as Eridu, which may have also been the later Sumerian nickname of Nun^{ki} as the Sumerian word for 'copper' was urudu (𒍐), and the city's primary industry was working the copper from the trade on the Euphrates. The copper trade in Eridu was so important to the Sumerian civilization that the Sumerian name of the Euphrates was ^{id}Buranun (𒀀𒇉𒄯𒄘𒉣), believed to mean 'source of copper. In this section of text, it appears the author misunderstood a cuneiform text about Eridu, which had the name both written as Nun^{ki} (𒉣𒆠) and then spelled phonetically as Eridu^{ki} (𒌓𒈗𒉣𒆠). This would have been necessary after the rise of the Old Babylonian Empire, as the name 'great place' (𒉣𒆠) was appropriated by Babylon. This also explains why Babylon (Βαβυλων / בָּבֶל) is listed as being in Sumer, as Nun^{ki} by itself meant 'Babylon' by the time the Aramaic translation was made.

Transliterated directly into Aramaic, the name Nun^{ki} Eridu^{ki} (𒉣𒆠 𒌓𒈗𒉣𒆠) is Nnrd (𐡍𐡍𐡓𐡃), as there was no E (𒌓) in Aramaic or Phoenician, and the KI (𒆠) would not have been transliterated. This can itself by transliterated into Greek as Nebrôd by misreading the second Aramaic N (𐡍), as the similarly shaped Aramaic B (𐡁), or into Hebrew as Nmrd, by misreading the second N (𐤍) in the Phoenician script as a similarly shaped M (𐤌). As all historical sources agree that the Septuagint was translated from Aramaic, while the Hebrew translation that later served as the source for the Masoretic Text was translated from older Judahite texts written in the Phoenician script, this seems a probable explanation for the differences between the Greek and Hebrew names. As this 'patriarch' has to have originally been Eridu, the name 'Nimrod' is corrected back to 'Eridu.'

26 Codex Alexandrinus: gigas epi tês gês (ΓΙΓΑϹΕΠΙΤΗϹΓΗϹ). Translation: Gigas on the earth (or land)

- Leningrad Codex: gibbor ba'aretz (גִּבֹּר בָּאָרֶץ). Translation: powerful (or strong) on earth (or land)

- Peshitta: gnbrâ bårôâ (ܟ݁ܢܒ݂ܪܐ ܒ݁ܐܪܥܐ).Translation: strong man (or giant, hero, Orion) on earth (or land, soil)

- Targum Onkelos: gibbar takkif be'ar'a (גִּבַּר תַּקִּיף בְּאַרְעָא). Translation: powerful (or strong) attacker on earth (or land, soil)

- Fragments Targum: gibbor betzayda bechet'ah (גְּבוֹר בְּצַיָּידָא בְּחֶטְאָה). Translation: powerful (or strong) inhuntingof sinners

- Targum Jerusalem: gibbar meroda (גְּבַר מְרוֹדָא). Translation: powerful (or strong) rebel (or mutineer)

In Greek mythology, the Gigantes were an ancient tribe of people or demigods who challenged the rule of the gods. The Greek translators appear to have interpreted this story as being much the same, using the word gigas essentially as 'apostate.' The Masoretic version is quite different, as it indicates the Aramaic term would have been gbrâ (אֲגַרָא), meaning 'husband,' 'owner,' or 'ruler.' This means the term translated from the Akkadian cuneiform precursor text would have been lugal (𒈗), also meaning 'lord,' 'master,' or 'king.'

According to various king lists recovered from archaeological digs in Iraq, Eridu was the original 'capital city' of Sumer, before a great flood destroyed all the cities of Sumer. Based on the archaeological evidence uncovered to date, the city was founded around 5400 BC, and reached a peak around 3000 BC. It later went into decline and was almost abandoned by 2000 BC, when King Amar-Sin of Ur began a massive reconstruction of the city, culminating in the unfinished Ziggurat of Amar-Sin. Therefore, the era when Eridu would have dominated Mesopotamia, would have probably been around 3000 BC.

27 Codex Alexandrinus: cynêgos enantion c̄u (ΚΥΝΗΓΟϹΕΝΑΝΤΙΟΝΚῩ). Translation: hunter opposing (or against) Lord

- LXX 15: cynêgos enanti Cyriou (ⲕⲩⲛⲏⲅⲟⲥ ⲉ̄ⲛⲁⲛⲧⲓ ⲕⲩⲣⲟⲩ). Translation: hunter before Lord

- LXX 125: cynêgos gigas enantion Cyriou tou theou (ⲕⲩⲛⲏⲅⲟⲥ ⲅⲓⲅⲁⲥ ⲉ̄ⲛⲁⲛⲧⲫⲟⲛ ⲕⲩⲣⲟⲩ ⲧⲟⲩ ⲑ̄ⲟⲩ). Translation: hunter of Gigas opposing (or against) Lord the god

- LXX 58: cynêgos enôpion Cyriou tou theou (ⲕⲩⲛⲏⲅⲟⲥ ⲉ̄ⲛⲁⲛⲧⲓⲟⲛ ⲕⲩⲣⲟⲩ ⲧⲟⲩ ⲑ̄ⲟⲩ). Translation:

Translation: hunter against Lord the god

- Leningrad Codex: gibbovr tzayid lifnei Yehvah (גִּבֹּר צַיִד לִפְנֵי יְהוָה). Translation: powerful (or strong) hunter in front of Yehwah

- Peshitta: nhšyrtnă qdm mryă (ܢܚܫܝܪܬܢܐ ܩܕܡ ܡܪܝܐ).Translation: divine inheritor before the master

- Targum Onkelos: gibbar takkif kodam yeyah (גִּבַּר תַּקִּיף קֳדָם יְיָ). Translation: powerful (or strong) attacker before Yah

- Fragments Targum: gibbor betzayda bechet'ah kadam yeyah (גִּבּוֹר בְּצַיְּידָא בְּחֶטְאָה קֳדָם יְיָ). Translation: powerful (or strong) in hunting of sinners before Yhŭ

- Targum Jerusalem: gibbar betzeida umeroda kodam yeyah (גִּבַּר בְּצֵידָא וּמְרוֹדָא קֳדָם יְיָ). Translation: powerful (or strong) in hunting and sinning before Yhŭ

The original Aramaic writer of the genealogy of nations appears to be attempting to explain the name of the first king in of Eridu: ensi Alulim (𒂗𒉈 𒀉𒇻𒅆). Ensi (𒂗𒉈) was the Sumerian word for 'lord' or 'governor,' while Alulim (𒀉𒇻𒅆) was composed of the logograms meaning 'strong' (𒀉), 'animal' (𒇻), and 'look for' (𒅆), resulting in this strange scribal note.

28 Codex Alexandrinus: Babulôn (ΒΑΒΥΛΩΝ). Translation: Babylon

- LXX 73: Babylô (βαυυλω)

- Leningrad Codex: Bavel (בָּבֶל). Translation: Babylon

- Peshitta: Bbl (ܒܒܠ). Translation: Babylon

- Targum Onkelos: Bavel (בָּבֶל). Translation: Babylon

- Fragments Targum: Bavel (בָּבֶל). Translation: Babylon

- Targum Jerusalem: bavel rabbeti (בָּבֶל רַבְּתִי). Translation: Babylon the Great

As this could not have been the later city of Babylon, which was not in Sumer, it must be assumed this is another reference to Eridu, which was also spelled as Nun[ki] (𒉣𒆠) in Akkadian cuneiform. For more information on Eridu see the previous note in this chapter.

29 Cotton Genesis: Orech (ⲟⲣⲉⲭ)

- LXX 707: Orach (Ⲟⲣⲁⲭ)

- LXX 75: Thoubech (Ⲑⲟⲩⲃⲉⲭ)

- LXX 129: Oreci (Ⲟⲣⲉⲩⲓ)

- LXX 426: Ôred (ⲱⲣⲉⲇ)

- LXX 82: Ôrech (ⲱⲣⲉⲭ)

- LXX 458: Thobel (Ⲑⲟⲩⲃⲗ)

- LXX 527: Ôrch (ⲱⲣⲭ)

- LXX 376: Erech (Ⲉⲣⲉⲭ)

- Leningrad Codex: Erech (אֶרֶךְ)

- Peshitta: Ôrk (ܐܘܪܟ)

- Targum Onkelos: Erech (אֶרֶךְ)

- Fragments Targum: Hadas (הֲדַס)

- Targum Jerusalem: Hadas (הֲדַס)

This name is generally accepted as referring to the ancient Sumerian city of Unug (�), using the Old Akkadian name of Uruk (𒌷𒀔).

30 Codex Alexandrinus: Archad (ⲁⲣⲭⲁⲇ)

- Cotton Genesis: Achad (ⲁⲭⲁⲇ)

- LXX 76: Archa (ⲁⲣⲭⲁ).

- LXX 761: Achath (ⲁⲭⲁⲑ)

- LXX 31: Archath (ⲁⲣⲭⲁⲑ)

- LXX 376: Arcamas (ⲁⲣⲕⲁⲙⲁⲥ)

- Leningrad Codex: Akkad (אַכַּד)

- Peshitta: Åkd (ܐܟܕ)

- Targum Onkelos: Akkad (אַכַּד)

- Fragments Targum: Netzivin (נְצִיבִין)

- Targum Jerusalem: Netzivin (נְצִיבִין)

Akkad[ki] (𒀝𒆠) was the capital of the Akkadian Empire which ruled Mesopotamia for a few centuries before the rise of the Neo-Sumerian Empire.

31 Codex Alexandrinus: Chalannê (ΧΑΛΑΝΝΗ)

- LXX 509: Galanni (Γαλαννι)

- LXX 55: Challanê (Χαλλανη)

- LXX 135: Chalanni (Χαλαννοι)

- LXX 707: Chalnan (Χαλναν)

- LXX 319: Chalanên (Χαλανην)

- LXX 58: Galannê (Γαλαννη)

- LXX 78: Chalanê (Χαλανη)

- LXX 527: Chalanê (Χαλανη)

- LXX 376: Chalan (Χαλαν)

- Leningrad Codex: Chalneh (כַּלְנֶה)

- Peshitta: Klyå (ܟܠܝܐ)

- Targum Onkelos: Chalneh (כַלְנֵה)

- Fragments Targum: Kitisfon (קְטִיסְפוֹן). Translation: Ctesiphon

- Targum Jerusalem: Ketispon (קְטִסְפוֹן). Translation: Ctesiphon

The location of Chalneh has been debated for thousands of years. The name is not known among the cities of Sumer, and therefore many, mostly anachronistic locations have been suggested. The 4th century AD Christian scholars Eusebius of Caesarea and of Stridon both identified Chalneh as Ctesiphon, near modern Baghdad, however Ctesiphon wasn't founded until the 120s BC, which was not only after the genealogy of nations was added to Cosmic Genesis, but after both the Greek and Hebrew translations had been made. In the Talmud (Yoma 10a) Chalneh is identified as being nufar ninfi (נוּפַר נִינְפִי), which has been interpreted by some as a reference to the ancient Sumerian city of Nippur[ki] (𒂗𒆤𒆠).

The word is accepted by some Christian groups as being a corruption of the Hebrew word kullanu (כֻּלָּנוּ), meaning 'everything,' meaning the sentence would have once read 'The beginning of his kingdom was Eridu, Uruk, Akkad, and everything in the land of Sumer.' Unfortunately, the 'Hebrew corruption' is also in the Greek translation, which was made from an Aramaic text. The equivalent term in Aramaic was klnå (ܟܠܢܐ), which is not the word found in the Masoretic Text, and the word that was transliterated as Chalannê appears to be based on Chalneh (כַלְנֶה), not klnå (ܟܠܢܐ) or kullanu (כֻּלָּנוּ). If the word in the Aramaic text was the same word retained in the Masoretic Text, then it was almost certainly a transliteration of kalûma (𒆗𒈠), also meaning 'everything.' Kalûma (𒆗𒈠), was the phonetic spelling of Kish (𒆧), one oldest and most famous ancient Sumerian cities. Kish is the Sumerian pronunciation of the city's name, however, it would have been pronounced as Kalûma in later Semitic cultures, therefore the more common Sumerian-derived English name of Kish is used.

32 Codex Alexandrinus: Sennaar (ⲤⲉⲚⲚⲀⲀⲣ)

- LXX 120: Ennaar (Ⲉⲛⲛⲁⲁⲣ)

- LXX 121: Senaar (Ⲥⲟⲛⲁⲁⲣ)

- LXX 129: Sinnaar (Ⲥⲟⲓⲛⲛⲁⲁⲣ)

- LXX 75: Sernnaar (Ⲥⲟⲣⲛⲛⲁⲁⲣ)

- LXX 343: Senar (Ⲥⲟⲛⲁⲣ)

- LXX 376: Naar (Ⲛⲁⲁⲣ)

- LXX 53: Seenar (Ⲥⲟⲟⲛⲁⲣ)

- LXX 527: Senaan (Ⲥⲟⲛⲁⲁⲛ)

- Leningrad Codex: Shin'ar (שִׁנְעָר)

- Peshitta: Snôr (ܣܢܥܪ)

- Targum Onkelos: Bavel (בָּבֶל)

- Bohairic manuscripts: Senaar (Ⲥⲉⲛⲁⲁⲣ)

33 Codex Alexandrinus: Assour (ⲁⲥⲥⲟⲨⲣ)

- LXX 17: Nassour (Ⲛⲁⲥⲥⲟⲩⲃ)

- LXX 127: Asour (ⲁⲥⲟⲩⲃ)

- LXX 400: Naassour (Ⲛⲁⲁⲥⲥⲟⲩⲃ)

- Leningrad Codex: Ashur (אַשּׁוּר). Translation: Assyria, Ashur

- Peshitta: Åtûryå (ܐܬܘܪܝܐ). Translation: Assyrians

- Targum Onkelos: Atura'ah (אָתוּרָאָה). Translation: Assyrians

- Fragments Targum: Atorayai (אָתוֹרִיָּיא)

- Targum Jerusalem: Attur (אַתּוּר). Translation: Assyria

- Armenian Bible: Asour (Ասուր). Translation: Ashur

Aššur (𒀭𒀸) was the national god of Assyria, normally anglicized as Ashur, while Aššur^ki (𒀸𒋩𒆠) was the original capital city of Assyria, normally anglicized as Assur. Unfortunately, both of these names were spelled the same in Aramaic, and other less complicated scripts, resulting this verse being rendered differently in Hebrew versus Greek. The Greek states that Ashur came from Sumer, and built the Assyrian cities, while the Hebrew does not specify who did it, implying it was the 'Nimrod' of the previous verse who went to Assur and built the cities of Assyria. However, later in the chapter Ashur is identified as being a Semite, not a Khuzite, which seems to confirm the Greek reading, that the Semite Assur had been living in the Khuzite cities before traveling north and founding Assyria.

Assyrian historical records do not record the city of Assur being founded by someone called Ashur, instead recording that the ancestors of the Assyrians original lived in tents, and later settled in a Hurrian city called Baltil, which later became Assur after the Assyrians became dominant. Therefore, if the genealogy of nations was originally written by an Assyrian, it was probably not a genealogy that claimed all people sprang from one small family, but a list of nations that had colonized the world in ancient times, which the Aramaic author simplified for some reason.

34 Cotton Genesis: Chalach (ⲭⲁⲗⲁⲭ)

- LXX 509: Chalec (ⲭⲁⲗⲉⲕ)

- LXX 75: Malach (Ⲙⲁⲗⲁⲭ)

- LXX 313: Chalam (ⲭⲁⲗⲁⲙ)

- LXX 615: Chalan (𝒳𝔞𝜆𝔞𝓃)

- LXX 82: Chalac (𝒳𝔞𝜆𝔞𝔲)

- LXX 54: Chalech (𝒳𝔞𝜆ϭ𝜒)

- LXX 72: Challac (𝒳𝔞𝜆𝜆𝔞𝔲)

- LXX 59: Chalaac (𝒳𝔞𝜆𝔞𝔞𝔲)

- LXX 44: Chalachach (𝒳𝔞𝜆𝔞𝜒𝔞𝜒)

- Leningrad Codex: Kalach (כֶּלַח)

- Peshitta: Klh (ܟܠܚ)

- Targum Onkelos: Kalach (כָּלַח)

- Fragments Targum: Charyait (חַרְיַית)

- Targum Jerusalem: Charyait (חַרְיַית)

- Bohairic manuscripts: Khalac (Ⲭⲁⲗⲁϭ)

The name is generally normalized as Kalhu in modern English, and is accepted as the city which once stood where the ruins of Nimrud lay today. The name Nimrud (ܢܡܪܘܕ / النمرود), was commonly applied to the ruins during the early late Classical era by Syriac Christians, based on the story of 'Nimrod' building a great city somewhere in the region, and was later adopted by the Muslims. The ruins continue to be known by both names in most languages. The following scribal note about Kalhu being the great city, is generally accepted as a reference to it being the capital of the Assyrian Empire, which places the origin of the scribal note between circa 864 BC and 706 BC. In approximately 864 BC, King Ashurbanipal II inaugurated Kalhu as the new capital of the Neo-Assyrian Empire, after approximately 15 years of rebuilding the large but dilapidated ancient city. It was the first time the capital of the Assyrians was moved from Assur in recorded history.

The capital was later moved to Dur Sharrukin by Sargon II in approximately 706 BC. Many biblical scholars accept this era as being when the genealogy of the nations was added to Cosmic Genesis, as the tribes listed are all recognizable from the era of the Neo-Assyrian Empire, including the Medes, Lydians, and Greeks, at the edge of the known world.

35 Codex Alexandrinus: Loudiim (ΛΟΥΔΙΙΜ)

- LXX 407: Loudiim (Λουδιιμ)

- LXX 15: Doudiim (Δουδιιμ)

- LXX 135: Louliim (Λουλιιμ)

- LXX 707: Loediim (Λοιδιιμ)

- LXX 319: Aoudiim (Αουδιιμ)

- LXX 426: Oylêd (Ουλλδ)

- LXX 343: Loudiêm (Λουδιλμ)

- LXX 82: Douliim (Δουλιιμ)

- LXX 376: Loudiôm (Λουδιωμ)

- Leningrad Codex: Ludim (לוּדִים). Translation: Lydians

- Peshitta: Lůdym (ܠܘܕܝܡ). Translation: Lydians

- Targum Onkelos: Luda'ei (לוּדָאֵי)

- Fragments Targum: Maryota'ei (מְרִיוֹטָאֵי)

- Targum Jerusalem: Givavta'ei (גִּיוַוטָאֵי)

The Hebrew term certainly means 'Lydians,' however, the Greeks appear to have not been sure about the translation, as they did not translated the well known name as lydicos (λυδικος). Lydia was an ancient kingdom in western Anatolia which became wealthy and powerful during the early iron age. It is plausible that the Assyrians viewed the Lydians as being an Egyptian colony, as both they had originally used a hieroglyphic script, like most ancient Anatolian cultures. There is no evidence that Egypt ever exerted any political control over Lydia, however, there certainly would have been a great deal of trade between the cultures.

Due to the improbability of Egypt colonizing western Anatolia, it is often suggested that this was a transcription error of 'Libyans' (לובים), which could have easily happened in either Aramaic, by reading a B (ב) as a D (ד), or in Phoenician, by reading a B (𐤁) as a D (𐤃). However, the scribe added a note later in the sentence stating that the Pelesets came from the region of the Chaslôniim / Kasluchim, which seems to confirm that the scribe interpreted this location as being in Anatolia. Additionally, the Caphthoriim / Kaftorim are generally accepted as being either the Minoans or an Anatolian people, and they are mentioned in the same list of Egyptian colonies. Like the Lydians, the Minoans originally used a hieroglyphic script, suggesting that the Assyrians viewed all the hieroglyphic writing civilizations as coming from Egypt.

36 Codex Alexandrinus: Aenemetiim (ΑΙΝΕΜΕΤΙΕΙΜ)

- LXX 407: Enemetiim (Ενϭμϭτιϭιμ)

- LXX 509: Enemetiin (Ενϭμϭτιϭιν)

- LXX 15: Nemetiim (Νϭμϭτιϭιμ)

- LXX 17: Enemitiim (Ενϭμπιϭιμ)

- LXX 55: Enaemitiim (Ενδιμπιϭιμ)

- LXX 135: Enematiim (Ενϭμδτιϭιμ)

- LXX 318: Enaemitiin (Ενδιμπιϭιν)

- LXX 392: Ainemitiim (Αινϭμπιϭιμ)

- LXX 319: Eniliim (Ενιλιϭιμ)

- LXX 16: Nematiim (Νϭμδτιϭιμ)

- LXX 120: Ainemitiin (Αινϭμπιϭιν)

- LXX 343: Enemêtiim (Ενϭμλ̄τιϭιμ)

- LXX 426: Senemiim (Cϭνϭμϭιμ)

- LXX 56: Enetiim (Ενϭτιϭιμ)

- LXX 79: Enaematiim (Ενδιμδτιϭιμ)

- LXX 82: Enimiim (Ενιμϭιμ)

- LXX 799: Anepitiêm (Ανϭππιλ̄μ)

- LXX 46: Enaemetiim (Ενδιμϭτιϭιμ)

- LXX 108: Ainiamiim (Αινϭιδμϭιμ)

- LXX 376: Enestisô (Ενϭστιꝏ)

- Leningrad Codex: Anamim (עֲנָמִים)

- Peshitta: Yôbym (ܝܘܒܝܡ)

- Targum Onkelos: Anama'ei (עֲנָמָאֵי)

- Fragments Targum: Pantepolita'ei (פַּנְטְפּוֹלִיטָאֵי)

- Targum Jerusalem: Martiyota'ei (מַרְטִיוֹטָאֵי)

- Bohairic manuscripts: Midiim (Ⲙⲓⲁⲓⲓⲙ)

This appears to be a reference to Upper Egyptians using a Semitic plural of the Egyptian name ḫn mnù (𓈖𓏏𓏤𓏏𓎡), later known as Chemmis (Χέμμις) in Greek, Khmim (Ϧⲙⲓⲙ) in Coptic, and Akhmim in Arabic (أخميم). Akhmim was a major city in Upper Egypt, and the source of the Akhmimic dialect of ancient Egyptian. Upper Egypt was the region north of Aswan, and south of Memphis, which had once been the heartland of Egypt, however, in the era the genealogy of nations was added to Cosmic Genesis, was viewed as being one of Egypt's children, which is mirrored in mirrored in the Greek records from the era, which claimed that Egyptian civilization began in Aethiopia (Kush), and colonized Upper and Lower Egypt.

37 Codex Alexandrinus: Labiim (Ⲗⲁⲃⲓⲓⲙ)

- LXX 407: Labiim (Ⲗⲁⲃⲓⲓⲙ)

- LXX 17: Labiem (Ⲗⲁⲃⲓⲉⲙ)

- LXX 392: Abiim (Ⲁⲃⲓⲓⲙ)

- LXX 18: Labiin (Ⲗⲁⲃⲓⲓⲛ)

- LXX 343: Elabiim (Ⲉⲗⲁⲃⲓⲓⲙ)

- LXX 56: Nephthaliim (Ⲛⲉⲫⲑⲁⲗⲓⲓⲙ)

- LXX 82: Lamiin (Ⲗⲁⲙⲓⲓⲛ)

- LXX 54: Dabiim (Ⲇⲁⲃⲓⲓⲙ)

- LXX 799: Labiêm (Ⲗⲁⲃⲓⲏⲙ)

- LXX 107: Damiim (Ⲇⲁⲙⲓⲓⲙ)

- LXX 664: Nephthalim (Ⲛⲉⲫⲑⲁⲗⲓⲙ)

- LXX 31: Labim (Ⲗⲁⲃⲓⲙ)

- Leningrad Codex: Lehavim (לְהָבִים)

- Peshitta: Lhbym (ܠܗܒܝܡ)

- Targum Onkelos: Lehava'ei (לְהָבָאֵי)

- Fragments Targum: Loseta'ai (לוֹסְטָאִי)

- Targum Jerusalem: Livavka'ei (לִיוַוקָאֵי)

This is generally accepted as a reference to Libyans, via the Egyptian word Lbu (𓃭𓃀𓅱𓈉). The term had been used in Egypt for hundreds of years by the time the genealogy of nations was added to the text, however, it is not clear how it would have been spelled in Assyrian or early Aramaic. In the Classical era, the Neo-Aramaic Syriac spelling of Libya was Lǔbå (ܠܘܒܐ), however, this would have been influenced by Greek. In the Neo-Assyrian era, the Egyptian term referred to the Libyan (Berber) peoples of North Africa west of the Nile. This included Put, which was mentioned separately earlier, suggesting that only the inland Libyans of the oases were being referred to. It is equally possible that more distant Libyans were being referred to, as Libyans (Berber) tribes were reported living right across North Africa, from Sudan to Morocco.

38 Codex Alexandrinus: Nephthaliim (ΝΕΦΘΑΛΙΙΜ)

- Cotton Genesis: Nephthadiim (ΝΕΦΘΑΔΙΕΙΜ)

- LXX 509: Nephthalim (Νεφθαλϵιμ)

- LXX 56: Labiim (Λαβιϵιμ)

- LXX 15: Nephthabiim (Νεφθαβιϵιμ)

- LXX 318: Naephthabiim (Ναιφθαβιϵιμ)

- LXX 707: Nathaliim (Ναθαλιϵιμ)

- LXX 58: Nephabiim (Νεφαβιϵιμ)

- LXX 129: Nephthalêm (Νεφθαλλημ)

- LXX 134: Nephthalim (Νεφθαλιμ)

- LXX 75: Mephthabiim (Μεφθαβιϵιμ)

- LXX 458: Mephthariim (Μεφθαριϵιμ)

- LXX 53: Ladibiim (Λαδιβιϵιμ)

- LXX 54: Nephthamiim (Νόφθαμόιμ)

- LXX 72: Neuthaliim (Νόυθαλίιμ)

- LXX 376: Nephthalsim (Νόφθαλσόιμ)

- LXX 664: Ladiimbiim (Λαδιόιμμιόιμ)

- Leningrad Codex: Naftuchim (נַפְתֻּחִים)

- Peshitta: Yptuḥym (ܢܦܬܘܚܝܡ)

- Targum Onkelos: Naftucha'ei (נַפְתּוּחָאֵי)

- Fragments Targum: not mentioned in the verse

- Targum Jerusalem: Pantaskina'ei (פֶּנְטַסְכִּינָאֵי)

- Bohairic manuscripts: Saphthabiim (Сафѳавіім)

The Hebrew name appears to be a reference to Lower Egyptians, using the name Nefertem (𓄤𓏏𓐝, transliteration: nfr tm, or nfl tm). Nefertem was a god mainly worshiped in Memphis, and believed to be the son of Ptah, the god the city was named after. During the era when Kush ruled Egypt, Memphis was the northern capital of the Kingdom of Kush, while Napata in modern Sudan, was the southern capital. The Memphitic dialect of Egyptian dominated Lower Egypt, ultimately giving rise to the Bohairic dialect of Coptic. It appears that the author of the genealogy of nations, or an Assyrian predecessor, interpreted Nefertem as the founding patriarch of Memphis, however, there is no evidence the Egyptians viewed him that way.

39 Berlin Genesis: Patrosonnii (ΠΑΤΡΟϹΟΝΝΙΕΙ)

- LXX 961: Patrosoniim (ΠΑΤΡΟϹΟΝΙΕΙΜ)

- Codex Alexandrinus: Patrosôniim (ΠΑΤΡΟϹѠΝΙΕΙΜ)

- LXX 509: Patrosonoem (Πατροσονοόιμ)

- LXX 17: Patrossoniim (Πατροσσονιόιμ)

- LXX 707: Patrosonim (Πατροσονόιμ)

- LXX 730: Patronôsiim (Πατρονωοσιόιμ)

- LXX 58: Prosoniim (Προσονιόιμ)

- LXX 128: Paprosson (Παπροσσον)

- LXX 129: Patrosônoem (Πατροσωνοб́ιμ)

- LXX 313: Patrossonim (Πατροσσονιμ)

- LXX 458: Patrôsôniim (Πατροσωσωνιб́ιμ)

- LXX 799: Patrosôniêm (Πατροσωνίꞁμ)

- LXX 53: Patrosôim (Πατροσωσб́ιμ)

- LXX 46: Patrôsôniim (Πατροσωσωνιιμ)

- LXX 54: Patrosthôniim (Πατροσθωνιб́ιμ)

- LXX 74: Patrosôniim (Πατροσωνιιμ)

- LXX 376: Pathrousim (Πаθρουσб́ιμ)

- LXX 664: Patronoem (Πατρονοб́ιμ)

- Leningrad Codex: Patrusim (פַּתְרֻסִֽים)

- Peshitta: Ptrůsym (ܦܬܪܘܣܝܡ)

- Targum Onkelos: Patrusa'ei (פַּתְרוּסָאֵי)

- Fragments Targum: Pilosa'ei (פִּילוֹסָאֵי)

- Targum Jerusalem: Nasyota'ei (נְסִיוֹטָאֵי)

- Bohairic ms.: Patrosomiim (Ⲡⲁⲧⲣⲟⲥⲟⲙⲓⲓⲙ)

This is term referred to the people of southernmost Egypt, which the Assyrians called Patúrisi (𒉺𒌓𒊑𒋛) in the Annals of Esarhaddon. The name was adopted from the Demotic Egyptian name På-tårsy (𓊪𓏏𓏤𓈅/𓊪𓏏𓂋𓋴), meaning 'southern land.' This region was northern Nubia during the Old Kingdom era, and although colonized by Egyptians appears to have remained mainly Nubian until the recent past. The Persians and Greeks both referred to the region as variations of 'Nubia' or 'Kush.' The modern English equivalent to Ptrsym (פתרסים) would be Aswani, as the region is administered by the Aswan governorate, however, the term Nubia appears to be more historically accurate.

40 Codex Alexandrinus: Chasmôn (Ⲭⲁⲥⲙⲱⲛ)

- LXX 407: Chaslôniim (Ⲭⲁⲥⲗⲱⲛιб́ιμ)

- LXX 509: Chaloem (Ⲭⲁⲗοб́ιμ)

- LXX 135: Chaslon (χλσλον)

- LXX 318: Nephthabiim (χλλοονισμ)

- LXX 17: Chasdon (χλσδον)

- LXX 346: Chasaon (χλσδον)

- LXX 128: Chalôriim (χλλοοβισμ)

- LXX 56: Chalon (χλλον)

- LXX 79: Chasloriim (χλσλοβισμ)

- LXX 82: Challôn (χλλλοον)

- LXX 130: Chalôn (χλλοον)

- LXX 46: Chalôniim (χλλοονιιμ)

- LXX 74: Chaslôniim (χλσλοονιιμ)

- LXX 54: Chaelôn (χλιλοον)

- LXX 72: Caniim (Κλνισμ)

- LXX 376: Chaslôm (χλσλοομ)

- LXX 799: Chasloniêm (χλσλονιℓμ)

- LXX 106: Chelon (χϭλον)

- LXX 664: Chalonoem (χλλονοσμ)

- LXX 31: Chasmon (χλσμον)

- Leningrad Codex: Kasluchim (כַּסְלֻחִים)

- Peshitta: Kslûḥym (ܟܣܠܘܚܝܡ)

- Targum Onkelos: Patrusa'ei (פְּתְרוּסָאֵי)

- Fragments Targum: Penatsachna'ei (פְּנַטְסְכְנָאֵי)

- Targum Jerusalem: Pantepolota'ei (פַּנְטְפּוֹלוֹטָאֵי)

This location is widely debated as there are no known references to the land earlier than the Greco-Roman era mention of a land of Kasluḥet on the Temple of Kom Ombo in Aswan, and that dates to a century after Cosmic Genesis was translated into Greek. In

Josephus' 1st century AD Jewish Antiquities, he mentioned that the Chaslôniim were an ancient Nubian people who were destroyed during Thutmose II's wars in Kush, circa 1500 BC. However, this would be a reference to the destruction of Kerma, the first Kushite capital. If so, the Kasluchim were the Kushites themselves. This view appears to have been repeated in the Bereshít Rabbah a few of centuries later, which referred to Kasluchim as Pekusim (פְּקוּסִים), which would be a transliteration of the Demotic Egyptian på Kåsh (𓂝𓎡𓈉), meaning 'land of Kush,' in the Hebrew plural form, and therefore the 'land of the Kushites.' The probable origin of the word 'Kasluchim' was the Assyrian ᵏᵘʳKasi āliūtum (𒆳𒁹𒀸𒄿𒀠𒌋𒌈), meaning 'land of Kush's citizens,' a reference to the ethnic Kushites, as opposed to the rest of the Egyptians. While this may have been what the earlier Assyrian author of the genealogy of nations was referring to, this interpretation is impossible if the 'father' 'Egypt/Mitzrayim' is interpreted as Kush, which the Aramaic author has clearly done.

The scribal note added, which claims the Pelesets originated in this land, means it was clearly not identified as Kush by the Aramaic author. The Pelesets were a Mediterranean or Anatolian people and not an African people, based on both the Egyptian records of their invasion, and the archaeological evidence. In this case, the author appears to have confused the term with the similar name ᵏᵘʳKaskatum (𒆳𒃻𒁹𒀠𒌈), commonly translated into English as Kaskians. The Kaskians lived in Anatolia north of the Lydians, in the region where the Palaa (𒉺𒆷𒀀) had lived before migrating away at the end of the bronze age. It is believed that the Kaskians may have pushed the Palaa out of their homeland, however, another interpretation is that they simply migrated into the region after the Palaa abandoned it. In any event, the scribal note indicating the homeland of the Pelesets indicates that the Aramaic author believed the reference was to the Kaskians. Nevertheless, the Kaskians were an Indo-European people who would have been included with the decedents of Gomer, and cannot be interpreted as being an Egyptian colony by any interpretation of the term, therefore, the term is interpreted via the Assyrian meaning in this translation.

41 Codex Alexandrinus: Phylistiim (ϕϒλιϲτιειμ)

- LXX 392: Phylêstiim (Φυλλͅοτιϭιμ)

- LXX 72: Philistiim (Φιλιϲτιϭιμ)

- LXX 376: Philisthêim (Φιλιϲθλϭιμ)

- LXX 799: Philistiêm (Φιλιϲτιλͅμ)

- Leningrad Codex: Pelishtim (פְּלִשְׁתִּים). Translation: Philistines (or Palestinians,

Pelesets)

- Peshitta: Plštyå (ܦܠܫܬܝܐ)

- Targum Onkelos: Pelishta'ei (פְּלִשְׁתָּאֵי)

- Fragments Targum: Pelishta'ei (פְּלִישְׁתָּאֵי)

- Targum Jerusalem: Pelishta'ei (פְּלִישְׁתָּאֵי)

The Pelesets were an ancient people based in the region of the modern Gaza Strip of the Palestinian Territories. The earliest surviving mention of them is from the reliefs of the Temple of Ramses III at Medinet Habu in Egypt that dates back to some time between 1186 and 1155 BC, in which they were called Půlåsåtî (𓂋𓏤𓊪𓃭𓋴𓍘𓈖). They were also known in Middle Babylonian as the ᵏᵘʳPalastu (𒆳𒉺𒆷𒀸𒌅). It is unclear where they came from, however, one theory is that they were the Pala, a Luwian people from the Black Sea coast of Anatolia.

The region was an independent country called Palaa (𒉺𒆷𒀀) in the Neshite (Hittite) records from the 1600s BC, however, have become part of the Nesite Empire by the 1500s BC. Around the time the Pelesets invaded Canaan, the Pala were driven from their homeland by the neighboring Kaskians from northeast Anatolia, which supports the connection between the groups, however, it has yet to be proven conclusively. The presence of the Pelesets in Southern Canaan during the time of Abraham and Isaac is anachronistic, and therefore this section of text, describing the origin of the Semitic tribes, found in both the Septuagint and the Masoretic Text, likely dates to the original Phoenician translation in the early Iron Age.

42 Berlin Genesis: Caphthôr (ⲕⲁⲫⲑⲱⲣ)

- LXX 961: Caphthoriim (ⲕⲁⲫⲑⲟⲣⲓⲉⲓⲙ)

- Codex Alexandrinus: Chaphth (ⲭⲁⲫⲑ)

- LXX 318: Chaphthoriin (ⲭⲁϥⲑⲟⲣⲓⲥⲓⲛ)

- LXX 56: Caphthar (ⲕⲁϥⲑⲁⲣ)

- LXX 134: Caphthoriim (ⲕⲁϥⲑⲟⲣⲓⲓⲙ)

- LXX 370: Cauphth (ⲕⲁⲩϥⲑ)

- LXX 799: Caphthoriêm (ⲕⲁϥⲑⲟⲣⲓⲏⲙ)

- LXX 458: Chalaphthoniim (ⲭⲁⲗⲁϥⲑⲟⲛⲓⲥⲓⲙ)

- LXX 376: Camphthôrim (ⲕⲁⲙϥⲑⲟⲱⲣⲥⲓⲙ)

- LXX 107: Camphthôr (ⲕⲁμⲫⲑⲟⲟⲣ)

- LXX 56: Chaphthar (ⲭⲁⲫⲑⲁⲣ)

- LXX 31: Gaphth (ⲅⲁⲫⲑ)

- LXX 44: Camphôr (ⲕⲁμⲫⲟⲟⲣ)

- Leningrad Codex: Kaftorim (כַּפְתֹּרִים). Translation: Caphtorites

- Peshitta: Qpûdqyå (ܩܦܘܕܩܝܐ)

- Targum Onkelos: Kapputeka'ei (קַפּוֹטְקָאֵי)

- Fragments Targum: Kapputeka'ei (קַפּוֹטְקָאֵי)

- Targum Jerusalem: Kappudeka'ei (קַפּוֹדְקָאֵי)

Caphtor was mentioned in several surviving ancient texts from the 2nd millennium BC, including the Mari Tablets, dated to circa 1770 BC, Thutmose III's *Hymn of Victory*, from circa 1450 BC, and the *Ras Sharma Texts* from Ugarit, dated to circa 1340 BC. Cosmic Genesis refers to Caphtor as a son of Mizraim (Egypt), which implies a colony of Egypt, while the Ras Sharma Texts uses the name Caphtor as the name of the home of the Canaanite god Kothar-wa-Khasis, which is believed to be the Canaanite version of the Egyptian god Ptah. The location of Caphtor was already long lost and debated by the time the Septuagint was translated at the Library of Alexandria, which supports the antiquity of Cosmic Genesis. At the time, Greek translators believed it was in Cappadocia, which was the translation used in the Septuagint's Deuteronomy. Cappadocia was in central modern Turkey, however, the Egyptian records that mention Caphtor (𓎡𓏏𓅱), list it as being a port city, and Cappadocia was an inland nation. This identification of Caphtor with Cappadocia is based on its location in Thutmose III's biography, from circa 1450 BC, which placed Caphtor as Thutmose's northernmost conquest, and his Empire had conquered all of Canaan, and extended to the border of Cappadocia. Jewish scholars have traditionally rejected Cappadocia as the location of Caphtor. In the 1st century AD, the Jewish historian and general Josephus wrote in his Antiquities of the Jews, that the Caphtorites were an Egyptian people whose city was destroyed in a war with the Aethopians (Kushites) and migrated to Philistia (the modern Gaza Strip).

Other Jewish sources, such as Maimonides, in the 12th century AD, have placed Caphtor in the Nile Delta. Early Christians accepted the Greek identification of Caphtor as Cappadocia, and Cappadocia was the translation of Caphtor that Jerome chose for the Vulgate in the 4th century. Modern scholars have debated the issue, with many locations suggested, including Cicilia (southern Turkey), Cyprus, Crete, or some other island in the Aegean Sea. Currently, the academic view is that either Cicilia or Crete are the most likely locations of Caphtor, however, the archaeological evidence from Crete shows that some major force burnt almost every town in Crete during the life of Thutmose III, which his biography claims he did to Caphtor, and therefore, the terms Crete and Minoan are used in this translation.

43 Berlin Genesis: Chetin (ⲭⲉⲧⲉⲓⲛ)

- LXX 961: Chettiim (ⲭⲉⲧⲧⲓⲉⲓⲙ)

- LXX 407: Chettaeon (ⲭⲟⲧⲧⲁⲓⲟⲛ)

- LXX 18: Chaett (ⲭⲁⲓⲧⲧ)

- LXX 129: Chettaeôn (ⲭⲟⲧⲧⲁⲓⲟⲟⲛ)

- LXX 458: Gett (ⲅⲟⲧⲧ)

- LXX 550: Chetaeon (ⲭⲟⲧⲁⲓⲟⲛ)

- Leningrad Codex: Chet (חֵת). Translation: Cyprus

- Peshitta: Ḥytyå (ܟܬܝܐ). Translation: Cypriots

- Targum Onkelos: Chet (חֵת). Translation: Cyprus

- Targum Jerusalem: Chet (חֵת). Translation: Cyprus

This term has created a great deal of confusion since the misidentification of the ruins of the Neshites as being 'Hittite' in the 1800s. The modern archaeological name 'Hittite,' is not derived from an ancient name for the culture applied by themselves, or anyone else, but rather adopted from the biblical reference to a then-unknown civilization somewhere in the region. There was an ancient culture in the region called the Hattians, however, they were conquered by the Nesites before 1700 BC, and subsequently disappeared from the historic records. The name was applied to culture today referred to as 'Hittites,' before the 'Hittite' language had been translated, and is incorrect. Since 1906, excavations at Boğazköy, the ancient 'Hittite' capital Hattusa have uncovered more than 10,000 'Hittite' texts, including the royal achieve. The actual name of the 'Hittite' language and people was Nešili (𒉈𒅆𒇷), which is now rendered in some academic literate as Nesite or Neshite. As early as the mid-1800s some scholars disputed the identification of the Nesites as the Biblical Hittites, including the Orientalist Max Müller, who was one of many claiming the Biblical Hittites were ancient Greeks or some other Mediterranean people.

Later in the Septuagint's translation of the Maccabees, the similar term Chettiim (Χεττιιμ) as a reference to all Greek-speaking lands, and therefore the Biblical Hittites were likely the Minoans or the Achaean Greeks. In the 1st century AD, the Jewish historian Josephus reported that Cethima was the name of Cyrus in Aramaic, and the Chettim were the descendants of Noah's grandson Chethimus, who had settled on Cyprus. Josephus reported that the name was preserved in the Greek name of the town Cition (Κίτιον). Most historians view it as more likely that the Aramaic name was derived from the city-state of Cition, which was known as Kâtjây (𒀸 𒊹𒅆 𒈦) in Egyptian records from the New Kingdom Era in the late Bronze Age, and Kt (𐤊𐤕) or Kty (𐤊𐤕𐤉) in Phoenician records from the early Iron Age. While this may be the origin of the term, by the era of the Neo-Assyrian era, the term must have also referred to other Greek islands, as both the prophets Isaiah and Ezekiel used the term 'Islands of Kittim.' As the term referred to people from Cyprus in Aramaic, the translations of 'Cypriots' is used.

44 LXX 407: Eyaeon (Ευαιον)

- LXX 318: Neuaeon (Νευαιον)

- LXX 107: Ebaeon (Ευαιον)

- Leningrad Codex: Chavilah (חֲוִילָֽה)

- Peshitta: Ḥůylâ (ܚܘܝܠܐ)

- Targum Onkelos: Chavilah (חֲוִילָה)

- Fragments Targum: Teripola'ei (טְרִיפּוֹלָאֵי)

- Targum Jerusalem: Chiva'ei (חִוָאֵי)

The various Greek names used here do not correlate with either each other or the Hebrew version. The Greek term Eyaeon (Ευαιον) is usually mirrored in the Hebrew translation with Chivvi (חִוִּי), which is used interchangeably with the term Chori (חֹרִי). Chori is accepted as referring to the Hurrians, which the Egyptians called Ḥârů (𓉔𓄿𓂋𓅱𓈉), and the Babylonians called Ḫuurri (𒄷𒌷𒊑). The Hurrians were one of the oldest cultures in the Middle East, however, became largely a slave cutlure within the Akkadian and Old Babylonian empires. Under the Mitanni empire, they rose to a position of wealth, and formed the noble caste. The Greek transliteration of this term was Chorrhaeous (Χορραιους), which, like the Hebrew term, was used interchangeably in the texts with Eyaeon (Ευαιον) / Chivvi (חִוִּי), although that term generally applied to the rules and priests.

The ultimate origin of the terms Eyaeon (Ευαιον) and Chivvi (חִוִּי), both appear to be the cuneiform word Éan (𒂍), meaning temple or sacred. In the Amarna Letters, which date to the 1330s BC, the term Éan (𒂍) was the name of a people, who appear to be the Mitanni, or a group within the Mitanni. A similar correlation between the terms is found in the Septuagint's 1ˢᵗ Paralipomenon and Masoretic Divrei-hay Yamim, where the Greek translation uses Beithani (Βαιθανι), however, the Hebrew uses the term Mitni (מִתְנִי). This term also refers to a group of people, meaning the underlying Edomite text the Greeks translated would have been 'people of the House of Ån (𐤉𐤀+𐤕𐤉), a direct Canaanite translation of É An (𒂍𒀭).

While Mitni was the transliteration used in the Edomite text that formed the basis of the Hebrew translation of Divrei-hayYamim, it was replaced with Chivvi (חִוִּי) in the Judahite texts, which served as the basis of most of the Masoretic texts. This likely originated in a Judahite copy of the text, after the Aramaic translation had been made, where an n (𐤍) was replaced with a w (𐤅). The Aramaic translation would have already been made in the time of King Manasseh, were the term was transliterated as Hyån (𐡇𐡉𐡀𐡍), itself a transliteration of the early Canaanite Hyån (𐤉𐤀+𐤉𐤂).

The term Ebaeon (Εβαιον), which is found as a substitute for Eyaeon (Ευαιον) in some copies of the Septuagint for term, must have originated in an intentional alteration to the text, as there are no similar letters for b (𐤁 ,𐤊 ,𐤐) and y (' ,^ ,𐤆) in the Semitic alphabets the text was previously in. This probable origin was an Ebionite translation in the first century AD. The Ebionites were an early Judeo-Christian sect based in Judea before the First Jewish-Roman war. Many fled east to Mesopotamia with the Mandeans and other smaller Judahite religious groups, while others fled south into Arabia. The Arabian Ebionites are generally viewed as shaping the Islamic view of the prophet Jesus (عيسَى).

45 LXX 833: Alam (ܐܠܡ)

- LXX 407: Ailam (ܐܝܠܡ)

- LXX 509: Ailad (ܐܝܠܕ)

- LXX 15: Elam (Ελαμ)

- LXX 128: Elim (Ελϭιμ)

- LXX 82: Iaelam (ιΔιλΔμ)

- LXX 130: Maelam (ΜΔιλΔμ)

- LXX 551: Ailêm (ܐܝܠܚܡ)

- LXX 59: Celam (ΚϭλΔμ)

- Leningrad Codex: Eilam (עֵילָם). Translation: Elam

- Peshitta: Åylm (ܚܠܡ)

- Targum Onkelos: Eilam (עֵילָם)

- Targum Jerusalem: Eilam (עֵילָם)

- Bohairic manuscripts: Elam (Ⲉⲗⲁⲙ)

- Armenian Bible: Kheŭats̈in (Խեւացին). Translation: Khuzestan

Elam being listed as a Semitic nation is strange, as the Elamite language was not a Semitic language. This suggests that the author was not classifying them as Semitic based on their spoken language, but their written script, which was a derivative of Akkadian cuneiform. The Elamites being listed as a Semitic nation also confirms that the author was not referring to them as the Khuzites who founded the cities of Sumer, even though in later centuries their descendants became known as Khuze.

46 Codex Alexandrinus: Caenan (ⲔⲀⲒⲚⲀⲚ)

- LXX 135: Caenam (Καιναμ)

- LXX 72: Caeêl (Καιηλ)

- Leningrad Codex: not mentioned

- Peshitta: not mentioned

- Targum Onkelos: not mentioned

- Armenian Bible: not mentioned

- Ge'ez manuscripts: Caenam (ቃይናም)

The Cainan are not mentioned in this verse of Noah, but are mentioned a couple of verse later, where they also appear in Cosmic Genesis. They are later mentioned in both versions of Exodus, and Moses married his daughter to one of them. Joshua was also reported to have allowed them to leave the cities that the Israelites were besieging before killing everyone else in the city, suggesting they were viewed as important in the era right after the Exodus. The name translates as 'smiths,' suggesting they were a guild or caste of metal-workers. It is unclear why the Cainan would have been removed from the Hebrew translation, however, it appears at one point they were generally redacted from the Israelite texts, as while initially being important, virtually no mention of them survives in the texts. This redaction found in the Masoretic Text, suggests they were still being redacted a late as the time of King Josiah, circa 625 BC, who would have probably been responsible for the original translation of the genealogy of nations into Judahite when he published his authorized version of the Torah.

47 Like the previous mention of Cainan (ᴋᴀɪɴᴀɴ), this one is missing from the geneology of Noah.

Cosmic Genesis: Chapter 11

In all the land was one language, and there was one language for all. It happened as they moved from the east, they found a plain in the land of Sumer, and they lived there. A man said to his neighbor, "Come, let us make bricks and bake them with fire."

The brick was for them like stone, and their mortar was bitumen. They said, "Come, let us build for ourselves a city and tower, whose top will be in the sky, and let us make a name for ourselves before we are scattered across the face of all the land."

The Lord came down to see the city and the tower, which the sons of men built.

The Lord said, "Look, there are one people, and one language for all, and they have begun to do this. Now nothing will stop them, in anything that they may have decided to do. Come, let's go down and confuse their language, that they may not understand each one the voice of his neighbor."

The Lord scattered them from there over the face of all the land, and they stopped building the city and the tower. (On this account, its name was called Babylon,[1] because the Lord confused the languages of all the land there, and the Lord scattered them on the surface of all the land from there.)

These are the generations of Shem: and Shem was a hundred years old when he fathered Arphaxad, the second year after the flood. Shem lived, after he had fathered Arphaxad, five hundred years, and fathered sons and daughters, and died.

Arphaxad lived a hundred and thirty-five years and fathered Cainan. Arphaxad lived after he had fathered Cainan, four hundred years, and fathered sons and daughters, and died.

Cainan lived a hundred and thirty years and fathered Salah, and Cainan lived after he had fathered Salah, three hundred and thirty years, and fathered sons and daughters, and died.

Salah lived a hundred and thirty years and fathered Eber. Salah lived after he had fathered Eber, three hundred and thirty years, and fathered sons and daughters, and died.

Eber lived a hundred and thirty-four years and fathered Peleg. Eber lived after he had fathered Peleg two hundred and seventy years, and fathered sons and daughters, and died.

Peleg lived a hundred and thirty years and fathered Reu. Peleg lived after he had fathered Reu, two hundred and nine years, and fathered sons and daughters, and died.

And Reu lived a hundred and thirty-two years and fathered Serug. And Reu lived after he had fathered Serug, two hundred and seven years, and fathered sons and daughters, and died.

Serug lived a hundred and thirty years and fathered Nahor. Serug lived after he had fathered Nahor, two hundred years, and fathered sons and daughters, and died.

Nahor lived a hundred and seventy-nine years and fathered Terah. Nahor lived after he had fathered Terah, a hundred and twenty-five years, and fathered sons and daughters, and he died.

And Terah lived seventy years and fathered Abram, Nahor, and Harran. These are the generations of Terah. Terah fathered Abram, Nahor, and Harran. Harran fathered Lot. Harran died in the presence of Terah his father, in the land in which he was born, in the country of the Chaldeans.

Abram and Nahor took for themselves wives, and the name of the wife of Abram was Sarai, and the name of the wife of Nahor, Milcah, daughter of Harran, and he was the father of Milcah, the father of Iscah. Sarai was barren and did not bear children. And Terah took Abram his son, and Lot the son Harran, the son of his son, and Sarai his daughter-in-law, the wife of Abram his son, and led them out of the land of the Chaldeans, to go into the land of Canaan, and they came as far as Harran, and he lived there. All the days of Terah in the land of Harran were two hundred and five years, and Terah died in Harran.

Cosmic Genesis: Chapter 11 Notes

1 Codex Alexandrinus: synchysis (ⲥⲩⲅⲭⲩⲥⲓⲥ). Translation: revolt (or confounding, disturbing, overthrow)

- Leningrad Codex: Bavel (בָּבֶל). Translation: Babylon

- Peshitta: Bbl (ܒܒܠ). Translation: Babylon (or Babylonia)

- Targum Onkelos: Bavel (בָּבֶל). Translation: Babylon (or Babylonia)

As this could not have been the later city of Babylon, which was not in Sumer, it must be assumed this is another reference to Eridu, which was also spelled as Nun^{ki} (𒉣𒆠) in Akkadian cuneiform. For more information on Eridu see the note in chapter 10. This explanation of the name of 'Babylon' does not make sense, as the name translates as 'gateway of god' in Semitic languages. It suggests that the explanation of the meaning of the name was already in the cuneiform text that the genealogy of nations was translated from, and interpreted the city of Nun^{ki} as the 'first place' (𒉣𒆠). The tower in question was probably Amar-Sin's unfinished ziggurat, from circa 2000 BC.

When he began building the ziggurat, Ur controlled most of the world they knew of, including most of modern Iraq, and Syria, and a large section of Iran. After Amar-Sin's early death, work on the ziggurat appears to been halted while his heir Shu-Sin dealt with a rebellion in Syria. After his death just seven years into his reign, possibly fighting in southern Canaan, Ur's power was weakened, and his heir Ibbi-Sin fought a long series of revolts among the Amorites and Elamtes, before finally being conquered by Elam.

As a result, work never resumed on Ziggurat of Amar-Sin. The building of the ziggurat would have been controversial at the time, as it was built on top of an ancient temple complex dedicated to Enki / Ia. The 18 ancient temples appear to have remained in use even after most of Eridu was abandoned, suggesting that one of the reasons the ziggurat was not completed after Amar-Sin's death was due to local outrage in Eridu, which Shu-Sin didn't also want to rebel, like the Amorites in Syria. The interpretation of 'Babylon' as meaning 'revolt' or 'confusion,' likely originated in the Greek translation at Alexandria, as the Egyptian name of 'Babylon' was Beber (𓃀𓃀𓂋𓈖), which is very similar to the Greek bar-bar (βαρ-βαρ), meaning 'foreign language,' and Sanskrit barbara (बर्बर), meaning 'stammering,' or 'idiot.'

Cosmic Genesis: Chapter 12

The Lord said to Abram, "Go out of your land and away from your families, and out of the house of your father, and come into the land which I will show you. I will make you a great nation, and I will bless you and magnify your name, and you will be blessed. I will bless those that bless you, and curse those that curse you, and in you will all the tribes of the land be blessed."

Abram went as the Lord told him, and Lot departed with him, and Abram was seventy-five years old when he went out of Harran. Abram took Sarai his wife, and Lot the son of his brother, and all their possessions, as many as they had got, and every mind which they had gotten in Harran, and they left to go to the land of Canaan. Abram traversed the land lengthwise as far as the place Shechem,[1] to the high oak, and the Canaanites then inhabited the land.

The Lord appeared to Abram and said to him, "I will give this land to your descendants. Abram built an altar there to the Lord who appeared to him." He departed there to the mountain east of the House of El,[2] and there he pitched his tent at the Temple of El near the sea, with the government office[3] to the east, and there he built an altar to the Lord, and called on the name of the Lord. Abram departed and went and camped in the wilderness.

There was a famine in the land, and Abram went down to Egypt to stay there because the famine prevailed in the land. It happened when Abram drew near to enter into Egypt, Abram said to Sarai his wife, "I know that you are a beautiful woman. It will come to pass then that when the Egyptians will see you, they will say, 'This is his wife,' and they will kill me, and they will keep you alive. Say, therefore, 'I am his sister,' that it may be well with me on account of you, and my mind will live because of you."

It happened when Abram entered into Egypt, the Egyptians saw his wife, that she was very beautiful, and when the princes of Pharaoh saw her they praised her to Pharaoh and brought her into the house of Pharaoh. They treated Abram well on her account, and he had sheep, calves, donkeys, menservants, women-servants, mules, and camels. God afflicted Pharaoh with great and severe afflictions, and also his house, because of Sarai, Abram's wife. Pharaoh having called Abram, said, "What is this you have done to me, that you did not tell me that she was your wife? Why did you say, 'She is my sister?' and I took her as a wife for myself? Now, look! Your wife is before you, take her and go quickly away."

Pharaoh gave orders to men concerning Abram, to join in sending him away, and his wife, and all that he had, and also Lot with him.

Cosmic Genesis: Chapter 12 Notes

1 Codex Alexandrinus: Sychem (ⲤⲨⲬⲈⲘ)

- LXX 343: Synchem (ⲤⲨⲛⲬⲟ́ⲙ)

- LXX 31: Sêchem (Ⲥⲏ̣Ⲭⲟ́ⲙ)

- Leningrad Codex: Shechem (שְׁכֶם)

- Peshitta: Škym (ܫܟܝܡ)

- Targum Onkelos: Shechem (שְׁכֶם)

- Sahidic manuscripts: Sekhem (Ⲥⲉⲭⲉⲙ)

Shechem was an ancient city at the foot of Mount Gerizim, on the outskirts of modern Nablus in the northern Palestinian West Bank. It was mentioned in the Elba Tablets from the 3rd millennium BC, and continuously inhabited until 67 AD when it was destroyed during the First Jewish-Roman War.

2 Codex Alexandrinus: Baethêl (ⲃⲀⲓⲑⲎⲗ)

- LXX 343: Bethêl (ⲃⲉ́ⲑⲏⲗ)

- LXX 130: Caethêl (ⲕⲀⲓⲑⲣⲗ)

- Leningrad Codex: Veit-El (בֵּית־אֵל). Translation: house (or temple) of El (or god)

- Peshitta: Byt Âyl (ܒܝܬ ܐܝܠ). Translation: house (or temple) of El (or god)

- Targum Onkelos: Beit-El (בֵּית־אֵל). Translation: house (or temple) of El (or god)

- Targum Jerusalem: Beit El (בֵּית אֵל). Translation: house (or temple) of El (or god)

The term Bethel meant several things in ancient Canaan. The term translates as 'house of god,' which can be translated as either 'Temple of God (or El)' or 'sky.' Bethel was worshiped as a god by the ancient Canaanites, the brother of El and Dagon according to Sanchuniathon, who referred to him as Baitylos, which is the name used in this translation when the god is denoted. The term can also be translated as 'meteorite' as meteorites were believed to be parts of the god Baitylos that had fallen to the Earth, and shrines were built around them.

3 Codex Alexandrinus: angae (ⲁⲅⲅⲁⲓ)

- LXX 75: ange (ⲁⲅⲅⲉ)

- Leningrad Codex: ha'ai (הָעָי)

- Peshitta: åy (ܥܝ)

- Targum Onkelos: ay (עַי)

- Fragments Targum: ay (עַי)

- Bohairic manuscripts: agge (ⲁⲅⲅⲉ)

The Greek translators also transliterated this name as Gai (Γαι) in some of the later books of the Septuagint. The Hebrew term is often translated as 'ruins' however, the place is inhabited during the era of Joshua, indicating 'ruins' is an incorrect interpretation. If the original book of Abraham was in Egyptian, the term used would have been ḥå (𓉐𓂝𓏤), the Egyptian word for 'government office.' As Sarai was later married to the King of Egypt, she would have needed to have been the daughter of a high-priest, and Abram's building an altar to his god between the Temple of El and the Egyptian government office would explain how he made contact with the Egyptian government. Marrying the daughters of the high priests was seen as a way for the king to legitimize his 'godhood' by marrying into the families that represented the gods on Earth.

The practice of the king marrying the daughter(s) of the high priest(s) of the god(s) was later adopted by the kings of Israel, and continued until the Babylonian captivity. Several locations in Canaan were referred to as Gai, suggesting several regional administrative offices were active in Canaan at the time. If the Egyptians were already in control of Canaan at the time, it indicates that Abram traveled through Canaan while the Middle Kingdom still ruled the region, which is consistent with the later timeline of Jacob and Joseph settling in Egypt as the Middle Kingdom collapsed, and Moses leading the exodus 400 years later at the end of the Second Intermediate Period.

Cosmic Genesis: Chapter 13

Abram went up out of Egypt, he and his wife, and all that he had, and Lot with him, into the wilderness. Abram was very rich in livestock, and silver, and gold. He went back to the place from where he had come from, into the wilderness as far as the House of El, as far as the place where his tent was before, between the Temple of El and the government office, to the place of the altar, where he had pitched his tent, and Abram there called on the name of the Lord. Lot, who went out with Abram had sheep, and livestock, and tents. The land was not large enough for them to live together, because their possessions were great, and the land was not large enough for them to live together.

There was a struggle between the herders of Abram's livestock, and the herders of Lot's livestock, and the Canaanites and the Perizzites who then inhabited the land. Abram said to Lot, "Let there not be strife between me and you, and between my herders and your herders, for we are men. Look! Is not the whole land before you? Separate yourself from me. If you go to the left, I will go to the right, and if you go to the right, I will go to the left."

Lot, having lifted his eyes saw all the country around the Jordan, that it was all watered, (before God overthrew Sodom and Gomorrah), like the paradise of the Lord, and like the land of Egypt until you come to Zoar. Lot chose for himself all the country around Jordan, and Lot went to the east, and they were separated each from his brother. Abram lived in the land of Canaan. Lot lived in a city of the neighboring people and pitched his tent in Sodom. But the men of Sodom were evil, and exceedingly sinful before God. God said to Abram after Lot was separated from him, "Look up with your eyes, and Look from the place where you now are, northward and southward, and eastward and seaward, for all the land which you see, I will give it to you and your descendants forever. I will make your descendants like the sand of the land, if anyone could count the dust of the land, then your descendants will be counted. Arise and traverse the land, both in the length of it and in the breadth, for to you will I give it, and to your descendants forever."

Abram having lived at a distance, came and lived by the oak of Mamre, which was in Hebron, and he there built an altar to the Lord.[1]

Cosmic Genesis: Chapter 13 Notes

1 Berlin Genesis: cyriô (ⲕⲨⲢⲓⲱ). Translation: lord

- LXX 551: cyriô tô theô (ⲕⲩⲣⲓ̂ⲱ ⲧⲱ ⲑⲉ̂ⲱ). Translation: lord the god

- Leningrad Codex: Yhvah (יְהֹוָה)

- DSS 4QGen[b]: Yhůh (𐤉𐤄𐤅𐤉)

- Peshitta: mryå (ܡܪܝܐ). Translation: master (lord)

- Targum Onkelos: yeyah (??). Translation: Yhů

- Targum Jerusalem: yeyah (??). Translation: Yhů

Cosmic Genesis: Chapter 14

It happened in the kingdom of the Amorite shepherds,[1] the king of Sumer and Uruk,[2] Amar son of Shulgi,[3] King of Elam and Thargal,[4] and King of the Guti,[5] went to war with Barak, king of Sodom,[6] and with Barsa, King of Gomorrah,[7] and King Sennaar of Adama,[8] and King Shemaeber of Bet Rabim,[9] and King Balac of Shasziru.[10] All these agreed with one consent at the salt valley, (this is now the sea of salt). Twelve years they served Shulgi, and for thirteenth years[11] they revolted.

In the fourteenth year, Shulgi's representative returned, and the kings with him, and cut to pieces the Raphites in Astaroth Karnaim, and Shaszi[12] with them, and the Gomorrhans[13] in the city of Shaveh, and the Hurrians[14] in the mountains of Seir, to the turpentine tree of Paran which is in the desert. Having turned back they came to the well of judgment (this is Kadesh), and they cut in pieces all the princes[15] of Amalek, and the Amorites dwelling in Hazezon-Tamar. The king of Sodom went out, and the king of Gomorrah, and the king of Adama, and the king of Bet Rabim, and the king of Shasziru, and they organized themselves into a formation against them, to battle in the Salt Valley, against Shulgi's representative, the King of Elam and Thargal, King of the Guti and the Amorite shepherds, King of Sumer and Uruk, King of the four lands,[16] against the five. Now the Salt Valley consists of slime-pits, and the king of Sodom fled, and the king of Gomorrah, and they fell there, and those who were left, fled to the mountain country.

They took all the cavalry of Sodom and Gomorrah, and all their provisions, and departed. They also took Lot the son of Abram's brother, and his property, and departed, as he lived in Sodom. One of those who had been rescued came and told Abram, then in the courthouse,[17] who governed for Elon the lord of the Amorites,[18] the brother of Eschol, and the brother of Onan, who were allied with Abram. Abram having heard that Lot his nephew had been taken captive, organized his three hundred and eighteen home-born slaves, and chased after them to Dan. He came on them in the night, he and his slaves, and he attacked them and chased them as far as Hobah, which is on the left of Damascus. He captured all the cavalry of Sodom, and he captured Lot his nephew, and all his possessions, and the women and the people. The king of Sodom went out to meet him after he returned from the slaughter of Chedorlaomer, and the kings with him, to the valley of Shaveh, (this was the plain of the kings).

King Melchizedek of Salem brought out loaves and wine, as he was the priest of the Highest God.[19] He blessed Abram, and said, "Blessed, be Abram, by the Highest God, who made Shamayim and Eretz, and blessed is the Highest God who delivered your enemies into your hand." Abram gave him a tenth of everything.

The king of Sodom said to Abram, "Give me the men, and take the cavalry for yourself."

Abram said to the king of Sodom, "I will stretch out my hand to the Lord, the Highest God, who made Shamayim and Eretz, that I will not take from all your goods, from a string to a shoe-lace, in case you should say, 'I have made Abram rich.' Except for the things the young men have eaten, and the portion for the men that went with me from Eschol, Onan, and Mamre. These will take a portion."

Cosmic Genesis: Chapter 14 Notes

1 Berlin Genesis: -marabel (-ΜΑΡΑΒΕΛ). The papyrus is damaged at the beginning of the name, however, it is believed to have read 'Amarabel.'

- LXX 961: Amarphad (ΑΜΑΡΦΑΔ)
- LXX 64: Amarphal (ΑμΑΡΦΑΛ)
- LXX 135: Armaphaa (ΑΡμΑΦΑΑ)
- LXX 25: Armaphal (ΑΡμΑΦΑΛ)
- LXX 120: Marphal (ΜΑΡΦΑΛ)
- LXX 128: Marphar (ΜΑΡΦΑΡ)
- LXX 426: Iamorphad (ΙΑμοΡΦΑΔ)
- LXX 413: Amalphar (ΑμΑΛΦΑΡ)
- LXX 799: Amardad (ΑμΑΡΔΑΔ)
- LXX 59: Armaphan (ΑΡμΑΦΑΝ)
- Leningrad Codex: Amrafel (אַמְרָפֶל)
- Peshitta: Åmrpyl (ܐܡܪܦܝܠ)

- Targum Onkelos: Amrafel (אַמְרָפֶל)

- Fragment Targums: Amrafel (אַמְרָפֶל)

- Targum Jerusalem: Amrafel (אַמְרָפֶל)

- Coptic manuscripts: Marphar (Μαρφαρ)

This term is generally read as the name of a king, however, later in the chapter is treated as the name of a kingdom. If the term originated in Old Akkadian, it would have been Amurru palu (𒀀𒈬𒌨𒊒 𒉺𒇻), meaning 'Amorite shepherds.' Amurru was generally viewed as the western-most region of Mesopotamian civilization, and one of the four regions of the Akkadian and Neo-Sumerian empires along with Elam in the east, Subartu (Assyria) in the north, and Akkad-Sumer in the south. The king of this empire at the time, was almost certainly Amar-Sin of Ur, who is the only king of Sumer in the general era that fits the story. Amar-Sin was the king of Ur circa 2000 BC, with different Assyriologists giving a range of dates between 2046 and 1973 BC for his 9 year long reign. During his era, Ur established an empire across most of modern Iraq and Syria, as well as across southern and western Iran. His empire included Uruk and other ancient Sumerian and Akkadian cities, as well as the Assyrian city of Assur, although the exact extent is not clear. One of the subject peoples of his empire was the Guti of the Zagros mountains, whom many scholars believe are the Goyim listed among his subject nations. Another subject nation was Elam, which is also listed.

According to the scant surviving records of his campaigns, he defeated the Marhashi in southern modern Iran, as well as the Lullubi and Hamazi in west-central Iran, Irabel in northern Iraq, and suppressed a rebellion in Assur, appointing the Akkadian Zariqum as governor. Among his many conquests is a list of five cities that have yet to be identified, named Šasíru (�𒈦𒊒), Šurudum (𒊒𒅗𒌇), Bitum-Rabium (𒉣 𒂍𒄖), Íabru (𒌀𒍝𒊒), and Úḫnuru (𒌋𒅆𒉣). Given the similarity of the names, they are probably the cities mentioned in this verse.

2 LXX 961: basileôs Sennaar Ariôch (ΒΑϹΙΛΕωϹϹΕΝΝΑΑΡ ΑΡΙωΧ). Translation: king of Sennaar Arioch

- LXX 509: basileus Senaar Ariôch (ⲙⲁⲥⲓⲗⲧ̄ⲟⲟⲥ ⲥⲟⲛⲁⲁⲣ ⲁⲣⲓⲟⲟⲭ). Translation: king of SenaarArioch

- LXX 135: basileôs Sennaar Ariô (ⲙⲁⲥⲓⲗⲧ̄ⲟⲟⲥ ⲥⲟⲛⲛⲁⲁⲣ ⲁⲣⲓⲟⲟ). Translation: king of Sennaar Ariw

- LXX 129: basileôs Sennaar Ôriôch (ⲙⲁⲥⲓⲗⲧ̄ⲟⲟⲥ ⲥⲟⲛⲛⲁⲁⲣ ⲱⲣⲓⲟⲟⲭ). Translation: king of Sennaar Orioch

- LXX 426: basileôs Sennaar Ariôd (ⲩⲁⲥⲓⲗⲧⲟⲟⲥ ⲥϬⲛⲛⲁⲁϼ ⲁϼⲓⲟⲟⲁ). Translation: king of Sennaar Ariôd

- LXX 82: basileôs Senaar cae Ariôch (ⲩⲁⲥⲓⲗⲧⲟⲟⲥ ⲥϬⲛⲛⲁⲁϼ ⳑⲁⲓ ⲁϼⲓⲟⲟⲭ). Translation: king of Sennaar and Arioch

- LXX 458: basileôs Ennaar Ariôch (ⲩⲁⲥⲓⲗⲧⲟⲟⲥ ⲉⲛⲛⲁⲁϼ ⲁϼⲓⲟⲟⲭ). Translation: king of EnnaarArioch

- LXX 72: basileôs Sanaar Ariôch (ⲩⲁⲥⲓⲗⲧⲟⲟⲥ ⲥⲁⲛⲁⲁϼ ⲁϼⲓⲟⲟⲭ). Translation: king of SanaarArioch

- LXX 376: basileôs Sennaar Argôch (ⲩⲁⲥⲓⲗⲧⲟⲟⲥ ⲥϬⲛⲛⲁⲁϼ ⲁϼⲅⲟⲟⲭ). Translation: king of Sennaar Argoch

- Leningrad Codex: melech shin'ar aryoch (מֶלֶךְ שִׁנְעָר אַרְיוֹךְ). Translation: king of Shniar Aryok

- Peshitta: mlkå dSnôr ůÅryůk (ܡܠܟܐ ܕܣܢܥܪ ܘܐܪܝܘܟ). Translation: king of Snor Aryok

- Targum Onkelos: malka deVavel Aryoch (מַלְכָּא דְבָבֶל אַרְיוֹךְ). Translation: king of Babylon Aryok

- Targum Jerusalem: malka dePunetos Aryoch (מַלְכָּא דְפוּנְטוֹס אַרְיוֹךְ). Translation: king of PontusAryok

- Bohairic manuscripts: basileôs Senaar nemAriôkh (ⲃⲁⲥⲓⲗⲉⲩⲥ ⲥⲉⲛⲁⲁⲣ ⲛⲉⲙ ⲁ̀ⲣⲓⲱⲭ). Translation: king of Senaar and Ariokh.

- Sahidic manuscripts: basileôs Senaar Arimakh (ⲃⲁⲥⲓⲗⲉⲩⲥ ⲥⲉⲛⲁⲁⲣ ⲁ̀ⲣⲓⲙⲁⲭ). Translation: king of SenaarArimakh.

The text are largely divided into two interpretations, either this is 'Sumer and Uruk,' as found in LXX 82, the Peshitta, and Bohairic manuscripts, or it is just 'Sumer,' and the word Uruk is viewed as the name of the following king. In the Neo-Sumerian era, Uruk did maintain its autonomy within the empire. Amar-Sin held both the titles of 'King of Sumer and Akkad,' as well as 'King of Uruk,' therefore, this translation follows the 'Sumer and Uruk' manuscripts.

3 LXX 961: basileôs Sellasaar Chodollag (ⲃⲁⲥⲓⲗⲉⲱⲥⲥⲉⲗⲗⲁⲥⲁⲁⲣ ⲭⲟⲇⲟⲗⲗⲁⲅ). Translation: king of Sellasaar Chodollag

- Codex Alexandrinus: basileus Sellasar o Chodollogomor (ⲃⲁⲥⲓⲗⲉⲩⲥ ⲥⲉⲗⲗⲁⲥⲁⲣ ⲟ ⲭⲟⲇⲟⲗⲗⲟⲅⲟⲙⲟⲣ). Translation: king of Sellasaar the Chodollogomor

- Cotton Genesis: -odolla- (-ⲟⲇⲟⲗⲗⲁ-). LXX D was burned in 1731, and only part of the name '[Ch]odolla[g]' survives in this verse. LXX D also uses the variant Cholodog (ⲭⲟⲇⲁⲗⲗ) twice later in the surviving sections of the chapter

- LXX 17: basileus Ellasar Chodolag (ⲩⲁⲥⲓⲗⲉ́ⲩⲥ Ελλⲇⲥⲁⲃ́ ⲭⲟⲇⲟⲗⲁⲅ). Translation: king of Ellasar Chodolag

- LXX 55: basileus Selasar Chodollag (ⲩⲁⲥⲓⲗⲉ́ⲩⲥ ⲥⲟⲗⲇⲥⲁⲃ́ ⲭⲟⲇⲟⲗⲗⲁⲅ). Translation: king of Selasar Chodollag

- LXX 64: basileus Ellasar cae Chodollogomor (ⲩⲁⲥⲓⲗⲉ́ⲩⲥ Ελλⲇⲥⲁⲃ́ ⲓⲁⲓ ⲭⲟⲇⲟⲗⲗⲟⲅⲟⲙⲟⲃ́). Translation: king of Ellasar and Chodollogomor

- LXX 318: basileus Sellasar Chodall (ⲩⲁⲥⲓⲗⲉ́ⲩⲥ ⲥⲟⲗⲗⲇⲥⲁⲃ́ ⲭⲟⲇⲇⲗⲗ). Translation: king of Sellasar Chodall. LXX 318 also uses the variant Chodallogomôr (ⲭⲟⲇⲇⲗⲗⲟⲅⲟⲙⲟⲟⲃ́) for the rest of the chapter supporting the original text switching from 'Shulgi' to 'Shulgi's representative' after the first mention of his name.

- LXX 57: basileus Ellasar Chollodog (ⲩⲁⲥⲓⲗⲟ́ⲩⲥ Ελλⲇⲥⲁⲃ́ ⲭⲟⲗⲗⲟⲗⲟⲅ). Translation: king of Ellasar Chollodog. LXX 57 also uses the variant Cholodog (ⲭⲟⲗⲟⲇⲟⲅ) later in the chapter.

- LXX 343: basileôs Elassar Selaasar Chodologemor (ⲩⲁⲥⲓⲗⲟ́ⲟⲥ Ελⲇⲥⲥⲁⲃ́ ⲥⲟ́ⲗⲗⲇⲥⲁⲃ́ ⲭⲟⲇⲟⲗⲟⲅⲟ́ⲙⲟⲃ́). Translation: king of Elassar (Selaasar) Chodologemor. LXX 343 also uses the variants Chodollasomor (ⲭⲟⲇⲟⲗⲗⲇⲥⲟⲙⲟⲃ́), Cholagomor (ⲭⲟⲗⲇⲅⲟⲙⲟⲃ́), Godollag (ⲅⲟⲇⲟⲗⲗⲇⲅ), and Chodollag (ⲭⲟⲇⲟⲗⲗⲇⲅ) later in the chapter.

- LXX 370: basileus Sallasar Cholodog (ⲩⲁⲥⲓⲗⲉ́ⲩⲥ ⲥⲇⲗⲗⲇⲥⲁⲃ́ ⲭⲟⲗⲟⲇⲟⲅ). Translation: king of Sallasar Cholodog. LXX 370 also uses the variants Chollodog (ⲭⲟⲗⲗⲟⲇⲟⲅ) and Godollag (ⲅⲟⲇⲟⲗⲗⲇⲅ) later in the chapter.

- LXX 426 basileus Ellasar Chôdollogomôr (ⲩⲁⲥⲓⲗⲉ́ⲩⲥ Ελλⲇⲥⲁⲃ́ ⲭⲟⲟⲇⲟⲗⲗⲟⲅⲟⲙⲟⲟⲃ́). Translation: king of Ellasar Chôdollogomôr. LXX 426 also uses the variants Chôdolagomôr (ⲭⲟⲟⲇⲟⲗⲇⲅⲟⲙⲟⲟⲃ́) and Chodolagomôr (ⲭⲟⲇⲟⲗⲇⲅⲟⲙⲟⲟⲃ́) later in the chapter.

- LXX 75: basileus Ellasar Chodollagomô (ⲩⲁⲥⲓⲗⲉ́ⲩⲥ Ελλⲇⲥⲁⲃ́ ⲭⲟⲇⲟⲗⲗⲇⲅⲟⲙⲟⲟ). Translation: king of Ellasar Chodollagomô. LXX 75 also uses the variant Chologomôr (ⲭⲟⲗⲟⲅⲟⲙⲟⲟⲃ́) later in the chapter.

- LXX 78: basileus Salasar Chodologobor (ⲩⲁⲥⲓⲗⲉ̄ⲩⲥ ⲥⲁⲗⲁⲥⲁⲣ ⲭⲟⲇⲟⲗⲟⲅⲟⲩⲟⲩⲟⲣ). Translation: basileus Salasar Chodologobor. LXX 78 also uses the variants Chodolog (ⲭⲟⲇⲟⲗⲟⲅ) and Cholodog (ⲭⲟⲗⲟⲇⲟⲅ) later in the chapter.

- LXX 72: basileus Elasar cae Chodollag (ⲩⲁⲥⲓⲗⲉ̄ⲩⲥ ⲉⲗⲁⲥⲁⲣ ⲩⲁⲓ ⲭⲟⲇⲟⲗⲗⲁⲅ). Translation: king of Elasar and Chodollag. LXX 72 also uses the variants Chodollogomor (ⲭⲟⲇⲟⲗⲗⲟⲅⲟⲩⲟⲣ), Cholag (ⲭⲟⲗⲁⲅ), and Chollag (ⲭⲟⲗⲗⲁⲅ) later in the chapter.

- LXX 107: basileus Ellasar cae Chodollogomor (ⲩⲁⲥⲓⲗⲉ̄ⲩⲥ ⲉⲗⲗⲁⲥⲁⲣ ⲩⲁⲓ ⲭⲟⲇⲟⲗⲗⲟⲅⲟⲩⲟⲣ). Translation: king of Ellasar and Chodollogomor. LXX 107 also uses the variants Todolog (ⲧⲟⲇⲟⲗⲟⲅ) and Cholodog (ⲭⲟⲗⲟⲇⲟⲅ) later in the chapter.

- LXX 414: basileus Elassar Chodollogomor (ⲩⲁⲥⲓⲗⲉ̄ⲩⲥ ⲉⲗⲁⲥⲥⲁⲣ ⲭⲟⲇⲟⲗⲗⲟⲅⲟⲩⲟⲣ). Translation: king of Elassar Chodollogomor. LXX 414 also uses the variant Chologodomor (ⲭⲟⲗⲟⲅⲟⲇⲟⲩⲟⲣ) later in the chapter.

- LXX 664: basileus Elassar Cholodog (ⲩⲁⲥⲓⲗⲉ̄ⲩⲥ ⲉⲗⲁⲥⲥⲁⲣ ⲭⲟⲗⲟⲇⲟⲅ). Translation: king of Elassar Cholodog. LXX 664 also uses the variants Chodologomôr (ⲭⲟⲇⲟⲗⲟⲅⲟⲩⲟⲟⲣ) ⲁⲛⲇ Chodolog (ⲭⲟⲇⲟⲗⲟⲅ) later in the chapter.

- LXX 122: basileus Ellasar Cholodog (ⲩⲁⲥⲓⲗⲉ̄ⲩⲥ ⲉⲗⲗⲁⲥⲁⲣ ⲭⲟⲗⲟⲇⲟⲅ). Translation: king of Ellasar Cholodog. LXX 664 also uses the variant Chollomor (ⲭⲟⲗⲗⲟⲩⲟⲣ) later in the chapter.

- Leningrad Codex: melech Ellasar Kedarela'omer (מֶלֶךְ אֶלָּסָר כְּדָרְלָעֹמֶר). Translation: king of Ellasar Kedarela'omer. The Leningrad Codex also uses the variant Chedarela'omer (כְדָרְלָעֹמֶר) later in the chapter.

- Peshitta: mlkå dDlsr ŭKrdlômr (ܡܠܟܐ ܕܕܠܣܪ ܘܟܪܕܠܥܡܪ). Translation: king of Dlsr and Krdlômr

- Targum Onkelos: malka de'Ellasar Kedarela'omer (מַלְכָּא דְאֶלָסָר כְּדָרְלָעֹמֶר). Translation: king of Ellasar Kedarelaomer

- Targum Jerusalem: malka deTalsar Kedarela'omer (מַלְכָּא דְתַלְסָר כְּדָרְלָעוֹמֶר). Translation: king of Talsar Kedarelaomer

- Bohairic manuscripts: basileôs Ellasar nem Khodolog (ⲃⲁⲥⲓⲗⲉⲩⲥ ⲉⲗⲗⲁⲥⲁⲣ ⲛⲉⲙ ⲭⲟⲇⲟⲗⲟⲅ). Translation: king of Ellasar and Khodolog.

- Sahidic manuscripts: basileôs Sellaar Khodollogomor (ⲃⲁⲥⲓⲗⲉⲩⲥ ⲥⲉⲗⲗⲁⲁⲣ ⲭⲟⲇⲟⲅⲩⲗⲗⲁⲅⲟⲙⲟⲣ). Translation: king of Sellaar Khodoullagomor. The Sahidic manuscriptsalso use the variant Kholodog (Χολοδογ) later in the chapter.

The somewhat garbled string of words has been interrupted several ways. The most common interpretation is that 'Sellasaar' and 'Chodollag' are the name of two kings or city-states. 'Sellasaar' is generally interpreted as a garbled translation of the name of the city of Larsaki (◁〓◀⟨⊕⟩), while 'Chodollag' is interpreted as the name of a king. The alternate common interpretation, as recorded in LXX 64 and 72, the Peshitta, and the Bohairic manuscripts, is that 'king of Ellasar and Chodollogomor' is a continuation of the titles of the king. The Codex Alexandrinus includes a third variant, as 'king of Sellasaar of Chodollogomor,' which then suggests that 'Sellassar' was either from, or the son of 'Chodollogomor.' Based on the described events, this appears to be a reference to King Amar-Sin, and his father king King Shulgi of the Neo-Sumerian empire's Ur III dynasty, with the original text reading 'Amar bīnum Shulgi (✳⟨⊂ 〓▷◁ ✳⟩⊞卅⟩), meaning 'Amar son of Shulgi.' Shulgi (✳⟩⊞卅⟩) was the king most responsible for the expansion of the Neo-Sumerian empire, conquering most of modern Iraq, and Syria, as well as most of southern Iran. His son Amar-Sin (✳⟨⊂✳▐⊞) ruled at the height of the Neo-Sumerian empire, which began contracting after his death, and collapsed under his grandson's reign. Without the vowel markings added in the late-classical era, the name Ålsr (אלסר), found in the Masoretic Text, is a direct transliteration of Amar (✳⟨⊂) using Canaanite phonetics: ÅL (✳) SUR (⟨⊂).

The Hebrew transliteration of Kedarela'omer (כְּדָרְלָעֹמֶר), and earliest Greek transliteration as Chodollag (χολολλαλγ) do not appear directly related, however, the Greek translations are not consistent, with both variations of Chodollag and Chodollogomor being used. Some manuscripts use both is different verses, while others are consistent in the term used. This suggests that the Aramaic texts the Greeks translated included both a variant of the name 'Chodollag,' and a form of 'Chodollag's' åmr (אמר), meaning 'Chodollag's speaker or representative. In any event, the wars of Shulgi and Amar-Sin are being described in the text. In Shulgi's 37th regal year, the Amorites revolted, and he built the 'Wall of the Land,' to keep them from overrunning his entire empire. Shulgi's primary focus were his wars to conquer the Zagros mountains and Iranian plateau, and he never led an army to reconquer Amurru.

According to this verse, he sent his son Amar to reconquer the Amorties, and he failed. The verse suggests he returned in his 3rd year as king to reconquer the Amorites, however, settled for destroying the five cities in the Dead Sea region instead. Amar-Sin's chronicle omits mentioning what he did in his 3rd and 4th regal year, however, in his 5th year, he appointed a new high-priest at the temple of Inanna in Uruk, indicating whatever he was doing in his 3rd and 4th years was not successful. According to the chronicles from the Ur III dynasty, the Amorites would not be reconquered for another 29 years. Instead, Amar-Sin appears to have changed tactics in year 6 and 7 of his reign, and he destroyed the cities of Šaszíru (⊟◀⊞⟨Σ), Šurudum (⊢⫫◁〓⊞), Bitum-Rabium

(𒐲 𒂍‐𒈗), Íabru (𒌋 𒀹𒀭), and Úḫnuru (𒀸𒋫𒀭𒀭), which appear to be the five cities mentioned as being allied to the Amorites. This was also recorded as the second time he destroyed Šaszíru (𒂦𒌅𒊺𒀭), indicating that he must have campaigned in the region during Shulgi's reign, as the city would not have been rebuilt in just a year or two.

Based on this story in Cosmic Genesis, it appears that the Amorite rebellion was backed by the Egyptian government, as Terah's faction appears to have fled Ur early in Shulgi's reign, and Abram ultimately became the brother-in-law of the king of Egypt, and a judge among the Amorites. Terah and Abram are both recorded as leading armies that were apparently loyal to them, not Egypt or Amurru, suggesting they represented an alternate royal line or priestly line before leaving Ur. The Chronicle of the Early Kings, which was compiled centuries later in the Middle Babylonian era, records that Shulgi was punished by Marduk for stealing from the temple of Marduk in Babylon, however, Babylon had not been built yet, and Marduk does not appear to have been a god yet, so this must have been the temple of Nergal at nearby Kutha, where Shulgi was recorded as initiating religious reforms. As the terms 'Sellasaar,' 'Chodollag,' and 'Chodollogomor' appear to have originated with the names 'Amar'(-Sin) and Shulgi, and the term 'Shulgi's representative,' those terms are restored in this translation.

4 LXX 961: basileôs Aelam Thargal (ΒΑϹΙΛΕѠϹΑΙΛΑΜΘΑΡΓΑΛ). Translation: king of Aelam Thargal

• Codex Alexandrinus: basileus Aelam Thalga (ΒΑϹΙΛΕΥϹΑΙΛΑΜΘΑΛΓΑ). Translation: king of Aelam Thalga

• Cotton Genesis: basileus Saelam Thalgal (ΒΑϹΙΛΕΥϹϹΑΙΛΑΜΘΑΛΓΑΛ). Translation: king of Saelam Thalgal

• LXX 15: basileus Ailam Oargal (ϋασιλόϋϲ Αιλᾱμ Ο αβγαλ). Translation: king of Ailam Oargal

• LXX 55: basileus Ailam Oarchal (ϋασιλόϋϲ Αιλᾱμ Ο αβχαλ). Translation: king of Ailam Oarchal

• LXX 319: basileus Ailam Tharga (ϋασιλόϋϲ Αιλᾱμ Θ αβγα). Translation: land Ailam Tharga

• LXX 120: basileus Aidam Thargal (ϋασιλόϋϲ Αι∆αμ Θ αβγαλ). Translation: king of Aidam Thargal

• LXX 128: basileus Aidam Tharagal (ϋασιλόϋϲ Αι∆αμ Θ αβαγαλ). Translation: king of Aidam Tharagal

- LXX 129: basileus Ailam Thergal (uдσιλδυc Ацλдμ Θбↅγдλ). Translation: king of Ailam Thergal

- LXX 343: basileôs Balaam de Thargal (uдσιλδωc βдλддμ дↅ ΘдⱤγдλ). Translation: king of Balaam the Thargal

- LXX 426: basileus Elam Thargad (uдσιλδυc Ελдμ ΘдⱤγдд). Translation: king of Elam Thargad

- LXX 78: basileus Ailam Thelgar (uдσιλδυc Ацλдμ ΘбλγдⱤ). Translation: king of Ailam Thelgar.

- LXX 71: basileus Ailam Thagal (uдσιλδυc Ацλдμ Θдγдλ). Translation: king of Ailam Thelgar

- LXX 72: basileus Elam Thargan (uдσιλδυc Ελдμ ΘдⱤγдₙ). Translation: king of Elam Thargan.

- LXX 799: basileus Edam Thargal (uдσιλδυc Εддμ ΘдⱤγдλ). Translation: king of Edam Thargal

- LXX 527: basileus Ailam Thagar (uдσιλδυc Ацλдμ ΘдγдⱤ). Translation: king of Ailam Thagar.

- LXX 53: basileus Ailam Therchal (uдσιλδυc Ацλдμ Θбↅχдλ). Translation: king of Ailam Therchal

- LXX 59: basileus Selam Thargam (uдσιλδυc Cбλдμ ΘдⱤγдμ). Translation: king of Selam Thargam

- Leningrad Codex: melech Eilam veTid'al (מֶלֶךְ עֵילָם וְתִדְעָל). Translation: king of Elam and Tidal

- Peshitta: mlkå dÔylm ûTrôyl (ܡܠܟܐ ܕܥܝܠܡ ܘܬܪܥܠ). Translation: king of Ôylm and Trôyl

- Targum Onkelos: malka de'Eilam veTid'al (מַלְכָּא דְעֵילָם וְתִדְעָל). Translation: king of Elam and Tidal

- Targum Jerusalem: malka de'Eilam veTid'al (מַלְכָּא דְעֵילָם וְתִדְעָל). Translation: king of Elam and Tidal

- Bohairic manuscripts: basileôs Elam Thargar (ⲃⲁⲥⲓⲗⲉⲩⲥ Ⲉⲗⲁⲙ Ⲑⲁⲣⲅⲁⲣ). Translation: king of Elam Thargar

• Sahidic manuscripts: basileôs Elam Thargal (ⲃⲁⲥⲓⲗⲉⲩⲥ Ⲉⲗⲁⲙ Ⲑⲁⲣⲅⲁⲗ). Translation: king of Elam Thargal

Elam was the nation on the northern coast of the Persian in Gulf at the time, while the variations of Thargal/Tidāl were likely a reference to Dilmun. The earliest recorded name of Dilmun was the Sumerian pictogram 𒉆, which was spelled phonetically as Nitukᵏⁱ (𒉌𒋻𒆠) by Sumerians, however, is believed to have been pronounced as Dilmun or Telmun in Old Akkadian. The pronunciation is unknown during the Neo-Sumerian era, however, as the earlier Akkadian king Sargon had claimed to have conquered Dilmun into his empire, and the later Sealand Dynasty, the last Neo-Sumerian dynasty appears to have been based in Dilmun, it is unlikely it was not also occupied by the Neo-Sumerian Empire.

While the local name of Dilmun is not known today, when the Greeks ruled the region, they recorded the local name as Tharrhô (Θαρρώ), which is quite similar to the name found in the Greek and Syriac translations, suggesting it was similar to the name in the earlier Aramaic translation.

5 Codex Alexandrinus: basileus ethnôn (ⲃⲁⲥⲓⲗⲉⲩⲥⲉⲑⲛⲱⲛ). Translation: king of nations (or tribes, peoples)

• LXX 135: basileôs ethnôn (υλσιλϭοος ϭθνοον). Translation: king of nations (or tribes)

• Leningrad Codex: melech goyim (מֶלֶךְ גּוֹיִם). Translation: king of Goys (or non-Semites)

• Peshitta: mlkå dglyå (ܡܠܟܐ ܕܓܠܝܐ). Translation: king of Goys (or non-Semites)

• Targum Onkelos: malka de'ammei (מַלְכָּא דְעַמְמֵי). Translation: king of people

• Targum Jerusalem: rama'ah keta'ala malka de'ammaya mishtam'in leih (רְמָאה כְּתַעֲלָא מַלְכָּא דְעַמְמַיָּא מְשְׁתַּמְעִין לֵיהּ). Translation: high ascended king of the peoples (or nations) inherited by (or allotted to) him

The origin of the Hebrew word Gwy (גוי) is unclear, as the term does not appear to be Semitic. In Hebrew, the term traditionally meant Indo-European peoples, including Medes, Persians, Scythians, Greeks, and Romans. One proposal to explain the term is that it is an East Semitic loanword, as the Assyrians and Babylonians were using the word Guti (𒄖𒋾 / 𒄖𒌓) as a term to represent the Medes, Persian, and Scythians during the 1ˢᵗ millennium BC.

The original Guti nation, that inhabited the Zagros mountains in the 3ʳᵈ millennium BC, are not believed to have been Indo-Europeans, however, the Medes settled in the same region during the early 1ˢᵗ millennium BC, resulting the name being applied to the them as well. In the late 3rd millennium BC, the Akkadians conquered the land of the Guti, known as Gutium^{ki} (𒆳𒄖𒌅𒌝𒆠), however, the Guti rebelled and conquered the Akkadian empire late in the 3rd millennium BC, and ruled Mesopotamia for almost a century. They were eventually driven out of Mesopotamia by Amar-Sin's great-grandfather, who then reunited the Sumero-Akkadian city-states and laid the foundations of the Empire of Ur. During the rule of Amar-Sin, the Guti were part of his empire, explaining why he held the title 'King of the Guti.'

6 LXX 961: Barac basileôs Sodomôn (ΒΑΡΑΚΒΑϹΙΛΕΩϹϹΟΔΟΜΩΝ). Translation: Barac king of Sodomon

• Codex Alexandrinus: Balla basileôs Sodomôn (ΒΑΛΛΑΒΑϹΙΛΕΩϹϹΟΔΟΜΩΝ). Translation: Balla king of Sodomon

• LXX 17: Balak basileus Sodomôn (βαλλαk υασιλϬυς Cοδομοον). Translation: Balak king of Sodomon

• LXX 64: Bara basileus Sodomôn (βαρα υασιλⲅⲟⲟⲥ Cοδομοον). Translation: Bara king of Sodomon

• LXX 392: Balba basileôs Sodomôn (βαλυα υασιλⲅⲟⲟⲥ Cοδομοον). Translation: Balba king of Sodomon

• LXX 75: Bara basileôs Sodomôn (βαρα υασιλⲅⲟⲟⲥ Cοδομοον) Translation: Bara king of Sodomon

• LXX 18: Marla basileus Sodomôn (Μαρλα υασιλⲅⲟⲟⲥ Cοδομοον). Translation: Marla king of Sodomon

• LXX 120: Bara basileôs Sodômôn (βαρα υασιλⲅⲟⲟⲥ Cοδοομοον). Translation: Bara king of Sodômôn

• LXX 500: Barlam basileôs Sodomôn (βαρλαμ υασιλⲅⲟⲟⲥ Cοδομοον). Translation: Barlam king of Sodomon

• LXX 370: Barlak basileus Sodomôn (βαρλαλ υασιλϬυς Cοδομοον). Translation: Barlak king of Sodomon

• LXX 246: Bara basileus Sodomon (βαρα υασιλϬυς Cοδομον). Translation: Bara king of Sodomon

• LXX 54: Malak basileus Sodomôn (Μαλαλ υασιλϬυς Cοδομοον). Translation: Malak king of Sodomon

- LXX 527: Bala basileus Sodomôn (βαλα υΔσιλό̄υc cοΔομοον). Translation: Bala king of Sodomon

- Leningrad Codex: Bera melech Sedom (בֶּ֣רַע מֶ֣לֶךְ סְדֹ֔ם). Translation: Bera king of Sedom

- Peshitta: Brô mlkå dSdům (ܟܢܒ ܡܠܟܐ ܕܣܕܘܡ). Translation: Bro king of Sdum

- Targum Onkelos: Bera malka diSdom (בֶּרַע מַלְכָּא דִסְדֹם). Translation: Bera king of Sdom

- Targum Jerusalem: Bera de'ovedoy bevish malka diSdom (בֶּרַע דְעוֹבְדוֹי בְּבִישׁ מַלְכָּא דִסְדוֹם). Translation: Bera, the worker of evil, king of Sdom

- Sahidic manuscripts: Balak basileôs Sodomôn (Βαλακ βαcιλεγc Cοδομωn). Translation: Balak king of Sodomon

This city is most likely the city called Šurudum (𒋗𒊒𒁺𒌝), which Amar-Sin claimed to have destroyed in year six of his reign. The 𒋗 logogram represented both the ŠUR and SUR sounds, however the Canaanites did not have a letter in either the Ugaritic or Phoenician scripts representing either ŠUR or SUR, and therefore the R sound was probably not recognized within the name, resulting in the transliteration of Sdm (𐤎𐤃𐤌). The common Greek and Coptic represents an Aramaic plural form, indicating the word was Sdůmn (𐤎𐤃𐤅𐤌𐤍) in Aramaic, meaning 'Sodomites.

7 LXX 961: Barsa basileôs Gomorrhas (ΒΑΡCΑΒΑCΙΛΕШCΓΟΜΟΡΡΑC). Translation: Barsa king of Gomorrhas

- LXX 707: Barsa basileôs Gomoras (βαρσΔ υΔσιλ̄q∞c Γομοβλc). Translation: Barsa king of Gomoras

- LXX 730: Barsaba basileôs Gomorrhas (βΔβσΔυΔ υΔσιλq∞c Γομοββλc). Translation: Barsabaking of Gomorrhas

- LXX 370: Gabrabasileôs Gomorrhas (ΓΔβυΔ υΔσιλq∞c Γομοββλc). Translation: Gabra king of Gomorrhas

- LXX 799: Barga basileôs Gomorrhas (βΔβγΔ υΔσιλq∞c Γομοββλc). Translation: Bar-gaking of Gomorrhas

- LXX 53: Barsa basileôs Gomorrhas (βΔβσΔϭ υΔσιλq∞c Γομοββλc). Translation: Barsae king of Gomorrhas

- Leningrad Codex: Birsha melech Amorah (בִּרְשַׁע מֶ֣לֶךְ עֲמֹרָה). Translation: Birsha king Amourah

• Peshitta: Bršô mlkå dÔmůrå (ܐܘܡܘܪܐ ܡܠܟܐ ܒܪܫܘ). Translation: Brshow king of Omourah

• Targum Onkelos: Birsha malka da'Amorah (בִּרְשַׁע מַלְכָּא דַעֲמֹרָה). Translation: Birsha king of Amourah

• Targum Jerusalem: Birsha de'ovedoy birshi'a malka da'Amorah (בִּרְשַׁע דְעוֹבְדוֹי בִּרְשִׁיעָא מַלְכָּא דַעֲמוֹרָה). Translation: Birsha, the worker of evil, king of Amourah

Based on the Hebrew, Aramaic, and Syriac spelling, this city is most likely the city called Úḫnuru (𒌷𒄯𒉡) in the list of cities conquered by Amar-Sin, as a similar consonant shift between N and M took place in the word Sumer, which is represented as Šinôār / Sennaar earlier in the verse.

8 LXX 509: Sennaar basileôs Sadama (ⲥⲉⲛⲛⲁⲁⲣ ⲩⲁⲥⲓⲗⲧⲟⲟⲥ ⲥⲁⲁⲁⲙⲁ). Translation: Sennaar king of Sadama

• LXX 15: Sennaab basileôs Adama (ⲥⲉⲛⲛⲁⲁⲩ ⲩⲁⲥⲓⲗⲧⲟⲟⲥ ⲁⲁⲁⲙⲁ). Translation: Sennaab king of Adama

• LXX 64: Sennaar basileôs Adama (ⲥⲉⲛⲛⲁⲁⲣ ⲩⲁⲥⲓⲗⲧⲟⲟⲥ ⲁⲁⲁⲙⲁ). Translation: Sennaar king of Adama

• LXX 319: Sennaa basileôs Adama (ⲥⲉⲛⲛⲁⲁ ⲩⲁⲥⲓⲗⲧⲟⲟⲥ ⲁⲁⲁⲙⲁ). Translation: Sennaa king of Adama

• LXX 314: Sennar basileôs Adama (ⲥⲉⲛⲛⲁⲣ ⲩⲁⲥⲓⲗⲧⲟⲟⲥ ⲁⲁⲁⲙⲁ). Translation: Sennar king of Adama

• LXX 14: Senaar basileôs Adama (ⲥⲉⲛⲁⲁⲣ ⲩⲁⲥⲓⲗⲧⲟⲟⲥ ⲁⲁⲁⲙⲁ). Translation: Senaar king of Adama

• LXX 426: Sennaar basileôs Adana (ⲥⲉⲛⲛⲁⲁⲣ ⲩⲁⲥⲓⲗⲧⲟⲟⲥ ⲁⲁⲁⲛⲁ). Translation: Sennaar king of Adana

• LXX 54: Senagar basileôs Adama (ⲥⲉⲛⲁⲅⲁⲣ ⲩⲁⲥⲓⲗⲧⲟⲟⲥ ⲁⲁⲁⲙⲁ). Translation: Senagar king of Adama

• LXX 376: Ennaab basileôs Adama (ⲉⲛⲛⲁⲁⲩ ⲩⲁⲥⲓⲗⲧⲟⲟⲥ ⲁⲁⲁⲙⲁ). Translation: Ennaab king of Adama

• Leningrad Codex: Shin'av. Melech Admah (שִׁנְאָב ׀ מֶלֶךְ אַדְמָה). Translation: Shinaab king of Admah

- Peshitta: Šnåb mlkå dÅdmå (ܐܬܢܒ ܡܠܟܐ ܕܐܕܡܐ). Translation: Shnab king of Admah

- Targum Onkelos: Shin'av malka de'Admah (שִׁנְאָב מַלְכָּא דְאַדְמָה). Translation: Shinab king of Admah

- Targum Jerusalem: Shin'av da'afilu le'avoy havah shanei malka de'admah (שִׁנְאָב דַּאֲפִילוּ לְאָבוֹי הֲוָה שָׁנֵי מַלְכָּא דְאַדְמָה). Translation: Shinab, who even rejected his ancestors, king of Admah

- Bohairic manuscripts: Sanaar basileôs Adama (Ⲥⲁⲛⲁⲁⲣ ⲃⲁⲥⲓⲗⲉⲩⲥ ⲇⲁⲁⲙⲁ). Translation: Sanaar king of Adama

- Sahidic manuscripts: Senaar basileôs Adama (Ⲥⲉⲛⲁⲁⲣ ⲃⲁⲥⲓⲗⲉⲩⲥ ⲇⲁⲁⲙⲁ). Translation: Senaar king of Adama

This city is not listed as one of the five cities destroyed by Amar-Sin in his 6th and 7th years, instead the name Íabru ($\Psi \rightleftarrows \Sigma$) is used for the fifth city. The term ådmh (אדמה), is an unlikely name for a city, as it was the Amorite, Hurrian, and Edomite word for 'land,' and/or the 'earth goddess,' suggesting that either the name of the city was replaced with the word 'land,' or was never in the original Israelite version of the story, in which case Sennaar / Shinaab was being referred to as the king of 'the land.'

The city of Íabru ($\Psi \rightleftarrows \Sigma$), which Amar-Sin destroyed circa 2000 BC, may be the same place as the 'ruin of the Hebrews' (העברים בעיי) that Moses led the Israelites to in Masoretic Numbers. This name was rendered as Achelgae (Αχελγαι) in the Septuagint's Numbers, and so it is not clear if the term was originally in Numbers and redacted by the Aramaic translator, or if an older term was replaced by the Hasmonean translators, however, it is unlikely the Hasomeans would have added the 'ruin of the Hebrews,' as it seems incongruous with the rest of the narrative. Moreover the beginning of the Greek name does appear to be a transliteration of Hôy (העי), which was transliterated as Aggai (Αγγαι) when it was a separate word.

This suggests that the Aramaic text the Greeks translated used the name Hôy Ôlgy ($^\wedge \Lambda \mathcal{L}^\upsilon \, ^{\wedge \upsilon} \eta$), meaning 'ruins of Ôlgy.' This appears to have resulted from a transcription error when translating the Phoenician script Hôy Ôbry (𐤆𐤀𐤔𐤏 𐤆𐤏𐤀), however it is difficult to imagine how the translator mistranscribed 'Hebrew,' suggesting it was an intentional alteration. However the name was spelled, the ruins were described as being in the desert to the east of Moab, in eastern modern Jordan, which is likely along Amar-Sin's route from Ur.

As the earliest records of the Ḫabiru ($\natural\natural \rightleftarrows \natural \triangleright \Sigma$) were from around 300 years after Amar-Sin attacked Íabru ($\Psi \rightleftarrows \Sigma$), it is plausible that Íabru was the ancestral homeland of the Ḫabiru, somewhere in the desert of eastern modern Jordan. It would have been impossible to translate Íabru ($\Psi \rightleftarrows \Sigma$) into Egyptian without rendering the name Ôprù

(𓀀 𓃾), which was the Egyptian form of Habiru, however, referred to slaves from Edom, making the city's name the Egyptian equivalent of 'Slave.' As both the Greek and Hebrew translations used the name Adama, the original substitution of Adama for Íabru, probably took place in the Egyptian translation, with the name Iduma (𓈙𓏏𓂋𓈖𓏤) replacing Íabru (𐤅𐤌𐤋Σ). This would have replaced the word 'slave' with the name of the land the slaves were from in the Egyptian translation. As both the Septuagint and Masoretic Text used the name Adama, that name is used in this translation, regardless of the name of the city in the records of Amur-Sin.

9 LXX 64: Symobor basileôs Sebôim (ⲥⲩⲙⲟⲩⲟⲃ ⲩⲁⲥⲓⲗⲧⲟⲟⲥ Ⲥⲟⲩⲟⲟⲓⲙ). Translation: Symobor king of Seboim

• LXX 707: Barsa basileôs Gomoras (ⲥⲩⲙⲙⲩⲃ ⲩⲁⲥⲓⲗⲧⲟⲟⲥ Ⲥⲟⲩⲟⲟⲓⲙ). Translation: Symbyr basileôs Sebôim. Translation: Symbyr king of Seboim

• LXX 319: Symôr basileôs Seboen (ⲥⲩⲙⲟⲟⲃ ⲩⲁⲥⲓⲗⲧⲟⲟⲥ Ⲥⲟⲩⲟⲟⲓⲛ). Translation: Symor king of Seboen

• LXX 343: Oymobor basileôs Sebboem (Ⲟⲩⲙⲟⲩⲟⲃ ⲩⲁⲥⲓⲗⲧⲟⲟⲥ Ⲥⲟⲩⲙⲟⲓⲙ). Translation: Oymobor king of Sebboem

• LXX 344: Oymobor basileôs Sebôim (ⲥⲩⲙⲟⲃ ⲩⲁⲥⲓⲗⲧⲟⲟⲥ Ⲥⲟⲩⲟⲟⲓⲙ). Translation: Oymobor king of Seboim

• LXX 426: Symobor basileôs Seboêm (ⲥⲩⲙⲟⲩⲟⲃ ⲩⲁⲥⲓⲗⲧⲟⲟⲥ Ⲥⲟⲩⲟⲗⲙ). Translation: Symobor king of Seboêm

• LXX 75: Symobor basileôs Sebônim (ⲥⲩⲙⲟⲩⲟⲃ ⲩⲁⲥⲓⲗⲧⲟⲟⲥ Ⲥⲟⲩⲟⲟⲛⲟⲓⲙ). Translation: Symobor king of Sebonim

• LXX 422: Symobôr basileôs Sebôim (ⲥⲩⲙⲟⲩⲟⲟⲃ ⲩⲁⲥⲓⲗⲧⲟⲟⲥ Ⲥⲟⲩⲟⲟⲓⲙ). Translation: Symobôr king of Seboim

• LXX 458: Symobor basileôs Sebonim (ⲥⲩⲙⲟⲩⲟⲃ ⲩⲁⲥⲓⲗⲧⲟⲟⲥ Ⲥⲟⲩⲟⲛⲟⲓⲙ). Translation: Symobôr king of Sebonim

• LXX 71: Symeôn basileus Seboem (ⲥⲩⲙⲥⲟⲟⲛ ⲩⲁⲥⲓⲗⲥⲩⲥ Ⲥⲟⲩⲟⲥⲓⲙ). Translation: Symeon king of Seboem

• LXX 72: Sybôr basileus Seboên (ⲥⲩⲩⲟⲟⲃ ⲩⲁⲥⲓⲗⲥⲩⲥ Ⲥⲟⲩⲟⲗⲛ). Translation: Sybor king of Seboen

- LXX 76: Symobor basileus Seboem (Cυμοιωοβ uλσιλόνc cόuοιμ). Translation: Symobor king of Seboen

- LXX 108: Simor basileôs Sebôim (Cιμοβ uλσιλσ⁻οoc cόuοιμ). Translation: Simor king of Seboim

- LXX 664: Symmobor basileôs Sebôim (Cυμμοιωοβ uλσιλσ⁻οoc cόuοιμ). Translation: Symmobor king of Seboim

- Leningrad Codex: Shem'ever melech Tzevoyim K [Tzevovyim Q] (שְׁמְאֶבֶר מֶלֶךְ צְבֹיִים כ [צְבוֹיִים ק]). Translation: Shemeber king of Seboyim (K) [Seboyim (Q)]

- Peshitta: Šmåyr mlkå dSbůåym (ܘܫܡܐܝܪ ܡܠܟܐ ܕܨܒܘܐܝܡ). Translation: Shmayr king of Sbuaym

- Targum Onkelos: Shem'ever malka diTzvoyim (שְׁמְאֶבֶר מַלְכָּא דִצְבוֹיִם). Translation: Shemeber king of Sboyim

- Targum Jerusalem: Shem'ever dimchabbel eivreih lizneih malka diTzvoyim (שְׁמְאֶבֶר דִמְחַבֵּל אֵיבְרֵיה לִיזְנֵיה מַלְכָּא דִצְבוֹיִם). Translation: Shemeber, attacker (or terrorizer) of Ebereh (or crossers, Eberites, Hebrew, Habirus, Íabrus) who wandered, king of Sboyim

- Bohairic manuscripts: Sunobor basileôs Sebôim (Cүnoвор вαcιλεүc Ceвшıм). Translation: Sunobor king of Seboim

- Sahidic manuscripts: Semobor basileôs Seboem (Ceмoвор вαcιλεүc Ceвoeм). Translation: Semobor king of Seboem

If Sebôim / Sbyym was one of the five unknown cities attacked by Amar-Sin in his final two years, it was likely the city known as Bitum-Rabium (𒂍 𒂷𒊏). This name appear to be the Akkadian spelling of a Canaanite name Bt Rbm (𐤁𐤕 𐤓𐤁𐤌), meaning 'Great House.' Bitum (𒂍) was the Akkadian Cuneiform spelling of the Canaanite word bt (𒂍 / 𐤁𐤕), which meant 'house,' 'temple,' or 'palace,' depending on context, and continues to be the Hebrew word báyit (בַּיִת) and Arabic bayt (بَيْت). During the Egyptian rule of Canaan it was spelled as båyt (𓉐𓏭𓏭𓉐). Rbm (𐤓𐤁𐤌) was a Canaanite word, documented in the Ammonite and Phoenician dialects, but not in Eastern Semitic languages, were the parallel term was rapāšum (𒊏𒉺𒀸𒌝), indicating that the city that Amar-Sin attacked was somewhere in Canaan east of the Jordan, as Egypt controlled west of the Jordan.

Due to the fact that Egyptians represented the 'R' and 'L' sounds using the same glyphs, it would have been impossible to translate Bitum-Rabium (𒂍 𒂷𒊏) into Egyptian without rendering the name as Båyt Rbů (𓏭𓉐 𓂋𓃀), meaning 'House of the Libyans,' a geographical impossibility. Therefore, it appears that the Egyptian translators substituted a term often used for Canaanites: Sbiů (𓃀𓈖𓇋𓃀), meaning 'rebels,' making the name Bâyt Sbiŭ (𒁹𒋲𒌋𒁺 𒁹𒌋𒊏), meaning 'House of the Rebels.'

The term Bâyt was probably also dropped before the name was translated back into cuneiform, as campaigns to suppress the Sbiŭ were common during the New Kingdom era. This would have left the Middle Babylonian cuneiform translator with the word Sbiŭ, the plural of Sbj to transliterate back into Canaanite, resulting in Szebiim (𒐊𒁹𒁹𒊏𒆷—), which was later translated into Canaanite as Sbyym (𐤑𐤁𐤉𐤉𐤌) in the early iron age. Given the other parallels between the campaigns of the King of Ur Amar-Sin, and this king of Sumer Amarpel, the older name is restored from the records of Amar-Sin throughout Cosmic Genesis as Bet Rabim.

10 Berlin Genesis (LXX 911): basileôs Bala autê estin Sêgôr (ΒΑϹΙΛΕѠϹΒΑΛΛΑΥΤΗ ΕϹΤΙΝϹΗΓѠΡ). Translation: King Bala this is Segor.

- LXX 15: basileôs Bala hautê estin Sigôr (μλσιλq·οος βλλλ λυτλ ϭοτιν Cιγοοβ). Translation: King Bala this is Sigor.

- LXX 25: basileôs Sala hautê estin Sêgôr (μλσιλq·οος Cλλλ λυτλ ϭοτιν Cλγοοβ). Translation: King Sala this is Segor.

- LXX 343: basileôs Balaac hautê estin Sitôr (μλσιλq·οος βλλλλι λυτλ ϭοτιν Cιτοοβ). Translation: King Balaac this is Sitor

- LXX 79: basileôs Bala hautê estin Sêgor (μλσιλϭοος βλλλ λυτλ ϭοτιν Cλγοβ). Translation: King Bala this is Segor

- LXX 53: basileôs Sabak hautê estin Sêgôr (μλσιλq·οος Cλμλι λυτλ ϭοτιν Cλγοοβ). Translation: King Sabak this is Segor.

- Leningrad Codex: melech Bela hi-Tzo'ar (מֶלֶךְ בֶּלַע הִיא־צֹעַר). Translation: King Bela it-Soar

- Peshitta: mlkå dBlô hy hy Sôr (ܡܠܟܐ ܕܒܠܥ ܗܝ ,ܗܝ ܨܥܪ). Translation: king the Blow it is Sor

- Targum Onkelos: malka deVela hi Tzo'ar (מַלְכָּא דְבֶלַע הִיא צֹעַר). Translation: king of Belait's Soar

- Targum Jerusalem: malka dekarta divla'at dayraha hi zo'ar (מַלְכָּא דְקַרְתָּא דִּבְלָעַת דַּיְירָהָא הִיא זֹעַר). Translation: king of the city of Blaatthe archer (or shooter, thrower) it's Zoar

This city appears to be the city called Šaszíru (𒂠𒊓𒅗𒊏), which Amar-Sin claimed to have destroyed in year six of his reign. The name appears to have been transliterated directly into Egyptian hieratic, and then transliterated incorrectly when the text was restored to Canaan during the New Kingdom era as Šuszíru (𒂅𒈬𒌅𒀭Σ), which was then transliterated into the confusing 'it's Sor' (הִיא צֹער), as hyå (הִיא) was the Hebrew translation of the Middle Babylonian term šū (𒂅𒈬). Based on the Hebrew and Greek translations of 'it's Sôr / Sêgôr,' the city is a generally accepted as being the Edomite city known as Sôr / Sêgôr / Zoara, from the classical era.

Significant archaeological digs have been undertaken in at the ruins of the city since the 1970s, however, to date only iron age or more recent artifacts have been found, suggesting that Šasíru was not Sôr. Given the other parallels between the campaigns of the King of Ur Amar-Sin, and this king of Sumer Amarpel, the older name is restored from the records of Amar-Sin throughout Cosmic Genesis as Shasziru for both 'it's Sêgôr' and Sêgôr, as Sêgôr / Sôr would have to be an update to whatever was in the text in the interpretation were 'it's Sêgôr' is a scribal note.

11 Codex Alexandrinus: tô triscaedecatô eti (ΤѠΤΡΙΣΚΑΙΔΕΚΑΤѠΕΤΕΙ). Translation: the thirteenth year

• Leningrad Codex: ushelosh esreh shanah (וּשְׁלֹשׁ עֶשְׂרֵה שָׁנָה). Translation: for thirteen years

• Samaritan Torah: ûbšlš ôšrh šgh (ᎯᎨᏇ ᎯᎬᏇᎾ Ꮗ፝ᏇᏇᎯᎢ). Translation: and in thirteenth year

• Peshitta: ûbdtlt ôšrå šnyn (ܫܢܝܢ ܟܡܐܐ ܕܬܠܬܐ܂). Translation: and in thirteenth year

• Targum Onkelos: utelat asrei shenin (וּתְלָת עֲשְׂרֵי שְׁנִין). Translation: and for thirteen years

• Targum Jerusalem: uvitlasrei shenin maradu (וּבְתְלָסְרֵי שְׁנִין מָרְדוּ). Translation: and for thirteen years (or ages, eras)

Amar-Sin, the King of the Four Regions, claimed he conquered or destroyed four similarly named cities in his sixth and seventh regal years, before dying in his ninth regal year. His successor Shu-Sin then ruled for nine years, meaning that the rebellion, if in the thirteenth year, would have been in the first year of the following king's reign: Ibbi-Sin, who was the last king of the Neo-Sumerian Empire. During Ibbi-Sin's reign, the Amorites revolted from his rule in Canaan, and after he was unable to reconquer them, Elam and other regions revolted, leading to the collapse of the Neo-Sumerian empire.

According to Cosmic Genesis / Bereshít, the Amorites were ruling parts of Syria and Canaan at the time, north and east of the Egyptian controlled regions, and appear to have been allied to Egypt, based on Abram's position as a judge of the Amorites, and his being the Egyptian king's brother-in-law. The difference between the Hebrew version, and the Greek, Syriac, and Samaritan versions is generally viewed by non-Jewish academics as a translation error within the Masoretic text, which must have happened after the Aramaic translation was made, presumably when the text was standardized in the Aramaic 'Hebrew' script under the Hasmonean dynasty. An alternate interpretation is that the Hebrew version is older, and the alternate wording found in the Greek, Syriac, and Samaritan versions originated in Hezekiah's Aramaic translation of the Torah.

12 Codex Alexandrinus: ethnê ischyra ama autoes (ϵϴNHICXYPAAMAAYTOIC). Translation: nation (or tribe) strong (or Ischyra) together with them

- LXX 392: ethnê ischyrotera hama autoes (ϵϴνϞ ισχυϟοτόϟϪ ϪμϪ Ϫυτοιc). Translation: nation (or tribe) powerful together with them.

- Leningrad Codex: hazZuzim beham (הַזּוּזִים בְּהָם). Translation: the Zuzes among

- Peshitta: ůlôšynådbhyn (ܘܠܐܫܝܢܐ ܕܒܗܘܢ). Translation: and the Oshyna of them

- Targum Onkelos: veyat takkifayya divhemta (וְיָת תַּקִּיפַיָּא דִּבְהֶמְתָּא). Translation: and the assaulters among them

- Targum Jerusalem: veyat takifaya divhemta (וְיָת תַּקִּיפַיָא דִּבְהֶמְתָּא). Translation: and the assaulters among them

The Masoretic term appears to be a reference to the people from the town of Shasziru (𒂼𒈨𒌓𒍢𒊏) which Amar-Sin reported destroying in his 6th year. The Greek translators or their Aramaic precursors appear to have not understood the reference, as the Greek phrase is not related. Based on the general usage for the word ischyros (ἰσχῡρός) in the Septuagint, as a translation of the name El found in the Masoretic Text, it appears that the Aramaic text read 'nation of El,' which probably seemed anachronistic to the Greek translators, resulting in the substitution. As the Shaszi have already been mentioned in the text as one of the peoples involved in the war, the name Zûzîm is imported from the Masoretic Text, and normalized to Shaszi based on the Akkadian spelling of the name.

13 Yale Genesis: Sommaeous (COMMAIOYC)

- Codex Alexandrinus: Somaeous (COMAIOYC)

- LXX 15: Sêmm (CϞμμ)

- LXX 55: Sonaeous (CONϪιουc)

- LXX 64: Ommaeous (ΟμμϪϕουc)

- LXX 707: Symeous (Cυμϟουc)

- LXX 319: Sômaeous (Cooμⲇⲓⲟⲩⲥ)

- LXX 343: Omoeous (Oμⲟⲓⲟⲩⲥ)

- LXX 130: Amm (ⲁμμ)

- LXX 71: Someous (Ⲥⲟμⳓⲟⲩⲥ)

- LXX 314: Ommeous (Oμμⳓⲟⲩⲥ)

- LXX 551: Ompsaeous (Oμⲯⲇⲓⲟⲩⲥ)

- LXX 799: Ômmeous (ⲱμμⳓⲟⲩⲥ)

- LXX 53: Oimm (Oⲓμμ)

- LXX 376: Sêmaeous (Ⲥⳑμⲇⲓⲟⲩⲥ)

- LXX 59: Sômmaeous (Cooμμⲇⲓⲟⲩⲥ)

- Leningrad Codex: eimim (אֵימִים). Translation: terrors

- Peshitta: åmnå (ܐܡܢܐ). Translation: evil

- Targum Onkelos: Eimtanei (אֵימְתָנֵי)

- Fragment Targums: Emetanayan (אֶמְתָנַיָאן)

- Targum Jerusalem: Eimtanei (אֵימְתָנֵי)

- Bohairic manuscripts: Someos (Ⲥⲟⲙⲉⲟⲥ)

As the Greek term was a transliteration of the term used in the Masoretic Text, the Masoretic term is translated here. Based on the rest of the differences between the translations, the word Êmîm, may have originated in the name of the people from the town of Úḫnuru (𒌑𒄷𒉡𒉌𒌷) which Amar-Sin reported destroying in his 7th year. Uru (𒌷) meant 'city,' and therefore, the people from the city would have been the Úḫnim. As the name Úḫnuru ultimately became the Hebrew Ômrh (עמרה) and Greek Gomorrhas (Γομορρας), the English name of the people would be the Gomorrhans.

14 Codex Alexandrinus: Chordaeous (ⲭⲟⲣⲇⲁⲓⲟⲩⲥ)

- LXX 55: Chôrrhaeous (ⲭⲟⲟⲣⲣⲇⲓⲟⲩⲥ)

- LXX 64: Chorrhaeous (ⲭⲟⲣⲣⲇⲫⲟⲩⲥ)

- LXX 343: Charrhaeous (ⲭⲇⲣⲣⲇⲓⲟⲩⲥ)

- LXX 400: Choraeous (χοβΔιουϲ)

- LXX 72: Chorrheous (χοββϬουϲ)

- LXX 77: Orrhaeous (ΟββΔιουϲ)

- LXX 799: Chôreous (χ∞βϬουϲ)

- LXX 31: Choraeas (χοβΔιΔϲ)

- LXX 59: Chôraeous (χ∞βΔιουϲ)

- Leningrad Codex: Chori (חֹרִי)

- Peshitta Manuscript 5b1: Hůå (ܟܘ)

- Peshitta Manuscript 7a1: Hůrnå (ܣܢܝܟ)

- Targum Onkelos: Chora'ei (חוֹרָאֵי)

- Fragment Targums: Chorava'ei (חוֹרְוָאֵי)

- Targum Jerusalem: Chora'ei (חוֹרָאֵי)

These appear to be the people the Egyptians called the Hårů (𓉗𓄿𓂋𓅱), which are known as the Hurrians in modern history books. The Hurrians were an ancient people in the Middle East, known as Harru (𒄯𒌋) in Akkadian Cuneiform, native to Northern Iraq, Syria, and eastern Turkey before the Semitic and Persian tribes migrated into the region. While they appear to have become a slave race for centuries under the rule of the Old Babylonian and Old Assyrian kingdoms, they became the dominant ethnic group of the Mitanni Empire between 1600 and 1300 BC, after being freed by the Indo-Aryan Mitanni.

The variations found in Peshitta Manuscripts 5b1, from the 5th century, and 7a1, from the 7th century, are generally interpreted as part of the ongoing work to synchronize the Peshitta with the Masoretic Text. The term Hůå (ܟܘ), used in 5b1, is the Syriac translation of 'Mitanni' (Ευαιον / חֲוִילָה), while Hůrnå (ܣܢܝܟ), used in 7a1 is the Syriac translation of 'Hurrian' (Χορραίους / חֹרִי). See note 44 in Cosmic Genesis: Chapter 10 for more information. Comparisons between the Septuagint and Masoretic Text show the terms were used interchangeably in the Aramaic source text for the Septuagint, and the existence of the deviation from both the Greek and Hebrew in 5b1 suggests that the Peshitta was also based an older Aramaic text.

15 Codex Alexandrinus: archontas (ᴀⲢⲬⲟⲚⲦⲀⳅ). Translation: archons (or princes, rulers)

- Leningrad Codex: sedeh (שָׂדֶה). Translation: field

- Peshitta: ršnå (ܪ̈ܫܢܐ). Translation: rulers (or chiefs)

- Targum Onkelos: chakal (חֲקַל). Translation: field

- Targum Jerusalem: chaklei (חַקְלִי). Translation: field

16 Berlin Genesis: basilea elasar oe tesgar (ᴃᴀⳉⳒⲉᴀⲉᴧᴧⳅᴀⲢⲟⳓⲦⲉⳅⳓᴀⲢ). Translation: king Elasar the Tesgar

- Codex Alexandrinus: basilea Elasar oe tessares (ᴃᴀⳉⳒⲉᴀⲉᴧᴧⳅᴀⲢⲟⳓⲦⲉⳅⳅᴀⲢⲉⳅ). Translation: king Elasar the four

- LXX 64: basilea Ellasar hoe tessares (ⳓᴧⲟⳉⳋᴧ Ⲉᴧᴧᴧⲟᴧᶄ ⲟⳓ ⲧⳍⲟⲟᴧᶋⳍⳓ). Translation: king Ellasar the four

- LXX 318: basilea Sellasar hoe tessares (ⳓᴧⲟⳉⳋᴧ Ⳍⲟᴧᴧᴧⲟᴧᶄ ⲟⳓ ⲧⳍⲟⲟᴧᶋⳍⳓ). Translation: king Sellasar the four

- LXX 707: basilea Ellasar hoe tessares (ⳓᴧⲟⳉⳋᴧ Ⲉᴧᴧᴧⲟᴧⳅ ⲟⳓ ⲧⳍⲟⲟᴧᶋⳍⳓ). Translation: king Ellasar the four

- LXX 343: basilea Selasar hoe tessares (ⳓᴧⲟⳉⳋᴧ Ⳍⲟᴧᴧⲟᴧᶄ ⲟⳓ ⲧⳍⲟⲟᴧᶋⳍⳓ). Translation: king Selasar the four

- LXX 426: basilea Lasar hoe tessares (ⳓᴧⲟⳉⳋᴧ ᴧᴧⲟᴧᶄ ⲟⳓ ⲧⳍⲟⲟᴧᶋⳍⳓ). Translation: king Lasar the four

- LXX 19: basilea Elasar hoe tessares (ⳓᴧⲟⳉⳋᴧ Ⲉᴧᴧᴧⲟᴧᶄ ⳓᴧⳓ ⲟⳓ ⲧⳍⲟⲟᴧᶋⳍⳓ). Translation: king Elasar and the four

- LXX 799: basilea Elasôr hoe tessares (ⳓᴧⲟⳉⳋᴧ Ⲉᴧᴧⲟⲟⲟᶄ ⲟⳓ ⲧⳍⲟⲟᴧᶋⳍⳓ). Translation: king Elasor the four

- Leningrad Codex: melech ellasar arba'ah (מֶלֶךְ אֶלָּסָר אַרְבָּעָה). Translation: king Ellasar four

- Peshitta: mlkå ddlsr årbôå mlkyn (ܡܠܟܐ ܕܕܠܣܪ ܐܪܒܥܐ ܡܠܟܝܢ). Translation: king of Dlsr four kings

- Targum Onkelos: malka de'ellasar arbe'ah (מַלְכָּא דְּאֶלָּסָר אַרְבְּעָה). Translation: king of Ellasar four

• Fragment Targums: malka de'elasar arba (מַלְכָּא דְאֶלְסָר אַרְבַּע). Translation: king of Elasar four

• Targum Jerusalem: malka ditlasar arba'at (מַלְכָּא דְתְלָסָר אַרְבַּעַת). Translation: king of Tlasar four

This phrase appears to be a transliteration of the Neo-Sumerian title lugal an kišurra arbaim (𒈗 𒀭 𒆧𒊏 𒐏𒁾𒀀), meaning 'king of everything under the sky in the four (lands).' If this was the origin of the phrase, it would have to have been translated into Egyptian before being translated back into Canaanite in order to transition from kišurra to ellāsār. As the phrase fell out of common use after the fall of the Neo-Sumerian empire, it indicates the original text must have been written sometime between approximately 2330 and 2000 BC.

17 Codex Alexandrinus: Abram tô peratê (ΑΒΡΑΜΤΩΠΕΡΑΤΗ). Possible translations: Abram the end, Abram then at extremity, Abram then in the courthouse (via Egyptian)

• Leningrad Codex: Avram ha'Ivri (אַבְרָם הָעִבְרִי). Translation: Abram the Hebrew (or Eberite, crosser)

• Peshitta: Åbrm ôbryå (ܐܒܪܡ ܥܒܪܝܐ). Translation: Abram crosser (or Eberite)

• Targum Onkelos: Avram ivra'ah (אַבְרָם עִבְרָאָה). Translation: Abram ferryman (or crosser, wrathful)

• Targum Jerusalem: Avram ivra (אַבְרָם עִיבְרָא). Translation: Abram ferryman (or crosser, wrathful)

The differences between the word Hebrew and Perate cannot be accounted for by a transliteration error. The term found in the Masoretic Text is the word meaning 'Hebrew,' referring to either an individual Hebrew or the Hebrew language. The Aramaic version of the word is identical ôbry (עֵבְרַי), however, meant both 'Hebrew' and 'Aramean' or 'Aramaic.' The Greek term peratê is more obscure. It could be interpreted as a variation on the Attican Greek dialect's perate (περατε), meaning 'end,' or 'extremity,' however, this interpretation does not fit the context, and like the Hebrew translation, the term is treated as a proper name. The term is a Middle Egyptian word per-ôâti (𓉐𓂋𓄿𓏏) for 'courthouse' in the Heliopolite dialect, however, meant 'house of lepers' or 'hospital' in other Egyptian dialects. The two variations were based on the name of the goddess Ôâti (𓄿), whose name meant 'leper' but was the judge of the dead in the Heliopolite theology.

The Heliopolite dialect was the official dialect of Egypt during the late Middle Kingdoms Canaanite dynasty, when the capital was in Iûnû (𓉺𓊖), as well as during the subsequent Canaanite dynasty, when the city was mentioned in Genesis and Exodus as

On (Ὠν) and Ȧûn (אֹן), and was later renamed Heliopolis by the Greeks (Ἡλίου πόλις). During the subsequent Hyksos dynasty, the capital was moved to Avaris, and then the New Kingdom's capital was in Thebes, meaning that the term has to be an artifact of a Middle Egyptian book of Abram or Israel, predating the Hyksos Dynasty. While the Heliopolite dialect's 'courthouse' makes more sense than Abram judging from a hospital, it is likely that the Akkadian Cuneiform translators did not know the Heliopolite dialect, and did not want to write that Abram was living in a house of lepers, and so simply transliterated the word. The substitution of 'the Hebrew' in the Masoretic text appears to be part of the Hasmonean redaction of circa 140 BC, when the Judahite dialect of Canaanite became the 'Hebrew' language.

18 Cotton Genesis: tê drui tê Mambrê o Amorrhis (ΤΗΔΡΥΙΤΗΜΔΜΒΡΗΟΔΜΟΡΡΙϹ). Translation: the oak the Mambre the Amorrhis

• LXX 509: tê drui tê Mambrê o Amoris (Τλ Δβυι Τλ Μδμμβλ ο Δμοβιϲ). Translation: the oak the Mambre the Amorite

• LXX 55: tê drui tê Mambrê ho Olmoris (Τλ Δβυι Τλ Μδμμβλ ο Ολμοβιϲ). Translation: the oak the Mambre the Olmoris

• LXX 127: tê drui tê Mabrê o Amoris (Τλ Δβυι Τλ Μδμβλ ο Δμοβιϲ). Translation: the oak the Mabre the Amorite

• LXX 707: tê drui tê Mabri o Gauros (Τλ Δβυι Τλ Μδμβι ο Γδυβοϲ). Translation: the oak the Mabri the Gauros

• LXX 313: tê drui tê Mambrên o Amoris (Τλ Δβυι Τλ Μδμμβι ο Δμοβιϲ). Translation: the oak the Mambren the Amorite

• LXX 426: tên dryn tên Mambrên ho Omoros (Τλν Δβυν Τλν Μδμμβλν ο Ομοβοϲ). Translation: the oak the Mambrên the Omoros

• LXX 19: tê drui tê Mambrê o Ammôr (Τλ Δβυι Τλ Μδμμλ ο Δμμοοβ). Translation: the oak the Mambre the Ammor

• LXX 82: tê drui tê Maurê ho Omoros (Τλ Δβυι Τλ Μδυβλ ο Ομοβοϲ). Translation: the oak the Maurethe Omoros

• LXX 458: tê drui tê Mambrê ho Amôris (Τλ Δβυι Τλ Μδμμβλ ο Δμοοβιϲ). Translation: the oak the Mambre the Amorite

• LXX 246: tê drui tê Mambrê o Amoris (Τλ Δβυι Τλ Μδμμλ ο Δμοβιϲ). Translation: the oak the Mambre the Amorite

- LXX 46: tê drui tê Mambrê ho Omôris (τﾚ ᴁﾚuι τﾚ Mᴀﾚﾟﾟﾟﾟﾟﾟﾟﾟﾟ o Oﾟﾟﾟﾟﾟﾟﾟﾟﾟﾟﾟ). Translation: the oak the Mambrethe Omoris

- LXX 72: tê drui tê Mambrê ho Gambros (τﾚ ᴁﾚuι τﾚ Mᴀﾚﾟﾟﾟﾟﾟﾟﾟﾟﾟ o Γᴀﾟﾟﾟﾟﾟﾟﾟﾟﾟﾟoc). Translation: the oak the Mambre the Gambros

- LXX 108: tê drui tê Mambrê ho Amôr (τﾚ ᴁﾚuι τﾚ Mᴀﾚﾟﾟﾟﾟﾟﾟﾟﾟﾟ o ᴧﾟﾟﾟﾟﾟ). Translation: the oak the Mambre the Amor

- LXX 314: tê drui tê Mambrê ho Ammor (τﾚ ᴁﾚuι τﾚ Mᴀﾚﾟﾟﾟﾟﾟﾟﾟﾟﾟ o ᴧﾟﾟﾟﾟﾟ). Translation: the oak the Mambre the Ammor

- LXX 799: tên dryn tên Maurên ho Ammoris (τﾚN ᴁﾚuN τﾚN MᴀuﾟﾟﾟﾟﾟﾟN o ᴧﾟﾟﾟﾟﾟﾟﾟﾟc). Translation: the oak the Maurên the Amorite

- Leningrad Codex: be'Elonei Mamre ha'emori (בְּאֵלֹנֵי מַמְרֵא הָאֱמֹרִי). Translation: at Elone for Mrea the speaker

- Peshitta: blůtå dmmrå åmůryå (ܒܠܘܛܐ ܕܡܡܪܐ ܐܡܘܪܝܐ). Translation: oak (or acorn) for Mmrå the speaker

- Targum Onkelos: bemeishrei Mamre Emora'ah (בְּמֵישְׁרֵי מַמְרֵא אֱמֹורָאָה). Translation: plains of Mamre the Amorite

- Targum Jerusalem: bechezvei Mamre Emora'ah (בְּחֶזְוֵי מַמְרֵא אֱמֹורָאָה). Translation: insight of Mamre the Amorite

The Greek and Hebrew translations are noticeably different, however, both include Aramaic loanwords or transliterations. The word the Greeks translated as 'oak' should have been åylnå (ܐܝܠܢܐ), however, that was neither translated nor transliterated into Hebrew, instead, the similar word ålny (אלני), was used. The Hebrew spelling of oak is ålůn (אלון), and therefore, the word in the Masoretic Text is neither Hebrew nor Aramaic, suggesting a proper name in another dialect. The Greek term 'Mambre the Amoris' appears to be a transliteration of the same terms found in the Masoretic Text as mmrå håmry (ממרא האמרי), which is a transliteration of the Aramaic term 'for the lord of the Amorites.' Along with the rest of the sentence regarding 'oak's' brothers, it indicates that the Aramaic text was about 'Elon, Lord of the Amorites.'

19 Codex Alexandrinus: theô tô ypsistô (ΘΕΩΤΩΥΨΙϹΤΩ). Translation: god the highest

- LXX 458: theô tô hypsistô (θεω του υψιστου). Translation: god the highest

- Leningrad Codex: El elyovn (אֵל עֶלְיֹון). Translation: god highest

- Peshitta: ålhå mrymå (ܐܠܗܐ ܡܪܝܡܐ). Translation: god of Miriam

- Targum Onkelos: El illa'ah (אֵל עִלָּאָה). Translation: god ascended

- Targum Jerusalem: Elaha ila'ah (אֱלָהָא עִילָאָה). Translation: god highest

The Greek term Highest God (θεω τω υψιστω) shows up several Second Temple Era Jewish texts, including 1ˢᵗ Ezra, Judith, 3ʳᵈ Maccabees, Psalms, and the Wisdom of Joshua ben Sira. Most of these texts were not redacted during the Hasmonean period and were not copied by the Masorites, however, Psalms does appear to have been redacted, as the Masoretic version has the term Yehvah Elyom which strongly supports the Hasmonean redactors as having replaced El with Yehvah. The term El Elyon is known to have been a major god of the Canaanites, called ål ůålyn in the Sefire Treaty from circa 750 BC. The quotes of Sanchuniathon's writing that have survived to the present, from circa 1200 BC, referred to the god called Elioun as the primordial creator-god of the Canaanites. Jews, Christians, Muslims, and non-religious historians and archaeologists all consider Elyon (highest) to be an epithet and not a proper name.

Cosmic Genesis: Chapter 15

After these things the word of the Lord came to Abram in a vision, saying, "Don't be afraid Abram, I shield you, and your reward will be very great."

Abram said, "Master,[1] what will you give me? Whereas I am departing without a child, except the son of Masek my home-born female slave, this Eliezer of Damascus."

Abram said, "I am sad because you have given me no descendant, but my home-born will succeed me."

Immediately there was a voice of the Lord to him, saying, "This will not be your heir, but he that will come out of you will be your heir."

He took him out and said, "Look up to the sky, and count the stars, if you will be able to count them fully," and he said, "So will your descendants be."

Abram believed God,[2] and it was counted as righteousness for him. He said to him, "I am the god who led you out of the land of the Chaldeans, to give you this land to inherit."

He asked, "Despot, how will I know that I will inherit it?"

He answered him, "Take for me a heifer in her third year, and a female-goat in her third year, and a ram in his third year, a dove and a pigeon." So he took to him all these, and divided them in the middle, and set them opposite to each other, but the birds he did not divide. Birds came down on the bodies, even on the divided parts of them, and Abram drove them away. About sunset, a trance fell on Abram, and Look! A great gloomy terror fell on him.

It was said to Abram, "You will surely know that your descendants will be travelers in a land not their own, and they will enslave them, and afflict them, and humble them four hundred years. The nation whom they will serve, I will judge, and after this, they will come out here with much property. But you will depart to your fathers in peace, nourished in a good old age. In the fourth generation, they will return here, for the sins of the Amorites are not yet completed, even until now."

When the sun was about to set, there was a flame, and a smoking furnace and lamps of fire, which passed between these divided pieces. On that day, the Lord made a covenant with Abram, saying, "To your descendants, I will give this land, from the river of Egypt[3] to the great river Euphrates, from the Kenites, Kenizzites, Kadmonites, Cypriots, Perizzites, Raphites, Amorites, Canaanites, Mitanni, Girgashites, and the Jebusites."

Cosmic Genesis: Chapter 15 Notes

1 Codex Alexandrinus: despota (ᗡеᴄΠΟΤᗅ). Translation: despot (or tyrant, lord, master)

• Vienna Genesis: despota (ᗡеᴄΠΟΤᗅ). Translation: despot (or tyrant, lord, master)

• LXX 319: Despota cyrie (Δϙσπотᗅ ᴡฬβιϭ). Translation: despot (or tyrant, lord, master) lord

• LXX 57: C_x^e (ϗ⳹). Translation: Lord.

• Leningrad Codex: adonai Yehvih (אֲדֹנָי יֱהוִה). Translation: Lord Yehvih

• Peshitta: mryå ålhå (ܐܠܗܐ ܡܪܝܐ). Translation: master (or lord) god

• Targum Onkelos: El illa'ah (אֵל עִלָּאָה). Translation: god ascended

• Fragment Targums: yeyah elohim (יְיָ אֱלֹהִים). Translation: Yhŭ gods (or god via Neo-Assyrian)

• Targum Jerusalem: yeyah elohim (יְיָ אֱלֹהִים). Translation: Yhŭ gods (or god via Neo-Assyrian)

• Sahidic manuscripts: kuros (ⲕ ⲩⲣⲟⲥ). Translation: lord

2 LXX 961: cae episteusen abram is t̅h̅n̅ (ΚᗅΙЄΠΠΙᴄΤЄⲨᴄЄΝᗅΒΡᗅΜЄΙᴄ̅Ο̅Ν̅). Translation: and believed Abram of god

• LXX 509: cae episteusen Abram tô theô (ᴋᗅι ϭπϕστϭυσϭᴎ ᗅυβᗅᴍ тоо θϭоо). Translation: and believed Abram the god

• LXX 108: cae episteusai Abram tô theô (ᴋᗅι ϭπϕστϭυσᗅι ᗅυβᗅᴍ тоо θϭоо). Translation: and believed Abram the god

• LXX 344: cae episteusen Abraam tô theô (ᴋᗅι ϭπϕστϭυσϭᴎ ᗅυβᗅᗅᴍ тоо θϭоо). Translation: and believed Abraham the god

• Leningrad Codex: vehe'emin baIhvah (וְהֶאֱמִן בַּיהוָה). Translation: and he believed in Ihvah

- Peshitta: ůhymn Åbrm bålhå (ܐܠܗܐ ܐܒܪܡ ܘܗܝܡܢ). Translation: and believed Abram the god

- Targum Onkelos: veheimin bemeimra dayya (וְהֵימִין בְּמֵימְרָא דַיְיָ). Translation: and believed in the name of Yhů

- Targum Neofiti: ůhyymn åbrm bšm mmrå dyyy (והיימן אברם בשם ממרא דייי). Translation: and believed Abram in name Lord the Yhů

3 Berlin Genesis: potamou Aegyptou (ΠΟΤΑΜΟΥΑΙΓΥΠΤΟΥ). Translation: river Egyptian

- LXX 75: potamou tou Aigyptou (ποτᾰμου του Αιγᾖπτου). Translation: river the Egyptian

- Leningrad Codex: nehar Mitzrayim (נְהַר מִצְרָיִם). Translation: river Egyptians

- Peshitta Manuscript 5b1: årôå dMṣryn (ܐܪܥܐ ܕܡܨܪܝܢ). Translation: land the Egyptians

- Peshitta Manuscript 7a1: nhrå dMṣryn (ܢܗܪܐ ܕܡܨܪܝܢ). Translation: river the Egyptians

- Targum Onkelos: nahara deMitzrayim (נַהֲרָא דְמִצְרָיִם). Translation: river of Egypt

- Targum Jerusalem: Nilos deMitzrayim (נִילוֹס דְמִצְרָיִם). Translation: Nile of Egypt

The variations found in Peshitta Manuscripts 5b1, from the 5th century, and 7a1, from the 7th century, are generally interpreted as part of the ongoing work to synchronize the Peshitta with the Masoretic Text. As few early copies of the Septuagint's Cosmic Genesis survive, and those that do show signs of massive rewriting in the early Christian era, it is unclear if the original Septuagint and Aramaic source text referred to the 'land of Egypt,' or 'river of Egypt.'

Cosmic Genesis: Chapter 16

Sarai the wife of Abram carried him no children, and she had an Egyptian maid whose name was Hagar. So Sarai said to Abram, "Look, the Lord has restrained me from bearing, therefore, go into my maid, that I may get children for myself through her."

Abram listened to the voice of Sarai. So Abram had lived ten years in the land of Canaan when Sarai the wife of Abram having taken Hagar the Egyptian, her handmaid, gave her to Abram her husband as a wife to him. He went into Hagar and she conceived and learned that she was with child, and her mistress was ashamed before her.

Sarai said to Abram, "I am injured by you. I gave my handmaid into you, and when I saw that she was with child, I was embarrassed before her. The Lord judge between me and you."

Abram said to Sarai, "Look your handmaid is in your hands, use her as it may seem good to you."

Sarai chastised her, and she fled from her presence. The messenger of the lord[1] found her by the fountain of water in the wilderness, by the fountain in the way to Zur. The messenger of the lord asked her, "Hagar, Sarai's maid, where are you coming from, and where are you going?"

She answered, "I am fleeing from the presence of my mistress Sarai."

The messenger of the lord said to her," Return to your mistress, and submit yourself under her hands."

The messenger of the lord said to her, "I will surely multiply your descendants, and it will not be numbered for multitude."

The messenger of the lord said to her, "Look you are with child, and will carry a son, and will call his name Ishmael, for the Lord has listened to your humiliation. He will be a wild man, his hands against all, and the hands of all against him, and he will live in the presence of all his brothers."

She called the name of the Lord the god who spoke to her, you are God who sees me," for she said, "I have openly seen him that appeared to me."

Therefore she called the well, 'The well of him whom I have openly seen.' (Look, it is between Kadesh and Bered.) Hagar carried a son for Abram, and

Abram called the name of his son which Hagar carried to him, Ishmael. Abram was eighty-six years old when Hagar carried Ishmael for Abram.

Cosmic Genesis: Chapter 16 Notes

1 Codex Alexandrinus: angelos c̅u̅ tou t̅h̅u̅ (ⲀⲅⲅⲈⲖⲟⲥⲔ̅Ⲩ̅ⲧⲟⲨⲐ̅Ⲩ̅). Translation: messenger lord the god

- LXX 707: angelon Cyriou tou theou (Ἀγγόλον Κυβφου του θόου). Translation: messenger lord the god

- Leningrad Codex: mal'ach Yehvah (מַלְאַךְ יְהֹוָה). Translation: messenger Yehvah

- Peshitta: mlåkh dmryå (ܡܠܐܟܗ ܕܡܪܝܐ). Translation: messenger the master (or lord)

- Targum Onkelos: mal'acha dayya (מַלְאָכָא דַיְיָ). Translation: messenger the Yhů

- Targum Jerusalem: mal'acha dayya (מַלְאָכָא דַיְיָ). Translation: messenger of Yhů

Cosmic Genesis: Chapter 17

Abram was ninety-nine years old, and the Lord appeared to Abram and said to him, "I am the god Resheph.[1] Be very pleasing before me, and be blameless. I will establish my covenant between me and you, and I will multiply you greatly."

Abram fell on his face, and God said to him, "Look! My covenant is with you, and you will be the father of many nations. Your name will no longer be Abram, but your name will be Abraham, for I have made you a father of many nations. I will increase you very greatly, and I will make nations from you, and kings will come out of you. I will establish my covenant between you and your descendants after you, for all their generations, as an eternal covenant, to be your god, and a god of your descendants after you. I will give you and your descendants after you, the land in which you stay, including all the land of Canaan as an eternal possession, and I will be a god to them."

God said to Abraham, "You will also fully follow my covenant, you and your descendants after you, for all their generations. This is the covenant, that you will fully keep between me and you, and between your descendants after you for all their generations, every male among you will be circumcised. You will be circumcised in the flesh of your foreskin, and it will be as a sign of a covenant between me and you. The child will be circumcised by you at eight days old, every male throughout your generations, and the slave born in the house, and he that is bought with silver, of every son of a stranger, who is not of your descendants. He who is born in your house, and he that is bought with silver will surely be circumcised, and my covenant will be on your flesh as an eternal covenant. The uncircumcised male, who will not be circumcised in the flesh of his foreskin on the eighth day, that mind will be utterly destroyed from its family, for he has broken my covenant."

God said to Abraham, "Sarai your wife, her name will not be called Sarai, Sarah will be her name. I will bless her and give you a son through her, and I will bless him and he will become nations, and kings of nations will come from him."

Abraham fell on his face and laughed, and asked in his heart, "Will there be a child to one who is a hundred years old? Will Sarah who is ninety years old, become pregnant?"

Abraham said to God, "Let this Ishmael live before you."

God said to Abraham, "Yes, watch, Sarah your wife will carry a son for you, and you will call his name Isaac, and I will establish my covenant with him, as an eternal covenant, to be a god to him and his descendants after him. Concerning Ishmael, see, I have heard you, and, watch, I have blessed him, and will increase him and multiply him greatly. He will father twelve nations, and I will make him a great nation. But I will establish my covenant with Isaac, whom Sarah will carry for you at this time, in the next year."

He stopped speaking with him, and God went up from Abraham. Abraham took Ishmael his son, and all his home-born slaves, and all those bought with silver, and every male of the men in the house of Abraham, and he circumcised their foreskins immediately that day, following what God had told him. Abraham was ninety-nine years old when his foreskin was circumcised. Ishmael his son was thirteen years old when his foreskin was circumcised. At that time, Abraham was circumcised, and Ishmael his son, and all the men of his house, both those born in the house and those bought with silver from alien nations.

Cosmic Genesis: Chapter 17 Notes

1 Codex Alexandrinus: Egô imi o theos sou (ⲉⲅⲱⲉⲓⲙⲓⲟⲑⲉⲟⲥⲥⲟⲩ). Translation: I am the god of you

• LXX 17: Egô imi Cyrios o theos sou (ⲉⲅⲱ ⲉⲓⲙ ⲕⲩⲃⲓⲟⲥ ⲟ ⲑⲉⲟⲥ ⲥⲟⲩ). Translation: I am Lord the god of you

• Leningrad Codex: ani-el shaddai (אֲנִי־אֵל שַׁדַּי). Translation: I'm god Šadday

• Peshitta: ånå ånå åylšdy ålhå (ܐܠܗܐ ,ܐܝܠܫܕܝ ܐܢܐ ܐܢܐ). Translation: I am Åylšdy god

• Targum Onkelos: ana el shaddai (אֲנָא אֵל שַׁדַּי). Translation: I'm god Shadday

• Targum Jerusalem: ana el shadai (אֲנָא אֵל שַׁדַּי). Translation: I'm god Shadday

The Greek, Hebrew, Hebrew and Aramaic translations often differ in regards to the name or title Shadday, suggesting that the early Aramaic and Canaanite (Judahite or Samaritan) source texts they worked from differed in regards to this word. The term was omitted throughout Cosmic Genesis, however, is in the Peshitta and Targums, suggesting that when the word was first encountered the Greeks did not know how to interpret it. It is equally possible that it was the Aramaic translator who had omitted it, however, it was almost certainly in the Canaanite version the translator worked from, as it is used consistently in the rest of Bereshít, and is mentioned again when Moses god's name Ān is introduced in the Septuagint's Exodus.

In the Peshitta, the term is interpreted as the proper name of the god speaking, while in the Targums and Masoretic Text, it could either be a name or a description. The cause of the confusion over the term Shadday, is likely due to the difference between the meaning of the word in Canaanite versus Aramaic. In Akkadian cuneiform, which was adopted as the written script by many cultures, the term was ^{deity}šēdu (✳⊏⧾), however, it referred to a 'protective spirit' or 'lesser god.' In the later Aramaic language, the word became šydå (𐡍𐡉𐡔𐡏), meaning 'demon' in the classical sense, as a type of muse or nymph. Whereas in Canaanite, šd (𐤔𐤃) took on a different meaning, generally interpreted as 'powerful' by the Early Classical Era, which is likely where the Greeks ultimately derived the term 'omnipotent' (παντοκράτορος), which was used later in the Septuagint where the Masoretic Text generally uses the term shadday.

This alternate interpretation of the šd (𐤔𐤃) in Canaanite is likely due to the Egyptian New Kingdom era rule over Canaan, when Shed (𓈙𓂧𓀜, transliteration: šd), was worshiped in the region. Shed, who was often referred to as 'the savior,' was virtually identical to the earlier Canaanite god Resheph who was largely suppressed after the fall of the Hyksos dynasty. In the Masoretic Book of Job, Eliphaz referred to humanity as the 'sons of Resheph' (בני-רשף) instead of the 'sons of Adam,' and then refers god as šdy (שדי). This usage is consistent throughout Masoretic Job, indicating that at some point the name Resheph was updated to Shadday, likely during the New Kingdom era, when Resheph worship was suppressed due to his associated with the earlier Hyksos dynasty.

During the early New Kingdoms era, holy texts about Resheph would have been updated to Shed (𓈙𓂧𓀜), which would have been transliterated into Canaanite using the Akkadian Cuneiform script in the late New Kingdom era as ^{deity}šēdu (✳⊏⧾), before being translated into Canaanite using the Phoenician script in the early iron age as šdy (𐤆𐤃𐤔), resulting in the confusing 'god of demons' (𐡍𐡉𐡔𐡏) in Aramaic. In the former Amorite lands of northern Canaan, where Aramaic later became dominant, the Hurrians living under the rule of the Mitanni Empire called him Ablu (𒀊𒇷), generally accepted as a shortened version of aplu ^{ilu}Ellil (𒀊𒇷 ✳𒆗𒂗𒆤), an epithet of Nergal, the son of the Old Babylonian god Ellil. Like Resheph and Nergal, Ablu was a god of both plague and healing. He was also imported to the Neshite (Hittite) and Trojan civilizations, as the god Apaliunas (𒀀𒉺𒇷𒌋𒈾𒀸) was mentioned in a peace treaty between the civilizations in 1280 BC.

Homer reported in the Illiad that Apollôn (Απολλων) was the god that built the wall of Troy, which confirms that the Greeks did view Apaliunas as Apollo. In the Illiad, a priest of Apollo called Chryses, referred to Apollo as the 'Lord of Mice' as he was believed to protect from plagues of mice. This indicates that the Pelesets viewed Shadday as a version of Apaliunas when they captured the box of the covenant in 1st Kingdoms (Masoretic Samuel), as they returned it with golden statues of mice after their cities were plagued by swarms of mice. In this particular verse, the term ^{god}šēdu (✳⬚) is transliterated directly into Hebrew as âl šdy (אל שדי), which has to have been in the Akkadian Cuneiform version of the text, and is therefore imported to this translation. As the term has to either be interpreted as 'god of demons,' from a the Akkadian ^{deity}šēdu (✳⬚), or 'god Resheph,' from the Egyptian Shed (𓂋𓈙𓏤), and Resheph is consistent with the rest of the books of the Septuagint, as well as the archaeological record, the term Resheph is used.

Cosmic Genesis: Chapter 18

God appeared to him by the oak of Mamre, as he sat by the door of his tent at noon. He lifted his eyes and saw, and saw three men stood before him, and having seen them he ran to meet them from the door of his tent and bowed to the ground.

He said, "Lord, if I have found favor in your sight, do not overlook your servant. Let water now be brought and let them wash your feet, and refresh yourselves under the tree. I will bring bread, and you will eat, and after this, you will depart on your journey, on account of which refreshment you have turned aside."

He said, "So do as you have said."

Abraham hurried to the tent to Sarah, and said to her, "Hurry, and knead three measures of fine flour, and make cakes."

Abraham ran to the cows, and took a young calf, tender and good, and gave it to his servant, and he hurried to dress it. He took butter and milk, and the calf which he had prepared, and he set them before them, and they did eat, and he stood by them under the tree.

He asked him, "Where is Sarah your wife?"

He answered and said, "Look! In the tent."

He answered, "I will return and visit you in the same season, and Sarah your wife will have a son."

Sarah heard at the door of the tent, being behind him. Abraham and Sarah were old, advanced in days, and the custom of women ceased with Sarah. Sarah laughed in herself, saying, "The thing has not as yet happened to me, even until now, and my lord is old."

The Lord said to Abraham, "Why is it that Sarah has laughed to herself, saying, 'Will I really become pregnant? I am already old.' Will anything be impossible for God? At this time I will return to you in the season, and Sarah will have a son."

But Sarah denied it, saying, "I did not laugh," because she was afraid.

He answered her, "No, but you did laugh."

The men having risen from there looked towards Sodom and Gomorrah. Abraham went with them, attending them on their journey. The Lord said, "Will I hide from Abraham my servant the things I intend to do? But Abraham will become a great and populous nation, and in him will all the nations of the land be blessed. For I know that he will command his sons, and his house after him, that they will keep the ways of the Lord, to do justice and judgment, that the Lord may bring on Abraham all things whatever he has spoken to him."

The Lord said, "The cries from Sodom and Gomorrah have been increasingly reported to me, and their sins are very great. So I will go down and see if they correspond with the cry which is reported to me, and if not, that I may know."

The men having departed from there came to Sodom, and Abraham was still standing before the Lord. Abraham approached and asked, "Would you destroy the righteous with the wicked, and will the righteous be like the wicked? If there are fifty righteous in the city, will you destroy them? Won't you spare the whole place for the sake of the fifty righteous if they are in it? By no means will you do this thing, to destroy the righteous with the wicked so the righteous will be like the wicked. By no means. You who judges the whole earth, will you not do right?"

The Lord answered, "If there are in Sodom fifty righteous in the city, I will spare the whole city and the whole region for their sake."

Abraham asked, "Now I have begun to speak to my Lord, and I am dirt and ashes. But if the fifty righteous should be only forty-five, will you destroy the whole city because of the five missing?"

He answered, "I will not destroy it if I find forty-five there."

He continued to question him still, "But if there are forty found there?"

He answered, "I will not destroy it for the sake of forty."

He asked, "Will there be anything against me, Lord, if I speak? But if there are thirty found there?"

He answered, "I will not destroy it for the sake of thirty."

He asked, "Since I am able to speak to the Lord, what if there are twenty found there?"

He answered, "I will not destroy it if I find twenty there."

He asked, "Will there be anything against me, Lord, if I speak once more? But if there are ten found there?"

He answered, "I will not destroy it for the sake of the ten."

The Lord departed when he ended speaking with Abraham, and Abraham returned to his home.

Cosmic Genesis: Chapter 19

The two messengers came to Sodom in the evening. Lot sat by the gate of Sodom, and Lot having seen them, rose up to meet them, and he worshiped with his face to the ground, and said, "Look! My lords turn aside into the house of your servant. Rest from your journey and powder your feet. When you rise early in the morning, you can depart on your journey."

They answered, "No, we will stay in the street."

He constrained them, and they turned aside to him, and they entered into his house, and he made a feast for them, and baked unleavened cakes for them, and they ate. But before they went to sleep, the men of the city, the Sodomites, surrounded the house, both young and old, all the people together. They called out Lot, and said to him, "Where are the men that came to you tonight? Bring them out to us, so we can be with them."

Lot went out to them to the porch, and he shut the door behind him, and said to them, "By no means, brothers! Do not act wickedly! Instead, I have two daughters who have not yet known a man. I will bring them out to you, and you can use them however you please. Only, do not injure these men, who came under the shelter of my roof to avoid this."

They replied to him, "Stand back! You came to reside here, and now you judge? Now then, we will harm you even more than them!"

They pushed hard against Lot, and they were close to breaking the door. The men reached out their hands and pulled Lot to them inside the house, and shut the door of the house. They struck the men that were at the door of the house with blindness, both small and great, and they grew tired of searching for the door. The men asked Lot, "Have you sons-in-law here, or sons, or daughters, or if you have any other friend in the city, bring them out of this place. For we are going to destroy this place, for their cry has been raised before the Lord, and the Lord has sent us here to destroy."

Lot went out, and spoke to his sons-in-law, who had married his daughters, and said, "Rise, and depart out of this place, for the Lord is about to destroy the city!"

But what he said seemed absurd to his sons-in-law. When it was morning, the messengers rushed Lot, saying, "Rise and take your wife, and your two daughters that you have, and go out, in case you are also destroyed with the iniquities of the city."

They were troubled, and the messengers[1] grabbed his hand, and the hand of his wife, and the hands of his two daughters, because the Lord had spared him. When they brought them out, they said, "Save your life by any means. Don't look around to that which is behind, or stay in any of the country around it, escape to the mountain, in case, perhaps you are overtaken together with them."

Lot said to them, "I beg, Lord, since your servant has found mercy before you, and you have magnified your righteousness in what you do towards me, in that my mind may live, but, I will not be able to escape to the mountain, in case perhaps the destruction overtakes me and I die. Look, this city is near for me to escape to, it is a small one, and there I will be safe. Is it not small? My mind will survive because of you."

He answered him, "Look, I have respected your opinion also about this thing, that I should not overthrow the city which you have spoken of. Hurry and escape to there, for I will not be able to do anything until you have arrived there."

(Therefore he called the name of that city, Zoar.)[1]

The sun had risen above the land when Lot entered into Zoar. The Lord rained brimstone and fire out of the sky, from the Lord, on Sodom and Gomorrah.[3] He overthrew those cities, and all the country around it, and all that lived in the cities, and the plants growing out of the ground.

His wife turned back, and she became a pillar of salt. Abraham rose up early to go to the place where he had stood before the Lord. He looked towards Sodom and Gomorrah, and the surrounding country, and saw that a flame went up from the land like the smoke of a furnace.

It happened that when God destroyed all the cities and the region around them, God remembered Abraham, and sent Lot out of the middle of the destruction, when the Lord destroyed those cities in which Lot lived. Lot left Zoar and lived in the mountain with his two daughters, for he was afraid to live in Zoar. He lived in a cave with his two daughters.

The elder said to the younger, "Our father is old, and there is no one on the land who will come into us, as it is done in all the land. Come, and let us make our father drink wine, and let us sleep with him, and let us raise children from our father."

They made their father drink wine that night, and the elder went in and lay with her father that night, and he did not know when he slept and when he rose up. It happened in the morning, that the elder said to the younger, "Look, I slept last night with our father, let us make him drink wine in tonight also, and you go in and sleep with him, and let us raise descendants from our father."

They made their father drink wine that night also, and the younger went in and slept with her father, and he did not know when he slept, nor when he arose. The two daughters of Lot conceived by their father. The elder carried a son and called his name Moab, saying, "He is of my father."

This is the father of the Moabites to this present day. The younger also carried a son, and called his name Benammi, saying, "The son of my family." This is the father of the Ammonites to this present day.

Cosmic Genesis: Chapter 19 Notes

1 Codex Alexandrinus: angeloe (Ⲁⲅⲅⲉⲗⲟⲓ). Translation: messengers (or angels)

• Leningrad Codex: anashim (אֲנָשִׁים). Translation: men (or husbands)

• Peshitta Manuscript 5b1: gbrå (ܓܒ̈ܪܐ). Translation: heroes

• Peshitta Manuscript 7a1: mlåôå (ܡܠܐܟ̈ܐ). Translation: messengers (or angels)

• Targum Onkelos: guvrayya (גֻבְרַיָּא). Translation: heroes

• Targum Jerusalem: mal'achaya dahavo medamyain legavraya (מַלְאֲכַיָּא דַהֲווֹ מְדַמְיָין לְגֻבְרַיָּא). Translation: messengers who were disguised as heroes

This variation found in Peshitta Manuscripts 5b1, from the 5th century, and 7a1, from the 7th century, is generally interpreted as part of the ongoing work to synchronize the Peshitta with the Septuagint.

2 This scribal note appears to confirm that the name was recorded as Šuszíru (𒂍𒈨𒈾𒊬) before being transcribed into the Phoenician Canaanite script, as šū szíru (𒂍𒈨 𒈾𒊬) translates as 'it is seed (or semen, offspring, descendants).' This note was probably added by the Akkadian cuneiform translator in the late New Kingdom era who first interpreted the name this way. For more information on Shasziru, see the note in chapter 14.

3 LXX 64: Sodoma cae Gomorrha (Coλομ ̇ ̈λι Γομοϱϱ̇). Translation: Sodoma and Gomorrha

- LXX 319: Sodôma cae Gomora (Coλooμ ̈λι Γομοϱ̇). Translation: Sodôma and Gomora

- LXX 75: Sôdomôn cae Gomorrha (Cooλομooν ̈λι Γομοϱϱ̇). Translation: Sôdomôn and Gomorrha

- LXX 500: Sôdoma and Gomorrha (Cooλομ ̈λι Γομοϱϱ̇). Translation: Sôdoma and Gomorrha

- Leningrad Codex: Sedom ve'al-Amorah (סְדֹם וְעַל־עֲמֹרָה). Translation: Sedom and the Amora

- Peshitta: Sdûm ûôl Ômûrâ (ܣܕܘܡ ܘܥܠ ܥܡܘܪܐ). Translation: Sdwm and the Omwra

- Targum Onkelos: Sedom ve'al Amorah (סְדוֹם וְעַל עֲמוֹרָה). Translation: Sedom and the Amora

- Fragment Targums: Sedom va'Amorah (סְדוֹם וַעֲמוֹרָה). Translation: Sedom and Amora

- Targum Jerusalem: Sedom ve'al Amorah (סְדוֹם וְעַל עֲמוֹרָה). Translation: Sedom and the Amora

The Tall el-Hammam archaeological site at the foot of Mount Sodom, in Jordan, dates back to circa 1700 BC and shows widespread damage caused by intense heat. It is theorized that the meteor impacted and burst in the atmosphere, leveling towns across a 200 square mile (500 km²) area. While the damage is evident from the archaeological record, the cause is unclear, and no impact site has been found. Some scholars believe this destruction may have been the source of the story of Sodom and Gomorrah.

Cosmic Genesis: Chapter 20

Abraham left there for the southern country, and lived between Kadesh and Zoar, and stayed in Gerar. Abraham said concerning Sarah his wife, "She is my sister," as he was afraid to say, "She is my wife," in case at any time the men of the city should kill him for her sake. So Abimelech king of Gerar sent and took Sarah.

God came to Abimelech by night in sleep, and said, "Look, you die for the woman, whom you have taken, has lived with a husband."

However Abimelech had not touched her, and he begged, "Lord, will you destroy an ignorant sinner and just nation? Didn't he tell me, 'She is my sister,' and didn't she say to me, 'He is my brother?' With a pure heart and in with clean hands have I done this."

God said to him in sleep, "Yes, I knew that you did this with a pure heart, and I spared you, so that you should not sin against me, therefore I did not allow you to touch her. But now return the man his wife, for he is a prophet and will pray for you, and you will live. But if you don't restore her, know that you and all yours will die."

Abimelech rose early in the morning and called all his servants, and he told them these words, and all the men were terrified. Abimelech called Abraham and demanded of him, "What is this that you have done to us? Have we sinned against you? You have brought on me and my kingdom a great sin! You have done to me something no one should do."

Abimelech asked Abraham, "What have you seen in me that you have done this?"

Abraham answered, "Well I thought, 'Surely God is not worshiped in this place, and they will kill me for my wife.' For truly she is my sister by my father, but not by my mother, and she became my wife. It happened when God brought me out of the house of my father, that I said to her, 'This righteousness you will perform for me, in every place into which we enter, say about me, He is my brother.'"

Abimelech took a thousand didrachmas, and sheep, and calves, and servants, and maidservants, and gave them to Abraham, and he returned him Sarah his wife. Abimelech said to Abraham, "Look, my land is before you, live wherever it may please you."

To Sarah, he said, "Look, I have given your brother a thousand didrachmas, those will be for you, the price of your discretion. To all the women you speak with, tell the truth in all things."

Abraham prayed to God, and God healed Abimelech, and his wife, and his women servants, and they carried children. Because the Lord had sealed every womb in the house of Abimelech, because of Sarah Abraham's wife.

Cosmic Genesis: Chapter 21

The Lord visited Sarah, as he said, and the Lord did to Sarah, as he spoke. She conceived and carried for Abraham a son in old age, at the set time the Lord had told to him. Abraham called the name of his son that was born to him, who Sarah gave birth to, Isaac. Abraham circumcised Isaac on the eighth day, as God commanded him. Abraham was a hundred years old when Isaac his son was born to him. Sarah said, "The Lord has made laughter for me, for whoever will hear will rejoice with me."

She asked, "Who will tell Abraham that Sarah suckles a child? I have born a child in my old age!"

The child grew and was weaned, and Abraham made a great feast the day that his son Isaac was weaned. When Sarah saw the son of Hagar the Egyptian, who was born to Abraham, playing with Isaac her son, she said to Abraham, "Throw out this slave-woman and her son, for the son of this slave-woman will not inherit along with my son Isaac."

But the matter appeared very difficult before Abraham, concerning his son. But God said to Abraham, "Let it not be hard for you concerning the child and concerning the slave-woman. In all things whatever Sarah will say to you, listen to her voice, as from Isaac will your descendants come. Moreover, I will make the son of this slave-woman a great nation because he is your descendant."

Abraham rose up in the morning and took loaves and a skin of water, and gave them to Hagar, and he put the child on her shoulder and sent her away, and after she departed, she wandered in the wilderness near Beersheba. The water was emptied from the skin, and she placed the child under a fir tree. She departed and sat down opposite him at the distance of a bow-shot, as she said, "I can't see the death of my child."

She sat opposite him, and the child cried out loud, and wept. God heard the voice of the child from the place where he was, and The messenger of the lord called down to Hagar, out of the sky, and said to her, "What is it Hagar? Don't be afraid, for God has heard the voice of the child from the place where he is. Rise up, and take the child, and hold him in your hand, for I will make him a great nation."

God opened her eyes, and she saw a well of living water, and she went and filled the skin with water, and gave the child drink. God was with the child, and he grew and lived in the wilderness, and became an archer. He lived in the wilderness, and his mother chose him a wife from Paran in Egypt.

It happened at that time that Abimelech spoke to Abraham, along with Ochozath his friend, and Phichol the chief captain of his army, saying, "God is with you in all things, whatever you may do. Now, therefore, swear to me by God that you will not injure me, nor my descendants, nor my name, but according to the righteousness which I have performed with you you will deal with me, and with the land in which you have stayed."

Abraham answered, "I will swear."

Abraham reproved Abimelech because of the wells of water, which the servants of Abimelech took away. Abimelech said to him, "I don't know who has done this thing to you. You did not tell it to me, and I didn't hear of it before today."

Abraham took sheep and calves and gave them to Abimelech, and both made a covenant. Abraham set seven ewe lambs by themselves. Abimelech asked Abraham, "What are these seven ewe lambs that you have set alone?"

Abraham said, "You will receive the seven ewe lambs from me, that they may be for me as a witness, that I dug this well."

Therefore he named the name of that place, 'The Well of the Oath,' as they both swore there. They made a covenant at the Well of the Oath, and then Abimelech rose up, and Ochozath his friend, and Phichol the commander-in-chief of his army, and they returned to the land of the Pelesets.[1] Abraham planted a field at Beersheba[2] and called there on the name of the Lord the god Eternal.[3] Abraham stayed in the land of the Pelesets many days.

Cosmic Genesis: Chapter 21 Notes

1 Codex Alexandrinus: Phylistiim (ΦΥΛΙϹΤΙΕΙΜ)

• LXX 131: Phylêst (Φυλλοτ)

• LXX 392: Phil (Φιλ)

• LXX 108: Philyst (Φιλυοτ)

• LXX 799: Philêstêim (Φιλλοτλοτμ)

- LXX 376: Philylist (Φιλυλιστ)

- Leningrad Codex: Pelishtim (פְּלִשְׁתִּים)

- Peshitta: plštyå (ܦܠܫܬܝܐ)

- Targum Onkelos: Pelishta'ei (פְּלִשְׁתָּאֵי)

- Targum Jerusalem: Pelishta'ei (פְּלִישְׁתָּאֵי)

The Peleseti were an ancient people based in the region of the modern Gaza Strip of the Palestinian Territories. The earliest surviving mention of them is from the reliefs of the Temple of Ramses III at Medinet Habu in Egypt that dates back to some time between 1186 and 1155 BC, in which they were called Půlåsåtî (𓊪𓍯𓂋𓏏𓈖𓀀𓏥). They were also known in cuneiform as the ᵏᵘʳPalastu (𒆳𒉺𒆷𒀸𒌓).

It is unclear where they came from, however, one theory is that they were the Pala, a Luwian people from the Black Sea coast of Anatolia. The region was an independent country called Palaa (𒉺𒆷𒀀) in the Hittite records from the 1600s BC, however, have become part of the Nesite Empire by the 1500s BC. Around the time the Pelesets invaded Canaan, the Pala were driven from their homeland by the neighboring Kaskians from northeast Anatolia, which supports the connection between the groups, however, it has yet to be proven conclusively. The presence of the Pelesets in Southern Canaan during the time of Abraham and Isaac is anachronistic, and therefore this section of text, describing the origin of the Semitic tribes, found in both the Septuagint and the Masoretic Text, likely dates to the original Phoenician translation in the early Iron Age.

2 LXX 961: phreati tou orcismou (ΦΡΕΑΤΙΤΟΥΟΡΚΙϹΜΟΥ). Translation: well of the administration of the oath

- Codex Alexandrinus: phreati tou orcou (ΦΡΕΑΤΙΤΟΥΟΡΚΟΥ). Translation: well of the oath

- LXX 19: phrear tou horcismou (φρέαρ του ορμισμου). Translation: well of the oath

- LXX 56: phrea tou horcismou (φρέα του ορμισμου). Translation: well of the oath

- LXX 610: phrear tou horcismou (φρέατος του ορμισμου). Translation: well of the oath

- Leningrad Codex: ve'er shava (בְּאֵר שֶׁבַע). Translation: well of the oath (or Beersheba)

- Peshitta: br šbå (ܒܪ ܫܒܥ). Translation: well of the oath (or Beersheba)

- Targum Onkelos: ve'er shava (בְּאֵר שְׁבַע). Translation: well of the oath (or Beersheba)

- Fragment Targums: ve'er shava (בְּאֵר שְׁבַע). Translation: well of the oath (or

Beersheba)

• Targum Jerusalm: beira desheva churefan (בֵּירָא דְשְׁבַע חוּרְפַּן). Translation: well of seven lambs

As the Greek term was a translation of the Hebrew name, the name of the town is restored in this translation. The region around the modern Beersheba has been inhabited since before 3000 BC.

3 LXX 961: onoma tou c̄u t̄h̄s aeônios (ΟΝΟΜΑΤΟΥΚΥΘϹΑΙѠΝΙΟϹ). Translation: name of the Lord god of centuries (or eons, time)

• LXX 509: anoma Cyriou theos aeônios (ονομα Κυρθου θϵοϲ ΑιѠνιοϲ). Translation: name of Lord god of centuries (or eons, time)

• LXX 121: onomati Cyriou theos aeônios (ονοματι Κυρθου θϵοϲ ΑιѠνιοϲ). Translation: name of Lord god of centuries (or eons, time)

• LXX 130: anoma cyriou theos aeônos (ονομα Luρθου θϵοϲ Αιωνοϲ). Translation: name lord god of centuries (or eons)

• Leningrad Codex: shem Yehvah El ovlam (שֵׁם יְהוָה אֵל עוֹלָם). Translation: name Yehwah God of the World (or universe, eternity)

• Peshitta: šmh dmrå ålhå dôlmå (ܫܡܗ ܕܡܪܐ ܐܠܗܐ ܕܥܠܡܐ). Translation: name of the master god of the age (or world)

• Targum Onkelos: shema dayya elaha de'alma (שְׁמָא דַיְיָ אֱלָהָא דְעָלְמָא). Translation: name of the Yhů god of the age (or world)

• Fragment Targums: shem meimra dayya elaha de'alma (שֵׁם מֵימְרָא דַיְיָ אֱלָהָא דְעָלְמָא). Translation: name command (or word) of Yhů god of the age (or world)

• Targum Jerusalm: shem meimra daYayah olaha alma (שֵׁם מֵימְרָא דַיְיָ אֱלָהָא עָלְמָא). Translation: name command (or word) of Yhů god forever

This verse does not survive in any of the Dead Sea Scrolls, however, the Greek word Aeônios (αἰώνιος) does appear to be a translation of the Hebrew word ôwlm (עולם) proving the word was present in the text the Greeks translated.

Cosmic Genesis: Chapter 22

It happened after these things that God tempted Abraham, and called to him, "Abraham! Abraham?"

He answered, "Look! I am here."

He said, "Take your son, the beloved one, whom you love, Isaac, and go into the highland,[1] and offer him there as a whole burnt offering, on one of the mountains which I will tell you."

Abraham got up in the morning and saddled his donkey, and he took with him two servants, and Isaac his son, and took split wood for a whole burnt offering, he arose and departed, and came to the place that God told him. On the third day, Abraham looked with his eyes, saw the place far away. Abraham told his servants, "Sit here with the donkey, and I and the boy, will go further, and after we worship, we will return to you."

Abraham took the wood of the whole burnt offering and laid it on Isaac his son, and he took in his hands both the fire and the dagger, and the two traveled together. Isaac said to Abraham his father, "Father?"

He replied, "What is it, son?"

He asked, "Look, the fire and the wood, where is the sheep for a whole burnt offering?"

Abraham answered, "God will provide himself a sheep for a whole burnt offering, my son."

Both traveled together and came to the place where God told him. There Abraham built the altar, and laid the wood on it, and having bound the feet of Isaac his son together, he laid him on the altar, on the wood. Abraham stretched out his hand to take the dagger to kill his son. The messenger of the lord called him out of the sky saying, "Abraham! Abraham?"

He answered, "Look, I am here."

He ordered, "Don't lay your hand on the child or do anything to him. Now I know that you fear God and for my sake, you have not spared your beloved son."

Abraham lifted up his eyes and saw a ram caught by his horns in a thicket of Sabec, and Abraham went and took the ram, and offered him up for a whole burnt offering in the place of Isaac his son. Abraham called the name of that place,

'The Lord has seen,' that they might say today, 'In the mountain, the Lord was seen.'

The messenger of the lord visited Abraham a second time out of the sky, saying, "I have sworn by myself," the Lord says, "because you have done this thing on my account, and have not spared your beloved son, surely I will bless you, and I will multiply your descendants like the stars of the sky, and like the sand of the seashore, and your descendants will inherit the cities of their enemies. In your descendants will all the nations of the land be blessed, because you have listened to my voice."

Abraham returned to his servants, and they arose and went together to the well of the oath, and Abraham lived at the well of the oath. It happened after these things, that it was reported to Abraham, "Men are saying, 'Look, Milcah herself too has born sons to Nahor your brother, Huz the firstborn, and Baux his brother, and Kemuel the father of the Syrians, Chesed, Hazo, Phaldes, Jidlaph, and Bethuel, and Bethuel fathered Rebekah.'" These are eight sons which Milcah carried for Nahor the brother of Abraham. His concubine whose name was Reumah, who also carried Tebah, Gaham, Tochos, and Mocha.

Cosmic Genesis: Chapter 22 Notes

1 Codex Alexandrinus: gên tên hypsêlên (ΓΗΝΤΗΝΥϮΗΛΗΝ). Translation: land that is high

- Leningrad Codex: El-eretz hammoriyyah (אֶל־אֶרֶץ הַמֹּרִיָּה). Translation: rebellious (or disobedient) land

- Peshitta: årôâ dåmûryå (ܐܪܥܐ ܕܡܘܪܝܐ). Translation: land is rebelling (or disobedient)

- Targum Onkelos: ar'a pulechana (אַרְעָא פּוּלְחָנָא). Translation: land of ritual (or rite, or cult)

- Fragment Targums: tur moriyah (טוּר מוֹרִיָּה). Translation: mount Morriya

- Targum Jerusalm: ara pulechana (אֲרַע פּוּלְחָנָא). Translation: land of ritual (or rite, or cult)

The Greek translation does not reflect the meaning of the Hebrew text, as the meaning of hammoriyyah (הַמֹּרִיָּה) is disobedience, rebelliousness, or defiance.

Cosmic Genesis: Chapter 23

The life of Sarah was a hundred and twenty-seven years. Sarah died in the city of Arboc, which is in the valley. This is Hebron in the land of Canaan. Abraham came to lament for Sarah and to mourn. Abraham stood up from before his dead, and Abraham spoke to the sons of the Cypriots, saying, "I am a traveler and a stranger among you, therefore, give me ownership of a burying-place among you, so I can bury my dead away from me."

The sons of the Cypriots answered Abraham, saying, "Not so, lord, but hear us. You are among us, a king from God. Bury your dead in our best sepulchers, for none of us will by any means withhold his sepulcher from you so that you should not bury your dead there."

Abraham got up and bowed to the people of the land, to the sons of the Cypriots. Abraham spoke to them, saying, "If you have it in your mind that I should bury my dead out of my sight, listen to me, and speak for me to Ephron the son of Zohar. And let him give me the double cave which he has, which is in a part of his field, let him give it to me for the silver it is worth, to possess a burying-place among you."

Now Ephron was sitting in the middle of the children of the Cypriots, and Ephron the Cypriot answered Abraham and spoke in front of the sons of the Cypriots, and of all who entered the city, saying, "Be with me, my lord, and hear me, I give to you the field and the cave which is in it. I have given it to you before all my countrymen. Bury your dead."

Abraham bowed before the people of the land. He said to Ephron before the people of the land, "Since you are on my side, hear me. Take the price of the field from me, so I can bury my dead there."

But Ephron answered Abraham, saying, "No, my Lord. I have heard, the land is worth four hundred silver shekels,[1] but what can this be between me and you? No, go bury your dead."

Abraham listened to Ephron, and Abraham gave to Ephron the silver, which he mentioned in front of the sons of the Cypriot, four hundred shekels of silver approved with merchants. The field of Ephron, which was in Double Cave, which is opposite Mamre, the field and the cave, which was in it, and every tree which was in the field, and whatever is in its borders around it, were made sure to Abraham for a possession, before the sons of the Cypriots, and all that entered into the city. After this, Abraham buried Sarah his wife in the double cave in the field, which is opposite Mamre, (this is Hebron in the land of Canaan). So the field and the cave which was in it were secured as Abraham's possession, as a burial place, by the sons of the Cypriot.

Cosmic Genesis: Chapter 23 Notes

1 Codex Alexandrinus: didrachmôn (ⲇⲓⲇⲣⲁⲭⲙⲱⲛ)

- LXX 318: didragmôn (ⲇⲓⲁⲃⲁⲅⲙⲟⲟⲛ)

- LXX 707: didragma (ⲇⲓⲁⲃⲁⲅⲙⲁ)

- LXX 16: dênariôn (ⲇⲏⲛⲁⲃⲓⲟⲟⲛ)

- LXX 128: dragmôn (ⲁⲃⲅⲙⲟⲟⲛ)

- LXX 246: ditragma (ⲇⲓⲧⲃⲁⲅⲙⲁ)

- LXX 129 didragma (ⲇⲓⲁⲃⲁⲅⲙⲁ)

- LXX 108: didrachmon (ⲇⲓⲁⲃⲁⲭⲙⲟⲛ)

- LXX 799: didragma (ⲇⲓⲁⲃⲁⲅⲙⲁ)

- LXX 664: didrachma (ⲇⲓⲁⲃⲁⲭⲙⲁ)

- Leningrad Codex: shekel (שֶׁקֶל). Translation: shekel

- Peshitta: tql (ܬܩܠ). Translation: weight (or shekel)

- Targum Onkelos: kaspa (כַּסְפָּא). Translation: silver

The shekel was a unit of weight used throughout the Middle East for thousands of years, weighing approximately 8.6 grams of silver. The Greek drachma was a coin weighing approximately half a shekel, and therefore under Greek rule of the Middle East, a two-drachma coin was used. As the Greeks clearly translated shekel into didrachma, the term shekel is restored in this translation.

Cosmic Genesis: Chapter 24

Abraham was old, advanced in days, and the Lord blessed Abraham in all things. Abraham said to his slave, the elder of his house, who had command over all his possessions, "Put your hand under my thigh, and I will have you swear an oath by the Lord, the god of the sky and the god of the land,[1] that you don't take a wife for my son Isaac from the daughters of the Canaanites, among whom I live. But you will go instead to my country, where I was born, and to my tribe, and you will take from there, a wife for my son Isaac."

The slave asked him, "Should I take back your son to the land you came from, if the woman is not willing to return with me to this land?"

Abraham answered him, "Make sure that you don't take my son back there. The Lord, the god Shamayim, and the god Eretz, who brought me out of my father's house, and out of the land from where I sprang, who spoke to me, and who swore to me, saying, 'I will give this land to you and to your descendants,' he will send his messenger before you, and you will take a wife for my son from there. If the woman should not be willing to come with you into this land, you will be clear from my oath, only don't take my son back there."

The slave put his hand under the thigh of his master Abraham and swore to him about this. The slave took ten camels from among his master's camels, and he took some of all the goods of his master with him, and he arose and went into Mesopotamia to the city of Nahor. He let his camels sleep outside the city, by the well of water in the evening, when girls go out to draw water.

He said, "Lord the god of my master Abraham, bring success to my travels today, and deal mercifully with my master Abraham. See I stand by the well of water, and the daughters of those that live in the city come out to collect water. It will be, the young girl to which I will ask, 'Lower your pitcher, that I may drink,' and she will reply, 'Drink and I will give your camels water, until they are finished drinking,' this is the one you have prepared for your slave Isaac, and so I will know that you have thought mercifully with my master Abraham."

It happened before he had done speaking in his mind, that Rebekah the daughter of Bethuel, the son of Milcah, the wife of Nahor, the brother of Abraham, came out with a pitcher on her shoulders. The young girl was very beautiful in appearance. She was a virgin and a man had not known her, and she went down to the well, and filled her pitcher, and came up. The slave ran up to meet her, and said, "Give me a little water to drink out of your pitcher."

She replied, "Drink Sir," and she hurried to lower the pitcher on her arm, and gave it to him, to drink from, until his thirst was sated. She said, "I will also collect water for your camels until they have all drank."

She hurried, and emptied the pitcher into the trough, and ran to the well to draw again, and drew water for all the camels. The man paid close attention to her but remained silent to know whether the Lord had made his way prosperous or not. When all the camels had finished drinking, the man took golden earrings, each a beka² in weight, and he put two bracelets on her hands, their weight was ten pieces of gold. He asked her, "Whose daughter are you? Tell me if there is room for us to lodge with your father."

She told him, "I am the daughter of Bethuel the son of Milcah, whom she carried for Nahor," and she told him, "We have both straw and much provisions, and a place for resting."

The man was very pleased, and worshiped the Lord, saying, "Blessed is the Lord the god of my master Abraham, who has not allowed his righteousness to fail, nor held his truth from my master, and the Lord has brought me successfully to the house of my lord's brother."

The girl ran and reported these words in the house of her mother. Rebekah had a brother whose name was Laban, and Laban ran out to meet the man at the well. It happened when he saw the earrings and the bracelets in the hands of his sister, and when he heard the words of Rebekah his sister, saying, 'The man spoke to me like this,' that he went to the man, as he stood by the camels at the well. He said to him, "Come in here, you blessed of the Lord, why do you stand outside, when I have prepared the house and a place for the camels?"

The man entered into the house, and unloaded the camels, and gave the camels straw and provisions, and water to wash his feet, and the feet of the men that were with him. He placed before them loaves to eat, but he said, "I will not eat until I have said my words."

He answered, "So speak."

He said, "I am a slave of Abraham, and the Lord has blessed my master greatly, and he is exalted, and he has given him sheep and calves, silver and gold, men-slaves and slave-women, camels and donkeys. Sarah my master's wife carried one son for my master after he had grown old, and he gave him whatever he had. And my master made me swear, 'You will not take a wife for my son from the daughters of the Canaanites, among whose land I live. But you will go to the house of my father, and to my tribe, and you will take a wife for my son from there.'

I asked my master, 'What if the woman will not go with me.' He said to me, 'Lord the god, to whom I have been acceptable in his presence, will send out his messenger with you and will bless your journey, and you will take a wife for my son, from my tribe, and from the house of my father. Then you will be clear from my curse, for if you have gone to my tribe, and they did not give her to you, then you will be clear from my oath.'

Having come today to the well, I said, 'Lord the god of my master Abraham, if you bless my journey that I am now on, look, I stand by the well of water, and the daughters of the men of the city come out to draw water, and it will be that the girl to whom I will say, 'Give me a little water to drink out of your pitcher,' and she will say to me, 'Drink and I will also draw water for your camels,' this will be the wife whom the Lord has prepared for his own slave Isaac, and hereby will I know that you have worked mercy with my master Abraham. It happened before I had done speaking in my mind, immediately Rebekah came out, having her pitcher on her shoulders, and she went down to the well and drew water, and I asked her, 'Give me something to drink.'

She hurried and let down her pitcher on her arm from herself, and said, 'You drink, and I will give your camels water, and I drank, and she gave the camels water.'

I asked her, 'Whose daughter are you? Tell me,' and she said, 'I am the daughter of Bethuel, the son of Nahor, whom Milcah carried for him,' and I put on her the earrings and the bracelets on her hands. Being very happy I worshiped the Lords, and I blessed the Lord the god of my master Abraham, who has helped me succeed in finding the correct road so that I should take the daughter of my master's brother for his son. If you will then deal mercifully and justly with my lord, tell me, and if not, tell me if I should turn to the right or to the left."

Laban and Bethuel answered and said, "This matter has come from the Lord, we will not be able to answer you bad or good. Look, Rebekah is before you, take her and leave, and let her be wife to the son of your master, as the Lord has said."

When the slave of Abraham heard these words, he bowed himself to the Earth before the Lord.[3] The slave had brought out jewels of silver and gold and clothing and gave them to Rebekah and gave gifts to her brother and her mother. Then he and the men traveling with him ate and drank and went to sleep. He rose in the morning and asked, "Send me away, so I may return to my master."

Her brothers and her mother said, "Let the young girl remain with us for ten days,[4] and after that, she will depart."

But he said to them, "Don't delay me, for the Lord has blessed the journey for me. Send me away, that I may return to my master."

They replied, "Let's call the girl, and ask her."

They called Rebekah, and asked her, "Will you go with this man?"

She answered, "I will go."

So, they sent out Rebekah their sister, and her goods, with the slave of Abraham, and his attendants. They blessed Rebekah, and said to her, "You are our sister. Become tens of millions and let your descendants possess the cities of their enemies."

Rebekah rose up with her women, and they mounted the camels and went with the man, and the slave took Rebekah and departed. Isaac went through the wilderness to the well of the vision, and he lived in the land towards the south. Isaac went out into the plain in the evening to meditate, and having lifted up his eyes, he saw camels coming. And Rebekah lifted up her eyes and saw Isaac, and she quickly climbed down from the camel, and said to the slave, "Who is that man that walks in the plain to meet us?"

The slave answered, "This is my master, and she took her veil and covered herself."

The slave told Isaac all the things that he had done. Isaac went into the house of his mother and took Rebekah, and she became his wife, and he loved her, and Isaac was comforted by Sarah his mother.

Cosmic Genesis: Chapter 24 Notes

1 Codex Alexandrinus: c̄n ton t̄h̄n tou ōunou cae ton t̄h̄n tês gês (K̄NTON⊖N̄TOY O̅Y̅NOY̅KAITON⊖N̄THCΓHC). Translation: Lord the god the sky and the god earth

• Leningrad Codex: Yhovah elohei hashamayim velohei ha'aretz (יְהֹוָה אֱלֹהֵי הַשָּׁמַיִם וֵאלֹהֵי הָאָרֶץ). Translation: Yhovah god the skies (or Shamayim) and god the land (or Eretz)

• Peshitta: mryå ålhå dšmyå ůålhå dårôå (ܡܪܝܐ ܐܠܗܐ ܕܫܡܝܐ ܘܐܠܗܐ ܕܐܪܥܐ). Translation: master god the sky and god the land

• Targum Onkelos: meimra dayya elaha dishmayya velaha de'ar'a (מֵימְרָא דַיְיָ אֱלָהָא דִשְׁמַיָּא וֵאלָהָא דְאַרְעָא). Translation: command (or word) the Yhů god the sky and god the land

• Targum Jerusalem: meimra dayya elaha demoteveih bishmei meroma hu elaha deshuletaneih al ar'a (מֵימְרָא דַיְיָ אֱלָהָא דְמוֹתְבֵיהּ בִּשְׁמֵי מְרוֹמָא הוּא אֱלָהָא דְשׁוּלְטָנֵיהּ עַל אַרְעָא). Translation: command (or word) of the Yhů god of sky above also the dominater of the earth

Based on the Masoretic reading, these were probably originally three different gods. Both the Canaanite god of the skies Shamayim (שָׁמַיִם), and the Canaanite god of the earth Eretz (אֶרֶץ), were called on separately in other sections of the Torah and Tanakh, including as witnesses of the oaths between the Lord and humanity. By the beginning of the Christian era, the verse appears to been interpreted as a long title of the Lord.

2 LXX 961: dracmên (ΔΡΑΚΜΗΝ)

• Codex Alexandrinus: drachmês (ΔΡΑΧΜΗC)

• LXX 509: drachmên (ΔΡάχμ̱Ν)

• LXX 630: dragmên (ΔΡάγμ̱Ν)

• LXX 318: drachmê (ΔΡάχμ̱)

• LXX 730: didrachmone-dach (ΔΙΔΡάχμονϬ-ΔΔΧ)

• LXX 30: dragmon (ΔΡάγμον)

- LXX 129: didragmênedid (ⲆⲓⲆⲢⲀⲅⲙⲗ ⲛⲟⲆⲟⲓⲆ)

- LXX 246: didragmês (ⲆⲓⲆⲢⲀⲅⲙⲗⲥ)

- LXX 54: didrachmôn (ⲆⲓⲆⲢⲀⲭⲙⲟⲟⲛ)

- LXX 569: didragmon (ⲆⲓⲆⲢⲀⲅⲙⲟⲛ)

- LXX 107: drachmon (ⲆⲢⲀⲭⲙⲟⲛ)

- LXX 664: drachmôn (ⲆⲢⲀⲭⲙⲟⲟⲛ)

- LXX 59: didrachmên (ⲆⲓⲆⲢⲀⲭⲙⲗⲛ)

- Leningrad Codex: beka (בֶּקַע). Translation: half-shekel

- Peshitta: mtqlå (ܡܬܩܠܐ). Translation: weight (or shekel, beka)

- Targum Onkelos: sil'in (סִלְעִין). Translation: selas

- Fragment Targums: sal'in (סַלְעִין). Translation: selas

- Targum Jerusalem: sal'in (סַלְעִין). Translation: selas

The drachma was a Greek coin used from around 1100 BC, worth approximately 4.3 grams of silver. The beka was the half-shekel measurement used in ancient Canaan. As 'drachma' was the Greek translation of beka, the term beka is restored in this translation.

3 Berlin Genesis: gên tô cô (ⲅⲏⲛⲧⲱⲕ̄ⲱ). Translation: Earth the lord

- LXX 961: gên cô (ⲅⲏⲛⲕ̄ⲱ). Translation: Earth lord

- Codex Alexandrinus (LXX A): gên cô (ⲅⲏⲛⲕ̄ⲱ). Translation: Earth lord

- Cotton Genesis: gên tô cô (ⲅⲏⲛⲧⲱⲕ̄ⲱ). Translation: Earth the lord

- LXX 31: pêgên cyriô (πⲗⲅⲗⲛ ⲕⲩⲣⲫⲟⲟ). Translation: well (or fountain) lord

- Leningrad Codex: artzah laIhvah (אַרְצָה לַיהוָה). Translation: Earth to (or for) Ihvah

- Peshitta: årôå qdm mryå (ܐܪܥܐ ܩܕܡ ܡܪܝܐ). Translation: land before lord

- Targum Onkelos: ar'a kodam yeyah (אַרְעָא קֳדָם יְיָ). Translation: land before Yhů

- Targum Jerusalem: ar'a kodam yeyah (אַרְעָא קֳדָם יְיָ). Translation: land before Yhů

4 Codex Alexandrinus: hêmeras hôsi deca (ΗΜΕΡΑϹѠϹΕΙΔΕΚΑ). Translation: days until ten

- LXX 56: hêmeras ôs hêmeras deca (ℏμɖβⲁc ⲟⲟc ℏμɖβⲁc Δɖⲗⲁ). Translation: days as days ten

- Leningrad Codex: yamim ov asovr (יָמִים אוֹ עָשׂוֹר). Translation: days or ten

- Peshitta Manuscript 5b1: ymn ôrn bôrn åů ôhrå yrḥn (ܟ̈ܐܪ ܐ ܐܕܪ ܟܪܢ ܐܕܪ ܥܢ ܐܕܪ ܝܢ܂). Translation: days season (or time) until season (or time) or ten months (or moons)

- Peshitta Manuscript 7a1: ôrn yrḥ yůmyn (ܝܘܡܝܢ ܝܪܚ ܐܪܢ). Translation: time (or season) month (or moon) days

- Targum Onkelos: ôymnå ôydn bôydn åů ôsrh yrhyn (עימנא עידן בעידן או עסרה ירהין). Translation: day eon (or age, time) in (or with) eon (or age, time) or for ten months (or moons)

- Targum Jerusalem: shatta chada o ashar yarchin (שַׁתָּא חֲדָא אוֹ עֲשַׂר יַרְחִין). Translation: year or for ten months (or moons)

This verse has been unclear since before the Greek and Hebrew translations were made. The similarity of the Targum Onkelos from the 2nd century AD, and Peshitta Manuscript 5b1 from the 5th century indicates that the Aramaic text was different from both the Greek and Hebrew translations. The surviving Greek copies of Cosmic Genesis, including the Berlin Genesis papyrus from the 2nd century AD, all show signs of being reworked to synchronize with the Hebrew translation of Bereshít the Jews were using at the time. The Targum Onkelos, which is generally dated to sometime between 100 and 120 AD, is according to the Megillah tractate in the Talmud, a restoration of an Aramaic language version of the Torah in circulation before the time of Ezra the Scribe, circa 350 BC. The Targum Onkelos is attributed to Onkelos, a convert to Judaism, who, based on the interchangeable usage of the names in the Megillah tractates of the Jerusalem and Babylonian Talmuds, appears to have been Aquila of Sinope, a disciple of Rabbi Akiva. According to Epiphanius' *De Ponderibus et Mensuris*, Aquila was a Christian relative of the Roman emperor Hadrian, who was sent to Jerusalem to rebuild the city after the First Jewish-Roman War. In Jerusalem he was rejected by the Christians for practicing astrology, as so converted to Judaism.

The similarities between the Targum Onkelos and the Peshitta Manuscript 5b1 suggest that both manuscripts drew from an older Aramaic text of Bereshít which was different from the surviving Hebrew and Greek translations. If the Aramaic source contained the original text, then the confusing surviving Hebrew translation would have been a simplification of the original text. Based on the verse found in Onkelos and 5b1, the original text probably read, 'until the new year, in ten months.' This reading would be based a precursor to the Aramaic translation using the Egyptian term msût-rå where Onkelos uses the term 'day eon' (עימנא עידן). Msût-rô (𓇌𓏤𓂝𓏏𓇳𓏤) was the name of the Egyptian New Years festival, which translates as 'birth (or expected time) of Ra (or day).'

By the New Kingdom it had also become the name of the last month of the Egyptian Civil Calendar, however, in this usage it appears to been a reference to the new year, not the month. If the original text did read 'the new year, in ten months,' then the earliest Aramaic translation must have been made before the simplified Hebrew translation that survives in the Masoretic Text. The origin of 'day eon' as a translation for mswt-rå, likely dates to the New Kingdom era cuneiform translation of Cosmic Genesis, when the term would have probably been rendered as úmuum ådunum (𒌓𒈬𒌝 𒀀𒁺𒉡𒌢), meaning 'sun (or days) appointed time (or period).'

Cosmic Genesis: Chapter 25

Abraham took another wife, whose name was Chettura. She carried for him Zimran, Jokshan, Medan, Midian, Ishbak, and Shuah.

Jokshan fathered Sheba and Dedan.

The sons of Dedan were the Assyrians, the Latusians, and the Leums.

The sons of Midian were Gephar, Epher, Enoch, Abida, and Eldaah, and all these were sons of Chettura.

Nevertheless, Abraham gave all his possessions to Isaac his son.

To the sons of his concubines, Abraham gave gifts, and while he was still living, he sent them east, into the country of the east, away from his son Isaac.

These were the years of the days of the life of Abraham as many as he lived, a hundred and seventy-five years, and Abraham died at a good old age, an old man full of days, and was added to his people. Isaac and Ishmael his sons, buried him in the double cave, in the field of Ephron, the son of Zohar the Cypriot, which is near Mamre, the field and the cave that Abraham bought from the sons of the Cypriot, and there they buried Abraham and Sarah his wife.

After Abraham was dead, God blessed Isaac his son, and Isaac lived by the 'well of the vision.'

These are the generations of Ishmael, the son of Abraham, whom Hagar the Egyptian, the woman-slave of Sarah carried for Abraham. These are the names of the sons of Ishmael, and the names of their generations. The firstborn of Ishmael were Nebajoth, Kedar, Adbeel, Mibsam, Masma, Duma, Mesha, Hadar, Teman, Jetur, Naphish, and Kedemah.

These are the sons of Ishmael, and these are their names, in their tents and in their dwellings, twelve princes according to their nations. These are the years of the life of Ishmael, a hundred and thirty-seven years, and he died and was added to his family. He lived from Havilah to Zur, which is opposite Egypt until one comes to the Assyrians, and he lived in the presence of all his brothers.

These are the generations of Isaac the son of Abraham. Abraham fathered Isaac. Isaac was forty years old when he took Rebekah as a wife, the daughter of Bethuel the Syrian, from Syrian Mesopotamia, the sister of Laban the Syrian.

Isaac prayed to the Lord concerning Rebekah, his wife, because she was barren, and the Lord heard him, and his wife Rebekah conceived in her womb. The babies moved within her, and she said, "If it is so for me, why is this happening to me?"

She went to inquire of the Lord, and the Lord said to her, "There are two nations in your womb, and two peoples will be separated from your belly, and one people will excel the other, and the greater will serve the less."

The days were fulfilled that she should deliver, and she had twins in her womb. The first came out red, and hairy all over like an animal skin, and she called his name Esau. After this, his brother came out, and his hand grabbed the heel of Esau, and she called his name Jacob. Isaac was sixty years old when Rebekah carried them. The boys grew, and Esau was a man skilled in hunting and living in the country, while Jacob was a simple man living in a house. Isaac loved Esau because his food was venison, but Rebekah loved Jacob. Jacob cooked a stew, and Esau came in from the plain collapsing.

Esau said to Jacob, "Let me eat that red stew because I am collapsing," and so his name was called Edom.

Jacob said to Esau, "Sell me your birthright today."

Esau replied, "Look, I am going to die, and what good is this birthright that belongs to me?"

Jacob said to him, "Swear to me today," and he swore to him, and Esau sold his birthright to Jacob. Jacob gave bread to Esau, and lentil stew and he ate and drank, and he arose and departed, and so Esau slighted his birthright.

Cosmic Genesis: Chapter 26

There was a famine in the land, besides the earlier famine which was during the time of Abraham, and Isaac went to Abimelech the king of the Pelesets to Gerar. The Lord appeared to him and said, "Don't go down to Egypt but stay in the land that I will tell you. Stay in this land and I will be with you, and bless you. I will give you and your descendants all this land, and I will establish my oath which I swore to your father Abraham. I will multiply your descendants like the stars of the sky, and I will give to your descendants all this land, and all the nations of the land will be blessed in your descendants. Because Abraham your father listened to my voice and kept my injunctions, and my commandments, and my ordinances, and my statutes."

Isaac lived in Gerar, and when the men of the place questioned him about Rebekah his wife, he said, 'She is my sister,' as he was afraid to say, 'She is my wife,' in case the men of the land should kill him because of Rebekah, because she was beautiful. He remained there a long time, and Abimelech the king of Gerar leaned to look through the window and saw Isaac playing with Rebekah his wife. Abimelech called Isaac, and asked, "Is she your wife? Why have you said, 'She is my sister?'"

Isaac answered him, "I did so because I thought, 'At some point, I may die because of her.'"

Abimelech said to him, "Why have you done this to us? One of my family may have laid with your wife in the near future, and you would have brought a sin of ignorance on us."

Abimelech commanded all his people, "Every man that touches this man and his wife will die."

Isaac sowed in that land, and he found in that year the barley grew a hundred-fold, and the Lord blessed him. The man was praised and increased until he became very famous. He had flocks of sheep, and herds of oxen, and many tilled fields, and the Pelesets envied him. All the wells, which the servants of his father had dug in the time of his father, the Pelesets filled up with dirt.

Abimelech said to Isaac, "Leave from among us, as you have become much stronger than we are."

Isaac departed from there, and traveled to the valley of Gerar, and lived there. Isaac re-dug the wells of water, which the servants of his father Abraham had dug, which the Pelesets had filled in after the death of his father Abraham, and he called them by the names that his father had named them. The servants of Isaac dug in the valley of Gerar, and they found there a well of living water. The shepherds from Gerar fought with the shepherds of Isaac, saying that the water was theirs, and they called the name of the well, 'Injury,' for they had injured him. After departing there, he dug another well, and they fought also for that one, and he named it 'Enmity.'

After leaving there they dug another well, and they did not fight over that one so he named it 'Room,' saying, "Because now the Lord has made room for us, and has increased us on the land."

He traveled from there to the 'Well of the Oath.' The Lord appeared to him that night, and said, "I am the god of Abraham your father. Don't be afraid, for I am with you, and I will bless you, and multiply your descendants for the sake of Abraham your father."

He built an altar there and called on the name of the Lord. He pitched his tent there, and the servants of Isaac dug a well there, in the valley of Gerar. Abimelech came to him from Gerar, and so did Ochozath his friend, and Phichol the commander-in-chief of his army.

Isaac asked them, "Why have you come to me? Before you hated me and sent me away from you."

They replied, "We have certainly seen that the Lord was with you, and we said, 'Let there be an oath between us and you,' and we will make a covenant with you, so you will do no wrong to us, as we have not hated you, and as we have treated you well, and have sent you away peacefully, now you are blessed by the Lord."

He made a feast for them, and they ate and drank. They rose in the morning and swore to each other, and Isaac sent them away, and they departed from him in safety.

It happened on that day, that the servants of Isaac came and told him of the well which they had dug, and they said, "We have not found water."

He called it, 'Oath.' Therefore he called the name of that city, the 'Well of Oath,' until today.

Esau was forty years old, and he took as wife Ioudin,[1] the daughter of Beoch the Cypriot, and Bashemath, daughter of Helon the Cypriot, and they were provoking to Isaac and Rebekah.

Cosmic Genesis: Chapter 26 Notes

1 Berlin Genesis: Ioudin (ιΟΥΔΕΙΝ)

- LXX 15: Ioudith (ιουΔⲋⲧθ)

- LXX 18: Ioudên (ιουΔⳑⲛ)

- LXX 64: Ioudin (ιουΔιⲛ)

- LXX 135: Ioudith (ιουΔⲓθ)

- LXX 55: Ioudêth (ιουΔⳑⲛθ)

- LXX 370: Ohydên (Ο υⲆⳑⲛ)

- LXX 56: Adan (ⲝⲆⲆⲛ)

- LXX 569: Ioud (ιουⲆ)

- LXX 53: Addan (ⲝⲆⲆⲆⲛ)

- Leningrad Codex: Yehudit (יְהוּדִית)

- Peshitta: Yhůdyt (ܝܗܘܕܝܬ)

- Targum Onkelos: Yehudit (יְהוּדִית)

- Targum Jerusalem: Yehudit (יְהוּדִית)

- Bohairic manuscripts: Ioudim (ΙογⲆⲓⲙ)

The Hebrew and Aramaic Yehudit (יְהוּדִית) is the name generally transliterated as Judith in English, however, the earliest surviving Greek and Coptic manuscripts used the name Ioudin / Ioudim (Ιουδειν / ΙογⲆⲓⲙ), indicating the early Aramaic translation likely used a different name. As the name Yhwdyt was the Canaanite name for a Judahite woman, and Judah did not exist in the time of Esau, it appears to be a Hasmonean era alteration to the text.

Cosmic Genesis: Chapter 27

After Isaac was old, his eyes were blinded and he could not see, and he called Esau, his elder son, and said to him, "My son?"

He answered, "Know that I am here."

He said, "Know that I have grown old, and don't know the day of my death. Now then take the weapons, both your quiver and your bow, and go into the plain, and get me venison, and make me meats as I like them, and bring them to me so I can eat, that my mind will bless you before I die."

Rebekah heard Isaac speaking to Esau his son, and Esau went to the plain to procure venison for his father. Rebekah said to Jacob, her younger son, "Know that I heard your father speaking to Esau your brother, saying, 'Bring me venison, and prepare me meats, that I may eat and bless you before the Lord before I die.' Now then my son, listen to me, as I command you. And go to the livestock and take for me there two kids, tender and good, and I will make them meats for your father, as he likes. And you will bring them to your father, and he will eat, that your father may bless you before he dies."

Jacob said to his mother Rebekah, "Esau, my brother, is a hairy man while I am a smooth man. Suppose my father feels me, and he will know that I am a liar, and I will bring on a curse on myself, and not a blessing."

His mother said to him, "Your curse is on me son. Only listen to my voice, and go and bring them to me."

So he went and brought them to his mother, and his mother made meats as his father liked them. And Rebekah took the fine clothing of her elder son Esau which was with her in the house, put it on Jacob her younger son. She put on his arms the skins of the sheep, and on the bare parts of his neck. She gave the meats, and the loaves which she had prepared, into the hands of Jacob her son.

He brought them to his father, and said, "Father?"

He replied, "Look I am here. Who are you son?"

Jacob said to his father, "I am Esau, your firstborn, and have done as you told me. Rise and sit, and eat of my venison, so your mind may bless me."

Isaac asked his son, "What is this, that you have found so quickly?"

He answered, "That which the Lord, your god brought to me."

Isaac told Jacob, "Come near to me, so I can feel you son, if you are my son Esau."

Jacob approached his father Isaac, and he felt him, and said, "The voice is Jacob's voice, but the hands are the hands of Esau."

He did not know him, as his hands were hairy like the hands of his brother Esau, and he blessed him, asking, "Are you my son Esau?"

He answered, "I am."

He said, "Bring it here, and I will eat of your venison son, so my mind may bless you," and he brought it to him, and he ate, and he brought him wine, and he drank.

Isaac his father, said to him, "Approach me and kiss me son."

He approached and kissed him, and smelled the odor of his garments, and blessed him, and said, "I know the smell of my son is like the smell of an abundant field, which the Lord has blessed. May God give to you of the dew of the sky, and the oil of the land, and an abundance of grain and wine. Let nations serve you, and princes bow down to you, and may you be the lord of your brother, and may the sons of your father do reverence to you, and accursed is he who curses you and blessed is he who blesses you."

After Isaac had finished blessing his son Jacob, right after Jacob had left the presence of Isaac his father, it happened that Esau his brother returned from hunting. He also prepared meats and brought them to his father, and he asked his father, "Let my father get up, and eat his son's venison, so that your mind may bless me."

Isaac his father asked him, "Who are you?"

He answered, "I am your firstborn son Esau."

Isaac was bewildered, and asked, "Who then is it that has procured venison for me and brought it to me? I already ate it before you came, and I have blessed him, and he will be blessed."

When Esau heard the words of his father Isaac, he cried out greatly and bitterly, saying, "I beg you, bless me also father!"

He answered him, "Your brother has come with subterfuge, and stolen your blessing."

He said, "He was named Jacob rightly! Know that this is the second time he has supplanted me. He has taken both my birthright and now he has taken my blessing!"

Esau asked his father, "Have you no blessing left for me father?"

Isaac answered Esau, "If I have made him your lord, and have made all his brothers his servants, and have strengthened him with grain and wine, then what will I do for you, son?"

Esau said to his father, "Have you only one blessing father? I beg you, bless me also father."

Isaac was troubled, and Esau cried aloud and wept. Isaac his father answered and said to him, "Know that your life will be of the oil of land, and of the dew of the sky from above. You will live by your sword and will serve your brother, and there will be a time when you will break and loosen his shackle from off your neck."

Esau was angry with Jacob because of the blessing, that his father blessed him, and Esau thought, 'Let the days of my father's mourning draw near, that I may kill my brother Jacob.'

The words of Esau her elder son were reported to Rebekah, and she sent and called Jacob her younger son, and said to him, "Know that Esau, your brother, threatens to kill you. Now then my son, listen to my voice, and get up and leave quickly into Mesopotamia, to Laban my brother in Harran. Live with him some days, until your brother's anger and rage against you subsides, and he forgets what you have done to him, and I will send and fetch you there, in case at any time I should be bereaved of you both in one day."

Rebekah said to Isaac, "I am tired of my life, because of the daughters of the sons of the Cypriots. If Jacob takes a wife of the daughters of this land, why should I live?"

Cosmic Genesis: Chapter 28

Isaac called Jacob, and he blessed him, and commanded him, "You will not take a wife from the daughters of the Canaanites. Rise and leave quickly to Mesopotamia, to the house of Bethuel the father of your mother, and take for yourself from there a wife from the daughters of Laban your mother's brother. May the god Resheph[1] bless you, and increase you, and multiply you, and you will become a number of nations. May he give you the blessing of my father Abraham, both you and your descendants after you, to inherit the land of your travels, which God gave to Abraham.

So Isaac sent Jacob away, and he went into Mesopotamia, to Laban the son of Bethuel the Syrian, the brother of Rebekah the mother of Jacob and Esau. Esau saw that Isaac had blessed Jacob, and sent him away to Syrian Mesopotamia as he blessed him, to fetch a wife for himself from there, when he ordered him, "You will not take a wife of the daughters of the Canaanites," and Jacob listened to his father and his mother, and went to Syrian Mesopotamia.

When Esau realized that the daughters of Canaan were evil in the eyes of Isaac, Esau went to Ishmael and took Mahalath the daughter of Ishmael, the son of Abraham, the sister of Nebajoth, as a wife in addition to his other wives.

Jacob left the Well of the Oath and traveled to Harran, and came to a certain place and slept there, as the sun had gone down, and he took one of the stones of the place, and put it at his head, and lay down to sleep in that place. He dreamed and saw a ladder fixed on the land whose top reached to the sky, and the messengers of God ascended and descended on it.[2]

The Lord stood on it, and said, "I am the god of your father Abraham, and the god of Isaac. Don't be afraid. I will give you and your descendants the land on which you lie. Your descendants will be like the sand of the land, and it will spread out to the sea, and the south, and the north, and to the east, and through you and your descendants will all the tribes of the land be blessed. Understand that I am with you to protect you forever in all the paths that you will travel, and I will bring you back to this land. I will not desert you until I have done all that I have told you."

Jacob awoke from his sleep, and said, "The Lord is in this place, and I did not know it."

He was afraid, and said, "How terrible is this place! This is none other than the house of God, and this is the gateway to the sky."

Jacob rose up in the morning and took the stone that had laid there by his head, and he set it up as a pillar and poured oil on the top of it. He named that place: Beth El. (The name of the town had previously been Luz.) Jacob vowed a vow, "If the Lord the god will be with me, and guard me throughout this journey which I am going on, and give me bread to eat, and clothing to put on, and bring me back in safety to the house of my father, then the Lord will be my god. This stone, which I have set as a pillar for you, will be the Temple of God for me, and of everyone, whatever you will give me, I will tithe a tenth for you."

Cosmic Genesis: Chapter 28 Notes

1 Codex Alexandrinus: t͞h͞s c͞s mou (ⲐⲤⲔⲤⲘⲞⲨ). Translation: god lord of mine

- LXX 64: theos mou (θεὸς μου). Translation: god of mine.

- Leningrad Codex: el shaddai (אֵל שַׁדַּי). Translation: god Šadday

- Peshitta: Åylšdy (ܐܠܫܕܝ,)

- Targum Onkelos: el shaddai (אֵל שַׁדַּי). Translation: god Šadday

- Targum Jerusalem: el shaddai (אֵל שַׁדַּי). Translation: god Šadday

This is the second deviation between Cosmic Genesis and Bereshít regarding the god Shaddai, and the second time the name or title Shaddai is missing entirely from the Septuagint's translation. The name Shaddai is imported from the Masoretic version and restored to Resheph to correct for the New Kingdom era redaction. For more information on the god Shadday and Resheph see the note in Cosmic Genesis: Chapter 17.

2 This story of a ladder reaching up into the sky was also found in the creation mythology of Heliopolis, in which Osiris climbed a ladder up into Nut (Night-sky). As a result, Egyptian tombs often included a ladder, and had the ceiling of the crypt, or interior or the lid of the sarcophagus painted blue with stars, representing Nut. The story involving Osiris appeared in the fifth dynasty, supplanting the an older version of the story in which Horus the Elder was assisted to climb the ladder into the sky by his four sons. As the Egyptian story is much older than the Israelite version, it seems likely that the story, of Jacob's dream itself, was based on the story from the creation mythology of Heliopolis.

Cosmic Genesis: Chapter 29

Jacob having lifted up his feet went to the land of the east to Laban, the son of Bethuel the Syrian, and the brother of Rebekah, mother of Jacob and Esau. He looked and found a well in the plain. There were three flocks of sheep resting at it, as out of that well they watered the flocks, but there was a great stone at the mouth of the well. There were all the flocks gathered, and they used to roll away the stone from the mouth of the well, and water the flocks, and set the stone again in its place on the mouth of the well.

Jacob asked them, "Brothers, where are you from?" They answered, "We are from Harran."

He asked them, "Do you know Laban the son of Nahor?"

They answered, "We do know him."

He asked them, "Is he well?"

They answered, "He is well. Look Rachel his daughter came with the sheep."

Jacob said, "It is still midday, it is not yet time for the flocks to be gathered together. Water your flocks, and leave and feed them."

They replied, "We will not be able to until all the shepherds are gathered together, and they roll away the stone from the mouth of the well. Then we will water the flocks."

While he was still speaking to them, Rachel the daughter of Laban came with her father's sheep, as she fed the sheep of her father. When Jacob saw Rachel the daughter of Laban, his mother's brother, and the sheep of Laban, his mother's brother, he came and rolled the stone away from the mouth of the well, and watered the sheep of Laban, his mother's brother. Jacob kissed Rachel, and cried with a loud voice, and wept. He told Rachel that he was the close relative of her father and the son of Rebekah, and she ran and reported to her father according to these words. It happened when Laban heard the name of Jacob, his sister's son, he ran to meet him, and embraced and kissed him, and brought him into his house, and he told Laban all these things.

Laban said to him, "You are of my bones and of my flesh," and he was with him a month.

Laban said to Jacob, "Surely you will not serve me for nothing, because you are my brother. Tell me what your reward is to be."

Now Laban had two daughters, the name of the elder was Leah, and the name of the younger, Rachel. The eyes of Leah were weak. But Rachel was beautiful in appearance, and very beautiful in attitude. Jacob loved Rachel, and offered, "I will serve you seven years for your younger daughter Rachel."

Laban replied to him, "It is better that I should give her to you, than that I should give her to another man. Live with me."

Jacob served for Rachel seven years, and they seemed to him like just a few days, because of his love of her. Jacob said to Laban, "Give me my wife, for my days are completed, that I may go into her."

Laban gathered together all the men of the land and held a marriage feast. However, he took his daughter Leah and brought her to Jacob, and Jacob went into her. Laban gave his daughter Leah, Zilpah his woman-slave, to be her woman-slave. In the morning Jacob realized it was Leah, and Jacob demanded from Laban, "What is this that you have done to me? Did I not serve you for Rachel? Why have you deceived me!"

Laban answered, "In our country, we do not give the younger before the elder! Work another seven years, and I will give her to you also, in return for your labor."

Jacob did so, and worked another seven, and Laban gave him his daughter Rachel as a wife. Laban gave to his daughter his woman-slave Bilhah, as a woman-slave for her.

He went into Rachel, and he loved Rachel more than Leah, and he served him another seven years. When the Lord the god saw that Leah was hated, he opened her womb, but Rachel was barren. Leah conceived and carried a son for Jacob, and she called his name, 'Reuben,' saying, "Because the Lord has looked on my humiliation, and has given me a son, now my husband will love me."

She conceived again and carried a second son for Jacob, and she said, "Because the Lord has heard that I am hated, he has given to me this one also," and she called his name, 'Simeon.'

She conceived yet again, and carried a son, and said, "Now my husband will be with me, for I have born him three sons." Therefore she called his name, 'Levi.'

Having conceived yet again, she carried a son, and said, "Now yet again I will give thanks to the Lord."

Therefore she called his name, 'Judah,' and stopped becoming pregnant.

Cosmic Genesis: Chapter 30

When Rachel saw that she carried no children for Jacob, she was jealous of her sister, and said to Jacob, "Give me children, or I will kill myself!"

Jacob was angry with Rachel, and said to her, "Am I in the place of the god who has deprived you of the fruit of the womb?"

Rachel said to Jacob, "See my woman-slave Bilhah, go into her, and she will bear on my knees, and I also will have children through her."

She gave him Bilhah her slave, as a wife for him, and Jacob went into her. Bilhah, Rachel's slave, conceived and carried Jacob a son, and Rachel said, "God has given judgment for me, and listened to my voice, and has given me a son," therefore she called his name, 'Dan.'

Bilhah, Rachel's slave, conceived again and carried a second son for Jacob, and Rachel said, "God has helped me. I competed with my sister and won," and she called his name, 'Naphtali.'

Leah saw that she stopped becoming pregnant, and she took Zilpah her slave, and gave her to Jacob as a wife, and he went into her. Zilpah the slave of Leah conceived and carried Jacob a son, and Leah said, "It is joyous," and she called his name, 'Gad.'

Zilpah, the slave of Leah conceived again and carried Jacob a second son, Leah said, "I am blessed, and the women will pronounce me blessed," and she called his name, 'Asher.'

Reuben went out on the day of the barley harvest, and found apples of mandrakes in the field, and brought them to his mother Leah, and Rachel said to Leah her sister, "Give me from your son's mandrakes."

Leah asked, "Is it not enough for you that you have taken my husband, will you also take my son's mandrakes?"

Rachel answered, "Not so. Let him lie with you tonight, in trade for your son's mandrakes."

Jacob came in out of the field at even, and Leah went out to meet him, and said, "You will come to me today, for I have hired you for my son's mandrakes," and he lay with her that night.

God listened to Leah, and she conceived and carried Jacob a fifth son. Leah said, "God has given me my reward because I gave my slave to my husband," and she called his name 'Issachar,' which means 'Reward.'

Leah conceived again and carried Jacob a sixth son, and Leah said, "God has given me a good gift at this time. My husband will prefer me, for I have carried him six sons," and she called his name, 'Zebulun.'

After this, she carried a daughter, and she called her name, 'Dinah.' God remembered Rachel, and God listened to her, and he opened her womb. She conceived and carried Jacob a son, and Rachel said, "God has taken away my shame."

She called his name Joseph, saying, "Let God add to me another son."

It happened after Rachel had born Joseph, Jacob said to Laban, "Send me away, that I may go to my place and to my land. Give my wives and my children, for whom I have served you, that I may depart, for you know the service which I have done for you."

Laban said to him, "If I have found favor in your sight, stay, perhaps understood well, for the Lord has blessed me at your coming in. State your wages to me, and I will give them."

Jacob replied, "You know in what ways I have served you, and how much of your livestock is with me. You had little before my time, and it has increased to a great multitude, and the Lord the god has blessed you at my feet. Now then, when will I set up also my own house?"

Laban asked him, "What will I give you?"

Jacob answered him, "You will not give me anything. If you will do this for me, I will again tend your flocks and look after them. Let all your sheep pass by today, and separate out every gray sheep from the rams, and everyone speckled and spotted goat, and this will be my reward. And my righteousness will listen to me in the morning, for it is my reward before you. Whatever will not be spotted and speckled among the goats, and gray among the rams will be taken with me."

Laban said to him, "Let it be as you've said." He separated in that day the spotted and speckled male-goats, and all the spotted and speckled female-goats, and all that was gray among the rams, and everyone that was white among them, and he gave them into the hand of his sons. He set a distance of a three days' journey between them and between Jacob. Jacob tended the livestock of Laban that were left behind.

Jacob took for himself green sticks of styrax trees and walnut and other trees, and Jacob peeled in them white stripes, and as he drew off the green, the white stripe which he had made appeared alternate on the sticks. He laid the sticks which he had peeled, in the hollows of the watering-troughs, that whenever the livestock should come to drink, as they should have come to drink before the sticks, the livestock might conceive at the sticks. So the livestock conceived at the sticks, and the livestock brought out young speckled and streaked and spotted with ash-colored spots. Jacob separated the lambs and set before the sheep a speckled ram, and every variegated one among the lambs, and he separated flocks for himself alone and did not mingle them with the sheep of Laban. It happened in the time in which the livestock became pregnant, conceiving in the belly, Jacob put the sticks before the livestock in the troughs, that they might conceive by the sticks. But he did not put them in indiscriminately whenever the livestock happened to bring out, but the unmarked ones were Laban's, and the marked ones were Jacob's. The man became very rich, and he had many livestock, and oxen, and servants, and woman-slaves, and camels, and donkeys.

Cosmic Genesis: Chapter 31

Jacob heard the words of the sons of Laban, saying, "Jacob has taken all that was our father's, and from our father's property he has received all this glory."

Jacob saw the attitude of Laban, and saw it was not towards him as it had been before. The Lord said to Jacob, "Return to the land of your father, and to your family, and I will be with you."

Jacob sent, and called Leah and Rachel to the plain where the flocks were. He said to them, "I see the face of your father, that it is not towards me as before, but the god of my father is with me. You too know, that with all my might I have served your father. But your father deceived me and changed my wages for the ten lambs, yet God gave him no power to hurt me. If he should say, 'The speckled will be your reward, then all the livestock would carry speckled,' and if he should say, 'The white will be your reward, then all would the livestock carry white.' So God has taken away all the livestock of your father, and given them to me. It happened when the livestock conceived and were with young, that I saw with my eyes while sleeping, and I saw the male-goats and the rams leaping on the sheep and the female-goats, speckled and variegated and spotted with ash-colored spots. The messenger of God said to me while I slept, 'Jacob,' and I asked, 'What is it?' He said, 'Look up with your eyes, and see the male-goats and the rams leaping on the sheep and the female-goats, speckled and variegated and spotted with ash-colored spots, for I have seen all things that Laban does to you. I am the God who appeared to you in the house of God, where you anointed a pillar to me, and vowed to me. Now then arise and depart out of this land, return to the land of your birth, and I will be with you.'"

Rachel and Leah answered, "Have we still a part or inheritance in the house of our father? Are we not considered strangers to him? He sold us and consumed our silver. All the wealth and the glory which God has taken from our father, it will be ours' and our childrens'. Now then do whatever God has told you."

Jacob rose and placed his wives and his children up on the camels. He took away all his possessions and all his stores, which he had received in Mesopotamia, and all that belonged to him, to depart to Isaac his father in the land of Canaan. Laban went to shear his sheep, and Rachel stole her father's icons. Jacob hid the matter from Laban the Syrian, so as not to tell him that he ran away. He departed with all that belonged to him, and passed over the river, and went into the mountains of Gilead.

But it was told to Laban the Syrian on the third day, that Jacob had fled, and he took his brothers with him, and chased after him a journey of seven days, and caught up to him in the mountains of Gilead. God came to Laban the Syrian in sleep at night, and said to him, "Pay attention that you don't at any time speak evilly to Jacob."

Laban caught up with Jacob, where Jacob pitched his tent in the mountains, and Laban stationed his brothers in the mountains of Gilead. Laban asked Jacob, "What have you done? Why did you run away secretly, and rob me and lead away my daughters like captive slaves? If you had told me, I would have sent you away with joy, and with songs, and timbrels, and harp. Was I not considered worthy to embrace my children and my daughters? Now then, you have worked foolishly. Now my hand has the power to hurt you, but the god of your father spoke to me yesterday, saying, 'Pay attention that you don't at any time speak evilly to Jacob.' Now then go on your way, for you have earnestly desired to depart to the house of your father. But why have you stolen my gods?"

Jacob answered Laban, "I was afraid, as I thought that at any point you might take away your daughters from me, and all my property."

Jacob continued, "With whoever you will find your gods, he will not live in the presence of our brothers. Take note of whatever I have of your property and take it," and he found nothing with him, but Jacob did not know that his wife Rachel had stolen them.

Laban went in and searched in the house of Leah, and did not find them, and he went out of the house of Leah, and searched in the house of Jacob, and in the house of the two woman-slaves, and did not find them, and he went also into the house of Rachel. Rachel took the icons, and placed them among the camel's packs, and sat on them. She said to her father, "do not be angry lord. I can't rise up before you, for it is with me according to the manner of women."

Laban searched in all the house and did not find his icons. Jacob was angry and argued with Laban, and Jacob answered and said to Laban, "What is my injustice, and what is my sin, that you have chased after me, and that you have searched all the furniture of my house? What have you found of all the furniture from your house? Set it here between your relations and my relations, and let them decide between us. For twenty years I have been with you, your sheep and your female-goats have not failed in carrying, and I did not eat the rams from your livestock. That which was stolen from your animals I did not report to you, and I made good from my own, both the thefts of the day and the thefts of the night. I was parched with heat by day and chilled with frost by night, and my sleep departed from my eyes. For twenty years have I been in your house. I served you fourteen years for your two daughters, and six years as a shepherd, and you falsely rated my pay for ten lambs. Unless I had the god of my father Abraham, and the fear of Isaac, now you would have sent me away empty. God saw my humiliation, and the labor of my hands, and rebuked you yesterday."

Laban answered Jacob, "The daughters are my daughters, and the sons my sons, and the livestock are my livestock, and all things which you see are mine, and the property of my daughters. What will I do to them today, or their children which they carried? Now then come, let me make a covenant, both I and you, and it will be as a witness between me and you."

He said to him, "Understand, there is no one with us. See God is a witness between me and you."

Jacob took a stone and set it up for a pillar. Jacob said to his brothers, "Gather stones," and they gathered stones and made a stack, and ate there on the stack.

Laban said to him, "This stack witnesses between me and you today."

Laban called it, the 'Stack of Testimony,' and Jacob called it, the 'Witness Stack.'

Laban said to Jacob, "See this stack and the pillar which I have set between me and you. This stack witnesses, and this pillar witnesses."

Therefore its name was called, the 'Stack Witnesses.'

The witness of which he spoke was, "Let God see it between me and you, because we are about to depart from each other. If you will humiliate my daughters, if you should take wives in addition to my daughters, see, there is no one with us watching, but God is witness between me and you."

Laban said to Jacob, "Know this stack and this pillar are a witness. For if I should not cross over to you, neither should you cross over to me, for mischief beyond this stack and this pillar. The god of Abraham and the god of Nahor judge between us," and Jacob swore by the fear of his father Isaac.

He offered a sacrifice in the mountain and called his brothers, and they ate and drank, and slept in the mountain. Laban rose up in the morning, and kissed his sons and his daughters, and blessed them, and Laban having turned back, departed to his place.

Cosmic Genesis: Chapter 32

Jacob left for his journey, and looking up, he saw the camp of the army of God, and the messengers of God met him. When he saw them Jacob said, "This is the Camp of God, and he called the name of that place, 'Encampments.'

Jacob sent messengers before him to Esau his brother to the land of Seir, in the country of Edom. He ordered them, saying, "Say this to my Lord Esau. So says your servant Jacob, 'I have stayed with Laban and waited until now. There were born to me oxen, and donkeys, and sheep, and men-slaves and women-slaves, and I sent word to my Lord Esau, that your servant might find favor in your sight.'"

The messengers returned to Jacob and reported, "We came to your brother Esau, and he comes to meet you with four hundred men."

Jacob was greatly terrified and was confused, and he divided the people that were with him, and the cows, and the camels, and the sheep, into two camps. Jacob said, "If Esau should come to one camp, and attack it, the other camp will be safe."

Jacob said, "God of my father Abraham, and god of my father Isaac, Lord, you are he who said to me, 'Depart quickly to the land of your birth, and I will do good for you.' Let there be for me a sufficiency of all the justice and all the truth which you have worked with your servant. For with this, my wand, I passed over this Jordan. Now I have become two camps. Save me from the hand of my brother, from the hand of Esau, for I am afraid of him, in case he should come and slaughter me, and the mothers of the children. But you said, 'I will do you good, and will make your descendants like the sand of the sea, which will not be a countable number.'"

He slept there that night, and took of the gifts which he carried with him, and sent out to Esau his brother, two hundred female-goats, twenty male-goats, two hundred sheep, twenty rams, thirty camels milking their foals, forty cows, ten bulls, twenty donkeys, and ten colts. He gave them to his servants and separated the groups, and he said to his servants, "Go out ahead of me, and put a space between the two groups."

He ordered the first, "If Esau my brother meets you, and asks you, 'Who are you? Where do you go, and whose are these possessions advancing before you?' You will answer, 'Your servant Jacob. He has sent gifts to my lord Esau, and he follows behind us.'"

He ordered the first and the second and the third, and all that went before him after these flocks, saying, "You will speak to your master Esau when you find him, and you will say, 'See, your servant Jacob follows us.'"

As he thought, 'I will reduce his anger with the gifts going to his presence, and afterward I will see his face, and perhaps he will accept me.'

So, the presents went on before him, but he himself stayed that night in the camp. He rose up in that night, and took his two wives and his two servant-maids, and his eleven children, and crossed over the ford of Jabbok. He took them, and passed over the torrent, and brought over all his possessions. Jacob was left alone, and a man wrestled with him until the morning. He saw that he could not prevail against him, and he touched the broad part of his thigh, and the broad part of Jacob's thigh was numbed during his wrestling with him.

He said to him, "Let me go, the day has dawned."

But he said, "I will not let you go, unless you bless me."

He asked him, "What is your name?"

He answered, "Jacob."

He said to him, "Your name will no longer be called Jacob. Your name will be Israel. You have prevailed with God, and will be mighty among men."

Jacob asked, "Tell me your name,"

He replied, "Why do you ask my name?" and he blessed him there.

Jacob called the name of that place, 'Face of God,' as, he said, 'I have seen God, face to face, and my life was saved.'"

The sun rose on him when he passed the Face of God, and he halted on his thigh. Therefore, the children of Israel will not eat the sinew which was benumbed, which is on the broad part of the thigh, until today, because the messenger had touched the broad part of the thigh of Jacob, the sinew which was numbed.

Cosmic Genesis: Chapter 33

Jacob looked up with his eyes and saw Esau his brother coming with four hundred men with him, and Jacob divided the children with Leah and Rachel, and the two slave-women. He put the two slave-women and their children first, and Leah and her children behind, and Rachel and Joseph last. He approached them and bowed to the ground seven times until he drew near to his brother. Esau ran on to meet him, and embraced him, and fell on his neck, and kissed him, and they both wept. Esau looked up and saw the women and the children, and asked, "Who are these to you?"

He answered, "The children with which God has mercifully blessed your servant."

The woman-slaves and their children approached and did reverence. Leah and her children approached and did reverence, and after this Rachel and Joseph approached and did reverence.

He asked, "What are these companies that I have met?"

He answered, "Gifts that your servant might find favor in your sight, my Lord."

Esau stated, "I have much my brother. Keep your own."

Jacob offered, "If I have found favor in your sight, receive the gifts through my hands. As I have seen your face, I have seen the face of God, and you will be very pleased with me. Receive my blessings, which I have brought you because God has had mercy on me, and I have all things," and he constrained him, and he took them.

He said, "Let us leave, and proceed right now."

He replied to him, "My Lord knows, that the children are very young, and the flocks and the herds with me are young. If I will drive them hard one day, all the livestock will die. Let my Lord go on before his servant, and I will have strength on the road according to the ease of the journey before me, and according to the speed of the children until I come to my lord at Seir."

Esau offered, "I will leave some of my people with you."

He asked, "Why? It is enough that I have found favor before you my lord."

Esau left that day on his journey to Seir. Jacob departed to his tents, and he made houses for himself there, and for his livestock he made stalls, therefore he called the name of that place, 'Booths.' Jacob came to Salem, a city of Shechem, which is in the land of Canaan when he departed out of Mesopotamia in Syria, and pitched his tent in front of the city. He bought the portion of the field, where he pitched his tent, from Hamor the father of Shechem, for a hundred lambs. He set up there an altar and called on God of Israel.

Cosmic Genesis: Chapter 34

Dinah, the daughter of Leah, whom she carried for Jacob, went out to see the daughters of the inhabitants. Shechem the son of Hamor the Mitannian, the ruler of the land, saw her, and took her and lay with her, and embarrassed her. He was attached to the mind of Dinah the daughter of Jacob, and he loved the girl, and he spoke to her according to the heart of the girl. Shechem spoke to Hamor his father, saying, "Take for me this girl as a wife."

Jacob heard that the son of Hamor had defiled Dinah his daughter while his sons were with his livestock in the plain. Jacob was silent until they came. Hamor the father of Shechem went out to Jacob, to speak to him. The sons of Jacob came from the plain, and when they heard, the men were deeply pained, and it was very grievous to them, because the man worked folly in Israel, having lain with the daughter of Jacob, which was not to be. Hamor spoke to them, saying, "Shechem my son has chosen in his heart your daughter. Give her therefore to him for a wife, and intermarry with us. Give us your daughters, and take our daughters for your sons. And live among us. And, Look, the land is spacious before you, live in it, and trade, and get possessions in it."

Shechem said to her father and to her brothers, "I would find favor with you, and we will give whatever you will name. Demand a large of dowry, and I will give accordingly as you ask me, only give me this girl for a wife."

The sons of Jacob answered Shechem and Hamor his father dishonestly and spoke to them because they had defiled Dinah their sister. Simeon and Levi, the brothers of Dinah, said to them, "We will not be able to do this thing, to give our sister to a man who is uncircumcised, for it is a reproach to us. Only on these terms will we conform to you, and live among you, if you also will be as we are, in that every male of you be circumcised. And we will give our daughters to you, and we will take of your daughters for wives to us, and we will live with you, and we will be as one race. But if you will not listen to us to be circumcised, we will take our daughter and depart."

The words pleased Hamor, and Shechem the son of Hamor. The young man did not delay to follow this instruction, for he was much attached to Jacob's daughter, and he was the most honorable of all in his father's house. Hamor and Shechem his son came to the gate of their city, and spoke to the men of their city, saying, "These men are peaceful, let them live with us on the land, and let them trade in it, and Look the land is extensive before them. We will take their daughters for us as wives, and we will give them our daughters. Only on these terms will the men conform to us to live with us to be one people, if every male among us is circumcised, as they also are circumcised. And will not their live-stock and their quadrupeds, and their possessions, be ours? Only in this let us conform to them, and they will live with us."

All that went in at the gate of their city listened to Hamor and Shechem his son, and they were circumcised in the flesh of their foreskin every male. It happened on the third day, when they were in pain, the two sons of Jacob, Simeon and Levi, Dinah's brothers, took each man his sword, and came on the city safely, and killed every male. They killed Hamor and Shechem his son with the edge of the sword, and took Dinah out of the house of Shechem, and left. The sons of Jacob came and slaughtered and ravaged the city in which they had defiled Dinah their sister. They took their sheep, oxen, and donkeys, and all things whatever were in the city, and whatever were in the plain. They took as slaves all the people from there, and all their goods, and their wives, and plun-dered both whatever was in the city, and whatever was in the houses.

Jacob said to Simeon and Levi, "You have made me villainous, and I will be hated by all the people in the land, both among the Canaanites and the Perizzites, and I am few in number. They will gather themselves against me and cut me in pieces, and I will be utterly destroyed, and my house."

They replied, "They will not treat our sister like a whore!"

Cosmic Genesis: Chapter 35

God said to Jacob, "Rise, go up to Bethel and live there, and build an altar there to the god that appeared to you when you fled from the face of Esau your brother."

Jacob said to his house, and to all that were with him, "Remove the alien gods[1] from among you, and purify yourselves, and change your clothes. Let us rise and go up to Bethel, and let us there make an altar to God who hears me in the day of trouble, who was with me, and saved me throughout in the journey on which I went."

They gave to Jacob the gods of the foreigners, which were in their hands, and the earrings which were in their ears, and Jacob hid them under the turpentine tree which is in Shechem and destroyed them to today. So Israel departed from Shechem, and the fear of God was on the cities around them, and they did not chase after the children of Israel. Jacob came to Luz, which is in the land of Canaan, (which is Beth El), he and all the people that were with him. He built there an altar and called the name of the place the House of God, for there God appeared to him when he fled from the face of his brother Esau.

Deborah, Rebekah's nurse, died and was buried below Bethel under the oak, and Jacob named it, 'The Oak of Mourning.'

God appeared to Jacob once more in Luz, when he came out of Mesopotamia in Syria, and God blessed him. God said to him, "Your name will not be called Jacob, but Israel will be your name," and he renamed him Israel.

God said to him, "I the god Resheph.[2] Increase and multiply, for nations and gatherings of nations will be of you, and kings will come out of your loins. The land which I gave to Abraham and Isaac, I have given it to you, and it will come to pass that I will give this land also to your descendants after you."

God went up from him, from the place where he spoke with him. Jacob set up a pillar in the place where God spoke with him, even a pillar of stone, and offered a libation on it, and poured oil on it. Jacob called the name of the place in which God spoke with him, Bethel.

Jacob moved from Bethel and pitched his tent beyond the Tower of Gader, and it happened when he drew near to Chabratha, to enter into Ephrath, Rachel gave birth, and her birthing was hard labor. It was such a difficult labor that the midwife said to her, "Be of good courage, for you will also have this son."

It happened during her giving up the spirit, for she was dying, that she called his name, Ben-Anu,[3] but his father called his name Benjamin. So Rachel died and was buried on the road to Ephrath (this is Bethlehem).[4] Jacob set up a pillar on her tomb, and this is the pillar on the tomb of Rachel, until today.

It happened when Israel lived in that land, that Reuben went and lay with Bilhah, the concubine of his father Jacob, and Israel heard, and the thing appeared grievous before him.

The sons of Jacob were twelve. The sons of Leah were the firstborn of Jacob: Reuben, Simeon, Levi, Judah, Issachar, Zebulun. The sons of Rachel were Joseph and Benjamin. The sons of Bilhah, the woman-slave of Rachel, were Dan and Naphtali. The sons of Zilpah, the woman-slave of Leah, were Gad and Asher. These are the sons of Jacob, which were born to him in Mesopotamia in Syria.

Jacob came to Isaac his father to Mamre, to a city of the plain, (this is Hebron in the land of Canaan), where Abraham and Isaac stayed. The days of Isaac which he lived were a hundred and eighty years. Isaac gave up the spirit and died, and was laid to his family, old and full of days, and Esau and Jacob his sons buried him.

Cosmic Genesis: Chapter 35 Notes

1 Codex Alexandrinus: theous tous allotrious (ⲐⲈⲞⲨⲤⲦⲞⲨⲤⲀⲗⲗⲞⲦⲢⲒⲞⲨⲤ). Translation: gods of strangers (or foreigners, aliens)

• Leningrad Codex: elohei hannechar (אֱלֹהֵי הַנֵּכָר). Translation: god strange (or foreign, alien)

• Peshitta: âlhâ mn byntkûn (ܐܠܗܐ ܡܢ ܒܝܢܬܟܘܢ). Translation: god of the foreigners

• Targum Onkelos: ta'avat ammayya (טָעֲוָת עַמְמַיָּא). Translation: error (or mistaken) of nations (or peoples)

• Targum Jerusalem: ta'avat ammaya (טָעֲוָת עַמְמַיָּא). Translation: error (or mistaken) of nations (or peoples)

2 Codex Colberto-Sarravianus: egô o t̄h̄s sou icanos (ⲈⲅⲰⲞⲐⲤⲤⲞⲨⲒⲔⲀⲚⲞⲤ). Translation: I'm the god of your skill

• Vienna Genesis: egô o t̄h̄s̄ sou icanos (ⲉⲅⲱⲟⲑⲥ̄ⲥⲟⲩ). Translation: I'm the god of you

• LXX 135: egô ho theos sou icanôs (ⲉⲅⲱ ⲟ ⲑⲉ̄ⲥ̄ⲥ ⲥⲟⲩ ⲓⲕⲁⲛⲟⲟⲥ). Translation: I'm the god of your skill

• LXX 82: egô ho theos sou icanousthô (ⲉⲅⲱ ⲟ ⲑⲉ̄ⲥ̄ⲥ ⲥⲟⲩ ⲓⲕⲁⲛⲟⲩⲥⲑⲱ). Translation: I'm the god of your sufficiency

• Leningrad Codex: ani el shaddai (אֲנִי אֵל שַׁדַּי). Translation: I'm god Shadday

• Peshitta: ånå ånå åylšdy ålhå (ܐܠܗܐ ,ܐܝܠܫܕܝ ܐܢܐ ܐܢܐ). Translation: I am Åylšdy god

• Targum Onkelos: ana el shaddai (אֲנָא אֵל שַׁדַּי). Translation: I'm god Shadday

• Targum Jerusalem: ana el shadai (אֲנָא אֵל שַׁדַּי). Translation: I'm god Shadday

This is the third deviation between Cosmic Genesis and Bereshít regarding the god Shadday, and the third time the name or title Shadday is missing entirely from the Septuagint's translation. The name Shadday is imported from the Masoretic version and restored to Resheph to correct for the New Kingdom era redaction. For more information on the god Shadday and Resheph, see the note in chapter 17.

3 Codex Alexandrinus: huios odynês mou (ⲨⲒⲟⲥⲟⲆⲨⲚⲎⲥⲘⲟⲨ). Translation: son of pain of mine.

• Leningrad Codex: ben-ovni (בֶּן־אוֹנִי). Translation: son of power

• Peshitta: br kåby (ܟܐܒܝ ܒܪ). Translation: son of pain (or wound, disease)

• Targum Onkelos: bar devai (בַּר דְּוָי). Translation: son of the woe

• Targum Jerusalem: bar devuyi (בַּר דְּווּיִי). Translation: son of the woe

The Greek translation appears to be partially an interpretation of ånå (אנא), meaning 'I,' however, it is not clear where the term 'pain' came from. The Hebrew term åúny (אוני) is not a proper term, however, is considered to be a decedent of the older Ugaritic Canaanite word ån (𐎀𐎐) meaning power, and closely related to the Akkadian word ān (𒀭), meaning 'god' or 'star.' The differences between the names that Rachel and Jacob gave the child represent the difference between the Akkadian Ān and Egyptian Amen (𓇋𓏠𓈖, transliteration: jmn) names, indicating that when the text was written, Ān and Amen were considered the same god. As the Greeks appear to have mistranslated the name, the older name is restored from the Masoretic Text.

4 LXX 961: ephratha autê estin Baethêleem (ⲈⲪⲢⲀⲐⲀⲀⲨⲦⲎⲈⲤⲦⲒⲚⲂⲀⲒⲐⲎⲚⲈⲈⲘ). Translation: Ephratha this is Bethlehem.

• Codex Alexandrinus: ephratha autê estin Bêthleem (ⲈⲪⲢⲀⲐⲀⲀⲨⲦⲎⲈⲤⲦⲒⲚ ⲂⲎⲐⲚⲈⲈⲘ). Translation: Ephratha this is Bethlehem.

• Vienna Genesis: Ephratha autê estin Bêthêle- (ⲈⲪⲢⲀⲐⲀ ⲀⲨⲦⲎ ⲈⲤⲦⲒⲚ ⲂⲎⲐⲎⲚⲈ-). The name Bethlehem is damaged, however, is believe to have originally read Bêthêleem (ⲂⲎⲐⲎⲚⲈⲈⲘ).

• LXX 131: Ephratha hautê estin Bêthlem (Εϐρⲁθⲁ ⲁⲩⲧⲏ ϭⲟⲧⲓⲛ βⲓⲑⲗϭϭμ). Translation: Ephratha this is Bêthlem.

• LXX 346: Eyphratha hautê estin Baethêl (Ευϐρⲁθⲁ ⲁⲩⲧⲏ ϭⲟⲧⲓⲛ βⲁⲓⲑⲓⲗ). Translation: Eyphtatha this is Bethel.

• LXX 25: Eyphratha hautê estin Bithleem (Ευϐρⲁθⲁ ⲁⲩⲧⲏ ϭⲟⲧⲓⲛ βⲓⲑⲗϭϭμ). Translation: Eyphtatha this is Bethlehem.

• LXX 57: Ephthara hautê estin Bêthleem (Εϐθⲁρⲁ ⲁⲩⲧⲏ ϭⲟⲧⲓⲛ βⲓⲑⲗϭϭμ). Translation: Ephthara this is Bethlehem.

• LXX 128: Eyphratha hautê estin Bêthleem (Ευϐρⲁθⲁ ⲁⲩⲧⲏ ϭⲟⲧⲓⲛ βⲓⲑⲗϭϭμ). Translation: Eyphtatha this is Bethlehem

• LXX 370: Ephrantha hautê estin Bithleem (Εϐρⲁⲛθⲁ ⲁⲩⲧⲏ ϭⲟⲧⲓⲛ βϭⲓⲑⲗϭϭμ). Translation: Ephrantha this is Bethlehem.

• LXX 56: Ephrath hautê estin Bêthleem (Εϐρⲁθ ⲁⲩⲧⲏ ϭⲟⲧⲓⲛ βⲓⲑⲗϭϭμ). Translation: Ephrath this is Bethlehem.

• LXX 79: Eyphrantha hautê estin Bêthleem (Ευϐρⲁⲛθⲁ ⲁⲩⲧⲏ ϭⲟⲧⲓⲛ βⲓⲑⲗϭϭμ). Translation: Eyphrantha this is Bethlehem.

• LXX 346: Ephratha hautê estin Baethêl (Εϐρⲁθⲁ ⲁⲩⲧⲏ ϭⲟⲧⲓⲛ βⲁⲓⲑⲓⲗ). Translation: Ephratha this is Bethel.

• LXX 107: Ephrantha hautê estin Bêthleem (Εϐρⲁⲛθⲁ ⲁⲩⲧⲏ ϭⲟⲧⲓⲛ βⲓⲑⲗϭϭμ). Translation: Ephrantha this is Bethlehem

• Leningrad Codex: Efratah hi beit lachem (אֶפְרָתָה הִוא בֵּית לָחֶם). Translation: Eprata it's Bethlehem (or 'house of bread,' Temple of Lehem)

• Peshitta: åprt: hy hy byt lhm (ܐܦܪܬ: ܗܝ, ܗܝ, ܒܝܬ ܠܚܡ). Translation: Aprt: it is Bethlehem (or house of bread, Temple of Lehem)

- Targum Onkelos: Efrat hi beit lachem (אֶפְרָת הִיא בֵּית לָחֶם). Translation: Eprat it's Bethlehem (or 'house of bread,' Temple of Lehem)

- Fragment Targums: Efrat (אֶפְרָת)

- Targum Jerusalem: Efrat (אֶפְרָת)

The Hebrew and Aramaic name of Eprātâ appears to be a corrupted Canaanite transliteration of the Egyptian name r-pr-t (𓂋 𓉐 𓏏 𓊹), which translates as 'temple of bread,' one meaning of the Canaanite name bêt leḥem (𐤁𐤉𐤕 𐤋𐤄𐤌). This suggests this section of text was a written in, or translated into Egyptian, and later translated into Canaanite, when the scribal note was added.

Cosmic Genesis: Chapter 36

These are the generations of Esau; this is Edom. Esau took to himself wives of the daughters of the Canaanites; Adah, the daughter of Helon the Cypriot, and Aholibamah, daughter of Anah the son of Zibeon, the Mitannian, and Bashemath, daughter of Ishmael, sister of Nebajoth. Adah carried to him Eliphaz, and Bashemath carried Deuel. Aholibamah carried Jeush, and Jaalam, and Korah; these are the sons of Esau, which were born to him in the land of Canaan.

Esau took his wives, and his sons, and his daughters, and all the persons of his house, and all his possessions, and all his livestock, and all that he had got, and all things whatever he had acquired in the land of Canaan, and Esau went out from the land of Canaan, from the face of his brother Jacob. For their substance was too great for them to live together, and the land of their residence could not bear them, because of the abundance of their possessions. Esau lived in mount Seir; Esau, he is Edom.

These are the generations of Esau, the father of Edom in Mount Seir. These are the names of the sons of Esau. Eliphaz, the son of Adah, the wife of Esau, and Deuel, the son of Bashemath, wife of Esau.

The sons of Eliphaz were Teman, Onam, Shophan, Gatam, and Kenez. And Timnath was a concubine of Eliphaz, the son of Esau, and she carried Amalek to Eliphaz. These are the sons of Adah, the wife of Esau.

These are the sons of Deuel; Nahath, Zerah, Shammah, and Mizzah. These were the sons of Bashemath, wife of Esau. These are the sons of Aholibamah, the daughter of Anah, the son of Zibeon, the wife of Esau, and she carried to Esau, Jeush, and Jaalam, and Korah.

These are the chiefs of the son of Esau, even the sons of Eliphaz, the firstborn of Esau; chief Teman, chief Onam, chief Shophan, chief Kenez, chief Korah, chief Gatam, chief Amalek. These are the chiefs of Eliphaz, in the land of Edom, the sons of Adah. These are the sons of Deuel, the son of Esau; chief Nahath, chief Zerah, chief Shammah, chief Mizzah. These are the chiefs of Deuel, in the land of Edom; these are the sons of Bashemath, wife of Esau.

These are the sons of Aholibamah, wife of Esau; chief Jeush, chief Jaalam, chief Korah. These are the chiefs of Aholibamah, daughter of Anah, wife of Esau.

These are the sons of Esau, and these are the chiefs; these are the sons of Edom.

These are the sons of Seir, the Hurrians, who inhabited the land; Lotan, Shobal, Zibeon, Anah, and Dishon, and Ezer, and Rison. These are the chiefs of the Hurrians, the son of Seir, in the land of Edom.

The sons of Lotan were Hori and Hemam, and the sister of Lotan, Timnath.

These are the sons of Shobal: Golam, and Manahath, and Ebal, and Shophan, and Onam.

These are the sons of Zibeon: Ajah and Anah. This is the Anah who found Jimna in the wilderness when he tended the animals of his father Zibeon.

These are the sons of Anah: Dishon and Aholibamah was the daughter of Anah.

These are the sons of Dishon: Hemdan, and Eshban, and Ithran, and Harran.

These are the sons of Ezer: Balaam, and Zaavan, and Akan.

These are the sons of Rison: Huz, and Aran.

These are the chiefs of Hurrians: chief Lotan, chief Shobal, chief Zibeon, chief Anah, chief Dishon, chief Ezer, chief Rison. These are the chiefs of the Hurrians, in their principalities in the land of Edom.

these are the kings which reigned in Edom before a king reigned in Israel. And Riblah, son of Beor, reigned in Edom, and the name of his city was Dinhabah. And Riblah died, and Jobab, son of Zerah, from Bosorrha reigned in his place.

Jobab died, and Hushim, from the land of the Temanites, reigned in his place.

Hushim died, and Hadad son of Bered, who cut off Midian in the plain of Moab, ruled in his place, and the name of his city was Getthaim.

Hadad died, and Samlah of Masrekah reigned in his place.

Samlah died, and Saul of Rehoboth by the river reigned in his place.

Saul died, and Baalhanan the son of Achbor reigned in his place.

And Baalhanan the son of Achbor died, and Arad the son of Bered reigned in his place, and the name of his city was Peor, and the name of his wife was Mehetabel, daughter of Matred, son of Mezahab.

These are the names of the chiefs of Esau, in their tribes, according to their place, in their countries, and in their nations: chief Timnath, chief Gola, chief Jetheth, chief Aholibamah, chief Elah, chief Pinon, chief Kenez, chief Teman, chief Mazar, chief Magediel, chief Zaphoin. These are the chiefs of Edom in their dwelling-places in the land of their possession; this is Esau, the father of Edom.

Jacob lived in the land where his father stayed, in the land of Canaan.

Cosmic Genesis: Chapter 37

These are the generations of Jacob. Joseph was seventeen years old, feeding the sheep of his father with his brothers. He was young compared to the sons of Bilhah, or the sons of Zilpah, the wives of his father, and Joseph brought to Israel, their father, the hateful reproach of his brothers. Jacob loved Joseph more than all his sons because he was to him the son of old age, and he made a coat for him of many colors. His brothers had seen that his father loved him more than all his sons, and hated him, and could not say anything nice to him.

Joseph had a dream and reported it to his brothers. He told them, "Hear this dream which I have had. I thought you were binding sheaves in the middle of the field, and my sheaf stood up and was erect, and your sheaves turned around and bowed to my sheaf."

His brothers said to him, "Will you indeed reign over us, or will you be Lord over us?" They hated him even more for his dreams and for telling them.

He had another dream, and related it to his father and his brothers, saying, "Look, I have had another dream, and in it, the sun, the moon, and the eleven stars bowed to me."

His father rebuked him, and said to him, "What is this dream that you have dreamed? Will both I and your mother and your brothers come and bow before you to the ground?

His brothers envied him, but his father observed it. His brothers went to feed the sheep of their father at Shechem. Israel said to Joseph, "Don't your brothers feed their flock in Shechem? I will send you to them."

He replied to him, "Look, I am here."

Israel said to him, "Go and see if your brothers and the sheep are well, and bring me word," and he sent him out of the Valley of Hebron, and he came to Shechem.

A man found him wandering in the field, and the man asked him, "What do you seek?" He answered, "I am seeking my brothers. Tell me where they feed their flocks."

The man said to him, "They have departed here. I heard them saying, 'Let us go to Dothan,'" and Joseph went after his brothers, and found them in Dothan.

They spied him from a distance before he drew near to them, and they wickedly took counsel to kill him. And each said to his brother, "Look, the dreamer comes. Now then, come and let's kill him, and throw him into one of the pits, and we will say, "An evil wild animal has devoured him, and we will see what his dreams will be."

When Reuben heard it, he rescued him out of their hands by saying, "Let us not strike the life from him." Reuben said to them, "Don't shed blood. Throw him into one of these pits in the wilderness but do not lay your hands on him," that he might rescue him out of their hands, and return him to his father.

It happened, when Joseph came to his brothers, that they stripped Joseph of his many-colored coat that was on him. They took him and cast him into the pit, and the pit was empty, it had no water. They sat down to eat bread and having lifted up their eyes they saw Ishmaelite travelers coming from Gilead, and their camels were heavily loaded with spices, and resin, and stacte, and they went to bring them to Egypt.

Judah said to his brothers, "What profit is it if we kill our brother, and hide his blood? Come, let's sell him to these Ishmaelites, but let's not turn our hands against him, because he is our brother and our flesh, and his brothers listened."

The men, the merchants of Madian, went by, and they drew and lifted Joseph out of the pit, and the Ishmaelites sold Joseph to for twenty pieces of gold, and they brought Joseph down into Egypt.

And Reuben returned to the pit and didn't see Joseph in the pit, and he tore his garments. He returned to his brothers and said, "The boy is gone, and where am I to go?"

Having taken the coat of Joseph, they killed a goat kid and stained the coat with its blood. They took the coat of many colors, and brought it to their father, and said, "We have found this. Know if it is your son's coat or not."

He recognized it, and said, "It is my son's coat, an evil wild animal has eaten him. A wild animal has carried off Joseph!"

Jacob tore his clothes, and put sackcloth on his loins, and mourned for his son many days. All his sons and his daughters gathered themselves together and came to comfort him, but he would not be comforted, saying, "I will go down to my son mourning to Hades, and his father wept for him."

The Midianites sold Joseph in Egypt to Pehtiefra,[1] the emissary[2] of Pharaoh,[3] captain of the guard.

Cosmic Genesis: Chapter 37 Notes

1 Codex Alexandrinus: Petrephê (ⲡⲉⲧⲣⲉⲫⲏ).

- LXX 84: Petephrê (ⲡⲟⲧⲟⲫⲣⲏ)

- LXX 127: Pentephrê (ⲡⲟⲛⲧⲟⲫⲣⲏ)

- LXX 16: Pettephrê (ⲡⲟⲧⲧⲟⲫⲣⲏ)

- LXX 75: Pentephris (ⲡⲟⲛⲧⲟⲫⲣⲓⲥ)

- LXX 408: Pettephri (ⲡⲟⲧⲧⲟⲫⲣⲓ)

- Leningrad Codex: Fotifar (פּוֹטִיפַר).

- Peshitta: Pûtypr (ܦܘܛܝܦܪ)

- Targum Onkelos: Fotifar (פּוֹטִיפַר)

- Fragment Targums: Fotifar (פּוֹטִיפַר)

- Targum Jerusalem: Fotifar (פּוֹטִיפַר)

- Bohairic manuscripts: Petephrê (Πετεφρη)

This appears to be a transliteration of the Egyptian name Phtî-f-rô (𓊪𓏏𓎛𓆑𓂋𓇳), meaning 'he has the strength of the sun.' See the note on Pehtiefra in chapter 39 for alternate transliterations.

2 Codex Alexandrinus: sparonti (ⲥⲡⲁⲣⲟⲛⲧⲓ)

- LXX 84: spadonti (ⲥⲡⲁⲇⲟⲛⲧⲓ)

- LXX 135: eunouchô (ⲉⲩⲛⲟⲩⲭⲱ). Translation: eunuch.

- LXX 392: epadonti (ⲉⲡⲁⲇⲟⲛⲧⲓ). Translation: sing.

- LXX 75: adonti (ⲁⲇⲟⲛⲧⲓ). Translation: please.

- LXX 72: paedonti (ⲡⲁⲓⲇⲟⲛⲧⲓ)

- LXX 799: speudonti (ⲥⲡⲟⲩⲇⲟⲛⲧⲓ). Translation: set going

- LXX 664: spendonti (σπόνδοντι). Translation: make a drink offering

- Leningrad Codex: seris (סָרִיס). Translation: eunuch

- Peshitta: dhšā (ܕܗܫܐ). Translation: attendant

- Targum Onkelos: rabba (רַבָּא). Translation: great

- Fragment Targums: shalita (שְׁלִיטָא)

- Targum Jerusalem: rabba (רַבָּא). Translation: great

None of the source texts agree on the word, with most of the Greek manuscripts including a transliteration of a word that Greeks found in the Aramaic text they translated. Some Greek, Hebrew, and Aramaic manuscripts include translations of the term as 'eunuch' or 'singer,' however, only the Masoretic Text and LXX 135 use the same term as later in chapter 37, which confirms that the early Aramaic translation used a different term. The original title was probably ủpủtj (𓏲𓊪𓏭𓂋), the Middle Egyptian word for 'messenger,' and the title of the king's personal emissary. The phonetic spelling of the Middle Egyptian pronunciation of the word in cuneiform would have been úapùàtiti (𒀀𒉺𒌑𒀀𒋾𒋾), however, 𒀀 can be transliterated as either Ú or SAM, 𒀀 can be transliterated as Å or HUD, and 𒋾 can be transliterated as TI or TENG. As the Canaanite script did not include letters representing the SAM, HUD, or TING sounds, the 𒀀 would have been transliterated as S (𐤔), 𒀀 would have been transliterated as D (𐤃), and 𒋾𒋾 could have been transliterated as NT (𐤍𐤕), resulting in the Canaanite spelling as spdnt (𐤔𐤐𐤃𐤍𐤕), which appears to be the origin of Greek transliterations.

3 Codex Alexandrinus: Pharaô (ΦΑΡΑѠ)

- Leningrad Codex: Par'oh (פַּרְעֹה). Translation: Pharaoh

- Peshitta: Prôûn (ܦܪܥܘܢ). Translation: Pharaoh

- Targum Onkelos: Par'oh (פַּרְעֹה). Translation: Pharaoh

- Bohairic manuscripts: Pharaô (Φαραѡ). Translation: Pharaoh

Both the Greek and Hebrew terms were the equivalent of the modern term Pharaoh, a title of the King of Egypt, however, this translation is anachronistic to the era the story it set in. Both the Greek and Hebrew terms are ultimately derived from the Egyptian word per-åô (𓉐𓉻), meaning 'big house,' or 'palace.'

During the New Kingdom era, the term became the title of the king of Egypt, which was adopted into Akkadian Cuneiform as Pirāú (𒉿𒊏𒌑), Canaanite as Prôh (𐤐𐤓𐤏𐤄), Aramaic as Prôû (𐡐𐡓𐡏𐡅), Greek as Pharaô (Φαραω), and Hebrew as Par'oh (פַּרְעֹה). The story is set during the Middle Kingdom era, when the king of Egypt's title was Nesut (transliterated hieroglyphs: nsůt. Spelled variously as †ₐ𝕄, †ₐ𝒹, or †ₐ𝒴 depending on context). As the term 'Pharaoh' is found in all copies of Cosmic Genesis and Bereshít, it likely originated with a reference to the palace, not the king himself.

Cosmic Genesis: Chapter 38

It happened at that time, that Judah went down from his brothers and came as far as to a certain man of Adullamite, whose name was Hirah. Judah saw there the daughter of a Canaanite man, whose name was Shuah, and he took her and went into her. She conceived and carried a son, and called his name, Ur. She conceived and carried a son again, and called his name, Onan. She again carried a son and called his name Shelah. She was in Cozbi when she carried them. Judah took a wife for Ur his firstborn, whose name was Tamar. Ur, the firstborn of Judah, was wicked before the Lord, and God killed him. Judah said to Onan, "Go into your brother's wife, and marry her as her brother-in-law, and bring up descendants for your brother."

Onan, knowing that the descendants would not be his, pulled out when he went into his brother's wife, that he spilled it on the ground so that he should not give seed to his brother's wife. This appeared evil before God, and he killed him also.

Judah said to Tamar, his daughter-in-law, "You sit a widow in the house of your father-in-law until Shelah my son is grown. He said, "In case he also dies like his brothers," and Tamar departed and sat in the house of her father.

The days were fulfilled, and Shuah the wife of Judah died, and Judah, being comforted, went to them that sheared his sheep, himself and Hirah his shepherd the Adullamite, to Timnath. It was told to Tamar his daughter-in-law, saying, "Look, your father-in-law goes up to Timnath, to shear his sheep."

Having taken off the garments of her widowhood from her, she put on a veil, and ornamented her face, and sat by the gates of Enan, which is along the road to Timnath, for she saw that Shelah was grown, but he gave her not to him for a wife. And when Judah saw her, he thought her to be a whore for she covered her face, and he did not know her. He went out of his way to her, and said to her, "Let me come into you," for he did not know that she was his daughter-in-law.

She asked, "What will you give me if you come into me?"

He answered, "I will send you a goat kid from my flock."

She asked, "Well, will you give me collateral until you send it?"

He inquired, "What collateral will I give you?"

She answered, "Your ring, and your bracelet, and the wand in your hand," and he gave them to her and went into her, and she conceived by him. She arose and departed, and took her veil off her, and put on the garments of her widow-hood.

Judah sent the goat kid by the hand of his shepherd the Adullamite, to receive the pledge from the woman, and he did not find her. He asked the men of the place, "Where is the whore who was in Enan by the roadside?"

They said, "There was no whore here."

He returned to Judah, and said, "I have not found her, and the men of the place say, 'There is no whore here.'"

Judah said, "Let them have her, but let's not be insulted! I sent this kid, and you have not found her." After three months, it was told to Judah, "Tamar your daughter-in-law has grievously played the whore, and look, she is pregnant from prostitution."

Judah ordered, "Bring her out, and let her be burnt."

As they were bringing her, she sent a message to her father-in-law, saying, "I am with child by the man who owns these things," and she said, "Find out who owns this ring, bracelet, and wand."

Judah knew them, and said, "Tamar is cleared rather than I, inasmuch as I gave her not to Shelah my son," and he was not with her again.

It happened when she was in labor, that she also had twins in her womb. It happened as she was giving birth, one thrust out his hand, and the midwife having taken hold of it, tied on his hand a scarlet thread, saying, "This one will come out first."

He drew back his hand, then immediately his brother came out, and she asked, "Why has the barrier been cut through because of you?" and she called his name, Pharez. After this came out his brother, on whose hand was the scarlet thread, and she called his name, Zerah.

Cosmic Genesis: Chapter 39

Joseph was brought down to Egypt, and Pehtiefra[1] the official[2] of Pharaoh, the captain of the guard, an Egyptian, bought him from the hands of the Ishmaelites, who brought him down there. The Lord was with Joseph, and he was a prosperous man, and he was in the house with his lord, the Egyptian. His master knew that the Lord was with him, and the Lord blessed his hands at whatever he happened to do.

Joseph found favor in the presence of his master and was very pleasing to him, and he set him over his house and all that he had he gave into the hand of Joseph. It happened after that he was set over his house, and over all that he had, that the Lord blessed the house of the Egyptian for Joseph's sake, and the blessing of the Lord was on all his possessions in the house, and in his field. He committed all that he had into the hands of Joseph, and he did not know of anything that belonged to him, except the bread which he himself ate. Joseph was handsome in form and exceedingly beautiful in attitude. It happened after these things, that his master's wife cast her eyes on Joseph, and said, "Lie with me."

But he would not, and said to his master's wife, "If because of me, my master knows nothing in his house and has given into my hands all things that belong to him, and in this house, there is nothing above me, nor has anything been kept back from me, except you, because you are his wife, how then will I do this wicked thing, and sin against God?"

She talked with Joseph each day, but he didn't listen and sleep with her, or be with her. It happened one day, when Joseph went into the house to do his business, there was no one from the household there, and she caught hold of him by his clothes, and said, "Lie with me," and he fled leaving his clothes in her hands. When she saw that he had left his clothes in her hands, and fled, and gone away, that she called those that were in the house, and said, "See, he has brought to us a Habiru slave[3] to mock us. He came into me, saying, 'Lie with me,' and I cried with a loud voice, and when he heard I raised my voice and cried, he fled and left his clothes with me."

She left the clothes by her until the master came to his house, and then told him, "The Habiru slave, whom you brought to us, came to me and mocked me, and said, 'I will lie with you.' When he heard me raised my voice and cry, he fled leaving his clothes with me."

When his master heard what his wife said, when she said, 'Your servant did this to me,' he was very angry. His master took Joseph, and threw him into the prison, into the place where the king's prisoners are kept.

The Lord was with Joseph and poured down mercy on him, and he gave him favor in the sight of the chief prison guard. The chief prison guard gave the prison into the hand of Joseph, and all the men led away to prison, and all things whatever they did there, he did them. Because of him, the chief prison guard knew nothing, for all things were in the hand of Joseph, because the Lord was with him, and whatever things he did, the Lord made them prosper in his hands.

Cosmic Genesis: Chapter 39 Notes

1 Codex Alexandrinus: Petephrê (ⲡⲉⲧⲉⲫⲣⲏ)

• LXX 630: Petephrês (ⲡⲟⲧⲟϥⲃⲗⲁⲥ)

• LXX 730: Patronôsiim (ⲡⲁⲧϼⲟⲛⲟⲟⲥⲓϭⲓⲙ)

• LXX 56: Pettephrê (ⲡⲟⲧⲧⲟϥⲃⲗ)

• LXX 121: Pentephrê (ⲡⲟϥⲛⲧⲟϥⲃⲗ)

• LXX 16: Pettephrês (ⲡⲟⲧⲧⲟϥⲃⲗⲁⲥ)

• LXX 75: Pentephris (ⲡⲟϥⲛⲧⲟϥⲃⲡⲓⲥ)

• LXX 19: Petephris (ⲡⲟⲧⲟϥⲃⲡⲓⲥ)

• Leningrad Codex: Fotifar (פּוֹטִיפַר).

• Peshitta: Pŭtypr (ܦܘܛܝܦܪ)

• Targum Onkelos: Fotifar (פּוֹטִיפַר)

• Targum Jerusalem: Fotifar (פּוֹטִיפַר)

• Bohairic manuscripts: Petephrê (Πετεφρη)

This appears to be a transliteration of the Egyptian name Phti-f-rô (𓀏𓇌𓇋𓈖𓏏𓇳), meaning 'he has the strength of the sun.' See the note on Pehtiefra in chapter 37 for alternate transliterations.

2 Codex Alexandrinus: eunouchos (ⲉⲩⲛⲟⲩⲭⲟⲥ)

- Leningrad Codex: seris (סָרִיס). Translation: eunuch

- Peshitta: dhšå (ܪܗܘܣܐ). Translation: attendant

- Targum Onkelos: rabba (רַבָּא). Translation: great

Both the Greek and Hebrew terms appear to be mistranslations based on the shifting meaning of the Aramaic term xâje (خواجه) during the Persian-era. The term originally meant 'lord' or 'vizier,' however, after the dynastic revolution of Darius the Great, the government began to promote homosexuals and eunuchs over married men as they were viewed as less likely to attempt to overthrow the government, meaning that xâje meant 'eunuch,' or 'gentlemen' by the end of the Persian era. This shift in the meaning of the Persian term caused a similar shift in the cuneiform title šu rēšu (𒇽𒊷𒇡), meaning 'the head' in Akkadian cuneiform, but meaning 'eunuch,' or 'nobleman' by the end of the Persian era. The Aramaic and Canaanite transliterations of Akkadian cuneiform term also shifted, resulting in the mistranslations found in the Greek and Hebrew texts. As the term would have meant 'official' originally, that term is used in this translation.

3 Codex Alexandrinus: paeda ebrae (ⲡⲁⲓⲇⲁⲉⲃⲣⲁⲓ).Translation: slave (or child, son, daughter, servant) ebrae (transliteration of the Aramaic 𐤏𐤁𐤓𐤉 meaning 'crosser')

- LXX 400: paeda Ebraeon (παιδα Εὐβραιον). Translation: slave (or child, son, daughter, servant) Hebrew (or Israelite, Aramean, Eberite)

- Leningrad Codex: ish Ivri (אִישׁ עִבְרִי). Translation: man (or husband) Hebrew (or Eberite)

- Peshitta: ôbdå ôbryå (ܥܒܪܝܐ ܗ ܥܒܕܐ). Translation: servant (or slave) crosser

- Targum Onkelos: gavra ivra'ah (גְּבְרָא עִבְרָאָה). Translation: man (or husband) crosser

If the Aramaic text of Genesis was based on an Akkadian Cuneiform source text, then this term must have been in the Cuneiform version as it is in both the Hebrew and Greek translations. The likely term would have been ḫabiru (𒄩𒁉𒊒), meaning 'dusky,' which was a word used to describe groups of marauders in the Middle East in the era. The term was in use from approximately 1800 to 1200 BC, however, does not appear to have been an ethnic term, but was generally used to describe rebels, mercenaries, outlaws, raiders, servants, and slaves. The people in question were also known as Middle Egyptian as Ôprů (𓂝𓊪𓂋), meaning the term could have been in an Egyptian precursor to the Cuneiform book of Genesis.

Cosmic Genesis: Chapter 40

It happened after these things, that the chief cupbearer of the king of Egypt and the chief baker trespassed against their lord, the king of Egypt. Pharaoh was angry with his two officials, with his chief cupbearer, and with his chief baker. He put them into the prison, into the place where Joseph had been led to. The chief prison guard committed them to Joseph, and he stood by them, and they were some days in the prison. They both had a dream in one night, and the vision of the dream of the chief cupbearer and chief baker, who belonged to the king of Egypt, who were in the prison, was this. Joseph went to them in the morning and saw them, and they had been troubled. He asked the officials of Pharaoh who were with him in the prison with his master, saying, "Why is it that your moods are sad today?"

They said to him, "We have seen a dream, and there is no interpreter of it."

Joseph said to them, "Is not the interpretation of them through God? Tell them than to me."

The chief cupbearer related his dream to Joseph, and said, "In my sleep, a vine was before me. In the vine were three stems, and it budding shot forth blossoms; the clusters of grapes were ripe. The cup of Pharaoh was in my hand, and I took the bunch of grapes, and squeezed it into the cup, and gave the cup into Pharaoh's hand."

Joseph said to him, "This is the interpretation of it. The three stems are three days. In three days, Pharaoh will remember your office, and he will restore you to your place of chief cupbearer, and you will give the cup of Pharaoh into his hand, according to your former high place, as you were used to be cupbearer. But remember me when it is good with you, and deal mercifully with me, and mention me to Pharaoh, and bring me out of this dungeon. I was stolen away out of the land of the Habirus, and here I have done nothing, but they have thrown me into this pit."

The chief baker saw that he interpreted correctly, and he said to Joseph, "I also saw a dream, and I thought I put up on my head three baskets of mealy food. In the upper basket, there was the work of the baker of every kind which Pharaoh eats, and the fowls of the air ate them out of the basket that was on my head."

Joseph answered him, "This is the interpretation of it. The three baskets are three days. In three days, and Pharaoh will take away your head from off you, and will hang you on a tree, and the birds of the sky will eat your flesh from off you."

It happened on the third day that it was Pharaoh's birthday, and he made a banquet for all his servants, and he remembered the office of the cupbearer and the office of the baker in the middle of his servants. He restored the chief cupbearer to his office, and he gave the cup into Pharaoh's hand. He hanged the chief baker, as Joseph had interpreted to them. Yet the chief cupbearer did not remember Joseph, but forgot him.

Cosmic Genesis: Chapter 41

After two years, Pharaoh had a dream, and he thought he stood on the bank of the river and as watched there came up, as it were, out of the river, seven cows, beautiful in appearance, and choice of flesh, and they fed on the sedge. Another seven cows came up after these, out of the river, ill-favored and lean-fleshed, and fed by the other cows on the bank of the river. The seven ill-favored and lean cows devoured the seven greatly favored and choice of flesh cows, and Pharaoh woke up.

He dreamed again, and saw seven ears came up on one stalk, choice and good. And then saw seven thin ears, blasted with wind, grew up after them. The seven thin ears, blasted with the wind, devoured the seven choice and full ears, and Pharaoh woke up, and it was a dream. In the morning his mind was troubled, and he sent and called all the interpreters in Egypt, and all her wise men, and Pharaoh told them his dream, and there was no one to explain it to Pharaoh.

The chief cupbearer said to Pharaoh, "I remember today my mistake. When Pharaoh was angry with his servants, and put us in prison in the house of the captain of the guard, both me and the chief baker. And we saw a dream, both in one night, I and he, and we saw each his own dream. There was there with us a young man, a Habiru slave of the captain of the guard, and we told him our dreams, and he interpreted them for us. It happened as he interpreted them to us, exactly so it happened, both that I was restored to my office, and that he was hanged.

Pharaoh called for Joseph, and they brought him out from the prison, and shaved him, and changed his clothes, and he came to Pharaoh. Pharaoh said to Joseph, "I have seen a vision, and there is no one to interpret it. But, I have heard men say that you can hear dreams and interpret them."

Joseph answered Pharaoh, "Without God, a true answer will not be given to Pharaoh."

Pharaoh spoke to Joseph, saying, "In my dream, I thought I stood by the bank of the river, and there came up, as it were, out of the river, seven cows greatly favored and choicest flesh, and they fed on the sedge. Then seven other cows came up after them, out of the river, evil and ill-favored and lean-fleshed, so terrible that I have never seen any like them in all the land of Egypt. The seven ill-favored and thin cows ate up the seven first good and choice cows. They went into their bellies, and they were not perceptible that they had gone into their bellies, and their appearance was as terrible looking as they had been before, and after I awoke, I fell asleep and dreamed again, and in my sleep seven ears grew up on one stem, full and good. Another seven thin ears, and blasted with the wind, grew up close to them. The seven thin and blasted ears devoured the seven fine and full ears. So I told the interpreters, and there was no one to explain it to me."

Joseph said to Pharaoh, "The dreams of Pharaoh are the same. Whatever God does, he has shown to Pharaoh. The seven good cows are seven years, and the seven good ears are seven years. The dreams of Pharaoh are the same. The seven thin cows that came up after them are seven years, and the seven thin and blasted ears are seven years, there will be seven years of famine. As for the word which I have told Pharaoh, whatever God intends to do, he has shown to Pharaoh. Watch, for seven years there will be plenty in all the land of Egypt. But there will come seven years of famine after these, and they will forget the plenty that will be in all Egypt, and the famine will consume the land."

"The plenty will not be remembered in the land because of the famine that will come after this, for it will be very terrible. Concerning the repetition of the dream, coming to Pharaoh twice, it is because God is saying it will come true, and God will rush to accomplish it. Now then, search out a wise and prudent man, and set him over the land of Egypt. Let Pharaoh appoint local governors over the land, and let them take up the fifth part of all the produce of the land of Egypt for the seven years of the plenty. Let them gather all the food of these seven good years that are coming, and let the grain be gathered under the hand of Pharaoh, and let food be kept in the cities. The stored food will be for the land against the seven years of famine, which will be in the land of Egypt and the land will not be utterly destroyed by the famine."

The words were pleasing in the sight of Pharaoh, and in the sight of all his servants. Pharaoh said to all his servants, "Will we find such a man as this, who has the spirit of God in him?"

Pharaoh said to Joseph, "Since God has shown you all these things, there is not a wiser or more prudent man than you. You will be over my house, and all my people will be obedient to your mouth. I will only be greater than you when it comes to the throne."

Pharaoh said to Joseph, "Understand, I set you today over all the land of Egypt."

Pharaoh took his ring off his hand, and put it on the hand of Joseph, and put a robe of fine linen on him, and put a necklace of gold around his neck. He mounted him on the second of his chariots, and a herald made a proclamation before him, and he set him over all the land of Egypt, and made him his cupbearer.

Pharaoh said to Joseph, "I am Pharaoh, without you, no one will lift up his hand in all the land of Egypt."

Pharaoh called the name of Joseph, Psonthom Phanech,[1] and he gave him Aseneth, the daughter of Pehtiefra, priest of Heliopolis,[2] to marry.

Joseph was thirty years old when he stood before Pharaoh, king of Egypt. Joseph left the presence of Pharaoh and traveled through the land of Egypt. The land produced, in the seven years of plenty, whole handfuls of grain. He gathered all the food of the seven years during which was plenty in the land of Egypt, and he stored up the food in the cities, and the food of the fields of a city around it he stored up in it. Joseph gathered a great deal of grain. like the sand of the sea until it could not be counted, as there was no way of counting it.

To Joseph were born two sons, before the seven years of famine came, which Aseneth, the daughter of Pehtiefra, priest of Heliopolis, carried for him. Joseph called the name of the firstborn Manasseh. "For God," he said, "has made me forget all my difficulties, and all things belong to my father."

He called the name of the second Ephraim. "For God," he said, "has increased me in the land of my humiliation."

The seven years of plenty passed away, which were in the land of Egypt. The seven years of famine began to come, as Joseph said, "and there was a famine in all the land, but in all the land of Egypt there was bread."

All the land of Egypt was hungry, and the people cried to Pharaoh for bread. Pharaoh said to all the Egyptians, "Go to Joseph, and do whatever he tells you."

The famine was on the face of all Eretz, and Joseph opened all the granaries and sold to all the Egyptians. All countries came to Egypt to buy of Joseph, for the famine prevailed in all the land.

Cosmic Genesis: Chapter 41 Notes

1 Codex Alexandrinus: Psonoomphanêch (ⲧⲟⲛⲟⲟⲙⲫⲁⲛⲏⲭ)

- LXX 15: Psomthomphanêc (Ⲩⲟⲙⲑⲟⲙ𝄢ⲁⲛⲑⲓ)

- LXX 17: Psomthomphanêch (Ⲩⲟⲙⲑⲟⲙ𝄢ⲁⲛⲑⲭ)

- LXX 135: Apsomthomphanêch (ⲁⲨⲟⲙⲑⲟⲙ𝄢ⲁⲛⲑⲭ)

- LXX 318: Psonthophanêch (Ⲩⲟⲛⲑⲟ𝄢ⲁⲛⲑⲭ)

- LXX 319: Psonthomphanêc (Ⲩⲟⲛⲑⲟⲙ𝄢ⲁⲛⲑⲓ)

- LXX 73: Psomphthomphanêch (Ⲩⲟⲙ𝄢ⲑⲟⲙ𝄢ⲁⲛⲑⲭ)

- LXX 121: Psonthômphanêch (Ⲩⲟⲛⲑⲱⲙ𝄢ⲁⲛⲑⲭ)

- LXX 343: Psonthomphanêch (Ⲩⲟⲛⲑⲟⲙ𝄢ⲁⲛⲑⲭ)

- LXX 426: Psomphthomphanê (Ⲩⲟⲙ𝄢ⲑⲟⲙ𝄢ⲁⲛⲑ)

- LXX 79: Psomthoumphanêch (Ⲩⲟⲙⲑⲟⲩⲙ𝄢ⲁⲛⲑⲭ)

- LXX 413: Psomthophanêc (Ⲩⲟⲙⲑⲟ𝄢ⲁⲛⲑⲓ)

- LXX 458: Psonthomphanic (Ⲩⲟⲛⲑⲟⲙ𝄢ⲁⲛⲓⲓ)

- LXX 72: Psonthonphaniêl (Ⲩⲟⲛⲑⲟⲛ𝄢ⲁⲛⲓⲑⲗ)

- LXX 618: Psonthomphanêm (Ⲩⲟⲛⲑⲟⲙ𝄢ⲁⲛⲑⲙ)

- LXX 527: Psomthomphanec (Ⲩⲟⲙⲑⲟⲙ𝄢ⲁⲛ𝕲ⲓ)

- LXX 59: Psonthômphanêch (Ⲩⲟⲛⲑⲱⲙ𝄢ⲁⲛⲑⲭ)

- Leningrad Codex: Tzafenat pa'neach (צָפְנַת פַּעְנֵחַ)

- Peshitta: Spnt pônh (ܨܦܢܬ ܦܘܢܚ)

- Targum Onkelos: gavra demittamran galeyan leih (גַּבְרָא דְּמִטַּמְרָן גַּלְיָן לֵיהּ). Translation: man to whom hidden things are revealed

- Targum Jerusalem: gavra ditmiran mefarsem (גַּבְרָא דְּטְמִירָן מְפַרְסֵם). Translation: man of famous secrets

- Bohairic ms.: Psonthômphanêkh (Ⲡⲥⲟⲛⲑⲱⲙⲫⲁⲛⲏⲭ)

- Sahidic ms.: Psothomphanêkh (Ⲡⲥⲟⲑⲟⲙⲫⲁⲛⲏⲭ)

The meaning of this name was lost until Egyptologists deciphered Ancient Egyptian. The 1st century AD Jewish historian Josephus believed it meant 'a finder of mysteries,' which was later adopted by Protestant Christian translators. In the 4th century, Jerome translated it as 'savior of the world' when he translated the first official Latin Bible. Since hieroglyphics were deciphered, the name had been reconstructed as 'the god speaks [and] he lives' (transliterated hieratic: ôḏd pô nṯr iů.f ånḫå) by Georg Steindorff in 1889, which is now widely accepted.

2 Codex Alexandrinus: Iou poleôs (ΙΟΥΠΟΛΕѠC)

- LXX 15: Iliou poleôs (ιλιου πȣλό̄ϲ)

- LXX 343: Hêliou poleôs (Ηλϕου πȣλό̄ϲ)

- Leningrad Codex: On (אוֹן)

- Peshitta: Åun (ܐܘܢ)

- Targum Onkelos: On (אוֹן)

- Targum Jerusalem: Tanis (טָנִיס)

- Bohairic manuscripts: On (Oн)

The city of Iůnů (𒀭) was the northern major religious center of Egypt. During the Second Intermediate era it became known by the shortened form Iůn (𒀭) in hieratic, which served as the basis of the Canaanite Åun (אֻן), which was later adopted as the classical Hebrew Åun (און), and then medieval Hebrew On (אוֹן).

The city was called Heliopolis by the Greeks, meaning 'Sun-City,' as most of the gods worshiped there were Solar gods, including the creator-god Atum, the solar-disk Aten, the sun Ra, and the scarab-beetle god Khepri. The major exception was the lunar-god Iôhů. Joseph having been given the daughter of a high-priest to wed would become a priest as well, although the text does not clarify which god he was the priest of. Nevertheless, he is never connected to the Sun in any way, and as an interpreter of dreams, the moon makes more sense as Joseph's god, implying he was the priest of Iôhů.

Cosmic Genesis: Chapter 42

Jacob heard that there was grain for sale in Egypt, and said to his sons, "Why are you indolent? Understand that I have heard that there is grain in Egypt. Go down there, and buy us some food so we may survive, and not starve."

The ten brothers of Joseph went down to buy grain out of Egypt. But Jacob did not send Benjamin, the brother of Joseph with his brothers. As he thought, 'Perhaps disease might infect him.'

The sons of Israel traveled to buy with those that traveled, for the famine was in the land of Canaan. Joseph was the ruler of the land and sold to all the people of the land. After arriving, the brothers of Joseph did reverence to him, bowing with their faces to the ground. When Joseph saw his brothers, he recognized them, but acted like a stranger to them, and spoke hard words to them, asking, "Where have you come from?"

They answered, "From the land of Canaan, to buy food."

Joseph recognized his brothers, but they did not recognize him. Joseph remembered his dream, that he saw, and he said to them, "You are spies. You have come to spy out the boundaries of the land."

But they replied, "No lord, we are your servants, and have come to buy food. We are all sons of one man. We are peaceful. Your servants are not spies."

He said to them, "No! You have come to see the boundaries of the land."

They said, "We are your servants, and are twelve brothers, from the land of Canaan. The youngest is with our father today, and the other one no longer exists."

Joseph said to them, "It is like I said to you, when I said, 'You are spies,' and here you will be known as such. By the health of Pharaoh, you will not leave here unless your younger brother comes here. Send one of you to get your brother, while you go into prison until it is clear if you are speaking the truth or not. But, if not, by the health of Pharaoh, you are proven to be spies."

He put them in prison for three days, and on the third day, he said to them, "Do this, and you will live, for I fear God. If you are peaceful, leave one of your brothers in prison, but you go and take back grain you've purchased. Bring your younger brother to me, and your words will be believed. But if not, you will die," and they did so.

Each said to his brother, "Yes, we are at fault concerning our brother, when we disregarded the anguish of his mind when he implored us, and we did not listen to him, and therefore this punishment has come on us."

Reuben said to them, "Didn't I tell you, 'Don't hurt the boy?' Yet you didn't listen to me! Now see, his blood is required."

They did not know that Joseph understood them, for there had been an interpreter between them. Joseph left them and cried, then returned and spoke to them, and he took Simeon from them and chained him before their eyes. Joseph gave orders to fill their sacks with grain, and to return their silver, to each into his sack, and to give them provision for the road, and it was done for them. After putting the grain on the donkeys, they departed there. One opened his sack to feed his donkeys when they stopped to rest, and saw also his bundle of silver, as it was in the mouth of his sack. He said to his brothers, "My silver has been returned to me, and look, it is in my sack."

Their hearts were amazed, yet they were troubled, saying to each other, "What is this that God has done to us?"

They returned to their father Jacob, in the land of Canaan, and reported to him all that had happened to them, saying, "The man, the lord of the land, spoke harshly to us, and put us in prison, like spies in the land. We said to him, 'We are men of peace. We are not spies. We are twelve brothers, sons of our father. One no longer exists, and the youngest is with his father today in the land of Canaan.' The man, the lord of the land, said to us, 'So I will know that you are peaceful, leave one brother here with me, and take the grain you have purchased for your family, and leave. Bring to me your younger brother, and then I will know that you are not spies, but that you are men of peace, and I will return your brother to you, and you may trade in the land.'"

It followed as they were emptying their sacks, there was each man's bundle of silver in his sack, and they and their father saw their bundles of silver and were afraid. Their father Jacob said to them, "You have saddened me. Joseph is gone, Simeon is gone, and you will take Benjamin? All these things have come on me."

And Reuben said to his father, "Murder my two sons if I don't bring him back to you! Give him to me, and I will bring him back to you!"

But he said, "My son will not go down with you, because his brother is dead, and only he is left, and suppose it will happen that he is afflicted on the way when you travel, then you will bring down my old age with sorrow to Hades."

Cosmic Genesis: Chapter 43

The famine continued in the land, and when they had finished eating the grain that they had brought out of Egypt, their father said to them, "Go back, and buy us a little food."

Judah said to him, "The man, the lord of the country, swore to us, 'You will not see my face unless your younger brother is with you.' If then, you send our brother with us, we will go down and buy food for you, but if you don't send our brother with us, we will not go, for the man said to us, 'You will not see my face unless your younger brother is with you.'"

Israel asked, "Why did you harm me when you told the man that you had a brother?"

They answered, "The man intensely interrogated us about our family, asking, 'Does your father still live?' and 'Do you have a brother?' We answered his questions, and did not know that he would tell us, 'Bring your brother.'"

Judah said to his father Israel, "Send the boy with me, and we will rise and leave, so we may live and not die, both we and you and our property. I swore by my hand before him, 'If I don't bring him to you, and place him before you, I will be guilty before you forever.' "If we had not delayed, we should have already returned twice by now."

Israel, their father, said to them, "If it is so, do this, and take the fruits of Eretz in your packs and carry down to the man presents of gum and honey, and frankincense, and stacte, and turpentine, and walnuts. Take twice the silver in your hands, and also the silver that was returned in your packs take back with you, in case, perhaps, it is a mistake. Take your brother, and rise and return to the man. May the god Resheph[1] give you favor in the sight of the man, and may he send away your other brother, and also Benjamin, as I have been bereaved, and am bereaved."

The men took these presents, and double the silver, and took in their hands also Benjamin, and they rose up and went down to Egypt, and stood before Joseph. Joseph saw them and his brother Benjamin, born of the same mother, and he said to the steward of his household, "Bring the men into the house, and kill animals and prepare them, for the men are to eat bread with me at noon."

The man did as Joseph had said, and he brought the men into the house of Joseph. The men, when they had realized that they were brought into the house of Joseph, said, "We are brought in because of the silver that was returned in our packs before. So they can organize charges against us, and take us as slaves, and also our donkeys."

After approaching the man who was over the house of Joseph, they asked him on the porch of the house, "We beg you, lord. We came down before to buy food. It happened, when we went to unpack and opened our packs, there was also the silver of each of us in his pack. We have now brought back in our hands, the weight of the silver, and we have brought more silver with us to buy food. We don't know who put the silver into our packs."

He said to them, "God dealt mercifully with you. Don't be afraid. Your god, and god of your fathers, has given you treasures in your packs, and I have enough of your good silver."

He brought Simeon out to them, and he brought water to wash their feet and fed their donkeys. They prepared their gifts until Joseph came at noon, for they heard that he was going to dine there. Joseph entered the house, and they brought him the gifts which they had in their hands, into the house, and they did him reverence with their face to the ground. He asked them, "How are you?" and he asked them, "Is your father, the old man of whom you spoke, healthy? Is he still alive?"

They answered, "Your servant, our father is well. He is still alive."

He said, "Blessed be that man by God," and they bowed, and did him reverence.

Joseph looked up with his eyes and saw his brother Benjamin, born of the same mother, and he asked, "Is this your younger brother, whom you spoke of bringing to me?" and he said, "God have mercy on you, my son."

Joseph was troubled, for his bowels yearned over his brother, and he wanted to cry, and he went into his room and cried. He washed his face and came out, and held back himself, and said, "Set out bread."

They set out bread before him alone, and for them by themselves, for the Egyptians eating with him, ate by themselves, for the Egyptians could not eat bread with the Hebrews. It is an abomination to the Egyptians. They sat down before him, the firstborn according to his seniority, and the younger according to his youth, and the men were amazed, everyone looking at his brother. They took their portions from him for themselves. But Benjamin's portion was five times the size of the others' portions. They drank their fill with him.

Cosmic Genesis: Chapter 43 Notes

1 Codex Vaticanus: t̄h̄s mou (ⲐⳞⲘⲞⲨ). Translation: god of mine

- Leningrad Codex: el shaddai (אֵל שַׁדָּי). Translation: god Shadday

- Peshitta: Åylšdy (ܐܠܫܕܝ)

- Targum Onkelos: el shaddai (אֵל שַׁדָּי). Translation: god Shadday

- Targum Jerusalem: el shadai (אֵל שַׁדָּי). Translation: god Shaday

This is the fourth deviation between Cosmic Genesis and Bereshít regarding the god Shaddai, and the fourth time the name or title Shaddai is missing entirely from the Septuagint's translation. The name Shaddai is imported from the Masoretic version and restored to Resheph to correct for the New Kingdom era redaction. For more information on the god Shadday and Resheph, see the note in chapter 17.

Cosmic Genesis: Chapter 44

Joseph ordered the steward of his house, "Fill the men's packs with food, as much as they can carry, and put the silver of each in the opening of his pack. Put my silver cup into the pack of the youngest, along with the price of his grain."

It was done according to the words of Joseph, as he had ordered.

The morning dawned, and the men were sent away, along with their donkeys. When they had left the city, and were not far away, Joseph said to his steward, "Rise, and chase after the men, and you will capture them, and demand of them, 'Why have you repaid evil for good? Why have you stolen my silver cup? Is it not this, in which my lord drinks? He divines omens with it! You have accomplished evil in doing this.'"

He found them and said these words. They asked him, "Why does our lord say these words? Your servants would never do this! If we brought back from the land of Canaan, the silver which we found in our packs, why would we steal silver or gold out of the house of your lord? With whoever of your servants you find this cup, let him die! Moreover, we will be slaves to our lord."

He replied, "Now then, it will be as you say. With whoever the cup will be found, he will be my slave, but you will be clear."

They hurried, and each man took down his pack and placed them on the ground, and they opened their packs. He searched, beginning with the oldest until he came to the youngest, and he found the cup in Benjamin's pack. They tore their garments, and each man laid his pack on his donkey and returned to the city. Judah and his brothers came to Joseph, while he was still there, and fell on the ground before him.

Joseph said to them, "What is this, that you have done? Don't you know that a man like me can divine the truth?"

Judah said, "What will we say to our lord? What will we say that could be justified when God has discovered the unrighteousness of your servants! See, we are slaves to our lord, both we and he with whom the cup has been found."

Joseph said, "Far be it from me to do this! The man with whom the cup has been found will be my slave. But you may return in safety to your father."

Judah approached him, and said, "I beg, lord, let your servant say a few words before you, and do not be angry with your servant, for you are next to Pharaoh. Lord, you asked your servants, asking, 'Do you have a father or a brother?' We answered my lord, 'We have a father, an old man, and he had a son in his old age, a young one, and his brother is dead, and he alone has been left behind to his mother, and his father loves him.' You said to your servants, 'Bring him down to me, and I will take care of him.' and we said to my lord, 'The child will not be able to leave his father, but if he should leave his father, he will die.' But you said to your servants, 'Only if your younger brother comes down with you, will you see my face again.'"

"When we went up to your servant, our father, we reported to him the words of our lord, and our father said, 'Go back and buy us a little food.' We said, 'We will not be able to go down unless our younger brother goes down with us, we will go down. We will not be able to see the man's face if our younger brother is not with us.' Your servant, our father, said to us, 'You know that my wife carried me two sons, and one has departed from me, and you said that he was eaten by wild animals, and I have not seen him until now."

"If you take this one also from my presence, and an affliction happens to him on the road, then you will bring down my old age with sorrow to Hades.' Now then, if I should go to your servant, our father, and the boy should not be with us, and his life depends on this boy's life, it will happen that when he sees the boy is not with us, he will die, and your servants will bring down the old age of your servant, our father, with sorrow to Hades. Your servant has received the boy, in charge from his father, saying, 'If I don't return him to you, and place him before you, I will be guilty to my father forever.' Now then, I will remain a slave with you, instead of the boy, a domestic slave of my lord. Just let the boy return with his brothers. How will I return to my father, and say, 'The boy is not with us?' If I will see the evil that will befall my father?"

Cosmic Genesis: Chapter 45

Joseph could not contain himself when all were standing by him, but said, "Dismiss all from me," and no one stood near Joseph when he made himself known to his brothers. He spoke with sobbing in his voice and all the Egyptians heard, and it was reported to the house of Pharaoh. Joseph said to his brothers, "I am Joseph. Does my father still live?"

His brothers could not answer him, as they were troubled. Joseph said to his brothers, "Come close to me," and when they drew near he said, "I am your brother Joseph, whom you sold into Egypt. Now then, don't be sad, and don't let it be difficult for you, in that you sold me here, for God sent me before you, for life. This is the second year that there is famine in the land, and there are still five more years remaining in which there is going to be neither plowing nor harvesting. God sent me before you, that there might be left among you a remnant in the land, to feed a great remnant of you. Now then, you did not send me here, but God did, and he has made me like a father to Pharaoh, and lord of all his house, and ruler of all the land of Egypt. Rise, therefore, and return to my father, and say to him, 'Your son Joseph says the following, "God has made me lord of all the land of Egypt. Therefore, come down to me, and don't delay, and you will live in the land of Goshen of Arabia, and you will be near me, you and your sons, and your grandsons, your sheep, oxen, and whatever things are yours. I will feed you there as the famine will continue for five more years. Otherwise, you be consumed, and your sons, and all your possessions. See with your eyes, and the eyes of my brother Benjamin, that it is my mouth that speaks to you.'" Report to my father all my glory in Egypt, and all things that you have seen, and rush to bring my father down here.

He fell on his brother Benjamin's neck and cried on him, and Benjamin cried on his neck. He kissed all his brothers and cried on them, and after these things, his brothers said to him. The report was carried into the house of Pharaoh, saying, "Joseph's brothers have come," and Pharaoh was glad, and also his household.

Pharaoh said to Joseph, "Tell your brothers, 'Fill your wagons, and depart to the land of Canaan. Pick up your father, and your possessions, and come to me, and I will give you some of all the goods of Egypt, and you will eat the marrow of the land.' Order them also, that they should take for themselves wagons out of the land of Egypt, 'for your little ones, and for your wives, and carry your father,' and then return. Do not be sparing, regarding your property, as all the wealth of Egypt will be yours."

The children of Israel did so, and Joseph gave them wagons, as per the words spoken by King Pharaoh, and he gave them provisions for the journey. He gave them each two sets of clothing, but for Benjamin, he gave three hundred pieces of gold, and five changes of clothing. For his father, he sent the same amount of present, and ten donkeys carrying some of all the good things of Egypt, and ten mules, carrying bread, for his father's journey. He sent away his brothers, and they left, and he said to them, "Don't be angry on the road."

They left Egypt, and traveled into the land of Canaan, to Jacob their father. They reported to him, "Your son Joseph is alive, and he is ruler over all the land of Egypt," and Jacob was amazed, and he did not believe them. They told him all the words said by Joseph, everything he had said to them, and having seen the wagons which Joseph sent to take him up, the spirit of Jacob their father revived.

Israel said, "It is a wonderful thing for me if Joseph my son is still alive. I will go see him before I die."

Cosmic Genesis: Chapter 46

Israel departed, he and all that he had, and traveled to the Well of the Oath, and he offered a sacrifice to the god of his father Isaac. God spoke to Israel in a night vision, "Jacob! Jacob?"

He asked, "What is it?"

He answered him, "I am the god of your fathers. Don't be afraid to go down to Egypt, for I will make you a great nation there. I will go down with you into Egypt, and I will bring you up at the end, and Joseph will put his hands on your eyes."

Jacob rose up from the well of the oath, and the sons of Israel carried their father, and the property, and their wives, on the wagons that Joseph had sent to carry them. They carried their goods and all their property which they had gotten in the land of Canaan, and they came into the land of Egypt, Jacob, and all his descendants with him. The sons, and the sons of his sons with him, his daughters, and the daughters of his daughters, and he brought all his descendants into Egypt.

These are the names of the sons of Israel that went into Egypt with their father Jacob; Jacob and his sons.

The firstborn of Jacob was Reuben.

The sons of Reuben were Enoch, Phallu, Hezron, and Carmi.

The sons of Simeon were Jemuel, Jimna, Ohad, Jachin, Zohar, and Saul, the sons of a Canaanite woman.

The sons of Levi were Gershon, Kohath, and Merari.

The sons of Judah were Er, Onan, Shelah, Pharez, and Zerah, however, Er and Onan had died in the land of Canaan.

The sons of Pharez were Hezron and Hamul.

The sons of Issachar were Tola, Pua, Asum, and Shimron.

The sons of Zebulun were Sered, Elon, and Achoel.

These are the sons of Leah, which she carried for Jacob in Mesopotamia in Syria, and Dinah his daughter. All the minds, sons and daughters, thirty-three.

The sons of Gad were Zephon, Haggi, Shuni, Ezbon, Aedis, Arodi, and Areli.

The sons of Asher were Jimnah, Ishuah, Isui, Beriah, and Serah their sister.

The sons of Beriah were Chobor and Malchiel.

These are the sons of Zilpah, which Laban gave to his daughter Leah, who carried these for Jacob, sixteen minds.

The sons of Rachel, the wife of Jacob, were Joseph and Benjamin.

There were sons born to Joseph in the land of Egypt, who Aseneth, the daughter of Pehtiefra, priest of Heliopolis, carried for him, including Manasseh and Ephraim.

There were sons born to Manasseh, which the Syrian concubine carried for him, including Machir.

Machir fathered Gilead.

The sons of Ephraim, the brother of Manasseh were Sutalaam and Gaham.

The sons of Sutalaam were Edom.

The sons of Benjamin were Belah, Becher, and Asbel.

The sons of Belah were Gera, Naaman, Ehi, Rosh, and Muppim, and Gera fathered Arad.

These are the sons of Rachel, which she carried for Jacob; all the minds were eighteen.

The son of Dan was Hushim.

The sons of Naphtali were Jahzeel, Guni, Izhar, and Shillem.

These are the sons of Bilhah, who Laban gave to his daughter Rachel, who carried these for Jacob; all the minds were seven.

All the minds that came with Jacob into Egypt, who came out of his thighs, besides the wives of the sons of Jacob, including all the minds were sixty-six.

The sons of Joseph, who were born for him in the land of Egypt, were nine minds; all the minds of the house of Jacob who came with Joseph into Egypt were seventy-five minds. He sent Judah before him to Joseph, to meet him face to face at the Temple of Atum in Pi-Ramesses.[1]

Joseph harnessed his chariots and went up to meet Israel his father, in Per-Atum, and after appearing before him, fell on his neck, and wept with abundant weeping.

Israel said to Joseph, "After this, I will die happily as I have seen your face, and you are still alive!"

Joseph said to his brothers, "I will go and tell Pharaoh, 'My brothers, and my father's house, who were in the land of Canaan, have come to me. The men are shepherds, and they have been herders of livestock, and they have brought with them their livestock, and their cows, and all their property.' If then Pharaoh calls you, and asks you, 'What is your occupation?' You will say, 'We, your servants, are herdsmen from our youth until now, both we and our fathers,' so that you may live in the land of Goshen of Arabia, for every shepherd is an abomination to the Egyptians."

Cosmic Genesis: Chapter 46 Notes

1 Cotton Genesis: Êrôôn polin is gên Ramessê (ⲎⲢⲱⲱⲚⲦⲦⲟⲗⲓⲚⲉⲓⲥⲅⲎⲚⲢⲀⲘⲉⲥⲥⲎ). Translation: Heroöpolis (or Pithom, Per-Atum, Heroes' city) in land Ramesses

• LXX 509: Hêrôôn polin is gên Ramessê (ⲎⲣⲁⳒⲟⲟⲛ ⲡⲟⲗⲓⲛ ⲥⲓⲥ ⲅⲗⲛ ⲢⲀⲙⲟⲥⲟⲟⲗ). Translation: Heroöpolis (or Pithom, Per-Atum, Heroes' city) in land Ramesses

• LXX 392: Êroôn polin is gên Ramessê (Ⲏⲣⲟⲟⲟⲛ ⲡⲟⲗⲓⲛ ⲥⲓⲥ ⲅⲗⲛ ⲢⲀⲙⲟⲥⲟⲟⲗ). Translation: Heroöpolis (or Pithom, Per-Atum, Heroes' city) in land Ramesses

• LXX 346: Hêrôôn polin pros gên Racessê (ⲎⲣⲁⳒⲟⲟⲛ ⲡⲟⲗⲓⲛ ⲡⲣⲟⲥ ⲅⲗⲛ ⲢⲀⳑⲟⲟⲟⲗ). Translation: Heroöpolis (or Pithom, Per-Atum, Heroes' city) towards land Racessê

• LXX 17: Hêrôôn polin is tên Ramesê (ⲎⲣⲁⳒⲟⲟⲛ ⲡⲟⲗⲓⲛ ⲥⲓⲥ ⲧⲗⲛ ⲢⲀⲙⲟⲟⲗ). Translation: Heroöpolis (or Pithom, Per-Atum, Heroes' city) inthe Ramesê

• LXX 25: Hêrôôn polin is gên Rem (ⲎⲣⲁⳒⲟⲟⲛ ⲡⲟⲗⲓⲛ ⲥⲓⲥ ⲅⲗⲛ Ⲣⲟ⳩). Translation: Heroöpolis (or Pithom, Per-Atum, Heroes' city) in land Rem

• LXX 75: Hêrôôn polin is gên Ramaesi (ⲎⲣⲁⳒⲟⲟⲛ ⲡⲟⲗⲓⲛ ⲥⲓⲥ ⲅⲗⲛ ⲢⲀⲙⲀⲓⲥⲓ). Translation: Heroöpolis (or Pithom, Per-Atum, Heroes' city) in land Ramaesi

• LXX 408: Hêrôôn palin en gê Ramesê (ⲎⲣⲁⳒⲟⲟⲛ ⲡⲟⲗⲓⲛ ⲥⲓⲥ ⲅⲗⲛ ⲢⲀⲙⲟⲟⲟⲓ). Translation: Heroes' city in land Ramesses

• LXX 76: Iroôn polin is gên Ramesê (ιϼοοοɴ πȣλιɴ ϭιϲ ɣℎɴ ℙλμϭϭℎ). Translation: Heroöpolis (or Pithom, Per-Atum, Heroes' city) in land Ramesses

• LXX 527: Hêrôôn palin en gê Ramesê (Hϼℸοοɴ πλλιɴ ϭɴ ɣℎ ℙλμϭϭℎ). Translation: Heroes' city in land Ramesses

• LXX 44: Hêrôôn polin is gên Ramesên (Hϼℸοοɴ πȣλιɴ ϭιϲ ɣℎɴ ℙλμϭϭℎɴ). Translation: Heroöpolis (or Pithom, Per-Atum, Heroes' city) in land Ramesên

• LXX 376: Hêrôôn polin is gên Ramesae (Hϼℸοοɴ πȣλιɴ ϭιϲ ɣℎɴ ℙλμϭϭλι). Translation: Heroöpolis (or Pithom, Per-Atum, Heroes' city) in land Ramesae

• LXX 610: Hêrôôn palin is gên Ramesê (Hϼℸοοɴ πλλιɴ ϭιϲ ɣℎɴ ℙλμϭϭℎ). Translation: Heroes' city backin land Ramesses

• Leningrad Codex: goshenah vayyavo'u artzah goshen (גֹּשְׁנָה וַיָּבֹאוּ אַרְצָה גֹּשֶׁן). Translation: goshenah and will come (or import) land Goshen

• Peshitta: Gšn ůåtů lårôå dGšn (ܓܫܢ ܘܐܬܘ ܠܐܪܥܐ ܕܓܫܢ). Translation: Gšn and will come to the land the Gšn

• Targum Onkelos: lefanna'ah kodamohi legoshen va'ato le'ar'a degoshen (לְפַנָּאָה קֳדָמוֹהִי לְגֹשֶׁן וַאֲתוֹ לְאַרְעָא דְגֹשֶׁן). Translation: clear a place before him in Goshen. They then came to the land of Goshen.

• Fragment Targums: Goshena (גּוֹשְׁנָא)

• Targum Jerusalem: Goshena ve'ato le'ar'a deGoshen (גּוֹשְׁנָא וְאָתוֹ לְאַרְעָא דְגֹשֶׁן). Translation: goshena and traveled to (or in the proximity of) Gshen

The terms found in the Septuagint and Masoretic Text do not correlate, suggesting the Aramaic version of Genesis read differently than the Paleo-Hebrew version. The meaning of the terms found in the Leningrad Codex, goshenah / goshen (גֹּשֶׁן / גֹּשְׁנָה) have been debated for thousands of years, and many attempts to identify it had been made. If the word was based on an Egyptian term, it was probably the Egyptian word gesen (𓈒𓈖), meaning 'oil of.' In 1885, the Egyptologist Édouard Naville identified this as the name of the Egyptian district that encompassed the region of Wadi Tumilat, Pithom, and the city of Ramesses, during the 26th Dynasty, between 672 and 525 BC, suggesting the name was updated to Goshen when the Judahite version of Genesis was compiled for King Josiah's Torah circa 625 BC.

The Aramaic version of Genesis could not have included the words goshenah / goshen as the Greeks did not transliterate the terms, instead, translating the terms they found as Êrôôn polin and Ramesses. Êrôôn polin (Ηρωων πολιν), meaning 'Hero's city' in Greek, was the Greek name of the city known as Per-Atum (transliterated hieratic: pr-tm) in

Egyptian, meaning the 'Temple of Atum.' The other term found in the Septuagint is unusual, as the Greeks should have translated the term as 'land of Ramesses' (χωρα των Ραμεσση) if that was the intent.

The Greek translation indicates the Aramaic text they worked from read ârq rômsîs (𐤔𐤀𐤉𐤊𐤅𐤉 𐤐𐤉𐤀), meaning 'land Ramesses.' This is one possible direct Aramaic translation of the Egyptian name Pi-Ramesses (𓉐 𓇋𓅓𓁷𓂝), meaning 'House,' 'Palace,' 'Temple;' or 'Domain' of Ramesses. Pi-Ramesses was the name of a major city in northern Egypt during the New Kingdom Era, founded by King Ramesses II (1279–1213 BC), near the site of the older Hyksos capital of Hut-Waret (𓉺𓏏𓄿𓈉), meaning 'mansion of the region,' more commonly transliterated as Avaris from the later Greek transliteration of Αυαρις.

As Pi-Ramesses was only known as Pi-Ramesses during the New Kingdom Era, this means the Aramaic version had to have been translated from a Cuneiform version of Abraham / Cosmic Genesis translated sometime before the 12th century BC. As this book of Abraham appears to have been written in Egyptian, the original local was likely Hut-Waret / Avaris. As the original text could not have been referring to the city of Per-Atum within the city of Pi-Ramesses (or Avaris), the alternate translation of Temple of Atum in Pi-Ramesses is used.

Cosmic Genesis: Chapter 47

Joseph went to Pharaoh and said, "My father and my brothers, and their livestock, oxen, and all their possessions, have come out of the land of Canaan, and see, they are in the land of Goshen."

He took from among his brothers, five men and brought them before Pharaoh.

Pharaoh asked the brothers of Joseph, "What is your occupation?"

They answered Pharaoh, "Your servants are herders, both we and our father," and they said to Pharaoh, "We have come to stay in the land, for there is no pasture for the flocks of your servants, for the famine has prevailed in the land of Canaan. So now, let us live in the land of Goshen."

Pharaoh said to Joseph, "Let them live in the land of Goshen, and if you know that there are able men among them, make them overseers of my livestock."

So Jacob and his sons came into Egypt, to Joseph, and Pharaoh the king of Egypt heard of it. Pharaoh spoke to Joseph, saying, "Your father, and your brothers, have come to you. See, the land of Egypt is before you. Settle your father and your brothers in the best land."

Joseph brought Jacob his father and set him before Pharaoh, and Jacob blessed Pharaoh. Pharaoh asked Jacob, "How many years have you lived?"

Jacob answered Pharaoh, "I have lived a hundred and thirty years. Few and evil have been the days of the years of my life. They have not attained the length of days of my fathers, that they lived." Jacob blessed Pharaoh and departed from him. Joseph settled his father and his brothers, and gave them a possession in the land of Egypt, in the best land, in the land of Ramesses, as Pharaoh commanded.

Joseph gave provisions to his father, and his brothers, and to all the house of his father, enough grain for each person. There was no grain in all the land, for the famine was great. Both the land of Egypt and the land of Canaan fainted from the famine. Joseph gathered all the silver that was found in the lands of Egypt and Canaan, in return for the grain which they bought, and he distributed grain to them, and Joseph brought all the silver into the house of Pharaoh. The economy in the land of Egypt failed, and in the land of Canaan, and all the Egyptians came to Joseph, saying, "Give us bread, and why do we die in your presence? For our silver is spent."

Joseph said to them, "Bring your livestock, and I will give you bread for your livestock if your silver is spent."

They brought their livestock to Joseph, and Joseph gave them bread in return for their horses, and for their sheep, and for their oxen, and for their donkeys, and Joseph provided them with bread, for all their livestock in that year. That year ended and they came to him in the second year, and said to him, "Must we then be consumed before our lord? If our silver has failed, and our possessions, and our livestock, was brought to you, our lord, and there has not been left to us, before our lord, more than our own bodies, and our land, we are indeed destitute. In order, then, that we don't die before you, and the land is made desolate, buy us, and our land, for bread, and we and our land will be slaves to Pharaoh. Give seed that we may sow, and live and not die, and so our land will not be made desolate."

Joseph bought all the land of the Egyptians for Pharaoh, as the Egyptians sold their land to Pharaoh, for the famine prevailed against them, and the land became Pharaoh's. He brought the people into slavery to him, as slaves, from one frontier of Egypt to the other, excepting only the land of the priests, Joseph did not buy this, for Pharaoh gave a portion as a gift to the priests, and they ate their portion which Pharaoh gave them, and therefore, they did not sell their land. Joseph said to all the Egyptians, "Understand, I have bought you and your land today for Pharaoh. Take seed with you, and sow the land. There will be fruits from it, and you will give a fifth part to Pharaoh, and the four remaining parts will be for yourselves, as seed for the land, and as food for you, and all that are in your houses."

They answered, "You have saved us, and we have found favor before our lord, and we will be slaves to Pharaoh."

Joseph appointed it to them as an ordinance until today, to reserve the fifth part for Pharaoh, on the land of Egypt, excepting only the land of the priests, that was not Pharaoh's. Israel lived in Egypt, in the land of Goshen, and they gained an inheritance on it, and they increased and multiplied greatly. Jacob survived seventeen years in the land of Egypt, and Jacob's days of the years of his life were a hundred and forty-seven years.

The days of Israel drew near for him to die, and he called his son Joseph, and said to him, "If I have found favor before you, put your hand under my thigh, and you will execute mercy and truth towards me, so as not to bury me in

Egypt. But I will sleep with my fathers, and you will carry me up out of Egypt, and bury me in their sepulcher."

He answered, "I will do according to your word."

He continued, "Swear to me," and he swore to him. Israel worshiped the highest with the wand.

Cosmic Genesis: Chapter 48

After this, that it was reported to Joseph, "See, your father is ill." and he took his two sons, Manasseh and Ephraim, to Jacob.

It was reported to Jacob, "Look, your son Joseph comes to you," and Israel strengthened himself and sat up on the bed.

Jacob said to Joseph, "The god Resheph[1] appeared to me in Luz, in the land of Canaan, and blessed me, and said to me, 'Look, I will increase you, and multiply you, and will make of you multitudes of nations, and I will give this land to you, and to your descendants after you, as an eternal possession.' Now then your two sons, who were born to you in the land of Egypt, before I came to you in Egypt, are mine. Ephraim and Manasseh, like Reuben and Simeon, they will be mine. The children which you will father from now on will be in the name of their brothers. They will be named after their inheritances. As for me, when I came out of Mesopotamia in Syria, Rachel, your mother, died in the land of Canaan, as I approached the horse-track of Chabratha, in the land of Canaan, en route to Ephrath, and I buried her in the road of the track." (This is Bethlehem.)

And when Israel saw the sons of Joseph, he asked, "Who are these to you?"

Joseph answered his father, "They are my sons, whom God gave me here."

Jacob said, "Bring me them, that I may bless them."

Now the eyes of Israel were dim through age, and he could not see, and he brought them near to him, and he kissed them and embraced them. Israel said to Joseph, "I have not been deprived of seeing your face, and God has shown me your descendants also."

Joseph brought them out from between his knees, and they did reverence to him, with their face to the ground. Joseph took his two sons, both Ephraim in his right hand, but on the left of Israel, and Manasseh on his left hand, but on the right of Israel, and brought them near to him. But Israel stretched out his right hand, laid it on the head of Ephraim who was the younger, and his left hand on the head of Manasseh, crossing his arms. He blessed them and said, "God, in whose sight my fathers were very pleasing, including Abraham and Isaac, God who continues to feed me from my youth until today. The messenger who delivers me from all evils, bless these boys, and my name will be called on them, and the name of my fathers, Abraham and Isaac, and let them be increased to a great multitude on the land."

Joseph having seen that his father put his right hand on the head of Ephraim, it seemed grievous to him, and Joseph took hold of the hand of his father, to remove it from the head of Ephraim to the head of Manasseh. Joseph said to his father, "Not so, father. This is the firstborn, lay your right hand on his head."

He would not, and said, "I know it, son, I know it. He also will be a people, and he will be exalted, but his younger brother will be greater than he, and his seed will become a multitude of nations."

He blessed them on that day, saying, "Through you, Israel will be blessed. God will make you like Ephraim and Manasseh," and he set Ephraim before Manasseh.

Israel said to Joseph, "See, I die, and God will be with you, and restore you to the land of your fathers. I give you Shechem, a select portion above your brothers, which I took out from the hands of the Amorites with my sword and bow."

Cosmic Genesis: Chapter 48 Notes

1 Codex Vaticanus: t̄h̄s mou (ⲐⲤⲘⲞⲨ). Translation: god of mine

- Leningrad Codex: el shaddai (אֵל שַׁדַּי). Translation: god Šadday

- Peshitta: Åylšdy (ܐܠܫܕܝ)

- Targum Onkelos: el shaddai (אֵל שַׁדַּי). Translation: god Shadday

- Targum Jerusalem: el shadai (אֵל שַׁדַּי). Translation: god Shadday

This is the fifth deviation between Cosmic Genesis and Bereshít regarding the god Shadday, and the fifth time the name or title Shadday is missing entirely from the Septuagint's translation. The name Shadday is imported from the Masoretic version and restored to Resheph to correct for the New Kingdom era redaction. For more information on the god Shadday and Raphesh, see the note in chapter 17.

Cosmic Genesis: Chapter 49

Jacob called his sons, and said to them, "Assemble yourselves, so I may tell you what will happen to you in future days. Gather around, and hear me, sons of Jacob. Listen to Israel; listen to your father."

"Reuben, my firstborn. You are my strength and the first of my children. Hard to put up with. Hard and self-willed. You were insolent like water. Don't explode with violence, for you went up to the bed of your father, and then you defiled the couch, where you went."

"Simeon and Levi, brothers. Accomplished the injustice of their cutting off. Don't let my mind come into their counsel and don't let my inward parts contend in their conspiracy, for in their anger they killed men, and in their passion, they hamstringed a bull. Cursed be their anger, for it was willful, and their anger, for it was aggravated. I will divide them from Jacob, and scatter them from Israel."

"Judah, your brothers have praised you, and your hands will be on the back of your enemies. Your father's sons will do you reverence. Judah, is a lion's cub, from the tender plant, my son, you are gone up, having couched you lie like a lion, and like a cub, who will stir him up? A ruler will not fail from Judah, nor a prince from his thighs, until there come the things stored up for him, and he is the expectation of nations. Binding his foal to the vine, and the foal of his donkey to the branch of it, he will wash his robe in wine, and his garment in the blood of the grape. His eyes will be more cheering than wine, and his teeth whiter than milk."

"Zebulun will live on the coast, and he will be a haven of ships and will extend to Sidon."

"Issachar has desired that which is good, resting between the inheritances. Having seen the resting place that it was good, and the land that it was fertile, he subjected his shoulder to labor, and became a farmer."

"Dan will judge his people, and Israel too, like one tribe. Let Dan be a serpent on the road, besetting the road, biting the heel of the horse, and the rider will fall backward, waiting for the salvation of the Lord."

"Gad, a plundering army will plunder him, but he will plunder them, chasing closely after them."

"Asher, fat will be his bread, and he will surrender the weak to princes."

"Naphtali is a spreading stem, bestowing beauty on its fruit."

"Joseph is a son increased. My dearly loved son is increased, my youngest son, return to me. Against whom men taking evil counsel reproached him, and the archers pressed hard on him. But their bow and arrows were mightily consumed, and the sinews of their arms were slackened by the hand of the mighty one of Jacob, and there is he, that strengthened Israel from the god of your father, and with Resheph[1] helped you and he blessed you with the blessing of Shamayim above, and the blessing of Eretz possessing all things, because of the blessing of the breasts and of the womb, the blessings of your father and your mother; it has prevailed above the blessing of the lasting mountains, and beyond the blessings of the eternal hills, and they will be on the head of Joseph and on the head of the brothers of whom he took the lead."

"Benjamin, like a ravenous wolf will still eat in the morning, and at evening he gives food."

All these are the twelve sons of Jacob, and their father spoke these words to them, and he blessed them. He blessed each of them according to his blessing. He said to them, "I am added to my people, you will bury me with my fathers in the cave, which is in the field of Ephron the Cypriot, in the double cave which is opposite Mamre, in the land of Canaan, the cave which Abraham bought of Ephron the Cypriot, for a possession of a sepulcher. There, they buried Abraham and Sarah his wife. There, they buried Isaac and Rebekah his wife, and there they buried Leah in the portion of the field, and of the cave that was in it, purchased from the sons of the Cypriots. Jacob finished giving orders to his sons and lifted up his feet onto the bed, and he died and was gathered to his people.

Cosmic Genesis: Chapter 49 Note

1 Codex Vaticanus: o t̄h̄s̄ o emos (ⲟⲐⲤⲞⲈⲘⲞⲤ). Translation: the god of mine

- Leningrad Codex: et shaddai (אֵת שַׁדַּי). Translation: with (or you) Shadday

- Peshitta: Åylšdy (ܐܝܠܫܕܝ)

- Targum Onkelos: yat shaddai (יָת שַׁדַּי). Translation: self Shadday

This is the sixth deviation between Cosmic Genesis and Bereshít regarding the god Shadday, and the sixth time the name or title Shadday is missing entirely from the Septuagint's translation. The name Shaddai is imported from the Masoretic version and restored to Resheph to correct for the New Kingdom era redaction. In this verse, the word åt (את) appears to be a translation of itti (𒀉𒋾), meaning 'with,' which is one of åt's more archaic interpretations. In most cases, the Masoretic Text uses åt (את) the same way as the Phoenician åyt (𐤀𐤉𐤕) and Aramaic yt (𐡉𐡕), both meaning 'you,' however, that interpretation is not valid in this verse.

Cosmic Genesis: Chapter 50

Joseph fell on his father's face, and wept and kissed him. Joseph commanded his servants, the embalmers, to embalm his father, and they embalmed Israel. They waited the forty days for him, which are the days that embalming takes, and Egypt mourned for him seventy days. And when the days of mourning were past, Joseph said to the princes of Pharaoh, "If I have found favor in your sight, speak concerning me to Pharaoh, saying, 'My father commanded me,' saying, 'In the sepulcher which I dug for myself in the land of Canaan you will bury me.' Now then I will go up and bury my father, and return again."

Pharaoh replied to Joseph, "Go up and bury your father, as he forced you to swear," and so Joseph went up to bury his father, and all the servants of Pharaoh went up with him, and the elders of his house, and all the elders of the land of Egypt, and all the household of Joseph, and his brothers, and all the house of his father, and his families, but they left behind the sheep and oxen in the land of Goshen. There went up with him also chariots and cavalry, and there was a very great company. They came to the threshing floor of Atad, which is beyond Jordan, and they mourned him with great lamentation, and he sat shiva for his father seven days. The inhabitants of the land of Canaan saw the mourning at the floor of Atad, and said, "This is a great mourning for the Egyptians," therefore he called its name, 'The mourning of Egypt,' which is beyond Jordan.

His sons did this for him. His sons carried him up into the land of Canaan and buried him in the double cave, which cave Abraham bought for possession of a burying place from Ephrom the Cypriot, near Mamre. Then Joseph returned to Egypt, he and his brothers, and those that had gone up with him to bury his father. When the brothers of Joseph saw that their father was dead, they said, "Let's keep watch, in case at any time Joseph remembers our the evil against him and pays us back all the evils which we have done against him."

They came to Joseph, and said, "Your father commanded us before his death, saying, 'Tell Joseph, 'Forgive them their injustice and their sin, in all the evil they have done to you.' Now accept the injustice of the servants of the god of your father.'"

Joseph wept while they spoke to him, then they came to him and said, "We, these persons, are your servants."

Joseph consoled them, "Don't be afraid, for I am God's. You took counsel against me for evil, but God took counsel for me for good, that the matter might be as it is today, and many people might be fed." He said to them, "Don't be afraid, I will maintain you, and your families," and he comforted them and spoke kindly to them.

Joseph lived in Egypt, he and his brothers and all the family of his father, and Joseph lived a hundred and ten years. Joseph saw the children of Ephraim to the third generation, and the sons of Machir, the son of Manasseh, were borne on the thigh of Joseph. Joseph spoke to his brothers, saying, "I die, but God will surely visit you and will bring you out of this land to the land that God swore to our fathers, Abraham, Isaac, and Jacob."

Joseph commanded the sons of Israel, saying, "When God visits you, then you will carry my bones up with you."

Joseph died at a hundred and ten years, and they buried him in a coffin in Egypt.

Exodus: Chapter 1

These are the names of the sons of Israel that entered Egypt with Jacob their father. They each entered with their whole family: Reuben, Simeon, Levi, Judah, Issachar, Zebulun, Benjamin, Dan, Naphtali, Gad, Asher, and Joseph was in Egypt. All the lives born from Jacob were seventy-five. Joseph died, and all his brothers, and all from that generation.

The Israelites increased and multiplied, and became numerous and grew powerful, and the land multiplied them. There arose up another king in Egypt, who had not known Joseph. He said to his nation, "Look, the descendants of Israel are a great multitude and are stronger than we have become, so let us deal cunningly with them, in case at any time they increase, and when war comes against us, they ally with our enemies, and once defeating us in war, they will leave out of the land."

He set over them taskmasters, who should punish them in their works, and they built strong cities for Pharaoh,[1] in Pithom,[2] Ramesses,[3] and On[4] (which is now Heliopolis). But as they humbled them, so much they multiplied and grew exceedingly strong, and the Egyptians greatly hated the Israelites. The Egyptians tyrannized the Israelites with force. They antagonized their lives of hard labor, in the clay and in brick-making, and all the works in the plains, according to all the works, in which they caused them to serve with violence.

The king of the Egyptians spoke to the midwives of the Habirus.[5] The name of the one was Shiphrah, and the name of the second, Pua. He said, "When you midwife for the Habiru women deliver a child, if it is a male, kill it. But if a female, save it."

However, the midwives feared God[6] and did not do as the king of Egypt ordered them, and they saved the male children. The king of Egypt called the midwives, and asked them, "Why have you have done this, and saved the male children?"

The midwives answered Pharaoh, "The Habiru women are not like the women of Egypt. They deliver before the midwives get to them." So they carried children.

God treated the midwives well, and the people multiplied and grew very strong. As the midwives feared God, they established for themselves families.

Pharaoh ordered all his people, "Any male child born to the Habirus, throw into the river, and every female, keep it alive."

Exodus: Chapter 1 Notes

1 Codex Vaticanus: pharaô (ⲫⲁⲣⲁⲱ)

- Leningrad Codex: far'oh (פַּרְעֹה). Translation: Pharaoh

- Peshitta: prôun (ܦܪܥܘܢ). Translation: Pharaoh

- Targum Onkelos: malka (מַלְכָּא). Translation: king

- Fragment Targums: malka (מַלְכָּא). Translation: king

- Targum Jerusalem: milich (מְלִיךְ). Translation: ruler

- Coptic manuscripts: Pharaô (Φαραω)

Both the Greek and Hebrew terms were the equivalent of the modern term Pharaoh, a title of the King of Egypt, however, this translation is anachronistic to the era the story it set in. Both the Greek and Hebrew terms are ultimately derived from the Egyptian word per-âô (𓉐), meaning 'big house,' or 'palace.' During the New Kingdom era, the term became the title of the king of Egypt, which was adopted into Akkadian Cuneiform as Pirāú (𒉺𒆠𒈦), Canaanite as Prôh (𐤐𐤓𐤏𐤄), Aramaic as Prôu (פרעו), Greek as Pharaô (Φαραω), and Hebrew as far'oh (פַּרְעֹה). The story is set during the Middle Kingdom era, when the king of Egypt's title was nesut (transliterated hieroglyphs: nsût, spelled variously as 𓇓𓏏𓈎, 𓇓𓏏𓂋, or 𓇓𓏏𓆑 depending on context). As the term 'Pharaoh' is found in all copies of Exodus, it likely originated with a reference to the palace, not the king himself.

2 Codex Alexandrinus: Pithôm (ⲡⲓⲑⲱⲙ)

- Codex Ambrosiano A 147: Pithôth (ⲡⲓⲑⲱⲑ)

- LXX 509: Pisôn (ⲡⲓⲥⲱⲛ)

- LXX 15: Phithôm (Φιθωμ)

- LXX 64: Pithôph (ⲡⲓⲑⲱϥ)

- LXX 135: Phimôth (Φιμωθ)

- LXX 318: Phithom (Φιθομ)

- LXX 55: Pithô (ⲡⲓⲑⲱ)

- LXX 392: Phithôn (Ⲫⲓⲑⲱⲛ)

- LXX 730: Pithôm (Ⲡⲟ́ⲓⲑⲱⲙ)

- LXX 56: Pepithô (Ⲡⲟ́ⲡⲟ́ⲓⲑⲱ)

- LXX 121: Thô (Ⲑⲱ)

- LXX 75: Pithôn (Ⲡⲓⲑⲱⲛ)

- LXX 78: Pithôph (Ⲡⲟ́ⲓⲑⲱ𝄢)

- LXX 82: Pithôn (Ⲡⲟ́ⲓⲑⲱⲛ)

- LXX 458: Plê (ⲡⲗ̔ⲗ̔)

- LXX 54: Pithoph (Ⲡⲟ́ⲓⲑⲟ𝄢)

- LXX 72: Plinthon (ⲡⲗⲓ𝈍ⲑⲟ𝈍)

- LXX 799: Phithôn (Ⲫⲟ́ⲓⲑⲱⲛ)

- LXX 53: Poethô (Ⲡⲟⲓⲑⲱ)

- LXX 376: Phithôm (Ⲫⲟ́ⲓⲑⲱⲙ)

- LXX 59: Bithôr (Ⲃⲓⲑⲱ𝞺)

- LXX 619: Bithôm (Ⲃⲓⲑⲱⲙ)

- Leningrad Codex: Pitom (פִּתֹם)

- DSS 4QExodᶜ: ptm (פתם)

- Peshitta: Pytwm (ܦܝܬܘܡ)

- Targum Onkelos: Pitom (פִּיתוֹם)

- Fragment Targums: Tanis (טָנִיס)

- Targum Jerusalem: Taneis (טָאנִיס)

- Bohairic manuscripts: Pethom (Ⲡⲉⲑⲟⲙ)

- Fayyumic manuscripts: Phithôth (Ⲫⲓⲑⲱⲑ)

- Sahidic manuscripts: Pithôm (Ⲡⲓⲑⲱⲙ)

This is generally accepted as the city of Per-Atum (𓉐 𓇼𓐰�), later called Heroöpolis by the Greeks. The location of both the Egyptian and Greek cities remains unclear, however, several sites have been located that appear to have been known as Per-Atum at various times in Egyptian history. The difficulty locating the 'city' is likely because the name is actually a reference to a temple, the Temple of Atum, which periodically relocated, and as a result the name of the community it was in changed as well. Excavations at the Tel El Maskhuta complex, in the western Nile Delta, show a Hyksos era (15th dynasty) settlement that was likely Per-Atum, although the site was later abandoned until the era of Pharaoh Necho II (26th dynasty, circa 600 BC).

The city of Tanis, included in the Jerusalem and Jonathan Targums, was located in the northeastern Nile Delta. During the 19th dynasty (1200s BC), the town of Tanis was the capital of the 14th district of Egypt, however, there are no earlier records of the city.

3 Codex Ambrosiano A 147: Ramesê (𐌐𐌀𐌌𐌄𐌂𐌇)

- LXX 707: Shn (ⲥⲏⲛ)

- LXX 313: Rem (Ρϭμ)

- LXX 72: Ramessê (Ρϫμϭϭⲟⲑ)

- LXX 125: Ramesi (Ρϫμϭϭⲓ)

- Leningrad Codex: Ra'amses (רַעְמְסֵס)

- Peshitta: Rômsys (ܪܥܡܣܝܣ)

- Targum Onkelos: Ra'amses (רַעְמְסֵס)

- Fragment Targums: Pilusin (פִּילוּסִין). Translation: Pelusium

- Targum Jerusalem: Pilusin (פִּילוּסִין). Translation: Pelusium

The location of Ramesses has been a matter of debate since before the Septuagint was translated, and the translators were not sure which ancient Egyptian city the name Ramesses was referring to. The historic city of Ramesses was built in the era of Pharaoh Shoshenq I (943 to 922 BC) and was still a major city when the stories found in Numbers were most likely compiled into a book under King Hezekiah (715 to 687 BC). The Late-Period city of Ramesses was a rebuilding of the New Kingdom era city of Pi-Ramesses, and as the city of Pi-Ramesses was never called Ramesses during the New Kingdom era, it must be assumed that the name was updated when the Torah was updated under Josiah.

The city of Pi-Ramesses, which was founded in 1290 BC, was itself a rebuilding of Avaris, the Hyksos capital, which had been destroyed when the Hyksos were driven from Egypt in circa 1550 BC, meaning it is not clear if the name Avaris or Pi-Ramesses was updated to Ramesses. Both Avaris and Pi-Ramesses had served as imperial capital cities when Egypt had ruled Canaan, and so either could be the city in the text, however, if one accepts that Pi-Ramesses was the city called Ramesses, then it dates the events in Exodus to the 1200s BC, immediately before the Bronze Age Collapse, yet there are already reports from a century earlier of the Shasu (Nomads) of Yhů in the Seir Region of modern Jordan, which are generally accepted as a reference to the Israelites, meaning the original name was probably Avaris, which had become obscure by Josiah's time, and was updated to the contemporary name.

The city of Pelusium, mentioned in the Jerusalem and Jonathan Targums, was the easternmost major city in the Nile Delta during the Greco-Roman era. The city had existed since the Old Kingdom era, and therefore it is plausible that if was the original city in the text, however, that is unlikely. The original name of the city was Sin (𒁺) in the Old Kingdom era, however, which continued to b used alongside later names that were applied to the city, and was the common name of the city in languages using the Akkadian Cuneiform script, commonly spelled as Sin (𒊺𒄀𒈨), the name of the Akkadian moon-god, later spelled as Syån (𐤎𐤉𐤍), Saen (Σαιν), Sin (סִין), and Sin (Cɪɴ) during the Classical era.

During the New Kingdom era, the name of the city was changed to Per-Amen (𓉐𓇋𓏠𓈖), meaning the 'house of Amen,' which also continued to be used, resulting in the Coptic Peremoun (Ⲡⲉⲣⲉⲙⲟⲩⲛ). During the early Iron Age, the name Per-Sin (𐤎𐤓𐤐) developed, which was later transliterated into Greek as Pelousion (Πηλουσιον), and then adopted into Hebrew and Judean-Aramaic as Pilusin (פִּילוּסִין), meaning the name could not have been in the early Aramaic translation of Exodus. Nevertheless, it is clear that the city was not viewed as being the historic city of Ramesses by the Judeans in the early-Christian era.

4 Codex Vaticanus: Om (ⲟⲙ)

- LXX 707: Ôn (ⲱⲛ)

- LXX 58: Ôr (ⲱⲣ)

The Masoretic Text, Peshitta, and Targums do not mention Heliopolis at this point. In Bereshít, it was called On (אוֹן). The Egyptian name Iůnů (𓉺𓊖) means 'the pillars,' and was one of the ancient holy cities of Egypt since predynastic times. It is currently located in the Ayn Shams district of Greater Cairo. It was the cult-center for several gods, mostly associated with the Sun, which is why the Greeks renamed it Heliopolis. The solar gods worshiped there include the creator-god Atum, the solar-disk Aten, the sun Ra, and the scarab-beetle god Khepri. The major exception was the lunar god Iôhů.

As Joseph was given the daughter of a high-priest to wed in Genesis, he would become a high-priest as well, although Genesis does not clarify which god he was the priest of. Nevertheless, he is never connected to the Sun in any way, and as an interpreter of dreams, the moon makes more sense as Joseph's god, implying he was the priest of Îôhů, which is likely the source of the Israelite god Yhů also called Yahweh.

5 Codex Vaticanus: ebraeas (ЄΒΡΛΙΑϹ)

- LXX 59: ebraeaes (ϬυβΛΙΔιϲ)

- Leningrad Codex: Ivriyyot (עִבְרִיֹּת). Translation: female Eberite

- Peshitta: Ôbrytå (ܥܒܪܝܬܐ). Translation: female crosser

- Targum Onkelos: Yehudayata (יְהוּדְיָתָא). Translation: Judahite

- Targum Jerusalem: Yehodayta (יְהוֹדְיָיתָא). Translation: Judahite

The Greek term is a translation of Hebrew, using the Second Temple era interpretation of the word, however, the Masoretic spelling is not the correct spelling of Hebrewess, Ôbryt (עברית), but the Aramaic word for a female Eberite, Ôbryůt (ܥܒܪܝܬ). The Eberites were the descendants of the patriarch Eber, an ancestor of Abraham who lived in Ur, in southern Iraq, according to Genesis. The term ôbr (ܥܒܪ / עבר) means 'to cross over' in both Hebrew and Aramaic, indicating that these Eberites were the people otherwise known to the Egyptians as Habiru. The earliest surviving mention of the Habiru (𒄩𒁉𒊒), was from the time of King Rim-Sin I of Larsa between approximately 1822 and 1763 BC, who reported they were an Aramean tribe living in southern Iraq.

Over the next 600 years, they were reported in hundreds of surviving documents ranging across the Middle East and Egypt, generally as marauders, although some were reported to be mercenaries, and those in Egypt were generally slaves. They disappeared around the end of the Bronze Age, shortly before the emergence of the Aramean Empire around Damascus and Hama, in the early Iron Age. As this reference is to the Habirus, that name is restored in this text. As there is no common feminine form of the name, the gender neutral form of Habiru is used.

6 Codex Vaticanus: o ths (ΟΘϹ). Translation: the god

- Leningrad Codex: ha'elohim (הָאֱלֹהִים). Translation: the gods (Aramaic), the goddesses (Hebrew)

This verse has not survived intact in any of the fragments found among the Dead Sea Scrolls, however, the word ålhym does survive in other verses that have survived among the Dead Sea Scrolls.

- DSS 4QGen-Exodᵃ: Ålhym (אלהים)

- DSS 4QpaleoGen-Exodˡ: Ålhym (𐤀𐤋𐤄𐤉𐤌)

- DSS 4QExodᵇ: Ålûhym (אלוהים)

- DSS 4QExodᶜ: the term is missing in complete text, meaning it was not there. The Masoretic verse has Yehvah elohim (יְהוָה אֱלֹהִים), while Dead Sea Scroll 4QExodᶜ has ådny Yhůh (אדני יהוה) which translates as my lord Yahweh. The Septuagint only has 'the god' (o θεος) in this verse, which means that 4QExodᶜ does not correspond to either the Septuagint or Masoretic version of Exodus.

- DSS 4QpaleoExodᵐ: Ålhym (𐤀𐤋𐤄𐤉𐤌). Translation: gods, Elohim

- Peshitta: ålhå (ܐܠܗܐ). Translation: God

- Targum Onkelos: yeyah (??). Translation: Yhů

- Targum Jerusalem: yeyah (??). Translation: Yhů

The term ålhym (𐤀𐤋𐤄𐤉𐤌), and ålhym (𐡀𐡋𐡄𐡉𐡌), are also direct transcriptions of the Neo-Assyrian word elium (𒀭𒇷𒌝), which by the Iron Age meant 'god,' indicating that text had previously been written in cuneiform, and was translated into Aramaic or Phoenician during the iron age. During the bronze age, the Old Babylonian word was Alium (𒀭𒇷𒌝), and referred to a specific god, ᵈᵉⁱᵗʸAn (𒀭𒀭) the highest god, and father of the other gods. His Old Akkadian name was derived from the word elûm (𒀭𒊑𒌝), meaning 'higher,' as the term was intended to convey the meaning of 'highest.' He was believed to live in the polar region of the sky, where the modern constellation of Draco is located, making him the highest in the sky, around which all the gods (stars) circled.

The term el elyovn (אֵל עֶלְיוֹן), meaning 'highest god,' was translated into Hebrew in Genesis Exodus: Chapter 14, where the Greeks translated it as theô tô ypsistô (Θεω τω υψιστω), also meaning 'highest god.' El Elyon is known to have been a major god of the Canaanites, called ål ůålyn (𐡀𐡋 𐡅𐡀𐡋𐡉𐡍), meaning 'God and Highest' in an Aramaic language Sefire Treaty from circa 750 BC. The Greek translations of Sanchuniathon's bronze age writing that has survived to the present, referred to the primordial creator god of the Canaanites as Elioun (Ελιουν), which appears to be the same god.

According to Sanchuniathon, Elioun was the highest (υψιστος) god, who made the sky and the land, and they made the rest of the gods. During the Old Babylonian and Old Assyrian eras, the gods Marduk and Ashur, the national gods of Babylon and Assyria, replaced the Akkadian Ān as the primary god of the Mesopotamian pantheons, and by the iron age, the word elium had came to mean 'god,' explaining why the Aramaic term ålhym (𐡀𐡋𐡄𐡉𐡌) would have been interpreted as 'god,' by the Greeks.

Exodus: Chapter 2

There was a certain man of the tribe of Levi, who took as wife one of the daughters of Levi. She conceived, and carried a male child, and having seen that he was fair, they hid him three months. When they could no longer hide him, his mother took an box for him, and smeared it with vegetable oil, and placed the child into it, and put it in the slime by the river. His sister was watching from a distance, to find out what would happen to him.

The daughter of Pharaoh came down to the river to bathe, and her girls walked by the river's side, and seeing the box in the slime, she sent her girl and picked it up. Having opened it, she saw the baby crying in the box, and the daughter of Pharaoh had compassion on it, and said, "This is one of the Habirus children."

His sister asked the daughter of Pharaoh, "Would you like for me to call a nurse of the Habirus for you, to suckle the child for you?"

The daughter of Pharaoh commanded, "Go!" and the young woman went and called the mother of the child. The daughter of Pharaoh ordered her, "Take care of this child and suckled it for me, and I will pay you," and the woman took the child and suckled it.

When the boy was grown, she brought him to the daughter of Pharaoh, and he became her son, and she called his name, 'Moses,'[1] saying, "I took him out of the water."

It happened in the length of time, that Moses grow up and went out to his brothers the sons of Israel, and saw their distress. He saw an Egyptian striking one of his Habiru brothers, the Israelites, and after looking around and seeing no one watching, and he killed the Egyptian and hid him in the sand. Going out a second day he saw two Habiru men fighting, and he asked the injurer, "Why do you hit your neighbor?"

He answered, "Who made you a ruler and a judge over us? Will you kill me like you killed the Egyptian yesterday?"

Then Moses was concerned, and said, "This matter has become known."

Pharaoh heard this matter and wanted to kill Moses, and Moses departed from the presence of Pharaoh, and traveled to the land of Midian,[2] and having entered the land of Midian, sat by the well. The priest of Midian had seven daughters, feeding the flock of their father Jethro, and they came and drew water until they filled their pitchers, to water the flock of their father Jethro. The shepherds came and were driving them away, and Moses rose up and rescued them, and drew water for them, and watered their sheep. They returned to Jethro their father, and he said to them, "Why have you come so quickly today?"

They answered, "An Egyptian saved us from the shepherds, and drew water for us and watered our sheep."

He said to his daughters, "Where is he? Why have you left the man? Call him, therefore, that he may eat bread."

Moses was established with the man, and he gave Shiphrah his daughter to Moses as a wife. The woman conceived and carried a son, and Moses called his name 'Gershom,' saying, "I am a traveler in a strange land."

In those days after a length of time, the king of Egypt died, and the Israelites groaned because of their tasks and cried, and their cry because of their tasks went up to God. God heard their groaning, and God remembered his covenant made with Abraham and Isaac and Jacob. God looked on the Israelites and was made known to them.

Exodus: Chapter 2 Notes

1 Codex Vaticanus: Môysên (ⲘⲱⲨⲤⲎ). LXX B also uses the spelling of Môysês (ⲘⲱⲨⲤⲎⲤ) later in Exodus.

- Codex Ambrosiano A 147: Môysên (ⲘⲱⲨⲤⲎⲚ)

- Codex Alexandrinus: Môysê (ⲘⲱⲨⲤⲎ)

- LXX 135: Môsê (Ⲙⲟⲟⲗ). LXX 135 also uses the spelling of Môysin (Ⲙⲟⲟⲩⲥⲓⲛ) later in Exodus.

- LXX 53: Môsês (Ⲙⲟⲟⲗⲥ)

- LXX 68: Môyssên (Ⲙⲟⲟⲩⲥⲟⲗⲛ). LXX 135 also uses the spelling of Môyssês (Ⲙⲟⲟⲩⲥⲟⲗⲥ) later in Exodus.

- Leningrad Codex: Mosheh (מֹשֶׁה)

- DSS 4QpaleoGen-Exod[l]: Mšh (𐤌𐤔𐤄)

This verse does not survive in most of the fragments found among the Dead Sea Scrolls, however, the name 'Moses' does survive in later verses that have survived among the

Dead Sea Scrolls.

- DSS 4QExod-Lev^f: Mšh (משה)
- DSS 4QGen-Exod^a: Mšh (משה)
- DSS 4QpaleoExod^m: Mšh (𐤌𐤔𐤄)
- DSS 2QExod^a: Mûšh (מושה)
- DSS 2QExod^b: Mûšh (מושה)
- DSS 4QExod^c: Mûšh (מושה)
- DSS 4QExod^b: Mûšh (מושה)
- DSS 1QExod: Mšh (משה)
- DSS Mur1: Mšh (משה)
- Peshitta: Mûšå (ܡܘܫܐ)
- Targum Onkelos: Mosheh (מֹשֶׁה)
- Fragment Targums: verse not included. In other verses the name is spelled as Mosheh (מֹשֶׁה)
- Targum Jerusalem: Mosheh (מֹשֶׁה)

It is generally accepted that at some point before the Septuagint was translated, half of Moses' name was redacted from the text. This theory is based on the similarity of the Egyptian term msi (𓄟𓋴), meaning 'give birth to,' or 'created by,' which was a common element of Egyptian names. Many kings of Egypt were known as the 'mesi' of a god, including Ramses (𓇳𓄟𓋴), Ahmose (𓇋𓄟𓋴), Tuthmose (𓅝𓄟𓋴), Amenmose (𓇋𓏠𓋴𓄟), and Ptahmose (𓁹𓄟𓋴𓏏𓎛). A theory that has been circulating since at least the time of Josephus in the 1st century AD, is that Moses' original name was Hapymoses, meaning the 'Nile created him.'

If this is the origin of the name, the name of the god that created Moses was likely dropped from the name very early in Israelite history, as there are no known surviving texts with the full name. The latest this is likely to have happened would have been during the Aramaic translation of King Hezekiah, however, it may have happened much earlier. An alternate interpretation is that the name is complete, and is derived from the Egyptian term mů-šåô (𓈗𓈖𓇋𓈘), meaning 'beginning on water,' which appears to be what the princess is stating.

2 Codex Vaticanus: Madiam (ΜΑΔΙΑΜ)

- Leningrad Codex: Midyan (מִדְיָן)

- Peshitta: Mdyn (ܡܕܝܢ)

- Targum Onkelos: Midyan (מִדְיָן)

- Targum Jerusalem: Midyan (מִדְיָן)

The land of Midiam is generally accepted as being in the Midiyan Mountains in the Hijaz area of Saudi Arabia, east of the Gulf of Aqaba. There is some debate regarding this location, as some scholars in the 1800s preferred the Sinai Peninsula in Egypt, and some preferred regions of Syria. Most of the ruins in the Hijaz date to after 800 BC, which caused some concern, however, earlier levels of civilization have been found dating back to the 1300s, including pottery described as 'Midianite Pottery' or 'Qurayyah Painted Ware.'

This pottery is widespread, ranging from the Qurayyah region in Hejaz as far north as Israel, Jordan, and the West Bank. The style is similar to the Mycenaean pottery of the era, suggesting that the Midianites may have been Sea Peoples that settled in the area, related to the Pelest (Philistines) in the Gaza Strip, and the Tribe of Dan. There is also older Minoan style pottery found in the region, suggesting the Minoans and later Mycenaean Greeks were using the region as a transshipment center between the Mediterranean and Red Seas for many centuries in the late Bronze Age and early Iron Age. If one accepted the dating for this story in either circa 1300s BC, or 1600s BC, then Midian would have been the closest land to the Nile Delta that Moses could have escaped to that was not under the rule of Egypt.

Exodus: Chapter 3

Moses was shepherding the flock of Jethro his father-in-law, the priest of Midian, and he brought the sheep to the edge of the wilderness and came to Mount Horeb. The messenger of the lord[1] appeared to him in the fire of flame out of the bush, and he saw that the bush was burning with fire, but was not consumed. Moses said, "I will approach and see this great sight, and why the bush is not burned up."

When the Lord saw him approach to watch, the Lord called him out of the bush, calling, "Moses, Moses!"

He asked, "What is it?"

He answered, "Don't come near here. Remove the sandals from your feet, as this place is holy ground." He continued, "I am the God of your father, the God of Abraham, and the God of Isaac, and the God of Jacob," and Moses turned away his face, as he was afraid to look at God.

The Lord said to Moses, "I have surely seen the suffering of my people that are in Egypt, and I have heard their cry caused by their taskmasters, for I know their suffering. I have come down to deliver them out of the hand of the Egyptians, and to bring them out of that land, and to bring them into a good and wide land, into a land flowing with milk and honey, into the land of the Canaanites, Cypriots,[2] Amorites, Perizzite, Girgashites, Mitanni,[3] and Jebusites. Now see, the cry of the Israelites has come to me, and I have seen the suffering with which the Egyptians punish them. Now come, I will send you to Pharaoh, king of Egypt, and you will bring out my people the Israelites from the land of Egypt."

Moses asked God, "Who am I, that I should go to Pharaoh king of Egypt, and that I should bring out the Israelites from the land of Egypt?"

God answered Moses, "I will be with you, and this will be the sign to you that I will send you out, when you bring out my people from Egypt, then you will serve the God on this mountain."

Moses asked God, "Look, I will go to the Israelites, and will say to them, 'the God of our fathers has sent me to you,' and they will ask me, 'What is his name?' How will I answer them?"

God answered Moses, "I am Resheph,"[4] and he added, "So will you tell the Israelites, 'Resheph has sent me to you.'"

God continued speaking to Moses, and said, "You will say this to the sons of Israel, 'Lord the god[5] of our fathers, the God of Abraham, and the God of Isaac, and the God of Jacob, has sent me to you. This is my name forever, and my memorial to generations and generations.' Go then and gather the elders of the Israelites, and you will say to them, 'The Lord God of our fathers has appeared to me, the God of Abraham, and the God of Isaac, and the God of Jacob, saying, I have surely seen you, and all the things which have happened to you in Egypt.'"

He continued, "'I will bring you up out of the suffering under the Egyptians to the land of the Canaanites and the Cypriots, and Amorites and Perizzite, and Girgashites, and Mitanni, and Jebusites, to a land flowing with milk and honey.' They will listen to your voice, and you and the elders of Israel will go to Pharaoh king of Egypt, and you will say to him, 'the God of the Habirus has called us. We will go on a journey of three days into the wilderness, that we may sacrifice to our God.' But I know that Pharaoh king of Egypt will not let you go, except with a mighty hand, and I will stretch out my hand, and strike the Egyptians with all my wonders, which I will work among them, and after, that he will send you out. I will give these people favor in the sight of the Egyptians, and when you escape, you will not depart empty. But every woman will ask of her neighbor and fellow lodger, articles of gold and silver, and apparel, and you will put them on your sons and your daughters, and plunder the Egyptians."

Exodus: Chapter 3 Notes

1 Codex Vaticanus: angelos cu (ΑΓΓΕΛΟΣΚῩ). Translation: messenger lord

- Leningrad Codex: mal'ach yehovah (מַלְאַךְ יְהֹוָה). Translation: messenger Yahoveh

- Peshitta: mlåkh dmryå (ܡܠܐܟܗ ܕܡܪܝܐ). Translation: messenger of master (or lord)

- Targum Onkelos: mal'acha dayeyah (מַלְאֲכָא דַיְיָ). Translation: messenger of Yah

2 Codex Vaticanus: Chettaeôn (ΧΕΤΤΑΙΩΝ)

- LXX 58: Chetgaeôn (Χϭτγλιοον)

- Leningrad Codex: Chitti (חִתִּי). Translation: Cypriots

- Peshitta: Ḥtyå (ܚܬܝܐ)

- Targum Onkelos: Chitta'ei (חִתָּאֵי)

• Targum Jerusalem: Chita'ei (חִיתָּאֵי)

This term has created a great deal of confusion since the misidentification of the ruins of the Neshites as being 'Hittite' in the 1800s. The modern archaeological name 'Hittite,' is not derived from an ancient name for the culture applied by themselves, or anyone else, but rather adopted from the biblical reference to a then-unknown civilization somewhere in the region. There was an ancient culture in the region called the Hattians, however, they were conquered by the Nesites before 1700 BC, and subsequently disappeared from the historic records.

The name was applied to culture today referred to as 'Hittites,' before the 'Hittite' language had been translated, and is incorrect. Since 1906, excavations at Boğazköy, the ancient 'Hittite' capital Hattusa have uncovered more than 10,000 'Hittite' texts, including the royal achieve. The actual name of the 'Hittite' language and people was Nešili (𒉈𒅆𒇷), which is now rendered in some academic literate as Nesite or Neshite. As early as the mid-1800s some scholars disputed the identification of the Nesites as the Biblical Hittites, including the Orientalist Max Müller, who was one of many claiming the Biblical Hittites were ancient Greeks or some other Mediterranean people. Later in the Septuagint's translation of the Maccabees, the similar term Chettiim (Χεττιιμ) as a reference to all Greek-speaking lands, and therefore the Biblical Hittites were likely the Minoans or the Achaean Greeks.

In the 1ˢᵗ century AD, the Jewish historian Josephus reported that Cethima was the name of Cyrus in Aramaic, and the Chettim were the descendants of Noah's grandson Chethimus, who had settled on Cyprus. Josephus reported that the name was preserved in the Greek name of the town Cition (Κίτιον). Most historians view it as more likely that the Aramaic name was derived from the city-state of Cition, which was known as Kâtjảy (𓈎𓂝𓏏𓏭𓊖) in Egyptian records from the New Kingdom Era in the late Bronze Age, and Kt (𐤊𐤕) or Kty (𐤊𐤕𐤉) in Phoenician records from the early Iron Age. While this may be the origin of the term, by the era of the Neo-Assyrian era, the term must have also referred to other Greek islands, as both the prophets Isaiah and Ezekiel used the term 'Islands of Kittim.' As the term referred to the entire island of Cyprus in Aramaic, the translations of 'Cyprus' and 'Cypriots' are used here.

3 Codex Vaticanus: Euaeôn (ΕΥΑΙωΝ)

• LXX 44: Ebaeôn (Ευᾱιοον)

• Leningrad Codex: Chivvi (חִוִּי)

• Peshitta: Ḥûyả (ܚܘܝܐ)

• Targum Onkelos: Chiva'ei (חִוָּאֵי)

- Targum Jerusalem: Chivavei (חִיוָואֵי)

The term is believed to have been derived from the name of the Hurrians, however, is derived separately from the other term Chori (חֹרִי). Chori is accepted as referring to the Hurrians, which the Egyptians called Hårů (𓍯𓈖𓂋𓈖), and the Babylonians called Ḫuurri (𒄷𒌨𒊑). The Hurrians were one of the oldest cultures in the Middle East, however, became largely a slave culture within the Akkadian and Old Babylonian empires. Under the Mitanni empire, they rose to a position of wealth, and formed the noble caste. The Greek transliteration of this term was variations of Chorrhaeous (Χορραιους), which, like the Hebrew term, was used interchangeably in the texts with Eyaeon (Ευαιον) / Chivvi (חִוִּי), although that term generally applied to the rules and priests.

The ultimate origin of the terms Eyaeon (Ευαιον) and Chivvi (חִוִּי), both appear to be the cuneiform word Éan (𒂍𒀭), meaning temple or sacred. In the Amarna Letters, which date to the 1330s BC, the term Éan (𒂍𒀭) was the name of a people, who appear to be the Mitanni, or the Mitanni-Aryan priesthood within the Mitanni. A similar correlation between the terms is found in the Septuagint's 1st Paralipomenon and Masoretic Divrei-hay Yamim, where the Greek translation uses Beithani (Βαιθανι), however, the Hebrew uses the term Mitni (מִתְנִי). This term also refers to a group of people, meaning the underlying Edomite text the Greeks translated would have been 'people of the House of Ån' (𐤉𐤕𐤁𐤄), a direct Canaanite translation of É An (𒂍𒀭).

While Mitni was the transliteration used in the Edomite text that formed the basis of the Hebrew translation of Divrei-hayYamim, it was replaced with Chivvi (חִוִּי) in the Judahite texts, which served as the basis of most of the Masoretic texts. This likely originated in a Judahite copy of the text, after the Aramaic translation had been made, where an N (𐤍) was replaced with a Ů (𐤅). The Aramaic translation would have already been made in the time of King Manasseh, were the term was transliterated as Hyån (𐤇𐤉𐤀𐤍), itself a transliteration of the early Canaanite Hyån (𐤉𐤕𐤁𐤄).

The term Ebaeôn (Εβαιων), which is found as a substitute for Eyaeon (Ευαιον) in some copies of the Septuagint for term, must have originated in an intentional alteration to the text, as there are no similar letters for b (ב ,כ ,פ) and y (י ,ע ,ז) in the Semitic alphabets the text was previously in. This probable origin was an Ebionite translation in the first century AD. The Ebionites were an early Judeo-Christian sect based in Judea before the First Jewish-Roman war. Many fled east to Mesopotamia with the Mandeans and other smaller Judahite religious groups, while others fled south into Arabia. The Arabian Ebionites are generally viewed as shaping the Islamic view of the prophet Jesus (عيسَى).

4 Codex Vaticanus: egô imi o Ôm (ⲉⲅⲱⲉⲓⲙⲓⲟⲱⲙ). Translation: I am the Ôm

• LXX 318: Hegô ipen ho ôn (ⲉⲅⲱ ⲋⲓⲡⲉⲛⲟ ⲟⲟⲛ). Translation: I speak the real

• Leningrad Codex: ehyeh asher ehyeh (אֶהְיֶה אֲשֶׁר אֶהְיֶה). Translation: I will exist (or happen to be, own) that (or which, who, whom) I will exist (or happen to be, own)

• DSS 4QGen-Exodᵃ: -hyh ǎšr ǎhyh (-אֿהֿיֿה אֿשֿר אֿהֿיֿה)

• Peshitta: ǎhyh ǎšrhyh (ܐܗܝܗ ܐܫܪܗܝܗ). Translation: I will be Asrhyh

• Targum Onkelos: ehyeh asher ehyeh (אֶהְיֶה אֲשֶׁר אֶהְיֶה). This is a direct copy of the phrase found in the Masoretic text.

• Fragment Targums: dein de'amar le'alma hevei vahavah ve'atid lemeimar leih hevei vahavah (דֵין דְּאָמַר לְעָלְמָא הֲוֵי וַהֲוָה וְעָתִיד לְמֵימַר לֵיהּ הֲוֵי וַהֲוָה). Translation: he who said to the word 'be,' and it was, and he who will saw to the world 'be,' and it will be. The Fragment Targums also includes the phrase "Tell the sons of Israel "Ehyeh sent me to you" (כְּדֵין תֵּימַר לִבְנֵי יִשְׂרָאֵל אֶהְיֶה שְׁלַחַנִי לִפְנֵיכֶם) at the end of the verse, repeating the Masoretic and Onkelos versions. In this Targum, Ehyê is used as a proper name, although does not appear to be one.

• Targum Jerusalem: dein de'amar vahavah alma amar vahavah kula (דֵין דְּאָמַר וַהֲוָה עָלְמָא אָמַר וַהֲוָה כּוּלָא). Translation: he who spoke and the world existed, who spoke all things existed. The Targum Jerusalem also includes 'Tell the sons of Israel "Ana, he in proper conduct and in good standing sent me to you" (כְּדָנָא תֵּימַר לִבְנֵי יִשְׂרָאֵל אֲנָא הוּא דְּהַוֵינָא וְעָתִיד לְמֶהֱוֵי שַׁדְרַנִי לְוָותְכוֹן), at the end of the verse. This Targum seems to mirror the Septuagint's use of Ôn as a name, however, that could also be interpreted as something like "Behold..."

• Armenian Bible: Es em Astoůats or ēn (Ես եմ Աստուած որ էս). Translation: I am God (or the sun) that is

The meaning of the variations of this verse has caused a great deal of debate since the early-Christian era. The various Septuagint manuscripts all include either the word ôm (ωμ) or ôn (ων), with most early copies using ôm, and Byzantine and later copies using ôn. Theodotian's Greek translation of the Hebrew text from circa 150 AD, also used the term ôm (ωμ), indicating that there was a Hebrew or Aramaic translation in common use that included the term. Theodotian's translation of Daniel included transliterations of Hebrew words in sections of text that survive in Aramaic in the Masoretic Text, indicating that he used an alternate Hebrew source text from the Masoretes.

Additional early Greek variations of the phrase are accepted as having existed, as several early Christian scholars quoted the verse differently, in some cases mirroring the Armenian or Coptic variations. The Armenian version added the word 'god' to the verse, while the Coptic translation appears to be a more direct translation of the existing

Hebrew text. In most verses where the Septuagint's Exodus used the name 'Ôm' or term 'ôn,' the Masoretic text reads Shaddai (שַׁדָּי), however, in this case contains a completely different phrase. The Masoretic term translates as essentially 'I will be what I will be,' and appears to be part of the redaction of the name Shaddai from the era of the Judahite kings Hezekiah and Manasseh. This is not the same translation of 'Shaddai' that is generally used in the Septuagint. The term El Šdy was used 48 times in the Masoretic Text, including 31 times in the book of Job, 6 times in Bereshít (Masoretic Cosmic Genesis), and once in Exodus. Both the Cosmic Genesis and Masoretic Exodus appear to have been redacted in regards to the identity of El Šdy, as there is no reference to El Šdy in Cosmic Genesis, and there is no reference to Ôn in Masoretic Exodus.

The Septuagint and Masoretic translations often differ in regards to the name or title Šdy, suggesting that the Aramaic and Canaanite (Judahite and Samaritan) source texts they worked from differed in regards to this word. The cause of the confusion over the term šdy, is likely due to the difference between the meaning of the word in Canaanite versus Aramaic. In Akkadian cuneiform, which was adopted as the written script by many cultures, the term was ^{deity}šēdu (✳⌖), however, it referred to a 'protective spirit' or 'lesser god.' In the later Aramaic language, the word became šydå (𐤍𐤉𐤃𐤔), meaning 'demon' in the classical sense, as a type of muse or nymph. Whereas in Canaanite, šdy (𐤆𐤀𐤅) took on different meaning, generally interpreted as 'powerful' by the Early Classical Era, which is likely where the Greeks ultimately derived the term 'omnipotent' (παντοκράτορος), which was used later in the Septuagint where the Masoretic Text generally uses the term šdy.

This alternate interpretation of the šdy (𐤆𐤀𐤅) in Canaanite is likely due to the Egyptian New Kingdom era rule over Canaan, when Shed (🝔, transliteration: šd), was worshiped in the region. Shed, who was often referred to as 'the savior,' was virtually identical to the earlier Canaanite god Resheph who was largely suppressed after the fall of the Hyksos dynasty. During the Hyksos Dynasty, Resheph was generally associated with the Egyptians gods of war, Set and Montu, however, one cult in Iůnů (Heliopolis), viewed him as the Amorite version of Atum. This belief abruptly disappeared from Egypt with the fall of the Hyksos dynasty, suggesting that Moses was a member of that cult.

In the Masoretic Book of Job, Eliphaz referred to humanity as the 'sons of Resheph' (בני-רשף) instead of the 'sons of Adam,' and then uses Shaddai as the name of a god. This god Šdy was explicitly listed alongside the god El in Masoretic Job, whereas in the Septuagint's Job they are not explicitly listed as two separate gods. The Greek translation of Shaddai (שדי) in Job is consistent with most of the Septuagint, using a term that translates as 'omnipotent' (παντοκράτορος), however, the name El (אל) is generally translated as a word meaning 'strong' (ισχυρος). It is likely because the Masoretic Text lists them side by side, as 'god El and god Shaddai,' (אל-אל ואל-שדי), which the Greek translators did not do, instead routinely dropping the second reference to a god when they were listed together.

The terms 'god Shaddai' (אל-שדי) and 'god El' (אל-אל) are repeatedly found in Masoretic Job, and are themselves direct translations of the same terms in Akkadian Cuneiform: ^{deity}šēdu (✳⊡) and ^{deity}Ān (✳✳). Unfortunately, the Akkadian meaning of the word šēdu was 'demonic,' which is likely the cause of it's redaction. Based on the linguistics of Masoretic Job, the text book existed in a Hieratic or Proto-Canaanite form during the Hyksos Dynasty, and therefore the name Resheph is not out of place, as Resheph was one of the main gods of the Hyksos rulers. During subsequent the New Kingdom era, Resheph worship was suppressed due to his associated with the earlier Hyksos dynasty. During the early New Kingdom era, holy texts about Resheph would have been updated to Shed (𓈙𓂝𓆓), which would have been transliterated into Canaanite using the Akkadian Cuneiform script in the late New Kingdom era as ^{god}šēdu (✳⊡), before being translated into Canaanite using the Phoenician script in the early iron age as šdy (𐤔𐤃𐤉), resulting in the confusing 'demonic' god in Aramaic.

The earliest Aramaic terms within the Masoretic text is found in Bereshít (Masoretic Cosmic Genesis), in the genealogy of nations, which is internally dated to between 713 and 708 BC, meaning it would have been composed during the life of King Hezekiah. According to the Tractate Sanhedrin (103a) in the Talmud, Hezekiah's heir King Manasseh removed 'the name' from the Torah, and while this is generally assumed to be the name Yahweh, the archaeological record shows that Yahwism continued to grow throughout the era, indicating it was a different name he removed. As these changes to the text appear to have been more prevalent in the Aramaic text, it is likely that it was the name Shaddai that he removed, likely substituting the Neo-Asssyrian word ån (✳ / אן), meaning 'god,' which later resulted in the strange Greek translation. As the Masoretic version of Exodus uses the name Shaddai in the other places where Greek Exodus uses Ôm/ôn, and Shaddai was the early Canaanite interpretation of Shed, the late bronze age interpretation off Resheph, that name is restored in this translation.

5 Codex Vaticanus: c̄s o t̄h̄s (ⲔⲤ Ⲟ ⲐⲤ). Translation: Lord the god

- Leningrad Codex: Yehvah elohei (יְהֹוָה אֱלֹהֵי). Translation: Yahweh god

- DSS 4QGen-Exodᵃ: -ålhy (-אלהי). Translations: - god. The name is missing due to damage to the text

- DSS 4QExodᵇ: Yhůh ål- (ויהוה אל-). Translation: Yahweh God-. The word god is damaged, however, the text does appear to be the same as the Aleppo Codex

- Peshitta: mryå ålhå (ܡܪܝܐ ܐܠܗܐ). Translation: master (or lord) god

- Targum Onkelos: yeyah elaha (יְיָ אֱלָהָא). Translation: Yah god

- Targum Jerusalem: yeyah elaha (יְיָ אֱלָהָא). Translation: Yah god

The name Iaw (Masoretic יְהֹוָה) was transliterated as Ιαω in the Septuagint, which was later transliterated as 'Iaw' by the Pre-Christian Romans. In later copies of the Septuagint, the name was replaced by the name written in Canaanite (𐤉𐤄𐤅𐤄) or Assyrian script (יהוה). The name Iaw is found in fragments of the 3rd century AD Papyrus Oxyrhynchus 1007, however, is represented by a double Yod ("), meaning it was copied from a later Hebrew or Aramaic text from that era. After the sixth century AD, the occasional copy of the Septuagint is found which uses the name, either written as Iaw (Ιαω) or a Greek approximation of יהוה (ΠΙΠΙ), however, all of these can be traced back to the Hexapla, Quinta, Sextus, and/or Septima, which attempted to retranslate and harmonize the Old Testament in the 3rd through 6th centuries AD.

There are no early surviving copies of the Septuagint's version of Exodus which have the name Iaw (Ιαω / יְהֹוָה) in it, like some of the other books of the Septuagint, and therefore it cannot be proven conclusively if the name was in the Septuagint's Exodus or not, however, a number of other books in the Septuagint appear to retain older versions of the Israelite scriptures that pre-date the redaction during the Hasmonean dynasty, which replaced many older names of gods with Yahweh or Yahweh Sabaoth, the national god of Hasmonean Judea.

The Aramaic sections of Masoretic Daniel that were not translated into Hebrew maintain the term adonai ha'elohim (אֲדֹנָי הָאֱלֹהִים), meaning the 'Lord the gods' where the Septuagint has 'Lord the god' (Κύριον τον θεον), however, the Hebrew sections have Yahweh elohim (יְהֹוָה אֱלֹהִים) where the Septuagint has 'Lord the god,' suggesting the Greek more accurately reflects the Aramaic source texts than the Hebrew translation. According to some records from the time, this was to repair the damage King Manasseh had done 600 years earlier when he removed the name Yahweh from the Israelite Texts, however, no evidence has survived from the era of Manasseh or earlier that proves the name was originally in the text, suggesting it was an attempt by the first Hasmonean High-Priest/King Simon the Zealot to create a national Judean religion with a god having a name similar to the Roman god Jove. As Cyrios ho theos (Κύριος ο θεος) translates directly as Lord the god, that term is used in this translation.

Exodus: Chapter 4

Moses asked, "If they don't believe me and don't listen to my voice, and they say, 'God has not appeared to you,' what will I say to them?"

The Lord asked him, "What is it that is in your hand?"

He answered, "A wand."

He ordered, "Throw it on the ground."

When he threw it on the ground, it became a serpent, and Moses fled from it. The Lord ordered Moses, "Stretch out your hand, and grab its tail." So he stretched out his hand and grabbed the tail, and it became a wand in his hand. "So they will believe you, that the God of your fathers has appeared to you, the God of Abraham, and the God of Isaac, and the God of Jacob."

The Lord continued speaking to him, "Touch your hand to your chest," and touched his hand to his chest, and brought his hand away from his chest, and his hand had become like snow. He said again, "Put your hand to your chest," and he put his hand to his chest, and brought his hand away from his chest, and it was again restored to the color of his other skin. "If they will not believe you, or listen to your voice after the first sign, they will believe your voice after the second sign. If they will not believe you after these two signs, and will not listen to your voice, then you will take water from the river and pour it on the dry land, and the water which you will take from the river will become blood on the dry land."

Moses said to the Lord, I pray, "Lord, I have not been sufficient in the past, that you have begun to speak to your servant. I am weak in speech, and slow-tongued."

The Lord said to Moses, "Who has given a mouth to man, and who has made the very hard of hearing, and the deaf, the seeing and the blind? Haven't I, God? Now go and I will open your mouth, and will instruct you in what you will say."

Moses said, "I beg you, Lord, appoint an able person who you will send."

The Lord was enraged by Moses, and said, "Look! Is not Aaron the Levite your brother? I know that he will surely speak to you. Look, he will come out to meet you, and seeing you he will celebrate within himself. You will speak to him, and you will put my words into his mouth, and I will open your mouth and his mouth, and I will instruct you in what you will do. He will speak for you to the people, and he will be your mouth, and you will be for him in things about God. This wand that was turned into a serpent you will take in your hand, where you will work miracles."

Moses went and returned to Jethro his father-in-law, and said, "I must leave and return to my brothers in Egypt, and will see if they are still alive."

Jethro replied to Moses, "Go in health."

In those days after some time, the king of Egypt died, and the Lord told Moses in Midian, "Go, leave for Egypt, for all that wanted your life are dead."

Moses took his wife and his children, and mounted them on the animals, and returned to Egypt, and Moses took the wand which he received from God in his hand. The Lord said to Moses, "When you go and return to Egypt, see all the miracles I have put into your hands, you will work before Pharaoh. I will harden his heart, and he will certainly not send away the people. You will say to Pharaoh, 'The Lord said, Israel is my firstborn, and I say to you, Send my people away, that they may serve me. If you will not send them away, know, I will kill your firstborn son.'"

It happened that the messenger of the lord met him along the road at an inn, and wanted to kill him. Shiphrah took a stone and cut off the foreskin of her son, and fell at his feet saying, "The blood of the circumcision of my son has stopped," and he departed from them because she had said, "The blood of the circumcision of my son has stopped."

The Lord told Aaron, "Go into the wilderness to meet Moses," and he went and met him in the Mountain of God, and they kissed each other. Moses reported to Aaron all the words of the Lord, which he sent, and all the things which he ordered him.

Moses and Aaron went and gathered the elders of the Israelites. Aaron spoke all these words, which God had said to Moses, and worked the miracles before the people. The people believed and rejoiced, because God had visited the Israelites and because he saw their suffering, and the people bowed and worshiped.

Exodus: Chapter 5

After this Moses and Aaron went to Pharaoh and said to him, "These things the Lord, the God of Israel has said, 'Send my people away, that they may have a feast to me in the wilderness.'"

Pharaoh asked, "Who is he that I should listen to his voice and that I should send away the Israelites? I do not know the Lord, and I will not let Israel go!"

They said to him, "The God of the Habirus has called us to him. We will go on a three days' journey into the wilderness, that we may sacrifice to God, in case at any time death or slaughter happens to us."

The king of Egypt asked them, "Why do you, Moses and Aaron, turn the people from their work? Return each of you to your work!" Pharaoh said, "Now look, the people are very numerous. Let's not give them rest from their work." The Pharaoh gave orders to the taskmasters of the people and the accountants, "You will no longer give straw to the people for brick-making as before, but let them go themselves, and collect straw for themselves. You will impose on them daily the quota of brick-making which they perform. You will not abate anything, for they are lazy. Therefore have they cried, saying, 'Let us rise and perform sacrifices to our God.' Let the works of these men be made grievous, and let them care for these things, and not care for vain words."

The taskmasters and the accountants hurried them, and they said to the people, "So says Pharaoh, 'I will give you straw no longer.' Go you, yourselves, get for yourselves straw whenever you can find it, for nothing is diminished from your quota."

So the people were dispersed in all the land of Egypt, to gather stubble for straw, and the taskmasters hurried them, saying, "Fulfill your regular daily tasks, even as when straw was given you."

The accountants of the race of the Israelites, who were set over them by the masters of Pharaoh, were scourged, men saying, "Why have you not fulfilled your quotas of brick-making as previously, today also?" The accountants of the Israelites went in and cried to Pharaoh, saying, "Why do you act so to your servants? Straw is not given to your servants, and they tell us to make bricks, and see your servants have been whipped. You will, therefore, injure your people."

He said to them, "You are lazy, you are idlers! Therefore you say, 'Let us go and sacrifice to our God.' Now then go and work, for straw will not be given to you, yet you will return the quota of bricks."

The accountants of the Israelites saw themselves in a terrible plight, men saying, "You will not fail from the brick-making to deliver that which belongs to each day."

They met Moses and Aaron coming out to meet them as they returned from Pharaoh, and they said to them, "The Lord will look on you and judge you, for you have made our savior abominable before Pharaoh, and before his servants, to put a sword into his hands to kill us."

Moses turned to the Lord, and said, "I beg Lord, why have you afflicted these people? And also why have you sent me? From the time that I went to Pharaoh to speak in your name, he has punished these people, and you have not delivered your people."

Exodus: Chapter 6

The Lord said to Moses, "Now you will see what I will do to Pharaoh. He will send them away with a mighty hand, and with a high arm will he throw them out of his land."

God said to Moses, "I'm Lord,[1] and I appeared to Abraham, Isaac, and Jacob, as their god Resheph,[2] and I did not tell them my name was Lord. I established my covenant with them, to give them the land of the Canaanites, the land in which they stayed, in which previously they lived as strangers. I listened to the groaning of the Israelites the affliction with which the Egyptians enslave them and I remembered your covenant. Go, speak to the Israelites, and say, 'I am the Lord, and I will lead you out from the tyranny of the Egyptians, and I will deliver you from slavery, and I will ransom you with a high arm, and great judgment. I will take you to be a people for myself, and will be your God, and you will know that I am Lord the god, who brought you out from the tyranny of the Egyptians. I will bring you into the land concerning which I stretched out my hand to give it to Abraham and Isaac and Jacob, and I will give it to you for an inheritance. I am the Lord.'"

Moses spoke so to the sons of Israel, and they did not listen to Moses for fearfulness and their hard tasks.

The Lord said Moses, "Go speak to Pharaoh, king of Egypt, tell him that he must send out the Israelites from his land."

Moses replied to the Lord "Look, the Israelites did not listen to me, so why will Pharaoh listen to me? I am not eloquent."

The Lord spoke to Moses and Aaron and gave them an order for Pharaoh king of Egypt, that he should send out the Israelites out of the land of Egypt.

These are the heads of the houses of their families: the sons of Reuben the firstborn of Israel; Enoch and Phallu, Hezron, and Carmi, this is the families of Reuben.

The sons of Simeon: Jemuel and Jimna, and Ohad, and Jachin and Zohar, and Saul the son of a Phoenician woman, these are the families of the sons of Simeon.

These are the names of the sons of Levi according to their families, Gershon, Kohath, and Merari, and the years of the life of Levi were a hundred and thirty-seven. These are the sons of Gershon: Libni, and Shimei, the houses of their family. The sons of Kohath: Amram and Izhar, Hebron, and Uzziel, and the years of the life of Kohath were a hundred and thirty-three years.

The sons of Merari: Mahali, and Mushi, these are the houses of the families of Levi, according to their families. Amram took as wife Jochebed the daughter of his father's brother, and she carried to him both Aaron and Moses, and Mariam their sister: and the years of the life of Amram were a hundred and thirty-two[3] years.

The sons of Izhar: Korah, and Nepheg, and Zichri.

The sons of Uzziel: Mishael, and Elizaphan, and Zithri.

Aaron took for himself as wife Elisabeth, the daughter of Amminadab's sister Nahshon, and she carried for him Nadab, Abihu, Eleazar, and Ithamar.

The sons of Korah: Assir, and Elkanah, and Abiasaph, these are the generations of Korah.

Eleazar the son of Aaron took to himself for a wife one of the daughters of Phutiel, and she carried to him Phinehas. These are the heads of the family of the Levites, according to their generations.

This is Aaron and Moses, who God told to bring the Israelites out of the land of Egypt with their forces. These are those who spoke with Pharaoh, king of Egypt, and Aaron himself and Moses brought out the Israelites from the land of Egypt, in the day in which the Law spoke to Moses in the land of Egypt. Then the Lord said to Moses, "I am the Lord. Tell Pharaoh, king of Egypt whatever I tell you."

Moses replied to the Lord, "Look, I am not good at speech, and why will Pharaoh listen to me?"

Exodus: Chapter 6 Notes

1 Codex Vaticanus: egô cs (ⲉⲅⲱⲕⲥ). Translation: I'm Lord

• Leningrad Codex: ani yehvah (אֲנִי יְהֹוָה). Translation: I'm Yehwah

• Peshitta: ånå ånå mryå (ܡܪܝܐ ܐܢܐ ܐܢܐ). Translation: I'm ana master (or lord)

• Targum Onkelos: ana yeyah (אֲנָא ??). Translation: I'm Yah

• Targum Jerusalem: ana yeyah (אֲנָא ??). Translation: I'm Yah

This verse was viewed as evidence of the redaction of the name of Lord during the Hasmonean dynasty. It was believed to have happened during the rule King Massaneh, however, the reference to Kalhu as the capital of Assyria in Genesis' genealogy of nations, dates the Aramaic translation to sometime before 706 BC. Additionally, the presence of the Ashkenaz in the genealogy of nations places the origin of that section of text to sometime after 715 BC, when the Ashkenaz were first documented by the Assyrians, meaning that the Aramaic translation appears to have been made during the rule of King Hezekiah of Judah. King Hezekiah is recorded in 4th Kingdoms (Masoretic Kings) as initiating a number of reforms to the religion of Judah, including destroying the bamahs which Moses instructed the Israelites to worship at, as well as destroying the statue of the serpent that Moses had made, and which Solomon had erected in the temple in Jerusalem, suggesting that it was Hezekiah who removed the name from the text. If so, the name removed would not have been Yhŭ/Yahweh, the god that Hezekiah worshiped, suggesting an Egyptian serpent god was originally named in the text.

2 Codex Vaticanus: ths Ôm (ⲐⲤⲰⲘ). Translation: god Om

- LXX 318. theos ôn (θόος ∞ν)

- Leningrad Codex: el shaddai (אֵל שַׁדָּי). Translation: god Shaddai (or powerful)

- Peshitta: Åylšdy (ܐܠܫܕܝ)

- Targum Onkelos: el shaddai (אֵל שַׁדָּי). Translation: god Shaddai (or demonic, ghoulish)

- Fragment Targums: elaha shemaya (אֱלָהָא שְׁמַיָּא). Translation: god sky

- Targum Jerusalem: el shadai (אֵל שַׁדָּי). Translation: god Shaddai (or demonic, ghoulish)

See the note on Resheph in Exodus: chapter 3 for more information on the relationship between Ôm/ôn, Shaddai, Shed, and Resheph.

3 Codex Vaticanus: ecaton triaconta dyo (ⲈⲔⲀⲦⲞⲚⲦⲢⲒⲀⲔⲞⲚⲦⲀⲆⲨⲞ). Translation hundred thirty two (132)

- Codex Alexandrinus: ecaton triaconta ex (ⲈⲔⲀⲦⲞⲚⲦⲢⲒⲀⲔⲞⲚⲦⲀⲈⲌ). Translation hundred thirty six (136)

- Leningrad Codex: sheva usheloshim ume'at (שֶׁבַע וּשְׁלֹשִׁים וּמְאַת). Translation: seven and thirty and hundred (137)

- Peshitta: måå ûtltyn ûšbô (ܡܐܐ ܘܬܠܬܝܢ ܘܫܒܥ). Translation: hundred and thirty and seven (137)

• Targum Onkelos: me'ah utelatin usheva (מְאָה וּתְלָתִין וּשְׁבַע). Translation: hundred and thirty and seven (137)

• Targum Jerusalem: me'ah utelatin usheva (מְאָה וּתְלָתִין וּשְׁבַע). Translation: hundred and thirty and seven (137)

Exodus: Chapter 7

The Lord told Moses, "I have given you the words of God for Pharaoh, and Aaron your brother will be your spokesman. You will say to him all things that I order you, and Aaron your brother will tell Pharaoh, that he should send the Israelites out of his land. I will harden the heart of Pharaoh, and I will multiply my signs and wonders in the land of Egypt. Pharaoh will not listen to you, and I will lay my hand on Egypt and will bring out my people the Israelites with my power out of the land of Egypt with great vengeance. All the Egyptians will know that I am the Lord, stretching out my hand on Egypt, and I will bring out the Israelites out of the middle of them."

Moses and Aaron did as the Lord commanded them. Moses was eighty years old, and Aaron his brother was eighty-three years old when they spoke to Pharaoh. The Lord spoke to Moses and Aaron, saying, "Now if Pharaoh should speak to you, saying, 'Give us a sign or a wonder,' then will you say to your brother Aaron, 'Take your wand and throw it on the ground before Pharaoh,' and before his servants, and it will become a serpent."

Moses and Aaron went in before Pharaoh, and before his servants, and they did so, as the Lord commanded them, and Aaron threw down his wand before Pharaoh, and before his servants, and it became a serpent. But Pharaoh called together the wise men of Egypt, and the sorcerers and the charmers also of the Egyptians did likewise with their sorcery. They each threw down their wands, and they became serpents, but the wand of Aaron swallowed up their wands. And the heart of Pharaoh was hardened, and he did not listen to them, as the Lord had commanded.

The Lord said to Moses, "The heart of Pharaoh is made hard so that he would not let the people go. Go to Pharaoh early in the morning. Look, he goes out to the water, and you will meet him on the bank of the river, and you will take in your hand the wand that was turned into a serpent. You will say to him, 'The Lord, the God of the Habirus has sent me to you, saying, Send my people away, that they may serve me in the wilderness, and, see, until now you have not listened.' The Lord says, 'So will you know that I am the Lord, look, I strike with the wand that is in my hand on the water which is in the river, and it will change it into blood. The fish that are in the river will die, and the river will stink afterward, and the Egyptians will not be able to drink water from the river.'"

The Lord said to Moses, "Say to your brother Aaron, 'Take your wand in your hand and stretch out your hand over the waters of Egypt, and their rivers, and their canals, and their ponds, and all their standing water,' and it will become blood. There was blood in all the land of Egypt, both in vessels of wood and of stone."

Moses and Aaron did as the Lord commanded them, and Aaron having lifted his hand with his wand, struck the water in the river before Pharaoh, and before his servants, and changed all the water in the river into blood. The fish in the river died, and the river stank thereupon, and the Egyptians could not drink water from the river, and the blood was in all the land of Egypt. The charmers also of the Egyptians did so with their sorcery, and the heart of Pharaoh was hardened, and he did not listen to them, even as the Lord said. Pharaoh turned and entered into his house, and he did not pay attention even to this. All the Egyptians dug round about the river, to drink water, as they could not drink water from the river, and seven days passed after the Lord has struck the river.

Exodus: Chapter 8

The Lord said to Moses, "Go to Pharaoh, and say to him, 'the Lord says, send out my people, that they may serve me. If you will not send them away, I punish all your coasts with frogs, and the river will swarm with frogs, and they will go up and enter into your houses, and into your bedrooms, and on your beds, and on the houses of your servants, and of your people and on your dough, and on your ovens. On you, and on your servants, and on your people, will the frogs come up.'"

The Lord said to Moses, "Tell Aaron your brother, 'Stretch out your hand and wand over the rivers, and the canals, and the pools, and bring up the frogs.'"

Aaron stretched out his hand over the waters of Egypt and brought up the frogs, and the frogs were brought up and covered the land of Egypt. The charmers of the Egyptians also did likewise with their sorcery and brought up the frogs on the land of Egypt. Pharaoh called Moses and Aaron, and said, "Pray for me to the Lord, and let him take away the frogs from me and my people, and I will send them away, and they will sacrifice to the Lord."

Moses said to Pharaoh, "Pick a time for me, when I will pray for you and your servants, and your people, to make the frogs disappear from you, and your people, and your houses, only in the river will they be left behind."

He replied, "Tomorrow!"

He said, therefore, "As you have said. That you may know, that there is no other god but the Lord. The frogs will be removed away from you, and from your houses and villages, and your servants, and your people, they will only be left in the river. Moses and Aaron left Pharaoh, and Moses cried to the Lord concerning the restriction of the frogs, as Pharaoh appointed him. The Lord did as Moses said, and the frogs died out of the houses, and out of the villages, and out of the fields. They gathered them together in heaps, and the land stank.

When Pharaoh saw that there was relief, his heart was hardened, and he did not listen to them, as the Lord had said. The Lord said to Moses, "Tell Aaron, 'Stretch out your wand in your hand and strike the dust of the land, and there will be lice both on man, and on quadrupeds, and in all the land of Egypt.'"

So Aaron stretched out his wand with his hand and struck the dust of the land, and the lice were on men and quadrupeds, and there were lice in all the dust of the land. The charmers also did so with their sorcery, to bring up the lice, and they could not. The lice were both on the men and the quadrupeds. So the charmers said to Pharaoh, "This is the finger of God."

But the heart of Pharaoh was hardened, and he did not listen to them, as the Lord had said. The Lord said to Moses, "Rise early in the morning, and stand before Pharaoh, and Look, he will go out to the water, and you will say to him, 'The Lord says, Send away my people, that they may serve me in the wilderness. If you will not let my people go, I send to you, and your servants, and your people, and your houses, the dog-fly, and the houses of the Egyptians will be filled with the dog-fly, all throughout the land.[1] I will distinguish marvelously in that day the land of Goshen, on which my people dwell, in which the dog-fly will not be, that you may know that I am the Lord, the god of all the land. I will put a difference between my people and your people, and tomorrow will this be on the land.'"

The Lord did so, and the dog-fly came in abundance into the houses of Pharaoh, and the houses of his servants, and across all the land of Egypt, and the land was destroyed by the dog-fly. Pharaoh called Moses and Aaron, saying, "Go and sacrifice to your God in the land."

Moses said, "It can't be so, for we will sacrifice to our Lord God before the abominations of the Egyptians, as if we sacrifice before the abominations of the Egyptians, we will be stoned. We will go on a journey of three days into the wilderness, and we will sacrifice to our Lord God, exactly as we were told."

Pharaoh said, "I will let you go, and you sacrifice to your God in the wilderness, but do not go very far away. Pray then for me to the Lord."

Moses said, "I will go out from you and pray to God, and the dog-fly will depart both from your servants, and from your people tomorrow. Do not, Pharaoh, deceive again, and not send the people away to do sacrifice to the Lord."

Moses went out from Pharaoh and prayed to God. The Lord did as Moses asked, and removed the dog-fly from Pharaoh, and his servants, and his people, and there were none left. Pharaoh hardened his heart, even on this occasion, and he would not send the people away.

Exodus: Chapter 8 Notes

1 This plague seems to be related to the Ugaritic Text's story of Ba'al's ability to control flies. This Canaanite story likely gave rise to the Zeus Apomyios cult in Greece, in which Zeus was believed to protect people from flies. The Canaanite term likely also gave rise to the Baalzebub (Βααλζεβουβ) and Baal muian (Βααλ μυιαν) of the Septuagint's 2nd Kingdoms, and ba'al zevuv (בַּעַל זְבוּב) from the Masoretic Kings, who was one of the gods the new god Yhŭ did not people worshiping anymore.

Exodus: Chapter 9

The Lord said to Moses, "Go to Pharaoh and say to him, "These things says the Lord, the god of the Habirus, 'Send my people away so they may serve me. If however, you will not send my people away, but yet detain them, the hand of the Lord will be on your livestock in the fields, the horses, donkeys, camels, oxen, and sheep, a very great death. I will make a marvelous distinction in that time between the livestock of the Egyptians, and the livestock of the Israelites, nothing will die of all that is of the children of Israel. God fixed a limit, saying, tomorrow the Lord will do this thing on the land.'"

The Lord did this the next day, and all the livestock of the Egyptians died, but none of the livestock of the Israelites died. When Pharaoh saw that none of all the livestock of the Israelites had died, the heart of Pharaoh was hardened, and he did not let the people go.

The Lord said to Moses and Aaron, "Take handfuls of ashes from a furnace and let Moses throw it towards the sky in front of Pharaoh his servants. Let it become dust over all the land of Egypt, and there will be inflamed sores breaking out both on men and animals across all the land of Egypt."

So he took of the ashes from a furnace before Pharaoh, and Moses scattered it towards the sky, and it became inflamed sore breaking out both on men and animals. The sorcerers could not stand before Moses because of the sores, for the sores were on the sorcerers, and in all the land of Egypt. The Lord hardened Pharaoh's heart, and he did not listen to them, as the Lord appointed.

The Lord said to Moses, "Rise early in the morning and stand before Pharaoh, and say to him, 'The Lord, God of the Habirus, says 'Send away my people that they may serve me. Until now I sent out all my plagues into your heart and the heart of your servants and your people, so you may know that there is not another like me in all the land. Now, I will stretch out my hand and strike you and kill your people, and you will be consumed from off the land. For this purpose have you been preserved, that I might display in you my strength and that my name might be published in all the land. Do you then yet work to hinder my people, and not to let them go? Look, tomorrow at this hour I will rain intense hail, such as has not been in Egypt from the time it was created until this day. Now then hurry to gather your livestock, and all that you have in the fields, for all the men and livestock as many as will be found in the fields, and will not enter into a house, will die.'"

Those of the servants of Pharaoh that feared the words of the Lord gathered his livestock into his houses. Those that did not listen in his mind to the word of the Lord, left the livestock in the fields. The Lord said to Moses, "Stretch out your hand to the sky, and there will be hail through all the land of Egypt, both on the men and the livestock, and all the plants in the land. Moses stretched out his hand to the sky, and the Lord sent thunder and hail, and the fire ran along on the ground, and the Lord rained hail on all the land of Egypt. There was hail and flaming fire mingled with the hail, and the hail was more intense than before in Egypt or from then onward.[1] The hail struck in all the land of Egypt both man and animal, and the hail struck all the grass in the field, and the hail broke in pieces all the trees in the field. Only in the land of Goshen where the Israelites were, it did not hail.

Pharaoh sent and called Moses and Aaron, and said to them, "I have sinned this time. The Lord is righteous, and I and my people are wicked. Pray then for me to the Lord, and let him cause the thunder of God to stop, and the hail and the fire, and I will send you out and you will no longer be here."

Moses said to him, "When I will have departed from the city, I will stretch out my hands to the Lord, and the thunder will stop and the hail and the rain will stop, that you may know that the land is the Lord's, but as for you and your servants, I know that you still do not fear the Lord."

The flax and the barley were struck, for the barley was in the ear, and the flax was seeding. But the wheat and the rye were not struck, for they were late. Moses went out from the city of Pharaoh and stretched out his hands to the Lord, and the thunders ceased and the hail and the rain did not fall on the land. When Pharaoh saw that the rain and the hail and the thunders stopped, he continued to sin, and he hardened his heart and the hearts of his servants. The heart of Pharaoh was hardened, and he did not send away the Israelites, as the Lord had told Moses.

Exodus: Chapter 9 Notes

1 This plague of hail and fiery hail, along with the preceding plague of ash, and the subsequent plague of darkness all seem to indicate a massive volcanic eruption in the northern hemisphere, such as the Minoan eruption of the island of Thera (Santorini) which took place during the rule of Ahmose I, circa 1550 BC. The Tempest Stele of Ahmose I depicts a time of storms like the ones depicted in Exodus, and likely weakened the Hyksos enough that Ahmose could conquer them. The Minoan eruption was one of the largest in recorded history, with over 100 km^3 of debris thrown into the sky. Ahmose I was the founder of the 18th Dynasty that reunited Egypt after the previous Hyksos dynasty had been driven out of Lower Egypt.

The 1st century Jewish General and Historian Josephus claimed the ancestors of the Israelites were the Hyksos, and the Torah's history had become corrupted, and therefore, if one accepted his claims, the Pharaoh in Exodus would have been Ahmoses I, and Moses would have likely been Khamudi, the last of the Hyksos kings in northern Egypt. This claim has been rejected by almost all scholars, and it is not clear why Josephus would have believed this, and it is assumed to be wishful thinking, as unless the Israelite were the Hyksos, there are no records in Egyptian history that align with the Exodus.

An alternate theory would be that the Pharaoh in Exodus was Khamudi, whose kingdom was then conquered by the Upper Egyptian Pharaoh Ahmose I after he died in the Papyrus Sea incident, whatever it was. This would explain some of the strange events but would mean that the era of the Exodus was significantly earlier than the estimated life of Moses between 1391 and 1271 BC by Rabbinical Jews, although would correspond with the estimated life circa 1592 BC by Jerome, and circa 1571 by James Ussher, and the dating found in the Septuagint, of circa 1547 BC.

Exodus: Chapter 10

The Lord said to Moses, "Go to Pharaoh, for I have hardened his heart and the hearts of his servants, that these signs may come on them, in order that you may tell your children, and your children's children, in how many ways I have insulted the Egyptians, and my wonders which I worked among them, and you will know that I am the Lord."

Moses and Aaron went in before Pharaoh, and they said to him, "The Lord, the God of the Habirus said, 'How long do you refuse to obey me? Send my people away, that they may serve me. But if you will not send my people away, Look, at this hour tomorrow, I will bring an abundance of locusts on all your lands. They will cover the face of the land, and you will not be able to see the land, and they will devour all that is left of the abundance of the land, which the hail has left you, and will devour every tree that grows for you on the land. Your houses will be filled, and the houses of your servants, and all the houses in all the land of the Egyptians, things which your fathers have never seen, nor their forefathers, from the day that they were on the land until this day.'"

Moses turned away and departed from Pharaoh, and the servants of Pharaoh said to him, "How long will this be a snare to us? Send away the men, that they may serve their god. Will you have Egypt be destroyed?"

They brought back both Moses and Aaron to Pharaoh, and he said to them, "Go and serve your god. But, who are those that are going with you?"

Moses answered, "We will go with the young and the old, with our sons and daughters, and sheep and oxen, for it is a feast of the Lord."

He replied to them, "So let the Lord go with you. I'll send you away, but must I send away your property also? I see that evil has attached itself to you. No, just let the men go and serve your god, as that is what you are seeking," and they threw them out from the presence of Pharaoh.

The Lord said to Moses, "Stretch out your hand over the land of Egypt, and let locusts come across the land, and they will devour every plant in the land, and all the fruit of the trees, which the hail left."

Moses lifted his wand towards the sky, and the Lord brought a south wind on the land, all that day and all that night. The morning dawned, and the south wind brought up the locusts and deposited them all over the land of Egypt. They landed in large numbers over all the territory of Egypt. Before then there were never so many locusts, and neither will there be again. They covered the face of the land, and the land was wasted, and they devoured all the plants of the land, and all the fruit of the trees, which was left by the hail, there was nothing green left on the trees, nor all the shrubs of the field, in all the land of Egypt.

Pharaoh rushed to call Moses and Aaron, saying, "I have sinned before Lord the god, and against you. Accept therefore my sin again this time, and pray to Lord the god, and let him take away from me this death."

Moses went out from Pharaoh and prayed to God, and the Lord brought in the opposite direction a strong wind from the sea, and took up the locusts and threw them into the Papyrus Sea, and there were no locusts left along all the coasts of Egypt. The Lord hardened the heart of Pharaoh again, and he did not send away the Israelites.

The Lord said to Moses, "Stretch out your hands to the sky, and let there be darkness across the land of Egypt, a darkness that may be felt."

Moses stretched out his hand to the sky, and there was darkness, including a storm over all the land of Egypt for three days. For three days no man saw his brother, and no man rose up from his bed for three days, but all the Israelites had light in all the places where they were.

Pharaoh called Moses and Aaron, saying, "Go, serve your Lord God, only leave behind your sheep and your oxen, and let your other property go with you."

Moses replied, "Not unless you will give us whole burnt offerings and sacrifices, which we will sacrifice to our Lord God. Our livestock will go with us, and we will not leave a hoof behind, as from them we will sacrifice to our Lord God. We won't know in what manner we will serve our Lord God until we arrive there."

But the Lord hardened the heart of Pharaoh, and he would not let them go, and Pharaoh said, "Leave me, beware of seeing me again because on that day you will die."

Moses replied, "As you have said, I will not come before you again."

Exodus: Chapter 11

The Lord said to Moses, "I will bring one more plague on Pharaoh and Egypt, and after that, he will send you away, and when he sends you out with everything, he will indeed drive you out. Speak therefore secretly in the ears of the people, and let everyone borrow from his neighbor jewels, silver, gold, and clothing."

The Lord gave his people favor in the sight of the Egyptians, and they lent to them as the man Moses was very important before the Egyptians, and before Pharaoh and his servants.

Moses said, "The Lord said, 'About midnight I go out into the middle of Egypt, and every firstborn in the land of Egypt will die, from the firstborn of Pharaoh who sits on the throne, to the firstborn of the slave-woman that is by the mill, and to the firstborn of all livestock. There will be a great cry through all the land of Egypt, such as has not been, and such will not be repeated again. But among all the Israelites will not a dog snarl with his tongue, either at man or animal, that you may know how wide a distinction the Lord will make between the Egyptians and Israel. All these your servants will come down to me, and do me reverence, saying, 'Go out, you and all the people over whom you preside, and afterward I will go out.'"

Moses left Pharaoh in anger, and the Lord told Moses, "Pharaoh will not listen to you, and I will greatly increase my signs and wonders in the land of Egypt."

Moses and Aaron worked all these signs and wonders in the land of Egypt before Pharaoh, and the Lord hardened the heart of Pharaoh, and he did not listen to send out the Israelites out of the land of Egypt.

Exodus: Chapter 12

The Lord said to Moses and Aaron in the land of Egypt, "This month will be the beginning of the year for you. It is the first for you among the months of the year. Tell all the congregation of the Israelites, "On the tenth day of this month let them take each man a sheep according to the houses of their families, every man a lamb for his household. If they are few in a household so that there are not enough for the lamb, he will invite a neighbor that lives near to him, as to the number of minds, every one according to that which suffices him will make a reckoning for the lamb. It will be an unblemished lamb, a year old male. You will take it from the lambs and the kids.'"

"'It will be kept by you until the fourteenth of this month and all the multitude of the congregation of the Israelites will kill it towards evening. They will take some of the blood and will put it on the two doorposts, and on the lintel, in the houses where they will eat them. They will eat the flesh this night roasted with fire, and they will eat unleavened bread with bitter plants. You will not eat it raw or boiled in water but only roasted with fire, the head with the feet, and the rest. Nothing will be left of it in the morning, and you will not break a bone of it. That which is left of it until the morning you will burn with fire. You will eat it with your loins clothed, and your sandals on your feet, and your wands in your hands. You will eat it quickly. It is a Passover to the Lord.'"

"'I will go throughout the land of Egypt in that night, and will strike every firstborn in the land of Egypt both man and animal, and on all the gods of Egypt will I execute vengeance. I am the Lord. The blood will be for a sign to you on the houses in which you are, and I will see the blood and will protect you, and there will not be on you the plague of destruction when I strike the land.'"

"'This day will be to you a memorial, and you will keep it a feast to the Lord through all your generations, and you will keep it a feast for a perpetual ordinance. Seven days you will eat unleavened bread, and from the first day, you will utterly remove leaven from your houses. Whoever will eat leaven, that mind will be utterly destroyed from Israel, from the first day until the seventh day. The first day will be called holy, and the seventh day will be called holy to you. You will do no servile work on them, only the things as are necessary for everyone, will you do. You will keep this commandment, for on this day will I bring your forces out of the land of Egypt, and you will make this day a perpetual ordinance for you throughout your generations. Beginning the fourteenth day of the first month, you will eat unleavened bread from the evening, until the twenty-first day of the month, until evening. Seven days leaven will not be found in your houses, but whoever will eat anything leavened, that mind will be cut off from the congregation of Israel, both among the occupiers of the land and the original inhabitants. You will eat nothing leavened, but in every habitation of yours you will eat unleavened bread.'"

Moses called all the elders of the Israelites, and said to them, "Go away and take to yourselves a lamb according to your families and kill the Passover lamb. You will take a bunch of hyssops, and having dipped it into some of the blood that is by the door, you will touch the lintel, and will put it on both doorposts, including of the blood which is by the door. You will not go out, everyone from the door of his house until the morning. The Lord will pass by to strike the Egyptians, and will see the blood on the lintel, and on both the doorposts, and the Lord will pass by the door, and will not allow the destroyer to enter into your houses to strike you. Follow this as an ordinance for yourself and your children forever. If you should enter into the land, which the Lord will give you, as he has spoken, keep this service. It will happen, if your sons say to you, 'What is this service?' Then you will answer them, 'This Passover is a sacrifice to the Lord, who defended the houses of the Israelites in Egypt when they struck the Egyptians but delivered our houses.'"

The people bowed and worshiped, and the Israelites departed and did as the Lord had commanded Moses and Aaron. It happened at midnight that the Lord struck all the firstborn in the land of Egypt, from the firstborn of Pharaoh who sat on the throne, to the firstborn of the slave-woman in the dungeon, and the first-born of all livestock. Pharaoh rose up at night, and his servants, and all the Egyptians, and there was a great cry in all the land of Egypt, for there was not a house in which there was not someone dead. Pharaoh called Moses and Aaron that night, and said to them, "Rise and depart from my people, both you and the Israelites. Go and serve Lord the god, even as you said. Take with you, your sheep and your oxen. Bless me also, I beg you."

The Egyptians grabbed the people, and they threw them out of the land quickly, as they said, "We all will die."

The people took their dough before their lumps of meal were leavened, bound up as it were in their garments, on their shoulders. The Israelites did as Moses commanded them, and they asked of the Egyptians articles of silver and gold and apparel. The Lord gave his people favor in the sight of the Egyptians, and they had loaned to them, and they plundered the Egyptians. The Israelites departed from Ramesses and went to the corrals, six hundred thousand infantry, counting the men, besides the slaves. A great mixed company went up with them, and sheep and oxen, and a large amount of livestock. They baked the dough which they brought out of Egypt, unleavened cakes, for it had not been leavened, as the Egyptians threw them out, and they could not remain, and they did not prepare provisions for the journey.

The time of the Israelites, which they stayed in the land of Egypt and the land of Canaan, was 430 years. It happened after the four hundred and thirty years, all the forces of the Lord came out of the land of Egypt by night. It is a watch kept to the Lord, so that he should bring them out of the land of Egypt, and that very night a watch was kept to the Lord so that it should be for all the Israelites to their generations.

The Lord said to Moses and Aaron, "This is the law of the Passover, and no stranger will eat of it. Every slave or servant bought with silver, you will circumcise, and then he may eat of it. A traveler or employee will not eat of it. In one house will it be eaten, and you will not carry the flesh out from the house, and a bone of it you will not break. All the congregation of the Israelites will keep it. If any convert will join you to keep the Passover of the Lord, you will circumcise every male of him, and then will he approach and sacrifice it, and he will be even as the original inhabitant of the land. No uncircumcised person will eat of it. There will be one law to the native, and the convert coming among you."

The Israelites did as the Lord commanded Moses and Aaron for them to do. It happened on that day that the Lord brought the Israelites out from the land of Egypt with their forces.

Exodus: Chapter 13

The Lord said to Moses, "Sacrifice to me every firstborn, first produced, opening every womb among the Israelites, both from man and animal. It is mine."

Moses said to the people, "Remember this day, in which you came out of the land of Egypt, out of the house of slavery, for with a strong hand the Lord brought you out of there, and leaven will not be eaten. For on this day you go out in the month of new grain. It will happen when Lord the god will have brought you into the land of the Canaanites, Cypriots, Amorites, Mitanni, Jebusites, Girgashites, and Perizzites, which he swore to your fathers to give you, a land flowing with milk and honey, that you will perform this service in this month. Six days you will eat unleavened bread, and on the seventh day is a feast to the Lord. Seven days will you eat unleavened bread; nothing leavened will be seen with you, neither will you have leaven in all your lands."

"You will tell your son in that day, saying, 'The Lord did this to me, as I was going out of Egypt.' It will be to you a sign on your hand and a memorial before your eyes, that the law of the Lord may be in your mouth, for with a strong hand Lord the god brought you out of Egypt. Keep this law according to the times of the seasons, from days to days. It will happen when Lord the god will bring you into the land of the Canaanites, as he swore to your fathers, and will give it to you, that you will dedicate every offspring opening the womb, the males to the Lord, every one that opens the womb out of the herds or among your livestock, as many as you will have, you will dedicate the males to the Lord. "E

"very offspring opening the womb of the donkeys you will exchange for a sheep, and if you will not exchange it, you will redeem it. Every firstborn male of your sons will you redeem. If your son should ask you from now on, saying, 'What is this?' Then you will say to him, 'With a strong hand the Lord brought us out of Egypt, out of the house of slavery. When Pharaoh hardened his heart so as not to send us away, he killed every firstborn in the land of Egypt, both the firstborn of men and the firstborn of animals, and therefore I sacrifice every offspring that opens the womb, the males to the Lord, and every firstborn of my sons I will redeem. It will be for a sign on your hand, and immovable before your eyes, for with a strong hand the Lord brought you out of Egypt."

(When Pharaoh sent out the people, God did not lead them on the road to the land of the Pelesets,[1] which was near, as God thought, 'In case at any time the people repent when they see war and return to Egypt.')

God led the people along the road through the wilderness, to the Papyrus Sea. In the fifth generation, the Israelites left the land of Egypt. Moses took the bones of Joseph with him, for he had solemnly adjured the Israelites, saying, "God will surely visit you, and you will carry up my bones here with you."

The Israelites departed from the corrals and camped in Etham[2] by the wilderness. God led them, in the day by a pillar of cloud, to show them the way, and in the night by a pillar of fire. The pillar of cloud did not fail by day, or the pillar of fire at night, before all the people.

Exodus: Chapter 13 Notes

1 Codex Vaticanus: Phylistiim (ϕⲨⲗⲓⲥⲧⲓⲓⲙ). Translation: Philistines (or Palestinians, Pelesets)

- Leningrad Codex: Pelishtim (פְּלִשְׁתִּים). Translation: Palestinians (or Pelesets)

- Peshitta: plštyå (ܦܠܫܬܝܐ). Translation: Palestinians

- Targum Onkelos: Felishta'ei (פְּלִשְׁתָּאֵי). Translation: Palestinians (or Pelesets)

- Targum Jerusalem: Pelishta'ei (פְּלִישְׁתָּאֵי). Translation: Palestinians (or Pelesets)

The Pelesets were an ancient people based in the region of the modern Gaza Strip of the Palestinian Territories. The earliest surviving mention of them is from the reliefs of the Temple of Ramses III at Medinet Habu in Egypt that dates back to some time between 1186 and 1155 BC, in which they were called Pelesets (𓊪𓏲𓂋𓏤𓏲𓈙𓏏𓀭). They were also known in Middle Babylonian as the [kur]Palastu (𒆳𒉺𒆷𒀸𒌇). It is unclear where they came from, however, one theory is that they were the Pala, a Luwian people from the Black Sea coast of Anatolia. The region was an independent country called Palaa (𒉺𒆷𒀀) in the Neshite (Hittite) records from the 1600s BC, however, have become part of the Nesite Empire by the 1500s BC. Around the time the Pelesets invaded Canaan, the Pala were driven from their homeland by the neighboring Kaskians from northeast Anatolia, which supports the connection between the groups, however, it has yet to be proven conclusively. The presence of the Pelesets in Southern Canaan during the time of Abraham and Isaac is anachronistic, and therefore this section of text, describing the origin of the Semitic tribes, found in both the Septuagint and the Masoretic Text, likely dates to the original Phoenician translation in the early Iron Age.

The presence of the Pelesets in Southern Canaan during the time of Moses and Aaron is anachronistic, and therefore this section of text, found in both the Septuagint and the Leningrad Codex, was likely an addition made in the Iron Age, when the Phoenician translation was made. It is an unusual text, as it purports to explain the thoughts of God, and reads like a note to explain why the Israelites did not encounter the Pelesets by a scribe that did not know the Pelesets arrived in the region much later.

2 Codex Vaticanus: Othom (ΟΘΟΜ)

- Leningrad Codex: Etam (אֵתָם)

- Peshitta: Åtm (ܐܬܡ)

- Targum Onkelos: Etam (אָתָם)

- Fragment Targums: name not mentioned in the verse

- Targum Jerusalem: Eitam (אִיתָם). Translation: orphan (or completed)

This is believed to represent 'Khetam,' one of the Egyptian fortresses that sat between the Mediterranean coast and the Gulf of Suez.

Exodus: Chapter 14

The Lord said to Moses, "Speak to the Israelites, and let them stop and camp at the village, between Migdol[1] and the sea, near Ba'al Zephon.[2] Between them, you will camp by the sea. Pharaoh will say to his people, 'As for these Israelites, they are wandering in the land, as the wilderness has trapped them.' I will harden the heart of Pharaoh, and he will pursue them, and I will be glorified in Pharaoh, and all his armies and all the Egyptians will know that I am the Lord," and they did so.

It was reported to the king of the Egyptians that the people had fled, and the heart of Pharaoh was turned, and that of his servants against the people, and they said, "What have we done, letting the Israelites go, so that they no longer serve us?"

So Pharaoh harnessed his chariots, and led off all his people with himself, and took six hundred chosen chariots, and all the cavalry of the Egyptians, and rulers over all. The Lord hardened the heart of Pharaoh, king of Egypt and his servants, and he pursued after the Israelites, and the Israelites went out with a strong arm. The Egyptians chased after them and found them camped by the sea, and all the horse of the chariots of Pharaoh, and the cavalry, and his army were near the settlement of Ba'al Zephon.

Pharaoh approached, and the Israelites looked up and saw, and the Egyptians camped behind them, and they were terrified. The Israelites cried to the Lord, and asked Moses, "Have you brought us out to kill us in the wilderness because there were no graves in the land of Egypt? What is this that you have done to us, having brought us out of Egypt? Is not this the words which we said to you in Egypt, saying, 'Leave us alone that we may serve the Egyptians.' It was better for us to serve the Egyptians than to die in this wilderness!"

Moses said to the people, "Be courageous! Stand and see salvation from the Lord, which he will work for us this day. As you have seen the Egyptians today, you will never see them again forever. The Lord will fight for you, and you will hold your peace."

The Lord asked Moses, "Why do you call me? Speak to the Israelites, and let them harness the horses again. Lift your hand with your wand, and stretch out your hand over the sea, and divide it, and let the Israelites enter into the middle of the sea on the dry land. I will harden the heart of Pharaoh and all the Egyptians, and they will go after them, and I will be glorified before Pharaoh, and on all his armies, and his chariots and his horses. All the Egyptians will know that I am the Lord when I am glorified before Pharaoh and his chariots and his horses."

The messenger of God that went before the camp of the Israelites moved and went behind, and the pillar of the cloud also moved from before them and stood behind them. It went between the camp of the Egyptians and the camp of Israel and stood, and there was darkness and blackness, and the night passed, and they did not come near to one another during the whole night. Moses stretched out his hand over the sea, and the Lord carried back the sea with a strong south wind all night and made the sea dry, and the water was divided. The Israelites went into the middle of the sea on the dry land, and the water of it was a wall on the right hand and a wall on the left. The Egyptians pursued them and went in after them, and every horse of Pharaoh, and his chariots, and his horsemen, into the middle of the sea.

It happened in the morning watch that the Lord looked out on the camp of the Egyptians through the pillar of fire and cloud, and troubled the camp of the Egyptians, and caught the axles of their chariots, and caused them to travel with difficulty, and the Egyptians said, "Let us flee from the face of Israel, for the Lord fights for them against the Egyptians."

The Lord told Moses, "Stretch out your hand over the sea and let the water return to its place and let it cover the Egyptians, covering both the chariots and the riders. Moses stretched out his hand over the sea, and the water returned to its place of the day, and the Egyptians fled from the water, and the Lord shook off the Egyptians in the middle of the sea. The water returned and covered the chariots and the riders, and all the forces of Pharaoh, who entered after them into the sea. There was none left of them, not even one, but the Israelites went along dry land in the middle of the sea, and the water was to them a wall on the right hand and a wall on the left.

So the Lord delivered Israel that day from the hands of the Egyptians, and Israel saw the Egyptians dead by the shore of the sea. Israel saw the mighty hand, the things which the Lord did to the Egyptians, and the people feared the Lord, and they believed in God and Moses, his servant.

Exodus: Chapter 14 Notes

1 Codex Vaticanus: Magdôlou (ⲘⲀⲄⲆⲰⲀⲞⲨ)

- Leningrad Codex: Migdol (מִגְדֹּל). Translation: tower, fortification, platform

- Peshitta: Mgdûl (ܡܓܕܘܠ)

- Targum Onkelos: Migdol (מִגְדּוֹל)

- Fragment Targums: Migdol (מִגְדּוֹל)

- Targum Jerusalem: Migdol (מִגְדּוֹל)

A Ptolemaic-era geographical text housed at the Cairo Museum lists four border fortresses along the Greek-era Arsinoe Canal, including Migdol and Ba'al Zephon. It seems likely these later fortresses were named after the fortresses in the Torah, which the Ptolemys had paid to have translated at the Library of Alexandria. Most scholars associate the Migdol with El Qantara, a city that today lays along the Suez Canal, between the Mediterranean Port Said and the Bitter Lakes. This location is possible, however, the term is generic enough to refer to any fortified tower.

2 Codex Vaticanus: Beelsepphôn (ⲂⲈⲈⲀⲤⲉⲡⲧⲫⲰⲚ)

- Leningrad Codex: ba'al tzefon (בַּעַל צְפֹן)

- Peshitta: bôlspûn (ܒܥܠܨܦܘܢ)

- Targum Onkelos: be'eil tzefon (בְּעֵיל צְפוֹן). Translation: Lord Zephon

- Fragment Targums: ta'avavt tzefon (טַעֲווֹת צְפוֹן). Translation: mistakes (or errors) of Zephon

- Targum Jerusalem: ta'avat tzefon demishtayyeir mikkol ta'avavn demitzrayim begin deyemerun mitzra'ei bachir hu ba'al tzefon mikkol ta'avavta de'ishtayyeir vela laka deyeitun lemisgod leih (טַעֲוַת צְפוֹן דְּמִשְׁתַּיֵּיר מִכָּל טַעֲווֹן דְּמִצְרַיִם דְּיֵמְרוּן מִצְרָאֵי בָּחִיר הוּא בַּעַל צְפוֹן מִכָּל טַעֲווֹתָא דְּאִשְׁתַּיֵּיר וְלָא לְקָא דְּיֵיתוּן לְמִסְגּוֹד לֵיה). Translation: mistakes of Zephon, the last place of all the mistakes of the Egyptians, for protection of the rebels of Egypt. Chosen was Baal Zephon from all mistakes because it remained and was not destroyed, the final place of worship of Yah.

Ba'al Zephon was a Canaanite god mentioned in the Ugaritic Texts from the 1300 BC. The origin of the name appears to have been Mount Zephon in on the modern Syrian-Turkish border at the northern-most frontier of Canaan. Its usage in Egypt appears to be based on a group of Canaanites settling in the area of Lake Bardawil on the north coast of the Sinai Peninsula, a shallow saline lake with a surface area of 147,000 acres (59,500 hectares). Ba'al Zephon continued to be worshiped in the region well into the Greek era.

The story of the sea being blown away so the Israelites could walk across it, only to return and drown the Egyptian army is reminiscent of the Greek story of the Serbonian Bog, also called Lake Serbonis, which had a deceptive appearance of looking solid, but was a bog that swallowed people that tried to pass through it. The Serbonian Bog myth has been identified with Lake Bardawil since the Greeks ruled Egypt. In ancient Egyptian records, Lake Bardawil was described as a quagmire that whole armies had been swallowed up by.

Given that Ba'al Zephon is identified in this chapter, and is known to refer to Lake Bardawil, it is clear that this unusual event took place in Lake Bardawil, and not in the Red Sea, as later writers assumed. It isn't clear where the longer verse found in the Targum Jerusalem came from, however the author is believed to have copied his longer verses from a variety of older copies of the Torah. Unlike the much shorter Jerusalem Targum, it does not appear to have originated with a specific sect of Israelites. There do not appear to have ever been any Greek translations that incorporated this longer verse.

Exodus: Chapter 15

Then Moses and the Israelites sang this song to God, "Sing of the Lord who has gloriously thrown the horse and rider into the sea! My assistant and protector in my salvation. This is my God and I will glorify him, my father's God, and I will praise him."

"Lord destroys armies! Lord is his name![1] He has thrown the chariots of Pharaoh and his army into the sea, the chosen mounted captains! They were swallowed up in the Papyrus Sea.[2] He covered them with the sea. They sank to the depth like a stone. Your right hand, God! Has been glorified in strength. Your right hand, God! Has broken the enemies. In the abundance of your glory, you have broken the adversaries to pieces. You sent out your anger, it devoured them like stubble. By the breath of your anger the water parted asunder, the waters were congealed like a wall, the waves were congealed in the middle of the sea. The enemy said, 'I will pursue, I will overtake, I will divide the plunder. I will satisfy my mind! I will destroy with my sword, and my hand will have dominion!' You sent out your wind, and the sea covered them. They sank like lead in the mighty water."

"Who is like you among the gods, Lord? Who is like you? Glorified in holiness, marvelous in glories, doing wonders. You stretched out your right hand, and Eretz[3] swallowed them up. You have guided in your righteousness this your people whom you have redeemed, by your strength you have called them into your holy resting-place. The nations heard and were angry, pangs have seized on those under obligation to the Pelesets.[4] Then the princes of Edom and the chiefs of the Moabites ran as trembling took hold on them, and all the inhabitants of Canaan melted away. Let trembling and fear fall on them. By the greatness of your arm, let them become like a stone until your people pass over, Lord! Until these, your people pass over, who you purchased. Bring them in and plant them in the mountain of their inheritance, in your prepared habitation, which you, Lord, have prepared, the sanctuary of the Lord, which your hands have prepared. Lord, reigning forever and ever and ever. For the horse of Pharaoh went in with the chariots and cavalry into the sea, and the Lord brought on them the water of the sea, but the Israelites walked through dry land in the middle of the sea."

Then Mariam the prophetess, the sister of Aaron, took a timbrel in her hand, and danced with all the women, each with timbrels. Mariam led them, saying, "Sing of the Lord who has gloriously thrown the horse and rider into the sea!"

Then Moses brought up the Israelites from the Papyrus Sea and brought them into the Wilderness of Shur,[5] and they went three days in the wilderness and found no water to drink. They came to Marah,[6] and could not drink at Marah, for it was bitter, therefore he named the name of that place, Bitterness.[7] The people murmured against Moses, saying, "What will we drink?"

Moses cried to the Lord, and the Lord showed him a tree, and he threw it into the water, and the water was sweetened. There he established for him ordinances and judgments, and there he tested him, and said, "If you will indeed listen to the voice of Lord the god, and do things pleasing before him, and will listen to his commands, and keep all his ordinances, no disease which I have brought on the Egyptians will I bring on you, for I am Lord the god who heals you."

They came to Elim,[8] and there were there twelve fountains of water, and seventy stems of palm-trees and they camped there by the waters.

Exodus: Chapter 15 Notes

1 Codex Vaticanus: cssyntribôn polemous csonoma autô (ⲔⲤⲤⲨⲚⲦⲢⲓⲂⲱⲚⲠⲞⲗⲉⲙⲞⲨⲤ ⲔⲤⲞⲚⲞⲙⲀ ⲀⲨⲦⲱ). Translation: lord (or main, chief, dominant, master) catastrophes (or destructions, demolitions) battles (or wars) lord name his

• Leningrad Codex: Yehvah ish milchamah Yehvah shemov (יְהֹוָה אִישׁ מִלְחָמָה יְהֹוָה שְׁמוֹ). Translation: Yehvah man (or husband) of wars (or battles). Yehvah is his name.

• Peshitta: mryå gnbrå ûqrbtnå mryå šmyh (ܡܪܝܐ ܓܢܒܪܐ ܘܩܪܒܬܢܐ ܡܪܝܐ ܫܡܗ). Translation: master (or lord) Orion (or 'giant,' hero, strongman) and Ursa Minor (or the 'bed,' the four stars: Kochab, Pherkad, Anwar al Farkadain, and Akhfa al Farkadain), master of the sky

• Targum Onkelos: yeyah marei nitzchan keravaya yeyah shemeh (יְיָ מָרֵי נִצְחָן קְרָבַיָא יְיָ שְׁמֵהּ). Translation: Yah. Translation: Yah lord of splendors (or eternities, perfections) to be near (or to fight, to make war). Yah of desolation (or 'is his name.')

• Fragment Targums: yeyah bikar shechinteih hu da'aveid lechon nitzchanei keraveichon bechol dar vadar moda gevureteih le'ama beit yishra'el adonai shemo ki chishmeih ken gevureteih yehe shemeih meshabbach le'almei almin (יְיָ בִּיקַר שְׁכִינְתֵּיה

הוּא דַּעֲבֵיד לְכוֹן נִצְחָנֵי קְרָבֵיכוֹן בְּכָל דַּר וְדַר מוֹדַע גְּבוּרְתֵּיה לְעַמָּא בֵּית יִשְׂרָאֵל יְיָ שְׁמוֹ כִּי כִשְׁמֵיה כֵּן גְּבוּרְתֵּיה יְהֵא שְׁמֵיה מְשַׁבַּח לְעָלְמֵי עָלְמִין). Translation: Yah honored in (or heavy is, visiting) his dwelling that was made (or served, slaved, done) to direct victories in wars (or battles), to generally dwell in, and to exist as a notice (or advertisement) for the people of the house of Israel. Yah is his name, because like his name is the power (or force). Let sky gusts from the virgin (or unmarried girl, Virgo) forever.

• Targum Jerusalem: merin benei yishra'el yeyah gavra aveid keraveinan bechol dar vadar minda gevureteih le'ammeih beit yishra'el yeyah shemeih kishmeih ken gevureteih yehei shemeih mevarach le'alemei almin (אָמְרִין בְּנֵי יִשְׂרָאֵל יְיָ נַבְרָא עָבֵיד קְרָבֵינָן בְּכָל דַּר וְדַר מִנְדַע גְּבוּרְתֵּיה לְעַמֵּיה בֵּית יִשְׂרָאֵל יְיָ שְׁמֵיה כִּשְׁמֵיה כֵּן גְּבוּרְתֵּיה יְהֵי שְׁמֵיה מְבָרַך לְעָלְמֵי עָלְמִין). Translation: It has been said by the children of Israel, "Yah man (or husband) makes prosperous (or labors in, produces) all who circle (or orbit, go around), and to dwell in knowledge (or intelligence) as a notice (or advertisement) for the people of the house of Israel. Yah of sky (in Hebrew, or 'towards name' in Aramaic), because like his name is the power (or force). Let exist sky blessings from the virgin (or unmarried girl, Virgo) forever.

There are no surviving early fragments of the Septuagint's Exodus that include the name Iaw (Ιαω), the Greek form of Yhŭ (וח^), suggesting the word in the early Aramaic version of Exodus was ådny (^ץ1N), which meant 'lord,' and was also the name of a god in the Canaanite religion, especially in the region around Baalbek, in modern Lebanon. Like the Samaritan Yhŭ, Ådny was the son of Asherah and El, suggesting they were regional variants of the same god. Unlike in Samaria and Judah, the Phoenician version of the god never became the supreme god among his worshipers, as his father El continued to fill that role until the rise of Christianity and Islam supplanted the traditional religion of Baalbek.

The use of the term 'Lord' in the Jerusalem and Jonathan Targums where yeyah (יְיָ) has been substituted, also makes more sense than the name Yah, suggesting the original Aramaic source texts of both used the term ådny (^ץ1N). If the earlier Aramaic translation did read 'Lord shemu,' and did originate in Egyptian, then it does not read 'Lord is my name,' but 'Lord of Shemu.' Shemu (≡ ♪⊕) was an Egyptian meaning 'harvest,' and was the name of the summer season: shemu (≡○). The Lord of the Harvest could have been a reference to Lord Lehem in Canaan, the god that Bethlehem is named after, however, the pronunciation of 'shemu' is Middle Egyptian, meaning this could not have been added to the text in the New Kingdom era or later. During the New Kingdom the pronunciation transitioned to Shom, which continued to be used as the Coptic šôm (ϣⲱⲙ) in the Classical era.

The translators of the Peshitta may have understood the reference to the Egyptian season of shemu, as Sah (Gabbarå / Orion) was the constellation that the Egyptians watched during shemu, waiting for the heliacal rising of Sopdet (Sirius), when the following season would begin. Shemu was followed by the dangerous intercalary week, when the annual floods may begin at anytime, following which came the flood season: akhet (𓈖𓏭𓇋). If this originated in during the Hyksos dynasty, then the reference to the 'Lord of Orion' would have been ^{deity}An (✳✳), who was also represented by the constellation today known as Orion.

The correlation of the word šmů (שׁמֹר) and the season šôm (ϣⲱⲙ) was probably first noted by Egyptian Israelites in the Classical era, as the reference to Virgo makes no sense astronomically or astrologically. The Canaanite goddess Anat was also known as 'the virgin,' and she was married to Yhů in the early-Persian era Israelite religion, as the Elephantine papyri have demonstrated. Likewise, Sopdet (Sirius) was viewed as the wife of Sah (Gabbarå / Orion) in the Egyptian religion. Therefore, the pairing of Orion and the Virgin would only make sense to early-Persian era Egyptian Israelites. It seems the Christian translator of the Peshitta did not accept the reference to the 'virgin,' and substituted the nearby constellation of the 'bed,' today known as Ursa Minor.

2 Codex Vaticanus: erythra thalassê (ⲉⲣⲩⲟⲣⲁⲟⲁⲗⲗⲁⲥⲥⲏ). Translation: Erythrean Sea (the Red Sea, Gulf of Aden, Persian Gulf, and Indian Ocean)

- Leningrad Codex: yam-Suf (יַם־סוּף). Translation: sea of papyrus (or reeds)

- Peshitta: ymå dsůp (ܝܡܐ ܕܣܘܦ). Translation: sea of papyrus (or reeds)

- Targum Onkelos: yama desuf (יַמָּא דְסוּף)

- Fragment Targums: yama desuf (יַמָּא דְסוּף). Translation: sea of papyrus (or reeds)

- Targum Jerusalem: yama desuf (יַמָּא דְסוּף). Translation: sea of papyrus (or reeds)

The Greek term is not geographically specific, allowing for the Israelites to have passed from Egypt to the wilderness at any point in the Red Sea or even the Gulf of Aden. The Greek name appears to be a translation of the Persian term Erostras, which referred to the entire Persian Gulf, Red Sea, and the Indian Ocean. The Greeks were likely referring to the Gulf of Suez, however, this was known to the ancient Egyptians as the 'Sea of Calm,' which is what the Israelites would have called it if that was where they were.

The Greeks transliterated the name as the Sea of Siph (Θαλάσσης Σιφ) in the Codex Vaticanus' translation of Judges, confirming that the name Swf was in the Aramaic text they worked from. The Aramaic term sůf (סוּף) and Phoenician term sůf (𐤎𐤅𐤐), both meaning papyrus plants were adopted from the Egyptian term tjůfî (�), which referred to papyrus, papyrus plants, and papyrus marshes. The Egyptian term continued to be used into the Classical era as the Coptic words čoouf (ϫⲟⲟⲩϥ), conf (ϭⲟⲛϥ), and comf (ϭⲟⲙϥ), all meaning papyrus. Conversely, the Egyptian name of the Red Sea was the Sea of Ḥeh (𓁌), meaning 'very large sea' from the Middle Kingdom era onward, however, it is believed to have originally been named after the ancient Egyptian frog god Heh (𓁨). As the Greek translation of Erythrean Sea is anachronistic, the translation of Papyrus Sea is imported from the Masoretic Text. As the Greek translation of Erythrean Sea is anachronistic, the translation of Papyrus Sea is imported from the Masoretic Text. The Hebrew term 'Sea of papyrus' is not geographically specific either, however, does match the description of the shallow Lake Bardawil which has been a major source for papyrus reeds throughout Egyptian history.

3 Codex Vaticanus: Gê (ⲅⲏ). Translation: Ge (or land, earth, country)

- Leningrad Codex: aretz (אֶרֶץ). Translation: Eretz (or land, earth, country, soil)

- Peshitta: årôå (ܐܪܥܐ). Translation: land

- Targum Onkelos: ar'a (אַרְעָא). Translation: land

- Fragment Targums: ar'a (אַרְעָא). Translation: land

- Targum Jerusalem: ar'a (אַרְעָא). Translation: land

The Earth (Eretz / Ge) is depicted as the same type of primordial deity in the Septuagint as it was in the Greek myths and called on to witness blessings and curses, implying consciousness. She is described as opening her mouth to swallow things more than once in the Torah, and in other Classical Era Israelite texts she spoke and had free will, meaning she continued to be seen as a type of goddess by some Israelites. In both the Targums Jerusalem and Jonathan, this verse is preceded by a debate between Ara (land) and Yama (sea) about which of them should consume the Egyptians, ultimately resulting in Ara opening her mouth and consuming them. Strangely, all versions of the story agree that it was the sea that consumed them, and all versions of the song agree that it was the land.

4 Codex Vaticanus: catoecountas Phylistiim (ⲕⲁⲧⲟⲓⲕⲟⲩⲛⲧⲁⲥⲫⲩⲗⲓⲥⲧⲓⲓⲙ). Translation: under-obligation to the Philistines (or Palestinians)

- Leningrad Codex: yoshevei Pelashet (יֹשְׁבֵי פְּלָשֶׁת). Translation: inhabitants of Palestine (or Philistia, Peleset)

- Peshitta: lytbh dplšt (ܠܝܬܒܗ ܕܦܠܫܬ). Translation: settlement of Pelesets (or Palestinians)

- Targum Onkelos: ledahavo yatevin biflashet (לְדַהֲווֹ יָתְבִין בִּפְלָשֶׁת). Translation: those who inhabited Plashet (or Palestine, Philistia, Peleset)

- Targum Jerusalem: dayrei ar'ahon dippelishta'ei (דַיְירֵי אַרְעָהוֹן דִּפְלִשְׁתָּאֵי). Translation:

the fires ruling (or pasturing in) the Pelisht (or Palestinian) land

The text refers to the Moabites, Edomites, and other Canaanites as being under obligation to the Pelesets (or Philistines, Palestinians) which is anachronistic as the Pelesets did not arrive in the region for another 300 years. This suggests that the word replaced another older term when the Phoenician translation was made. The Targum Onkelos includes the curious deviation of 'those who lived in Philistia,' indicating that Onkelos knew that they were not the Pelesets.

At the time, the region was under the rule of the Hyksos (𓋴𓀭), whose regional capital was at Sharuhen, in the modern Palestinian Gaza strip. The Hyksos were driven from the region within a decade of the Septuagint's dating of the exodus, and therefore their name would have meant nothing 400 years later, when the Canaanite translation was made. The Targum Jerusalem includes the strange reference to the 'fires' who 'ruled Philistia,' which appears to be a mistranslation of a Middle Egyptian version of the verse. Most Egyptologists currently view the Hyksos nobility as being Amorites, who the Egyptians called the Åmů (𓄿𓀭), a homonym of åmů (𓄿𓄿𓂧𓏏), meaning 'fires.'

5 Codex Vaticanus: erêmon Sour (ЄʀHMONCOYʀ). Translation: desert of Sour

• Leningrad Codex: midbar-Shur (מִדְבַּר־שׁוּר). Translation: desert (or pastureland) or Shur

• Peshitta: mdbrå dšůd (ܡܕܒܪܐ ܕܫܘܕ). Translation: desert (or wilderness, steppe, leader, guide) of robbery (or piracy)

• Targum Onkelos: madbera dechagra (מַדְבְּרָא דְחַגְרָא). Translation: desert (or wilderness, steppe, leader, guide) of limping

• Fragment Targums: orecha dechalutza (אוֹרְחָא דְחָלוּצָא). Translation: road of Chalutza (possibly meaning 'purification' from the Arabic kalaṣa – خلص)

• Targum Jerusalem: madbera dechalutza (מַדְבְּרָא דְחָלוּצָא). Translation: desert (or wilderness, steppe, leader, guide) of Chalutza (possibly meaning 'purification' from the Arabic kalaṣa - خلص)

The location of the 'Wilderness of Shur' is debated, however, the location of 'Shur' is known. Shur is the Canaanite pronunciation of the Egyptian name šå-hr (𓈌𓄿), meaning the 'plains of Horus,' a region on the Mediterranean coast between the Nile Delta and Lake Bardawil. This indicates the Wilderness of Shur was the Northern Sinai Peninsula, which seems to be supported in the following paragraphs which discuss the 'Bitter Waters.' This means the Israelites headed south from Lake Bardawil.

6 Codex Vaticanus: Merra (Ⲙⲉⲣⲣⲁ)

- Leningrad Codex: marah (מָרָה). Translation: bitter

- Peshitta: Mûrt (ܡܘܪܬ)

- Targum Onkelos: marah (מָרָה). Translation: bitter

- Targum Jerusalem: marah (מָרָה). Translation: bitter

The Greek translation deviates from the Hebrew and Aramaic versions in that both transliterates and translates the Hebrew and Aramaic word for 'bitter,' treating it as the toponym Merra (Μερρα), but thn switching to the translation of picria (πικρια), meaning 'bitter' in Greek. The location of this bitter water has been debated, and is largely dependent on where the events involving the Papyrus Sea and Mount Sinai took place. Based on the Papyrus Sea being Lake Bardawil, the bitter waters would be the Bitter Lakes, half-way between the Mediterranean coast and the Gulf of Suez. The larger of the two Bitter Lakes, the Great Bitter Lake had dried out completely by the time the Suez Canal was constructed in the late 1800s, which now connects these two lakes, as well as linking them to the Mediterranean and Gulf of Suez. The Pyramid Texts, which date back to the Old Kingdom era, mention the Great Bitter Lake, implying the existence of one or more Small Bitter Lake(s), and therefore the name is very ancient, long preceding the era of Moses.

It seems unlikely that there would have been another area of bitter waters in the region that the Egyptians somehow never noticed through thousands of years of occupation, and therefore, the Bitter Lakes are almost certainly the place being described in this chapter. If this interpretation is correct, it would mean the Israelites started moving east along the coastal road to Canaan, and then turned back and headed south into the Sinai Peninsula after the events at the Papyrus Sea.

7 Codex Vaticanus: Pikria (ⲡⲓⲕⲣⲓⲁ). Translation: bitter

- Leningrad Codex: marah (מָרֹה). Translation: bitter

- Peshitta: Mûrt (ܡܘܪܬ)

- Targum Onkelos: marah (מָרָה). Translation: bitter

- Targum Jerusalem: marah (מָרָה). Translation: bitter

See the previous note for more information.

8 Codex Vaticanus: Ailim (ΑΙΛΙΜ)

- Leningrad Codex: Eilima (אֵילִ֗מָה)

- Peshitta: Åylm (ܐܝܠܡ)

- Targum Onkelos: Eilim (אֵילִם)

- Targum Jerusalem: Elim (אֵלִים)

The word is Semitic for 'stags' or 'rams,' written in Akkadian as ayyalum (𒀀𒈠𒇻), Ugaritic as åylm (𐎀𐎊𐎍𐎎), Phoenician as åylm (𐤀𐤉𐤋𐤌), Sabean åylm (𐩱𐩺𐩡𐩣), Aramaic as åylåm (𐡀𐡉𐡋𐡌), Hebrew åylym (אילים), and Syriac as åylåm (ܐܝܠܡ). While the word is phonetically the same as the word for stags, neither the Greek nor Hebrew translations translate the term directly, treating it as a toponym.

The location of Elim is debated, like the other stations along the route the Israelites took out of Egypt. Its location is largely based on the assumptions about the events of the Papyrus Sea, the location of the Bitter Waters, and ultimately the location of the Wilderness of Sin and Mount Sinai. It is traditionally identified by Muslims as the Oyun Musa (عيون موسى), meaning 'Spring of Moses' in the western Sinai, where there are twelve ancient wells. It is not clear when the location was named, and it is plausible that this location was named after Moses by Emperor Constantine's mother, Helena Augusta, when she named Mount Sinai and the Sinai Peninsula in the 330s AD. As the Greek translators did not identify the town, it could not have been widely known as the 'Moses' Spring' circa 250 BC. Another theory is the Elim may have referred to the Wadi Gharandel in the Sinai peninsula, again this is based on the theory that Exodus' Mount Sinai was the large mountain range named Sinai by Helena Augusta in the 330s AD.

If the Israelites were trying to leave Egypt, and one would assume Moses was leading them towards Midian, where he first encountered the fire-messenger, then the logical direction was east following the southern road across the Sinai Peninsula, which runs east from the Bitter Lakes to the modern town of An-Nekhel in central Sinai, before continuing on to mountains of Hashem El Tarif in eastern Sinai. An-Nekhel is known to have been used as a watering hole along the southern road since Pharaonic times. It is postulated to have been a Canaanite town, founded during the Hyksos era, named after the Canaanite goddess Nikkal, meaning 'Great lady of the Fruitful,' who was the goddess of orchards.

If this theory is correct, then there must have been a settlement with orchards in the region, matching to some degree the Exodus' description of a place of wells and trees. Nikkal was the wife of the Canaanite moon god Yarikh, which supports the town being somewhere the Sinai Desert, if the Sinai was named after the Akkadian moon god Sin.

Exodus: Chapter 16

They departed from Elim, and all the congregation of the Israelites came to the Wilderness of Sin,[1] which is between Elim and Sinai,[2] and on the fifteenth day, in the second month, after they left the land of Egypt, all the congregation of the Israelites murmured against Moses and Aaron. The Israelites said to them, "If only we had died, struck down by the Lord in the land of Egypt, when we sat by the fleshpots, and ate bread to satisfaction! You have brought us out into this wilderness, to starve us all to death!"

The Lord said to Moses, "Look, I will rain bread on you out of the sky, and the people will go out, and they will gather their daily portion each day, so I may test them, whether they follow my commandments or not. It will happen on the sixth day that they will prepare whatever they have brought in, and it will be double of what they will have gathered for the day, in previous days."

Moses and Aaron said to all the congregation of the Israelites, "So you will know that the Lord has brought you out of the land of Egypt, in the morning you will see the glory of the Lord, as he has heard your murmuring against God. Who are we, that you continue to murmur against us?"

Moses said, "This is the day when the Lord gives you flesh to eat in the evening, and bread in the morning until you are full because the Lord has heard your murmuring, which you murmur against us. Who are we? Your murmuring is not against us, but God!"

Moses said to Aaron, "Tell all the congregation of the Israelites, 'Come before God because he has heard your murmuring.'"

When Aaron spoke to all the congregation of the Israelites, and they turned towards the wilderness, then the glory of the Lord appeared in a cloud. The Lord said to Moses, "I have heard the murmuring of the Israelites. Tell them, 'Towards evening you will eat flesh, and in the morning you will be satisfied with bread, and you will know that I am Lord the god.'"

It was evening, and quails came up and covered the camp, in the morning it happened as the dew ceased around the camp, that they saw the face of the wilderness was covered in a small thing like white coriander seed, like frost on the land. When the Israelites saw it, they said one to another, "What is this?" As they did not know what it was.

Moses told them, "This is the bread which the Lord has given you to eat. This is that which the Lord has said, 'Gather of it each man for his family, a measure for each person, by the head according to the number of your minds, gather each of you with his neighbors.'"

The Israelites did so, and gathered, some more and some less. Having measured the measure full, he who gathered more had nothing left over, and he who had gathered less had no shortage. Each gathered just sufficient for the need of those who belonged to him.

Moses told them, "Let no man leave any of it until the morning." But they did not listen to Moses, and some left it until the morning, and it bred worms and stank, and Moses was irritated with them. They gathered it every morning, each man what he needed, and when the sun grew hot it melted. It happened on the sixth day, they gathered double what was needed, two measures for one man, and all the chiefs of the congregation went in and reported it to Moses.

Moses said to them, "Is this not the word that the Lord said? Tomorrow is the sabbath, a holy rest to for the Lord. Bake, you who bake, and see what you will see. All that is left over leave is to be stored for tomorrow." They left it until the morning as Moses commanded them, and it did not stink and there were no worms in it.

Moses commanded, "Eat that today, for today is a sabbath to the Lord. It will not be found in the plain. Six days you will gather it, and on the seventh day is a sabbath, as there will be none on that day."

It happened on the seventh day that some of the people went out to gather, and found none. The Lord said to Moses, "How long are you unwilling to listen to my commands and my law? See, the Lord has given you this day, the sabbath, therefore he has given you on the sixth day the bread of two days. You will sit each of you in your houses, let no one go out from his place on the seventh day."

The people kept sabbath on the seventh day. The Israelites called the name of it manna, and it was as white coriander seed, and the taste of it was like a wafer with honey. Moses said, "The Lord has commanded, 'Fill a measure with manna, to be stored up for your generations, that they may see the bread which you ate in the wilderness when the Lord led you out of the land of Egypt.'"

Moses said to Aaron, "Take a golden pot and gather into it one full measure of manna, and you will store it near God, to be kept for your generations," as the

Lord commanded Moses. Aaron stored it near the testimony. The Israelites ate manna forty years until they came to the land of Phoenicia. Now the measure was the tenth part of three measures.

Exodus: Chapter 16 Notes

1 Codex Vaticanus: Sin (ϲιν)

- Leningrad Codex: Sin (סִ֖ין)

- Peshitta: Syn (ܣܝܢ)

- Targum Onkelos: Sin (סִין)

- Targum Jerusalem: Sin (סִין)

The Wilderness of Sin (Σιν) is the translation in the Septuagint for both the Masoretic Wilderness of Sin (סִין) in Exodus and the Wilderness of Tzin (צִן) in Numbers, which was followed by Jerome in the Latin Vulgate as the Wilderness of Sin. This suggests that the Aramaic version of the Torah did not differentiate between the two. As the book of Numbers was likely organized into its current state during the era of King Hezekiah's reforms, and it was almost certainly written in the Phoenician script that was in use in Judah at the time, it is likely that it more accurately records the two locations as separate places. In Numbers chapter 33, they are both listed in the long sequence of stops the Israelites made as they traveled from Egypt, confirming that the Hebrew translator, and probably the Judahite or Moabite compiler of the original book of Numbers viewed them as separate places.

Conversely, Exodus shows clear signs of having been written in Akkadian cuneiform, which is likely where the pronunciation of Sin is derived, ultimately from the Akkadian spelling of Sîn (𒂗𒍪), which was spelled in Aramaic as Syn (𒋀𒌈), the direct transliteration of the Hebrew Syn (סין). While the Aramaic spelling would have been standardized by the common spelling of the name of the moon god, there was nothing to standardize the spelling of the toponym in the Phoenician script, resulting in both toponyms being rendered phonetically by the scribes that unified the stories found in Numbers into a book circa 700 BC.

The locations of these wildernesses have been a matter of debate for more than 2000 years, and early Christians era scholars widely debated this issue, with the majority favoring the region around Petra, in Jordan, or the Midian Mountains in northwestern Saudi Arabia. The Wilderness of Sin is identified within the Torah, as being between Elim and Mount Sinai, however, both locations are debated today. The Wilderness of Sinai is identified as including the site of Kadesh Barne, however, this location is also debated. Emperor Constantine's mother, Helena Augusta, named the Sinai Peninsula and

Mount Sinai of Egypt in the 330s AD to resolve this issue, however, few scholars agree with this location today, as other references indicate the Israelites were wandering in northwest Saudi Arabia, Jordan, southern Syria.

Currently, Christian and Islamic scholars treating the Exodus as history, prefer Petra in Jordan, as the site of Kadesh, and Jebel al-Madhbah near Petra as Mount Sinai. This mountain has the Valley of Moses, called Wadi Musa in Arabic, which has an ancient staircase leading to the top of the mountain. It was clearly an ancient religious site, housing rain-fed cisterns, and two gigantic obelisks. At the entrance to the Valley of Moses is the Spring of Moses, which is believed to be the location that Moses struck the rock with his wand and caused water to flow. Based on the 1st century Josephus' claim that Kadesh Barnea was at Petra, the Wilderness of Sinai appears to be another name for the southern Arabah, the mostly dry valley running north from the Gulf of Aqaba to the Dead Sea. By extension, if Sinai and Sin are not two different spellings of the same place, then the location of the Wilderness of Sin would have to be the Sinai Desert, between An-Nekhel (Elim), and Hashem El Tarif (Rephidim).

2 Codex Vaticanus: Sina (ⲥⲓⲛⲁ)

• Leningrad Codex: Sinai (סִינַי)

• Peshitta: Syny (ܣܝܢܝ)

• Targum Onkelos: Sinai (סִינַי)

• Targum Jerusalem: Sinai (סִינַי)

As this name is generally spelled as 'Sinai' in English, that transliteration is used. See the previous note for a more information on Sin and Sinai.

Exodus: Chapter 17

All the congregation of the Israelites departed from the Wilderness of Sin, according to their encampments, by the command of the Lord, and they camped in Rephidim,[1] but there was no water for the people to drink. The people reviled Moses, saying, "Give us water, that we may drink."

Moses said to them, "Why do you hate me, and why do you tempt the Lord?"

The people thirsted there for water, and there the people murmured against Moses, saying, "Why is this? Have you brought us out of Egypt to kill us and our children and our livestock by thirst?"

Moses cried to the Lord, saying, "What will I do with this people? In a little while they will stone me."

The Lord answered Moses, "Go before these people and take with you the elders of the people, and the wand with which you struck the river, take it in your hand. Go and look, and I will stand there before you come, on the rock with a heavy plow,[2] and you will strike the rock, and water will come out from it, and the people will drink."

Moses did so before the sons of Israel, and he called the name of that place, Temptation and Reviling,[3] because of the reviling of the Israelites, and because they tempted the Lord, saying, "Is the Lord among us or not?" Amalek came and fought with Israel in Rephidim. Moses said to Joshua, "Choose out for yourself mighty men, and go out and set the army in formation against Amalek tomorrow, and, watch I will stand on the top of the hill, and the wand of God will be in my hand."

Joshua did as Moses told him, and he went out and set the army in formation against Amalek, and Moses and Aaron and Hur went up to the top of the hill. It happened when Moses lifted his hands, Israel prevailed, and when he let down his hands, Amalek prevailed. But the hands of Moses were heavy, and they took a stone and put it under him, and he sat on it, and Aaron and Hur supported his hands one on this side, and the other on that, and the hands of Moses were supported until the sun went down.

Joshua routed Amalek and all his people with the slaughter of the sword. The Lord commanded Moses, "Write this as a memorial in a book, and tell to Joshua, 'I will utterly blot out the memory of Amalek from under the sky.'"

Moses built an altar to the Lord, and called the name of it, 'the Lord my Refuge,'[4] for with a secret hand the Lord wages war on Amalek to all generations.

Exodus: Chapter 17 Notes

1 Codex Vaticanus: Raphidin (ⲢⲀⲪⲒⲆⲒⲚ)

• Leningrad Codex: Refidim (רְפִידִים)

• Peshitta: Rpydyn (ܪܦܝܕܝܢ)

• Targum Onkelos: Refidim (רְפִידִים)

• Targum Jerusalem: Refidim (רְפִידִים)

This location is generally associated with the Wadi Feiran, or the Feiran Oasis within it. The Wadi Feiran is an 81-mile (130 km) long wadi (seasonal river) which runs down the Jebel Musa to the Gulf of Suez. The Feiran Oasis, also called El Hesweh, is approximately 3 miles (4.8 km) long, and generally habitable year-round. The Greek geographer and polymath Claudius Ptolemy identified this as the location of Paran from the Torah, which is likely where the Arabic name came from.

The assumption that Wadi Feiran is Rephidim is again predicated on Jebel Musa being Mount Sinai, or at least in the vicinity of Mount Sinai, however, if Horeb is Sinai, then Sinai would have to be near or in Midian, as that was where Moses first encountered the fire-messenger that sent him back to Egypt, and a location in southern Sinai seems highly improbable for a Midianite shepherd, especially one trying to avoid Egyptians, who were mining in the region. If the Israelites had followed the southern road across the Sinai Peninsula en route to Mount Sinai/Horeb/Seir, they would have passed the An-Nekhel in central Sinai, and then proceeded east to the mountains of Hashem El Tarif in eastern Sinai, before following the Arabah north towards Jebel al-Madhbah. The likely location of this event along the route is at Hashem El Tarif, which did at one point have a spring flowing down from the top of the summit. The location of Rephidim at Hashem El Tarif is supported by the subsequent attack of the Amalekites, who, according to the Book of Numbers lived in the Negev, south of Judea, which is directly north of Hashem El Tarif.

2 Codex Vaticanus: epi tês petras en chôrêb (ⲈⲠⲒⲦⲎⲤⲠⲈⲦⲢⲀⲤⲈⲚⲬⲰⲢⲎⲂ). Translation: on (or at, near, before) the rock (or Petra) in Horeb

• Leningrad Codex: al-hatzur bechorev (עַל־הַצּוּר בְּחֹרֵב). Translation: on (or above) the rock (or Tyre, Petra) in (or with, during, among) Horeb (or sword, war, plow)

- Peshitta: ôl trnå bḥùryb (ܟܘܪܝܒ ܐܠ ܛܘܪܐ). Translation: on (or towards, against, about) rock (or flint) in (or at, with) Horeb (or sword, war, plow)

- Targum Onkelos: al tinara bechorev (עַל טִנָרָא בְּחוֹרֵב). Translation: on (or towards, against, about) rock (or flint) in (or at, with) Horeb (or sword, war, plow)

- Targum Jerusalem: be'atra detechemei roshem rigla bechorev (בְּאַתְרָא דְתֶחֱמֵי רוֹשֶׁם רִיגְלָא בְּחוֹרֵב). Translation: in country (or place, region) of the seeing impression (or sketch, outline) foot (or leg, foot soldier, foot stool, hoof, base) in (or at, with) Horeb (or sword, war, plow)

The Greek translators translated the Aramaic text as 'in Horeb,' which is also how the Hebrew translation could be interpreted, supporting the Aramaic text as being essentially the same as the Hebrew, and reading as bhrb (בחרב).

Unfortunately, the Greek translation does not make sense, as they were not near Mount Horeb at the time. An alternate reading of the Hebrew and Aramaic translations would be 'with a sword,' or 'with a plowshare,' neither of which probably made sense to the Greek translators, and so they opted for Horeb. Pseudo-Jonathan likely used a text that referred to a foot-plow, but did not understand the meaning, resulting in his broken translation.

This appears to be a misunderstanding of the underlying Akkadian cuneiform text, in which the word ḫarbum (𒄯𒁉𒌝) referred to a specialized heavy plow used to break up hard dry soil, as opposed to a lighter plow which was used to make furrows in fields. The name of this tool was spelled as ḥrb (חרב) in Aramaic, however, that word also meant any form of plow, sword, or spear. In this case, the Lord was apparently offering Moses a tool to breakup the hard soil and allow the water to flow. As the Greek translation is clearly incorrect, the translation of 'with a heavy plow' is imported from the Masoretic Text.

3 Codex Vaticanus: pirasmos cae loedorêsis (ΠΕΙΡΑϹΜΟϹΚΑΙΛΟΙΔΟΡΗϹΙϹ). Translation: temptation and reviling (ridicule).

- Leningrad Codex: massah umerivah (מַסָּה וּמְרִיבָה)

- Peshitta: nså: ûmrybå (ܢܣܐ: ܘܡܪܝܒܐ). Translation: tempted (or tested) and dispute (or quarrel)

- Targum Onkelos: niseita umatzuta (נְסֵיתָא וּמַצּוּתָא). Translation: standing banners (or fleeing place, existing miracle) and commandment

- Targum Jerusalem: nisyona umatzuta (נְסִיוֹנָא וּמַצּוּתָא). Translation: temptation (or trial) and commandment

4 Codex Vaticanus: cs mou cataphugê (ΚϹΜΟΥΚΑΤΑΦΥΓΗ). Translation: Lord my refuge

• Leningrad Codex: Yehvah. Nissi (נִסִּי \ יְהוָה). Translation: Yahweh. My miracle (or flag, banner, pole)

• DSS 4QpaleoExod^m: yhůh nsy (𐤆𐤇𐤉 𐤀𐤉𐤄𐤆). DSS 4QpaleoExod^m dates to the Hasmonean Dynasty (140 to 37 BC), and appears to be an early copy of the restored Samaritan Torah developed after General Pompey released the Samaritans from slavery under the Hasmoneans in 69 BC.

• Peshitta: mryå nsy (ܢܣܝ ܡܪܝܐ). Translation: Lord my miracle (or flag, banner, pole)

• Targum Onkelos: yeyah da'avad leh nisin (יְיָ דַּעֲבַד לֵהּ נִסִּין). Translation: Yhů who (or that, of) serves for (or of) miracles (or banners, poles).

• Targum Jerusalem: meimra dayeyah dein nisa (מֵימְרָא דַּיְיָ דֵּין נִיסָא). Translation: word of master that Yhů judgment (or deliberation) sign (or symbol, constellation, appearance)

The term found in the Masoretic Text and DSS 4QpaleoExod^m cannot be the original term in the verse, as nsy (ܢܣܝ / נִסִּי / 𐤆𐤉) was adopted from Persian word nišåni (𐎴𐎡𐏁𐎠𐎴), meaning 'flag,' or 'banner.' It was adopted into Judahite and Aramaic during the Persian Empire, centuries before the oldest surviving copies of this verse. Based on the context and phonetics, the original word was likely našû (𐎴𐎠𐎿𐎢), meaning to 'raise up,' 'support,' or 'deliver,' making the original verse read 'Lord (or Iaw) delivers,' which is similar to the Greek interpretation.

Exodus: Chapter 18

Jethro the priest of Midian, the father-in-law of Moses, heard of all that the Lord did to his people Israel, as the Lord brought Israel out of Egypt. Jethro the father-in-law of Moses, took Shiphrah the wife of Moses after she had been sent away, and her two sons, the name of the one was Gershom, when his father said, "I was a traveler in a strange land," and the name of the second Eliezer, when he said, "For the god of my father is my helper, and he has rescued me out of the hand of Pharaoh."

Jethro the father-in-law of Moses, and his sons and his wife, went out to Moses into the wilderness, where he camped on the mount of God. It was told to Moses, saying, "Look, your father-in-law Jethro is coming to you, and your wife and two sons with him."

Moses went out to meet his father-in-law, and did him reverence, and kissed him, and they embraced each other, and he brought them into the tent. Moses related to his father-in-law all things that the Lord did to Pharaoh and all the Egyptians for Israel's sake, and all the struggle that had happened to them in the road, and that the Lord had rescued them out of the hand of Pharaoh, and out of the hand of the Egyptians. Jethro was amazed at all the good things which the Lord did to them since he rescued them out of the hand of the Egyptians and out of the hand of Pharaoh and Jethro said, "Blessed be the Lord because he has rescued them out of the hand of the Egyptians and out of the hand of Pharaoh. Now know I that the Lord is greater than all gods, because of this, in which they attacked them."

Jethro the father-in-law of Moses took whole burnt offerings and sacrifices for God, for Aaron and all the elders of Israel came to eat bread with the father-in-law of Moses before God. It happened after the morning that Moses sat to judge the people, and all the people stood by Moses from morning until evening. Jethro having seen all that was done to the people, said, "What is this that you do to the people? You sit alone, and all the people stand by you from morning until evening?"

Moses told his father-in-law, "Because the people come to me to seek judgment from God. For whenever there is a dispute among them, and they come to me, I give judgment on each, and I teach them the ordinances of God and his law."

423

The father-in-law of Moses said to him, "You don't do this thing correctly, you will wear away with intolerable weariness, both you and all these people that are with you. This thing is hard, you will not be able to endure it yourself alone. Now then listen to me, and I will advise you, and God will be with you. You are to the people, all the things concerning God, and you bring their words to God. You testify to them the ordinances of God and his law, and you show to them the way that they will walk, and the works which they will do."

"Do you look out for yourself out of all the people able men, fearing God, righteous men, hating pride, and you will set over them captains of thousands and captains of hundreds, and captains of fifties, and captains of tens. They will judge the people at all times, and the too burdensome matter they will bring to you, but they will judge the smaller cases, so they will relieve you and help you. If you will do this, God will strengthen you, and you will be able to pay attention, and all these people will return in peace into his own place."

Moses listened to the voice of his father-in-law and did as he advised him. Moses picked able men out of all Israel, and he made them captains of thousands and captains of hundreds, and captains of fifties and captains of tens over them. They judged the people at all times, and every too burdensome matter they brought to Moses, but every light-matter they judged themselves. Moses dismissed his father-in-law, and he returned to his own land.

Exodus: Chapter 19

In the third month of the departure of the Israelites from the land of Egypt, on the same day, they came into the Wilderness of Sinai. They departed from Rephidim and came into the Wilderness of Sinai, and there Israel camped before the mountain. Moses went up to the mount of God, and God called him out of the mountain, saying, "These things will you say to the house of Jacob, and you will report them to the Israelites. You have seen all that I have done to the Egyptians, and I took you up as on eagles' wings, and I brought you near to myself. Now if you will indeed hear my voice, and keep my covenant, you will be for me a peculiar people above all nations, for the whole land is mine. You will be for me a royal priesthood and a holy nation, these words will you speak to the Israelites."

Moses came and called the elders of the people, and he set before them all these words, which God appointed them. All the people answered with one voice, and said, "All things that God has spoken, we will do and listen to," and Moses reported these words to God.

The Lord said to Moses, "Look! I come to you in a pillar of a cloud, that the people may hear me speaking to you, and may believe you forever," and Moses reported the words of the people to the Lord.

The Lord told Moses, "Go down and solemnly order the people, and sanctify them today and tomorrow, and let them wash their garments. Let them be ready against the third day, for on the third day the Lord will descend on Mount Sinai before all the people. You will separate the people saying, 'Pay attention to yourselves that you go not up into the mountain or touch any part of it.' Everyone that touches the mountain will die. A hand will not touch it, for everyone that touches will be stoned with stones or shot through with a dart, whether animal or whether man, it will not live. When the voices and trumpets and cloud depart from off the mountain, they may come up the mountain."

Moses went down from the mountain to the people and sanctified them, and they washed their clothes. He said to the people, "Be ready and for three days don't go near a woman."

It happened on the third day, as the morning drew near, there were voices and lightning and dark clouds on Mount Sinai, and the voice of the trumpet sounded loud, and all the people in the camp trembled. Moses led the people out of the camp to meet God, and they stood by under the camp. Mount Sinai was smoking because God had descended on it in fire, and the smoke went up like the smoke of a furnace, and the people were amazed. The sounds of the trumpet were growing very much louder, and when Moses spoke, God answered him with a voice.

The Lord came down on Mount Sinai on the top of the mountain, and the Lord called Moses to the top of the mountain, and Moses went up. God said to Moses, "Go down and solemnly order the people, in case at any time they come close to see God, and a number of them fall. Let the priests that draw near to our Lord God to sanctify themselves, in case some are removed by the Lord."

Moses said to God, "The people will not be able to approach to Mount Sinai, for you have solemnly ordered us, saying, 'Set bounds to the mountain and sanctify it.'"

The Lord said to him, "Go, descend, and return with Aaron, but don't let the priests and the people force their way up to God, in case the Lord destroys some of them."

Moses went down to the people and said to them.

Exodus: Chapter 20

The Lord said all these words: "I am Lord the god, who brought you out of the land of Egypt, out of the house of slavery."

"You will worship no other gods beside me. You will not make for yourself an idol, or an image of anything which is in the sky above, or which is in the land below, or which is in the waters under the land."

"You will not bow down to them, or serve them, for I am Lord the god, a jealous God, repaying the sins of the fathers on the children, to the third and fourth generation to them that hate me, and bestowing mercy on them that love me to thousands of them, and on them that keep my commandments."

"You will not take the name of Lord the god in vain, for Lord the god will not forgive him who takes his name in vain."

"Remember the sabbath day to keep it holy. Six days you will labor and will perform all your work. But on the seventh day is the sabbath of Lord the god, and you will do no work on it, or your son, your daughter, your servant, your slave-girl, your ox, your donkey, or any livestock of yours, or even the stranger that stays with you. For in six days, the Lord made the sky and the land, and the sea and all things in them, and then rested on the seventh day. Therefore, the Lord blessed the seventh day, and it is sacred."

"Honor your father and your mother, so it may go well with you, and so you may live long on the good land, which Lord the god gives to you."

"You will not commit adultery."

"You will not steal."

"You will not kill."

"You will not bear false witness against your neighbor."

"You will not covet your neighbor's wife. You will not covet your neighbor's house, or his field, or his servant, or his maid, or his ox, or his donkey, or any of his livestock, or whatever belongs to your neighbor."

All the people saw the voice, and the flashes, and the voice of the trumpet, and the mountain smoking, and all the people were afraid and stood far away, and said to Moses, "You speak to us, and don't let God speak to us, in case we die."

Moses said to them, "Be courageous, for God is come to you to try you, that his fear may be among you, that you don't sin."

The people stood far away, and Moses went into the darkness where God was. The Lord told Moses, "Say this to the house of Jacob, and report it to the Israelites, 'You have seen that I have spoken to you from the sky. You will not make for yourselves gods of silver, and gods of gold you will not make to yourselves. You will make for me an altar of dirt, and on it, you will sacrifice your whole burnt offerings, and your peace-offerings, and your sheep and your calves in every place, where I will record my name, and I will come to you and bless you. If you will make for me an altar of stones, you will not build them cut stones, for you have lifted your tools on them, and they are defiled. You will not go up to my altar by steps, that you may not uncover your nakedness on it."

Exodus: Chapter 21

"These are the ordinances which you will set before them. If you buy a Habiru slave, he will serve you for six years, and in the seventh year he will go out free for nothing. If he should have come in alone, he will also go out alone, and if his wife should have gone in together with him, his wife also will go out. Moreover, if his master gave him a wife, and she had born him sons or daughters, the wife, and the children will be his master's and he will leave by himself. If the slave should say, 'I love my master and wife and children, and I will not leave,' his master will bring him to the judgment-seat of God, and then will he bring him to the door, to the doorpost, and his master will pierce his ear through with an awl, and he will serve him forever."

"If anyone sells his daughter as a slave, she will not depart like the slave-girls depart. If she is not pleasing to her master, who has betrothed herself to him, he will let her go free, but he is not at liberty to sell her to a foreign nation, because he has trifled with her. If he should have betrothed her to his son, he will do to her according to the right of daughters. If he takes another for himself, he will not deprive her of necessaries and her apparel, and her companionship with him. If he will not do these three things to her, she will go out free without silver."

"If any man strikes another and he dies, let him be certainly put to death. But as for he that did not do it intentionally, but God delivered him into his hands, I will give you a place where the slayer may flee. If anyone lies in wait for his neighbor, to kill him by craft, and he goes for refuge, you will take him from my altar to put him to death. Whoever hits his father or his mother, let him be certainly put to death. He that reviles his father or his mother will surely die. Whoever steals one of the Israelites, and prevails over him and sells him, and he is found with him, let him certainly die. If two men revile each other and strike each other with a stone or fist, and he doesn't die, but is laid up in his bed. If the man arises and walks around on his stick, he that struck him will be clear. He will only pay for his loss of time, and for his healing. If a man strikes his slave or his slave-girl, with a wand, and the party dies under his hands, he will be surely punished. But if the servant continues to live a day or two, don't let the master be punished, for he is his property."

"If two men fight and strike a woman with child, and her child is born deformed, he will be forced to pay a penalty that the woman's husband may lay on him, he will pay with a valuation. But if it is perfectly formed, he will give life for life, eye for eye, tooth for tooth, hand for hand, foot for foot, burning for burning, wound for wound, stripe for stripe."

"If one hits the eye of his slave, or the eye of his slave-girl, and put it out, he will let them go free for their eye's sake. If he should strike out the tooth of his slave, or the tooth of his slave-girl, he will send them away free for their tooth's sake."

"If a bull gores a man or woman and he or she dies, the bull will be stoned with stones, and his flesh will not be eaten, but the owner of the bull will be innocent. If the bull should have been given to goring in former time, and men should have told his owner, and he has not removed him, but he should have slain a man or woman, the bull will be stoned, and his owner will die also. If a ransom should be imposed on him, he will pay for the ransom of his mind as much as they will lay on him. If the bull gores a son or daughter, let them do to him according to this ordinance. If the bull gores a slave or slave-girl, he will pay to their master thirty silver shekels,[1] and the bull will be stoned. If anyone opens a pit or digs a cavity in stone, and does not cover it, and an ox or a donkey falls in there, the owner of the pit will make compensation. He will give silver to their owner, and the dead will be his own."

"If any man's bull gore the bull of his neighbor, and it dies, they will sell the living bull and divide the silver, and they will divide the dead bull. But if the bull is known to have been given to goring in time past, and they have testified to his owner, and he has not removed him, he will repay bull for bull, but the dead will be his own."

Exodus: Chapter 21 Note

1 Codex Vaticanus: argyriou triaconta didrachma (ΑΡΓΥΡΙΟΥ ΤΡΙΑΚΟΝΤΑ ΔΙΔΡΑΧΜΑ). Translation: silver coins thirty two-drachmas

• Leningrad Codex: kesef | sheloshim shekalim (כֶּסֶף ׀ שְׁלֹשִׁים שְׁקָלִים). Translation: silver. Thirty shekels

• Peshitta: kspå (ܟܣܦܐ). Translation: silver

• Targum Onkelos: kesef sheloshim shekalim (כְּסַף תְּלָתִין סִלְעִין). Translation: silver thirty rocks (or stones)

• Targum Jerusalem: kesef sheloshim shekalim (כְּסַף תְּלָתִין סִלְעִין). Translation: silver thirty rocks (or stones)

The shekel was a unit of weight used throughout the Middle East for thousands of years, weighing approximately 8.6 grams of silver. The Greek drachma was a coin weighing approximately half a shekel, and therefore under Greek rule of the Middle East a two-drachma coin was used. As the Greeks clearly translated shekel into didrachma, the term shekel is restored in this translation.

Exodus: Chapter 22

"If someone steals a calf or a sheep, and kills it or sells it, he will repay five calves for the calf, and four sheep for the sheep. If the thief is found breaking in by himself and is struck and dies, there will not be blood shed for him. But if the sun rises on him, he is guilty, he will die, and if he has nothing, let him be sold in compensation for what he has stolen. If the thing stolen is left and is in his hand alive, whether ox or sheep, he will repay them twice as much.

If anyone should feed down a field or a vineyard, and should send his animal to feed down another field, he will make compensation of his own field according to his produce, and if he will have fed down the whole field, he will pay for compensation the best of his own field and the best of his vineyard."

"If a fire has spread and caught thorns, and should also set on fire threshing-floors or ears of grain or a field, he that started the fire will make compensation."

"If anyone loans to his neighbor silver or goods to keep, and they are stolen out of the man's house, and the thief is found he will repay double. But if the thief is not be found, the master of the house will come forward before God and will swear that he has not worked deviously against his neighbor's deposit, according to every alleged injury, whether concerning a calf, or a donkey, or a sheep, or a garment, and every alleged loss, whatever it may be. The judgment of both will proceed before God, and he that is convicted by God will repay his neighbor double."

"If anyone loans his neighbor a calf or sheep or any animal to keep, and it is wounded or dies or is taken, and no one knows, an oath of God will be between both, each swearing that he is not at all guilty in the matter of his neighbor's deposit, and so his master will accept him guiltless, and he will not make compensation. If it is stolen from him, he will make compensation to the the Lord. If it was killed by animals, he will take him to see the body, and he will not make compensation."

"If anyone borrows from his neighbor, and it is wounded or dies or is carried away, and it is not returned to the owner, he will make compensation. But if it is returned to the owner, he will not make compensation, but if the borrower is an employee, he will have the ruined animal instead of his employee."

"If anyone deceives a virgin that is not engaged to be married, and lays with her, he will surely take her for a wife. If her father positively refuses, and will not consent to give her to him as a wife, he will pay silver to her father according to the amount of the dowry of virgins."

"You will not save the lives of sorcerers."

"Everyone that lies with an animal you will put to death."

"He that sacrifices to any gods other than to the Lord will be killed."

"You will not hurt a stranger, nor mistreat him, as you were strangers in the land of Egypt."

"You will not hurt a widow or orphan. If you should hurt them through ill-treatment, and they should cry aloud to me, I will surely hear their voice. I will be very angry and will kill you with the sword, and your wives will be widows and your children orphans."

"If you should lend silver to your poor brother, you will not be hard on him you will not demand interest from him. If you take your neighbor's garment for a pledge, you will restore it to him before sunset. For this is his clothing, this is the only covering of his nakedness. In what will he sleep? If then he will cry to me, I will listen to him, for I am merciful."

"You will not hate the gods, nor speak ill of the ruler of your people."

"You will not hold back the first fruits of your threshing floor and press. The firstborn of your sons you will give to me. You will do so with your calf and your sheep and your donkey. Seven days will it be under the mother, and the eighth day you will give it to me."

"You will be holy men for me, and you will not eat the flesh of animals, you will cast it to the dogs."

Exodus: Chapter 23

"You will not receive a false report. You will not agree with the unjust man to become an unjust witness. You will not follow with the multitude into evil. You will not follow a multitude to turn aside with the majority to shut out judgment. You will not spare a poor man in judgment."

"If you find your enemy's ox or his donkey going astray, you will turn them back and return them to him. If you see your enemy's donkey fallen under its burden, you will not pass by it, but will help to raise it with him."

"You will not take away the sentence of the poor in his judgment. You will abstain from every unjust thing. You will not kill the innocent and just, and you will not justify the wicked for gifts. You will not receive gifts, for gifts blind the eyes of the seeing, and corrupt just words."

"You will not punish a stranger, for you know the heart of a stranger, as you were yourselves strangers in the land of Egypt. Six years you will sow your land, and gather in the fruits of it. But in the seventh year, you will let it rest, and leave it, and the poor of your nation will feed, and the wild animals of the field will eat that which remains. You will do this to your vineyard and your oliveyard."

"Six days you will work, and on the seventh day there will be rest, so your ox and your donkey can rest, and that the son of your slave-girl and the stranger may be refreshed."

"Observe all things I have commanded you, and do not mention the names of other gods. They will not be heard out of your mouth."

"Hold a feast for me three times a year. Pay attention to keep the feast of unleavened bread: seven days you will eat unleavened bread, as I ordered you at the season of the month of new grain, for in it you came out of Egypt, and you will not appear before me empty. You will keep the feast of the harvest of first-fruits of your labors, whatever you will have sown in your field, and the feast of completion at the end of the year in the gathering in of your works out of your field. Three times in the year will all your males appear before Lord the god."

"For once I will have thrown out the nations from before you, and will have widened your borders, you will not offer the blood of my incense offering with leaven, neither must the fat of my feast remain until the morning. You will bring the first-offerings of the first fruits of your land into the house of the Lord the god. You will not seethe a lamb in its mother's milk. And, Look, I send my messenger before your face, that he may keep you in the way, that he may bring you into the land which I have prepared for you. Pay attention to yourself and listen to him, and don't disobey him. For he will not give way to you, for my name is on him."

"If you will hear my voice, and if you will do all the things I will order you, and keep my covenant, you will be for me a peculiar people above all nations, for the whole land is mine, and you will be for me a royal priesthood and a holy nation. These words will you speak to the Israelites, 'If you will indeed hear my voice, and do all the things I will tell you, I will be an enemy to your enemies, and an adversary to your adversaries.' For my messenger will go as your leader, and will bring you to the Amorite, and Cypriot, and Perizzite, and Canaanite, and Girgasite, and Mitanni, and Jebusite, and I will destroy them. You will not worship their gods, nor serve them. You will not do according to their works, but will utterly destroy them, and break to pieces their pillars. You will serve Lord the god, and I will bless your bread and your wine and your water, and I will turn away sickness from you."

"There will be no one on your land that is impotent or barren. I will surely fulfill the number of your days. I will send terror before you, and I will strike with amazement all the nations to which you will come, and I will make all your enemies flee. I will send hornets before you, and you will drive out the Amorites and the Mitannian, and the Canaanites and the Cypriots from you."

"I will not throw them out in one year, or the land may become desolate, and the animals of the field may multiply against you. Little by little I will drive them out from before you until you will be increased and inherit the land. I will set your borders from the Papyrus Sea to the sea of the Pelesets, and from the wilderness to the great river Euphrates, and I will give into your hand those that live in the land and will drive them out from you. You will make no covenant with them and their gods. They will not dwell in your land, in case they cause you to sin against me, and for if you should serve their gods, these will be an offense to you."

Exodus: Chapter 24

To Moses was said, "Go up to the Lord, you and Aaron, and Nadab, and Abihu, and seventy of the elders of Israel, and they will worship the Lord from a distance. Moses alone will draw near to God, and they will not draw near, and the people will not come up with them.

Moses went in and related to the people all the words of God and the ordinances, and all the people answered with one voice, saying, "All the words which the Lord has spoken, we will do and listen."

Moses wrote all the words of the Lord, and Moses rose up early in the morning, and built an altar under the mountain, and set up twelve stones for the twelve tribes of Israel. He sent out the young men of the Israelites, and they offered whole burnt offerings, and they sacrificed young calves as a peace-offering to the gods. Moses took half the blood and poured it into bowls, and half the blood he poured out on the altar. He took the book of the covenant and read it in the ears of the people, and they said, "All things whatever the Lord has spoken we will do and listen therein."

Moses took the blood and sprinkled it on the people, and said, "Look the blood of the covenant, which the Lord has made with you concerning all these words."

Moses went up, and Aaron, and Nadab and Abihu, and seventy of the elders of Israel. They saw the place where the god of Israel stood, and under his feet was as it were a work of sapphire slabs, and as it were the appearance of the firmament of the sky in its purity. Of the chosen ones of Israel, there was not even one missing, and they appeared where God was and did eat and drink. the Lord said to Moses, "Come up to me into the mountain, and I will give you the tablets of stone, the law, and the commandments, which I have written to give them laws."

Moses rose up with Joshua his attendant, and they went up into the mount of God. To the elders, they said, "Rest there until we return to you, and look, Aaron and Hur are with you. If any man has a cause to be tried, let them go to them."

Moses and Joshua went up to the mountain, and the cloud covered the mountain. The glory of God came down on Mount Sinai, and the cloud covered it six days, and the Lord called Moses on the seventh day out of the cloud. The appearance of the glory of the Lord was as burning fire on the top of the mountain before the Israelites. Moses went into the middle of the cloud, and went up to the mountain, and was there in the mountain forty days and forty nights.

Exodus: Chapter 25

The Lord said to Moses, "Speak to the Israelites, and take first fruits of all, who may be disposed in their heart to give, and you will take my first fruits. This is the offering which you will take of them, and gold and silver and brass, and blue, and purple, and double scarlet, and finespun linen, and goats' hair, and rams' skins dyed red, and blue skins, and incorruptible wood, and oil for the light, incense for anointing oil, and for the composition of incense, and carnelian stones, and stones for the carved work of the shoulder-piece, and the full-length robe."

"You will make a sanctuary for me, and I will appear among you. You will make for me according to all things which I show you in the mountain, even the pattern of the tabernacle, and the pattern of all its furniture: so will you make it. You will make the box of the testimony of incorruptible wood; the length of two cubits and a half, and the width of a cubit and a half, and the height of a cubit and a half. You will gild it with pure gold, you will gild it within and without, and you will make for it golden wreaths twisted around it."

"You will cast four golden rings for it and will put them on the four sides, two rings on the one side, and two rings on the other side. You will make staffs of incorruptible wood and will coat them with gold. You will put the staffs into the rings on the sides of the box, to bear the box with them. The staffs will remain fixed in the rings of the box."

"You will put into the box the testimonies which I will give you." You will make a lid, a lid of pure gold. The length of two cubits and a half, and the width of a cubit and a half. You will make two sphinxes[1] graven in gold, and you will put them on both sides of the lid. They will be made, one cherub on this side, and another cherub on the other side of the lid, and you will make the two sphinxes on the two sides. The sphinxes will stretch out their wings above, overshadowing the lid with their wings, and their faces will be towards each other, the faces of the sphinxes will be towards the lid. You will set the lid on the top of the box, and you will put into the box the testimonies which I will give you."

"I will make myself known to you from there, and I will speak to you from above the lid, between the two sphinxes, which are on the box of the testimony. In all things which I order you concerning the Israelites."

"You will make a table of pure gold, two cubits in length, and a cubit in width, and a cubit and a half in height. You will make for it golden wreaths twisted around about, and you will make for it a crown of a hand-width around it. You will make a twisted wreath for the crown around about. You will make four golden rings, and you will put the four rings on the four parts of its feet under the crown. The rings will be for bearings for the staffs, that they may bear the table with them. You will make the staffs of incorruptible wood, and you will gild them with pure gold, and the table will be borne with them."

"You will make its dishes and its censers, and its bowls, and its cups, with which you will offer drink-offerings. You will make them of pure gold. You will place show-bread on the table before me continually. You will make a candlestick of pure gold, you will engrave the candlestick: its stem and its branches, and its bowls and its knobs and its lilies will be of it. Six branches proceeding sideways, three branches of the candlestick from one side of it, and three branches of the candlestick from the other side."

"Three bowls fashioned like almonds, on each branch a knob and a lily; so to the six branches proceeding from the candlestick, and in the candlestick four bowls fashioned like almonds, in each branch knobs and the flowers of it. A knob under two branches out of it, and a knob under four branches out of it. So to the six branches proceeding from the candlestick, and in the candlestick four bowls fashioned like almonds. Let the knobs and the branches be of one piece, altogether graven of one piece of pure gold. You will make its seven lamps: and you will set on it the lamps, and they will shine from one front. You will make its funnel and its snuff-dishes of pure gold. All these articles will be a talent of pure gold. See, you will make them according to the pattern shown you in the mount."

Exodus: Chapter 25 Notes

1 Codex Vaticanus: cheroubim (ΧΕΡΟΥΒΙΜ)

- Leningrad Codex: keruvim (כְּרֻבִים). Translation: cherubs (or griffins, sphinxes)

- Peshitta: krůbå (ܟ̈ܪܘܒܐ). Translation: cherubs (or griffins, sphinxes)

- Targum Onkelos: keruvin (כְּרוּבִין). Translation: cherubs (or griffins, sphinxes)

- Targum Jerusalem: keruvin (כְּרוּבִין). Translation: cherubs (or griffins, sphinxes)

The word 'cherub' (ܟܪܘܒܐ / כרוב / 𐤊𐤓𐤁 / 𐩫𐩧𐩨) was the West Semitic term for the mythical creature generally called a 'griffin' today. Based in the archaeological record of Canaan, it appears that the concept of the cherub was based on the Egyptian sphinx, as the earliest cherub statues found in Canaan were Egyptian statues of sphinxes.

Archaeologists are not sure if the griffins of Anatolia were based on the Canaanite cherub, or the Egyptian sphinxes directly, however, all three mythical beings are closely related in the archaeological record. The term cherub was for some reason reinterpreted as 'baby angels' by Christians, although in the Books of the Kingdoms God was described as riding on cherubs, and it is not clear why any god would ride around on 'baby angels,' and therefore the alternate translation of 'sphinxes' is used.

Exodus: Chapter 26

"You will make the tabernacle, ten curtains of finely spun linen, and blue and purple, and spun scarlet with sphinxes. You will make them with the work of a weaver. One curtain will be forty-eight cubits long, and one curtain will be four cubits wide. There will be the same measurement for all the curtains. The five curtains will be joined one to another, and the other five curtains will be closely connected to one another. You will make for them loops of blue on the edge of one curtain, on one side for the coupling, and so will you make on the edge of the outer curtain for the second coupling. Fifty loops will you make for one curtain, and fifty loops will you make on the part of the curtain answering to the coupling of the second, opposite each other, corresponding to each other at each point. You will make fifty golden rings, and you will join the curtains to each other with the rings, and it will be one tabernacle."

"You will make for a covering of the tabernacle from skins with the hair still on. You will make them from eleven skins. The length of one skin thirty cubits, and the width of one skin four cubits: there will be the same measure to the eleven skins. You will join the five skins together, and the six skins together, and you will double the sixth skin in front of the tabernacle. You will make fifty loops on the border of one skin, which is in the middle for the joints, and you will make fifty loops on the edge of the second skin that joins it. You will make fifty bronze rings, and you will join the rings by the loops, and you will join the skins, and they will be one."

"The end of the skins of the tabernacle you will fix so the half of the skin that is left you will fold over, and the extra skins of the tabernacle you will fold it over behind the tabernacle. A cubit on this side, and a cubit on that side of that which remains of the skins, of the length of the skins of the tabernacle. It will fold over the sides of the tabernacle on this side and that side, and so may cover it. You will make for a covering of the tabernacle rams' skins dyed red, and blue skins as coverings above. You will make the posts of the tabernacle of incorruptible wood. Of ten cubits will you make one post, and the width of one post of a cubit and a half. Two joints will you make in one post, answering the one to the other: so will you do to all the posts of the tabernacle. You will make posts to the tabernacle, twenty posts on the north side. You will make for the twenty posts forty silver sockets. Two sockets on each post on both its sides, and two sockets on the other post for both its sides. For the next side, towards the south, twenty posts, and their forty silver sockets. Two sockets for one post on each of its sides, and two sockets for the other post on each of its sides. On the back of the tabernacle at the part which is towards the west, you will make six posts. You will make two posts on the corners of the tabernacle behind. It will be equal below, they will be equal towards the same part from the heads to one joining, so will you make to both the two corners, let them be equal."

"There will be eight posts and their sixteen silver sockets. Two sockets to one post on both its sides and two sockets to the other post. You will make bars of incorruptible wood; five to one post on one side of the tabernacle, and five bars to one post on the second side of the tabernacle, and five bars to the hinder posts, on the side of the tabernacle towards the sea."

"Place the bar in the middle, between the posts, going through from the one side to the other side. You will gild the posts with gold, and you will make golden rings, into which you will introduce the bars, and you will gild the bars with gold. You will set up the tabernacle according to the pattern shown you in the mount. You will make a veil of blue and purple and scarlet woven, and fine linen spun: you will make it sphinxes in woven work. You will set it on four posts of incorruptible wood coated with gold, and their tops will be gold, and their four sockets will be of silver."

"You will put the veil on the posts, and you will carry within the veil, the box of the testimony, and the veil will make a separation for you between the holy and the holy of holies. You will screen with the veil the box of the testimony in the holy of holies. You will set the table outside the veil, and the candlestick opposite the table on the south side of the tabernacle, and you will put the table on the north side of the tabernacle. You will make a screen for the door of the tabernacle of blue, and purple, and spun scarlet and fine linen spun, the work of the embroiderer. You will make for the veil five posts, and you will gild them with gold, and their chapiters will be gold, and you will cast for them five bronze sockets.

Exodus: Chapter 27

"You will make an altar from incorruptible wood, five cubits in the length, and five cubits in the width. The altar will be square, and the height of it will be three cubits. You will make the horns on the four corners; the horns will be of it, and you will overlay them with brass. You will make a rim for the altar, and its covering and its cups, and its meat hooks, and its fire-pan, and all its vessels will you make of brass."

"You will make for it a bronze grate with netting, and you will make for the grate four bronze rings under the four sides. You will put them below under the grate of the altar, and the grate will extend to the middle of the altar."

"You will make for the altar staffs from incorruptible wood, and you will cover them with brass. You will put the staffs into the rings, and let the staffs be on the sides of the altar to carry it. You will make it hollow with boards: according to what was shown you in the mount, so you will make it. You will make a court for the tabernacle, curtains of the court of fine linen spun on the south side, the length of a hundred cubits for one side."

"The twenty pillars and twenty bronze sockets from them, and their rings and their silver clasps. So there will be on the side towards the north curtains of a hundred cubits in length, and their pillars twenty, and their sockets twenty of brass, and the rings and the clasps of the pillars, and their sockets coated with silver. In the width of the tabernacle towards the west curtains of fifty cubits, their pillars ten and their sockets ten. In the width of the tabernacle towards the south, curtains of fifty cubits; their pillars ten, and their sockets ten. The height of the curtains will be fifty cubits for the one side of the gate, with three pillars, and three sockets. For the second side the height of the curtains will be of fifteen cubits, and their pillars three, and their sockets three. A veil for the door of the court, the height of it of twenty cubits of blue linen, and purple, and spun scarlet, and of fine linen spun with the are of the embroiderer; their pillars four, and their sockets four. All the pillars of the court round about coated with silver, and their chapiters silver and their brass sockets."

"The length of the court will be a hundred cubits on each side and the width fifty on each side, and the height five cubits of fine linen spun, and their sockets of brass. All the furniture and all the instruments and the pins of the court will be of brass. Do you order the Israelites, and let them take for you refined pure olive oil beaten to burn for light, that a lamp may burn continually in the tabernacle of the testimony, outside the veil that is over the box of the covenant, will Aaron and his sons burn it from evening until morning, before the Lord, and it is a perpetual ordinance to your generations of the Israelites."

Exodus: Chapter 28

"Take with yourself both Aaron your brother, and his sons, them of the Israelites. So that Aaron, and Nadab and Abihu, and Eleazar and Ithamar, sons of Aaron, may minister to me. You will make holy apparel for Aaron your brother, for honor and glory. Speak to all those who are wise in understanding, whom I have filled with the breath of wisdom and perception,[1] and they will make the holy apparel of Aaron for the sanctuary, in which apparel he will minister to me as a priest. These are the garments which they will make: the breastplate, and the shoulder-piece, and the full-length robe, and the tunic with a fringe, and the brimmed hat, and the girdle, and they will make holy garments for Aaron and his sons to minister to me as priests."

They will take the gold, and the blue, and the purple, and the scarlet, and the fine linen. They will make the shoulder-piece of fine linen spun, the woven work of the embroiderer. The work will have two shoulder-pieces joined together, fastened on the two sides. The woven work of the shoulder-pieces which is on it will be of one piece according to the work, of pure gold and blue and purple, and spun scarlet and fine twined linen. You will take the two stones, the stones of emerald, and you will engrave on them the names of the Israelites. Six names on the first stone, and the other six names on the second stone, according to their births."

"It will be the work of the stone-engravers, as will engraving a seal on the two stones with the names of the Israelites. You will put the two stones on the shoulders of the shoulder-piece: they are memorial stones for the Israelites: and Aaron will bear the names of the Israelites before the Lord on his two shoulders, a memorial for them. You will make little shields of pure gold, and you will make two fringes of pure gold, decorated with wreathed flowers. You will put the wreathed fringes on the circlets, fastening them on their shoulder-pieces in the front."

"You will make the oracle of judgment, the work of the embroiderer: in keeping with the vest, you will make it of gold, and blue and purple, and spun scarlet, and fine spun linen. You will make it square: it will be double; of a span the length of it, and a span the width. You will interweave with it a texture of four rows of stone; there will be a row of stones, a carnelian, a topaz, and emerald, the first row. The second row, a carbuncle, a sapphire, and a jasper. The third row, a lapis lazuli, an agate, an amethyst: and the fourth row, a chrysolite, and a beryl, and an onyx stone, set round with gold, bound together with gold, and let them be in each row."

"Let there be twelve stones with the names of the Israelites engraved as seals: let them be for the twelve tribes each according to the name. You will make on the oracle woven fringes, a chain-work of pure gold. Aaron will take the names of the Israelites, on the oracle of judgment on his breast; a memorial before God for him as he goes into the sanctuary. You will put the fringes on the oracle of judgment, and you will put the wreaths on both sides of the oracle, and you will put the two circlets on both the shoulders of the vest in front. You will put the lights and perfections on the oracle of judgment, and it will be on the breast of Aaron when he goes into the holy place before the Lord, and Aaron will bear the judgments of the Israelites on his breast before the Lord continually."

"You will make the full-length tunic entirely of blue. The opening of it will be in the middle having a fringe round about the opening, the work of the weaver, woven together in the joining of the same piece that it might not be tore. Under the fringe of the robe below, you will make as it were pomegranates of a flowering pomegranate tree, of blue, and purple, and spun scarlet, and fine linen spun, under the fringe of the robe round about: golden pomegranates of the same shape, and bells around about between these. A bell by the side of a golden pomegranate, and flower-work on the fringe of the robe around it."

"Aaron will speak when he administers, when he goes into the sanctuary before the Lord and as he goes out, so he doesn't die. You will make a plate of pure gold, and you will engrave on it as the graving of a signet, Holiness of the Lord. You will put it on the spun blue cloth, and it will be on the miter: it will be in the front of the miter. It will be on the forehead of Aaron, and Aaron will bear away the sins of their holy things, all that the Israelites will sanctify of every gift of their holy things, and it will be on the forehead of Aaron continually acceptable for them before the Lord."

"The fringes of the garments will be of fine linen, and you will make a turban of fine linen, and you will make a girdle, the work of the embroiderer. For the sons of Aaron, you will make tunics and girdles, and you will make for them brimmed hats for honor and glory. You will put them on Aaron your brother, and his sons with him, and you will anoint them and consecrate them: and you will sanctify them, that they may minister to me in the priest's office. You will make for them linen drawers to cover the nakedness of their flesh; they will reach from the loins to the thighs. Aaron will have them, and his sons, whenever they enter into the tabernacle of witness, or when they will advance to the altar of the sanctuary to minister, so they will not bring sin on themselves, in case they die. It is a perpetual statute for him, and for his seed after him."

Exodus: Chapter 28 Notes

1 Codex Vaticanus: pneumatos aesthêseôs cae poeêsousin (ΠΝΕΥΜΑΤΟC ΑΙCΘΗCΕΩC ΚΑΙ ΠΟΙΗCΟΥCΙΝ). Translation: air (or wind, breath, life, spirit) of discernment (or perception, senses)

• Leningrad Codex: ruach chochmah (רוּחַ חָכְמָה). Translation: wind (or air, atmosphere, direction, spirit, mind, demon) wisdom (or counsel, knowledge)

• Peshitta: rûhå dḥkmtå (ܪܘܚܐ ܕܚܟܡܬܐ). Translation: spirit (or specter, breath, wind, smell, pain) of wisdom (or science, philosophy, judgment, expertness

• Targum Onkelos: ruach chachemeta (רוּחַ חָכְמְתָא). Translation: wind (or air, direction, spirit, mind) wisdom (or counsel, knowledge)

• Targum Jerusalem: rucha dechachemeta (רוּחָא דְחָכְמְתָא). Translation: wind (or air, direction, spirit, mind) wisdom (or counsel, knowledge)

Exodus: Chapter 29

"These are the things which you will do with them. You will sanctify them so that they will serve me in the priesthood, and you will take one young calf from the herd, and two unblemished rams, and unleavened loaves kneaded with oil, and unleavened cakes anointed with oil. You will make them of fine flour of wheat. You will put them in one basket, and you will offer them on the basket, and the young calf and the two rams. You will bring Aaron and his sons to the doors of the tabernacle of the testimony, and you will wash them with water. Having taken the garments, you will put on Aaron your brother both the full-length robe and the vest and the oracle, and you will join for him the oracle to the vest."

"You will put the miter on his head, and you will put the plate, the Holiness, on the miter. You will take from the anointing oil, and you will pour it on his head and anoint him, and you will bring his sons, and put garments on them. You will gird them with the girdles, and put the brimmed hats on them, and they will have a priestly office to me forever, and you will make perfect the hands of Aaron and the hands of his sons."

"You will bring the calf to the door of the tabernacle of witness, and Aaron and his sons will lay their hands on the head of the calf, before the Lord, by the doors of the tabernacle of witness. You will kill the calf before the Lord, by the doors of the tabernacle of witness. You will take of the blood of the calf, and put it on the horns of the altar with your finger, but all the rest of the blood you will pour out at the foot of the altar. You will take all the fat that is on the belly, and the lobe of the liver, and the two kidneys, and the fat that is on them and will put them on the altar. But the flesh of the calf, and his skin, and his dung will you burn with fire outside of the camp; for it is an offering on account of sin."

"You will take one ram, and Aaron and his sons will lay their hands on the head of the ram. You will kill it, and take the blood and pour it on the altar and around it. You will divide the ram by his several limbs, and you will wash the inward parts and the feet with water, and you will put them on the divided parts with the head. You will offer the whole ram on the altar, a whole burnt offering to the Lord for a sweet-smelling savor. It is an offering of incense to the Lord."

"You will take the second ram, and Aaron and his sons will lay their hands on the head of the ram. You will kill it, and take of the blood of it, and put it on the tip of Aaron's right ear, and on the thumb of his right hand, and on the big toe of his right foot, and on the tips of the right ears of his sons, and on the thumbs of their right hands, and on the big toes of their right feet. You will take of the blood from the altar, and of the anointing oil, and you will sprinkle it on Aaron and his garments, and his sons and on his sons' garments with him, and he will be sanctified and his apparel, and his sons and his sons' apparel with him: but the blood of the ram you will pour round about on the altar. You will take from the ram its fat, both the fat that covers the belly, and the lobe of the liver, and the two kidneys, and the fat that is on them, and the right shoulder, for this is an accomplishment."

"One cake made with oil, and one cake from the basket of unleavened bread set out before the Lord. You will place them all in the hands of Aaron, and the hands of his sons, and you will separate them for a separation before the Lord. You will take them from their hands, and will offer them up on the altar of whole burnt offering for a sweet-smelling savor before the Lord, and it is an offering to the Lord. You will take the breast from the ram of consecration which is Aaron's, and you will separate it as a separate offering before the Lord, and it will be to you for a portion. You will sanctify the separated breast and the shoulder of removal which has been separated, and which has been removed from the ram of consecration, of the portion of Aaron and of that of his sons."

"It will be a perpetual statute of the Israelites to Aaron and his sons, for this is a separate offering, and it will be a special offering from the Israelites, from the peace-offerings of the Israelites, a special offering to the Lord. The apparel of the sanctuary which is Aaron's will be his son's after him, for them to be anointed in them, and to fill their hands. The priest his successor from among his sons who will go into the tabernacle of witness to minister in the holies will put them on seven days. You will take the ram of consecration, and you will boil the flesh in the holy place. Aaron and his sons will eat the flesh of the ram, and the loaves in the basket, by the doors of the tabernacle of witness. They will eat the offerings with which they were sanctified to fill their hands, to sanctify them, and a stranger will not eat of them, for they are holy. If anything is left of the flesh of the sacrifice of consecration and the loaves until the morning, you will burn the remainder with fire. It will not be eaten, for it is a holy thing.

So you will do for Aaron and his sons according to all things that I have commanded you. Seven days will you fill their hands. You will sacrifice the calf of the sin-offering on the day of purification, and you will purify the altar when you do sanctify it, and you will anoint it to sanctify it. Seven days will you purify the altar and sanctify it, and the altar will be most holy, everyone that touches the altar will be hallowed. These are the offerings that you will offer on the altar: two unblemished lambs of a year old daily on the altar continually, a constant offering. One lamb you will offer in the morning, and the second lamb you will offer in the evening.

The tenth measure of fine flour mingled with the fourth part of a hin[1] of beaten oil, and a drink-offering the fourth part of a hin of wine for one lamb. You will offer the second lamb in the evening, the same way as the morning-offering, and according to the drink-offering of the morning lamb. You will offer it an offering to the Lord for a sweet-smelling savor, a perpetual sacrifice to your generations, at the door of the tabernacle of witness before the Lord, and in which I will be known to you from there, to speak to you.

I will there give orders to the Israelites, and I will be sanctified in my glory. I will sanctify the tabernacle of the testimony and the altar, and I will sanctify Aaron and his sons, to minister as priests to me. I will be named among the Israelites and will be their God. They will know that I am the Lord their God, who brought them forth out of the land of Egypt, to be named by them, and to be their God.

Exodus: Chapter 29 Notes

1 Codex Vaticanus: in (ιN)

- Leningrad Codex: hin (הִין)

- Peshitta: hmynå (ܗܡܝܢܐ). Translation: belt

- Targum Onkelos: hina (הִינָא)

- Targum Jerusalem: hina (הִינָא)

The hin was ancient Samaritan and Judahite unit of measurement estimated around 3.7 liters (3.9 quarts).

Exodus: Chapter 30

You will make the altar of incense of incorruptible wood. You will make it a cubit in length, and a cubit wide: it will be square, and the height of it will be of two cubits, and its horns will be part of it. You will gild its grate with pure gold, and its sides around it, and its horns, and you will make for it a wreathed border of gold around it. You will make under its wreathed border two rings of pure gold. You will make it to the two corners on the two sides, and they will be bearings for the staffs, to bear it with them. You will make the staffs of incorruptible wood and will gild them with gold. You will set it before the veil that is over the box of the testimonies, in which I will make myself known to you from there."

"Aaron will burn on it fine compound incense every morning. Whenever he trims the lamps he will burn incense on it. When Aaron lights the lamps in the evening, he will burn incense on it; a constant incense-offering always before the Lord for their generations. You will not offer strange incense on it, nor an offering made by fire, nor a sacrifice, and you will not pour a drink-offering on it. Once in the year Aaron, will make atonement on its horns, he will purge it with the blood of purification for their generations. This is most holy to the Lord."

The Lord said to Moses, "If you take account of the Israelites in the surveying of them, and they will give everyone a ransom for his mind to the Lord, then there will not be among them a fall in the visiting of them. This is what they will give, as many as pass the survey, half a coin which is according to the coin of the sanctuary. Twenty gerahs[1] go into the shekel, but a half shekel is the offering to the Lord. Everyone that passes the survey from twenty years old and upwards will give the offering to the Lord. The rich will not give more, and the poor will not give less than the half shekel in giving the offering to the Lord, to make atonement for your minds. You will take the silver of the offering from the Israelites, and will give it for the service of the tabernacle of the testimony, and it will be to the Israelites a memorial before the Lord, to make atonement for your minds."

The Lord said to Moses, "Make a bronze layer, and a bronze base for it, to wash one's self, and you will put it between the tabernacle of witness and the altar, and you will pour forth water into it. Aaron and his sons will wash their hands and their feet with water from it. Whenever they will go into the tabernacle of witness, they will wash with water, so they will not die, whenever they advance to the altar to do service and to offer the whole burnt offerings to the Lord. They will wash their hands and feet with water, whenever they will go into the tabernacle of witness. They will wash with water, that they don't die, and it will be for them a perpetual statute, for him and his generations after him."

The Lord said to Moses, "Also take sweet plants, the flower of choice myrrh five hundred shekels, and the half of this two hundred and fifty shekels of sweet-smelling cinnamon, and two hundred and fifty shekels of sweet-smelling calamus and of iris, five hundred shekels to the sanctuary, and a hin of olive oil. You will make it a holy anointing oil, a perfumed ointment tempered by the skill of the perfumer: it will be a holy anointing oil. You will anoint with it the tabernacle of witness, and the box of the tabernacle of witness, and all its furniture, and the candlestick and all its furniture, and the altar of incense, and the altar of whole burnt offerings and all its furniture, and the table and all its furniture, and the layer. You will sanctify them, and they will be most holy. Everyone that touches them will be hallowed. You will anoint Aaron and his sons, and sanctify them that they may minister to me as priests. You will speak to the Israelites, saying, This will be to you a holy anointing oil throughout your generations. It will not be poured on man's flesh, and you will not make any for yourselves according to this composition: it is holy, and will be holiness to you. Whoever will make it in like manner, and whoever will give of it to a stranger, will be destroyed from among his people."

The Lord said to Moses, "Take for yourself sweet plants, stacte, onycha, sweet galbanum, and transparent frankincense. There will be an equal to equal. They will make with it perfumed incense, tempered with the are of a perfumer, a pure holy work. Of these, you will beat some small, and you will put it before the testimonies in the tabernacle of the testimony, from where I will make myself known to you, and it will be for you the holiest incense. You will not make any for yourselves according to this composition, and it will be to you a holy thing for the Lord. Whoever will make any in like manner, to smell in it, will perish from his people."

Exodus: Chapter 30 Notes

1 Codex Vaticanus: oboloe (ΟΒΟΛΟΙ). Translation: obols

• Leningrad Codex: gerah (גֵּרָה). Translation: gerah

- Peshitta: zŭzyn (ܙܘܙܝܢ). Translation: zuzes

- Targum Onkelos: ma'in (מָעִין). Translations: m'ahs

- Targum Jerusalem: ma'in (מָעִין). Translations: m'ahs

The obol was a Greek coin used from around 1100 BC, worth ⅙ of a drachma, approximately 0.72 grams of silver. The gerah was a measurement equaling one twentieth of a shekel. The zuz mentioned in the Peshitta was a coin used in the middle east from the era of the Old Akkadian empire until th Greco-Roman era, however, was valued at ½ a shekel. The mah mentioned in the Targum was the Phoenician coin equivalent to the obol, suggesting it is the term in the Aramaic text that the Greeks translated. As the Greek obol is not one twentieth of a shekel, the name gerah is imported from the Masoretic text.

Exodus: Chapter 31

The Lord said to Moses, "I have called by name Bezaleel the son of Uri the son of Hur, of the tribe of Judah. I have filled him with a divine spirit of wisdom, and understanding, and knowledge, to invent in every work, and as to the frame work, to labor in gold, and silver, and brass, and blue, and purple, and spun scarlet, and works in stone, and for artificers' work in wood, to work at all works."

"I have given him and Eliab the son of Achisamach of the tribe of Dan, and to everyone understanding in heart I have given understanding, and they will work in all things as many as I have appointed you, the tabernacle of witness, and the box of the covenant and the lid that is on it, and the furniture of the tabernacle, and the altars, and the table and all its furniture, and the pure candlestick and all its furniture, and the layer and its base, and Aaron's robes of ministry, and the robes of his sons to minister to me as priests, and the anointing oil and the compound incense of the sanctuary, according to all that I have commanded you will they make them."

The Lord said to Moses, "Do you also order the Israelites, saying, pay attention and keep my sabbaths, as they are a sign for me and among you throughout your generations, that you may know that I am the Lord who sanctifies you. You will keep the sabbaths because this is holy to the Lord for you, he that profanes it will surely be put to death. Everyone who will do work on it, that mind will be destroyed from among his people. Six days you will do works, but the seventh day is the sabbath, a holy rest to the Lord, and everyone who will do work on the seventh day will be put to death. The Israelites will keep the sabbaths, to observe them throughout their generations. It is a perpetual covenant with me and the Israelites, it is a perpetual sign with me."

For in six days the Lord made the sky and the land, and on the seventh day he stopped and rested. He gave to Moses when he left off speaking to him in Mount Sinai the two tablets of the testimony, tablets of stone written on with the finger of God.

Exodus: Chapter 32

When the people saw that Moses delayed to come down from the mountain, the people combined against Aaron, and said to him, "Rise and make us gods who will lead us. For this Moses, the man who brought us out of the land of Egypt, we do not know what is become of him."

Aaron replied to them, "Take off the golden earrings which are in the ears of your wives and daughters, and bring them to me." All the people took off the golden earrings that were in their ears and brought them to Aaron. He received them at their hands and formed them with a graving tool, and he made them a molten calf, and said, "These are your gods, Israel, which have brought you up out of the land of Egypt." Aaron after seeing it built an altar before it and Aaron made a proclamation saying, tomorrow is a feast of the Lord. Having risen early in the morning, he set on the altar whole burnt offerings and offered a peace-offering, and the people sat down to eat and drink and rose up to play.

The Lord said to Moses, "Go quickly, descend here, for your people whom you brought out of the land of Egypt have transgressed. They have quickly gone out of the way which you commanded. They have made for themselves a calf, and worshiped it, and sacrificed to it, and said, 'These are your gods, Israel, who brought you up out of the land of Egypt.' Now leave me alone, and I will be very angry with them and consume them, and I will make you a great nation."

Moses prayed before Lord the god, "Why, the Lord, are you very angry with your people, whom you brought out of the land of Egypt with great strength, and with your high arm? Be careful or at some point the Egyptians say, "With evil intent, he brought them out to kill them in the mountains, and to consume them from off the land. Stop from your wrathful anger, and be merciful to the sin of your people, remembering Abraham and Isaac and Jacob your servants, to whom you have sworn by yourself, and have spoken to them, saying, 'I will greatly multiply your seed as the stars of the sky for multitude, and all this land which you spoke of to give to them so that they will possess it forever.'"

The Lord was prevailed on to preserve his people. Moses turned and went down from the mountain, and the two tablets of the testimony were in his hands, tablets of stone written on both their sides. They were written within and without. The tablets were the work of God and the writing of God written on the tablets.

Joshua, after hearing the voice of the people crying, said to "Moses, There is a noise of war in the camp."

Moses replied, "It is not the voice of them that begin the battle, nor the voice of them that begin the cry of defeat, but the voice of them that begin the banquet of wine do I hear." When he drew near to the camp, he saw the calf and the dances, and Moses became very angry and threw the two tablets out of his hands, and broke them to pieces at the foot of the mountain. Having taken the calf which they made, he consumed it with fire, and ground it very small, and scattered it on the water, and made the Israelites drink it. Moses said to Aaron, "What have these people done to you, that you have brought on them a great sin?"

Aaron answered Moses, "Do not be angry, my lord, for you know the impulsiveness of this people. For they say to me, 'Make us gods, which will go before us, for as for this man Moses, who brought us out of Egypt, we do not know what is become of him.' I said to them, 'If anyone has golden ornaments, take them off, and they gave them to me,' and I throw them into the fire, and there came out this calf."

When Moses saw that the people were scattered, for Aaron had scattered them to be rejoicing to their enemies, then Moses stood at the gate of the camp, and said, "Who is on the Lord's side? Let him come to me."[1]

Then all the sons of Levi came to him, and he said to them, "The Lord God of Israel says, 'Put everyone his sword on his waist, and go through and return from gate to gate through the camp, and kill everyone his brother, and everyone kill his neighbor, and everyone kill whoever is closest to him.'

The sons of Levi did as Moses spoke to them, and there fell of the people in that day to the number of three thousand men. Moses said to them, "You have filled your hands this day to the Lord, each one against his son or his brother, so that blessing should be given to you."

It happened after the morning had begun that Moses said to the people, "You have sinned a great sin, and now I will go up to God, that I may make atonement for your sin." Moses returned to the Lord and said, "I pray, Lord, these people have sinned a great sin, and they have made for themselves golden gods. Now if you will forgive their sin, forgive it, and if not, blot me out of your book, which you have written."

The Lord said to Moses, "If anyone has sinned against me, I will blot them out of my book. Now go, descend, and lead these people into the place of which I spoke to you. Look, my messenger will go before your face, and in the day when I will visit I will bring on them their sin."

The Lord killed the people for the creation of the calf, which Aaron made.

Exodus: Chapter 32 Notes

1 This battle between the two sides, 'the Lord's side' and Aaron's calf-god's side is often ignored by Jews and Christians, as Aaron's calf-god had to be Yahweh, meaning Moses 'Lord' was not Yahweh. Yahweh has been found depicted as a calf until the time of King Josiah's reforms, which seems to have continued the calf-god motif. Second-Temple-Era descriptions of Yahweh include horns and cloven feet, which along with his abode of fire and brimstone were adopted by the early Christians as depictions of the devil. While Aaron's calf-god shows no signs of his solar-calf descendant, he is clearly the Yahweh calf of Asherah, found on a pithos sherd found at Kuntillet Ajrud, near Hashem El Tarif dated to circa 800 BC. Moses' subsequent statement that the massacre was for the 'Lord,' confirms that Aaron's calf-god, was not the 'Lord' at that time, yet he was an Elohim by 800 BC, supporting the connection to Yahweh (Iaw/Îôhů).

As Asherah was the goddess of the sky, the calf of Asherah was likely a lunar god, as many Middle Eastern and Mediterranean lunar gods were depicted as being bovine or having horns, which represented the crescent moon. Obvious examples include virtually all depictions of the Greek Selene, Roman Luna, Hurrian Kushuh, and Luwian Arma. Additionally, the earliest statue of Osiris-Îôhů discovered to date, which is accepted as representing the ancient appearance of Îôhů, has prominent horns, and appears to be almost identical to the Southern Egyptian lunar god Khonsu.

Other shards found at Kuntillet Ajrud show the Yahweh was, circa 800 BC, part of the Canaanite pantheon, listing him with Ba'al, El, and Asherah, however, does also refer to him as the Yahweh of Samaria, and the Yahweh of the Teman, supporting the idea that he was worshiped in Samaria, as well as in Teman, which is believed to have been a town near Petra based on references in the books of Jeremiah, Ezekiel, Obadiah, Amos, Habakkuk, and Baruch. Eusebius reported in his Onomasticon that there was a town called Temen 15 miles from Petra, which could have been the original site of Kadesh Barnea as Petra itself had not been built yet. The radical shift of Yahweh from lunar to solar deity must have taken place between 800 and 600 BC, during the reforms and counter-reforms that seem to have been primarily driven by the religious reforms in Assyria.

Exodus: Chapter 33

The Lord said to Moses, "Go forward, you and your people, whom you brought out of the land of Egypt, to the land which I swore to Abraham, Isaac, and Jacob, saying, 'I will give it to your seed. I will send at the same time my messenger before your face, and he will throw out the Amorite and the Cypriot, and the Perizzite and Girgasite, and Mitannian, and Jebusite, and Canaanite. I will bring you into a land flowing with milk and honey. I will not go up with you, in case I consume you along the way because you are a stubborn people.'"

The people had heard this terrible saying, mourned in mourning apparel. For the Lord said to the Israelites, "You are a stubborn people. Pay attention in case I bring on you another plague, and destroy you. Now then take off your glorious apparel, and your ornaments, and I will show you what I will do to you."

So the sons of Israel took off their ornaments and their array from Mount Horeb. Moses took his tabernacle and pitched it outside of the camp, at a distance from the camp, and it was called the tabernacle of the testimony: and it happened that everyone that wanted the Lord went out to the tabernacle which was outside of the camp. Whenever Moses went into the tabernacle outside of the camp, all the people stood everyone watching by the doors of his tent, and when Moses departed, they took notice until he entered into the tabernacle. When Moses entered into the tabernacle, the pillar of the cloud descended and stood at the door of the tabernacle, and God talked to Moses."

"All the people saw the pillar of the cloud standing by the door of the tabernacle, and all the people stood and worshiped everyone at the door of his tent. The Lord spoke to Moses face to face, as one would speak to his friend, and he retired to the camp. But his servant Joshua the son of Nun, a young man, did not leave the tabernacle. Moses said to the Lord, "Look! You told me, 'Lead these people,' but you have not shown me whom you will send with me, but you have said to me, 'I know you above all, and you have favor with me.' If then I have found favor in your sight, reveal yourself to me, that I may evidently see you. That I may find favor in your sight, and that I may know that this great nation is your people."

He replied, "I will go before you, and give you rest."

He said to him, "If you don't go up with us yourself, don't bring me up here. How will it be surely known, that both I and this people have found favor with you unless you go with us? So both I and your people will be glorified beyond all the nations, as many as are on the land."

The Lord said to Moses, "I will also do this thing for you, which you have spoken. You have found grace before me, and I know you above all."

Moses stated, "Manifest yourself to me."

God said, "I will pass by before you with my glory, and I will be called by my name, the Lord, before you, and I will have mercy on whom I will have mercy, and will have pity on whom I will have pity."

God said, "You will not be able to see my face. For no man will see my face and live."

The Lord said, "Look, there is a place by me. You will stand on the rock, and when my glory will pass by, then I will put you into a hole of the rock, and I will cover you over with my hand until I will have passed by. I will remove my hand, and then will you see my back parts, but my face will not appear to you."

Exodus: Chapter 34

The Lord said to Moses, "Carve for yourself two tablets of stone, like the first were, and come up the mountain to me, and I will write on the tablets the words, which were on the first tablets, which you broke. Be ready in the morning, and you will go up Mount Sinai, and stand there before me on the top of the mountain. Let no one go up with you, nor be seen in all the mountain, and don't let the sheep and oxen feed near that mountain."

Moses carved two tablets of stone, as also the first were, and Moses having arisen early, went up to Mount Sinai, as the Lord appointed him, and Moses took the two tablets of stone. The Lord descended in a cloud, and stood near him there, and called the name of the Lord. The Lord passed by before his face, and proclaimed, "The Lord of the gods, pitiful and merciful, restraint and very compassionate, and true, and keeping justice and mercy for thousands, taking away iniquity, and unrighteousness, and sins, and he will not clear the guilty, bringing the iniquity of the fathers on the children, and to the children's children, to the third and fourth generation."

Moses rushed, and bowed to the ground and worshiped and said, "If I have found grace before you, let the Lord go with us. For the people is stubborn, and you will take away our sins and our iniquities, and we will be yours."

The Lord said to Moses, "Look, I establish a covenant with you in the presence of all your people. I will do glorious things, which have not been done in all the land, or any nation. All the people among you will see the works of the Lord, that they are wonderful, which I will do for you."

"Pay attention to all things whatever I command you. Look, I throw out from before you the Amorite and the Canaanite and the Perizzite, and the Cypriot, and Mitanni, and Girgasite and Jebusite. Pay attention to yourself, in case at any time you make a covenant with the residents in the land to which you are entering, in case it becomes for you a stumbling block among you. You will destroy their altars, and break in pieces their pillars, and you will cut down their Asherahs,[1] and the graven images of their gods you will burn with fire. For you will not worship strange gods, for Lord the god, a jealous name, is a jealous God, in case at any time you make a covenant with the residents in the land, and they go whoring after their gods and sacrifice to their gods, and they call you, and you should eat of their feasts, and you should take of their daughters for your sons, and you should give of your daughters to their sons, and your daughters should

467

go a whoring after their gods, and your sons should go a whoring after their gods. You will not make to yourself molten gods."

"You will keep the feast of unleavened bread, seven days will you eat unleavened bread, as I have ordered you, at the season in the month of new grain, for in the month of new grain you came out from Egypt. The males are mine, everything that opens the womb, every firstborn of a calf, and every firstborn of sheep. The firstborn of a donkey you will redeem with a sheep, and if you will not redeem it you will pay a price, every firstborn of your sons will you redeem. You will not appear before me empty."

"Six days you will work, but on the seventh day, you will rest. There will be rest in seed-time and harvest. You will make for me the feast of weeks, the beginning of wheat harvest, and the feast of harvesting in the middle of the year. Three times in the year will every male of you appear before the Lord, the God of Israel. For when I will have driven out the nations before you and will have enlarged your coasts, no one will desire your land, whenever you may go up to appear before Lord the god, three times in the year."

"You will not mix the blood of my incense-offerings with leaven, neither will the sacrifices of the feast of the Passover remain until the morning. The first fruits of your land will you put into the house of Lord the god. You will not boil a lamb in his mother's milk."

The Lord said to Moses, "Write these words for yourself, for on these words I have established a covenant with you and with Israel."

Moses was there before the Lord forty days and forty nights. He did not eat bread, and he did not drink water, and he wrote on the tablets these words of the covenant, the ten sayings. When Moses went down from the mountain, and there were the two tablets in the hands of Moses, as then he went down from the mountain, Moses did not know that the appearance of the skin of his face was glorified, when he spoke to him. Aaron and all the elders of Israel saw Moses, and the appearance of the skin of his face was made glorious, and they feared to approach him.

Moses called them, and Aaron and all the rulers of the community turned towards him, and Moses spoke to them. Afterward, all the Israelites came to him, and he commanded them all things, whatever the Lord had commanded him on Mount Sinai. When he ceased speaking to them, he put a veil on his face. Whenever Moses went in before the Lord to speak to him, he took off the veil until he went out, and he went out and spoke to all the Israelites whatever the Lord commanded him. The Israelites saw the face of Moses, that it was glorified, and Moses put the veil over his face until he went in to speak with him.

Exodus: Chapter 34 Notes

1 Codex Vaticanus: alsê (ⲁⲗⲥⲏ). Translation: grove (or woods, park)

- Leningrad Codex: asherav (אֲשֵׁרָיו). Translation: happiness

- Peshitta: ḥlthûn (ܚܠܬܘܢ). Translation: ossuaries

- Targum Onkelos: ashereihon (אֲשֵׁרֵיהוֹן). Translations: asherahs

- Targum Jerusalem: ashereihon (אֲשֵׁרֵיהוֹן). Translations: asherahs

The Greek translation indicates that the word Åšrh (אשרה) was used in the Aramaic translation. Asherah was the Aramaic and Hebrew name of the Bronze Age Canaanite goddess of fertility, who merged with the Egyptian goddess Hathor (𓉽𓏏) during the New Kingdom Era, and became a sky goddess. In the Bronze Age, she was one of the two wives of El, and known as Åṯrt (𐎀𐎘𐎗𐎚) in the Ugaritic Text. In Akkadian she was a god known as [deity]Asdartú (𒀭𒊍𒁯𒌈),while in Babylonian she was known as [deity]Ištar (𒀭𒈹). She appears to have been worshiped by planting oak trees, like here Middle Kingdom era Egyptian equivalent Iusaaset, who was worshiped by planting acacia trees. Like Asherah, Atum's wife Iusaaset was merged with Hathor during the New Kingdom Era. This reference to the Asherahs being cut down is almost certainly a reference to the oak trees that the ancient Canaanites used to mark important graves.

Exodus: Chapter 35

Moses gathered all the congregation of the Israelites together, and said, "These are the words which the Lord has spoken for you to do. 'Six days will you perform works, but on the seventh day will be rest, a holy sabbath, a rest for the Lord. Everyone that does work on it, let him die. You will not burn a fire in any of your dwellings on the sabbath-day. I am the Lord.'"

Moses spoke to all the congregation of the Israelites, saying, "This is what the Lord has appointed for you, saying, 'Take of yourselves an offering for the Lord, everyone that engages in his heart they will bring the first fruits to the Lord, gold, silver, brass, blue, purple, double spun scarlet, and fine spun linen, goats' hair and rams' skins dyed red, and skins dyed blue, and incorruptible wood, and carnelian stones, and stones for engraving for the vest and full-length robe. Every man that is wise in heart among you, let him come and work all things whatever the Lord has commanded. The tabernacle, and the cords, and the coverings, and the rings, and the bars, and the posts, and the box of the testimony, and its staffs, and its lid, and the veil, and the curtains of the court, and its posts, and the emerald stones, and the incense, and the anointing oil, and the table and all its furniture, and the candlestick for the light and all its furniture, and the altar and all its furniture; and the holy garments of Aaron the priest, and the garments in which they will do service, and the garments of priesthood for the sons of Aaron and the anointing oil, and the compound incense.'"

All the congregation of the Israelites went out from Moses. In whoever's heart prompted them, and to whoever it seemed good in their mind, they brought an offering. They brought an offering to the Lord for all the works of the tabernacle of witness, and all its services, and all the robes of the sanctuary. The men, including everyone to whom it seemed good in his heart, brought from the women seals and earrings, and finger-rings, and chains, and bracelets, every article of gold. All brought ornaments of gold to the Lord, and with whatever fine linen was found, and they brought skins dyed blue, and rams' skins dyed red. Everyone that offered an offering brought silver and brass, the offerings to the Lord, and they with whom was found incorruptible wood, and they brought offerings for all the works of the preparation. Every woman skilled in her heart to spin with her hands, they brought spun articles, the blue, and purple, and scarlet and fine linen. All the women to whom it seemed good in their heart in their wisdom, spun the goats' hair.

The rulers brought the emerald stones, and the stones for setting in the vest, and the oracle, and the compounds both for the anointing oil, and the composition of the incense. Every man and woman whose mind inclined them to come in and do the works, all that Lord appointed them to do through Moses, they, the Israelites brought an offering to the Lord.

Moses said to the Israelites, "Look, God has called by name Bezaleel the son of Uri the son of Hur, of the tribe of Judah, and has filled him with a divine spirit of wisdom and understanding, and knowledge of all things, to labor skillfully in all works of precise workmanship, to form the gold and the silver and the brass, and to work in stone, and to fashion the wood, and to work by every work of wisdom."

God gave improved understanding both to him and to Eliab the son of Achisamach of the tribe of Dan. God filled them with wisdom, understanding, and perception, to understand to work all the works of the sanctuary, and to weave the woven and embroidered work with scarlet and fine linen, to do all work of curious workmanship and embroidery.

Exodus: Chapter 36

Bezaleel worked, and Eliab and every one wise in understanding, to whom was given wisdom and knowledge, to understand to do all the works according to the holy offices, according to all things which the Lord appointed. Moses called Bezaleel and Eliab, and all that had wisdom, to whom God gave knowledge in their heart, and all who were freely willing to come forward to the works, to perform them. They received from Moses all the offerings, which the Israelites brought for all the works of the sanctuary to do them, and they continued to receive the gifts brought, from those who brought them in the morning. There came all the wise men who worked the works of the sanctuary, each according to his work, which they worked. One said to Moses, "The people bring an abundance too great in proportion to all the works which the Lord has appointed them to do."

Moses commanded, and proclaimed in the camp, saying, "Let neither man nor woman any longer labor for the offerings of the sanctuary," and the people were restrained from bringing any more. They had works sufficient for making the furniture, and they left some besides. Every wise one among those that worked made the robes of the holy places, which belong to Aaron the priest, as the Lord commanded Moses. They made the vest of gold, and blue, and purple, and spun scarlet, and fine spun linen. The plates were divided, the threads of gold, to interweave with the blue and purple, and with the spun scarlet, and the fine spun linen, they made it a woven work, shoulder-pieces joined from both sides, a work woven by mutual twisting of the parts into itself. They made it of the same material according to the making of it, of gold, and blue, and purple, and spun scarlet, and fine spun linen, as the Lord commanded Moses, and they made the two emerald stones clasped together and set in gold, graven and cut after the cutting of a seal with the names of the Israelites, and he put them on the shoulder-pieces of the vest, as stones of memorial of the Israelites, as the Lord appointed Moses.

They made the oracle, a work woven with embroidery, according to the work of the vest, of gold, and blue, and purple, and spun scarlet, and fine spun linen. They made the oracle square and double, the length of a span, and the width of a span, double. There was interwoven with it a woven work of four rows of stones, a series of stones, the first row, a carnelian, topaz, and emerald. The second row, a carbuncle, sapphire, and jasper. The third row, lapis lazuli, agate, and amethyst. The fourth row chrysolite, beryl, onyx surrounded with gold, and fastened with gold. The stones were twelve according to the names of the Israelites, graven according to their names for seals, each according to his name for the twelve tribes. They made on the oracle turned wreaths, wreathed work, of pure gold, and they made two golden circlets and two golden rings.

They put the two golden rings on both the upper corners of the oracle, and they put the golden wreaths on the rings on both sides of the oracle, and the two wreaths into the two couplings. They put them on the two circlets, and they put them on the shoulders of the vest opposite each other in front. They made two golden rings and put them on the two projections on the top of the oracle, and on the top of the under part of the vest within. They made two golden rings, and put them on both the shoulders of the vest under it, in front by the coupling above the connection of the vest. He fastened the oracle by the rings that were on it to the rings of the vest, which were fastened with a blue string, joined together with the woven work of the vest; that the oracle should not be loosed from the vest, as the Lord commanded Moses.

They made the tunic under the vest, woven work, all of blue. The opening of the tunic in the middle woven closely together, the opening having a fringe round about, that it might not be tore. They made on the border of the tunic below pomegranates as of a flowering pomegranate tree, of blue, and purple, and spun scarlet, and fine spun linen. They made golden bells, and put the bells on the border of the tunic around it between the pomegranates: a golden bell and a pomegranate on the border of the tunic around it, for the ministration, as the Lord commanded Moses. They made vestments of fine linen, a woven work, for Aaron and his sons, and the brimmed hats of fine linen, and the miter of fine linen and the drawers of fine spun linen, and their girdles of fine linen, and blue, and purple, and scarlet spun, the work of an embroiderer, according as the Lord commanded Moses.

They made the golden plate, a dedicated thing of the sanctuary, of pure gold, and he wrote on it graven letters as of a seal, 'Gift of the Holy.' They gave it a blue border, so that it should be on the miter above, as the Lord commanded Moses.

Exodus: Chapter 37

They made ten curtains for the tabernacle, each one twenty-eight cubits long and four cubits wide. They made the veil of blue, and purple, and spun scarlet, and fine spun linen, the woven work with sphinxes. They put it on four posts of incorruptible wood coated with gold, and their chapiters were gold, and their four sockets were silver. They made the veil of the door of the tabernacle of the testimony from blue, purple, and scarlet finely spun linen, woven work with sphinxes, and their posts five, and the rings, and they gilded their chapiters and their clasps with gold, and they had five sockets of brass.

They made the court towards the south. The curtains of the court of fine spun linen, a hundred cubits on each side, with their twenty posts, and their twenty sockets, and on the north side a hundred each way, and on the south side a hundred each way, with their twenty posts and their twenty sockets. On the west side curtains fifty cubits long, with ten posts and ten sockets. On the east side, curtains fifty cubits long and fifteen cubits high, with three pillars and three sockets. At the second back on this side and on that by the gate of the court, curtains fifteen cubits high, with three pillars and three sockets. All the curtains of the tabernacle of fine spun linen. The sockets of their pillars were brass, and their hooks were silver, and their chapiters were coated with silver, and all the posts of the court were coated with silver. The veil of the gate of the court, the work of an embroiderer, was blue, and purple and spun scarlet, and fine spun linen. Its length was twenty cubits, and its height and the width of five cubits, made the same as the curtains of the court. Their four pillars, and their four sockets were brass, and their hooks were silver, and their chapiters were coated with silver. All the pins of the court around it were brass, and they were coated with silver.

This was the appointment of the tabernacle of witness, accordingly as it was appointed to Moses, so that the public service should belong to the Levites, through Ithamar the son of Aaron the priest. Bezaleel the son of Uri of the tribe of Judah, did as the Lord commanded Moses. Eliab the son of Achisamach of the tribe of Dan was there, who was chief artificer in the woven works and needle-works and embroideries, to weave with the scarlet and fine linen.

Exodus: Chapter 38

Bezaleel made the box and coated it with pure gold both inside and outside, and he cast four golden rings for it, two on the one side, and two on the other, wide enough for the staffs so that men could carry it with them. He made the lid over the box of pure gold, and the two sphinxes of gold, one sphinx on the one end of the lid, and another sphinx on the other end of the lid, overshadowing the lid with their wings. He made the set table of pure gold and cast four rings for it, two on the one side and two on the other side, broad, so that men should lift it with the staffs in them. He made the staffs of the box and the table and gilded them with gold. He made the furniture of the table, both the dishes, and the censers, and the cups, and the bowls with which he would offer drink-offerings, from gold.

He made the candlestick which gives light, of gold, the stem solid, and the branches from both its sides, and blossoms proceeding from its branches, three on this side, and three on the other, made equal to each other. As to their lamps, which are on the ends, knobs like walnuts proceeded from them, and sockets proceeding from them, that the lamps might be on them, and the seventh socket, on the top of the candlestick, on the summit above, entirely of solid gold.

On it the candlestick seven golden lamps, and its snuffers gold, and its snuff-dishes gold. He coated the posts with silver, and cast for the posts golden rings, and gilded the bars with gold, and he gilded the posts of the veil with gold and made the hooks from gold. He made also the rings of the tabernacle from gold, and the rings of the court, and the rings for drawing out the veil above from brass. He cast the silver chapiters of the tabernacle, and the bronze chapiters of the door of the tabernacle, and the gate of the court, and he made silver hooks for the posts, he coated them with silver on the posts. He made the pins of the tabernacle and the pins of the court from brass. He made the bronze altar of the bronze censers, which belonged to the men engaged in sedition with the gathering of Korah. He made all the vessels of the altar and its fire-pan, and its base, and its bowls, and the bronze meat hooks. He made an appendage for the altar of netting under the grate, beneath it as far as the middle of it, and he fastened to it four bronze rings on the four parts of the appendage of the altar, wide enough for the bars, to bear the altar with them. He made the holy anointing oil and the composition of the incense, the pure work of the perfumer. He made the bronze layer, and the bronze base of it of the mirrors of the women that fasted, who fasted by the doors of the tabernacle of witness, in the day in which he set it up. He made the layer, that of it Moses and Aaron and his sons might wash their hands and their feet: when they went into the tabernacle of witness, or whenever they should advance to the altar to do service, they washed, as the Lord commanded Moses.

Exodus: Chapter 39

All the gold that was employed for the works according to all the fabrication of the holy things, was of the gold of the first fruits, twenty-nine talents, and seven hundred and twenty shekels according to the holy shekel. The offering of silver from the men that were numbered of the congregation a hundred talents, and a thousand and seven hundred and seventy-five shekels, one beka[1] each, the half-shekel, according to the holy shekel. Everyone that passed the survey from twenty years old and upwards to the number of six hundred thousand, and three thousand and five hundred and fifty. The one hundred talents of silver went to the casting of the hundred chapiters of the tabernacle, and to the chapiters of the veil, a hundred chapiters to the hundred talents, a talent to a chapiter. The thousand and seven hundred and seventy-five shekels he formed into hooks for the pillars, and he gilded their chapiters and adorned them.

The brass of the offering was seventy talents, and a thousand and five hundred shekels and they made of it the bases of the door of the tabernacle of witness, and the bases of the court round about, and the bases of the gate of the court, and the pins of the tabernacle, and the pins of the court round about, and the bronze appendage of the altar, and all the vessels of the altar, and all the instruments of the tabernacle of witness. The Israelites did as the Lord commanded Moses. From the gold that remained of the offering they made vessels to minister with before the Lord.

The blue that was left, and the purple, and the scarlet they made into garments of ministry for Aaron so that he should minister with them in the sanctuary, and they brought the garments to Moses, and the tabernacle, and its furniture, its bases and its bars and the posts; and the box of the covenant, and its bearers, and the altar and all its furniture. They made the anointing oil, and the incense of composition, and the pure candlestick, and its lamps, lamps for burning, and oil for the light, and the table of show-bread, and all its furniture, and the show-bread on it, and the garments of the sanctuary which belong to Aaron, and the garments of his sons, for the priestly ministry, and the curtains of the court, and the posts, and the veil of the door of the tabernacle, and the gate of the court, and all the vessels of the tabernacle and all its instruments: and the skins, even rams' skins dyed red, and the blue coverings, and the coverings of the other things, and the pins, and all the instruments for the works of the tabernacle of witness.

Whatever things the Lord appointed Moses, so did the Israelites make all the possession. Moses saw all the works, and they had done them all as the Lord commanded Moses, so had they made them, and Moses blessed them.

Exodus: Chapter 39 Notes

1 Codex Vaticanus: drachmê (ΔΡΑΧΜΗ). Translation: drachma

- Leningrad Codex: beka (בֶּקַע)

- Peshitta: mtqlå (ܡܬܩܠܐ). Translation: scales (or shekel, beqa)

- Targum Onkelos: tikla (תִּקְלָא). Translations: scales (or shekel, beqa)

The drachma was a Greek coin used from around 1100 BC, worth approximately 4.3 grams of silver. The beka was the half-shekel measurement used in ancient Canaan. As 'drachma' was the Greek translation of beka, the term beka is restored in this translation.

Exodus: Chapter 40

The Lord said to Moses, "On the first day of the first month, at the new moon, you will set up the tabernacle of witness, and you will place in it the box of the testimony and will cover the box with the veil, and you will bring in the table and will set out that which is to be set out on it, and you will bring in the candle-stick and place its lamps on it. You will place the golden altar, to burn incense before the box, and you will put a covering of a veil on the door of the tabernacle of witness. You will put the altar of burnt offerings by the doors of the tabernacle of witness, and you will set up the tabernacle around about, and you will hallow all that belongs to it around about.

You will take the anointing oil, and will anoint the tabernacle, and all things in it, and will sanctify it, and all its furniture, and it will be holy. You will anoint the altar of burnt offerings and all its furniture, and you will hallow the altar, and the altar will be most holy. You will bring Aaron and his sons to the doors of the tabernacle of witness, and you will wash them with water. You will put on Aaron the holy garments, and you will anoint him, and you will sanctify him, and he will minister to me as a priest. You will bring up his sons and will put garments on them. You will anoint them as you did anoint their father, and they will minister to me as priests, and it will be that they will have an everlasting anointing of the priesthood, throughout their generations. Moses did all things whatever the Lord commanded him, so did he. It happened in the first month, in the second year after their going forth out of Egypt, at the new moon, that the tabernacle was set up.

Moses set up the tabernacle, and put on the chapiters, and put the bars into their places, and set up the posts. He stretched out the curtains over the taber-nacle and put the veil of the tabernacle on it above as the Lord commanded Moses. He took the testimonies and put them into the box, and he put the staffs under the sides of the box. He brought the box into the tabernacle, and put on it the covering of the veil, and covered the box of the testimony, as the Lord commanded Moses. He put the table in the tabernacle of witness, on the north side outside the veil of the tabernacle. He put on it the show-bread before the Lord, as the Lord commanded Moses. He put the candlestick into the tabernacle of witness, on the side of the tabernacle towards the south. He put on it its lamps before the Lord, as the Lord had commanded Moses.

He put the golden altar in the tabernacle of witness before the veil; and he burnt on it incense of composition, as the Lord commanded Moses. He put the altar of the burnt offerings by the doors of the tabernacle. He set up the court round about the tabernacle and the altar, and Moses accomplished all the works. The cloud covered the tabernacle of witness, and the tabernacle was filled with the glory of the Lord. Moses was not able to enter into the tabernacle of the testimony, because the cloud overshadowed it, and the tabernacle was filled with the glory of the Lord. When the cloud went up from the tabernacle, the Israelites packed to depart again with their baggage. If the cloud did not go up, they did not prepare to depart, until the day when the cloud went up. For a cloud was on the tabernacle by day, and a fire was on it by night before all Israel, in all their preparations.

Leviticus: Chapter 1

Moses[1] was again called by Iaw,[2] and told from the tabernacle of witness, "Speak to the children of Israel, and say to them, 'If any man among you brings gifts to Iaw, you will bring your gifts of the livestock and the oxen and the sheep. If his gift is a whole burnt offering, he will bring an undamaged male of the herd to the door of the tabernacle of witness. He will bring it as acceptable before Iaw. He will lay his hand on the head of the burnt offering as a thing acceptable for him, to make atonement for him. They will kill the calf before Iaw, and the sons of Aaron the priests will bring the blood, and they will pour the blood around the altar, which is at the doors of the tabernacle of witness. Having flayed the whole burnt offering, they will divide it by its limbs."

"The sons of Aaron the priests will place fire on the altar and will stack the wood on the fire. The sons of Aaron the priests will pile up the divided parts, and the head, and the fat on the wood on the fire, the wood which is on the altar. The entrails and the feet they will wash in water, and the priests will put all on the altar. It is a burnt offering, a sacrifice, a smell of sweet savor to Iaw."

"If his gift to Iaw is a sheep, a lamb, or a kid, for the whole burnt offering, he will bring a male without imperfection. He will lay his hand on its head, and they will kill it by the side of the altar, towards the north before Iaw, and the sons of Aaron the priests will pour its blood on the altar and around it. They will divide it by its limbs, and its head and its fat, and the priests will place them up on the wood which is on the fire, on the altar. They will wash the entrails and the feet with water, and the priest will bring all the parts and put them on the altar. It is a burnt offering, a sacrifice, a smell of sweet savor to Iaw. If he brings his gift, a burnt offering to Iaw, from the birds, then he will bring his gift of doves or pigeons. The priest will bring it to the altar and will twist off its head, and the priest will put it on the altar and will wring out the blood at the bottom of the altar. He will take away the crop with the feathers, and will throw it out by the altar towards the east to the place of the ashes. He will break it off from the wings and will not separate it, and the priest will put it on the altar on the wood which is on the fire. It is a burnt offering, a sacrifice, a sweet-smelling savor to Iaw."

Leviticus: Chapter 1 Notes

1 Codex Vaticanus: Môysên (Ⲙⲱⲩⲥⲏⲛ)

- Leningrad Codex: Mosheh (מֹשֶׁה)

This verse does not survive in most of the fragments found among the Dead Sea Scrolls, however, the name 'Moses' does survive in later verses that have survived among the Dead Sea Scrolls.

- DSS 6QpaleoLev: Mšh (𐤌𐤔𐤄)

- DSS 4QLev[b]: Mšh (משה)

- DSS 4QLev-Num[a]: Mšh (משה)

- DSS 11QpaleoLev[a]: Mšh (𐤌𐤔𐤄)

- DSS 4QLev[c]: Mšh (משה)

- Peshitta: Mûšâ (ܡܘܫܐ)

- Targum Onkelos: Mšê (מֹשֶׁה)

- Fragment Targums: Mšê (מֹשֶׁה)

- Targum Jerusalem: Mšê (מֹשֶׁה)

It is generally accepted that at some point before the Septuagint was translated, half of Moses' name was redacted from the text. This theory is based on the similarity of the Egyptian term msî (𓄟𓋴), meaning 'give birth to,' or 'created by,' which was a common element of Egyptian names. Many kings of Egypt were known as the 'msî' of a god, including Ramses (𓇳𓄟𓋴), Ahmose (𓇋𓄟𓋴), Tuthmose (�𓄟𓋴), Amenmose (𓇋𓏠𓈖𓄟𓋴), and Ptahmose (𓏤𓁹𓄟𓋴). A theory that has been circulating since at least the time of Josephus in the 1st century AD, is that Moses' original name was Hapymoses, meaning the 'Nile created him.'

If this is the origin of the name, the name of the god that created Moses was likely dropped from the name very early in Israelite history, as there are no known surviving texts with the full name. The latest this is likely to have happened would have been during the Aramaic translation of King Hezekiah, however, it may have happened much earlier. An alternate interpretation is that the name is complete, and is derived from the Egyptian term mû-šâô (𓈗𓈘𓄿𓈖), meaning 'beginning on water,' which appears to be what the princess stated when she found him.

2 Codex Vaticanus: c̄s (κ̄c̄). Translation: lord

- Leningrad Codex: Yehvah (יְהוָֹה)

This verse does not survive in most of the Dead Sea Scrolls, however, the name does survive in later sections of Leviticus.

- LXX 4QpapLXXLev[b]: Iaô (ιλΩ)

- DSS 1QpaleoLev: Yhůh (𐤉𐤄𐤅𐤄)

- DSS 4QLev-Num[a]: Yhůh (𐤉𐤄𐤅𐤄)

- DSS 4QLev[b]: Yhůh (𐤉𐤄𐤅𐤄)

- DSS 4QLev[c]: Yhůh (יהוה)

- DSS 4QLev[d]: Yhůh (יהוה)

- DSS 4QLev[e]: Yhůh (יהוה)

- DSS 11QpaleoLev[a]: Yhůh (𐤉𐤄𐤅𐤄)

- DSS 11QLev[b]: Yhůh (𐤉𐤄𐤅𐤄)

- DSS MasLev[a]: Yhůh (יהוה)

- DSS MasLev[b]: Yhůh (יהוה)

- Peshitta: mryå (ܡܪܝܐ). Translation: master (or lord)

- Targum Onkelos: yeyah (??). Translation: Yhů

- Fragment Targums: yeyah (??). Translation: Yhů

- Targum Jerusalem: yeyah (??). Translation: Yhů

The surviving fragments of Leviticus in Septuagint Manuscript 4QpapLXXLev[b] from the Hasmonean Dynasty (140 to 37 BC) render the name as Iaô (ιλΩ) in chapters 3 and 4. This transliteration of the name is based on the Aramaic Yhů (יהו), and not the Hebrew Yhůh (יהוה), indicating that Manuscript 4QpapLXXLev[b] was translated from an Aramaic source, like most of the books that comprised the Septuagint.

While it cannot be proven at this time that the original Septuagint's translation of Leviticus used the name Iaô, most scholars believe Leviticus was written by the Levites as an amendment to the Laws of Moses found in Exodus, and to cement their claims to the priesthood of Solomon's Temple, which had been overseen by the Sons of Korah since the time of Solomon. These new laws removed human sacrifice entirely, rather than simply allowing a substituted animal, which strongly implies the Israelites were settled in cities by that time when inherent inequity would have left the poor without the ability to redeem their firstborn.

Child sacrifice was denounced by the Prophet Jeremiah circa 650 BC, and banned by King Josiah in 4th Kingdoms (Masoretic Kings) circa 625 BC, meaning Israelites were practicing child sacrifice then, and therefore, Leviticus could not have been an accepted text until after that time. As Yhŭ (Yahweh) was the god of both Jeremiah and Josiah, Yhŭ was likely the original god in the book of Leviticus. The name Iaô (Ιαω) was translated as 'Iaw' in Latin texts during the Classical Era.

The name was removed from the Christian copies of the Septuagint during the 2nd and 3rd century Christian-Gnostic debates over whether Iaw was the devil or not. The term 'Lord' replaced Iaw during the debates, however, before that, the various versions of the Septuagint used either Iaô (Ιαω) or the 'sacred name' written in the Hebrew or Phoenician (Paleo-Hebrew) scripts. According to Origen of Alexandria in the late 2nd century AD, the Canaanite (Phoenician script) was the most accurate. According to Theodoret of Cyprus in the 5th century, Samaritans pronounced the name as Iabe (Ιαβε) or Iabae (Ιαβαι). Hebrews substitute the word 'HaShem' in all non-scriptural contexts, which is accepted within rabbinical Judaism as meaning 'the name.' Christians have traditionally translated several ways including Jehovah, Jehova, and Jova.

The two names Yhŭ (יהו‎^) and Yhŭh (יהוה‎), are prophetically identical to the names of the Egyptian lunar-god of Heliopolis: Îôh and Îôhŭ, which is likely of origin of the twin names found in the Canaanite scriptures, assuming one accepts the historicity of Joseph as the priest of Heliopolis in Genesis, and the Exodus of Moses, Aaron, and the Israelites from Egypt. As Manuscript 4QpapLXXLev[b] is the oldest partially surviving copy of the Septuagint's Leviticus, the name is transliterated the traditional Latin way as Iaw.

Leviticus: Chapter 2

"If a mind brings a gift as a sacrifice to Iaw, his gift will be fine flour, and he will pour oil on it and will put frankincense on it. It is a sacrifice. He will bring it to the priests the sons of Aaron, and having taken from it a handful of the fine flour with the oil, and all its frankincense, then the priest will put the memorial of it on the altar, it is a sacrifice, an odor of sweet savor to Iaw. The remainder of the sacrifice will be for Aaron and his sons, the holiest portion from the sacrifices of Iaw. If he brings as a gift a sacrifice baked from the oven as a gift to Iaw of fine flour, he will bring unleavened bread kneaded with oil, and unleavened cakes covered in oil."

"If your gift is a sacrifice from a pan, it is fine flour mingled with oil, unleavened offerings. You will break them into fragments and pour oil on them. It is a sacrifice to Iaw. If your gift is a sacrifice from the stove, it will be made of fine flour with oil. He will offer this sacrifice to Iaw and will bring it to the priest. The priest will approach the altar and will remove a memorial piece from it, and will place the remained on the altar."

"A burnt offering, a smell of sweet savor to Iaw. That which is left of the sacrifice will be for Aaron and his sons, holiest from the burnt offerings of Iaw. You will not leaven any sacrifice which you will bring to Iaw, for as to any leaven or honey, you will not bring it to offer a gift to Iaw. You will bring them in the way of fruits to Iaw, but they will not be offered on the altar for a sweet-smelling savor to Iaw."

"Every gift of your sacrifice will be seasoned with salt. Omit not the salt of the covenant of Iaw from your sacrifices, on every gift of yours you will offer salt to Iaw your god. If you would offer a sacrifice of first-fruits to Iaw, it will be new grains ground and roasted for Iaw, so will you bring the sacrifice of the first fruits. You will pour oil on it and will place frankincense on it. It is a sacrifice. The priest will offer the memorial taken from the grains with the oil and all its frankincense. It is a burnt offering to Iaw."

Leviticus: Chapter 3

"If his gift to Iaw is a peace-offering, if he brings an ox, whether male or female, he will bring it undamaged before Iaw. He will lay his hands on the head of the sacrifice and will kill it before Iaw, by the doors of the tabernacle of witness. The priests, the sons of Aaron will pour the blood on the altar of burnt offerings around it. They will bring of the peace-offering a burnt sacrifice to Iaw, the fat covering the belly, and all the fat on the belly. The two kidneys and the fat that is on them. He will take away that which is on the thighs, and the caul above the liver together with the kidneys. The priests, the sons of Aaron will offer them on the altar on the burnt offering, on the wood which is on the fire on the altar: it is a burnt offering, a smell of sweet savor to Iaw. If his gift is from the sheep, a peace-offering to Iaw, male or female, he will bring it undamaged."

"If he brings a lamb for his gift, he will bring it before Iaw. He will lay his hands on the head of his offering and kill it by the doors of the tabernacle of witness, and the priests the sons of Aaron will pour out the blood on the altar and around it. He will bring of the peace-offering a burnt sacrifice to God.[1] The fat and the hinder part undamaged he will take away with the loins, and having taken away all the fat that covers the belly, and all the fat that is on the belly, and both the kidneys and the fat that is on them, and that which is on the thighs, and the caul which is on the liver with the kidneys, the priest will offer these on the altar. It is a sacrifice of sweet savor, a burnt offering to Iaw."

"If his offering is from the goats, then he will bring it before Iaw, and he will lay his hands on its head, and they will kill it before Iaw by the doors of the tabernacle of witness, and the priests the sons of Aaron will pour out the blood on the altar and around it. He will offer it a burnt offering to Iaw, including the fat that covers the belly, and all the fat that is on the belly. Both the kidneys, and all the fat that is on them, that which is on the thighs, and the caul of the liver with the kidneys, will he take away. The priest will offer it on the altar. It is a burnt offering, a smell of sweet savor to Iaw. All the fat belongs to Iaw. It is a perpetual statute throughout your generations, in all your habitations. You will eat no fat and no blood."

Leviticus: Chapter 3 Notes

1 Codex Vaticanus: tô thô (ΤѠＯⲎ). Translation: the god

- Leningrad Codex: laIhvah (לִיהָוֶה). Translation: to (or for) Yhwa

- Peshitta: lmryå (ܠܡܪܝܐ). Translation: to (or for, of) master (or lord)

- Targum Onkelos: kodam yeyah (קֳדָם יֹי). Translation: before (or 'in front of') Yhů

- Targum Jerusalem: kodam yeyah (קֳדָם יֹי). Translation: before (or 'in front of') Yhů

Based on the deviation between the Greek and Hebrew translations, it seems likely that the Judahite original read hålhym (𐤄𐤀𐤋𐤄𐤉𐤌), meaning 'the ålhym.' The phrase remains in some of the later chapters of Leviticus, where it is mirrored by 'god' in Greek. This suggests that the Hebrew translators were substituting lyhwh (ליהוה) for hålhym and not just 'the lord'.

Leviticus: Chapter 4

Iaw said to Moses, "Say to the children of Israel, 'If a mind will sin unwillingly before Iaw, in any of the commandments of Iaw concerning things which he should not do, and does some of them or if the anointed priest sin causes the people to sin, then he will bring for his sin, which he has sinned, an undamaged calf of the herd to Iaw for his sin.'"

"He will bring the calf to the door of the tabernacle of witness before Iaw, and he will put his hand on the head of the calf before Iaw and will kill the calf in the presence of Iaw. The anointed priest who has been consecrated, having received the blood of the calf will then bring it into the tabernacle of witness. The priest will dip his finger into the blood, and sprinkle of the blood seven times before Iaw, over against the holy veil. The priest will put of the blood of the calf on the horns of the altar of the compound incense which is before Iaw, which is in the tabernacle of witness, and all the blood of the calf will he pour out by the foot of the altar of whole burnt offerings, which is by the doors of the tabernacle of witness, and all the fat of the calf of the sin-offering will he take off from it; the fat that covers the insides, and all the fat that is on the insides, and the two kidneys, and the fat that is on them, which is on the thighs, and the caul that is on the liver with the kidneys, them will he take away, as he takes it away from the calf of the sacrifice of peace-offering, so will the priest offer it on the altar of burnt offering. They will take the skin of the calf, and all his flesh with the head and the extremities and the belly and the dung, and they will carry out the whole calf from the camp into a clean place, where they pour out the ashes, and they will burn it with fire there on wood. It will be burnt on the ashes poured out.'"

"If the whole congregation of Israel ignorantly trespasses, and it should escape the notice of the congregation, and they should do something forbidden in any of the commands of Iaw, which should not be done, and should transgress, and the sin in which they have sinned should become known to them, then will the congregation bring an undamaged calf of the herd for a sin-offering, and they will bring it to the doors of the tabernacle of witness. The elders of the congregation will lay their hands on the head of the calf before Iaw, and they will kill the calf before Iaw. The anointed priest will bring in some of the blood of the calf into the tabernacle of witness."

"The priest will dip his finger into some of the blood of the calf and will sprinkle it seven times before Iaw, in front of the veil of the sanctuary. The priest will put some of the blood on the horns of the altar of the incense of composition, which is before Iaw, which is in the tabernacle of witness, and he will pour out all the blood at the bottom of the altar of whole burnt offerings, which is by the door of the tabernacle of witness. He will take away all the fat from it, and will offer it up on the altar. He will do to the calf as he did to the calf of the sin-offering, so will it be done, and the priest will make atonement for them, and the trespass will be forgiven them. They will carry out the calf whole throughout the camp, and they will burn the calf as they burnt the previous calf. It is the sin-offering of the congregation.'"

"If a ruler sins, and breaks one of the commands of Iaw his god, doing the thing which should not be done, unwillingly, and will sin and trespass, and his trespass in which he has sinned, becomes known to him, then will he offer for his gift a kid of the goats, a male without imperfection. He will lay his hand on the head of the kid, and they will kill it in the place where they kill the victims for whole burnt offerings before Iaw. It is a sin-offering. The priest will smear with his finger some of the blood of the sin-offering onto the horns of the altar of whole burnt offering, and he will pour out all its blood at the bottom of the altar of whole burnt offerings. He will offer up all his fat on the altar, as the fat of the sacrifice of peace-offering, and the priest will make atonement for him concerning his sin, and it will be forgiven him.'"

"'If a mind of the people of the land should sin unwillingly, in doing a thing contrary to any of the commandments of Iaw, and his sin should become known to him, then he will bring a kid of the goats, a female without imperfection he will bring for his sin, which he has sinned. He will lay his hand on the head of his sin-offering, and they will kill the kid of the sin-offering in the place where they kill the victims for whole burnt offerings. The priest will take its blood with his finger, and will smear it on the horns of the altar of whole burnt offerings, and all its blood he will pour out at the foot of the altar. He will take away all the fat, like the fat is taken away from the sacrifice of peace-offering, and the priest will offer it on the altar for a smell of sweet savor to Iaw, and the priest will make atonement for him, and his sin will be forgiven him."

"If he should offer a lamb for his sin-offering, he will offer a female without imperfection. He will lay his hand on the head of the sin-offerings, and they will kill it in the place where they kill the whole burnt offerings. The priest will take of the blood of the sin-offering with his finger, and will put it on the horns of the altar of whole burnt offerings, and he will pour out all its blood by the bottom of the altar of whole burnt offering. He will take away all his fat, as the fat of the lamb of the sacrifice of peace-offering is taken away, and the priest will put it on the altar for a whole burnt offering to Iaw, and the priest will make atonement for him for the sin which he sinned, and it will be forgiven him.'"

Leviticus: Chapter 5

"'If a mind sins and hears the voice of swearing, and he is a witness or has seen or been conscious if he does not report it, he will bear his iniquity. That mind[1] which will touch any unclean thing, or carcass, or that which is unclean being taken of animals, or the dead bodies of abominable reptiles which are unclean, or carcasses of unclean livestock, or should touch the uncleanness of a man, or whatever kind, which he may touch and be defiled by, and it should have escaped him, but afterward, he should know, then he has transgressed.'"

"That unrighteous mind, which determines with his lips to do evil or to do good according to whatever a man may determine with an oath, and it has escaped his notice, and he will afterward know it, and so he should sin in any one of these things, then will he declare his sin in the things in which he has sinned by that sin. He will bring for his transgressions against Iaw, for his sin which he has sinned, a ewe lamb of the flock, or a kid of the goats, for a sin-offering, and the priest will make an atonement for him for his sin which he has sinned, and his sin will be forgiven him.'"

"'If he can't afford a sheep, he will bring for his sin which he has sinned, two turtledoves or two young pigeons to Iaw, one for a sin-offering, and the other for a burnt offering. He will bring them to the priest, and the priest will bring the sin-offering first, and the priest will pinch off the head from the neck, and will not divide the body. He will sprinkle of the blood of the sin-offering on the side of the altar, but the rest of the blood he will drop at the foot of the altar, for it is a sin-offering.'"

"He will make the second a whole burnt offering, as it is fit, and the priest will make atonement for his sin which he has sinned, and it will be forgiven him. If he can't afford a pair of turtledoves or two young pigeons, then he will bring as his gift for his sin, a tenth of a bushel of fine flour for a sin-offering, he will not pour oil on it, nor will he put frankincense on it, because it is a sin-offering. He will bring it to the priest, and the priest having taken a handful of it, will lay the memorial of it on the altar of whole burnt offerings to Iaw, it is a sin-offering. The priest will make atonement for him for his sin, which he has sinned in one of these things, and it will be forgiven him, and that which is left will be the priest's, as an offering of fine flour.'"

Iaw said to Moses, "The mind which will be really unaware and will sin unwillingly in any of the holy things of Iaw, will also bring to Iaw for his transgression a ram from the flock without imperfection, valued according to shekels of silver according to the shekel of the sanctuary, for his transgression in which he transgressed. He will make compensation for that in which he has sinned in the holy things, and he will add the fifth part to it, and give it to the priest, and the priest will make atonement for him with the ram of transgression, and his sin will be forgiven."

"The mind which will sin, and do one thing against any of the commandments of Iaw, which it is not right to do, and has not known it, and has transgressed, and has contracted guilt, he will even bring a ram without imperfection from the flock, valued at a price of silver for his transgression to the priest, and the priest will make atonement for his trespass of ignorance, in which he ignorantly trespassed, and he did not know it, and it will be forgiven. For he has surely been guilty of transgression before Iaw."

Leviticus: Chapter 5 Notes

1 Codex Vaticanus: psychê (ΨΥΧΗ). Translation: psyche (or personality, mind)

• Leningrad Codex: nefesh (נֶפֶשׁ). Translation: mind (or person)

• Peshitta: npšå (ܢܦܫܐ). Translation: mind

• Targum Onkelos: enash (אֱנַשׁ). Translation: human

• Targum Jerusalem: bar nash (בַר נָשׁ). Translation: son of human

Leviticus: Chapter 6

Iaw said to Moses, "The mind which has sinned, and intentionally ignored the commandments of Iaw, and has dealt falsely in the affairs of his neighbor in the matter of a deposit, or concerning fellowship, or concerning plunder, or has in anything wronged his neighbor, or has found that which was lost, and has lied about it, and has sworn dishonestly concerning anyone regarding anything, whatever a man does to sin, it will come to pass, whenever he has sinned, and transgressed, that he will restore the plunder which he has seized, or redress the injury which he has committed, or restore the deposit which was entrusted to him, or the lost article which he has found of any kind, about which he swore dishonestly, he will even restore it in full, and he will add to it the fifth part besides."

"He will restore it to him whose it is in the day in which he happens to be convicted. He will bring to Iaw for his trespass, a ram of the flock, without imperfection, of value to the amount of the thing in which he trespassed. The priest will make atonement for him before Iaw, and he will be forgiven for all the things which he did and trespassed in it."

Iaw said to Moses, "Tell Aaron and his sons, 'This is the law of whole burnt offering. This is the whole burnt offering, which will burn on the altar all night until the morning, and the fire of the altar will burn it, and it will not be put out. The priest will put on the linen tunic, and he will put the linen trousers on his body and will take away that which has been thoroughly burnt, which the fire has consumed, including the whole burnt offering from the altar, and he will put it near the altar. He will take off his robe, and put on another robe, and he will take out the offering that has been burnt out of the camp into a clean place. The fire on the altar will be kept burning on it, and will not be extinguished, and the priest will burn on it wood every morning, and will heap on it the whole burnt offering, and will lay on it the fat of the peace-offering. The fire will always burn on the altar. It will not be extinguished.'"

"'This is the law of the sacrifice, which the sons of Aaron will bring before Iaw and the altar. He will take from it a handful of the fine flour of the sacrifice with its oil, and with all its frankincense, which are on the sacrifice, and he will offer up on the altar a burnt offering as a sweet-smelling savor, a memorial it to Iaw. Aaron and his sons will eat that which is left from it. It will be eaten outside leaven in a holy place, they will eat it in the court of the tabernacle of witness. It will not be baked with leaven. I have given it to them, as a portion of the burnt offerings of Iaw. It is holiest, as the offering for sin, and as the offering for trespass. Every male of the priests will eat it. It is a perpetual ordinance throughout your generations for the burnt offerings of Iaw. Whoever will touch them will be sacred.'"

Iaw said to Moses, "This is the gift for Aaron and his sons, which they will offer to Iaw in the day in which you will anoint him: a tenth of a bushel of fine flour for a sacrifice continually, half of it in the morning, and half of it in the evening. It will be made with oil in a frying pan. He will offer it kneaded and in rolls, an offering of fragments, an offering of a sweet savor to Iaw. The anointed priest who is in his place, one of his sons, will offer it. It is a perpetual statute, it will all be consumed. Every sacrifice of a priest will be thoroughly burnt, and will not be eaten."

Iaw said to Moses, saying, "Tell Aaron and his sons, 'This is the law of the sin-offering: In the place where they kill the whole burnt offering, they will kill the sin-offerings before Iaw: they are holiest. The priest that offers it will eat it. It will be eaten in a holy place, in the court of the tabernacle of witness. Everyone that touches the flesh, will be holy, and on whoever's garment any its blood has been sprinkled, whoever has it sprinkled, will be washed in the holy place. The earthen vessel, in whichever it has been dirtied, will be broken, and if it has been dirtied in a brazen vessel, he will scour it and wash it with water. Every male priest will eat it. It is holiest to Iaw. No offerings for sin, of whose blood there will be brought any into the tabernacle of witness to make atonement in the holy place, will be eaten: they will be burnt with fire.'"

"'This is the law of the ram for the trespass-offering. It is sacred. In the place where they kill the whole burnt offering, they will kill the ram of the trespass-offering before Iaw, and he will pour out the blood at the bottom of the altar and around it. He will offer all the fat from it, and the loins, and all the fat that covers the insides, and all the fat that is on the insides, and the two kidneys, and the fat that is on them, that which is on the thighs, and the caul on the liver with the kidney, he will take them away."

"The priest will offer them on the altar a burnt offering to the Lord, it is for trespass. Every male of the priest will eat them, in the holy place they will eat them: they are sacred. Like the sin-offering, so also is the trespass-offering. There is one law for them, the priest who will make the atonement with it, it will be his. As for the priest who offers a man's whole burnt offering, the skin of the whole burnt offering which he offers will be his. Every sacrifice which will be prepared in the oven, and everyone which will be prepared on the stove, or in a frying-pan, it is the property of the priest that offers it. It will be his. Every sacrifice made up with oil, or not made up with oil, will belong to the sons of Aaron, an equal portion to each.'"

Leviticus: Chapter 7

"This is the law of the sacrificial peace-offering, which they will bring to Iaw. If a man wants to offer it for praise, then he will bring for the sacrifice of praise, loaves of fine flour made up with oil, and unleavened cakes coated with oil, and fine flour kneaded with oil. With leavened bread, he will offer his gifts, with the peace-offering of praise. He will bring one of all his gifts, a separate offering to Iaw: it will belong to the priest who pours out the blood of the peace-offering. The flesh of the sacrifice of the peace-offering of praise will be his, and it will be eaten in the day in which it is offered: they will not leave it until the morning. If it is a vow, or he offers his gift by his own will, on whatever day he will offer his sacrifice, it will be eaten, and in the morning, that which is left of the flesh of the sacrifice until the third day will be consumed with fire. If he does at all eat of the flesh on the third day, it will not be accepted for him that offering."

"It will not be considered by him, it is pollution, and whatever mind will eat it, will bear his iniquity. Whatever flesh has touched anything unclean, it will not be eaten. It will be burned with fire. Everyone who is clean will eat the flesh. Whatever mind will eat of the flesh of the sacrifice of the peace-offering which is Iaw's and become unclean, that mind will perish from his people. Whatever mind will touch anything unclean, either of the uncleanness of a man, or unclean quadrupeds, or any unclean abominable thing, and will eat of the flesh of the sacrifice of the peace-offering, which is Iaw's, that mind will perish from his people."

Iaw said to Moses, "Tell the children of Israel, 'You will eat no fat of oxen or sheep or goats. The fat of animals that have died by themselves, or have been killed by animals, may be employed for any work, but it will not be eaten for food. Everyone that eats the fat of the animals, from which he will bring a burnt offering to Iaw, that mind will perish from his people. You will eat no blood in all your houses, either of animals or birds. Every mind that will eat blood, that mind will perish from his people.'"

Iaw said to Moses, "You will also tell the children of Israel, 'He that offers a sacrifice of peace-offering, will bring his gift to Iaw also from the sacrifice of peace-offering. His hands will bring the burnt offerings to Iaw, the fat which is on the breast and the lois from the liver, he will bring them, to set them for a gift before Iaw. The priest will offer the fat on the altar, and the breast will be Aaron's and his sons, and you will give the right shoulder as a choice piece to the priest of your sacrificial peace-offering. He that offers the blood of the peace-offering, and the fat, of the sons of Aaron, his will be the right shoulder for a portion.'"

"'For I have taken the wave-breast and shoulder of separation from the children of Israel from your sacrificial peace-offerings, and I have given them to Aaron the priest and his sons, a perpetual ordinance due from the children of Israel. This is the anointing of Aaron, and the anointing of his sons, their portion of the burnt offerings of Iaw, in the day in which he brought them forward to minister as priests to Iaw, as Iaw commanded to give to them in the day in which he anointed them of the sons of Israel, a perpetual statute through their generations.'"

This is the law of the whole burnt offerings, and sacrifice, and sin-offering, and offering for transgression, and the sacrifice of consecration, and the sacrifice of peace-offering, as Iaw commanded Moses in the Mount Sinai, in the day in which he commanded the children of Israel to offer their gifts before Iaw in the Wilderness of Sinai.

Leviticus: Chapter 8

Iaw said to Moses, "Take Aaron and his sons, and his robes and the anointing oil, and the calf for the sin-offering, and the two rams, and the basket of unleavened bread, and assemble the whole congregation at the entrance of the tabernacle of witness."

Moses did as Iaw appointed him, and he assembled the congregation at the door of the tabernacle of witness. Moses said to the congregation, "This is what Iaw has commanded you to do."

Moses brought near Aaron and his sons, and washed them with water, and put on him the coat, and girded him with the girdle, and clothed him with the tunic, and put on him the vest, and dressed him in a girdle according to the make of the vest, and clasped him closely with it: and put on it the oracle, the Manifestation and the Truth. He put the miter on his head, with the golden plate in the front, the holiest thing, as Iaw commanded Moses. Moses took of the anointing oil, and sprinkled it seven times on the altar, and anointed the altar, and hallowed it, and all things on it, and the layer, and its foot, and sanctified them, and anointed the tabernacle and all its furniture, and hallowed it. Moses poured the anointing oil on the head of Aaron, and he anointed him and sanctified him.

Moses brought the sons of Aaron near, and put on them, coats and girded them with girdles, and put turbans on them as Iaw commanded Moses. Moses brought near the calf for the sin-offering, and Aaron and his sons laid their hands on the head of the calf of the sin-offering. He killed it, and Moses took of the blood and put it on the horns of the altar round about with his finger, and he purified the altar, and poured out the blood at the bottom of the altar, and sanctified it, to make atonement on it.

Moses took all the fat that was on the insides, and the lobe on the liver, and both the kidneys, and the fat that was on them, and Moses offered them on the altar. But the calf's hide, flesh, and dung, he burnt with fire outside the camp, as Iaw commanded Moses. Moses brought near the ram for a whole burnt offering, and Aaron and his sons laid their hands on the head of the ram.

Moses killed the ram, and Moses poured the blood on the altar and around it. He divided the ram by its limbs, and Moses offered the head, the limbs, and the fat, and he washed the belly and the feet with water. Moses offered up the whole ram on the altar. It is a whole burnt offering for a sweet-smelling savor, it is a burnt offering to Iaw, as Iaw commanded Moses.

Moses brought the second ram, the ram of consecration, and Aaron and his sons laid their hands on the head of the ram, and he killed him. Moses took some of his blood and put it on the tip of Aaron's right ear, and the thumb of his right hand, and the big toe of his right foot. Moses brought near the sons of Aaron, and Moses put of the blood the tips of their right ears, and on the thumbs of their right hands, and the big toes of their right feet and Moses poured out the blood on the altar and around it. He took the fat, and the rump, and the fat on the belly, and the liver, and the two kidneys, and the fat that is on them, and the right shoulder. From the basket of consecration, which was before Iaw, he also took one unleavened loaf, and one loaf made with oil, and one cake, and put them on the fat, and the right shoulder, and put them all in the hands of Aaron, and in the hands of his sons, and offered them up as an offering before Iaw.

Moses took them at their hands, and Moses offered them on the altar, on the whole burnt offering of consecration, which is a smell of sweet savor. It is a burnt offering to Iaw. Moses took the breast, and separated it for a heave-offering before Iaw, from the ram of consecration, and it became Moses' portion, as Iaw commanded Moses. Moses took of the anointing oil, and of the blood that was on the altar, and sprinkled it on Aaron, and his garments, and his sons, and the garments of his sons with him. He sanctified Aaron and his garments, and his sons, and the garments of his sons with him.

Moses said to Aaron and his sons, "Boil the flesh in the tent of the tabernacle of witness in the holy place, and there you will eat it and the loaves in the basket of consecration, as it has been ordered to me, Iaw said, 'Aaron and his sons will eat them.' That which is left of the flesh and of the loaves burn with fire. You will not go out from the door of the tabernacle of witness for seven days until the end of the day; the day of your consecration. For in seven days will he consecrate you, as he did in this day on which Iaw commanded me to do so, to make an atonement for you. You will remain seven days at the door of the tabernacle of witness, day and night. You will observe the ordinances of Iaw, so you don't die. This has been commanded to me by Lord the god."[1]

Aaron and his sons performed all these commands that Iaw had commanded Moses.

Leviticus: Chapter 8 Notes

1 Codex Vaticanus: c̄s o t̄h̄s (ⲔⲤⲞⲐⲤ). Translation: Lord the god.

- Leningrad Codex: Yehovah (יְהֹוָה)

- Peshitta: mryå (ܡܪܝܐ). Translation: master

- Targum Onkelos: mera dayyah (מְרָא דַיְיָ). Translation: master (or lord) of Yhů

- Targum Jerusalem: mera dayyah (מְרָא דַיְיָ). Translation: master (or lord) of Yhů

Leviticus: Chapter 9

It happened on the eighth day, that Moses called Aaron and his sons, and the elders of Israel. Moses said to Aaron, "Take for yourself a young calf of the herd for a sin-offering, and a ram for a whole burnt offering, undamaged, and offer them before Iaw. Speak to the elders of Israel, saying, 'Take one kid of the goats for a sin-offering, and a young calf, and a spotless lamb a year old for a whole burnt offering, and a calf and a ram for a peace offering before Iaw, and fine flour mixed with oil, for today Iaw will appear among you.'"

They took what Moses commanded them before the tabernacle of witness, and all the congregation drew near, and they stood before Iaw. Moses declared, "This is what Iaw has said. Do it, and the glory of Iaw will appear among you."

Moses said to Aaron, "Approach the altar, and offer your sin-offering, and your whole burnt offering, and make atonement for yourself, and your house, and offer the gifts of the people, and make atonement for them, as Iaw commanded Moses."

Aaron approached the altar and killed the calf of his sin-offering. The sons of Aaron brought the blood to him, and he dipped his finger into the blood and put it on the horns of the altar, and he poured out the blood at the bottom of the altar. He offered up on the altar the fat and the kidneys and the liver of the sin-offering, as Iaw had commanded Moses. The flesh and the hide he burnt with fire outside of the camp. He killed the whole burnt offering, and the sons of Aaron brought the blood to him, and he poured it on the altar and around it. They brought the whole burnt offering, in its pieces. He put them and the head on the altar. He washed the belly and the feet with water, and he put them on the whole burnt offering on the altar.

He took the gift of the people, and took the goat of the sin-offering from the people, and killed it, and purified it also like the first. He brought the whole burnt offering and offered it in the same way. He brought the sacrifice and filled his hands with it, and laid it on the altar, besides the morning whole burnt offering. He killed the calf, and the ram of the sacrifice of peace-offering of the people, and the sons of Aaron brought the blood to him, and he poured it out on the altar and around it. He took the fat of the calf, and the hindquarters of the ram, and the fat covering the belly, and the two kidneys, and the fat on them, and the caul on the liver. He put the fat on the breasts and offered the fat on the altar. Aaron separated the breast and the right shoulder as a choice-offering before

Iaw, as Iaw commanded Moses. Aaron lifted his hands over the people and blessed them, and after he had offered the sin-offering, and the whole burnt offerings, and the peace-offerings, he came down.

Moses and Aaron entered into the tabernacle of witness, and they came out and blessed all the people, and the glory of Iaw appeared to all the people. Fire came out from Iaw and devoured the offerings on the altar, both the whole burnt offerings and the fat, and all the people saw, and were amazed, and fell on their faces.

Leviticus: Chapter 10

Aaron's two sons Nadab and Abihu, each took his censer, and put fire in it, and threw incense on it, and offered strange fire before Iaw, which Iaw did not command them, and fire came out from Iaw, and devoured them, and they died before Iaw.

Moses said to Aaron, "This is what Iaw said, 'I will be sanctified by those that draw near to me, and I will be glorified in the whole congregation,'" and Aaron was hurt in his heart.

Moses called Misadae and Elizaphan, the sons of Uzziel, the sons of the brother of Aaron's father, and said to them, "Approach and take your brothers from before the sanctuary out of the camp."

They approached and carried them in their coats out of the camp, as Moses had said.

Moses said to Aaron, and his remaining sons Eleazar and Ithamar, "You will not shave your heads, and you will not tear your clothes, or you may die, and then there would be anger on all the congregation, and your brothers, even all the house of Israel, would be saddened by the burning, that they were burnt by Iaw. You will not go out from the door of the tabernacle of witness, that you do not die, for Iaw's anointing oil is on you."

They did according to the word of Moses.

Iaw said to Aaron, "Whenever you enter into the tabernacle of witness or when you approach the altar, you will not drink wine or strong drink, you or your sons with you, so you will not die. It is a perpetual statute for your generations, to distinguish between sacred and profane, and between clean and unclean, and to teach the children of Israel all the commandments, which Iaw spoke to them by Moses."

Moses said to Aaron and his surviving sons Eleazar and Ithamar, "Take the sacrifice that is left of the burnt offerings of Iaw, and you will eat unleavened bread by the altar. It is sacred. You will eat it in the holy place, for this is a statute for you and a statute for your sons, of the burnt offerings to Iaw, for so it has been commanded to me. You will eat the breast of separation, and the shoulder of the choice-offering in the holy place, you and your sons and your house with you."

"It has been given as an ordinance for you and an ordinance for your sons, of the sacrificial peace-offering of the children of Israel. They will bring the shoulder of the choice-offering, and the breast of the separation on the burnt offerings of the fat, to separate for a separation before Iaw, and it will be a perpetual ordinance for you and your sons and your daughters with you, as Iaw commanded Moses."

Moses diligently searched for the goat of the sin-offering, but it had been consumed by fire, and Moses was angry with Eleazar and Ithamar the sons of Aaron that were left, demanding, "Why did you not eat the sin-offering in the holy place? Because it is sacred that he has given you this to eat, that you might take away the sin of the congregation, and make atonement for them before Iaw! The blood was not brought into the holy place! You will eat it inside, before Iaw, as Iaw commanded me!"

Aaron said to Moses, "If they have brought near today their sin-offerings, and their whole burnt offerings before Iaw and these events have happened to me, and yet I should eat today of the sin-offering, would it be pleasing to Iaw?"

Moses heard it, and it pleased him.

Leviticus: Chapter 11

Iaw said to Moses and Aaron, "Tell the sons of Israel, 'These are the animals which you may eat out of all animals that are on the land. Every animal that has split hooves and making divisions of two claws, and chewing the cud among animals, these you may eat. But these you may not eat, of those that chew the cud, and of those that have split hooves, and divide claws, the camel, because it chews the cud, but does not have split hooves, this is unclean to you. The rabbit, because it chews the cud, but does not have split hooves, this is unclean to you. The hare, because it does not chew the cud, and does not have split hooves, this is unclean to you. The hog, because this animal has split hooves and makes claws of the hoof, but it does not chew the cud, is unclean to you. You will not eat of their flesh, and you will not touch their carcasses, these are unclean to you."

"These are what you may eat of all that are in the waters: all things that have fins and scales in the waters, and the seas, and the brooks, these you may eat. All things which have no fins or scales in the water, or the seas, and the brooks, of all which the waters produce, and of every mind living in the water, are an abomination, and they will be abominations to you. You may not eat of their flesh, and you will detest their carcasses. All things that have no fins or scales of those that are in the waters, these are an abomination to you."

"These are the things which you will detest among birds, and they will not be eaten, they are an abomination: the eagle and the bearded vulture, and the sea-eagle. The vulture, and the falcon, and those like them, and the sparrow, and the owl, and the cormorant, and those like them, and every raven, and the birds like them, and the hawk and those like them, and the night-raven and the cormorant and the stork, and the red-bill, and the pelican, and swan, and the heron, and the lapwing, and those like them, and the hoopoe and the bat. All winged creatures that creep, which go on four feet, are abominations to you."

"But these you may eat of the creeping winged animals, which go on four feet, which have legs above their feet, to leap with on the land. These you may eat of them: the caterpillar and those like it, and the attacus and those like it, and the cantharus and those like it, and the locust and those like it."

"Every creeping thing from among the birds, which has four feet, is an abomination to you. These will defile you. Everyone that touches their carcasses will be unclean until the evening. Everyone that takes of their dead bodies will wash his garments and will be unclean until the evening."

"Whichever among the animal that has split hooves and makes claws, and does not chew the cud, will be unclean to you. Everyone that touches their dead bodies will be unclean until evening. All of the wild animals that move on four feet, is unclean to you. Everyone that touches their dead bodies will be unclean until evening. He that takes their dead bodies will wash his clothes and will be unclean until evening. These are unclean to you. These are unclean to you: the reptiles on the land, the weasel, and the mouse, and the lizard, the ferret, and the chameleon, and the salamander, and the newt, and the mole. These are unclean to you: all the reptiles which are on the land. Everyone who touches their carcasses will be unclean until evening."

"On whatever one of their dead bodies will fall it, will be unclean. Whatever wooden vessel, or garment, or skin, or sack it is, every vessel in which work should be done, will be dipped in water, and will be unclean until evening, and then it will be clean. Every earthen vessel into which one of these things will fall, whatever is inside it, will be unclean, and it will be broken. All food that is eaten, on which water will come from such a vessel, will be unclean, and every beverage which is drunk in any such vessel will be unclean. Everything on which there will fall of their dead bodies will be unclean; ovens and stands for jars will be broken down: these are unclean, and they will be unclean to you. Only if the water is from fountains of water or a pool, or confluence of water, it will be clean, but he who touches their carcasses will be unclean."

"If one of their carcasses should fall on any grain seed which is to be sown, it will be clean. But if water is poured on any seed, and one of their dead bodies falls on it, it is unclean to you."

"If one of the livestock dies, which it is lawful for you to eat, anyone that touches their carcasses will be unclean until evening. He that eats their carcasses will wash his garments, and be unclean until evening, and he that carries any of their carcasses will wash his garments, and bathe himself in water, and be unclean until evening."

"Every reptile that creeps on the land, will be an abomination to you. It will not be eaten. Every animal that creeps on its belly, and everyone that goes on four feet continually, which abounds with feet among all the reptiles creeping on the land, you will not eat it, for it is an abomination to you. You will not defile your minds with any of the reptiles that creep on the land, and you will not be polluted with them, and you will not be unclean by them."

"For I am Iaw the god, and you will be sanctified, and you will be holy, because I, Iaw your God, am holy, and you will not defile your minds with any of the reptiles creeping on the land. For I am Iaw who brought you up out of the land of Egypt to be your god, and you will be holy, for I Iaw am holy. This is the law concerning animals and birds and every living creature moving in the water, and every living creature creeping on the land, to distinguish between the unclean and the clean, and between those that give birth alive, that should be eaten, and those that give birth alive, that should not be eaten."

Chapter 11 Notes

1 Codex Vaticanus: hymôn ths (ΥΜѠΝΘΣ). Translation: your god

• Leningrad Codex: lachem lelohim (לָכֶם לֵאלֹהִים). Translation: for you the goddesses (in Hebrew, or 'gods' in Aramaic, or 'god' in Neo-Assyrian)

This paragraph has not survived intact in any of the fragments of Leviticus found among the Dead Sea Scrolls, however, the word âlhym is found in other fragments of Leviticus, confirming it was used in the same place that the Masoretic Text uses it.

• Dead Sea Scroll 1QpaleoLev: âlhym (ʰⱫⱫⱯⱢⱯ)

• Dead Sea Scroll 4QLev-Numᵃ: âlhym (םיהˡא)

• Dead Sea Scroll 4QLevᵇ: âlhym (םיהˡא)

• Dead Sea Scroll 11QpaleoLevᵃ: âlhym (ʰⱫⱫⱯⱢⱯ)

• Peshitta: âlhå (ܐܠܗܐ). Translation: god

• Targum Onkelos: elah (אֱלָה). Translation: god

• Targum Jerusalem: alaha (אלָהָא). Translation: God

The word in the Masoretic Text is commonly translated as 'God,' but is a plural form of the Aramaic âlhå (ܐܠܗܐ), meaning 'gods,' or a plural form of the Hebrew elah (אֱלָה) meaning 'goddesses.'

The term âlhym (ⱯⱢⱫⱫ), and âlhym (ℷ^תלﬦ), are also direct transcriptions of the Assyrian cuneiform word elium (𒀭𒇲𒌉), which by the Iron Age meant 'god,' indicating that text had previously been written in cuneiform, and was translated into Aramaic or Phoenician during the iron age. During the bronze age, the word was pronounced as Alium (𒀭𒇲𒌉), and referred to a specific god, ᵈᵉⁱᵗʸAn (✶✶) the highest god, and father of the other gods. His Akkadian name was derived from the word elûm (𒀭𒈨𒉡), meaning 'higher,' as the term was intended to convey the meaning of 'highest.' He was believed to live in the polar region of the sky, where the modern constellation of Draco is located, making him the highest in the sky, around which all the gods (stars) circled.

The term El elyovn (אֵל עֶלְיוֹן), meaning 'highest god,' was translated into Hebrew in Genesis Chapter 14, where the Greeks translated it as theô tô ypsistô (θεω τω υψιστω), also meaning 'highest god.' El Elyon is known to have been a major god of the Canaanites, called âl ûâlyn (𐤉𐤋𐤏𐤍 𐤋𐤀), meaning 'God and Highest' in an Aramaic language Sefire Treaty from circa 750 BC. The Greek translations of Sanchuniathon's bronze age writing that has survived to the present, referred to the primordial creator god of the Canaanites as Elioun (Ελιουν), which appears to be the same god. According to Sanchuniathon, Elioun was the highest (υψιστος) god, who made the sky and the land, and they made the rest of the gods.

During the Old Babylonian and Old Assyrian eras, the gods Marduk and Ashur, the national gods of Babylon and Assyria, replaced the Akkadian An as the primary god of the Mesopotamian pantheons, and by the iron age, the word elium had came to mean 'god,' explaining why the Aramaic term âlhym (𐤉𐤄𐤋𐤀) would have been interpreted as 'god,' by the Greeks.

Leviticus: Chapter 12

Iaw said to Moses, "Tell the children of Israel, 'Whichever woman has conceived and born a male child will be unclean seven days, she will be unclean according to the days of separation for her monthly flow. On the eighth day, she will circumcise the flesh of his foreskin. For thirty-three days she will continue in her unclean blood. She will touch nothing holy, and will not enter the sanctuary, until the days of her purification are fulfilled. But if she should have born a female child, then she will be unclean twice seven days, according to the time of her monthly flow, and for sixty-six days will she remain in her unclean blood."

"When the days of her purification has been fulfilled for a son or a daughter, she will bring an undamaged lamb of a year old for a whole burnt offering, and a young pigeon or turtle-dove for a sin-offering to the door of the tabernacle of witness, to the priest. He will present it before Iaw, and the priest will make atonement for her and will purge her from the fountain of her blood. This is the law of she who carries a male or a female. If she can't afford a lamb, then will she take two turtledoves or two young pigeons, one for a whole burnt offering, and one for a sin-offering, and the priest will make atonement for her, and she will be purified.'"

Leviticus: Chapter 13

Iaw said to Moses and Aaron, "If any man should have on the skin of his flesh a bright clear spot, and there should be on the skin of his flesh a plague of leprosy, he will be brought to Aaron the priest, or one of his sons the priests. The priest will view the spot in the skin of his flesh, and if the hair in the spot is changed to white, and the appearance of the spot is below the skin of the flesh, it is a plague of leprosy, and the priest will look on it, and pronounce him unclean. But if the spot is clear and white in the skin of his flesh, yet the appearance it is not deep below the skin, and its hair has not changed to white hair, but it is dark, then the priest will separate him that has the spot seven days, and the priest will look on the spot the seventh day."

"Look, if the spot remains as before, if the spot has not spread in the skin, then the priest will separate him the second time seven days. The priest will look at him the second time on the seventh day. And, Look, if the spot is dark, and the spot has not spread in the skin, then the priest will pronounce him clean. For it is just a mark, and the man will wash his garments and be clean. But if the bright spot should have changed and spread in the skin after the priest has seen him to purify him, then he will appear the second time to the priest, and the priest will look at him. Look, if the mark has spread in the skin, then the priest will pronounce him unclean. It is leprosy."

"If a man has a plague of leprosy, then he will come to the priest. The priest will look, and if it is a white spot in the skin, and it has changed the hair to white, and there is some of the sound part of the quick flesh in the sore it is leprosy growing old in the skin of the flesh, and the priest will pronounce him unclean and will separate him because he is unclean. If leprosy should have come out very evidently in the skin, and leprosy should cover all the skin of the patient from the head to the feet, wherever the priest will look, then the priest will see, and, leprosy has covered all the skin of the flesh, and the priest will pronounce him clean of the plague because it has changed all to white, it is clean."

"But on any day the quick flesh appears on him, he will be pronounced unclean. The priest will look on the sound flesh, and the sound flesh will prove him to be unclean, for it is unclean, it is leprosy. But if the sound flesh is restored and changed to white, then he will come to the priest, and the priest will see him, and if the plague is turned white, then the priest will pronounce the patient clean. He is clean. If the flesh should have become an ulcer in his skin and should be healed, and there should be in the place of the ulcer a white sore, or one looking white and bright, or fiery, and it will be seen by the priest; then the priest will look, and if the appearance is beneath the skin, and its hair has changed to white, then the priest will pronounce him unclean because it is leprosy, it has broken out in the ulcer."

"But if the priest looks, and there is no white hair on it, and it is not below the skin of the flesh, and it is dark-colored; then the priest will separate him seven days. But if it manifestly spread over the skin, then the priest will pronounce him unclean: it is a plague of leprosy. It has broken out in the ulcer. But if the bright spot should remain in its place and not spread, it is the scar of the ulcer, and the priest will pronounce him clean. If the flesh of his skin in a state of fiery inflammation, and there is in his skin the part which is healed from the inflammation, bright, clear, and white, mixed with red or very white, then the priest will look at him, and, if the white hair is changed to a bright color, and its appearance is lower than the skin, it is leprosy, it has broken out in the inflammation, and the priest will pronounce him unclean. It is a plague of leprosy."

"But if the priest should look, and there is no white hair in the bright spot, and it is not lower than the skin, and it is dark, then the priest will separate him seven days. The priest will look on him on the seventh day, and if the spot has spread in the skin, then the priest will pronounce him unclean. It is a plague of leprosy. It has broken out in the ulcer. But if the bright spot remains stationary, and has not spread in the skin, but the sore should be dark, it is a scar of inflammation, and the priest will pronounce him clean, for it is the mark of the inflammation."

"If a man or a woman have in them a plague of leprosy in the head or the beard; then the priest will look on the plague, and, if the appearance it is beneath the skin, and in it, there is thin yellowish hair, then the priest will pronounce him unclean. It is dandruff, it is the leprosy of the head or leprosy of the beard. If the priest should see the plague of dandruff, and, the appearance it is not beneath the skin, and there is no yellowish hair in it, then the priest will set apart him that has the plague of dandruff seven days."

"The priest will look at the plague on the seventh day, and if the dandruff is not spread, and there is no yellowish hair on it, and the appearance of dandruff is not hollow under the skin, then the skin will be shaven, but the dandruff will not be shaven, and the priest will set aside the person having the dandruff the second time for seven days. The priest will see the dandruff on the seventh day, and see if the dandruff has not spread in the skin after the man's being shaved, and the appearance of the dandruff is not hollow beneath the skin, then the priest will pronounce him clean, and he will wash his garments, and be clean. But if the dandruff is indeed spread in the skin after he has been purified, then the priest will look, and, if the dandruff is spread in the skin, the priest will not examine concerning the yellow hair, for he is unclean. But if the dandruff remains before him in its place, and a dark hair should have risen in it, the scurf is healed. He is clean, and the priest will pronounce him clean."

"If a man or woman should have on the skin of their flesh bright whiteness spots, then the priest will look, and there are bright spots of a bright whiteness in the skin of their flesh, it is eczema. It burst out in the skin of his flesh. He is clean.

"If anyone's head should lose the hair, he is only bald, he is clean. If his head should lose the hair in front, he is forehead bald. He is clean. If there should be in his baldness of head, or his baldness of forehead, a white or fiery plague, it is leprosy in his baldness of head or baldness of forehead. The priest will look on him, and if the appearance of the plague is white or inflamed in his baldness of head or baldness in front, as the appearance of leprosy in the skin of his flesh, he is a leprous man: the priest will surely pronounce him unclean, his plague is in his head. The leper in whom the plague is, let his garments be loosened, and his head uncovered, and let him have a covering put on his mouth, and he will be called unclean. The days in which the plague will be on him, being unclean, he will be considered unclean. He will dwell apart, his place of residence will be outside the camp."

"If a garment has in it the plague of leprosy, a garment of wool, or a garment of flax, either in the warp or in the woof, or the linen, or in the woolen threads, or skin, or in any workmanship of skin, and the plague is greenish or reddish in the skin, or in the garment, either in the warp, or in the woof, or in any utensil of skin, it is a plague of leprosy, and he will show it to the priest. The priest will look on the plague, and the priest will set apart that which has the plague seven days."

"The priest will look at the plague on the seventh day, and if the plague is spread in the garment, either in the warp or in the woof, or the skin, in whatever things may be used in their workmanship, the plague is confirmed leprosy. It is unclean. He will burn the garment, either the warp or woof in woolen garments or in flaxen or in any utensil of skin, in which there may be the plague; because it is confirmed leprosy; it will be burnt with fire."

"If the priest should see, and the plague has not spread in the garments, either in the warp or in the woof, or any utensil of skin, then the priest will give directions, and one will wash that on which there may have been the plague, and the priest will set it aside a second time for seven days. The priest will look on it after the plague has been washed, and if this, even the plague, has not changed its appearance, and the plague does not spread, it is unclean."

"It will be burnt with fire. It is fixed in the garment, in the warp, or in the woof. If the priest should look, and the spot is dark after it has been washed, he will tear it off from the garment, either from the warp or from the woof, or the skin. If it should still appear in the garment, either in the warp or in the woof, or any article of skin, it is leprosy bursting out. That which has the plague in it will be burnt with fire. The garment, or the warp, or the woof, or any article of skin, which will be washed, and the plague depart from it, will also be washed again, and will be clean. This is the law of the plague of leprosy of a woolen or linen garment, either of the warp, or woof, or any leather article, to pronounce it clean or unclean."

Leviticus: Chapter 14

Iaw said to Moses, "This is the law of the leper. In whatever day he has been cleansed, then will he be brought to the priest. The priest will come out of the camp, and the priest will look, and the plague of leprosy is removed from the leper. The priest will give directions, and they will take for him that is cleansed two clean live birds, and cedarwood, and spun scarlet, and hyssop. The priest will give direction, and they will kill one bird over an earthen vessel over running water. As for the living bird, he will take it, and the cedarwood, and the spun scarlet, and the hyssop, and he will dip them and the living bird into the blood of the bird that was slain over running water. He will sprinkle seven times on him that was cleansed of his leprosy, and he will be clean, and he will let go the living bird into the field."

"The man that has been cleansed will wash his garments, and will shave off all his hair, and will wash in water, and will be clean, and after that, he will go into the camp and will remain out of his house seven days. It will come to pass on the seventh day, he will shave off all his hair on his head, and his beard, and his eyebrows, even all his hair will he shave, and he will wash his garments, and wash his body with water, and will be clean. On the eighth day, he will take two undamaged one-year-old lambs, and an undamaged one-year-old ewe lamb, and three-tenths of fine flour for sacrifice kneaded with oil, and one small cup of oil. The priest that cleanses will present the man under purification, and these offerings before Iaw, at the door of the tabernacle of witness. The priest will take one lamb, and offer him for a trespass-offering, and the cup of oil, and set them apart for a special offering before Iaw."

"They will kill the lamb in the place where they kill the whole burnt offerings, and the sin-offerings, in the holy places, like it was a sin-offering or trespass-offering. It belongs to the priest, it is holiest. The priest will take of the blood of the trespass-offering, and the priest will put it on the tip of the right ear of the person under cleansing, and the thumb of his right hand, and the big toe of his right foot. The priest will take of the cup of oil, and will pour it on his own left hand. He will dip the finger of his right hand into some of the oil that is in his left hand, and he will sprinkle with his finger seven times before Iaw."

"The remaining oil that is in his hand, the priest will put on the tip of the right ear of him that is under cleansing, and on the thumb of his right hand, and the big toe of his right foot, in place of the blood of the trespass-offering. The remaining oil that is on the hand of the priest, the priest will put on the head of the cleansed leper, and the priest will make atonement for him before Iaw. The priest will sacrifice the sin-offering, and the priest will make atonement for the person under purification to cleanse him from his sin, and afterward, the priest will kill the whole burnt offering. The priest will offer the whole burnt offering, and the sacrifice the altar before Iaw and the priest will make atonement for him, and he will be cleansed. If he is poor, and can't afford much, he can take one lamb for his transgression for a separate-offering, to make appeasement for him, and a tenth measure of fine flour mingled with oil for a sacrifice, and one cup of oil, and two turtledoves, or two young pigeons, as he can afford, and the one will be for a sin-offering, and the other for a whole burnt offering. He will bring them on the eighth day, to purify him, to the priest, to the door of the tabernacle of witness before Iaw. The priest will take the lamb of the trespass-offering, and the cup of oil, and place them for a set-offering before Iaw."

"He will kill the lamb of the trespass-offering, and the priest will take of the blood of the trespass-offering, and put it on the tip of the right ear of him that is under purification, and the thumb of his right hand, and on the big toe of his right foot. The priest will pour the oil on his own left hand. The priest will sprinkle with the finger of his right hand some of the oil that is in his left hand seven times before Iaw. The priest will put of the oil that is on his hand on the tip of the right ear of him that is under purification, and on the thumb of his right hand, and the big toe of his right foot, on the place of the blood of the tres-pass-offering. That which is left of the oil which is on the hand of the priest he will put on the head of him that is purged, and the priest will make atonement for him before Iaw. He will offer one of the turtledoves or the young pigeons, as he can afford it, the one for a sin-offering, the other for a whole burnt offering with the meat-offering, and the priest will make atonement before Iaw for him that is under purification. This is the law for him in who is the plague of leprosy, and who can't afford the offerings for his purification."

Iaw said to Moses and Aaron, "When you enter into the land of the Canaanites, which I give you for a possession, and I will put the plague of leprosy in the houses of the land of your possession, then the owner of the house will come and report to the priest, saying, 'I have seen as it were a plague in the house.' The priest will give orders to remove the furniture from the house before the priest comes in to see the plague, and so none of the things in the house will become unclean, and afterward, the priest will go in to examine the house. He will look at the plague, and if the plague is in the walls of the house, he will see greenish or reddish cavities, and the appearance of them will is beneath the surface of the walls. The priest will exit the house by the door of the house, and the priest will quarantine the house seven days. The priest will return on the seventh day and view the house, and, if the plague is spread in the walls of the house, then the priest will give orders, and they will take away the stones in which the plague is, and will cast them out of the city into an unclean place. They will scrape the inside of the house and will pour out the dust scraped off outside the city into an unclean place. They will take other scraped stones, and put them in the place of the former stones, and they will take other plaster and plaster the house."

"If the plague should return, and break out in the house after they have taken away the stones and after the house is scraped, and after it has been plastered, then the priest will go in and see if the plague is spread in the house, it is confirmed leprosy in the house. It is unclean. They will take down the house, and its timbers and its stones, and they will carry out all the mortar outside of the city into an unclean place. He that goes into the house at any time, during its separation, will be unclean until evening. He that sleeps in the house will wash his garments, and be unclean until evening, and he that eats in the house will wash his garments, and be unclean until evening."

"If the priest will arrive and enter and see the plague has not at all spread in the house after the house has been plastered, then the priest will declare the house clean because the plague is healed. He will take to purify the house two clean living birds, and cedarwood, and spun scarlet, and hyssop. He will kill one bird in an earthen vessel over running water. He will take the cedarwood, and the spun scarlet, and the hyssop, and the living bird, and will dip it into the blood of the bird slain over running water, and with them, he will sprinkle the house seven times. He will purify the house with the blood of the bird, and with the running water, and with the living bird, and with the cedarwood, and with the hyssop, and with the spun scarlet. He will let the living bird go out of the city into the field, and will make atonement for the house, and it will be clean. This is the law concerning every plague of leprosy and dandruff, and leprosy of a garment, and a house, and a sore, and a clear spot, and a shining one, and of declaring in what day it is unclean, and in what day it will be purged."

This is the law of leprosy.

Leviticus: Chapter 15

Iaw said to Moses and Aaron, "Speak to the children of Israel, and you will say to them, 'Any man that has an issue out of his body, his issue is unclean. This is the law of his uncleanness. Whoever has gonorrhea coming out of his body, this is his uncleanness in him by reason of the issue, by which, his body is affected through the issue: all the days of the issue of his body, by which his body is affected through the issue, there is his uncleanness. Every bed on which he that has the issue will happen to lie is unclean, and every seat on which he that has the issue may happen to sit, will be unclean. The man who will touch his bed, will wash his garments, and bathe himself in water and will be unclean until evening."

"Whoever sits on the seat on which he that has the issue may have sat, will wash his garments, and bathe himself in water, and will be unclean until evening. He that touches the skin of him that has the issue, will wash his garments and bathe himself in water, and will be unclean until evening. If he that has the issue should spit on one that is clean, that person will wash his garments, and bathe himself in water, and be unclean until evening. Every donkey's saddle, on which the man with the issue has mounted, will be unclean until evening. Everyone that touches whatever has been under him will be unclean until evening, and he that takes them up will wash his garments, and bathe himself in water and will be unclean until evening."

"Whoever he that has the issue will touch, if he has not rinsed his hands in water, he will wash his garments, and bathe his body in water, and will be unclean until evening. The earthen vessel which he that has the issue will happen to touch will be broken, and a wooden vessel will be washed with water and will be clean. and if he that has the issue should be cleansed of his issue, then he will count for himself seven days for his purification, and he will wash his garments and bathe his body in water and will be clean. On the eighth day, he will take to himself two turtledoves or two young pigeons, and he will bring them before Iaw to the doors of the tabernacle of witness and will give them to the priest. The priest will offer them one for a sin-offering, and the other for a whole burnt offering, and the priest will make atonement for him before Iaw for his issue."

"The man whose seed of copulation will happen to come out from him will then wash his whole body and will be unclean until evening. Every garment and every skin on which there will be the seed of copulation will both be washed with water, and be unclean until evening. A woman, if a man lays with her and copulates with semen, they will both bathe themselves in water and will be unclean until evening. The woman whoever has an issue of blood, when her issue will be in her body, will be seven days in her separation, everyone that touches her will be unclean until evening. Everything on which she will lie in her separation will be unclean, and whatever she will sit on, will be unclean."|

"Whoever will touch her bed will wash his garments, and bathe his body in water, and will be unclean until evening. and everyone that touches any vessel on which she will sit, will wash his garments and bathe himself in water and will be unclean until evening. Whether it is while she is on her bed, or on a seat which she may happen to sit on when he touches her, he will be unclean until evening. If anyone will lie with her, and her uncleanness is on him, he will be unclean seven days, and every bed on which he has lain will be unclean."

"If a woman has an issue of blood many days, not in the time of her separation, if the blood should also flow after her separation, all the days of the issue of her uncleanness will be as the days of her separation. She will be unclean. Every bed on which she will lie all the days of her flow will be to her as the bed of her separation, and every seat on which she will sit will be unclean according to the uncleanness of her separation. everyone that touches it will be unclean, and he will wash his garments, and bathe his body in water, and will be unclean until evening. But if she will be cleansed from her flow, then she will count for herself seven days, and afterward, she will be considered clean. On the eighth day, she will take two turtledoves, or two young pigeons, and will bring them to the priest, to the door of the tabernacle of witness. The priest will offer one for a sin-offering, and the other for a whole burnt offering, and the priest will make atonement for her before Iaw for her unclean flow."

"You will make the children of Israel to beware of their uncleannesses, so they will not die for their uncleanness, in polluting my tabernacle that is among them."

This is the law of the man who has an issue, and if one discharge seed of copulation, so that he should be polluted by it. This is the law for her that has the issue of blood in her separation, and as to the person who has an issue of seed, in his issue: it is a law for the male and the female, and for the man who has lain with her that is set apart.

Leviticus: Chapter 16

Iaw spoke to Moses after the two sons of Aaron died when bringing strange fire before Iaw. Iaw said to Moses, "Speak to Aaron your brother, and let him not come in at all times into the holy place within the veil before the lid, which is on the ark of the testimony, and he will not die, for I will appear in a cloud on the lid. Aaron enter into the holy place: with a calf of the herd for a sin-offering, and having a ram for a whole burnt offering. He will put on the consecrated linen tunic, and he has on his flesh the linen trousers, and will gird himself with a linen girdle, and will put on the linen cap, they are holy garments, and he will bathe all his body in water, and will put them on."

"He will take of the congregation of the children of Israel two kids of the goats for a sin-offering, and one lamb for a whole burnt offering. Aaron will bring the calf for his own sin-offering and will make atonement for himself and his house. He will take the two goats, and place them before Iaw by the door of the tabernacle of witness. Aaron will cast lots on the two goats, one lot for Iaw, and the other for the scapegoat.[1] Aaron will bring forward the goat on which the lot for Iaw fell, and will offer him for a sin-offering. The goat on which the lot of the scapegoat came, he will present alive before Iaw, to make atonement on him, to send him away as a scapegoat, and he will send him into the wilderness."

"Aaron will bring the calf for his sin, and he will make atonement for himself and for his house, and he will kill the calf for his sin-offering. He will take his censer full of coals of fire off the altar, which is before Iaw, and he will fill his hands with fine compound incense and will bring it within the veil. He will put the incense on the fire before Iaw, and the smoke of the incense will cover the mercy-seat over the tables of testimony, and he will not die. He will take of the blood of the calf, and sprinkle with his finger on the mercy-seat towards the east: before the mercy-seat will he sprinkle seven times of the blood with his finger. He will kill the goat for the sin-offering that is for the people, before Iaw, and he will bring in its blood within the veil, and will do with its blood as he did with the blood of the calf, and will sprinkle its blood on the mercy-seat, in front of the mercy-seat. He will make atonement for the sanctuary on account of the uncleanness of the children of Israel, and their trespasses in the matter of all their sins, and thus will he do to the tabernacle of witness established among them in the middle of their uncleanness."

"There will be no man in the tabernacle of witness when he goes in to make atonement in the holy place, until he has come out. He will make atonement for himself, and his house, and all the congregation of the children of Israel. He will come out to the altar that is before Iaw, and he will make atonement on it, and he will take the blood of the calf, and the blood of the goat, and will put it on the horns of the altar and around it. He will sprinkle some of the blood on it seven times with his finger and will purge it, and hallow it from the uncleanness of the children of Israel. He will finish making atonement for the sanctuary and for the tabernacle of witness, and the altar, and he will make a cleansing for the priests, and he will bring the living goat. Aaron will lay his hands on the head of the live goat and he will declare over him all the iniquities of the children of Israel, and all their unrighteousness, and all their sins, and he will lay them on the head of the live goat and will send him by the hand of a ready man into the wilderness. The goat will bear their unrighteousness on him into a desert land, and Aaron will send away the goat into the wilderness."

"Aaron will enter into the tabernacle of witness and will take off the linen garment, which he had put on, as he entered into the holy place, and will lay it down. He will bathe his body in water in the holy place, and will put on his clothing, and will go out and offer the whole burnt offering for himself and the whole burnt offering for the people: and will make atonement for himself and for his house, and for the people, as for the priests. He will offer the fat for the sin-offering on the altar. He that sends forth the goat that has been set apart to be let go, will wash his garments, and bathe his body in water, and afterward will enter into the camp. The calf for the sin-offering, and the goat for the sin-offering, whose blood was brought in to make atonement in the holy place, they will carry out of the camp, and burn them with fire, even their skins and their flesh and their dung."

"He that burns them will wash his garments, and bathe his body in water, and afterward, he will enter into the camp. This will be a perpetual statute for you, in the seventh month, on the tenth day of the month, you will humble your minds, and will do no work, nor the native and the stranger who lives among you. For on this day he will make an atonement for you, to cleanse you from all your sins before Iaw, and you will be purged."

"This will be for you the holiest sabbath, a rest, and you will humble your minds; it is a perpetual ordinance. The priest whoever they will anoint will make atonement, and whoever they will consecrate to exercise the priestly office after his father, and he will put on the linen robe, the holy garment. He will make atonement for the holiest place, and the tabernacle of witness, and he will make atonement for the altar, and for the priests, and he will make atonement for all the congregation. This will be to you a perpetual statute to make atonement for the children of Israel for all their sins."

It will be done once in the year, as Iaw commanded Moses.

Leviticus: Chapter 16 Notes

1 Codex Vaticanus: chimarous (ⲭⲓⲙⲀⲣⲞⲨⲤ). Translation: male-goat-kid

- Leningrad Codex: se'irei (שְׂעִירֵי). Translation: hairy

- DSS 4QLev-Numᵃ: šôyry (שעירי)

- Peshitta: ôzå (ܥܙܐ). Translation: she-goat

- Targum Onkelos: tzefirei (צְפִירֵי). Translation: he-goats

- Targum Jerusalem: tzefirei (צְפִירֵי). Translation: he-goats

The Hebrew word is generally believed to be a variation of the Greek word satyr (σάτυρος), itself possibly based on an older Canaanite term, however, the Greeks did not use the word satyr, instead, translating the word as male-goat-kid (χιμάρους), indicating that they did not consider the sacrifice to be a satyr. Both the Peshitta and Targum Onkelos use the Aramaic word for 'she-goat(s).'

Leviticus: Chapter 17

Iaw said to Moses, "Speak to Aaron and to his sons, and to all the children of Israel, and say to them, 'This is the word which Iaw has commanded, saying, Every man of the children of Israel, or of the strangers dwelling among you, who will kill a calf, or a sheep, or a goat in the camp, or who will kill it out of the camp, and will not bring it to the door of the tabernacle of witness, to sacrifice it for a whole burnt offering or peace-offering to Iaw to be acceptable for a sweet-smelling savor: and whoever will kill it outside, and will not bring it to the door of the tabernacle of witness, to offer it as a gift to Iaw before the tabernacle of Iaw. Blood will be imputed to that man, as he has shed blood. That mind will be cut off from his people.'"

"'The children of Israel may offer their sacrifices, all that they will kill in the fields, and bring them to Iaw to the doors of the tabernacle of witness to the priest, and they will sacrifice them as a peace-offering to Iaw. The priest will pour the blood on the altar round about before Iaw by the doors of the tabernacle of witness and will offer the fat for a sweet-smelling savor to Iaw. They will no longer offer their sacrifices to vain gods after which they go a whoring, it will be a perpetual statute to you for your generations.'"

"You will say to them, 'Whatever man of the children of Israel, or the sons of the proselytes dwelling among you, will offer a whole burnt offering or a sacrifice, and will not bring it to the door of the tabernacle of witness to sacrifice it to Iaw, that man will be destroyed from among his people. Whatever man of the children of Israel, or the strangers dwelling among you, will eat any blood, I will even set my face against that mind that eats blood, and will destroy it from its people. For the life of the flesh is its blood, and I have given it to you on the altar to make atonement for your minds; for its blood will make atonement for the mind.'"

"'Therefore I said to the children of Israel, 'No mind of you will eat blood, and the stranger that lives among you will not eat blood.' Whatever man of the children of Israel, or the strangers dwelling among you will take any animal in hunting, animal, or bird, which is eaten, then he will pour out the blood, and cover it in the dust. For the blood of all flesh is its life, and I said to the children of Israel, 'You will not eat the blood of any flesh,' for the life of all flesh is its blood. Everyone that eats it will be destroyed. Every mind which eats that which has died itself, or is taken of animals, either among the natives or among the strangers, will wash his garments, and bathe himself in water, and will be unclean until evening: then will he be clean. But if he does not wash his garments, and do not bathe his body in water, then will he bear his iniquity.'"

Leviticus: Chapter 18

Iaw commanded Moses, "Speak to the children of Israel and say to them, 'I am Iaw the god. You will not do according to the ways of Egypt, in which you lived, and according to the ways of the land of Canaan, into which I bring you. You will not do, and you will not follow their ordinances. You will observe my judgments, and will keep my ordinances, and will follow them. I am Iaw the god! So you will keep all my ordinances, and all my judgments, and do them, which if a man does, he will live in them! I am Iaw the god!"

"No man will draw near to any of his near family members and uncover their nakedness! I am Iaw!"

"You will not uncover the nakedness of your father, or the nakedness of your mother, for she is your mother! You will not uncover her nakedness. You will not uncover the nakedness of your father's wife, it is your father's nakedness. You will not uncover the nakedness of your sister or your father or your mother, born at home or abroad. The nakedness of your grand-daughter you will not uncover because it is your nakedness. You will not uncover the nakedness of the daughter of your father's wife; she is your sister by the same father, you will not uncover her nakedness. You will not uncover the nakedness of your father's sister. She is near family to your father. You will not uncover the nakedness of your mother's sister. She is near family to your mother. You will not uncover the nakedness of your father's brother, and you will not go into his wife. She is your relation. You will not uncover the nakedness of your daughter-in-law, for she is your son's wife, you will not uncover her nakedness. You will not uncover the nakedness of your brother's wife. It is your brother's nakedness. The nakedness of a woman and her daughter will you not uncover, nor will you take her grand-daughter to uncover their nakedness. They are your family, and it is inappropriate."

"You will not take your wife's sister in addition to her while she is still alive, as a rival, to uncover their nakedness together. You will not go into a woman during her separation for her uncleanness, to uncover her nakedness. You will not lie with your neighbor's wife, to defile yourself with her. You will not give of your seed to serve Moloch[1] and you will not profane my holy name. I am Iaw."

"You will not lie with a male as with a woman, for it is an abomination. Neither will you lie with any quadruped for copulation, to be polluted with it.

533

Neither will a woman present herself before any quadruped to have intercourse with it, for it is an abomination."

"Do not defile yourselves with any of these things, for in all these things the nations are defiled, which I drive out before you. The land is polluted, and I have repaid their iniquity to them because of it, and the land is injured by those who live on it. You will keep all my statutes and all my ordinances, and you will do none of these abominations; neither the native, nor the stranger that joins himself with you. All these abominations the men of the land did who were before you, and the land was defiled, and the land may becomes injured by you in your polluting it, as it was injured by the nations before you."

"For whoever will do any of these abominations, the minds that do them will be destroyed from among their people. You will keep mine ordinances, that you may not do any of the abominable practices, which have taken place before your time, and you will not be polluted in them, as I am Iaw the god."

Leviticus: Chapter 18 Notes

1 Codex Vaticanus: archôn (ΑΡΧШΝ). Translation: ruler

• Leningrad Codex: Molech (מֹלֶךְ). Translation: Moloch

• Peshitta: lmbtnw nûkrytå (ܢܘܟܪ̈ܝܬܐ ܠܡܒܛܢܘ). Translation: the womb of (feminine) foreigners

• Targum Onkelos: Molech (מוֹלֶךְ). Translation: Moloch

• Targum Jerusalem: bat ammin (בַּת עַמְמִין). Translation: daughter of the (foreign) peoples

The meaning of this verse has been debated for thousands of years. The Greek translation treated the word as a human 'ruler,' suggesting a prohibition on sending one's children to fight for a ruler, presumably other than the king of Jerusalem. The Hebrew translation, and the Aramaic Targum Onkelos both use the name Molech, which is believed to have been the Judahite variant of the Ammonite god Milcom, although this is still debated. The Aramaic translations found in the Peshitta and Targum Jerusalem both read as prohibitions on interbreeding with non-Jews.

As Leviticus was almost certainly written in Judahite, the precursor to Classical Hebrew, the original word would have been mlk (𐤌𐤋𐤊), meaning 'king.' All records related to the translation indicate the Greek translation was made from an Aramaic translation, meaning the word would have been mlkå (𐡌𐡋𐡊), which means 'king' or 'ruler.' The significant deviation found in the Peshitta and Targum Jerusalem appears to be a substitution made after Molech worship had disappeared, and when the Judahite leaders were trying to suppress intermarriage with other nations. It may be a relic of Ezra's Aramaic Torah. As the name Molech is likely the original term used in the verse, the common English translation of Moloch is used in.

Leviticus: Chapter 19

Iaw said Moses, Speak to the congregation of the children of Israel, and you will say to them, 'You will be holy, for I, Iaw your God, am holy. Let every one of you respect his father and his mother, and you will keep my sabbaths. I am Iaw the god!'"

"'You will not worship idols, and you will not make molten gods for yourselves. I am Iaw the god!'"

"If you sacrifice a peace-offering to Iaw, you will offer it acceptable from yourselves. In whatever day you sacrifice it, it will be eaten, and on the following day, and if any it should be left until the third day, it will be thoroughly burnt with fire. If it should be at all eaten on the third day, it is unfit for sacrifice. It will not be accepted. He that eats it will bear his iniquity because he has profaned the holy things of Iaw, and the minds that eat it will be destroyed from among their people. When you reap the harvest of your land, you will not complete the reaping of your field with exactness, and you will not gather that which falls from your reaping. You will not go over the gathering of your vineyard, neither will you gather the remaining grapes of your vineyard. You will leave them for the poor and the stranger. I am Iaw the god!'"

"'You will not steal. You will not lie. You will not provide false witness as an informer against your neighbor. You will not swear unjustly by my name, and you will not profane the holy name of your god. I am Iaw the god!'

"'You will not injure your neighbor, nor will you rob him, nor will the wages of your employee remain with you overnight. You will not revile the deaf, neither will you put a stumbling block in the way of the blind, and you will fear Iaw the god. I am Iaw the god! You will not act unjustly in judgment. You will not accept the existence of poor people, nor admire mighty people. You will judge your neighbor justly. You will not walk deceitfully among your people. You will not rise against the blood of your neighbor. I am Iaw the god!'"

"'You will not hate your brother in your heart. You will not in any way rebuke your neighbor, so you will not bear sin on his account. Your hand will not avenge you, and you will not be angry with the children of your people. You will love your neighbor as yourself. I am Iaw!'"

"'You will observe my law. You will not let your livestock mate with one of a different kind, and you will not sow your vineyard with diverse seed, and you will not put on yourself a mingled garment woven of two materials. If anyone lay carnally with a woman, and she should be a home-servant kept for a man, and she has not been ransomed, and her freedom has not been given to her, they will be visited with punishment; but they will not die, because she was not set at liberty. He will bring for his trespass to Iaw to the door of the tabernacle of witness, a ram for a trespass-offering. The priest will make atonement for him with the ram of the trespass-offering, before Iaw, for the sin which he sinned, and the sin which he sinned will be forgiven him.'"

"'When you enter into the land which Iaw your God gives you, and will plant any fruit tree, then you will purge away its uncleanness. Its fruit will be unclean for you for three years, and will not be eaten. In the fourth year, all its fruit will be holy, a subject of praise to Iaw. In the fifth year, you will eat the fruit, its produce is an increase for you. I am Iaw the god!'"

"'Do not eat on the mountains, nor employ omens, nor divine by inspection of birds. You will not cut the hair of your head round, nor disfigure your beard. You will not make cuttings in your body for a dead body, and you will not tattoo on yourselves any marks. I am Iaw the god!'"

"'You will not profane your daughter and prostitute her, so the land will not go whoring, and the land become filled with iniquity. You will keep my sabbaths, and revere my sanctuaries: I am Iaw!'"

"'Do not follow your feelings, or you will pollute yourselves with them. I am Iaw the god.'"

"'You will rise up before the gray head, and honor the face of the old man, and will fear your God, I am Iaw your God.'"[1]

"'If a stranger should come to your land, you will not attack him. The stranger that comes to you will be among you as the native, and you will love him as yourself; for you were strangers in the land of Egypt: I am Iaw the god!'"

"'You will not act dishonestly in judgment, in measures and weights and scales. There will be among you just balances and just weights and just liquid measure. I am Iaw your God, who brought you out of the land of Egypt. You will keep all my law and all my ordinances, and you will do them. I am Iaw your God!'"

Leviticus: Chapter 19 Notes

1 Codex Vaticanus: cae phobêthêsê c̄n ton t̄h̄n sou. egô imi c̄s o t̄h̄s hymôn (ΚΑΙ ΦΟΒΗΘΗϹΗΚ̄Ν̄ΤΟΝΘ̄Ν̄ϹΟΥΕΓωΕΙΜΙΚ̄ϹΟΘ̄ϹΥΜωΝ) Translation: and fear lord the god of you. I am lord the god of you

- Leningrad Codex: veyareta me'eloheicha ani Yehvah (וְיָרֵאתָ מֵאֱלֹהֶיךָ אֲנִי יְהוָה). Translation: and fear god of yours I'm Yehvah

- Peshitta: âlå dḥl mn âlhå: ånå ånå mryå (ܐܠܐ ܕܚܠ ܡܢ ܐܠܗܐ: ܐܢܐ ܐܢܐ ܡܪܝܐ). Translation: unless being afraid of god: I am master

- Targum Onkelos: vetidchal me'elahach ana yeyah (וְתִדְחַל מֵאֱלָהָךְ אֲנָא יְיָ). Translation: and be afraid of god of yours I'm Yhů

- Targum Jerusalem: vetidchal me'elahach ana yeyah (וְתִדְחַל מֵאֱלָהָךְ אֲנָא יְיָ). Translation: and be afraid of god of yours I'm Yhů

Leviticus: Chapter 20

Iaw said to Moses, "You will also tell the children of Israel, 'If there are any of the children of Israel, or of those who have become proselytes in Israel, who give his seed to Moloch,[1] let him be put to death. The nation on the land will stone him with stones. I will set my face against that man and will cut him off from his people, because he has given of his seed to Moloch, to defile my sanctuary, and profane the name of them that are consecrated to me."

"If the natives of the land should in any way overlook that man in giving of his seed to Moloch, so as not put him to death, then I will set my face against that man and his family, and I will destroy him, and all who have been of one mind with him, so that he should go a whoring to the princes, from their people. The mind that will follow those who have in them divining spirits, or enchanters, to go a whoring after them; I will set my face against that mind and will destroy it from among its people. You will be holy, for I, Iaw your God, am holy.'"

"'You will observe my ordinances, and do them. I am Iaw who sanctifies you. Every man who will speak evil of his father or his mother, let him die the death. Has he spoken evil of his father or his mother? He will be guilty."

"Whatever man will commit adultery with the wife of a man, or whoever will commit adultery with the wife of his neighbor, let them die the death, the adulterer and the adulteress."

"If anyone should lie with his father's wife, he has uncovered his father's nakedness: let them both die the death, they are guilty. If anyone should lie with his daughter-in-law, let them both be put to death, for they have worked impiety, they are guilty."

"Whoever will lie with a male as with a woman, they have both worked abomination; let them die the death, they are guilty."

"Whoever will take a woman and her mother, it is iniquity: they will burn him and them with fire. So there will not be iniquity among you.'"

"Whoever lies with an animal, let him die the death, and you will kill the animal. Whatever woman approaches any animal to have intercourse with it, you will kill the woman and the animal. Let them die the death, they are guilty."

"Whoever will take his sister by his father or by his mother, and will see her nakedness, and she sees his nakedness, it is a reproach: they will be destroyed before the children of their family. He has uncovered his sister's nakedness, they will bear their sin."

"Whatever man will lie with a woman that is set apart for a flow, and will uncover her nakedness, he has uncovered her fountain, and she has uncovered the flow of her blood. They will both be destroyed from among their generation."

"You will not uncover the nakedness of your father's sister, or the sister of your mother. For that man has uncovered the nakedness of one near family: they will bear their iniquity."

"Whoever lies with his near relative, has uncovered the nakedness of one closely related to him. They will die childless. Whoever will take his brother's wife, it is uncleanness, he has uncovered his brother's nakedness, they will die childless."

"Keep all my ordinances, and my judgments, and you will do them, and the land will not be injured by you, which I bring you to live in. Don't follow in the customs of the nations which I drive out from before you; for they have done all these things, and I have abhorred them: and I said to you, You will inherit their land, and I will give it to you for a possession, a land flowing with milk and honey. I am Iaw your God, who has separated you from all people. You will make a distinction between the clean and the unclean livestock, and between clean and unclean birds, and you will not defile your minds with livestock, or with birds, or with any creeping things of the land, which I have separated for you because of uncleanness. You will be holy to me, because I, Iaw your God, am holy, who separated you from all nations, to be mine."

"As for a man or woman whoever of them has in them a divining spirit, or be an enchanter, let them both die the death. You will stone them with stones, they are guilty."

Leviticus: Chapter 20 Notes

1 Codex Vaticanus: archôn (ⲁⲣⲭⲱⲛ). Translation: ruler

• Dead Sea Scroll 11QpaleoLevᵃ: mlk (𐤌𐤋𐤊). Translation: king

• Leningrad Codex: Molech (מֹלֶךְ). Translation: Moloch

- Peshitta: nůkrytå (ܢܘܟܪܝܬܐ). Translation: (feminine) foreigners

- Targum Onkelos: Molech (מוֹלֶךְ). Translation: Moloch

- Targum Jerusalem: Molech (מוֹלֶךְ). Translation: Moloch

The meaning of this verse has been debated for thousands of years. The Greek translation treated the word as a human 'ruler,' suggesting a prohibition on sending one's children to fight for a ruler, presumably other than the king of Jerusalem. The Hebrew translation, and the Aramaic Targum Onkelos both use the name Molech, which is believed to have been the Judahite variant of the Ammonite god Milcom, although this is still debated. The Aramaic translations found in the Peshitta and Targum Jerusalem both read as prohibitions on interbreeding with non-Jews. As Leviticus was almost certainly written in Judahite, the precursor to Classical Hebrew, the original word would have been mlk (𐤌𐤋𐤊), meaning 'king,' as preserved in DSS 11QpaleoLev[a]. All records related to the translation indicate the Greek translation was made from an Aramaic translation, meaning the would would have been mlkå (𐤌𐤋𐤊𐤀), which means 'king' or 'ruler.' As the name Molech is likely the original term used in the verse, the common English translation of Moloch is used in.

Leviticus: Chapter 21

Iaw said to Moses, "Speak to the priests, the sons of Aaron, and you will tell them that they will not defile themselves in their nation for the dead, but they may mourn for a relative who is very near to them, for a father and mother, and sons and daughters, for a brother, and for a virgin sister that is near to one, that is not married to a man, for this one will defile himself. He will not defile himself suddenly among his people to profane himself."

"You will not shave your head for the dead with baldness on the top, and they will not shave their beard, neither will they cut gashes in their flesh. They will be holy to their god, and they will not profane the name of their god, for they offer the sacrifices of Iaw as the gifts of their god, and they will be holy. They will not take a woman who is a harlot and profaned, or a woman put away from her husband. Holy is Iaw the god. You will hallow him, he offers the gifts of Iaw your God. He will be holy, for I, Iaw that sanctify them, am holy."

"If the daughter of a priest should be profaned to go whoring, she profanes the name of her father, and she will be burnt with fire. The priest that is chief among his brothers, having had the oil poured on his head as the anointed one, and he having been consecrated to put on the garments, will not take the miter off his head, and will not rend his garments, neither will he go in to any dead body, neither will he defile himself for his father or his mother. He will not go forth out of the sanctuary, and he will not profane the sanctuary of his god, because the holy anointing oil of God is on him. I am Iaw! He will take as a wife a virgin from his own tribe. But a widow, or one that is divorced, or profaned, or a harlot, these he will not take. He will take as a wife a virgin of his own people. He will not profane his seed among his people. I am Iaw, who sanctifies him."

Iaw said to Moses, "Tell Aaron, 'A man of your tribe throughout your generations, who has an imperfection in him, will not draw near to offer the gifts of his god. No man who has an imperfection in him will draw near, a man blind, lame, with a disfigured nose or his ears cut, a man who has a broken hand or a broken foot, or humpbacked, or blear-eyed, or that has lost his eye-lashes, or a man who has a malignant ulcer, or eczema, or one that has lost a testicle. Whoever of the seed of Aaron the priest has an imperfection on him, will not come near to offer sacrifices to your god, because he has an imperfection on him. He will not come close and offer the gifts of god. The gifts of god are sacred, and he will eat of the holy things. Only he will not approach the veil, and he will not come close to the altar, because he has an imperfection, and he will not profane the sanctuary of his god, for I am Iaw, who sanctifies them.'" Moses spoke to Aaron and his sons, and all the children of Israel.

Leviticus: Chapter 22

Iaw said to Moses, "Speak to Aaron and his sons, and let them pay attention concerning the holy things of the children of Israel, so they will not profane my holy name in any of the things which they consecrate to me. I am Iaw! Say to them, 'Every man throughout your generations, whoever from all your seed will approach the holy things, whatever the children of Israel will consecrate to Iaw, while his uncleanness is on him, that mind will be cut off from me. I am Iaw the god!'"

"The man from the seed of Aaron the priest, if he should have leprosy or issue of the reins, will not eat of the holy things, until he is cleansed, and he that touches any uncleanness of a dead body, or the man whose semen has gone out from him, or whoever will touch any unclean reptile, which will defile him, or who will touch a man, whereby he will defile him according to all his uncleanness, whatever mind will touch them will be unclean until evening. He will not eat of the holy things unless he bathes his body in water, and the sun goes down, and then he will be clean, and then he will eat of all the holy things, for they are his bread. He will not eat that which dies itself or is taken of animals so that he should be polluted by them. I am Iaw!"

"They will keep my ordinances, that they do not bear iniquity because of them, and die because of them if they profane them. I am Iaw the god that sanctifies them!"

"No foreigner will eat holy things. One that resides with a priest, or an employee, will not eat the holy things. But if a priest should have a slave purchased for silver, he will eat of his bread, and they that are born in his house, they also will eat of his bread. If the daughter of a priest should marry a stranger, she will not eat of the offerings of the sanctuary. If the daughter of a priest should be a widow, or divorced, and have no seed, she will return to her father's house, as in her youth. She will eat of her father's bread, but no stranger will eat it. The man who will ignorantly eat holy things, will add the fifth part to it, and give the holy thing to the priest. They will not profane the holy things of the children of Israel, which they offer to Iaw. So they should bring on themselves the iniquity of trespass in their eating their holy things. I am Iaw the god, the sanctifier of this!"[1]

Iaw said to Moses, "Speak to Aaron and his sons, and all the congregation of Israel, and you will say to them, 'Any man of the children of Israel, or of the strangers that lives among them in Israel, who offers his gifts according to all their confession and according to all their choice, whatever they may bring to God whole burnt offerings your free will offerings will be males without imperfection of the herds, or the sheep, or the goats. They will not bring to Iaw anything that has an imperfection in it, for it will not be acceptable for you. Whichever man will offer a peace-offering to Iaw, discharging a vow, or in the way of free will offering, or an offering in your feasts, of the herds or of the sheep, it will be without imperfection for acceptance. There will be no imperfection in it."

"One that is blind, or broken, or has its tongue cut out, or is troubled with warts, or has a malignant ulcer, or eczema, they will not offer these to Iaw. Neither will you offer any of them for a burnt offering on the altar of Iaw. A calf or a sheep with the ears cut off, or that has lost its tail, you will kill them for yourself. But they will not be accepted for your vow. That which has broken testicles, or is crushed or gelded or mutilated, you will not offer them to Iaw, nor will you sacrifice them on your land. Neither will you offer the gifts of your god of all these things by the hand of a stranger, because there is corruption in them, an imperfection in them. These will not be accepted for you."

Iaw said to Moses, "As for a calf, or a sheep, or a goat, whenever it is born, then after it is seven days under its mother, and on the eighth day and after they will be accepted for sacrifices, a burnt offering to Iaw. A bullock and a ewe, it and it's young, you will not kill in one day. If you should offer a sacrifice, a vow of rejoicing to Iaw, you will offer it to be accepted for you. On that same day, it will be eaten. You will not leave some of the meat until the next day. I am Iaw!

You will keep my commandments and do them. You will not profane the sacred name,[2] and I will be sanctified in the middle of the children of Israel. I am Iaw that sanctifies you, who brought you out of the land of Egypt, to be your god. I am Iaw!"

Leviticus: Chapter 23 Notes

1 Codex Vaticanus: egô c̅s̅ o t̅h̅s̅ o agiazôn autous (ϵⲅⲱ ⲕ̅ⲥ̅ ⲟ ⲑ̅ⲥ̅ ⲟ ⲁⲅⲓⲁⲍⲱⲛ ⲁⲩⲧⲟⲩⲥ). Translation: I am Lord the god the sanctifier of this.

- Leningrad Codex: ani Yehvah mekaddesham (אֲנִי יְהוָה מְקַדְּשָׁם). Translation: I Yehvah of sanctuaries

• DSS 4QLev[b]: åny Yhůh mqdšm (טשיצפ אוהי וֹאַ). Translation: I Yhůh of sanctuaries.

• Peshitta: ånå ånå mryå dmqdš ånå lhůn (ܠܗܘܢ ܐܢܐ ܕܡܩܕܫ ܡܪܝܐ ܐܢܐ ܐܢܐ). Translation: I am master the temple (or sanctuary) I myself

• Targum Onkelos: tidḥal me'elahach ana yeyah (יְיָ אֲנָא מֵאֱלָהָךְ תִּדְחַל). Translation: be afraid of god of yours I'm Yhů of sanctuaries

• Targum Jerusalem: ana yeyah mekadishhon (מְקַדְּשָׁהוֹן יְיָ אֲנָא). Translation: I'm Yhů

This verse includes one of the two deviations between the Septuagint and Masoretic versions of Leviticus regarding the name of the author's god, assuming one accepts that Dead Sea Scroll 4QpapLXXLev[b] retains the original Greek translation of the Aramaic Yhů (𐤉𐤄𐤅) as Iaô (Ιαω). The Greek text indicates the Aramaic Text of Leviticus used the term adonai ha'elohim (הָאֱלֹהִים אֲדֹנָי), however, also restructured the verse slightly, likely because the Aramaic translator did not understand the Edomite word myqdšm (𐤌𐤔𐤃𐤒𐤌).

2 Codex Vaticanus: to onoma tou agiou (ΤΟΟΝΟΜΑΤΟΥΑΓΙΟΥ). Translation: the name of sacred (or saint)

• Leningrad Codex: et-shem kadeshi (קָדְשִׁי אֶת־שֵׁם). Translation: the name sacred (or Qetesh)

• Peshitta: šmå dqůdšy (ܕܩܘܕܫܝ ܫܡܐ). Translation: name of Qetesh (or sacred)

• Targum Onkelos: ana yeyah mekaddishchon (מְקַדְּשְׁכוֹן יְיָ אֲנָא). Translation: I'm yeyah (or Yhů) from sacredness

Leviticus: Chapter 23

Iaw said to Moses, "Speak to the children of Israel, and you will say to them, 'The feasts of Iaw which you will call holy assemblies, these are my feasts. Six days will you do works, but on the seventh day is the sabbath, a rest, a holy convocation to Iaw. You will not do any work, it is a sabbath to Iaw in all your dwellings. These are the feasts to Iaw, holy assemblies which you will call in their seasons. In the first month, on the fourteenth day of the month, between the evening times is Iaw's Passover. On the fifteenth day of this month is the feast of unleavened bread for Iaw, and for seven days will you eat unleavened bread."

"The first day will be a holy convocation to you, and you will do no servile work. You will offer whole burnt offerings to Iaw for seven days, and the seventh day will be a holy convocation to you, and you will do no servile work."

Iaw said to Moses, "Tell the children of Israel, 'When you will enter into the land which I give you, and reap the harvest it, then will you bring a sheaf, the first fruits of your harvest, to the priest, and he will lift the sheaf before Iaw, to be accepted for you. On the morning of the first day, the priest will lift it. You will offer on the day on which you bring the sheaf, a lamb without imperfection of a year old for a whole burnt offering to Iaw. Its meat-offering two tenth portions of fine flour mingled with oil: it is a sacrifice to Iaw, a smell of sweet savor to Iaw, and its drink-offering a quarter of a hin[1] of wine. You will not eat bread, or the new parched grain, until this same day, until you offer the sacrifices to your god. It is a perpetual statute throughout your generations in all your dwellings.'"

"'You will count for yourselves from the day after the sabbath, from the day on which you will offer the sheaf of the heave-offering, seven full weeks until the morning after the last week you will count fifty days and will bring a new meat-offering to Iaw. You will bring from your dwelling loaves, as a heave-offering, two loaves, they will be of two tenth portions of fine flour, they will be baked with the leaven of the first fruits for Iaw. You will bring with the loaves seven undamaged lambs, each a year old, and one calf of the herd, and two rams without imperfection, and they will be a whole burnt offering to Iaw. Their meat-offerings and their drink-offerings will be a sacrifice, a smell of sweet savor to Iaw. They will sacrifice one kid of the goats for a sin-offering, and two lambs, each a year old for a peace-offering, with the loaves of the first fruits.'"

"'The priest will place them with the loaves of the first-fruits, and offering before Iaw with the two lambs, they will be holy to Iaw. They will belong to the priest that brings them. You will call this day a convocation. It will be holy to you. You will do no servile work on it. It is a perpetual ordinance throughout your generations in all your habitations. When you will reap the harvest of your land, you will not fully reap the remainder of the harvest of your field when you reap, and you will not gather that which falls from your reaping. You will leave it for the poor and the stranger. I am Iaw your god!'"

Iaw said to Moses, "Tell the children of Israel, 'In the seventh month, on the first day of the month, you will rest with a celebration of trumpets. It will be for you a holiday. You will do no servile work, and you will offer a whole burnt offering to Iaw."

Iaw said to Moses, "Also on the tenth day of this seventh month is a day of atonement. It will be a holy convocation to you, and you will humble your minds, and offer a whole burnt offering to Iaw. You will do no work on this day, for this is a day of atonement for you, to make atonement for you before Iaw your god. Every mind that will not be humbled in that day, will be cut off from among its people. Every mind which will do work on that day, that mind will be destroyed from among its people. You will do no manner of work: it is a perpetual statute throughout your generations in all your habitations. It will be a holy sabbath to you, and you will humble your minds, from the ninth day of the month: from evening to evening you will keep your sabbaths."

Iaw said to Moses, "Tell the children of Israel, 'On the fifteenth day of this seventh month, there will be a feast of tabernacles seven days to Iaw. On the first day will be a holy convocation, and you will do no servile work. Seven days will you offer whole burnt offerings to Iaw, and the eighth-day will be a holy convocation to you, and you will offer whole burnt offerings to Iaw. It is a time of release, you will do no servile work. These are the feasts to Iaw, which you will call holy assemblies, to offer burnt offerings to Iaw, whole burnt offerings, and their meat-offerings, and their drink-offerings, that for each day on its day."

"Besides the sabbaths of Iaw, and your gifts, and all your vows, and your freewill offerings, which you will give to Iaw, on the fifteenth day of this seventh month, when you have completely gathered in the fruits of the land, you will keep a feast to Iaw seven days. On the first day there will be a rest and on the eighth day a rest. On the first day you will take good fruit of trees, and branches of palm trees, and thick boughs of trees, and willows, and branches of osiers from the brook, to rejoice before Iaw your God seven days in the year. It is a perpetual statute for your generations. In the seventh month, you will keep it. Seven days you will dwell in tabernacles: every native in Israel will dwell in tents, that your posterity may see, that I made the children of Israel dwell in tents when I brought them out of the land of Egypt. I am Iaw the god!"

So Moses recounted the feasts of Iaw to the children of Israel.

Leviticus: Chapter 23 Notes

1 Codex Vaticanus: in (ιℵ)

• Leningrad Codex: hin (הִין)

• Peshitta: hmynâ (ܗܡܝܢܐ). Translation: belt (a unit of measurement in the Persian empire)

• Targum Onkelos: hina (הִינָא)

• Targum Jerusalem: hina (הִינָא)

The hin was ancient Samaritan and Judahite unit of measurement estimated around 3.7 liters (3.9 quarts).

Leviticus: Chapter 24

Iaw said to Moses, "Order the children of Israel and let them take for you pure beaten olive oil for the light, to burn a lamp continually, outside the veil in the tabernacle of witness, and Aaron and his sons will burn it from evening until morning before Iaw continually, a perpetual statute throughout your generations. You will burn the lamps on the pure lamp-stand before Iaw until the morning. You will take fine flour, and make it twelve loaves; each loaf will be of two tenth parts. You will put them in two rows, each row containing six loaves, on the pure table before Iaw. You will put in each row pure frankincense and salt, and these things will be for loaves for a memorial, set out before Iaw."

"On the sabbath-day, they will be set out before Iaw continually before the children of Israel, for an eternal covenant. They will be for Aaron and his sons, and they will eat them in the holy place. For this is their sacred portion of the offerings made to Iaw, a perpetual statute. There went about a son of an Israelite woman, and he was the son of an Egyptian man among the sons of Israel, and they fought in the camp, the son of the Israelite woman, and a man who was an Israelite. The son of the Israelite woman cursed by the name, and they brought him to Moses. His mother's name was Salomith, daughter of Dabri of the tribe of Dan. They held him in a ward, to judge him by the command of Iaw.

Iaw said to Moses, "Bring him out who cursed outside the camp, and all who heard will lay their hands on his head, and all the congregation will stone him. Speak to the sons of Israel, and you will say to them, 'Whoever will curse God will bear his sin. He that names the name of Iaw, let him die the death. Let all the congregation of Israel stone him with stones, whether he is a stranger or a native, let him die for cursing the name of Iaw.'"

"Whoever strikes a man and he dies, let him die the death. Whoever will strike an animal, and it will die, let him return life for life. Whoever will inflict an imperfection on his neighbor, as he has done to him, so will it be done to himself in return: bruise for bruise, eye for eye, tooth for tooth. If anyone inflicts an imperfection on a man, so will it be rendered to him. Whoever will strike a man, and he will die, let him die the death."

"There will be one judgment for the stranger and the native, for I am Iaw your God!"

Moses spoke to the children of Israel, and they brought him that had cursed out of the camp, and stoned him with stones. The children of Israel did as Iaw commanded Moses.

Leviticus: Chapter 25

Iaw spoke to Moses on Mount Sinai, saying, "Tell the children of Israel, "Whenever you have entered into the land, which I give to you, then the land will rest which I give to you, for its sabbaths to Iaw. Six years you will sow your field, and six years you will prune your vine, and gather in its fruit. But in the seventh year will be a sabbath, it will be a rest to the land, a sabbath to Iaw. You will not sow your field, and you will not prune your vine. You will not gather the spontaneous produce of your field, and you will not gather fully the grapes of your dedication. It will be a year of rest to the land. The sabbaths of the land will be food for you, and for your man-slave, and your woman-slave, and your employee, and the stranger that lives with you. For your livestock, and for the wild beats that are in your land, will every fruit be for food."

"You will calculate for yourself seven sabbaths of years, seven times seven years, and they will be for you seven weeks of years, forty-nine years. In the seventh month, on the tenth day of the month, you will proclaim with the sound of a trumpet in all your land. On the day of atonement, you will proclaim with a trumpet in all your land. You will sanctify the year, the fiftieth year, and you will proclaim a release on the land for all that inhabit it. It will be given a year of release, a jubilee for you, and each one will depart to his possession, and you will go each to his family. This is a jubilee of release, the year will be for you the fiftieth year, you will not sow, nor reap the produce that comes itself from the land, neither will you gather its planted fruits. It is a jubilee of release. It will be holy to you, you will eat its fruits of the fields."

"In the year of the release, the jubilee, will each one return to his possession. If you should sell a possession to your neighbor, or if you should buy from your neighbor, don't let a man oppress his neighbor. According to the number of years after the jubilee, you will buy from your neighbor, according to the number of years of the fruits will he sell to you. If it is a greater number of years he will increase the value of his possession, and if there is a smaller number of years, he will decrease the value of his possession, according to the number of crops, so will he sell to you. Don't let a man oppress his neighbor, and you will fear Iaw your god. I am Iaw, your god!"

"You will keep all my ordinances, and all my judgments, and observe them, and you will keep them, and dwell securely in the land. The land will yield her increase, and you will eat to fullness and will dwell securely in it. If you should say, 'What will we eat in this seventh year, if we do not sow nor gather in our fruits?' Then will I send my blessing on you in the sixth year, and the land will produce enough fruits for three years. You will sow in the eighth year, and eat old fruits until the ninth year: until its fruit comes, you will eat old fruits of the old. The land will not be sold permanently as the land is mine, and because you were strangers and travelers before me."

"In every land of your possession, you will allow ransoms for the land. If your brother who is with you is poor, and should have sold part of his possession, and his relative who is near to him comes, then he will redeem the possession which his brother has sold. If one has no nearby relative, and he prospers with his hand, and he finds sufficient silver, enough for his ransom, then he will calculate the years of his sale, and he will give what is due to the man to whom he sold it, and he will return to his possession. But if his hand has not prospered sufficiently, so that he could restore the silver to him, then he who bought the possessions has them until the sixth year of the release, and it will go out in the release, and the owner will return to his possession. If anyone should sell an inhabited house in a walled city, then there will be the ransom on it, until the time is fulfilled. Its time of ransom will be a full year. If it isn't ransomed until a complete year, the house which is in the walled city will be surely confirmed to he who bought it, throughout his generations, and it will not go out in the release. But the houses in the villages which have no walls around them will be considered as the fields of the country. They will always be redeemable, and they will go out in the release.

The cities of the Levites, the houses of the cities in their possession, will always be redeemable to the Levites. If anyone will redeem a house of the Levites, then their purchase of the houses of their possession go out in the release, because the houses of the cities of the Levites are their possession among the children of Israel. The lands set apart for their cities will not be sold, because this is their perpetual possession."

"If your brother who is with you becomes poor, and he fails in resources with you, you will help him as a stranger and a traveler, and your brother will live with you. You will not charge him interest, nor increase, and you will fear your god. I am Iaw! Your brother will live with you. You will not lend your silver to him at interest, and you will not lend your meat to him to be returned with an increase. I am Iaw your God, who brought you out of the land of Egypt, to give you the land of Canaan, to be your God!"

If your brother near you is lowered, and is sold to you, he will not serve you with the servitude of a slave. He will be with you as an employee or a traveler. He will work for you until the year of release, and he will go out in the release, and his children with him, and he will go to his family, he will rush back to his patrimony. Because these are my servants, who I brought out of the land of Egypt, they will not be sold like a common slave. You will not oppress him with labor, and will fear Iaw, your god. However many men-slaves and woman-slaves you have, you will purchase your male and female slaves from the nations that are around you. Of the sons of the travelers that are among you, from these you will buy and of their relations, all that will be in your lands. Let them be a possession for you. You will distribute them to your children after you, and they will be for you permanent possessions forever. As to your brothers, the children of Israel, you will not oppress your brother with labor."

"If a stranger or traveler with you becomes rich, and your brother in distress is sold to the stranger or the traveler that is with you, or to a proselyte by extraction; after he is sold to him there will be redemption for him. One of his brothers will redeem him. A brother of his father or a son of his father's brother will redeem him, or let one of his near family of his tribe redeem him. If he should become rich and redeem himself, then he will calculate with his purchaser from the year that he sold himself to him until the year of release, and the silver of his purchase will be as that of an employee, he will be with him from year to year. If any have a greater number of years than enough, according to these he will pay his ransom out of his purchase-silver. If but a little time is left of the years until the year of release, then he will consider him according to his years and will pay his wages as an employee. He will be with him from year to year. You will not oppress him with labor before you. If he does not pay his ransom accordingly, he will go out in the year of his release, he and his children with him. The children of Israel are my servants. They are my attendants, whom I brought out of the land of Egypt."

Leviticus: Chapter 26

"I am Iaw your god! You will not make for yourselves gods made with hands or engraved. Neither will you set up a stele[1] for yourselves, neither will you set up a stone for an object in your land to worship it. I am Iaw the god!"

"You will keep my sabbaths, and revere my sanctuaries: I am Iaw! If you follow my ordinances, and keep my commandments, and do them, then I will give you the rain in its season, and the land will produce its fruits, and the trees of the field will yield their fruit. Your threshing time will surpass the vintage, and your vintage will surpass your seed time, and you will eat your bread to the full, and you will dwell safely on your land, and war will not go through your land. I will give peace in your land, and you will sleep, and none will make you afraid. I will destroy the evil animals out of your land, and you will chase your enemies, and they will fall before you in slaughter."

"Five of you will chase a hundred, and a hundred of you will chase tens of thousands, and your enemies will fall before you by the sword. I will look on you, and increase you, and multiply you, and establish my covenant with you. You will consume that which is old and very old, and drive out the old to make way for the new. I will set my tabernacle among you, and my mind will not hate you, and I will walk among you, and be your god, and you will be my people."

"I am Iaw your God, who brought you out of the land of Egypt, where you were slaves, and I broke the bands of your shackles, and brought you out openly. But if you will not listen to me, nor obey these my ordinances, but disobey them, and your mind should loathe my judgments, so that you should not keep all my commands, to break my covenant, then I will do this to you: I will even bring on you perplexity and the itch, and the fever that causes your eyes to waste away, and disease that consumes your life, and you will sow your seeds in vain, and your enemies will eat them."

"I will set my face against you, and you will fall before your enemies, and they who hate you will chase you, and you will flee with no one pursuing you. If you still refuse to listen to me, then I will punish you again another seven times for your sins. I will break down the haughtiness of your pride, and I will make your sky like iron, and your land like brass."

"Your strength will be in vain, and your land will not yield its seed, and the tree of your field will not yield its fruit. If after this you should walk perversely, and not be willing to obey me, I will further bring on you seven plagues according to your sins. I will send against you the wild animals of the land, and they will devour you and will consume your livestock, and I will make you few in number, and your roads will be desolate. If subsequently you are not corrected but walk perversely towards me, I also will walk with you with a perverse spirit, and I also will strike you seven times for your sins. I will bring on you a sword avenging the cause of my covenant, and you will flee for refuge to your cities, and I will send out death against you, and you will be delivered into the hands of your enemies."

"When I afflict you with a famine of bread, then ten women will bake your loaves in one oven, and they will render your loaves by weight, and you will eat, and not be satisfied. If after this you will not obey me, but walk perversely towards me, then I will walk with you with a prepared mind, and I will punish you seven-times, according to your sins. You will eat the flesh of your sons, and the flesh of your daughters you will eat."

"I will render your steles desolate, and will utterly destroy your wooden images made with hands, and I will lay your carcasses on the carcasses of your idols, and my mind will loathe you. I will lay your cities waste, and I will make your sanctuaries desolate, and I will not smell the savor of your sacrifices. I will lay your land desolate, and your enemies who dwell in it will wonder at it. I will scatter you among the nations, and the sword will come on you and consume you, and your land will be desolate, and your cities will be desolate. Then the land will enjoy its sabbaths all the days of its desolation. You will be in the land of your enemies; then the land will keep its sabbaths, and the land will enjoy its sabbaths all the days its desolation: it will keep sabbaths which it kept not among your sabbaths when you lived in it."

"To those who are left of you, I will bring slavery into their heart in the land of their enemies, and the sound of a shaken leaf will chase them, and they will flee as fleeing from war and will fall when none pursues them. Brother will disregard brother as in war when none pursues, and you will not be able to with-stand your enemies. You will perish among the Gentiles, and the land of your enemies will devour you. Those who are left of you will perish, because of their sins, and because of the sins of their fathers: in the land of their enemies will they consume away. They will confess their sins, and the sins of their fathers, that they have transgressed and neglected me, and that they have walked perversely before me, and I walked with them with a perverse mind, and I will destroy them in the land of their enemies. Then their uncircumcised heart will be ashamed, and then they will acquiesce in the punishment of their sins."

"I will remember the covenant of Jacob, and the covenant of Isaac, and the covenant of Abraham I will also remember. I will remember the land, and the land will be left of them; then the land will enjoy her sabbaths when it is deserted through them: and they will accept the punishment of their iniquities, because they neglected my judgments, and in their mind loathed my ordinances. Yet not even thus, while they were in the land of their enemies, did I overlook them, nor did I loathe them to consume them, to break my covenant made with them, for I am Iaw their god. I will remember their former covenant, when I brought them out of the land of Egypt, out of the house of slavery before the nation, to be their God. I am Iaw!"

These are my judgments and my ordinances, and the law which Iaw gave between himself and the children of Israel, in Mount Sinai, by the hand of Moses.

Leviticus: Chapter 26 Notes

1 Codex Vaticanus: stêlên (ⲥⲧⲏⲗⲏⲛ). Translation: stele (or pillar)

• Leningrad Codex: matzevah (מַצֵּבָה). Translation: pillar (or monument, tree-stump)

• Peshitta: qymtå (ܩܝܡܬܐ). Translation: columns (or statues, tree trunks, necromancy, resurrection)

• Targum Onkelos: tzelem (צְלֵם). Translation: idols

• Fragment Targums: even dit'u (אֶבֶן דְּטְעוּ). Translation: stone misleading (or idol)

• Targum Jerusalem: tzilmin (צִילְמִין). Translation: statue

Leviticus: Chapter 27

Iaw said to Moses, "Tell the children of Israel, 'Whoever will vow a vow as the value of his mind for Iaw, the value of a male from twenty years old to sixty years old will be his value will be fifty shekels[1] of silver by the standard of the sanctuary. The value of a female will be thirty shekels. If it is from five years old to twenty, the value of a male will be twenty shekels, and of a female ten shekels. From a month old to five years old, the value of a male will be five shekels, and of a female, three shekels of silver. If from sixty years old and upward, if it is a male, his value will be fifteen shekels of silver, and if a female, ten shekels. If the man is too poor for the value, he will stand before the priest, and the priest will value him: according to what the man who has vowed can afford, the priest will value him.'"

"If it is from the livestock that is offered as a gift to Iaw, whoever will offer one of these to Iaw, it will be holy. He will not change it, a good for a bad, or a bad for a good, and if he does at all change it, an animal for an animal, it and the substitute will be holy. If it is any unclean animal, of which none are offered as a gift to Iaw, he will set the animal before the priest. The priest will make a value between the good and the bad, and accordingly as the priest will value it, so will it stand. If the worshiper will at all redeem it, he will add the fifth part to its value. Whatever man will consecrate his house as holy to Iaw, the priest will make an evaluation of it between the good and the bad. As the priest will value it, so will it stand. If he that has sanctified it should redeem his house, he will add to it the fifth part of the silver of the value, and it will be his."

"If a man should offer to Iaw a part of the field of his possession, then the value will be according to its seed, fifty shekels of silver for a kor[2] of barley. If he should sanctify his field from the year of release, it will stand according to his value. If he should sanctify his field in the latter time after the release, the priest will reckon to him the silver for the remaining years, until the next year of release, and it will be deducted as an equivalent from his full value. If he who sanctified the field would redeem it, he will add to its value the fifth part of the silver, and it will be his."

"If he does not redeem the field but should sell the field to another man, he will not after redeem it. But the field will be holy to Iaw after the release, as separated land, the priest will possess it. If he should consecrate to Iaw of a field which he has bought, which is not of the field of his possession, the priest will reckon to him the full value from the year of release, and he will pay the value in that day as holy to Iaw.

"In the year of release, the land will be restored to the man of whom the other bought it, whose possession of the land was. Every value will be by holy weights: the shekel will be twenty gerahs.[3] Every firstborn which will be produced among your livestock will be Lord' and no man will sanctify it, whether calf or sheep, it is Lord'. But if he should redeem an unclean animal, according to its value, then he will add the fifth part to it, and it will be his, and if he does not redeem it, it will be sold according to its value. Every dedicated thing which a man will dedicate to Iaw of all that he has, whether man or animal, or of the field of his possession, he will not sell it, nor redeem it."

"Every devoted thing will be sacred to Iaw. Whatever will be dedicated to men, will not be ransomed, but will be surely put to death. Every tithe of the land, both of the seed of the land, and the fruit of trees, is Iaw's, it is holy to Iaw. If a man should at all redeem his tithe, he will add the fifth part to it, and it will be his. Every tithe of oxen, and sheep, and whatever may be counted under the wand, the tenth will be holy to Iaw. You will not change a good for a bad, or a bad for a good, and if you should at all change it, its equivalent also will be holy, it will not be redeemed."

These are the commandments that Iaw commanded Moses for the sons of Israel on Mount Sinai.

Leviticus: Chapter 27 Notes

1 Codex Vaticanus: didrachma (ⲆⲒⲆⲢⲀⲭⲘⲀ). Translation: two-drachmas

- Leningrad Codex: shekalim (שְׁקָלִים). Translation: shekels

- Peshitta: mtqlyn (ܡܬܩܠܝܢ). Translation: scales (or weight, shekel, beka)

- Targum Onkelos: sil'in (סִלְעִין). Translation: selas (or rocks)

- Targum Jerusalem: sil'in (סִלְעִין). Translation: selas (or rocks)

The shekel was a unit of weight used throughout the Middle East for thousands of years, weighing approximately 8.6 grams of silver. The Greek drachma was a coin weighing approximately half a shekel, and therefore under Greek rule of the Middle East, a two-drachma coin was used. As the Greeks clearly translated shekel into didrachma, the term shekel is restored in this translation. The sela, mentioned in the Targums, was a weight and coin although the value varied depending its metal.

2 Codex Vaticanus: corou (ΚΟΡΟΥ)

- Leningrad Codex: chomer (חֹמֶר)

- DSS 11QpaleoLevᵃ: hmr (𐤇𐤌𐤓)

- Peshitta: kůr (ܟܘܪ)

- Targum Onkelos: kur (כּוֹר)

- Fragment Targums: chomer (חוֹמֶר)

- Targum Jerusalem: kor (כּוֹר)

The Greek and Hebrew translations use different units of measurement which are considered equivalents in different languages. The Septuagint uses a transliteration of the Imperial Aramaic word kůrå (עיראַ), which was also the precursor to the Syriac word kůr (ܟܘܪ) in the Peshitta, and kur (כּוֹר) in the Onkelos and Jonathan Targums, referred to the ancient Mesopotamian unit of measurement known as the kurru (𒃻). The Masoretic text includes a direct transliteration of the Phoenician spelling of the word ḥmr (𐤇𐤌𐤓), the Canaanite equivalent of the kurru, which was also the term used in the Samaritan Dead Sea Scroll 11QpaleoLevᵃ from the Herodian dynasty. The existence of the Canaanite word confirms the text of Leviticus was almost certainly written in Judahite before the rise of the Neo-Babylonian Empire.

3 Codex Vaticanus: oboloe (ΟΒΟΛΟΙ). Translation: obols

- Leningrad Codex: gerah (גֵּרָה)

- Peshitta: môyn (ܡܥܝܢ). Translations: m'ahs

- Targum Onkelos: ma'in (מְעִין). Translations: m'ahs

- Targum Jerusalem: ma'in (מְעִין). Translations: m'ahs

The obol was a Greek coin used from around 1100 BC, worth ⅙ of a drachma, approximately 0.72 grams of silver. The gerah was a measurement equaling one-twentieth of a shekel. The mina mentioned in the Peshitta and Targum Onkelos was an ancient Mesopotamian coin and measurement, however, was much larger than the shekel, generally valued at 60 shekels. As the Greek translation translated the name of the measurement to obol, the name gerah is restored in this translation.

Numbers: Chapter 1

The Lord[1] spoke to Moses[2] in the Wilderness of Sinai,[3] at the tabernacle of witness, on the first day of the second month, in the second year after they departed from the land of Egypt, saying, "Count all the community of Israel according to their families, and according to the houses of their fathers' families, and according to their number by their names, and according to their heads. Every male twenty years old and up, everyone that went out in the army of Israel, count them with their strength, you and Aaron go count them. With you, there will be each one of the rulers according to the tribe of each, and they will be according to the houses of their families."

"These are the names of the men who will be present with you:

From the tribe of Reuben: Elizur the son of Shedeur.

From the tribe of Simeon: Shelumiel the son of Zurishaddai.

From the tribe of Judah: Nahshon the son of Amminadab.

"From the tribe of Issachar: Nethanel the son of Zuar.

From the tribe of Zebulun: Eliab the son of Helon.

From the tribe of the sons of Joseph: from Ephraim: Elishama the son of Ammihud, and from Manasseh: Gamaliel the son of Pedahzur.

From the tribe of Benjamin: Abidan the son of Gideoni.

From the tribe of Dan: Ahiezer the son of Ammishaddai.

From the tribe of Asher: Pagiel the son of Ochran.

From the tribe of Gad: Eliasaph the son of Deuel.

From the tribe of Naphtali: Ahira the son of Enan.

These were famous men of the community, heads of the tribes according to their families. These are heads of thousands in Israel. Moses and Aaron took these men who were called by name. They assembled all the community on the first day of the month in the second year, and they record them after their lineage, after their families, after the number of their names, from twenty years old and upwards, every male according to their number, and as the Lord commanded Moses, so they were counted in the Wilderness of Sinai.

The sons of Reuben the firstborn of Israel according to their families, according to their divisions, according to the houses of their families, according to the number of their names, according to their heads, all males from twenty years old and upward, everyone who went out with the army, the count of the tribe of Reuben was 46,400.

For the children of Simeon according to their families, according to their divisions, according to the houses of their families, according to the number of their names, according to their polls, all males from twenty years old and upward, everyone who went out with the army, the count of the tribe of Simeon was 59,300.

For the sons of Judah according to their families, according to their divisions, according to the houses of their families, according to the number of their names, according to their polls, all males from twenty years old and upward, everyone who went out with the army, the count of the tribe of Judah was 74,600.

For the sons of Issachar according to their families, according to their divisions, according to the houses of their families, according to the number of their names, according to their polls, all males from twenty years old and upward, everyone who went out with the army, the count of the tribe of Issachar was 54,400.

For the sons of Zebulun according to their families, according to their divisions, according to the houses of their families, according to the number of their names, according to their polls, all males from twenty years old and upward, everyone who went out with the army, the count of the tribe of Zebulun was 57,400.

For the sons of Joseph, the sons of Ephraim, according to their families, according to their divisions, according to the houses of their families, according to the number of their names, according to their polls, all males from twenty years old and upward, everyone who went out with the army, the count of the tribe of Ephraim was 40,500.

For the sons of Manasseh according to their families, according to their divisions, according to the houses of their families, according to the number of their names, according to their polls, all males from twenty years old and upward, everyone who went out with the army, the count of the tribe of Manasseh was 32,200.

For the sons of Benjamin according to their families, according to their divisions, according to the houses of their families, according to the number of their names, according to their polls, every male from twenty years old and upward, everyone who went out with the army, the count of the tribe of Benjamin was 35,400.

For the sons of Gad according to their families, according to their divisions, according to the houses of their families, according to the number of their names, according to their polls, all males from twenty years old and upward, everyone who went out with the army, the count of the tribe of Gad was 45,600.

For the sons of Dan according to their families, according to their divisions, according to the houses of their families, according to the number of their names, according to their polls, all males from twenty years old and upward, everyone who went out with the army, the count of the tribe of Dan was 62,700.

For the sons of Asher according to their families, according to their divisions, according to the houses of their families, according to the number of their names, according to their polls, every male from twenty years old and upward, everyone who went out with the army, the count of the tribe of Asher was 41,500.

For the sons of Naphtali according to their families, according to their divisions, according to the houses of their families, according to the number of their names, according to their polls, every male from twenty years old and upward, everyone who went out with the army, the count of the tribe of Naphtali was 53,400.

This is the count which Moses and Aaron and the rulers of Israel, being twelve men, conducted. There was a man for each tribe, they were according to the tribe of the houses of their family. The whole count of the children of Israel with their army from twenty years old and upward, everyone that went out to set himself in battle formation for Israel came to 603,550. But the Levites of the tribe of their family were not counted among the children of Israel.

The Lord said to Moses, "See, you will not muster the tribe of Levi, and you will not count their numbers, among the children of Israel. Set the Levites over the tabernacle of witness, and over all its furniture, and over all things that are in it. They will do service in it, and they will camp around the tabernacle. When moving the tabernacle, the Levites will take it down, and in pitching the tabernacle they will set it up, and let the stranger that advances to touch it die. The children of Israel will camp, every man in his own order, and every man according to his captain, with their army. But let the Levites camp round about the tabernacle of witness neighboring it, and so there will be no sin among the children of Israel. The Levites themselves will keep the guard of the tabernacle of witness."

The children of Israel did according to all that the Lord commanded Moses and Aaron, so did they.

Numbers: Chapter 1 Notes

1 Codex Vaticanus: c̄s (ᴋ̄ᴄ). Translation: lord

• DSS 4QLXXNum: Yhůh (𐤉𐤄𐤅𐤄) in later chapters. LXX 803 was a copy of Numbers in which the name Yhůh had been inserted in Judahite script.

• Leningrad Codex: Yehvah (יְהֺוָה)

This verse has not survived among the Dead Sea Scrolls, however, the name Yhůh is used later in the Dead Sea fragments of Numbers where the Masoretic Text has Yhůh and Septuagint retains 'Lord.'

• DSS 4QLev-Numᵃ: yhůh (𐤉𐤄𐤅𐤄)

• DSS 2QNumᵃ: yhůh (𐤉𐤄𐤅𐤄)

• DSS 4QNumᵇ: yhůh (𐤉𐤄𐤅𐤄)

• Peshitta: mryå (ܡܪܝܐ). Translation: master

• Targum Onkelos: yeyah (??). Translation: Yhů

• Targum Jerusalem: yeyah (??). Translation: Yhů

• Ketef Hinnom scroll 2: Yhůh (𐤉𐤄𐤅𐤄). KH2 is a silver scroll engraved with Judahite text similar to three verses in Numbers: Chapter 6. It is generally dated to between the 7th and 4th centuries BC, although some scholars have stated it could be as recent as the 2nd century BC. The text is similar to verses in Numbers chapter 6, but not identical, as they refer to Yhůh as 'the warrior.'

There are no early surviving copies of the Septuagint's version of Numbers which have the Greek translation of the name in them, Iaw (ιαω), like the early fragments of the Septuagint's Leviticus known as 4QpapLXXLevᵇ, and therefore it cannot be known conclusively if the name was ever in the Septuagint's Numbers or not. There are fragments of a copy of the Septuagint's version of Numbers known as 4QLXXNum which include the name, however, it is copied into the Greek text in the Judahite script (𐤉𐤄𐤅𐤄), indicating it was a redacted form of Septuagint's Numbers, in which someone had attempted to 'restore' the name to the text, suggesting it was not there in the original Greek translation. The original Phoenician script (Edomite, Paleo-Hebrew) version of Numbers likely used the word Adon (𐤀𐤃𐤍) which meant 'Lord.' The Aramaic sections of Masoretic Daniel that were not translated into Hebrew maintain the term adonai ha'elohim (אֲדֹנָי הָאֱלֹהִים), meaning the 'Lord the gods' where the Septuagint has 'Lord the god' (Κύριον τον θεόν). As most books of the Septuagint were translated from Aramaic texts, the Aramaic text almost certainly used the term adonay where the Septuagint has 'Lord.'

The name Yahweh appears to have been added to most of the books in the Masoretic Text when the texts were translated to Hebrew during the Hasmonean Dynasty of Judea, between 140 and 37 BC. According to the Talmud, this was to repair the damage King Manasseh had done 600 years earlier when he removed the name Yahweh from the Israelite Texts, however, no evidence has survived from the era of Manasseh or earlier that proves the name was originally in the text, suggesting it was an attempt by the first Hasmonean High-Priest/King Simon the Zealot to create a national Judean religion with a god having a name similar to the Roman god Jupiter, which was pronounced as Jove or Jova in common Latin.

The name Yahweh, in the Aramaic form of Yhŭ (𐡉𐡄𐡅), does appear to have originally been in some of the books of the Septuagint, such as Leviticus, which originated under the rule of King Josiah, and Yhŭ was a popular god among Judeans and Israelites under Persian and Greek rule. The translators at the Library of Alexandria transliterated this name as Iaw (Ιαω) in the books it was originally in, however, under the Hasmonean Dynasty it seems to have been added to all the books translated into Hebrew, creating some confusion among early Christians.

There were debates in the early Christian era about which version of the Israelite scriptures to use, the Greek, Hebrew, Samaritan, or Syriac translations, resulting in different versions of the scriptures being used by different churches. Some versions replaced the term Lord with Iaw in the Greek texts, either in the Greek form as Ιαω, or by copying in the Hebrew form of the name Yhŭh (יהוה) or the older Phoenician form of Yhŭh (𐤉𐤄𐤅𐤄), or by mocking the Hebrew with Greek letters as ΠΙΠΙ. This created a great deal of confusion among Christians, and ultimately the books of the Septuagint that had the name Iaw in them were redacted so all the books used the term Lord (Κύριοσ). Most Christian translations, as well as Jewish translations, have continued to use the term 'Lord' in place of the name Yahweh, due to the prohibition on using any names of God that was introduced during the Hasmonean dynasty.

2 Codex Vaticanus: Môysên (ⲘⲱⲨⲤⲏⲚ)

- LXX 318: Môysê (Ⲙⲟⲟⲩⲥⲏ)

- LXX 58: Môsên (Ⲙⲟⲟⲥⲏⲛ)

- LXX 72: Môsi (Ⲙⲟⲟⲥⲓ)

- Leningrad Codex: Mosheh (מֹשֶׁה)

- Peshitta: mûšå (ܡܘܫܐ)

- Targum Onkelos: Mosheh (מֹשֶׁה)

- Targum Jerusalem: Mosheh (מֹשֶׁה)

It is generally accepted that at some point before the Septuagint was translated, half of Moses' name was redacted from the text. This theory is based on the similarity of the Egyptian term msî (𓄛𓅱), meaning 'give birth to,' or 'created by,' which was a common element of Egyptian names. Many kings of Egypt were known as the 'msî' of a god, including Ramses (𓇳𓄛𓅱), Ahmose (𓇌𓄛𓅱), Tuthmose (𓅝𓄛𓅱), Amenmose (𓇋𓏠𓈖𓄛𓅱), and Ptahmose (𓎡𓏏𓎛𓄛𓅱). A theory that has been circulating since at least the time of Josephus in the 1st century AD, is that Moses' original name was Hapymoses, meaning the 'Nile created him.' If this is the origin of the name, the name of the god that created Moses was likely dropped from the name very early in Israelite history, as there are no known surviving texts with the full name. The latest this is likely to have happened would have been during the Aramaic translation of King Hezekiah, however, it may have happened much earlier.

An alternate interpretation is that the name is complete, and is derived from the Egyptian term mů-šåô (𓄿𓈗𓈘𓂝), meaning 'beginning on water,' which appears to be what the princess stated in Exodus, when she found Moses and named him.

3 Codex Vaticanus: Sina (ⲤⲈⲒⲚⲀ)

- LXX 18: Sinae (ⲤⲒⲚⲀⲒ)

- LXX 30: Sêna (ⲤⲏⲚⲀ)

- LXX 46: Sina (ⲤⲒⲚⲀⲱ)

- LXX 126: Sin (ⲤⲒⲚ)

- Leningrad Codex: Sinai (סִינָי)

- Peshitta: Syny (ܣܝܢܝ)

- Targum Onkelos: Sinai (סִינַי)

- Targum Jerusalem: Sinai (סִינַי)

The Wilderness of Sin (Σιν) is the translation in the Septuagint for both the Masoretic Wilderness of Sin (סִין) in Exodus, and the Wilderness of Tzin (צִן) in Numbers, which was followed by Jerome in the Latin Vulgate as the Wilderness of Sin. This suggests that the early Aramaic version of the Torah did not differentiate between the two. As the book of Numbers was likely organized into its current state during the era of King Hezekiah's reforms, and it was almost certainly written in the Phoenician script that was in use in Judah at the time, it is likely that it more accurately records the two locations as separate places.

In chapter 33, they are both listed in the long sequence of stops the Israelites made as they traveled from Egypt, confirming that the Hebrew translator, and probably the Judahite or Moabite compiler of the original book of Numbers viewed them as separate places. Conversely, Exodus shows clear signs of having been written in Middle Babylonian cuneiform, which is likely where the pronunciation of Sin is derived, ultimately from the Akkadian spelling of Sīn (𒀭𒌍), which was spelled in Aramaic as Syn (𐤎𐤉𐤍), the direct transliteration of the Hebrew Syn (סִין). While the Aramaic spelling would have been standardized by the common spelling of the name of the moon god, there was nothing to standardize the spelling of the toponym in the Phoenician script, resulting in both toponyms being rendered phonetically by the scribes that unified the stories found in Numbers into a book circa 700 BC.

The locations of these wildernesses have been a matter of debate for more than 2000 years, and early Christians era scholars widely debated this issue, with the majority favoring the region around Petra, in Jordan, or the Midian Mountains in northwestern Saudi Arabia. The Wilderness of Sin is identified within the Torah, as being between Elim and Mount Sinai, however, both locations are debated today. The Wilderness of Sinai is identified as including the site of Kadesh Barne, however, this location is also debated. Emperor Constantine's mother, Helena Augusta, renamed the Sinai Peninsula and Mount Sinai in Egypt in the 330s AD to resolve this issue, however, few scholars agree with this location today, as other references indicate the Israelites were wandering in northwest Saudi Arabia, Jordan, southern Syria.

Currently, Christian and Islamic scholars treating the Exodus as history, prefer Petra in Jordan, as the site of Kadesh, and Jebel al-Madhbah near Petra as Mount Sinai. This mountain has the Valley of Moses, called Wadi Musa in Arabic, which has an ancient staircase leading to the top of the mountain. It was clearly an ancient religious site, housing rain-fed cisterns, and two gigantic obelisks. At the entrance to the Valley of Moses is the Spring of Moses, which is believed to be the location that Moses struck the rock with his wand and caused water to flow. Based on the 1st century Josephus' claim that Kadesh Barnea was at Petra, the Wilderness of Sinai appears to be another name for the southern Arabah, the mostly dry valley running north from the Gulf of Aqaba to the Dead Sea. By extension, if Sinai and Sin are not two different spellings of the same place, then the location of the Wilderness of Sin would have to be the Sinai Desert, between An-Nekhel (Elim), and Hashem El Tarif (Rephidim).

Numbers: Chapter 2

The Lord said to Moses and Aaron, "Let the children of Israel camp near each other, every man keeping his rank, according to their standards, according to the houses of their families. The children of Israel will camp around the tabernacle of witness. Those that camp closest to the east will be the order of the camp of Judah with their army, and the prince of the sons of Judah, Nahshon the son of Amminadab. His forces were counted at 74,600."

"Those who camp next are from the tribe of Issachar, and the prince of the sons of Issachar will be Nethanel the son of Zuar. His forces were counted at 54,400."

"Those who camp next are from the tribe of Zebulun, and the prince of the sons of Zebulun will be Eliab the son of Helon. His forces were counted at 57,400. All that were counted of the camp of Judah were 186,400. They will move first with their forces."

"This is the order of the camp of Reuben, their forces will be towards the south, and the prince of the children of Reuben will be Elizur the son of Shedeur. His forces were counted at 64,500."

"Those who camp next to him are from the tribe of Simeon, and the prince of the sons of Simeon will be Shelumiel the son of Zurishaddai. His forces were counted at 59,300."

"Those who camp next to them is the tribe of Gad, and the prince of the sons of Gad, Eliasaph the son of Deuel. His forces were counted at 45,650. All who were counted of the camp of Reuben were 151,450. They with their forces will proceed in the second place."

"Then the tabernacle of witness will be set forward, and the camp of the Levites will be between the camps, as they will camp, so also will they commence their march, each one next in order to his fellow according to their companies. The station of the camp of Ephraim will be by the sea with their forces, and the head of the children of Ephraim will be Elishama the son of Ammihud. His forces were counted at 40,500. Those who camp next is from the tribe of Manasseh, and the prince of the sons of Manasseh, Gamaliel the son of Pedahzur. His forces were counted at 32,200."

"Those who camp next is from the tribe of Benjamin, and the prince of the sons of Benjamin, Abidan the son of Gideoni. His forces were counted at 35,400. All that were counted of the camp of Ephraim were 108,100. They with their forces will set out third."

"The order of the camp of Dan will be towards the north with their forces, and the prince of the sons of Dan, Ahiezer the son of Ammishaddai. His forces were counted at 62,700."

"Those who camp next to him will be the tribe of Asher, and the prince of the sons of Asher, Phagiel the son of Ochran. His forces were counted at 41,500.

"Those who camp next are from the tribe of Naphtali, and the prince of the children of Naphtali, Ahira the son of Enan. His forces were counted at 53,400.

"All that were counted of the camp of Dan were 157,600. They will set out last according to their order."

This is the number of the children of Israel according to the houses of their families. All the number in the camps with their forces was 603,550. However, the Levites were not counted with them, as the Lord commanded Moses. The children of Israel did all things that the Lord commanded Moses, and they camped in their order, and so they began their march in succession each according to their divisions, according to the houses of their families.

Numbers: Chapter 3

These are the generations of Aaron and Moses, on the day that the Lord spoke to Moses at Mount Sinai. These are the names of the sons of Aaron: Nadab the firstborn, and Abihu, Eleazar, and Ithamar. These are the names of the sons of Aaron, the anointed priests whom they consecrated to the priesthood. Nadab and Abihu died before the Lord, when they offered strange fire before the Lord, in the Wilderness of Sinai. They had no children. Eleazar and Ithamar ministered in the priests' office with Aaron their father.

The Lord said to Moses, "Take the tribe of Levi and set them before Aaron the priest, and they will minister for him and will keep his orders, and the orders of the children of Israel, before the tabernacle of witness, to do the works of the tabernacle. They will keep all the furniture of the tabernacle of witness, and the orders of the children of Israel conducting all the works of the tabernacle. You will give the Levites to Aaron, and his sons the priests. They are given as a gift to me from the children of Israel. You will appoint Aaron and his sons over the tabernacle of witness, and they will keep their order of priesthood, and all things belonging to the altar, and within the veil, and the stranger that touches them will die."

The Lord said to Moses, "Look, I have taken the Levites from among the children of Israel, instead of every male that opens the womb from among the children of Israel, they will be their price, and the Levites will be mine, as every firstborn is mine. In the day in which I struck every firstborn in the land of Egypt, I sanctified to myself every firstborn in Israel, both of man and beast, they will be mine. I am the Lord."

The Lord said to Moses in the Wilderness of Sinai, "Count the sons of Levi, according to the houses of their families, according to their divisions, count every male from a month old and upwards."

Moses and Aaron counted them by the word of the Lord, as the Lord commanded them. These were the names of the sons of Levi: Gershon, Kohath, and Merari. These are the names of the sons of Gershon according to their families; Libni and Shimei: and the sons of Kohath according to their families; Amram and Jezer, Hebron, and Uzziel. The sons of Merari according to their families, Mahali and Musi. These are the families of the Levites according to the houses of their families. To Gershon belongs the family of Libni, and the family of Shimei:

579

these are the families of Gershon. The counting of them according to the number, every male a month old and up, their count was 7,500."

"The sons of Gershon will camp westward behind the tabernacle. The ruler of the household of the family of Gershon was Eliasaph the son of Lael. The order of the sons of Gershon in the tabernacle of witness was the tent and the veil, and the covering of the door of the tabernacle of witness, and the curtains of the court, and the veil of the door of the court, which is by the tabernacle, and the remainder of all its works. To Kohath belonged one division, that of Amram, and another division, that of Jezer, and another division, that of Hebron, and another division, that of Uzziel: these are the divisions of Kohath, according to number. Every male from a month old and upward, 8,600, keeping the orders of the holy things."

"The families of the sons of Kohath will camp beside the tabernacle towards the south. The chief of the house of the families of the divisions of Kohath was Elizaphan the son of Uzziel. Their order was the box, and the table, and the candlestick, and the altars, and all the vessels of the sanctuary where they do holy service, and the veil, and all their works. The chief over the heads of the Levites was Eleazar the son of Aaron the priest, appointed to keep the orders of the holy things. To Merari belonged the family of Mahali, and the family of Musi: these are the families of Merari.

"The mustering of them according to number, every male from a month old and upwards, was 6,050. The head of the house of the families of the division of Merari was Zuriel the son of Abihail, and they will camp by the side of the taber- nacle northward. The oversight of the order of the sons of Merari included the chapiters of the tabernacle, and its bars, and its pillars, and its sockets, and all their furniture, and their works, and the pillars of the court round about, and their bases, and their pins, and their cords. Those who camp before the tabernacle of witness on the east will be Moses and Aaron and his sons, keeping the orders of the sanctuary according to the orders of the children of Israel, and the stranger that touches them will die. All the numbering of the Levites, whom Moses and Aaron counted by the word of the Lord, according to their families, every male from a month old and upwards, were 22,000."

The Lord said to Moses, "Count every firstborn male of the children of Israel a month old and up and record the number by name. You will take the Levites for me, I am the Lord, instead of all the firstborn of the sons of Israel, and the livestock of the Levites instead of all the firstborn among the livestock of the children of Israel."

Moses counted, as the Lord commanded him, every firstborn among the children of Israel. All the male firstborn in number by name, from a month old and upwards, were according to their numbering 22,273.

The Lord said to Moses, "Take the Levites instead of all the firstborn of the sons of Israel, and the livestock of the Levites instead of their livestock, and the Levites will be mine. I am the Lord! For the ransoms of the 273 which exceed the Levites in number of the firstborn of the sons of Israel, you will even take five shekels[1] per head. You will take them according to the holy shekel,[2] twenty gerahs[3] to the shekel. You will give the money to Aaron and to his sons, the ransom of those who exceed in number among them. Moses took the silver, the ransom of those that exceeded in number the redemption of the Levites. He took the silver from the firstborn of the sons of Israel, 1,365 shekels, according to the holy shekel. Moses gave the ransom of them that were over to Aaron and his sons, by the word of the Lord, as the Lord commanded Moses.

Numbers: Chapter 3 Notes

1 Codex Vaticanus: siclous (ϲΙΚΛΟΥϹ). Translation: shekels

• Leningrad Codex: shekalim (שְׁקָלִים). Translation: shekels

• Peshitta: mtqlyn (ܡܬܩܠܝܢ). Translation: scales (or weights, shekels, or gerahs)

• Targum Onkelos: sil'in (סִלְעִין). Translation: selas (or rocks)

• Targum Jerusalem: sil'in (סִלְעִין). Translation: selas (or rocks)

• Sahidic manuscripts: siklum (ϲΙΚΛΥΜ). Translation: shekels

The shekel was a unit of weight used throughout the Middle East for thousands of years, weighing approximately 8.6 grams of silver. The Greek drachma was a coin weighing approximately half a shekel, and therefore under Greek rule of the Middle East, a two-drachma coin was used. As the Greeks clearly translated shekel into didrachma, the term shekel is restored in this translation. The sela, mentioned in the Targums, was a weight and coin although the value varied depending on the metal it was made of.

2 Codex Vaticanus: didrachmon (ⲆⲒⲆⲢⲀⲭⲘⲞⲚ). Translation: two drachmas

• Codex Ambrosiano A 147: didragmon (ⲆⲒⲆⲢⲀⲅⲘⲞⲚ)

• LXX 30: didrachma (ⲆⲒⲆⲢⲀⲭⲘⲀ)

• LXX 130: didagmon (ⲆⲒⲆⲆⲅⲙⲟⲛ)

• LXX 320: didragman (ⲆⲒⲆⲢⲆⲅⲙⲆⲛ)

• LXX 246: dêdragmon (ⲆⲏⲆⲢⲆⲅⲙⲟⲛ)

• LXX 767: didragma (ⲆⲒⲆⲢⲆⲅⲙⲆ)

• LXX 321: didranchmon (ⲆⲒⲆⲢⲆⲅⲭⲙⲟⲛ)

• Leningrad Codex: shekalim (שְׁקָלִים). Translation: shekels

• Peshitta: mtqlyn (ܡܬܩܠܝܢ). Translation: scales (or weights, shekels, or gerahs)

• Targum Onkelos: sil'in (סִלְעִין). Translation: rocks

• Targum Jerusalem: sil'i (סִלְעִי). Translation: sela (or rocky)

• Sahidic manuscripts: siklum (ⲥⲓⲕⲗⲩⲙ). Translation: shekels

The shekel was a unit of weight used throughout the Middle East for thousands of years, weighing approximately 8.6 grams of silver. The Greek drachma was a coin weighing approximately half a shekel, and therefore under Greek rule of the Middle East, a two-drachma coin was used. In this verse, the Greek translators used by the transliteration of siclous (σίκλους) and the Greek translation of didrachmon (διδραχμον), while the Hebrew, Aramaic, and Coptic manuscripts consistently used the same term. As the Greeks clearly translated shekel into didrachma, the term shekel is restored in this translation.

3 Codex Vaticanus: obolous (ⲞⲂⲞⲗⲞⲨⲤ). Translation: obols

• LXX 833: oboloe (ⲟⲩⲟⲗⲟⲓ)

• LXX 72: oboloes (ⲟⲩⲟⲗⲟⲓⲥ)

• Leningrad Codex: gerah (גֵּרָה). Translation: gerah

• Peshitta: môyn (ܡܥܝܢ). Translations: mahs

• Targum Onkelos: ma'in (מְעִין). Translations: mahs

• Targum Jerusalem: ma'in (מְעִין). Translations: mahs

The obol was a Greek coin used from around 1100 BC, worth ⅙ of a drachma, approximately 0.72 grams of silver. The gerah was a measurement equaling one-twentieth of a shekel. The mah mentioned in the Targums was the Phoenician coin equivalent to the obol, suggesting it is the term in the Aramaic text that the Greeks translated. As the Greek translators substituted the obol, the name gerah is restored.

Numbers: Chapter 4

The Lord said to Moses and Aaron, "Take the number of the children of Kohath from among of the sons of Levi, after their families, according to the houses of their fathers' households, twenty-five years up until fifty years, everyone that goes in to administer, to do all the works in the tabernacle of witness. These are the works of the sons of Kohath in the tabernacle of witness. It is sacred. Aaron and his sons will go in, when the camp is about to move and will take down the shadowing veil, and will cover with it the ark of the testimony. They will put on it a cover, even a blue skin, and put on it above a garment all of blue, and will put the staffs through the rings.

They will put on the table set out for show-bread a purple cloth, and the dishes, and the censers, and the cups, and the vessels with which one offers drink offerings, and the continual loaves will be on it. They will put on it a scarlet cloth, and they will cover it with a blue covering of skin, and they will put the staffs into it. They will take a blue covering, and cover the candlestick that gives light, and its lamps, and its snuffers, and its funnels, and all the vessels of oil with which they minister. They will put it, and all its vessels, into a blue skin cover, and they will put it on bearers. They will put a blue cloth for a cover on the golden altar and will cover it with a blue skin cover, and put in its staffs. They will take all the instruments of service, with which they minister in the sanctuary: and will place them in a cloth of blue, and will cover them with blue skin covering, and put them on staffs."

"He will put the covering on the altar, and they will cover it with a purple cloth. They will put on it all the vessels with which they minister on it, and the fire-pans, and the fleshhooks, and the cups, and the cover, and all the vessels of the altar, and they will put on it a blue cover of skins and will put in its staffs, and they will take a purple cloth, and cover the laver and its foot, and they will put it into a blue cover of skin, and put it on bars. Aaron and his sons will finish covering the holy things, and all the holy vessels, when the camp begins to move, and afterward the sons of Kohath will go in to take up the furniture, but will not touch the holy things, or else they'll die. Then the sons of Kohath will carry in the tabernacle of witness. Eleazar the son of Aaron the priest is overseer, the oil of the light, and the incense of composition, and the daily sacrifice and the anointing oil, are his order. Even the oversight of the whole tabernacle, and all things that are in it in the holy place, in all the works."

The Lord said to Moses and Aaron, "You will not destroy the family of Kohath from the tribe of the Levites. This you do to them, and they will live and not die when they approach the holy of holies: Let Aaron and his sons advance, and they will place them each in his post for carrying. So they will by no means go in to look suddenly on the holy things, and die."

The Lord said to Moses, "Take the number of the children of Gershon, and these according to the houses of their lineage, according to their families. Take the number of them from twenty-five years old up until the age of fifty, everyone that goes in to minister, to do his business in the tabernacle of witness. This is the public service of the family of Gershon, to minister and to carry. The family will carry the skins of the tabernacle, and the tabernacle of witness, and its veil, and the blue cover that was on it above, and the cover of the door of the tabernacle of witness. All the curtains of the court which were on the tabernacle of witness, and the appendages, and all the vessels of service that they minister with they will attend to. According to the direction of Aaron and his sons will be the ministry of the sons of Gershon, in all their ministries, and all their works. You will take account of them by name in all things borne by them. This is the service of the sons of Gershon in the tabernacle of witness, and their order by the hand of Ithamar the son of Aaron the priest. The sons of Merari according to their families, according to the houses of their lineage, take the count of them. Take the count of them from twenty-five years old up until fifty years old, everyone that goes in to perform the services of the tabernacle of witness."

"These are the orders of the things done by them according to all their works in the tabernacle of witness: they will carry the chapiters of the tabernacle, and the bars, and its pillars, and its sockets, and the veil, and there will be their sockets, and their pillars, and the curtain of the door of the tabernacle. They will carry the pillars of the court round about, and there will be their sockets, and they will carry the pillars of the veil of the door of the court, and their sockets and their pins, and their cords, and all their furniture, and all their instruments of service, record their number by name and all the articles of the order of the things borne by them. This is the ministration of the family of the sons of Merari in all their works in the tabernacle of witness, by the hand of Ithamar the son of Aaron the priest. Moses and Aaron and the rulers of Israel took the number of the sons of Kohath according to their families, according to the houses of their lineage, from twenty-five years old and up to the age of fifty years, everyone that goes in to minister and do service in the tabernacle of witness. Their count according to their families was 2,750."

This is the numbering of the family of Kohath, everyone that ministers in the tabernacle of witness, as Moses and Aaron counted them by the word of the Lord, by the hand of Moses. The sons of Gershon were counted according to their families, according to the houses of their lineage, from twenty-five years old and upward until fifty years old, everyone that goes in to minister and to do the services in the tabernacle of witness. Their count according to their families, according to the houses of their lineage was 2,630. This is the numbering of the family of the sons of Gershon, everyone who ministers in the tabernacle of witness, whom Moses and Aaron counted by the word of the Lord, by the hand of Moses. Also, the family of the sons of Merari were counted according to their divisions, according to the house of their fathers; from twenty-five years old and upward until fifty years old, everyone that goes in to minister in the services of the tabernacle of witness. Their count according to their families, according to the houses of their lineage was 3,200.

This is the numbering of the family of the sons of Merari, whom Moses and Aaron counted by the word of the Lord, by the hand of Moses. All that were counted, whom Moses and Aaron and the rulers of Israel counted, namely, the Levites, according to their families and according to the houses of their lineage, from twenty-five years old and upward until fifty years old, everyone that goes in for the service of the works, and the order of the things that are carried in the tabernacle of witness. They who were counted were 8,580. He reviewed them according to the word of the Lord by the hand of Moses, appointing each man over their respective work, and their burdens. They were counted, as the Lord commanded Moses.

Numbers: Chapter 5

The Lord said to Moses, "Order the children of Israel, to send out of the camp every leper, and everyone who has gonorrhea, and everyone who is unclean in the mind.[1] Whether male or female, send them out of the camp, so they will not defile their camp in which I live among them."

The children of Israel did so and sent them out of the camp as the Lord said to Moses, so did the children of Israel. The Lord said to Moses, "Tell the children of Israel, "Every man or woman who will commit any sin that is common to man, or if that mind will in any way have neglected the commandment and transgressed, that person will confess the sin which he has committed and will make satisfaction for his trespass. He will pay the principal, and will add to it the fifth part, and will make restoration to him against whom he has trespassed. But if a man has no near relative to make satisfaction for his trespass to him, the trespass-offering paid to the Lord will be for the priest, besides the ram of atonement, by which he will make an atonement with it for him. Every first fruits in all the sanctified things among the children of Israel, whatever they will offer to the Lord, will be for the priest himself. The sacred things of every man will be his, and whatever a man will give to the priest, the gift will be his."

The Lord said to Moses, "Tell the children of Israel, "Whoever's wife transgresses against him, and slight and despise him, and supposing anyone will lie with her carnally, and it is hidden from the eyes of her husband, and she should conceal it and be herself defiled, and there be no witness with her. Should there come on him a spirit of jealousy, and he should be jealous of his wife, and she is defiled, or, there should come on him a spirit of jealousy, and he should be jealous of his wife, and she should not be defiled, then, will the man bring his wife to the priest, and will bring his gift for her, a tenth of an ephah[2] of barley. He will not pour oil on it, nor will he put frankincense on it, as it is a sacrifice of jealousy, a sacrifice of memorial reminding of sin."

"The priest will bring her, and make her stand before the Lord. The priest will take pure running water in an earthen vessel, and he will take from the dust that is on the floor of the tabernacle of witness, and the priest having taken it will cast it into the water. The priest will cause the woman to stand before the Lord, and will uncover the head of the woman, and will put into her hands the sacrifice of memorial, the sacrifice of jealousy, and in the hand of the priest will be the water of this conviction that brings the curse. The priest will adjure her, and will say to the woman, 'If no one has lain with you, and if you have not transgressed to be polluted, being under the authority of your husband, be free from this water of the conviction that causes the curse.' But if being a married woman you have transgressed, or been polluted, and anyone has lain with you, besides your husband.' Then the priest will adjure the woman by the oaths of this curse, and the priest will say to the woman, 'The Lord curse you under an oath among your people, in that the Lord should cause your thigh to rot and your belly to swell, and this water bringing the curse will enter into your womb to cause your belly to swell, and your thigh to rot.' The woman will say, 'Amen, Amen!'"[3]

"The priest will write these curses in a book and will write them in with the water of the conviction that brings the curse. He will cause the woman to drink the water of the conviction that brings the curse, and the water of the conviction that brings the curse will enter into her. The priest will take from the hand of the woman the sacrifice of jealousy, and will present the sacrifice before the Lord, and will bring it to the altar. The priest will take a handful of the sacrifice as a memorial of it and will offer it up on the altar, and afterward, he will cause the woman to drink the water. It will happen, if she is defiled, and have altogether escaped the notice of her husband, then the water of the conviction that brings the curse will enter into her, and she will swell in her belly, and her thigh will rot, and the woman will be cursed among her people. But if the woman has not been polluted, and is clean, then will she be guiltless and will conceive seed."

This is the law of jealousy, in which a married woman should happen to transgress and be defiled, or in the case of a man on whoever the spirit of jealousy should come, and he should be jealous of his wife, and he should place his wife before the Lord, and the priest will execute towards her all this law. Then the man will be clear from sin, and that woman will carry her sin.

Numbers: Chapter 5 Notes

1 Codex Vaticanus: acatharton epi psychê (ΑΚΑΘΑΡΤΟΝΕΠΙϯΥΧΗ). Translation: foul (or unclean, impure) in psyche (or mind, personality)

• LXX 318: acatharton epi psychên (ἀκαϙ/θάβτον Ϭπι Ψυχλ ̅ν). Translation: foul (or unclean, impure) in psyche (or mind, personality)

- LXX 319: acatharton apo psychê (ἀϰαϒθἀβτοℕ ἀπο Ψυχℏ). Translation: foul (or unclean, impure) from psyche (or mind, personality)

- LXX 16: acatharton tê psychê (ἀϰαϒθἀβτοℕ τℏ Ψυχℏ). Translation: foul (or unclean, impure) the psyche (or mind, personality)

- LXX 426: acatharton epi tychê (ἀϰαϒθἀβτοℕ ϭπι τυχℏ). Translation: foul (or unclean, impure) in action (or fate, providence)

- LXX 54: acatharton epi psychês (ἀϰαϒθἀβτοℕ ϭπι Ψυχℏc). Translation: foul (or unclean, impure) in psyche (or mind, personality)

- LXX 72: acatharton en tê psychê (ἀϰαϒθἀβτοℕ ϭℕ τℏ Ψυχℏ). Translation: foul (or unclean, impure) in the psyche (or mind, personality)

- Leningrad Codex: tame lanafesh (טָמֵא לָנֶפֶשׁ). Translation: ritually unclean to (or of) soul (or psyche, life, person, will)

- Peshitta: tmå bnpšh (ܛܡܐ ܒܢܦܫ). Translations: ritually unclean of ego (or breath, psyche)

- Targum Onkelos: temei nafsha de'enasha (טְמֵי נַפְשָׁא דֶאֱנָשָׁא). Translations: ritually unclean of ego (or breath, psyche) of man (or human, mortal)

- Targum Jerusalem: temei nafsha demit (טְמֵי נַפְשָׁא דְמִית). Translations: ritually unclean of ego (or breath, psyche) of man (or human, mortal)

2 Codex Vaticanus: oephi (οιϕι)

- Leningrad Codex: eifah (אֵיפָה). Translation: ephah

- Peshitta: såtå (ܣܐܬܐ). Translations: bowls (or measurements)

- Targum Onkelos: bitlat se'in (בִּתְלָת סָאִין). Translations: in three sahs

- Targum Jerusalem: bitlat se'in (בִּתְלָת סָאִין). Translations: in three sahs

The Septuagint includes a Greek transliteration of the Hebrew term âyph (איפה). The ephah was a unit of measurement adopted by the Canaanites and Arabs from the Egyptian oipe (𓇋𓊪𓏏). It continued to be used in Egypt during the classical era, where the word was spelled in Coptic as aeipe (ⲁⲉⲓⲡⲉ) in Akhmimic, aipi (ⲁⲓⲡⲓ) in Fayyumic, oeipe (ⲟⲉⲓⲡⲉ) in Sahidic, and ōipi (ⲱⲓⲡⲓ) in Bohairic, depending on dialect. The ephah was a dry measurement equalling 432 eggs, meaning the measurement in the text was the equivalent or 43.2 eggs.

3 Codex Vaticanus: genoeto genoeto (ΓΕΝΟΙΤΟΓΕΝΟΙΤΟ). Translation: Earth forbid Earth forbid

• Leningrad Codex: amen amen (אָמֵן \ אָמֵן). Translation: 'I agree' (or artist, master, craftsmen, creator, expert, foster parent, Amen) 'I agree'

• Peshitta: åmyn åmyn (ܐܡܝܢ ܐܡܝܢ)

• Targum Onkelos: amen amen (אָמֵן אָמֵן)

• Fragment Targums: amen dela ista'avit amen in ana atidah lemiste'ava (אָמֵן דְלָא אִסְתָּאֲבִית אָמֵן אִין אֲנָא עֲתִידָה לְמִסְתָּאֲבָא). Translations: Amen if not unclean Amen not will become unclean

• Targum Jerusalem: amen in iste'avit kad me'arsa amen in iste'avit kad nesivta (אָמֵן אִין אִסְתָּאֲבִית כַּד מֵאָרְסָא אָמֵן אִין אִסְתָּאֲבִית כַּד נְסִיבְתָא). Translations: Amen not unclean when married Amen not unclean when offered [in marriage]

As the original text could not have used the Greek expression, the term amen is imported from the Masoretic Text. If the Canaanite expression amen was not derived from the name of the supreme Egyptian god Amen's name during the Egyptian rule of Canaan when the Book of Numbers is set, it's possible it was based on the Akkadian word for artist, åummānu (𒌝𒈝𒉡), however, this seems less likely than the name of the Egyptian creator god. According to Egyptologists, during the New Kingdom era, Amen (𓇋𓏠𓈖) is believed to have been pronounced as Åman. Earlier, during the Middle Kingdom the name was pronounced as Jaman, explaining the pronunciation of Benjamin, and later during the Nubian dynasty, the name was pronounced as Åmon, explaining the pronunciation of King Amon's name.

Numbers: Chapter 6

The Lord said to Moses, tell the children of Israel, "Whatever man or woman should specially vow a vow to separate oneself with purity to the Lord, he will purely abstain from wine and strong drink. He will drink no wine or strong alcoholic drink. Whatever is made from grapes he will not drink, neither will he eat fresh grapes or raisins. All the days of his vow: he will eat none of all the things that come from the vine, wine from the grape-stones to the grape-stone. All the days of his separation, a razor will not come on his head, until the days are completed which he vowed to the Lord."

"He will be holy, cherishing a head of hair, even long hair, all the days of his vow to the Lord. He will not come near to any dead body, to his father or his mother, or his brother or his sister. He will not defile himself for them when they have died, because the vow of God is on him on his head. All the days of his vow he will be holy to the Lord. If anyone should die suddenly by him, immediately the head of his vow will be defiled, and he will shave his head in whatever day he will be purified. On the seventh day, he will be shaved. On the eighth day, he will bring two turtledoves, or two young pigeons, to the priest, to the doors of the tabernacle of witness."

"The priest will offer one as a sin offering, and the other as a whole burnt offering. The priest will make atonement for him in the things in which he sinned respecting the dead body, and he will sanctify his head in that day in which he was consecrated to the Lord, the days of his vow being interrupted, he will bring a year-old lamb for a trespass-offering, and the former days will not be counted, because the head of his vow was polluted. This is the law of he who has vowed. On whichever day he has fulfilled the days of his vow, he will himself bring his gift to the doors of the tabernacle of witness. He will bring his gift to the Lord, one year-old male lamb without imperfection for a whole burnt offering, and one year-old female lamb without imperfection for a sin offering, and one ram without imperfection for a peace offering, and a basket of unleavened bread of fine flour, including loaves kneaded with oil, and unleavened cakes covered with oil, and their sacrifice, and their drink offering."

"The priest will bring them before the Lord and will offer his sin offering, and his whole burnt offering. He will offer the ram as a sacrifice of peace offering to the Lord with the basket of unleavened bread, and the priest will offer its sacrifice and its drink offering. He that has vowed will shave the head of his consecration by the doors of the tabernacle of witness and will put the hairs on the fire which is under the sacrifice of peace offering. The priest will take the sodden shoulder of the ram, and one unleavened loaf from the basket, and one unleavened cake, and will put them in the hands of the Nazarene[1] after he has shaved off his vow. The priest will present them as an offering before the Lord, it will be the holy portion for the priest beside the breast of the heave-offering and beside the shoulder of the wave-offering, and afterward, the Nazarene will drink wine."

This is the law of the Nazarene who has vowed to the Lord his gift to the Lord, concerning his vow, besides what he may be able to afford according to the value of his vow, which he may have vowed according to the law of separation.

The Lord said to Moses, "Tell Aaron and to his sons, 'You will bless the children of Israel, saying them, 'The Lord bless you and keep you. The Lord make his face shine on you, and have mercy on you. The Lord lift his face on you and give you peace.'[2] They will put my name on the children of Israel, and I, the Lord will bless them."

Numbers: Chapter 6 Notes

1 LXX 963: eugmenou (ЄΥΓΜЄΝΟΥ)

- Codex Vaticanus: eugmenou (ΗΥΓΜЄΝΟΥ). Translation: devotee (or vower, prayer)

- Codex Colberto-Sarravianus: euchomenou (ЄΥΧΟΜЄΝΟΥ)

- Codex Ambrosiano A 147: euxamenou (ЄΥΞΑΜЄΝΟΥ)

- LXX 407: êgmenou (ἠγμένου)

- LXX 458: egmenou (ὀγμένου)

- LXX 72: êgnismenou (ἠγνισμένου)

- LXX 799: êêgmenou (ἠἠγμένου)

- Leningrad Codex: nazir (נָזִיר). Translation: separated (or monk)

- Peshitta: nzyrûtâ (ܢܙܝܪܘܬܐ)

- Targum Onkelos: neziru (נְזִירוּ)

- Targum Jerusalem: nezira (נְזִירָא)

The Greeks translated this term was 'devotee' in Numbers, suggesting the term was obscure when the Torah was translated circa 250 BC. In Judges, the same term was used for Sampson, who was described as being a nezir (נְזִיר) from birth in the Masoretic text, which was transliterated as nazir (ΝΑΖΙΡ) in the Codex Vaticanus and naziraeon (ΝΑΖΙΡΑΙΟΝ) in the Codex Alexandrinus. 1st Maccabees records that there was a community of naziraeous (ναζιραίους) in Judea during the revolt, which was between 165 and 140 BC. The word used in 1st Maccabees can be translated several ways, including Nazirites, Nazarenes, and Nasoreans, depending on the religious views of the translator, however, all would have been spelled as nzyr (נזיר) in Hebrew.

The Jewish interpretation, as defined in the Talmud, was a Jew that took vows to abstain from wine, not cut their hair, and not touch corpses, as described in Numbers. The Nazarene community in 1st Maccabees is sometimes theorized to be an early reference to the Essenes. The term Nazarene was used in the Christian gospels as a title of Jesus, and therefore became the Arabic and Hebrew term for 'Christian,' however, the Mandaeans claimed the term referred to their priesthood, which had once been led by John the Baptist, who had baptized Jesus.

In the case of Sampson, he judges the Israelites between approximately 1130 and 1110 BC, under the rule of the Pelesets, who the Egyptians had surrendered Canaan to. This means that the concept of the Nazir was already established by that era, supporting the antiquity of this section of Numbers. As the Greeks appear to have translated the term Nazir as 'devotee,' the most common English translation is used.

2 A similar phrase is found in Ketef Hinnom scroll 2, which is generally reconstructed as: "-hbrw. May be blessed he by Yhŭ[h], the warrior and the rebuker of [E]vil, may bless you, Yhŭh keep you. May shine, Yh[ŭ]h, his face [on] you and grant you p[ea]ce."

KH2 is a silver scroll inscribed in Judahite, that was found in an archaeological site near Jerusalem dating to the 4th century BC. It is generally considered a magical amulet to have been created sometime between the 7th and 4th century BC. It is unclear if it was a paraphrase of this verse in Numbers, or simply a similar phase, however, if it was a paraphrase from Numbers, it would mean the text of Numbers was different at the time, as Yhŭh is not referred to as 'the warrior,' in Numbers.

Numbers: Chapter 7

It came to pass on the day in which Moses finished setting up the tabernacle, that he anointed it, and consecrated it, and all its furniture, and the altar and all its furniture, he even anointed them and consecrated them. The princes of Israel brought gifts, twelve princes of their fathers' houses: these were the heads of tribes, these are they that presided over the numbering. They brought their gift before the Lord, six covered wagons, and twelve oxen, a wagon from two princes, and a calf from each, and they brought them before the tabernacle.

The Lord said to Moses, "Take from them, and they will be for the works of the services of the tabernacle of witness. You will give them to the Levites, to each one according to his administration. Moses took the wagons and the oxen and gave them to the Levites. He gave two wagons and four oxen to the sons of Gershon, according to their administrations. Four wagons and eight oxen he gave to the sons of Merari according to their administrations, by Ithamar the son of Aaron the priest. But to the sons of Kohath, he did not give, because they have the administrations of the sacred things. They will carry them on their shoulders.

The rulers brought gifts for the dedication of the altar on the day that he anointed it, and the rulers brought their gifts before the altar. The Lord said to Moses, "One chief each day, will offer their gifts a chief each day for the dedication of the altar."

On the first day Nahshon the son of Amminadab, prince of the tribe of Judah offered his gift. He brought his gift, one silver charger of 130 shekels in weight, one silver bowl, of 70 shekels according to the holy shekel, both full of fine flour kneaded with oil for a sacrifice. One golden censer of 10 shekels full of incense. One calf from the herd, one ram, one year-old male lamb for a whole burnt offering, and one goat kid for a sin offering. For a sacrifice of peace offering, two heifers, five rams, five male goats, five year-old female lambs. This was the gift of Nahshon the son of Amminadab.

On the second day Nethanel the son of Zuar, the prince of the tribe of Issachar, brought his offering. He brought his gift, one silver charger, weighing 130 shekels, one silver bowl of 70 shekels according to the holy shekel, both full of fine flour kneaded with oil for a sacrifice. One censer of 10 golden shekels, full of incense. One calf from the herd, one ram, one year-old male lamb for a whole burnt offering, and one goat kid for a sin offering. For a sacrifice, a peace offering, two heifers, five rams, five male goats, five year-old female lambs. This was the gift of Nethanel the son of Zuar.

On the third day the prince of the sons of Zebulun, Eliab the son of Helon. He brought his gift, one silver charger, weighing 130 shekels, one silver bowl of 70 shekels according to the holy shekel, both full of fine flour kneaded with oil for a sacrifice. One golden censer of 10 shekels, full of incense. One calf from the herd, one ram, one year-old male lamb for a whole burnt offering, and one goat kid for a sin offering. For a sacrifice of peace offering, two heifers, five rams, five male goats, five year-old female lambs. This was the gift of Eliab the son of Helon.

On the fourth day Elizur the son of Shedeur, the prince of the children of Reuben. He brought his gift, one silver charger, weighing 130 shekels, one silver bowl of 70 shekels according to the holy shekel, both full of fine flour kneaded with oil for a sacrifice. One golden censer of 10 shekels full of incense. One calf from the herd, one ram, one year-old male lamb for a whole burnt offering, and one goat kid for a sin offering. For a sacrifice of peace offering, two heifers, five rams, five male goats, five year-old female lambs. This was the gift of Elizur the son of Shedeur.

On the fifth day the prince of the children of Simeon, Shelumiel the son of Zurishaddai. He brought his gift, one silver charger, weighing 130 shekels, one silver bowl of 70 shekels according to the holy shekel, both full of fine flour kneaded with oil for a sacrifice. One golden censer of 10 shekels, full of incense. One calf from the herd, one ram, one year-old male lamb for a whole burnt offering, and one goat kid for a sin offering. For a sacrifice of peace offering, two heifers, five rams, five male goats, five year-old female lambs. This was the gift of Shelumiel the son of Zurishaddai.

On the sixth day the prince of the sons of Gad, Eliasaph the son of Deuel. He brought his gift, one silver charger, weighing 130 shekels, one silver bowl of 70 shekels according to the holy shekel, both full of fine flour kneaded with oil for a sacrifice. One golden censer of 10 shekels, full of incense. One calf from the herd, one ram, one year-old male lamb for a whole burnt offering, and one goat kid for a sin offering. For a sacrifice of peace offering, two heifers, five rams, five male goats, five year-old female lambs. This was the gift of Eliasaph the son of Deuel.

On the seventh day the prince of the sons of Ephraim, Elishama the son of Ammihud. He brought his gift, one silver charger, weighing 130 shekels, one silver bowl of 70 shekels according to the holy shekel, both full of fine flour kneaded with oil for a sacrifice. One golden censer of 10 shekels, full of incense. One calf from the herd, one ram, one year-old male lamb for a whole burnt offering, and one goat kid for a sin offering. For a sacrifice of peace offering, two heifers, five rams, five male goats, five year-old female lambs. This was the gift of Elishama the son of Ammihud.

On the eighth day the prince of the sons of Manasseh, Gamaliel the son of Pedahzur. He brought his gift, one silver charger, weighing 130 shekels, one silver bowl of 70 shekels according to the holy shekel, both full of fine flour mingled with oil for a sacrifice. One golden censer of 10 shekels, full of incense. One calf from the herd, one ram, one year-old male lamb for a whole burnt offering, and one goat kid for a sin offering. For a sacrifice of peace offering two heifers, five rams, five male goats, five year-old female lambs. This was the gift of Gamaliel the son of Pedahzur.

On the ninth day the prince of the sons of Benjamin, Abidan the son of Gideoni. He brought his gift, one silver charger, weighing 130 shekels, one silver bowl of 70 shekels according to the holy shekel, both full of fine flour mingled with oil for a sacrifice. One golden censer of 10 shekels, full of incense. One calf from the herd, one ram, one year-old male lamb for a whole burnt offering, and one goat kid for a sin offering. For a sacrifice of peace offering, two heifers, five rams, five male goats, five year-old female lambs. This was the gift of Abidan the son of Gideoni.

On the tenth day the prince of the sons of Dan, Ahiezer the son of Ammishaddai. He brought his gift, one silver charger, weighing 130 shekels, one silver bowl of 70 shekels according to the holy shekel, both full of fine flour kneaded with oil for a sacrifice. One golden censer of 10 shekels, full of incense. One calf from the herd, one ram, one year-old male lamb for a whole burnt offering, and one goat kid for a sin offering. For a sacrifice of peace offering, two heifers, five rams, five male goats, five year-old female lambs. This was the gift of Ahiezer the son of Ammishaddai.

On the eleventh day the prince of the sons of Asher, Phageel the son of Ochran. He brought his gift, one silver charger, weighing 130 shekels, one silver bowl of 70 shekels according to the holy shekel, both full of fine flour mingled with oil for a sacrifice. One golden censer of 10 shekels, full of incense. One calf from the herd, one ram, one year-old male lamb for a whole burnt offering, and one goat kid for a sin offering. For a sacrifice of peace offering, two heifers, five rams, five male goats, five year-old female lambs. This was the gift of Phageel the son of Ochran.

On the twelfth day the prince of the sons of Naphtali, Ahira the son of Enan. He brought his gift, one silver charger, weighing 130 shekels, one silver bowl of 70 shekels according to the holy shekel; both full of fine flour mingled with oil for a sacrifice. One golden censer of 10 shekels, full of incense. One calf from the herd, one ram, one year-old male lamb for a whole burnt offering, and one goat kid for a sin offering. For a sacrifice of peace offering, two heifers, five rams, five male goats, five year-old female lambs. This was the gift of Ahira the son of Enan. This was the dedication of the altar on the day in which Moses anointed it, by the princes of the sons of Israel, twelve silver chargers, twelve silver bowls, twelve golden censers, each one charger of 130 shekels, and each bowl of 70 shekels, all the silver of the vessels was 2,400 shekels, the shekels according to the holy shekel, as 12 golden censers full of incense, all the gold of the shekels being 120 shekels. All the livestock for whole burnt offerings, twelve calves, twelve rams, twelve year-old male lambs, and their sacrifice, and their drink offerings: and twelve male goat-kids for sin offering. All the livestock for a sacrifice of peace offering, twenty-four heifers, sixty rams, sixty male goats of a year-old, sixty year-old female lambs without imperfection."

This was the dedication of the altar. After that Moses filled his hands, and after he anointed him. When Moses went into the tabernacle of witness to speak to him, then he heard the voice of the Lord speaking to him from off the mercy-seat, which is on the ark of the testimony, between the two sphinxes,[1] and he spoke to him.

Numbers: Chapter 7 Notes

1 LXX 963: cheroubin (ⲭⲉⲣⲟⲩⲃⲉⲓⲛ)

• Codex Vaticanus: cheroubim (ⲭⲉⲣⲟⲩⲃⲉⲓⲙ)

• Codex Venetus: cheroubin (χόβουμιν)

• LXX 125: cheroubim o estin epi tês cibôtou tou martyriou (χόβουμφμ οϐοτιν ϐπι τλς ιμωτου του μάβτυβιου). Translation: cherubs that exist on the box of testimony (or martyrdom, evidence)

• LXX 376: chaeroubim (χλιβουμμ)

600

- Leningrad Codex: keruvim (כְּרֻבִים). Translation: cherubs (or griffins, sphinxes)

- Peshitta: krŭbyn (ܟ̈ܪܘܒܐ). Translation: cherubs (or griffins)

- Targum Onkelos: keruvayya (כְּרוּבַיָּא). Translation: cherubs (or griffins)

- Targum Jerusalem: keruvayya (כְּרוּבַיָּא). Translation: cherubs (or griffins)

The word 'cherub' (ܟ̈ܪܘܒܐ / כרוב / 𐤊𐤓𐤁 / 𐤊𐤓𐤁) was the West Semitic term for the mythical creature generally called a 'griffin' today. Based in the archaeological record of Canaan, it appears that the concept of the cherub was based on the Egyptian sphinx, as the earliest cherub statues found in Canaan were Egyptian statues of sphinxes.

Archaeologists are not sure if the griffins of Anatolia were based on the Canaanite cherub, or the Egyptian sphinxes directly, however, all three mythical beings are closely related in the archaeological record. The term cherub was for some reason reinterpreted as 'baby angels' by Christians, although in the Books of the Kingdoms God was described as riding on cherubs, and it is not clear why any god would ride around on 'baby angels,' and therefore the alternate translation of 'sphinxes' is used in this translation.

Numbers: Chapter 8

The Lord said to Moses, "Tell Aaron, "Whenever you will set the lamps in order, the seven lamps will give light opposite the candlestick." Aaron did so, on one side opposite the candlestick he lighted its lamps, as the Lord told Moses. This is the arrangement of the candlestick. It is solid gold, its stem and its lilies are all solid, according to the pattern which the Lord showed Moses, so he made the candlestick.

The Lord said to Moses, "Take the Levites out from among the children of Israel and purify them. You will perform their purification like so, you will sprinkle them with water of purification, and a razor will shave their whole body, and they will wash their garments and will be clean. They will take one calf from the herd, and its sacrifice, fine flour mingled with oil, and you will take a year-old calf from the herd for a sin offering. You will bring the Levites before the tabernacle of witness, and you will assemble all the community of the sons of Israel. Bring the Levites before the Lord, and the sons of Israel will lay their hands on the Levites. Aaron will separate the Levites as a gift before the Lord from the children of Israel, and they will be prepared to perform the works of the Lord. The Levites will lay their hands on the heads of the calves, and you will offer one for a sin offering, and the other for a whole burnt offering to the Lord, to make atonement for them. You will set the Levites before the Lord, and before Aaron, and before his sons, and you will give them as a gift before the Lord."

"Separate the Levites from among the sons of Israel, and they will be mine. Afterward, the Levites will go in to perform the works of the tabernacle of witness, and you will purify them, and present them before the Lord. For these are given to me as a present from among the children of Israel. I have taken them to myself instead of all the firstborn of the sons of Israel that open every womb. For every firstborn among the children of Israel is mine, whether of man or beast, in the day in which I struck every firstborn in the land of Egypt, I sanc- tified them to myself. I took the Levites in the place of every firstborn among the children of Israel. I gave the Levites as a gift to Aaron and his sons from among the children of Israel, to do the service of the children of Israel in the tabernacle of witness, and to make atonement for the children of Israel, so there will be none among the sons of Israel to draw near to the holy things."

Moses and Aaron, and all the community of the children of Israel, did to the Levites as the Lord commanded Moses concerning the Levites, so the sons of Israel did to them. So the Levites purified themselves and washed their garments, and Aaron presented them as a gift before the Lord, and Aaron made atonement for them to purify them. Afterward, the Levites went in to administer their service in the tabernacle of witness before Aaron, and before his sons. As the Lord appointed Moses concerning the Levites, so they did to them.

The Lord said to Moses, "This is the ordinance for the Levites. From twenty-five years old and upward, they will go in to do the work in the tabernacle of witness. From fifty years old the Levites will cease from the ministry, and will not work any longer. His brother will serve in the tabernacle of witness to keep orders, but he will not do works. So you will do to the Levites in their orders."

Numbers: Chapter 9

The Lord said to Moses in the Wilderness of Sinai, in the second year after they left the land of Egypt, in the first month, "Speak, and let the children of Israel keep the Passover in its season. On the fourteenth day of the first month, in the evening, you will keep it in its season. You will keep it according to its law, and according to its ordinance."

Moses ordered the children of Israel to sacrifice the Passover, on the fourteenth day of the first month in the Wilderness of Sinai, as the Lord appointed Moses, so the children of Israel did. There came men who were unclean because of a dead body, and they were not able to keep the Passover on that day, and they came before Moses and Aaron on that day. These men said to him, "We are unclean because of the dead body of a man. Will we, therefore, fail to offer the gift to the Lord in its season among the children of Israel?"

Moses said to them, "Stand there, and I will hear what order the Lord will give concerning you."

The Lord said to Moses, "Tell the children of Israel, 'Whatever man will be unclean because of a dead body, or on a journey far off, among you, or among your descendants, he will then keep the Passover to the Lord, in the second month, on the fourteenth day. In the evening they will offer it, with unleavened bread and bitter plants will they eat it. They will not leave it until the morning, and they will not break a bone of it. They will sacrifice it according to the ordinance of the Passover."

"Whatever man will be clean, and is not far off on a journey, and will fail to keep the Passover, that mind will be cut off from his people, because he has not offered the gift to the Lord in its season. That man will carry his iniquity. If there should come to you a stranger in your land and should keep the Passover to the Lord, he will keep it according to the law of the Passover and according to its ordinance. There will be one law for you, both for the stranger and for the native of the land."

"In the day in which the tabernacle was pitched the cloud covered the tabernacle, the house of the testimony, and in the evening there was on the tabernacle the appearance of fire until the morning. So it was continually, the cloud covered it by day and the appearance of fire by night. When the cloud went up from the tabernacle, then after that the children of Israel departed, and in whatever place the cloud rested, there the children of Israel camped. The children of Israel will camp by the command of the Lord, and by the command of the Lord, they will leave. All the days in which the cloud overshadows the tabernacle, the children of Israel will camp. Whenever the cloud will be drawn over the tabernacle for many days, then the children of Israel will follow the command of God[1] and they will not move."

"It will be, whenever the cloud overshadows the tabernacle several days, they will camp by the word of the Lord, and will move by the command of the Lord. It will happen, whenever the cloud remains from the evening until the morning, and in the morning the cloud will go up, then they will move by day or by night. When the cloud continues more than a month overshadowing the tabernacle, the children of Israel will camp, and will not depart. For they will depart by the command of the Lord."

They followed the order of the Lord by the command of the Lord by the hand of Moses.

Numbers: Chapter 9 Notes

1 Codex Vaticanus: thu (ⲐⲨ). Translation: God

• Leningrad Codex: Yehvah (יְהוָֹה)

• Peshitta: mryå (ܡܪܝܐ). Translation: master (or lord)

• Targum Onkelos: yeyah (??). Translation: Yhů

• Targum Jerusalem: yeyah (??). Translation: Yhů

Numbers: Chapter 10

The Lord said to Moses, "Make for yourself two silver trumpets. You will make them of beaten work, and they will be for you to call the assembly, and of moving the camps. You will sound with them, and all the community will be gathered to the door of the tabernacle of witness. If they will sound with one, all the rulers including the princes of Israel will come to you. You will sound an alarm, the camps pitched eastward will begin to move. You will sound a second alarm, and the camps pitched southward will move. If you sound a third alarm, and the camps pitched westward will move forward. If you sound a fourth alarm, and they that camp towards the north will move forward, they will sound an alarm at their departure."

"Whenever you will gather the assembly, you will sound, but not an alarm. The priests, the sons of Aaron will sound with the trumpets, and it will be a perpetual ordinance for you throughout your generations. If you will go out to war in your land against your enemies who oppose you, then you will sound with the trumpets, as a remembrance before the Lord, and you will be saved from your enemies. In the days of your gladness, and your feasts, and your new moons, you will sound with the trumpets at your whole burnt offerings and the sacrifices of your peace offerings. There will be a memorial for you before the god,[1] me Lord, your god."[2]

(And said Lord to Moses, "I am content to dwell in this mountain which is restored, and you shall be removed from it, and you shall enter into the mountain of the Amorites, and into their subject's mountains, and their subjects in Lebanon and to the coast of the sea of the Canaanites, and from Anti-lebanon to the great river Euphrates. I will concede in front of you the land where you enter, which will be distributed by lottery, the land which I handed to your forefathers Abraham, Isaac, and Jacob, and their descendants.")[3]

It happened in the second year, in the second month, on the twentieth day of the month, the cloud went up from the tabernacle of witness. The children of Israel set forward with their baggage in the Wilderness of Sinai, and the cloud rested in the Wilderness of Paran. The first rank departed by the word of the Lord by the hand of Moses. They first set in motion the order of the camp of the children of Judah with their army, and over their army was Nahshon, son of Amminadab. Over the army of the tribe of the sons of Issachar, was Nethanel the son of Zuar. Over the army of the tribe of the sons of Zebulun, was Eliab the son of Helon. They will take down the tabernacle, and the sons of Gershon will set forward, and the sons of Merari, who carry the tabernacle. The order of the camp of Reuben set forward with their army, and over their army was Elizur the son of Shedeur. Over the army of the tribe of the sons of Simeon, was Shelumiel the son of Zurishaddai. Over the army of the tribe of the children of Gad, was Eliasaph the son of Deuel.

The sons of Kohath set out carrying the holy things, and the others will set up the tabernacle when they arrive. The order of the camp of Ephraim set out with their forces, and over their forces was Elishama the son of Ammihud.

Over the forces of the tribes of the sons of Manasseh, was Gamaliel the son of Pedahzur. Over the forces of the tribe of the children of Benjamin, was Abidan the son of Gideoni. The order of the camp of the sons of Dan will set forward the last of all the camps, with their forces: and over their forces was Ahiezer the son of Ammishaddai. Over the forces of the tribe of the sons of Asher, was Phageel the son of Ochran. Over the forces of the tribe of the sons of Naphtali, was Ahira the son of Enan. These are the armies of the children of Israel, and they set forward with their forces.

Moses said to Jobab the son of Ragouel the Midianite, the son-in-law of Moses,[4] "We are going forward to the place which the Lord said, 'I will give you this.' Come with us, and we will treat you well, for Lord has spoken good concerning Israel."

He said to him, "I will not go, but I will return to my land and my families"

He said, "Dont' leave us, because you have been with us in the wilderness, and you will be an elder among us. It will happen if you will go with us, it will even happen that in whatever things Lord will do us good, we will also do you good."

They departed from the mount of the Lord a three days' journey, and the ark of the covenant of the Lord went before them a three days' journey to provide rest for them. The cloud overshadowed them by day when they departed from the camp. It came to pass when the ark set forward, that Moses said, "Rise, Lord, and let your enemies be scattered. Let all that hate you flee."

When resting he said, "Turn again, Lord, the thousands and tens of thousands of Israel."

Numbers: Chapter 10 Notes

1 Codex Vaticanus: thu (ΘΥ). Translation: God

- Leningrad Codex: Yehvah (יְהֹוָה)

- Peshitta: mryå (ܡܪܝܐ). Translation: master (or lord)

- Targum Onkelos: meimra dayya (מֵימְרָא דַיְיָ). Translation: command of the Yhů

- Targum Jerusalem: elahachon beram satana mit'arvev lekal yabbevutechon (אֱלָהְכוֹן בְּרַם סָטָנָא מִתְעָרֵב לְקָל יַבְּבוּתְכוֹן). Translation: your god however Satan (or adversary, devil) amazed trembling

2 Codex Vaticanus: egô cso thsymôn (ΕΓѠΚϹΟΘϹΥΜѠΝ). Translation: I'm lord the god of you

- Leningrad Codex: ani Yehovah eloheichem (אֲנִי יְהֹוָה אֱלֹהֵיכֶם). Translation: I'm Yehowa your god

- Peshitta: ånå ånå mryå ålhkůn (ܐܢܐ ܐܢܐ ܡܪܝܐ ܐܠܗܟܘܢ). Translation: I am master your god

- Targum Onkelos: ana yeyah elahachon (אֲנָא יְיָ אֱלָהְכוֹן). Translation: I'm Yhů your god

- Targum Jerusalem: ana hu yeyah elahachon (אֲנָא הוּא יְיָ אֱלָהְכוֹן). Translation: I'm he: Yhů your god

The phrase Lord God (Κύριος ο θεος) only appears a few times in Numbers, although does feature prominently in Genesis and Exodus. It is missing entirely from Leviticus, strongly suggesting that the Book of Numbers is older than Leviticus, or composed of fragments that are older than Leviticus. The Aramaic sections of Masoretic Daniel that were not translated into Hebrew maintain the term adonai ha'elohim (אֲדֹנָי הָאֱלֹהִים), meaning the 'Lord the gods' where the Septuagint has 'Lord the god' (Κύριος ο θεος). As most books of the Septuagint were translated from Aramaic texts, the Aramaic text almost certainly used the term adonai ha'elohim where the Septuagint has 'Lord the god.'

3 LXX 78: cae elalêsen cspros môsên legôn icanousthô ymin catoecin en tô ori touto epistraphêtae cae aparatae ymis cae isporeuesthae is oros amorrhaeôn cae pros pantas tous perioecous autou tous en tê paediadi is oros cae paedion cae pros liban cae paralian thalassês gên chananaeôn cae antilibanon eôs tou megalou potamou euphratou isselthate paradedôca enôpion ymôn tên gên iselthontae clironomêsatae tên gên ên ômosa toes

patrasin ymôn tô abraam cae isaac cae iacôb dounae tô spermati autou met' autous (ιλι
ϭλλλοϭν ιοπϸος μοοϧν λϭγοον ιιλνουϭθοο υμιν ιιλτοιιϭιν ϭν τοο οϸϭιτουτο ϭπιοτϸλϷϧτλι
ιιλι λπλϸλτλι υμϭιc ιιλι ϭιοποϸϭυϭϭθλι ϭιc οϸοc λμοϸϸλιοον ιιλι πϸοc πλντλc τουc πϭϸιοιιμουc λυτου
τουc ϭν τϧπλιϊιλϊι ϭιc οϸοc ιιλι πλιϊιον ιιλι πϸοc λιιλν ιιλιπλϸλλιλν θλλλοοϧc γϧν
χλνλνλιοον ιιλι λντιλιιλνον ϭοοc του μϭγλλου ποτλμου ϭυϷϸλτουϭιοοϭλθλτϭ πλϸλλϭλοοιιλ
ϭνοοπιον υμοον τϧν γϧν ϭιοϭλθοντλι ιιλιϸονομϧνολτλι τϧνγϧν ϧν οομοολ τοιc πλτϸλοιν υμοον
τοο λιιϸλλμ ιιλι ιολλι ιιλι ιλιιοοιι ϊουνλι τοο οπϭϸμλτι λυτου μϭτ λυτουc). Translation: and spoke
Lord to Moses, saying, "I am content to dwell in this mountain which is returned, and it
shall be removed from you, and you shall enter into the mountain of the Amorites, and
into their children's mountains (or subject's mountains), and children (or subjects, slaves)
to Lebanon and the coast of the sea of the Canaanites, and Anti-lebanon to the great river
Euphrates. Where you enter, I will concede in front of you the land, which will be
distributed by lottery, the land which I shouldered (or carried) to the forefathers
Abraham, Isaac, and Jacob, and their descendants."

• LXX 767: cae elalêsen cspros môsên legôn icanousthô ymin catoecin en tô ori touto
epistraphêtae cae aparatae ymis cae isporeuesthae is oros amorrhaeôn cae pros pantas tous
perioecous autou tous en tê paediadi is oros cae paedion cae pros liban cae paralian
thalassês gên chananaeôn cae antilibanon eôs tou megalou potamou euphratou isselthate
isselthatae paradedôca enôpion ymôn tên gên iselthontae clironomêsatae tên gên ên
ômosa toes patrasin ymôn tô abraam cae isaac cae iacôb dounae tô spermati autou met'
autous (ιλι ϭλλλοϭν ιοπϸος μοοϧν λϭγοον ιιλνουϭθοο υμιν ιιλτοιιϭιν ϭν τοο οϸϭι τουτο
ϭπιοτϸλϷϧτλι ιιλιλπλϸλτλι υμϭιc ιιλι ϭιοποϸϭυϭϭθλι ϭιc οϸοc λμοϸϸλιοον ιιλι πϸοc πλντλc τουc
πϭϸιοιιμουcλυτου τουc ϭν τϧ πλιϊιλϊι ϭιc οϸοc ιιλι πλιϊιον ιιλι πϸοc λιιλν ιιλι πλϸλλιλν
θλλλοοϧcγϧν χλνλνλιοον ιιλι λντιλιιλνον ϭοοc του μϭγλλου ποτλμου ϭυϷϸλτου ϭιοοϭλθλτλι
πλϸλλϭλοοιιλ ϭνοοπιονυμοον τϧν γϧν ϭιοϭλθοντλι ιιλιϸονομϧνολτλι τϧν γϧν ϧν οομοολ τοιc
πλτϸλοιν υμοον τοολιιϸλλμ ιιλι ιολλι ιιλι ιλιιοοιι ϊουνλι τοο οπϭϸμλτι λυτου μϭτ λυτουc).

Translation: and spoke Lord to Moses, saying, "I am content to dwell in this mountain
which is returned, and it shall be removed from you, and you shall enter into the
mountain of the Amorites, and into their children's mountains (or subject's mountains),
and children (or subjects, slaves) to Lebanon and the coast of the sea of the Canaanites, and
Anti-lebanon to the great river Euphrates. Where you enter, I will concede in front of
you the land, which will be distributed by lottery, the land which I shouldered (or
carried) to the forefathers Abraham, Isaac, and Jacob, and their descendants."

This verse is only found in two known Septuagint manuscripts, however, is consistent
with the Hasidic texts of the 2nd century BC, and may represent an alternate early

Aramaic translation of Numbers.

4 Codex Vaticanus: Obab uiô Ragouêl tô Madianitê tô gambrô Môysê (ΟΒΑΒ ΥΙѠ ΡΑΓΟΥΗΛ ΤѠΜΑΔΙΑΝΕΙΤΗ ΤѠ ΓΑΜΒΡѠ ΜѠΥCΗ). Translation: Obab son of Rhagouel the Midianite the groom (or son in law) of Moses

• Codex Alexandrinus: Ôbab uiô Ragouêl tô Madianiti tô gambrô Môysê (ѠΒΑΒ ΥΙѠ ΡΑΓΟΥΗΛ ΤѠΜΑΔΙΑΝΙΤΙ ΤѠΓΑΜΒΡѠΜѠΥCΗ). Translation: Obab son of Rhagouel the Midianite the groom (or son in law) of Moses

• Codex Ambrosiano A 147: Iôbab uiô Ragouêl tô Madianitê tô pentherô Môysê (ΙѠΒΑΒΥΙѠΡΑΓΟΥΗΛ ΤѠΜΑΔΙΑΝΙΤΗ ΤѠ ΠΕΝΘΕΡѠΜѠΥCΗ). Translation: Iobab son of Rhagouel the Midianite the fatherin law of Moses

• LXX 509: Olibath huiô Rhagouêl tô Madianitê tô gambrô Môysê (ΟλιυΔθ υιοο ΡΔγουλλ τοο ΜΔΔιΔνθτλ τοογΔμυβοο Μοουσλ). Translation: Olibath son of Rhagouel the Midianite the groom (or son in law) of Moses

• LXX 131: Ômab huiô Rhagouêl tô Madianitê tô gambrô Môysê (ωμΔu υιοο ΡΔγουλλ τοο ΜΔΔιΔνθτλ τοογΔμυβοο Μοουσλ). Translation: Omabson of Rhagouel the Midianite the groom (or son in law) of Moses

• LXX 319: Hôbab huiô Rhagouêl tô Maadanitê tô gambrô Môysê (ωuΔu υιοο ΡΔγουλλ τοο ΜΔΔΔΔνιτλ τοογΔμυβοο Μοουσλ). Translation: Hobab son of Rhagouel the Midianite the groom (or son in law) of Moses

• LXX 16: Hôbab huiô Rhagouêl tô Madianê tô gambrô autou (ωuΔu υιοο ΡΔγουλλ τοο ΜΔΔιΔνλ τοο γΔμυβοο Δυτου). Translation: Hobab son of Rhagouel the Madine the groom of him

• LXX 30: Hôbab huiô Rhagouêl tô Maniaditê tô gambrô Môysê (ωuΔu υιοο ΡΔγουλλ τοο ΜΔνιΔΔιτλ τοογΔμυβοο Μοουσλ). Translation: Hobab son of Rhagouel the Maniadite the groom (or son in law) of Moses

• LXX 58: Hôbab huiô Rhagouêl tô Madianiti tô gambrô Môysê (ωuΔu υιοο ΡΔγουλλ τοο ΜΔΔιΔνιτόι τοογΔμυβοο Μοουσλ). Translation: Hobab son of Rhagouel the Midianite the groom (or son in law) of Moses

• LXX 118: Hôbab huiô Rhagouêl tô Madiniatê tô gambrô Môysê (ωuΔu υιοο ΡΔγουλλ τοο ΜΔΔινιΔτλ τοογΔμυβοο Μοουσλ). Translation: Hobab son of Rhagouel the Midianite the groom (or son in law) of Moses

- LXX 19: Hôbab huiô Rhagouêl tô Madiniati tô gambrô Môysê (ⲱⲩⲁⲙ ⲩⲓⲟⲟ Ｐⲁⲅⲟⲩⲏλ ⲧⲟⲟ ｍⲁⲇⲓⲛⲓⲁⲧⲓ ⲧⲟⲟⲅⲇⲙⲩＰⲟⲟ Ｍⲟⲟⲩⲟⲏ). Translation: Hobab son of Rhagouel the Midianite the groom (or son in law) of Moses

- LXX 246: Iôabad huiô Rhagouêl tô Madianitê Môysê (ｌⲟⲟⲇⲩⲁⲁ ⲩⲓⲟⲟ Ｐⲁⲅⲟⲩλ ⲧⲟⲟ ｍⲁⲇⲓⲁⲛⲫⲧⲏ Ｍⲟⲟⲩⲟⲏ). Translation: Ioabadson of Rhagouel the Midianite the groom (or son in law) of Moses

- LXX 130: Abab huiô Rhagouêl tô Madianitê tô gambrô Môysê (ⲁⲩⲁⲙ ⲩⲓⲟⲟ Ｐⲁⲅⲟⲩλ ⲧⲟⲟ ｍⲁⲇⲓⲁⲛⲫⲧⲏ ⲧⲟⲟ ⲅⲇⲙⲩＰⲟⲟ Ｍⲟⲟⲩⲟⲏ). Translation: Abab son of Rhagouel the Midianite the groom (or son in law) of Moses

- LXX 458: Iôabab uiôn Rhagouêl tô Madianêti tô gambrô Môysê (ｌⲟⲟⲇⲩⲁⲙ ⲩⲓⲟⲟｎ Ｐⲁⲅⲟⲩλ ⲧⲟⲟ ｍⲁⲇⲓⲁⲛⲏⲧⲓ ⲧⲟⲟ ⲅⲇⲙⲩＰⲟⲟ Ｍⲟⲟⲩⲟⲏ). Translation: Ioabab son of Rhagouel the Midianite the groom (or son in law) of Moses

- LXX 72: Hôbab huiô Rhagouêl tô Madianê tô gambrô Môsê (ⲱⲩⲁⲙ ⲩⲓⲟⲟ Ｐⲁⲅⲟⲩλ ⲧⲟⲟ ｍⲁⲇⲓⲁｎⲏ ⲧⲟⲟ ⲅⲇⲙⲩＰⲟⲟ Ｍⲟⲟⲟⲏ). Translation: Hobab son of Rhagouel the Midianite the groom (or son in law) of Moses

- LXX 528: Ôbath huiô Rhagouêl tô Madianitê tô gambrô Môysê (ⲱⲩⲁθ ⲩⲓⲟⲟ Ｐⲁⲅⲟⲩλ ⲧⲟⲟ ｍⲁⲇⲓⲁⲛⲫⲧⲏ ⲧⲟⲟ ⲅⲇⲙⲩＰⲟⲟ Ｍⲟⲟⲩⲟⲏ). Translation: Obath son of Rhagouel the Midianite the groom (or son in law) of Moses

- LXX 44: Iôab huiô Rhagouêl tô Madianitê tô gambrô Môysê (ｌⲟⲟⲇⲩ ⲩⲓⲟⲟ Ｐⲁⲅⲟⲩλ ⲧⲟⲟ ｍⲁⲇⲓⲁⲛⲫⲧⲏ ⲧⲟⲟ ⲅⲇⲙⲩＰⲟⲟ Ｍⲟⲟⲩⲟⲏ). Translation: Ioabson of Rhagouel the Midianite the groom (or son in law) of Moses

- Leningrad Codex: Chovav ben-Re'u'el hamMidyani choten Mosheh (חֹבָב בֶּן־רְעוּאֵל הַמִּדְיָנִי חֹתֵן מֹשֶׁה). Translation: Chovav son of Reuel the Midianite groom (or son-in-law) of Moses

- Peshitta: Ḥûbb: br Rôûåyl Mdynyå ḥmûhy dMůšå (ܣܟܒ: ܟܝ ܐܟܪܐ ܠܟܪܐ ܡܕܝܢܝܐ, ܗܡܘܗܝ ܕܡܘܫܐ). Translation: Hubb son of Rouayl Midianite father-in-law of Moses

- Targum Onkelos: Chovav bar Re'u'el Midyana'ah chamuhi deMosheh (חֹבָב בַּר רְעוּאֵל מִדְיָנָאָה חֲמוּהִי דְמֹשֶׁה). Translation: Chovav son of Reuel Midianite father-in-law of Moses

- Targum Jerusalem: Chovav bar Re'u'el Midyana'ah chamoy deMosheh (חוֹבָב בַּר רְעוּאֵל מִדְיָנָאָה חֲמוֹי דְמֹשֶׁה). Translation: Chovav son of Reuel Midianite father-in-law of Moses

Jobab was also mentioned in Judges chapter 1, however, the texts don't always agree on who he was. In Judges, the Codex Alexandrinus refers to him as Jobab the blacksmith the father-in-law of Moses, while the Codex Vaticanus refers to Jethro the blacksmith son-in-law of Moses, and the Masoretic Text omit the name, simply referring to the blacksmith son-in-law of Moses. It is unclear why there are so many variants of the name and relationship in Judges, however, Numbers is generally consistent between the Septuagint and Masoretic Text in regards to the relationship, with most text reading 'son-in-law' (γαμβρω / חֹתֵן) of Moses, and only a few Septuagint manuscripts referring to him as the 'father-in-law' (πενθερω), or omitting the nature of the relationship. Conversely, both the Peshitta and Targum Onkelos agree that he was the father-in-law of Moses.

Numbers: Chapter 11

The people murmured sinfully before the Lord, and the Lord heard them and was very angry, and fire erupted among them from the Lord and devoured a part of the camp. The people cried to Moses, and Moses prayed to the Lord, and the fire was quenched. The name of that place was called Burning,[1] as a fire was started among them by the Lord.

The mixed multitude among them lusted a lust, and they and the children of Israel sat down and wept and said, "Who will give us flesh to eat? We remember the fish, which we ate in Egypt freely, and the cucumbers, and the watermelons, and the leeks, and the garlic, and the onions. But now our mind is dried up. Our eyes see nothing but the manna. The manna is like coriander seed, and it looks like hoarfrost."

The people went through the field, and gathered, and ground it in the mill, or pounded it in a mortar, and baked it in a pan, and made cakes of it. The sweetness of it was like the taste of wafer made with oil. When the dew came on the camp by night, the manna came down on it. Moses heard them weeping in their families, everyone in his door, and the Lord was very angry. It was evil in the sight of Moses.

Moses said to the Lord, "Why have you afflicted your servant, and why have I not found grace in your sight, that you should lay the weight of these people on me? Have I conceived all these people, or have I born them? That you say to me, 'Take them into your bosom, as a nurse would take her suckling, into the land which you swore to their fathers?' From where have I flesh to give to all these people? For they cry to me, saying, 'Give us flesh, that we may eat. I will not be able to carry these people alone, for this thing is too heavy for me. If you do this to me, kill me completely if I have found favor with you, that I may not see my affliction."

The Lord replied to Moses, "Gather me 70 men from the elders of Israel, whom you yourself know that they are the elders of the people, and their scribes, and you will bring them to the tabernacle of witness, and they will stand there with you. I will go down and speak there with you, and I will take of the spirit that is in you and will put it on them, and they will carry together with you the impetus of the people, and you will not carry them alone. To the people you will say, Purify yourselves for the morning, and you will eat flesh, for you wept before the Lord, saying, 'Who will give us flesh to eat? As it was better for us in Egypt,' and the Lord will allow you to eat flesh, and you will eat flesh. You will not eat one day, nor two, nor five days, nor 10 days, nor twenty days; you will eat for a full month until the flesh comes out of your nostrils, and it will be cholera to you, because you disobeyed the Lord, who is among you, and wept before him, saying, 'Why did we come out of Egypt?'"

Moses asked, "The people among whom I am, are an army of 600,000, and you said, 'I will give them flesh to eat, and they will eat a whole month. Will sheep and oxen be butchered for them, and will it be enough for them? Or will all the fish of the sea be gathered together for them, and will it be enough for them?"

The Lord answered Moses, "Will the hand of the Lord not be enough? Now you will know whether my word will take place or not."

Moses went out and spoke the words of the Lord to the people. He gathered 70 men of the elders of the people, and he set them around the tabernacle. The Lord came down in a cloud, and spoke to him, and took of the spirit that was on him, and put it on the 70 men that were elders, and when the spirit rested on them, they prophesied and then ceased. There were two men left in the camp, one named Elidad, and the other named Medad, and the spirit rested on them, and these were of the number of them that were enrolled, but they did not come to the tabernacle, and they prophesied in the camp.

A young man ran and told Moses, and spoke, saying, Elidad and Medad prophesy in the camp. Joshua the son of Nun, who attended on Moses, the chosen one, said, "My lord Moses, forbid them."

Moses asked him, "Are you jealous on my account? If only all the Lord's people were prophets, whenever the Lord will put his spirit on them."

Moses departed the camp along with the elders of Israel. A wind came out from the Lord, and brought quails in from the sea, and it brought them down on the camp a day's journey on this side, and a day's journey on that side, around the camp, as it were two cubits deep off the ground. The people rose up all day, and all night, and all the next day, and gathered quails. He who gathered little gathered 10 measures, and they refreshed themselves around the camp. The flesh was already between their teeth before it died, and the Lord became angry with the people, and the Lord struck the people with a very great plague. The name of that place was called the Graves of Desire,[2] for there they buried the people that lusted. The people departed from the Graves of Desire to Hazeroth, and the people arrived in Hazeroth.

Numbers: Chapter 11 Notes

1 Codex Vaticanus: empyrismos (ЄMΠΥΡICMOC). Translation: concentration

- LXX 799: emprismos (Ἐμπβισμος)

- LXX 376: Emprysmos (Ἐμπβυσμος)

- Leningrad Codex: tav'erah (תַּבְעֵרָה). Translation: conflagration, burning, fire

- Peshitta: yqdnå (ܝܩܕܢܐ). Translation: burnt offerings

- Targum Onkelos: delekta (דְּלֵקְתָּא). Translation: burnings (or inflammations)

- Targum Jerusalem: deleikta (דְּלֵיקְתָּא). Translation: burnings (or inflammations)

2 Codex Vaticanus: Mnêmata tês epithymias (MNHMATA THCЄΠΙΘΥΜΙΑC). Translation: graves of desire

- LXX 509: mnêma tês epithymias (μνημα της ὄπιθυμφὰc). Translation: memorials of desire

- LXX 73: bounon tês epithymiôn (ιουνον της ὄπιθυμιοον). Translation: hills (or altars) of desires (or wishes). This version of the verse was also quoted in the Clementine literature, dated to between the 1st and 3rd centuries AD.

- LXX 313: mnêmatos tês epithymias (μνημματοc της ὄπιθυμφὰc). Translation: memorials of desire.

- Leningrad Codex: kivrot hatta'avah (קִבְרוֹת הַתַּאֲוָה). Translation: Graves of Lust

- DSS 4QNum[b]: qb- (קב). Only the first two letters survive, however, they do match the letters in the Leningrad Codex.

- Peshitta: qbrå drgtå (ܩܒܪܐ ܕܪܓܬܐ). Translation: tombs (or sepulchers) of permanence

- Targum Onkelos: kivrei dimsha'alei (קִבְרֵי דִמְשַׁאֲלֵי). Translation: tombs (or sepulchers) of the lenders (or borrowers, demanders)

- Targum Jerusalem: kivrei dimshaylei bishra (קִבְרֵי דִמְשַׁיְילֵי בִּישְׂרָא). Translation: tombs (or sepulchers) of the lenders (or borrowers, demanders) of human-flesh (or human-skin)

Numbers: Chapter 12

Mariam and Aaron spoke against Moses, because of the Ethiopian woman that Moses took, as he had taken an Ethiopian woman. They said, "Has the Lord only spoken to Moses? Has he not also spoken to us?"

And the Lord heard it. The man Moses was very meek beyond all the men that were on the land. The Lord immediately called Moses and Aaron and Mariam, "Come up the three of you to the tabernacle of witness."

The three came up to the tabernacle of witness, and the Lord descended in a column of cloud and stood at the door of the tabernacle of witness. Aaron and Mariam were called, and both came forward. He said to them, "Hear my words. If there should be among you a prophet to the Lord, I will be made known to him in a vision, and in sleep will I speak to him. My servant Moses is not so. He is faithful in all my house. I will speak to him face to face openly, and not in dark speeches. He has seen the glory of the Lord. Why were you not afraid to speak against my servant Moses?"

The great anger of the Lord was on them, and he departed, and the cloud departed from the tabernacle. Mariam became leprous as snow, and Aaron looked at Mariam and saw she was leprous. Aaron said to Moses, "I beg you, my lord, do not lay sin on us, for we were ignorant in which we sinned. Let her not be as it were like death, as an abortion coming out of his mother's womb when the disease devours half of the flesh."

Moses cried to the Lord, "El,[1] I beg you, heal her."

The Lord said to Moses, "If her father had only spit in her face, will she not be ashamed seven days? Let her be set apart seven days outside the camp, and afterward, she may come in."

Mariam was separated outside the camp for seven days, and the people did not move forward until Mariam was cleansed.

Numbers: Chapter 12 Notes

1 Codex Vaticanus: ths (ΘC). Translation: god

- LXX 319: thee (θεε). Translation: god

- LXX 121: theos mou (θεὸς μου). Translation: my god

- Leningrad Codex: el (אֵל). Translation: El (or god)

- Peshitta: ålhå (ܐܠܗܐ). Translation: god

- Targum Onkelos: elaha (אֱלָהָא). Translation: god

- Fragment Targums: elaha (אֱלָהָא). Translation: god

- Targum Jerusalem: elaha (אֱלָהָא). Translation: god

This verse does not survive among the Dead Sea Scrolls. This verse shows the Greeks did translate the term El as 'God.' As El is a proper name, it is restored from the Masoretic Text in this translation.

Numbers: Chapter 13

Afterward, the people set out from Hazeroth, and camped in the Wilderness of Paran.[1] The Lord said to Moses, "Send for your men and let them spy the land of the Canaanites, which I give to the sons of Israel as a possession, one man for a tribe, you will send them away according to their families, every one of them a prince."

Moses sent them out of the Wilderness of Paran by the word of the Lord, all these were the princes of the sons of Israel. These are their names:

From the tribe of Reuben, Samuel the son of Zakkur.

From the tribe of Simeon, Shaphat the son of Hori.

From the tribe of Judah, Caleb the son of Jephunneh.

From the tribe of Issachar, Igal the son of Joseph.

From the tribe of Ephraim, Hoshea the son of Nun.

From the tribe of Benjamin, Palti the son of Raphu.

From the tribe of Zebulun, Geuel the son of Sodi.

From the tribe of Joseph of the sons of Manasseh, Gaddi the son of Susi.

From the tribe of Dan, Ammiel the son of Gemalli.

From the tribe of Asher, Sethur the son of Michael.

From the tribe of Naphtali, Nahbi the son of Sabi.

From the tribe of Gad, Geuel the son of Maki.

These are the names of the men that Moses sent to spy out the land. Moses called Hoshea the son of Nun, Joshua. Moses sent them to spy out the land of Canaan, and said to them, "Go up by this wilderness, and you will go up to the mountain, and you will see the land, what it is, and the people that live in it, whether it is strong or weak, or whether they are few or many. What the land is on which they live, whether it is good or bad, and what the cities are in which these live, whether they live in fortified cities or unfortified. What the land is, whether rich or neglected, whether there are trees in it or not, and you will persevere and take of the fruits of the land."

It was springtime, before the time of the grape. They went up and surveyed the land from the Wilderness of Sin[2] to Rehob, as men go into Ephaath.[3] They went up by the wilderness and departed as far as Hebron, and there were Ahiman, Sheshai, Talmai, the children of Anak. (Hebron was built seven years before Tanis[4] in Egypt.) They came to the valley of the cluster and surveyed it, and they cut down there a bough and one cluster of grapes on it and carried it on staffs, and they took of the pomegranates and the figs. They called that place, The valley of the cluster, because of the cluster which the children of Israel cut down from there.

They returned from there, having surveyed the land, after forty days. They proceeded and came to Moses and Aaron and all the community of the children of Israel, to the Wilderness of Paran Kadesh. They brought word to them and to all the community, and they showed the fruit of the land. They reported to him, "We came into the land into which you sent us, a land flowing with milk and honey, and this is the fruit of it. Only the nation that dwells on it is bold, and they have very great and fortified towns, and we saw there Anakites.[5] Amalekites live in the southern region of the land, and the Cypriots,[6] Mitannians,[7] Jebusites, and the Amorites live in the hill country. The Canaanites live by the sea, and by the Jordan River."

Caleb stopped the people from speaking to Moses, and said to him, "No, but we will go up by all means, and will inherit it, for we will surely prevail against them."

But the men that went up together with him said, "We do not go up, for we will not by any means be able to go up against the nation, for it is much stronger than we."

They brought a horror of that land which they surveyed on the children of Israel, saying, "The land which we passed by to survey it, is a land that eats up its inhabitants, and all the people whom we saw in it are men of extraordinary stature. There we saw the Gigantes (sons of Anak, from the Nepilim),[8] and we were like locusts before them. This is how we compared to them."

Numbers: Chapter 13 Notes

1 Codex Vaticanus: Pharan (ΦΑΡΑΝ)

- LXX 630: Phara (ΦΑΡΑ)

- Leningrad Codex: Paran (פָּארָן)

- Peshitta: Prn (ܦܪܢ)

- Targum Onkelos: Paran (פָּארָן)

- Fragment Targums: Paran (פָּארָן)

- Targum Jerusalem: Paran (פָּארָן)

- Bohairic manuscripts: Pharran (Ⲫⲁⲣⲣⲁⲛ)

The Wilderness of Paran was mentioned in Genesis, Numbers, Deuteronomy, and 3rd Kingdoms (Masoretic Kings), and Masoretic Habakkuk, however, the location of Paran is debated. The book of Numbers states that Paran was Kadesh, and the book of Deuteronomy locates it in the Arabah Desert of southern modern Jordan and Israel. In the second century AD, the Christian geographer Claudius Ptolemy located it in the southern Sinai Peninsula, at the region now called the Wadi Feiran, while Islamic scholars have interpreted it as the Hijaz region of western Saudi Arabia, around Mecca.

2 Codex Vaticanus: Sin (ⲥⲉⲓⲛ)

- Codex Venetus: Sina (ⲥⲓⲛⲁ)

- LXX 30: Sêna (ⲥⲏⲛⲁ)

- LXX 56: Sên (ⲥⲏⲛ)

- LXX 528: Sin (ⲥⲓⲛ)

- LXX 59: Sinr (ⲥⲓⲛⲣ)

- Leningrad Codex: Tzin (צִן)

- DSS 4QNum[b]: Tzyn (צין)

- Peshitta: Tzyn (ܨܝܢ)

- Targum Onkelos: Tzin (צִין)

- Targum Jerusalem: Tzin (צִין)

- Sahidic manuscripts: Sein (ⲥⲓⲉⲛ)

See the note in chapter 1 for more information on the Wilderness of Sin.

3 Codex Vaticanus: Ephaath (Ⲉⲫⲁⲁⲑ)

- Codex Colberto-Sarravianus: Eglaaam (Ⲉⲅⲗⲁⲁⲁⲙ)

- Codex Alexandrinus: Aemath (Ⲁⲓⲙⲁⲑ)

- LXX 28: Aitham (Ⲁⲓⲑⲁⲙ)

- LXX 318: Hemath (Ⲉⲙⲁⲱⲑ)

- LXX 319: Samath (Ⲥⲁⲙⲁⲑ)

- LXX 129: Emae (Ⲉⲙⲁⲋ)

- LXX 75: Emmaôth (Ⲉⲙⲙⲁⲱⲑ)

- LXX 246: Niphath (Ⲛⲓⲫⲁⲑ)

- LXX 799: Enphath (Ⲉⲛⲫⲁⲑ)

- LXX 56: Nephath (Ⲛⲋⲫⲁⲑ)

- Leningrad Codex: chamat (חֲמָת). Translation: fortress (or Hama)

- Peshitta: ḥmt (ܚܡܬ). Translation: fortress (or Hama)

- Targum Onkelos: chamat (חֲמָת). Translation: fortress (or Hama)

- Targum Jerusalem: Antucheya (אַנְטוּכְיָא). Translation: Antioch

- Bohairic manuscripts: Paath (Ⲡⲁⲁⲑ)

- Sahidic manuscripts: Emaath (Ⲉⲙⲁⲁⲑ)

The Greek and Hebrew translations differ here, with most Greek translations referring to a place generally called Ephaath, although there are many variants of the name in Greek. The Hebrew translation refers to either to a fortress, or the city of Hama in northern Syria. The Syrian city of Hama was known to the ancient Arameans and Canaanites as Ḥmt (חמת / חֵלָן / 𐤇𐤌𐤕), derived from the word 'fortress,' and has existed since before 5000 BC. Under the Seleucid Dynasty, the city was renamed Epiphania (Επιφανεια), which the Translators at the Library of Alexandria would have known how to spell, as it was the Greek word meaning 'manifestation.' Some Greek and Coptic manuscripts due use Greek transliterations of ḥmt (חמת). including the 5th century Codex Alexandrinus, however, the Alexandrinus is known to have included names transliterated from the Hebrew translations then in circulation.

The Greek term Ephaath (Εφααθ) is less clear, however, similar to the name Ephratha / Efratah (Εφραθα / אֶפְרָתָה) in Cosmic Genesis / Bereshít, which was identified as the old name of Bethlehem. The term in Cosmic Genesis / Bereshít appears to be corrupted Canaanite transliteration of the Egyptian name r-pr-t (𓏏 𓉐 𓆑 𓏏), which translates as 'temple of bread,' one meaning of the Canaanite name bêt leḥem (𐤁𐤉𐤕 𐤋𐤇𐤌). If Ephaath (Εφααθ) is a transliteration of the same name from an old Aramaic translationof Numbers, it would then be a reference to Bethlehem, not Hama. As the Greek and Hebrew texts appear to be referring to different places, the Greek name is used in this translation.

The name Antioch, found in the Targum Jonathan, referred to the city of Antakya in southernmost modern Turkey, which was founded by Seleucus I Nicator, one of Alexander the Great's generals in approximately 300 BC. It is unclear why anyone would have thought that Antioch was the city in the verse, however, it was built it was near mount Zephon. Prior to the Greek city, a Canaanite town was located on the site, named Meroe, where a major shrine to the virgin goddess Anat was located. This suggests the substitution was theological, not political, as Anat was the wife of Yhû in the early-Persian era.

4 Codex Vaticanus: Tanin (ⲦⲀⲚⲒⲚ). Translation: Tanis

- LXX 318: Taêan (Ταμαν)

- LXX 319: Tanin (Τανϭιν)

- LXX 509: Tani (Τανι)

- LXX 64: Tanis (Τανιc)

- LXX 55: Taêin (Ταλιν)

- LXX 128: Taneôs (Τανϭοοc)

- LXX 313: Tanên (Τανλν)

- LXX 381: Tês (Τλc)

- LXX 458: Tanyn (Τανυν)

- Leningrad Codex: Tzo'an (צֹעַן). Translation: Tanis

- Peshitta: Sôn (ܨܢ). Translation: Tanis

- Targum Onkelos: Tanas (טָנַס)

- Fragment Targums: Taneis (טָאנֵיס)

- Bohairic manuscripts: Khani (Ⲭⲁⲛⲓ)

- Sahidic manuscripts: Khaane (Ⲭⲁⲁⲛⲉ)

Tanis and Tzo'an were the Greek and Hebrew names for an ancient city in northeast Egypt, which is believed to have originally been named something like Khani (Χανι). This scribal note about Tanis is clearly a later addition to the text. Hebron is much older than Tanis, and Tanis was not significant in any way until the 19th dynasty (circa 1290 to 1190 BC) when it became the capital of the 14th nome (province). During the 21st and 22nd Dynasties, circa 1070 to 720 BC Tanis became the capital of Egypt, which is likely when this line was added. The 22nd dynasty Pharaoh Shoshenq I invaded Judea during the reign of King Rehoboam, circa 935 BC, while the later 22nd dynasty Pharaoh Osorkon II was an ally of Samaria during their war against Assyria circa 725 BC. The 22nd dynasty disintegrated into multiple competing dynasties after the Assyrians defeated the allied Samaritan-Egyptian forces, and Tanis was no longer a capital city, meaning this line could have been added at any point in ancient Israelite-Samaritan history up until circa 725 BC. Conversely, Hebron existed by 1800 BC, and according to the Book of Joshua, Joshua conquered Hebron circa 1500 BC in the traditional Christian chronology, such as the chronologies of Jerome and Ussher.

5 Codex Vaticanus: Enach (ЄΝΑΧ)

• Codex Colberto-Sarravianus: Enek (ЄΝЄΚ)

• Codex Alexandrinus: Aenac (ΑΙΝΑΚ)

• LXX 767: Inac (ΕιΝΑᴫ)

• LXX 16: Enaac (ΕΝΑΑᴫ)

• Leningrad Codex: Anak (עֲנָק). Translation: giant, huge, large, big, neck

• Peshitta: gnbrå (ܓܢܒܪܐ). Translation: heroes (or strong men, giants). Translation: heroes (or strong men, giants)

• Targum Onkelos: gibbarayya (גִּבָּרַיָּא). Translation: heroes (or strong men, giants). Translation: heroes (or strong men, giants)

• Targum Jerusalem: gibbara (גִּבָּרָא). Translation: heroes (or strong men, giants). Translation: heroes (or strong men, giants)

• Sahidic manuscripts: Enakh (Єνακx)

The Anakites (Anakim) were a tribe of people also referred to in the books of Deuteronomy, Joshua, and Judges. According to the book of Judges, they lived in Hebron. Egyptian execration texts from the Middle Kingdom Era, record a group of Canaanites in the region called the 'Anaq' who are generally considered to be the same people. They were reportedly the enemies of the Egyptians at the time.

6 Codex Vaticanus: Chettaeos (ϰεττλιος)

- LXX 120: Chegaeos (ϰϭγλιος)

- LXX 458: Achettaeos (λχϭττλιος)

- LXX 618: Chetaeos (ϰϭτλιος)

- Leningrad Codex: Chitti (חִתִּי). Translation: Cypriots

- Peshitta: Ḥytyå (ܚܬܝܐ). Translation: living (or animals, beasts, pure, vitals)

- Targum Onkelos: Chitta'ah (חִתָּאָה)

- Targum Jerusalem: Chitta'ei (חִתָּאֵי)

This term has created a great deal of confusion since the misidentification of the ruins of the Neshites as being 'Hittite' in the 1800s. The modern archaeological name 'Hittite,' is not derived from an ancient name for the culture applied by themselves, or anyone else, but rather adopted from the biblical reference to a then-unknown civilization somewhere in the region. There was an ancient culture in the region called the Hattians, however, they were conquered by the Nesites before 1700 BC, and subsequently disappeared from the historic records. The name was applied to a culture today referred to as 'Hittites,' before the 'Hittite' language had been translated, and is incorrect. Since 1906, excavations at Boğazköy, the ancient 'Hittite' capital Hattusa have uncovered more than 10,000 'Hittite' texts, including the royal achieve. The actual name of the 'Hittite' language and people was Nešili (𒉈𒅖𒇷), which is now rendered in some academic literate as Nesite or Neshite. As early as the mid-1800s some scholars disputed the identification of the Nesites as the Biblical Hittites, including the Orientalist Max Müller, who was one of many claiming the Biblical Hittites were ancient Greeks or some other Mediterranean people. Later in the Septuagint's translation of the Maccabees, the similar term Chettiim (Χεττιιμ) as a reference to all Greek-speaking lands.

In the 1ˢᵗ century AD, the Jewish historian Josephus reported that Cethima was the name of Cyrus in Aramaic, and the Chettim were the descendants of Noah's grandson Chethimus, who had settled on Cyprus. Josephus reported that the name was preserved in the Greek name of the town Cition (Κίτιον). Most historians view it as more likely that the Aramaic name was derived from the city-state of Cition, which was known as Kåtjåy (𓃰𓈖𓏏𓇌) in Egyptian records from the New Kingdom Era in the late Bronze Age, and Kt (𐤊𐤕) or Kty (𐤊𐤕𐤉) in Phoenician records from the early Iron Age. While this may be the origin of the term, by the era of the Neo-Assyrian era, the term must have also referred to other Greek islands, as both the prophets Isaiah and Ezekiel used the term 'Islands of Kittim.' As the term referred to the entire island of Cyprus in Aramaic, the translation of 'Cypriots' is used.

7 Codex Vaticanus: Eyaeos (ΕΥΑΙΟC)

- LXX 30: Ebaeos (Ευλιος)

- Bohairic manuscripts: Euaios (Ϭγλιος)

- Vetus Latina: Eucheus

The word is missing from this list of nations in the Masoretic Text, Peshitta, and Targums. In other verses, it is Ha'avvim (הָעַוִּים) or Chivvi (חִוִּי) in the Leningrad Codex. The term is believed to have been derived from a name of the Hurrians, however, is derived separately from the other term Chori (חֹרִי). Chori is accepted as referring to the Hurrians, which the Egyptians called Ḥårů (𓐍𓂋𓅱𓈖), and the Babylonians called Ḫuurri (𒄯𒊑). The Hurrians were one of the oldest cultures in the Middle East, however, became largely a slave culture within the Akkadian and Old Babylonian empires. Under the Mitanni empire, they rose to a position of wealth, and formed the noble caste. The Greek transliteration of this term was variations of Chorrhaeous (Χορραιους), which, like the Hebrew term, was used interchangeably in the texts with Eyaeon (Ευαιον) / Chivvi (חִוִּי), although that term generally applied to the rules and priests.

The ultimate origin of the terms Eyaeon (Ευαιον) / Eyaeos (Ευαιος) and Ha'avvim (הָעַוִּים) / Chivvi (חִוִּי), both appear to be the cuneiform word Éan (𒂍𒀭), meaning temple or sacred. In the Amarna Letters, which date to the 1330s BC, the term Éan (𒂍𒀭) was the name of a people, who appear to be the Mitanni, or the Mitanni-Aryan priesthood within the Mitanni. A similar correlation between the terms is found in the Septuagint's 1ˢᵗ Paralipomenon and Masoretic Divrei-hay Yamim, where the Greek translation uses Beithani (Βαιθανι), however, the Hebrew uses the term Mitni (מִתְנִי). This term also refers to a group of people, meaning the underlying Edomite text the Greeks translated would have been 'people of the House of Ån' (𐤏𐤍𐤕𐤁), a direct Canaanite translation of É An (𒂍𒀭).

While Mitni was the transliteration used in the Edomite text that formed the basis of the Hebrew translation of Divrei-hayYamim, it was replaced with Chivvi (חִוִּי) in the Judahite texts, which served as the basis of most of the Masoretic texts. This likely originated in a Judahite copy of the text, after the Aramaic translation had been made, where an N (𐤍) was replaced with a Ů (𐤅). The Aramaic translation would have already been made in the time of King Manasseh, were the term was transliterated as Hyån (𐡄𐡉𐡀𐡍), itself a transliteration of the early Canaanite Hyån (𐤄𐤉𐤀𐤍).

The term Ebaeôn (Εβαιων) / Ebaeos (Εβαιος), which is found as a substitute for Eyaeon (Ευαιον) / Eyaeos (Ευαιος) in some copies of the Septuagint for term, must have

originated in an intentional alteration to the text, as there are no similar letters for b (,ﭖ
ﭖ ,ﭖ) and y (ﭖ ,ﭖ ,ﭖ) in the Semitic alphabets the text was previously in. This probable
origin was an Ebionite translation in the first century AD. The Ebionites were an early
Judeo-Christian sect based in Judea before the First Jewish-Roman war. Many fled east
to Mesopotamia with the Mandeans and other smaller Judahite religious groups, while
others fled south into Arabia. The Arabian Ebionites are generally viewed as shaping the
Islamic view of the prophet Jesus (عِيسَى).

8 Codex Vaticanus: gigantas (ΓΙΓΑΝΤΑΣ). Translation: Gigantes

• Codex Colberto-Sarravianus: gigantas uious enac ec tôn gigantôn (ΓΙΓΑΝΤΑΣΥΙΟΥΣ
ΕΝΑΚΕΚΤΩΝΓΙΓΑΝΤΩΝ). Translation: Gigantes sons of Enak of the Gigantes

• LXX 128: gigantas uious gigantôn (γϕγαντας υιους γιγαντων). Translation: Gigantes
son of Gigantes

• LXX 18: gigantas uious Aenac ec tôn gigantôn (γϕγαντας υιους Αιναλι ϭι τωον
γιγαντων). Translation: Gigantes son of Aenac of the Gigantes

• Leningrad Codex: nefilim benei anak min-hannefilim (נְפִילִים בְּנֵי עֲנָק מִן־הַנְּפִלִים).
Translation: Nepilim sons of Anak from the Nepilim

• Peshitta: gnbrå: bny gnbrå: dmn gnbrå (ܓܢܒܪܐ: ܒܢܝ ܓܢܒܪܐ: ܕܡܢ ܓܢܒܪܐ).
Translation: heroes (or strong men, giants) sons of heroes (or strong men, giants) blood of
heroes (or strong men, giants)

• Targum Onkelos: gibbarayya benei Anak min gibbarayya (גִּבָּרַיָּא בְּנֵי עֲנָק מִן גִּבָּרַיָּא).
Translation: heroes (or strong men, giants) sons of Anaq of heroes (or strong men, giants)

• Fragment Targums: gavraya venei anak mignisat guveraya (גַבְרַיָא בְּנֵי עֲנָק מִגְנִיסַת
גּוּבְרַיָא). Translation: heroes (or strong men, giants) sons of Anaq of the family (or
decedents) of Guberaya (or Orion)

• Vetus Latina: gigantum. Translation: giants

The Aramaic translators appear to have simplified the text, as the Greeks would have
transliterated the names. The term Gigantes was used as a translation in the Septuagint
for the both of the words that were transliterated as Anak and Nephilim in the Masoretic
Text, suggesting the Aramaic translation generally used the same term for both. While
most Christian translations of both the Septuagint and the Masoretic Text translate this
word as 'giant,' neither the Greek nor Hebrew terms mean 'giant.'

The Anak (עֲנָק) mentioned in the Masoretic Text, were also recorded in the Middle
Kingdom era Execration texts, as the Anaq, a people that lived in the region around

Mount Hermon. The Hebrew term nefilim (נְפִילִים) is accepted as meaning 'fallen,' and, the term is likely related to the Aramaic name for the Orion constellation Npylyâ (ℵ^ᒪ^ᒋ). The term nefilim (נְפִילִים) likely originated as a description of the Orionid meteor shower that happens each year, between October 2 and November 7, as the Earth passes through the debris left by Halley's Comet. Peaks of 70 meteors a minute have been recorded, and these meteors fall from the region of the sky where Orion's upstretched arm is located. The region of the sky where the constellations Orion and Lepus are located was known as the asterism Sah (𝄜) in the religion of the Egyptian Old Kingdom, which represented Sah, the father of the gods. The Sumerian version of Sah was An (✳), who was also the father of the gods, and represented by the stars of Orion. The name Greek name Orion (Ὠρίων) is derived from the Akkadian Cuneiform name Uru-An (⟨Σ✳⊕), meaning 'Light of An,' as the early Greeks learned of the asterism from the Canaanites that had settled in Cyprus.

As the Greeks neither translated nor transliterated the term Nephilim, it is unlikely it was in the Aramaic text they translated, suggesting whatever term they found in the text was either conceptually or phonetically similar to the Greek Gigas (Γίγας). A more detailed version of this story appears in the Books of Enoch, where the term was translated into Ge'ez as ôyryn (ዐይርን) meaning 'watchers' or 'guardians'. A similar term, egirô (εγείρω) meaning 'awaken,' appears to have been used in the Greek translation of Secrets of Enoch, which was later transliterated into Old Slavonic as Grigori (Ҡьҁѿҡѳьѿ). This indicates the original term was likely something that meant 'watcher' and sounded like Gigas, and given the connections to Mount Hermon, the Orion constellation, and thereby the god An, and his children the [an]Anuna (✳I⊬⊕), the original term in the Cuneiform text was almost certainly Igigi (𒂊𒀭𒄀𒂊𒀭).

The Igigi were described as being a group of lesser gods that rebelled against the rule of the [an]Anuna, which translates as 'sons of the [deity]An/sky,' and their name was the homophone of the Akkadian word igigi (𒅅𒄀) meaning to 'observe and measure.' As the original Edomite text probably included the terms found in the Masoretic Text, the longer text is imported and placed in parentheses.

Numbers: Chapter 14

All the community lifted their voice and cried, and the people wept all that night. All the children of Israel murmured against Moses and Aaron, and all the community said to them, "We should have died in the land of Egypt! Or in this wilderness, we should have died! Why does the Lord bring us into this land to die in war? Our wives and our children will be victims. Now then it is better to return to Egypt."

They said one to another, "Let us choose a ruler, and return to Egypt."

Moses and Aaron fell on their face before all the community of the children of Israel. But Joshua the son of Nun, and Caleb the son of Jephunneh, of those who had spied out the land, tore their garments, and spoke to all the community of the children of Israel, saying, "The land which we surveyed is actually extremely good. If the Lord chooses us, he will bring us into this land, and give it to us. A land that flows with milk and honey! Only don't abandon the Lord, and don't fear the people of the land, for they are meat for us! For the season of prosperity has departed from them, but the Lord is among us. Don't fear them!"

All the community shouted, "Stone them with stones," and the glory of the Lord appeared in the cloud on the tabernacle of witness to all the children of Israel.

The Lord asked Moses, "How long will these people provoke me? How long will they don't believe me for all the signs which I have worked among them? I will strike them dow dead and destroy them, and I will make of you and your father's house a great nation, and much greater than this."

Moses replied to the Lord, "Then Egypt will hear, that you have brought up these people from them by your might. Moreover, all the residents in this land have heard that you are the Lord of these people, who, the Lord, have been seen by them face to face, and your cloud rests among them, and you go before them by day in a pillar of a cloud, and by night in a pillar of fire. If you will destroy this nation as one man, then all the nations that have heard your name will speak, saying, 'Because the Lord could not bring these people into the land which he swore to them, he has destroyed them in the wilderness.' Now, the Lord, let your strength be exalted, as you said. The Lord is restraint and merciful, and true, removing transgressions and iniquities and sins, and he will by no means clear the guilty, visiting the sins of the fathers on the children to the third and fourth generation. Forgive these people their sin according to your great mercy, as you were favorable to them from Egypt until now."

The Lord said to Moses, "I am gracious to them according to your word. But as I live and my name is living, so the glory of the Lord will fill all the land. For all the men who see my glory, and the signs which I worked in Egypt, and in the wilderness, and have tempted me this tenth time, and have not listened to my voice, surely they will not see the land, which I swore to their fathers, but their children which are with me here, as many as don't know good or evil, every inexperienced youth, to them will I give the land. But none who have provoked me will see it. My servant Caleb, because there was another spirit in him, and he followed me, I will bring him into the land into which he entered, and his seed will inherit it. But Amalekites and the Canaanites live in the valley. Tomorrow, turn and depart for the wilderness by the way of the Sea of Edom."[1]

The Lord said to Moses and Aaron, "How long will I endure this wicked community? I have heard their murmurings against me, even the murmuring of the children of Israel, which they have murmured concerning you. Say to them, 'As I live, says the Lord, surely as you spoke into my ears, so will I do to you. Your carcasses will fall in this wilderness, and all those of you that were surveyed, and those of you that were counted from twenty years old and up, all that murmured against me, you will not enter into the land for which I stretched out my hand to establish you on, except only Caleb the son of Jephunneh, and Joshua the son of Nun. Your little ones, who you said would become prey, them will I bring into the land, and they will inherit the land, from which you turned away. Your carcasses will fall in this wilderness. Your sons will be fed in the wilderness for forty years, and they will carry your fornication until your carcasses are consumed in the wilderness. According to the number of the days during which you spied the land, forty days, a day for a year, you will carry your sins forty years, and you will know my fierce anger. I, the Lord have said, 'Surely will I do this to this evil community that has risen together against me. In this wilderness, they will be completely consumed, and there they will die.'"

The men that Moses sent to spy out the land, and who came and murmured against it to the assembly to bring out evil words concerning the land, the men that spoke evil reports against the land, died of the plague before the Lord. Joshua the son of Nun and Caleb the son of Jephunneh still lived out of those men who went to spy out the land. Moses spoke these words to all the children of Israel, and the people mourned greatly. They rose early in the morning and went up to the top of the mountain, saying, "Look, these men that are here will go up to the place of which the Lord has spoken because we have sinned."

Moses asked, "Why do you transgress the word of the Lord? You will not prosper. Don't go up, for the Lord is not with you, and will you fall before the face of your enemies. For Amalek and the Canaanites are there before you, and you will fall by the sword, because you have disobeyed the Lord and turned aside, and the Lord will not be among you."

Having forced their way through, they went up to the top of the mountain, but the ark of the covenant of the Lord and Moses stirred would not leave the camp. The Amalekites and Canaanites that lived in that mountains came down, and routed them, and destroyed them to Herman, and they returned to the camp.

Numbers: Chapter 14 Notes

1 Codex Vaticanus: thalassan Erythran (ΘΑΛΑϹϹΑΝΕΡΥΘΡΑΝ). Translation: Erythrean Sea

- LXX 128: thalassês Erythras (θαλάσσης Ερυθράς). Translation: Erythrean Sea

- LXX 799: thalassê Erythra (θαλάσση Ερυθρά). Translation: Erythrean Sea

- Leningrad Codex: yam-suf (יַם־סוּף). General Translation: sea of papyrus (or reeds)

- Peshitta: ymå dsŭp (ܝܡܐ ܕܣܘܦ). Translation: sea of papyrus (or reeds)

- Targum Onkelos: yamma desuf (יְמָא דְסוּף). Translation: sea of papyrus (or reeds)

- Targum Jerusalem: yamma desuf (יְמָא דְסוּף). Translation: sea of papyrus (or reeds)

The Greek term is not geographically specific, however, by this point the Israelites should have been at the Gulf of Aqaba. The Greek name appears to be a translation of the Persian term Erostras, which referred to the entire Persian Gulf, Red Sea, and the Indian Ocean.

The Greeks were likely interpreting this as the Gulf of Aqaba, however, this was known to the ancient Egyptians as the 'Sea of Edom' (𓇋𓄿𓂧𓅓𓈖 𓇋𓄿𓂋𓅓𓈗) which is what the Israelites would have called it if that was where they were. The Egyptian name is accepted as being adopted from the Canaanite name of the Gulf of Aqaba, which was ym Ådm (𐎊𐎎 𐎀𐎄𐎎) in Ugaritic, ym Ådm (𐤉𐤌 𐤀𐤃𐤌) in Phoenician, and ymå hÅydm (𐡉𐡌𐡀 𐡄𐡀𐡃𐡌) in Aramaic, all of which translate as 'Sea of Edom.' As 'Edom' and 'red' were both spelled as ådm (𐤀𐤃𐤌) in Canaanite (Judahite, Samartian, Edomite), and åydm (ﬗﬗ) and Aramaic, the Aramaic texts that the Greeks translated probably used the name Sea of Edom/red, suggesting the Aramaic translator believed that the Sea of Papyrus was the Sea of Edom. Based on the writings of Jeremiah, the Sea of Papyrus was accepted as having been the Sea of Edom by the 600s BC, which was the earliest that the ancient collection of texts composing Numbers could have been complied and added to the Torah, based on their language. As the sea in the verse must have originally been the Sea of Edom, the name is restored in this translation.

Numbers: Chapter 15

The Lord said to Moses, "Tell the children of Israel, 'When you have come into the land of your habitation, which I give to you, and you will offer whole burnt offerings to the Lord, a whole burnt offering or a sacrifice to magnify a vow, or a free-will offering, or to offer in your feasts a sacrifice of sweet savor to the Lord, whether from the herd or the flock, then he that offers his gift to the Lord will bring a sacrifice of fine flour, a tenth part of a bushel mingled with oil, even with a quarter of a hin.[1] For a drink offering you will offer a quarter of a hin on the whole burnt offering or the sacrifice. For every lamb, you will offer so much, as a sacrifice, a smell of sweet savor to the Lord. For a ram, when you offer it as a whole burnt offering or as a sacrifice, you will prepare as a sacrifice two-tenths of fine flour mingled with oil, the third part of a hin.'"

"'You will offer for a smell of sweet savor to the Lord wine for a drink offering, a third of a hin. If you sacrifice a whole burnt offering or a sacrifice, to perform a vow or a peace offering to the Lord, then the worshiper will offer the calf as a sacrifice, three tenths of fine flour mixed with a half of oil. Wine for a drink offering the half of a hin, a sacrifice for a smell of sweet savor to the Lord. This you will do to one calf or one ram, or one lamb of the sheep or goat kid. According to the number of whatever you will offer, so will you do to each one, according to their number. Every native of the country will do this to offer such things as sacrifices for a smell of sweet savor to the Lord. If there should be a stranger among you in your land or one who should be born to you among your generations, and he will offer a sacrifice, a smell of sweet savor to the Lord as you do, so the whole community will offer to the Lord. There will be one law for you and the strangers living among you, a perpetual law for your generations. As you are, so will the stranger be before the Lord. There will be one law and one ordinance for you, and for the stranger that abides among you.'"

The Lord said to Moses, "Tell the sons of Israel, 'When you are entering into the land, into which I bring you, then it will happen when you will eat of the bread of the land, you will separate a wave-offering, a special offering to the Lord, the first fruits of your dough. You will offer your bread a heave-offering: as a heave-offering from the threshing floor, so will you separate it, even the first fruits of your dough, and you will give the Lord a heave-offering throughout your generations. But whenever you will transgress, and not perform all these commands, which the Lord spoke to Moses, as the Lord ordered you by the hand of Moses, from the day which the Lord ordered you and forward throughout your generations, then it will happen, if a trespass is committed unwillingly, unknown to the community, then will all the community offer a calf from the herd without imperfection for a whole burnt offering of sweet savor to the Lord, and its sacrifice and its drink offering according to the ordinance, and one goat kid for a sin offering."

"The priest will make atonement for all the community of the children of Israel, and the trespass will be forgiven them, because it is involuntary, and they have brought their gift, a burnt offering to the Lord for their trespass before the Lord, even for their involuntary sins. It will be forgiven as respects all the community of the children of Israel, and the stranger that is living among you, because it is involuntary to all the people.'"

"'If one mind sins unwillingly, he will bring one male goat of a year-old for a sin offering. The priest will make atonement for the mind that committed the trespass unwillingly, and that sinned unwillingly before the Lord, to make atonement for him. There will be the same law for the native among the children of Israel, and for the stranger that abides among them, whoever will commit a trespass unwillingly. Whichever mind either of the natives or the strangers will do anything with a presumptuous hand, he will provoke God, and that mind will be cut off from his people, for he has set at nothing the word of the Lord and broken his commands, that mind will be completely destroyed, his sin is on him.'"

The children of Israel were in the wilderness, and they found a man gathering sticks on the sabbath day. They who found him gathering sticks on the sabbath day brought him to Moses and Aaron, and all the community of the children of Israel. They placed him in custody, for they did not determine what they should do to him.

The Lord said to Moses, "Let the man be by all means put to death, let all the community stone him with stones."

All the community brought him out of the camp, and all the community stoned him with stones outside the camp, as the Lord commanded Moses.

The Lord said to Moses, "Speak to the children of Israel, and tell them, and let them make for themselves fringes on the borders of their garments throughout their generations. You will put on the fringes of the borders a lace of blue. It will be on your fringes, and you will look at them, and you will remember all the

commands of the Lord, and do them, and you will not turn back after your imag-
inations, and after the sight of your eyes in the things after which you go
whoring, that you may remember and perform all my commands, and you will
be holy to your god. I am Lord the god who brought you out of the land of
Egypt, to be your god. I am the Lord you god!"[2]

Numbers: Chapter 15 Notes

1 Codex Vaticanus: in (ιΝ)

- Leningrad Codex: hin (הִין)

- Peshitta: hmynå (ܗܡܝܢܐ). Translation: hmyna (or belt, girdle)

- Targum Onkelos: hina (הִינָא)

- Targum Jerusalem: hina (הִינָא)

The hin was an ancient Israelite and Judean unit of measurement. Estimated around 3.7
liters, or 3.9 quarts.

2 Codex Vaticanus: egô c̄s̄ o t̄h̄s̄ ymôn o exagagôn ymas ec gês Aigyptou inae ymôn
t̄h̄s̄, egô c̄s̄ o thsymôn (ЄΓѠ Κ̄Ϲ Ο Θ̄Ϲ ΥΜѠΝ Ο ЄΞΑΓΑΓѠΝ ΥΜΑϹ ЄΚ ΓΗϹ
ΑΙΓΥΠΤΟΥЄΙΝΑΙΥΜѠΝΘϹЄΓѠΚ̄ϹΟΘ̄ϹΥΜѠΝ). Translation: I am Lord the god of
you who exported you from the land Egypt to be your god. I am Lord the god of you.

- LXX 318: egô cyrios ho theos hymôn ho exagagôn hymas ec gês Aigyptou inae
hymôn theos, egô cyrios ho theos hymôn (ϭγω ϗⲱβιοϲ ο θϭοϲ υμοον ο ϭξⲁγⲁγοον υμⲁϲ
ϭξⲀⲅγⲅⲃπτου ϭινⲁι υμοον θϭ̄ϲ, ϭγω ϗⲱβιοϲ ο θϭοϲυμοον). Translation: I am Lord the god of
you who exported you from Egypt to be your god. I am Lord the god of you

- LXX 130: egô cyrios ho theos hymôn ho exagôn hymas ec gês Aigyptou inae hymôn
theos, egô cyrios ho theos hymôn (ϭγω ϗⲱβιοϲ ο θϭοϲ υμοον ο ϭξⲀγοον υμⲁϲ ϭⲓ γʰϲ
Ⲁⲅγⲃπτου ϭινⲁι υμοον θϭ̄ϲ, ϭγω ϗⲱβιοϲ ο θϭοϲ υμοον). Translation: I am Lord the god of
you who exported you from the land Egypt to be your god. I am Lord the god of you

- LXX 72: egô cyrios ho theos hymôn ho exagagôn hymas ec gês Aigyptou inae ymin
theos, egô cyrios ho theos hymôn (ϭγω ϗⲱβιοϲ ο θϭοϲ υμοον ο ϭξⲀγⲀγοονυμⲁϲ ϭⲓ γʰϲ
Ⲁⲅγⲃπτου ϭινⲁι υμιν θϭ̄ϲ, ϭγοοϗⲱβιοϲ ο θϭοϲ υμοον). Translation: I am Lord the god of you
who exported you from the land of Egypt to be your god. I am Lord the god of y'll

• LXX 528: egô cyrios ho theos hymôn ho exagagôn hymas ec tês Aigyptou inae hymôn theos, egô cyrios ho theos hymôn (ⲋⲅⲱⲗⲁⲃⲣⲓⲟⲥ ⲟ ⲑⲉ́ⲟⲥ ⲩⲙⲟⲟⲛ ⲟ ⲋ̇ⲝ̇ⲅ̇ⲅ̇ⲅ̇ⲱ̇ⲟⲛ ⲩⲙⲁⲥ ⲋⲓⲓ ⲧⲓ̅ⲥ ⲁⲓⲅⲟⲃⲡⲧⲟⲩ ⲋⲓⲛⲁⲓ ⲩⲙⲟⲟⲛ ⲑⲉ́ⲟ̅ⲥ, ⲋⲅⲱ ⲗⲁⲃⲣⲓⲟⲥ ⲟ ⲑⲉ́ⲟⲥ ⲩⲙⲟⲟⲛ). Translation: I am Lord the god of you who exported you from the Egypt to be your god. I am Lord the god of you

• Leningrad Codex: ani Yehvah eloheichem asher hovtzeti etchem me'eretz Mitzrayim lihyovt lachem lelohim ani Yehvah eloheichem (אֲנִי יְהוָה אֱלֹהֵיכֶם אֲשֶׁר הוֹצֵאתִי אֶתְכֶם מֵאֶרֶץ מִצְרַיִם לִהְיוֹת לָכֶם לֵאלֹהִים אֲנִי יְהוָה אֱלֹהֵיכֶם). Translation: I am Yhůh your god who removed you from the land of Egypt to be for you the elohim. I am Yhůh elohim of yours.

• Peshitta: ånå ånå mryå ålhkůn: dåpqtkůn mn årôå dmsryn: dåhůå lkůn ålhå: ånå ånå mryå ålhkůn (ܟܘܢ ܐ‍ܠ‍ܗܐ: ܐܢܐ ܐܢܐ ܡܪܝܐ ܐܠܗܟܘܢ: ܕܐܦܩܬܟܘܢ ܡ ܐܘܪܥܐ ܕܡܨܪܝܢ: ܐܠܗܟܘܢ ܐܢܐ ܐܢܐ ܡܪܝܐ ܐܠܗܟܘܢ). Translation: Translation: I am Master (or lord) your god who removed you from the land of Egypt to be for you god. I am Master (or lord) your god.

• Targum Onkelos: ana yeyah elahachon di appekit yatechon me'ar'a deMitzrayim lemehavei lechon le'elaha ana yeyah elahachon (אֲנָא יְיָ אֱלָהֲכוֹן דִּי אַפֵּקִית יָתְכוֹן מֵאַרְעָא דְמִצְרַיִם לְמֶהֱוֵי לְכוֹן לֵאֱלָהָא אֲנָא יְיָ אֱלָהֲכוֹן). Translation: I'm Yhů your god who exported you from the land of Egypt to be for you a god. I'm Yhů your god.

• Targum Jerusalem: ana hu yeyah elahachon di ferakit ve'appekit yatchon perikin me'ar'a deMitzrayim metol lemehevei lechon le'elaha ana hu yeyah elahachon (אֲנָא הוּא יְיָ אֱלָהֲכוֹן דִּי פְּרָקִית וְאַפֵּקִית יַתְכוֹן פְּרִיקִין מֵאַרְעָא דְמִצְרַיִם מְטוֹל לְמֶהֱוֵי לְכוֹן לֵאֱלָהָא אֲנָא הוּא יְיָ אֱלָהֲכוֹן). Translation: I'm he: Yhů your god, who separated and exported you spreading out from the land of Egypt, for the reason that is to be a god. I'm he: Yhů your god.

The word in the Masoretic Text is commonly translated as 'God,' but is a plural form of the Aramaic ålhå (𐡍𐡋𐡄𐡀), meaning 'gods,' or a plural form of the Hebrew elah (אֱלָה) meaning 'goddesses.' The term ålhym (𐡙𐡆𐡀𐡋𐡀), and ålhym (𐡙𐡀𐡍𐡋𐡀), are also direct transcriptions of the Neo-Assyrian word elium (𒀭𒈨𒇺𒈨𒌠), which by the Iron Age meant 'god,' indicating that text had previously been written in cuneiform, and was translated into Aramaic or Phoenician during the iron age. During the bronze age, the word was pronounced as Alium (𒀭𒈨𒇺𒈨𒌠), and referred to a specific god, [deity]An (𒀭𒀭) the highest god, and father of the other gods. His Akkadian name was derived from the word elûm (𒀭𒈨𒇺), meaning 'higher,' as the term was intended to convey the meaning of 'highest.'

During the Sumerian era, he was believed to live in the polar region of the sky, where the modern constellation of Draco is located, making him the highest in the sky, around which all the gods (stars) circled. By the Akkadian era, Ellil was believed to be the highest god, living in the polar region, however, the name 'Highest' continued to be used for An. By the Babylonian era be was believed to be the god governing the ecliptic, specifically the asterism later known as Orion, which was ultimately named after him in Greek from the Akkadian úru An (𒌷𒀭𒀭), meaning 'Light of An.' The term El elyovn (אֵל עֶלְיוֹן), meaning 'highest god,' was translated into Hebrew in Genesis Numbers: Chapter 14, where the Greeks translated it as theô tô hypsistô (θεῶ τῶ υψίστω), also meaning 'highest god.'

El Elyon is known to have been a major god of the Canaanites, called ȧl ůȧlyn (𐤋𐤀 𐤏𐤋𐤉𐤍), meaning 'God and Highest' in an Aramaic language Sefire Treaty from circa 750 BC. The Greek translations of Sanchuniathon's bronze age writing that has survived to the present, referred to the primordial creator god of the Canaanites as Elioun (Ελιουν), which appears to be the same god. According to Sanchuniathon, Elioun was the highest (υψιστος) god, who made the sky and the land, and they made the rest of the gods. During the Old Babylonian and Old Assyrian eras, the gods Marduk and Ashur, the national gods of Babylon and Assyria, replaced the Akkadian An as the primary god of the Mesopotamian pantheons, and by the iron age, the word elium had came to mean 'god,' explaining why the Aramaic term ȧlhym (𐤀𐤋𐤄𐤉𐤌) would have been interpreted as 'god,' by the Greeks.

Numbers: Chapter 16

Korah the son of Jezer the son of Kohath the son of Levi, and Dathan and Abiram, the sons of Eliab, and On the son of Peleth the son of Reuben, rose up and spoke before Moses, and 250 men of the sons of Israel, chiefs of the assembly, chosen councilors, and men of renown. They rose up against Moses and Aaron, and said, "Let it be enough for you that all the community are holy, and the Lord is among them. Why do you set up yourselves against the community of the Lord?"

When Moses heard it, he fell on his face. He said to Korah and all his assembly, "God has visited and known those that are his, and who are holy, and has brought them to himself. Whom he has chosen for himself, he has brought to himself. Do this, take for yourselves censers, Korah and all his company, and put fire in them, and put incense on them before the Lord tomorrow, and it will happen that the man whom the Lord has chosen, he will be holy. Let it be enough for you, you sons of Levi."

Moses said to Korah, "Listen to me, you sons of Levi. Is it a little thing for you, that God of Israel has separated you from the community of Israel, and brought you near to himself to minister in the services of the tabernacle of the Lord, and to stand before the tabernacle to minister for them? He has brought you near and all your brothers the sons of Levi with you, and do you seek to be priests also? So it is with you and all your community which is gathered together against God, and who is Aaron, that you murmur against him?"

Moses called Dathan and Abiram, the sons of Eliab, and they replied, "We will not go up. Is it a minor thing that you have brought us out of a land flowing with milk and honey, to kill us in the wilderness, and that you alone rule over us? You are a prince, but have you brought us into a land flowing with milk and honey, and have you given us an inheritance of land and vineyards? Would you have cut out the eyes of those men? We will not go up."

Moses was exceedingly indignant, and said to the Lord, "Pay no attention to their sacrifice. I have not taken away the desire of any one of them, neither have I hurt any one of them."

Moses said to Korah, "Sanctify your company and be ready before the Lord, you and Aaron and them, tomorrow. Take each man his censer, and you will put incense on them and will bring each one his censer before the Lord, 250 censers, and you and Aaron will bring each his censer."

Each man took his censer, and they put fire in them and laid incense on them, and Moses and Aaron stood by the doors of the tabernacle of witness. Korah raised against them all his company by the door of the tabernacle of witness, and the glory of the Lord appeared to all the community.

the Lord said to Moses and Aaron, "Separate yourselves from the middle of this community, and I will consume them at once."

They fell on their faces and asked, "El, god[1] of spirits and all flesh, if one man has sinned, will the anger of the Lord be on the whole community?"

The Lord said to Moses, "Tell the community, 'Depart from the company of Korah and around him."

Moses rose up and went to Dathan and Abiram, and all the elders of Israel went with him. He said to the community, "Separate yourselves from the tents of these stubborn men, and touch nothing that belongs to them, in case you are consumed with them in all their sin."

They stood apart from the tent of Korah and around it. Dathan and Abiram went out and stood by the doors to their tents, and their wives and their children and their store.

Moses said, "Now will you know that the Lord has sent me to perform all these works, that I have not done them of myself. If these men will die according to the death of all men, if also their visitation will be according to the visitation of all men, then the Lord has not sent me. But if the Lord will show by a vision, and Adamah[2] will open her mouth and swallow them up, and their houses, and their tents, and all that belongs to them, and they will go down alive into Hades, then you will know that these men have provoked the Lord."

When he finished saying these words, the ground ripped apart beneath them. The ground[3] opened and swallowed them up, and their houses, and all the men that were with Korah, and their livestock. They went down and all that they had, alive into Hades, and the ground covered them, and they perished from among the community. All Israel around them fled from the sound of them, saying, "In case the ground swallows us up also."

Fire went out from the Lord and devoured the 250 men that offered incense.

The Lord said to Moses, and to Eleazar the son of Aaron the priest, "Pick up the bronze censers from among the men that have been burnt, and scatter the strange fire, for they have sanctified the censers of these sinners against their minds, and make them beaten plates a covering for the altar, because they were brought before the Lord and consecrated, and they became a sign to the children of Israel. Eleazar the son of Aaron the priest took the bronze censers, which the men who had been burnt brought near, and they put them as a covering on the altar, a memorial to the children of Israel that no stranger might draw near, who is not of the seed of Aaron, to offer incense before the Lord, so he will not be as Korah and as they that conspired with him, as the Lord spoke to him by the hand of Moses.

The children of Israel murmured the next day against Moses and Aaron, saying, "You have killed the people of the Lord. It came to pass when the community united against Moses and Aaron, that they ran impetuously to the tabernacle of witness, and the cloud covered it, and the glory of the Lord appeared. Moses and Aaron went in, in front of the tabernacle of witness.

The Lord said to Moses and Aaron, "Depart out of the middle of this community, and I will consume them at once, and they fell on their faces.

Moses said to Aaron, "Take a censer, and put on it fire from the altar, and put incense on it, and carry it away quickly into the camp, and make atonement for them, for anger has gone out from the presence of the Lord, and it has begun to destroy the people."

Aaron took as Moses told him, and ran among the community, for already the plague had begun among the people, and he put on the incense and made an atonement for the people. He stood between the dead and the living, and the plague ceased. They who died in the plague were 14,700, besides those that died on account of Korah. Aaron returned to Moses to the door of the tabernacle of witness, and the plague ceased.

Numbers: Chapter 16 Notes

1 Codex Vaticanus: t̄h̄s t̄h̄s (ѲСѲС). Translation: god god

- Codex Colberto-Sarravianus: thee thee (ѲЄЄѲЄЄ). Translation: god god

- LXX 707: Theos o theos (Ѳ6̄8̄с о θ6̄ѵс). Translation: God the god

- LXX 75: Theos (ϴⲟ̅ⲥ). Translation: God

- Leningrad Codex: el elohei (אֵל אֱלֹהֵי). Translation: El (or god, strong) god

- Peshitta: åyl ålhå (ܐܝܠ ܐܠܗܐ). Translation: El (or god, strong) god

- Targum Onkelos: el elaha (אֵל אֱלָהָא). Translation: El (or god in Hebrew) god

- Fragment Targums: elaha (אֱלָהָא). Translation: god

- Targum Jerusalem: el elaha (אֵל אֱלָהָא). Translation: El (or god in Hebrew) god

- Sahidic manuscripts: noute (ⲛⲟⲩⲧⲉ). Translation: god

- Vetus Latina: deus deus fortis domine. Translation: god god powerful (or strong) lord

In this verse, the word Theos (Θεος) is being used as a proper name, and so El (אֵל) is restored from the Masoretic Text. El, which means 'God,' was also the name of the ancient Canaanite creator-god. El is also the name of the god that Jacob worshiped in Genesis, as he built the Temple of El near Shiloh, which continued to be the main temple in Samaria until Yahweh supplanted El shortly before the Assyrians conquered Samaria.

2 Codex Vaticanus: Gê (ⲅⲏ). Translation: Ge (the Earth goddess)

- Codex Venetus: Gê ê (ⲅⲏ ⲏ). Translation: Ge (the Earth goddess) she

- Leningrad Codex: Adamah (אֲדָמָה). Translation: Adama (the Elbaite, Hurrian, and Edomite Earth goddess)

- Peshitta: årôå (ܐܪܥܐ). Translation: land

- Targum Onkelos: ar'a (אַרְעָא). Translation: land

- Targum Jerusalem: ar'a (אַרְעָא). Translation: land

Adamma was the Elbaite name of an earth goddess, generally associated with the underworld, not the surface. In the 3rd millennium BC Elbaite texts, she was the wife the god Rašaap (𒀭𒊏𒊓𒀊), later known as Ršp (𒀭𒊏𒊓𒀊 / 𐤓𐤔𐤐) by the Amorites and Canaanites, more commonly known as Resheph (רֶשֶׁף / 𐤓𐤔𐤐) today, from the version of his name in the Masoretic Text. During the Hyksos Dynasty, Rašaap was also viewed as being the Egyptian god Atum (𓇋𓏏𓈘) by a cult based in Iͦͦunu (Heliopolis), although this association ended with the fall of the Hyksos dynasty. During the early New Kingdom era, his worship was suppressed in Egypt and Canaan, where he was replaced by Shed/Shaddai (𓈙𓂧𓀭 / 𐤔𐤃𐤅).

With the exception of Ishara, the Amorites did not view goddesses as important, however, the Hurrian culture which had been dominated by the Amorites continued to view Adamma as the wife of Rašaap after the fall of the Hyksos Dynasty. The fact that the name Adamma was mentioned supports the text of Numbers originating during the bronze age, as Adamma was not worshiped in Canaan during the iron age, having been supplanted by the Canaanite earth-goddess Eretz. The Earth (Eretz / Adamma) is depicted as the same type of primordial deity in the Septuagint as she was in the Greek myths and called on to witness blessings and curses, implying consciousness. As the goddess' name was Adamma, not Earth or Ge, that name is restored from the Leningrad Codex.

3 Codex Vaticanus: ênoechthê ê gê (ΗΝΟΙΧΘΗΗΓΗ). Translation: opened the Earth (or Ge, land)

- Leningrad Codex: tiftach ha'Aretz et-piha (תִּפְתַּח הָאָרֶץ אֶת־פִּיהָ). Translation: opened the Earth (or Eretz, dirt) it's (or his, her) mouth

- Peshitta: ptḥt ârôâ pùmh (ܘܦܬܚܬ ܐܪܥܐ ܦܘܡܗ). Translation: opened land's mouth

- Targum Onkelos: tiftach ha'Aretz et piha (תִּפְתַּח הָאָרֶץ אֶת פִּיה). Translation: opened land it's (or his, her) mouth

- Targum Jerusalem: fetachat ar'a yat pumah (פְּתָחַת אַרְעָא יַת פּוּמָה). Translation: opened land it's (or his, her) mouth

The Earth (Eretz / Adamma) is depicted as the same type of primordial deity in the Septuagint as she was in the Greek myths and called on to witness blessings and curses, implying consciousness. As the goddess' name was Eretz, not Earth or Ge, that name is restored from the Masoretic Text. The text varies between Eretz, the common Canaanite word for 'Mother Earth' and Adamma, the Elbaite, Amorite, and Hurrian name for 'Mother Earth,' both names are restored from the Masoretic Text in their respective places. The Greeks translated both as Gê (Γη), the name of the primordial Greek 'Mother Earth,' later renamed Gaia in the Roman Era.

Numbers: Chapter 17

The Lord said to Moses, "Speak to the children of Israel, and take wands from them, according to the houses of their families, a wand from all their princes, according to the houses of their families, twelve wands, and write the name of each on his wand. Write the name of Aaron on the wand of Levi, as it is one wand for each. They will give them according to the tribe of the house of their families. You will put them in the tabernacle of witness, before the testimony, where I will be made known to you. The wand will blossom for the man whom I choose, and I will remove the murmuring of the children of Israel, which they murmur against you."

Moses spoke to the children of Israel, and all their chiefs gave him a wand each, for one chief a wand, according to the house of their families, twelve wands, and the wand of Aaron was among the wands. Moses set up the wands before the Lord in the tabernacle of witness. It came to pass in the morning, that Moses and Aaron went into the tabernacle of witness, and saw the wand of Aaron for the house of Levi had blossomed, and put out a bud, and bloomed blossoms and produced almonds.

Moses brought out all the wands from before the Lord to all the sons of Israel, and they looked, and each one took his wand. The Lord said to Moses, "Set up the wand of Aaron before the testimonies to be kept as a sign for the children of the disobedient, and let their murmuring cease from me, and they will not die."

Moses and Aaron did as the Lord commanded Moses.

The children of Israel said to Moses, "Look, we are cut off, we are destroyed, we are consumed. Everyone that touches the tabernacle of the Lord, dies. Will we all die?"

Numbers: Chapter 18

The Lord said to Aaron, "You and your sons and your father's house will carry the sins of the holy things, and you and your sons will carry the iniquity of your priesthood. Take with yourself your brothers the tribe of Levi, the family of your father, and let them be joined to you, and let them minister to you, and you and your sons with you will minister before the tabernacle of witness. They will keep your orders and the orders of the tabernacle. Only they will not approach the holy vessels and the altar, so both they and you will not die."

"They will be joined to you and will keep the orders of the tabernacle of witness, in all the services of the tabernacle, and a stranger will not approach you. You will keep the orders of the holy things, and the orders of the altar, and so there will not be anger in the children of Israel. I have taken your brothers the Levites out of the middle of the children of Israel, a present given to the Lord, to minister in the services of the tabernacle of witness. You and your sons after you will keep up your priestly administration, according to the whole manner of the altar, and that which is within the veil, and you will minister in the services as the office of your priesthood, and the stranger that comes near will die."

The Lord said to Aaron, "Look! I have given you the order of the first fruits of all things consecrated to me by the children of Israel. I have given them to you as an honor, and to your sons after you for a perpetual ordinance. Let this be to you from all the holy things that are consecrated to me, even the burnt offerings, from all their gifts, and all their sacrifices, and every trespass-offering of theirs, and from all their sin offerings, whatever things they give to me of all their holy things, they will be yours and your sons.' In the holiest place will you eat them, every male will eat them, you and your sons, they will be holy to you."

"This will be for you of the first fruits of their gifts, of all the wave offerings of the children of Israel, to you have I given them and to your sons and your daughters with you, a perpetual ordinance. Every clean person in your house will eat them. Every first-offering of oil, and every first-offering of wine, their first fruits of grain, whatever they may give to the Lord, to you have I given them."

"All the first fruits that are in their land, whatever they will offer to the Lord, will be yours. Every clean person in your house will eat them. Every devoted thing among the children of Israel will be yours. Everything that opens the womb of all flesh, whatever they bring to the Lord, whether man or beast, will be yours. Only the firstborn of men will be surely redeemed, and you will redeem the firstborn of unclean livestock. The redemption of them will be from a month old, their valuation of five shekels, it is twenty gerahs according to the holy shekel. But you will not redeem the firstborn of calves and the firstborn of sheep and the firstborn of goats."

"They are holy, and you will pour their blood on the altar, and you will offer the fat as a burnt offering for a smell of sweet savor to the Lord. The flesh will be yours, as also the breast of the wave-offering and as the right shoulder, it will be yours. Every special offering of the holy things, whatever the children of Israel will especially offer to the Lord, I have given to you and your sons and your daughters with you, a perpetual ordinance. It is a covenant of perpetual salt forever before the Lord, for you and your seed after you."

The Lord said to Aaron, "You have no inheritance in their land, neither will you have any portion among them, for I am your portion and your inheritance among the children of Israel. And, Look, I have given to the sons of Levi every tithe in Israel for an inheritance for their services, whenever they perform ministry in the tabernacle of witness. The children of Israel will no longer draw near to the tabernacle of witness to incur fatal guilt. The Levite himself will perform the service of the tabernacle of witness, and they will carry their iniquities, it is a perpetual statute throughout their generations, and among the children of Israel, they will not receive an inheritance. Because I have given as a distinct portion to the Levites for an inheritance the tithes of the children of Israel, whatever they will offer to the Lord, therefore I said to them, 'Among the children of Israel they have no inheritance.'"

The Lord said to Moses, "You will also speak to the Levites, and will say to them, 'If you take the tithe from the children of Israel, which I have given you from them for an inheritance, then will you separate from it a heave-offering to the Lord, a tenth of the tenth. Your heave offerings will be reckoned to you as grain from the floor, and an offering from the winepress. So you will also separate them from all the offerings of the Lord out of all your tithes, whatever you will receive from the children of Israel, and you will give of them an offering to the Lord to Aaron the priest. Of all your gifts you will offer an offering to the Lord and of every first-fruit the consecrated part from it."

"You will say to them, When you will offer the first fruits from it, then will it be reckoned to the Levites as produce from the threshing floor, and as produce from the winepress. You will eat it in any place, you and your families, for this is your reward for your services in the tabernacle of witness. You will not carry sin because of it, because you have offered an offering of first fruits from it, and you will not profane the holy things of the children of Israel, that you don't die."

Numbers: Chapter 19

The Lord said to Moses and Aaron, "This is the constitution of the law, as the Lord has commanded, 'Speak to the sons of Israel and let them take for you a red heifer outside spots, that has no spot on her, and on which no yoke has been put. You will give her to Eleazar the priest, and they will bring her out of the camp into a clean place and kill her before his face. Eleazar will take of her blood, and sprinkle her blood seven times in front of the tabernacle of witness. They will burn her to ashes before him, and her skin and her flesh and her blood, with her dung, will be burnt. The priest will take cedarwood and hyssop and scarlet wool, and they will throw them onto the burning heifer."

"The priest will wash his garments, and bathe his body in water, and afterward, he can go into the camp, and the priest will be unclean until evening. He that burns her will wash his garments, and bathe his body, and will be unclean until evening. A clean man will gather up the ashes of the heifer, and lay them up in a clean place outside the camp, and they will be for the community of the children of Israel to keep. It is the water of sprinkling, a purification.'"

"'He that collects the ashes of the heifer will wash his garments and will be unclean until evening, and it will be a perpetual statute for the children of Israel and the strangers joined to them. He that touches the dead body of any man, will be unclean for seven days. He will be purified on the third day and the seventh day and will be clean, but if he is not be purged on the third day and the seventh day, he will not be clean. Everyone that touches the carcass of the body of a man, if he should have died, and the other not have been purified, has defiled the tabernacle of the Lord. That mind will be cut off from Israel because the water of sprinkling has not been sprinkled on him. He is unclean, and his uncleanness is yet on him.'"

"'This is the law. If a man dies in a house, everyone that goes into the house, and all things in the house, will be unclean for seven days. Every open vessel that had no lid covering it will be unclean. Everyone who touches a man slain by violence, or a corpse, or human bone, or sepulcher, will be unclean for seven days. They will take for the unclean of the burnt ashes of purification, and they will pour on them running water into a vessel. A clean man will take hyssop, and dip it into the water, and sprinkle it on the house, and the furniture, and all the minds that are therein, and on him that touched the human bone, or the slain man, or the corpse, or the tomb. The clean man will sprinkle the water on the unclean on the third day and on the seventh day, and on the seventh day he will purify himself and the other will wash his garments, and bathe himself in water, and will be unclean until evening.'"

"'Whichever man is defiled and will not purify himself, that mind will be cut off from among the community because he has defiled the holy things of the Lord because the water of sprinkling has not been sprinkled on him. He is unclean. It will be for you a perpetual statute, and he that sprinkles the water of sprinkling will wash his garments. He that touches the water of sprinkling will be unclean until evening. Whatever the unclean man will touch will be unclean, and the mind that touches it will be unclean until evening.'"

Numbers: Chapter 20

The entire community of the children of Israel came into the Wilderness of Sin, in the first month, and the people lived in Kadesh. Mariam died there and was buried there. There was no water for the community, and they gathered themselves together against Moses and Aaron. The people criticized Moses, saying, "We should have died in the destruction of our brothers before the Lord! Why have you brought the community of the Lord into this wilderness, to kill us and our livestock? Why is this? You have brought us out of Egypt, that we should come into this evil place where there is no sowing or figs, or vines, or pomegranates. There isn't even water to drink!"

Moses and Aaron went from before the assembly to the door of the tabernacle of witness, and they fell on their faces, and the glory of the Lord appeared to them. The Lord said to Moses, "Take your wand, and call the assembly, you and Aaron your brother, and speak to the rock before them, and it will give out its waters. You will bring water out of the rock for them, and give drink to the community and their livestock."

Moses took his wand which was before the Lord, as the Lord commanded. Moses and Aaron assembled the community before the rock, and said, "Hear me, you disobedient ones! Must we bring water out of this rock for you?" Moses lifted his hand and struck the rock with his wand twice, and a great deal of water came out, and the community drank, and their livestock.

The Lord said to Moses and Aaron, "Because you have not believed me to sanctify, me before the children of Israel, therefore you will not bring this community into the land which I have given them." This is the Water of Strife because the children of Israel spoke insolently before the Lord, and he was sanctified in them.

Moses sent messengers from Kadesh to the king of Edom, saying, "So says your brother Israel, 'You know all the trouble that has found us. How our fathers went down into Egypt, and we stayed in Egypt for many days, and the Egyptians afflicted us and our fathers. We cried to the Lord, and the Lord heard our voice, and sent a messenger and brought us out of Egypt. Now we are in the city of Kadesh, at the extremity of your frontiers. We will pass through your land, we will not go through the fields, nor through the vineyards, nor will we drink water out of your cistern. We will go by the king's highway. We will not turn aside to the right hand or the left until we have passed your borders.'"

Edom replied to him, "You will not pass through me, and if otherwise, I will go out to meet you in war."

The children of Israel said to him, "We will pass by the mountain, and if I and my livestock drink of your water, I will pay you, but it is no matter of importance, we will go by the mountain.

He replied, "You will not pass through me," and Edom went out to meet him with a great army, and a mighty hand. So Edom refused to allow Israel to pass through his borders, and Israel turned away from him. They departed from Kadesh, and the children of Israel, even the whole community, came to Mount Hor.[1]

The Lord said Moses and Aaron in Mount Hor, on the borders of the land of Edom, "Let Aaron be added to his people, for you will certainly not go into the land which I have given the children of Israel because you provoked me at the Water of Strife. Take Aaron, and Eleazar his son, and bring them up to Mount Hor before all the community, and take Aaron's apparel from off him and put it on Eleazar his son. Let Aaron die there and be added to his people."

Moses did as the Lord commanded him, and took him up to Mount Hor, before all the community. He took Aaron's garments off him and put them on Eleazar his son, and Aaron died on the top of the mountain, and Moses and Eleazar came down from the mountain. All the community saw that Aaron was dead, and they wept for Aaron thirty days, including all the house of Israel.

Numbers: Chapter 20 Notes

1 Codex Vaticanus: Ôr to oros (ⲱⲣⲧⲟⲟⲣⲟⲥ). Translation: Or the mountain

- LXX 416: Sôr to aros (Ⲥⲟⲟⲃ ⲧⲟ ⲟⲃⲟⲥ). Translation: Sor the mountain.

- LXX 126: aros Ôr (ⲟⲃⲟⲥ ⲱⲃ). Translation: Mount Or.

- Leningrad Codex: Hor hahar (הֹר הָהָר). Translation: Hor the mountain

- Peshitta: Ḥûr ṭûrå (ܛܘܪܐ ܗܘܪ). Translation: Ḥûr hill (or mountain)

- Targum Onkelos: Hor tura (הֹר טוּרָא). Translation: Hor hill (or mountain)

- Targum Jerusalem: Tavvros umanos (טַוְורוֹס אוּמָנוֹס). Translation: Nur mountains (from the Greek Taurus Amanus – Ταυρος Αμανός)

The book of Numbers includes two distinct mountains called Hor, one south of Edom, and the other to the far north, somewhere. The locations of both of these Mount Hors have been debated since the Second Temple Era, as they define the northern and southern borders of the lands the Israelites were to live in.

The southern Mount Hor was located on the 'edge of the land of Edom' according to Numbers and was where Aaron died. In the 1st century AD, Josephus identified this Mount Hor, as the mountain today called Jebel Nebi Harun, a mountain near Petra, which he claimed was Kadesh Barne. This location was adopted by Islamic historians, and today has a 'tomb' of the Prophet Harun (Aaron) on it.

While Mount Hor may be Jebel Nebi Harun, it is also notable that Mount Horeb (Χωρηβ / חֹרֵב) is not mentioned in Numbers, even though it played such a significant role in Exodus, and, therefore, Horeb may be another name of the southern Hor. Throughout most references to Mount Horeb and Mount Sinai they appear to be references to the same mountain, both in the Torah, and later in other works, such as 3rd Kingdoms (Masoretic Kings). To further complicate the geography, a third name was applied to it in the Book of Judges, which is considered by scholars to be the oldest surviving texts that have not been heavily redacted by later priesthoods. In Song of Deborah, found in Judges, the mountain where God came down to the Israelites is called Mount Seir, and the details of the story she repeats are the same as those of the Horeb/Sinai event. Fortunately, this does narrow the list of possible mountains to the southern Abarim mountains in modern Jordan, south of the Dead Sea.

The 1st century Jewish General and Historian Josephus, who was given the ancient scrolls from the Second Temple when Rome destroyed it, identified Kadesh Barnea as Petra, which he claimed was known as Rekem in ancient times. The location of Kadesh Barnea is central to identifying the location of Sinai, as the Israelites went to Kadesh Barnea after leaving Mount Sinai, and both were outside of Edomite territory, which by the 700s BC included the southern Abarim mountains. Nevertheless, Josephus reported that Petra was part of Midian during the Exodus, meaning the Edomites were still only in the northern Abarim mountains, east of the Dead Sea. Josephus' claims about ancient Petra being named Rekem has been confirmed by archaeology, as has the fact that the region was not Edomite until after 800 BC, meaning it could have been Midianite before that, and also could have been Kasdeh Barnea.

The Egyptian el-Amarna Letters, written between 1360 and 1332 BC do mention the Shasu of Sôr, which is translated as the 'nomads of Seir,' implying someone was living in the Seir region of the southern Abarim mountains. If Mount Seir was near Petra (Kadesh Barnea) in the 1300s BC, the mountain would have been Jebel al-Madhbah, which translates as 'The Mountain of the Altar.' The Mountain of the Altar has been associated with Moses since at least the pre-Christian era and includes a Valley of Mose and a Spring of Moses. The mountain's summit is covered in rock-cut ceremonial structures and is reached by a rock-cut staircase. There are two giant obelisks, carved out of the rocky surface, near a large rectangular promenade hollowed out so the edges for benches. The site also included large cisterns for collecting rainwater. It is unclear when this complex was carved out of the rock, as the site was later quarried for blue slate, which archaeologists believed once covered the site. This blue slate was likely what was later identified as sapphire in the Septuagint.

The northern Mount Hor is more difficult to identify, however, many attempts have been made. During the Second Temple Era, the most common northern Mount Hor was Mount Nur (also called Amanus, Amanah, Manus, Umanis), near the modern Turkish-Syrian border. The Targum Jonathan uses the Greek name of the Nur Mountains: Taurus Amanus (Ταυρος Αμανός) transliterated into Aramaic.

The text of Numbers supports the identification of the northern Hor being at Nur, as the mountain is described as being near Hama, the major city of the Syrian northwest, which has been inhabited constantly for more than 7000 years. Additionally, in other Hebrew scriptures, such as Isaiah, the northern border is called Zephon (צפון), which is known to have been the Canaanite name of a mountain in the Nur Mountains. The original version of Numbers likely used the name Zephon, which was then redacted to Hor in Josiah's 'authorized' version of the Torah, as he went to great lengths to purge the old gods from his country, and Mount Zephon was the holy mountain of the Canaanite god of thunder Ba'al Hadad. In order to simplify the reading of this translation, the southern Hor in translated as Mount Hor, while the northern Hor is called Mount Nur.

Numbers: Chapter 21

Arad the Canaanite king who lived by the wilderness heard that Israel came by the way of Atharin, and he made war against Israel and carried off many captives from among them. Israel vowed a vow to the Lord, and said, "If you will deliver these people into my power, I will devote it and its cities to you."

The Lord listened to the voice of Israel and delivered the Canaanites into his power, and Israel devoted him and his cities, and they called the name of that place Anathema. Having departed from Mount Hor by the way leading to the Sea of Edom, they circled the land of Edom, and the people lost courage along the way. The people spoke against God and Moses, saying, "Why is this? Have you brought us out of Egypt to kill us in the wilderness? There is no bread or water, and our minds hate this ruined bread."[1]

The Lord sent among the people deadly serpents, and they bit the people, and many people among the children of Israel died. The people came to Moses and said, "We have sinned, for we have spoken against the Lord, and against you. Pray to the Lord, and let him take away the serpent from us."

Moses prayed to the Lord for the people, and the Lord said to Moses, "Make a serpent, and put it on a signal-staff, and it will come to be that whenever a serpent bites a man, everyone bit that looks at it will live." Moses made a serpent of brass and put it on a signal-staff, and it happened that whenever a serpent bit a man, and he looked on the bronze serpent, he lived.

The children of Israel departed and camped in Oboth. Having departed from Oboth, they traveled past the ruins of the Habirus,[2] on the farther side in the wilderness beyond Moab to the east. There they departed and camped in the valley of Zared. They departed there and camped on the other side of Arnon in the wilderness, the country which extends from the frontiers of the Amorites, for Arnon is the borders of Moab, between Moab and the Amorites. Therefore it is said in a book, 'A war of the Lord has set on fire Zoob, and the brooks of Arnon.' He has appointed brooks to cause Ar to live there, and it lies near the border of Moab. There they came to the well, this is the well of which the Lord said to Moses, "Gather the people, and I will give them water to drink."

Then Israel sang this song at the well, 'Begin to sing of the well for it.' The princes dug it, the kings of the nations in their kingdom, in their lordship sank it in the rock, and they went from the well to Mattanah, and from Mattanah to

Nahaliel, and from Nahaliel to Bamoth, and from Bamoth to Janen, which is in the plain of Moab as seen from the top of the quarried rock that looks towards the wilderness.

Moses sent ambassadors to Sihon king of the Amorites, with peaceful words, saying, "We will pass through your land, we will go by the road. We will not turn aside to the field or the vineyard. We will not drink water out of your well. We will go by the king's highway until we have passed your boundaries."

Sihon did not allow Israel to pass through his borders, and Sihon gathered all his people and went out to set the battle formation against Israel into the wilderness, and he came to Jahaz and set the battle in array against Israel. Israel attacked him and slaughtered by the sword, and they became possessors of his land, from Arnon to Jabbok, as far as the children of Amman, for Jaazer is the borders of the children of Amman. Israel took all their cities, and Israel lived in all the cities of the Amorites, in Heshbon, and all cities belonging to it. Heshbon is the city of Sihon king of the Amorites, and he before fought against the king of Moab, and they took all his land, from Ar to Arnon.

Therefore they say, those who deal in dark speeches, "Come to Heshbon, that the city of Sihon may be built and prepared. For a fire has gone out from Heshbon, a flame from the city of Sihon, and has consumed as far as Moab, and devoured the pillars of Arnon. Woe to you, Moab. You are lost, you people of Chamos! Their sons are sold for preservation, and their daughters are captives to Sihon king of the Amorites. Their seed will perish from Heshbon to Dibon, and their women have yet further started a fire against Moab. Israel lived in all the cities of the Amorites. Moses sent to spy out Jaazer, and they took it, and its villages, and threw out the Amorites that lived there. Having returned, they went up the road that leads to Bashan, and Og the king of Bashan went out to meet them, and all his people to war to Edrei.

The Lord said to Moses, "Don't fear him, for I have delivered him and all his people, and all his land, into your hands, and you will do to him as you did to Sihon king of the Amorites, who lived in Heshbon."

He killed him and his sons, and all his people, until he left none of his to be taken alive, and they inherited his land.

Numbers: Chapter 21 Notes

1 Codex Vaticanus: artô tô diacenô (ᴀᴩᴛⲱᴛⲱⲇιᴀᴋᴇɴⲱ). Translation: bread the emptiness

- LXX 630: artô tô diacimenô (ᴀⲣᴛⲟⲟ ᴛⲟⲟ ⲇιⲇⳑⳋιⳑⳋⲛⲟⲟ). Translation: bread is to be served

- LXX 129: artô tô dicenô (ᴀⲣᴛⲟⲟ ᴛⲟⲟ ⲇιⳑⳋⲛⲟⲟ)

- LXX 646: archonti toutô tô diacenô (ᴀⲣⲭⲟⲛᴛι ᴛⲟⲟⲃᴛⲟⲟ ᴛⲟⲟ ⲇιⲇⳑⳋⲛⲟⲟ). Translation: ruler here is ruined

- LXX 767: artô tô diacenô cae couphô (ᴀⲣⲧⲟⲟ ᴛⲟⲟ ⲇιⲇⳑⳋⲛⲟⲟ ⳑⲇι ⳑⲟⲩⲫⲟⲟ). Translation: bread is ruined and lightweight

- Leningrad Codex: lechem hakkelokel (רְחֶם הַקְּלֹקֵל). Translation: bread the ruined

- Peshitta: lḥmå zôûrå (ܠܚܡܐ ܙܥܘܪܐ). Translation: bread the ruined

- Targum Onkelos: manna hadein demeichleih kalil (מַנָּא הָדֵין דְּמֵיכְלֵיהּ קְלִיל). Translation: manna troublesome (or legal) containers are lightweight

- Targum Jerusalem: mana hadein dimzoneih kalil (מָנָא הָדֵין דִּמְזוֹנֵיהּ קְלִיל). Translation: manna troublesome (or legal) food is lightweight

2 Codex Vaticanus: chalgli (ⲭⲇⳑⲅⲇⲉι)

- Codex Ambrosiano A 147: Achellae (ⲇⲭⲉⳑⳑⲇι)

- Codex Venetus: Iaêl (ιⲇⳑⳑλ)

- LXX 509: Achalgae (ⲇⲭⲇⳑⳋⲅⲇⳋι)

- LXX 392: Chelgi (ⲭⳋⳑⲅⳋι)

- LXX 319: Gae (ⲅⲇι)

- LXX 343: Achalchagi (ⲇⲭⲇⳑⲭⲇⲅι)

- LXX 426: Aeê (ⲇιⳑ)

- LXX 118: Achilim gaei (ⲇⲭιⳑⳋιⲙ ⲅⲇιⳋι)

- LXX 56: Achalgae (ⲇⲭⲇⳑⲅⲇι)

- LXX 82: Acheltaec (ⲇⲭⳋⳑᴛⲇιⳑ)

- LXX 417: Chalchae (χαλχαι)

- LXX 19: Achilim chaeim (Αχιλℑιμ χαιℑιμ)

- LXX 458: Achelsein en geêl (Αχℑλοℑℑιν ℑν γℑℓλ)

- LXX 767: Achelsein en gaein (Αχℑλοℑℑιν ℑν γαιℑιν)

- LXX 528: Achalchae (Αχαλχαι)

- LXX 799: Achelge (Αχℑλγℑ)

- LXX 53: Phachelgae (Φαχℑλγαι)

- Leningrad Codex: be'iyyei ha'Avarim (בְּעִיֵּי הָעֲבָרִים). Translation: ruins of the Hebrews (or Eberites)

- Peshitta: bôynâ dôbryå (ܟܘܒܐ ܕܒܪܝܐ). Translation: ruins of the Hebrews (or Eberites)

- Targum Onkelos: Avara'ei (עֲבָרָאֵי)

- Targum Jerusalem: megizta (מְגִזְתָּא). Translation: fortress

- Bohairic manuscripts: Akhin (ⲁⲭⲓⲛ)

- Sahidic manuscripts: Akhirgaein (ⲁⲭⲓⲣⲅⲁⲉⲓⲛ)

- Vetus Latina: Achiin

Multiple Greek versions of this name exist, some of which mirror the Hebrew and Aramaic terms, however, most do not. As the Masoretic version claims the Israelites camped at the 'ruins of the Hebrews,' it means the Hebrews were not considered to be Israelites at the time, which is not something the Hebrew translator would have likely added to the text. This suggests that the Hebrew translation was at least partially made from a Canaanite (Judahite or Samaritan) copy of Numbers which included this line. The Targum Onkelos contains a varient, in treating the term as a proper place: Avara'ei, implying that it was not universally viewed as the 'ruins of the Hebrews' by Aramaic speaking people in the early-Christian era.

This likely began as a reference to the ruins of Íabru (𒀭𒅎𒁺𒊑), a city destroyed by King Amar-Sin of Ur centuries earlier, during the life of Abraham. The location is not known, however, the city was associated with four cities in the Dead Sea region, and the name suggests it was somewhere in the desert between the Iraqi marshlands and the Dead Sea. In the aftermath of the destruction of Íabru, Habirus began raiding all regions bordering the Syrian desert. If Moses did lead the Israelites to the ruins of Íabru, it suggests they went a long way into the desert to escape the Egyptians, and possibly to

662

what they viewed as their ancestral homeland, as they appear to be a Habiru people. As some of the Septuagint manuscripts indicate the Aramaic text the Greeks translated included the same term that the Peshitta and Masoretic text use, it is imported.

Numbers: Chapter 22

The children of Israel departed and camped to the west of Moab by Jordan near Jericho. When Balak son of Zippor saw all that Israel did to the Amorites, then the Moabites were extremely afraid of the people because they were many, and Moab was worried before the face of the children of Israel. Moab said to the elders of Midian, "Now will this assembly eats up all that is around us, as a calf would eat up the green plants of the field."

Balak son of Zippor was king of Moab at that time. He sent ambassadors to Balaam the son of Beor, to Ur, which is in the river land, to the sons of his people,[1] to call him, saying, "Look, people have come out of Egypt, and have covered the surface of the land, and have camped close to me. Now come and help me curse these people, for they are stronger than we are. If we can kill some of them, I will drive them out of the land, as I know that whoever you bless, they are blessed, and whoever you curse, they are cursed."

The elders of Moab went, and the elders of Midian with their divining instruments in their hands. They went to Balaam and told him the words of Balak.

He replied to them, "Wait here tonight, and I will tell you what the Lord tells me," and the princes of Moab stayed with Balaam.

God came to Balaam, and asked him, "Who are these men with you?"

Balaam answered God, Balak son of Zippor, king of Moab, sent them to me, saying, "Look, people have come out of Egypt, and have covered the face of the land, and have camped near to me. Now come and curse them for me, so I will be able to hit them and cast them out of the land."

God said to Balaam, "You will not go with them or curse the people, for they are blessed."

Balaam rose in the morning, and told the princes of Balak, "Leave quickly to your lord, God does not permit me to go with you."

The princes of Moab rose, and returned to Balak, and told him, "Balaam will not come with us."

Balak sent more princes, more honorable princes than the first. They came to Balaam, and they said to him, "Balak the son of Zippor says, 'I beg you, don't delay coming to me. For I will greatly honor you and will do for you whatever you will say. Come then, curse these people for me."

Balaam answered the princes of Balak, "If Balak would give me his house full of silver and gold, I will not be able to go against the word of Lord the god, to make those people little or great in just my mind. Now, you also wait here this night, and I will hear what the Lord will say to me."

God came to Balaam by night, and said to him, "If these men have come to call you, rise and follow them, however, the word which I will speak to you, it will you do."

Balaam rose in the morning, and saddled his donkey, and went with the princes of Moab. God was very angry because he went, and the messenger of God rose up to stop him. He had mounted his donkey, and his two servants were with him. When the donkey saw the messenger of God standing in the way, with his sword drawn in his hand, then the donkey turned away and went into the field, and Balaam struck the donkey with his wand to direct her back along the way. The messenger of God stood in the avenues of the vines, fences being on both sides. When the donkey saw the messenger of God, she thrust herself against the wall and crushed Balaam's foot against the wall, and he struck her again. The messenger of God went farther, and came and stood in a narrow place where it was impossible to turn to the right or the left. When the donkey saw the messenger of God, she lay down under Balaam, and Balaam became angry and struck the donkey with his wand. God opened the mouth of the donkey, and she asked Balaam, "What have I done to you, that you have struck me this third time?"

Balaam answered the donkey, "You have mocked me, and if I had had a sword in my hand, I would now have killed you."

The donkey replied to Balaam, "Am I not your donkey on which you have ridden since your youth until today? Did I ever do this to you, completely ignore you?"

And he answered, "No."

God opened the eyes of Balaam, and he saw the messenger of God standing in the way, with his sword drawn in hand, and he kneeled down and worshiped on his face. The messenger of God said to him, "Why have you struck your donkey this third time? And, Look, I came out to stop you, as your path did not seem right to me, and when the donkey saw me she turned away from me this third time. If she had not turned away, I would have killed you, but would have left her alive."

Balaam replied to the messenger of God, "I have sinned, for I did not know that you were standing in the way to meet me, and now if you do not want me to go on, I will return."

The messenger of God said to Balaam, "Go with the men, however the words which I will speak to you, you will carefully repeat."

Balaam went with the princes of Balak. When Balak heard that Balaam had arrived, he went out to meet him, to a city of Moab, which is on the borders of Arnon, which is at the farthest part of the borders. Balak said to Balaam, "Didn't I send to you, and call you? Why haven't you come to me? Won't I be able to honor you?"

Balaam replied to Balak, "Look, I have now come to you. Will I be able to say something? God has put into my mouth words that I will speak."

Balaam went with Balak, and they came to the fortified city.[2] Balak offered sheep and calves and sent to Balaam and to his princes who were with him. It was morning, and Balak took Balaam, and brought him up to steles of Ba'al,[3] and showed him some of the people.

Numbers: Chapter 22 Notes

1 Codex Alexandrinus: Bathoura (ΒΑΘΟΥΡΑ). Translation: of olive oil

- LXX 318: Baethoura (βαιθουρα)

- LXX 120: Phathourrha (φαθουρρα)

- LXX 121: Phathouras (φαθουρας)

- LXX 129: Phathyra (φαθυρα)

- LXX 616: Phaboura (φαμουρα)

- LXX 75: Phathoura (φαθοϐρα)

- LXX 29: Pathoura (παθουρα)

- LXX 458: Para (παρα)

- LXX 550: Phathara (ⲫⲁⲑⲁⲣⲁ)

- LXX 528: Phththoura (ⲫⲑⲑⲟⲩⲣⲁ)

- LXX 618: Bathourô (ⲃⲁⲑⲟⲩⲣⲱ)

- LXX 664: Bathyra (ⲃⲁⲑⲩⲣⲁ)

- LXX 376: Phatoura (ⲫⲁⲧⲟⲩⲣⲁ)

- Leningrad Codex: Petovrah (פְּתוֹרָה). Translation: Petora

- Peshitta: Pšǔrå (ܦܣܘܪܐ)

- Targum Onkelos: Perat (פְּרָת). Translation: Euphrates

- Targum Jerusalem: Aram de'al Perat (אֲרָם דְּעַל פְּרָת). Translation: Aram (or Syria) on the Euphrates

- Sahidic manuscripts: Pharua (ⲫⲁⲣⲩⲁ)

The name of the city Petovrah (פְּתוֹרָה), appears to be a transliteration of the Babylonian cuneiform word paššūru (𒄑𒀊𒉽𒈥), which meant 'table.' The related Aramaic word was pāṭūrā (פתורא), the Syriac word was pāṭūrā (ܦܬܘܪܐ), and the related Arabic word is fāṭūr (فَاطُور), all of which mean 'table,' 'tray,' or 'platter.' The older Akkadian spelling was paššuru (𒆠), which was also the spelling of the name of the city of Ur, in southern modern Iraq. If the original text of this section of text was written before the development of the Phoenician alphabet, it would have been written in Akkadian Cuneiform, the script used in Canaan under Egyptian rule during the New Kingdom era, suggesting the transliteration error took place when the Phoenician translation was made in the early-Iron Age. Wherever 'Petora' was located, it was accepted in the Classical era as being somewhere along the Euphrates, as evidenced by the Targums.

2 Codex Vaticanus: polis epauleôn (ⲠⲞⲖⲈⲓⲤ ⲈⲠⲀⲨⲖⲈⲱⲚ). Translation: city of farming (or pasture, grassland)

- Codex Ambrosiano A 147: polin epauleôn (ⲠⲞⲖⲓⲚ ⲈⲠⲀⲨⲖⲈⲱⲚ). Translation: city of farming (or pasture, grassland)

- LXX 767: polis epauleôs (πⲃⲖⲟⲓⲥ ⲟπⲁⲩⲗⲟⲱⲥ).Translation: city of farming (or pasture, grassland)

- Leningrad Codex: kiryat chutzovt (קִרְיַת חֻצוֹת). Translation: city of midnight (or noon)

- Peshitta: qûryt hsrût (ܩܪܝܬ ܚܣܪܘܬ). Translation: the city of scribe's reeds (pens)

- Targum Onkelos: kiryat machozohi (קִרְיַת מְחוֹזוֹהִי). Translation: city in his territories

- Targum Jerusalem: karta desichon hi birosha (קַרְתָּא דְסִיחוֹן הִיא בִּירוֹשָׁא). Translation: city of Sihon it's Birosha (or of cypress)

The term in the Masoretic Text is not proper Hebrew, and appears to be an older Canaanite dialect transliterated into Hebrew. The term appears to be the Phoenician qårt hsrt (𐤒𐤓𐤕 𐤇𐤑𐤓𐤕), which means a 'fortified town,' in which a transcription error resulted in hsrt being copied as hswt. The Greek translation appears to have been from the Aramaic 'city of hsyrh (חצירה),' meaning the 'city of pasture,' or 'city of grass.' Both 'fortified' and 'pasture' were spelled similarly in Aramaic (חצירה and חצר) and Phoenician (𐤇𐤑𐤓𐤕 and 𐤇𐤑𐤓), suggesting that a translation error may have happened when the name was translated into Aramaic from Paleo-Hebrew, resulting in 'pasture' instead of 'fortified.' As the Greek and Hebrew names are not directly related, the Greek name is transliterated in this translation.

3 Codex Vaticanus: stêlên tou Baal (ϹΤΗΛΗΝΤΟΥΒΑΑΛ). Translation: steles (or columns) of Baal

- LXX 407: stêlên tou balal (στηλην του υαλαλ). Translation: steles (or columns) of Balal

- LXX 318: stêlên tou balaac (στηλην του υαλααc). Translation: steles (or columns) of Balaak

- LXX 29: stêlên tou balaam (στηλην του υαλααμ). Translation: steles (or columns) of Balaam

- LXX 458: stolên tou boual (στολην του υουαλ). Translation: robes (or equipment) of Boual

- LXX 46: stêlên tô balam (στηλην του υαλαμ). Translation: steles (or columns) of Balam

- LXX 72: stêlên tô baal (στηλην τοο υααλ). Translation: steles (or columns) of Baal

- LXX 528: stêlên tô balaal (στηλην του υαλααλ). Translation: steles (or columns) of Balaal

- LXX 664: stêlên tou balac (στηλην του υαλαc). Translation: steles (or columns) of Balak

- Leningrad Codex: bamovt ba'al (בָּמוֹת בָּעַל). Translation: bamahs of the Lord (or Baal)

- Peshitta: bmût bôlâ (ܟܘܡܬ ܒ ܒܥܠܐ). Translations: bamahs of the Lord (or master, husband)

- Targum Onkelos: ramat dachalteih (רָמַת דַּחַלְתֵּיהּ). Translations: hills of ossuary

- Targum Jerusalem: ramat dachalta dif'or (רָמַת דַּחֲלְתָּא דִּפְעוֹר). Translations: hills of the ossuary of Peor

- Vetus Latina: titulum suum ollus balac. Translation: his tablets (or inscriptions) of Balac

The ancient Canaanites used to worship the gods on mountaintops or hilltops, where they erected altars as Moses had described in Exodus, along with Asherah (oak) trees. In Phoenician and Hebrew, these were known as Bamahs, which the Greeks translated as steles. The term Greek word βααλ is clearly a transliteration of the Hebrew term בְּעֵל, which translates as Lord, however, was applied to many lords.

The Balaam ben Beor is known from the Deir Alla Inscription (KAI 312) to have been the prophet of multiple gods, including Elohim (𐤀𐤋𐤄𐤍), Shaddai (𐤔𐤃𐤉), Ishtar (𐤏𐤔𐤕𐤓), and Saggar (𐤔𐤂𐤓). While the inscription dates to the 800s BC, the inclusion of Saggar placed to origin of the list in the bronze age, as Saggar was a Mesopotamian god whose worship had disappeared in Canaan and Syria by the early iron age. Earlier in the 3rd millennium BC, he had been viewed as the husband of Ishara in Elba, however, like many older gods from the region, was not viewed as important to the Amorites. He later resurfaced in the Hurrian religion with Adamma and other older gods under the rule of the Mitanni Empire, however, his worship disappeared in Canaan and Syria after the fall of the Mitanni Empire. This suggests that the prophecy of Balaam was made no later than the 1300s BC.

The Targums use variations of the term dahaltêh, meaning ossuray, which is also used as a translation for Asherah in other verses. In Canaan, oak trees were planted above the graves of important kings as 'living gravestones,' and according to the Targum Jonathan, this was the ossuray of the Lord of Peor.

Numbers: Chapter 23

Balaam said to Balak, "Build seven altars for me here, and prepare more calves for me, and seven rams."

Balak did as Balaam told him, and he offered up a calf and a ram on each altar. Balaam said to Balak, "Stand by your sacrifice, and I will go and see if God will come and meet me, and the words which he will tell me, I will report to you."

Balak stood by his sacrifice. Balaam went to inquire of God, and he went straight forward, and God appeared to Balaam, and Balaam said to him, I have prepared the seven altars, and have offered a calf and a ram on every altar. God put a word into the mouth of Balaam, and said, "You will return to Balak, this is what you will say."

He returned to him, and moreover, he stood over his whole burnt offerings, and all the princes of Moab with him, and the Spirit of God came on him. He told his story, and said, "Balak king of Moab sent for me out of Mesopotamia, out of the mountains of the east, saying, 'Come, curse Jacob for me, and come, call a curse for me on Israel.' How will I pray if not calling down curse of the Lord, or what will I curse if not calling down the curse of god?[1] From the top of the mountains, I will see him, and from the hills, I will watch him. Look, the people will live alone, and will not be considered among the nations. Who has exactly calculated the seed of Jacob, and who will number the families of Israel? Let my mind die with the minds of the righteous, and let my seed be as their seed."

Balak said to Balaam, "What have you done to me? I called you to curse my enemies, and you have greatly blessed them!"

Balaam said to Balak, "Whatever the Lord will put into my mouth, won't I speak it exactly?"

Balak said to him, "Come with me to another place where you will not see them, and you will see only a part of them and will not see them all. Curse them from there." He took him to a high place of the field to the top of the quarried rock, and there he built seven altars, and offered a calf and a ram on each altar."

Balaam said to Balak, "Stand by your sacrifice, and I will go to inquire of God. God met Balaam, and put a word into his mouth, and said, "Return to Balak, and is what you will say."

He returned to him, and stood by his whole burnt sacrifice, and all the princes of Moab were with him, and Balak asked him, "What has the Lord said?"

He continued his parable, and said, "Rise Balak and hear, listen as a witness, you son of Zippor. God is not as man to waver, nor like a human[2] to be threatened. Won't he do what he says? Will he speak and not keep to his word? Look, I have received commandment to bless, and I will bless, and not turn back. There will not be trouble in Jacob, neither will sorrow be seen in Israel, Lord the god is with him, the glories of rulers are in him. It was God who brought him out of Egypt like the glory of his gazelle.[3] For there is no divination against Jacob, nor enchantment in Israel. In time, it will be told to Jacob and Israel what will God perform. The people will rise like a lion's cub who will exalt himself as a lion, he will not lie down until he has eaten the prey, and he will drink the blood of the slain."

Balak said to Balaam, "Neither curse him at all for me nor bless them at all."

Balaam answered and said to Balak, "Didn't I say to you, 'Whatever God will tell me, that will I do?'"

Balak said to Balaam, "Come, and I will move you to another place if it will please God, and curse them for me from there. Balak took Balaam to the top of Peor, which extends to the wilderness.

Balaam said to Balak, "Build here seven altars for me, and prepare seven calves from me, and seven rams."

Balak did as Balaam told him, and offered a calf and a ram on every altar.

Numbers: Chapter 23 Notes

1 Codex Vaticanus: ti arasômae on mê cataratae csê ti catarasômae on mê cataratae o ths (ΤΙΑΡΑϹШΜΑΙΟΝΜΗΚΑΤΑΡΑΤΑΙΚϹΗΤΙΚΑΤΑΡΑϹШΜΑΙΟΝΜΗΚΑΤΑΡΑΤΑΙΟ ΘϹ). Translation: what will I pray to if not call down curse of lord, or what will I call down curses if not calling down curse of god

• Codex Alexandrinus: ti arasomae on mê aratae o cs ê ti catarasomae on mê cataratae o ths (ΤΙ ΑΡΑϹΟΜΑΙ ΟΝ ΜΗ ΑΡΑΤΑΙ Ο ΚϹ Η ΤΙΚΑΤΑΡΑϹΟΜΑΙ ΟΝΜΗΚΑΤΑΡΑΤΑΙΟΘϹ). Translation: what will I pray to if not praying to the lord, or what will I call down curses if not calling down curse of god

- Codex Venetus: ti arasomae on mê aratae csê ti epicatarasomae on mê cataratae o ths (ΤΙ ΑΡΑϹΟΜΑΙ ΟΝ ΜΗ ΑΡΑΤΑΙ Κ͞Ϲ Η ΤΙ ΕΠΙΚΑΤΑΡΑϹΟΜΑΙ ΟΝ ΜΗ ΚΑΤΑΡΑΤΑΙ Ο Θ͞Ϲ). Translation: what will I pray to if not praying to lord, or what will I call down curses if not calling down curse of the god

- LXX 55: ti arasamae hon mê aratae cataratae o cyrios theos ê ti catarasomae hon mê cataratae ho theos (τῷ ἀβάσλμλι ον μλ κλτάβάτλι ο κᾶβίος θ̅ϭος λ τῷ κλτάβαγ/σομλι ον μλ κλτάβάτλι ο θ̅ϭ̅c). Translation: what will I pray to if not call down curse of lord god, or what will I call down curses if not calling down curse of god

- LXX 58: ti catarasomae hon mê aratae cataratae o cyrios ê ti arasomae hon mê cataratae ho theos (τῷ κλτάβάσομλι ον μλ κλτάβάτλι ο κᾶβίος λ τῷ ἀβάσομλι ον μλ ἀβάτλι ο θ̅ϭ̅c). Translation: what will I call down curses if not calling down curses of lord, or what will I pray to if not praying to the god

- LXX 73: ti arasomae hon mê aratae o csê ti cataratae cs ê ti arasomae hon mê aratae ho th[s] (τῷ ἀβαγ/σομλι ον μλ ἀβάτλι ο κcλ τι κλτάβάτλι κcλ τῷ ἀβάσομλι ον μλ ἀβάτλι ο θ̅[s]). Translation: what will I pray to if not praying to lord or calling down curses from lord, or what will I pray to if not praying to the god

- LXX 426: ti arasomae hon mê aratae csê ti catarasomae hon mê cataratae ho th[s] c[s] (τῷ ἀβαγ/σομλι ον μλ ἀβάτλι κcλ τῷ κλτάβαγ/σομλι ον μλ κλτάβάτλι ο θ̅[s] κ̅[s]). Translation: what will I pray to if not praying to lord or what will I call down curses to if not calling down curses from the god lord

- LXX 458: ti arasomae hon tropon mê cataratae o cyrios cae eti catarasomae hon mê cataratae ho theos (τῷ ἀβαγ/σομλι ον τρόπον μλ κλτάβάτλι ο κᾶβίος κλι ϭτι κλτάβαγ/σομλι ον μλ κλτάβάτλι ο θ̅ϭ̅c). Translation: what will I pray to if not decreeing down curses of lord, and furthermore will I bring down curses if not cursing by the god

- LXX 767: ti arasômae hon mê arasetae cyrios kai eti catarasômae hon mê catarasetae ho theos (τῷ ἀβάσοομλι ον μλ ἀβάσϭτλι κᾶβίος κλι ϭτι κλτάβάσοομλι ον μλ κλτάβάσϭτλι ο θ̅ϭ̅c). Translation: what will I pray to if not praying to lord, and what will I bring down curses from if not bringing down curses by the god

- Leningrad Codex: mah ekkov lo kabboh El umah ez'om lo za'am Yehvah (מָה אֶקֹּב לֹא קַבֹּה אֵל וּמָה אֶזְעֹם לֹא זָעַם יְהוָה). Translation: how will I declare something not declared by god (or El) and how do I curse not cursed by Yehwah

- Peshitta: mnå ålûtyûhy: dlå lth ålhå: ůmnå åûbdyůhy: dlå åûbdh mryå (ܡܢܐ ܐܠܘܛܝܘܗܝ܃ ܕܠܐ ܐܠܗܐ ܘܡܢܐ ܐܘܒܕܝܘܗܝ܃ ܕܠܐ ܐܘܒܕܗ ܡܪܝܐ܃). Translations:

how do I curse when not cursed by god and how do I curse when not cursed by master

• Targum Onkelos: ma aloteih dela latyeh el uma atarecheih dela tarecheih yeyah (מָא אֱלוֹטֵיה דְּלָא לַטְיֵיה אֵל וּמָא אֲתָרְכֵיה דְּלָא תָרְכֵיה יְיָ). Translations: how do I purifywhen not purifying by god (or El) and how do I divine anger when not enraging Yhù

• Fragment Targums: mah ana layit deveit ya'akv umeimra dayeyah mevarech yathon umah ana maz'eir deveit yishra'el umeimra dayeyah masgei yathon (מָה אֲנָא לָיִיט דְּבֵית יַעֲקֹב וּמֵימְרָא דַּיְיָ מְבָרֵךְ יַתְהוֹן וּמָה אֲנָא מַזְעֵיר דְּבֵית יִשְׂרָאֵל וּמֵימְרָא דַּיְיָ מַסְגֵּי יַתְהוֹן). Translation: what can I purify the house of Jacob and the command of Yhù himself, and how can I makesmall the house of Israel and the command of Yhù himself?

2 Codex Vaticanus: huios anthrôpou (ΥΙΟΣΑΝΘΡΩΠΟΥ). Translation: son of human

• Leningrad Codex: ben-adam (בֶן־אָדָם). Translation: son of Adam (or human)

• Peshitta: brnšǎ (ܒܪܢܫܐ). Translation: son of mortal (or human)

• Targum Onkelos: benei enasha (בְּנֵי אֱנָשָׁא). Translations: son of mortal (or human)

• Fragment Targums: benei enasha (בְּנֵי אֱנָשָׁא). Translations: son of mortal (or human)

• Targum Jerusalem: benei vishra (בְּנֵי בִישְׂרָא). Translation: sons of flesh (or meat, milk)

3 Codex Vaticanus: ôs doxa monocerôtos autô (ΩC ΔΟΞΑ ΜΟΝΟΚΕΡΩΤΟC ΑΥΤΩ). Translation: just like like glory (or splendor) unicorn (one-horn) his (or hers, its)

• Leningrad Codex: keto'afot re'em lo (כְּתוֹעֲפֹת רְאֵם לוֹ). Translation: like flying-symbol gazelle (or onyx) his

• Peshitta: bôŭšnh ŭbrŭmh (ܟܒܥܘܫܢܗ ܘܒܪܘܡܗ). Translation: with (or in, from) power (or strength, mass, firmness) and with (or in, from) glory (or elevation, height)

• Targum Onkelos: tukepa veruma dileih (תּוּקְפָּא וְרוּמָא דִּילֵיה). Translation: strength (or solidness) and greatness of the Yh

• Fragment Targums: tukefa vetushebachta verome-muta dideih hi (תּוּקְפָא וְתוּשְׁבַּחְתָּא וְרוֹמְמוּתָא דִּידֵיה הִיא). Translation: strength (or anger, attacking) and praise (or singing, wisdom) and great-death (or great Mot) which is his (or hers, its)

• Targum Jerusalem: tukefa veromemuta tushebecha ugevureta dideih hu (תּוּקְפָּא וְרוֹמְמוּתָא תּוּשְׁבְּחָא וּגְבוּרְתָא דִּידֵיה הוּא). Translation: strength (or anger, attacking) and and great-death (or great Mot) great glory (or praise) and superiority which are his (or hers, its)

• Vetus Latina: cujus fortitudo similis est unicornis. Translation: with strength like a unicorn (or one-horn)

• Vulgate: cujus fortitudo similis est rhinocerotis. Translation: with strength like a rhinoceros.

The Greek word monocerotos (μονοκέρωτος) referred to the Asian rhinoceros, which, unlike the African rhinoceros, only has one horn. This term was translated directly into the old Latin translation as unicornis, the origin of the English word unicorn. By the beginning of the 5th century, Greek influence in Persia and India had been lost, and the term monocerotos was rare enough that Jerome substituted the more common rhinoceros (rhinocerotis) in his Orthodox Latin translation.

The Greek interpretation of monocerotos for the animal referred to as raem (רְאֵם) in the Masoretic text, appears to be based on the description of the animal in the book of Job, which appears to have been translated either earlier than, or at the same time as the Torah, however, all commentators agree that the translation of 'Asian rhinoceros' is almost certainly incorrect in this verse. Most modern translations either use the term unicorn, from the Greek text, or gazelle or oryx from the Hebrew text. The Hebrew word re'em (רְאֵם) is descended from the Akkadian rimu (𒆠𒄷) meaning wild bull, and the Ugaritic rûm (𐎗𐎜𐎎) meaning gazelle or wild buffalo. The related Arabic word rīm (ريم) means oryx.

Based on the reference in Daniel, Raem was probably the old Canaanite name of a constellation, either Taurus or Aries, however, this is also probably not what this verse was in reference to. The gazelle or oryx was also the symbol of the Amorite god Resheph, and his subsequent reinterpretation as Shed during the Egyptian New Kingdom era. As Resheph, later reinterpreted as Shaddai, appears to be the god of Abraham and Moses, this would be a reference to his power leading the Israelites out of Egypt. The Targums and Peshitta interpret the term re'em differently, as ruma (רוּמָא), meaning 'great,' however, this interpretation is clearly not how the Greek and Hebrew translators viewed the term. It appears to have been part of the ongoing attempts to make the text fit the theology of the era. As the translations of rhinoceros and unicorn both appear to be incorrect, the term gazelle is imported from the Masoretic text.

Numbers: Chapter 24

When Balaam saw that it pleased God to bless Israel, he did not do according to his custom to cast the omens but turned his face towards the wilderness. Balaam lifted his eyes and saw Israel camped in their tribes, and the spirit of God came over him. He continued, and Balaam son of Beor said, "The man who sees honestly says; he who claims he hears the words of El, who sees Shaddayin,[1] he who sees in sleep with his eyes open says: How good are your habitations, Jacob, and your tents, Israel? Like shady groves, and like gardens by a river, and like tents which God pitched, and like cedars by the waters."

"There will come a man out of his seed, and he will rule over many nations, and be exalted over Agog[2] his king, and his kingdom will be increased. God led him out of Egypt like the glory of the gazelle! He will consume the nations of his enemies, and he will suck the marrow out of their fat bones, and with his darts, he will shoot through the enemy. He laid down, and he rested like a lion, and like a lion cub, who will stir him up? They who bless you are blessed. And they who curse you are cursed."

Balak was angry with Balaam and clasped his hands together. Balak said to Balaam, "I called you to curse my enemy, and Look! You have decidedly blessed him three times! Now flee to your home! I said, 'I will honor you,' but now the Lord has deprived you of glory."

Balaam said to Balak, "Did I not tell the messengers you sent to me, 'If Balak should give me his house full of silver and gold, I will not be able to go against the word of the Lord to make it good or bad by myself? Whatever things God will say, them will I speak. Now, Look, I return to my home. Come, I will advise you of what these people will do to your people in the last days."

He continued his parable and said, "Balaam the son of Beor says; the man who sees truly says; hearing the words of El, knowing knowledge from Elyon, (and seeing Shaddayin; who forecasts) with open eyes.[3] I will point to him, but not now. I bless him, but he does not come close. A star will rise out of Jacob, a man will spring out of Israel, and will crush the princes of Moab, and will ruin all the sons of Seth. Edom will be an inheritance, and Esau his enemy will be an inheritance of Israel, and Israel will be valiant. One will arise out of Jacob, and destroy out of the city he who escapes."

Having seen Amalek, he continued and said, "Amalek is the first of the nations, yet his seed will perish."

Having seen the blacksmiths,[4] he continued and said, "Your living-place is strong, yet though you should put your nest in a rock, and though Beor should have a nest of cunning, the Assyrians will carry you away captive."

He looked at Og, and continued his parable, and said, "Oh, oh, who will live, when God will put these things? A hand will come from Cyprus,[5] and will attack Assyria, and will attack the Habirus,[6] and they will die together."[7]

Balaam rose and departed and returned to his place, and Balak went to his own home.

Numbers: Chapter 24 Notes

1 Codex Vaticanus: phêsin acouôn logia thuostis orasin thu iden en ypnô, apocecalymmenoe oe ophthalmoe autou (ϕΗϹΙΝ ΑΚΟΥωΝ ΛΟΓΙΑ ΘΥ ΟϹΤΙϹ ΟΡΑϹΙΝ ΘΥ ΕΙΔΕΝ ΕΝ ΥΠΝω ΑΠΟΚΕΚΑΛΥΜΜΕΝΟΙ ΟΙ ΟϕΘΑΛΜΟΙ ΑΥΤΟΥ). Translation: says hears (or listens, understands) words (or logic) god who sees god perceives in sleep (or trance) revealed the eyes his

• Codex Alexandrinus: phêsin acouôn logia thuischyrou ostis orasin theou iden en ypnô apocecalymmenoe oe ophthalmoe autou (ϕΗϹΙΝ ΑΚΟΥωΝ ΛΟΓΙΑ ΘΥ ΙϹΧΥΡΟΥ ΟϹΤΙϹ ΟΡΑϹΙΝ ΘΥ ΕΙΔΕΝ ΕΝ ΥΠΝω ΑΠΟΚΕΚΑΛΥΜΜΕΝΟΙ ΟΙ ΟϕΘΑΛΜΟΙ ΑΥΤΟΥ). Translation: says hears (or listens, understands) words (or logic) strong who sees god strong perceives in sleep (or trance) revealed the eyes his

• Codex Ambrosiano A 147: phêsin ostis orasin thuiden en hypnô apocecalymmenoe oe ophthalmoe autou (ϕΗϹΙΝ ΟϹΤΙϹ ΟΡΑϹΙΝ ΘΥ ΕΙΔΕΝ ΕΝ ΥΠΝω ΑΠΟΚΕΚΑΛΥΜΜΕΝΟΙ ΟΙ ΟϕΘΑΛΜΟΙ ΑΥΤΟΥ). Translation: says words (or logic) god who sees god perceives in sleep (or trance) revealed the eyes his

• Codex Venetus: phêsin o acouôn logia theou hastis harasin theou iden en hypnô apocecalymmenoe hoe ophthalmoe autou (ϕλσιν ο ἀκοʒɔον λϑγιʒ θɤου οστις οϱʒσιν θɤου ϭιʒϬν ϭν υπνɔο, ἀποιϭιʒλυμμϥνοι οι οϑθʒλμοι ʒυτου). Translation: says the hears (or listens, understands) words (or logic) god who sees god perceives in sleep (or trance) revealed the eyes his

• LXX 616: phêsin acouôn logia ischyrôs hastis harasin theou iden en hypnô, apocecalymmenoe hoe ophthalmoe autou (ϕλσιν ἀκοʒɔον λϑγιʒ ισχυϱοος οστις οϱʒσιν θɤου ϭιʒϬν ϭν υπνɔο, ἀποιϭιʒλυμμϥνοι οι οϑθʒλμοι ʒυτου). Translation: says hears (or listens, understands) words (or logic) strong who sees god perceives in sleep (or trance) revealed the eyes his

- LXX 246: phêsin acouôn logia ischyrou phêsin o anthrôpos o alêthinôs orôn hastis harasin theou iden en hypnô, apocecalymmenoe hoe ophthalmoe autou (ϕησιν ᴧιιοϬοοℕ ᴧϵγιᴧ ισχυρου ϕησιν οᴧℕθϸοοπος οᴧᴧηθιℕοος οϸοοℕ οστις οϸᴧσιℕ θϬου ϬιᴧϬℕ Ϭℕ υπℕοο, ᴧποιϬιᴧᴧυμμϲⲧℕοι οι οϕθᴧᴧμοι ᴧυτου). Translation: says hears (or listens, understands) words (or logic) of strong speaks as human genuine (or truthful) watcher (or eyes) who sees god perceives in sleep (or trance) revealed the eyes his

- LXX 72: phêsin logia ischyra hastis harasin ischyra iden en hypnô, apocecalymmenoe hoe ophthalmoe autou (ϕησιν ᴧϵγιᴧ ισχυϸᴧ οστις οϸᴧσιℕ ισχυϸᴧϬιᴧϬℕ Ϭℕ υπℕοο, ᴧποιϬιᴧᴧυμμϲⲧℕοι οι οϕθᴧᴧμοι ᴧυτου). Translation: says hears (or listens, understands) words (or logic) strong who sees god perceives in sleep (or trance) revealed the eyes hisal

- LXX 59: phêsin cae acouôn logia ischyra hastis harasin theou iden en hypnô, apocecalymmenoe hoe ophthalmoe autou (ϕησιν ιᴧι ᴧιιοϬοοℕ ᴧϵγιᴧ ισχυϸᴧ οστις οϸᴧσιℕ θϬου ϬιᴧϬℕ Ϭℕ υπℕοο, ᴧποιϬιᴧᴧυμμϲⲧℕοι οι οϕθᴧᴧμοι ᴧυτου). Translation: says and hears (or listens, understands) words (or logic) of strength who sees god perceives in sleep (or trance) revealed the eyes his

- Leningrad Codex: ne'um shomea' imrei-El asher machazeh Shaddai yechezeh nofel ugelui einayim (נְאֻם שֹׁמֵעַ אִמְרֵי־אֵל אֲשֶׁר מַחֲזֵה שַׁדַּי יֶחֱזֶה נֹפֵל וּגְלוּי עֵינָיִם). Translation: declares hears pronouncement of El (or god) who sees Shaddai (or demonic) forecasts fall and manifest eyes

- Peshitta: åmr dšmô måmrå dålhå: ûhzûå dålhå ḥzå: kd rmå ûptyhn ôynûhy (ܐܡܪ ܕܫܡܥ ܡܐܡܪܐ ܕܐܠܗܐ: ܘܚܙܘܐ ܕܐܠܗܐ ܚܙܐ: ܟܕ ܪܡܐ ܘܦܬܝܚܢ ܥܝܢܘܗܝ,). Translation: he spoke the discourse of god, and prophesied for god visions, with wide open eyes

- Targum Onkelos: emar dishma meimar min kodam El vechezu min kodam Shaddai chazei shechiv umitgelei leih (אֲמַר דִּשְׁמַע מֵימַר מִן קֳדָם אֵל וְחֵזוּ מִן קֳדָם שַׁדַּי חֲזֵי שְׁכִיב וּמִתְגְּלֵי לֵיה). Translations: he spoke and heard the command (or word) proceeding from god (or El) and saw proceeding from god (or El) Shaddai (or powerful) and recognizes while laying down and revealed by Yh (or woe)

- Fragment Targums: eimar gavra dishma mamlel min kodam yeyah vedi chaza min kodam shadai chazei vechad havah ba'ei havah nishtatach al appoy verazei nevu'ata mitgalin leih vahavah mitnabbei al nafsheih dehu nafil becharba vesof nevu'ata lemitkayma (אֵימַר גַּבְרָא דִּשְׁמַע מְמַלֵּל מִן קֳדָם יְיָ וְדִי חֲזָא מִן קֳדָם שַׁדַּי חֲזֵי וְכַד הֲוָה בָּעֵי הֲוָה נִשְׁתַּטַּח עַל אַפּוֹי וְרָזֵי נְבוּאָתָא מִתְגַּלִּין לֵיה וַהֲוָה מִתְנַבֵּי עַל נַפְשֵׁיה דְּהוּא נָפִיל בְּחַרְבָּא וְסוֹף נְבוּאָתָא לְמִתְקַיְּימָא). Translation: spoke man the heard speech from before Yhû, and perceived knowledge from before Shaddai's vision (or aperture), and when he himself saw it, he stretched out on his face, and came to him revelation of Yh, and produced prophecies from the mind (or soul) of he, Orion's (or Napil's) sword (or dry gust). And he penned (or finished, wrote) his prophecy, and it will happen.

• Targum Jerusalem: eimar dishma meimar min kodam elaha chayai decheiziyu min kodam el shadai havah chamei vechad ba'ei demitgelei leih havah mishtatach al anpoy verazya setimaya mah de'itkasei min neviya mitgelei leih (אֵימַר דְּשְׁמַע מֵימַר מָן קֳדָם אֱלָהָא חַיָּיא דְּחֲיזִיו מָן קֳדָם אֵל שַׁדַּי הֲוָה חֲמֵי וְכַד בָּעֵי דְּמִתְגְּלֵי לֵיה הֲוָה מִשְׁתַּטַח עַל אַנפּוֹי וְרָזְיָא סְתִימַיָּא מָה דְּאִתְכַּסֵי מָן נְבִיָא מִתְגְּלֵי לֵיה). Translation: spoke the heard command (or word) from before god and perceived the heat within from god Shaddai, who produced the vision, and when he saw from Yh, he fell on his face, and a powerful (or strong) storm (or winter storm) of revelation departed the prophet praising to Yh.

The shortened Greek verse was almost certainly already in the Aramaic translations they worded from, as it is part of a pattern of redacting Shaddai from the version of the Torah that ended up in the Septuagint. The name was translated into Greek as Omnipotent (παντοκρατοροσ) in the Septuagint's book of Job, and transliterated directly in Greek as Saddai (Σαδδαι) like in Ezekiel, however, is entirely missing from Cosmic Genesis while appearing six times in the Bereshít, the Hebrew translation.

The term 'god Šdy' (אל-שדי) is used repeatedly in Masoretic Bereshít regarding the god of Abraham, Isaac, and Jacob, however, does not show up in the Septuagint's Cosmic Genesis, where 'the Lord' or 'god' are used instead. The term ål Šdy was only used 48 times in the Masoretic Text, including 31 times in the book of Job, 6 times in Bereshít, and once in Exodus, when Moses' god identified himself as the god of Jacob, however, the name Ān (Ων) is used the Septuagint's version of the verse. Both the Masoretic and Septuagint's versions of Cosmic Genesis and Masoretic Exodus appear to have been redacted in regards to the identity of ål Šdy, as there is no reference to ål Šdy in Cosmic Genesis, and there is no reference to Ān in Masoretic Exodus. In Numbers, it appears the Aramaic translator simply omitted it, as it appears twice in the Masoretic version, both times in the list of gods that Balaam was the prophet of, making it easy to omit.

The Septuagint and Masoretic translations often differ in regards to the name or title Shaddai, suggesting that the Aramaic and Canaanite (Judahite or Samaritan) source texts they worked from differed in regards to this word. The cause of the confusion over the term Shaddai, is likely due to the difference between the meaning of the word in Canaanite versus Aramaic. In Akkadian cuneiform, which was adopted as the written script by many cultures, the term was ^{deity}šedu (✳𒀭), however, it referred to a 'protective spirit' or 'lesser god.' In the later Aramaic language, the word became šydå (ܢܝܕܫ), meaning 'demon' in the classical sense, as a type of muse or nymph. Whereas in Canaanite, šdy (𐤔𐤃𐤉) took on different meaning, generally interpreted as 'powerful' by the Early Classical Era, which is likely where the Greeks ultimately derived the term 'omnipotent' (παντοκράτοροσ), which was used later in the Septuagint where the Masoretic Text generally uses the term šdy.

This alternate interpretation of the šdy (𐤔𐤃𐤉) in Canaanite is likely due to the Egyptian New Kingdom era rule over Canaan, when Shed (𓄞𓂧𓀭, transliteration: šd), was worshiped in the region. Shed, who was often referred to as 'the savior,' was virtually identical to the earlier Canaanite god Resheph who was largely suppressed after the fall of the Hyksos dynasty.

In the Masoretic Book of Job, Eliphaz referred to humanity as the 'sons of Resheph' (בני-רשף) instead of the 'sons of Adam,' and then uses Šdy as the name of a god. This god Šdy was explicitly listed alongside the god El in Masoretic Job, whereas in the Septuagint's Job they are not explicitly listed as two separate gods. The Greek translation of Šdy (שדי) in Job is consistent with most of the Septuagint, using a term that translates as 'omnipotent' (παντοκράτοροσ), however, the name El (אל) is generally translated as a word meaning 'strong' (ισχυροσ). It is likely because the Masoretic Text lists them side by side, as 'god El and god Šdy' (אל-אל ואל-שדי), which the Greek translators did not do, instead routinely dropping the second reference to a god when they were listed together. The terms 'god Šdy' (אל-שדי) and 'god El' (אל-אל) are repeatedly found in Masoretic Job, and are themselves direct translations of the same terms in Akkadian Cuneiform: ^{deity}šēdu (𒀭𒆘) and ^{deity}An (𒀭𒀭). Unfortunately, the Akkadian meaning of the word šēdu was 'demonic,' which is likely the cause of it's redaction. Based on the linguistics of Masoretic Job, the text book existed in a hieratic Canaanite form during the Hyksos Dynasty, and therefore the name Resheph is not out of place, as Resheph was one of the main gods of the Hyksos rulers.

During subsequent the New Kingdom era, Resheph worship was suppressed due to his associated with the earlier Hyksos dynasty. During the early New Kingdom era, holy texts about Resheph would have been updated to Shed (𓄞𓂧𓀭), which would have been transliterated into Canaanite using the Akkadian Cuneiform script in the late New Kingdom era as ^{deity}šēdu (𒀭𒆘), before being translated into Canaanite using the Phoenician script in the early iron age as šdy (𐤔𐤃𐤉), resulting in the confusing 'demonic' (𐡔𐡃𐡉𐡀) god in Aramaic.

This word has not survived among the Dead Sea Scrolls, however, 4QNum^{b} does have a partial copy of this verse which is significantly shorter than the Masoretic version, indicating that the verse was still being rewritten during the Hasmonean Dynasty (140 to 37 BC). As the Deir Alla Inscription (KAI 312), which was carved in Moabite between 880 and 770 BC confirms that Balaam was a prophet of several gods, including Šdyn (𐤔𐤃𐤉𐤍), generally anglicized as Shaddayin, the Moabite name of the god is restored in this translation, along with the names of El and Elyon from the Masoretic text.

2 Codex Vaticanus: Gôg (ⲅⲱⲅ)

- LXX 319: Ôg (ⲱⲅ)

- LXX 127: Agôg (ⲁⲅⲱⲅ)

- LXX 44: Gôb (ⲅⲟⲟⲩ)

- Leningrad Codex: Agag (אֲגַג)

- Peshitta: Ågg (ܐܓܓ)

- Targum Onkelos: Agag (אֲגַג)

- Fragment Targums: Agag (אֲגַג)

- Targum Jerusalem: Agag (אֲגַג)

- Bohairic manuscripts: Gôg (Ⲅⲱⲅ)

- Sahidic manuscripts: Gôg (Ⲅⲱⲅ)

- Vetus Latina: Gog

3 Codex Vaticanus: acouôn logia t̄h̄u epistamenos epistêmên para ypsistou cae orasin t̄h̄u idôn en ypnô apocecalymmenoe oe ophthalmoe autou (ⲀⲔⲞⲨⲰⲚ ⲗⲞⲅⲓⲀ ⲞⲨ̄ ⲈⲠⲒⲤⲦⲀⲘⲈⲚⲞⲤ ⲈⲠⲒⲤⲦⲎⲘⲎⲚ ⲠⲀⲢⲀⲨⳡⲒⲤⲦⲞⲨ ⲔⲀⲒ ⲞⲢⲀⲤⲒⲚ ⲞⲨ̄ ⲒⲆⲰⲚ ⲈⲚ ⲨⲠⲚⲰ ⲀⲠⲞⲔⲈⲔⲀⲗⲨⲘⲘⲈⲚⲞⲒ ⲞⲒ ⲞⲪⲐⲀⲗⲘⲞⲒ ⲀⲨⲦⲞⲨ). Translation: hear (or listen, understand) words of god knows knowledge highest and sees god perceives in sleep (or trance) revealed the eyes his

- LXX 55: acouôn logia cyepistamenos epistêmên hypsistou cae harasin theou iden en hypnô apocecalymmenoe hoe ophthalmoe aùtou (ⲇⲩⲟⲟⲟⲟⲛ ⲗⲅⲩⲓⲇ ⲓⲩⲟⲡⲓⲥⲧⲁⲛⲙⲟⲛⲟⲥ ⲟⲡⲓⲥⲧⲣⲙⲓⲛ ⲩⳡⲫⲟⲧⲟⲩ ⲓⲇⲓⲟⲣⲇⲥⲓⲛ ⲑⲟⲟⲩ ⲟⲓⲇⲟⲛ ⲟⲛ ⲩⲡⲛⲟⲟ ⲁⲡⲟⲓⲟⲓⲇⲗⲩⲙⲙⲁ︦ⲛⲟⲓ ⲟⲓ ⲟⲫⲑⲁⲗⲙⲟⲓ ⲇⲩⲧⲟⲩ).

Translation: hear (or listen, understand) words of lord knows knowledge highest and sees god perceives in sleep (or trance) revealed the eyes his

- LXX 551: acouôn logia theou epistamenos epistêmên hypsistou cae harasin theoū orôn en hypnô apocecalymmenoe hoe ophthalmoe aùtou (ⲇⲩⲟⲟⲟⲟⲛ ⲗⲅⲩⲓⲇ ⲑⲟⲟⲩ ⲟⲡⲓⲥⲧⲁⲛⲙⲟⲛⲟⲥ ⲟⲡⲓⲥⲧⲣⲙⲓⲛ ⲩⳡⲫⲟⲧⲟⲩⲓⲇⲓ ⲟⲣⲇⲥⲓⲛ ⲑⲟⲟⲩ ⲟⲣⲟⲟⲛ ⲟⲛ ⲩⲡⲛⲟⲟ ⲁⲡⲟⲓⲟⲓⲇⲗⲩⲙⲙⲁ︦ⲛⲟⲓ ⲟⲓ ⲟⲫⲑⲁⲗⲙⲟⲓ ⲇⲩⲧⲟⲩ).

Translation: hear (or listen, understand) words god knows knowledge god looks and sees god perceives in sleep (or trance) revealed the eyes his

- LXX 664: acouôn logia theou epistamenos epistêmên par hypsistou cae harasin theou idôn en hypnô apocecalymmenoe hoe ophthalmoe autou (ⲇⲩⲟⲟⲟⲟⲛ ⲗⲅⲩⲓⲇ ⲑⲟⲟⲩ σπιστα∧∧μϭνος σπιστρμℓℵ παℓβ υΨϕοτου ℓℶι οℓᴅσιℵ θϭου ιᴅωωℵ ϭℵ υπℵωω ᴅπολϭℶℶλυμμϭℵοι οι ιοℵ οϟθℶλμοι ᴅυτου). Translation: hear (or listen, understand) words god knows knowledge from the highest and sees god perceives in sleep (or trance) revealed the eyes his

- LXX 53: acouôn logia theou epistamenos epistêmên hypsistou cae harasin theou idôn en hypnô cecalymmenoe hoe ophthalmoe autou (ᴅℶιο϶ωωℵ λ϶γιᴅ θϭου σπιστα∧∧μϭνος σπιστρμℓℵ υΨϕοτου ℓℶι οℓᴅσιℵ θϭου ιᴅωωℵ ϭℵ υπℵωω ℓϭℶλυμμϭℵοι οι οϟθℶλμοι ᴅυτου). Translation: hear (or listen, understand) words god knows knowledge highest and sees god perceives in sleep (or trance) covered the eyes his

- Leningrad Codex: ne'um shomea' imrei-el veyodea' da'at Elyovn machazeh Shaddai yechezeh nofel ugelui einayim (נְאֻם שֹׁמֵעַ אִמְרֵי־אֵל וְיֹדֵעַ דַּעַת עֶלְיוֹן מַחֲזֵה שַׁדַּי יֶחֱזֶה נֹפֵל וּגְלוּי עֵינָיִם). Translation: declares hears pronouncement of El (or god) and knows mind Elyon (or highest) and sees Shaddai (or demonic) forecasts fall and manifest eyes

- Peshitta: åmr dšmô måmrå dålhå: ûydô mdôå dmrymå: ûhzůå dålhå ḥzå: kd rmå ûptyhn ôynůhy (ܐܡܪ ܕܫܡܥ ܡܐܡܪܐ ܕܐܠܗܐ: ܘܝܕܥ ܡܕܥܐ ܕܪܡܐ: ܘܚܙܐ ܕܐܠܗܐ ܚܙܐ: ܟܕ ܪܡܐ ܦܬܝܚܝܢ ܥܝܢܘܗܝ,). Translation: declares hears commandment from god and knows the mind of the heights, and sees from god visions with wide open eyes

- Targum Onkelos: emar dishma meimar min kodam el vida madda min kodam illa'ah chezu min kodam shaddai chazei shechiv umitgelei leih (אֲמַר דִּשְׁמַע מֵימַר מִן קֳדָם אֵל וִידַע מַדַּע מִן קֳדָם עִלָּאָה חֵזוּ מִן קֳדָם שַׁדַּי חֲזֵי שְׁכִיב וּמִתְגְּלֵי לֵיהּ). Translation: declares hears commandment proceeding from El (or god) and knows the intelligence proceeding from Elyon (or highest) and sees from Shaddai (or powerful) sees laying down from Yh

- Fragment Targums: amar gavra dishma mamlal min kodam yeyah vida de'ah min kodam ilaveih dachazei min kodam shadai havah chazei vechad havah ba'ei havah mishtatach al appoy verazei nevu'ata mitgalyain leih vahavah mitnabbe al nafsheih dehu nafil becharba vesof neviyuteih lemitkayma (אֲמַר גַּבְרָא דִּשְׁמַע מַמְלַל מִן קֳדָם יְיָ וִידַע דֵּעָה מִן קֳדָם עִילָּוֵיהּ דַּחֲזֵי מִן קֳדָם שַׁדַּי חֲזֵי וְכַד הֲוָה בָּעֵי הֲוָה מִשְׁתַּטַּח עַל אַפּוֹי וְרָזֵי נְבוּאֲתָא מִתְגַּלְיָין לֵיהּ וַהֲוָה מִתְנַבֵּא עַל נַפְשֵׁיהּ דְּהוּא נָפִיל בְּחַרְבָּא וְסוֹף נְבִיּוּתֵיהּ לְמִתְקַיְּימָא). Translation: spoke man the heardspeechfrom before Yhů, and perceived knowledge from before Elyon who saw from before Shaddai. He himself saw it, and when he himself saw, he stretched out on his face and came to him revelation of Yh, and produced prophecies from the mind (or soul) from Orion's (or Napil's) sword (or dry gust). And he penned (or finished, wrote) his prophecy from Yh, and it will happen.

- Targum Jerusalem: eimar deshama meimar min kodam elaha vida sha'ta deratach beih elaha ila'ah decheizu min kodam shadai chamei vechad havah ba'ei deyitgelei leih havah mishtatach unefal al appoy verazya setimaya mah de'itkasei min neviya havah mitgelei leih (אֵימַר דִּשְׁמַע מֵימַר מִן קֳדָם אֱלָהָא וִידַע שַׁעְתָּא דְּרָתַח בֵּיהּ אֱלָהָא עִלָּאָה דְּחֵיזוּ מִן קֳדָם

683

שַׁדַּי חָמֵי וְכַד הֲוָה בָּעֵי דְיִתְגְלֵי לֵיה הֲוָה מִשְׁתַּטַּח וּנְפַל עַל אַפּוֹי וְרַזְיָא סְתִימַיָא מָה דְאִתְכַּסֵּי מִן נְבִיָא
(הֲוָה מִתְגְלֵי לֵיה). Translation: spoke theheard command (or word) from before god and perceived the heat within Yh god highest, who saw before Shaddai's spectacle (or vision), when he himself saw the revelation of Yh, he himself bowed and lay down on his face, and strong (or powerful) storm (or winter storm) whichfrom throne came, the prophet disclosed for Yh

The Aramaic text the Greeks translated could not have read exactly as the Masoretic text reads, as there are specifically Hebrew and Moabite words in the Masoretic version that the Aramaic translator would have translated. Nevertheless, the difference is significant beyond the language used, as all references to Shaddai are again missing from the Greek version, suggesting that the Aramaic translator as unwilling to refer to the 'demonic god.' As the Deir Alla Inscription (KAI 312), which was carved in Moabite between 880 and 770 BC confirms that Balaam was a prophet of several gods, including Šdyn (𐤔𐤃𐤉𐤍), generally anglicized as Shaddayin, the Moabite name of the god is restored in this translation, along with the names of El and Elyon from the Masoretic Text.

4 Codex Vaticanus: Caeneon (ΚΕΝΑΙΟΝ)

• Codex Alexandrinus: Caeneon (ΚΑΙΝΕΟΝ)

• Codex Ambrosiano A 147: Canaeon (ΚΑΝΑΙΟΝ)

• LXX 509: Cananaeon (Κανανaιον)

• LXX 127: Cinaeon (Κϭιναιον)

• LXX 318: Chananaeon (Χανανaιον)

• LXX 707: Caenaeon (Καιναιον)

• LXX 319: Ceneôn (Κϭνϭων)

• LXX 246: Caenion (Καινιον)

• LXX 71: Caeneôn (Καινϭων)

• LXX 761: Chettiim (Χϭττιϭιμ)

• LXX 416: Cennaeon (Κϭνναιον)

• Leningrad Codex: keini (קֵינִי). Translation: smiths (or metalsmiths)

• Peshitta: qynyå (ܩܝܢܝܐ). Translation: smiths

• Targum Onkelos: Shalma'ah (שַׁלְמָאָה). Translation: Shalmites (an Arab tribe)

- Fragment Targums: Shalmaya (שַׁלְמַיָא). Translation: Shalmites (an Arab tribe)

- Targum Jerusalem: Yitro (יִתְרוֹ). Translation: Jethro

- Sahidic manuscripts: Kinnaios (ⲔⲒⲚⲚⲀⲒⲞⲤ)

5 Codex Alexandrinus: Cêtiaeôn (ⲔⲎⲦⲒⲀⲒⲰⲚ)

- LXX 15: Citieôn (ⲔⲒⲦⲒϭⲟⲟⲛ)

- LXX 127: Tettiim (ⲦϭⲦⲦϭⲓϭⲓμ)

- LXX 318: Cêtaeôn (ⲔⳑⲦⲀⲓⲟⲟⲛ)

- LXX 18: Cêtieôn (ⲔⳑⲦⲒϭⲟⲟⲛ)

- LXX 58: Citêaeôn (ⲔⲒⳑⲀⲓⲟⲟⲛ)

- LXX 75: Coetaeôn (ⲔⲟⲓⲦⲀⲓⲟⲟⲛ)

- LXX 767: Chettaeôn (ⲭϭⲦⲦⲀⲓⲟⲟⲛ)

- LXX 416: Citiaeôn (ⲔⲒⲦⲒⲀϕⲟⲟⲛ)

- LXX 610: Chetiim (ⲭϭⲦⲒϭⲓμ)

- Leningrad Codex: Kittim (כִּתִּים)

- Peshitta: Ktyå (ܟܬܝܐ)

- Targum Onkelos: Roma'ei (רוֹמָאֵי). Translation: Roman

- Fragment Targums: Livranaya min medinta rabbeta veyitzrefun imhon ligyonin sagyain min deRoma'ei (לִבְרַנַיָא מִן מְדִינְתָּא רַבְּתָא וְיִצְרְפוּן עִמְהוֹן לִגְיוֹנִין סַגְיִין מִן דְרוֹמָאֵי). Translation: Liburnia from the province (or city), great and combining with the legions spreading from Rome

- Targum Jerusalem: Lammebarneya ume'ara Italya veyitztarfun beligyonin deyifkun min Kusetantinei (לִמְבַּרְנְיָא וּמֵארַע אַטַלְיָא וְיִצְטַרְפוּן בְּלִגְיוֹנִין דְיִפְקוּן מִן קוּסְטַנְטִינֵי). Translation: Lombardy and attack the land of Italy and combining with legions commanded by Constantine

- Sahidic manuscripts: Khidre (ⲭⲒⲀⲣⲉ)

- Vetus Latina manuscripts 403 and 1964: Citheorum

- Codex Gothicus Legionensis (VL 91): Sethim

Kittim was a kingdom in eastern Cyprus, founded in the 13th century BC, and used by the Hebrews as the name of the island of Cyprus. The name was recorded during the Egyptian New Kingdom as Kåtjåy (𓈎𓏏𓇌𓅓𓈗), Phoenician as Kty (𐤊𐤕𐤉), and ancient Greek as Cition (Κίτιον). It was also applied to the Aegean islands and Greece in later periods. The Masoretic text refer to a fleet of ships (צִים) coming from Kittim, not 'a hand.' This land of Ktym was where the Kty came from who were mentioned in Genesis, Exodus, and earlier in Numbers.

6 Codex Vaticanus: Ebraeous (ЄΒΡΑΙΟΥC). Translation: Hebrews

• LXX 82: Ebaeous (Ευλιουc)

• Leningrad Codex: Ever (עֵבֶר). Translation: Eber

• Peshitta: ôbr (ܥܒܪ). Translation: crosser (or Habiru, Eber)

• Targum Onkelos: l'evar Perat (לְעֵבַר פְּרָת). Translation: those across the Euphrates

• Fragment Targums: benei Ever nahara (בְּנֵי עֵבֶר נַהֲרָא). Translation: sons of Eber (or Eberites) in Syria (or Aram, rivers)

• Targum Jerusalem: benoy de'Ever (בְּנוֹי דְעֵבֶר). Translation: sons of Eber

• Codex Gothicus Legionensis (VL 91): Heber

If the Canaanite text of Numbers was based on an Akkadian Cuneiform source text, then this term must have been ḫabiru (𒄩𒁉𒊒), meaning 'dusky,' which was a word used to describe groups of marauders in the Middle East in the era. The term was in use from approximately 1800 to 1200 BC, however, does not appear to have been an ethnic term, but was generally used to describe rebels, mercenaries, outlaws, raiders, servants, and slaves. The inclusion of the Habirus in the curse against the Assyrians, suggests the Israelites were not considered Habirus at the time, as Balaam was unable to curse the Israelites.

7 The reference to Assyria implies it is a major nation at the time, which dates the composition of the text to either before the collapse of the Old Assyrian Empire, circa 1392 BC, or during the era of the Neo-Assyrian Empire, between circa 911 and 612 BC. As the Habirus disappeared from the historic records in the 1100s BC, this indicates that the curse of Balaam dates to before 1392 BC.

Numbers: Chapter 25

Israel stayed in Shittim, and the people began going whoring after the daughters of Moab. They called them to the sacrifices of their idols, and the people ate from their sacrifices and worshiped their idols. Israel declared themselves sacred to Lord Peor,[1] and the Lord was very angry with Israel.

The Lord said to Moses, "Take all the heads of the people, and make them examples for the Lord against Shemesh,[2] and the anger of the Lord will be turned away from Israel."

Moses said to the tribes of Israel, "Everyone! Kill his friends who have been made sacred to Lord Peor!"

And a man of the children of Israel came and brought his brother and a Midianite woman before Moses, and before all the community of the children of Israel, and they were weeping at the door of the tabernacle of witness. Phinehas the son of Eleazar, the son of Aaron the priest, saw it, and rose out of the middle of the community, and took a dagger in his hand, and went in after the Israelite man into the furnace, and stabbed them both through, both the Israelite man, and the woman through her womb, and the violence was stopped among the children of Israel. Those that died in the violence were 24,000.

The Lord said to Moses, "Phinehas the son of Eleazar the son of Aaron the priest has caused my anger to cease from the children of Israel when I was exceedingly jealous with them, and so I did not consume the children of Israel in my jealousy. So say to him, 'Look, I give him a covenant of peace, and he and his seed after him have a perpetual covenant of the priesthood, because he was zealous for his God, and made atonement for the children of Israel.'"

The name of the murdered Israelite man, who was murdered with the Midianite woman, was Zambri the son of Salu, prince of a house of the tribe of Simeon. The name of the Midianite woman who was murdered, was Kozbi, daughter of Zur, a prince of the nation of Ommoth. It is a chief house among the people of Midian.

The Lord said to Moses, "Say to the children of Israel, "Attack the Midianites as enemies, and murder them, for they are enemies to you by the treachery in which they trap you through Peor and through Kozbi their sister, daughter of a prince of Midian, who was murdered in the day of the violence because of Peor.

Numbers: Chapter 25 Notes

1 Codex Vaticanus: Beelphegôr (ΒΕΕΛΦΕΓωΡ)

- LXX 121: Belphegôr (Βϭλϐϭγ∞ρ)

- LXX 128: Beelphebôr (Βϭϭλϐϭu∞ρ)

- LXX 618: Pheelphegôr (Φϭϭλϐϭγ∞ρ)

- LXX 53: Beelgôr (Βϭϭλγ∞ρ)

- Leningrad Codex: Baal Pe'ovr (בַּעַל פְּעוֹר). Translation: Lord Peor.

- Peshitta: Bôl Pôûr (ܒܥܠ ܦܥܘܪ). Translation: Lord Peor

- Targum Onkelos: Va'ala Pe'ovr (בְּעֵלָא פְּעוֹר). Translation: Lord Peor

- Fragment Targums: ta'avavta DipPe'or (טָעֲוָותָא דִּפְעוֹר). Translation: mistake of Peor

- Targum Jerusalem: Va'ala Pe'ovr (בְּעֵלָא פְּעוֹר). Translation: lord of Peor

- Bohairic manuscripts: Belphegôr (Βελφεϣρ)

- Sahidic manuscripts: Belphegôr (Βελφεϣρ)

Phagôr (Φαγωρ) was the name of a place that Joshua conquered in the Septuagint's version of the Book of Joshua. There are no known locations associated with the name Peor, which implies the location was abandoned after the events of Numbers chapter 25, or perhaps shortly afterward when Joshua conquered the city in Joshua chapter 13. Other Hebrew texts, such as Micah refer to the Lord of Peor in association with the Shittim Valley, however, this name appears to have been an insult directed towards Lord Hammon who was worshiped at Tell el-Hammam in the 800s BC. There is no clear link between Hammon and Peor, implying the worshipers of Peor disappeared around the time the Israelites traveled through the Shittim Valley.

The major ruins in the Shittim Valley, are found at Tell el-Hammam, which was occupied from at least 3600 BC until the beginning of the Late Bronze Age (circa 1500 BC) when the site was abandoned for unknown reasons. It was rebuilt in the 900s BC as a Samaritan city. As Tell el-Hammam is in the Shittim Valley, and was destroyed or abandoned when the Israelites moved through the region, using either the traditional Christian dating, or the Minoan Eruption and collapse of the Hyksos Dynasty from the Book of Exodus, the Bronze-Age city was likely Peor (Φαγωρ). The exact dating of the abandonment of the bronze-age city is unclear, and there is some evidence of occupation for a few decades after 1550 BC, but the site does appear to have been abandoned around 1500 BC.

2 Codex Vaticanus: Êliou (ΗΛΙΟΥ). Translation: Helios (or the sun)

- Codex Alexandrinus: laou (ΛΑΟΥ). Translation: people

- LXX 71: C$_x$^{y} (κ͞ς). Translation: lord

- Leningrad Codex: shamesh (שָׁמֶשׁ). Translation: Shemesh (or sun)

- Targum Onkelos: shimsha (שִׁמְשָׁא). Translation: sun

- Fragment Targums: shimsha (שִׁמְשָׁא). Translation: sun

- Targum Jerusalem: shimsha (שִׁמְשָׁא). Translation: sun

Helios and Shemesh were the Greek and Canaanite gods of the sun. The Septuagint and Masoretic Text have similar verses, however, the Masoretic Text are generally translated differently, with translators adding various words, for example:

> "And the LORD said unto Moses, Take all the heads of the people, and hang them up before the LORD against the sun, that the fierce anger of the LORD may be turned away from Israel."

> King James Edition

> "The LORD said to Moses, "Take all the ringleaders and have them publicly impaled before the LORD, so that the LORD's wrath may turn away from Israel."

> Tanakh (JPS 1985)

> "The LORD said to Moses, "Take all the leaders of the people and execute them in broad daylight before the LORD, so that the fierce anger of the LORD may turn away from Israel."

> New American Standard Bible

The term 'sun' has also been phased out of modern translations since it has been documented that the Shemesh was a Canaanite god, which this verse is clearly referring to.

The Masoretic verse is:

וַיֹּאמֶר יְהוָה אֶל־מֹשֶׁה קַח אֶת־כָּל־רָאשֵׁי הָעָם וְהוֹקַע אוֹתָם לַיהוָה נֶגֶד הַשָּׁמֶשׁ וְיָשֹׁב חֲרוֹן אַף־יְהוָה מִיִּשְׂרָאֵל

Which translates as:

> And said Yahweh to Moses, 'Take all the leaders of the people and denounce Yahweh against Shemesh, and bring and end the burning anger of Yahweh against Israel.

Numbers: Chapter 26

After the plague, the Lord said to Moses and Eleazar the priest, "Take a count of all the community of the children of Israel, from twenty years old and up, according to the houses of their fathers' families; every one that went out to set himself in formation.

Moses and Eleazar the priest said in Araboth of Moab at the Jordan by Jericho, "This is the count of every one from twenty years old and up as the Lord commanded Moses." The sons of Israel that came out of Egypt are as follows:

Reuben was the firstborn of Israel, and the sons of Reuben: Enoch and the family of Enoch, to Phallu belongs the family of the Phalluites, to Hezron belongs the family of Hezronite, to Karmi belongs the family of Karmites. These are the families of Reuben, and their count was 43,730.

The sons of Phallu were Eliab, and the sons of Eliab, Namuel, and Dathan, and Abiram. These were renowned men of the community, these were those who rose up against Moses and Aaron in the gathering of Korah, in the rebellion against the Lord. Eretz opened her mouth and swallowed them up and Korah, when their assembly perished the fire devoured the 250, and they were for a sign. But the Sons of Korah did not die.

The sons of Simeon, both the family of the sons of Simeon: to Namuel belonged the family of the Namuelites, to Jamin belonged the family of the Jimnites, to Jakin belonged the family of the Jakinites, to Zerah belonged the family of the Zerahites, to Saul belonged the family of the Saulites. These are the families of Simeon according to their count, 22,200.

The sons of Judah: Er and Onan, and Er and Onan died in the land of Canaan. These were the sons of Judah, according to their families: to Shelah belonged the family of the Shelanites, to Pharez belonged the family of the Pharzites, to Zerah belonged the family of the Zerahites. The sons of Pharez were: to Hezron belonged the family of the Hezronites, to Hamul belonged the family of the Hamulites. These are the families of Judah according to their count, 76,500.

The sons of Issachar according to their families: to Tola belonged the family of the Tolaites, to Pua belonged the family of the Punites, to Jashub belonged the family of the Jashubites, to Shimron belonged the family of the Shimronites. These are the families of Issachar according to their count, 64,400.

691

The sons of Zebulun according to their families: to Sered belonged the family of the Sardites, to Helon belonged the family of the Elonites, to Jahleel belonged the family of the Jahleelites. These are the families of Zebulun according to their count, 60,500.

The sons of Gad according to their families: to Zephon belonged the family of the Zephonites, to Haggi belonged the family of the Haggites, to Shuni belonged the family of the Shunites, to Ozni belonged the family of the Oznites, to Eri belonged the family of the Erites, to Arodi belonged the family of the Arodites, to Areli belonged the family of the Arelites. These are the families of the children of Gad according to their count, 43,500.

The sons of Asher according to their families: to Imnah belonged the family of the Imnites, to Jesus belonged the family of the Jesusites, to Beriah belonged the family of the Beriites. To Eber belonged the family of the Heberites, to Malchiel belonged the family of the Malchielites. The name of the daughter of Asher: Serah. These are the families of Asher according to their count, 43,400.

The sons of Joseph according to their families: Manasseh and Ephraim. The sons of Manasseh. To Makir belonged the family of the Makirites. Makir fathered Gilead, and to Gilead belonged the family of the Gileadites. These are the sons of Gilead: to Jeezer belonged the family of the Jeezerites, to Helek belonged the family of the Helekites. To Asriel belonged the family of the Asrielites. To Shechem, the family of the Shechemites. To Shemida belonged the family of the Shemidaites. To Hepher belonged the family of the Hepherites. To Zelophehad the son of Hepher there were no sons, but daughters: and these were the names of the daughters of Zelophehad: Mahlah, Noah, Hoglah, Milkah, and Tirzah. These are the families of Manasseh according to their count, 52,700.

These are the children of Ephraim: to Shuthelah belonged the family of the Shuthelahites, to Tanach belonged the family of the Tanachites. These are the sons of Shuthelah: to Eden the family of the Edenites. These are the families of Ephraim according to their count, 32,500. These are the families of the children of Joseph according to their families.

The sons of Benjamin according to their families: to Bala belonged the family of the Belaites, to Ashbel belonged the family of the Ashbelites, to Ahiram belonged the family of the Ahiramites. To Shupham, the family of the Shuphamites. The sons of Bala were Ard and Naaman: to Ard belonged the family of the Ardites, and to Naaman belonged the family of the Naamites. These are the sons of Benjamin by their families according to their count, 35,500.

The sons of Dan according to their families: to Shupham belonged the family of the Shuphamites. These are the families of Dan according to their families. All the families of Shupham according to their count, 64,400.

The sons of Naphtali according to their families; to Jahzeel belonged the family of the Jahzeelites, to Guni belonging the family of the Gunites. To Jezer belonged the family of the Jezerites, and to Shillem belonged the family of the Shillemites. These are the families of Naphtali, according to their count, 40,300.

This is the count of the children of Israel, 601,730.

The Lord said to Moses, "The land will be divided, so that they may inherit according to the count of the names. To the greater number, you will give the greater inheritance, and to the smaller number, you will give the lesser inheritance. To each one, as they have been counted, will their inheritance be given. The land will be divided among the names by lot, they will inherit according to the tribes of their families. You will divide their inheritance by lot between the many and the few.

The sons of Levi according to their families: to Gershon and the family of the Gedsonites, to Kohath and the family of the Kohathites, to Merari and the family of the Merarites. These are the families of the sons of Levi: the family of the Libnites, the family of the Hebronites, the family of the Coreites, and the family of the Mushites, and Kohath fathered Amram. The name of his wife was Jochebed, daughter of Levi, who carried these for Levi in Egypt, and she gave birth to Amram, Aaron, Moses, and Mariam their sister. To Aaron were born Nadab, Abihu, Eleazar, and Ithamar. Nadab and Abihu died when they offered strange fire before the Lord in the Wilderness of Sinai. There were according to their count, 23,000, every male from a month old and up, for they were not counted among the children of Israel, because they have no inheritance among the children of Israel.

This is the count of Moses and Eleazar the priest, who counted the children of Israel in Araboth of Moab, at Jordan by Jericho. Among these people, there was not a man counted by Moses and Aaron, who the children of Israel counted in the Wilderness of Sinai. For the Lord had said to them, "They will surely die in the wilderness, and there was not even one of them left, except Caleb the son of Jephunneh, and Joshua the son of Nun.

Numbers: Chapter 27

The daughters of Zelophehad the son of Hepher, the son of Gilead, the son of Makir, of the tribe of Manasseh, of the sons of Joseph, came near. These were their names: Maala, Noah, Hoglah, Milcah, and Tirzah. They stood before Moses, and before Eleazar the priest, and before the princes, and before all the community at the door of the tabernacle of witness, and said, "Our father died in the wilderness, and he was not among the community that rebelled against the Lord in the gathering of Korah. He died for his own sin, and he had no sons. Don't let the name of our father be blotted out from among his people, because he has no son. Give us an inheritance among our father's brothers."

Moses brought their case before the Lord. The Lord said to Moses, "The daughters of Zelophehad have spoken rightly. You will give them a possession of an inheritance among their father's brothers, and you will assign their father's inheritance to them. You will tell the children of Israel, 'If a man dies, and has no son, you will assign his inheritance to his daughter. If he has no daughter, you will give his inheritance to his brother. If he has no brothers, you will give his inheritance to his father's brother. If there be no brothers of his father, you will give the inheritance to his nearest relation of his tribe, to inherit his possessions."

This will be for the children of Israel an ordinance of judgment, as the Lord commanded Moses.

The Lord said to Moses, "Go up to the mountain that is in the country beyond Jordan (this is Mount Nebo),[1] and look at the land of Canaan, which I give to the sons of Israel for a possession. You will see it, and you also will be added to your people, like Aaron your brother was added to them in Mount Hor, because you transgressed my commandment in the Wilderness of Sin, when the community resisted and refused to sanctify me, you did not sanctify me at the water before them." (This is the water of Strife in Kadesh in the Wilderness of Sin.)

Moses said to the Lord, "Let Lord the god of spirits and all flesh appoint a man over this community. Who will go out before them? Who will come in before them? Who will lead them out? Who will bring them in? The community of the Lord will not be as sheep without a shepherd."

The Lord answered Moses, "Take with yourself Joshua the son of Nun, a man who has the Spirit in him, and you will lay your hands on him. You will set him before Eleazar the priest, and you will give him an order before all the community, and you will give an order concerning him before them. You will put your glory on him, that the children of Israel may listen to him. He will stand before Eleazar the priest, and consult for him the judgment of statements against the Lord, and they will go out at his word, and at his word they will come in, he and the children of Israel with one accord, and all the community."

Moses did as the Lord commanded him, and he took Joshua and set him before Eleazar the priest, and before all the community. He laid his hands on him and appointed him as the Lord ordered Moses.

Numbers: Chapter 27 Notes

1 Codex Vaticanus: oros Nabau (ΟΡΟϹΝΑΒΑΥ). Translation: Mount Nabau

- LXX 127: aros Nagau (οϼος Νἀγἀυ). Translation: Mount Nagau

- LXX 128: aros Nabab (οϼος Νᾶυᾶυ). Translation: Mount Nabab

- LXX 72: orous Naban (οϼους Νᾶυᾶν). Translation: Mount Naban

- LXX 528: aros Nauau (οϼος Νᾶυᾶυ). Translation: Mount Nauau

- LXX 126: orous Nabôn (οϼους Νᾶυοον). Translation: Mount Nabon

- Leningrad Codex: har ha'Avarim (הָר הָעֲבָרִים). Translation: Mountain of Abarim

- Peshitta: dÔbryå (ܪܒܥܒܐ). Translation: in Obrya

- Targum Onkelos: da'Avara'ei (דְּעַבְרָאֵי). Translation: in Abarae

- Targum Jerusalem: tavvra de'Avra'ei (טְוּוּרָא דְּעַבְרָאֵי). Translation: hill of Abrae

Mount Nebo is not listed in this verse in the Masoretic Text, Peshitta, or Targums, and appears to have been added to the Greek translation as a scribal note. It is mentioned in other verses of the Masoretic Text regarding these mountains, and they seem consistent that Nebo was in the Abarim Mountains.

Mount Nebo has been identified with the mountain now known as Mount Nebo, the highest mountain in the Abarim Mountains, since at least the 4th century AD when a Byzantine church was erected on the mountain. The church was abandoned sometime after the 6th century and rebuilt in the 20th century. There is some scholarly debate about whether this was the original Mount Nebo or not, however, at this time the Orthodox and Catholic churches accept it as the Mount Nebo from Numbers, as do Islamic scholars.

Numbers: Chapter 28

The Lord said to Moses, "Command the children of Israel, 'You observe offerings to me at my feasts and my gifts, my presents and my burnt offerings as a sweet-smelling savor.' You will say to them, 'These are the burnt offerings that you will bring to the Lord: two year-old lambs without imperfection every day, for a whole burnt offering perpetually. You will offer one lamb in the morning, and you will offer the second lamb towards the evening. You will offer a tenth of an ephah of fine flour for a sacrifice, mixed with a quarter of a hin oil. It is a perpetual whole burnt offering, a sacrifice offered in Mount Sinai as a sweet-smelling savor to the Lord. Its drink offering will be a quarter of a hin for each lamb."

"In the holy place will you pour a strong drink as a drink offering to the Lord. The second lamb you will offer towards evening, and you will offer it according to its sacrifice and according to its drink offering for a smell of sweet savor to the Lord. On the sabbath day, you will offer two year-old lambs without imperfection, and two tenths of fine flour mixed with oil for a sacrifice, and a drink offering. It is a whole burnt offering of the sabbaths on the sabbath days, besides the continued whole burnt offering, and its drink offering.'"

"At the new moons, you will bring a whole burnt offering to the Lord. Two calves from the herd, and one ram, and seven year-old lambs without imperfection. Three tenths of fine flour mixed with oil for one calf, and two tenths of fine flour mixed with oil for one ram. A tenth of fine flour mixed with oil for each lamb, as a sacrifice. A sweet-smelling savor, a burnt offering to the Lord. Their drink offering will be half a hin per calf, and a third of a hin per ram, and a quarter of a hin of wine per lamb. This is the whole burnt offering monthly throughout the months of the year. He will offer one goat kid for a sin offering to the Lord. It will be offered beside the continual whole burnt offering and its drink offering."

"In the first month, on the fourteenth day of the month, is the Passover to the Lord. On the fifteenth day of this month is a feast, and for seven days you will eat unleavened bread. The first day will be for you a holiday, and you will do no servile work. You will bring whole burnt offerings, as a sacrifice to the Lord: two calves from the herd, one ram, and seven year old lambs, and they will without imperfection. Their sacrifice will be fine flour mixed with oil, three tenths for one calf, and two tenths for one ram. You will offer a tenth for each lamb, for the seven lambs. You will offer one goat kid for a sin offering, to make atonement for you. Besides the perpetual whole burnt offering in the morning, which is a whole burnt sacrifice for a continuance. These you will offer daily for seven days, a gift, a sacrifice for a sweet-smelling savor to the Lord, beside the continual whole burnt offering, you will offer its drink offering. The seventh day will be for you a holiday. You will do no servile work in it."

"On the day of the new grain, when you offer a new sacrifice at the festival of weeks, to the Lord, there will be for you a holiday, and you will do no servile work. You will bring whole burnt offerings for a sweet-smelling savor to the Lord, two calves from the herd, and one ram, and seven lambs without imperfection. Their sacrifice will be fine flour mixed with oil, and there will be three tenths per calf, and two tenths per ram. A tenth for each lamb separately, for the seven lambs, and a goat kid, for a sin offering, to make atonement for you, besides the perpetual whole burnt offering, and you will offer to me their sacrifice. They will be for you undamaged, and you will offer their drink offerings."

Numbers: Chapter 29

"In the seventh month, on the first day of the month, there will be for you a holiday, and you will do no servile work. It will be for you a day of blowing the trumpets. You will offer whole burnt offerings for a sweet savor to the Lord, one calf from the herd, one ram, and seven year-old lambs without imperfection. Their sacrifice will be fine flour mingled with oil, three tenth amounts for one calf, and two tenth amounts for one ram. A tenth deal for each of the seven lambs. One goat kid for a sin offering, to make atonement for you. Besides the whole burnt offerings for the new moon, and their sacrifice, and their drink offerings, and their perpetual whole burnt offering, and their sacrifice and their drink offerings according to their ordinance for a sweet-smelling savor to the Lord. On the tenth of this month, there will be for you a holiday, and you will afflict your minds, and you will do no work."

"You will bring close the whole burnt offerings for a sweet-smelling savor to the Lord, burnt sacrifices to the Lord, one calf from the herd, one ram, seven year-old lambs, and they will be for you without imperfection. Their sacrifice will be fine flour mingled with oil, three tenth amounts for one calf, and two tenth amounts for one ram. A tenth deal for each lamb, for the seven lambs. One goat kid for a sin offering, to make atonement for you besides the sin offering for atonement, and the continual whole burnt offering, its sacrifice, and its drink offering according to its ordinance for a smell of sweet savor, a burnt sacrifice to the Lord."

"On the fifteenth day of this seventh month you have a holiday and will do no servile work, and you will keep it a feast to the Lord seven days. You will bring close whole burnt offerings, as a sacrifice for a smell of sweet savor to the Lord, on the first day thirteen calves from the herd, two rams, and fourteen year-old lambs, and they will be without imperfection. Their sacrifice will be fine flour mingled with oil, and there will be three tenth amounts for one calf, for the thirteen calves, and two tenth amounts for one ram, for the two rams. A tenth deal for every lamb, for the fourteen lambs. One goat kid for a sin offering, besides the continual whole burnt offering there will be their sacrifice and their drink offerings."

"On the second day, twelve calves, two rams, fourteen year-old lambs without imperfection. Their sacrifice and their drink offering will be for the calves and the rams and the lambs according to their number, according to their ordinance.

One goat kid for a sin offering, and besides the perpetual whole burnt offering, and their sacrifice and their drink offerings."

"On the third day, eleven calves, two rams, and fourteen year-old lambs without imperfection. Their sacrifice and their drink offering will be to the calves and the rams and the lambs according to their number, according to their ordinance. One goat kid for a sin offering, besides the continual whole burnt offering there will be their sacrifice and their drink offerings."

"On the fourth day, ten calves, two rams, and fourteen year-old lambs without imperfection. There will be their sacrifice and their drink offerings to the calves and the rams and the lambs according to their number, according to their ordinance. One goat kid for a sin offering, besides the continual whole burnt offering there will be their sacrifice and their drink offerings."

"On the fifth day, nine calves, two rams, and fourteen year-old lambs without imperfection. Their sacrifice and their drink offerings will be to the calves and the rams and the lambs according to their number, according to their ordinance. One goat kid for a sin offering, and beside the perpetual whole burnt offering there will be their sacrifice and their drink offerings."

"On the sixth day, eight calves, two rams, and fourteen year-old lambs without imperfection. There will be their sacrifice and their drink offerings to the calves and rams and lambs according to their number, according to their ordinance. One goat kid for a sin offering, besides the perpetual whole burnt offering there will be their sacrifice and their drink offerings."

"On the seventh day, seven calves, two rams, and fourteen year-old lambs without imperfection. Their sacrifice and their drink offerings will be to the calves and the rams and the lambs according to their number, according to their ordinance. One goat kid for a sin offering, besides the continual whole burnt offering, there will be their sacrifice and their drink offerings."

"On the eighth day, there will be for you a release. You will do no servile work on it. You will offer whole burnt offerings as sacrifices to the Lord, one calf, one ram, and seven year-old lambs without imperfection. There will be their sacrifice and their drink offerings for the calf and the ram and the lambs according to their number, according to their ordinance. One goat kid for a sin offering, and in addition, the continual whole burnt offering, and there will be their sacrifice and their drink offerings. These sacrifices will you offer to the

Lord in your feasts, besides your vows, and you will offer your free will offerings and your whole burnt offerings, and your sacrifice and your drink offerings, and your peace offerings."

Numbers: Chapter 30

Moses told the children of Israel everything that the Lord commanded Moses.

Moses told the heads of the tribes of the children of Israel, "This is that which the Lord has commanded. Whatever man will vow a vow to the Lord, or swear an oath, or bind himself with an obligation in his mind, he will not profane his word, all that will come out of his mouth he will do. If a woman will vow a vow to the Lord, or bind herself with an obligation in her youth in her father's house, and her father should hear her vows and her obligations, where she has bound her mind, and her father should hold his peace at her, then all her vows will stand, and all the obligations with which she has bound her mind will remain to her. But if her father straightly forbids her in the day in which he will hear all her vows and her obligations, which she has contracted in her mind, they will not stand. The Lord will hold her guiltless because her father forbade her. If she should be indeed married, and her vows are on her according to the utterance of her lips, the obligations which she has contracted in her mind, and her husband should hear, and hold his peace at her in the day in which he should hear, then this will all her vows be binding, and her obligations, which she has contracted in her mind will stand. If her husband should in any way forbid her in the day in which he should hear her, none of her vows or obligations which she has contracted in her mind will stand, because her husband has disallowed her, and the Lord will hold her guiltless."

"The vow of a widow or her who is divorced, whatever she will vow in her mind, will remain with her. If her vow was made in the house of her husband, or the obligation in her mind with an oath, and her husband should hear, and hold his peace at her, and not disallow her, then all her vows will stand, and all the obligations which she contracted in her mind, will stand against her. But if her husband should completely forbid the vow on the day in which he heard it, none of the things which will proceed out of her lips in her vows, and in the obligations contracted in her mind will remain with her, her husband has canceled them, and the Lord will hold her guiltless. Every vow, and every binding oath to afflict her mind, her husband will confirm it to her, or her husband will cancel it. But if he is wholly silent at her from day to day, then will he bind on her all her vows, and he will confirm to her the obligations which she has bound on herself because he held his peace at her in the day in which he heard her. If her husband should completely in any way cancel them after the day in which he heard them, then he will carry his iniquity."

These are the ordinances that the Lord commanded Moses, between a man and his wife, and between a father and daughter in her youth in the house of her father.

Numbers: Chapter 31

The Lord said to Moses, "Avenge the vengeance of the children of Israel on the Midianites, and then you will be added to your people."

Moses said to the people, "Arm men among yourselves, and set yourselves in array before the Lord against Midian, to inflict vengeance on Midian from the Lord. Send a thousand of each tribe from all the tribes of the children of Israel to set themselves in formation."

They counted out the thousands of Israel, a thousand of each tribe, twelve thousand, and armed them for war. Moses sent them away, a thousand from every tribe in their forces, and Phinehas the son of Eleazar the son of Aaron the priest, with the holy instruments, and the signal trumpets were in their hands. They set themselves in formation against Midian, as the Lord commanded Moses, and they killed every male. They killed the kings of Midian together with their subjects, including Evi, Rekem, Zur, Ur, and Reba, the five kings of Midian. They killed Balaam the son of Beor with their others slain. They took as captives the women of Midian, and their property, and their livestock, and all their possessions, and they plundered their people. They burnt with fire all their cities in the places of their habitation and they burnt their villages with fire. They took all their plunder, and all their spoils, both man and beast. They brought to Moses and Eleazar the priest, and all the children of Israel, the captives, and the spoils, and the plunder, to the camp to Araboth in Moab, which is by the Jordan near Jericho. Moses and Eleazar the priest and all the rulers of the community went out of the camp to meet them. Moses was angry with the captains of the army, the heads of thousands, and the heads of hundreds who came from the battle formation."

Moses asked them, "Why have you kept every female alive? For they were the cause of the children of Israel by the word of Balaam to revolt and despise the word of the Lord, because of Peor there was violence in the community of the Lord. Now then kill every male in all the spoils, kill every woman, who has been with a man. As for all the captive women, who have not been with men, keep them alive. You will camp outside the great camp seven days. Everyone who has killed and who touches a slain man, will purify himself on the third day, and you and your captives will purify yourselves on the seventh day. You will purify every garment and every leather utensil, and every work of goatskin, and every wooden vessel."

Eleazar the priest said to the men of the army that came from the battle forma-tion, "This is the ordinance of the law which the Lord has commanded Moses. Besides the gold, and the silver, and the brass, and the iron, and lead, and tin, everything that will pass through the fire will be clean, nevertheless, it will be purified with the water of sanctification, and whatever will not pass through the fire will pass through water. On the seventh day, you will wash your garments, and be clean, and afterward, you may come into the camp."

The Lord said to Moses, "Count the captives both the humans and animals, you and Eleazar the priest, and the heads of the families of the community. You will divide the spoils between the warriors that went out to battle, and the whole community. You will take a tribute for the Lord from the warriors that went out to battle, one mind out of 500 from the men and the livestock, including the oxen, sheep, and donkeys, and you will take from their half. You will give them to Eleazar the priest as the first fruits of the Lord. From the half belonging to the children of Israel, you will take one per 50 from the men, and the oxen, sheep, donkeys, and all the livestock, and you will give them to the Levites that keep the orders in the tabernacle of the Lord."

Moses and Eleazar the priest did as the Lord commanded Moses. That which remained of the spoil which the warriors took, was 675,000 sheep, 72,000 oxen, and 61,000 donkeys, and 32,000 captured virgin girls. The half, the whole portion of those that went out to war, from the number of the sheep, was 337,500, and those sacrificed to the Lord from the sheep were 675. The oxen, 630,000, and those sacrificed to the Lord were 72. The donkeys, 30,500, and those sacrificed to the Lord were 61. Of the people, 16,000, and those sacrificed of them to the Lord were 32.[1] Moses gave the sacrifice to the Lord, the heave-offering to God. To Eleazar the priest, as the Lord commanded Moses, from the half belonging to the children of Israel, whom Moses separated from the warriors. The half taken from the sheep, belonging to the community was 337,500, the oxen were 36,000, the donkeys were 30,500, and the humans were 16,000. Moses took the half belonging to the children of Israel, the one out of 50 of men and livestock, and he gave them to the Levites who keep the orders of the tabernacle of the Lord as the Lord commanded Moses. All those who were appointed to be officers of thou-sands of the army, captains of thousands and captains of hundreds, approached Moses, and said to Moses, "Your servants have counted the warriors with us and not one is missing. We have brought our sacrifice to the Lord, every man who has found an article of gold, whether an armlet, chain, ring, bracelet, or a hair-clasp, to make atonement for us before the Lord."

Moses and Eleazar the priest took the gold from them, including all the worked articles. All the worked gold, including the offering that they offered to the Lord, was 16,750 shekels from the captains of thousands and the captains of hundreds. The warriors took plunder, each one for himself. Moses and Eleazar the priest took the gold from the captains of thousands and captains of hundreds and brought them into the tabernacle of witness, a memorial of the children of Israel before the Lord.

Numbers: Chapter 31 Notes

1 This verse about human sacrifice to the Lord is also found in the Masoretic Text, but not always translated by modern translators:

וְנֶפֶשׁ אָדָם שִׁשָּׁה עָשָׂר אָלֶף וּמִכְסָם לַיהוָה שְׁנַיִם וּשְׁלֹשִׁים נָפֶשׁ

Compare translations:

> And the persons were sixteen thousand; of which the LORD'S tribute was thirty and two persons.

> King James Version (1769 revision)

> and 16,000 human beings.

> Tanakh (JPS 1985)

A direct translation of the Masoretic Text would be:

> and people, men: 16,000; levy to Yahweh: 32 people.

Numbers: Chapter 32

The children of Reuben and the children of Gad had vast herds of livestock, and they saw the land of Jazer, and the land of Gilead and the place was a good place for livestock. The children of Reuben and the children of Gad came and said to Moses, and Eleazar the priest, and the princes of the community, "Ataroth, Dibon, Jaazer, Nimrah, Heshbon, Elealeh, Shibmah, Nebo, and Beon, the land which the Lord has delivered up before the children of Israel, is pasture land, and your servants have livestock."

They said, "If we have found grace in your sight, let this land be given to your servants for a possession, and do not make us cross over Jordan."

Moses said to the sons of Gad and the sons of Reuben, "Will your brothers go to war, and will you sit here? Why do you pervert the minds of the children of Israel, that they should not cross over into the land, which the Lord gives them? Did your fathers not do this, when I sent them from Kadesh Barne to spy out the land? They went up to the valley of the cluster, and spied the land, and turned back the heart of the children of Israel, that they should not go into the land, which the Lord gave them. The Lord was very angry in that day and swore, saying, 'Surely these men who came up out of Egypt from twenty years old and up, who know good and evil, will not see the land which I swore to give to Abraham and Isaac and Jacob, for they have not closely followed after me,' except Caleb the son of Jephunneh, who was set apart, and Joshua the son of Nun, for they closely obeyed the Lord. The Lord was very angry with Israel, and for forty years he caused them to wander in the wilderness until all the generation which did evil in the sight of the Lord was dead. Look, you have risen in the place of your fathers, an evil race of sinful men, to increase yet farther the fierce anger of the Lord against Israel. For you will turn away from him to desert him yet once more in the wilderness, and you will sin against this whole community."

They came to him, and replied, "We will build corrals here for our livestock, and cities for our possessions, and we will arm ourselves and go as an advanced guard before the children of Israel, until we have brought them into their place, and our possessions will remain in walled cities because of the inhabitants of the land. We will not return to our houses until the children of Israel have been distributed, each to his own inheritance. We will no longer inherit with them from the other side of Jordan from now onward because we have our full inheritance on the east side of Jordan."

Moses said to them, "If you will do according to these words, if you will arm yourselves before the Lord for battle, and every one of you will pass over Jordan fully armed before the Lord until his enemy is destroyed from before his face, and the land will be subdued before the Lord, then afterward you will return, and be guiltless before the Lord, and as regards Israel, and this land will be for you for a possession before the Lord. But if you will not do so, you will sin against the Lord, and you will know your sin when afflictions will come on you. Build cities and storehouses for yourselves, and folds for your livestock, and that which you suggested."

The sons of Reuben and the sons of Gad said to Moses, "Your servants will do as our lord commands. Our storehouses, and our wives, and all our livestock will be in the cities of Gilead. But your servants will go over, all armed and set in order before the Lord to battle, as our lord says."

Moses appointed to them as judges Eleazar the priest, and Joshua the son of Nun, and the chiefs of the families of the tribes of Israel. Moses said to them, "If the sons of Reuben and the sons of Gad will pass over Jordan with you, everyone armed for war before the Lord, and you will subdue the land before you, then you will give to them the land of Gilead as a possession. But if they will not pass over armed with you to war before the Lord, then will you cause to pass over their possessions and their wives and their livestock before you into the land of Canaan, and they will inherit with you in the land of Canaan."

The sons of Reuben and the sons of Gad answered, "Whatever our lord says to his servants, that will we do. We will go over armed before the Lord into the land of Canaan, and you will give us our inheritance beyond Jordan."

Moses gave to them, to the sons of Gad and the sons of Reuben, and to the half-tribe of Manasseh of the sons of Joseph, the kingdom of Sihon king of the Amorites, and the kingdom of Og king of Bashan, the land and its cities with its frontiers, the cities of the land around it. The sons of Gad built Dibon, and Ataroth, and Aroer, and Shophan, and Jazer, they set them up, and Beth Nimrah, and Beth Haran, strong cities, and folds for sheep. The sons of Reuben built Heshbon, and Elealeh, and Kiriathaim, and Ba'al Meon, surrounded with walls, and Sibmah, and they called the names of the cities which they built, after their own names. A son of Makir the son of Manasseh went to Gilead, and took it, and destroyed the

Amorites who lived in it. Moses gave Gilead to Makir the son of Manasseh, and he lived there. Jair the son of Manasseh went and took their folds, and renamed them the Villages of Jair. Nobah went and took Kenath and her villages, and renamed them Nobah after his name.

Numbers: Chapter 33

These are the stages of the children of Israel, as they went out from the land of Egypt with their army by the hand of Moses and Aaron. Moses wrote their exodus and their stages, by the word of the Lord, and these are the stages of their travels. They departed from Ramesses[1] in the first month, on the fifteenth day of the first month. On the day after the Passover, the children of Israel went out defiantly in front of all the Egyptians. The Egyptians buried their dead, all that the Lord slaughtered, every firstborn in the land of Egypt, when the Lord executed vengeance on their gods.

The children of Israel departed from Ramesses and camped in the corrals,[2] and they departed from the corrals and camped in Etham,[3] which is a part of the wilderness.

They departed from Etham and camped at the mouth of the watercourse[4] which is opposite Ba'al Zephon,[5] and camped opposite Migdol.[6]

They departed from before the mouth of the river and crossed the middle of the sea into the wilderness, and they traveled three days through the wilderness and camped in the Bitter Lakes.[7]

They departed from the Bitter Lakes and went to Elim.[8] In Elim were twelve fountains of water and 70 palm trees, and they camped there by the water.

They departed from Elim and camped by the Sea of Edom.

They departed from the Sea of Edom and camped in the Wilderness of Sin.

They departed from the Wilderness of Sin and camped in Raphaca.[9]

They departed from Raphaca and camped in Alush.

They departed from Alush and camped in Rephidim,[10] and there was no water there for the people to drink.

They departed from Rephidim and camped in the Wilderness of Sinai.

They departed from the Wilderness of Sinai and camped at the Graves of Desire.

They departed from the Graves of Desire and camped in Hazeroth.

They departed from Hazeroth and camped in Rithmah.

They departed from Rithmah and camped in Rimmon Perez.

They departed from Rimmon Perez and camped in Libnah.

They departed from Libnah and camped in Rissah.

They departed from Rissah and camped in Kehelathah.

They departed from Kehelathah and camped in Shepher.

They departed from Shepher and camped in Haradah.

They departed from Haradah and camped in Makheloth.

They departed from Makheloth and camped in Tahath.

They departed from Tahath and camped in Terah.

They departed from Terah and camped in Mithkah.

They departed from Mithkah and camped in Hashmonah.

They departed from Hashmonah and camped in Moseroth.

They departed from Moseroth and camped in Bene Jaakan.

They departed from Bene Jaakan and camped in the mountain Gudgodah.

They departed from the mountain Gudgodah and camped in Jotbathah.

They departed from Jotbathah and camped in Abronah.

They departed from Abronah and camped in Ezion Geber.

They departed from Ezion Geber and camped in the Wilderness of Sin.

They departed from the Wilderness of Sin and camped in the Wilderness of Paran. This is Kadesh.

They departed from Kadesh and camped at Mount Hor near the land of Edom.

Aaron the priest went up by the command of the Lord, and died there in the fortieth year since the departure of the children of Israel from the land of Egypt, in the fifth month, on the first day of the month. Aaron was 123 years old when he died on Mount Hor. Arad the Canaanite king, who lived in the land of Canaan, heard when the children of Israel were entering the land.

They departed from Mount Hor and camped in Hashmonah. They departed from Hashmonah and camped in Punon.

They departed from Punon and camped in Oboth.

They departed from Oboth and camped in Gai, on the other side of the Jordan on the border of Moab.

They departed from Gai and camped in Dibon Gad.

They departed from Dibon Gad and camped in Almon Diblathaim.

They departed from Almon Diblathaim and camped on the mountains of Abarim, near Nebo.

They departed from the mountains of Abarim and camped to the west of Moab, at the Jordan near Jericho.

They camped by the Jordan between Beth Jeshimoth as far as Belsa to the west of Moab.

The Lord spoke to Moses at the west of Moab by Jordan at Jericho, saying, "Speak to the children of Israel and say to them, "You are to pass over Jordan into the land of Canaan. You will destroy all that live in the land before your face, and you will abolish their high places, and all their molten images you will destroy, and you will demolish all their pillars."

"You will destroy all the inhabitants of the land, and you will live in it, for I have given their land to you for an inheritance. You will inherit their land according to your tribes; to the greater number you will give the larger possession, and to the smaller, you will give the lesser possession. To whatever part his name will go out by lot, there will be his property. You will inherit according to the tribes of your families. But if you will not destroy the residents in the land from before you, then it will happen that whoever you spare will be thorns in your eyes, and darts in your sides and they will be enemies to you on the land on which you will live, and it will happen that as I had determined to do to them, I will also do to you."

Numbers: Chapter 33 Notes

1 Codex Vaticanus: Ramessôn (ⲣⲁⲙⲉⲥⲥⲱⲛ)

• Codex Alexandrinus: Ramessê (ⲣⲁⲙⲉⲥⲥⲏ)

• LXX 624: Ramesê (ⲣⲁⲙⲁⲥⲥⲏ)

- LXX 509: Ramessô (Ρⲁⲙⲉⲥⲥⲱ)

- LXX 318: Ramesi (Ρⲁⲙⲉⲥⲥⲓ)

- LXX 319: Rammesê (Ρⲁⲙⲙⲉⲥⲏ)

- LXX 16: Ramesê (Ρⲁⲙⲉⲥⲏ)

- LXX 426: Ramessês (Ρⲁⲙⲉⲥⲥⲏⲥ)

- LXX 75: Ramesi (Ρⲁⲙⲉⲥⲓ)

- LXX 82: Ramesês (Ρⲁⲙⲉⲥⲏⲥ)

- LXX 458: Remessê (Ρⲉⲙⲉⲥⲥⲏ)

- LXX 527: Ramesôn (Ρⲁⲙⲉⲥⲱⲛ)

- LXX 53: Cramessê (Κⲣⲁⲙⲉⲥⲥⲏ)

- LXX 619: Ramaesôn (Ρⲁⲙⲁⲓⲥⲱⲛ)

- Leningrad Codex: Ra'meses (רַעְמְסֵס).

- Peshitta: Rômsys (ܪܥܡܣܝܣ)

- Targum Onkelos: Ra'meses (רַעְמְסֵס)

- Targum Jerusalem: Pilusin (פִּילוּסִין). Translation: Pelusium

- Bohairic manuscripts: Ramesê (Ραⲙⲁⲥⲥⲏ)

The location of Ramesses has been a matter of debate since before the Septuagint was translated, and the translators were not sure which ancient Egyptian city the name Ramesses was referring to. The historic city of Ramesses (𓇋𓅓𓊪𓏏) was built in the era of Pharaoh Shoshenq I (943 to 922 BC) and was still a major city when the stories found in Numbers were most likely compiled into a book under King Josiah (640 to 609 BC). The Late-Period city of Ramesses was a rebuilding of the New Kingdom era city of Pi-Ramesses (𓂋𓉐𓇋𓅓𓊪𓏏), and as the city of Pi-Ramesses was never called Ramesses during the New Kingdom era, it must be assumed that the name was updated when the stories were compiled under Josiah.

The city of Pi-Ramesses, which was founded in 1290 BC, was itself a rebuilding of Avaris (𓉗𓏏𓉐𓈎𓊖), the Hyksos capital, which had been destroyed when the Hyksos were driven from Egypt in circa 1550 BC, meaning it is not clear if the name Avaris or Pi-Ramesses was updated to Ramesses. Both Avaris and Pi-Ramesses had served as imperial capital cities when Egypt had ruled Canaan, and so either could be the city in the text, however, if one accepts that Pi-Ramesses was the city called Ramesses, then it dates the events in Exodus to the 1200s BC, immediately before the Bronze Age Collapse, yet there are already reports from a century earlier of the Shasu (Nomads) of Yhů in the Seir Region of modern Jordan, which are generally accepted as a reference to the Israelites, meaning the original name was probably Avaris, which had become obscure by Josiah's time, and was updated to the contemporary name.

The city of Pelusium, mentioned in the Jerusalem and Jonathan Targums on Exodus and Numbers, was the easternmost major city in the Nile Delta during the Greco-Roman era. The city had existed since the Old Kingdom era, and therefore it is plausible that if was the original city in the text, however, that is unlikely.

The original name of the city was Sin (𓊖) in the Old Kingdom era, however, which continued to b used alongside later names that were applied to the city, and was the common name of the city in languages using the Akkadian Cuneiform script, commonly spelled as Sin (𒂗𒍪), the name of the Akkadian moon-god, later spelled as Syân (𐤎𐤉𐤍), Saen (Σαιν), Sin (סִין), and Sin (Ꮯ) during the Classical era. During the New Kingdom era, the name of the city was changed to Per-Amen (𓉐𓇋𓏠𓈖), meaning the 'house of Amen,' which also continued to be used, resulting in the Coptic Peremoun (Ⲡⲉⲣⲉⲙⲟⲩⲛ). During the early Iron Age, the name Per-Sin (𓉐𓋴𓈖) developed, which was later transliterated into Greek as Pelousion (Πηλουσιον), and then adopted into Hebrew and Judean-Aramaic as Pilusin (פִּילוֹסִין), meaning the name could not have been in the early Aramaic translation of Exodus and Numbers. Nevertheless, it is clear that the city was not viewed as being the historic city of Ramesses by the Judeans in the early-Christian era.

2 Codex Vaticanus: Sochôth (ⲥⲟⲭⲱⲑ)

- LXX 15: Socôth (ⲥⲟⲩⲟⲟⲑ)

- LXX 28: Occhôth (ⲟⲩⲭⲟⲟⲑ)

- LXX 82: Othom (Οθομ)

- LXX 130: Ochôth (Οχωθ)

- LXX 72: Socchôth (ⲥⲟⲩⲭⳉⲑ)

- LXX 527: Achchôth (ⲁⲭⲭⲟⲟⲑ)

- Leningrad Codex: sukkot (סֻכֹּת)

- Peshitta: skůt (ܣܟܘܬ)

- Targum Onkelos: sukkot (סֻכֹּת)

- Targum Jerusalem: sukkot (סֻכּוֹת)

- Bohairic manuscripts: Suchôuth (Cⲩⲭⲱⲩⲑ)

- Sahidic manuscripts: Sogchôuth (Coⲣⲭⲱⲩⲑ)

- Vetus Latina: Soccoth

The Septuagint and Masoretic Text both treat Sukkot as a place name, however, this is also the word for 'stables,' or 'corrals,' which implies the original text was about the Israelites retrieving their animals before leaving Egypt. In the 1800s the Biblical scholar and Egyptologist Edouard Naville identified the Hebrew word Sukkot with the ancient Egyptian word Tjeku, the name of the capital of the capital town of the Egyptian district that spanned the Wadi Tumilat during the New Kingdom Era, later called Per-Atum during the Late Period. This claim has not been endorsed by later Egyptologists, as no supporting evidence has been found.

In the Egyptian story the Voyage of Wenamen, set in the early Iron Age, the land of Canaan had been taken over by Tjeker, which appears to be the South Egyptian way of referring to worshipers of the North Egyptian creator God Atum, in reference to his temple in Tjeku. Naville's conclusions regarding Tjeku being Sukkot, may have been based on the assumption that the South Egyptians believed that the Israelites in Canaan were Atum worshipers.

3 Codex Vaticanus: Bouthan (ⲃⲟⲨⲐⲁⲛ)

- LXX 127: Southam (Coⲩⲑⲁμ)

- LXX 417: Mouthan (Moⲩⲑⲁⲛ)

- LXX 58: Boutham (βoⲩⲑⲁμ)

- LXX 426: Oytham (Oⲩⲑⲁμ)

- LXX 413: Boutha (βoⲩⲑⲁ)

- LXX 71: Bothan (βoⲑⲁⲛ)

- LXX 767: Bithan (βⲓⲑⲁⲛ)

- LXX 799: Otham (Oⲑⲁμ)

- Leningrad Codex: Etam (אֵתָם)

- Peshitta: Ǎtm (ܐܬܡ)

- Targum Onkelos: Etam (אֵתָם)

718

- Fragment Targums: Eitan (אֵיתָן)

- Targum Jerusalem: Eitam (אֵיתָם)

- Bohairic manuscripts: Buthai (Bⲩⲑⲁⲓ)

This is believed to represent 'Khetam,' one of the Egyptian fortresses that sat between the Mediterranean coast and the Gulf of Suez. In the Middle Kingdom's *Tale of Sinhue*, Sinhue reported sneaking past an Egyptian fort in the vicinity at night when he was escaping Egypt.

4 Codex Vaticanus: stoma Epirôth (ⲥⲧⲟⲙⲁⲉⲡⲓⲣⲱⲟ). Translation: mouth (or face, source) of Epiroth

- LXX 527: stoma Irôth (ⲥⲧⲟⲙⲁ ⲓⲣⲟⲟⲑ). Translation: mouth (or face, source) of Iroth

- LXX 318: stoma Êrôth (ⲥⲧⲟⲙⲁ ⲏⲣⲟⲟⲑ). Translation: mouth (or face, source) of Eroth

- LXX 58: stoma epi Airôth (ⲥⲧⲟⲙⲁ ⲉⲡⲓ ⲁⲟⲓⲣⲟⲟⲑ). Translation: mouth (or face, source) at (or near, on, upon) Airoth

- LXX 120: stoma Eirôn (ⲥⲧⲟⲙⲁ ⲉⲓⲣⲟⲟⲛ). Translation: mouth to Eiron

- LXX 529: stoma is Rôth (ⲥⲧⲟⲙⲁ ⲟⲓⲥ ⲣⲟⲟⲑ). Translation: mouth to Roth

- LXX 82: stoma Epirôth (ⲥⲧⲟⲙⲁ ⲉⲡⲟⲓⲣⲟⲟⲑ). Translation: mouth of Epiroth

- LXX 126: stoma hi Rôth (ⲥⲧⲟⲙⲁ ⲟⲓ ⲣⲟⲟⲑ). Translation: mouth (or face, source) if Roth

- Leningrad Codex: pi hachirot (פִּי הַחִירֹת). Translation: fold of the hirot

- Peshitta: pům Hårytå (ܦܘܡ ܚܪܝܬܐ). Translation: mouth (or entrance, riverbank) of Haryta

- Targum Onkelos: pum chirata (פּוּם חִירְתָא). Translation: mouth (or entrance, riverbank) of the heir (or interior)

- Fragment Targums: punedekei cheirata (פּוּנְדְקֵי חֵירָתָא). Translation: innkeepers of the heir (or interior)

- Targum Jerusalem: pumei chirata (פּוּמֵי חִירָתָא). Translation: mouth of the heir (or interior)

- Bohairic manuscripts: ro Pirôuth (ⲣⲟ Ⲡⲓⲣⲱⲩⲑ). Translation: mouth of Pirouth.

The name 'Hirot' is an ancient Egyptian word transliterated as ḥr-t, which meant both watercourse (𓇳𓏤𓈖) and Nile deposits (𓇳𓈖𓏥) depending on context. The term was generally used in the Nile Delta, where the watercourses moved regularly as sediment built up. This was most likely a reference to the mouth of the Pelusiac branch of the Nile River, the ancient eastern-most branch of the Nile.

5 Codex Vaticanus: Beelsepphôn (ΒΕΕλϹΕΠϜωΝ)

- LXX 509: Belselphôn (βϭλσϭλϛοoν)

- LXX 15: Beelsephphôn (βϭϭλσϭϛϛοoν)

- LXX 319: Beelsemphôr (βϭϭλσϭμϛοoρ)

- LXX 75: Beêlsepphôn (βϭϭλσϭμπϛοoν)

- LXX 458: Beelsepphôr (βϭϭλσϭπϛοoρ)

- LXX 246: Beelsemphôn (βϭϭλσϭμϛοoν)

- LXX 71: Beêlsepphôn (βϭʇλσϭπϛοoν)

- Leningrad Codex: Baal Tzefon (בַּעַל צְפֹן)

- Peshitta: Bôlspůn (ܒܥܠܨܦܘܢ)

- Targum Onkelos: Be'el Tzefon (בְּעֵל צְפוֹן)

- Fragment Targums: appei ta'avavta (אַפֵּי טַעֲוָותָא). Translation: cast perversions (idols)

- Targum Jerusalem: ta'avavt Tzefon (טַעֲוַות צְפוֹן). Translation: perversion of Zephon

- Bohairic manuscripts: Belsephôun (Βελϲεφωγ̄Ν)

- Sahidic manuscripts: Bersephôun (Βερϲεφωγ̄Ν)

Ba'al Zephon was a Canaanite god mentioned in the Ugaritic Texts from circa 1300 BC and considered to be the Canaanite version of Amen (Amun). The origin of the name appears to have been Mount Zephon on the modern Syrian-Turkish border at the northern-most frontier of Canaan. Its usage in Egypt appears to be based on a group of Canaanites settling in the area of Lake Bardawil on the north coast of the Sinai Peninsula, a shallow saline lake with a surface area of 147,000 acres (59,500 hectares). Ba'al Zephon continued to be worshiped in the region well into the Greek era.

The story of the sea being blown away so the Israelites could walk across it, only to return and drown the Egyptian army is reminiscent of the Greek story of the Serbonian Bog, also called Lake Serbonis, which had a deceptive appearance of looking solid but was a bog that swallowed people that tried to pass through it. The Serbonian Bog myth has been identified with Lake Bardawil since the Greeks ruled Egypt. In ancient Egyptian records, Lake Bardawil was described as a quagmire that whole armies had been swallowed up by. Given that Ba'al Zephon is identified in this chapter, and is known to refer to Lake Bardawil, it is clear that this unusual event took place in Lake Bardawil, and not in the Red Sea, as later writers assumed.

6 Codex Vaticanus: Magdôlou (ⲘⲀⲄⲆⲱⲖⲞⲨ)

- LXX 318: Magdolou (Μάγδολου)

- LXX 129: Macdôlou (Μάκδωλου)

- LXX 426: Magdalou (Μάγδαλου)

- Leningrad Codex: Migdol (מִגְדֹּל). Translation: tower, fortification, platform

- Peshitta: Mgdůl (ܡܓܕܘܠ)

- Targum Onkelos: Migdol (מִגְדֹּל)

- Targum Jerusalem: Migdol (מִגְדּוֹל)

- Bohairic manuscripts: Magdôulôun (ⲘⲀⲄⲆⲱⲨⲖⲱⲨⲚ)

- Sahidic manuscripts: Magdôun (ⲘⲀⲄⲆⲱⲨⲚ)

A Ptolemaic-era geographical text housed at the Cairo Museum lists four border fortresses along the Greek-era Arsinoe Canal, including Migdol and Ba'al Zephon. It seems likely these later fortresses were named after the fortresses in the Torah, which the Ptolemys had paid to have translated at the Library of Alexandria. Most scholars associate Migdol with El Qantara, a city that today lays along the Suez Canal, between the Mediterranean Port Said and the Bitter Lakes. This location is possible, however, the term is generic enough that any fortified tower may be indicated. In the Egyptian Middle Kingdom Era Tale of Sinhue, the hero Sinhue also described passing a fortification between the Nile and the Bitter Lakes as he fled Egypt, which suggests whatever the fortification was, it had been there for centuries by the time the Israelites passed it.

7 Codex Vaticanus: Picriaes (ⲠⲒⲔⲢⲒⲀⲓⲤ). Translation: bitter

- LXX 120: Picrias (Πικρίας)

- Leningrad Codex: Marah (מָרָה). Translation: bile

- Peshitta: můrt (ܡܘܪܬ)

- Targum Onkelos: Marah (מָרָה). Translation: bile

- Fragment Targums: Marah (מָרָה). Translation: bile

- Targum Jerusalem: Marah (מָרָה). Translation: bile

The Greek translation of this locale in Exodus both transliterated mrh (מרה) as Merrha (Μερρα), and translated it as picria (πικρια). In Numbers, they just translated the word as picriaes (πικρίαις) meaning 'bitter.' The location of this bitter water has been debated and is largely dependent on where the events involving the Papyrus Sea and Mount Sinai took place. This list of locations does mention the Israelites crossing the sea after reaching Ba'al Zephon but does not name the sea. The 'Erythrean Sea' was only mentioned later when it was mentioned the second time in Exodus. Based on the 'Papyrus Sea' event being at Lake Bardawil, the bitter waters would likely be the Bitter Lakes, halfway between the Mediterranean coast and the Gulf of Suez. The larger of the two Bitter Lakes, the Great Bitter Lake had dried out completely by the time the Suez Canal was constructed, which now connects these two lakes, as well as linking them to the Mediterranean and Gulf of Suez. The Pyramid Texts, which date back to the Old Kingdom era, mention the Great Bitter Lake, implying the existence of one or more Small Bitter Lake(s), and therefore the name is very ancient, long preceding the era of Moses.

It seems improbable that there would have been another area of bitter waters in the region that the Egyptians somehow never noticed through thousands of years of occupation, and therefore, the Bitter Lakes are almost certainly the place being described in this chapter. If this interpretation is correct, it would mean the Israelites started moving east along the coastal road to Canaan, and then turned back and headed south into the Sinai after leaving Lake Bardawil.

8 Codex Vaticanus: Ailim (ΑΙΛΙΜ)

- Codex Colberto-Sarravianus: Elim (ЄΛЄΙΜ)

- LXX 509: Salin (cΔΛ6ιɴ)

- LXX 84: Aelêm (ΔιΛɦμ)

- LXX 318: Elim (Єλιμ)

- LXX 82: Alim (ΔΛ6ιμ)

- LXX 458: Selim (c6Λ6ιμ)

- LXX 767: Selim (c6Λιμ)

- LXX 799: Elêm (ЄΛɦμ)

- Leningrad Codex: Eilim (אֵילִם)

- Peshitta: Åylm (ܐܠܝܡ)

- Targum Onkelos: Eilim (אֵילִם)

- Fragment Targums: Eilimah (אֵילִימָה)

- Targum Jerusalem: Eilim (אֵילִם)

- Bohairic manuscript Vatican Coptic 1: Ulim (Ⲩⲗⲓⲙ)

- Bohairic manuscript BnF Coptic 1: Elim (Ⲉⲗⲓⲙ)

- Sahidic manuscripts: Elim (Ⲉⲗⲓⲙ)

The location of Elim is debated, like the other stations along the route the Israelites took out of Egypt. Its location is largely based on the assumptions about the events of the Papyrus Sea, the location of the Bitter Waters, and ultimately the location of the Wilderness of Sin and Mount Sinai. It is traditionally identified by Muslims as the Oyun Musa (عيون موسى), meaning 'Moses Spring' in the western Sinai Peninsula, where there are twelve ancient wells. It is not clear when the location was named, and it is plausible that this location was named after Moses by Emperor Constantine's mother, Helena Augusta, when she named Mount Sinai and the Sinai Peninsula in the 330s AD. As the Greek translators did not identify the town, it could not have been widely known as the 'Moses Spring' circa 250 BC. Another theory is the Elim may have referred to the Wadi Gharandel in the Sinai Peninsula, again this is based on the theory that Exodus' Mount Sinai was the large mountain range named Sinai by Helena Augusta in the 330s AD.

If the Israelites were trying to leave Egypt, and one would assume Moses was leading them towards Midian, where he first encountered the fire-angel, then the logical direction was east following the southern road across the Sinai Peninsula, which runs east from the Bitter Lakes to the modern town of An-Nekhel in central Sinai, before continuing on to mountains of Hashem El Tarif in eastern Sinai. An-Nekhel is known to have been used as a watering hole along the southern road since Pharaonic times. It is postulated to have been a Canaanite town, founded during the Hyksos era, named after the Canaanite goddess Nikkal-wa-Ib, meaning 'Great lady of the Fruitful,' who was the goddess of orchards. If this theory is correct, then there must have been a settlement with orchards in the region, matching to some degree the Exodus' description of a place of wells and trees.

9 Codex Vaticanus: Raphaca (Ραφακα)

- Codex Alexandrinus: Raphacan (Ραφακαν)

- Codex Venetus: Rapha (Ραφϻα)

- LXX 58: Raphacae (Ραφαϰαι)

- LXX 120: Racapha (Ραϰαφα)

- LXX 343: Raphac (Ραφαϰ)

- LXX 29: Raphaen (Ραφαϭιν)

- LXX 767: Daphaca (Δαφαϰα)

- LXX 321: Raphec (Ραφϭϰ)

- Leningrad Codex: Dafekah (דָּפְקָה). Generally transliterated as Dophkah

- Peshitta: Rpqå (ܪܦܩܐ)

- Targum Onkelos: Dafekah (דִּפְקָה)

- Targum Jerusalem: Dafekah (דִּפְקָה)

- Sahidic manuscripts: Daphaga (Δαφαγα)

The town of Dophkah is believed to have been near modern Elat, on the coast of the Gulf of Aqaba. The difference in the spelling of the names found in the Greek and Syriac translations, versus the Hebrew and Coptic translations likely originated in either the Canaanite (Judahite or Samaritan) or early Aramaic translations, as both the Canaanite D (𐤃) and R (𐤓), and Aramaic D (𐡃) and R (𐡓) were similar in shape.

10 Codex Vaticanus: Raphidin (Ραφιδιν)

- LXX 426: Raphidim (Ραφιδιμ)

- LXX 616: Raphadin (Ραφααϭιν)

- LXX 75: Raphidên (Ραφιδην)

- LXX 761: Raphidim (Ραφιαϭιμ)

- LXX 767: Raphiadin (Ραφιααϭιν)

- LXX 416: Raphêdin (Ραφηδιν)

- Leningrad Codex: Refidim (רְפִידִם)

- Peshitta: Rpydyn (ܪܦܝܕܝܢ)

- Targum Onkelos: Refidim (רְפִידִם)

- Targum Jerusalem: Refidim (רְפִידִים)

- Bohairic manuscripts: Raphazin (Ραφαζιν)

- Sahidic manuscripts: Raphidin (Ραφιδιν)

This location is generally associated with the Wadi Feiran, or the Feiran Oasis within it. The Wadi Feiran is an 81-mile (130 km) long wadi (seasonal river) which runs down the Jebel Musa to the Gulf of Suez. The Feiran Oasis, also called El Hesweh, is approximately 3 miles (4.8 km) long, and generally habitable year-round. The Greek geographer and polymath Claudius Ptolemy identified this as the location of Paran from the Torah, which is likely where the Arabic name came from.

The assumption that Wadi Feiran is Rephidim is again predicated on Jebel Musa being Mount Sinai, or at least in the vicinity of Mount Sinai, however, if Horeb is Sinai, then Sinai would have to be near or in Midian, as that was where Moses first encountered the fire-messenger that sent him back to Egypt, and a location in southern Sinai seems highly improbable for a Midianite shepherd, especially one trying to avoid Egyptians, who were mining in the region.

If the Israelites had followed the southern road across the Sinai Peninsula en route to Mount Sinai/Horeb/Seir, they would have passed the An-Nekhel in central Sinai, and then proceeded east to the mountains of Hashem El Tarif in eastern Sinai, before following the Arabah north towards Jebel al-Madhbah. The likely location of this event along the route is at Hashem El Tarif, which did at one point have a spring flowing down from the top of the summit. The location of Rephidim at Hashem El Tarif is supported by the subsequent attack of the Amalekites, who, according to the Book of Numbers lived in the Negev, south of Judea, which is directly north of Hashem El Tarif.

Numbers: Chapter 34

The Lord said to Moses, "Order the children of Israel, 'You are entering into the land of Canaan. It will be an inheritance for you, the land of Canaan with its boundaries. Your southern border will be from the Wilderness of Sin to the border of Edom, and your southern border will be on the edge of the Dead Sea[1] in the east. Your border will go around you from the south to the ascent of Akrabbim, and will proceed by Ennac, and will follow southward to Kadesh Barnea, and it will go out to the village of Arad and will proceed by Azmon. The border will span from Azmon to the river of Egypt,[2] and the sea will be the end. You have your border on the sea, the Mediterranean Sea[3] will be the boundary. This will be for you the border on the west.'"

"This will be your northern border. From the Mediterranean Sea, you will measure for yourselves, by the side of the mountain. You will measure for yourselves the mountain from Mount Nur at the entrance into Hama, and the termination of it will be the frontiers of Sarada.[4] The border will go out to As-Safira,[5] and its termination will be at Hazar-enan.[6] This will be your border from the north. You will measure for yourselves the eastern border from Hazar-enan to the treeless land.[7] The border will go down the treeless land to Rablah[8] eastward to the fountains, and the border will go down from Rablah behind the Sea of Galilee[9] in the east. The border will go down the Jordan, and the end will be the Dead Sea. This will be your land and its borders around it."

Moses ordered the children of Israel, "This is the land which you will inherit by lot, even as the Lord commanded us to give it to the nine tribes and the half-tribe of Manasseh. The tribe of the children of Reuben, and the tribe of the children of Gad have received their inheritance according to the houses of their families, and the half-tribe of Manasseh have received their inheritances. Two tribes and half a tribe have received their inheritance beyond Jordan by Jericho to the southeast."

The Lord said to Moses, "These are the names of the men who will assign the land before you as an inheritance: Eleazar the priest and Joshua the son of Nun. You will take one ruler from each tribe to divide the land to you by lot. These are the names of the men:"

"From the tribe of Judah: Caleb the son of Jephunneh."

"From the tribe of Simeon: Shelumiel the son of Ammihud."

"From the tribe of Benjamin: Elidad the son of Kislon."

"From the tribe of Dan, the prince was Bukki the son of Jogli."

"From the sons of Joseph, among the tribe of the sons of Manasseh, the prince was Hanniel the son of Oufi, and from the tribe of the sons of Ephraim, the prince was Kemuel the son of Shiphtan."

"From the tribe of Zebulun, the prince was Elizaphan the son of Parnach."

"From the tribe of the sons of Issachar, the prince was Paltiel the son of Azzan."

"From the tribe of the children of Asher, the prince was Ahihud the son of Shelomi."

"From the tribe of Naphtali, the prince was Pedahel the son of Ammihud."

The Lord commanded these to distribute the inheritances to the children of Israel in the land of Canaan.

Numbers: Chapter 34 Notes

1 Codex Vaticanus: thalassês tês alycês (ΘΑΛΑCCHCΤHCΑΛΥΚHC). Translation: sea of salt (the modern Dead Sea)

• LXX 799: alycês thalassês (ἀλυκὴc θαλάσσηc). Translation: Salt Sea (the modern Dead Sea)

• LXX 416: thalattês tês halycês (θαλάττηc τὴc ἀλυκὴc). Translation: sea of salt (the modern Dead Sea)

• Leningrad Codex: yam-hammelach (יָם־הַמֶּלַח). Translation: sea of salt (the modern Dead Sea)

• Peshitta: ymå dmlhå (ܝܡܐ ܕܡܠܚܐ). Translation: sea of salt (the modern Dead Sea)

• Targum Onkelos: yamma demilcha (יַמָּא דְמִלְחָא). Translation: sea of salt (the modern Dead Sea)

• Fragment Targums: yama demilcha (יְמָא דְמִלְחָא). Translation: sea of salt (the modern Dead Sea)

2 Codex Vaticanus: chimarrhoun Aegyptou (ⲬⲈⲒⲘⲀⲢⲢⲞⲨⲚⲀⲒⲄⲨⲠⲦⲞⲨ). Translation: river of Egypt

• Codex Colberto-Sarravianus: chimarrhou Aegyptou (ⲬⲈⲒⲘⲀⲢⲢⲞⲨⲀⲒⲄⲨⲠⲦⲞⲨ). Translation: river of Egypt

• Codex Alexandrinus: chimarrhon Aigyptou (ⲬⲈⲒⲘⲀⲢⲢⲞⲚⲀⲒⲄⲨⲠⲦⲞⲨ). Translation: river of Egypt

• LXX 509: chimarrhoun Aigyptoun (χϭιμαⲛⲢⲢουⲛ Ⲁⲓⲅυπτουⲛ)

• LXX 127: chimarrhou Aigyptou (χιμⲀⲢⲢου Ⲁⲓⲅⲱⲡτου)

• LXX 392: chimarrhon Aigyptou (χιμⲀⲢⲢоⲛ Ⲁⲓⲅⲱⲡτου)

• LXX 30: chimaron Aigyptou (χϭιμⲀⲢоⲛ Ⲁⲓⲅⲱⲡτου)

• LXX 58: chimarrhou Aigyptou (χϭιμⲀⲢⲢου Ⲁⲓⲅⲱⲡτου). Translation: river of Egypt

• LXX 343: chimaron Aigyptou (χιμⲀⲢоⲛ Ⲁⲓⲅⲱⲡτου)

• LXX 72: chimarou Aigyptou (χϭιμⲀⲢου Ⲁⲓⲅⲱⲡτου)

• LXX 19: chimarrhoun ex Aigyptou (χϭιμⲁⲛⲢⲢουⲛ ϭ⳩ Ⲁⲓⲅⲱⲡτου). Translation: river on Egypt

• Leningrad Codex: nachlah Mitzrayim (נַחְלָה מִצְרָיִם). Translation: territory of Egyptians

• Peshitta: nhlå dmsryn (ܢܚܠܐ ܕܡܨܪܝܢ). Translation: river of the Egyptians

• Targum Onkelos: nachala deMitzrayim (נַחְלָא דְמִצְרָיִם). Translation: river of Egyptians

• Jerusalem Targum: Nilos Mitzrayim (נִילוֹס מִצְרָיִם). Translation: Nile of Egypt

• Jonathan Targum: Nilos deMitzra'ei (נִילוֹס דְמִצְרָאֵי). Translation: Nile of the Egyptians

This river was accepted as the Nile in ancient Hebrew and Aramaic interpretations, including the Jerusalem and Jonathan Targums.

3 Codex Vaticanus: thalassês tês megalês (ⲐⲀⲀⲀⲤⲤⲎⲤ ⲦⲎⲤ ⲘⲈⲄⲀⲀⲎⲤ). Translation: sea the great (or Mediterranean Sea)

• Leningrad Codex: hayyam haggadovl (הַיָּם הַגָּדוֹל). Translation: the sea the great

• Peshitta: ymå rbå (ܝܡܐ ܪܒܐ). Translation: sea great (or Mediterranean Sea)

- Targum Onkelos: yamma rabba (יַמָּא רַבָּא). Translation: sea great (or Mediterranean Sea)

- Fragment Targums: yama rabba (יְמָא רַבָּא). Translation: sea great (or Mediterranean Sea)

- Targum Jerusalem: yama rabba (יְמָא רַבָּא). Translation: sea great (or Mediterranean Sea)

4 Codex Vaticanus: Asadac (ᴀᴄᴀᴅᴀᴋ)

- Codex Colberto-Sarravianus: Sarada (ᴄᴀᴘᴀᴅᴀ)

- Codex Alexandrinus: Sadadac (ᴄᴀᴅᴀᴅᴀᴋ)

- Codex Ambrosiano A 147: Saradac (ᴄᴀᴘᴀᴅᴀᴋ)

- Codex Venetus: Sardach (ᴄᴀρᴀᴅχ)

- LXX 28: Sadac (ᴄᴅᴅᴅ𝗹)

- LXX 121: Sasadac (ᴄᴅσᴅᴅᴅ𝗹)

- LXX 127: Asaraddac (ᴀσᴅρᴅᴅᴅᴅ𝗹)

- LXX 318: o Adadac (o ᴀᴅᴅᴅᴅ𝗹). Translation: the Adadac.

- LXX 319: Aradac (ᴀρᴅᴅᴅ𝗹)

- LXX 30: Sardac (ᴄᴀρᴅᴅ𝗹)

- LXX 343: Saddac (ᴄᴅᴅᴅᴅ𝗹)

- LXX 56: Sadada (ᴄᴅᴅᴅᴅᴅ)

- LXX 422 Sedac (ᴄ6ᴅᴅ𝗹)

- LXX 59: Caddac (κᴅᴅᴅᴅ𝗹)

- Leningrad Codex: Tzedadah (צְדָדָה). Generally transliterated as Zedad.

- Peshitta: Ṣdd (ܨܕܕ)

- Targum Onkelos: Tzedad (צְדָד)

- Jerusalem Targum: Avvlas deKilka'ei (אַוְולָס דְקִילְקָאֵי). Translation: Awwlas of the Cilicians

- Jonathan Targum: Avelas deKilka'ei (אֲבְלָס דְקִילְקָאֵי). Translation: Abelas of the

Cilicians

- Bohairic manuscripts: Ararad (ⲁⲣⲁⲣⲁⲇ)

- Sahidic manuscripts: Sadarak (Ⲥⲁⲇⲁⲣⲁⲕ)

This is theorized as being the inland Syrian town of Sedad (صدد), east of northern Lebanon, however, Sarada was listed as being coastal, and therefore could not be Sedad. Based on the previous mention of Mount Nur and the city of Hama, Zedad was likely on the Mediterranean coast south of modern Samandagi, where both the Orontes River, which flows through Hama, and the Karusu River which flows down from the Nur mountains, empty in the Mediterranean. The interpretations found in the Targums generally placed it in Cilicia, northwest of the Nur Mountains.

5 Codex Vaticanus: Dephrôna (ⲇⲉⲫⲣⲱⲛⲁ)

- Codex Ambrosiano A 147: Zephrôna (ⲍⲉⲫⲣⲱⲛⲁ)

- Codex Venetus: Phrôna (ⲫⲣⲟⲟⲛⲁ)

- LXX 121: Zebrôna (ⲍⲟⲩⲫⲟⲟⲛⲁ)

- LXX 318: Zephrona (ⲍⲟⲟⲫⲟⲟⲛⲁ)

- LXX 707: Ephrôna (ⲉⲫⲫⲟⲟⲛⲁ)

- LXX 58: Sephrôna (ⲥⲟⲟⲫⲟⲟⲛⲁ)

- LXX 107: Ephônna (ⲉⲫⲟⲟⲛⲛⲁ)

- LXX 59: Ezephrôna (ⲉⲍⲟⲟⲫⲟⲟⲛⲁ)

- LXX 376: Ephrôn (ⲉⲫⲫⲟⲟⲛ)

- LXX 610: Ephrônna (ⲉⲫⲫⲟⲟⲛⲛⲁ)

- Leningrad Codex: Zifronah (זִפְרֹֽנָה)

- Peshitta: Zprŭn (ܙܦܪܘܢ)

- Targum Onkelos: Zifron (זִפְרֹן)

- Jerusalem Targum: Zafeirin (זְפֵירִין)

- Jonathan Targum: keren zechuta (קְרֵן זְכוּתָא). Translation: town of Zekuta

- Bohairic manuscripts: Sephrôna (Ⲥⲉⲫⲣⲱⲛⲁ)

- Sahidic manuscripts: Ephôunan (Ⲉⲫⲱⲩⲛⲁⲛ)

According to the Talmud, Rabbi Akiva ben Yosef lived in a Syrian town named As-Safira in the 1st century, which has subsequently been identified as the town of As-Safira (السفيرة) in northern Syria. Jerome called this town Zephyrium in the 4th century, and also identified it as the northern boundary of Canaan. It is unclear when As-Safira was founded, however, in 750 BC, a treaty was signed there now known as Sfire Treaty I, which listed a number of gods, including El Elyon (Highest God). This seems to confirm it is the town the Hebrews at the time called Ziphron, and therefore the name As-Safira is used.

6 Codex Vaticanus: Arsenaem (ΑΡϹΕΝΑΕΙΜ)

• Codex Colberto-Sarravianus: Asernaen (ΑϹΕΡΝΑΕΙΝ)

• Codex Venetus: Arsenaen (Αρϭναϭιν)

• LXX 407: Asernaem (Αϭϭρναϭιμ)

• LXX 527: Hasernaen (Αϭϭρναφν)

• LXX 64: Arsenaen (Αρϭναιν)

• LXX 707: Asenaem (Αϭϭναϭιμ)

• LXX 127: Arernaen (Αρϭρναϭιν)

• LXX 58: Asernaên (Αϭϭρναℓν)

• LXX 73: Arsernaen (Αρϭϭρναϭιν)

• LXX 426: Asarênan (Αϭαρℓναν)

• LXX 500: Sernaen (Cϭρναϭιν)

• LXX 56: Asernaam (Αϭϭρνααμ)

• LXX 29: Arsenasi (Αρϭναϭοι)

• LXX 72: Asernaê (Αϭϭρναℓ)

• LXX 82: Aserena (Αϭϭρϭνα)

• LXX 618: Arsenae (Αρϭναι)

• LXX 528: Sernaem (Cϭρναϭιμ)

- LXX 68: Asenaen (ᴀⲟⲋⲛⲁⲋⲓⲛ)

- LXX 610: Aseraen (ᴀⲟⲋⲣⲁⲓⲛ)

- LXX 619: Arsernaen (ᴀⲣⲟⲋⲣⲛⲁⲓⲛ)

- Leningrad Codex: Chatzar einan (חֲצַ֥ר עֵינָֽן). Generally Transliterated as Hazar-enan.

- Peshitta: Hsr ôynn (ܚܣܪ ܥܝܢܢ)

- Targum Onkelos: Chatzar einan (חֲצַר עֵינָן)

- Fragment Targums: yrat Aynuta (יְרַת עֵיְינוּתָא). Translation: gift (or dowry) of Ayynutah

- Targum Jerusalem: Chiraya deveit Sachal velimtzi'ut darata rabbeta dImMitz'a bein tirat invevta leveit Darmashek (כִירַיָא דְבֵית סָכָל וְלִמְצִיעוּת דָרְתָא רַבְּתָא דִמְמְצָעָא בֵּין טִירַת עֵיְנְוָותָא לְבֵית דַרְמָשָׁק). Translation: Kiraya of house of Sakal and to the middle of the great court which is Misah, between the tower of Inewwtah and the house of Darmaseq

  - Bohairic manuscripts: Asernen (ⲁⲥⲉⲣⲛⲉⲛ)

  - Sahidic manuscripts: Arsenaen (ⲁⲣⲥⲉⲛⲁⲉⲛ)

The location of this settlement is unknown, however, may be Hazarin (حزارين), in the Dead Cities (المدن الميتة) in northwest Syria. The settlement seems to have been abandoned between the 6th and 10th centuries, and re-inhabited during the Ottoman era. The 2nd century Targum Jonathan rendered Hazar-enan as 'walled suburb of the springs,' meaning the rabbi Jonathan ben Uzziel, believed the location was simply a settlement on the edge of the wilderness in northern Syria.

7 Codex Vaticanus: Semphamar (ⲥⲉⲙⲫⲁⲙⲁⲣ)

- Codex Colberto-Sarravianus: Sephama (ⲥⲉⲫⲁⲙⲁ)

- Codex Ambrosiano A 147: Sepphama (ⲥⲉⲡⲫⲁⲙⲁ)

- LXX 407: Sempphamar (ⲥⲋⲙⲡⲫⲁⲙⲁⲣ)

- LXX 127: Sephamar (ⲥⲋⲫⲁⲙⲁⲣ)

- LXX 630: Sepphamar (ⲥⲋⲡⲫⲁⲙⲁⲣ)

- LXX 18: Sephamar (ⲥⲋⲫⲁⲙⲁⲣ)

- LXX 56: Semphama (ⲥⲋⲙⲫⲁⲙⲁ)

- LXX 82: Asephama (ᴀⲟⲋⲫⲁⲙⲁ)

- LXX 416: Emphamar (Ἐμϐάμάϸ)

- LXX 53: Sepphagma (Cὀπϐάγμά)

- Leningrad Codex: Shefamah (שְׁפָמָה)

- Peshitta: Špm (ܫܦܡ)

- Targum Onkelos: Shefam (שְׁפָם)

- Fragment Targums: not mentioned in the verse

- Targum Jerusalem: Afmi'ah (אַפְמִיאָה)

- Bohairic Manuscripts: Semphamar (Семфамар)

- Sahidic Manuscripts: Sepharaman (Сефараман)

The Greek translation reads like the name of a town, which has shaped how the Masoretic Text are interpreted by both Christians and Jews, however, the Hebrew term שפמ simply means treeless land, which means the eastern border was the border of the Syrian Desert (Syrian Steppe, Jordanian Steppe, Badia), much as the western border was the Mediterranean Sea. The original meaning of the term שפמ is imported from the Masoretic Text in this translation.

8 Codex Vaticanus: Arbêla (Ἀρϐηλά)

- LXX 319: Arnaen (Ἀϸνάϭ𝜄ν)

- LXX 509: Bêla (Ϭηλά)

- LXX 129: Arbêl (Ἀϸμηλ)

- LXX 82: Arbala (Ἀϸμάλά)

- LXX 799: Arbola (Ἀϸμολά)

- Leningrad Codex: Rivlah (רִבְלָה). Generally Transliterated as Riblah

- Peshitta: Dblt (ܗܒܠܬ)

- Targum Onkelos: Rivlah (רִבְלָה)

- Fragment Targums: not mentioned in the verse

- Targum Jerusalem: Defanei (דְפָנֵי)

- Sahidic manuscripts: Bêura (Ϭηγρά)

The town of Rablah (رابلة) continues to exist rear the Syrian-Lebanese border. It was a significant site throughout the history of Canaan, as it sat along the main route between the Nile and Euphrates. Pharaoh Necho II established a camp in Rablah after defeating King Josiah's army in 609 BC, en route to his battle with the Assyrians. King Nebuchadnezzar of Babylon also set up a camp there during his invasion of Judah a few decades later. As the name of the town continues to be essentially the same, the modern name Rablah is used.

9 Codex Vaticanus: thalassês chennereth (ⲐⲀⲗⲗⲀⳜⳜⲎⳜ ⲭⲈⲚⲚⲈⲢⲉⲐ). Translation: Sea of Chinnereth

- Codex Colberto-Sarravianus: thalassēs khennanerethra (ⲐⲀⲗⲗⲀⳜⳜⲎⳜ ⲭⲈⲚⲚⲀⲚⲈⲢⲉⲐⲢⲀ)

- Codex Venetus (LXX V): thalassês Chenar (θαλασσης Χϭναβ)

- LXX 509: thalassês chenara (θαλασσης Χϭναβα)

- LXX 127: thalassês chennaara (θαλασσης Χϭννααβα)

- LXX 58: thalassês Chennara (θαλασσης Χϭνναβα)

- LXX 129: thalassês Chenera (θαλασσης Χϭνϭβα)

- LXX 343: thalassês Chereth (θαλασσης Χϭβϭβϭθ)

- LXX 82: thalassês Chelaenera (θαλασσης Χϭλαινϭβα)

- LXX 417: thalassês Chereneth (θαλασσης Χϭβϭνϭθ)

- LXX 527: thalassês Chinar (θαλασσης Χϭιναβ)

- LXX 59: thalassês Chereth (θαλασσης Χϭβϭθ)

- Leningrad Codex: yam-Kinneret (יָם־כִּנֶּרֶת). Translation: Sea of Chinnereth

- Peshitta: ymå dKnrt (ܝܡܐ ܕܟܢܪܬ). Translation: Sea of Chinnereth

- Targum Onkelos: yam Ginesar (יַם גִּנֵּסָר). Translation: Sea of Ginesar

- Fragment Targums: yama deGinusar (יַמָּא דְגִינוֹסָר). Translation: Sea of Ginusar

- Targum Jerusalem: yama diGneisar (יַמָּא דְגֵנֵיסָר). Translation: Sea of Gnesar

- Bohairic manuscripts: Iom Khenara (ⲓⲟⲙ ⲬⲉⲚⲀⲢⲀ). Translation: sea of Khenara

- Sahidic manuscripts: Eiom Khennara (ⲉⲓⲟⲙ ⲬⲉⲚⲚⲀⲢⲀ)

All of the variations found in the Greek, Hebrew, Syriac, Aramaic, and Coptic translations, are accepted as referring the Sea of Galilee, also called Lake Tiberius, on the modern Israeli-Golan Heights border. The oldest historically attested name for the lake and surrounding regions was 'Kinneret' which is found in Masoretic Numbers and Joshua, and also the Ugaritic texts and Egyptian records from the late bronze age, as well as the Peshitta. There was a major city in the region which is believed to have been the origin of the name. The earliest surviving record of it, was in the Annals of Thutmose III, from the 15th century BC, where it was known as Knnårtů (𓈖𓄿𓏏𓂧𓃭) in Egyptian during Egypt's rule of the region during the New Kingdom era, and Knrt (𐎋𐎐𐎗𐎚) in Ugaritic Canaanite from the same era. The variations of the name 'Chennereth' are accepted as a direct Greek transliteration of the names in the text they translated. From the Neo-Assyrian era onward, the sea was known as the Sea of Glyl (𐎁𐎍𐎍), which became Galilaeas (Γαλιλαίας) in Greek, the source of the modern English name Galilee. Under Roman rule it was renamed Lake Tiberius, however, became known as 'Ginesar' (גְּנֵּיסָר) in late-Classical Palestinian-Aramaic. The fact that Numbers and Joshua use the name that is otherwise only found in bronze age texts, support the antiquity of some of some sections of these books.

Numbers: Chapter 35

The Lord said to Moses to the west of Moab by Jordan near Jericho, "Give orders to the children of Israel, and they will give to the Levites cities to live in from the lots of their possession, and they will give to the Levites the suburbs of the cities around them. The cities will be for them to live in, and their districts will be for their livestock and all their beasts. The suburbs of the cities which you will give to the Levites will be from the wall of the city and out 2000 cubits around it. You will measure outside the city on the east side 2000 cubits, and on the south side 2000 cubits, and on the west side 2000 cubits, and on the north side 2000 cubits, and your city will be among this, and the suburbs of the cities as described."

"You will give the cities to the Levites, the six cities of refuge which you will give for the slayer to flee there, and in addition to these, forty-two cities. You will give to the Levites in all forty-eight cities, them and their suburbs. As for the cities which you will give out of the possession of the children of Israel, from those that have much you will give much, and from those that have less you will give less: they will give of their cities to the Levites each one according to his inheritance which they will inherit."

The Lord said to Moses, "Speak to the children of Israel, and you will tell them, 'You are to cross over Jordan into the land of Canaan. You will appoint to yourselves cities: they will be for you cities of refuge for the slayer to flee to, everyone who has struck a life unintentionally. The cities will be for you places of refuge from him that as relative represents the blood, and the slayer will not die until he stands before the community for judgment. The cities which you will assign, including the six cities, will be places of refuge for you. You will assign three cities on the other side of Jordan, and you will assign three cities in the land of Canaan. It will be a place of refuge for the children of Israel, and the stranger, and he that travels among you. These cities will be as a place of refuge for everyone to flee there who has unintentionally killed a man. If he should hit him with an iron instrument, and the man should die, he is a murderer, let the murderer be put to death. If he hits him with a stone thrown by his hand, which can kill a man, and he dies, he is a murderer, let the murderer be put to death. If he should hit him with an instrument of wood from his hand, which can kill a man, and he dies, he is a murderer, let the murderer be put to death."

"The avenger of blood himself will kill the murderer when he will meet him he will kill him. If he stabs him viciously or throws anything on him from an ambuscade, and the man dies, or if he hits him with his hand in anger, and the man dies, let the man that hit him be put to death, he is a murderer. Let the murderer be put to death. The avenger of blood will kill the murderer when he meets him. But if he should stab him suddenly, not viciously, or throw any vessel or weapon at him, not from an ambuscade, or hit him with any stone accidentally, and he dies, but he was not his enemy, nor wanted to hurt him, then the assembly will judge between the hitter and the avenger of blood, according to these judgments. The community will rescue the slayer from the avenger of blood, and the community will restore him to his city of refuge, to what place he fled for refuge, and he will live there until the death of the high priest, whom they anointed with the holy oil. But if the slayer should in any way go outside the limits of the city to which he fled for refuge, and the avenger of blood finds him, and the avenger of blood should kill the slayer, and he is not guilty."

"Let him remain in the city of refuge until the high priest dies, and after the death of the high priest, the slayer will return to his own land. These things will be for you for an ordinance of judgment throughout your generations in all your dwellings. Whoever takes a life, you will kill the murderer by the testimony of witnesses, and one witness will not testify against a mind that he should die. You will not accept ransoms for life from a murderer who is worthy of death, and he will be certainly put to death. You will not accept a ransom to excuse his fleeing to the city of refuge, so that he should again live in the land, until the death of the high priest. So will you not pollute the land in which you live with murder. This blood pollutes the land, and the land will not be purged from the bloodshed on it, but by the blood of he that shed it. You will not defile the land on which you live, on which I live among you. I am the Lord living among the children of Israel."

Numbers: Chapter 36

The heads of the tribe of the sons of Gilead the son of Makir the son of Manasseh, of the tribe of the sons of Joseph, came near and spoke to Moses and before Eleazar the priest, and before the heads of the houses of the families of the children of Israel: and they said, "The Lord commanded our lord to render the land of inheritance by lot to the children of Israel, and the Lord appointed our lord to give the inheritance of Zelophehad our brother to his daughters. They will become wives in one of the tribes of the children of Israel, so their inheritance will be taken away from the possession of our fathers, and will be added to the inheritance of the tribe into which the women will marry, and will be taken away from the portion of our inheritance. If there will be a release of the children of Israel, then will their inheritance be added to the inheritance of the tribe into which the women marry, and their inheritance will be taken away from the inheritance of our family's tribe."

Moses ordered the children of Israel by the commandment of the Lord, "The tribe of the children of Joseph says this. 'This is the thing which the Lord has appointed the daughters of Zelophehad, when he said, 'Let them be wives where they please,' only let them marry men of their father's tribe. So the inheritance will not go among the children of Israel from tribe to tribe, for the children of Israel will be cemented each in the inheritance of his family's tribe. Whatever daughter is an heiress to a property of the tribes of the children Israel, such women will be married each to one of her father's tribe, that the sons of Israel may each inherit the property of his father's tribe. The inheritance will not go about from one tribe to another, but the children of Israel will steadfastly continue each in his own inheritance.'"

As the Lord commanded Moses, so they did to the daughters of Zelophehad. So Tirzah, and Hoglah, and Milcah, and Noah, and Malaa, the daughters of Zelophehad, married their cousins, and they were married to men of the tribe of Manasseh of the sons of Joseph, and their inheritance was attached to the tribe of their father's family. These are the commandments, and the ordinances, and the judgments, which the Lord commanded by the hand of Moses, at the west of Moab, at Jordan by Jericho.

Deuteronomy: Chapter 1

These are the words which Moses[1] said to all of Israel on this side of the Jordan in the desert towards the west near the Sea of Edom,[2] between Paran,[3] (and Meson),[4] Tophel,[5] and Laban,[6] and Aulon,[7] and the gold works.[8] It is a journey of eleven days from Horeb[9] past Mount Seir[10] to Kadesh Barnea.[11] In the fortieth year, in the eleventh month, on the first day of the month, Moses spoke to all the children of Israel and told them all the things which the Lord[12] commanded him for them. After he had destroyed Sihon king of the Amorites who lived in Heshbon, and Og the king of Bashan who lived in Ashteroth and Edrei.

Beyond Jordan in the land of Moab, Moses began to declare this law, saying, "Lord the god[13] spoke to us in Horeb, saying, 'Let it be enough for you to live so long in this mountain. Turn and leave, and enter into the mountain of the Amorites, and go to all that live near Arabah,[14] to the mountain and the plain and to the south, and the land of the Canaanites near the sea, and Anti-lebanon, as far as the great river, the river Euphrates. See, delivered before you is the land, go in and inherit the land, which I swore to your fathers, Abraham, Isaac, and Jacob, to give it to them and to their descendants after them.'"

I said to you at that time, "I will not be able to bear you by myself. Lord the god has multiplied you, and, Look, today you are as many as the stars in the sky. Lord the god of your fathers increased you a thousand-fold more than you are and bless you as he has said to you. How will I alone be able to bear your labor, and your burden, and your disputes? Give to yourselves wise and understanding and prudent men from your tribes, and I will set your leaders over you."

You answered me, "That which you have told us to do is good."

So I took from you wise and understanding and prudent men, and I set them to rule over you as rulers of thousands, and rulers of hundreds, and rulers of fifties, and rulers of tens, and scribes to your judges. I ordered your judges at that time, "Hear cases between your brothers and judge rightly between a man and his brother, and the stranger that is with him. You will not have respect to a face in judgment, you will judge equally between small and great. You will not shrink from before the person of a man, for the judgment is God's. Whatever matter will be too hard for you, you will bring it to me, and I will hear it.

I ordered you at that time all the commands which you will perform. We departed from Horeb, and went through all that great and terrible wilderness, which you saw, by the way of the mountain of the Amorite, as our Lord the god ordered us, and we came as far as Kadesh Barnea. I said to you, "You have come as far as the mountain of the Amorite, which our Lord the god gives to you. Look, Lord the god has delivered to us the land ahead of you. Go in and inherit it as Lord the god of your fathers said to you. Don't be afraid, nor be fearful."

You all came to me, and said, "Let us send men before us, and let them go up to the land for us, and let them bring back to us a report of the way by which we will go up, and of the cities into which we will enter."

The suggestion pleased me, and I took of you twelve men, one man per tribe. They left and went up to the mountain, and they came as far as the valley of the cluster and surveyed it. They took in their hands of the fruit of the land, and brought it to you, and said, "The land is good which our Lord the god gives us."

Yet you would not go in but rebelled against the words of our Lord the god. You murmured in your tents, and said, "Because the Lord hated us, he has brought us out of the land of Egypt to deliver us into the hands of the Amorites, to destroy us. To what place do we go?"

Your brothers drew away your heart, saying, "It is a great nation and populous, and mightier than we, and there are cities great and walled up to the sky. Moreover, we saw there the sons of the Anaks."[15]

I said to you, "Don't be afraid, or be fearful of them, Lord the god is in front of you, he will fight against them together with you effectually, according to all that he worked for you in the land of Egypt, and in this wilderness which you saw, by the way of the mountain of the Amorite. How Lord the god will carry you as a nursling, like any man would nurse his child, along all the way which you have traveled until you have come to this place. In this matter you did not believe our Lord the god, who goes before you along the way to find you a place, guiding you in fire by night, showing you the way by which you go, and a cloud by day."

The Lord heard the sound of your words, and being greatly provoked he swore, "Not one of these men will see this good land, which I swore to their fathers, except Caleb the son of Jephunneh. He will see it, and to him, I will give the land on which he went up, and to his sons, because he obeyed closely the will of the Lord."

The Lord was angry with me for your sake, saying, "Neither will you by any means enter there. Joshua the son of Nun, who stands by you, he will enter in there. You strengthen him, for he will cause Israel to inherit it. Every young child who this day knows not good or evil, they will enter there, and to them, I will give it, and they will inherit it."

You turned and marched into the wilderness, in the way along the Red Sea. You answered and said, "We have sinned before our Lord the god. We will go up and fight according to all that our Lord the god has commanded us, and having taken everyone his weapons of war, and being gathered together, you went up to the mountain."

The Lord said to me, "Tell them, 'You will not go up and fight, for I am not with you, so you will not be destroyed before your enemies."

I spoke to you, and you did not listen to me, and you transgressed the commandment of the Lord, and you forced your way and went up into the mountain. The Amorites who lived in that mountain came out to meet you and chased you like bees do, and slaughtered you from Seir to Hormah. You sat down and wept before our Lord the god, and the Lord did not listen to your voice, neither did he pay attention to you. You lived in Kadesh many days, as many days as you lived there.

Deuteronomy: Chapter 1 Notes

1 Codex Vaticanus: Môysês (ⲘⲱⲨⲤⲏⲚ)

• LXX 58: Môsês (Ⲙⲟⲟⲗⲥ)

• Leningrad Codex: Mosheh (מֹשֶׁה)

• Peshitta: Mûšå (ܡܘܫܐ)

• Targum Onkelos: Mosheh (מֹשֶׁה)

• Fragment Targums: Mosheh (מֹשֶׁה)

• Targum Jerusalem: Mosheh (מֹשֶׁה)

• Codex Lugdunensis (LV 100): Moyses ex ore domini. Translation: Moses from the lord

• Shapira scrolls: Mšh ôl py Yhůh (𐤉𐤅𐤄𐤆 𐤆𐤋 𐤋𐤏 𐤅𐤅𐤔). Translation: Moses from (in Samaritan, or 'on top of' in Judaite and Hebrew, 'on the head' in Akkadian and Babylonian) mouth of Yhůh

It is generally accepted that at some point before the Septuagint was translated, half of Moses' name was redacted from the text. This theory is based on the similarity of the Egyptian term msî (𓄟𓇋), meaning 'give birth to,' or 'created by,' which was a common element of Egyptian names. Many kings of Egypt were known as the 'msî' of a god, including Ramses (𓇋𓄟𓇋), Ahmose (𓇏𓄟𓇋), Tuthmose (𓅝𓄟𓇋), Amenmose (𓇋𓏠𓈖 𓄟𓇋), and Ptahmose (𓏤𓇋𓄟𓇋𓏤). A theory that has been circulating since at least the time of Josephus in the 1st century AD, is that Moses' original name was Hapymoses, meaning the 'Nile created him.' If this is the origin of the name, the name of the god that created Moses was likely dropped from the name very early in Israelite history, as there are no known surviving texts with the full name. The latest this is likely to have happened would have been during the Aramaic translation of King Hezekiah, however, it may have happened much earlier. An alternate interpretation is that the name is complete, and is derived from the Egyptian term mů-šâô (𓈗𓈘𓈖𓈖), meaning 'beginning on water,' which appears to be what the princess stated in Exodus, when she found Moses and named him.

2 Codex Vaticanus: en tê erêmô pros dysmaes plêsion tês Erythras (ΕΝ ΤΗ ΕΡΗΜѠ ΠΡΟϹ ΔΥϹΜΑΙϹ ΠΛΗϹΙΟΝ ΤΗϹ ΕΡΥΘΡΑϹ). Translation: in the undefended (or abandoned, void, lonely) towards west near Erythras (or Red)

• LXX 407: en tê erêmô pros dysmas plêsion tês erythras (ϵν τη ϵρημω προς Δυσμας πλησφον της ϵρυθρας). Translation: in the undefended (or abandoned, void, lonely) towards west near Erythras (or Red)

• LXX 121: en tê gê erêmô pros dysmaes plêsion tês erythras (ϵν τη γη ϵρημω προς Δυσμαις πλησφον της ϵρυθρας). Translation: in the undefended (or abandoned, void, lonely) land towards west near Erythras (or Red)

• LXX 58: en tê erêmô pros dysmaes plêsion tês erythras thalassês (ϵν τη ϵρημω προς Δυσμαις πλησφον της ϵρυθρας θαλασσης). Translation: in the undefended (or abandoned, void, lonely) towards west near Erythras (or Red) Sea

• Leningrad Codex: bammidbar ba'aravah movl suf (בַּמִּדְבָּר בָּעֲרָבָה מֹול סוּף).
Translation: in the wilderness of Arabah (or plain, desert) opposite (or against, facing Sup (or papyrus, reeds)

744

- Peshitta: bmdbrå bôrbå lûqpl sûp (ܣܘܦ ܠܘܩܒܠ ܚܪܒܐ ܒܡܕܒܪܐ). Translation: in the wilderness in the west (or Arabah, guardian, groomsman, ram, sheep, lamb, sunset, guarantee) facing Sûp (or papyrus, reeds)

- Targum Onkelos: vemadbera ve'al de'argizu vemeishra lokovel yam suf (בְּמַדְבְּרָא וְעַל דְּאַרְגִּיזוּ בְּמֵישְׁרָא לָקֳבֵל יַם סוּף). Translation: in the wilderness and at the snake (or serpent) of correction (or retitude, uprightness) opposite the sea of Sup (or papyrus, reeds)

- Fragment Targums: Mosheh va'amar lehon hala bemadbera betura desinai ityehivat lechon orayta uvemeishra demo'av itparshat lechon kammah nisin ugevuran avad lechon meimra dayya kad haveitun kaymin al yama desuf (מֹשֶׁה וַאֲמַר לְהוֹן הֲלָא בְּמַדְבְּרָא בְּטוּרָא דְּסִינַי אִתְיְהִיבַת לְכוֹן אוֹרַיְיתָא וּבְמֵישְׁרָא דְמוֹאָב אִתְפַּרְשַׁת לְכוֹן כַּמָּה נִסִין וּגְבוּרָן עֲבַד לְכוֹן מֵימְרָא דַיְיָ כַּד הֲוֵיתוּן קַיְימִין עַל יַמָא דְסוּף). Translation: Moses said to them, "Wasn't it in the wilderness of the Mountof Sinai that was given to you the instruction(or Torah, law), and in the plains (or valleys) of Moab where separated and corrected and tested, but heroes worshiped firmly the command of Yhû. When wounded for you at the Sea of Papyrus (or reeds)..."

- Targum Jerusalem: va'amar lehon hala bemadbera betavra desinai ityehivat lechon orayta uvemeishraya demo'av itparshat lechon kammah nisin uferishan avad lechon kudesha berich hu mizman da'avartun al geif yama desuf (וַאֲמַר לְהוֹן הֲלָא בְּמַדְבְּרָא בְּטוּרָא דְּסִינַי אִתְיְהִיבַת לְכוֹן אוֹרַיְיתָא וּבְמֵישְׁרַיָא דְמוֹאָב אִתְפַּרְשַׁת לְכוֹן כַּמָּה נִיסִין וּפֵרִישָׁן עֲבַד לְכוֹן קוּדְשָׁא בְּרִיךְ הוּא מִזְמָן דַּעֲבַרְתוּן עַל גֵּיף יַמָא דְסוּף). Translation: ...and said to them, "Wasn't it in the wilderness of the Mount of Sinai that was given to you the instruction (or Torah, law), and in the plains (or level places) of Moab where explained (or corrected) how many miracles (or camps, libations) and explanations were given from Qetesh (or holiness), blessed by He (or she, it), caused for the Abartus (or Oberites) on the shore of the Sea of Sup (or papyrus, reeds)

- Codex Lugdunensis (LV 100): in solitudine campestri Moab contra mare Rubrum. Translation: in secluded (or solitude, lonely) countries (or rural lands) of Moab against the Red Sea.

- Shapira scrolls: bmdbr bôbr hyrdn bôrbh (𐤁𐤌𐤃𐤁𐤓 𐤁𐤏𐤁𐤓 𐤄𐤉𐤓𐤃𐤍 𐤁𐤏𐤓𐤁𐤄). Translation: in the wilderness beyond (or across) the Jordan in the plain (or Arabah). This verse suggests the Shapira scroll was written in Samaria or Judah, not Moab, where it was supposedly discovered.

The Greek and Hebrew translations differ here, indicating that the Imperial Aramaic translation must have read the same as the Syriac, as in Aramaic, the term ôrbå (עֲרָבָ / ܥܪܒܐ) could be interpreted as either 'west,' as the Greeks translated, or as 'Arabah,' as the Hebrew translations reads. The earlier meanings of the word were the Akkadian cuneiform erēbu (𒀀𒊏𒁍), meaning 'to arrive' and Ugaritic ôrb (𐎓𐎗𐎁), meaning 'to enter,' suggesting that in the bronze age, the verse referred to the Israelite arriving at the Sea of Papyrus (סוף), not being in Arabah, the southern region of modern Israel and Jordan. Most of the surviving manuscripts do not include the word 'sea' (θαλασσης). It is not found in any of the Hebrew or Syriac manuscripts, and only a few Greek manuscripts. It is however, found in the Vetus Latina and Coptic manuscripts, as well as the Targums, indicating that this was the common interpretation by both Jews and Christians in the Roman era.

The Greek name Erythras (Ερυθρας) is not geographically specific. The Greek name appears to be a translation of the Persian term Erostras, which referred to the entire Persian Gulf, Red Sea, and the Indian Ocean. The Greeks were likely referring to the Gulf of Suez, however, this was known to the ancient Egyptians as the 'Sea of Calm' (𓏴𓈖𓏭𓈖𓏤𓈖), which is what the Israelites would have called it if that was where they were. The Hebrew translation places the event in the Gulf of Aqaba, however, this was known to the ancient Egyptians as the 'Sea of Edom' (𓏴𓈖𓏭𓈖𓏤) which is what the Israelites would have called it if that was where they were. The Egyptian name is accepted as being adopted from the Canaanite name of the Gulf of Aqaba, which was ym Ådm (𐎊𐎎 𐎀𐎄𐎎) in Ugaritic, ym Ådm (𐤉𐤌 𐤀𐤃𐤌) in Phoenician, and ymå hÅydm (𐡉𐡌𐡀 𐡀𐡃𐡌) in Aramaic, all of which translate as 'Sea of Edom.' As 'Edom' and 'red' were both spelled as ådm (𐤀𐤃𐤌) in Canaanite (Judahite, Samartian, Edomite), and åydm (𐡀𐡃𐡌) and Aramaic, the Aramaic texts that the Greeks translated probably used the name Sea of Edom/red, suggesting the Aramaic translator believed that the Sea of Papyrus was the Sea of Edom. Based on the writings of Jeremiah, the Sea of Papyrus was accepted as having been the Sea of Edom by the 7th century BC. In the 6th century BC, Arabs began settling in southern Edom, during the 5th century BC southern region of Edom bordering the Gulf of Aqaba was annexed by the kingdom of Lihyan. By the 4th century BC, when the Greeks conquered the Persian Empire, the Gulf of Aqaba was known as the Gulf of Lihyan, meaning the older term 'Sea of Edom' no longer made sense, and was interpreted by the Arameans and Greeks as the 'Sea of Red.'

Based on this verse, and the transition of the word ôrb (𒂍𒇲) in the bronze age, to ôrbh (𐤀𐤓𐤁𐤄) in the iron age, it is likely that the Samaritan, Judahite, and Edomite priests and scribes believed that the Sea of Papyrus was the old name of the Gulf of Aqaba, which is at the southern end of the Arabah valley.

The Greeks transliterated the name as the Sea of Siph (ΘΑΛΑϹϹΗϹ ϹΙΦ) in the Codex Vaticanus' translation of Judges, confirming that the name Swf was in the Aramaic text they worked from. The Aramaic term sůf (סוף) and Phoenician term sůf (𐤑𐤅𐤐), both meaning 'papyrus plants,' were adopted from the Egyptian term tjůfî (𓄿𓏤𓈖𓏏), which referred to papyrus, papyrus plants, and papyrus marshes. The Egyptian term continued to be used into the Classical era as the Sahidic word čoouf (ϫⲟⲟⲩϥ), and Bohairic words conf (ϭⲟⲛϥ) and comf (ϭⲟⲙϥ), all meaning papyrus. Conversely, the Egyptian name of the Red Sea was the Sea of Heh (𓁨), meaning 'very large sea' from the Middle Kingdom era onward, however, it is believed to have originally been named after the ancient Egyptian frog god Heh (𓁭). In the early Classical era it was also known as the Sea of Khôr (⌐⁶), meaning anger, however, it was never referred to as the Sea of 'Papyrus' in surviving Dynastic Egyptian documents.

The Hebrew term 'Sea of papyrus' is not geographically specific either, however, does match the description of the shallow Lake Bardawil which has been a major source for papyrus reeds throughout Egyptian history. As there are two 'Papyrus Seas' in the Hebrew translation, however, a Sea of Siph (Papyrus) and a Sea of in Erythras (Red, Edom) in the Greek texts, the two seas are named either Papyrus Sea or Sea of Edom in this translation, based on their location along the route the Israelites traveled out of Egypt.

3 Codex Vaticanus: Pharan (ΦΑΡΑΝ)

• Leningrad Codex: Paran (פָּארָן)

• Peshitta: byt Prn (ܒܝܬ ܦܪܢ). Translation: house (or temple, abode) of Prn

• Targum Onkelos: Paran de'ittappalu al manna (פָּארָן דְּאִתַּפָּלוּ עַל מַנָּא). Translation: Paran where they insulted the mana

• Fragment Targums: madbera deFaran (מַדְבְּרָא דְפָאָרָן). Translation: wilderness (or desert) of Paran

• Targum Jerusalem: Paran (פָּארָן)

• Bohairic manuscripts: Pharran (Φαρραν)

The Wilderness of Paran was mentioned in Genesis, Numbers, Deuteronomy, and 3rd Kingdoms (Masoretic Kings), and Masoretic Habakkuk, however, the location of Paran is debated. The book of Numbers states that Paran was Kadesh, while the Masoretic version of Deuteronomy locates it in the Arabah Desert of southern modern Jordan and Israel. In the second century AD, the Christian geographer Claudius Ptolemy located it in the southern Sinai Peninsula, at the region now called the Wadi Feiran, while Islamic scholars have interpreted it as the Hijaz region of western Saudi Arabia, around Mecca.

4 LXX 118: cae ana Meson (ϲαι ανα Μεϲον)

The addition of Meson is found in several Greek manuscripts, as well as Arabic translations, and appears to have originated in the Syriac Hexapla.

5 Codex Vaticanus: Tophol (ΤΟΦΟΛ)

• Codex Ambrosiano A 147: Tophel (ΤΟΦΕΛ)

• Codex Freer Greek MS. V: Gophal (ΓΟΦΟΛ)

• LXX 509: Tophoa (ΤοβοΛ)

• LXX 392: Tophan (Τοβλν)

• LXX 58: Tophôl (Τοβωλ)

• LXX 426: Thophol (Θοβολ)

• LXX 767: Tophal (Τοβλλ)

• LXX 55: Tophôn (Τοβων). LXX 55 places Tophôn after Aylôn.

• LXX 761: Tophor (Τοβορ)

• Leningrad Codex: Tofel (תֹּפֶל)

• Peshitta: byt tpl (ܒܝܬ ܬܦܠ). Translation: house (or temple, abode) of Tpl

• Targum Onkelos: Tappalu (תַּפְּלוּ)

• Fragment Targums: not mentioned in the verse

• Targum Jerusalem: Tefaltun (טְפַלְתּוּן)

• Sahidic manuscripts: Tophor (Τοφορ)

• Codex Lugdunensis (LV 100): Hobol

6 Codex Vaticanus: Lobon (ΛΟΒΟΝ)

• Codex Ambrosiano A 147: Laban (ΛΑΒΑΝ)

• LXX 16: Lôbon (Λωυλον)

• LXX 318: Lobôn (Λουωον)

• LXX 82: Dobon (Δουλον)

• LXX 72: Lôbôn (Λωυλωον)

• LXX 59: Labôn (Λαυλωον)

• LXX 376: Lob (Λου)

- Leningrad Codex: Lavan (לָבָן)

- Peshitta: Lbnn (لبن)

- Targum Onkelos: not mentioned in the verse

- Fragment Targums: not mentioned in the verse

- Targum Jerusalem: not mentioned in the verse

- Bohairic manuscripts: Lobona (Λοβονα)

- Sahidic manuscripts: Lobôn (Λοβων)

This location is generally considered unknown, however, based on its generally location, is likely the same place the Egyptians called Rbn during the New Kingdom era, as Egyptians did not distinguish between Ls and Rs like Semitic peoples.

7 Codex Vaticanus: Aulôn (ΑΥΛΩΝ)

- LXX 509: Aulon (Αυλον)

- LXX 528: Ayton (Αυτον)

- Leningrad Codex: Chatzerot (וַחֲצֵרֹת)

- Peshitta: Ḥsrût (ܚܨܪܘܬ)

- Targum Onkelos: not mentioned in the verse

- Fragment Targums: Chatzerot (חֲצֵרוֹת)

- Targum Jerusalem: Chatzerot (חֲצֵרוֹת)

8 Codex Vaticanus: Catachrysea (ΚΑΤΑΧΡΥCΕΑ)

- Codex Venetus: Catachrysaea (ΚΑΤΑΧΡΥCΑΙΑ)

- LXX 14: Catachryseôn (Κατάχρυσεων)

- LXX 52: Catôchrysea (Κατωχρυσεα)

- LXX 58: cata ta chrysea (κατα τα χρυσεα). Translation: with the gold

- Leningrad Codex: di zahav (דִּי זָהָב). Translation: enough (of sufficient) gold

- Peshitta: dyzhb (ܕܝܗܒ). Translation: that gold (or coins, money, goldsmith)

- Targum Onkelos: egal didhav (עֵגֶל דִּדְהַב). Translation: calf of gold

- Fragment Targums: dahava senina (דְּהָבָא סְנִינָא). Translation: golden bush

- Targum Jerusalem: eigal dahava (עִינַל דְּהָבָא). Translation: calf of gold

Based on the general geography described, this 'enough gold,' was likely the cradle of gold near modern Medina in Saudi Arabia, which was a large gold mining center in Arabia for over 6000 years.

9 Codex Vaticanus: Chôrêb (ⲭⲱⲣⲏⲃ)

- LXX 318: Chorêb (χοβ̄ηⲩ)

- LXX 55: Chôrib (χωβ̄ιⲩ)

- LXX 130: Chôrên (χωβ̄ηⲛ)

- LXX 767: Chôrêth (χωβ̄ηθ)

- Leningrad Codex: Chorev (חֹרֵב)

- Peshitta: Ḥůryb (ܚܘܪܝܒ)

- Targum Onkelos: Chorev (חֹרֵב)

- Fragment Targums: tura deChorev (טוּרָא דְחוֹרֵב). Translation: mountain of Horeb

- Targum Jerusalem: Chorev (חוֹרֵב)

- Shapira scrolls: Ḥrb (𐤇𐤓𐤁)

Throughout most references to Mount Horeb and Mount Sinai, they appear to be references to the same mountain, both in the Torah, and later in other works, such as 3rd Kingdoms (Masoretic Kings). The two names are believed to be derived from the names of the Sun and the Moon. The name Horeb is believed to be derived from the word for glowing/heat, while the name Sinai is derived from the name of the Semitic moon-god Sin. Various Jewish and Christian scholars have tried to resolve the issue of the same stories happening on two mountains. In the Middle Ages, the Rabbi Abraham ibn Ezra suggested that there was only one mountain, with two peaks, while later during the Protestant Reformation John Calvin suggested it was one mountain where the eastern side was named Sinai, while the western side was named Horeb.

Biblical scholars in the 1800s and 1900s developed the alternate hypothesis that two names are derived from two Torah traditions, one Solar and one Lunar, which were then united into a single Torah under the rule of King Josiah or earlier. Subsequent theories have suggested the unification of the two Torahs could have taken place later, under the Persian or even Greek rule of Judea, however, it seems unlikely to have happened that late as the Samaritan Torah has virtually identical twin stories about

Horeb/Sinai, and the schism between the Jews and Samaritans appears to have happened during the life of Ezra the Scribe, circa 350 BC. The term Horeb is generally associated with Moses, while Sinai is more often found in texts about Aaron, which implies that whatever the origin of the story, two versions have developed by the time of Josiah, one focused on Moses' Solar-Snake god, and the other focused on Aaron's Lunar-Calf god. When the two Torahs were harmonized it created several parallel statements and stories, often with different geographical locations.

To further complicate the geography, a third name was applied to it in the Book of Judges, which is considered by scholars to be the oldest surviving texts that have not been heavily redacted by later priesthoods. In Song of Deborah, found in Judges, the mountain where God came down to the Israelites is called Mount Seir, and the details of the story she repeats are the same as those of the Sinai event. Fortunately, this does narrow the list of possible mountains to the southern Abarim mountains in modern Jordan, south of the Dead Sea. In this verse, the author identified Horeb as being eleven days away from Mount Seir, which supports Horeb and Sinai being different locations, with Horeb being to the west of the Aravah, likely at Hashem El Tarif, near the modern Egyptian-Israeli border.

The 1st century Jewish General and Historian Josephus, who was given the ancient scrolls from the Second Temple when Rome destroyed it, claimed that ancient records indicated that Mount Sinai was in the Roman province of Arabia Petra, and was between Egypt and Arabia. This itself does little to clarify where it was, as Arabia Petra encompassed the entire Sinai Peninsula, as well as southern modern Israel, Jordan, and northwest Saudi Arabia, however, it does appear to have been an accurate report of what the ancient scrolls recorded as the disciple Paul reported the same thing. Paul was a Pharisee before his conversion to Christianity and quoted a lot of obscure Jewish texts in support of his ideology. Paul's claim that Sinai was in Arabia, is generally accepted as meaning the Roman province of Arabia Petra, as he was a Roman citizen, as does not appear to have ever left the empire. In order to simplify the reading of this translation, the southern Hor is called Hor, while the northern Hor is called Nur.

10 Codex Vaticanus: Sêir (ϹΗΙΡ)

- LXX 630: Siir (ϹΙϬΙΡ)

- LXX 318: Sêêr (ϹΗΗΡ)

- LXX 108: Siir (ϹϬΙϬΙΡ)

- LXX 19: Setir (ϹϬΤϬΙΡ)

- LXX 72: Siêr (ϹΙΗΡ)

- LXX 106: Sêr (ⲥⲏ̅ⲣ)

- LXX 618: Sêêir (ⲥⲏ̅ⲏ̅ⲓⲣ)

- Leningrad Codex: Se'ir (שֵׂעִיר)

- Dead Sea Scroll 4QDeut[h]: Šôyr (שעיר)

- Peshitta: Sôyr (ܣܥܝܪ)

- Targum Onkelos: Se'ir (שֵׂעִיר)

- Fragment Targums: Gavla (גַבְלָא)

- Targum Jerusalem: Gavla (גַבְלָא)

- Bohairic manuscripts: Sêir (ⲤⲎⲒⲢ)

- Sahidic manuscripts: Seir (ⲤⲈⲒⲢ)

- Shapira scrolls: -ôyr (-ⲣⲟⲍ) in a later verse; this verse was not in the scroll. The scroll was damaged, however, likely read Šôyr (ⲣⲟⲍⲱ) before being damaged.

Mount Seir was identified as being in Edom in the Book of Genesis, where Abraham's son Esau's descendants lived. Mount Seir was not mentioned in Exodus, Leviticus, or Numbers, but was mentioned in the Song of Deborah, found in Judges, as the mountain where God came down to the Israelites, and the details of the story she repeats are the same as those of the Sinai Event, implying Seir was another name for Sinai. Seir was also mentioned in the Egyptian el-Amarna Letters, written between 1360 and 1332 BC, were the Nomads (Shasu) of Sôr lived, somewhere in the Abarim mountains of modern southwest Jordan.

11 Codex Vaticanus: Cadês Barnê (ⲔⲀⲆⲎⲤⲄⲀⲢⲚⲎ)

- LXX 319: Caddês Barnê (Ⲕⲁⲇⲇⲗ̅ⲥ βⲁⲣ̅ⲛⲣ)

- LXX 669: Cadês Barni (Ⲕⲁⲇⲗ̅ⲥ βⲁⲣ̅ⲛⲋ̅ⲓ)

- LXX 71: Caddês Barni (Ⲕⲁⲇⲇⲗ̅ⲥ βⲁⲣ̅ⲛⲓ)

- LXX 53: Caddês Barnôs (Ⲕⲁⲇⲇⲗ̅ⲥ βⲁⲣ̅ⲛⲟⲟⲥ)

- Leningrad Codex: Kadesh Barnea' (קָדֵשׁ בַּרְנֵעַ). Translation: Sacred Barnea (or Varnea)

- Dead Sea Scroll 4QDeut[h]: Qdš Brnô (קדש ברנו). Translation: sacred Brnow (or Vrnow)

- Peshitta: rqm dḥyå (ܪܩܡ ܕܚܝܐ). Translation: various (or numbers of) life

- Targum Onkelos: rekam gei'ah (רְקַם גֵּיאָה). Translation: various (or numbers of) gorges (or ravines)

- Fragment Targums: rekam degei'a (רְקַם דְּגֵיעָא). Translation: numbers (or various) of gorges (or ravines)

- Targum Jerusalem: rekam gei'ah (רְקַם גֵּיאָה). Translation: various (or numbers of) gorges (or ravines)

- Shapira scrolls: qdš brnô (𐤒𐤃𐤔 𐤁𐤓𐤍𐤅) in a later verse; this verse was not in the scroll.

The location of Kadesh Barnea has been debated since the Second Temple Era. The Jewish general and historian Josephus reported that the sacred books salvaged from the Second Temple when it was destroyed by the Romans placed Kadesh Barnea at Petra, in modern Jordan. He also claimed that Mount Sinai was nearby, which is the source of the claim that Mountain of the Altar (Jebel al-Madhbah) was Mount Sinai. The name Kadesh Barnea is undoubtedly named after an ancient deity, as the first word, kadesh (קדש), means holy or sacred. The name Barnea, more commonly pronounced as Varne'a in Hebrew, is presumably the name of the deity in question, and is quite similar to the name Mitannian Indo-Aryan (Vedic) god Varuna.

As Deuteronomy chapter 2 goes on to report that there were Hurrians living in Seir before the Edomites killed them and inhabited the region, this would support the name Varuna being the source of Barnea, as the Hurrians were the major population base of the Mitanni Empire. This connection between the Mitannian Indo-Aryan Varuna worshipers at Mount Seir would also explain how the name Mitra-Varuna (𐎐𐎛𐎓) entered into Judaism, as his earliest recorded Hebrew name Mttrůn (מטטרון) is essentially the same as the Mitannian Miitra-Aruna, and played the same role in the Vedic Texts as Metatron did in Second Temple Era Judaism. Subsequent Hebrew pronunciations of the name from the Medieval Era, Mttrůn (מטטרון), Metateron (מֶטַטְרוֹן), Metatron (מְטַטְרוֹן), Meitatron (מֵיטַטְרוֹן), Mitatron (מִיטַטְרוֹן), and Mattatron (מַטַטְרוֹן), as well as the Arabic Mītatrūn (ميططرون), are all influenced by the Greek pronunciation of the name Metà-thrónos (Μετα-θρόνος), which means 'next to the throne.'

12 Papyrus Fouad 266 (LXX 847, 848 and 942): Yhůh (יהוה). Papyrus Fouad 266 dates from the Hasmonean Dynasty (140 to 37 BC). It is a fragment of the Septuagint with the name יהוה written in Hebrew in gaps that are the correct length to write Κύριος, indicating it was part of the Hasmonean redaction of Deuteronomy.

- Codex Vaticanus: Cₓˢ (Ҟ). Translation: lord

- Leningrad Codex: Yehvah (יְהוָה)

This verse does not survive intact in any fragments of the Dead Sea Scrolls, however, the name Yahweh is found in different verses that have survived from among the Dead Sea Scrolls, mostly from the Hasmonean Dynasty or later, however.

- Dead Sea Scroll 1QDeutᵃ: yhůh (𐤉𐤄𐤅𐤄)
- Dead Sea Scroll 1QDeutᵇ: yhůh (𐤉𐤄𐤅𐤄)
- Dead Sea Scroll 4QDeutᵃ: yhůh (𐤉𐤄𐤅𐤄)
- Dead Sea Scroll 4QDeutᵇ: yhůh (𐤉𐤄𐤅𐤄)
- Dead Sea Scroll 4QDeutᶜ: yhůh (𐤉𐤄𐤅𐤄)
- Dead Sea Scroll 4QDeutᵈ: yhůh (𐤉𐤄𐤅𐤄)
- Dead Sea Scroll 4QDeutᵉ: yhůh (𐤉𐤄𐤅𐤄)
- Dead Sea Scroll 4QDeutᶠ: yhůh (𐤉𐤄𐤅𐤄)
- Dead Sea Scroll 4QDeutᵍ: yhůh (𐤉𐤄𐤅𐤄)
- Dead Sea Scroll 4QDeutʰ: yhůh (𐤉𐤄𐤅𐤄)
- Dead Sea Scroll 4QDeutⁱ: yhůh (𐤉𐤄𐤅𐤄)
- Dead Sea Scroll 4QDeutʲ: yhůh (𐤉𐤄𐤅𐤄)
- Dead Sea Scroll 4QDeutᵏ¹: yhůh (𐤉𐤄𐤅𐤄)
- Dead Sea Scroll 4QDeutᵏ²: yhůh (𐤉𐤄𐤅𐤄)
- Dead Sea Scroll 4QDeutˡ: yhůh (𐤉𐤄𐤅𐤄)
- Dead Sea Scroll 4QDeutᵐ: yhůh (𐤉𐤄𐤅𐤄)
- Dead Sea Scroll 4QDeutⁿ: yhůh (𐤉𐤄𐤅𐤄)
- Dead Sea Scroll 4QDeutᵒ: yhůh (𐤉𐤄𐤅𐤄)
- Dead Sea Scroll 4QDeutᵖ: yhůh (𐤉𐤄𐤅𐤄)
- Dead Sea Scroll 4QDeutᑫ: yhůh (𐤉𐤄𐤅𐤄)
- Dead Sea Scroll 4QpaleoDeutʳ: yhůh (𐤉𐤄𐤅𐤄)
- Dead Sea Scroll 5QDeut: yhůh (𐤉𐤄𐤅𐤄)
- Peshitta: mryå (ܡܪܝܐ). Translation: master
- Targum Onkelos: yeyah (ײַ). Translation: Yhů
- Fragment Targums: not mentioned in the verse

- Targum Jerusalem: yeyah (??). Translation: Yhŭ

- Shapira scrolls: Yhŭh (𐤉𐤄𐤅𐤄) in otherverses; this verse was not in the scroll.

The name Yahweh (יהוה) was transliterated as Iaw (Ιαω) in some later books of the Septuagint, however, no early copies of Deuteronomy survive that include the name Iaw (Ιαω). The Papyrus Fouad 266 is an early copy of the Septuagint in which the name Yhŭh (יהוה) was placed into the Greek text in Assyrian (Hebrew) script. The gaps in the Greek text where the Yhŭh was written, were six characters long, meaning the Greek text was copied from a copy of the Septuagint that had the word cyrios (κύριοσ), and the Greek scribe left gaps where a Hebrew scribe later wrote the name in the Assyrian script. This manuscript has been dated to the era of the Hasmonean Dynasty and therefore is consistent with the Hasmoneans' attempt to replace El with Yahweh in the ancient scriptures.

The name Yhŭh (𐤉𐤄𐤅𐤄 / יהוה) is in almost all fragments of Deuteronomy found among the Dead Sea Scrolls, however, almost all of these scrolls have been dated to the Hasmonean Dynasty or later, and most are in the Assyrian 'block' script, the official script of the Hasmonean Dynasty. There are a few exceptions though, 4QpaleoDeut^r is a fragment of Deuteronomy written in the Phoenician (Samaritan / Paleo-Hebrew script) that includes the name Yhŭh (𐤉𐤄𐤅𐤄), however, also dates to the Hasmonean Dynasty, and was therefore likely a copy written for the Samaritans, who continued using the old script. 4QDeut^{k2} is an Assyrian script text from the later Herodian dynasty that uses the name Yhŭh in the Phoenician script, which indicates that by the Hasmonean Dynasty Jews were accepting that the name was always in Deuteronomy.

5QDeut is the only fragment of Deuteronomy currently dated to before the Hasmonean Dynasty that includes the name, however, is written in the Assyrian script indicating it was likely written during the Maccabean Revolt that created the Hasmonean Dynasty. The dating of 1QDeut^a and 1QDeut^b also remain unclear, and may be earlier than the Romans Era (6 to 390 AD), however, as they are also in the Assyrian script, are unlikely to date to earlier than the Hasmonean Dynasty. Based on the six-space gaps in Papyrus Fouad 266, it does seem clear that the original Greek translation included the word 'Lord' (ΚΥΡΙΟΣ) where the Masoretic Text currently use the name Yehvah (יְהוָֹה), and therefore the word Lord is used in this translation.

13 Codex Vaticanus: c̄s o t̄h̄s hêmôn (ΚϹΟΘϹΗΜШΝ). Translation: Lord the god of mine

- LXX 19: Cyrios o theos hêmôn (Κ ⲁⲃριος ο θϲ̅ος ο θϲ̅ος ⳑμοον). Translation: Lord the god the god of mine

- LXX 71: Cyrios ho theos ymôn (κ ᾱβριος ο θεός υμωον). Translation: Lord the god of y'all

- Westminster Leningrad Codex: Yehvah eloheinu (יְהוָה אֱלֹהֵינוּ). Translation: Yehwah our god

This phrase survives in part or full, in multiple Dead Sea Scrolls, although in later verses as most do not have the beginning of Deuteronomy chapter 1.

- Dead Sea Scroll 1QDeut[b]: -h ålhy (אלהי ה-) survives. Translations [Yhů]h god

- Dead Sea Scroll 4QDeut[h]: yhůh ålhy (והוהi אלהי). Translation: Yhůh god

- Peshitta: mryå ålhn (ܡܪܝܐ ܐܠܗܢ). Translation: master gods

- Targum Onkelos: yeyah elahana (יְיָ אֱלָהַנָא). Translation: Yhů our god

- Targum Jerusalem: yeyah elahein (יְיָ אֱלָהִין). Translation: Yhů gods

- Shapira scrolls: ålhm ålhnů (𐤀𐤋𐤄𐤌 𐤀𐤋𐤄𐤍𐤅). Translation: goddesses (in Judahite, 'gods' in Aramaic, 'god' in Judahite-Aramaic) our goddess (in Judahite, 'gods' in Aramaic, 'god' in Judahite-Aramaic)

The Aramaic sections of Masoretic Daniel that were not translated into Hebrew maintain the term adonai ha'elohim (אֲדֹנָי הָאֱלֹהִים), meaning the 'Lord the gods' where the Septuagint has 'Lord the god' (Κύριοσ ο θεοσ). As most books of the Septuagint were translated from Aramaic texts, the Aramaic text almost certainly used the term donai ha'elohim where the Septuagint has 'Lord the god.' The name Yahweh appears to have been added to most of the books in the Masoretic Text when the texts were translated to Hebrew during the Hasmonean Dynasty of Judea, between 140 and 37 BC. According to the records from the time, this was to repair the damage King Manasseh had done 600 years earlier when he removed the name Yahweh from the Israelite Texts, however, no evidence has survived from the era of Manasseh or earlier that proves the name was originally in the text, suggesting it was an attempt by the first Hasmonean High-Priest/King Simon the Zealot to create a national Judean religion with a god having a name similar to the Roman god Jove.

The name Yahweh, in the Aramaic form of Yhů (𐤉𐤄𐤅) does appear to have originally been in some of the books of the Septuagint, such as Leviticus, which originated under the rule of King Josiah or later, and Yhů was a popular god among Judeans and Israelites under Persian and Greek rule. The translators at the Library of Alexandria transliterated this name as Iaw (Ιαω) in the books it was originally in, however, under the Hasmonean Dynasty it seems to have been added to all the books translated into Hebrew, creating some confusion among early Christians.

There were debates in the early Christian era about which version of the Israelite scriptures to use, the Greek, Hebrew, Samaritan, or Syriac translations, resulting in different versions of the scriptures being used by different churches. Some versions replaced the name Lord with Iaw in the Greek texts, either in the Greek form as Ιαω, or by copying in the Hebrew form of the name Yhůh (יהוה) or the older Phoenician form of Yhůh (𐤉𐤄𐤅𐤄), or by mocking the Hebrew with Greek letters as ΠΙΠΙ. This created a great deal of confusion among Christians, and ultimately the books of the Septuagint that had the name Iaw in them were redacted so all the books used the term Lord (Κύριοσ). Most Christian translations, as well as Jewish translations, have continued to use the term 'Lord' in place of the name Yahweh, due to the prohibition on using any names of God that was introduced during the Hasmonean dynasty.

There are no early surviving copies of the Septuagint's version of Deuteronomy which have the name Iaw (Ιαω / 𐤉𐤄𐤅) in them, like some of the other books of the Septuagint, and therefore it cannot be proven if the name was in the Septuagint's Genesis or not, however, the terms used in Septuagint's Genesis are consistent with the surviving Aramaic sections of Masoretic Daniel, strongly suggesting the Aramaic source text the Greek translators used, included the term Adonai h'elahin, and not Yhů h'elahin. The Aramaic term likely meant 'Lord of the gods,' however, has been interpreted several ways within monotheistic religions, including the Jewish 'powers of Yahweh' and Christian 'Lord of the Trinity.' As Κυριος ο Θεος translates directly as Lord the god (or Lord the god), that term is used in this translation.

14 Codex Vaticanus: Araba (ΑΡΑΒΑ)

- LXX 246: Arouba (Αβουυλ)

- LXX 422: Arrhaba (Αββλυλ)

- LXX 120: Ara (Αβλ)

- LXX 767: Saraba (Cλβλυλ)

- Leningrad Codex: Aravah (עֲרָבָה). Translation: plain

- Peshitta: Ôrbå (ܥܪܒܐ)

- Targum Onkelos: meishrayya (מֵישְׁרַיָּא). Translation: plain (or even, straight)

- Targum Jerusalem: meishra (מֵישְׁרָא). Translation: plain (or even, straight)

- Bohairic manuscripts: Areba (ⲁⲣⲉⲃⲁ)

- Sahidic manuscripts: Abra (ⲁⲃⲣⲁ)

- Codex Lugdunensis (LV 100): Arabin

- Shapira scrolls: Ôrbh (𐤀𐤓𐤁𐤄)

Arabah was the name for the region south of the Dead Sea.

15 Codex Vaticanus: uious gigantôn (ΥΙΟΥΟΙΓΑΝΤΩΝ). Translation: sons of Gigantes (in ancient Greek, or giants in modern Greek)

- LXX 28: uios Gigantôn (υιος Γιγαννντοον). Translation: son of Gigantes

- Leningrad Codex: benei Anakim (בְּנֵי עֲנָקִים). Translation: sons of Anakites (or neck, necklace, or giant in modern Hebrew)

- Peshitta: bny gnbrå (ܒܢܝ ܓܢܒܪܐ). Translation: sons of heroes

- Targum Onkelos: benei gibbara'ei (בְּנֵי גִבָּרָאֵי). Translation: sons of heroes

- Targum Jerusalem: benei Efron gibbara chameina (בְּנֵי עֶפְרוֹן גִּבְּרָא חֲמֵינָא). Translation: sons of Ephron hero of his kind

The Anaks were transliterated as Enach (Εναχ) in the Book of Numbers, and Enacim (Ενακιμ) later in Deuteronomy, but translated as Gigantes in this verse, implying the Greeks considered the Anaks to be like the Gigantes of ancient Greece, who fought a war against the Olympian gods, and lost. The Anaks (Anakim) were a tribe of people also referred to in the books of Joshua and Judges. According to the book of Judges, they apparently lived in Hebron.

The Egyptian Execration Texts from the Middle Kingdom (circa 2050 to 1650 BC) record a group of Canaanites called the 'ly Anaq' who are generally considered to be the same people. The name Anaks is restored in this translation from the Masoretic Text, as that does appear to be their name. Based on the name of the Anak, the original term was probably a reference to the Éanak (𒂍𒀭𒈹), the name of the worshipers of Inanna, the Queen of Heaven, the Sumerian deification of the planet Venus.

Deuteronomy: Chapter 2

We turned and departed into the wilderness, by the road from the Sea of Edom, as the Lord told me, and we surrounded Mount Seir for many days.

The Lord said to me, "You have encompassed this mountain long enough, turn therefore toward the north. Order the people, "You are going through the borders of your brothers the children of Esau, who live in Seir, and they will fear you, and dread you greatly. Do not engage in war against them, for I will not give you their land even enough to set your foot on, for I have given mount Seir to the children of Esau as an inheritance. Buy food from them for silver and eat, and you will receive water from them by measure for silver, and drink."

Our Lord the god has blessed you in every work of your hands. Consider how you traveled through that great and terrible wilderness. Look, Lord the god has been with you forty years, you did not lack anything. We passed by our brothers the children of Esau, who lived in Seir, by the way of Arabah from Aelon and from Eziongaber, and we turned and passed by the way of the desert of Moab.

The Lord said to me, "Do not you quarrel with the Moabites, and do not engage in war with them, for I will not give you of their land as an inheritance, for I have given Ar to the children of Lot to inherit. Formerly the Emims lived in it, a great and numerous nation and powerful, like the Anaks. These also will be counted as Rephaim[1] like the Anaks[2] (who the Moabites call Emims).[3] The Hurrians[4] lived in Seir before, and the sons of Esau destroyed them, and completely consumed them from before them. They lived in their place, as Israel did in the land of his inheritance, which the Lord gave to them.

Now then I said, "Arise and depart, and cross the valley of Zered."

The days in which we traveled from Kadesh Barnea until we crossed the Valley of Zered, were thirty-eight years, until the whole generation of the men of war failed, dying out of the camp as Lord the god swore to them. The hand of the Lord was on them to destroy them out from among the camp until they were consumed. It came to pass when all the men of war died out from among the people, that the Lord spoke to me, saying, "Today you will pass over the borders of Moab to Aroer, and you will come close to the children of Amman.[5] Do not quarrel with them, or wage war against them, for I will not give you the land of the children of Amman as an inheritance, because I have given it to the children of Lot as an inheritance. It will be counted as a land of Raphain, for the

Raphain lived there before, (the Ammonites call them Zamzums).[6] A great nation and populous, and mightier than you, like the Anaks, yet the Lord destroyed them out from before them, and they inherited their land, and they lived there instead of them until this day. As they did to the children of Esau that live in Seir, even as they destroyed the Hurrians from before them, and inherited their country, and lived there instead of them until this day."

"The Mitanni[7] who live between Azzah and Gaza,[8] and the Minoans[9] who came out of Crete,[10] destroyed them and lived in their space. Now then, arise and depart, and pass through the valley of Arnon. Look, I have delivered into your hands Sihon the king of Heshbon the Amorite, and his land. Begin to inherit it. Engage in war with him today. Begin to put your terror and your fear on the face of all the nations under the sky, who will be troubled when they have heard your name, and will be in anguish before you."

I sent ambassadors from the wilderness of Kedemoth to Sihon king of Heshbon with peaceable words, saying, "I will pass through your land. I will go by road. I will not turn aside to the right hand or to the left. You will sell me food for silver, and I will eat, and you will sell me water for silver, and I will drink. I will only go through on my feet, as the sons of Esau allowed me, who lived in Seir, and the Moabites who lived in Aroer, until I have crossed the Jordan into the land which our Lord the god gives us."

Sihon king of Heshbon would not agree that we should pass by, because our Lord the god hardened his spirit, and made his heart stubborn, that he might be delivered into your hands, as on this day. The Lord said to me, "Look, I have begun to deliver before you Sihon the king of Heshbon the Amorite, and his land, and begin to inherit his land. Sihon the king of Heshbon came out to meet us, he and all his people to war at Jahaz. Our Lord the god delivered him before our face, and we destroyed him, and his sons, and all his people. We took possession of all his cities at that time, and we completely destroyed every city in succession, and their wives, and their children. We left no living victims, except we took the livestock captive and took the spoil of the cities. From Aroer, which is by the brink of the Arnon River, and the city which is in the valley, and as far as Mount Gilead, there was not a city that escaped us. Our Lord the god delivered all of them into our hands. Only we did not come close to the children of Amman, even all the parts bordering on the brook of Jabbok, and the cities in the mountain country, as our Lord the god ordered us.

Deuteronomy: Chapter 2 Notes

1 Codex Vaticanus: Raphaen (ΡΑΦΑΙΝ)

• LXX 509: Raphaem (ΡΑϨΑϬιμ)

• LXX 59: Raphaên (ΡΑϨΑλ̄ν)

• Leningrad Codex: Refa'im (רְפָאִים). Translation: long-dead (or a tribe generally transliterated as Rephaites)

• Peshitta: gnbrå (ܓܢܒܪܐ). Translation: heroes (or giants)

• Targum Onkelos: gibbara'ei (גִבָּרָאֵי). Translation: heroes

• Targum Jerusalem: gibbaraya (גִבָּרַיָא). Translation: heroes (or giants)

• Bohairic manuscripts: Raphain (Ραφαιν)

• Shapira scrolls: Rpåm (𐤓𐤐𐤌)

The Raphites (𐤓𐤐𐤀𐤌) were semi-deified by the 1200s BC, as the Ugaritic Texts include the so-called Rephaim Text. They appear to be an ancient people that had been deified and were believed to live in the underworld. The word's etymology implies they were healers.

2 Codex Vaticanus: Enac (ΕΝΑΚ)

• Codex Freer Greek MS. V: Aenac (ΑΙΝΑΚ)

• LXX 509: Ennac (Εͷͷαϫ)

• LXX 426: Enacim (Εͷαϫιϻ)

• LXX 72: Senak (CϬͷαϫ)

• Leningrad Codex: Anakim (עֲנָקִים). Translation: Anakites (or neck, necklace, or giant in modern Hebrew)

• Peshitta: gnbrå (ܓܢܒܪܐ). Translation: heroes (or giants)

• Targum Onkelos: gibbara'ei (גִבָּרָאֵי). Translation: heroes

• Targum Jerusalem: ginberaya (גִנְבְּרַיָא)

• Sahidic manuscripts: Anak (ⲁⲛⲁⲕ)

• Codex Lugdunensis (VL 100): Senak

• Munich Palimpsest (VL 104): Aenac et unianimes sunt. Translation: Aenac and they are unanimous

3 Codex Vaticanus: Ommin (ΟΜΜΙΝ)

- Codex Alexandrinus: Oommin (ΟΟΜΜΕΙΝ)

- Codex Ambrosiano A 147: Emmin (ΕΜΜΕΙΝ)

- LXX 630: Omin (Ομϭιν)

- LXX 318: Ommên (Ομμλν)

- LXX 426: Ommim (Ομμμ)

- LXX 125: Omin (Ομν)

- LXX 646: Ommiin (Ομμϭιν)

- LXX 537: Êmmin (Ημμϭιν)

- LXX 59: Omiên (Ομλν)

- LXX 376: Ommiim (Ομμϭιμ)

- Leningrad Codex: emim (אֵמִים). Translation: terrors (or threateners, frighteners)

- Peshitta: Åmnå (ܐܡܢܐ). Translation: task(or art, evil, carefreeness)

- Targum Onkelos: Eimtanei (אֵימְתָנֵי)

- Targum Jerusalem: Eimtanei (אֵימְתָנֵי)

- Bohairic manuscripts: Ommin (ΟΜΜΙΝ)

- Sahidic manuscripts: Ommiein (ΟΜΜΙΕΙΝ)

- Codex Lugdunensis (VL 100): Omitte

- Shapira scrolls: Åmm (𐤉𐤉𐤕)

The scribal note suggests that the text was used in Moab, and the note was added for the Moabites. The book of Deuteronomy is sometimes interpreted as an anti-Moabite text that had been written to discredit the prophet Balaam and the gods of Moab. This note, and other Moabite translations in the book, indicate that there was an earlier version of the book before it was used in Moab.

4 Codex Vaticanus: Chorraion (ΧΟΡΡΑΙΟΝ)

- LXX 30: Chôrrhaeon (χωρραιον)

- LXX 46: Choraeon (χοραιον)

- LXX 610: Amorrhaeon (Αμορραιον)

- LXX 767: Chôraeon (χωραιον)

- Leningrad Codex: Chorim (חֹרִים). Translation: Hurrians

- Peshitta: Ḥůryå (ܚܘܪܝܐ)

- Targum Onkelos: Chora'ei (חֹרָאֵי)

- Targum Jerusalem: Genusaya (גְנוּסָיָא)

- Shapira scrolls: Ḥrm (𐤇𐤓𐤌)

These appear to be the people the Egyptians called the Ḥårů (𓉔𓄿𓂋𓅱𓈉), which are known as the Hurrians in modern history books. The Hurrians were an ancient people in the Middle East, native to Northern Iraq, Syria, and eastern Turkey before the Semitic and Persian tribes migrated into the region. While they appear to have become a slave race for centuries under the rule of the Old Babylonian and Old Assyrian kingdoms, they became the dominant ethnic group of the Mitanni Empire between 1600 and 1300 BC, after being freed by the Indo-Aryan Mitanni people.

5 LXX 963: ymôn amman (ΥΜΩΝΑΜΜΑΝ). Translation: sons of Amman

- Codex Vaticanus: ymôn Ammôn (ΥΙΩΝΑΜΜΩΝ). Translation: sons of Ammon

- LXX 616: huiôn Ammô (υιον Αμμω). Translation: sons of Ammo

- LXX 59: huiôn Amôn (υιον Αμων). Translation: sons of Amon

- LXX 527: ymôn Amban (υμων Αμυαν). Translation: sons of Amban

- Leningrad Codex: benei Ammon (בְּנֵי עַמּוֹן). Translation: sons of Ammon

- Peshitta: bny Ômůn (ܒܢܝ ܥܡܘܢ). Translation: sons of Ammôn

- Targum Onkelos: benei Ammon (בְּנֵי עַמּוֹן)

- Targum Jerusalem: benei Ammon (בְּנֵי עַמּוֹן)

- Bohairic manuscripts: šēri Ammôn (ϣⲏⲣⲓ ⲁⲙⲙⲱⲛ). Translation: sons of Ammon

- Codex Lugdunensis (VL 100): filiorum Ammon. Translation: son of Ammon

- Shapira scrolls: Ômnm (𐤏𐤌𐤌𐤏). Translation: Ammonites

Amman was one of the nations to the east of Israel and later Judah, in modern Jordan, around the modern capital, Amman, which is named after the ancient Kingdom. As Amman is the modern city's name, Amman is used in this translation.

6 LXX 963: Zozomen (ΖΟΖΟΜΕΝ)

- Codex Vaticanus : Zochomin (ΖΟΧΟΜΕΙΝ)

- Codex Ambrosiano A 147: Zommin (ΖΟΜΜΕΙΝ)

- Codex Freer Greek MS. V: Zozommin (ΖΟΖΟΜΜΕΙΝ)

- Codex Venetus: Nozommin (Νοζομμιν)

- LXX 407: Ommin (Ομμɛιν)

- LXX 509: Zochammin (Ζοχαμμɛιν)

- LXX 55: Zozommin (Ζοζομμιν)

- LXX 64: Zomzommin (Ζομζομμϕν)

- LXX 730: Zamzommin (Ζαμζομμιν)

- LXX 318: Oozzommên (Οοζζομμλν)

- LXX 16: Zomzomin (Ζομζομιν)

- LXX 58: Zomzomin (Ζομζομɛιν)

- LXX 121: Zoommin (Ζοομμɛιν)

- LXX 134: Zonzimmin (Ζονζιμμιν)

- LXX 313: Zomzomphim (Ζομζομϕɛιμ)

- LXX 343: Zômzommin (Ζωμζομμιν)

- LXX 426: Zomzommim (Ζομζομμιμ)

- LXX 707: Zômmin (Ζωμμɛιν)

- LXX 125: Zonzomin (Ζονζομιν)

- LXX 130: Zomzompi (Ζομζομπɛι)

- LXX 646: Zômzombim (Ζωμζομιϭιμ)

- LXX 71: Zozomin (Ζοζομιν)

- LXX 71: Zommin (Ζομμιν)

- LXX 767: Zozomin (Ζοζομϭιν)

- LXX 107: Zonzommin (Ζονζομμιν)

- LXX 52: Zomzombim (Ζομζομιϭιμ)

- LXX 106: Conzommin (Κονζομμιν)

- LXX 321: Zomzompi (Ζομζομπι)

- LXX 527: Zêzomên (Ζhζομhν)

- LXX 46: Zomphim (Ζομϕϭιμ)

- LXX 59: Zomzommên (Ζομζομμhν)

- LXX 68: Zomnin (Ζομνϭιν)

- Leningrad Codex: Zamzummim (זַמְזֻמִּים)

- Peshitta: Zmzyn (ܙܡܙܝܢ)

- Targum Onkelos: Chushbanei (חֻשְׁבָּנֵי)

- Targum Jerusalem: Zeimtanei (זֵימְתָנֵי)

- Bohairic manuscripts: Zozommin (Ⲍⲟⲍⲟⲙⲙⲓⲛ)

- Sahidic manuscript Sa 17: Zozomein (Ⲍⲟⲍⲟⲙⲉⲓⲛ)

- Codex Lugdunensis (VL 100): Zozomin

- Shapira scrolls: Ôzmzmm (𐤌𐤌𐤆𐤌𐤆𐤀)

The scribal note suggests that the text was used in Moab, and the note was added for the Moabites. The book of Deuteronomy is sometimes interpreted as an anti-Moabite text that had been written to discredit the prophet Balaam and the gods of Moab. This note, and other Moabite translations in the book, indicate that there was an earlier version of the book before it was used in Moab.

7 Codex Vaticanus: Eyaeoe (ϵΥΛΙΟΙ)

• LXX 106: Euae (Ευλι)

• Leningrad Codex: Avvim (עַוִּים)

• Peshitta: Ôûyå (ܟܘܐ)

• Targum Onkelos: Avva'ei (עַוָּאֵי)

• Targum Jerusalem: she'ar peleitat Kena'ana'ei (שְׁאָר פְּלֵיטַת כְּנַעֲנָאֵי). Translantion: escaped remnants of the Canaanites

• Codex Lugdunensis (VL 100): Ebeu

The Greek term Eyaeoe (Ευαιοι) is a variation of Eyaeon (Ευαιον), which is usually mirrored in the Hebrew translation with Chivvi (חִוִּי), however, in Deuteronomy it mirrored by Avvim (עַוִּים). In the Hebrew translation, Chivvi (חִוִּי) is used interchangeably with Chori (חֹרִי). Chori is accepted as referring to the Hurrians, which the Egyptians called Hårů (𓉔𓄿𓂋𓅱), and the Babylonians called Huurri (𒄷𒌝�[...]). The Hurrians were one of the oldest cultures in the Middle East, however, became largely a slave culture within the Akkadian and Old Babylonian empires. Under the Mitanni empire, they rose to a position of wealth, and formed the noble caste. The Greek transliteration of this term was Chorrhaeous (Χορραιους), which, like the Hebrew term, was used interchangeably in the texts with Eyaeon (Ευαιον) / Chivvi (חִוִּי), although that term generally applied to the rules and priests.

The ultimate origin of the terms Eyaeon (Ευαιον) Avvim (עַוִּים), and Chivvi (חִוִּי), both appear to be the cuneiform word Éan (𒂍𒀭), meaning temple or sacred. In the Amarna Letters, which date to the 1330s BC, the term Éan (𒂍𒀭) was the name of a people, who appear to be the Mitanni, or a group within the Mitanni. A similar correlation between the terms is found in the Septuagint's 1ˢᵗ Paralipomenon and Masoretic Divrei-hay Yamim, where the Greek translation uses Beithani (Βαιθανι), however, the Hebrew uses the term Mitni (מִתְנִי). This term also refers to a group of people, meaning the underlying Edomite text the Greeks translated would have been 'people of the House of Ån (𐤀𐤍), a direct Canaanite translation of É An (𒂍𒀭).

While Mitni was the transliteration used in the Edomite text that formed the basis of the Hebrew translation of Divrei-hayYamim, it was replaced with Chivvi (חִוִּי) in the Judahite texts, which served as the basis of most of the Masoretic texts. This likely originated in a Judahite copy of the text, after the Aramaic translation had been made, where an N (𐤍) was replaced with a Ů (𐤅). The Aramaic translation would have already been made in the time of King Manasseh, were the term was transliterated as Hyån (חֿיןֿ), itself a transliteration of the early Canaanite Hyån (𐤇𐤉𐤍). The term Avvim (עַוִּים) found in Deuteronomy, which originated in Samaritan, appears to have maintained a closer transliteration of the cuneiform Éan (𒂍𒀭), based on the Neo-Sumerian pronouciation of Ay.am.

8 LXX 963: Asêrôth eôs Gazês (ⲁⲥⲏⲣⲱⲑⲉⲱⲥⲅⲁⲍⲏⲥ). Translation: Aseroth before Gaza

- Codex Vaticanus: Asêdôth heôs Gazês (ⲁⲟⲏⲇⲱⲑ ⲟⲟⲥ ⲅ ⲁ/ⲍ/ⲏⲥ). Translation: Asedoth before Gaza

- LXX 52: Asirôth heôs Gazês (ⲁⲟⲓⲣⲱⲑ ⲟⲟⲥ ⲅ ⲁ/ⲍ/ⲏⲥ). Translation: Asiroth before Gaza

- LXX 120: Asirôth heôs Gazis (ⲁⲟⲟⲓⲣⲱⲑ ⲟⲟⲥ ⲅⲁⲍ,ⲟⲓⲥ). Translation: Asiroth before Gaza

- LXX 767: Pasêrôth heôs Gazês (ⲡⲁⲟⲏ ⲣⲱⲑ ⲟⲟⲥ ⲅ ⲁ/ⲍ/ⲏⲥ). Translation: Paserothbefore Gaza

- LXX 527: Pasêrôth heôs Gazês (ⲛⲁⲟⲏ ⲣⲣⲱⲑ ⲟⲟⲥ ⲅ ⲁ/ⲍ/ⲏⲥ). Translation: Nasêrrhôth heôs Gazês

- Leningrad Codex: chatzerim ad-Azzah (חֲצֵרִים עַד־עַזָּה). Translation: yards (or courtyards) to (or on, until) Gaza

- Peshitta: ḥṣrym ûôdmâ lÔâzâ (ܥܕܡܐ ܘܥܕܡܐ ܠܐܙܐ). Translation: yards (or courtyards) and until Gaza

- Targum Onkelos: Defiach ad Azzah (דְּפִיחַ עַד עַזָּה)

- Targum Jerusalem: Difria' ad Azzah (דְּפְרִיעַ עַד עַזָּה)

- Codex Lugdunensis (VL 100): Asaroth usque Gazan. Translation: Asaroth all the way to Gazan

9 Codex Vaticanus: Cappadoces (ⲕⲁⲡⲡⲁⲇⲟⲕⲉⲥ). Translation: Cappadocians

- LXX 376: Cappodoces (ⲕⲁⲡⲡⲟⲇⲟⲩⲟ́ⲥ)

- LXX 646: Cappadocae (ⲕⲁⲡⲡⲁⲇⲟⲩⲁⲓ)

- LXX 46: Cappadocis (ⲕⲁⲡⲡⲁⲇⲟⲩⲟⲓⲥ)

- LXX 619: Cappadocoe (ⲕⲁⲡⲡⲁⲇⲟⲩⲟⲓ)

- LXX 707: Cappadôces (ⲕⲁⲡⲡⲁⲇⲟⲟⲩⲟ́ⲥ)

- LXX 767: Campadoces (ⲕⲁⲙⲡⲁⲇⲟⲩⲟ́ⲥ)

- Leningrad Codex: Kaftorim (כַּפְתֹּרִים). Translation: Caphtorites

- Peshitta: Qpûdqyå (ܩܦܘܕܩܝܐ)

- Targum Onkelos: Kapputeka'ei (קַפּוֹטְקָאֵי)

- Targum Jerusalem: she'ar peleitat Kena'ana'ei (שְׁאָר פְּלֵיטַת כְּנַעֲנָאֵי). Translantion: escaped remnants of the Canaanites

This translation accepts the common translation of Caphtor as Crete, meaning the Caphtorites would have been the Minoans. Archaeological and genetic evidence has proven that the Minoans traded and settled the coastal regions of the eastern Mediterranean between 2500 and 1500 BC, including northern Egypt and ancient Canaan as far south as the Midian Mountains of northwest Saudi Arabia. The Mandean messenger/angel Ptahil (ܦܬܐܗܝܠ) is generally viewed as being based on the Egyptian creator god Ptah (𓁹𓏏𓎛), whom the Egyptians claimed originated in Minoan Crete, suggesting the Kaftorim in Canaan may have referred to a cult, not the ethnic group themselves.

10 LXX 963: Cappadocias (ΚΑΠΠΑΔΟΚΙΑϹ). Translation: Cappadocia

- Codex Ambrosiano A 147: Capadocias (Καπαδολιλc)

- LXX 707: Capadôcias (Καπαδοολιλc)

- LXX 313: Cappodocias (Καππολολιλc)

- LXX 767: Campadoces (Καμπαδολιλc)

- LXX 75: Cappadôcias (Καππαδοολιλc)

- LXX 53: Ppadocias (Ππαδολιλc)

- Leningrad Codex: Kaftovr (כַּפְתֹּור). Translation: Caphtor (or Minoan Crete)

- Peshitta: Qpdûqy (ܩܦܕܘܩܝ)

- Targum Onkelos: Kapputekayya (קַפּוֹטְקַיָּא)

- Targum Jerusalem: Kapputekeya'ah (קַפּוֹטְקְיָאה)

Caphtor was mentioned in several surviving ancient texts from the 2nd millennium BC, including the Mari Tablets, dated to circa 1770 BC, Thutmose III's Hymn of Victory, from circa 1450 BC, and the Ras Sharma Texts from Ugarit, dated to circa 1340 BC. Cosmic Genesis / Bereshít refers to Caphtor as a son of Mizraim (Egypt), which implies a colony of Egypt, while the Ras Sharma Texts uses the name Caphtor as the name of the home of the Canaanite god Kothar-wa-Khasis, which is accepted as the Canaanite version of the Egyptian god Ptah.

The location of Caphtor was already long lost and debated by the time the Septuagint was translated at the Library of Alexandria, which supports the antiquity of the Book of Deuteronomy. At the time, Greek translators believed it was in Cappadocia, in central modern Turkey, most likely associating it with the civilization today referred to as the Neshites (Hittites), however, the Egyptian records that mention Kftyŭ (𓎛𓄿𓅱), list it as being a port city, and Cappadocia was an inland nation. This identification of Caphtor with Cappadocia is based on its location in Thutmose III's biography, from circa 1450 BC, which placed Caphtor as Thutmose's northernmost conquest, and his Empire had conquered all of Canaan, and extended to the border of Cappadocia.

Jewish scholars have traditionally rejected Cappadocia as the location of Caphtor. In the 1st century AD, the Jewish historian and general Josephus wrote in his Antiquities of the Jews, that the Caphtorites were an Egyptian people whose city was destroyed in a war with the Aethopians (presumably Kushites) and migrated to Philistia (the modern Gaza Strip). Other Jewish sources, such as Maimonides, in the 12th century AD, have placed Caphtor in the Nile Delta.

Early Christians accepted the Greek identification of Caphtor as Cappadocia, and Cappadocia was the translation of Caphtor that Jerome chose for the Vulgate in the 4th century. Modern scholars have debated the issue, with many locations suggested, including Cicilia (southern Turkey), Cyprus, Crete, or some other island in the Aegean Sea.

Currently, the academic view is that either Cicilia or Crete are the most likely locations of Caphtor, however, the archaeological evidence from Crete shows that some major force burnt almost every town in Crete during the life of Thutmose III, which his biography claims he did to Caphtor, and therefore, the terms Crete and Cretan are used in this translation.

Deuteronomy: Chapter 3

We turned and went by the path leading to Bashan, and Og[1] the king of Bashan came out to meet us, he and all his people, to battle at Edrei. The Lord said to me, "Don't fear him, for I have delivered him and his people and land, into your hands, and you will do to him as you did to Sihon king of the Amorites who lived in Heshbon."

Our Lord the god delivered him into our hands, even Og the king of Bashan, and all his people, and we destroyed him until we left none of his seed. We conquered all his cities at that time, there was not a city which we did not take from the. Sixty cities and all the country around Lajat, belonging to king Og in Bashan: all of which were strong cities, with high walls, gates, and bars. As well as many cities of the Perizzites. We completely destroyed them as we dealt with Sihon the king of Heshbon, so we completely destroyed every city in order, and the women and the children, and all the livestock, and we took as conquest for ourselves the spoil of the cities. At that time we took the land out of the hands of the two kings of the Amorites, who were beyond the Jordan, extending from the Arnon[2] River all the way to Hermon.[3] (The Phoenicians[4] call Hermon Sanior,[5] and the Amorites called it Shenir.)[6]

All the cities of Misor,[7] and all Gilead,[8] and all Bashan[9] as far as Salkhad[10] and Daraa,[11] cities of the kingdom of Og in Bashan. For only Og the king of Bashan was left of the Raphain. His bed was a bed of iron, it is in the citadel city of the children of Ammon, the length of it is nine cubits, and the width of it four cubits, according to the cubit of a man. We inherited that land at that time from the ruins[12] that are by the edge of the Arnon River, and half the hills of Gilead. I gave his cities to Reuben and to Gad. The rest of Gilead, and all Bashan the kingdom of Og I gave to the half-tribe of Manasseh, and all the country around Lajat,[13] all of Bashan, it will be counted as the land of Raphain. Jair the son of Manasseh took all the country around Lajat as far as the borders of Geshuri and Maachathi: he called them by his name Bashan Thavoth Jair until this day.

To Machir I gave Gilead. To Reuben and to Gad I gave the land under Gilead as far as the Arnon River, the border between the river and as far as Jabbok, the river is the border to the children Amman. Arabah and Jordan are the boundaries of the Sea of Galilee[14] and east of the Sea of Arabah (the Sea of Salt),[15] past Asedoth east of the Phasga.[16] I ordered you at that time, "Lord the god has given you this land by lot. Arm yourselves, everyone that is powerful, and go before your brothers the children of Israel. Only your wives and your children and your livestock (I know that you have much livestock), let them remain in the cities which I have given you. Until Lord the god gives your brothers rest, as also has he given to you, and they also will inherit the land, which our Lord the god gives them on the other side of Jordan. then you will return, each one to his inheritance which I have given you."

I commanded Joshua at that time, "Your eyes have seen all things, which our Lord the god did to these two kings, so will our Lord the god will do to all the kingdoms against which you meet over there. You will not be afraid of them, because our Lord the god himself will fight for you."

I implored the Lord at that time, "Lord the god, you have begun to show to your servant your strength, and your power, and your mighty hand, and your high arm: for what god is there in the sky or on the earth, who will do as you have done, and according to your might? I will, therefore, go over and see this good land that is beyond Jordan, this good mountain and Anti-lebanon. Because of you, the Lord did not regard me or listened not to me."

The Lord replied to me," Let it be enough for you, don't speak of this matter to me anymore. Go up to the top of the quarried rock, and look with your eyes westward, and northward, and southward, and eastward, and look at it with your eyes, for you will not go over this Jordan. Order Joshua, and strengthen him, and encourage him, as he will go before the face of these people, and he will give them the inheritance of all the land which you have seen."

We lived in the valley near the house of Peor.

Deuteronomy: Chapter 3 Notes

1 LXX 963: Og (ⲱⲅ)

• Codex Vaticanus: Gôg (ⲅⲱⲅ)

• LXX 767: Nôg (Nⲱⲅ)

• Leningrad Codex: Og (עֹוג)

• Peshitta: Åug (ܐܘܓ)

• Targum Onkelos: Og (עוֹג)

• Targum Jerusalem: Og (עוֹג)

- Shapira scrolls: Åg (𐤉𐤏)

2 Codex Vaticanus: Arnôn (ΑΡΝѠΝ)

- Leningrad Codex: Arnon (אַרְנֹן)

- Peshitta: Årnůn (ܐܪܢܘܢ)

- Targum Onkelos: Arnon (אַרְנֹן)

- Targum Jerusalem: Arnona (אַרְנוֹנָא)

- Shapira scrolls: Årnn (𐤀𐤓𐤍𐤍)

Generally identified as Wadi Mujib in Jordan, a river canyon that flows into the Dead Sea.

3 LXX 963: Aermôn (ΑΕΡΜѠΝ)

- Codex Ambrosiano A 147: orous Aermôn (ΟΡΟΥϹΑΕΡΜѠΝ). Translation: Mount Hermon

- Codex Colberto-Sarravianus: orous Ermôn (ΟΡΟΥϹΕΡΜѠΝ). Translation: Mount Hermon

- Leningrad Codex: har Chermovn (הַר חֶרְמוֹן). Translation: Mount Hermon

- Peshitta: tůrå dHrmůn (ܛܘܪܐ ܕܚܪܡܘܢ). Translation: mount of Hermon

- Targum Onkelos: tura deChermon (טוּרָא דְחֶרְמוֹן). Translation: mount of Hermon

- Targum Jerusalem: tavvra deChermon (טַוְורָא דְחֶרְמוֹן). Translation: mount of Hermon

Mount Hermon is still known, as the southernmost major peak in the Anti-Lebanon mountain range, on the border of Syria, Lebanon, and the Israeli-occupied Golan Heights. The peak is currently occupied by a UN Peace Keeping Force.

4 Codex Vaticanus: Phoenices (ΦΟΙΝΙΚΕϹ). Translation: Phoenicians

- LXX 75: Phinices (ΦΙΝΙΚΕϹ)

- LXX 318: Phynices (ΦΥΝΙΚΕϹ)

- Leningrad Codex: Tzidonim (צִידֹנִים). Translation: Sidonians

- Peshitta: Sydnyå (ܨܝܕܢܝܐ). Translation: Sidonians

- Targum Onkelos: Tzidona'ei (צִידֹנָאֵי)

- Fragment Targums: Tzidona'ei (צִידוֹנָאֵי)

- Targum Jerusalem: Tzidona'ei (צִידוֹנָאֵי)

The Sidonians were a Canaanite people from the city of Sidon. Phoenician was the Greek name for the Canaanites.

5 LXX 920: Saniôr (ⲥⲁⲛⲓⲱⲣ)

- Codex Freer Greek MS. V: Saniôr (ⲥⲁⲛⲉⲓⲱⲣ)

- LXX 422: Sanêôr (ⲥⲁⲛⲏⲱⲣ)

- LXX 75: Sanaôr (ⲥⲁⲛⲁⲱⲣ)

- LXX 59: Aniôr (ⲁⲛⲓⲱⲣ)

- LXX 767: Sanriôn (ⲥⲁⲛⲣⲓⲱⲛ)

- LXX 53: Saniôn (ⲥⲁⲛⲓⲱⲛ)

- LXX 53: Sariôn (ⲥⲁⲣⲓⲱⲛ)

- Leningrad Codex: Siryon (שִׂרְיֹן)

- Peshitta: Sryůn (ܣܪܝܘܢ)

- Targum Onkelos: Siryon (סִרְיֹן)

- Fragment Targums: ar'a masrei peirohi (אַרְעָא מַסְרֵי פֵּירוֹהִי). Translation: land of mouth-watering (or fruit producing) sin

- Targum Jerusalem: tavvra demasrei peiroy (טָוָורָא דְמַסְרֵי פֵּירוֹי). Translation: mountain of sinful fruit

- Codex Lugdunensis (VL 100): Seir

6 LXX 920: Sanir (ⲥⲁⲛⲉⲓⲣ)

- LXX 963: Anir (ⲁⲛⲉⲓⲣ)

- Codex Venetus: Saniir (ⲥⲁⲛⲓⲉⲓⲣ)

- LXX 407: Saniêr (ⲥⲁⲛⲓⲏⲣ)

- LXX 46: Sanir (ⲥⲁⲛⲫⲣ)

- LXX 15: Sanêr (ⲥⲁⲛⲏⲣ)

- LXX 392: Samir (ⲤⲀⲙⲓⲣ)

- LXX 319: Samior (ⲤⲀⲙⲓⲟⲣ)

- LXX 458: Samior (Ⲁⲙⲓⲣ)

- LXX 59: Aniêr (Ⲁⲛⲓⲩⲣ)

- Leningrad Codex: Senir (שְׂנִיר)

- Peshitta: Snyr (ܣܢܝܪ)

- Targum Onkelos: tur Talga (טוּר תַּלְגָּא). Translation: Mount Snow

- Fragment Targums: ar'a marbei peirei ilana (אַרְעָא מַרְבֵּי פֵּירֵי אִילָנָא). Translation: land of best fruit trees

- Targum Jerusalem: tavavr talga (טָוָור תַּלְגָּא). Translation: mount Snow

- Bohairic manuscripts: Saniôur (ⲤⲀⲛⲓⲱⲩⲣ)

- Sahidic manuscript Sa 17: Saneir (ⲤⲀⲛⲉⲓⲣ)

- Codex Lugdunensis (VL 100): Sanis

7 LXX 963: Misôr (ⲙⲉⲓⲤⲱⲣ)

- Codex Vaticanus: Misôr (ⲙⲓⲤⲱⲣ)

- LXX 707: Mêsôr (Ⲙⲏⲥⲱⲣ)

- LXX 59: Miôr (Ⲙⲓⲱⲣ)

- Leningrad Codex: mishor (מִישֹׁר). Translation: plain (or level country, table land)

- Peshitta: pqôtå (ܦܩܥܬܐ). Translation: plain (or level country, table land)

- Targum Onkelos: meishra (מֵישְׁרָא). Translation: plains (or valleys, lowlands)

- Targum Jerusalem: meishra (מֵישְׁרָא). Translation: plains (or valleys, lowlands)

- Bohairic manuscripts: Nisôur (Ⲛⲓⲥⲱⲩⲣ)

- Codex Lugdunensis (VL 100): Mysorum

Misôr was also the name of a Canaanite god. The Greeks interpreted it as a land named after Misôr, while the Hebrew translation can simply be read as 'table land.'

8 Codex Vaticanus: Galaad (ܓܠܥܕ)

- LXX 509: Balaan (βαλααν)

- Leningrad Codex: Gil'ad (גִּלְעָד)

- Peshitta: Glôd (ܓܠܥܕ)

- Targum Onkelos: Gil'ad (גִּלְעָד)

- Targum Jerusalem: Gil'ad (גִּלְעָד)

- Codex Lugdunensis (VL 100): Galatia

Gilead was land now located in the Irbid, Ajloun, Jerash and Balqa Governorates of northwest Jordan. Galatia, the translation used in Vetus Latina manuscripts, was an unrelated land in central Anatolia, suggesting the early Latin translator did not know the geography of the region.

9 LXX 920: Basan (ΒΑϹΑΝ)

- LXX 30: Bassan (βασσαν)

- LXX 121: Bassan (βασα)

- Leningrad Codex: Bashan (בָּשָׁן)

- Peshitta: Mtnyn (ܡܬܢܝܢ). Translation: Mitanni

- Targum Onkelos: Matnan (מַתְנָן)

- Targum Jerusalem: Matnan (מַתְנָן)

- Bohairic manuscripts: Basan (Ⲃⲁⲥⲁⲛ)

- Codex Lugdunensis (VL 100): Chasan

- Shapira scrolls: Bšn (𐤁𐤔𐤍)

Bashan was the name off the rocky land located in modern southern Syria and the Golan Heights. The Aramaic Targums and Peshitta use the alternate term Mitanni, which does refer to the nation ruling the region in the bronze age, however, it is unclear where the name entered into the Aramaic translations, as it is not found in the Hebrew, Greek, Coptic, or Latin translations. The term was forgotten by the beginning of the iron age, and not rediscovered until the 1800s, suggesting it may have been used in an older Samaritan version of Deuteronomy, and replaced at some point by Bashan.

10 LXX 920: Elcha (ελχα)

- LXX 407: Elchan (Ελχαν)

- LXX 58: Selca (ceλυα)

- LXX 72: Elca (ελυα)

- LXX 73: Lacha (λαχα)

- LXX 120: Melcha (Μελχα)

- LXX 730: Selcha (ceλχα)

- Leningrad Codex: Salchah (סַלְכָה)

- Peshitta: Slkå (ܣܠܩܐ)

- Targum Onkelos: Salchah (סַלְכָה)

- Targum Jerusalem: Salvavki (סַלְוְוקִיא). Translation: Seleucia

- Bohairic manuscripts: Sella (Сελλα)

- Codex Lugdunensis (VL 100): Chelchat

- Shapira scrolls: Slkh (𐤔𐤋𐤊)

Salkhad is city in southern Syria, and the capital of Salkhad district, in as-Suwayda
Governorate. The Targum Jerusalem's substitution of Seleucia (סַלְוְוקִיא) is strange as the
targum is in Palestinean-Aramaic, meaning it originated in Palestine, and nearby Salkhad
has never been abandoned. Selucia was the capital of the Selucid Greek empire, between
305 and 240 BC, suggesting the substitution happened during the era, however, it is not
found in the Fragment Targums, which are in Judean-Aramaic and share a lot of
otherwise unique material with the Targum Jerusalem.

11 Codex Vaticanus: Edraem (εδραειμ)

- LXX 64: Edraen (Εδραϊν)

- LXX 59: Edraên (Εδραην)

- LXX 767: Aidraen (Αιδραϊν)

- LXX 376: Edran (Εδραν)

- LXX 707: Edrae (Εδραϊ)

- LXX 82: Edra (ΕΔΡΔ)

- LXX 71: Esdrain (ΕσΔΡΔιΝ)

- LXX 56: Esdraen (ΕσΔΡΔϬιΝ)

- LXX 53: Esdraem (ΕσΔΡΔϬιμ)

- LXX 319: Eudraen (ΕυΔΡΔϬιΝ)

- LXX 58: Esdrae (ΕσΔΡΔϬι)

- Leningrad Codex: Edre'i (אֶדְרֶעִי)

- Peshitta: Ȧrdôy (ܐܪܕܥܝ)

- Targum Onkelos: Edre'i (אֶדְרֶעִי)

- Targum Jerusalem: Edre'at (אֶדְרֶעָת)

- Bohairic manuscripts: Edrain (ΕΔΡΔιΝ)

- Codex Lugdunensis (VL 100): Chebrain

- Shapira scrolls: Ȧrdôy (𐤆𐤅𐤉𐤀𐤕)

Edraem/Edrei is the ancient name for Daraa, a city in southern Syria, and the capital of Daraa district, and Daraa Governorate.

12 LXX 920: Aroêr (ΔΡΟΗΡ)

- LXX 58: Edraên (ΔΡοωहΡ)

- LXX 30: Aroer (ΔΡοϬιΡ)

- LXX 46: Aroên (ΔΡοहΝ)

- LXX 314: Roêr (ΡοहΡ)

- LXX 527: Asêr (ΔσहΡ)

- Leningrad Codex: aro'er (עֲרֹעֵר). Translation: ruins

- Peshitta: Ȧrnûn (ܐܪܢܘܢ)

- Targum Onkelos: aro'er (עֲרֹעֵר)

- Targum Jerusalem: aro'er (עֲרוֹעֵר)

- Sahidic manuscripts: Naroêur (ΝΔρΟΗγΡ)

- Shapira scrolls: Ôrôr (𐤀𐤅𐤀𐤅) in a different verse.

This is generally accepted as a reference to ancient ruins on the shore of the Arnon River, now known as the Wadi Mujib in Jordan. In chapter 2 Aroer was described as being on the banks of the Arnon, which would explain why the names are used interchangeably.

13 Codex Vaticanus: Argob (ΑΡΓΟΒ)

- LXX 407: Argôb (Ἀργωου)

- LXX 53: Argô (Ἀργω)

- LXX 318: Argôm (Ἀργωομ)

- LXX 699: Arboc (Ἀβιοϲ)

- LXX 610: Argê (Ἀργη)

- LXX 527: Araarboc (Ἀβααβιοϲ)

- Leningrad Codex: Argov (אַרְגֹּב)

- Peshitta: Årgůb (ܐܪܓܘܒ)

- Targum Onkelos: Terachona (טְרָכוֹנָא)

- Fragment Targums: Atarchuna (אֲטַרְכוּנָא)

- Targum Jerusalem: Targona (טַרְגוֹנָא)

- Bohairic manuscripts: Arkôub (ⲁⲣⲕⲱⲩⲃ)

- Shapira scrolls: Årgb (𐤀𐤓𐤂𐤁)

Argob was an ancient name for the Lajat lava field in southern Syria, on the border of the Daraa and as-Suwayda Governorates.

14 LXX 920: Machanarath (ΜΑΧΑΝΑΡΑΘ)

- Codex Vaticanus: Machanareth (ΜΑΧΑΝΑΡΕΘ)

- Codex Alexandrinus: Machenereth (ΜΑΧΕΝΕΡΕΘ)

- Codex Freer Greek MS. V: Machanarad (ΜΑΧΑΝΑΡΑΔ)

- Codex Venetus: Chenereth (ΧΕΝΕΡΕΘ)

- LXX 407: Machanereth (Μαχανɛρɛθ)

- LXX 527: Machanarat (ΜΑΧΑΝΑΡΑΤ)

- LXX 619: Machanatar (ΜΑΧΑΝΑΤΑΡ)

- LXX 76: Manarath (ΜΑΝΑΡΑΘ)

- LXX 75: Machandrad (ΜΑΧΑΝΑΡΔΔ)

- LXX 458: Machandrad (ΜΑΧΑΝΡΔΔ)

- LXX 54: Machandrad (ΜΑΧΔΔΡΔΔ)

- LXX 376: Chanarath (ΧΑΝΑΡΑΘ)

- LXX 68: Machanereth (ΜΑΧΑΝΘΡΘΘ)

- LXX 83: Machaenereth (ΜΑΧΑΙΝΘΡΘΘ)

- LXX 59: Macheneth (ΜΑΧΘΝΘΘ)

- LXX 30: Machanarad (ΜΑΧΑΝΑΡΔΔ)

- LXX 85: Machenered (ΜΑΧΘΝΘΡΘΔ)

- LXX 73: Machenerd (ΜΑΧΘΝΘΡΔ)

- LXX 16: Chenered (ΧΘΝΘΡΘΔ)

- LXX 53: Chanereth (ΧΑΝΘΡΘΘ)

- LXX 72: Chaneth (ΧΑΝΘΘ)

- Leningrad Codex: mikkinneret (מִכִּנֶּרֶת). Translation: the Kinneret

- Peshitta: mn Knrt (ܡܢ ܟܢܪܬ). Translation: the Kinneret

- Targum Onkelos: migGenosar (מִגְּנוֹסַר)

- Fragment Targums: min Ginosar (מִן גְּנוֹסַר)

- Targum Jerusalem: miGnisar (מִגְנִיסַר)

- Bohairic manuscripts: Makhanareth (Μαχαναρεθ)

- Codex Lugdunensis (VL 100): Malechanaret

Kinneret is an alternate name for the Sea of Galilee, also known as Lake Tiberius.

15 LXX 963: thalassês Araba thalassês alycês (ΘΑΛΑϹϹΗϹΑΡΑΒΑΘΑΛΑϹϹΗϹ ΑΛΥΚΗϹ). Translation: Sea of Araba sea of salt

• Codex Ambrosiano A 147: thalassês tou araba thalassês alycês (ΘΑΛΑϹϹΗϹΤΟΥ ΑΡΑΒΑΘΑΛΑϹϹΗϹΑΛΥΚΗϹ). Translation: Sea of the Araba sea of salt

• LXX 44: thalassês Araba thalassês halycês (θλαϙοσολς Αββⲇⲙⲇ θλαϙοσολς ⲇλυⲗⲗς). Translation: Sea of Arraba sea of salt

• LXX 46: thalassês Ara thalassês halycês (θλαϙοσολς Αβⲇ θλαϙοσολς ⲇλυⲗⲗς). Translation: Sea of Ara sea of salt

• LXX 71: escha cae Araba eôs thalassês halycês (ⲋοχⲇ ⲗⲇⲓ Αβⲇⲙⲁϙ ⲋοⲟⲥ θλαϙοσολς ⲇλυⲗⲗς). Translation: slit and Arabah from the sea of salt

• LXX 707: thalassês Raba thalassês halycês (θλαϙοσολς Ρⲇⲙⲇ θλαϙοσολς ⲇλυⲗⲗς). Translation: Sea of Raba sea of salt

• LXX 767: thalassês Saraba thalassês halycês (θλαϙοσολς ⲥⲇβⲇⲙⲇ θλαϙοσολς ⲇλυⲗⲗς). Translation: Sea of Saraba sea of salt

• Leningrad Codex: yam ha'Aravah yam hammelach (יָם הָעֲרָבָה יָם הַמֶּלַח). Translation: Sea the Plain sea the salt

• Peshitta: ymâ dÔrbâ ymâ dmlhâ (ܝܡܐ ܕܥܪܒܐ ܝܡܐ ܕܡܠܚܐ). Translation: sea of Arabah sea of salt

• Targum Onkelos: yamma demeishra yamma demilcha (יַמָּא דְמֵישְׁרָא יַמָּא דְמִלְחָא). Translation: sea of the plain sea of salt

• Fragment Targums: yama demeishra yama demilcha (יַמָּא דְמֵישְׁרָא יַמָּא דְמִלְחָא). Translation: sea of the plain sea of salt

• Targum Jerusalem: yamma demeshera (יַמָּא דְמֶשְׁרָא). Translation: sea of salt

The Sea of Arabah was an ancient name for the Dead Sea. The fact that both the Greek and Hebrew translations include the same scribal note indicating that the Sea of Arabah was the Sea of Salt indicates that the Aramaic translator did not believe the term Sea of Arabah was no longer commonly understood when the Aramaic translation was made.

This indicates that the translation was either made outside of Judea, or by immigrants, as the book of Ezra claims the Samaritan population was by the late Persian Era. It also indicates that the book must have been translated from an older version, presumably in Phoenician (Samaritan, Judahite, Ammonite, Moabite or Edomite) which used the older name.

16 LXX 963: apo Asêdôth tên Phasga anatolôn (ΑΠΟΑϹΗΔѠΘΤΗΝΦΑϹΓΑ ΑΝΑΤΟΛѠΝ). Translation: under (or past, near) Asedoth the Phasga eastward

• Codex Ambrosiano A 147: ypo tês Asêdôth tên Pharanga anatolôn (ΥΠΟ ΤΗϹ ΑϹΗΔѠΘ ΤΗΝ ΦΑΡΑΓΓΑ ΑΝΑΤΟΛѠΝ). Translation: under (or past, near) the Asedoth the Pharanga eastward

• Codex Venetus: apo Sêdôth tên Pharanga anatolôn (ΑΠΟϹΗΔѠΘΤΗΝΦΑΡΑΓΓΑ ΑΝΑΤΟΛѠΝ). Translation: under (or past, near) Sedoth the Pharanga eastward

• LXX 422: apo Asidôn tên Phasgath anatolôn (Ἀπο Ασιλοον την Φασγαθ ανατολοον). Translation: under (or past, near) Asidon the Pharanga eastward

• LXX 53: hypo Asidôth tên Pharanga anatolôn (υπο Ασιλοοθ την Φαβαγγα ανατολοον). Translation: under (or past, near) Asidoth the Pharanga eastward

• LXX 392: hypo Asidôo tên Phasga anatolôn (υπο Ασιλοοο την Φασγα ανατολοον). Translation: under (or past, near) Asidôo the Pharanga eastward

• LXX 72: hypo Asidôd tên Phasga anatolôn (υπο Ασιλοολ την Φασγα ανατολοον). Translation: under (or past, near) Asidod the Pharanga eastward

• LXX 767: hypo Asidôn tên Phaga anatolôn (υπο Ασιλοον την Φαγα ανατολοον). Translation: under (or past, near) Asidon the Pharanga eastward

• LXX 319: hypo Asidôn tên Phasgad anatolôn (υπο Ασιλοον την Φασγαλ ανατολοον). Translation: under (or past, near) Asidon the Pharanga eastward

• LXX 59: hypo Asêdôth tên Pharangan anatolôn (υπο Ασηλοοθ την Φαβαγγαν ανατολοον). Translation: under (or past, near) Asedoth the Pharangan eastward

• Leningrad Codex: tachat ashdot happisgah mizrachah (תַּחַת אַשְׁדֹּת הַפִּסְגָּה מִזְרָחָה). Translation: beneath the peak (or summit) the peak eastern

• Peshitta: dthyt Åšdůd ůpsgå dbrmtå mn mdnhå (ܕܬܚܝܬ ܐܫܕܘܕ ܘܦܣܓܐ ܕܒܪܡܬܐ ܡܢ ܡܕܢܚܐ). Translation: beneath Ashdod and peak of bar-mata (meaning 'outside native land' in Aramaic) in the east (or of sunshine)

• Targum Onkelos: techot mashpach meramata madincha (תְּחוֹת מַשְׁפַּךְ מְרָמָתָא מַדִינְחָא). Translation: beneath the ravines of the peak of the province

• Fragment Targums: techot beit shefichot kitma min maddincha (תְּחוֹת בֵּית שְׁפִיכוּת קִיטְמָא מִן מַדִינְחָא). Translation: beneath the house of pouring of powder from the province

- Targum Jerusalem: techot shafchut maya meramata maddincha (תְּחוֹת שַׁפְכוּת מַיָא מֵרָמָתָא מַדִינְחָא). Translation: beneath the pouring of house of the deceiver of the east

Deuteronomy: Chapter 4

Now Israel, hear the ordinances and judgments, all that I teach you today to do: that you may live, and be multiplied, and that you may go in and inherit the land, which the Lord the god of your fathers gives you. You will not add to the word which I command you, and you will not take from it. Keep the commandments of our Lord the god, all that I command you this day. Your eyes have seen all that our Lord the god did in the case of Ba'al Peor, for every man that went to Ba'al Peor, Lord the god has completely destroyed him from among you. But you that kept close to Lord the god are all alive today.

Look, I have shown you ordinances and judgments as the Lord commanded me, that you should do so in the land into which you go to inherit. You will keep and do them, for this is your wisdom and understanding before all nations, as many as will hear all these ordinances, and they will say, "Look, this great nation is a wise and understanding people." For what manner of nation is so great, and which has a god so near to them as our Lord the god is in all things in whatever we may ask of him? What manner of nation is so great, which has righteous ordinances and judgments according to all this law, which I set before you this day? Pay attention to yourself, and keep your mind diligent. Don't forget any of the things, which your eyes have seen, and don't let them depart from your heart all the days of your life.

You will teach your sons and your sons' sons, all the things that happened in the day in which you stood before our Lord the god in Horeb in the day of the assembly, for the Lord said to me, "Gather the people to me, and let them hear my words, that they may learn to fear me all the days which they live on the earth, and they will teach their sons."

You came close and stood under the mountain, and the mountain burned with fire up to the sky. There was darkness, blackness, and lightning. The Lord spoke to you out of the middle of the fire a voice of words, which you heard: and you saw nothing like it, you only heard a voice. He announced to you his covenant, which he commanded you to keep, including the ten commandments, and he wrote them on two tablets of stone. The Lord commanded me at that time, to teach you ordinances and judgments, that you should do them in the land which you go to inherit. Pay close attention to your hearts, as you saw no vision in the day in which the Lord spoke to you in Horeb in the mountain out of the middle of the fire. If you transgress and make for yourselves a carved image, any kind of figure, the figure of male or female, the figure of any animal that is on the earth, the figure of any winged bird which flies under the sky, the figure of any reptile which creeps on the earth, the figure of any fish of those which are in the waters under the earth, and in case having looked up to the sky, and having seen the sun and the moon and the stars, and all the order of the sky, you should go astray and worship them, and serve them, who Lord the god has distributed to all the nations under the sky. But God took you, and led you out of the land of Egypt, out of the iron furnace of Egypt, to be for him a people of inheritance, as you become today.

Lord the god was angry with me for the things you said and swore that I should not cross the Jordan and that I should not enter into the land, which the Lord the god gives you for an inheritance. I die in this land, and will not cross over the Jordan, but you are to cross over and will inherit this good land. Pay attention to yourselves, in case you forget the covenant of our Lord the god, which he made with you, and you transgress and make for yourselves a carved image of any of the things concerning which the Lord the god commanded you. For Lord the god is a consuming fire, a jealous god. When you have fathered sons, and have grandsons, and you have lived a long time in the land, and have transgressed, and made a carved image of anything, and have done wickedly before Lord the god to provoke him, I call the sky and earth this day to witness against you, that you will certainly die-off from the land, into which you go across the Jordan to inherit. You will not prolong your days on it but will be completely cut off.

The Lord will scatter you among all nations, and you will be left few in number among all the nations, among which the Lord will bring you. You will serve other gods there, the works of the hands of men, wood and stones, which shall not see, nor can they hear, nor eat, nor smell. There you will seek Lord the god, and you will find him whenever you will seek him with all your heart, and with all your mind in your affliction. All these things will come on you in the last days, and you will return to Lord the god and will listen to his voice. Because Lord the god is a god of pity, he will not forsake you, nor destroy you. He will not forget the covenant of your fathers, which the Lord swore to them.

Ask about the former days which were before you, from the day when God created man on the earth, and beginning at the one end of the sky to the other end of the sky, if there has happened anything like this great event if such a thing has been heard when a nation has heard the voice of the living God speaking out of the middle of the fire, as you have heard and have lived. If God has decided to go and take for himself a nation out of the middle of another nation with trials and with signs, and with wonders, and with war, and with a mighty hand, and with a high arm, and with great sights, according to all the things which our Lord the god did in Egypt in your sight. So that you should know that Lord the god is god, and there is none beside him. His voice was made audible from the sky to instruct you, and he showed you on the earth his great fire, and you heard his words out of the middle of the fire.

Because he loved your fathers, he also chose you as their seed after them, and he brought you with his great strength out of Egypt, to destroy nations greater and stronger than you in front of you, to bring you in, to give you their land to inherit, as you have it this day. You will know this day, and will consider in your heart, that Lord the god is god in the sky above, and on the earth beneath, and there is no one else but him. Keep his commandments, and his ordinances, all that I command you this day, that it may go well with you, and with your sons after you, that you may be long-lived on the land, which the Lord the god gives you forever.

Then Moses separated three cities beyond Jordan in the east, that the slayer might flee there, who should have slain his neighbor unintentionally, who he did not hate previously, and he will flee to one of these cities and live: Bosor in the wilderness, in the plain country of Reuben, and Ramoth in Gilead belonging to the Gadites, and Gaulon in Bashan belonging to Manasseh. This is the law that Moses set before the children of Israel. These are the testimonies, and the ordinances, and the judgments, which Moses spoke to the sons of Israel, when they came out of the land of Egypt, on the east side of Jordan, in the valley near the house of Peor, in the land of Sihon king of the Amorites, who lived in Heshbon, whom Moses and the sons of Israel destroyed when they came out of the land of Egypt. They inherited his land, and the land of Og king of Bashan, two kings of the Amorites, who were to the east of Jordant. From the ruins, which are on the edge of the Arnon River, even to Mount Sihon, which is Hermon. All Arabah east of Jordan under Azzah, quarried in the rock.

Deuteronomy: Chapter 5

Moses called all of Israel, and said to them, "Listen, Israel, to the ordinances and judgments, everything that I speak in your ears this day, and you will learn them, and observe and do them. Lord the god made a covenant with you in Horeb. The Lord did not make this covenant with your fathers, but with you: you are all here alive this day. The Lord spoke to you face to face in the mountain out of the middle of the fire. I stood between the Lord and you at that time to report to you the words of the Lord, (because you were afraid before the fire, and you did not go up to the mountain) saying, "I am Lord the god, who brought you out of the land of Egypt, out of the house of slavery. You will have no other gods before my face. You will not make for yourself an image, nor likeness of anything in the sky above, or whatever is in the earth beneath, and whatever is in the waters under the earth. You will not bow down to them, nor will you serve them; for I am Lord the god, a jealous god, visiting the sins of the fathers on the children to the third and fourth generation to those who hate me, and doing mercifully to thousands of them that love me, and that keep my commandments."

"You will not take the name of Lord the god in vain, for Lord the god will certainly not acquit him that takes his name in vain. Keep the sabbath day to sanctify it, as Lord the god commanded you. Six days you will work, and you will do all your works, but on the seventh day is the sabbath of Lord the god. You will do in it no work, you, nor your son, or your daughter, your man-slave or your woman-slave, your ox or your donkey, or all your livestock, or the foreigner who lives among you. Your man-slave may rest, and your woman-slave, and your ox, as well as you."

Remember that you were a slave in the land of Egypt, and Lord the god brought you out there with a mighty hand, and a high arm: therefore the Lord appointed you to keep the sabbath day and to sanctify it. Honor your father and your mother, as Lord the god commanded you. that it may be well with you, and that you may live long on the land, which the Lord the god gives you. You will not commit murder. You will not commit adultery. You will not steal. You will not bear false witness against your neighbor. You will not covet your neighbor's wife; you will not covet your neighbor's house, nor his field, nor his man-slave, nor his maid, nor his ox, nor his donkey, nor any animal of his, nor anything that is your neighbor's.

The Lord spoke these words to all the assembly of you, in the mountain out of the middle of the fire, there was darkness, blackness, storm, a loud voice, and he added no more, and he wrote them on two tablets of stone, and he gave them to me. It came to pass when you heard the voice out of the middle of the fire, for the mountain burned with fire, that you came to me, even all the heads of your tribes, and your elders, and you said, "Look, our Lord the god has shown us his glory, and we have heard his voice out of the middle of the fire: this day we have seen that God will speak to man, and he will live. Now let us not die, for this great fire will consume us, if we will hear the voice of our Lord the god anymore, and we will die. For what flesh is there which has heard the voice of the living God, speaking out of the middle of the fire, as we have heard, and will live? You go close and hear all that our Lord the god will say, and you will tell us all things whatever our Lord the god will tell you, and we will hear and obey."

The Lord heard the voice of your words as you spoke to me, and the Lord said to me, "I have heard the voice of the words of these people, even all things that they have said to you. They have said well all that they have spoken. If only there was such a heart in them, that they should fear me and keep my commands always, that it might be well with them and with their sons forever. Go, say to them, 'Return to your houses,' but stand here with me, and I will tell you all the commands, and the ordinances, and the judgments, which you will teach them, and let them do so in the land which I give them for an inheritance.

You will pay attention and do as Lord the god commanded you. You will not turn aside to the right hand or the left, from all the ways which the Lord the god commanded you to walk in, that he may give you peace, and that it may be well with you, and you may prolong your days on the land which you will inherit.

Deuteronomy: Chapter 6

These are the commands, and the ordinances, and the judgments, as many as Lord our god gave commandment to do in the land on which you enter to inherit it. That you will fear Lord the god, keep you all his ordinances, and his commandments, which I command you today, you, and your sons, and your grandsons, all the days of your life, that you may live many days. Therefore, listen Israel, and observe them, that it may be well with you, and that you may be greatly multiplied, as Lord the god of your fathers said that he would give you a land flowing with milk and honey.

These are the ordinances, and the judgments, which the Lord commanded the children of Israel in the wilderness when they had gone out from the land of Egypt. "Listen Israel, our Lord the god is one the Lord. You will love Lord the god with all your mind, and with all your mind, and all your strength. These words, all that I command you this day, will be in your heart and your mind. You will teach them to your children, and you will speak of them sitting in the house, and walking by the way, and lying down, and rising. You will fasten them for a sign on your hand, and it will be immovable before your eyes. You will write them on the lintels of your houses and of your gates. It will come to pass when Lord the god has brought you into the land which he swore to your fathers, to Abraham, and Isaac, and to Jacob, to give you great and beautiful cities which you did not build, houses full of all good things which you did not fill, pools dug in the rock which you did not dig, vineyards and olive-yards which you did not plant, then having eaten and been filled, beware in case you forget that it was Lord the god that brought you out of the land of Egypt, out of the house of slavery."

"You will fear Lord the god, and him only will you serve. You will cling to him, and by his name, you will swear. Don't follow other gods of the nations around you, as Lord the god among you is a jealous god, in case Lord the god becomes very angry with you, and destroys you from off the face of the earth. You will not tempt Lord the god, as you tempted him in the temptation. You will, by all means, keep the commands of Lord the god, the testimonies, and the ordinances, which he commanded you. You will do that which is pleasing and good before Lord the god, that it may be well with you, and that you may go in and inherit the good land, which the Lord swore to your fathers, to chase all your enemies from in front of you, as the Lord foretold."

"It will come to pass when your son will ask you tomorrow, 'What are the testimonies, and the ordinances, and the judgments, which our Lord the god has commanded us?'

Then you will answer your son, "We were slaves to Pharaoh in the land of Egypt, and the Lord brought us out there with a mighty hand, and with a high arm. The Lord gave signs and great and evil wonders in Egypt, Pharaoh, and his house in front of us. He brought us out there to give us this land, which he swore to give to our fathers. The Lord ordered us to observe all these ordinances, to fear our Lord the god, that it may be well with us forever, that we may live, as even today. There will be mercy for us if we pay attention to keep all these commands before our Lord the god, as he has commanded us."

Deuteronomy: Chapter 7

When Lord the god brings you into the land which you go to possess, he will remove great nations from before you, the Cypriots,[1] Girgashites, Amorites, Canaanites, Perizzites, Mitannians, and Jebusites, seven nations more numerous and stronger than you, and Lord the god will deliver them into your hands, then you will destroy them. You will completely destroy them. You will not make a peace treaty with them, neither will you feel compassion for them, neither will you agree to marry them. You will not give your daughter to his son, and you will not take his daughter for your son. For he will draw away your son from me, and he will serve other gods. The Lord will be very angry with you, and will soon completely destroy you. You will do this to them: you will destroy their altars, and will break down their columns, and will cut down their groves, and will burn with fire the carved images of their gods.

You are a sacred people to Lord the god, and Lord the god chose you to be for him a unique people beyond all nations that are on the face of the earth. It was not because you are more numerous than all other nations that the Lord preferred you. The Lord chose you, as you are fewer in number than all other nations. Because the Lord loved you, and in keeping the oath which he swore to your fathers, the Lord brought you out with a strong hand, and the Lord redeemed you from the house of slavery, out of the hand of Pharaoh king of Egypt. You will know, therefore, that Lord the god is god, a faithful god, who keeps covenant and mercy for them that love him, and for those that keep his commandments to a thousand generations, and who recompenses them that hate him to their face, to destroy them completely. Will not be relaxed with those that hate him: he will repay them to their face.

You will, therefore, obey the commands, and the ordinances, and the judgments, which I command you to do today. It will happen that when you have heard these ordinances, and have kept and done them, that Lord the god will keep the covenant and the mercy with you, which he swore to your fathers. He will love you, and bless you, and multiply you, and he will bless the offspring of your belly, and the fruit of your land, your grain, and your wine, and your oil, the herds of your oxen, and the flocks of your sheep, on the land which the Lord swore to your fathers to give to you. You will be blessed beyond all nations. There will not be among you an impotent or barren one, or among your livestock. Lord the god will remove from you all sickness, and none of the evil diseases of Egypt, which you have seen, and all that you have known, will he infect you with. He will infect them on all that hate you.

You will eat all the spoils of the nations which the Lord the god gives you, your eye will not spare them, and you will not serve their gods for this is an offense for you. But if you should say in your heart, "This nation is greater than I, how will I be able to destroy them completely?" You will not fear them, you will certainly remember all that Lord the god did to Pharaoh and all the Egyptians: the great temptations which your eyes have seen, those signs and great wonders, the strong hand, and the high arm, how Lord the god brought you out. Likewise, Lord the god will do to all the nations, who you fear in their presence. Lord the god will send against them the hornets until they that are left and they that are hidden from you be completely destroyed. You will not be wounded by them, because Lord the god is among you, is a great and powerful god. Lord the god will consume these nations before you by little and little.

You will not be able to consume them quickly, in case the land becomes desert, and the wild beasts of the field are multiplied against you. Lord the god will deliver them into your hands, and you will destroy them with great destruction until you have completely destroyed them. He will deliver their kings into your hands, and you will destroy their name from that place. None will stand in opposition before you until you have completely destroyed them. You will burn with fire the carved images of their gods. You will not covet their silver, neither will you take for yourself gold from them, in case you should offend, because it is an abomination to Lord the god. You will not bring an abomination into your house, or you should be an accursed thing like it. You will completely hate it, and altogether despise it, because it is a cursed thing.

Deuteronomy: Chapter 7 Notes

1 LXX 963: Chettaeon (ΧΕΤΤΑΙΟΝ)

• LXX 46: Chetaeon (Χέταιον)

• Leningrad Codex: Chitti (חִתִּי). Translation: Cypriots

• Peshitta: Ḥytyå (ܚܬܝܐ)

• Targum Onkelos: Chitta'ei (חִתָּאֵי)

• Targum Jerusalem: Chitta'ei (חִתָּאֵי)

This term has created a great deal of confusion since the misidentification of the ruins of the Neshites as being 'Hittite' in the 1800s. The modern archaeological name 'Hittite,' is not derived from an ancient name for the culture applied by themselves, or anyone else, but rather adopted from the biblical reference to a then-unknown civilization somewhere in the region.

There was an ancient culture in the region called the Hattians, however, they were conquered by the Nesites before 1700 BC, and subsequently disappeared from the historic records. The name was applied to culture today referred to as 'Hittites,' before the 'Hittite' language had been translated, and is incorrect. Since 1906, excavations at Boğazköy, the ancient 'Hittite' capital Hattusa have uncovered more than 10,000 'Hittite' texts, including the royal achieve. The actual name of the 'Hittite' language and people was Nešili (𒉈𒅆𒇷), which is now rendered in some academic literate as Nesite or Neshite. As early as the mid-1800s some scholars disputed the identification of the Nesites as the Biblical Hittites, including the Orientalist Max Müller, who was one of many claiming the Biblical Hittites were ancient Greeks or some other Mediterranean people. Later in the Septuagint's translation of the Maccabees, the similar term Chettiim (Χεττιιμ) as a reference to all Greek-speaking lands, and therefore the Biblical Hittites were likely the Minoans or the Achaean Greeks.

In the 1st century AD, the Jewish historian Josephus reported that Cethima was the name of Cyrus in Aramaic, and the Chettim were the descendants of Noah's grandson Chethimus, who had settled on Cyprus. Josephus reported that the name was preserved in the Greek name of the town Cition (Κίτιον). Most historians view it as more likely that the Aramaic name was derived from the city-state of Cition, which was known as Kâtjây (𓎡𓏏𓇋𓇌𓈉) in Egyptian records from the New Kingdom Era in the late Bronze Age, and Kt (𐤊𐤕) or Kty (𐤊𐤕𐤉) in Phoenician records from the early Iron Age. While this may be the origin of the term, by the era of the Neo-Assyrian era, the term must have also referred to other Greek islands, as both the prophets Isaiah and Ezekiel used the term 'Islands of Kittim.' As the term referred to the entire island of Cyprus in Aramaic, the translations of 'Cyprus' and 'Cypriots' are used here.

Deuteronomy: Chapter 8

You will observe all the commands which I order you today, that you may live and be multiplied, and enter in and inherit the land, which the Lord the god swore to give to your fathers. You will remember all the ways that Lord the god led you in the wilderness, when he punished you, and tried you, to test your in your heart whether you would keep his commandments or not. He punished you and straightened you with hunger, and fed you with manna, which your fathers did not know to teach you that man does not live by bread alone, but by every word that proceeds out of the mouth of God does man live. Your garments did not grow old and fall from you, your shoes were not worn out, your feet were not painfully hardened, these entire forty years!

You know in your heart, that as if any man should chastise his son, so Lord the god will chastise you. You will keep the commands of Lord the god, to follow his ways, and to fear him. For Lord the god will bring you into a good and exten-sive land, where there are torrents of waters, and fountains issuing of deep places through the plains and the mountains. A land of wheat and barley, in which are vines, figs, pomegranates. A land of olive oil and honey. A land on which you will not eat your bread with poverty, and you will not want anything. A land whose stones are iron, and out of its mountains you will dig brass. You will eat and be filled and will bless Lord the god on the good land, which he has given you.

Pay attention to yourself that you don't forget Lord the god, and don't keep his commands, and his judgments, and ordinances, which I command you this day, in case when you have eaten and are full, and have built good houses, and lived in them, and your oxen and your sheep are multiplied to you, and your silver and your gold are multiplied to you, and all your possessions are multiplied to you, you should be exalted in heart, and forget Lord the god, who brought you out of the land of Egypt, out of the house of slavery, who brought you through that great and terrible wilderness, where is the biting serpent, and scorpion, and drought, where there was no water, who brought you a fountain of water out of the flinty rock, who fed you with manna in the wilderness, which you did not know, and your fathers did not know, that he might punish you, and thoroughly test you, and you'll do good in your latter days.

In case you should say in your heart, "My strength and the power of my hand have worked for me this great wealth." But you will remember Lord the god, that he gives you the strength to get wealth, so that he may establish his covenant, which the Lord swore to your fathers, and on this day. It will come to pass if you do at all forget Lord the god, and should go after other gods, and serve them, and worship them, I call the sky and earth to witness against you this day, that you will certainly perish. As also the other nations which the Lord the god destroys in front of you, so will you perish, because you did not listen to the voice of Lord the god.

Deuteronomy: Chapter 9

Listen Israel! You go this day across the Jordan to inherit nations greater and stronger than yourselves, cities great and walled up to the sky. A great people and many and tall, the sons of Anakites, whom you know. Regarding whom you have heard it said, "Who can stand before the children of Anakites?"

"You will know today, that Lord the god will go before you. He is a consuming fire, and he will destroy them, and he will turn them back before you and will destroy them quickly, as the Lord said to you, 'Don't say in your heart, when Lord the god has destroyed these nations in front of you, 'Because my righteousness, Lord brought me in to inherit this good land.'" Not for your righteousness, or the holiness of your heart, do you go in to inherit their land, but because of the wickedness of these nations the Lord will destroy them from before you, and that he may establish the covenant, which the Lord swore to our fathers, to Abraham, Isaac, and Jacob. You will know today, that it is not for your righteousness that Lord the god gives you this good land to inherit, for you are a stubborn people.

Don't forget how much you provoked Lord the god in the wilderness, from the day that you came out of Egypt, even until you came into this place, you continued to be disobedient toward the Lord. Also in Horeb you provoked the Lord, and the Lord was angry enough with you to destroy you. When I went up into the mountain to receive the tablets of stone, the tablets of the covenant, which the Lord made with you, and I was in the mountain forty days and forty nights, I ate no bread and drank no water. The Lord gave me the two tablets of stone written with the finger of God, and on them, there had been written all the words which the Lord spoke to you in the mountain on the day of the assembly. It happened after forty days and forty nights, the Lord gave me the two tablets of stone, the tablets of the covenant. The Lord said to me, "Rise, go down quickly from here. Your people, whom you brought out of the land of Egypt, have transgressed. They have quickly abandoned the way which I commanded them, and have made themselves a molten image."

The Lord said to me, "I have said to you before, 'I have seen this people, and, look, it is a stubborn people. Now allow me to completely destroy them, and I will blot out their name from under the sky, and will make of you a nation great and strong, and more numerous than this.'"

"I turned and went down from the mountain, and the mountain burned with fire to the sky, and the two tablets of the testimonies were in my two hands. When I saw that you had sinned against Lord the god, and had made for yourselves a molten image, and had gone astray from the way, which the Lord commanded you to do, I took hold of the two tablets, and threw them out of my two hands, and broke them before you. I made my petition before the Lord as also in the first forty days and forty nights. I ate no bread and drank no water, on account of all your sins which you sinned in doing evil before Lord the god to provoke him. I was greatly terrified because of the rage and anger because the Lord was provoked with you completely to the point of destroying you, yet the Lord listened to me at this time also. He was angry enough with Aaron to destroy him completely, and I prayed for Aaron also at that time. Your sin which you had made, the calf, I took, and burnt it with fire, and pounded it and ground it down until it became fine, and it became like dust, and I threw the dust into the brook that descended from the mountain."

Also at Burning, and at Temptation, and at the Graves of Desire, you provoked the Lord. When the Lord sent you out from Kadesh Barnea, saying, "Go up and inherit the land which I give to you," then you disobeyed the word of Lord the god, and did not believe him, and did not listen to his voice. You were disobedient towards the Lord from the day in which he became known to you.

I prayed before the Lord forty days and forty nights, the number that I prayed before, for the Lord said that he would completely destroy you. I prayed to god, and said, "Lord Ba'al, King of gods,[1] don't destroy your people and your inheritance, who you did redeem, who you brought out of the land of Egypt with your great power, and with your strong hand, and with your high arm. Remember Abraham, Isaac, and Jacob your servants, to whom you swore by yourself. Look not at the hardness of heart of these people, and their impieties, and their sins. In case the inhabitants of the land from where you brought us out say, 'Because the Lord could not bring them into the land of which he told them, and because he hated them, has he brought them out to slay them in the wilderness.' These are your people and your portion, who you brought out of the land of Egypt with your great strength, and with your mighty hand, and with your high arm."

Deuteronomy: Chapter 9 Notes

1 Codex Vaticanus: c̄e basileu tôn theôn (ⲔⲈⲂⲀⳠⲒⲀⲈⲨⲦⲰⲚⲐⲈⲰⲚ). Translation: lord king of the gods

- Codex Alexandrinus: cyrie cyrie basileu tôn theôn (ⲔⲨⲢⲒⲈⲔⲨⲢⲒⲈⲂⲀⳠⲒⲀⲈⲨⲦⲰⲚ ⲐⲈⲰⲚ). Translation: lord lord king of the gods

- LXX 799: Cyrie cyrie basileus tôn ethnôn (ⲕ ⲁ̅ⲃ̅ⲓⳠ ⳑⲁ̅ⲃ̅ⲓⳠ ⳙⲁⲥⲓⳑⳛⳡⲥ ⲧⲟⲟⲛ ⳝⲑⲛⲟⲟⲛ). Translation: Lord lord king of the nations

- LXX 707: Cyrie cyrie basileus tôn aeônôn (ⲕ ⲁ̅ⲃ̅ⲓⳠ ⳑⲁ̅ⲃ̅ⲓⳠ ⳙⲁⲥⲓⳑⳛⳡⲥ ⲧⲟⲟⲛ ⳑⲓⲟⲟⲛⲟⲟⲛ). Translation: Lord lord king of the ages (or centuries)

- Leningrad Codex: Adonai Yehwih (אֲדֹנָי יְהוִה). Translation: Lord Yehvih

- Peshitta: mryå ålhå ll (ܠܠ ܐܠܗܐ ܡܪܝܐ). Translation: lord god of night (or Lil)

- Targum Onkelos: yeyah elahim (יְיָ אֱלֹהִים). Translation: Yhǔ gods

- Targum Jerusalem: yeyah elahachon (יְיָ אֱלָהְכוֹן). Translation: Yhǔ your god

This verse has not survived among the Dead Sea Scrolls. The differences between these two verses show a clear difference between the Aramaic text the Greeks translated circa 250 BC, and the Hebrew text the Masoretes began copying them in the 4th century AD. The removal of references to other gods is consistent with the Hasmonean redaction.

The term 'King of the Gods' is clearly polytheistic, which points to this section of Deuteronomy being older than Leviticus, which was essentially monotheistic. In the Canaanite religion, which El was central to, Ba'al Hadad became the King of the Gods after El left the world, and this verse seems to be about him. Lord Lord (Κύριε Κύριε) appears to be a Greek translation of ådn bôlå (אדן בעל) meaning Lord Ba'al. The term King of the Gods would have been mlkå hålhyn (אלהין מלכא) in Aramaic, meaning the line would have read ådn bôlå mlkå hålhyn, which would be translated as Lord Ba'al King of the Elohim in Hebrew, which would have certainly been removed by a Hasmonean redactor. The general implication of this line is that Lord Ba'al was the Lord speaking to Moses according to the author, and that he was also called the King of the Gods, which would indicate the author was familiar with the Ba'al Cycle, and he expected his readers to also be familiar with it. Both the prophets Hosea and Zephaniah denounced the Israelite worship of Ba'al, along with other gods. Hosea lived in Samaria before it was conquered by the Assyrians, while Zephaniah lived in Judah during the time of Josiah, shortly before Egypt conquered Judah.

The Samaritan prophet Ezekiel, who lived before King Josiah's reforms, prophesied on behalf of Lord Ba'al (Κύριε Κύριε), whom he identified as coming from Zephon, where Ba'al Hadad's temple was built in the Ugaritic Texts, and denounced the worship of the gods of the Temple of Jerusalem, suggesting that worship of Lord Ba'al was widespread at the time. The inclusion of the term 'King of the gods' suggests that Lord Ba'al was also the god the Ammonites called Mlkm (𐤌𐤋𐤊𐤌), which the author of 4ᵗʰ Kingdoms (Masoretic Kings) called 'King' (מלך), transliterated as Moloch (Μολοχ) in the Septuagint, and accented as Mōlek (מֹלֶךְ) by the Masoretes, whom the Judahites were recorded as sacrificing their firstborn to before King Josiah's reforms. This supports the origin of Deuteronomy in the Kingdom of Samaria before it was conquered by the Assyrians, and the book's usage in Judah before the reforms.

Deuteronomy: Chapter 10

At that time the Lord said to me, "Cut for yourself two stone tablets like the first, and come up to me in the mountain, and make for yourself a wooden box.[1] You will write on the tablets the words which were on the first tablets which you broke, and you will put them into the box."

So I made a box of boards of incorruptible wood, and I cut tablets of stone like the first, and I went up to the mountain, and the two tablets were in my hand. He wrote on the tablets like the first, writing the ten commandments, which the Lord spoke to you in the mountain out of the middle of the fire, and the Lord gave them to me. I turned and came down from the mountain, and I put the tablets into the box which I had made, and they were there, as the Lord commanded me.

The children of Israel departed from Beeroth of the sons of Jaakan to Mosera, where Aaron died, and there he was buried, and Eleazar his son became priest in his place. They departed there to Gudgodah and traveled from Gudgodah to Jotbath, a land in which are torrents of water. At that time the Lord separated the tribe of Levi, to carry the box of the covenant of the Lord, and to stand near before the Lord and minister and bless in his name until this day. Therefore the Levites have no part of the inheritance among their brothers. The Lord himself is their inheritance, as he said to them. I stood on the mount forty days and forty nights, and the Lord heard me at that time also, and the Lord would not destroy you.

The Lord said to me, "Go, set out before these people, and let them go in and inherit the land, which I swore to their fathers to give to them."

Now, Israel, what does Lord the god require of you, except to fear Lord the god, and to follow all his ways, and to love him, and to serve Lord the god with all your heart, and with all your mind, to keep the commandments of Lord the god, and his ordinances, all that I order you today, that it may go well with you? See your Lord the god Shamayim. The skies of Shamayim and the earth, and everything on it are his.[2] Only the Lord chose your fathers to love them, and he chose their descendants after them, including you, above all nations, like today. Therefore you will circumcise the hardness of your heart, and you will not harden your neck.

Lord the god is God of gods, and the Lord of lords, the great, and strong, and terrible God, who does not wonder at persons, nor will he by any means accept a bribe. Executing judgment for the stranger and orphan and widow, and he loves the stranger and gives him food and clothing. You will love the stranger, for you were strangers in the land of Egypt. You will fear Lord the god, and serve him, and will cleave to him, and will swear by his name. He is your pride, and he is your god, who has worked among you these great and glorious things, which your eyes have seen. With seventy minds your fathers went down into Egypt, but Lord the god has made you as the stars of the sky in multitude.

Deuteronomy: Chapter 10 Notes

1 Codex Vaticanus: cibôton (ΚΙΒШΤΟΝ). Translation: box

- Leningrad Codex: aron (אָרֹן). Translation: cupboard (or closet, cabinet)

- Peshitta: qbůrtå (ܩܒܘܪܬܐ). Translation: coffin (or urn, sarcophagus)

- Targum Onkelos: arona (אֲרוֹנָא). Translation: cupboard (or closet, cabinet)

- Targum Jerusalem: arona (אֲרוֹנָא). Translation: cupboard (or closet, cabinet)

- Shapira scrolls: Årn (𐤀𐤓𐤍). Translation: box

2 Codex Vaticanus: idou c̄s o th̄s sou o ounos cae o ounos tou ounou, ê gê cae panta, osa estin en autê (ΙΔΟΥ Κ̄C̄ Ο Θ̄C̄ CΟΥ Ο ΟΥΝΟC ΚΑΙ Ο ΟΥΝΟC ΤΟΥ ΟΥΝΟΥ Η ΓΗ ΚΑΙ ΠΑΝΤΑ ΟCΑ ΕCΤΙΝ ΕΝ ΑΥΤΗ). Translation: "See Lord the god of your vaulted-sky (or Uranus), and the vaulted-sky (or Uranus) of the vaulted-sky (or Uranus), the earth (or Ge) and everything there are his."

- LXX 767: idou cyriou tou theou sou ouranos cae yranos tou ouranou, hê gê cae panta, hasa estin en autê (ιΔου ͆ͱͲ͂ου του θ͂ου σου ουϼΑΝΟC ͱΑΙ υϼΑΝΟC του ουϼΑΝΟΥ, ʒͷ γ͆ͷ ͱΑΙ παͶ͵ΝΤΑ, οσΑ ͷοτιΝ ͷΝ Αͷτͷ). Translation: "See Lord thegod of you, and Uranus of the skies of Uranus, the earth and everything there are his."

- LXX 318: idou cyriou tou theou sou ouranos cae yranos tou oủranou, hê gê cae panta, hasa estin en autê (ιΔου ͆ͱͲ͂ου του θ͂ου σου ουϼΑΝΟC του ουϼΑΝΟΥ, ʒͷ γ͆ͷ ͱΑΙ παͶ͵ΝΤΑ, οσΑ ͷοτιΝ ͷΝ Αͷτͷ). Translation: "See Lord thegod of you, skies of sky, the earth and everything there are his."

- LXX 83: idou cyriou toũ theoũ sou cae ta dicaeômata autou osa egô entellomae soe sêmeron ho oủranos cae ho oủranos toũ oủranoũ, hê gẽ cae panta, hasa estin en aủtẽ (ιΔου ⲕⲩⲣⲫⲟⲩ ⲧⲟⲩ ⲑ̄ⲟⲩ ⲥⲟⲩ ⲕ̄ⲁ̄ⲓ ⲧⲁ ⲇ̄ⲓⲕ̄ⲁⲓⲟⲟⲙⲁⲧⲁ ⲁⲩⲧⲟⲩ ⲟⲥⲁ ⲟ̄ⲅⲱ ⲟ̄ⲛⲧⲟ̄ⲗⲗⲟⲙⲁⲓ ⲥⲟⲓ ⲥ̄ⲏ̄ⲙⲟ̄ⲣⲟⲛ ⲟ ⲟⲩⲣⲁ̄ⲛⲟⲥ ⲕ̄ⲁ̄ⲓ ⲟ ⲟⲩⲣⲁ̄ⲛⲟⲥ ⲧⲟⲩ ⲟⲩⲣⲁ̄ⲛⲟⲩ, ⲏ̄ ⲅ̄ⲏ ⲕ̄ⲁ̄ⲓ ⲡⲁ̄ⲛⲧⲁ, ⲟⲥⲁ ⲟ̄ⲥⲧⲓⲛ ⲟ̄ⲛ ⲁⲩⲧⲏ̄). Translation: "See Lord thegod of you, and the authority of his as far as I declare to you today, the skies and the skies of the sky, the earth and everything there are his."

• Leningrad Codex: hen laIhvah eloheicha hashamayim ushemei hashamayim ha'aretz vechol-asher-bah (הֵן לַיהוָה אֱלֹהֶיךָ הַשָּׁמַיִם וּשְׁמֵי הַשָּׁמָיִם הָאָרֶץ וְכָל־אֲשֶׁר־בָּהּ) Translation: "seethe Yhwah your god Shamayim and the sky of Shamayim the earth and everything in her."

• Dead Sea Scroll 4QDeut^l: the verse is damaged, however -hårs ůkl åš- (- אארץ וכל אש) survives. Translation: "-land and everything-"

• Peshitta: dmryå ånůn ålhk šmyå ušmy šmyå ůårôå wkl dåyt bh (ܕܡܪܝܐ ܐܢܘܢ ܐܠܗܟ ܫܡܝܐ ܘܫܡܝ ܫܡܝܐ ܘܐܪܥܐ ܘܟܠ ܕܐܝܬ ܒܗ). Translation: master of ours, our god Shamyya (or sky) and name Shamyya (or sky) and land and everything that exists in it

• Targum Onkelos: ha dayeyah elahach shemayya ushemei shemayya ar'a vechol di vah (הָא דַּיְיָ אֱלָהָךְ שְׁמַיָּא וּשְׁמֵי שְׁמַיָּא אַרְעָא וְכָל דִּי בַהּ). Translation: see the Yhů, your god sky (or Shemayyah), land, and everything in it

• Targum Jerusalem: ha dayeyah elahachon shemaya ushemei shemaya vechittei mal'achaya divhon limshamshin kodamoy ar'a vechol de'it bah (הָא דַּיְיָ אֱלָהְכוֹן שְׁמַיָּא וּשְׁמֵי שְׁמַיָּא וְכִתֵּי מַלְאֲכַיָּא דִבְהוֹן לִמְשַׁמְשִׁין קֳדָמוֹי אַרְעָא וְכָל דְּאִית בָּהּ). Translation: Translation: see the Yhů, your gods sky (or Shemayyah) and the name Shemeyyah (or sky), land, and chicken-messenger (possibly the peacock-angel), their bear, the servants of ancient land and everything in it

The difference between the Septuagint's version and the Masoretic version of this verse is significant, and the Septuagint's reading is generally used by translators of the Masoretic Text. The Greek translation is consistent with the Greek concept of the sky circa 250 BC, wherein there was a sky under the vaulted dome covering the earth, above which lived the gods. This structure is similar to the Second Temple Era description of the vaulted sky found in the Books of Enoch, except there were seven skies in the Jewish version, one above the other. This seven-skied world was drawn from the concept of the celestial spheres, in which each visible planet moved in its own spherical sky.

As there is no evidence of the Israelites ever believing in a single vaulted sky, the Septuagint's version is likely a Greek reinterpretation that assumed the word ushemei (ושמי) was a transcription error. If the Masoretic version is similar to what the Greeks translated, it appears to be a partial redaction of a version of Deuteronomy in which

Shamayim was the Lord. This would point clearly to Deuteronomy's composition in Samaria under Assyrian rule, as the Canaanite god Shamayim was regarded as the local variant of Asshur, the national god of Assyria, who by that time was known as to Ansar (⸬⸬), the 'Whole Sky.' It cannot be determined from this fragment in the Masoretic Text if the original author was a Shamayim worshiper, or if an older text had Shamayim's name inserted, however, the worship of Shamayim was widespread in Samaria and Judah in the 8th and 7th centuries BC, as reported by Hosea, Zephaniah, and Jonah. King Josiah ultimately banned the worship of Shamayim in Judah circa 625 BC.

Deuteronomy: Chapter 11

You will love Lord the god and will follow his appointments, and his ordinances, and his commandments, and his judgments, always. You will know today, for I speak not to your children, who don't know and have not seen the discipline of Lord the god, and his wonderful works, and his strong hand, and his high arm, and his miracles, and his wonders, which he worked in Egypt against Pharaoh king of Egypt, and all his land, and what he did to the army of the Egyptians, and their chariots, and their cavalry, and their infantry. How he made the water of the Papyrus Sea to overwhelm the face of them as they pursued after you, and the Lord destroyed them until today. All the things which he did to you in the wilderness until you came into this place, and all the things that he did to Dathan and Abiram the sons of Eliab the son of Reuben, whom the earth opening her mouth swallowed up, and their houses, and their tents, and all their substance that was with them among all Israel. For your eyes have seen all the mighty works of the Lord, which he worked among you today.

You will keep all his commandments, all I command you today, that you may live, and be multiplied, and that you may go in and inherit the land, into which you go across the Jordan to inherit, so you may live long on the land, which the Lord swore to your fathers to give to them, and to their seed after them, a land flowing with milk and honey.

The land into which you go to inherit is not like the land of Egypt, where you came out of, where they sow the seed, and water it with their feet, as a garden of plants. The land into which you go to inherit is a land of mountains and plains, it will drink the rainwater from the sky. A land which the Lord the god surveys continually, the eyes of Lord the god are on it from the beginning of the year to the end of the year. Now if you will indeed listen to all the commands which I order you today, to love Lord the god, and to serve him with all your heart, and with all your mind, then he will give to your land the early and late rain in its season, and you will bring in your grain, and your wine, and your oil. He will give food in your fields to your livestock, and when you have eaten and are full, pay attention to yourself that your heart does not be puffed up, and you transgress, and serve other gods, and worship them. The Lord will be angry with you, and hold back the sky, and there will not be rain, and the earth will not yield its fruit. You will perish quickly from off the good land, which the Lord has given you.

You will keep these words in your heart and your mind, and you will bind them as a sign on your hand, and it will be fixed before your eyes. You will teach them to your children, to speak about them when you sit in the house, and when you walk, and when you sleep, and when you rise. You will write them on the lintels of your houses, and your gates, that your days may be long, and the days of your children, in the land which the Lord swore to your fathers to give to them, as the days of the sky on the earth. It will come to pass, that if you will indeed listen to all these commands, which I order you to observe today, to love our Lord the god, and to follow all his ways, and to cling close to him, then the Lord will throw out all these nations before you, and you will inherit great nations, stronger than yourselves. Every place on which the sole of your foot will tread will be yours, from the wilderness and Anti-lebanon, and the great river, the river Euphrates, even as far as the west sea will be your frontiers. No one will stand before you, and Lord the god will put the fear of you and the dread of you on the face of all the land, in which you will tread, as he told you.

See, I set before you today the blessing and the curse, the blessing, if you listen to the commands of Lord the god, all that I command you today, and the curse if you do not listen to the commands of our Lord the god, all I command you today, and you wander from the way which I have commanded you, having gone to serve other gods, which you don't know. It will come to pass when Lord the god has brought you into the land into which you go over to inherit it, then you will put a blessing on Mount Gerizim, and a curse on Mount Ebal. See! Are not these beyond the Jordan, to the west in the land of Canaan, which lies near the circle[1] by the high oak? For you are passing over the Jordan, to go in and inherit the land, which our Lord the god gives you to inherit always, and you will live in it. You will pay attention to do all his ordinances, and these judgments, as many as I set before you today.

Deuteronomy: Chapter 11 Notes

1 Codex Vaticanus: Golgol (ⲅⲟⲗⲅⲟⲗ)

• Codex Colberto-Sarravianus: Golgôn (ⲅⲟⲗⲅⲱⲛ)

• Codex Ambrosiano A 147: Golgod (ⲅⲟⲗⲅⲟⲇ)

• Codex Venetus: Godgod (ⲅⲟⲇⲅⲟⲇ)

• LXX 407: Golgôd (ⲅⲟλγⲱⲇ)

- LXX 82: Golgô (Γολγω)

- LXX 630: Golgon (Γολγον)

- LXX 58: Galgal (Γαλγαλ)

- LXX 321: Goggol (Γογγολ)

- LXX 75: Golgol (Γολγολ)

- Leningrad Codex: gilgal (גִּלְגָּל). Translation: circle

- Dead Sea Scroll 1QDeutᵃ: glgl (𐤂𐤋𐤂𐤋)

- Peshitta: glôlå (ܓܠܝܠܐ)

- Targum Onkelos: gilgela (גִּלְגְּלָא)

- Targum Jerusalem: gulgela (גֻּלְגְּלָא)

- Shapira scrolls: glgl (𐤂𐤋𐤂𐤋)

This was generally assumed to be a reference to a town in previous centuries, however, archaeologists have discovered several ceremonial stone circles in Canaan that were used between 1200 and 1000 BC for gatherings that are assumed to be religious in nature. As these stone circles are found down in the valleys, unlike the bamah altars at the tops of hills where the Canaanites worshiped, and 'circles' (גלגל) are mentioned throughout the old Hebrew texts, it is assumed they are early Israelite religious centers from before the First Temple was built.

Deuteronomy: Chapter 12

These are the ordinances and the judgments, which you will observe and do in the land, which the Lord the god of your fathers gives you for an inheritance, all the days which you live on the land. You will completely destroy all the places in which they served their gods in the land you inherit, on the high mountains and the hills, and under the thick tree. You will destroy their altars, and break to pieces their pillars, and you will cut down their groves, and you will burn with fire the carved images of their gods, and you will abolish their name out of that place. You will not do so to Lord the god, but in the place which the Lord the god will choose, in one of your cities to name his name there, and to be called on, you will even seek him out and go there.

You will take there your whole burnt offerings, and your sacrifices, and your first fruits, and your vows, and your freewill offerings, and your offerings of thanksgiving, the firstborn of your herds, and your flocks. You will eat there before Lord the god, and you will rejoice in all the things on which you will lay your hand, you and your houses, as Lord the god has blessed you. You will not do altogether as we do here today, every man doing what is pleasing in his own sight. Until now you have not arrived at your rest and the inheritance, which our Lord the god gives you. You will go over the Jordan and will live in the land, which our Lord the god takes as an inheritance for you.

He will give you rest from all your enemies, and you will live safely. There will be a place which the Lord the god will choose for his name to be called there, there will you bring all things that I order you today, your whole burnt offerings, and your sacrifices, and your tithes, and the first fruits of your hands, and every choice gift of yours, whatever you will vow to Lord the god. You will rejoice before Lord the god, you and your sons, and your daughters, and your men-servants and your woman-slaves, and the Levite that is at your gates, because he has no portion or inheritance with you. Pay attention to yourself that you don't offer your whole burnt offerings in any place which you will see, except in the place which the Lord the god will choose. In one of your tribes, there you will offer your whole burnt offerings, and there you will do all things whatever I order you today.

You will kill according to all your desire and will eat flesh according to the blessing of Lord the god, which he has given you in every city, the unclean that are with you, and the clean will eat it on equal terms, like the doe or the stag.

Only, you will not eat the blood, you will pour it out on the ground like water. In your cities, you will not be able to eat the tithe of your grain, and your wine, and of your oil, the firstborn of your herd and of your flock, and all your vows as many as you have vowed, and your thanks-offerings, and the first fruits of your hands. Before Lord the god, you will eat it, in the place which the Lord the god will choose for himself, you, and your son, and your daughter, your man-slave, and your woman-slave, and the stranger that is within your gates, and you will rejoice before Lord the god, on whatever you will lay your hand. Pay attention to yourself that you do not desert the Levites in all the time that you live on the earth.

If Lord the god expands your borders, as he said to you, and you will say, "I will eat flesh," if your mind should desire to eat flesh, you will eat all the flesh you desire in your mind. If the place that Lord the god will choose for himself where his name is called on, is far from you, then you will kill from your herd and of your flock which God has given you, even as I commanded you, and you will eat in your cities according to the desire of your mind. As the doe and the stag are eaten, so will you eat it, the unclean in you and the clean will eat it the same way. Pay diligent attention that you eat no blood, for blood is the life of it, and the life will not be eaten with the flesh. You will not eat it, you will pour it out on the ground like water. You will not eat it, that it may go well with you and with your sons after you if you will do that which is good and pleasing before Lord the god.

You will take your holy things, if you have any, and your vowed offerings, and come to the place which the Lord the god will choose to have his name placed on it. You will sacrifice your whole burnt offerings, you will offer the flesh on the altar of Lord the god, but the blood of your sacrifices you will pour out at the foot of the altar of Lord the god, and the flesh you may eat. Beware and listen, and you will do all the commands which I order you, that it may go well with you and with your sons forever if you will do that which is pleasing and good before Lord the god. If Lord the god will completely destroy the nations from before you where you go to inherit their land, and you will inherit it and live in their land. Pay attention to yourself that you don't seek to follow them after they are destroyed before you, saying, "How do these nations worship their gods? I will do the same."

You will not do so to your god, for they have sacrificed among their gods, the abominations of the Lord which he hates, for they burn their sons and their daughters in the fire of their gods. Every word that I command you today, you will observe it: you will not add to it, nor take from it.

Deuteronomy: Chapter 13

If there appears among you a prophet or one who dreams a dream, and he predicts a sign or a wonder, and the sign or the wonder happens as he told you, and he says, "Let's go and serve other gods," who you don't know. You will not listen to the words of that prophet, or the dreamer of that dream, because Lord the god tests you, to know whether you love your god with all your heart and with all your mind. You will obey Lord the god, and fear him, and you will hear his voice, and attach yourselves to him. That prophet or that dreamer of a dream will die, for he has spoken to make you error from Lord the god who brought you out of the land of Egypt, who redeemed you from slavery, to draw you away from the way that Lord the god commanded you to walk. You will abolish the evil from among you.

If your brother by your father or mother, or your son, or daughter, or your wife in your heart, or friend who is equal to your own mind, says to you secretly, "Let us go and serve other gods," which neither you nor your fathers have known, from the gods of the nations that are around you, whether they are from near you or at a distance from you, from one end of the earth to the other, you will not agree with him, neither will you listen to him. Your eye will not spare him, and you will feel no regret for him, nor will you at all protect him. You will certainly report concerning him, and your hands will be on him among the first to slay him, and the hands of all the people will follow. They will stone him with stones, and he will die, because he wanted to draw you away from Lord the god who brought you out of the land of Egypt, out of the house of slavery.

All Israel will hear, and fear, and will not again do this evil thing among you. If in one of your cities which the Lord the god gives you to live in, you hear men saying, "Evil men have gone out from you, and have caused all the inhabitants of their land to fall away, saying, 'Let us go and worship other gods,' whom you did not know, then you will inquire and ask, and search diligently, and look, if it is clearly true, and this abomination has taken place among you, you will completely destroy all the residents in that land with the edge of the sword. You will solemnly curse it, and all things in it. All its spoils you will gather into its public roads, and you will burn the city with fire, and all its spoils publicly before Lord the god. It will remain uninhabited forever, and it will not be built again. There will be none of the cursed thing left in your hand that the Lord may turn from his fierce anger, and give you mercy and pity you, and multiply you, as he swore to your father, if you listen to the voice of Lord the god, to keep his commandments, all that I order you today, to do that which is good and pleasing before Lord the god.

Deuteronomy: Chapter 14

You are the children of Lord the god. You will not shave any baldness between your eyes for the dead. For you are a holy people to Lord the god, and Lord the god has chosen you to be a unique people to himself of all the nations on the face of the earth. You will not eat any abominable thing. These are the beasts which you will eat: the calf from the corral, the lamb from the herd, the goat kid, the red deer, the gazelle, the antelope, the wild donkey,[1] and white-tail,[2] and oryx,[3] and giraffe.[4] Every animal that has split-hoofs, and makes claws of two divisions, and that chews the cud among beasts, these you will eat. These you will not eat from these that chew the cud, and of those that divide the hoofs, and make distinct claws: the camel, and the hare, and the rabbit, because they chew the cud, but do not have divided-hoofs, so these are unclean to you. As for the swine, because they have divided hoofs and makes claws of the hoof, yet he does not chew the cud, it is unclean for you. You will not eat their flesh, or touch their dead bodies.

These you may eat of all that are in the water. You may eat all that have fins and scales. All that do not have fins and scales you will not eat, as they are unclean for you. You may eat every clean bird. These of the birds you may not eat: the eagle, and the bearded vulture, and the sea-eagle, and the vulture, and the kite and these like them, and the sparrow, and the owl, and the seagull, and the heron, and the swan, and the stork, and the cormorant, and the hawk, and similar to them, and the hoopoe, and the raven, and the pelican, and the heron and those like them, and the flamingo and the bat. All winged animals that creep are unclean to you, and you will not eat them. You may eat every clean bird. You will eat nothing that spontaneously dies; it will be given to the traveler in your cities and he will eat it, or you will sell it to a stranger because you are a holy people to Lord the god.

You will not boil a lamb in his mother's milk. You will tithe a tenth of all the produce of your seed, the fruit of your field year by year. You will eat it in the place which the Lord the god will choose to have his name called there, you will bring the tithe of your grain and your wine, and your oil, the firstborn of your herd and your flock, that you may learn to fear Lord the god always. If the journey is too far for you, and you are not able to bring them, because the place is far from you which the Lord the god will choose to have his name called there, because Lord the god will bless you, then you will sell them for silver, and you will take the silver in your hands, and you will go to the place which the Lord the god will choose. You will give the silver for whatever your mind will desire, for oxen or sheep, or wine, or you will lay it out on strong drink, or on whatever your mind may desire, and you will eat there before Lord the god, and you will rejoice and your house, and the Levite that is in your cities, because he has no portion or inheritance with you. After three years you will bring out all the tithes of your fruits, in that year you will lay it up in your cities. The Levites will come because they have no part or lot with you, and the stranger, and the orphan, and the widow which is in your cities. They will eat and be filled, that Lord the god may bless you in all the works which you will do.

Deuteronomy: Chapter 14 Notes

1 Codex Vaticanus: tragelaphon (ΤΡΑΓΕΛΑΦΟΝ). Translation: goat-deer

- Leningrad Codex: akko (אַקּוֹ)

- Peshitta: yôlå (ܝܥܠܐ). Translation: ibex

- Targum Onkelos: ya'la (יַעְלָא). Translation: ibex

- Targum Jerusalem: ya'alin (יַעְלִין). Translation: ibexes

The Greek translation uses the name tragelaphus, which was a mythical animal in Greek writing that Aristotle used as an example a thing that was knowable even though it did not exist. The term used in the Masoretic Text is not proper Hebrew, but is accepted as referring to a wild goat. The Masoretic term was likely a transliteration of the Akkadian cuneiform word akanu (𒀭𒆜𒄷), meaning wild donkey.

2 Codex Vaticanus: pygargon (ΠΥΓΑΡΓΟΝ). Translation: white-tail

- Codex Alexandrinus: pydargon (ΠΥΔΑΡΓΟΝ)

- LXX 509: pyrargon (πυβάβγον)

- LXX 407: pygagron (πυγάγβον)

- LXX 319: pygarrhon (πυγάββον)

- LXX 52: pygaron (πυγάβον)

- LXX 458: pyrgargon (πυβγάβγον)

- LXX 318: pyrtagon (πυβτάγον)

- LXX 529: pygarton (πυγᾰβτον)

- LXX 500: pyrgalon (πυβγᾰλον)

- LXX 527: pelargon (πὅλᾰβγον)

- Leningrad Codex: dishon (דִישֹׁן)

- Peshitta: rymå (ܪܘܡܐ). Translation: buffalo (or unicorn, Asian rhinoceros)

- Targum Onkelos: reima (רֵימָא). Translation: buffalo (or unicorn, Asian rhinoceros)

- Targum Jerusalem: rimnin (רִימְנִין). Translation: buffaloes (or unicorns, Asian rhinoceroses)

The Greek term is a generic reference to a white-tail deer, however, the Masoretic term is less clear, as is does not appear to be Hebrew, Aramaic, or Akkadian. The closest term in the region is ḥiṣān (حِصَان) the Hijazi Arabic term for horse. As the Masoretic term is unclear, the Greek term is translated.

3 Codex Vaticanus: oryga (ΟΡΥΓΑ). Translation: oryx

- LXX 54: ogrega (ογβὅγᾰ)

- Leningrad Codex: te'o (תְּאֹו). Translation: buffalo

- Peshitta: dyså (ܕܝܣܐ)

- Targum Onkelos: torebala (תֹורְבָּלָא). Translation: auroch (or Lebanese buffalo)

- Targum Jerusalem: torei bar (תֹורֵי בַּר). Translation: bollocks of the forest (or open space)

4 Codex Vaticanus: camêlopardalin (ΚΑΜΗΛΟΠΑΡΔΑΛΙΝ). Translation: camel-lepard (or giraffe)

- LXX 54: calopardalên (ɫᾰλοπᾰβᾰᾰλ̔ν)

- LXX 72: camêlopardalon (ɫᾰμ̔λοπᾰβᾰᾰλον)

- LXX 29: camêloparthalin (ɫᾰμ̔λοπᾰβθᾰλιν)

- LXX 509: camêlonpardalin (ɫᾰμ̔λονπᾰβᾰᾰλιν)

- Leningrad Codex: zamer (זֶמֶר). Translation: sing

- Peshitta: årnå (ܐܪܢܐ). Translation: mountain goat

- Targum Onkelos: ditza (דִּיצָא)

- Targum Jerusalem: ditzin (דִּיצִין)

The Masoretic term zmr is generally accepted as being the same word as zmr (𐎇𐎎𐎗) in the Ugaritic, however, it is not clear which animal the word referred to. It is generally assumed to be some kind of antelope. As the Masoretic term is unclear, the Greek term is translated.

Deuteronomy: Chapter 15

Every seven years you will have a general release. This is the ordinance of the release: you will remit every private debt which your neighbor owes you, and you will not ask payment of it from your brother, as it has been called a release by Lord the god. From a stranger, you will still ask whatever he has of yours, but for your brother, you will remit his debt to you. Doing this will ensure there will not be a poor person among you, for Lord the god will certainly bless you in the land which the Lord the god gives you by inheritance, that you should inherit it.

If you will listen to the voice of Lord the god, to keep and do all these commandments, all I order you this day, (for Lord the god has blessed you in the way in which he spoke to you,) then you will lend to many nations, but you will not borrow, and you will rule over many nations, but they will not rule over you. If there is among you a poor man from your brothers in one of your cities in the land which Lord the god gives you, you will not harden your heart, nor will you close your hand from your brother who is in need. You will certainly open your hands to him and will lend to him as much as he wants according to his need. Pay attention to yourself, that there is not a secret thought in your heart thinking, "The seventh year, the year of release, draws near," and your eye will be evil to your brother that is in need, and you will not give to him, and he will cry against you to the Lord, and there will be a great sin in you. You will certainly give to him, and you will lend him as much as he wants, according to his need. You will not grudge in your heart as you give to him, because on this account Lord the god will bless you in all your works, and in all things on which you will lay your hand.

The poor will never cease from your land, therefore I order you this, "You will certainly open your hands to your poor brother, and to he, that is distressed on your land. If your brother or sister, a Habiru or a female Habiru[1] is sold to you, they will serve you six years, and in the seventh year you will send him out free from you. When you send him out free from you, you will not send him out empty-handed. You will give him provision for the journey from your flock, grain, and wine. As Lord the god has blessed you, so you will give him. You will remember that you were a servant in the land of Egypt, and Lord the god redeemed you from there, therefore I order you to do this thing. If he should say to you, "I will not leave you," because he continues to love you and your house, as he is happy with you, then you will take a spike and pierce his ear through at the door, and he will be your servant forever. You will do the same with your woman-slave. It will not seem difficult for you when they are sent out free from you, because your servant has served you six years according to the annual hire of an employee, so Lord the god will bless you in all things whatever you may do.

Every firstborn that will be born among your cows and your sheep, you will sanctify the males to Lord the god, you will not work with your firstborn calf, and you will not shear the firstborn of your sheep. You will eat it before the Lord year after year in the place which the Lord the god will choose, you and your house. If there is in it an imperfection, if it is lame or blind, an evil imperfection, you will not sacrifice it to Lord the god. You will eat it in your cities, the unclean in you and the clean will eat it as equals, like the doe or the stag. Only you will not eat the blood, you will pour it out on the earth like water.

Deuteronomy: Chapter 15 Notes

1 Codex Vaticanus: Ebraeos cae êEbraea (ЄВΡΑΙΟϹΚΑΙΗЄΒΡΑΙΑ). Translation: Hebrew and the Hebrewess

• Codex Colberto-Sarravianus: Ebraeos ê Êbraea (ЄΒΡΑΙΟϹΗΗΒΡΑΙΑ). Translation: Hebrew or Hebrewess

• Codex Venetus: Ebraeos ê Ebraea (ЄΒΡΑΙΟϹΗЄΒΡΑΙΑ). Translation: Hebrew or Hebrewess

• LXX 76: Ebraeos ê hêEbaea (Ευβαιος ι̅ ι̅ Ευαια). Translation: Ebraeos or the Hebrewess

• LXX 376: Ebeos ê hêEbraea (Ευϭος ι̅ ι̅ Ευβαφα). Translation: Ebeos or the Hebrewess

• LXX 616: Ebaeos ê hêEbraea (Ευαιος ι̅ ι̅ Ευβαφα). Translation: Ebeos or the Hebrewess

• Leningrad Codex: ha'Ivri ov ha'Ivriyyah (הָעִבְרִי אוֹ הָעִבְרִיָּה). Translation: the Hebrew (or Eberite, crosser) or the Hebrewess (or Eberitess, female-crosser)

• Peshitta: Ôbryâ åů Ôbrytå (ܥܒܪܝܐ ܐܘ ܥܒܪܝܬܐ). Translation: Hebrew or Hebrewess

• Targum Onkelos: bar Yisra'el o bat Yisra'el (בַּר יִשְׂרָאֵל אוֹ בַּת יִשְׂרָאֵל). Translation: sons of Israel or daughters of Israel

- Targum Jerusalem: bar Yishra'el o vat Yishra'el (בַּר יִשְׂרָאֵל אוֹ בַת יִשְׂרָאֵל). Translation: sons of Israel or daughters of Israel

The Eberites were the descendants of the patriarch Eber, an ancestor of Abraham who lived in Ur, in southern Iraq, according to Genesis. Many Semitic nations were believed to have been his descendants, including the Arameans, suggesting that this section of text was added during the early Iron Age, when Samaria ruled Aram. The term ôbr (עבר / ﬠﬠ) means 'to cross over' in both Hebrew and Aramaic, indicating that these Eberites were the people otherwise known to the Mesopotamians and Egyptians as Habiru. The earliest surviving mention of the Habiru (𒄩𒁉𒊒), was from the time of King Rim-Sin I of Larsa between approximately 1822 and 1763 BC, who reported they were an Aramean tribe living in southern Iraq.

Over the next 600 years, they were reported in hundreds of surviving documents ranging across the Middle East and Egypt, generally as marauders, although some were reported to be mercenaries, and those in Egypt were generally slaves. They disappeared around the end of the Bronze Age, shortly before the era of the Samaritan Empire that briefly controlled the Aramean cities of Damascus and Hama. As this reference is to the Habirus, that name is restored in this text. As there is no common feminine form of the name, the term 'female Habiru' is used.

Deuteronomy: Chapter 16

Observe the month of new grain, and you will sacrifice the Passover to Lord the god, because in the month of new grain you came out of Egypt at night. You will sacrifice the Passover to Lord the god, both sheep and oxen in the place which the Lord the god will choose to have his name called. You will not eat leaven with it, seven days will you eat unleavened bread with it, the bread of affliction, because you came out of Egypt in a hurry, so you may remember the day that you came out of the land of Egypt all the days of your life. Leaven will not be seen by you in all your borders for seven days, and there will not be left any of the flesh which you will sacrifice in the evening on the first day until the next morning. You will not have power to sacrifice the Passover in any of the cities, which the Lord the god gives you, but in the place which the Lord the god will choose, to have his name called there, you will sacrifice the Passover at the setting of the sun, the same time when you came out of Egypt.

You will boil and roast and eat it in the place, which the Lord the god will choose, and you will return in the morning, and go to your houses. Six days you will eat unleavened bread, and on the seventh day is a holiday, a feast to Lord the god. You will not do any work on it, except what must be done by a mind. Seven weeks will you count for yourself, when you have begun to put the sickle to the grain, you will begin to count seven weeks. You will keep the feast of weeks to Lord the god, accordingly as your hand has power in as many things as Lord the god will give you. You will rejoice before Lord the god, you and your son, and your daughter, your man-slave and your woman-slave, and the Levites, and the stranger, and the orphan, and the widow who lives among you, in whatever place Lord the god will choose, that his name should be called there.

You will remember that you were a servant in the land of Egypt, and you will observe and do these commands. You will keep for yourself the feast of tabernacles seven days when you gather your produce from your grain floor and your winepress. You will rejoice in your feast, you, and your son, and your daughter, your man-slave, and your woman-slave, and the Levites, and the stranger, and the orphan, and the widow that is in your cities. Seven days you will keep a feast to Lord the god in the place which the Lord the god will choose for himself, and if Lord the god will bless you in all your fruits, and in every work of your hands, then you will rejoice. Three times in the year will all your males appear before Lord the god in the place which the Lord will choose in the feast of unleavened bread, and in the feast of weeks, and in the feast of taberna-cles. You will not appear before Lord the god empty-handed. Each one according to his ability, according to the blessing of Lord the god which he has given you.

You will make for yourself judges and officers in your cities, which the Lord the god gives you in your tribes, and they will judge the people with righteous judgment: they will not seize judgment for favor persons, nor receive gifts, because gifts blind the eyes of the wise, and pervert the words of the righteous. You will justly pursue justice, that you may live, and go in and inherit the land which the Lord the god gives you. You will not raise for yourself an Asherah,[1] you will not plant for yourself any tree near the altar of your god. You will not set up for yourself a stele,[2] which the Lord the god hates.

Deuteronomy: Chapter 16 Notes

1 Codex Vaticanus: alsos (ⲁⲗⲥⲟⲥ). Translation: grove (or woods)

- LXX 82: assos (Ασσος)

- Leningrad Codex: Asherah (אֲשֵׁרָה). Translation: Asherah

- Peshitta: štltå (ܫܬܠܬܐ). Translation: seedlings (or saplings)

- Targum Onkelos: Asherat (אֲשֵׁרַת). Translation: Asherah (or permit, license)

- Targum Jerusalem: Asheirata (אֲשֵׁירָתָא). Translation: Asherah (or permit, license)

Asherah was the name of an Israelite goddess before the time of Elijah in the 9th century BC, described as the mother of Yhůh, and the wife of El. According to the books of the Kingdoms (Masoretic Kings), she was worshiped in the King Solomon's Temple along with a Ba'al, presumably Ba'al Shalim, who Jerusalem and Solomon was named after. Like Atum, the Egyptian version of Shalim, the god's wife was associated with the night sky and worshiped by planting a sacred tree, and known as the title 'Hand of god.' In the case of Asherah, her sacred tree was the oak tree, which is a self-pollinating 'virgin' tree. Important Canaanite graves were marked by planting oak acorns, which grew into 'living tombstones.' As the Greek term alsos was a translation of Asherah, the name is restored from the Masoretic Text.

2 Codex Vaticanus: stêlên (ⲥⲧⲏⲗⲏⲛ). Translation: stele (or column, pile, pillar)

- Leningrad Codex: matzevah (מַצֵּבָה). Translation: gravestone

- Peshitta: qymtå (ܩܝܡܬܐ). Translation: tombstone (or tree stump, resurrection)

- Targum Onkelos: kama (קָמָא). Translation: pillar (or statue)

- Targum Jerusalem: kama (קָמָא). Translation: pillar (or statue)

Deuteronomy: Chapter 17

You will not sacrifice to Lord the god a calf or a sheep, in which there is an imperfection, or any evil thing, for it is an abomination to Lord the god. If there should be found in any one of your cities, which the Lord the god gives you, a man or a woman who will do that which is evil before Lord the god, to transgress his covenant, and they should go to serve and worship other gods, Shemesh,[1] Yarikh,[2] any of those from the worlds of the sky which I do not command.[3] If it is reported to you, and you have inquired diligently, and, know the thing really took place, and this abomination has been done in Israel, then you will bring out that man or woman, and you will stone them with stones, and they will die. He will die on the testimony of two or three witnesses, a man who is put to death will not be put to death according to one witness. The hand of the witnesses will be among the first to put him to death, and the hands of the other people will follow, and so will you remove the evil one from among yourselves.

If a matter will be too hard for you to judge, blood between blood, cause between cause, stroke between stroke, and contradiction between contradiction, or other matters of judgment in your cities, then you will rise and go up to the place which Lord the god will choose, and you will come to the priests the Levites, and to the judge who will exist in those days, and they will study the matter and report the judgment to you. You will act according to the things which they will report to you out of the place which Lord the god will choose, and you will observe all that has been commanded in the law. You will do according to the law and to the judgment which they will declare to you. You will not swerve to the right hand or the left from any sentence which they will report to you.

The man that will act in haughtiness, and not listen to the priest who stands to minister in the name of Lord the god, or the judge who will preside in those days, that man will die, and you will remove the evil one out of Israel. All the people will hear and fear, and will no longer lack reverence.

When you enter into the land which the Lord the god gives you, and will inherit it and live in it, and will say, "I will set a king[4] over me, as also the other nations around me." You will certainly set over you the king who Lord the god will choose, from your brothers you will set a king over you. You will not set over you a stranger who is not your brother. He will not multiply for himself horses, and he will not return the people to Egypt. If he should multiply for himself horses, for the Lord said, "You will not anymore return that way."

He will not multiply for himself wives, in case his heart changes, and he will not greatly multiply for himself silver and gold. When he has been established in his government, then he will copy for himself the law into a book by the hands of the priests the Levites, and it will be with him, and he will read it all the days of his life, that he may learn to fear Lord the god, and keep all these command-ments, and to observe these ordinances so that his heart does not become elevated from his brothers, and so that he doesn't depart from the commandments on the right hand or the left. Then he and his sons may reign long in his dominion among the children of Israel.

Deuteronomy: Chapter 17 Notes

1 Codex Vaticanus: êliô (ΗλΙω). Translation Helios (or sun)

- Leningrad Codex: Shemesh (שֶׁמֶשׁ). Translation: Shemesh (or sun)

- Peshitta: šmšå (ܫܡܫܐ). Translation: sun

- Targum Onkelos: shimsha (שִׁמְשָׁא). Translation: sun

- Targum Jerusalem: shimsha (שִׁמְשָׁא). Translation: sun

Shemesh (𐤔𐤌𐤔) was the Canaanite god of the sun, the equivalent of the Akkadian Shamshu (𒀭), Greek Helios (Ηλίω), and Egyptian Ra (☉𓏤𓁛). By the era of King Josiah, the sun gods were dominant throughout the region, with the Babylonians worshiping deityMarduk (𒀭𒀫𒌓) the 'sun-calf god' as the supreme God, and the Egyptians worshiping Amen (𓇋𓏠𓈖) as the sun god, father god in the Theban trinity, and supreme God of Egypt. Based on 1st Ezra, after the king of Egypt killed King Josiah, he restored the worship of the 'Lord,' which had to have been been Shemesh, as Egyptian records report he was a worshiper Ra, Amen, and Atum, the Egyptian sun gods.

2 Codex Vaticanus: selênê (ϹΕΛΗΝΗ). Translation: Selene (or moon)

- Leningrad Codex: Yareach (יָרֵחַ). Translation: Yarikh (or moon)

- Peshitta: shrå (ܣܗܪܐ). Translation: crescent (or moon, silver)

- Targum Onkelos: sihara (סִיהֲרָא). Translation: crescent (or moon, silver)

- Targum Jerusalem: sihara (סִיהֲרָא). Translation: crescent (or moon, silver)

Yrḫ / Yrh (𐤉𐤓𐤇 / 𐤁𐤀𐤆) was the Canaanite god of the moon, the equivalent of the Sabaen Ůrḫ (𐩥𐩧𐩭), Aramaic Yrhå (ירחא), Sumerian ᵃⁿNanna (𒀭𒋀𒆠), Akkadian Sin (𒂗𒍪), North Egyptian Îôhů (𓇋𓂝𓎛𓇳), South Egyptian Khonsu (𓊨𓈖𓇳), and Greek Selene (Σελήνη).

The moon god may have been dominant in Southern Canaan and Hejaz Mountains, which the Neo-Babylonian king Nabonidus believed, however, that would have been long before the era of Josiah. The city of Jericho appears to have been named after the Canaanite moon god Yrh, and was one of the major fortified cities in the region for thousands of years before it was destroyed around 1500 BC. Nabonidus attempted to restore the worship of the moon god briefly, however, lost his empire to the Persians.

3 Codex Vaticanus: panti tôn ec tou cosmou tou ounoua ou prosetaxen (ΠΑΝΤΙ ΤΩΝ ΕΚ ΤΟΥ ΚΟϹΜΟΥ ΤΟΥ ΟΥΝΟΥ Α ΟΥ ΠΡΟϹΕΤΑΞΕΝ). Translation: any (or all, each) those from (or out, of) the cosmos (or worlds, universe) the vaulted-sky (or Uranus) which not command

- Codex Alexandrinus: panti tôn cosmô tô ec ouranou a ou prosetaxa (ΠΑΝΤΙ ΤΩΝ ΚΟϹΜΩ ΤΩ ΕΚ ΟΥΡΑΝΟΥ Α ΟΥ ΠΡΟϹΕΤΑΞΑ). Translation: any (or all, each) the cosmos (or worlds, universe) those from the vaulted-sky (or Uranus) which not command

- Codex Venetus: panti tôn cosmou tô ec ouranou a ou proetaxa soe (ΠΑΝΤΙ ΤΩΝ ΚΟϹΜΟΥ ΤΩ ΕΚ ΟΥΡΑΝΟΥ Α ΟΥ ΠΡΟΕΤΑΞΑ ϹΟΙ). Translation: any (or all, each) the cosmos (or worlds, universe) those from the vaulted-sky (or Uranus) which not command you

- LXX 707: panti to ec tou cosmou tou ouranou ha ou prosetaxa (πλντι το ϭμ του μϭσμου του ουϸλνου λ ου πϸοσϙτλξλ). Translation: any (or all, each) those from (or out, of) the cosmos (or worlds, universe) the vaulted-sky (Uranus) which not command

- LXX 29: panti tôn en tou cosmô tou ouranou ha ou prosetaxa (πλντι τοον ϭν του μοσμοο του ουϸλνου λ ου πϸοσϙτλξλ). Translation: any (or all, each) those in the cosmos (or worlds, universe) of the vaulted-sky (or Uranus) which not command

- LXX 130: panti tôn en tou cosmou tou ouranou ha ou prosetaxae (πλντι τοον ϭν του μϭσμου του ουϸλνου λ ου πϸοσϭτλξλι). Translation: any (or all, each) those in the cosmos (or worlds, universe) of the vaulted-sky (or Uranus) which not command

- Leningrad Codex: lechol-tzeva hashamayim asher lo-tzivviti (לְכֹל־צְבָא הַשָּׁמַיִם אֲשֶׁר לֹא־צִוִּיתִי). Translation: every (or all, whole) military (or army) the skies (or Shamayim) which not I ordered

• Peshitta: lkl ḥylůtå dšmyå dlå pqdt (ܦܩܕܬ ܕܠܐ ܕܫܡܝܐ ܚܝܠܘܬܐ ܠܟܠ). Translation: every (or all, whole) military (or army) of the sky which not I command

• Targum Onkelos: lechol cheilei shemayya di la fakkedit (לְכָל חֵילֵי שְׁמַיָּא דִּי לָא פַּקֵּדִית). Translation: every (or all, whole) army (or valor) of the sky which not I command

• Targum Jerusalem: lechol cheila shemaya dela fakkeidit (לְכָל חֵילָא שְׁמַיָּא דְלָא פַּקֵּידִית). Translation: every (or all, whole) army (or valor) of the sky which not I command

As the Greek and Hebrew texts do not correlate, the Greek text is followed.

4 Codex Alexandrinus: archontas (ΑΡΧΟΝΤΑϹ). Translation: king (or ruler)

• LXX 848: archonta (Άρχοντα). Translation: king (or ruler)

• Leningrad Codex: melech (מֶלֶךְ). Translation: king

• Peshitta: mlkå (ܡܠܟܐ). Translation: king

• Targum Onkelos: malka (מַלְכָּא). Translation: king

• Targum Jerusalem: malka (מַלְכָּא). Translation: king

Deuteronomy: Chapter 18

The priests, the Levites, including the whole tribe of Levi, have no part nor inheritance with Israel. The burnt offerings of the Lord are their inheritance, and they will eat them. They have no inheritance among their brothers. The Lord himself has his portion as he said. This is the due of the priests in the things coming from the people from those who offer sacrifices, whether it be a calf or a sheep, and you will give the shoulder to the priest, and the cheeks, and the great intestine, and the first fruits of your grain, and of your wine, and of your oil, and you will give to him the first fruits of the fleeces of your sheep.

The Lord has chosen them out of all your tribes, to stand before Lord the god, to minister and bless in his name, himself, and his sons among the children of Israel. If a Levite comes from one of the cities of all the children of Israel, where he lives, accordingly as his own desires, to the place which he has chosen, he will minister in the name of Lord his god, as all his brothers the Levites, who stand there present before Lord the god. He will eat an allotted portion, besides the sale of his hereditary property.

When you have entered into the land which the Lord the god gives you, you will not learn to do according to the abominations of those nations. There will not be found among you one who purges his son or his daughter with fire, one who divines, who deals with omens, and augury, a sorcerer employing incantation, one who has in him a divining spirit, and observer of signs, questioning the dead. For everyone that does these things is an abomination to Lord the god, because all of these abominations the Lord will destroy them from in front of you. You will be perfect before Lord the god. For all these nations whose land you will inherit, they listen to omens and divination, which Lord the god has not permitted you to do.

Lord the god will raise for you a prophet from your brothers, like me. You will listen to him, according to all things which you did desire of Lord the god in Horeb in the day of the assembly, saying, "We will not hear again the voice of Lord the god, and we will not anymore see this great fire, and so we will not die."

The Lord said to me, "They have spoken rightly, all that they have said to you. I will raise for them a prophet from their brothers, like you. I will put my words in his mouth, and he will speak them as I command him. Whatever man will not listen to whatever words that prophet says in my name, I will take vengeance on him. But the prophet whoever will impiously speak in my name a word which I have not commanded him to speak, and whoever will speak in the name of other gods, that prophet will die. But if you will say in your heart, 'How will we know which words the Lord has not spoken?' Whatever words that prophet will speak in the name of the Lord, and they will not come true, and not come to pass, this is the thing which the Lord has not spoken. That prophet has spoken wickedly. You will not spare him."

Deuteronomy: Chapter 19

When Lord the god has destroyed the nations which God gives you, all the land, and you will inherit them, and live in their cities, and in their houses, you will separate for yourself three cities among your land, which the Lord the god gives you. Take a survey of your way, and you will divide the coasts of your land, which the Lord the god apportions to you, into three parts, and there will be there a refuge for every murderer. This will be the ordinance of the murderer, who will flee there, and will live, whoever has killed his neighbor ignorantly and he didn't hate him previously. Whoever will enter in the woods with his neighbor, to gather wood, and if the hand of him cutting wood with the ax should be violently shaken, and the ax-head falls off from the handle and should land on his neighbor, and he should die, he will flee to one of these cities to live.

In case the avenger of blood chases after the slayer because his heart is hot, and catches him because the way is too long, and slays him, even though there is on this man no sentence of death because he didn't hate him previously. Therefore I order you, "You will separate for yourself three cities. If the Lord will enlarge your borders, as he swore to your fathers, and the Lord will give you all the land which he said he would give to your fathers, if you will listen to do all these commands, which I order you today, to love Lord the god, and to follow all his ways continually, you will add for yourself yet three cities to these three. So innocent blood will not be spilled in the land, which the Lord the god gives you to inherit, and there will not be in you one guilty of blood."

But if there should be among you a man, hating his neighbor, and he should lay in wait for him, and rise up against him, and kill him so that he dies, and he should flee to one of these cities, then the elders of his city will send, and take him from there and they will deliver him into the hands of the avengers of blood, and he will die. Your eye will not spare him, and you will purge the innocent blood from Israel, and it will go well with you.

You will not move the landmarks of your neighbor, which your fathers set in the inheritance, in which you have obtained a share in the land, which the Lord the god gives you to inherit. One witness will not stand to testify against a man for any iniquity, or for any fault, or for any sin which he may commit, by the mouth of two witnesses, or by the mouth of three witnesses, will every ruling be established. If an unjust witness rises against a man, alleging iniquity against him, then will the two men between whom the controversy is, stand before the Lord, and before the priests, and before the judges, who may exist in those days. The judges will make a diligent investigation, if an unjust witness has given false testimony, and has stood against his brother, then you will do to him as he wickedly devised to do against his brother, and you will remove the evil from yourselves. The rest will hear and fear and do no more of this evil among you. Your eye will not spare him. You will exact life for life, eye for an eye, tooth for tooth, hand for hand, and foot for foot.

Deuteronomy: Chapter 20

If you should go out to war against your enemies and should see cavalry, and a more numerous people than yourself, you will not be afraid of them, for Lord the god is with you, who brought you up out of the land of Egypt. It will come to pass whenever you will come close to battle that the priest will come close and speak to the people and will say to them, "Listen Israel, you are going this day to battle against your enemies. Don't let your heart faint, don't be afraid, nor be confused, nor turn aside from their face. For it is Lord the god who advances with you, to fight with you against your enemies, and to save you."

The scribes will say to the people, "What man is he that has built a new house, and has not dedicated it? Let him go and return to his house, in case he dies in the war, and another man dedicates it. What man has planted a vineyard, and not been made happy with it? Let him go and return to his house, in case he dies in the battle, and another man be made happy with it. What man is betrothed a wife, and has not taken her? Let him go and return to his house, in case he dies in the battle, and another man takes her."

The scribes will speak further to the people, and say, "What man fears and is cowardly in his heart? Let him go and return to his house, in case he makes the heart of his brother fail, like his own."

It will come to pass when the scribes have ceased speaking to the people, that they will appoint generals of the army to be leaders of the people. If you will come close to a city to conquer them by war, then call them out peaceably. If then they should answer peaceably to you, and open to you, it will be that all the people found in it will be tributary and slaves to you. But if they will not listen to you, but wage war against you, you will besiege it, until Lord the god delivers it into your hands, and you will kill every male from it with the edge of the sword, except the women and the stock, and all the livestock, and whatever will be in the city, and all the plunder you will take as spoil for yourself, and will eat all the plunder of your enemies whom Lord the god gives you.

This you will do to all the cities that are very far away from you, not being of the cities of these nations which the Lord the god gives you to inherit. Of these you will not take anything alive; but you will certainly curse them, the Cypriots, and the Amorites, and the Canaanites, and the Perizzites, and the Mitanni, and the Jebusites, and the Girgashites, as Lord the god commanded you. That they may not teach you to do all their abominations, which they did for their gods, and so you should sin before Lord the god. If you should besiege a city many days to prevail against it by war to take it, you will not destroy its trees, by applying an iron tool to them, but you will eat of it, and will not cut it down. Is the tree that is in the field a man, to enter against you into the work of the siege? But the tree which you know to not be fruit-bearing, this you will destroy and cut down, and you will construct a mound against the city, which makes war against you until it is delivered up.

Deuteronomy: Chapter 21

If one is found slain with the sword in the land, which the Lord the god gives you to inherit, having fallen in the field, and they do not know who has killed him, your elders and your judges will come out and will measure the distances of the cities around the slain man. It will be that the city which is nearest to the slain man the elders of that city will take a heifer from the herd, which has not labored, and which has not pulled a yoke.

The elders of that city will bring down the heifer to a rough valley, which has not been tilled and is not sown, and they will cut the sinews of the heifer in the valley. The priests, the Levites, will come because Lord the god has chosen them to stand by him, and to bless in his name, and by their word will every controversy and every stroke be decided. All the elders of that city who come close to the slain man will wash their hands over the head of the heifer which was slain in the valley, and they will answer and say, "Our hands have not shed this blood, and our eyes have not seen it. Be merciful to your people Israel, whom you have redeemed, Lord, that innocent blood may not be on your people Israel," and the blood will be atoned for by them. You will take away the inno-cent blood from among you if you should do that which is good and pleasing before Lord the god.

If when you go out to war against your enemies, Lord the god should deliver them into your hands, and you should take their spoil, and should see among the spoil a woman beautiful in appearance, and should think about her, and take her for yourself for a wife, and should bring her within your house, then you will shave her head, and pare her nails, and will take away her garments of captivity from off her, and she will live in your house and will mourn her father and mother for a month, and afterward, you will go into her and live with her, and she will be your wife. If you do not delight in her, you will send her away free, and she will not by any means be sold for silver, you will not treat her contemp-tuously, because you have humbled her.

If a man has two wives, the one loved and the other hated, and both the loved and the hated should have born him children, and the son of the hated should be firstborn, then it will be that whenever he will divide by inheritance his goods to his sons, he will not be able to give the right of the firstborn to the son of the loved one, having ignored the son of the hated, which is the firstborn. But he will acknowledge the firstborn of the hated one and give to him double of all things which will be found by him, because he is the beginning of his children, and to him belongs the birthright.

If any man has a disobedient and contentious son, who does not listen to the voice of his father and the voice of his mother, and they should correct him, and he should not listen to them, then his father and his mother will take hold of him and bring him to the elders of his city, and the gate of the place and they will say to the men of their city, "Our son is disobedient and contentious, and he does not listen to our voice. He is a reveler and a drunkard." The men of his city will stone him with stones, and he will die. You will remove the evil one from your-selves, and the rest will hear and fear.

If there is sin in anyone, and the judgment of death be on him, and he is put to death, and you hang him in a tree, his body will not remain all night on the tree, but you will, by all means, bury it in that day, for everyone that is hanged in a tree is cursed by God, and you will by no means defile the land which the Lord the god gives you for an inheritance.

Deuteronomy: Chapter 22

When you see the calf of your brother or his sheep wandering in the road, you will not ignore them, you will, by all means, return them to your brother, and you will restore them to him. If your brother does not come to you, and you do not know him, you will bring it into your house within, and it will be with you until your brother will seek them, and you will restore them to him. This you will do with his donkey, and you this will do to his garment, and this you will do to everything that your brother has lost, whatever has been lost by him, and you have found, which you will not ignore.

You will not see the donkey of your brother, or his calf, fallen on the road. You will not ignore them, you will certainly help raise them.

The clothing of a man will not be worn by a woman, neither will a man put on a woman's dress, for everyone that does these things is an abomination to Lord the god.

If you should come across a nest of birds in front of you along the road, or in a tree, or on the ground, young or eggs and the mother who is brooding on the young or the eggs, you will not take the mother with the young ones. You will let the mother go, but you will take the young for yourself, that it may go well with you, and that you may live long.

If you should build a new house, then you will make a parapet to your house, so you will not bring blood-guiltiness to your house if one should in any way fall from it.

You will not sow your vineyard with diverse seeds, in case the fruit is devoted to whatever seed you may sow with the fruit of your vineyard.

You will not plow with an ox and a donkey together.

You will not wear a false garment, wool, and linen together.

You will make fringes on the four borders of your garments, with whatever you may be clothed.

If anyone should take a wife, and live with her, and hate her, and use terrible words against her, and bring against her an evil name, and say, "I took this woman, and when I came to her I found in her no tokens of virginity," then the father and the mother of the girl will take and bring out the girl's tokens of virginity to the elders of the city to the gate.

The father of the girl will say to the elders, "I gave my daughter to this man as a wife, and now he hates her, and uses terrible words against her, saying, 'I have not found tokens of virginity with your daughter.' Yet these are the tokens of my daughter's virginity." They will unfold the garment before the elders of the city. The elders of that city will take that man, and will chastise him, and will fine him a hundred shekels, and will give them to the father of the girl, because he has brought out an evil name against a virgin of Israel, and she will be his wife. He will never be able to divorce her. But if this report is true, and the tokens of virginity are not found for the girl, then will they bring out the girl to the doors of her father's house, and will stone her with stones, and she will die, because she has worked folly among the children of Israel, to defile the house of her father by whoring, and so you will remove the evil one from among you.

If a man is found sleeping with a woman married to another man, you will kill them both, the man that slept with the woman, and the woman, and so you will remove the wicked one out of Israel.

If there is a young girl married to a man, and a man found her in the city and has slept with her, you will bring them both out to the gate of their city, and they will be stoned with stones, and they will die, the girl, because she did not cry out in the city, and the man, because he humbled his neighbor's spouse, and so you will remove the evil one from yourselves.

But if a man finds out in the field, a girl that is engaged and he should rape her, you will slay the man that raped her only. The girl has not committed a sin worthy of death, like when a man should rise against his neighbor, and slay him, so is this thing, because he found her in the field, and the betrothed girl cried out, and there was none to help her.

If anyone should find a young virgin who has not been engaged and should rape her, and be caught, the man who raped her will give to the father of the girl fifty silver didrachms,[1] and she will be his wife because he has humbled her. He will never be able to divorce her.

A man will not take his father's wife, and will not uncover his father's skirt.

Deuteronomy: Chapter 22 Notes

1 Codex Alexandrinus: pentêconta didrachma argyriou (ΠΕΝΤΗΚΟΝΤΑ ΔΙΔΡΑΧΜΑ ΑΡΓΥΡΙΟΥ). Translation: fifty double-drachmas of silver

• Codex Ambrosiano A 147: pentêconta didragma argyriou (ΠΕΝΤΗΚΟΝΤΑ ΔΙΔΡΑΓΜΑ ΑΡΓΥΡΙΟΥ). Translation: fifty double-drachmas of silver

• LXX 82: pentêconta argyriou didrachma (πέντρμοντα ἀργυρβου διαβαχμα). Translation: fifty silver double-drachmas

• Leningrad Codex: chamishim kasef (חֲמִשִּׁים בֶּסֶף). Translation: fifty silvers

• Peshitta: ḥmšyn dkspå (ܟܣܦܐ ܚܡܫܝܢ). Translation: fifty of silvers

• Targum Onkelos: chamshin sil'in dichsaf (חַמְשִׁין סִלְעִין דִּכְסַף). Translation: fifty selas of silver

• Targum Jerusalem: chamshin sil'in dichsaf (חַמְשִׁין סִלְעִין דִּכְסַף). Translation: fifty selas of silver

The Greek translation includes the measurement of didrachma, which is missing from the Masoretic Text. In other books of the Septuagint, the term didrachma is mirrored in the Masoretic Text by shekel, which imported into this translations as it must have been in the Aramaic source texts the Greeks used. In the later Aramaic targums, the translation of 'selas' was used, however, this was a different coin and unit of measurement.

Deuteronomy: Chapter 23

He who is damaged or mutilated in his private parts will not enter into the assembly of the Lord. One born of a harlot will not enter into the assembly of the Lord. The Ammonite and Moabite will not enter into the assembly of the Lord, even until the tenth generation he will not enter into the assembly of the Lord, even forever, because they did not meet you with bread and water along the road, when you went out of Egypt, and because they hired Balaam the son of Beor of Mesopotamia[1] to curse you. But Lord the god would not listen to Balaam, and Lord the god changed the curses into blessings because Lord the god loved you. You will not speak peaceably or profitably to them all your days forever.

You will not hate an Edomite, because he is your brother. You will not hate an Egyptian, because you were a stranger in his land. If sons are born to them, in the third generation they will enter into the assembly of the Lord.

If you should go out to engage with your enemies, then you will keep away from every wicked thing. If there should be among you a man who is not clean because of his issue by night, then he will go out of the camp, and he will not enter into the camp. It will come to pass toward evening he will wash his body with water, and when the sun has gone down, he will go into the camp.

You have a place outside of the camp, and you will go out there, and you have a trowel on your girdle, and it will come to pass when you would relieve yourself outside, that you will dig with it, and will bring back the dirt and cover your waste.

Because Lord the god walks in your camp to deliver you and to give up your enemy in front of you, your camp will be holy, and there will not appear among you a disgraceful thing, or he will turn away from you.

You will not return a slave to his master, who running from his master attaches himself to you. He will live with you, he will live among you where he will please. You will not punish him.

There will not be a harlot from the daughters of Israel, and there will not be a fornicator from the sons of Israel. There will not be a healer[2] among the daughters of Israel, and there will not be an initiate[3] among the sons of Israel.

You will not bring the wages of a whore,[4] or the price of a dog[5] into the Temple of Lord the god, for any vow because both are an abomination to Lord the god.

You will not lend to your brother on interest of silver, or interest of meat, or interest of anything which you may lend out. You may lend on interest to a stranger, but to your brother, you will not lend on interest, that Lord the god may bless you in all your works on the land, into which you are entering to inherit.

If you will vow a vow to Lord the god, you will not delay paying it, for Lord the god will certainly require it of you, and otherwise, it will be a sin for you. But if you should be unwilling to vow, it is not a sin for you. You will remember the words that come from between your lips, and as you have vowed a gift to Lord the god, you will do that which you have said with your mouth.

Deuteronomy: Chapter 23 Notes

1 Codex Vaticanus: Mesopotamias (ΜΕϹΟΠΟΤΑΜΙΑϹ). Translation: Mesopotamia

• LXX 376: Mesôpotamias (Μϭσωποτᾁμᾁϲ). Translation: Mesopotamia

• LXX 44: Mesopotamias (Μϭσοποτᾁμϭιᾁϲ). Translation: Mesopotamia

• Leningrad Codex: petovr aram naharayim (פְּתוֹר אֲרַם נַהֲרַיִם). Translation: Petovr Aram Rivers

• Peshitta: Pytûr dÅrm nhryn (ܦܬܘܪ ܕܐܪܡ ܢܗܪܝܢ). Translation: Pytûr of Aram Rivers

• Targum Onkelos: petor aram di al perat (פְּתוֹר אֲרָם דִּי עַל פְּרָת). Translation: Petor Aram that on Euphrates

• Targum Jerusalem: Petor chelmaya demitbanya be'ara Aram de'al Perat (פְּתוֹר חֶלְמָיָא דְּמִתְבַּנְיָא בְּאַרַע אֲרָם דְּעַל פְּרָת). Translation: Petor Helmaya (or dreamer) which is built in the land of Aram on the Euphrates

Mesopotamia is the Greek translation of Aram-Naharayim, however, the Septuagint does not include a translation of Petor in this verse. The verses in Numbers that refer to Balaam, call his hometown Phathoura (Φαθουρα) in the Septuagint, and Petovrah (פְּתוֹרָה) in the Masoretic Text, both of which are similar to the term used in the Masoretic version of this verse.

The name of the city Petovrah (פְּתוֹרָה), appears to be a transliteration of the Babylonian cuneiform word paššūru (𒄑𒁀𒀭�), which meant 'table.' The related Aramaic word was pāṭūrā (פָּתוּרָא), the Syriac word was pāṭūrā (ܦܳܬܘܪܐ), and the related Arabic word is fāṭūr (فَاطُور), all of which mean 'table,' 'tray,' or 'platter.' The older Akkadian spelling of paššūru (𒊬), which was also the spelling of the name of the city of Ur, in southern modern Iraq. If the original text of this section of text was written before the development of the Phoenician alphabet, it would have been written in Akkadian Cuneiform, the official script used in Canaan under Egyptian rule during the New Kingdom era, suggesting the transliteration error took place when the Phoenician translation was made in the early Iron Age.

2 Codex Vaticanus: telesphoros (ΤΕΛΕϹΦΟΡΟϹ). Translation: healer

- LXX 75: telosphoros (τέλοσφορος)

- LXX 458: telosphôros (τέλοσφῶρος)

- Leningrad Codex: kedeshah (קְדֵשָׁה). Translation: holiness (or sanctify, saintliness)

- Peshitta: znytå (ܙܢܝܬܐ). Translation: fornicator

- Targum Onkelos: zannita (זַנִּיתָא). Translation: fornicator

- Fragment Targums: zenu (זְנוּ). Translation: fornication

- Targum Jerusalem: te'ita (טְעִיתָא). Translation: prostitute

This verse has been generally accepted as referring to female sacred-sex-workers, involved in sex-rites at the temples of Qetesh. There was a Palace of Qetesh reported to have been near the Temple of El in Shiloh, and another near the Temple in Jerusalem.

Various alternate theories are also suggested by researchers, including that the word simply meant Priestess of Qetesh, as the word appears to be derived from the Akkadian word 'qadishu' (𒆖𒁲𒋗), meaning 'nun,' and a separate word was used for prostitute, zonoh (זוֹנָה), which is used in the next verse. Ritualistic sex acts were documented in the Temples of Qetesh (under her various names) across the Middle East dating back to Sumerian times (before 3000 BC), however, most recent archaeological evidence supports the idea that the prostitutes were males, transvestites, or transgender in modern parlance. Given the debate over the meaning of kedeshah (קְדֵשָׁה), the Greek translation healer (τελεσφόρος) is used in this translation.

3 Codex Vaticanus: teliscomenos (ΤΕΛΙϹΚΟΜΕΝΟϹ). Translation: abstinent-initiate

• Codex Alexandrinus: telescomenos pasan euchên (ΤΕΛΕϹΚΟΜΕΝΟϹΠΑϹΑΝ ΕΥΧΗΝ). Translation: abstinent-initiate every prayer

• LXX 407: teliscomenos is pasan euchên (τέλισϗομέϗνος ϲιϲ πλσλϗ ϛυχͷν). Translation: abstinent-initiate into every prayer

• LXX 19: teliscomenos is pasan euchên (τέλισϗομέϗνος πϟοϲ πλσλσλϗ). Translation: abstinent-initiate everyone similar

• Leningrad Codex: kadesh (קָדֵשׁ). Translation: Kadesh (or holiness)

• Peshitta: znâ (ܙܢܐ). Translation: fornication

• Targum Onkelos: gavra mibbenei Yisra'el itteta ama (גַּבְרָא מִבְּנֵי יִשְׂרָאֵל אִתְּתָא אָמָא). Translation: husband of the sons of Israel to a slave-woman

• Fragment Targums: nefak bar (נְפַק בַּר). Translation: exiled son

• Targum Jerusalem: gavra bar Yishra'el yat garmeih biznu (גַּבְרָא בַּר יִשְׂרָאֵל יַת גַּרְמֵיהּ בִּזְנוּ). Translation: husband son of Israel himself to cause through fornication (or 'Israelite pimps')

This verse has been generally accepted as referring to male sacred-sex-workers, involved in sex-rites at the temples of Qetesh by Christians. There was a Palace of Qetesh reported to have been near the Temple of El in Shiloh, and another near the Temple in Jerusalem.

Ritualistic sex acts were documented in the Temples of Qetesh (under her various names) across the Middle East dating back to Sumerian times (before 3000 BC), however, most recent archaeological evidence supports the idea that the prostitutes were males, transvestites or transgender in modern parlance. These males, often eunuch, prostitutes were documented into the Roman era, however, had become rare. While the traditional translations of 'Sodomite' or 'male-prostitute' may be an accurate description of the kadesh themselves, the verse does not appear to be referring to the sex-acts, but rather the group itself, and therefore the word 'initiate' (τελισκόμενος) is used in this translation. Curiously, the author is not stating that the kedeshah and kadesh should be banned, just that Israelites should not be kedeshah and kadesh, implying it was acceptable for other nationalities to be kedeshah and kadesh. This would date the authorship of the verse to either before King Josiah's reforms or place the authorship outside of Judah.

Alternatively, the targums that developed parallel to the Christian interpretation take several alternative viewpoints, including the statement that Israelite men could not marry slave women, not tolerate exiles, and not be pimps. Given the diversity of opinions, this translation uses the original Greek meaning of the word.

4 Codex Vaticanus: pornês (ΠΟΡΝΗС). Translation: whore

- LXX 16: pornê (πορνᾳ)

- Leningrad Codex: zonah (זוֹנָה). Translation: whore (or prostitute, slut, harlot)

- Dead Sea Scroll 4QDeutᵍ: zǔnh (זונה)

- Peshitta: znytå (ܙܢܝܬܐ). Translation: fornicator

- Targum Onkelos: zannita (זַנִּיתָא). Translation: fornicator

- Fragment Targums: zenu (זְנוּ). Translation: fornication

- Targum Jerusalem: te'ita (טָעִיתָא). Translation: prostitute

This verse is generally linked with the previous statement about kedeshah and kadesh, however, uses a derogatory term for the prostitutes, implying it is a separate statement about not offering clean things to God. As the offering is silver being offered at the Temple of the Lord the god, it is clear the date of authorship is after the Israelites had settled in Canaan, and after there was both coinage and a Temple of the Lord the god, meaning after the time of King Solomon circa 950 BC.

5 Codex Vaticanus: cynos (ΚΥΝΟС). Translation: female dog

- LXX 16: coenos (ʟοɪνοс). Translation: public

- LXX 767: coenôs (ʟοɪνωс). Translation: public

- LXX 509: cynon (ʟυνον). Translation: cynic

- LXX 54: cyros (ʟυρος). Translation: supreme power (or authority, Cyrus)

- LXX 72: gynaecos (γυναικος). Translation: woman

- Leningrad Codex: keleb (כֶּלֶב). Translation: male dog

- Peshitta: klbå (ܟܠܒܐ). Translation: dog (or wild, mad, wind, Sirius)

- Targum Onkelos: kalba (כַּלְבָּא). Translation: dog (or wild, mad, wind, Sirius)

- Fragment Targums: keleb (כֶּלֶב). Translation: male dog

- Targum Jerusalem: keleb (כָלֶב). Translation: male dog

The term 'dog' is often assumed to be related to the word 'whore' earlier in the verse, and the term 'initiate' in the previous verse, resulting in the mistranslation 'male prostitute' in some translations, assuming the word 'dog' was a slanderous term for homosexual males. The verse is simply about not offering silver acquired in unclean ways to God. Dogs were unclean animals that the Israelites nevertheless kept, and bought and sold, but did not eat.

Deuteronomy: Chapter 24

If you should go into the grain field of your neighbor, then you may gather the ears with your hands, but you will not put the sickle to your neighbor's grain.

If you should go into the vineyard of your neighbor, you will eat grapes sufficient to satisfy your desire, but you may not put them into a vessel.

If anyone should take a wife and live with her, then it will come to pass if she should not have found favor before him, because he has found something unpleasant in her, that he will write for her a letter of divorcement, and give it to her and send her out of his house. If she should go away and be married to another man, and the second husband should hate her, and write for her a letter of divorcement, and give it to her hands, and send her out of his house, and the second husband should die, who took her to himself as a wife, the former husband who sent her away will not be able to return and take her for himself as a wife after she has been defiled, because it is an abomination before Lord the god, and you will not defile the land, which the Lord the god gives you to inherit.

If anyone should have recently taken a wife, he will not go out to war, neither will anything be laid on him, he will be guiltless in his house for one year, he will celebrate his wife whom he has taken.

You will not take for a pledge the under millstone, nor the upper millstone, for this man who does so takes life for a pledge.

If a man should be caught kidnapping a child of Israel, and having captured him he should sell him, that thief will die, and so will you remove that evil one from yourselves.

Pay attention to yourself in regarding the plague of leprosy. You will pay great attention to do according to all the laws, which the priests, the Levites will report to you. Pay attention to do, as I have ordered you. Remember all that Lord the god did to Mariam along the road, when you were going out of Egypt.

If your neighbor owes you a debt, any debt whatever, you will not go into his house to take his pledge. You will stand outside, and the man who is in your debt will bring the pledge out to you. If the man is poor, you will not keep his pledge overnight. You will certainly restore his pledge at sunset, and he will sleep in his garment, and he will bless you, and it will be mercy shown by you before Lord the god.

You will not unjustly withhold the wages of the poor and needy of your brothers, or of the strangers who are in your cities. You will pay him his wages the same day, the sun will not go down on it, because he is poor and he trusts in it, and he will cry against you to the Lord, and it will be sin in you.

The fathers will not be put to death for the children, and the sons will not be put to death for the fathers. Everyone will die for his own sin.

You will not wrest the judgment of the stranger and the fatherless, and widow. You will not take the widow's garment for a pledge.

You will remember that you were a slave in the land of Egypt, and Lord the god redeemed you from there, therefore I order you to do this thing. When you have reaped grain in your field, and have forgotten a sheaf in your field, you will not return to take it. It will be for the stranger, and the orphan and the widow, that Lord the god may bless you in all the works of your hands.

If you should gather your olives, you will not return to collect the remainder, it will be for the stranger, and the fatherless, and the widow, and you will remember that you were a slave in the land of Egypt, therefore I command you to do this thing.

Whenever you gather the grapes of your vineyard, you will not glean what you have left, it will be for the stranger, and the orphan, and the widow, and you will remember that you were a slave in the land of Egypt, therefore I command you to do this thing.

Deuteronomy: Chapter 25

If there should be a dispute between men, and they should come forward for judgment, and the judges judge, and justify the righteous, and condemn the wicked, then it will come to pass, if the unrighteous should be worthy of stripes, you will lay him down before the judges, and they will whip him before them according to his iniquity. They will whip him with forty lashes, they will not inflict more, for if you should whip him with more lashes beyond these, your brother will be disgraced before you.

You will not muzzle the ox that treads out the grain.

If brothers should live together, and one of them should die, and should not have a child, the wife of the deceased will not marry out of the family to a man not related. Her husband's brother will go into her and will take her for himself as a wife, and will live with her. It will come to pass that the child which she will bear, will be constituted by the name of the deceased, and his name will not be blotted out of Israel. If the man should not be willing to take his brother's wife, then the will woman go up to the gate to the elders, and she will say, "My husband's brother will not raise up the name of his brother in Israel. My husband's brother has not been willing." The elders of his city will call him, and speak to him, and if he stands and says, "I will not take her," then his brother's wife will come forward before the elders, and will remove one shoe from off his foot, and will spit in his face, and will answer and say, "This will they do to the man who will not build his brother's house in Israel." His name will be called in Israel, "The house of him that has had his shoe removed."

If men should fight, a man with his brother and the wife of one of them should approach to rescue her husband out of the hand of he that kills him, and she should stretch out her hand, and take hold of his private parts, you will cut off her hand. Your eye will not spare her. You will not have in your bag diverse weights, a great and a small. You will not have in your house diverse measures, a great and a small. You have a true and just weight, and a true and just measure, that you may live long on the land which the Lord the god gives you for an inheritance. For everyone that does this is an abomination to Lord the god, everyone that does injustice.

Remember what Amalek did to you along the road, when you left from the land of Egypt, how he blocked your way and attacked your backs, even those that were weary behind you, and you did hunger and were weary, and he did not fear god. It will come to pass whenever Lord the god has given you rest from all your enemies around you, in the land which the Lord the god gives you to inherit, you will blot out the name of Amalek from under the sky, and will not forget to do it.

Deuteronomy: Chapter 26

When you have entered into the land, which Lord the god gives you to inherit, and you have inherited it, and you have lived in it, you will take the first of the fruits of your land, which Lord the god gives you, and you will put them into a basket, and you will go to the place which Lord the god will choose to have his name called there. You will come to the priest who will exist in those days, and you will say to him, "I testify today by Lord the god, that I have come into the land which the Lord swore to our fathers to give to us."

The priest will take the basket out of your hands, and will set it before the altar of Lord the god, and he will answer and say before Lord the god, "My father abandoned Syria, and went down into Egypt, and stayed there with a small number, and became there a mighty nation and a great multitude. The Egyptians punished us, and humbled us, and imposed hard tasks on us. We cried out to our Lord the god, and the Lord heard our voice and saw our humiliation, and our labor, and our affliction. The Lord brought us out of Egypt himself with his great strength, and his mighty hand, and his high arm, and with great visions, and with signs, and with wonders. He brought us into this place and gave us this land, a land flowing with milk and honey. Now, Look, I have brought the first of the fruits of the land, which you gave me, Lord, a land flowing with milk and honey."

You will leave it before Lord the god, and you will worship before Lord the god, and you will rejoice in all the good things, which the Lord the god has given you, you and your family, and the Levites, and the aliens that are among you.

When you have completed all the tithings of your fruits in the third year, you will give the second tenth to the Levites, and stranger, and fatherless, and widow, and they will eat it in your cities, and be merry. You will say before Lord the god, "I have fully collected the holy things out of my house, and I have given them to the Levites, and the stranger, and the orphan, and the widow, according to all commands which you did command me: I did not transgress your command, and I did not forget it. In my distress I did not eat of them, I have not gathered of them for an unclean person, I have not given them to the dead. I have listened to the voice of our Lord the god, I have done as you have commanded me. Look down from your sacred temple in the sky,[1] and bless your people Israel, and the land which you have given them, as you did swear to our fathers, to give to us a land flowing with milk and honey."

On this day the Lord, your god ordered you to keep all the ordinances and judgments, and you will observe and do them, with all your heart, and with all your mind. You have chosen a god today to be your god, and to follow all his ways, and to observe his ordinances and judgments, and to listen to his voice. The Lord has chosen you this day that you should be to him a unique people, as he said, to keep his commands, and that you should be above all nations, as he has made you renowned, and a pride, and glorious, that you should be a holy people to Lord the god, as he has spoken.

Deuteronomy: Chapter 26 Notes

1 Codex Vaticanus: oecou tou hagiou sou ec tou ounou (ΟΙΚΟΥΤΟΥΑΓΙΟΥϹΟΥΕΚ ΤΟΥΟΥΝΟΥ). Translation: temple the sacred (or saint, holy) yours from the sky (or Uranus)

• LXX 376: oecou so hagiou sou ec tou ouranou (οιιου σο αγφου σου ὅιι του ουβἀνου). Translation: temple yours sacred yours from the sky

• LXX 664: oecou sou tou hagiou sou (οιιου σου του αγφου σου). Translation: temple of yours the sacred of yours

• Leningrad Codex: mimme'ovn kodshecha min-hashamayim (מִמְּעֹוֹן קָדְשְׁךָ מִן־הַשָּׁמַיִם). Translation: from abode (or home, temple) holiness (sacred, Qetesh), from the skies (or Shamayim)

• Peshitta: dqůdšk mn šmyå (ܩܘܕܫܟ ܡܢ ܫܡܝܐ). Translation: of holiness (or sanctity, shrine, temple) from sky

• Targum Onkelos: mimmedor kadeshach min shemayya (מִמְדוֹר קָדְשָׁךְ מִן שְׁמַיָּא). Translation: from your circle (or circuit, dwelling) sacred in the sky

• Fragment Targums: mimdor beit shechinat yekarach vekudeshach min shemaya (מִמְדוֹר בֵּית שְׁכִינַת יְקָרָךְ וְקוּדְשָׁךְ מִן שְׁמַיָּא). Translation: from your circle (or circuit, dwelling) house (or temple, abode) where you live (or shechinah) honored (or heavy, precious, cold) and sanctified (or holy) from sky

• Targum Jerusalem: mimdor beit shechinat kudeshach min shemaya (מִמְדוֹר בֵּית שְׁכִינַת קוּדְשָׁךְ מִן שְׁמַיָּא). Translation: from your circle (or circuit, dwelling) house (or temple, abode) where you live (or shechinah) sanctified (or holy) from sky

Deuteronomy: Chapter 27

Moses and the elders of Israel commanded, "Keep all these commands, all that I command you today. It will come to pass in the day when you will cross over the Jordan into the land which the Lord the god gives you, that you will set up for yourself great stones, and will plaster them with plaster. You will write on these stones all the words of this law, as soon as you have crossed Jordan, when you have entered into the land, which the Lord the god of your fathers gives you, a land flowing with milk and honey, as Lord the god of your fathers said to you. It will be as soon as you are gone over the Jordan, you will set up these stones, which I command you today, on Mount Ebal, and you will plaster them with plaster."

"You will build there an altar to Lord the god, an altar of stones, and you will not use iron on it. You will build an altar to Lord the god from whole stones, and you will offer on it whole burnt offerings to Lord the god. You will offer a peace-offering there, and you will eat and be filled, and rejoice before Lord the god. You will write on the stones all this law very plainly."

Moses and the priests the Levites said to all Israel, "Be silent and listen Israel, today you have become the people of Lord the god. You will listen to the voice of Lord the god and will do all his commands, and his ordinances, as many as I command you today."

Moses ordered the people on that day, "These will stand to bless the people on mount Gerizim having gone over the Jordan: Simeon, Levi, Judas, Issachar, Joseph, and Benjamin. These will stand for cursing on mount Ebal: Reuben, Gad, Asher, Zebulun, Dan, and Naphtali. The Levites will answer and say to all Israel with a loud voice, 'Cursed is the man whoever will make a carved or molten image, an abomination to the Lord, the work of the hands of craftsmen, and will put it in a secret place, and all the people will love Amen.'[1]

'Cursed is the man that dishonors his father or his mother, and all the people will praise Amen.'

'Cursed is he that removes his neighbor's landmarks, and all the people will praise Amen.'

'Cursed is he that makes the blind to wander in the road, and all the people will praise Amen.'

'Cursed is everyone that will pervert the judgment of the stranger, and orphan, and widow, and all the people will praise Amen/'

'Cursed is he that lies with his father's wife, because he has uncovered his father's skirt, and all the people will praise Amen.'

'Cursed is he that lies with any animal, and all the people will praise Amen.'

'Cursed is he that lies with his sister by his father or his mother, and all the people will praise Amen.'

'Cursed is he that lies with his daughter-in-law, and all the people will praise Amen.'

'Cursed is he that lies with his wife's sister, and all the people will praise Amen.'

'Cursed is he that kills his neighbor secretly, and all the people will praise Amen.'

'Cursed is he whoever has taken payment to take the life of an innocent man, and all the people will praise Amen.'

'Cursed is every man that continues not in all the words of this law to do them, and all the people will praise Amen.'

Deuteronomy: Chapter 27 Notes

1 Codex Vaticanus: apocrithis o laos erousin Genoeto (ΑΠΟΚΡΙΘΕΙϹΟΛΛΟϹ ΕΡΟΥϹΙΝΓΕΝΟΙΤΟ). Translation: reply (or judge) the people will love (or praise) Genoeto

• Codex Alexandrinus: apocrithis laos erousin Genoeto (ΑΠΟΚΡΙΘΕΙϹΠΛϹΟΛΛΟϹ ΕΡΕΙΓΕΝΟΙΤΟ). Translation: reply (or judge) the people will love (or praise) Genoeto

• LXX 44: apocrithis erousin genoeto pas o laos (ἀπολιβιθόϛιϲ ὅρουσιν γόνοιτο πλϲ ο λλοϲ). Translation: to choose (or to judge) love (or praise) Genoeto all the people

• LXX 75: apocrithentes pas ho laos erousin Genoeto (ἀπολιβιθόϛντόϲ πλϲ ο λλοϲ ὅρουσιν Γϙνοιτο). Translation: set apart (or seperate) all the people will love (or praise) Genoeto

• LXX 376: apocrithentes pas ho laos erousin Genoeto (ἀπολιβιθόϛιϲ πλϲ ο λλοϲ οτι Γϙνοιτο). Translation: set apart (or seperate) all the people will love (or praise) Genoeto

- Leningrad Codex: anu chol-ha'am ve'ameru amen (עָנוּ כָל־הָעָם וְאָמְרוּ אָמֵן). Translation: reply (or answer) all the nation will say (or see, witness in Akkadian) agreed (or Amen)

- Peshitta: nônûn klh ômå ûnåmrûn åmyn (ܢܥܢܘܢ ܟܠܗ ܥܡܐ ܘܢܐܡܪܘܢ ܐܡܝܢ). Translation: answeredall the nation and will command (or Aries, lamb) agreed (or Amen)

- Targum Onkelos: vitivun kol amma veyeimrun Amen (וִיתִיבוּן כָּל עַמָּא וְיֵימְרוּן אָמֵן). Translation: returned all the people and said agreed (or Amen)

- Fragment Targums: ve'ilein ve'amerin Amen (וְאִילֵין וְאָמְרִין אָמֵן). Translation: and those and said agreed (or Amen)

- Targum Jerusalem: veshavei vetumera havon anyain kulehon kachada ve'amerin Amen (וְשָׁוֵי בְטוּמְרָא הֲווֹן עַנְיִין כּוּלְהוֹן כַּחֲדָא וְאָמְרִין אָמֵן). Translation: and leavinga secret hiding place producing (or residing, falling) poverty (or delayed) all rejoiced and said agreed (or Amen)

- Shapira scrolls: ûônû kl hôm ûåmrû åmn (𐤀𐤌𐤍 𐤅𐤉𐤀𐤌𐤓𐤅 𐤏𐤌 𐤊𐤋 𐤅𐤏𐤍𐤅). Translation: and humble all the nation and pronounce Amen (or agreement)

The Greek translation is quite different from the Hebrew, suggesting the Aramaic was different. Genoeto (Γένοιτο) was a Greek expression, meaning 'Earth forbid,' which was used as a translation of 'amen,' the Jewish expression meaning 'agreed.'

Deuteronomy: Chapter 28

It will come to pass, if you will indeed hear the voice of Lord the god, to observe and do all these commands, which I order you this day, that Lord the god will set you on high above all the nations of the earth, and all these blessings will come on you and will find you. If you will indeed hear the voice of Lord the god, blessed you will be in the city, and blessed you will be in the field. Blessed will be the offspring of your belly, and the fruits of your land, and your oxen herds, and your sheep flocks. Blessed will be your barns and your stores. Blessed will you be in your coming in, and blessed will you be in your going out.

The Lord will deliver your enemies who resist you, completely broken in front of you. They will come out against you one way, and they will flee from before you seven ways. The Lord will send on you his blessing in your barns, and on all on which you will put your hand, in the land which the Lord the god gives you. The Lord raises you up for himself as a holy people, as he swore to your fathers, if you will hear the voice of Lord the god, and follow all his ways. All the nations of the earth will see that the name of the Lord is called on by you, and they will stand in awe of you.

Lord the god will multiply you for good, and in the offspring of your belly, and in the offspring of your livestock, and in the fruits of your land, on your land which the Lord swore to your fathers to give to you. May the Lord open to you his good treasury in the sky, to give rain to your land in season, may he bless all the works of your hands, so you will lend to many nations, but you will not borrow, and you will rule over many nations, but they will not rule over you.

Lord the god will make you the head, and not the tail, and you will then be above and you will not be below, if you will listen to the voice of Lord the god, in all things that I order you this day to observe. You will not turn aside from any of the commandments, which I order you today, to the right hand or to the left, to follow other gods to serve them.

But it will happen, if you will not listen to the voice of Lord the god, to observe all his commandments, as many as I order you today, then all these curses will come on you, and destroy you. You will be cursed in the city and You will be cursed in the field. Your barns and your stores will be cursed. Your offspring will be cursed, and the fruits of your land, your herds of oxen, and your flocks of sheep. You will be cursed in your coming in and you will be cursed in your going out.

The Lord sends against you poverty, and famine, and wasting of all things on which you will put your hand until he has completely destroyed you, and until he has consumed you quickly because of your evil devices, because you have forsaken me.

The Lord causes pestilence to cling to you until he has consumed you off the land into which you go to inherit.

The Lord plague you with distress, and fever, cold, inflammation, blighting, and paleness, and they will pursue you until they have destroyed you.

You have over your head a sky of brass, and the earth under you will be iron. Lord the god will make the rain in your land dust, and dust will come down from the sky until it has destroyed you, and until it has quickly consumed you.

The Lord gives you up for slaughter before your enemies. You go out against them one way and flee from before them seven ways, and you will be a diaspora in all the kingdoms of the earth. Your dead men will be food for the birds of the sky, and to the beasts of the earth, and there will be none to scare them away.

The Lord plague you with the ulcer of Egypt, and hemorrhoids, and with malignant scabs, and itch, so that you can not be healed.

The Lord plague you with insanity, and blindness, and astonishment of mind. You will grope at midday, as a blind man would grope in the darkness, and you will not prosper in your ways, and then you will be unjustly treated and plundered continually, and there will be no helper.

You will take a wife, and another man will have her.

You will build a house, and you will not live in it.

You will plant a vineyard, and will not gather the grapes of it.

Your calf will be slain before you, and you will not eat of it.

Your donkey will be violently taken away from you, and will not be restored to you.

Your sheep will be given to your enemies.

You will have no helper.

Your sons and your daughters will be given to another nation.

Your failing eyes will look for them.

Your hand has no strength.

A nation which you don't know will eat the produce of your land, and all your labors.

You will be injured and crushed always.

You will be distracted, because of the sights of your eyes which you will see.

The Lord kills you with an evil sore, on the knees and the legs, so that you will not be able to be healed from the sole of your foot to the crown of your head.

The Lord carry away you and your kings, who you will elect above you, to a nation which neither you nor your fathers know, and there you will serve other gods of wood and stone. And you will be there for a wonder, and a parable, and a tale, among all the nations, to which the Lord the god will carry you away.

You will carry out much seed into the field, and you will bring in little because the locust will devour it.

You will plant a vineyard, and dress it, and will not drink the wine, neither will you delight yourself with it, because the worm will devour them.

You have olive trees in all your borders, and you will not anoint yourself with oil, because your olive will completely drop its fruit.

You will father sons and daughters, and they will not be yours, for they will be sold into captivity.

All your trees and the fruits of your land will be consumed in blight.

The stranger that is among you will be raised up very high, and you will come down very low. He will lend to you, and you will not lend to him. He will be the head, and you will be the tail.

All these curses will come on you, and will pursue you, and will destroy you until he has consumed you, and until he has destroyed you, because you did not listen to the voice of Lord the god, to keep his commands and his ordinances which he has commanded you.

These things will be signs for you, and wonders among your descendants forever, because you did not serve Lord the god with gladness and a good heart, because of the abundance of all things. You will serve your enemies, which the

Lord will send out against you, in hunger, and in thirst, and in nakedness, and in the want of all things, and you will wear on your neck a yoke of iron until he has destroyed you.

The Lord will bring on you a nation from the extremity of the earth, like the swift flying of an eagle, a nation whose voice you will not understand, a nation bold in countenance, which will not wonder at the body of the aged and will not pity the young.

He will eat up the young of your livestock, and the fruits of your land, so as not to leave to you grain, wine, oil, your ox herds, and your sheep flocks, until he has destroyed you, and has completely crushed you in your cities, until the high and strong walls in which you trust are destroyed, throughout all your land, and he will plague you in your cities, which he has given to you.

You will eat the fruit of your belly, the flesh of your sons and of your daughters, all that he has given you, in your straightness and your affliction, with which your enemy will torment you.

He that is tender and very delicate among you will look with an evil eye on his brother, and the wife in his chest, and the children that are left, which may have been left to him, so as not to give to one of them of the flesh of his children, whom he will eat, because of his having nothing left him in your straightness, and in your affliction, with which your enemies will afflict you in all your cities.

She that is tender and delicate among you, whose foot has not assayed to go on the earth for delicacy and tenderness, will look with an evil eye on her husband in her chest, and her son and her daughter, and her afterbirth that comes out between her feet, and the child which she will carry, for she will eat them because of the want of all things, secretly in your straightness, and in your affliction, with which your enemy will afflict you in your cities. If you will not listen to all the words of this law, which have been written in this book, to fear this glorious and wonderful name, Lord the god, then the Lord will magnify your plagues, and the plagues of your seed, great and wonderful plagues, and evil and abiding diseases.

He will bring on you all the evil pain of Egypt, of which you were afraid, and they will cling to you. The Lord will bring on you every sickness, and every plague that is not written, and everyone that is written in the book of this law until he has destroyed you.

You will be left few in number, whereas you were as the stars of the sky in number because you did not listen to the voice of Lord the god. It will come to pass that as the Lord rejoiced to do you good and to multiply you, so the Lord will rejoice to destroy you, and you will be quickly removed from the land into which you go to inherit.

Lord the god will scatter you among all nations, from one end of the earth to the other, and there you will serve other gods of wood and stone, which you have not known, nor your fathers. Moreover, among those nations he will not give you quiet, nor will the sole of your foot have rest, and there the Lord will give you another and a misgiving heart, and failing eyes, and a wasting mind. Your life will be in suspense before your eyes, and you will be afraid by day and by night, and you will have no assurance of your life. In the morning you will say, "If only it were evening!" and in the evening you will say, "If only it were morning!" for the fear of your heart with which you will fear, and for the sights of your eyes which you will see.

The Lord will bring you back to Egypt in ships, by the way of which I said, "You will not see it again, and you will be sold there to your enemies as slave-men and slave-women, but none will buy you."

Deuteronomy: Chapter 29

These are the words of the covenant, which the Lord commanded Moses to make with the children of Israel in the land of Moab, besides the covenant which he made with them in Horeb. Moses called all the sons of Israel and said to them, "You have seen all things that the Lord did in the land of Egypt before you to Pharaoh and his servants, and all his land, the great temptations which your eyes have seen, the signs, and those great wonders. Yet Lord the god has not given you the heart to know, and eyes to see, and ears to hear, until this day. He led you forty years in the wilderness, your garments did not grow old, and your sandals were not worn away off your feet. You did not eat bread, you did not drink wine or strong drink, that you might know that I am Lord the god. You came as far as this place, and there came out Sihon king of Heshbon, and Og king of Bashan, to meet us in war. We destroyed them and took their land, and I gave it as an inheritance to Reuben and Gad, and the half-tribe of Manasseh.

You will make sure to do all the words of this covenant, that you may understand all things that you will do. You all stand today before Lord the god, the heads of your tribes, and your elders, and your judges, and your officers, every man of Israel, your wives, and your children, and the stranger who is among your camp, from your lumberjack to your water collector, that you should enter into the covenant of Lord the god and his oaths, as many as Lord the god appoints you today. He will appoint you for himself as a people, and he will be your god, as he said to you, and as he swore to your fathers, Abraham, and Isaac, and Jacob.

I do not appoint to you alone this covenant and this oath, but to those also who are here with you today before Lord the god, and to those who are not here with you today. For you know how we lived in the land of Egypt, and how we came through the middle of the nations through whom you came. You saw their abominations, and their idols, wood and stone, silver and gold, which are among them. In case there be among you man, or woman, or family, or tribe, whose heart has turned aside from Lord the god, having gone to serve the gods of these nations. If there is among you a root springing up with gall and bitterness.

It will be if one will hear the words of this curse, and will flatter himself in his heart, saying, "Let good happen to me, for I will walk in the error of my heart," in case the sinner destroy the guiltless with him, god will by no means be willing to pardon him, but then the anger of the Lord and his jealousy will flame out against that man, and all the curses of this covenant will attach themselves to him, which are written in this book, and the Lord will blot out his name from under the sky. The Lord will separate that man for the evil of all the children of Israel, according to all the curses of the covenant that are written in the book of this law.

Another generation will say, even your sons who will rise after you, and the stranger who will come from a land far away, and will see the plagues of that land and their diseases, which the Lord has sent on it, brimstone and burning salt, (the whole land will not be sown, neither will any green thing spring, nor rise on it, as Sodom and Gomorrah were destroyed, and Admah and Zeboiim which the Lord overthrew in his rage and anger) and all the nations will say, "Why has the Lord done this to this land? What is this great fierceness of anger?"

Men will say, "Because they abandoned the covenant of Lord the god of their fathers, the things which he appointed to their fathers when he brought them out of the land of Egypt, and they went and served other gods, which they did not know, and he did not assign them to them. The Lord was exceedingly angry with that land to bring on it according to all the curses which are written in the book of this law. The Lord removed them from their land in rage and anger, and very great indignation, and threw them out into another land," as at present. The secret things belong to our Lord the god, but the things that are revealed belong to us and to our children forever to follow all the words of this law.

Deuteronomy: Chapter 30

It will come to pass when all these things have happened to you, the blessing and the curse, which I have set in front of you, and you will receive them into your heart among all the nations, in which the Lord has scattered you, and will return to Lord the god, and will listen to his voice, according to all things which I order you this day, with all your heart, and with all your mind, then the Lord will heal your iniquities, and will pity you, and will again gather you out from all the nations, among which the Lord has scattered you. If your dispersion is from one end of the sky to the other, there Lord the god will gather you, and there will Lord the god take you. Lord the god will bring you in from there into the land which your fathers have inherited, and you will inherit it, and he will treat you well, and multiply you more than your fathers.

The Lord will purge your heart, and the heart of your seed, to love Lord the god with all your heart, and with all your mind, that you may live. Lord the god will put these curses on your enemies, and on those that hate you, who have persecuted you. You will return and listen to the voice of Lord the god and will keep his commands, all that I order you this day. Lord the god will bless you in every work of your hands, in the offspring of your belly, and the offspring of your livestock, and in the fruits of your land, because Lord the god will again rejoice over you for good, as he rejoiced over your fathers. If you will listen to the voice of Lord the god, to keep his commandments, and his ordinances, and his judgments written in the book of this law, if you turn to Lord the god with all your heart, and with all your mind.

This command which I give you this day is not difficult, neither is it far from you. It is not in the sky above, as if someone was asking, "Who will go up for us into the sky, and will take it for us, and we will hear and do it?" Neither is it beyond the sea, saying, "Who will go over for us to the other side of the sea, and take it for us, and make it known to us, and we will do it?" The word is very near you, in your mouth, and your heart, and in your hands to do it. Look, I have set before you this day life and death, good and evil. If you will listen to the commands of Lord the god, which I command you this day, to love Lord the god, to follow all his ways, and to keep his ordinances, and his judgments, and then you will live and will be many in number, and Lord the god will bless you in all the land into which you go to inherit it.

But if your heart changes, and you will not listen, and you will go astray and worship other gods, and serve them, I declare to you this day, that you will completely perish, and you will by no means live long on the land, into which you cross over the Jordan to inherit. I call both the sky and earth to witness this day against you, I have set before you life and death, the blessing and the curse. Choose your life, that you and your seed may live, to love Lord the god, to listen to his voice, and cling to him, for this is your life, and the length of your days, that you should live on the land, which the Lord swore to your fathers, Abraham, and Isaac, and Jacob, to give to them.

Deuteronomy: Chapter 31

Moses finished speaking all these words to all the children of Israel, and said to them, "I am today a hundred and twenty years old. I will not be able any longer to come in or go out. The Lord said to me, 'You will not go over this Jordan.' Lord the god who goes before you will destroy these nations before you, and you will inherit them. It will be Joshua that leads you, as the Lord has said. Lord the god will do to them as he did to Sihon and Og the two kings of the Amorites, who were beyond Jordan, and to their land, as he destroyed them. The Lord has delivered them to you, and you will do to them, as I ordered you. Be courageous and strong. Don't be afraid or cowardly before them, as it is Lord the god that advances with you, among you, and he will not abandon you or desert you."

Moses called Joshua, and said to him before all Israel, "Be courageous and strong, for you will go in before these people into the land which the Lord swore to give to your fathers, and you will give it to them for an inheritance. The Lord that goes with you will not betray you or abandon you, and don't be afraid," therefore don't be afraid.

Moses wrote the words of this law in a book and gave it to the priests the sons of Levi who carry the box of the covenant of the Lord, and to the elders of the sons of Israel. Moses ordered them in that day, "After seven years, in the time of the year of release, in the feast of tabernacles, when all Israel comes together to appear before Lord the god, in the place which the Lord will choose, you will read this law before all Israel, having assembled the people, the men, and the women, the children, and the stranger that is in your cities, that they may hear, and that they may learn to fear Lord the god. They will listen to all the words of this law. Their sons who have not known will hear, and will learn to fear Lord the god all the days that they live on the land, into which you go over Jordan to inherit."

The Lord said to Moses, "Look, the days of your death are at hand, call Joshua, and stand by the doors of the tabernacle of testimony, and I will give him an order."

Moses and Joshua went to the tabernacle of testimony and stood by the doors of the tabernacle of testimony. The Lord descended in a cloud and stood by the doors of the tabernacle of testimony, and the pillar of the cloud stood by the doors of the tabernacle of testimony. The Lord said to Moses, "Look, you will sleep with your fathers, and these people will rise and go whoring after the alien gods of the land, into which they are entering, and they will forsake me, and break my covenant, which I made with them. I will be very angry with them on that day, and I will leave them and turn my face away from them, and they will be devoured. Many evils and plagues will come on them, and they will say in that day, 'Because my Lord the god is not with me, these evils have come on me.' I will certainly turn away my face from them in that day, because of all their evil doings which they have done, because they turned aside after alien gods. Now write the words of this song, and teach it to the children of Israel, and you will put it into their mouth, that this song may witness for me among the children of Israel to their face. For I will bring them into the good land, which I swore to their fathers, to give to them a land flowing with milk and honey, and they will eat and be filled and satisfy themselves. Then they will turn aside after other gods, and serve them, and they will provoke me, and break my covenant. This song will stand up to witness against them, for they will not forget it out of their mouth, or out of the mouth of their seed. I know their wickedness, what they are doing here today before I have brought them into the good land, which I swore to their fathers."

Moses wrote this song on that day and taught it to the children of Israel. He ordered Joshua, "Be courageous and strong, for you will bring the sons of Israel into the land, which the Lord swore to them, and he will be with you."

When Moses finished writing all the words of this law in a book, even to the end, then he ordered the Levites who bear the box of the covenant of the Lord, "Take the book of this law, and you will put it inside of the box of the covenant of Lord the god, and it will be there among you as a testimony. For I know your provocation, and your stiff neck, for yet during my life with you at this day, you have been provoking in your conduct toward god, so how will you not also be so after my death? Gather together to me the heads of your tribes, and your elders, and your judges, and your officers, that I may speak in their ears all these words, and I call both the sky and earth to witness against them. For I know that after my death you will completely transgress, and turn aside out of the way which I have commanded you, and evils will come on you at the end of days because you will do evil before the Lord, to provoke him to anger by the works of your hands."

Moses spoke all the words of this song even to the end, in the ears of the whole assembly.

Deuteronomy: Chapter 32

Watch Shamayim,[1] and I will speak, and let Eretz[2] hear the words out of my mouth. Let my speech be looked for like the rain, and my words come down as dew, as the shower on the plants, and as snow on the grass. For I have called on the name of the Lord, "Assign you greatness to our God. As for God, his works are true, and all his ways are judgments, God is faithful, and there is no unrighteousness in him. Just and holy is the Lord. They have sinned, not pleasing him, spotted children, a contrary and perverse generation. Do you, therefore, repay the Lord? Are the people so foolish and unwise? Did not your father purchase you, and make you, and form you?"

Remember the days of old, consider the ages of ages. Ask your father, and he will tell you, your elders, and they will tell you. When the Highest[3] divided the nations, when he separated the sons of Adam, he divided the borders of the nations according to the number of the messengers of God. The people of Jacob became the portion of the Lord, and Israel was the line of his inheritance. He maintained him in the wilderness, in burning thirst and dry land. He led him about and instructed him, and kept him as the apple of his eye. As an eagle would watch over his brood and yearns over his young, and receives them having spread his wings, and takes them up on his back. The Lord alone led them, there was no alien god with them.

He brought them up on the strength of the land. He fed them with the fruits of the fields. They sucked honey out of the rock, and oil out of the solid rock. Butter of cows, and milk of sheep, with the fat of lambs and rams, of calves and kids, with the fat of kidneys of wheat, and he drank wine, the blood of the grape. So Jacob ate and was filled, and the beloved one kicked, he grew fat, he became thick and broad. Then he abandoned the god that made him and departed from God his savior. They provoked me to anger with alien gods, with their abominations, they bitterly angered me. They sacrificed to devils, and not to God, but to gods whom they did not know. New and fresh gods came in, who their fathers did not know.

You have forsaken the God who fathered you and forgotten El[4] who feeds you. The Lord saw, and was jealous, and was provoked by the anger of his sons and daughters, and said, "I will turn away my face from them, and will show what will happen to them in the last days, for it is a perverse generation, sons with no faith. They have provoked me to jealousy with that which is not God, they have exasperated me with their idols, and I will provoke them to jealousy with them that are no nation, I will anger them with a nation void of understanding. For a fire has been started out of my anger, it will burn to Hades below, it will devour the land and the fruits of it. It will set on fire the foundations of the mountains. I will gather evils on them and will paralyze them with my weapons. They will be wasted by hunger and devoured by Resheph,[5] and destroyed bitterly. I will send out against them the teeth of a hippopotamus,[6] with the rage of serpents creeping on the ground. Outside, the sword will bereave them of children, and terror will issue out of the secret chambers. The young man will perish with the virgin, the suckling with he who has grown old."

I said, "I will scatter them, and I will cause their memorial to cease from among men. Were it not for the anger of the enemy, in case they should live long, in case their enemies should combine against them, in case they should say, 'Our own high arm, and not the Lord, has done all these things.'"

It is a nation that has lost counsel, and there is no understanding in them. They had no sense to understand. Let them reserve these things against the time to come. How should one pursue a thousand, and two chase tens of thousands, if God had not sold them, and the Lord delivered them up? For their gods are not like our god, but our enemies are void of understanding. For their vine is of the vine of Sodom, and their vine-branch of Gomorrah, their grape is a grape of gall, their cluster is one of bitterness. Their wine is the rage of serpents and the incurable rage of asps.

Look! Are not these things stored up by me, and sealed among my treasures? In the day of vengeance, I will repay, whenever their foot will be tripped up. The day of their destruction is near to them, and the judgments at hand are close to you. The Lord will judge his people and will be comforted over his servants. For he saw that they were paralyzed, and failed in the hostile invasion, and were become feeble.

The Lord asked, "Where are their gods in whom they trusted? The fat of whose sacrifices you ate, and you drank the wine of their drink offerings? Let them rise and help you, and be your protectors. Look, Look that I am he, and there is no god beside me. I kill, and I will make live. I will kill, and I will heal. None will deliver out of my hands. For I will lift my hand to the sky, and swear by my right hand, and I will say, I live forever. I will sharpen my sword like lightning, and my hand will take hold of judgment. I will render judgment to my enemies and will repay them that hate me. I will make my weapons drunk with blood, and my sword will devour flesh, it will glut itself with the blood of the wounded, and from the captivity of the heads of their enemies that rule over them."

Celebrate Shamayim with him, and worship him all the sons of God. Celebrate nations, with all your people, and strengthen him all messengers of God.[7] He will avenge the blood of his sons, and he will render vengeance, and repay justice to his enemies, and will reward them that hate him, and the Lord will purge the land of his people.

Moses wrote this song on that day and taught it to the children of Israel, and Moses went in and spoke all the words of this law in the ears of the people, he and Joshua the son of Nun. Moses finished speaking to all Israel. He said to them, "Pay attention with your heart to all these words, which I testify to you this day, which you will command your sons, to observe and do all the words of this law. For this is no vain word to you, for it is your life, and because of this word you will live long on the land, into which you go over Jordan to inherit."

The Lord said to Moses in this day, "Go up to Mount Abarim, (this is Mount Nebo which is in the land of Moab near Jericho), and see the land of Canaan, which I give to the sons of Israel, and die in the mountain where you are going, and be added to your people, as Aaron your brother died on Mount Horeb and was added to his people. Because you disobeyed my word among the children of Israel, at the waters of Temptation of Kadesh in the wilderness of Sin, because you did not praise me among the sons of Israel. You will see the land before you, but you will not enter into it."

Deuteronomy: Chapter 32 Notes

1 Codex Vaticanus: ourane (ΟΥΡΑΝΕ). Translation: sky (or Uranus)

• Aleppo Codex: Šmym (שמים). Translation: Shamayim (or skies)

• Leningrad Codex: Shamayim (שָׁמָיִם). Translation: Shamayim (or skies)

• Peshitta: šmyå (ܫܡܝܐ). Translation: sky

• Targum Onkelos: shemayya (שְׁמַיָּא). Translation: sky

• Fragment Targums: shamayim (שָׁמַיִם). Translation: skies

- Targum Jerusalem: shemaya (שְׁמַיָּא). Translation: sky

Shamayim was depicted as the same type of primordial deity in the Septuagint as Uranus was in the Greek myths and called on to witness blessings and curses, implying consciousness. Based on the writings of Jonah and Zephaniah, as well as 4th Kingdoms (Masoretic Kings), Shamayim was a major god in Samaria and Judea before King Josiah's reforms and therefore his name is restored from the Masoretic Text, as he was not known as Uranus.

2 Codex Vaticanus: Gê (ΓΗ). Translation: Ge (or land, dirt, earth)

- Aleppo Codex: års (אָרֶץ). Translation: Eretz (or land, earth, dirt)

- Leningrad Codex: Aretz (אֶרֶץ). Translation: Eretz (or land, earth, dirt)

- Peshitta: årôâ (ܐܪܥܐ). Translation: land

- Targum Onkelos: ar'a (אַרְעָא). Translation: land

- Fragment Targums: ar'a (אַרְעָא). Translation: land

- Targum Jerusalem: ar'a (אַרְעָא). Translation: land

The Earth (Eretz / Ge) is depicted as the same type of primordial deity in the Septuagint as it was in the Greek myths and called on to witness blessings and curses, implying consciousness. As her name was not Earth or Ge, the Hebrew (and Canaanite) name Eretz is restored from the Masoretic text. The fact that she is called on by Moses, along with Shamayim, means the Song of Moses is much older than the rest of Deuteronomy, and must, if nothing else, date to before King Josiah banned the worship of Shamayim, in circa 625 BC.

3 Codex Vaticanus: hypsistos (ΥΨΙΣΤΟΣ). Translation: highest

- Aleppo Codex: ôlyůn (עֶלְיוֹן). Translation: highest

- Leningrad Codex: elyon (עֶלְיוֹן). Translation: highest

- Peshitta: mrymå (ܡܪܝܡܐ). Translation: command

- Targum Onkelos: illa'ah (עִלָּאָה). Translation: highest

- Fragment Targums: ilaya (עִילָיָא)

- Targum Jerusalem: ila'ah alma (עִלָּאָה עָלְמָא). Translation: highest enteral

El Elyon (Highest God) was God of Melchizedek, the king of Salem (either Jerusalem or the city of Salem in Samaria) when Abraham passed through Canaan. The term El

Elyon is known to have been a major god of the Canaanites, called Âl wôlyn in the Sefire Treaty from circa 750 BC. The quotes of Sanchuniathon's writing that have survived to the present, from circa 1200 BC, referred to the god called Elioun as the primordial creator-god of the Canaanites.

4 Codex Vaticanus: thu (ΘY̅). Translation: god

- LXX 246: Thᵘ sou (Θᵘ σου). Translation: god yours

- Aleppo Codex: Âl (אל). Translation: El (or God)

- Leningrad Codex: El (אֵל). Translation: El (or God)

- Peshitta: âlhå (ܐܠܗܐ). Translation: god

- Targum Onkelos: elaha (אֱלָהָא). Translation: highest

- Fragment Targums: yeyah (??). Translation: Yhû

- Targum Jerusalem: yeyah (??). Translation: Yhû

This verse shows the Greeks did translate the term El as God (θεοῦ). As El is a proper name, it is restored from the Masoretic Text in this translation.

5 Codex Vaticanus: orneôn (ΟΡΝΕѠΝ). Translation: raptor (or bird of prey)

- Aleppo Codex: ršp (רשף). Translation: Resheph (or pestilence)

- Leningrad Codex: Reshef (רֶשֶׁף). Translation: Resheph

- Peshitta: rûhå byštå (ܪܘܚܐ ܒܝܫܬܐ). Translation: wind (or spirit) of evil

- Targum Onkelos: ruchin bishan (רוּחִין בִּישָׁן). Translation: winds (or spirits) of evil

- Fragment Targums: charba (חַרְבָּא). Translation: sword (or dagger)

- Targum Jerusalem: lilin umeravvchei revavchin bishin (לִילִין וּמְרְוֹחֵי רְוֹחִין בִּישִׁין). Translation: night-demons and rebellious winds (or spirits) of evil

Resheph was the Amorite god of both pestilence and healing, whose name was recorded as Rašaap (𒊏𒊭𒀊) in tablets from Ebla dating to the 3ʳᵈ millennium BC, as well as Reshpu (𓂋𓈙𓊪𓅱) in Egyptian. Resheph's name was later recorded as Ršp (𐎗𐎌𐎔) in Ugaritic Canaanite from the 1300s BC, and Ršp (𐤓𐤔𐤐) in Phoenician Canaanite from the early iron age, both of which are direct transliterations of the Classical Hebrew Ršp (רשף). Resheph was recorded as the husband of Adamma, the Amorite, and later Hurrian and Edomite goddess of the earth, the name used in Numbers for the Israelite earth goddess.

877

Resheph was one of the major gods of the Hyksos dynasty, considered the equivalent of the Babylonian god Nergal (✴🐦▷🚩⊟) and Egyptian Sutekh (𓃮𓊖), originally pronounced as Setesh (transliterated hieroglyphs: stš) before the New Kingdom era, and later as Setekh (transliterated hieroglyphs: stḫ), which resulted in the later Greek transliteration of Sêth (Σηθ). After the collapse of the Hyksos dynasty, the worship of both Sutekh and Resheph was suppress during the New Kingdom era, and a new god named Shed (🐍𓂷𓊖) largely replaced Resheph in Canaan, which appears to be the origin of the Canaanite term shed (𐤔𐤃) and the Israelite name Šdy (𐤔𐤃𐤉). The inclusion of the name in the Song of Moses indicates that the song was likely composed before the suppression of Resheph during the New Kingdom era.

6 Codex Vaticanus: thêriôn (ΘΗΡΙѠΝ). Translation: wild animal (or Lupus)

• Aleppo Codex: bhmt (בהמת). Translation: animal (or livestock)

• Leningrad Codex: behemot (בְּהֵמוֹת). Translation: behemoth

• Peshitta: ḥyůty šnå (ܚܝܘܬ, ܫܢܐ). Translation: animals (or living) tusks (or teeth)

• Targum Onkelos: cheivat bara (חֵיוַת בָּרָא). Translation: animal of forest (or prairie)

• Fragment Targums: cheivat bera (חֵיוַת בְּרָא). Translation: animal of forest (or prairie)

• Targum Jerusalem: Akkuim dinchitin veshineihon heich cheivavt bera (עַכּוּיִם דְּנָכְיתִין בְּשִׁינֵיהוֹן הֵיךְ חֵיוַות בָּרָא). Translation: Acreans who bite with teeth like animals of the forest

The Septuagint and two versions of the Masoretic Text differ at this point. The Aleppo Codex uses the Canaanite and Hebrew word meaning 'livestock' or 'animals,' which is documented in Ugaritic Canaanite as bhmt (𐎁𐎅𐎎𐎚), from the 1300s BC. However, both the Septuagint and Westminster Leningrad Codex use a singular form, as 'wild animal' (θηρίων) or Behemoth (בְּהֵמוֹת). This suggests that the Aramaic translation was the same as the Westminster Leningrad Codex, and the word was later simplified to 'animals' in the Aleppo Codex. The word Behemoth was also spelled as behemot (בְּהֵמוֹת) in the Westminster Leningrad Codex's book of Job, and as bhmůt (בהמות) in the Aleppo Codex's book of Job, indicating that the word was in the older text that was translated into Classical Hebrew. The word was transliterated into Classical Syriac as bhmůt (ܒܗܡܘܬܐ), indicating that the earlier Imperial Aramaic spelling was almost certainly bhmůt (בהמות), the plural form of bhmw (בהמו), however, that word is not found in any known Aramaic text. For almost 2000 years, linguists have considered this a transliteration of the Ancient Egyptian word for 'water ox' (𓃲𓁹𓈗). This translation was worked out during the Early Christian Era, and assumed to be a reference to a hippopotamus, based on the conceptually similar words meaning hippopotamus in Greek,

Arabic, Persian, Hebrew, and Coptic, all of which are composed of words meaning 'horse' and either 'water' or 'river.'

The link between the Ancient Egyptian word for 'water buffalo' and the Aramaic term 'bhmw' was worked out in the Late-Classical Era, and therefore influenced the languages within the Byzantine and Russian Empires, resulting in the words for 'hippopotamus' being derived from behemoth in many languages, including Armenian begemot (բեգեմոտ), Azerbaijani begemot, Belarusian bjehjemót (бегемóт), Bulgarian begemót (бегемóт), Chuvash begemot (бегемот), Georgian behemoti (ბეჰემოთი), Hebrew behemot (בְּהֵמוֹת), Kazakh begemot (бегемот), Kyrgyz begemot (бегемот), Latvian behemots, Lithuanian begemotas, Ossetian begemot (бегемот), Russian begemót (бегемóт), Tajik bahmut (бахмут), Turkmen begemot, Ukrainian behemót (бегемóт), Uyghur bëgëmot (بېگېموت), and Uzbek begemot. In some of these languages, the term is now considered dated and has been replaced with words based on the Greek word hippopotamos (ιπποπόταμος).

The Ancient Egyptians had several names for 'hippopotamus,' however, generally called it a ḥåb (𓎛𓄿𓃀𓃯), and therefore, it suggests that the Song of Moses was composed in an Egyptianized Canaanite dialect earlier than the New Kingdom era, when the term ss yåwr (𐤎𐤎 𐤉𐤀𐤅𐤓), meaning 'horse of the Nile,' was adopted by the Canaanites as a name for the hippopotamus.

The earliest documented Canaanite word for horse, was the late Bronze Age ŝŝů (𐎝𐎝𐎆) in Ugaritic, which was imported to Egyptian as ssm (𓊃𓅓𓃗), meaning 'horse.' Conversely, yåůr (𐤉𐤀𐤅𐤓) was imported to Canaanite from the Egyptian ỉtrů (𓇋𓏏𓂋𓅱𓈗), meaning 'great river,' and specifically referring to the Nile.

The Egyptian term continued in use until the Classical era, when it was spelled as htho ior (ϩⲑⲟ ⲓⲟⲣ), meaning 'horse' and 'Nile' in Coptic Egyptian. The Canaanite term was imported to Median and Persian as 'aspa ap' from the Avestan words aspa (𐬀𐬯𐬞𐬀) and ap (𐬀𐬞), meaning 'horse' and 'water,' and continues today in the Persian term for hippopotamus, asb-e âbi (اسب آبی). The Persian term appears to have been the basis of the Greek and Arabic terms hippopotamos (ιπποπόταμος) and faras nahr (فرس نهر), both of which combine the words for 'horse' and 'river.'

In this verse, the Greek translation could also be interpreted as a reference to the constellation Lupus, however, it is unlikely that the original Canaanite song of Moses was referring to an asterism, and so the translation of 'hippopotamus' is imported from the Westminster Leningrad Codex via the accepted Middle Egyptian interpretation of the word.

7 Codex Vaticanus: euphranthête ouranoe hama autô cae proscynêsatôsan autô pantes huioe thu (ΕΥΦΡΑΝΘΗΤΕ ΟΥΡΑΝΟΙ ΑΜΑ ΑΥΤΩ ΚΑΙ ΠΡΟϹΚΥΝΗϹΑΤΩϹΑΝ ΑΥΤΩΠΑΝΤΕϹΥΙΟΙΘῩ). Translation: Praise skies (or Uranus) together with him and worship him all the sons of god

- LXX 58: euphranthête oe ouranoe hama autô cae proscynêsatôsan autô pantes huioe theou (ϭυϐβαννθϞτϭ οι ουβανοφ ἀμἀ ἀυτοο ϻἀι πϱοϭϻυνϞσἀτοοσἀν ἀυτοο παννντϭ υιοι θϭου). Translation: praise the skies (or Uranus) together with him and worship him all the sons of god

- LXX 407: euphranthête ouranoe hama autoes cae proscynêsatôsan auton pantes huioe theou (ϭυϐβαννθϞτϭ ουβανοφ ἀμἀ ἀυτοιϲ ϻἀι πϱοϭϻυνϞσἀτοοσἀν ἀυτον παννντϭ υιοι θϭου). Translation: praise the skies (or Uranus) together with themand worship him all the sons of god

- LXX 313: euphranthête ouranoe hama autô cae proscynêsatôsan autô pantes oe huioe theou oe theou (ϭυϐβαννθϞτϭ ουβανοφ ἀμἀ ἀυτοο ϻἀι πϱοϭϻυνϞσἀτοοσἀν ἀυτοο παννντϭ οι υιοι θϭου οι θϭου). Translation: praise the skies (or Uranus) together with them and worship him all the sons of god the god

This verse is not found in the Masoretic text, Peshitta, or Targums. The name Shamayim is used as it was the Masoretic translation of Uranus in other verses.

Deuteronomy: Chapter 33

This is the blessing with which Moses the man of God blessed the children of Israel before his death. He said, "The Lord has come from Sinai, and has appeared from Seir to us, and has rushed out of the Mount of Paran, with the ten thousands of Kadesh, on his right hand were his messengers with him. He spared his people, and all his sanctified ones are under your hands, and they are under you, and he received from his words the law which Moses ordered us, an inheritance to the assemblies of Jacob. He will be king with the beloved one when the kings of the people are gathered together with the tribes of Israel. Let Reuben live, and not die, and let him be many in number.

This is the blessing of Judah, "Hear the Lord, the voice of Judah, and you visit his people, his hands will contend for him, and you will be a help from his enemies."

To Levi, he said, "Give to Levi his manifestations, and his truth to the holy man, whom they tempted in the temptation. They criticized him at the water of strife. Who says to his father and mother, I have not seen you, and he did not know his brothers, and he refused to know his sons. He kept your oracles and observed your covenant. They will declare your ordinances to Jacob, and your law to Israel: they will place incense in the time of your anger continually on your altar. Bless, the Lord, his strength, and accept the works of his hands, break the loins of his enemies that have risen against him, and don't let them that hate him rise."

To Benjamin, he said, "The beloved of the Lord will live in confidence, and god overshadows him always, and he rested between his shoulders."

To Joseph, he said, "His land is of the blessing of the Lord, of the seasons of sky and dew, and of the deeps of wells below, and of the fruits of the changes of the sun in season, and of the produce of the months, from the top of the ancient mountains, and from the top of the eternal hills, and of the fullness of the land in season, and let the things pleasing to him that lived in the bush come on the head of Joseph, and on the crown of him who was glorified above his brothers. His beauty is as the firstborn of his bull, his horn is the horn of a rhinoceros,[1] with them he will thrust the nations at once, even from the end of the earth, these are the ten thousands of Ephraim, and these are the thousands of Manasseh."

To Zebulun, he said, "Rejoice Zebulun, in your going out, and Issachar in his tents. They will completely destroy the nations, and you will call men there, and there offer the sacrifice of righteousness, for the wealth of the sea will suckle you, and so will the marts of them that live by the sea-coast."

To Gad he said, "Blessed be he that enlarges Gad: as a lion he rested, having broken the arm and the ruler. He saw his first fruits, that there the land of the kings gathered with the chiefs of the people divided. The Lord worked right-eousness and his judgment with Israel."

To Dan, he said, "Dan is a lion's cub, and will leap out of Bashan."

To Naphtali, he said, "Naphtali has the fullness of good things, and let him be filled with the blessings of the Lord. He will inherit the west and the south."

To Asher, he said, "Asher is blessed with children, and he will be acceptable to his brothers. He will dip his foot in oil. His sandal will be iron and brass; as your days, so will be your strength. There is not any such as the god of the beloved, who mounts the sky assists you, and the magnificence of the framework."

The rule of God will protect you, and that under the strength of the eternal arms, and he will throw out the enemy from in front of you, saying, "Perish. Israel will live in confidence alone on the land of Jacob, with grain and wine, and the sky will be misty with dew on you. Blessed are you, O Israel, who is like to you, people saved by the Lord? Your helper will hold his shield over you, and his sword is your boast, and your enemies will speak falsely to you, and you will tread on their neck."

Deuteronomy: Chapter 33 Notes

1 Codex Vaticanus: monocerôtos (**ΜΟΝΟΚΕΡѠΤΟϹ**). Translation: Asian rhinoceros (or unicorn, narwhal)

- Aleppo Codex: råm (רֵאם). Translation: oryx

- Leningrad Codex: re'em (רְאֵם). Translation: oryx

- Peshitta: rymå (ܪܝܡܐ). Translation: buffalo (or unicorn)

- Targum Onkelos: Ruma (רוּמָא). Translation: Rome (or haughty)

- Fragment Targums: rimna (רִימְנָא). Translation: pomegranate

- Targum Jerusalem: rivvavta (רְבְוותָא). Translation: great-stork (or Cygnus)

- Vulgate: rhinocerotis. Translation: rhinoceros

The word re'em (רְאֵם) is descended from the Akkadian rimu (𒉈𒌝) meaning wild bull, and the Ugaritic rŭm (𒊑𒌑𒌝) meaning wild buffalo. The related Arabic word rīm (ريم) means oryx, however, based on the reference in Daniel, Re'em was probably the old name of the constellation Taurus or Ares, which is probably what the author intended, as it is difficult to imagine an oryx being described so gloriously. The translators of the Targums had diverse opinions on what this verse was about, including Romans, pomegranates, and the constellation Cygnus.

The Greek unicorn was a semi-mythical creature reported to live in India, almost certainly the Asian rhinoceros, which, unlike the African rhinoceros, only has one horn. This is the translation used in the Latin Vulgate, however, 'unicorn' or 'oryx' are often used in modern English translations, as it is not clear what the re'em (רְאֵם) actually was.

Deuteronomy: Chapter 34

Moses went up from Araboth Moab to the mount of Nebo, to the top of Phasga, which is near Jericho, and the Lord showed him all the mountains of Gilead to Dan, and all the land of Naphtali, and all the land of Ephraim and Manasseh, and all the land of Judah to the farthest sea, and the wilderness, and the country round about Jericho, the city of palm-trees, to Zoar.

The Lord said to Moses, "This is the land of which I swore to Abraham, and Isaac, and Jacob, saying, 'To your seed will I give it,' and I have shown it to your eyes, but you will not go in there."

So Moses the servant of the Lord died in the land of Moab by the word of the Lord. They buried him in Gai near the Temple of Peor, and no one has seen his sepulcher to this day. Moses was a hundred and twenty years old at his death, yet his eyes were not dimmed, nor were his natural powers destroyed. The children of Israel wept for Moses in Araboth of Moab at the Jordan near Jericho for thirty days, and the days of the sad mourning for Moses were completed.

Joshua the son of Nun was filled with the spirit of knowledge, for Moses had laid his hands on him, and the children of Israel listened to him, and they did as the Lord commanded Moses. There did not rise another prophet in Israel like Moses, whom the Lord knew face to face, in all the signs and wonders, which the Lord sent him to work in Egypt against Pharaoh and his servants and all his land, and the great wonders, and the mighty hand which Moses displayed before all Israel.

Joshua: Chapter 1

After the death of Moses, the Lord[1] said to Joshua the son of Nun, the minister of Moses, "Moses my servant is dead. Now then rise, go across the Jordan, you and all these people, into the land which I give them. Every place on which you will step I will give to you, as I told Moses. The wilderness and Anti-Lebanon, as far as the great river, the river Euphrates, and as far as the farthest sea, your coasts will be at the setting of the sun. Not a man will stand against you all the days of your life, and as I was with Moses, so will I also be with you, and I will not fail you, or neglect you. Be strong and act like a man, as you will divide the land among these people, which I swore to give to your fathers."

"Be strong, therefore, and act like a man, and observe and do as Moses my servant commanded you. You will not turn from them to the right hand or the left, that you may be wise in whatever you may do. The book of this law will not leave out of your mouth, and you will meditate on it day and night, that you may know how to do all the things that are written in it. Then you will prosper, and make your ways prosperous, and then you will be wise. Look! I have commanded you 'Be strong and courageous, do not be cowardly nor fearful, for Lord the god[2] is with you in all places, to wherever you go.'"

Joshua commanded the scribes of the people, "Go into the middle of the camp of the people, and command the people, 'Prepare provisions, for in three days you will go across the Jordan, enter into and take possession of the land, which Lord the god of your fathers gives to you."

To Reuben, and to Gad, and to the half-tribe of Manasseh, Joshua said, "Remember the words that Moses the servant of the Lord commanded you, 'The Lord the god has caused you to peace, and has given you this land. Let your wives and your children and your livestock live in the land which he has given you, but you will cross well-armed before your brothers, every one of you who is strong, and you will fight on their side, until Lord the god has given your brothers peace, like you, and they have inherited the land that Lord the god gives them. Then you will leave, each one to his inheritance that Moses gave you to the east of the Jordan."

They answered Joshua, "We will do all things which you command us, and we will go everywhere you will send us. As we listened to Moses, we will listen to you. Only let Lord the god be with you, as he was with Moses.

Whoever will disobey you, and whoever will not listen to your words as you will command him, let him die, but you be strong and courageous."

Joshua: Chapter 1 Notes

1 Codex Vaticanus: c̄s (K͞C). Translation: lord

• Aleppo Codex: Yhůh (יהוה)

• Leningrad Codex: Yehvah (יְהוָה)

• Targum Jerusalem: yeyah (יְיָ). Translation: Yhů

This verse does not survive in the Dead Sea Scrolls, however, the name does show up in later verses that have survived.

• Dead Sea Scroll 4QJosh^a: Yhůh (יהוה)

• Dead Sea Scroll 4QJosh^b: Yhůh (יהוה)

The Septuagint's version of the Joshua was translated before 200 BC, as it was carried south by the Israelite community, who left Egypt for Kush (modern Sudan) during the Judean Rebellion against the Ptolemys in 200 BC. This means it predates the Hasmonean redaction and contains the term Lord (Κύριοσ) instead of Iaô (Ιαω), which, if correctly translated from the Aramaic source texts, would have read ådny (אדני). The Greeks are believed to have transliterated Yhů (יהו), the Aramaic version of the name Yehvah/Yehvah, as Iaô (Ιαω) in the Book of Leviticus, published circa 250 BC, as evidenced by the Dead Sea Scroll Septuagint fragment 4QpapLXXLev^b, which dates from Hasmonean era Judea. 4QpapLXXLev^b could be interpreted as a Hasmonean redaction of the Septuagint, however, Leviticus appears to have been written during the rule of King Josiah, and his God was Yhů, supporting the existence of Yhů in the Book of Leviticus.

The Aramaic sections of Masoretic Daniel that were not translated into Hebrew maintain the term adonai ha'elohim (אֲדֹנָי הָאֱלֹהִים), meaning the 'Lord the gods' where the Septuagint has 'Lord the god' (Κύριον τὸν θεὸν), however, the Hebrew sections have Yahweh elohim (יְהוָה אֱלֹהִים) where the Septuagint has 'Lord the god,' suggesting the Greek more accurately reflects the Aramaic source texts than the Hebrew translation. According to some records from the time, this was to repair the damage King Manasseh had done 600 years earlier when he removed the name Yahweh from the Israelite Texts, however, no evidence has survived from the era of Manasseh or earlier that proves the name was originally in the text, suggesting it was an attempt by the first Hasmonean High-Priest/King Simon the Zealot to create a national Judean religion with a god having a name similar to the Roman god Jove.

In the 3rd century AD, the Christians redacted the Septuagint removing the name Iaô, both in Greek, and in Latin translations which transliterated Iαω as Iaw, replacing it with 'Lord.' This resolved the debate with the Gnostics about whether Iaw was the devil or not. Before that, the various versions of the early Christian-era Septuagint books that included the name, either used Iαω, or the name written in Hebrew or Phoenician (Paleo-Hebrew) scripts. According to Origen of Alexandria in the late 2nd century AD, the Phoenician (most ancient script) was the most accurate. According to Theodoret of Cyprus in the 5th century, the Samaritans, who never switched to the Assyrian block letter 'Hebrew,' pronounced the name as Iabe (Iαβε) or Iabae (Iαβαι). Hebrews substitute the word 'hasheim,' meaning 'the name,' in all non-scriptural contexts since the Hasmoneans banned the pronunciation of the names of God. Christians have traditionally translated several ways including Jehovah, Jehova, and Jova. As the original Greek translation of Joshua does not appear to have included the name, the term Lord is used in this translation.

2 Codex Vaticanus: c̄s o t̄h̄s (ᴋᴄoᴇ̄ᴄ) . Translation: Lord the god

- Aleppo Codex: Yhŭh ålhyk (יהוה אלהיך). Translation: Yhŭh your god

- Leningrad Codex: Yehvah eloheicha (יְהוָה אֱלֹהֶיךָ). Translation: Yehwah your god

- Targum Jerusalem: dayeyah elahachon (דַיְיָ אֱלָהְכוֹן). Translation: the Yhŭ your god

This verse does not survive in the Dead Sea Scrolls, however, a similar term does show up in later verses that have survived.

- Dead Sea Scroll 4QJosh[a]: Yhŭh ålhy (יהוה אלהי). Translations: Yhŭh my god

The Septuagint's version of the Joshua was translated before 200 BC, as it was carried south by the Israelite community, who left Egypt for Kush (modern Sudan) during the Judean Rebellion against the Ptolemys in 200 BC. This means it predates the Hasmonean redaction and contains the term Lord (Κύριοσ) instead of Iaô (Iαω), which, if correctly translated from the Aramaic source texts, would have read ådny (אדני). The Greeks are believed to have transliterated Yhŭ (יהו), the Aramaic version of the name Yehvah/Yehwah, as Iaô (Iαω) in the Book of Leviticus, published circa 250 BC, as evidenced by the Dead Sea Scroll Septuagint fragment 4QpapLXXLev[b], which dates from Hasmonean era Judea. 4QpapLXXLev[b] could be interpreted as a Hasmonean redaction of the Septuagint, however, Leviticus appears to have been written during the rule of King Josiah, and his God was Yhŭ, supporting the existence of Yhŭ in the Book of Leviticus.

The Aramaic sections of Masoretic Daniel that were not translated into Hebrew maintain the term adonai ha'elohim (אֲדֹנָי הָאֱלֹהִים), meaning the 'Lord the gods' where the Septuagint has 'Lord the god' (Κύριον τὸν θεὸν), however, the Hebrew sections have Yahweh elohim (יְהוָה אֱלֹהִים) where the Septuagint has 'Lord the god,' suggesting the Greek more accurately reflects the Aramaic source texts than the Hebrew translation. According to some records from the time, this was to repair the damage King Manasseh had done 600 years earlier when he removed the name Yahweh from the Israelite Texts, however, no evidence has survived from the era of Manasseh or earlier that proves the name was originally in the text, suggesting it was an attempt by the first Hasmonean High-Priest/King Simon the Zealot to create a national Judean religion with a god having a name similar to the Roman god Jove.

In later copies of the Septuagint, the name was replaced by the name written in Phoenician (𐤉𐤄𐤅𐤄) or Hebrew script (יהוה). The name Iaw is found in fragments of the 3rd century AD Papyrus Oxyrhynchus 1007, however, is represented by a double Yod (״), meaning it was copied from a later Hebrew or Aramaic text from that era. After the sixth century AD, the occasional copy of the Septuagint is found which uses the name, either written as Ιαω or a Greek approximation of יהוה (ΠΙΠΙ), however, all of these can be traced back to the Hexapla, Quinta, Sextus, and/or Septima, which attempted to retranslate and harmonize the Old Testament in the 3rd through 6th centuries AD. There are no early surviving copies of the Septuagint's version of Joshua which have the name Iaw (Ιαω / 𐤉𐤄𐤅) in it like some of the other books of the Septuagint. As Κυριοσ ο θεοσ translates directly as Lord God (or Lord the God), that term is used.

Joshua: Chapter 2

Joshua the son of Nun, sent two young men from Shittim[1] to spy on the land, ordering, "Go up, and view the land around Jericho."

The two young men went to Jericho, and entered into the house of a prostitute, whose name was Rehob, and lodged there. It was reported to the king of Jericho, "Men of the sons of Israel have come in here to spy the land."

The king of Jericho sent and spoke to Rehob, ordering, "Bring out the men that entered into your house tonight, as they have come to spy on the land."

The woman took the two men and hid them, and replied to the messengers, "The men came into me, but after the gate was shut in the dark, the men left. I don't know where they've gone. Chase after them, and you may catch them."

She had taken them up onto the roof to the house, and hidden them in flax-stalks that were spread on her on the roof. The left and men chased after them along the road to ford on the Jordan, where the gate was shut. After the men pursuing them had left, and before the spies had gone to sleep, she went up to them on the top of the house, and said, "I know that the Lord has given you the land, as the fear of you, has fallen on us. For we have heard that Lord the god dried up the Papyrus Sea[2] before you, when you came out of the land of Egypt, and all that he did to the two kings of the Amorites, who were beyond Jordan, to Sihon and Og, whom you completely destroyed. When we heard it we were amazed in our heart, and there was no longer any spirit in any of us because of you, for Lord the god is the god in the sky above and on the land below. Now swear to me by Lord the god, since I dealt mercifully with you, you will also deal mercifully with the house of my father, and save the house of my father, my mother, and my brothers, and all my house, and all that they have, and you will rescue my mind from Mot.[3]

The men answered her, "Our life for yours even to death."

She confirmed, "When the Lord has delivered the city to you, you will deal mercifully and truly with me."

She let them down out her window, and she said to them, "Go into the hill-country, in case the pursuers find you, and hide there for three days until your pursuers return from looking for you, and afterward you can leave on your way."

The men said to her, "This is our oath. Look, we will enter into a part of the city, and you will set the sign: you will bind this scarlet cord in the window, by which you have let us down, and you will bring into your house with yourself, your father, and your mother, and your brothers, and all the family of your father. It will come to pass that whoever will be outside the door of your house, his guilt will be on him, and we will be free of this, your oath. We will be responsible for all that will be found with you in your house. But if anyone should injure us, or betray these our matters, we will be free of this, your oath."

She said to them, "Let it be as you have said," and she sent them out, and they departed. They came to the hill-country and remained there for three days, and the pursuers searched all the roads and did not find them. The two young men returned and came down out of the mountain, and they went over to Joshua the son of Nun, and told him all things that had happened to them. They said to Joshua, "The Lord has delivered all the land into our power, and all the inhabitants of that land tremble because of us."

Joshua: Chapter 2 Notes

1 Codex Vaticanus: Sattin (ϲⲀⲦⲦⲓⲛ)

• Aleppo Codex: Štym (שטים)

• Leningrad Codex: Shittim (שִׁטִּים)

• Targum Jerusalem: Shitin (שטין)

The location of the Shittim Valley is generally accepted as Khirbet el-Kafrayn, in Jordan. Other Israelite texts, such as Micah refer to the Lord of Peor in association with the Shittim Valley, however, this name appears to have been an insult directed towards Lord Hammon who was worshiped at Tell el-Hammam in the 800s BC. There is no clear link between Hammon and Peor, implying the worshipers of Peor disappeared around the time the Israelites traveled through the Shittim Valley.

The major ruins in the Shittim Valley, are found at Tell el-Hammam, which was occupied from at least 3600 BC until the beginning of the Late Bronze Age (1550 to 1200) when the site was abandoned for unknown reasons. It was rebuilt in the 900s BC as a Samaritan city. As Tell el-Hammam is in the Shittim Valley, and was destroyed or abandoned when the Israelites moved through the region, using either the traditional Christian dating or the Minoan Eruption and collapse of the Hyksos Dynasty from the Book of Exodus, the Bronze-Age city was likely Peor (Φαγωρ). The exact dating of the abandonment of the bronze-age city is unclear, and there is some evidence of occupation for a few decades after 1550 BC, but the site does appear to have been abandoned by 1500 BC.

2 Codex Vaticanus: erythran thalassan (ЄΡΥΘΡΑΝΘΑΛΑϹϹΑΝ). Translation: Erythrean (or Red) Sea

- Aleppo Codex: ym sůp (ים סוף). Translation: sea of reeds (or papyrus)
- Leningrad Codex: yam-suf (יַם־סֽוּף). Translation: sea of reeds (or papyrus)
- Targum Jerusalem: yama deSuf (יַמָּא דְסוּף). Translation: sea of reeds (or papyrus)

The Greek term is not geographically specific, as it is a translation of the Persian term Erostras, which referred to the entire Persian Gulf, Red Sea, and the Indian Ocean. The Greeks were likely referring to the Gulf of Suez, however, this was known to the ancient Egyptians as the 'Sea of Calm,' which is what the Israelites would have called it if that was where they were. The original Sea of Reeds was almost certainly Lake Bardawil on the north coast of the Sinai Peninsula, a shallow saline lake with a surface area of 147,000 acres (59,500 hectares).

The Greeks transliterated the name as the Sea of Siph (ΘΑΛΑϹϹΗϹϹΙΦ) in the Codex Vaticanus' translation of Judges, confirming that the name Swf was in the Aramaic text they worked from. Both the Aramaic term sůf (סוף) and Phoenician term sůf (𐤎𐤅𐤐), both meaning papyrus plants were adopted from the Egyptian term tjůfi (𓍿𓅱𓆑𓇗𓏥), which referred to papyrus, papyrus plants, and papyrus marshes. The Egyptian term continued to be used into the Classical era as the Coptic words čoouf (ϫⲟⲟⲩϥ), conf (ϭⲟⲛϥ), and comf (ϭⲟⲙϥ), all meaning papyrus. Conversely, the Egyptian name of the Red Sea was the Sea of Ḥeḥ (𓁨), meaning 'very large sea' from the Middle Kingdom era onward, however, it is believed to have originally been named after the ancient Egyptian frog god Heh (𓎛𓎛𓅱).

As the Greek translation of Erythrean Sea is anachronistic, the translation of Papyrus Sea is imported from the Masoretic Text. Based on the described journey out of Egypt, the original Papyrus Sea would have been Lake Bardawil on the north coast of the Sinai Peninsula, a shallow saline lake with a surface area of 147,000 acres (59,500 hectares).

3 Codex Vaticanus: Thanatou (ΘΑΝΑΤΟΥ). Translation: Thanatos (or death, corpse)

- Aleppo Codex: Mwt (מות). Translation: Mot (or 'to die' in Aramaic, 'death' in Hebrew)
- Leningrad Codex: Mavet (מָוֶת). Translation: Mot (or 'death' in Hebrew)

Mot (ד— / ‎+ﬡ) was the Canaanite god of death, which the Greeks interpreted as the local version of Thanatos, the Greek god of death. The Israelites viewed Mot as the angel of Death in the era of the prophets, which resulted in Thanatos becoming the Christian angel of death in the early centuries of the Christian era.

Joshua: Chapter 3

Joshua rose early in the morning and left Shittim, and they came as far as the Jordan and lodged there before they crossed over. After three days, the scribes went through the camp, and they ordered the people, "When you see the box[1] of the covenant of Lord the god, and our priests and the Levites carrying it, you will leave from your places, and you will follow it, but keep a distance from it. You will stand at least two thousand cubits from it. Do not approach it, that you may know which way you are to go, as you have not gone this way previously."

Joshua said to the people, "Sanctify yourselves against tomorrow, for tomorrow the Lord will do wonders among you." Joshua said to the priests, "Take up the box of the covenant of the Lord, and go before the people."

The priests picked up the box of the covenant of the Lord and went before the people. The Lord said to Joshua, "Today I begin to exalt you before all the Israelites, that they may know that as I was with Moses, so will I also be with you. Now order the priests that carry the box of the covenant, 'As soon as you enter on a part of the water of Jordan, then you will stand in the Jordan.'"

Joshua said to the Israelites, "Come here and listen to the word of Lord the god. By this you will know that the living God is among you, and will completely destroy from before us the Canaanites, Cypriots,[2] Perizzites, Mitanni,[3] Amorites, Girgashites, and Jebusites. Look, the box of the covenant of the Lord crosses the Jordan. Choose among yourselves twelve men of the sons of Israel, one from each tribe. It will come to pass, when the feet of the priests that carry the box of the covenant of the Lord enter into the water of the Jordan, the water of Jordan below will stop, and the water coming down from above will stop."

The people packed up their tents to cross the Jordan, and the priests carried the box of the covenant of the Lord before the people. When the priests that carried the box of the covenant of the Lord entered on Jordan, and the feet of the priests that carried the box of the covenant of the Lord were stepped into the water of the Jordan, (now the Jordan, its whole channel overflowed all its banks as in the days of the wheat harvest.) Then the waters that came down from above stopped, frozen and exceedingly violent, as far off as the region of Kariathiarim, and that which came down to the Dead Sea (the salt sea),[4] until it completely failed, and the people stood opposite Jericho. The priests that carried the box of the covenant of the Lord stood on dry land in the middle of Jordan, and all the Israelites went through on dry land until all the people had completely crossed the Jordan.

Joshua: Chapter 3 Notes

1 Codex Vaticanus: cibôton (ΚΙΒѠΤΟΝ). Translation: box (or chest)

- Aleppo Codex: årůn (ארון). Translation: box

- Leningrad Codex: aron (אֲרֹון). Translation: box

- Targum Jerusalem: aron (אֲרֹון). Translation: box

The Greek term cibôton (κιβωτὸν) was based on the Aramaic word tybůtå (מק^ביתא), however, the Hebrew translation uses a different word, also meaning 'box.' The reason for the Hebrew substitution is likely due to the Aramaic word being based on the Egyptian word djebåt (𓆓𓃀𓏏), meaning 'sarcophagus,' since the classical era, which has resulted in many strange translations. The Egyptian word is accepted as being adopted into Canaanite during the New Kingdom Era, when it was pronounced as debåt (𓂦𓃀𓏏), indicating that the Egyptian word was likely the original in the text. By the Classical era, when the Hebrew text was translated, the related Coptic Egyptian word taibe (ⲧⲁⲓⲃⲉ) had come to mean coffin, meaning the 'box of god' would have become the 'coffin of god' explaining the Hebrew substitution of årůn (ארון).

2 Codex Vaticanus: Chettaeon (ΧΕΤΤΑΙΟΝ)

- Aleppo Codex: Hty (חתי). Translation: Cypriots

- Leningrad Codex: Chitti (חִתִּי). Translation: Cypriots

- Targum Jerusalem: Chitta'ei (חִתָּאֵי). Translation: Cypriots

This term has created a great deal of confusion since the misidentification of the ruins of the Neshites as being 'Hittite' in the 1800s. The modern archaeological name 'Hittite,' is not derived from an ancient name for the culture applied by themselves, or anyone else, but rather adopted from the biblical reference to a then-unknown civilization somewhere in the region. There was an ancient culture in the region called the Hattians, however, they were conquered by the Nesites before 1700 BC, and subsequently disappeared from the historic records.

The name was applied to culture today referred to as 'Hittites,' before the 'Hittite' language had been translated, and is incorrect. Since 1906, excavations at Boğazköy, the ancient 'Hittite' capital Hattusa have uncovered more than 10,000 'Hittite' texts, including the royal achieve. The actual name of the 'Hittite' language and people was

Nešili (☰⟨⟩⟨⟩), which is now rendered in some academic literate as Nesite or Neshite. As early as the mid-1800s some scholars disputed the identification of the Nesites as the Biblical Hittites, including the Orientalist Max Müller, who was one of many claiming the Biblical Hittites were ancient Greeks or some other Mediterranean people. Later in the Septuagint's translation of the Maccabees, the similar term Chettiim (Χεττιιμ) as a reference to all Greek-speaking lands, and therefore the Biblical Hittites were likely the Minoans or the Achaean Greeks.

In the 1st century AD, the Jewish historian Josephus reported that Cethima was the name of Cyrus in Aramaic, and the Chettim were the descendants of Noah's grandson Chethimus, who had settled on Cyprus. Josephus reported that the name was preserved in the Greek name of the town Cition (Κίτιον). Most historians view it as more likely that the Aramaic name was derived from the city-state of Cition, which was known as Kåtjåy (☰) in Egyptian records from the New Kingdom Era in the late Bronze Age, and Kt (☰) or Kty (☰) in Phoenician records from the early Iron Age. While this may be the origin of the term, by the era of the Neo-Assyrian era, the term must have also referred to other Greek islands, as both the prophets Isaiah and Ezekiel used the term 'Islands of Kittim.'

As the term referred to the entire island of Cyprus in Aramaic, the translations of 'Cyprus' and 'Cypriots' are used here.

3 Codex Vaticanus: Euaion (ΕΥΑΙΟΝ)

- Aleppo Codex: Ḥůy (חוי)

- Leningrad Codex: Chivvi (חִוִּי)

- Targum Jerusalem: Chiva'ei (חִוָאֵי)

The term is believed to have been derived from the name of the Hurrians, however, is derived separately from the other term Chori (חֹרִי). Chori is accepted as referring to the Hurrians, which the Egyptians called Håru (☰), and the Babylonians called Ḥuurri (☰). The Hurrians were one of the oldest cultures in the Middle East, however, became largely a slave culture within the Akkadian and Old Babylonian empires. Under the Mitanni empire, they rose to a position of wealth, and formed the noble caste. The Greek transliteration of this term was variations of Chorrhaeous (Χορραιους), which, like the Hebrew term, was used interchangeably in the texts with Eyaeon (Ευαιον) / Chivvi (חִוִּי), although that term generally applied to the rules and priests.

The ultimate origin of the terms Eyaeon (Ευαῖον) and Chivvi (חִוִּי), both appear to be the cuneiform word Éan (☰), meaning temple or sacred. In the Amarna Letters, which date to the 1330s BC, the term Éan (☰) was the name of a people, who appear to be the Mitanni, or the Mitanni-Aryan priesthood within the Mitanni. A similar correlation between the terms is found in the Septuagint's 1ˢᵗ Paralipomenon and Masoretic Divrei-hay Yamim, where the Greek translation uses Beithani (Βαιθανι), however, the Hebrew uses the term Mitni (מִתְנִי). This term also refers to a group of people, meaning the underlying Edomite text the Greeks translated would have been 'people of the House of Ån' (𐤉𐤗𐤕𐤋𐤆𐤏), a direct Canaanite translation of É An (𒂍𒀭).

While Mitni was the transliteration used in the Edomite text that formed the basis of the Hebrew translation of Divrei-hayYamim, it was replaced with Chivvi (חִוִּי) in the Judahite texts, which served as the basis of most of the Masoretic texts. This likely originated in a Judahite copy of the text, after the Aramaic translation had been made, where an N (𐤍) was replaced with a Ů (𐤅). The Aramaic translation would have already been made in the time of King Manasseh, were the term was transliterated as Hyån (𐤉𐤍𐤇𐤕), itself a transliteration of the early Canaanite Hyån (𐤉𐤗𐤕𐤆).

4 Codex Vaticanus: thalassan Araba thalassan alos (ΘΑΛΑϹϹΑΝΑΡΑΒΑΘΑΛΑϹϹΑΝ ΑΛΟϹ). Translation: Sea of Arabah Sea of Salt

• Aleppo Codex: ym hôrbh ym hmlh (יס הערבה יס המלח). Translation: Sea of the Plain sea of salt

• Leningrad Codex: yam ha'aravah yam-hammelach (יְם הָעֲרָבָה יְם־הַמֶּלַח). Translation: Sea of the Plain sea of salt

• Targum Jerusalem: leyama demeishra leyama demilcha (לְיַמָּא דְמֵישְׁרָא לְיַמָּא דְמִלְחָא). Translation: the sea of the valley the sea of salt

The Sea of Arabah was an ancient name for the Dead Sea. The scribal notes clarifying that the Sea of Arabah was the salt sea appears to have been included in the Aramaic source text that both the Septuagint and Masoretic versions of Joshua were translated from. The fact that the Aramaic translator needed to clarify which sea the Sea of Arabah was, suggests the Aramaic translation of Joshua was made in the north, likely in Gilead or Aram. This note also means the original Book of Joshua was not written in Aramaic, but translated from another language, and, clearly written earlier, when the term Sea of Arabah was commonly used.

Joshua: Chapter 4

When the people had completely crossed the Jordan, the Lord said to Joshua, "Take men from the people, one from each tribe, and organize them, and you will take out of the middle of the Jordan twelve existing stones, and having carried them across together with yourselves, place them in your camp, where you will camp for the night."

Joshua called twelve distinguished men among the Israelites, one of each tribe, and said to them, "Advance before me in the presence of the Lord into the middle of Jordan, and each pick up a stone from there, let him carry it on your shoulders, according to the number of the twelve tribes of Israel. These may be for you continually an appointed sign, so when your son asks you in the future, 'What are these stones to us?' Then you may explain to your son, 'The river Jordan was dried up from before the box of the covenant of the Lord when it passed it, and these stones will be as a memorial for you for the Israelites forever."

The Israelites did so, as the Lord commanded Joshua. They picked up twelve stones out of the middle of Jordan, (as the Lord commanded Joshua when the Israelites had completely crossed over,) and carried these stones with them into the camp, and laid them down there. Joshua set also another twelve stones in Jordan itself, in the place that was under the feet of the priests that carried the box of the covenant of the Lord, and there they are to this day. The priests that carried the box of the covenant stood in Jordan until Joshua had finished all that the Lord commanded him to report to the people, and the people rushed and crossed over. When all the people had passed over, that the box of the covenant of the Lord crossed over, and the stones before them. The sons of Reuben, and the sons of Gad, and the half-tribe of Manasseh crossed equipped before the Israelites, as Moses commanded them. Forty thousand armed for battle went over before the Lord to war, to the city of Jericho. On that day the Lord magnified Joshua before all the people of Israel, and they were afraid of him, like they had been of Moses, as long as he lived.

The Lord said to Joshua, "Order the priests that carry the box of the covenant of the testimony of the Lord, to come up out of Jordan."

Joshua ordered the priests, "Come up out of Jordan."

When the priests who carried the box of the covenant of the Lord had come up out of Jordan and set their feet on the land, the water of the Jordan returned rapidly to its place and went as before over all its banks. The people came out of the Jordan on the tenth day of the first month, and the Israelites camped at the circle[1] in the region eastward from Jericho. Joshua set these twelve stones which he took out of Jordan, in a circle, and said, "When your sons ask you, 'What are these stones? Tell your sons, that Israel came over the Jordan on dry land when Lord the god had dried up the water of Jordan from before them until they had passed over. As Lord the god did to the Papyrus Sea, which Lord the god dried up from before us until we passed over. That all the nations of the earth might know, that the power of the Lord is mighty and that you might worship Lord the god in every work."

Joshua: Chapter 4 Notes

1 Codex Vaticanus: Galgaloes (ΓΑΛΓΑΛΟΙϹ)

• Aleppo Codex: glgl (גלגל). Translation: circle

• Leningrad Codex: gilgāl (גִּלְגָּל). Translation: circle

• Targum Jerusalem: gilgala (גִלְגָלָא). Translation: wheel

Gilgal (גִּלְגָּל) is the Hebrew word for circle. Archaeologists have discovered several ceremonial stone circles in Canaan that were used between 1200 and 1000 BC for gatherings that are assumed to be religious in nature. As these stone circles are found down in the valleys, unlike the altars at the tops of hills where the Canaanites worshiped, and 'circles' (גלגל) are mentioned throughout the old Israelite texts, it is assumed they are early Israelite religious centers from before the First Temple was built.

Joshua: Chapter 5

When the kings of the Amorites who were beyond Jordan heard, and the kings of Phoenicia[1] by the sea, that Lord the god had dried up the river Jordan from before the Israelites when they passed over, that their hearts failed, and their minds melted, and there was no sense in them in the face of the Israelites.

About this time the Lord said to Joshua, "Make yourself stone knives from sharp stone, and sit down and circumcise the Israelites the second time."

Joshua made sharp knives of stone, and circumcised the Israelites at the place called the 'Hill of Foreskins.' This is how Joshua purified the Israelites, as many as were born in the way, and as many as were uncircumcised of them that came out of Egypt, all these Joshua circumcised. For forty-two years Israel wandered among the abandoned places of desert-dwellers.[2] Therefore most of the fighting men that came out of the land of Egypt were uncircumcised, those who disobeyed the commands of God, concerning who he determined should not see the land, which the Lord swore to give to their fathers, a land flowing with milk and honey. In their place he raised up their sons, who Joshua circumcised, because they were uncircumcised, having been born long the way. When they had been circumcised they rested sitting there in the camp until they were healed.

The lord[3] said to Joshua the son of Nun, "On this day have I removed the reproach of Egypt from you," and he called the name of that place Gilgal.

The Israelites kept the Passover on the fourteenth day of the month in the evening, to the west of Jericho on the opposite side of the Jordan in the plain. They ate the grain of the earth unleavened and new grain. On this day the manna stopped after they had eaten of the grain of the land, and the Israelites no longer had manna. They took the fruits of the land of the Phoenicians in that year. When Joshua was in Jericho, that he looked up with his eyes and saw a man standing before him, and there was a drawn sword in his hand, and Joshua approached and said to him, "Are you with us, or on the side of our enemies?"

He answered him, "I have now come, the Generalissimo of the army of the Lord."[4]

Joshua fell on his face to the earth, and said to him, "Lord, what do you command of your servant?"

The Generalissimo of the Lord said to Joshua, "Remove your shoes off your feet, for the place on which you now stand is sacred."

Joshua: Chapter 5 Notes

1 Codex Vaticanus: Phoenicês (ϕΟΙΝΙΚΗϹ). Translation: Phoenicia

• Aleppo Codex: Knôny (כנעני). Translation: Canaan

• Leningrad Codex: Kena'ani (כְּנַעֲנִי). Translation: Canaan

• Targum Jerusalem: Chena'ana'ah (כְּנַעֲנָאָה). Translation: Canaan

Phoenicia and Canaan were two names of the same land and culture. Phoenicia is believed to be derived from the Egyptian name of the people, which then sped through the Mediterranean. Canaan is believed to be derived from the Akkadian name for the people, which was mainly used in Semitic languages of the Middle East. Both terms are believed to be derived from the name 'purple people,' as the Canaanites were mass exporters of purple dye and fabric throughout most of their civilization.

2 Codex Vaticanus: tê erêmô tê Madbaritidi (ΤΗΕΡΗΜѠΤΗΜΑΔΒΑΡΙΤΙΔΙ). Translation: the desert the Madbarites

• Aleppo Codex: mdbr (מדבר). Translation: the desert

• Leningrad Codex: midbar (מִדְבָּר). Translation: the desert

• Targum Jerusalem: madbera (מַדְבְּרָא). Translation: the desert

The Greek translation deviates from the Hebrew and Judeo-Aramaic translations, which simply refer to the desert. The Greek could either be read as the 'desert of the Madbarites,' or the 'abandoned places of the Madbarites.' The term Madbaritidi (Μαδβαριτιδι) is a synthesis of the Aramaic mdbrå (מדברא) meaning 'desert' and the Greek -itidi (-ιτιδι), meaning 'people of,' the precursor to the modern English '-ites.' This means the term had to be adopted from a term in the Aramaic text which translates as 'desert dweller.' Based on the context, the Aramaic word was likely mdbråyn (מדבריין), meaning 'desert-dweller.' This means the Aramaic text either read the redundant 'desert of the desert-dwellers,' or 'abandoned places of the desert-dwellers,' which is the interpretation used in this translation. As desert-dwellers are nomadic, is suggested the Israelites had occupied their settlements while they were elsewhere.

3 Codex Vaticanus: c̄s (κ̄c̄). Translation: lord

- Aleppo Codex: Yhůh (יהוה)

- Leningrad Codex: Yehvah (יְהֹוָה)

- Targum Jerusalem: yeyah (יְיָ). Translation: Yhů

Based on the requirement to re-institute the Egyptian practice of circumcision, in order to remove the 'reproach of Egypt,' this appears to be describing the Israelites rejoining Egyptian civilization, which would make the 'lord' in the text King Thutmose I, before the Hasmoneans carelessly changed him to Yahweh.

4 Codex Vaticanus: archistratêgos dynameôs c̄u (ΑΡΧΙCΤΡΑΤΗΓΟCΔΥΝΑΜΕωCΚ̄Ῡ). Translation: Generalissimo (or high strategist, supreme commander) of the forces of the Lord

- Aleppo Codex: šr ṣbå yhůh (שר צבא יהוה). Translation: minister of the army of Yhůh

- Leningrad Codex: sar-tzeva-Yehvah (שַׂר־צְבָא־יְהֹוָה). Translation: minister of the army of Yehwah

- Targum Jerusalem: Mal'ach sheliach min kodam yeyah (מַלְאַךְ שְׁלִיחַ מִן קֳדָם יְיָ). Translation: messenger-agent from before Yhů

While the Greeks gave the 'Generalissimo' an impressive rank, the Masoretic texts simply call him a minister or secretary, and the later Jerusalem Targum labels him as a messenger-agent. Assuming that this was not a reference to a supernatural being, or some extraterrestrial being, it was likely the commander of the Egyptian army who was campaigning in Canaan in the year this story is set according to the Septuagint's chronology. Jericho was destroyed, its walls pulled down around the time that the Egyptian army passed through the region, and most Egyptologists accept that the Egyptian army destroyed the city, regardless of whatever the Israelites were doing there.

Joshua: Chapter 6

Now Jericho was closely sealed up and besieged, and none went out of it, and none came in.

The Lord said to Joshua, "Look, I deliver Jericho into your power, and its king in it, and its mighty men. Set the warriors around it. It will be that when you will sound with the trumpet, all the people will shout together. When they have shouted, the walls of the city will fall by themselves, and all the people will enter, each one rushing directly into the city."

Joshua the son of Nun went to the priests, and said to them, "Let seven priests having seven sacred trumpets proceed before the Lord, and let them sound loud, and let the box of the covenant of the Lord follow. Order the people to go round, and circle the city, and let your warriors pass by armed before the Lord. Let the warriors proceed before, and the priests bringing up the rear behind the box of the covenant of the Lord proceed sounding the trumpets."

Joshua commanded the people, saying, don't cry out, nor let anyone hear your voice until he himself declares to you the day to cry out, and then you will cry out. The box of the covenant of God having gone around immediately returned into the camp and lodged there. On the second day Joshua rose in the morning, and the priests picked up the box of the covenant of the Lord. The seven priests bearing the seven trumpets went on before the Lord, and afterward, the warriors went on, and the remainder of the multitude went after the box of the covenant of the Lord, and the priests sounded with the trumpets. All the rest of the multitude circled the city six times from within a short distance and went back again into the camp. They did this for six days.

On the seventh day, they rose early and circled the city on that day seven times. It happened at the seventh circuit the priests blew the trumpets, and Joshua said to the Israelites, "Shout, for the Lord has given you the city. The city will be cursed and, and all things that are in it, to Lord Sabaoth,[1] only save Rehob the prostitute, and all things in her house. But keep yourselves strictly from the cursed things, in case you change your mind and take the cursed things, and you make the camp of the Israelites a cursed thing and destroy us. All the silver, or gold, or brass, or iron, will be holy to the Lord. It will be carried into the treasury of the Lord."

The priests sounded with the trumpets, and when the people heard the trumpets, all the people shouted at once with a loud and strong shout, and all the walls fell around it, and all the people went up into the city. Joshua devoted it to destruction and all things that were in the city, man and woman, young man and old, and calf and donkey, by the edge of the sword.[2]

Joshua said to the two young men who had acted as spies, "Go into the house of the woman, and bring her out here, she and all that she has."

The two young men who had spied out the city entered into the house of the woman, and brought out Rehob the prostitute, and her father, and her mother, and her brothers, and her families, and all that she had, and they took her out to the camp of Israel. The city was burnt with fire with all things that were in it, only the silver, and gold, and brass, and iron, they brought into the treasury of the Lord. Joshua saved Rehob the prostitute, and all the house of her father, and allowed her to live in Israel until this day because she hid the spies which Joshua sent to spy out Jericho. Joshua adjured them on that day before The Lord, saying, "Cursed be the man who will build that city, he will lay the foundation of it in his firstborn, and he will set up the gates of it in his youngest son."

(As did Hozan of the Temple of El. He laid the foundation with Abiram, his firstborn, and set up the gates of it with his youngest surviving son.)

The Lord was with Joshua, and his name was in all the land.

Joshua: Chapter 6 Notes

1 Codex Vaticanus: Cyriô Sabaôth (ⲕⲩⲣⲓⲱ ⲥⲁⲃⲁⲱⲑ). Translation: Lord Sabaoth (or 'forces' in Hebrew, 'desires' in Aramaic)

- Aleppo Codex: Yhŭh (יהוה). Translation: Yhŭh

- Leningrad Codex: Yehvah (יְהֹוָה). Translation: Yehwah

- Targum Jerusalem: yeyah (??). Translation: Yhŭ

This reference to Lord Sabaoth is clearly earlier than the Hasmonean redaction, which replaced most referenced to the various Lords of Canaan with Yhŭh. In this case, the entire term Lord Sabaoth was replaced by Yahweh in the Hasmonean redaction, indicating that they considered Lord Sabaoth to be a proper name, and not a title. According to Greek and Roman records from the era, as well as the books of Maccabees, the Judahites worshiped Lord Sabaoth during the Greek rule of Judea. The Greeks associated Lord Sabaoth with Dionysus, while the Romans associated Lord Sabaoth with

Bacchus. Immediately after the Maccabean Revolt had successfully driven out the Greeks and established the Hasmonean Dynasty, the Judeans sent an emissary to Rome to request an alliance against the Greeks, but Roman records indicate that the result was all Judeans being evicted from Rome because the Judean emissaries claimed that their god 'Jupiter Sabazious' was the Roman god Jupiter. As this was the earliest Roman records of a Judean god with a name like Jupiter's (Latin: Iuppiter or Iovis), it seems the first Hasmonean King/High-Priest Simon the Zealot was responsible for the resurgence of the name Yhŭh, which completely replaced Lord Sabaoth before the end of the Hasmonean dynasty.

2 The walled city of Jericho, which has been identified as Tell es-Sultan since 1869, was destroyed sometime circa 1500 BC, and the site was virtually unoccupied until after 1000 BC. The site has been studied extensively, with various dates given for its destruction ranging from 1700 to 1400 BC. The cause of the collapse of the walls is unknown, however, it is theorized, depending on when the walls fell, that they may have been ripped down by the Egyptians circa 1500 BC, as Thutmose I's army campaigned all the way to the Euphrates, however, according to Thutmose I's records, they found no one to fight in Canaan, implying someone had recently campaigned in the region. He claimed that the Canaanite chieftains had pledged loyalty to Egypt, however, archaeological evidence shows after 1500 BC fortifications began being built throughout Canaan.

Joshua: Chapter 7

But the Israelites committed a great crime and plundered some of the cursed things. Achan the son of Carmi, the son of Zabdi, the son of Zerah, of the tribe of Judah, took of the cursed things, and the Lord was very angry with the Israelites. Joshua sent men to the government office, which is by the Temple of El, ordering, "Spy out the government office,"[1] and the men went up and spied on Gai.

They returned to Joshua, and reported to him, "Don't send all the people up, but send about two or three thousand men up to capture the city by siege. Don't send up there all the people, as the enemy are few."

About three thousand men when up, and they fled from the men of Gai. The men of Gai killed thirty-six of them, and chased them from the gate, and drove them from the steep hill, and the heart of the people was alarmed and became like water. Joshua tore his garments and fell to the earth on his face before the Lord until evening, both he and the elders of Israel, and they threw dirt on their heads.

Joshua said, "I beg, Lord, has your servant brought these people across the Jordan to deliver them to the Amorites to destroy us? We should have remained and settled ourselves beyond Jordan. What will I say since Israel has turned his back before his enemy? When the Canaanites and all the inhabitants of the land hear it, they will surround us and destroy us from off the land. What will you do for your great name?"

The Lord answered Joshua, "Get up! Why have you fallen on your face? The people have sinned and transgressed the covenant which I made with them. They have stolen cursed things and put them into their store. The Israelites will not be able to stand before their enemies. They will turn their back before their enemies, as they have become a cursed thing! I will no longer be with you unless you remove the cursed thing from yourselves. Rise! Sanctify the people and tell them to sanctify themselves for the morning, so says Lord the god of Israel. The cursed thing is among you. You will not be able to stand before your enemies until you have removed the cursed things from among you. You will all be gathered together by your tribes in the morning, and the tribe which the Lord will indicate, you will bring by families. The family which the Lord will indicate, you will bring by household, and the household which the Lord will indicate, you will bring man by man. The man who will be pointed out will be burnt with fire, and all that he has, because he has transgressed the covenant of the Lord, and has worked wickedness in Israel."

Joshua rose early and brought the people by their tribes, and the tribe of Judah was indicated. It was brought by their families, and the family of the Zerahites was indicated. It was brought man by man, and Achan the son of Zabdi the son of Zerah was indicated. Joshua said to Achan, "Give glory this day to Lord the god of Israel, and make a confession, and tell me what you have done, and don't hide it from me."

Achan answered Joshua, "Indeed I have sinned against Lord the god of Israel. I did this: I saw in the spoil an embroidered mantle, and two hundred shekels[2] of silver, and one golden wedge of fifty shekels, and I wanted them and took them, and look, they are hidden in my tent, and the silver is hidden under them."

Joshua sent messengers, and they ran to the tent in the camp, and these things were hidden in his tent, and the silver under them. They brought them out of the tent and brought them to Joshua and the elders of Israel, and they laid them before the Lord. Joshua took Achan the son of Zerah and brought him to the valley of Achor, and his sons, and his daughters, and his calves, and his donkeys, and all his sheep, and his tent, and all his property, and all the people were with him. He brought them to Emec Achor. Joshua asked Achan, "Why have you destroyed us? The Lord will destroy you today."

All Israel stoned him with stones. They set up over him a great heap of stones, and the Lord ceased from his fierce anger. Therefore he called the place Emecachor until this day.

Joshua: Chapter 7 Notes

1 Codex Vaticanus: Gai (ܓܝ)

- Aleppo Codex: Hôy (הֺעי)

- Leningrad Codex: Ha'ai (הָעַי)

- Targum Jerusalem: ay (עי). Translation: ruins

The Greek translators transliterated this word two different ways from the Aramaic texts they translated. In Genesis it was transliterated as Aggai (Αγγαι), however, both the geographic location and the Hebrew translation of Hôy (העי) confirm it is the same location. The Hebrew term is often translated as 'ruins' however, the place is inhabited during the era of Joshua, indicating 'ruins' is an incorrect interpretation. The term appears to have originated with the Middle Egyptian word ḥå (𓉿𓈙𓂋), meaning 'government office,' and several 'ḥås' are mentioned as existing in Canaan. This 'government office' was the one Abram had built an altar near when he first entered Canaan.

As Canaan had been under the control of the Egyptians during the Middle Kingdom era, as well as during the Canaanite and Hyksos dynasties of the Second Intermediate Period, the colonial offices appear to have been continuously occupied. In the year the story is set, 1504 BC, the armies of Thutmose I had just marched through Canaan, however, he does not appear to have reclaimed the old 'government office' in Samaria, and based on the Israelites attacking 'Gai' immediately after removing the 'reproach of Egypt,' by re-instituting the Egyptian custom of circumcision, and attacking Jericho with the 'Generalissimo of the forces of the Lord,' it suggests that the Israelites attacked the 'government office' for the Egyptians. By the era of Joshua, this Gai appears to have become a town, and the term is used as a proper name.

2 Codex Vaticanus: didrachma (ΔΙΔΡΑΧΜΑ). Translation: two-drachmas

• Aleppo Codex: šqlym (שְׁקָלִים). Translation: shekels

• Leningrad Codex: shekalim (שְׁקָלִים). Translation: shekels

• Targum Jerusalem: sal'in (סַלְעִין). Translation: selas

The shekel was a unit of weight used throughout the Middle East for thousands of years, weighing approximately 8.6 grams of silver. The Greek drachma was a coin weighing approximately half a shekel, and therefore under Greek rule of the Middle East, a two-drachma coin was used. As the Greeks clearly translated shekel into didrachma, the term shekel is restored in this translation. The term sela, used as the Targum Jerusalem, was a similarly sized coin and weight from the late classical era.

Joshua: Chapter 8

The Lord said to Joshua, "Don't be afraid or nervous. Take with you all the warriors, and rise, and go up to Gai. I have given into your hands the king of Gai and his land. You will do to Gai, as you did to Jericho and its king, and you will take for yourself the spoils of its livestock. Set an ambush behind the city."

Joshua and all the warriors rose to go up to Gai, and Joshua chose out thirty thousand mighty men, and he sent them away by night. He ordered them, "You lie in ambush behind the city, near the city, and you will all remain ready. I and all with me will come close to the city, the inhabitants of Gai will come out to meet us like before, and we will flee from before them. When they will come out after us, we will draw them away from the city. They will say, 'These men flee from before us, like before.' You will rise up out of the ambuscade, and go into the city. You will do according to this word. Look, I have commanded you."

Joshua sent them, and they went to lie in ambush, and they lay between the Temple of El[1] and the government office, to the west of Gai.

Joshua rose early in the morning and reviewed the people, and he went up, he and the elders before the people to Gai. All the warriors went up with him, and they went forward and approached the city from the east. The ambuscade was on the west side of the city. When the king of Gai saw it, he rushed and went out to meet them immediately in battle, he and all the people that were with him, and he did not know that there was an ambuscade positioned against him behind the city. Joshua and Israel saw them and retreated from before them, and they chased after the Israelites, and traveled a distance from the city. There was no one left in Gai who did not chase after Israel, and they left the city open when they chased after Israel.

The Lord said to Joshua, "Stretch out your hand with the spear towards the city, for I have delivered it into your hands, and those laying in wait will rise quickly from their place."

Joshua stretched out his hand and his spear towards the city, and the ambuscade rose quickly out of their place, and entered into the city and captured it. They quickly set the city on fire. When the inhabitants of Gai looked around them, then they saw the smoke going up out of the city to the sky, and they were no longer able to flee this way or that way. Joshua and all Israel saw that the ambuscade had taken the city and that the smoke of the city went up to the sky, and they turned and attacked the men of Gai. These came out of the city to meet them, and they were in the middle of the army, some being on this side, and some on that, and they slaughtered them until there was none left of them who survived and escaped.

They took the king of Gai alive and brought him to Joshua. When the Israelites had finished slaying all that were in Gai, and in the fields, and in the mountain on the descent, from where they pursued them even to the end, then Joshua returned to Gai and struck it with the edge of the sword. They who died on that day, men and women were twelve thousand, all the inhabitants of Gai. Beside the spoils that were in the city, all things which the Israelites took as spoil for themselves according to the command of the Lord, as the Lord commanded Joshua. Joshua burnt the city with fire, he made it an uninhabited heap forever, even to this day.

He hanged the king of Gai on a doubletree, and he remained on the tree until evening. When the sun went down, Joshua gave the order, and they took down his body from the tree and threw it into a trench, and they set over him a heap of stones until this day.

Joshua: Chapters 8 Notes

1 Codex Vaticanus: Baethêl (ΒΑΙΘΗΛ)

• Aleppo Codex: byt âl (בית אל). Translation: house (or temple) of El (or god)

• Leningrad Codex: veit-el (בֵית־אֵל). Translation: house (or temple) of El (or god)

• Targum Jerusalem: beit el (בֵּית אֵל). Translation: house (or temple) of El (or god)

The term Bethel meant several things in ancient Canaan. The term translates as 'house of god,' which can be translated as either 'Temple of God (or El)' or 'sky/heaven.' Bethel was worshiped as a god by the ancient Canaanites, the brother of El and Dagon according to Sanchuniathon, who referred to him as Baitylos, which is the name used in this translation when the god is denoted. The term can also be translated as 'meteorite' as meteorites were believed to be parts of the god Baitylos that had fallen to the Earth, and shrines were built around them. A Temple of El was built in the region by Jacob in Genesis and appears to have been a major town by the time of Joshua.

Joshua: Chapter 9

When the kings of the Amorites on the other side of Jordan, who were in the mountain country, and in the plain, and in all the coast of the great sea, and those who were near Anti-Lebanon, and the Cypriots, Canaanites, Perizzite, Mitanni, Amorites, Girgashites, and Jebusites heard, they came in an alliance to make war against Joshua and Israel.

Then Joshua built an altar to Lord the god of Israel on Mount Ebal, as Moses the servant of the Lord commanded the Israelites, as it is written in the law of Moses, an altar of uncarved stones, against which iron had not been lifted. There he offered whole burnt offerings to the Lord and a peace offering. Joshua wrote on the stones a copy of the law of Moses, before the Israelites. All Israel, and their elders, and their judges, and their scribes passed on one side and on the other before the box. The priests and the Levites took up the box of the covenant of the Lord. The foreigners and the natives were there, who were half of them near Mount Gerizim and half near Mount Ebal, as Moses the servant of the Lord commanded at first, to bless the people.

Afterward, Joshua read accordingly all the words of this law, the blessings, and the curses, according to all things written in the law of Moses. There was not a word of all that Moses ordered Joshua, which Joshua read not in the ears of all the assembly of the Israelites, the men, and the women, and the children, and the strangers that joined themselves to Israel.

The inhabitants of Gibeon heard of all that the Lord did to Jericho and Gai. They worked cunningly, and they went and made provisions and prepared themselves, and having taken old sacks on their shoulders, and old and tore and patched bottles of wine, and the upper part of their shoes and their sandals old and clouted on their feet, and their old garments on them, and the bread in their provisions was dry, moldy, and partially eaten.

They came to Joshua at the camp of Israel at the circle, and said to Joshua and Israel, "We have come from a far off land, now then make a covenant with us."

The Israelites replied to the Hurrians,[1] "Suppose you live among us, how should I make a covenant with you?"

They replied to Joshua, "We are your servants."

Joshua asked them, "Where are you from, and where have you come from?"

They answered, "Your servants have come from a very far country in the name of Lord the god, for we have heard his name, and all that he did in Egypt, and all that he did to the kings of the Amorites, who were beyond Jordan, to Sihon king of the Amorites, and Og king of Bashan, who lived in Ashteroth and in Edrei. Our elders and all that inhabit our land when they heard said to us, 'Take with yourselves provision for the journey and go to meet them, and you will say to them, 'We are your servants, and now make a covenant with us.' These are the loaves we took hot for our journey on the day on which we came out to come to you, and now they are dried and have become moldy. These are the skins of wine which we filled when new, and they are torn, and our garments and our shoes are worn out because of the very long journey."

The chiefs took of their provision and asked no counsel of the Lord. Joshua made peace with them, and they made a covenant with them to protect them, and the princes of the congregation swore to them. Three days after they had made the covenant with them, they heard that they were near neighbors and that they lived among them. The Israelites departed and came to their cities, and their cities were Gibeon, and Kefireh,[2] and Beirut,[3] and the cities of Ye'arim,[4] and the Israelites did not fight with them, because all the princes swore to them by Lord the god of Israel, and all the congregation murmured at the princes.

The princes said to all the congregation "We have sworn to them by Lord the god of Israel, and now we will not be able to touch them. We will do this, we will capture them alive, and we will preserve them, so there will be no anger against us, because of the oath which we swore to them. They will live and will be lumberjacks and drawers of water for all the congregation," as the princes swore to them.

Joshua called them together and asked them, "Why have you deceived me, saying, 'We live very far from you, whereas you are fellow-countrymen of those who live among us? Now you are cursed. There will not be any of you that is not a slave, or a lumberjack, or a drawer of water for me and my god."

They answered Joshua, "It was reported to us that Lord the god ordered his servant, Moses, to give you this land, and to destroy us and all that lived on it before you. We were very afraid for our lives because of you, and therefore we did this thing. Now look, we are in your power. Do to us as it is pleasing to you, and as it seems good to you."

They did so to them, and Joshua rescued them on that day out of the hands of the Israelites, and they did not kill them. Joshua made them on that day lumber-jacks and drawers of water to the whole congregation, and for the altar of God. Therefore the inhabitants of Gibeon became lumberjacks and drawers of water for the altar of God until this day, even for the place which the Lord should choose. Then Joshua built an altar to Lord the god of Israel on Mount Ebal, as Moses the servant of the Lord commanded the Israelites, as it was written in the law of Moses, an altar of uncarved stones, on which iron had not been lifted, and he offered there whole burnt offerings to the Lord, and a piece offering. Joshua wrote on the stones a copy of the law of Moses, before the Israelites. All Israel, and their elders, and their judges, and their scribes passed on one side and on the other, before the box, and the priests, the Levites took up the box of the covenant of the Lord. The stranger and the native were there, who were half of those near Mount Ebal, as Moses the servant of the Lord commanded before, to bless the people.

Joshua: Chapter 9 Notes

1 Codex Vaticanus: Chorrhaeon (ΧΟΡΡΑΙΟΝ). This is a Greek transliteration of Chori (חֹרִי), the term generally believed to refer to the Hurrians.

- Aleppo Codex: Ḥůy (חוי)

- Leningrad Codex: Chivvi (חִוִּי)

- Targum Jerusalem: Chiva'ah (חִוָאָה)

There were two terms used in the Septuagint and Masoretic Text for the Hurrians: Chorrhaeon / Chori (Χορραῖον / חֹרִי) and Euaion / Chivvi (Εὐαῖον / חִוִּי), however, in this case, the names do not match between the Septuagint and Masoretic Text, indicating that there were two versions of Joshua in circulation. The terms are both believed to derive from the same culture, however, are not interchangeable.

The name Chorrhaeon / Chori, often transliterated as Horite, referred to the Hurrian people, while the term Euaion / Chivvi, referred to the Mitanni-Aryan nobility or Vedic priests. This difference between the Greek and Hebrew texts cannot be accounted for through a transliteration error, or the assumption that the Greeks decided to use the same term for both people, as Euaion (Εὐαῖον) was already used in the Book of Joshua. Hurrians are documented in southern Canaan at the time, as the Adbi-Heba, the chieftain of Jerusalem, had a Hurrian name in the Amarna Letters, circa 1335 BC.

2 Codex Vaticanus: Cephira (ΚΕΦΙΡΑ)

- Aleppo Codex: Kpyrh (כפירה)

- Leningrad Codex: Kefirah (כְּפִירָה)

- Targum Jerusalem: Chefirah (כְפִירָה)

This is believed to be Khirbet Kefireh in the West Bank of Palestinian Territories.

3 Codex Vaticanus: Bêrôth (ΒΗΡѠΘ)

- Aleppo Codex: Bårůt (בארות)

- Leningrad Codex: Ve'erot (בְאֵרוֹת)

- Targum Jerusalem: Ve'erot (בְאֵרוֹת)

The location of this town is disputed. Some sources claim it is Al-Bireh, while others claim it is Biddu, both in the West Bank of Palestinian Territories. The Hebrew name is identical to the Phoenician name of Beirut, Bårt (𐤕𐤓𐤀𐤁), however, the modern Hebrew spelling of Beirut is Byyrůt (ביירות), derived from the Arabic Bayrūt (بيروت).

The term used in the Septuagint is not the Greek name for Beirut, which is Bêrytos (Βηρυτός), however, all sources agree that the terms found in the Masoretic Text and Septuagint are variant spellings of Beirut, although the town in question is believed to have been in the West Bank, and not Lebanon.

4 Codex Vaticanus: Iarin (ΙΑΡΙΝ)

- Aleppo Codex: Qryt Yôrym (קרית יערים)

- Leningrad Codex: Qiryat Ye'arim (קִרְיַת יְעָרִים)

- Targum Jerusalem: Qiryat Ye'arim (קִרְיַת יְעָרִים)

The location of this town is generally assumed to be at the same location as the modern town of Kiryat Ye'arim in Israel.

Joshua: Chapter 10

When King Adonibezec[1] of Jerusalem heard that Joshua had taken Gai and had destroyed it. That as he'd done to Jericho and its king, he had also done to Gai and its king, and that the inhabitants of Gibeon had gone over to Joshua and Israel, then they were greatly terrified by them, for the king knew that Gibeon was a great city, one of the mother cities, and all its men were mighty. So King Adoni-bezek of Jerusalem sent messages to King Hoham of Hebron, and King Piram of Jarmuth, and King Japhia of Lachish, and King Debir of Adullam, saying, "Come up here to me, and help me, and let us take Gibeon, because the Gibeonites have gone over to Joshua and to the Israelites."

The five kings of the Jebusites went up, the king of Jerusalem, and the king of Hebron, and the king of Jarmuth, and the king of Lachish, and the king of Adullam, they and all their people, and camped around Gibeon, and besieged it. The inhabitants of Gibeon sent word to Joshua at the camp by the circle, saying, "Do not delay from your servants. Come up quickly to us, and help us and save us. All the kings of the Amorites who live in the hill country are gathered against us."

Joshua went up from the circle, he and all the warriors with him, everyone mighty in strength. The Lord said to Joshua, "Don't fear them, for I have delivered them into your hands. There will not be one of them left."

When Joshua came suddenly on them, he had advanced all night from the circle. The Lord struck them with terror before the Israelites, and the Lord destroyed them in a great slaughter at Gibeon, and they chased them by the road going up to the House of Horon,[2] and they slaughtered them to Azekah and to Makkedah. When they fled from the face of the Israelites at the descent of Temple of Horon, then the Lord threw hailstones on them from the sky to Azekah, and more died by the hailstones, than those who the Israelites killed with the sword in the battle.

Then Joshua spoke to the Lord, in the day in which the Lord delivered the Amorites into the power of Israel when he destroyed them in Gibeon, and they were destroyed from before the Israelites. Joshua said, "Let the sun stand over Gibeon and the moon over the valley of Ayalon."

The sun and the moon stood still until God executed vengeance on their enemies, and the sun stood still in the middle of the sky. It did not proceed to set until the end of one day. There was not a day like it either before or after, that god should listen to man because the Lord fought on the side of Israel. The five kings fled, and hid in a cave in Makkedah.

Joshua was told, "The five kings have been found hidden in the cave in Makkedah." Joshua said, "Roll stones to the mouth of the cave and set men to watch over them. Don't stand still, but chase after your enemies and seize of them, and do not allow them to enter into their cities, for Lord the god has delivered them into our hands."

When Joshua and all Israel stopped slaughtering them, they that escaped took refuge in the fortified cities. All the people returned healthy to Joshua at Makkedah, and none of the Israelites murmured with his tongue. Joshua said, "Open the cave, and bring out these five kings from the cave."

They brought the five kings out of the cave, the king of Jerusalem, and the king of Hebron, and the king of Jarmuth, and the king of Lachish, and the king of Adullamite. When they brought them out to Joshua, he called together all Israel, and the chiefs of the army that went with him, and said to them, "Come forward and set your feet on their necks," and they came and set their feet on their necks.

Joshua said to them, "Do not fear them or be cowardly. Be courageous and strong, as the Lord will do this to all your enemies against who you fight."

Joshua killed them and hanged them on five trees, and they hung on the trees until the evening. Towards the setting of the sun, Joshua commanded, and they took them down from the trees and threw them into the cave which they had fled for refuge, and they rolled stones into the cave, which remain until this day. They took Makkedah on that day and killed the inhabitants with the edge of the sword, and they completely destroyed every living thing that was in it, and there was none left in it that was preserved and had escaped. They did to the king of Makkedah, as they did to the king of Jericho. Joshua and all Israel with him departed out of Makkedah to Libnah and besieged Libnah. The Lord delivered it into the hands of Israel, and they took it and its king and killed the inhabitants with the edge of the sword, and everything breathing in it. Nothing was left in it that survived and escaped, and they did to its king as they did to the king of Jericho. Joshua and all Israel with him departed from Libnah to Lachish, and he camped around it and besieged it.

The Lord delivered Lachish into the hands of Israel, and they took it on the second day, and they put the inhabitants to death with the edge of the sword, and completely destroyed it, as they had done to Libnah. Then Horam the king of Gezer went up to help Lachish, and Joshua slaughtered him and his people with the edge of the sword until there was none left of him that was safe and escaped. Joshua and all Israel with him departed from Lachish to Adullam, and he besieged it and attacked it. The Lord delivered it into the hand of Israel, and he took it on that day, and killed the inhabitants with the edge of the sword, and killed everything breathing in it, as they did to Lachish.

Joshua and all Israel with him departed to Hebron and camped around it. He struck it with the edge of the sword, and all the living creatures that were in it. There was no one left alive. They destroyed it and all things in it, as they did to Adullam. Joshua and all Israel returned to Debir, and they camped around it, and they took it, and its king, and its villages. He struck it with the edge of the sword, and they destroyed it, and everything breathing in it. They did not leave in it anyone alive.

They did to Hebron and her king, as they did to Debir and her king. Joshua struck all the land of the hill country, and Negev and the plain country, and Azzah, and her kings, they did not leave of them one alive. They completely destroyed everything that had the breath of life, as Lord the god of Israel commanded, from Kadesh Barnea[3] to Gaza, all Goshen, as far as Gibeon. Joshua slaughtered, once for all, all their kings, and their land, because Lord the god of Israel fought on the side of Israel.

Joshua: Chapter 10 Notes

1 Codex Vaticanus: Adônibezec (ΑΔΩΝΙΒΕΖΕΚ)

- Aleppo Codex: ådny Ṣdq (אדני צדק). Translation: Lord Sydyk (or of Justice)

- Leningrad Codex: Adoni-Tzedek (אֲדֹנִי־צֶדֶק). Translation: Lord Sydyk (or of Justice)

- Targum Jerusalem: Adoni Tzedek (אֲדֹנִי צֶדֶק). Translation: Lord Sydyk (or of Justice)

The Greek translators treated the term as a name, Adônibezec, however, the Hebrew translation treats it as a title 'Lord of Justice.' The two translations also deviate on whether it was bezec (βεζεκ) or tzedek (צֶדֶק), which cannot simply be a transliteration error, as the Greeks knew of the Canaanite god Sydyk, and transliterated his name as Sydyc (Συδυκ). Adônibezec is a transliteration of a Semitic term, meaning essentially the

'My Lord in Strength' in Canaanite and Aramaic. During the Roman era, Sydyk was viewed as the Canaanite version of Jupiter, the supreme God of the Roman Empire. As the Septuagint does not agree with the Masoretic Text, the Greek name is used in this translation.

2 Codex Vaticanus: Ôrônin (ⲱⲣⲱⲛⲓⲛ)

- Aleppo Codex: byt Hŭrn (בית חורן). Translation: House (or Temple) of Horon

- Leningrad Codex: veit-Chovron (בֵּית־חֹורֹן). Translation: House (or Temple) of Horon

- Targum Jerusalem: veit Choron (בֵּית חֹורֹון). Translation: House (or Temple) of Horon

Horon was one of the Canaanite underworld gods. He was one of the sons of Mot (Death), who himself later became the Israelite messenger of death Mot, and early Christian angel of death Thanatos. Hŭårn (𓉔𓂋𓈖𓏤𓅱) was also a god of death in ancient Egypt, and the source of the Greek psychopomp Charon (Χάρων) according to Diodorus Siculus. The town around the Temple of Horon is also listed in the inscriptions at the Temple of Karnak, in Egypt, as 'Batae Houarn' in Egyptian hieroglyphs, one of the towns that Pharaoh Sheshonq I attacked, circa 925 BC, which was later recorded in the 3rd Kingdoms (Masoretic Kings). During the era of the two kingdoms, the twin towns of Upper and Lower Beth-Horon served as border towns. These towns have been identified as the Palestinian villages of Beit Ur al-Fauqa and Beit Ur al-Tahta, in the West Bank.

3 Codex Vaticanus: Cadês Barnê (ⲕⲁⲇⲏⲥⲃⲁⲣⲛⲏ)

- Aleppo Codex: qdš brnô (קדש ברנע). Translation: Sacred Barnea

- Leningrad Codex: Kadesh Barnea' (קָדֵשׁ בַּרְנֵעַ). Translation: Sacred Barnea

- Targum Jerusalem: Rekam gei'ah (רְקָם גֵּיאָה). Translation: Petra (or stony, rocky) hills

The location of Kadesh Barnea has been debated since the Second Temple Era. The Jewish general and historian Josephus reported that the sacred books salvaged from the Second Temple when it was destroyed by the Romans placed Kadesh Barnea at Petra, in modern Jordan. He also claimed that Mount Sinai was nearby, which is the source of the claim that Mountain of the Altar (Jebel al-Madhbah) was Mount Sinai. The name Kadesh Barnea is undoubtedly named after an ancient deity, as the first word, Kadesh (קָדֵשׁ), means holy or sacred. The name Barnea is presumably the name of the deity in question, and the general Hebrew pronunciation of the name as Varne'a is quite similar to the name Mitannian god Aruna, the equivalent of the Vedic god Varuna.

As Deuteronomy chapter 2 reports that Hurrians were living in Seir before the Edomites killed them and inhabited the region, this would support the name Aruna being the source of Barnea, as the Hurrians were the major population base of the Mitanni Empire. This connection between the Mitannian Indo-Aryan Varuna worshipers at Mount Seir would also explain how Mitra-Varuna (𒀀𒊑 𒇻𒈪) entered into Judaism, as his earliest recorded Hebrew name Mṭṭrûn (מטטרון) is essentially the same as the Mitannian god of covenants Miitra-Aruna, and played the same role in the Vedic Texts as Metatron did in Second Temple Era Judaism. Subsequent Hebrew pronunciations of the name from the Medieval Era, Mṭṭrûn (מטטרון), Metateron (מֶטְטְרֹון), Metatron (מְטַטְרֹון), Meitatron (מֵיטַטְרֹון), Mitatron (מִיטַטְרֹון), and Mattatron (מַטַּטְרֹון), as well as the Arabic Mītaṭrūn (ميططرون), are all influenced by the Greek pronunciation of the name Metà-thrónos (Μετὰ-θρόνος), which means 'next to the throne.'

Joshua: Chapter 11

When King Jabin of Hazor heard, he sent word to King Jobab of Madon, and to the king of Shimron, and the king of Achshaph, and the kings who were by the Sidon the Great,[1] to the hill country and to Arabah across Chinneroth, and to the plain, and to Phenaeddor, and to the Canaanites on the coast to the east, and to the Amorites on the coast, and the Cypriots, and the Perizzites, and the Jebusites in the mountain, and the Mitanni, and those living at the foot of Mount Hermon in the land of Mizpeh. They went out with their kings, like the sand of the sea in numbers, with horses, and a great many chariots. All the kings assembled in person, and came to the same place, and camped at the waters of Madon to make war with Israel.

The Lord said to Joshua, "Do not be afraid of them, for tomorrow at this time I will make them run from Israel. You will hamstring their horses, and burn their chariots with fire."

Joshua and all the warriors suddenly attacked them at the water of Madon and followed them into the hill country. The Lord delivered them into the power of Israel, and they struck them and chased them to Sidon the Great,[2] and to Maseron,[3] and to the plains of Mizpeh in the east. They destroyed them until there was not one of them left that survived. Joshua did to them, as the Lord commanded him, he mutilated their horses, and burnt their chariots with fire.

Joshua returned after that and took Hazor and her king. Previously Hazor was the chief of these kingdoms. They killed with the sword all that breathed in it and completely destroyed them all, and there was nothing living left in it. They burnt Hazor with fire. Joshua took all the cities of the kingdoms, and their kings, and killed them with the edge of the sword, and completely killed them, as Moses the servant of the Lord commanded.

But Israel did not burn all the walled cities, only Hazor was burnt. The Israelites took all its spoils for themselves, and they killed all the men with the edge of the sword, until they destroyed them, and they left none of them breathing. As the Lord commanded his servant Moses, Moses also commanded Joshua, and this Joshua did, he transgressed no law of all that Moses commanded him. Joshua took all the hill country, and all the land of Negev, and all the land of Goshen, and the plain country, and that towards the west, and the mountain of Israel and the low country by the mountain, from the mountain of Halak, and that which goes up to Seir, and as far as Ba'al Gad,[4] and the plains of Lebanon under Mount Hermon.

He took all their kings and destroyed and killed them. For many days, Joshua waged war with these kings. There was no city which Israel did not capture. They took it all in war. For the Lord had hardened their hearts to go out to war against Israel, so they might be completely destroyed, and mercy should not be granted to them, but that they should be completely destroyed, as the Lord told Moses.

Joshua came at that time, and completely destroyed the Anaks[5] out of the hill country, from Hebron and from Debir, and from Anab, and from all the race of Israel, and from all the mountain of Judah with their cities, and Joshua completely destroyed them. There was not anyone left of the Anaks near the Israelites, there were only some of them in Gaza, and in Gath, and in Ashdod. Joshua took all the land, as the Lord commanded Moses, and Joshua gave it for an inheritance to Israel by division according to their tribes, and the land war ended.

Joshua: Chapter 11 Notes

1 Codex Vaticanus: Sidôna tên megalên (ϹΙΔѠΝΑΤΗΝΜΕΓΑΛΗΝ). Translation: Sidon the great

• Aleppo Codex: Ṣpûn bhr (צפון בהר). Translation: Zephon (or north) on mountain

• Leningrad Codex: Tzefovn bahar (צְפוֹן בָּהָר). Translation: Zephon (or north) on mountain

• Targum Jerusalem: Tzepuna betura (צְפוּנָא בְּטוּרָא). Translation: Zephon at mountain

The Greek and Hebrew translations differ at this point. The reference to Sidon as the great city, found in the Greek at this point, and also the Hebrew and Aramaic Targums later in the chapter, would date the original text to earlier than circa 980 BC, when Sidon was the mother city of the Phoenicians. Between 980 and 947 BC, King Hiram of Tyre, led the Tyrians in challenging the dominance of Sidon. The Hebrew translation of Mount Zephon (צפון בהר) instead of Sidon is unlikely to have been a Hasmonean redaction, and is something that was likely retained in the Judahite (or Samaritan) texts that the Hebrew translators worked from. Mount Zephon was the holy mountain of northern Canaan, where the temple of the storm-god Ba'al Hadad was located.

2 Codex Vaticanus: Sidônos tês megalês (ϹΙΔѠΝΟϹΤΗϹΜΕΓΑΛΗϹ). Translation: Sidon the great

• Aleppo Codex: Ṣydûn rbh (צידון רבה). Translation: great Sidon

- Leningrad Codex: Tzidovn Rabbah (צִידְוֹן רַבָּה). Translation: great Sidon

- Targum Jerusalem: Tzidovn rabbeta (צִידוֹן רַבְּתָא). Translation: great Sidon

3 Codex Vaticanus: Maserôn (ΜΑϹΕΡѠΝ)

- Aleppo Codex: mšrpůt mym (משרפות מים). Translation: crematoria waters

- Leningrad Codex: misrefovt mayim (מִשְׂרְפוֹת מַיִם). Translation: crematoria waters

- Targum Jerusalem: chartzei yama (חַרְצֵי יַמָּא). Translation: sharps (or sharp things, cutting things, cuts) seas

This is considered an unknown location at the southern border of Sidonian control on the Mediterranean coast. It is most likely a reference to the glass production facilities of Sidon, which were the city's largest export during the Late-Bronze Age. As this trade disappeared in the early Iron Age, it would place the origin of the Book of Joshua before the Bronze Age Collapse.

4 Codex Vaticanus: Baalgad (ΒΑΑΛΓΑΔ)

- Aleppo Codex: Bôl Gd (בעל גד)

- Leningrad Codex: Ba'al Gad (בְּעַל גָּד)

- Targum Jerusalem: shar Gad (שַׂר גָד). Translation: prince (or commander) Gad

Ba'al Gad was an ancient Canaanite god, the god of luck, and the god that Jacob's son Gad was named after, and therefore the entire tribe of Gad.

5 Codex Vaticanus: Enacim (ΕΝΑΚΙΜ)

- Aleppo Codex: Ônqym (ענקים). Translation: giant, huge, large, big, neck, necklace, Anaks (an ancient tribe of Canaan)

- Leningrad Codex: Anakim (עֲנָקִים). Translation: giant, huge, large, big, neck, necklace, Anaks (an ancient tribe of Canaan)

- Targum Jerusalem: gibbaraya (גִבָּרַיָּא). Translation: strong men (or giants, heroes)

The Anaks were transliterated as Enach (Εναχ) in the Book of Numbers, but translated as Gigantes (Γιγάντων) in the Book of Deuteronomy, implying the Greeks considered the Anaks to be like the Gigantes of ancient Greece, who fought a war against the Olympian gods, and lost. The Anaks were a tribe of people also referred to in the book of Judges. According to the book of Judges, they apparently lived in Hebron. The Egyptian

Execration Texts from the Middle Kingdom record a group of Canaanites called the 'Anaq' who are generally considered to be the same people.

Joshua: Chapter 12

These are the kings of the land, whom the Israelites killed, and inherited their land beyond Jordan from the east, from the valley of Arnon to Mount Hermon, and all the land of Arabah on the east. Sihon king of the Amorites, who lived in Heshbon, ruling from Arnon, which is in the valley, on the slope of the valley, and half of Gilead as far as Jabbok, the borders of the Ammonites. Arabah as far as the sea of Galilee[1] to the east, and as far as the Dead Sea, the salt sea to the east by the way to Asimoth, from Teman under Azzah Phasga. King Og of Bashan, who lived in Ashteroth and in Edrei, was what remained of the Gigantes[2] ruling from Mount Hermon and from Salcah, and over all the land of Bashan to the borders of Gergesi, and Machi, and the half of Gilead of the borders of Sihon king of Heshbon. Moses the servant of the Lord and the Israelites struck them down, and Moses gave them by way of inheritance to Reuben, and Gad, and to the half-tribe of Manasseh.

These are the kings of the Amorites, who Joshua and the Israelites killed beyond Jordan by the sea of Ba'al Gad in the plain of Lebanon, and as far as the mountain of Halak, as men go up to Seir, and Joshua gave it to the tribes of Israel to inherit according to their portion, in the mountain, and in the plain, and in Arabah, and in Azzah, and in the wilderness, and the Negev, the Cypriots, Amorites, Canaanites, Perizzites, Mitanni, and Jebusites.

The king of Jericho, and the king of Gai, which is near the Temple of El, the king of Jerusalem, the king of Hebron, the king of Jarmuth, the king of Lachish, the king of Eglon, the king of Gezer, the king of Debir, the king of Geder, the king of Hormah, the king of Arad, the king of Libnah, the king of Adullam, the king of Elath, the king of Tappuah, the king of Hepher, the king of Aphek of Aroc, the king of Hushim, the king of Shimron, the king of Mambroth, the king of Achshaph, the king of Kadesh, the king of Zachac, the king of Maredoth, the king of Jecom of Carmel, the king of Adullam belonging to Phennealdor, the king of Gei of Galilee, and the king of Tirzah. All these were twenty-nine kings.

Joshua: Chapter 12 Notes

1 Codex Vaticanus: Chenereth (ⲭⲉⲛⲉⲣⲉⲑ)

• Aleppo Codex: Knrût (**כנרות**)

• Leningrad Codex: Kinarot (כִּנֲרוֹת)

- Targum Jerusalem: Ginosar (גִינוֹסַר)

These are all alternate names for the region around the Sea of Galilee.

2 Codex Vaticanus: gigantôn (ΓΙΓΑΝΤШΝ). Translation: Gigantes

- Aleppo Codex: Rpåym (רפאים). Translation: long-dead (in Canaanite), giants (modern Hebrew), Rephaites (theoretical ancient tribe)

- Leningrad Codex: Refa'im (רְפָאִים). Translation: long-dead (in Canaanite), giants (modern Hebrew), Rephaites (theoretical ancient tribe)

- Targum Jerusalem: gibbaraya (גִבָּרַיָא). Translation: strong men (or giants, heroes)

The Rpåm (𐤓𐤐𐤀𐤌) were a semi-deified long-dead people by the 1200s BC, as the Ugaritic Texts include the so-called Rephaim Text. They appear to be an ancient people that had been deified and were believed to live in the underworld. The word's etymology implies they were healers. The fact that they were described as 'ruling from Mount Hermon' implies they were the 'watchers' from the Enochian tradition.

The similarities between the name Enach / Ônq (Εναχ / עָנָק) and Enôch / Hnûk (Ενωχ / חֲנוֹך) may have led to the confusion in the translation, resulting in both Ônqym (עֲנָקִים) and Rpåym (רפאים) as Gigantes in different places in the books of Numbers, Deuteronomy, and Joshua. As the Books of Enoch had to have been translated also before the Beta Israel community left Egypt during the rebellion of 200 BC, the Books of Enoch must have been translated at the same time, and likely by the same translators.

Joshua: Chapter 13

When Joshua was old and advanced in years, the Lord said to Joshua, "You are advanced in days, and there is much land left to inherit. This is the land that remains: the borders of the Pelesets,[1] the Geshurites, and the Canaanite, from the wilderness near Egypt, as far as the borders of Ekron on the left of the Canaanites the land is reckoned to the five principalities of the Pelesets, to the inhabitants of Gaza, Ashdod, Ashkelon, Gath, and Ekron, and to the Mitanni from Teman, to all the land of Canaan before Gaza, and the Sidonians as far as Aphek, as far as the borders of the Amorites."

"All the land of Giblites of the Pelesets, and all Lebanon east of the circle, under Mount Hermon as far as the entering in of Hamath, everyone that inhabits the hill country from Lebanon as far as Masereth Memphomaim. All the Sidonians, I will destroy them from before Israel, but you give them by inheritance to Israel, as I ordered you. Now divide this land by lot to the nine tribes, and to the half-tribe of Manasseh. From Jordan to the Mediterranean Sea in the west, you will give it to them. The Mediterranean Sea will be the boundary."

"But to the two tribes and to the half-tribe of Manasseh, to Reuben and to Gad Moses gave an inheritance beyond Jordan, Moses the servant of the Lord gave it to them eastward, from Aroer, which is on the bank of the brook of Arnon, and the city in the middle of the valley, and all Misor from Medeba. All the cities of Sihon king of the Amorites, who reigned from Heshbon to the borders of the Ammonites, and the region of Gilead, and the borders of the Geshurites and the Maachathites, the whole of Mount Hermon, and all the land of Bashan to Acha. All the kingdom of Og in the region of Bashan, who reigned in Ashteroth and in Edrei, he was left of the Raphites, and Moses killed him and destroyed him."

But the Israelites did not destroy the Geshurites and the Maachathites and the Canaanites, and the king of the Geshurites and the Maachathites lived among the Israelites until this day. Only no inheritance was given to the tribe of Levi, Lord the god of Israel is their inheritance, as the Lord told them. This is the division that Moses made to the Israelites in Araboth Moab, on the other side of Jordan, by Jericho. Moses gave the land to the tribe of Reuben according to their families. Their borders were from Aroer, which is opposite the brook of Arnon, and theirs is the city that is in the valley of Arnon; and all Misor, to Heshbon, and all the cities in Misor, and Debir, and Bamoth-Ba'al, and the house of Baal-Meon, and Bashan, and Bakedmoth, and Maephaad, and Kariathaim, and Shibmah, and

931

Serada, and Sior on Mount Emak,[2] and the House of Peor,[3] and Azzah Phasga, and the House of Jeshimoth, and all the cities of Misor, and all the kingdom of Sihon king of the Amorites, who Moses killed, both he and the princes of Midian,[4] Evi,[5] Petra,[6] Zur,[7] and Hur,[8] and Prince Reba of the remnants of Sihon, and the inhabitants of the land.

Balaam the son of Beor the prophet they killed in the battle. The borders of Reuben were at the Jordan, which was the boundary. This is the inheritance of the children of Reuben according to their families, these were their cities and their villages. Moses gave an inheritance to the sons of Gad according to their families. Their borders were Jazer, all the cities of Gilead, and half the land of the Ammonites to Arabah, which is before Arad. From Heshbon to Araboth by Massepha, and Betonim, and Mahanaim to the borders of Debir, and Enadom, and Othargai, and the House of Nimrah, and Succoth, and Zaphon, and the rest of the kingdom of Sihon king of Heshbon, and Jordan will be the boundary as far as part of the Sea of Galilee,[9] beyond Jordan to the east. This is the inheritance of the children of Gad according to their families and according to their cities. According to their families, they will turn their backs before their enemies, because their cities and their villages were according to their families.

Moses gave to half the tribe of Manasseh according to their families. Their borders were from Mahanaim, and all the kingdom of Bashan, and all the kingdom of Og king of Bashan, and all the villages of Jair, which are in the region of Bashan, sixty cities, and the half of Gilead, and in Ashteroth, and in Edrei, royal cities of Og in the land of Bashan, Moses gave to the sons of Machir the sons of Manasseh, including to the half-tribe sons of Machir the sons of Manasseh, according to their families. These are those who Moses allowed to inherit beyond the Jordan, in Araboth Moab, and beyond Jordan east of Jericho.

Joshua: Chapter 13 Notes

1 Codex Vaticanus: Phylistiim (ⲫⲨⲗⲓⲥⲧⲓⲓⲙ). Translation: Philistines (or Pelesets, Pelesets)

- Aleppo Codex: Plštym (פלשתים). Translation: Philistines (or Palestinians, Pelesets)

- Leningrad Codex: Pelishtim (פְּלִשְׁתִּים). Translation: Philistines (or Palestinians, Pelesets)

- Targum Jerusalem: Pelishta'ei (פְּלִשְׁתָּאֵי). Translation: Philistines (or Palestinians,

Pelesets)

The Pelesets were an ancient people based in the region of the modern Gaza Strip of the Palestinian Territories. The earliest surviving mention of them is from the reliefs of the Temple of Ramses III at Medinet Habu in Egypt that dates back to some time between 1186 and 1155 BC, in which they were called Půlåsåtî (𓊪𓏳𓃭𓇋𓋴𓍿𓏭), commonly anglicized as Pelesets. They were also known in Middle Babylonian as the ᵏᵘʳPalastu (𒆳𒉺𒆷𒅖𒌅).

It is unclear where they came from, however, one theory is that they were the Pala, a Luwian people from the Black Sea coast of Anatolia. The region was an independent country called Palaa (𒆳𒉺𒆷𒀀) in the Neshite (Hittite) records from the 1600s BC, however, have become part of the Nesite Empire by the 1500s BC. Around the time the Pelesets invaded Canaan, the Pala were driven from their homeland by the neighboring Kaskians from northeast Anatolia, which supports the connection between the groups, however, it has yet to be proven conclusively.

The presence of the Pelesets in Southern Canaan during the time of Joshua is anachronistic, as the Egyptians recorded the Pelesets arriving in the 1200s BC. At the time, the Egyptians recorded that the Hanubu were the dominant population in Sinai, which is believed to have been a reference to the Minoans, however, they disappeared from the region shortly after the Minoan erruption. Therefore this section of text, describing the origin of the Semitic tribes, found in both the Septuagint and the Masoretic text, likely dates to the original Phoenician translation in the early Iron Age, by which time the name Hanubu was no longer recognized.

2 Codex Vaticanus: Emac (ЄΜΑΚ)

- Aleppo Codex: ômq (עמק). Translation: valley (or vale, lowland, open country)

- Leningrad Codex: emek (עֵמֶק). Translation: valley (or vale, lowland, open country)

- Targum Jerusalem: meishra (מֵישְׁרָא). Translation: plain (or valley)

3 Codex Vaticanus: Baethphogôr (ΒΑΙΘΦΟΓΩΡ)

- Aleppo Codex: Byt Pôůr (בית פעור). Translation: House (or Temple) of Pwr

- Leningrad Codex: Veit Pe'ovr (בֵית פָּעוֹר). Translation: House (or Temple) of Peor

- Targum Jerusalem: Veit Pe'or (בֵית פְּעוֹר). Translation: House (or Temple) of Peor

This verse has not survived among the Dead Sea Scrolls. There are no known locations associated with the name Peor, which implies the location was abandoned after the events of Joshua. Other Israelite texts, such as Micah refer to the Lord of Peor in association with the Shittim Valley, however, this name appears to have been an insult directed towards Lord Hammon who was worshiped at Tell el-Hammam in the 800s BC.

There is no clear link between Hammon and Peor, implying the worshipers of Peor disappeared around the time the Israelites passed through the Shittim Valley. The major ruins in the Shittim Valley, are found at Tell el-Hammam, which was occupied from at least 3600 BC until the beginning of the Late Bronze Age (1550 to 1200) when the site was abandoned for unknown reasons. It was rebuilt in the 900s BC as a Samaritan city. As Tell el-Hammam is in the Shittim Valley and was destroyed or abandoned when the Israelites moved through the region, using either the traditional Christian dating or the Minoan Eruption and collapse of the Hyksos Dynasty from the Book of Exodus, it is likely that the Bronze-Age city was Peor (Φαγωρ). The exact dating of the abandonment of the bronze-age city is unclear, and there is some evidence of occupation for a few decades after 1550 BC, but the site does appear to have been abandoned around 1500 BC, meaning Joshua would have had to have destroyed it around them.

4 Codex Vaticanus: Madiam (ΜΑΔΙΑΜ). Translation: Midian

- Aleppo Codex: Mdyn (מדין). Translation: Midian

- Leningrad Codex: Midyan (מִדְיָן). Translation: Midian

- Targum Jerusalem: Midyan (מִדְיָן). Translation: plain (or valley)

5 Codex Vaticanus: Eui (ϵΥι)

- Aleppo Codex: Åůy (אוי)

- Leningrad Codex: Evi (אֱוִי)

- Targum Jerusalem: Evi (אֱוִי)

6 Codex Vaticanus: Rocom (ΡΟΚΟΜ)

- Aleppo Codex: rqm (רקם). Translation: Petra

- Leningrad Codex: reqem (רֶקֶם). Translation: Petra

- Targum Jerusalem: reqem (רֶקֶם). Translation: Petra

Raqmu was the ancient name of Petra, in modern southwest Jordan. By the era of the kingdoms of Judah and Samaria, the region was known as Sela (סֶלַע), suggesting this section of text is older.

7 Codex Vaticanus: Sour (ⲤⲞⲨⲢ)

- Aleppo Codex: Ṣûr (צור). Translation: Zur (or rock)

- Leningrad Codex: Tzur (צֻור). Translation: Zur (or rock)

- Targum Jerusalem: Tzur (צור). Translation: Zur (or rock)

Based on the other locations in southern Canaan, this is probably a reference to Beth-Zur, in the West Bank, south of Jerusalem.

8 Codex Vaticanus: Oyr (ⲞⲨⲢ)

- Aleppo Codex: ḥûr (חור). Translation: white

- Leningrad Codex: chur (חור). Translation: white

- Targum Jerusalem: chur (חור). Translation: watch (or look)

This appears to be a reference to Tell es-Safi near Hebron, an ancient fortress from the Bronze Age, built on a hill composed of white cliffs. The site has been occupied continuously since the 5th millenium BC.

9 Codex Vaticanus: thalassês Chenereth (ⲐⲀⲖⲀⲤⲤⲎⲤ ⲬⲈⲚⲈⲢⲉⲐ). Translation: Sea of Chinnereth

- Aleppo Codex: ym Knrt (ים כנרת). Translation: Sea of Chinnereth

- Leningrad Codex: yam-Kinneret (יָם־כִּנֶרֶת). Translation: Sea of Chinnereth

- Targum Jerusalem: yam Ginosar (יַם גִּינוֹסָר). Translation: sea of Ginosar

These are all alternate names for the Sea of Galilee, also known as Lake Tiberius.

Joshua: Chapter 14

These are those of the Israelites that received their inheritance in the land of Canaan, to who Eleazar the priest, and Joshua the son of Nun, and the heads of the families of the tribes of the Israelites, gave inheritance. They inherited according to their lots, as the Lord commanded by the hand of Joshua to the nine tribes and the half-tribe, on the other side of Jordan. But to the Levites, he gave no inheritance among them. For the sons of Joseph were two tribes, Manasseh and Ephraim, and there was no inheritance in the land given to the Levites, only cities to live in, and their suburbs separated for the livestock, and their livestock. As the Lord commanded Moses, so the Israelites did when they divided the land.

The children of Judah came to Joshua at the circle, and Caleb the son of Jephunneh the Kenezite said to him, "You know the word that the Lord spoke to Moses the man of God concerning me and you in Kadesh Barnea. For I was forty years old when Moses the servant of God sent me out of Kadesh Barnea to spy out the land, and I returned him an answer according to his mind."

"My brothers that went up with me turned away the heart of the people, but I chose to follow the Lord, my God. Moses swore on that day, 'The land on which you have gone up, it will be your inheritance and your children's forever, because you have chosen to follow Lord the god.' Now the Lord has kept me alive as he said."

"This is the forty-fifth year since the Lord spoke that word to Moses, and Israel journeyed in the wilderness, and now look, I am on this day eighty-five years old. I am still strong this day, like when the Lord sent me. Just as strong am I now to go out and to come in for war. Now I ask of you this mountain, as the Lord said on that day, for you heard this word on that day, and now the Anaks are there, cities great and strong. If then the Lord should be with me, I will completely destroy them, as the Lord told me."

Joshua blessed him and gave Hebron to Caleb the son of Jephunneh the son of Kenez for an inheritance. Therefore Hebron became the inheritance of Caleb the son of Jephunneh the Kenezite until this day because he followed the command-ment of Lord the god of Israel. The name of Hebron was previously the city Argob, it was the mother city of the Anaks, and the land rested from war.

Joshua: Chapter 15

The borders of the tribe of Judah according to their families were from the borders of Edom from the Wilderness of Zin, as far as Kadesh to the south. Their borders were from the south as far as a part of the salt sea from the high country that extends to the south. They follow from the ascent of Akrabbim, and go out around Zenan, and go up from the south to Kadesh Barnea, and go out to Hezron, and proceed up to Adar, and go out by the way that is west of Karkaa. They go out to Zalmonah and start at the valley of Egypt, and the end of its boundaries will be at the sea. These are their boundaries to the south.

Their boundaries to the east are along the salt sea and the Jordan. The borders in the north are from the seacoast, and part of the Jordan, the borders go up to the House of Hoglah, and continue along the north to the House of Arabah, and up to the stone of Bohan the son of Reuben. The borders continue on to the quarter of the valley of Achor, and go down to the circle which is at the approach to Adummim, which is to the south in the valley, and terminate at the water of the Fountain of Shemesh,[1] and from there go to the Fountain of Rogel. The borders go up to the valley of Hinns,[2] behind Jebus to the south (this is Jerusalem). The borders terminate at the top of the mountain, which is before the valley of Hinns towards the west, (which is next to the land of the Raphites of the north). The border going out from the top of the mountain terminates at the fountain of the water of Nephtoah and terminates at Mount Ephron, and the border will lead to Baalah (this is the city of Jarim).

The border will go around Baalah to the sea and will go on to Mount Seir behind the city of Jearim to the north (this is Chesalon). It will come down to the Temple of Shemesh and will go on to the south. The border terminates behind Ekron to the north, and the borders will terminate at Booths, and the borders will go on to the south and will terminate at Libnah, and the start of the borders will be at the sea. Their borders will be at the sea, the great sea will be the boundary. These are the borders of the children of Judah according to their families.

To Caleb the son of Jephunneh, he gave a portion in the middle of the children of Judah by the command of God. Joshua gave him the city of Arboc the mother-city of Anaks (this is Hebron). Caleb the son of Jephunneh destroyed the three sons of the Anaks there: Susi, and Tholami, and Achima.

Caleb went up there to the inhabitants of Debir. (The name of Debir was previously the City of Letters before.)[3]

Caleb offered, "Whoever will take and destroy the City of Letters, and conquer it, to him will I give my daughter Acsah as a wife."

Othniel the son of Kenaz the brother of Caleb took it, and he gave Acsah his daughter to him as a wife. As she left she counseled him, "I will ask of my father a field, and she called from her donkey."

Caleb asked her, "What do you have to say?"

She answered him, "Give me a blessing, as you have set me to the land of Negev. Give me Botthanis."

He gave her Upper Gonaethla, and Lower Gonaethla. This is the inheritance of the tribe of the children of Judah.

The cities belonging to the tribe of the children of Judah on the borders of Edom by the wilderness where: Kabzeel, Ara, Hazor, Icam, Regma, Aruel, Kadesh, Asorionain, Maenam, Balmaenan, and their villages, and the cities of Hezron: Hazor, Sen, Salmaa, Molada, Seri, Bethpalet, Hazarshual, and Beersheba, and their villages, and their hamlets: Baalah, Bacoc, Hushim, Eltolad, the Temple of El, Hormah, Ziklag, Macharim, Sethennac, Lebaoth, Sale, and Eromoth. Twenty-nine cities, and their villages.

In the plain country: Eshtaol, Raa, Assa, Ramen, Tano, Iluthoth, Maeani, Jermuth, Adullam, Membra, Socoh, Jazeca, Sharaim, and Gederah and its villages; fourteen cities and their villages.

Zenan, Hadashah, Migdalgad, Dilean, Mizpeh, Joktheel, Bozkath, Ideadalea, Chabra, Maches, Maachos, Gederoth, Temple of Dagon, Naamah, Makkedah; sixteen cities, and their villages.

Libnah, Ether, Anoch, Jana, Nezib, Keilah, Achzib, Kezib, Bathesar, and Elon; ten cities and their villages.

Ekron and her villages, and their hamlets. From Ekron: Gemna and all the cities that are near Azzah, and their villages.

Asiedoth, and her villages and hamlets.

Gaza, and its villages and hamlets as far as the river of Egypt, and the Mediterranean Sea[4] is the boundary.

In the hill country: Shamir, Jetheth, Socha, Renna, and the City of Letters (this is Debir),[5] and Anon, Es, Anim, Aesam, Goshen, Chalu, Channa, Giloh; eleven cities, and their villages.

Aerem, Remna, Soma, Janum, Bethtappuah, Aphekah, Humtah, and the city Arboc, (this is Hebron) and Zior; Nine cities and their villages.

Maon, Carmel, Ozib, Itan, Jezreel, Aricam, Zacanaim, Gibeah, and Thimnathah; nine cities, and their villages.

Halhul, House of Zur, Gedor, Maarath, the Temple of Anat, Eltekon; six cities, and their villages.

Theco, Ephrath, this is House of Lehem, Phagor, Aetan, Culon, Tatam, Thobes, Carem, Galem, Thether, and Manocho; eleven cities, and their villages.

The Town of Baal (this is the city of Jarim), and Sotheba; two cities and their villages.

Baddargeis, Tharabaam, Aenon, Aeochioza, Naphlazon, and the cities of Sadon, and Ancades, seven cities, and their villages.

The Jebusite lived in Jerusalem, and the children of Judah could not destroy them. (The Jebusites live in Jerusalem to this day.)

Joshua: Chapter 15 Notes

1 Codex Vaticanus: Êliou (ΗΛΙΟΥ). Translation: Helios (or sun)

- Aleppo Codex: šmš (שמש). Translation: Shemesh (or sun)

- Leningrad Codex: shemesh (שֶׁמֶשׁ). Translation: Shemesh (or sun)

- Targum Jerusalem: shemesh (שְׁמֶשׁ). Translation: Shemesh (or sun)

Shemesh was the Canaanite sun god, whose worship was later banned by King Josiah.

2 Codex Vaticanus: pharanga Onom (ΦΑΡΑΓΓΑΟΝΟΜ). Translation: abyss (or ravine) of Onom

- Aleppo Codex: gy vn hnm (גי בן הנם). Translation: Valley of the sons of Hnm

- Leningrad Codex: gei ven-Hinnom (גֵּי בֶן־הִנֹּם). Translation: Valley of the sons of Hinnom

- Targum Jerusalem: lecheilat bar Hinom (לְחֵילַת בַּר הִנֹם). Translation: the stength of the sons of Hinom

The Septuagint includes a different name in chapter 18, reading 'Forest of Sonnam' (ναπης Σονναμ) where the Masoretic text reads Valley of the Sons of Hinnom (גֵּי בֶן־הִנֹּם). The misreading of an H (𐤄) for a S (𐤑) indicates a transcription error when a Samaritan or Judahite version of the book was translated into Aramaic, however, the substitution of 'forest' for 'valley of the sons...' is clearly not a translation error. The combination of 'valley/abyss' and 'forest' suggests it is a reference to a gravesite, and not a physical valley. At the time, Canaanites marked gravesites by planting trees, usually oak, which was known as the 'Asherah' tree, because it could self-pollinate, and was therefore seen as a 'virgin' tree.

The origin of the word is likely a plural of hinn (حِنّ), a reference to an ancient extinct type of being that once lived on the Earth in Semitic folklore. The hinns continue to be part of the Islamic and Druze religions, although their roles in the religions vary. It is agreed that they are extinct, however, it isn't clear what they were. Many sources describe the hinn and binn as powerful, gigantic primordial creatures, suggesting they were influenced by finding the bones of extinct animals. Conversely, the Revelations of 'Abdullah Al-Sayid Muhammad Habib claims the hinns were air creatures, and their enemies the binns were water creatures, while the medieval Islamic historian al-Tabari claimed they were created from poisonous fire (سموم). In most versions of the stories, they fought in part of a series of wars for control of the earth before the creation of humanity, and most of the ancient species became extinct, including the hinns.

In the context of a gravesite, it is likely that the term 'sons of hinns' did not refer to some known people, but an ancient gravesite of a by then unknown people. Oak trees are known to live over 1000 years, and reproduce, so the gravesite in question could have already been thousands of years old. Later during the reforms of King Josiah, ancient graves and Asherah groves near Jerusalem were destroyed, and he was specifically recorded as destroying a statue in the valley of the sons of Hinns, implying that this was the gravesite he destroyed.

3 Codex Vaticanus: Dabir an to proteron Polis grammatôn (ΔΑΒΙΡΗΝΤΟΠΡΟΤΕΡΟΝ ΠΟΛΙϹΓΡΑΜΜΑΤѠΝ). Translation: Dabir it was previously City of Letters (or writing)

- Aleppo Codex: dbr lpnym qryt spr (דבר לפנים קרית ספר). Translation: Dbr was formerly Village Book (or scroll)

- Leningrad Codex: debir lefanim kiryat-sefer (דְּבִר לְפָנִים קִרְיַת־סֵפֶר). Translation: Debir was formerly Village of Book (or scroll)

- Targum Jerusalem: debar milkadmin kiryat archei (דְּבַר מִלְקַדְמִין קִרְיַת אַרְכֵּי).
Translation: Debar was in old days village of chief

The location of this city is unclear, however, it is often identified with Khirbet Rabud in the West Bank of Palestinian Territories.

4 Codex Vaticanus: thalassa ê megalê (ΘΛΛΛϹϹΛΗΜΕΓΛΛΗ). Translation: sea the great

- Aleppo Codex: hym hgbŭl [hgdŭl] (חיס הגבול [הגדול]). Translation: sea the edge [the great]

- Leningrad Codex: hayyam haggavovl K [haggadovl Q] (הַיָּם הַגְּבוֹל כ [הַגָּדוֹל ק]). Translation: sea the edge (K) [the great (Q)]

- Targum Jerusalem: yama Rabbah (יַמָּא רַבָּה). Translation: sea great

The Great Sea was a name for the Mediterranean.

5 Codex Vaticanus: polis grammatôn autê estin Dabir (ΠΟΛΙϹΓΡΑΜΜΑΤΩΝΑΥΤΗ ΕϹΤΙΝΔΛΒΙΡ). Translation: city of letters this is Dabir

- Codex Alexandrinus: Polis grammatôn hautê Dabir (ΠΟΛΙϹΓΡΑΜΜΑΤΩΝΑΥΤΗ ΔΛΒΙΡ). Translation: city of letters it's Dabir

- Aleppo Codex: qryt snh hyå dbr (קרית סנה היא דבר). Translation: village of bush (or bramble) it is Debir

- Leningrad Codex: kiryat-sannah hi devir (קִרְיַת־סַנָּה הִיא דְּבִר). Translation: village of bush (or bramble) it is Debir

- Targum Jerusalem: kiryat sanah hi devir (קִרְיַת סַנָה הִיא דְּבִיר). Translation: village of bush (or bramble) it's Debir

Joshua: Chapter 16

The borders of the children of Joseph were from the Jordan by Jericho to the east, and they went up from Jericho to the hill country, to the wilderness, to the Temple of El in Luza,[1] and they will go out to the Temple of El and continue to the borders of the Archites. They go across to the sea to the borders of Japhletites, as far as the borders of Lower House of Horon, and from there the border will be the sea. The sons of Joseph, Ephraim, and Manasseh took their inheritance.

The borders of the children of Ephraim were according to their families, and the borders of their inheritance were to the east of Ataroth, and Eroc as far as Upper House of Horon, and Gazara. The borders continue to the sea to Icasmon north of Therma, and they go east to Taanath and Sellesa and pass on eastward to Janohah, and to Macho, and Ataroth, these are their villages, and they will come to Jericho and will start at Jordan. The borders will proceed from Tappuah to the sea by Kanah, and the end will be at the sea. This is the inheritance of the tribe of Ephraim according to their families.

The cities separated to the Ephramites were among the inheritance of the sons of Manasseh, all the cities and their villages. Ephraim did not destroy the Canaanites who lived in Gezer, and the Canaanites lived in Ephraim until Pharaoh the king of Egypt went up and took it, and burnt it with fire. The Canaanites and Perizzite, and the residents in Gaza were destroyed, and Pharaoh gave them as a dowry to his daughter.

Joshua: Chapter 16 Notes

1 Codex Vaticanus: Baethêl Louza (ΒΑΙΘΗΛΛΟΥΖΑ)

• Aleppo Codex: Byt Ål lûzh (בית אל לוזה). Translation: House (or Temple) of El (or God) in Luza

• Leningrad Codex: Veit-Ēl lûzâ (בֵּית־אֵל לוּזָה). Translation: House (or Temple) of El (or God) in Luza

• Targum Jerusalem: Veit Ēl (בֵית אֵל). Translation: House (or Temple) of El

Joshua: Chapter 17

The borders of the tribe of the children of Manasseh, (as he was the firstborn of Joseph,) assigned to Machir the firstborn of Manasseh the father of Gilead, as he was a warrior, were the lands of Gilead and of Bashan. There was land assigned to the other sons of Manasseh according to their families. To the sons of Jezi and to the sons of Kelez, and to the sons of Asriel, and to the sons of Shechem, and to the sons of Symarim, and to the sons of Hepher, these are the males according to their families.

Zelophehad the sons of Hepher had no sons but daughters, and these are the names of the daughters of Zelophehad: Maala, Noah, Hoglah, Milcah, and Tirzah. They stood before Eleazar the priest, and before Joshua, and before the rulers, and said, "God gave an order by the hand of Moses, to give us an inheritance among our brothers," so there was given to them by the command of the Lord an inheritance among the brothers of their father. Their lot fell to them from Manasseh, and to the plain of Labec of the land of Gilead, which is beyond Jordan. For the daughters of the sons of Manasseh inherited a portion among their brothers, and the land of Gilead was assigned to the remainder of the sons of Manasseh.

The borders of the sons of Manasseh were Delanath, which was before the sons of Anath, and it proceeded to the borders even to Jamin and Jassib to the Fountain of Tappuah. It belonged to Manasseh, and Tappuah on the borders of Manasseh belonged to the Ephramites. The borders went down to the valley of Kanah southward by the valley of Jezreel (there is a turpentine tree belonging to Ephraim between that and the city of Manasseh), and the borders of Manasseh are north to the brook, and the sea will be its end. To the south, the land belonged to Ephraim, and north to Manasseh and the sea was their border. To the north, they bordered Asher, and to the east Issachar.

Manasseh had in the portion of Issachar: Asher, the House of Shean and their villages, and the inhabitants of Dor, and its villages, and the inhabitants of Megiddo, and its villages, and the third part of Mapheta, and its villages. The sons of Manasseh were not able to destroy these cities, and the Canaanites began to live in that land. It happened that when the Israelites were strong, they made the Canaanites subject, but they did not completely destroy them. The sons of Joseph asked Joshua, "Why have you caused us to inherit one inheritance and one line? We are a great people, and God has blessed us."

Joshua replied to them, "If you are a great people, go up to the forest, and clear the land for yourself, if Mount Ephraim is too little for you."

They answered, "Mount Ephraim does not please us, and the Canaanites living in it in the House of Shean, and in its villages, and in the valley of Jezrael, have the best cavalry and iron."

Joshua said to the sons of Joseph, "If you are a great people, and have great strength, you will not have only one inheritance. For you have the wood, for there is a forest and you will clear it, and the land will be yours. Then you will completely destroy the Canaanites, for they have the best cavalry, yet you are stronger."

Joshua: Chapter 18

All the congregation of the Israelites was assembled at Shiloh, and there they pitched the tabernacle of witness, and the land was subdued by them. The sons of Israel remained, all those who had not received their inheritance, seven tribes.

Joshua said to the sons of Israel, "How long will you wait to inherit the land that Lord the god has given you? Appoint for yourselves three men from each tribe, and let them rise up and go through the land, and let them describe it to me, as it would be best to divide it. They came to him and he divided to them seven portions, saying, "Judah will be for them a southern border, and the sons of Joseph will be for them a northern border. Divide the land into seven parts, and bring the description here to me, and I will bring your lot before Lord the god. The Levites have no part among you, for the priesthood of the Lord is his portion. Gad, Reuben, and the half-tribe of Manasseh have received their inheritance beyond the Jordan to the east, which Moses the servant of the Lord gave to them.

The men rose and went out, and Joshua ordered the men who went to walk through the land, saying, "Go and explore the land and come to me, and I will bring your lot here before the Lord in Shiloh."

They went and explored the land, and they viewed it, and described it according to the cities, seven parts in a book, and brought the book to Joshua. Joshua cast the lot for them in Shiloh before the Lord. The lot of the tribe of Benjamin came out first according to their families, and the borders of their lot came out between the children of Judah and the children of Joseph. Their borders were to the north from the Jordan near Jericho to the mountain in the west, and the start of it will be the Temple of An[1] of the desert-dwellers.[2]

The borders will go out there to Luz, to the south of Luz, (this is the Temple of El). The borders will go down to Ataroth Addar, to the hill country, which is southward of Lower House of Horon. The borders will pass through and proceed to the part that looks towards the sea, on the south, from the mountain in front of House of Horon southward, and its termination will be at the town of Ba'al, this is the town of Jearim, a city of the children of Judah towards the west.

The south side on the part of the town of Ba'al and the borders will go across to Gasin, to the fountain of the water of Nephtoah. The borders will extend down on one side, this is in front of the Forest of Hinns[3] (which is the Valley of

Raphites of the north),[4] and go down the Valley of Hinns[5] south of the Jebusites. It will come down to the Fountain of Rogel. The borders will go across to the Fountain of the Temple of Shemesh, and will proceed to Geliloth, which is on the way to Adummim, and they will come down to the stone of Bohan of the sons of Reuben, and will pass to the north of the House of Arabah, and will go down to the borders to the north of the sea. The termination of the borders will be at the creek of the salt sea northward to the south side of the Jordan. These are their southern borders. The Jordan will be their boundary on the east. This is the inheritance of the children of Benjamin, these are their borders according to their families.

The cities of the children of Benjamin according to their families were Jericho, the House of Hoglah, the Valley of Keziz, the House of Arabah, Sarai, Besana, Avim, Phara, Ophrah, Carapha, Cephira, Moni, Geba; twelve cities and their villages.

Gibeon, Ramah, Beeroth, Mizpah, Miron, Amoke, Phira, Caphan, Nacan, Selecan, Taralah, Jebus (this is Jerusalem), Gibeah; thirteen cities, and their villages.

This is the inheritance of the sons of Benjamin according to their families.

Joshua: Chapter 18 Notes

1 Codex Vaticanus: Baethôn (ⲃⲁⲓⲉⲱⲛ)

• Aleppo Codex: Byt Åůn (בית און)

• Leningrad Codex: Veit Aven (בֵּית אָוֶן)

• Targum Jerusalem: Veit Aven (בֵּית אָוֶן)

The Temple of Ôn / Aven was still being used in the time of Hosea, in the 700s BC, as he warned Israelites not to worship there. On was also the name of Moses' god in the Septuagint's book of Exodus, which claims that Ôn (Ων) was the name that he was known to by Abram, Isaac, and Jacob. This implies that the original name of Abram's god was Anu (✳), the Mesopotamian version of El, which would support his origin story in the city of Ur.

2 Codex Vaticanus: Madbaritis (ΜΑΔΒΑΡΙΤΙϹ). Translation: Madbarites

- Aleppo Codex: mdbr (מדבר). Translation: desert (or wilderness)

- Leningrad Codex: midbara (מִדְבָּר). Translation: desert (or wilderness)

- Targum Jerusalem: madbar (מַדְבַּר). Translation: desert (or wilderness)

Similar to the transliteratidi of Madbaritidi (Μαδβαρῖτις) in chapter 5, this a synthesis of the Aramaic mdbrå (מדברא) meaning 'desert' and the Greek '-itis' (-ῖτις), meaning 'people of,' the precursor to the modern English '-ites.' Again, the Greek appears to have translated the Aramaic word mdbråyn (מדבראין), meaning 'desert-dweller,' which is a deviation from the simpler term 'desert' found in the Hebrew and Judeo-Aramaic translations. The deviation likely occurred because the term desert-dwellers could be a reference to the Israelites themselves during the era, and the Hebrew translators wanted to clarify that it was a temple in the desert, not in Samaria.

3 Codex Vaticanus: napês Sonnam (ΝΑΠΗϹϹΟΝΝΑΜ). Translation: woodland (or grove) of Sonnam

- Aleppo Codex: gy vn hnm (גי בן הנם). Translation: Valley of the sons of Hnm

- Leningrad Codex: gei ven-Hinnom (גֵּי בֶן־הִנֹּם). Translation: Valley of the sons of Hinnom

- Targum Jerusalem: cheilat bar Hinom (חֵילַת בַּר הִנֹם). Translation: stength of the sons of Hinom

The Septuagint includes a different name in chapter 18, reading 'abyss of Onom' (φαραγγα ονομ) where the Masoretic text reads Valley of the Sons of Hinnom (גֵּי בֶן־הִנֹּם), indicating the Aramaic translation used shorter names than the Judahite and Samaritan versions. The difference between in the names Sonnam and Hinnom in this verse likely originated when the Aramaic translation was created, as the Canaanite's script, which was used for Samaritan and Judahite in the early iron age, had similar shapes for the H (𐤀) and the Ś (𐤙). While the Aramaic script did not have a similar H (𐡄) and Ś (𐡎), the early Greek alphabet did have a similar H (ϵ) and Š (ϲ), and therefore, the error could be interpreted as a Greek copying error. However, a virtually identical error is found in the Judahite Apocalypse of Ezra, which rendered the Sea of Edom as the Sea of Sodom. In that case, it was the word 'the/of' in between 'sea' and 'Edom' that was misread as an S, indicating the error took place in the Canaanite script.

The origin of the name Hnm (הנם) is likely a plural of hinn (حِنّ), a reference to an ancient extinct type of being that once lived on the Earth in Semitic folklore. The hinns continue to be part of the Islamic and Druze religions, although their roles in the religions vary. It is agreed that they are extinct, however, it isn't clear what they were.

Many sources describe the hinns and binns as powerful, gigantic primordial creatures, suggesting they were influenced by finding the bones of extinct animals. Conversely, the Revelations of 'Abdullah Al-Sayid Muhammad Habib claims the hinns were air creatures, and the binns were water creatures, while the medieval Islamic historian al-Tabari claimed they were created from poisonous fire (سموم). In most versions of the stories, they fought in part of a series of wars for control of the earth before the creation of humanity, and most of the ancient species became extinct, including the hinns.

The substitution of 'forest' or 'woodland' for 'valley of the sons...' is clearly not a translation error. The combination of 'valley/abyss' and 'forest/woodland' suggests it is a reference to a gravesite, and not a physical valley. At the time, Canaanites marked gravesites by planting trees, usually oak, which was known as the 'Asherah' tree, because it could self-pollinate, and was therefore seen as a 'virgin' tree. In the context of a gravesite, it is likely that the term 'sons of hinns' did not refer to some known people, but an ancient gravesite of a by then unknown people. Oak trees are known to live over 1000 years, and reproduce, so the gravesite in question could have already been thousands of years old. Later during the reforms of King Josiah, ancient graves and Asherah groves near Jerusalem were destroyed, and he was specifically recorded as destroying a statue in the valley of the sons of Hinns, implying that this was the gravesite he destroyed.

4 Codex Vaticanus: merous Emecraphaen apo borrha (ΜΕΡΟΥϹΕΜΕΚΡΑΦΑΕΙΝ ΑΠΟΒΟΡΡΑ). Translation: region of Emecraphaen of the north

- Aleppo Codex: åshr vômk rfåm tzfvnh (אשר בעמק רפאים צפונה). Translation: exists the valley of Raphaim northern

- Leningrad Codex: asher be'emek refa'im tzafovnah (אֲשֶׁר בְּעֵמֶק רְפָאִים צָפוֹנָה). Translation: exists the valley Raphaim northern

- Targum Jerusalem: bemeishar gibbaraya tzifuna (בְּמֵישַׁר גִּבְּרַיָּא צָפוֹנָא). Translation: straight of the husband of the north

As the Greek includes a transliteration of the Hebrew, the Hebrew is imported. This scribal note seems to confirm that the 'Forest of Hinns' was the 'valley of the Raphiam,' supporting the term 'valley/abyss of hinns' referring to a graveyard. The two terms translated as 'Hinns' and 'Raphites' are not generally found in the same ancient literature, with hinns being mostly found in Arabic literature, and Raphites being mostly found in Canaanite literature. This scribal note, in both the Greek and Hebrew translations, indicates the scribe was trying to let a northern reader understand that a Hinn was a Raphite. This shows that the original language of the text was more influenced by Arabic than Canaanite, supporting the claims that the people following Joshua had previously been in the Arabian desert. The scribal note must date back to an earlier copy of the text, as there would have been no reason to add it to both the Aramaic and Judahite translations, which later served as the basis for the Greek and Hebrew. The Aramaic translators would have simply used the correct Aramaic term, and left the Judahite text unaltered. It probably originated in the Samaritan version of the text, as at its height, the Kingdom of Israel was reported to have spanned the Levant from Edom to Hama.

At other points in the Septuagint, the Valley of Raphim is translated as the Valley of Gigantes (κοιλαδι των γιγαντων), indicating that the Greeks were not clear on who the sons of the Raphim were. It is likely that this was not being used as a reference to a tribe by the time the scribal note was added, as the Raphites (𐤓𐤐𐤀𐤌) were already viewed as residing in the underworld in Ugaritic Texts from the mid-1300s BC.

5 Codex Vaticanus: Gaeenna (ⲅⲁⲓⲉⲛⲛⲁ). Translation: Gaeenna

- Aleppo Codex: gy hnm (**גי הנם**). Translation: valley Hnm

- Leningrad Codex: gei Hinnom (גֵּי הִנֹּם). Translation: valley Hinnom

- Targum Jerusalem: lecheilat bar hinom (לְחֵילַת בַּר הִנֹם). Translation: the army (or strength, force) of the sons of Hinom

As the Greek includes a transliteration of the Hebrew 'valley of Hinns,' the Hebrew is imported.

Joshua: Chapter 19

The second lot came out for the children of Simeon, and their inheritance was in the middle of the lots of the children of Judah. Their lot was Beersheba, Sheba, Caladam, Arsola, Balah, Jason, Erthula, the Temple of El, Hormah, Ziklag, the House of Marcaboth, the Yard of Susah, the House of Lebaoth, and their fields; thirteen cities, and their villages.

Rimmon, Thalcha, Jetheth, and Ashan; four cities and their villages around the cities as far as Balec as men go south to Bameth.

This is the inheritance of the tribe of the children of Simeon according to their families. The inheritance of the tribe of the children of Simeon was a part of the lot of Judah, for the portion of the children of Judah was greater than theirs, and the children of Simeon inherited in the middle of their lot.

The third lot came out to Zebulun according to their families. The borders of their inheritance will be: Esedekgola will be their border, the sea, and Magelda, and it will reach towards the House of Arabah in the valley, which is opposite Jokneam. The border returned from Sedduc in a contrary direction eastward from the Temple of Shemesh, to the borders of Chisloth Tabor, and will pass on to Daberath, and will proceed upward to Phangai. There it will come around in the opposite direction eastward to Gebere to the city of Kazin, and will go on to Rimmon Ammatharim Annoua.[1] The borders will come north to Hannathon, and will continue on to Jiphthah El, Kattath, Nahalal, Shimron, Jericho, and the House of Lehem. This is the inheritance of the tribe of the sons of Zebulun according to their families, these cities and their villages.

The fourth lot came out to Issachar. Their borders were Jezreel, Chesulloth, Shunem, Agin, Shion, Reeroth, Anaharath, Dabiron, Kishion, Abez, Remeth, Jeon, Tomman, Aemarec, and Bersaphes. The boundaries will border on Gaethbor, and on Salim westward, and the Temple of Shemesh, and the extremity of his border will be the Jordan. This is the inheritance of the tribe of the children of Issachar according to their families, the cities and their villages.

The fifth lot came out to Asher according to their families. Their borders were Helkath, Hali, Bathok, Achshaph, Alammelech, Ammi-El, and Maasa, and the lot bordered on Carmel in the west, and on Sihon and Libnath. It will return westward from the Temple of Dagon, and will join Zebulun and the valley of Iphtah-El to the north, and the borders will come to the north Beth Emek, and Neiel, and will go on to Cabul on the left, including Ebron, Rehob, Hammon, and Kanah to Sidon the Great. The borders will turn back to Ramah, and to the Fountain of Masphassat, and the Tyrians and the borders will return to Hosah, and their end will be the sea by Apoleb, Achzib, Archob, Aphek, and Rehob. This is the inheritance of the tribe of the sons of Asher according to their families, the cities and their villages.

The sixth lot came out to Naphtali. Their borders were Moolam, Mola, Besemiin, Arme, Nekeb, Jephthamai, as far as Dodam, and ended at the Jordan. The coasts returned westward by Athabor, and go out from there to Jacana, and border on Zebulun to the south, and Asher will join it to the west, and the Jordan to the east. The walled cities of the Tyrians: Tyre, Omathadaketh, Kenereth, Armaith, Areal, Hazor, Kadesh, Assari, the well of Hazor, Iron, Migdal El, the Temple of Anath, and the Temple of Shemesh. This is the inheritance of the tribe of the children of Naphtali.

The seventh lot came out to Dan. Their borders were Zorah, Asa, the City of Shemesh, Salamin, Ammon, Jethlah, Elon, Timnah, Ekron, Eltekeh, Begethon, and Gebeelan, Azor, Bene-berak, and Gath Rimmon. West of Hieracon the border was near to Jaffa. This is the inheritance of the tribe of the children of Dan, according to their families, these are their cities and their villages.

The children of Dan did not drive out the Amorites who attacked them in the mountains, and the Amorites would not allow them to come down into the valley, but they forcibly took from them the border of their portion. The sons of Dan went and fought against Leshem, and took it, and slaughtered it with the edge of the sword, and they lived in it and called the name of it Leshem Dan. The Amorites continued to live in Edom and in Salamin, and the hand of Ephraim prevailed against them, and they became a tribute for them.

They proceeded to take possession of the land according to their borders, and the Israelites gave an inheritance to Joshua the son of Nun among them, by the command of God, and they gave him the city which he asked for, Timnath Serah, which is on Mount Ephraim, and he built the city and lived in it. These are the divisions which Eleazar the priest divided by lot, and Joshua the son of Nun, and the heads of families among the tribes of Israel, according to the lots, in Shiloh before the Lord by the doors of the tabernacle of testimony, and they went to take possession of the land.

Joshua: Chapter 19 Notes

1 Codex Vaticanus: Remmôn Ammatharim Annoua (ρεμμωναμμαθαριμ αννογα)

- Aleppo Codex: Rmůn hmtår hnôh (רמון המתאר הנעה)

- Leningrad Codex: Rimmovn hammeto'ar hanne'ah (רמּוֹן הַמְּתֹאָר הַגְּעָה)

- Targum Jerusalem: Rimon dimto'ar umittaman mistechar lene'ah (רְמוֹן דְּמְתוֹאַר וּמִתַּמָן מִסְתְּחַר לְנֶעָה). Translation: desert (or wilderness)

In this case, the Greeks transliterated a word similar to hammeto'ar (הַמְּתֹאָר) as Ammatharim (Αμμαθαριμ). As 'hammesoor' translates as 'that describes' it is possible that the text originated by the scribal note "(which is Annoua)" however, that cannot be known for sure. As it is, neither the Greek nor Hebrew translations make sense in this verse.

Joshua: Chapter 20

The Lord said to Joshua, "Tell the Israelites, 'Assign the cities of refuge, of which I told you through Moses. A refuge for the slayer who has struck a man unintentionally. The cities will be refuges for you, and the slayer will not be put to death by the avenger of blood until he has stood before the congregation for judgment.'"

Joshua separated Kadesh in Galilee on Mount Naphtali, and Shechem on Mount Ephraim, and the city of Arba (this is Hebron), in the mountains of Judah. Beyond the Jordan, he appointed Bezer in the wilderness in the plain out of the tribe of Reuben, and Ramoth in Gilead out of the tribe of Gad, and Golan in the country of Bashan out of the tribe of Manasseh.

These were the cities selected for the sons of Israel, and for the stranger living among them, that everyone who kills a mind unintentionally should flee there, that he should not die by the hand of the avenger of blood until he should stand before the congregation for judgment.

Joshua: Chapter 21

The heads of the families of the Levites approached Eleazar the priest and Joshua the son of Nun, and to the heads of families of the tribes of Israel. They said to them in Shiloh in the land of Canaan, "The Lord gave commandment by Moses to give us cities to live in, and the country around it for our livestock."

The Israelites gave the Levites their inheritance by the command of the Lord, the cities, and the country around them. The lot came out for the Kohathites, and the sons of Aaron, the priests the Levites, had by lot thirteen cities out of the tribes of Judah, Simeon, and Benjamin. To the sons of Kohath that were left were given by lot ten cities, out of the tribes of Ephraim and Dan, and out of the half-tribe of Manasseh. The sons of Gershon had thirteen cities, out of the tribes of Issachar, Asher, Naphtali, and out of the half-tribe of Manasseh in the land of Bashan. The sons of Merari according to their families had by lot twelve cities, out of the tribes of Reuben, Gad, and Zebulun. The Israelites gave to the Levites the cities and their suburbs by lot, as the Lord commanded Moses.

The tribe of the children of Judah, and the children of Simeon, and part of the tribe of the children of Benjamin gave these cities, and they were assigned to the sons of Aaron of the family of Kohath of the Levites, for the lot fell to these. And they gave to them the town of Arba, the mother-city of the sons of Anaks (this is Hebron), in the mountainous country of Judah, and the suburbs around it. But the lands of the city and its villages Joshua gave to the sons of Caleb the son of Jephunneh for a possession. To the sons of Aaron, he gave the city of refuge for the slayer, Hebron, and the suburbs belonging to it, and Libnah, and the suburbs belonging to it, and Elon and its suburbs, and Teman and its suburbs, Gella and its suburbs, and Debir and its suburbs, and Asa and its suburbs, and Tany and its suburbs, and the Temple of Shemesh and its suburbs; nine cities from these two tribes.

From the tribe of Benjamin, Gibeon and its suburbs, Geba and its suburbs, Anathoth and its suburbs, Almon and its suburbs; four cities. All the cities of the sons of Aaron the priests, thirteen. To the families, including the sons of Kohath the Levites, that were left of the sons of Kohath, there was given their priests' city, out of the tribe of Ephraim, and they gave them the slayer's city of refuge Shechem, and its suburbs, and Gezer and its suburbs, and House of Horon and its suburbs; four cities. From the tribe of Dan: Eltekeh and its suburbs, Gibbethon and its suburbs, Ayalon and its suburbs, Gath Rimmon and its suburbs; four cities.

Out of the half-tribe of Manasseh: Taanach and its suburbs, and Jebatha and its suburbs; two cities. In all were given ten cities, and the suburbs of each belonging to them, to the families of the sons of Kohath that remained. Joshua gave to the sons of Gershon the Levites out of the other half-tribe of Manasseh cities set apart for the slayers, Golan in the country of Bashan, and its suburbs, and Bosora and its suburbs; two cities.

Out of the tribe of Issachar: Kishion and its suburbs, Daberath and its suburbs, Remmath and its suburbs, and the Well of Letters, and its suburbs; four cities.

Out of the tribe of Asher: Basella and its suburbs, and Abdon and its suburbs, and Helkath and its suburbs, and Rehob and its suburbs; four cities.

Of the tribe of Naphtali: the city set apart for the slayer, Kadesh in Galilee, and its suburbs, and Hammoth Dor, and its suburbs; and Themmon and its suburbs; three cities. All the cities of the Gershonites according to their families were thir-teen cities. To the family of the sons of Merari the Levites that remained, he gave out of the tribe of Zebulun, Mahanaim and its suburbs, Kadesh and its suburbs, and Zillah and its suburbs: three cities.

Beyond the Jordan near Jericho, out of the tribe of Reuben: the city of refuge for the slayer, Bezer in the wilderness, Miso and its suburbs, Jahaz and its suburbs, Kedemoth and its suburbs, Mephaath and its suburbs; four cities.

Out of the tribe of Gad the city of refuge for the slayer, both Ramoth in Gilead, and its suburbs, Mahanaim and its suburbs, Heshbon and its suburbs, Jazer and its suburbs: the cities were four in all. All these cities were given to the sons of Merari according to the families of them that were left out of the tribe of Levi, and their limits were the twelve cities. All the cities of the Levites among the possession of the Israelites, were forty-eight cities, and their suburbs around these cities, a city and the suburbs round about the city to all these cities: and Joshua ceased dividing the land by their borders: and the Israelites gave a portion to Joshua because of the commandment of the Lord: they gave him the city which he asked: they gave him Timnath Serah on Mount Ephraim, and Joshua built the city and lived in it. Joshua took the knives of stone, which he circumcised the Israelites that were born in the desert along the way, and put them in Timnath Serah. So the Lord gave to Israel all the land which he swore to give to their fathers: and they inherited it, and lived in it. The Lord gave them the rest around at, as he swore to their fathers: not one of all their enemies maintained his ground against them. The Lord delivered all their enemies into their hands. Not one of the good things which the Lord said to the Israelites failed. All happened.

Joshua: Chapter 22

Then Joshua called together the sons of Reuben, and the sons of Gad, and the half-tribe of Manasseh, and said to them, "You have heard all that Moses the servant of the Lord commanded you, and you have listened to my voice in all that he commanded you. You have not deserted your brothers these many days. Until this day you have kept the commandment of Lord the god. Now Lord the god has given our brothers rest, as he told them. Now then, return and leave to your homes, and to the land of your possession, which Moses gave you on the other side of the Jordan. But take great heed to do the commands and the law, which Moses the servant of the Lord commanded you to do: to love Lord the god, to walk in all his ways, to keep his commands, and to cling to him, and serve him with all your mind, and with all your mind."

Joshua blessed them and dismissed them, and they went to their homes. To one half of the tribe of Manasseh Moses gave a portion in the land of Bashan, and to the other half, Joshua gave a portion with his brothers on the west side of the Jordan. When Joshua sent them away to their homes, then he blessed them. They departed with much wealth to their houses, and they divided the spoil of their enemies with their brothers, a great deal of livestock, silver, gold, iron, and many clothes. So the sons of Reuben, and the sons of Gad, and the half-tribe of Manasseh, departed from the Israelites in Shiloh in the land of Canaan, to go away into Gilead, into the land of their possession, which they inherited by the command of the Lord, by the hand of Moses.

They came to Gilead of Jordan, which is in the land of Canaan. The children of Reuben, and the children of Gad, and the half-tribe of Manasseh built an altar there by the Jordan, a great altar to look at. The Israelites were heard to say, "Look, the sons of Reuben, Gad, and the half-tribe of Manasseh have built an altar at the borders of the land of Canaan at Gilead of Jordan, on the opposite side as the Israelites." All the Israelites gathered together to Shiloh, to go up and fight against them. The Israelites sent to the sons of Reuben, Gad, and the half-tribe of Manasseh in the land of Gilead, both Phinehas the son of Eleazar the son of Aaron the priest, and ten of the chiefs with him, one chief of every household out of all the tribes of Israel, (the heads of families are the captains of thousands in Israel.)

They came to the sons of Reuben, Gad, and the half-tribe of Manasseh in the land of Gilead, and said to them, "The whole congregation of the Lord says, 'What is this transgression that you have done before the God of Israel, to turn away today from the Lord, in that you have built for yourselves an altar so that you should be apostates from the Lord? Is the sin of Peor too little for you, whereas we have not been cleansed from it until this day, though there was a plague among the congregation of the Lord? You have this day rebelled from the Lord. It will come to pass if you revolt this day from the Lord, that tomorrow there will be anger on all Israel."

"Now if the land of your possession is too little, cross over to the land of the possession of the Lord, where the tabernacle of the Lord lives, and receive your inheritance among us. Do not become apostates from God, neither become apostates from the Lord, because of your having built an altar apart from the altar of Lord the god. Look! did not Achan the son of Zerah commit a trespass taking of the cursed thing, and there was anger on the whole congregation of Israel? Yet he himself died alone in his own sin."

The sons of Reuben, Gad, and the half-tribe of Manasseh answered the captains of the thousands of Israel, "The god of gods is Lord, and the god of gods, Lord himself knows[1] and judges Israel. If we have transgressed before the Lord by apostasy, let him not save us this day. If we have built for ourselves an altar, to apostatize from Lord the god, to offer on it a sacrifice of whole burnt offerings, to offer on it a sacrifice of peace offering, the Lord will require it. But we have done this for the sake of precaution concerning this thing, saying, 'In case from now on your sons should say to our sons, 'What have you to do with Lord the god of Israel? The Lord has set boundaries between us and you, even the Jordan, and you have no portion in the Lord,' and your sons will alienate our sons, that they should not worship the Lord.'"

"We gave orders to do this, to build this altar, not for burnt offerings, nor for meat-offerings, but that this may be a witness between you and us, and between our posterity after us, that we may do service to the Lord before him, with our burnt offerings and our meat-offerings and our peace offerings. So your sons will not say to our sons, from now on, 'You have no portion in the Lord.' We said, 'If ever it should come to pass that they should speak so to us, or to our posterity from now on, then will they say, 'Look the likeness of the altar of the Lord, which our fathers made, not for the sake of burnt offerings, nor for the sake of meat-offerings, but it is a witness between you and us, and between our sons.' Far be it from us therefore that we should turn away from the Lord this day to apostatize from the Lord, so that we should build an altar for burnt offerings, and for peace offerings, besides the altar of the Lord which is before his tabernacle."

Phinehas the priest and all the chiefs of the congregation of Israel who were with him heard the words which the children of Reuben, Gad, and the half-tribe of Manasseh spoke, and it pleased them. Phinehas the priest said to the sons of Reuben, Gad, and to the half-tribe of Manasseh, "Today we know that the Lord is with us, because you have not trespassed grievously against the Lord, and because you have delivered the Israelites out of the hand of the Lord."

So Phinehas the priest and the princes departed from the children of Reuben, Gad, and the half-tribe of Manasseh, out of Gilead to the land of Canaan to the Israelites, and reported the words to them. It pleased the Israelites, and they spoke to the Israelites, and blessed the God of the Israelites, and told them to not go up to war against the others and destroy the land of the children of Reuben, Gad, and the half-tribe of Manasseh. Joshua gave a name to the altar of the children of Reuben, Gad, and the half-tribe of Manasseh, and said, "It is a testimony among them, that the Lord is their God."

Joshua: Chapter 22 Notes

1 Codex Vaticanus: o ths ths estin cs, cae o ths ths cs autòs oĩden (ΟΘϹΘϹΕϹΤΙΝΚϹ ΚΑΙΟΘϹΘϹΚϹΑΥΤΟϹΟΙΔΕΝ). Translation: the god god is lord, and the god god lord himself knows

• Aleppo Codex: ål ålhym yhůh ål ålhym yhůh hůå ydô (אל אלהים יהוה אל אלהים יהוה הוא ידע). Translation: the (or god, El) gods (or elohim) Yhůh the (or god, El) gods (or elohim) Yhůh he knows

• Leningrad Codex: el | elohim | Yehvah el | elohim | Yehvah hu yodea' (אֵ֥ל \ אֱלֹהִ֨ים \ יְהוָ֗ה אֵ֣ל \ אֱלֹהִ֤ים \ יְהוָה֙ ה֣וּא יֹדֵ֔עַ). Translation: god (or El) – gods (or elohim) – Yehwah god (or El) – gods (or elohim) – Yehwah he knows

• Targum Jerusalem: el elohim yeyah el elohim yeyah kodamohi yedia' (אֵל אֱלֹהִים יְיָ אֵל אֱלֹהִים יְיָ קֳדָמוֹהִי יְדִיעַ). Translation: god (or El) gods Yhů god (or El) gods Yhů he knows

As neither the Greek nor Hebrew text makes sense here, and clearly were not understood by the Masoretes due to their punctuation marks, it is assumed that the Greeks translated both 'el' and elohim as 'god,' as they did in other sections of the Septuagint. If the term elohim originally meant 'gods' in this verse, which is its Aramaic meaning, then the Aramaic precursor text would have read 'the god of gods is Lord (possibly Adonay or Ba'al), and the god of gods, Lord himself, knows..."

Joshua: Chapter 23

Many days after the Lord had given Israel rest from all his enemies, when Joshua was old and advanced in years. Joshua called together all the Israelites, and their elders, and their chiefs, and their judges, and their officers, and said to them, "I am old and advanced in years. You have seen all that Lord the god has done to all these nations before us. It is Lord the god who has fought for you. See, that I have given to you these nations that are left to you by lots to your tribes, all the nations beginning at the Jordan. Some I have destroyed, and the boundaries will be at the great sea to the west."

"The Lord the god, will destroy them before us until they completely perish, and he will send against them the wild beasts until he has completely destroyed them and their kings from before you, and you will inherit their land, as Lord the god promised you. Therefore strive diligently to observe and do all things written in the book of the law of Moses, that you do not turn to the right or to the left, that you do not go in among these nations that are left, and the names of their gods will not be named among you. Neither will you serve them, neither will you bow down to them. But you will cling to Lord the god, as you have done until this day. The Lord will destroy them before you, even great and strong nations. No one has stood before us until this day. One of you has chased a thousand, because Lord the god, he fought for you, as he said to us."

"Pay close attention to love Lord the god. For if you will turn aside and attach yourselves to these nations that are left with you, and make marriages with them, and become mingled with them and they with you, know that the Lord will no longer destroy these nations from before you, and they will be to you snares and stumbling blocks, and nails in your heels, and darts in your eyes until you are destroyed from off this good land, which Lord the god has given you. But I quickly go the way of death, as all that are on the earth also do, and you know in your heart and in your mind, that not one word has fallen to the ground of all the words which Lord the god has spoken respecting all that concerns us".

"There has not one of them failed. It will come to pass, that as all the good things have come on us which Lord the god will bring on you all the evil things until he has destroyed you from off this good land, which the Lord has given you, when you transgress the covenant of Lord the god, which he has ordered us, and go and serve other gods, and bow down to them."

Joshua: Chapter 24

Joshua gathered all the tribes of Israel to Shiloh, and assembled their elders, and their officers, and their judges, and set them before God. Joshua said to all the people, "Lord the god of Israel says, 'Your fathers at first stayed beyond the river, including Terah, the father of Abraham and the father of Nahor, and they served other gods. I took your father Abraham from the other side of the river, and I guided him through all the land, and I multiplied his seed, and I gave to him Isaac, and to Isaac Jacob and Esau. I gave to Esau Mount Seir for him to inherit, and Jacob and his sons went down to Egypt and became a great and populous and mighty nation there, and the Egyptians attacked them. I struck Egypt with the wonders that I worked among them.'"

"Afterward God brought out our fathers from Egypt, and you entered into the Papyrus Sea, and the Egyptians pursued after our fathers with chariots and horses into the Papyrus Sea. We cried aloud to the Lord, and he put a cloud and darkness between us and the Egyptians, and he brought the sea on them and covered them. Your eyes have seen all that the Lord did in the land of Egypt, and you were in the wilderness many days. He brought us into the land of the Amorites that lived beyond the Jordan, and the Lord delivered them into our hands, and you inherited their land, and completely destroyed them from before you. Balak, king of Moab, son of Zippor, rose, and made war against Israel, and sent and called Balaam to curse us. But Lord the god would not destroy you, and he greatly blessed us, and rescued us out of their hands, and delivered them to us. You crossed across the Jordan and came to Jericho, and the inhabitants of Jericho fought against us, the Amorites, Canaanites, Perizzites, Mitanni, Jebusites, Cypriots, and Girgasite, but the Lord delivered them into our hands. He sent out hornets before you, and he drove them out from before you, all twelve kings of the Amorites, not with your sword, nor with your bow."

"He gave you a land on which you did not labor and cities which you did not build, and you were settled in them. You eat of vineyards and olive yards which you did not plant. Now fear the Lord, and serve him in righteousness and justice, and remove the strange gods, which our fathers served beyond the river, and in Egypt, and serve the Lord. But if it does not seem good to you to serve the Lord, choose for yourselves today who you will serve, whether the gods of your fathers that were on the other side of the river, or the gods of the Amorites, among whose land you live in, but I and my house will serve the Lord, for he is holy."

The people answered and said, "Far be it from us to forsake the Lord, to serve other gods. Lord the god, he is God. He brought us and our fathers out from Egypt and protected us along the roads on which we walked, and among all the nations through which we passed. The Lord threw out the Amorites and all the nations that inhabited the land from before us. Yes, we will serve the Lord, for he is our god."

Joshua said to the people, "Indeed you will not be able to serve the Lord, for God is holy, and he being jealous will not forgive your sins and your transgressions. Whenever you will forsake the Lord and serve other gods, then he will come on you and afflict you, and consume you, because he has done good for you."

The people said to Joshua, "No, but we will serve the Lord."

Joshua said to the people, "You are witnesses against yourselves, that you have chosen the Lord to serve him. Now take away the strange gods that are among you, and set your heart right towards Lord the god of Israel."

The people replied to Joshua, "We will serve the Lord, and we will listen to his voice."

So Joshua made a covenant with the people on that day and gave them a law and an ordinance in Shiloh before the tabernacle of the God of Israel. He wrote these words in the book of the laws of God. Joshua took a great stone and set it up under the turpentine tree before the Lord. Joshua said to the people, "Look, this stone will be among you as a witness, for it has heard all the words that have been spoken to it by the Lord. He has spoken to you today, and this stone will be among you as a witness in the last days, whenever you will deal falsely with Lord the god."

Joshua dismissed the people, and they went every man to his place. It happened after these things that Joshua the son of Nun the servant of the Lord died, at the age of a hundred and ten years. They buried him by the borders of his inheritance in Timnath Serah on Mount Ephraim, north of Mount Gilead. There they put with him into the tomb in which they buried him, the knives of stone with which he circumcised the Israelites at the circle, when he brought them out of Egypt, as the Lord appointed them, and there they are to this day.

Israel served the Lord all the days of Joshua and all the days of the elders that lived as long as Joshua, and all that knew all the works of the Lord which he worked for Israel. The Israelites brought up the bones of Joseph out of Egypt, and buried them in Shechem, in the portion of the land which Jacob bought of the Amorites who lived in Shechem for a hundred ewe-lambs, and he gave it to Joseph for a portion. It happened afterward that Eleazar the high-priest the son of Aaron died and was buried in the hill of Phinehas his son, which he gave him on Mount Ephraim.

On that day the Israelites took the box of God and carried it around among them, and Phinehas exercised the priest's office in place of Eleazar his father until he died, and he was buried in his own place Gabaar, but the Israelites departed every one to their place, and to their own city, and the Israelites worshiped Asherah and Astarte,[1] and the gods of the nations around them, and the Lord delivered them into the hands of Eglom king of Moab and he ruled over them eighteen years.[2]

Joshua: Chapter 24 Notes

1 Codex Vaticanus: Astartên cae Astaróth (ΑϹΤΑΡΤΗΝΚΑΙΑϹΤΑΡѠΘ). Translation: Asherah and Astarte

This verse, is not found in the Masoretic Text. The two goddesses mentioned are the wives of El from the Ugaritic Texts: Aṯrt (𐎀𐎘𐎗𐎚), later called Asherah (אשרה) by the Israelites; and Ôṯtrt-ym (𐎓𐎘𐎚𐎗𐎚𐎊𐎎), later called Ôštrt (𐤏𐤔𐤕𐤓𐤕) by the Phoenicians, Astarte (Ἀστάρτη) by the Greeks, and Ashtoret (עַשְׁתֹּרֶת) by the Israelites. The names in the Septuagint are transliterations of the Aramaic names, not the Greek names, indicating that they were in the Aramaic version of Joshua. The more common English names are used.

2 This verse is not found in the Masoretic Text, indicating that the Septuagint's Joshua was made from a Samaritan text, and not a Judahite text, as Eglom king of Moab only conquered Gilead and Samaria, not Judah or Edom.

Judges: Chapter 1

After the death of Joshua, the Israelites asked the Lord,[1] "Who will go up for us first against the Canaanites, to fight against them?"

The Lord answered, "Judah will go up. Watch, I have delivered the land into his hand."

Judah said to his brother Simeon, "Come up with me into my allotted territory and let us ally ourselves against the Canaanites, and I also will go with you into your allotted territory," and Simeon went with him. Judah went up, and the Lord delivered the Canaanite and the Perizzite into their hands, and they slaughtered ten thousand men in Bezek.[2] They defeated the Lord of Bezek[3] in Bezek and fought against him, and they attacked the Canaanites and the Perizzites. The Lord of Bezek fled, and they chased after him, and caught him, and cut off his thumbs and his big toes.

The Lord of Bezek said, "Seventy kings collected their food from my table after I cut their thumbs and their big toes off. As I have done, God has repaid me."

They brought him to Jerusalem, and he died there.

The children of Judah attacked Jerusalem and plundered it, and slaughtered by the edge of the sword, and burnt the city with fire. Afterward, the children of Judah went down to fight with the Canaanites living in the hill country, and the Negev, and the plain country.

Judah went to the Canaanites who lived in Hebron and Hebron came out against him. (Previously, Hebron was called the village of Arbaseifer.) They slaughtered Sheshai, Ahiman, and Tamlai, the descendants of Anaks.

They went up from there to the inhabitants of Debir. (Debir was previously called the village of Seifer [City of Letters.])[5]

Caleb said, "Whoever will attack the village of Seifer, and will capture it first, I will give him my daughter Acsah as a wife."

Othniel the younger son of Kenez the brother of Caleb captured it, and Caleb gave him his daughter Acsah as a wife. It happened as she went in, that Othniel urged her to ask for a field from her father, and she whined and cried from her donkey, "You have sent me out into a southern land."

Caleb asked her, "What is your request?"

Acsah answered him, "Give me a blessing, I beg of you, for you have sent me out to a southern land, and you will give me the prize of water," and Caleb gave her according to her heart the prize of the upper springs and the low springs.

The children of Jobab the blacksmith[6] the son-in-law of Moses went up from the city of palm-trees[7] with the children of Judah, to the wilderness that is to the south of Judah, which is at the descent of Arad, and they lived with the people. Judah went with Simeon his brother and slaughtered the Canaanites that inhabited Zephath, and they completely destroyed them, and they called the name of the city Anathema.[8] But Judah did not inherit Gaza and her coast, or Ashkelon and her coast, or Ekron and her coast, or Ashdod and the lands around it. The Lord was with Judah, and he inherited the mountain, as they were not able to destroy the inhabitants of the valley, for Rechab[9] prevented them. They gave Hebron to Caleb, as Moses said, and there he inherited the three cities of the children of Anaks. But the Benjaminites did not take the inheritance of the Jebusites who lived in Jerusalem, and the Jebusites lived with the Benjaminites in Jerusalem until this day.

The sons of Joseph also went up to the Temple of El[10] and the Lord was with them. They camped and surveyed the Temple of El (the name of the town was Luz[11] then). The spies looked and saw a man go out of the city, and they captured him, and said, "Show us the way into the city, and we will deal mercifully with you."

He showed them the way into the city, and they slaughtered the city with the edge of the sword, but they let the man and his family go. The man went into the land of the Cypriots,[12] and built a city there called Luz,[13] and this is its name until this day.

Manasseh did not drive out the inhabitants of the House of She'an[14] (which is Scythopolis), or her towns and her suburbs, nor Ti'inik[15] and her towns, nor the inhabitants of Dor[16] and her suburbs and towns, or the inhabitants of Balak[17] and her suburbs and her towns, or the inhabitants of Megiddo[18] and her suburbs and towns, or the inhabitants of Belameh[19] and her suburbs and towns. The Canaanites began to live in this land. It happened when Israel was strong, that he made the Canaanites tributary, but did not completely drive them out.

Ephraim did not drive out the Canaanites that lived in Gezer, and the Canaanites lived among them in Gezer and became tributary.

Zebulun did not drive out the inhabitants of Kitron, nor the inhabitants of Domana,[20] and the Canaanites lived among them and became tributary to them.

Asher did not drive out the inhabitants of Acco who became tributary to him, or the inhabitants of Dor,[21] Sidon,[22] Ahlab,[23] Achazib,[24] Helbah, Nai,[25] or Ereo.[26] Asher lived among the Canaanites who inhabited the land, for they could not drive them out.

Naphtali did not drive out the inhabitants of House of Shemesh,[27] or the inhabitants of House of Anat,[28] and Naphtali lived among the Canaanites who inhabited the land, but the inhabitants of House of Shemesh and House of Anat became tributary to them.

The Amorites drove out the children of Dan into the mountains, and they did not allow them to come down into the valley. The Amorites began to live in the clay mountains,[29] where there are bears and foxes, in Myrsinoni[30] and Sha'alvim.[31] The hand of the house of Joseph was heavy on the Amorites, and they became tributary to them. The border of the Amorites was from the ascent of Akrabbim,[32] from the Petra[33] and upwards.

Judges: Chapter 1 Notes

1 Codex Vaticanus: tou cyriou (ΤΟΥΚΥΡΙΟΥ). Translation: the Lord

• Codex Alexandrinus: en cyriô (ΕΝΚΥΡΙѠ). Translation: of Lord

• Aleppo Codex: byhůh (בִּיהוה). Translation: in (or with, while, among, on) Yhůh

• Leningrad Codex: baYhvah (בַּיהוָה). Translation: in (or with, while, among, on) Yhvah

• Targum Jerusalem: dayeyah (דְיֵי). Translation: of (or from) Yhů

This chapter does not survive among the Dead Sea Scrolls, however, the name Yhůh does survive in later sections of Judges that have survived among the Dead Sea Scrolls.

• Dead Sea Scroll 4QJudg[a]: Yhůh (𐤉𐤄𐤅𐤄)

• Dead Sea Scroll 4QJudg[b]: Yhůh (𐤉𐤄𐤅𐤄)

The Septuagint's version of the Judges was translated before 200 BC, as it was carried south by the Beta Israel community, who left Egypt for Kush (modern Sudan) during the Jewish Rebellion against the Ptolemys in 200 BC. This means it predates the Hasmonean redaction and contains the term Lord (Κύριος) instead of Iaw (Ιαω), which, if correctly translated from the Aramaic source texts, would have read ådny (𐤀𐤃𐤍𐤉). The

Greeks are believed to have transliterated Yhů (יהו), the Aramaic version of the name Yhvah/Yehvah, as Iaô (Ιαω) in the Book of Leviticus, published circa 250 BC, as evidenced by the Dead Sea Scroll Septuagint fragment 4QpapLXXLev[b], which dates from Hasmonean era Judea. 4QpapLXXLev[b] could be interpreted as a Hasmonean redaction of the Septuagint, however, Leviticus appears to have been written during the rule of King Josiah, and his God was Yhů, supporting the existence of Yhů in the Book of Leviticus. The Aramaic sections of Masoretic Daniel that were not translated into Hebrew maintain the term adonai ha'elohim (אֲדֹנָי הָאֱלֹהִים), meaning the 'Lord the gods' where the Septuagint has 'Lord the god' (Κύριον τὸν θεὸν), however, the Hebrew sections have Yehvah elohim (יְהֹוָה אֱלֹהִים) where the Septuagint has 'Lord the god,' suggesting the Greek more accurately reflects the Aramaic source texts than the Hebrew translation. According to the Talmud, this was to repair the damage King Manasseh had done 600 years earlier when he removed the name Yehvah from the Israelite Texts, however, no evidence has survived from the era of Manasseh or earlier that proves the name was originally in the text, suggesting it was an attempt by the first Hasmonean High-Priest/King Simon the Zealot to create a national Judean religion with a god having a name similar to the Roman god Jove.

In the 3rd century AD, the Christians redacted the Septuagint removing the name Iaô, both in Greek, and in Latin translations which transliterated Ιαω as Iaw, replacing it with 'Lord.' This resolved the debate with the Gnostics about whether Iaw was the devil or not. Before that, the various versions of the early Christian-era Septuagint books that included the name, either used Ιαω, or the name written in Hebrew or Phoenician (Paleo-Hebrew) scripts. According to Origen of Alexandria in the late 2nd century AD, the Phoenician (most ancient script) was the most accurate. According to Theodoret of Cyprus in the 5th century, the Samaritans, who never switched to the Assyrian block letter 'Hebrew,' pronounced the name as Iabe (Ιαβε) or Iabae (Ιαβαι). Hebrews substitute the word 'hasheim,' meaning 'the name,' in all non-scriptural contexts since the Hasmoneans banned the pronunciation of the names of God. Christians have traditionally translated several ways including Jehovah, Jehova, and Jova. As the original Greek translation of Joshua does not appear to have included the name, the term Lord is used in this translation.

2 Codex Vaticanus: Bezec (ΒΕΖΕΚ)

- Aleppo Codex: bzq (בזק)

- Leningrad Codex: bezeq (בֶזֶק)

- Targum Jerusalem: bezeq (בֶזֶק)

The location of Bezek is debated. Currently, the majority of scholars believe it was at the village of Ibziq in the northern Palestinian West Bank, while others had suggested it was at the nearby village of Salhab.

3 Codex Vaticanus: Adônibezec (ΑΔѠΝΙΒΕΖΕΚ)

- Aleppo Codex: ådny bzq (אדני בזק). Translation: Lord of Bezek

- Leningrad Codex: adoni bezeq (אֲדֹנִי בֶזֶק). Translation: Lord of Bezek

- Targum Jerusalem: adoni bezeq (אֲדֹנִי בֶזֶק). Translation: Lord of Bezek

While the Septuagint treats Adonibezec as a proper name, it is clear from the Masoretic Text that is was simply his title. The fact that this 'Lord' who had defeated 70 kings was not considered a king himself, supports the dating for the invasion of southern Canaan circa 1500 BC, after Pharaoh Thutmose's armies had passed through the territory, and the local chieftains had sworn allegiance to him. As the region was in chaos between the collapse of the Hyksos Dynasty circa 1540 BC, and the Pharaoh Thutmose's army pacifying the region in 1505 BC, it is entirely possible that a would be successor to the Hyksos may have captured and mutilated 70 other would-be kings, before submitting to the Egyptians and consolidating his position within the new empire as a local lord.

4 Codex Vaticanus: Cariatharboxepher (ΚΑΡΙΑΘΑΡΒΟΞΕΦΕΡ)

- Codex Alexandrinus: Cariatharbocsepher (ΚΑΡΙΑΘΑΡΒΟΚΣΕΦΕΡ)

- Aleppo Codex: qryt årbô (קרית ארבע). Translation: Village of Labor

- Leningrad Codex: kiryat arba (קִרְיַת אַרְבַּע). Translation: Village of Labor

- Targum Jerusalem: kiryat arba (קִרְיַת אַרְבַּע). Translation: Village of four

The Greek καριαθαρβοξεφερ and καριαθαρβοκσεφερ are not transliterations of kiryat arba (קִרְיַת אַרְבַּע), but a transliteration of kiryat arba sefer (קִרְיַת אַרְבַּע סָפֶּר), meaning 'village of working books,' or 'village of the library.' As the word was removed from the text after 200 BC, the Hasmoneans are the most likely redactors.

5 Codex Vaticanus: Cariathsôphar polis grammatôn (ΚΑΡΙΑΘΣѠΦΑΡΠΟΛΙΣ ΓΡΑΜΜΑΤѠΝ). Translation: Cariathsôphar, city of letters

- Codex Alexandrinus: Polis grammatôn (ΠΟΛΙΣΓΡΑΜΜΑΤѠΝ). Translation: City of Letters

- Aleppo Codex: qryt spr (קרית ספר). Translation: Village Book (or scroll)

- Leningrad Codex: kiryat-sefer (קִרְיַת־סֵפֶר). Translation: Village Book (or scroll)

- Targum Jerusalem: kiryat archei (קִרְיַת אַרְכֵי). Translation: Village of Arke

The Greek καριαθσωφαρ is a transliteration of the Hebrew term found in the Masoretic Text. The Greeks added a translation 'city of the letters,' meaning they considered the name of the town to imply a communications hub. These two cities being burnt imply that the Judeans and Simeonites were targeting centers for higher learning within Canaan. These towns would have likely served as the main communications centers, as, prior to telegraphs being invented in the 1800s AD, the primary form of long-distance communication was letters. Cities where scribes studied writing and pigeon handling were found throughout the Middle East and the Mediterranean, such as Sumerian (and later Babylonian) Zimbar (later Sippar), a name also translating a 'Letters,' in Babylonian, although originally meaning 'birds' in Sumerian.

6 Codex Vaticanus: Iothor tou Cinaeou tou gambrou Môyseôs (ΙΟΘΟΡΤΟΥΚΙΝΑΙΟΥ ΤΟΥΓΑΜΒΡΟΥΜѠΥϹΕѠϹ). Translation: Jethro the Kenite the son-in-law of Moses

- Codex Alexandrinus: Iôbab tou Cinaeou pentherou Môysê (ΙѠΒΑΒΤΟΥΚΙΝΑΙΟΥ ΠΕΝΘΕΡΟΥΜѠΥϹΗ). Translation: Jobab the Kenite father-in-law of Moses

- Aleppo Codex: qyny htn mšh (קֵינִי חֹתֵן מֹשֶׁה). Translation: smith (or metalworker) son-in-law (or brother-in-law) of Moses

- Leningrad Codex: keini choten Mosheh (קֵינִי חֹתֵן מֹשֶׁה). Translation: smith (or metalworker) son-in-law (or brother-in-law) of Moses

- Targum Jerusalem: Shalma'ah chamuhi deMosheh (שַׁלְמָאָה חֲמוּהִי דְמֹשֶׁה). Translation: Shalmaite (Arabic tribe) of the house of (or his daughter's father-in-law) of Moses

Three variations of this text are known, two in the Septuagint codices, and one in the Masoretic Text. The two Septuagint versions name the man in question as either Jethro (Ιοθορ) or Jobab (Ιωβαβ), while the Masoretic Text omits the name. The one version of the Septuagint and the Masoretic Text agree that he was Moses' son-in-law or brother-in-law (Γαμβρου / חֹתֵן), while the other Septuagint version claims father-in-law (Πενθερου). Of all these sources, the Codex Vaticanus is the oldest, dating to the 4th century AD, which calls him Jethro the blacksmith son-in-law of Moses.

The Codex Alexandrinus dates to the 5th century AD and is believed to be based on the revision made by Lucian the Martyr circa 300 AD, who redacted the Septuagint to make it more like the Hebrew texts that were then in circulation. Strangely, the Codex Alexandrinus claims Jobab was Moses' father-in-law, while the Masoretic Text claims the unnamed blacksmith was Moses' son-in-law. As the Masoretic Text omit the name, there were likely different versions of Judges in circulation at the time the Masorites began copying the text, and they omitted the name in order to not pass on the wrong name. Regardless of what the Masoretic Text state, almost all English translations of them, refer to this blacksmith as Moses' father-in-law.

As two of the sources, Codex Vaticanus and the Masoretic Text agree he was Moses' son-in-law, the term son-in-law is used in this translation. Additionally, Moses' father-in-law Jethro was not a blacksmith, but a shepherd, and therefore it seems clear that Moses married his daughter to a blacksmith, although that story has not survived to the present. The man is named both Jethro and Jobab in this chapter of the surviving Septuagint codices, however, all three source texts call him 'Jobab the son-in-law of Moses' in Judges chapter 4.

7 Codex Vaticanus: poleôs tôn phoenicôn (ΠΟΛΕѠΣΤѠΝΦΟΙΝΙΚѠΝ). Translation: city the Phoenicians (or palm trees, dates, Phoenix)

- Aleppo Codex: môyr htmrym (**מֵעִיר הַתְּמָרִים**). Translation: dates (or date palm trees in Hebrew), or blinking (in Aramaic)

- Leningrad Codex: me'ir hattemarim (מֵעִיר הַתְּמָרִים). Translation: dates (or date palm trees)

- Targum Jerusalem: karta Yericho (קַרְתָּא יְרִיחוֹ). Translation: city of Jericho

As this flows from the Judahites capturing the 'city of letters,' suggesting that 'city of palm trees' was an alternate translation of the same location. The term used in the Masoretic Text is Hebrew, however, the word was adopted into Hebrew from the Aramaic word tmrå (קמלְרָא) in the Iron Age, meaning it cannot have been the name used in the text before the Phoenician translation was made in the Kingdom of Samaria or Israel in the early Iron Age. The translator of the Targum Jerusalem seems to have recognized the anachronism, and substituted 'Jericho.' If 'palm' was the alternate translation of 'letters,' it suggests the Phoenician translation of Judges was made from an Egyptian language text, as 'book,' 'scroll,' 'papyrus,' and 'palm plants' was the same word in Egyptian: bât (𓃭𓏤𓈖𓏛), while the words were not synonyms in Semitic languages.

8 Codex Vaticanus: Anathema (ΑΝΑΘΕΜΑ)

- Codex Alexandrinus: Hexolethreusis (ΕΞΟΛΕΘΡΕΥΣΙΣ)

- Aleppo Codex: hrmh (**חרמה**). Translation: the highlands (or the heights)

- Leningrad Codex: charemah (חָרְמָה). Translation: the highlands (or the heights)

- Targum Jerusalem: charemah (חָרְמָה). Translation: destruction

As all three source texts use a different name, the name Anathema is used from the Codex Vaticanus, the oldest of the surviving translations.

9 Codex Vaticanus: Rêchab (ΡΗΧΑΒ)

- Aleppo Codex: rkb brzl (רכב ברזל). Translation: chariots of iron

- Leningrad Codex: rekeb barzel (רֶכֶב בַּרְזֶל). Translation: chariots of iron

- Targum Jerusalem: detichin devarzela (דְתִיכִין דְבַרְזְלָא). Translation: in the judgment of iron

The Greek translation, Masoretic text, and Targum Jerusalem each interpret this sentence quite differently. The Greek translation interpreted Rechab as the name of a town or people, and is likely the same town or people mentioned in Psalms chapter 86 as Raab (Ρααβ), which was listed alongside other lands and cities that had defeated the Israelites, including Babylon, Tyre, Kush, and the Philistines. The term shows up in the parallel verse in the Masoretic Text as rhb (רהב), generally transliterated as Rahob, which was also the name of a sea monster in ancient Israelite myths. The prophet Isaiah, who lived around the time that the Phoenician translation of Judges was probably made, also used the term to refer to Egypt, suggesting the original text read that 'Egypt' had stopped Judah from destroying the people living in the valley. The translators of the Septuagint also translated rhb (רהב) as Cetus (Κητη) in Job chapter 9, indicating that they viewed Rechab as the ancient Israelite asterism of Cetus. Another term also translated as Cetus was Tanninim (תַּנִּינֵם) in Genesis which was also translated as dragons (δρακοντα) in Psalms, while the term Livyatan (לִוְיָתָן), generally transliterated as Leviathan was also translated as a dragon (δρακων).

The term Leviathan was used in the book of Isaiah, in a reference to the Ugaritic Texts which substituted the name Leviathan for Lotan. As such, this verse could the read either as the people of a town named Rêchab (Ρηχαβ) repulsing the Israelite attack, or the Egyptians forbidding the attack, or the god-monster itself defeating them, and presumably their god. Clearly, the Hasmonean redactors did not like this implication, and so changed this to read rkb brzl (רכב ברזל), meaning either chariots of iron, or the Egyptian's iron, depending on the interpretation of rekeb (רֶכֶב).

The translator of the Targum Jerusalem seemed to have recognized the double meaning of rekeb, and therefore substituted 'the judgment of iron' (דְתִיכִין דְבַרְזְלָא), however, iron is generally not viewed as being in wide use before the beginning of the iron age, and so these 'iron chariots,' are often viewed as an anachronism. If the 'iron chariots' were part of an older version of the story which had been lost in the Aramaic translation that the Greeks worked from, the 'iron' was probably the metal the ancient Egyptians called djôm (𓈖𓏤), which they recorded building chariots from during the

New Kingdom era. Egyptologists generally believe this metal was electrum, as it is reported as coming from the 'gold' mines of southeast Egypt, where the 'gold' veins are rich in silver. The Egyptians had separate terms for both gold and silver, and referred to djôm as if it was some other kind of metal. As the gold veins in the region also contain small amounts of iron and nickle, it is possible that djôm was the residue left over from smelting the gold and sliver out of the raw metal, meaning that 'iron' would be an appropriate translation.

The New Kingdom king Tutankhamen was buried with an iron-nickel dagger, indicating that the residue from the gold and silver processing was being used to make weaponry during the New Kingdom era, however, it has not been proven that this was the metal known as djôm which was used to make chariots. Additionally, the Egyptians were smithing iron mined at Site 200 in the Timna Valley, in southern Israel's Arabah region during the New Kingdom era, presumably for weaponry. Nevertheless, it is more likely that the original reference was simply to Egypt itself, and the term 'iron' was an addition made in the early classical era, as the Greeks certainly knew what iron was, and would have translated it if it was in the texts they worked from, and it is improbable that the Aramaic translator would have removed the word.

10 Codex Vaticanus: Baethêl (ΒΑΙΘΗΛ)

• Aleppo Codex: byt âl (בֵּית אֵל). Translation: house (or temple) of El (or god), Baitylos (or meteorite)

• Leningrad Codex: beit-El (בֵּית־אֵל). Translation: house (or temple) of El (or god), Baitylos (or meteorite)

• Targum Jerusalem: veit El (בֵית אֵל). Translation: house (or temple) of El

The term Bethel meant several things in ancient Canaan. The term translates as 'house of god,' which can be translated as either 'Temple of God/El' or 'sky/heaven.' Bethel was worshiped as a god by the ancient Canaanites, the brother of El and Dagon according to Sanchuniathon, who referred to him as Baitylos, which is the name used in this translation when the god. The term can also be translated as 'meteorite' as meteorites were believed to be parts of the god Baitylos that had fallen to the Earth, and shrines were built around them.

11 Codex Vaticanus: Louza (ΛΟΥΖΑ)

• Aleppo Codex: Lûz (לוז)

• Leningrad Codex: Luz (לוּז)

- Targum Jerusalem: Luz (לוז)

The Samaritan city at the foot of Mount Gerizim is still known as Luza.

12 Codex Vaticanus: Chettiin (ⲬⲉⲦⲦⲓⲓⲛ)

- Codex Alexandrinus: Chettiim (ⲬⲉⲦⲦⲓⲓⲙ)

- Aleppo Codex: Ḥtym (חתים). General Translation: Cypriots

- Leningrad Codex: Chittim (חִתִּים). Translation: Cypriots

- Targum Jerusalem: Chitta'ei (חִתָּאֵי). Translation: Cypriots

This term has created a great deal of confusion since the misidentification of the ruins of the Neshites as being 'Hittite' in the 1800s. The modern archaeological name 'Hittite,' is not derived from an ancient name for the culture applied by themselves, or anyone else, but rather adopted from the biblical reference to a then-unknown civilization somewhere in the region. There was an ancient culture in the region called the Hattians, however, they were conquered by the Nesites before 1700 BC, and subsequently disappeared from the historic records. The name was applied to culture today referred to as 'Hittites,' before the 'Hittite' language had been translated, and is incorrect. Since 1906, excavations at Boğazköy, the ancient 'Hittite' capital Hattusa have uncovered more than 10,000 'Hittite' texts, including the royal achieve. The actual name of the 'Hittite' language and people was Nešili (𒉈𒅆𒇷), which is now rendered in some academic literate as Nesite or Neshite. As early as the mid-1800s some scholars disputed the identification of the Nesites as the Biblical Hittites, including the Orientalist Max Müller, who was one of many claiming the Biblical Hittites were ancient Greeks or some other Mediterranean people.

Later in the Septuagint's translation of the Maccabees, the similar term Chettiim (Χεττιιμ) as a reference to all Greek-speaking lands, and therefore the Biblical Hittites were likely the Minoans or the Achaean Greeks. In the 1st century AD, the Jewish historian Josephus reported that Cethima was the name of Cyrus in Aramaic, and the Chettim were the descendants of Noah's grandson Chethimus, who had settled on Cyprus. Josephus reported that the name was preserved in the Greek name of the town Cition (Κίτιον). Most historians view it as more likely that the Aramaic name was derived from the city-state of Cition, which was known as Kåtjåy (𓎡𓃀𓏏𓍿𓃀) in Egyptian records from the New Kingdom Era in the late Bronze Age, and Kt (𐤊𐤕) or Kty (𐤊𐤕𐤉) in Phoenician records from the early Iron Age. While this may be the origin of the term, by the era of the Neo-Assyrian era, the term must have also referred to other Greek islands, as both the prophets Isaiah and Ezekiel used the term 'Islands of Kittim.' As the term referred to the entire island of Cyprus in Aramaic, the translations of 'Cyprus' and 'Cypriots' are used here.

13 Codex Vaticanus: Louza (ⲗⲟⲨⲌⲁ)

- Aleppo Codex: Lůz (לוז)

- Leningrad Codex: Luz (לוֹז)

- Targum Jerusalem: Luz (לוז)

The Greek spelling of Louza (Λουζα) is a transliteration of the Aramaic spelling of the name, Lůzå (לוזא), indicating the Greek translation was made from an Aramaic source text. It is not clear which city of Luz/Louza the man built. There are a number of ancient cities across the Mediterranean bearing the name, including the Minoan city of Liso/Lissus (Λισο/Λισσος) on Crete, the ancient Greek city of Laüs (Λαος) in southern Italy, and the ancient Portuguese town of Lousã, as well as ancient records of towns with similar names in Carthaginian Tunisia and Algeria. The town of Liso in Crete is believed to date back to late-Minoan times, before 1100 BC, making it the most likely city being referred to.

The Canaanites (Phoenicians and Carthaginians) were present in southern Italy, northwest Africa, and Iberia long before the Greeks, however, it is not clear that any of the other settlements date back to before 1000 BC. The Greeks had occupied Laüs before 500 BC, however, it is not clear who founded the city or when. Ruins of the Portuguese town of Lousã have been found dating back to the Roman era, and the locations of the towns in Tunisia and Algeria are no longer known.

14 Codex Vaticanus: Baethsan (ⲃⲁⲓⲑⲤⲁⲛ)

- Aleppo Codex: byt šån (בית שאן). Translation: House (or temple) of She'an

- Leningrad Codex: beit-She'an (בֵּית־שְׁאָן). Translation: House (or temple) of She'an

- Targum Jerusalem: beit She'an (בֵּית שְׁאָן). Translation: House (or temple) of wishes

The city of Beth She'an was officially annexed by the Egyptians around 1457 BC, when the army of Thutmose III occupied Canaan en route to Syria. The city was an Egyptian city in Canaan until the collapse of the Egyptian New Kingdom, circa 1150 BC, when the city was burnt down. It was rebuilt a few decades later as a Canaanite city and the ruins of the new city show no evidence of being culturally connected to Egypt. The Assyrians burnt down the city again when they occupied Samaria circa 732 BC, and it remained largely unoccupied until sometime in the Persian era, when Scythians settled at the site, resulting in the Greek name Scythopolis.

While the Greeks added the reference to the contemporary name of Scythopolis, the Masoretic Text does not include that reference, and the city in question is the city of Beth She'an that was burned down in 1150 BC. The book of Judge's claims that Beth She'an was not occupied by the Israelites is true, the Egyptians recorded that the city was under their control and there are no records of it being attacked. These Egyptian records are found on the monuments in Karnak and are supported by the archaeological evidence of an Egyptian city at the site between 1450 and 1150 BC. Based on the Egyptian records, the main god worshiped at the Beth She'an was a god called Mekal, which appears to be a precursor to the Jewish messenger Michael.

15 Codex Vaticanus: Thanak (ΘΑΝΑΚ).

• Codex Alexandrinus: Ecthanaad (ΕΚΘΑΝΑΑΔ)

• Aleppo Codex: Tônk (תַעְנך)

• Leningrad Codex: Ta'nach (תַּעְנַךְ)

• Targum Jerusalem: Ta'anach (תַּעֲנַךְ)

As the Codex Vaticanus and Masoretic Text agree, most translations of the Septuagint prefer the name Thanak (or Taanach) over Ecthanaad. The modern village is called Ti'inik, and is located in the northern-most region of the Palestinian West Bank. Ti'inik was occupied by the Egyptians between 1457 and 1150 BC.

16 Codex Vaticanus: Dôr (ΔΩΡ)

• Aleppo Codex: Dŭr (דּוֹר)

• Leningrad Codex: Dor (דּוֹר)

• Targum Jerusalem: Dor (דּוֹר)

The city of Dor was occupied by the Egyptians during the New Kingdom era, between 1457 and 1150 BC. The city of Djr (𓂧𓂋𓈉) was mentioned in several Egyptian texts from the New Kingdom era, and featured in the Voyage of Wenamen set circa 1050 BC, after the city had broken away from Egyptian control. The city was located as the mound today called Tel Dor on the Mediterranean coast of Israel between Haifa and Hadera.

17 Codex Vaticanus: Balak (ΒΑΛΑΚ)

- Codex Alexandrinus: Balaam (ΒΑΛΑΑΜ)

- Aleppo Codex: Yblôm (יבלעם)

- Leningrad Codex: Yivle'am (יִבְלְעָם)

- Targum Jerusalem: Yivle'am (יִבְלְעָם)

The Septuagint's list of cities also includes Ieblaam (Ιεβλααμ) at the end, which also appears to be a transliteration of Yivle'am (יִבְלְעָם) from the Masoretic text. As Belameh (Βαλααμ / בְּלְעָם) also appears at the end of the list, Balak is used in this translation. The name Balak (Βαλακ) appears to be a translation of the Hebrew name Balak (בָּלָק), which was the name of the Moabite king in Numbers, which implies the land of Balak was Moab. Moab was occupied by the Egyptians during the New Kingdom, however, does not appear in their records until the Canaanite campaigns of Ramesses II circa 1275 BC. By the time of Ramesses II, Moab was a petty kingdom allied to Egypt, however, it is likely that it was officially annexed in 1457 BC when Thutmose III's armies annexed the rest of Canaan.

18 Codex Vaticanus: Magedô (ΜΑΓΕΔΩ)

- Codex Alexandrinus: Magedôn (ΜΑΓΕΔΩΝ)

- Aleppo Codex: Mgdû (מגדו)

- Leningrad Codex: Megiddov (מְגִדּוֹ)

- Targum Jerusalem: Megido (מְגִדוֹ)

The town of Megiddo was listed as a town occupied by the armies of Thutmose III's army in 1457 BC. Some records from Megiddo have survived among the Amarna Letters. Amarna Letter EA245 mentioned the governor Biridiya, from circa 1350 BC.

19 Codex Vaticanus: Ieblaam (ΙΕΒΛΑΑΜ)

The Masoretic Text does not contain another name after Meggido in this list, however, the Greek Ieblaam (Ιεβλααμ), which is found in both the Vaticanus and Alexandrinus versions of Judges, appears to be a translation of yiVle'am (יִבְלְעָם), meaning 'of Vle'am,' which is listed earlier in the Masoretic Text. The city of Balaam is generally accepted as the city of Belameh, listed as one of the towns occupied by Pharaoh Thutmose III's army circa 1450 BC. The town was occupied throughout Israelite and Judahite history, and was known as Belemoth during the Greco-Roman era.

20 Codex Vaticanus: Dômana (ᴅᴄᴏᴍᴀɴᴀ)

- Codex Alexandrinus: Enaala (ᴇɴᴀᴀᴧᴀ)

- Aleppo Codex: Nhll (נחלל)

- Leningrad Codex: Nahalol (נַהֲלֹל)

- Targum Jerusalem: Nahalol (נַהֲלֹל)

The Codex Alexandrinus' Enaala appears to be a transliteration of the Hebrew Nahalal, however, was most likely part of Lucian's redaction circa 300 AD, meaning the original Septuagint probably used the name Domana. There is an Israeli community called Nahalal in northern Israel today, however, there is no archaeological evidence connecting it to the ancient settlement.

21 Codex Vaticanus: Dôr (ᴅᴄᴏᴩ)

The Masoretic Text does not mention Dor a second time here, however, it was previously listed among the cities that Manasseh did not drive the inhabitants out of.

22 Codex Vaticanus: Sidôna (ᴄɪᴅᴄᴏɴᴀ)

- Aleppo Codex: Sydůn (צידון)

- Leningrad Codex: Tzidovn (צִידֹון)

- Targum Jerusalem: Tzidovn (צִידֹון)

Sidon (𐤑𐤃𐤍) was one of the most ancient Canaanite cities, and arguably the mother-city of all of Canaanite culture. Tyre also claimed to be Phoenicia's mother-city, however, it was originally a colony of Sidon. Egyptian records from the 1300s BC listed the city as Djedunå (𓂧𓏏𓈖𓍯) while it was part of the Egyptian New Kingdom. It was likely occupied by Thutmose III with the rest of Canaan in 1457 BC.

23 Greek: Aalaph (ᴀᴀᴧᴀφ)

- Aleppo Codex: Åhlb (אחלב)

- Leningrad Codex: Achlav (אֲחְלָב)

- Targum Jerusalem: Achlav (אֲחְלָב)

24 Codex Vaticanus: Aschazi (ⲀⲤⲬⲀⲌⲒ)

- Codex Alexandrinus: Achazib (ⲀⲬⲀⲌⲒⲂ)

- Aleppo Codex: Åkzyb (אכזיב)

- Leningrad Codex: Achziv (אַכְזִיב)

- Targum Jerusalem: Achziv (אַכְזִיב)

Achzib was a major Canaanite city during the Egyptian New Kingdom Era. It was originally built between two rivers, however, by the Middle Bronze Age, the city extended from one river to the other, and the Canaanites dug a moat between the two rivers, effectively making the city into an island. The city was later transferred to King Hiram of Tyre by King Solomon and appears to have been independent of Israelite (Samaritan and Judahites) control until the Assyrians conquered it in 701 BC under King Sennacherib. The city of Achzib was located along the Mediterranean coast of modern Israel, north of Acre.

25 Codex Vaticanus: Nai (ⲚⲀⲒ)

- Codex Alexandrinus: Aphec (ⲀⲪⲈⲔ)

- Aleppo Codex: Åpyq (אפיק)

- Leningrad Codex: Afik (אֲפִיק)

- Targum Jerusalem: Afik (אֲפִיק)

The Codex Alexandrinus' Aphec appears to be a transliteration of the Hebrew åpyq, however, was most likely part of Lucian's redaction circa 300 AD, meaning the original Septuagint probably used the name Nai.

26 Codex Vaticanus: Ereô (ⲈⲢⲈⲰ)

- Codex Alexandrinus: Roôb (ⲢⲞⲰⲂ)

- Aleppo Codex: Rhb (רחב)

- Leningrad Codex: Rechov (רְחֹב)

- Targum Jerusalem: Rechov (רְחוֹב)

This location is not known today. There are the remains of another place called Rehob near Beth She'an, however, the ruins in question are not believed to be associated with this Rehob. There is also not an ancient site known as Ereo. The general assumption is that the location of this Rehob (or Ereo) was in Lebanon somewhere. As the name Roôb found in the Codex Alexandrinus is likely part of Lucian's redaction, and Ereo was likely the original name in the Septuagint, Ereo is used in this translation.

27 Greek: Baethsamys (ΒΑΙΘϹΑΜΥϹ)

• Aleppo Codex: Byt Šmš (בית שמש). Translation: house (or temple) of Shemesh (or sun)

• Leningrad Codex: veit-Shemesh (בֵית־שֶׁמֶשׁ). Translation: house (or temple) of Shemesh (or sun)

• Targum Jerusalem: veit Shemesh (בֵית שֶׁמֶשׁ). Translation: house (or temple) of Shemesh (or sun)

The modern city of Beit Shemesh (بيت شيمش / בֵּית שֶׁמֶשׁ) is located near the ancient site of the town, today called Tel Beit Shemesh. Shemesh was the Canaanite sun god, influenced by the Mesopotamian solar-god Shamesh. King Josiah of Judah banned the worship of Shemesh in circa 625 BC, along with the other Canaanite and early Israelite gods.

28 Codex Vaticanus: Baethanath (ΒΑΙΘΑΝΑΘ)

• Codex Alexandrinus: Baetheneth (ΒΑΙΘΕΝΕΘ)

• Aleppo Codex: Byt ônt (בית ענת). Translation: house (or temple) of Anat

• Leningrad Codex: veit-Anat (בֵית־עֲנָת). Translation: house (or temple) of Anat

• Targum Jerusalem: veit Anat (בֵית עֲנָת). Translation: house (or temple) of Anat

The location of Beth Anat is unknown today. Sites have been suggested in Lebanon, Galilee, and at the foot of Mount Hermon. Anat (𐤏𐤍𐤕) was a war goddess, and one of the major deities of Canaan. Anat was one of the key motivators of her brother Ba'al Hadad's rebellion against Yam (Sea) in the Canaanite Ba'al Cycle literature, dated to between 1450 and 1200 BC. She was also central to Ba'al's resurrection during his conflict with Mot (Death). Her worship had already been imported to Egypt during the Second Intermediate Period, currently dated to between 1650 and 1580 BC, and was part of Pharaoh Anat-Har's name, showing how important she was at the time.

She was integrated into the Egyptian pantheon as the daughter of Ptah, the creator-god. It is unclear which dynasty Anat-Har was a Pharaoh of, however, his name suggests he was a Canaanite or Hyksos Pharaoh. There are remains of temples dedicated to her dating from the Hyksos Dynasty in the ruins of Avaris (later Pi-Ramesses, and then Ramesses) and Memphis (now Cairo) in Egypt, and Beth She'an (later called Scythopolis) in Israel. The Temple of Anat in Avaris was taken over by later dynasties and expanded within the renamed city of Pi-Ramesses, and she continued to be a major Egyptian goddess throughout the New Kingdom. Anat later became synonymous with her Canaanite title Qetesh in Canaan, although Qetesh was adopted as a separate Goddess by the Egyptians. Qetesh was widely worshiped by the Israelites before King Josiah banned her worship in Judah circa 625 BC. The name Anat continued to be used by the Israelites in addition to her title Qetesh (Holiness), and was treated as the wife of Yhǔ (Yehvah) until at least the 5th century BC, as evidenced by the Elephantine papyri, which listed her as Anat-Yhǔ.

29 Codex Vaticanus: ori tô ostracôdi (ΟΡΕΙΤѠΟϹΤΡΑΚѠΔΕΙ). Translation: Mountains of earth (or pottery)

• Codex Alexandrinus: ori tou Myrsinônos (ΟΡΕΙ ΤΟΥ ΜΥΡϹΙΝѠΝΟϹ). Translation: Mountains of Myrsinônos (or myrtle)

• Aleppo Codex: bhr ḥrs (בהר חרס). Translation: mountain of destruction (or clay)

• Leningrad Codex: behar-cheres (בְּהַר־חֶרֶס). Translation: mountain of destruction (or clay)

• Targum Jerusalem: tur cheres (טוּר חֶרֶס). Translation: Mount Heres

As the name Codex Vaticanus is similar to the 'Mount Heres' of the Masoretic Text, that name is imported. However, it is not entirely clear what the name Heres means, as it is sometimes a reference to the underworld in Canaanite literature, but sometimes a reference to the sun or a sun-god in early Israelite literature. This may be an alternate or earlier translation of the northern Mount Hor from the Book of Joshua.

30 Codex Vaticanus: Myrsinôni (ΜΥΡϹΙΝѠΝΙ)

• Codex Alexandrinus: does not mention the Μυρσινωνι Mountains a second time, however, does mention the name earlier in the verse.

• Aleppo Codex: Åylǔn (אילון)

• Leningrad Codex: Ayyalovn (אַיָּלוֹן)

• Targum Jerusalem: Ayalon (אַיָלוֹן)

Ajalon was listed by Governor Adbi-Heba of Jerusalem as a town destroyed by invaders in the El-Amarna Letters circa 1330 BC. Prior to this, the town was considered Egyptian territory, however, this attack on Ayalon appears to be part of an ongoing process of territorial losses by the New Kingdom. Pharaoh Sheshonk I recaptured the region in 925 BC after the collapse of the United Kingdom of Israel.

31 Codex Vaticanus: Thalabin (ΘΑΛΑΒΙΝ).

• Codex Alexandrinus: does not mention the name Thalabin, Shaalbim, or any other variation in this verse.

• Aleppo Codex: Šôlbym (שעלבים)

• Leningrad Codex: Sha'alvim (שַׁעַלְבִים)

• Targum Jerusalem: Sha'alvim (שַׁעַלְבִים)

The ruins near the modern Israeli town of Šôlbym are believed to be the ruins of Shaalbim. As the Greek Thalabin appears to be a transliteration of Shaalbim, and the modern town is called Sha'alvim, that name is used in this translation.

32 Codex Vaticanus: Acrabin (ΑΚΡΑΒΙΝ)

• Aleppo Codex: ôqrbym (עקרבים). Translation: scorpions

• Leningrad Codex: akrabbim (עַקְרַבִּים). Translation: scorpions

• Targum Jerusalem: akra bim (עֲקַר בִּים). Translation: barren (or sterile) among

The location of the Ascent of Akrabbim has been debated for over 2000 years. The 1st century AD Jewish historian Flavius Josephus described the Ascent of Akrabbim as lying between Judea and Galilee in Samaria in *The Wars of the Jews* circa 75 AD:

> Now as to the country of Samaria, it lies between Judea and Galilee; it begins at a village that is in the great plain called Ginea, and ends at the Acrabbene toparchy, and is entirely of the same nature with Judea; for both countries are made up of hills and valleys, and are moist enough for agriculture, and are very fruitful.

33 Codex Vaticanus: Petras (ΠΕΤΡΑΣ). Translation: Petra (or stone)

• Aleppo Codex: Slô (סלע). Translation: stone

• Leningrad Codex: Sela (סֶלַע). Translation: stone

• Targum Jerusalem: keifa (כֵּיפָא). Translation: pressure

It is not clear from the Masoretic Text if the original author intended the city of Petra or not, however, the Greek translators did translate the term as the name of the city. The 1st century AD Jewish historian Flavius Josephus located the Torah's Kadesh Barnea at

Petra, which would mean that Petra was in the Hebrew texts before the era of Judges. A town called Sela was listed in the Amarna Letters from circa 1330 BC, which appears to be Petra. In the Amarna Letters, Sela was occupied by the Egyptians, however, does not appear to have been part of the Egyptian Empire before that time.

Judges: Chapter 2

The messenger of the lord[1] went up from the circle[2] to Bokim,[3] the Temple of El, and to the Temple of Israel,[4] and said to them, "The Lord says, 'I brought you up out of Egypt, and I brought you into the land which I swore to your fathers and I promised, "I will never break my covenant that I have made with you. You will make no covenant with those that live in this land, neither will you worship their gods. Instead, you will destroy their carved images, you will pull down their altars." But, you did not listen to my voice, and you did these things, and I said, "I will not drive them out from before you, but they will be distresses to you, and their gods will be an offense to you."'"

When the messenger of the lord spoke these words to the Israelites, the people raised their voices and wept. They renamed that place Bokim. They sacrificed to the Lord there, and Joshua dismissed the people, and they went each man to his inheritance, to inherit the land. The people served the Lord all the days of Joshua, and all the days of the elders that lived many days with Joshua, as many as knew all the great works of the Lord, what things he had worked in Israel. Joshua the son of Nun, the servant of the Lord, died at a hundred and ten years old. They buried him in the border of his inheritance, in Timnath Heres, in the mountains of Ephraim, on the north side of Mount Gaash. All that generation was laid with their fathers, and another generation rose up after them, who did not know the Lord, nor the work which he did for Israel. The Israelites worked evil before the Lord and served the Ba'als.[5] They forgot the Lord God[6] of their fathers, who brought them out of the land of Egypt, and followed other gods, the gods of the nations around them, and they worshiped them. They provoked the Lord, and forgot him, and served Ba'al[7] and Astarte.[8] The Lord was very angry with Israel, and he gave them into the hands of plunderers, and they ruined them. He sold them into the hands of their enemies around them, and they could no longer resist their enemies, among whoever they went, and the hand of the Lord was evilly against them. As the Lord had promised, and as the Lord had sworn to them, he punished them greatly. Then the Lord raised up judges, and the Lord saved them out of the hands of those that plundered them, and yet they did not listen to the judges, and they went whoring after other gods and worshiped them. They turned quickly from how their fathers walked when they listen to the words of the Lord. The Lord raised judges among them, and the Lord was with the judges and saved them out of the hand of their enemies all the days of the judges because the Lord was moved by their moaning caused by those that besieged them and attacked them. When the judges died, they went back and again corrupted themselves worse than their fathers, going after other gods to serve them and to worship them. They did not abandon their devices or their stubborn ways. The Lord was very angry with Israel, and said, "Since this nation has forgotten my covenant which I commanded their fathers, and has not listened to my voice, I will never again drive out a man from the nations in front of them, which Joshua the son of Nun left in the land."

The Lord left them to see if Israel would keep the way of the Lord, and follow it like their fathers had or not. So the Lord left these nations and did not drive them out suddenly, and he did not deliver them into the hand of Joshua.

Judges: Chapter 2 Notes

1 Codex Vaticanus: angelos cyriou (ΑΓΓΕΛΟΣΚΥΡΙΟΥ). Translation: messenger lord

- Aleppo Codex: mlǎk Yhủh (מלאך יהוה). Translation: messenger Yhủh

- Leningrad Codex: mal'ach-Yehvah (מַלְאַד־יְהֹוָה). Translation: messenger Yehwah

- Targum Jerusalem: kodam yeyah (קֳדָם יְי?). Translation: advance of Yhủ

2 Codex Vaticanus: Galgal (ΓΑΛΓΑΛ)

- Aleppo Codex: glgl (גלגל). Translation: circle

- Leningrad Codex: gilgal (גִּלְגָּל). Translation: circle

- Targum Jerusalem: gilgela (גִּלְגְּלָא)

Gilgal (גִּלְגָּל) is the Hebrew word for circle. Archaeologists have discovered several ceremonial stone circles in Canaan that were used between 1200 and 1000 BC for gatherings that are assumed to be religious in nature. As these stone circles are found down in the valleys, unlike the altars at the tops of hills where the Canaanites worshiped, and 'circles' (גלגל) are mentioned throughout the old Hebrew texts, it is assumed they are early Israelite religious centers from before the First Temple was built. According to the Book of Joshua, the Israelites built a stone circle in Samaria after invading Canaan in approximately 1508 BC.

3 Codex Vaticanus: Clauthmôna (ΚΛΑΥΘΜΩΝΑ). Translation: weepings

- Aleppo Codex: bkym (**בכים**). Translation: cryings

- Leningrad Codex: bochim (בֹּכִים). Translation: cryings

- Targum Jerusalem: Bochim (בּוֹכִים)

As the Greek translation appears to be a translation of the Hebrew name, the Hebrew name is used in this translation.

4 Codex Vaticanus: oecon Israêl (ΟΙΚΟΝΙϹΡΑΗΛ). Translation: home (or house, or temple) of Israel

This reference is missing from the Masoretic version of Judges, however, as it was referring to the Samaritan temple on or near Mount Gerizim, it would have been removed. Assuming this is part of the original text of Judges, it supports the Samaritan claim that the original Israelite temple built in Canaan was on Mount Gerizim, before the building of King Solomon's Temple. Conversely, this may be viewed as evidence that the Greeks translated a Samaritan copy of Judges, however, it is unlikely that any Samaritan copies have been translated into Aramaic, as the Samaritans never abandoned the old Canaanite dialect of Samaria or the Phoenician script.

5 Greek: Baalim (ΒΑΑΛΙΜ)

- Aleppo Codex: bôlym (**בעלים**). Translation: the lords (or the masters, the husbands)

- Leningrad Codex: be'alim (בְּעָלִים). Translation: the lords (or the masters, the husbands)

- Targum Jerusalem: ba'alaya (בַּעֲלַיָּא). Translation: lords

The term Ba'al was an ancient Semitic term that was used to denote lords or gods of Canaan.

6 Codex Vaticanus: ton c̄n ton t̄h̄n (ΤΟΝΚ̄ΝΤΟΝΘ̄Ν). Translation: the Lord the God

- Codex Alexandrinus: ton cyrion theon (ΤΟΝΚΥΡΙΟΝΘΕΟΝ). Translation: the Lord God

- Aleppo Codex: åt yhůh ålhy (**את יהוה אלהי**). Translation: the Yhůh god

- Leningrad Codex: et-Yehvah | elohei (אֶת־יְהוָה \ אֱלֹהֵי). Translation: the Yehwah. God

- Targum Jerusalem: dayeyah elaha (דַיְי אֱלָהָא). Translation: from Yhů god

The name Yhŭ (יהו) was transliterated as Iaô (Ιαω) in some books of the Septuagint, which was later transliterated as Iaw by the Pre-Christian Romans. In later copies of the Septuagint, the name was replaced by the name written in Canaanite (𐤉𐤄𐤅𐤄) or Assyrian script (יהוה). There are no early surviving copies of the Septuagint's version of Judges which have the name Iaô (Ιαω) in it, like some of the other books of the Septuagint, and therefore it cannot be proven conclusively if the name was in the Septuagint's Judges or not, however, a number of other books in the Septuagint appear to retain older versions of the Hebrew scriptures that pre-date the redaction during the Hasmonean dynasty, which replaced many older names of gods with Yehvah or Yehvah tzeva'ovt, the national god of Hasmonean Judea. The Aramaic sections of Masoretic Daniel that were not translated into Hebrew maintain the term adonai ha'elohim (אֲדֹנִי הָאֱלֹהִים), meaning the 'Lord the gods' where the Septuagint has 'Lord the god' (Κύριον τὸν θεὸν), however, the Hebrew sections have Yehvah elohim (יְהוָה אֱלֹהִים) where the Septuagint has 'Lord the god,' suggesting the Greek more accurately reflects the Aramaic source texts than the Hebrew translation.

According to tractate Sanhedrin (103b) in the Talmud, King Manasseh was blamed for removing the name, however, as his grandson Josiah 'restored' the Torah circa 625 BC, one would expect that he would have restored the name as well, if it had have been in Exodus to begin with. Furthermore, the early Torah appears to have already been translated into Aramaic during the era of Manasseh's father king Hezekiah, suggesting that he removed the name during his religious reforms.

7 Codex Vaticanus: Ba'al (ΒΑΑΛ)

- Aleppo Codex: bôl (בעל). Translation: lord (or master, or husband)

- Leningrad Codex: ba'al (בָּעַל). Translation: lord (or master, or husband)

- Targum Jerusalem: va'ala (בְעָלָא). Translation: lord (or master, or husband)

While Ba'al was a title applied to many Canaanite gods, when used as a name, it referred to Ba'al Hadad, the storm god, and hero of the Ba'al Cycle literature of ancient Canaan.

8 Codex Vaticanus: Astartaes (ΑϹΤΑΡΤΑΙϹ)

- Aleppo Codex: Ôštrŭt (עשתרות)

- Leningrad Codex: Ashtarovt (עַשְׁתָּרֹות)

- Targum Jerusalem: Ashtarata (עֲשְׁתָּרְתָא)

Astarte was the Greek name the Canaanite of Ashtoreth and Mesopotamian Ishtar. Ashtoreth was the Canaanite goddess of love, sex, war, and the planet Venus. Local versions of her were worshiped throughout the Middle East and the Mediterranean Sea. In Akkadian, he was a god known as Asdartu, while in Babylonia she was known as Ishtar, in Ugaritic she was known as 'Athtart, and in Etruscan, she was known as Uni-Astre. The Greek goddess Aphrodite appears to be derived from an early version of her, while the Roman goddess appears to be derived indirectly through the Etruscan Uni-Astre. The Aramean transgender deity Atargatis appears to be another early offshoot that maintained the early male aspect of the god from the Akkadian era while accepting that the god had become a goddess. During the New Kingdom era of Egyptian history, circa 1549 tom 1077 AD, Astarte was incorporated into the Egyptian pantheon as one of the daughters of Ra, as she appeared in the book entitled the 'Contest between Horus and Set.' According to the Phoenician scholar Sanchuniathon, who supposedly lived circa 1200 BC, Astarte's sister was Asherah, who was also known as Anat. The word Asherah also appears in the Septuagint many times and appears to be widely worshiped by the early Israelites.

Judges: Chapter 3

These are the nations which the Lord left to test Israel with, all that had not known the wars of Canaan, for the sake of the generations of Israel, to teach them war. The men before them did not know them. The five lords of the foreigners,[1] and all the Canaanites, Sidonians, and Mitanni[2] who lived in Lebanon from Mount Hermon[3] to the entrance of Hama.[4] This was done to test Israel, to know whether they would obey the commands of the Lord, which he ordered their fathers through the hand of Moses. The Israelites lived among the Canaanites, Cypriots, Amorites, Perizzites, Mitannians, and Jebusites. They took their daughters as wives for themselves, and they gave their daughters to their sons and served their gods.

The Israelites did evil in the sight of the Lord, and forgot the Lord God, and served Ba'als and Asherahs.[5] The Lord was very angry with Israel and sold them into the hand of the Kassite Barattarna,[6] king of the Syrian rivers,[7] and the Israelites served the Kassite Barattarna eight years. The Israelites cried to the Lord, and the Lord raised a savior for Israel, and he saved them, Othniel the son of Kenez, the younger brother of Caleb. The spirit of the Lord came on him, and he judged Israel, and he went out to war against the Kassite Barattarna, and the Lord delivered into his hand the Kassite Barattarna king of the Syrian rivers, and his hand prevailed against the Kassite Barattarna. The land was peaceful for forty years, and Othniel the son of Kenez died.

The Israelites continued to do evil before the Lord, and the Lord strengthened Moab against Israel because they had done evil before the Lord. He gathered to himself all Ammonites and Amalekites, and went and attacked Israel, and occupied the city of palm-trees. The Israelites served Eglon the king of Moab for eighteen years. The Israelites cried to the Lord, and he raised for them a savior, Ehud the son of Gera, a Benjamite, a man who used both hands alike, and the Israelites sent gifts by his hand to Eglon king of Moab. Ehud made himself a double-edged dagger a span long, and he hid it under his cloak on his right thigh. He went and brought the presents to Eglon king of Moab, and Eglon was a very fat man.[8] When Ehud had finished offering his gifts, he dismissed those that brought the gifts. He returned from the quarries that were by the circle, and Ehud said, "I have a secret message for you, king!"

Eglon replied to him, "Be quiet, and he sent away from his presence all who waited on him."

Ehud went to him, and they sat in his upper summer chamber all alone, and Ehud said, "I have a message from God for you, my king," and Eglon rose up from his throne near him. As he arose, Ehud stretched out his left hand, and took the dagger from his right thigh, and plunged it into his stomach, and drove in also the haft behind the blade, and the fat closed in on the blade, as he did not pull out the dagger from his belly. Ehud went out to the porch, and collapsed out by the guards stationed there, and shut the doors of the chamber on him, and locked them. He went out, and Eglon's servants came and saw, and the doors of the upper chamber were locked, and they asked, "Does he not uncover his feet in the summer chamber? They waited until they were embarrassed, and no one opened the doors of the upper chamber. They took the key, and opened them, and found their lord had fallen dead on the ground.

Ehud escaped while they were in chaos, and no one paid attention to him, and he passed the quarries and escaped to Seirah.[9] It happened when Ehud came into the land of Israel, that he blew the horn on Mount Ephraim, and the Israelites came down with him from the mountain. He led them and said, "Come down after me, for the Lord God has delivered our enemies, Moab, into our hands!"

They went down after him and occupied the fords of the Jordan en route to Moab, and he did not allow a man to pass over. They slaughtered about ten thousand Moabites on that day, every lusty person and every mighty man, and not a man escaped. Moab was humbled on that day under the hand of Israel, and the land had peace for eighty years, and Ehud judged them until he died.

After him rose up Shamgar the son of Anat, and slaughtered six hundred Pelesets with a plowshare, like one drawn by oxen, and he too saved Israel.

Judges: Chapter 3 Notes

1 Greek: allophylôn (ΑΛΛΟΦΥΛΩΝ). Translation: foreigners (or strangers, aliens)

• Aleppo Codex: plštym (פלשתים). Translation: Philistines (or Palestinians, Peleset)

• Leningrad Codex: Felishtim (פְּלִשְׁתִּים). Translation: Philistines (or Palestinians, Peleset)

• Targum Jerusalem: Pelishta'ei (פְּלִשְׁתָּאֵי). Translation: Philistines (or Palestinians, Peleset)

The Pelesets were an ancient people based in the region of the modern Gaza Strip of the Palestinian Territories. The earliest surviving mention of them is from the reliefs of the Temple of Ramses III at Medinet Habu in Egypt that dates back to some time between 1186 and 1155 BC, in which they were called Pelesets (𓊪𓃭𓈙𓏏𓈖𓀀𓏥). They were also known in Middle Babylonian as the ᵏᵘʳPalastu (𒆳𒉺𒆷𒀸𒌈). It is unclear where they came from, however, one theory is that they were the Pala, a Luwian people from the Black Sea coast of Anatolia. The region was an independent country called Palaa (𒆳𒉺𒆷𒀀) in the Neshite (Hittite) records from the 1600s BC, however, have become part of the Nesite Empire by the 1500s BC. Around the time the Pelesets invaded Canaan, the Pala were driven from their homeland by the neighboring Kaskians from northeast Anatolia, which supports the connection between the groups, however, it has yet to be proven conclusively. The presence of the Pelesets in Southern Canaan during the time of Abraham and Isaac is anachronistic, and therefore this section of text, describing the origin of the Semitic tribes, found in both the Septuagint and the Masoretic Text, likely dates to the original Phoenician translation in the early Iron Age.

2 Greek: Euaion (ΕΥΑΙΟΝ)

- Aleppo Codex: Hůy (חוי)

- Leningrad Codex: Chivvi (חִוִּי)

- Targum Jerusalem: Chiva'ei (חִוָאֵי). Translation: farmer

The term is believed to have been derived from the name of the Hurrians, however, is derived separately from the other term Chori (חֹרִי). As the Hivites are routinely reported to be rulers, the term appears to represent the Mitanni-Aryan nobility or Vedic priests. As the Mitanni Empire lost its Canaanite territory circa 1350 BC, the original text of Judges must date back to before that time.

3 Codex Vaticanus: orous tou Aermôn (ΟΡΟΥΣΤΟΥΑΕΡΜΩΝ). Translation: mountain of Hermon

- Codex Alexandrinus: orous tou Balaermôn (ΟΡΟΥΣΤΟΥΒΑΛΑΕΡΜΩΝ). Translation: mountain of Balaermon

- Aleppo Codex: hr Bôl Hrmůn (הר בעל חרמון). Translation: mountain of Lord Hermon

- Leningrad Codex: har Ba'al Chermovn (הַר בַּעַל חֶרְמֹון). Translation: mountain of Lord Hermon

- Targum Jerusalem: tur meishar Chermovn (טור מֵישַׁר חֶרְמֹון). Translation: mountain of the prince (or commander) of Hermon

The location of Ba'al-Hermon in the Masoretic Text and Codex Alexandrinus is unclear, however, the Codex Vaticanus indicates it was Mount Hermon, on the modern Israeli-

Lebanese-Syrian border. Mount Hermon was the location where the Watchers descended to Earth in the Enochian Book of the Watchers. It is also the location of the Anaks in the Book of Joshua, which appears to be a reference to the descendants of the Watchers. The Egyptians listed a people known as the Anaq living in the region between 2300 and 1700 BC, which are accepted as being the same people the Israelites called the Anaks. The ruins of over 30 temples have been discovered on Mount Hermon, including a rock-cut temple of the summit called Qasr Antar, which may date back to the Anak civilization.

4 Codex Vaticanus: Labôemath (ΛΑΒωΕΜΑΘ)

• Codex Alexandrinus: Lobôêmath (ΛΟΒωΗΜΑΘ)

• Aleppo Codex: lbůå Ḥmt (לְבוֹא חמת). Translation: entrance to Hama

• Leningrad Codex: levov Chamat (לְבוֹא חֲמָת). Translation: entrance to Hama

• Targum Jerusalem: ma'alana daChamat (מְעַלְנָא דַחֲמָת). Translation: gateway of Hama

The Greeks transliterated the word meaning 'entrance' as part of the name, and therefore the Masoretic version of the name is used in this translation. Hama is a major city in western Syria north of Lebanon that had been inhabited since around 6000 BC. It was under the control of the Mitanni Empire between 1500 and 1350 BC.

5 Codex Vaticanus: toes alsesin (ΤΟΙϹΑΛϹΕϹΙΝ). Translation: the sacred groves

• Aleppo Codex: åšrůt (אשרות). Translation: Asherahs

• Leningrad Codex: Asherovt (אֲשֵׁרוֹת). Translation: Asherahs

• Targum Jerusalem: Asharata (אֲשֵׁרָתָא). Translation: Asherahs

Asherah was the wife of the Canaanite god El, and Mesopotamian god An (Anu), and the mother of the Canaanite gods. The Asherahs in question were likely sacred oak trees dedicated to Asherah, similar to the sacred acacia trees dedicated to Iusaaset in Egypt. Iusaaset was the wife of Atum, the Egyptian creator god of Heliopolis that served as the basis of Moses' creator god, and Egyptian equivalent of Ba'al Shalim, the Canaanite god that Jerusalem was named after.

6 Codex Vaticanus: Chousarsathaem (ΧΟΥϹΑΡϹΑΘΑΙΜ)

• Codex Alexandrinus: Chousarsathôm (ΧΟΥϹΑΡϹΑΘωΜ)

• Aleppo Codex: kůšn ršôtym (כושן רשעתים)

- Leningrad Codex: kushan rish'atayim (כּוּשַׁן רִשְׁעָתַיִם)

- Targum Jerusalem: Kushan chayava (כּוּשָׁן חַיָּבָא). Translation: Kushan sinner (or debtor, stammerer, legal heir)

While the Hebrew term Kush (כוש) referred to the land of Kush, south of Egypt, whose people were known as the Kushi (כּוּשִׁי), Kushan (כּוּשָׁן) was a different term, which the Greeks did not recognize, and therefore transliterated as Chousa (Χουσα). As the term referred to someone who was the king in thee rivers of Aram (Syria), the origin of the word was almost certainly Kasium (𒅗𒀸𒅆𒌑𒈬), today translated as Kassite. The Kassites were the rulers of Babylonia in the late bronze age from some time in the 1500s BC, until 1155 BC, when they were conquered by the Elamites. The Hebrew term rishatayim (רִשְׁעָתַיִם) is not proper Hebrew, Canaanite, or Aramaic, however, may be a corruption of the term resha'im (רְשָׁעִים), meaning 'criminals.' Alternatively, this may be the ancient Canaanite spelling of the name of king Paarshataar (𒉺𒅈𒊭𒋫𒀀𒌚), more commonly transliterated as Barattarna today, king of the Mitanni Empire circa 1485 BC. Barattarna is recorded as occupying northern Canaan during the reign of Hatshepsut by establishing a series of puppet states across the region, and gaining access to the Mediterranean Sea.

In circa 1479 BC, the Egyptian king Thutmose II died, and his former queen Hatshepsut seized the throne in the name of his two year old son Thutmose III. Hatshepsut was not the mother of Thutmose III, another wife Iset was, whom Hatshepsut married after officially changing her sex to male. After changing genders Hatshepsut declared himself to be Thutmose III's regent, although later assumed the role of king himself until his death, when Thutmose III inherited the throne. While Hatshepsut was a very unpopular king, his rule established the dominant architectural style of the New Kingdom. The entire concept of a female king was rejected by many, with graffiti mocking King Hatshepsut's gender appearing in archaeological records of the era. Most of Kush appears to have rejected Hatshepsut, and rebelled against his rule. After inheriting the throne in circa 1458 BC, Thutmose III attempted to erase Hatshepsut's rule from Egyptian records, claiming to have ruled continuously from the death of Thutmose II in circa 1479 BC. While her role as queen of Thutmose II was never erased, the era when Hatshepsut ruled Egypt was, and his era as king was not rediscovered until the 1800s.

It is clear that there was a rebellion against King Hatshepsut in Syria, backed by the Mitanni, and control of all territory north of Megiddo was lost, as the first thing Thutmose III did after assuming the throne was march north into Canaan, where he fought the battle of Megiddo against the rebelling Syrian kings, and their Mitanni allies. The Battle of Megiddo was the largest battle recorded in Egyptian records up until that time, with both the Egyptians and Canaanite rebels estimated to have fielded around

1,000 chariots and 10,000 infantry. After defeating the Canaanites in the initial battle, the Egyptians plundered 924 chariots and 200 suits of armor. The Canaanite kings fell back to the fortified city of Kadesh, which the Egyptians then besieged for seven months. According to the records at Karnak, when the city surrendered the Egyptians captured 340 Canaanite and Mitanni princes, 2,041 mares, 191 foals, 6 stallions, 924 chariots, 200 suits of armor, 502 bows, 1,929 cattle, and 22,500 sheep.

Between 1458 and 1425 BC, Thutmose III fought a series of campaigns in Canaan, pushing Egyptian control north to the Euphrates River, and then crossed it into the Mitanni empire, where he plundered the country, which apparently had not rebuilt its defenses after the loss at Megiddo. After securing Canaan, Thutmose III marched his army south into Nubia, recapturing territory as far as the fourth cataract, all of which had been lost under the rule of Hatshepsut.

It is unclear why the author would have referred to Barattarna as a Kassite unless it was actually written at the time. The Mitanni rulers are often linked to the Kassites culturally, however, the peoples they ruled were not culturally similar. During the wars of Thutmose III in Canaan, the term Mitanni become common, however, earlier records simply called the land Naharin, meaning 'Rivers,' and called the people Hurrians. While the Hurrians were the primary population of the Mitanni Empire, the rulers were an unrelated group of Indo-Aryans, who spoke a language similar to Sanskrit, and worshiped the Vedic gods. They appear to have seized power over the Hurrians in the Khabur river region in the 1550s BC, from which they expanded in every direction until the Battle of Megiddo.

The Mitanni relationship with the Kassites is unclear, as the Kassites are not viewed as being Indo-Aryans, however, may have been Hurrians. The two cultures were close at the time, and it is plausible that the earliest Mitanni to arrive in the region were viewed as being Kassites by the Canaanites. Nevertheless, by 1457 BC the term would have already been anachronistic, as the term Mitanni would have replaced it, suggesting this verse was written between 1472 and 1457 BC. As the actions of King Barattarna correlate with what Rishatayim is described as doing in the verse, his name is used in this translation, however, it is plausible it was simply a reference to the rebels.

7 Codex Vaticanus: basileôs Syrias potamôn (ΒΑϹΙΛΕΩϹϹΥΡΙΑϹΠΟΤΑΜΩΝ). Translation: king of the Syrian rivers

- Aleppo Codex: mlk Årm nhrym (מלך ארם נהרים). Translation: king of Aram's rivers

- Leningrad Codex: melech Aram naharayim (מֶלֶךְ אֲרַם נַהֲרָיִם). Translation: king of Aram's rivers

- Targum Jerusalem: malka da'Aram di al Perat (מַלְכָּא דַאֲרָם דִי עַל פְּרָת). Translation:

king of Aram (or Syria) on the Euphrates

The region in question is northern-most modern Syria, and south-east Turkey north of Syria, which was occupied by the Egyptians between 1505 and 1480 BC, and again between 1457 and 1350 BC. The Egyptian name was Naharin, which had been adopted from the local Aramaic word meaning 'rivers.' At the time specified in the Septuagint's chronology, between 1480 and 1472 BC, this was the Mitanni king Barattarna.

8 Codex Vaticanus: Eglôm anêr astios sphodra (ⲉⲅⲗⲱⲙ ⲁⲛⲏⲣ ⲁⲥⲧⲉⲓⲟⲥ ⲥⲫⲟⲇⲣⲁ). Translation: Elgom was a very handsome (or cosmopolitan, elegant) man

• Aleppo Codex: ôglŭn åyš bryå måd (עֶגְלוֹן אִישׁ בָּרִיא מְאֹד). Translation: Eglon was a very healthy (or very fat, lusty) man

• Leningrad Codex: Eglovn ish bari me'od (עֶגְלוֹן אִישׁ בָּרִיא מְאֹד). Translation: Eglon was a very healthy (or very fat, lusty) man

• Targum Jerusalem: Eglon gevar fatim lachada (עֶגְלוֹן גְּבַר פַּטִים לַחֲדָא). Translation: Eglon was a powerful (or strong) perfumed (or fat) one

The Greeks appear to have translated fat (בָּרִיא) as handsome (αστειος) assuming this was a homosexual encounter, however, the Hebrew term implies the man was either healthy or fat or lusty, and later he is confirmed as being very fat.

9 Codex Vaticanus: Setirôtha (ⲥⲉⲧⲓⲣⲱⲑⲁ)

• Codex Alexandrinus: Sirôtha (ⲥⲉⲓⲣⲱⲑⲁ)

• Aleppo Codex: Šôyrth (שְׂעִירָתָה)

• Leningrad Codex: Se'iratah (שְׂעִירָתָה)

• Targum Jerusalem: Se'irata (שְׂעִירָתָא)

The Greek and Hebrew names appear to be transliterations of the same name, assumed to be an ancient town in the mountains of Ephraim.

Judges: Chapter 4

The Israelites continued to do evil against the Lord after Ehud was dead. The Lord sold the Israelites into the hand of Jabin the king of Canaan who ruled from Hazor,[1] and the chief of the army was Siazara,[2] who lived in the Forge-of-the-Foreigners.[3] The Israelites cried to the Lord because he had nine hundred iron chariots, and he mightily oppressed Israel twenty years. Deborah was a prophetess and the wife of Lapidoth who judged Israel at that time. She sat under the Palm Tree of Deborah between Ramah[4] and Bethel in the mountains of Ephraim, and the Israelites went up to her for judgment.

Deborah sent and called Barak the son of Abinoam out of Kadesh Naphtali, and she asked him, "Has not the Lord God of Israel commanded you, 'Go to Mount Tabor, and take ten thousand men of the Naphtalites and Zebulonites. I will bring to you to the Kishion river, where Siazara the captain of the army of Jabin and his chariots and his multitude are, and I will deliver them into your hands?'"

Barak answered her, "If you will go with me, I will go, and if you will not go, I will not go, as I don't know the day to which the Lord sends his messenger to me."

She replied, "I will certainly go with you, but know that your victory will not depend on the expedition you undertake, for the Lord will sell Siazara into the hands of a woman."

Deborah left Kadesh with Barak. Barak called the Zebulonites and Naphtalites out of Kadesh, and 10,000 men went up with him, and Deborah also went up with him. Eber the blacksmith[5] who remained of the blacksmiths,[6] descended from the sons of Jobab, the son-in-law of Moses,[7] pitched his tent by the oak of the covetous ones, which is near Kedesh. Siazara was told that Barak the son of Abinoam had gone up to Mount Tabor. Siazara summoned all his chariots, nine hundred iron chariots, and all the people with him from the Forge-of-the-Foreigners to the Kishion river.

Deborah said to Barak, "Rise, for this is the day on which the Lord has delivered Siazara into your hand. The Lord will go out before you," and Barak went down from Mount Tabor and 10,000 men with him.

The Lord discomfited Siazara, and all his chariots, and army, with the edge of the sword before Barak, and Siazara fell off his chariot and fled on foot. Barak chased after the chariots and army, to the Forge-of-the-Foreigners, and the whole army of Siazara fell by the edge of the sword, and there was no one left. Siazara fled on foot to the tent of Jael the wife of Eber the blacksmith his friend, for there was peace between Jabin king of Hazor and the house of Eber the blacksmith. Jael went out to meet Siazara, and said to him, "Turn aside my lord, turn aside to me, don't be afraid."

He turned aside to her into the tent, and she covered him with a mantle. Siazara said to her, "Give me, I beg you, a little water to drink, for I am thirsty," and she opened a jug of milk, and gave it to him drink, and covered him.

Siazara told her, "Stand now by the door of the tent, and it will come to pass if any man comes to you, and asks, 'Is there a man here?' Then answer, 'There is not.'"

Jael the wife of Eber took a tent spike and a hammer in her hands, and went secretly to him and held the spike to his temple and drove it through into the ground, and he collapsed, and darkness fell on him and he died. Barak was chasing Siazara, and Jael went out to meet him, and said to him, "Come, and I will take you to the man who you are looking for."

He went with her and saw Siazara was dead, and the spike was in his temple. So God destroyed Jabin king of Canaan on that day before the Israelites. The hand of the Israelites prevailed more and more against King Jabin of Canaan until they completely destroyed King Jabin of Canaan.

Judges: Chapter 4 Notes

1 Codex Vaticanus: Asôr (ᴀⲥⲱⲣ)

- Aleppo Codex: Hṣŭr (חצור)

- Leningrad Codex: Chatzovr (חָצֹ֖ור)

- Targum Jerusalem: Chatzovr (חָצֹור)

Hazor was a major town north of the Sea of Galilee for thousands of years, from at least 2700 BC to the Greek era. The town was mentioned in the Egyptian Execration Texts from the 1700s BC, the Mari Archive of the 1600s BC, the Annals of Thutmoses III in the 1400s BC, the Amarna Letters of the 1300s, and the Papyrus Anastasi I from the 1200s BC. Between 1800 and 1550 BC, the town was a vassal of the city of Qatna, in modern Syria. Hazor was officially annexed by the New Egyptian Empire in 1457 BC when Pharaoh Thutmose III's armies passed through Canaan en route to Syria, however, continued to be governed by local kings subject to the empire. The Amarna Letters include correspondence between the King of Hazor and Pharaoh Akhenaten, specifically EA227 and EA228, the second one mentioning the name of the King of Hazor as being Abdi-Tirshi of 'Hasura.'

These Letters are broadly dated with the rest as being written between 1350 and 1330 BC. According to the chronology of the Septuagint, the era that Jabin of Hazor ruled the Israelites was 1334 to 1314 BC, implying he was appointed by Smenkhkare, Neferneferuaten, or Tutankhamen in the aftermath of Akhenaten's reign (1351 to 1334 BC), or by Siazara when he claimed the throne. This implies that the Judges Ehud and Shamgar were close to the Egyptian crown during their periods as Judge, which would have taken place during the reigns of Amenhotep II, Thutmose IV, Amenhotep III, and Akhenaten.

2 Codex Vaticanus: Sisara (ϲιϲαρα)

- Aleppo Codex: Sysrå (סיסרא)

- Leningrad Codex: Sisra (סִיסְרָא)

- Targum Jerusalem: Sisra (סִיסְרָא)

This name appears to have been the Egyptian name Siazârô (𓋴𓄿𓇳𓏤), meaning 'recognized son of Ra,' however, this specific name would have denoted a king from either southern Egypt or Nubia, and Siazara is otherwise unknown from regal records. As Siazara is described as commanding an army with 900 iron chariots, this appears to be the Egyptian army stationed in Canaan. Based on the chronologies in the Septuagint's Exodus, Joshua, and Judges, Siazara would have been the commander of the Egyptian forces in Canaan sometime between 1334 to 1314 BC. Iron weapons and chariots had been introduced by the Hyksos dynasty, and the Egyptians of the New Kingdom did use some iron weapons for their military, however, it is not clear if they were still using iron chariots, or have reverted to bronze chariots. It is not known where they were smithing their iron weapons, however, it was not in Egypt and believed to have been somewhere in Canaan or Nubia. This may have been at Site 200 in the Timna Valley, in southern Israel's Arabah region. Site 200 is an iron smelting site worked by Egyptians during the Egyptian New Kingdom era.

3 Codex Vaticanus: Arisôth tôn ethnôn (αριϲωθτωνεθνων). Translation: Arisoth the Nations

- Aleppo Codex: hršt hgůym (חרשת הגוים)

- Leningrad Codex: charoshet hagGovyim (חֲרֹשֶׁת הַגּוֹיִם). Translation: the forge of the foreigners

- Targum Jerusalem: tekof kerakkei ammaya (תְּקוֹף כְּרַכֵּי עַמְמַיָא). Translation: fortified (or strong) large city of the commoners (or peoples)

The term govyim (גּוֹיִם), translated as 'tribes' (εθνων) in Greek and 'commoners' (עַמְמַיָא) in the Targum Jerusalem, was originally adopted from the Akkadian name of the Gutium (𒆳𒄖𒋾𒌝) tribe who lived in the Zagros mountains during the Akkadian and Neo-Sumerian eras. During the Middle Babylonian era, the setting of Judges, the term began being applied to the Indo-European tribes that entered Mesopotamia from the Zagros mountains, including the Kassites, who seized control of Babylon, and then ruled Babylonia for centuries. The only peoples in Canaan likely to be identified as Gutium were the Hyksos and Mitanni. The Smith of the Gutium is described as being the fortress that Siazara's army was based out of. It seems likely the fortress was inherited from the Hyksos Dynasty which built several fortresses in Canaan.

4 Codex Vaticanus: Rama (ρΑΜΑ)

- Aleppo Codex: Rmh (רמה)

- Leningrad Codex: Ramah (רָמֶה)

- Targum Jerusalem: Yricho pardesin beramata zeitin avedin meshach bevik'ata beit shakya (יְרִיחוֹ פַּרְדְסִין בְּרָמָתָא זֵיתִין עָבְדִין מְשַׁח בְּבִקְעָתָא בֵּית שָׁקְיָא). Translation: Jericho's orchards (or walled gardens) and Ramah's olives, creators of perfume in the valley of Beth Shakya

A town called Ramah was located near Gibeah in the Book of Joshua.

5 Codex Vaticanus: Chaber o Cinaeos (ΧΑΒΕρΟΚΙΝΑΙΟϹ). Translation: Chaber the Cinaeos

- Codex Alexandrinus: plêsion tou Cinaeou (ΠΛΗϹΙΟΝΤΟΥΚΙΝΑΙΟΥ). Translation: near the Cinaeou

- Aleppo Codex: Ḥbr hqyny (חבר הקיני). Translation: Ḥbr the Kenite (or smith)

- Leningrad Codex: Chever hakkeini (חֶבֶר הַקֵּינִי). Translation: Ḥeber the Kenite (or smith)

- Targum Jerusalem: Chever Shalma'ah (חֶבֶר שַׁלְמָאָה). Translation: Ḥeber Shalmaite

As the term Kenite means blacksmith, he is referred to him as 'Heber the blacksmith' in this translation. The Shalmaites mentioned in the Jerusalem Targum were a tribe of arabs from the late-Classical era, 2000 years after the era the book is set in.

6 Codex Vaticanus: Caena (ΚΑΙΝΑ)

- Codex Alexandrinus: the term is omitted from the verse

- Aleppo Codex: qyn (קֵיִן). Translation: smith, metalworker, blacksmith

- Leningrad Codex: kayin (קַיִן). Translation: smith, metalworker, blacksmith

- Targum Jerusalem: Shalma'ei (שַׁלְמָאֵי). Translation: Shalmaites

7 Codex Vaticanus: Iôbab gambrou Môysê (ΙΩΒΑΒΓΑΜΒΡΟΥΜΩΥϹΗ). Translation: Jobab bridegroom of Moses

- Aleppo Codex: Ḥbb ḥtn Mšh (חבב חתן משה). Translation: Hbb groom Moses

- Leningrad Codex: Chovav choten Mosheh (חֹבָב חֹתֵן מֹשֶׁה). Translation: Hobab groom Moses

- Targum Jerusalem: Chovav chamuhi deMosheh (חוֹבָב חֲמוּהִי דְמֹשֶׁה). Translation: Hobab in the house of Moses

Judges: Chapter 5

Deborah and Barak ben Abinoam, sang on that day:

A revelation was made in Israel when the people were made willing!

Praise you, Lord!

Listen you kings! Listen governors,[1] and I will sing!

I will sing to the Lord! I will!

I will sing a psalm to the Lord God of Israel!

Lord, in your going out on Seir, when you went out of the land of Edom, the earth quaked and the sky dropped dew, and the cloud rained.

The mountains were shaken before the face of the Lord, the Sinai before the face of the Lord God of Israel.

In the days of Shamgar son of Anath, in the days of Jael, they deserted the ways and became perverse.

The mighty men in Israel failed, they failed until Deborah arose as a mother for Israel.

They chose new gods, then the rulers of cities fought, and there was no shield or spear seen among forty thousand Israelites.

My heart listens to the orders given in Israel, you that are willing among the people, bless the Lord.

You who move as Aten the sun god at midday,[2] sitting in judgment, and following the path, and riding the pathway, declare from the noise of disturbers among the drawers of water and retell the righteous acts of the Lord. Increase righteous acts in Israel, then the people of the Lord will go down to the cities.

Awake, awake, Deborah! Awake, awake, sing a song!

Rise, Barak, and catch captives, son of Abinoam.

Then the survivors went down against the nobles, the people of the Lord went down for him among the mighty ones from me. Ephraim rooted them out in Amalek, then Benjamin with your people from Machir came down with me hunting out the enemy, and from Zebulun came those that write with the scribe's pen to record.

Princes of Issachar were with Deborah and Barak, so she sent Barak on foot into the valley to the portions of Reuben. Great pangs reached the heart.

Why did they sit between the sheepfolds to hear the bleating of flocks for the divisions of Reuben? There was great searching of hearts. Gilead is on the other side of Jordan where he pitched his tents. Why does Dan remain in ships? Asher sat down on the sea-coasts, and he will camp at his ports. The people of Zebulun exposed their mind to death, and Naphtali went to the high places of their land.

Kings set themselves in formation, and then the kings of Canaan fought in Ti'inik at the water of Megiddo, and they took no bribe of money. The stars from the sky set themselves in formation, they left their paths to fight with Siazara. The brook of Kishion swept them away, the ancient brook, the brook Kishion.

"My mighty mind will trample him down. When the hoofs of the horse were entangled, his mighty ones earnestly rushed to curse Southern Egypt.[3] Curse it," said the messenger of the lord, "Cursed is everyone who dwells in it, because they did not come to help the Lord, to help him among the mighty."

"Blessed among women be Jael the wife of Eber the blacksmith. Let her be blessed above women in tents. He asked for water, and she gave him milk in a dish, she brought butter of princes, she stretched out her left hand to the spike, and her right to the hand workman's hammer and she struck Siazara with it, she nailed through his head and murdered him!"

"She nailed through his temples! He rolled down between her feet, and he fell and lay between her feet. He collapsed and fell, where he collapsed, there he fell dead."

"The mother of Siazara looked down through the window out of the loophole, saying, 'Why was his chariot ashamed? Why did the wheels of his chariots wait?'"

"Her wise ladies answered her, and she returned answers to herself, 'Won't they find him dividing the plunder? He will certainly be gracious to every man! There are spoils of dyed garments for Siazara, spoils of various dyed garments, dyed embroidered garments, they are the spoils for his neck.'"

"So let all your enemies perish, Lord! They who love him will be like the sun[4] coming in his strength."

The land had peace for forty years.[5]

Judges: Chapter 5 Notes

1 Codex Vaticanus: satrapae (ϹΑΤΡΑΠΑΙ). Translation: satraps

• Codex Alexandrinus: satrapae dynatoe (ϹΑΤΡΑΠΑΙΔΥΝΑΤΟΙ). Translation: satraps of power (or forces)

• Aleppo Codex: {R} rznym {S} ånky (רֹזְנִים (ס) אָנֹכִי {ר})

• Leningrad Codex: rozenim anochi (רֹזְנִים אָנֹכִי)

• Targum Jerusalem: shiltonaya (שִׁלְטוֹנַיָּא). Translation: sultans

The Greeks substituted the word in the Old Aramaic text as 'satraps,' the Persian word for governors, however, that is not a translation of the term in the Hebrew translation. Likewise, the translator of the Targum Jerusalem substituted 'sultans.' The Aleppo Codex indicates that the terms 'rznym' and 'ånky' were found in two different source texts, however the Leningrad Codex later treats them as continuous string of words. Neither term is actually Hebrew, however, rznym (רזנים) is generally assumed to be scribal error of rbnym (רבנים), meaning 'great ones' which may be the source of the Greek 'satraps,' however, it is more likely that 'satraps' was already added to the Aramaic text the Greeks translated, as they had no reason to substitute a Persian word.

Assuming that rznym is a scribal error of rbnym, this error must have taken place when the cuneiform text of Judges, or possibly just a book of Deborah and Barak was translated into Canaanite. The Akkadian cuneiform BÈ (𒁉) was part of the ZÁ (𒍝), along with the UD (𒌓). As the UD also held the phonetic value of U, it would have simply meant the original Canaanite cuneiform word in the text was a plural of rabbu (𒊏𒁉𒌓), which mirrors the reconstructed pronunciation of the word rabbu (𒊏𒁍), the in Ugaritic Canaanite version of the word from the same era.

None of the other scripts that the book could have been written in had similar letters for B and Z, including Egyptian hieroglyphics as used to spell Canaanite words: B (𓃀) and Z (𓊃), Paleo-Canaanite: B (𐤁) and Z (=), Phoenician Canaanite: B (𐤁) and Z (𐤆), and Aramaic: B (𐡁) and Z (𐡆). The translation of 'satraps of power,' found in the Codex Alexandrinus, indicates that the two words were already in a combined form of the text by the 5th century, and that the Greeks interpreted Ånky (אנכי) as a reference to the Anaki (עֲנָקִי). The Ånåkî (𓂝𓈖𓈎) were also recorded in Egyptian records from the Middle Kingdoms as having lived in the region of mount Hermon and mount Carmel, however, they do not appear to have still been around in the New Kingdom era, suggesting it was an attempt to interpret the word rznym after the script had been translated into Proto-Canaanite or Canaanite. As the original term in the text was probably 'rabbu' which is essentially the bronze age version of the Septuagint's 'satrap,' and Targum Jerusalem's 'sultan,' the term 'governor' is used in this translation.

2 Codex Vaticanus: epibebêcotes epi onou thêlias mesêmbrias cathêmenoe epi critêriou cae poreuomenoe epi odous synedrôn eph odô (ЄΠΙΒЄΒΗΚΟΤЄС ЄΠΙ ΟΝΟΥ ΘΗΛЄΙΑС ΜЄСΗΜΒΡΙΑС ΚΑΘΗΜЄΝΟΙ ЄΠΙ ΚΡΙΤΗΡΙΟΥ ΚΑΙ ΠΟΡЄΥΟΜЄΝΟΙ ЄΠΙ ΟΔΟΥС СΥΝЄΔΡωΝЄφΟΔω). Translation: "You who rides on a single female at noon, sitting in judgment, and following the path, and riding the pathway."

• Codex Alexandrinus: epibebêcotes epi ypozygiôn cathêmenoe epi lampênôn (ЄΠΙΒЄΒΗΚΟΤЄС ЄΠΙ ΥΠΟΖΥΓΙωΝ ΚΑΘΗΜЄΝΟΙ ЄΠΙ ΛΑΜΠΗΝωΝ). Translation: "You who ride on a beast of burden and covered chariots."

• Aleppo Codex: rkby åtnŭt shrŭt {s} yšby {r} ôl mdyn ŭhlky ôl drk--šyhŭ {s} (**רכבי** {ס} **שיחו--על דרך והלכי על מדין {ר} ישבי {ס} צחרות אתנות**). Translation: "You who mount tribes [S] inhabitants [R] in Midian and travel along the path, speak [S]"

• Leningrad Codex: rochevei atonovt tzechorovt yoshevei al-middin veholechei al-derech sichu (**רֹכְבֵי אֲתֹנוֹת צְחֹרוֹת יֹשְׁבֵי עַל־מִדִּין וְהֹלְכֵי עַל־דֶּרֶךְ שִׂיחוּ**). Translation: "You who ride on white donkeys, and sit in Midian and travel along the path, speak."

The verse had been a mystery for thousands of years, as God should not be described as riding a 'female at noon,' 'beasts of burden and covered chariots,' or 'white donkeys.' Åtnŭt (**אתנות**) appears to be an ancient attempt to transliterate Aten (𐡀𐡕𐡍) into Aramaic and then Hebrew via the Akkadian Cuneiform Iaati ᵃⁿUtu (𒀭𒌓), meaning 'Aten god of the Sun.' This would mean the verse was something like: "You who move as Aten the sun god at midday, sitting in judgment, and following the path, and riding the pathway."

Aten was the Egyptian solar-god during the reign of Akhenaten (1353 to 1336 BC), whose name translates in Egyptian as 'disk.' The name Aten fell out of use in Egypt during the restoration of the old gods by Pharaoh Horemheb (1319-1292 BC), implying the Song of Deborah and Barak date to before the end of this era. Based on the dating of the Book of Judges found in the Septuagint, the song would have been sung in 1314 BC, five years into Horemheb's reign.

3 Codex Vaticanus: Mêrôz (ΜΗΡωΖ)

• Codex Alexandrinus: Marôz (ΜΑΡωΖ)

• Aleppo Codex: Mrŭz (**מרוז**)

• Leningrad Codex: Meroz (**מֵרוֹז**)

• Targum Jerusalem: Meroz (**מֵרוֹז**)

Interpretations of what Merez was, differ wildly. Some associate it with the village of Mitzr (**כְּפַר מְצָר**) in northern Israel, southwest of the Sea of Galilee. The Village of Misr was founded at some point by Egyptian settlers in Canaan, however, it is unclear when. The oldest ruins discovered in the village only date back to the Roman era, however, the name is Arabic, indicating that this community was founded long after the time of Deborah.

A commentary in the Talmud (Moed Katan 16a) claims that Meroz is a planet that refused to help the Israelites in their time of trouble, however, the name Meroz does not correlate with the Canaanite name of any planet. The author of Moed Katan was probably conflating the Hebrew word from Judges with the Roman name Mars, which would have been anachronistic, as even if a precursor to the Latin language existed in the late Bronze Age, there is no reason an Israelite would have used the proto-Latin name.

None of the known variants of the Semitic name of Egypt are a close match to Meroz/Maroz, however, the Egyptian name Marēs, is almost phonetically identical. Mâô-rsî (𓂝𓂓𓂋 𓇌𓈖) was an ancient Egyptian name for Southern Egypt, which translates as approximately 'Southern Place.' It continued to be used until the Classical era, when it was pronounced as Marēs (Μαρης). The exact pronunciation of ancient Egyptian names is debated before the development of the Demotic script, and therefore it cannot be known how the Egyptians pronounced Marēs during the era of Deborah, however, it is documented in Late Egyptian Demotic as being Mâôrs (𐎟/𐎟𐎟), supporting the New Kingdom era pronunciation as being very similar to the term used by Deborah.

The simplest explanation is that the word Mrûz (מרוז) referred to Southern Egypt itself, and not the village named 'Egypt.' At the time, the Egyptian imperial capital was in Thebes, the capital of Southern Egypt. Therefore, the implication is that King Jabin and the Egyptian General Siazara, were rebelling against Egypt, and the Egyptians did not send relief into Canaan to help their subjects. As the Septuagint dates their rule over Canaan to between 1334 and 1314 BC, this means they seized control when Akenhaten died, and ruled throughout the brief reigns of Smenkhkare (1335-1334 BC), Neferneferuaten (1334-1332 BC), Tutankhamen (1334-1325 BC), and Ay (1332-1319 BC), as well as the first five years of Horemheb (1319-1292 BC). This was a chaotic period in Egyptian history, and it is possible the entire Egyptian army in Canaan rebelled, as it wasn't entirely clear who the Pharaoh actually was during most of this period. General Siazara may have not seen his army as being in rebellion if he did not see the government in Egypt as valid.

By year five of Horemheb's reign, it would have been clear that the government had been restored in Egypt, and his position in Canaan would have become a clear case of rebellion, which would explain why his army had become so ineffective as his troops abandoned him to return to Egypt. As the word does appear to be s reference to Southern Egypt, that name is restored in this translation.

4 Codex Vaticanus: Êliou (Hλιογ). Translation: Helios

- Codex Alexandrinus: tou Êliou (ΤΟΥHλιΟΥ). Translation: the sun

- Aleppo Codex: hšmš (השמש). Translation: the sun

- Leningrad Codex: hashemesh (הַשֶּׁמֶשׁ). Translation: the sun

- Targum Jerusalem: shimsha (שׁמְשָׁא). Translation: sun

Shemesh was the Canaanite sun god, whose worship was later banned by King Josiah. The presence of a sun-god in the text supports the earlier reading of åtnût (אתנות) as Aten, as Aten was the dominant Egyptian solar-god at the time, and Canaan was part of the Egyptian Empire at the time.

5 Based on the chronology of the Septuagint, these forty years of peace ended in 1279 BC, when Ramesses II launched his first campaign against Syria.

Judges: Chapter 6

The Israelites did evil in the sight of the Lord, and the Lord gave them into the hand of Midian for seven years. The hand of Midian prevailed against Israel, and the Israelites made for themselves the caves in the mountains, and the dens, and the holes in the rocks because of Midian. It happened when the Israelites sowed, that the Midianites, Amalekites, and Nesites[1] went up together. They camped against them and destroyed their fruits as far as Gaza, and they did not leave the support of life in the land of Israel, and not even an ox or donkey among the herds. They brought their animals and came with their tents in great numbers like the locusts, and there was no counting them and their camels. They came to the land of Israel and laid waste to it.

Israel was greatly impoverished because of Midian and the Israelites cried to the Lord because of Midian. The Lord sent a prophet to the Israelites, and he said to them, "The Lord God of Israel says, 'I am he who brought you up out of the land of Egypt, and I brought you up out of the house of your slavery. I delivered you out of the hands of Egypt, and out of the hands of all that attacked you, and I drove them out before you, and I gave you their land. I said to you, 'I am the Lord God, you will not fear the gods of the Amorites in whose land you live,' but you did not listen to my voice."

The messenger of the lord came and sat down under the fir tree, which was in Ephrath in the land of Joash the father of Esdri. Gideon his son was threshing wheat in a wine press to escape from the face of Midian. The messenger of the lord appeared to him and said to him, "The Lord is with you, and you are mighty in strength."

Gideon replied to him, "Be gracious with me, my lord, but if the Lord is with us, why have these evils found us? Where are all his miracles, which our fathers have told us about, when they said, 'Did not the Lord bring us up out of Egypt?' Now he has abandoned us and given us into the hand of Midian."

The messenger of the lord turned to him and said, "Go in your strength, and you will save Israel out of the hand of Midian. Look, I have sent you."

Gideon asked him, "Be gracious with me, my lord. How will I save Israel? Look, my thousand[2] are weak among Manasseh, and I am the least in my father's house."

The messenger of the lord answered him, "The Lord will be with you, and you will slaughter Midian like one man."

Gideon said to him, "If I have found mercy in your eyes, and you will do for me all that you have said to me today, don't leave here until I come to you, and I will bring an offering and offer it to you."

He replied, "I will remain until you return."

Gideon went and prepared a goat-kid and a bushel of fine unleavened flour, and he put the meat in the basket, and poured the broth into the pot, and brought them out to him under the turpentine tree, and approached.

The messenger of God said to him, "Take the meat and the unleavened cakes, and put them on that rock, and pour out the broth nearby," and he did so. The messenger of the lord stretched out the end of the wand that was in his hand and touched the flesh and the unleavened bread, and fire came up out of the rock and consumed the flesh and the unleavened bread, and the messenger of the lord vanished from his sight.

Gideon understood that he was the messenger of the lord, and Gideon said, "Oh my Lord God! I have seen the messenger of the lord face to face!"

The Lord said to him, "Peace be to you, and don't be afraid, as you will not die."

Gideon built an altar there to the Lord, and called it Lord Shalim.[3] Until this day, as it is still in Ephrath of the father of Esdri. It happened that night, that the Lord said to him, "Take the young bull which your father has, the second bull which is seven years old, and destroy the altar of Ba'al which your father has, and the Asherah which is by it, you will also destroy. You will build an altar to the Lord God on the top of the rocky mountain[4] in the appointed place, and you will take the second bull and will offer up whole burnt offerings with the wood of the grove, which you will destroy."

Gideon took ten men from his servants and did as the Lord had told him, and as he was afraid of what the house of his father and the men of the city would do if he did it in the daytime, so he did it at night. The men of the city rose up early in the morning and saw the altar of Ba'al had been demolished, and the Asherah next to it had been destroyed, and they saw the second bull which Gideon offered on the altar that had been built. Men asked their neighbors, "Who has done this?" and they inquired and searched, and learned that Gideon the son of Joash had done this thing.

The men of the city demanded of Joash, "Bring out your son, and let him die because he has destroyed the altar of Ba'al and because he has destroyed the Asherah that was by it."

Gideon the son of Joash said to all the men who rose up against him, "Do you now plead for Ba'al? Will you save him? Whoever will plead for him, let him be murdered this morning! If he is a god, let him plead for himself, because someone has torn down his altar."

He called it on that day Jerubbaal, saying, "Let Ba'al plead because his altar has been overthrown."

All Midian and Amalek, and the Nesites themselves together and camped in the valley of Jezreel.[5] The wind of the Lord came on Gideon, and he blew with the horn, and Abiezer came to follow him. Gideon sent messengers to all Manasseh, Asher, and Zebulun, and Naphtali, and he went up to meet them. Gideon said to God, "If you will save Israel by my hand, as you have promised, I have put the fleece of wool in the threshing floor, and if there is dew on the fleece only, and the rest of the ground is dry, I will know that you will save Israel by my hand, as you have said."

It was so, and he rose up early in the morning and wrung the fleece, and dew dropped from the fleece, filling a full bowl of water.

Gideon said to God, "I beg you, don't become angry with me, and I will speak again. I will   make one more test with the fleece. Let the fleece only be dry, and let there be dew on all the ground."

God made it so that night, and only the fleece was dry, and on all the ground there was dew.

Judges: Chapter 6 Notes

1 Codex Vaticanus: uioe anatolôn (ΥΙΟΙΑΝΑΤΟΛΩΝ). Translation: sons of the east

- Aleppo Codex: bny qdm (בני קדם). Translation: sons of the east (or ancients)

- Leningrad Codex: venei-kedem (בְנֵי־קֶדֶם). Translation: sons of the east (or ancients)

- Dead Sea Scroll 4QJudgᵃ: bny qdm (בני קדם). Translation: sons of the east (or ancients)

• Targum Jerusalem: venei madincha (בְּנֵי מַדִינְחָא). Translation: sons of the country (or city, Medina)

The 'East' in ancient Canaan referred to Mesopotamia, meaning that the Israelites were referring to a Mesopotamian people plundering the land with the support of the Midianites and Amalekites. The Septuagint's chronology places this 7-year period in approximately 1274 to 1267 BC. This time period corresponds to Ramesses II's campaigns in Canaan against the Nesites (𓉔𓏏𓊖), often misidentified as Hittites, between 1274 and 1269 BC. By Ramesses II's reign, the Egyptians had lost control of northern Canaan to the Nesites, and in 1274 BC Ramesses launched an invasion of northern Canaan, attempting to recapture Kadesh. The first campaign, in 1274 BC, was a failure, although Egypt did weaken the Nesite army in the south. The second campaign, in 1273 BC, was also a failure, although the Egyptians did reach the outskirts of Kadesh. The third campaign, in 1271 BC, successfully captured Kadesh, and pushed the Nesites out of Canaan. In the following years, Egypt consolidated control over Canaan, occupying Edom, Seir, Moab, Jerusalem, Jericho, Heshbon, and Damascus, most of which submitted to Egypt peacefully. This consolidation of Egyptian authority in Canaan is believed to have only taken until 1269 BC according to Egyptologists, however, the Book of Judges reports it took until 1267 BC. The conflict with the Nesites did continue after 1269 BC, and the peace treaty between Egypt and the Nesites was not signed until 1258 BC. This indicates the people referred to in Judges as 'sons of the East,' were Nesites, which is the term used in this translation.

2 Codex Vaticanus: chilias (ΧΙΛΙΑC). Translation: thousand

• Aleppo Codex: ålpy (אלפי). Translation: thousands

• Leningrad Codex: alpi (אַלְפִּי). Translation: thousands

• Targum Jerusalem: zar'iti (זַרְעִיתִי). Translation: families

3 Codex Vaticanus: eirênê cu (ΕΙΡΗΝΗΚῩ). Translation: peace lord

• Aleppo Codex: Yhůh šlům (יהוה שלום). Translation: Yhůh peace (or Shalim)

• Leningrad Codex: Yehvah shalovm (יְהֹוָה שָׁלֹום). Translation: Yehwah peace

• Targum Jerusalem: yeyah da'avad leih shelam (יְיָ דַעֲבַד לֵיהּ שְׁלָם). Translation: Yhů serves the Yah to be complete (or to be Shalim, until evening)

As the Greek translation predates the Hasmonean redaction of circa 140 BC that inserted Yehvah, it reads 'Lord' instead of Yehvah. The Aramaic version of Judges likely read ådny šlmå (אדני שלמא), meaning 'Lord Peace,' which was both the Greek translation and the Masoretic interpretation of the Hebrew translation. The Hebrew term šlûm (שלום) is a transliteration of the Phoenician term šlm (שלמ), which can be translated as either 'peace' or 'Shalim,' the name of the god of the evening, known as Atum in Egyptian, and the name of the god that Jerusalem was named after. As Shalim was one of the ancient Canaanite Lords at the time, it is likely that the earlier Phoenician text read Ba'al Shalim (בעל שלמ). The Hasmoneans redacted most instances of Adon and Ba'al to Yehvah around 140 BC, resulting in the strange expression 'Yehvah Peace' in the Masoretic Text, however, there is no evidence of a community named after 'Yehvah Peace' in Canaan in the 1200s BC.

4 Codex Vaticanus: Maouec (ΜΑΟΥΕΚ)

- Codex Alexandrinus: Maôz (ΜΑωΖ)

- Aleppo Codex: môûz (מעוז). Translation: rock (or stone)

- Leningrad Codex: ma'ovz (מָעוֹז). Translation: rock (or stone)

- Targum Jerusalem: tukefa (תּוּקְפָא). Translation: power

The Greeks transliterated the Aramaic word for 'rock' which is used in this translation.

5 Codex Vaticanus: Ezereel (ΕΖΕΡΕΕλ)

- Codex Alexandrinus: Iezrael (ΙΕΖΡΑΕλ)

- Aleppo Codex: Yzrôål (יזרעאל)

- Leningrad Codex: Yizre'el (יִזְרְעֶאל)

- Targum Jerusalem: Yizre'el (יִזְרְעֶאל)

The Jazreel Valley is in northern Israel and was along the over land route between Egypt and Syria. Some scholars believe the name Jezreel was the origin of the name Israel, as the valley runs through ancient Samaria. If the Nesites pushed as far south as Jazreel, it would have likely been between Ramesses II's first Syrian campaign in 1273 BC, and the Battle of Kadesh in 1269 BC when Ramesses II pushed the Nesites out of Canaan.

Judges: Chapter 7

Jerubbaal rose early, as did Gideon and all the people with him, and camped at the Fountain of Arad. The camp of Midian was to the north of him, reaching from the Hill of Moreh, in the valley.

The Lord said to Gideon, "The people with you are many, so many that I may not deliver Midian into their hand, in case at any time Israel boasts against me, saying, 'My own hand has saved me.' Now tell the people, 'Whoever is afraid and fearful? Let him turn and leave Mount Gilead,'" and twenty-two thousand people left, leaving ten thousand.

The Lord said to Gideon, "The people are still too numerous, bring them down to the water, and I will purge them there for you. It will happen that whoever I will say to you, 'This one will go with you,' he will go with you, and of whoever I will say to you, 'This one will not go with you,' he will not go with you."

He brought the people down to the water, and the Lord said to Gideon, "Whoever will lap of the water with his tongue like a dog, you will set him apart, and also whoever will kneel on his knees to drink."

The count of those that lapped with their hand to their mouth was three hundred men, and all the rest of the people knelled on their knees to drink water. The Lord said to Gideon, "I will save you by the three hundred men that lapped, and I will give Midian into your hand, and all the rest of the people will go everyone to his home."

They took the provisions of the people in their hands and their horns, and he sent away every man of Israel each to his tent, and he strengthened the three hundred, and the army of Midian was beneath him in the valley. In that night the Lord said to him, "Rise, go down into the camp, for I have delivered it into your hand. If you are afraid to go down, go down with Pharaoh's servant[1] to the soldiers' camp. You will hear what they will say, and afterward, your hands will be strong, and you will go down into the camp."

He and Pharaoh's servant went down to the extremity of the companies of fifty, which were in the camp. Midian and Amalek and all the Nesites were scattered in the valley like locusts in multitude, and there was no counting their camels, and they were like the sand of the seashore for multitude. Gideon came and heard a man describing a dream to his neighbor. He said, "Look, I have dreamed a dream, in which a cake of barley bread rolled into the camp of Midian, and it came as far as a tent and hit it, and it fell, and it turned over, and the tent fell."

His neighbor replied, "This is none other than the sword of Gideon, son of Joash, an Israelite. God has delivered Midian and all the army into his hand."

When Gideon heard the account of the dream and the interpretation of it, he worshiped the Lord and returned to the camp of Israel, and said, "Rise, for the Lord has delivered the camp of Midian into our hand."

He divided the three hundred men into three companies and put horns in the hands of all, and empty pitchers, and torches in the pitchers, and he said to them, "You will watch me, and this is what you will do. I will go into the army, and as I do, you will also do. I will blow with the horn, and all you with me will blow with the horn around the whole camp, and you will shout, "For the Lord and Gideon."

Gideon and the hundred men that were with him came to the outskirts of the army at the beginning of the midnight watch, and they completely roused the guards and sounded with the horns, and they broke the pitchers that were in their hands, and the three companies sounded with the horns, and broke the pitchers, and held the torches in their left hands, and in their right hands their horns to sound with. They cried out, "A sword for the Lord and Gideon."

Every man stood in his place around the army, and all the army ran, and sounded an alarm, and fled. They sounded with the three hundred horns, and the Lord set every man's sword in all the army against his neighbor. The army fled as far as the Temple of Seth in Garagatha,[2] Abel-meholah,[3] and Tabbath, and the Israelites from Naphtali, Asher, and Manasseh came to help and chased after Midian. Gideon sent messengers into all the mountains of Ephraim, saying, "Come down to meet Midian, and capture for yourselves the water as far as the House of Barah on the Jordan."

Every Ephraimite cried out, and they captured the water all the way to the House of Barah on the Jordan. They captured the princes of Midian, including Oreb and Zeeb. They killed Oreb in Sur Oreb, and killed Zeeb at the winepress of Zeeb,[4] and they crushed Midian and brought the heads of Oreb and Zeeb to Gideon from beyond the Jordan.

Judges: Chapter 7 Notes

1 Codex Vaticanus: Phara to paedarion (ΦΑΡΑΤΟΠΑΙΔΑΡΙΟΝ). Translation: Phara the child (or servant)

- Aleppo Codex: prh nôrk (פרה נערך). Possible translation: carrying (or cow, Purah) boy (or servant, youth)

- Leningrad Codex: furah na'archa (פֻּרָה נַעֲרֶךָ). Possible translation: carrying (or cow, Purah) boy (or servant, youth)

- Targum Jerusalem: furah ulemach (פוּרָה עוּלֵמָךְ). Translation: framework (or wine press) the world

Based on the context, this strange sentence appears to be a reverence to an Egyptian overseer stationed by Pharaoh among the Tribe of Manasseh. The Phoenician spelling of 'pharaoh' was prôh (𐤐𐤓𐤏𐤄), while the Aramaic spelling was prôûn (פרעון), neither of which is an exact match for the transliterated words prh (פרה) and phara (φαρα), indicating that neither the Paleo-Hebrew nor Aramaic texts included the word 'pharaoh' but a similar sounding word. This suggests that the word, along with the Song of Deborah, was transliterated from another script, likely Akkadian Cuneiform or Egyptian.

The Akkadian Cuneiform spelling of 'pharaoh' was pirôû (𒉺𒊒) during the late Bronze Age, while the Egyptian spelling was pr-ôâ (𓉐𓉻) during the late Bronze era and early Iron Age. While either script could have been used at the time, the cuneiform name is pronounced almost exactly like the term found in the Hebrew translation, while the Egyptian is pronounced slightly differently, suggesting the original text was in cuneiform.

2 Codex Vaticanus: Bêthseedta Garagatha (ΒΗΘCΕΕΔΤΑΓΑΡΑΓΑΘΑ)

- Codex Alexandrinus: Baethasetta (ΒΑΙΘΑCΕΤΤΑ)

- Aleppo Codex: byt hšth srrth (בית השטה צררתה)

- Leningrad Codex: beit hashittah tzereratah (בֵּית הַשִּׁטָּה צְרֵרָתָה)

- Targum Jerusalem: beit shitah litzreirat (בֵּית שִׁיטָה לִצְרֵירַת)

The term vyt hoshth (בית השטה) translates as House of 'sth,' which appears to be a transliterated name, possibly Seth, the Egyptian god that had been widely worshiped by the Hyksos. Shth (שטה) could also be a spelling error of shvth (שוטה), meaning 'fool,' or shyth (שיטה), meaning 'system.' As Seth is a direct translation, the term 'House of Seth in Garagatha,' is used. Zererah is spelled in various ways in the Masoretic Text and transliterated in various ways, including Zaretan, Zarethan, Zeredathah, Zartanah, or

Zarthan. It is believed the town was in the Jordan valley, south of the Sea of Galilee. It is unclear if Garagatha was an alternate name for Zererah or another location, however, as the names are noticeably different the Greek term is used.

3 Codex Vaticanus: Abômeoula (ΑΒѠΜΕΟΥΛΛ)

- Codex Alexandrinus: Abelmeoula (ΑΒΕΛΜΕΟΥΛΛ)

- Aleppo Codex: Åbl mhůlh (אבל מחולה)

- Leningrad Codex: Avel mechovlah (אָבֵל מְחוֹלָה)

- Targum Jerusalem: Avel mechovlah (אָבֵל מְחוֹלָה)

Abel-meholah would later be the birth town of the prophet Elisha. It was described as being near the Jordan River, south of the House of She'an (Beit She'an), which would seem to confirm that Zererah was somewhere in the area.

4 Codex Vaticanus: Iacephzêph (ΙΑΚΕΦΖΗΦ)

- Codex Alexandrinus: Iacephzêb (ΙΑΚΕΦΖΗΒ)

- Aleppo Codex: byqb zåb (ביקב זאב). Translation: wine press of Zeeb

- Leningrad Codex: veyekev-Ze'ev (בְּיֶקֶב־זְאֵב). Translation: wine press of Zeeb

- Targum Jerusalem: meishar Ze'ev (מֵישַׁר זְאֵב). Translation: level (or upright) of Zeeb

As the Greeks transliterated the word 'wine press of Zeeb' as Ιακεφζηφ or Ιακεφζηβ, the Hebrew translation is imported from the Masoretic Text.

Judges: Chapter 8

The Ephraimites said to Gideon, "What is this that you have done to us, in that you did not call us when you went to fight with Midian?"

They rebuked him sharply, and later when their spirit calmed towards him, he replied to them, "What have I now done in comparison to you? Is not the gleaning of Ephraim better than the vintage of Abiezer? The Lord has delivered into your hand the princes of Midian, both Oreb and Zeeb, and what could I do in comparison to you?"

Gideon came to Jordan, and went over, himself and the three hundred with him, hungry, yet still chasing. He said to the men of Succoth, "Give, I beg you, bread to feed these people that follow me, because they are tired, and look, I am chasing after Zebah and Zalmunna, the kings of Midian."

The princes of Succoth asked, "Are the hands of Zebah and Zalmunna now in your hand, that we should give bread to your army?"

Gideon answered, "When the Lord gives Zebah and Zalmunna into my hand, then I will scourge your flesh with the thorns of the wilderness, and briers.

He went up from there to Penuel and spoke to them the same way, and the men of Penuel answered him as the men of Succoth had answered him. Gideon said to the men of Penuel, "When I return in victory, I will break down this tower."

Zebah and Zalmunna were in Karkor, and their army was with them, about fifteen thousand, all that were left of the army of the Neshites,[1] and they that fell were a hundred and twenty thousand men that drew the sword. Gideon went up by the way of them that lived in tents, east of Nobah and Jogbehah, and he struck the army, and the army was secure. Zebah and Zalmunna fled, and he chased after them, and took the two kings of Midian, Zebah, and Zalmunna, and discomfited all the army.

Gideon the son of Joash returned from the battle, from the Ascent of Heres.[2] He took as prisoner a boy from Succoth and questioned him, and he wrote for him the names of the princes of Succoth and their elders, seventy-seven men. Gideon came to the princes of Succoth, and said, "Look Zebah and Zalmunna, who you teased me about, saying, 'Are the hands of Zebah and Zalmunna now in your hand, that we should give bread to your men that are faint?'"

He took the elders of the city and he scourged them with the thorns of the wilderness and the briers. He torn down the tower of Penuel and killed the men of the city. He asked Zebah and Zalmunna, "Where are the men who you killed in Tabor?"

They answered, "Like you, they were in the ranks of the sons of the king."[3]

Gideon said, "They were my brothers and the sons of my mother. As the Lord lives, if you had kept them alive, I would not murder you."

He said to Jetheth his firstborn, "Rise and kill them," but the boy did not draw his sword, for he was afraid, as he was still very young.

Zebah and Zalmunna said, "Rise and attack us, for your strength is like that of a man," and Gideon rose, and killed Zebah and Zalmunna, and he took the round ornaments that were on the necks of their camels.

The men of Israel said to Gideon, "Rule, my lord, over us. Both you, and your son, and your son's son, for you have saved us out of the hand of Midian."

Gideon said to them, "I will not rule, and my son will not rule over you. The Lord will rule over you."

Gideon said to them, "I will make a request of you, that you each give me an earring out of your plunder, as they had golden earrings because they were Ishmaelites."

They said, "We will certainly give them," and he opened his garment, and each man tossed into it an earring from his plunder. The weight of the golden earrings which he asked, was a thousand and seven hundred pieces of gold, besides the crescents, and the chains, and the garments, and the purple cloths that were on the kings of Midian, and besides the chains that were on the necks of their camels. Gideon made a vest from it and set it in his city in Ephrath.

All Israel went whoring after it there, and it became a stumbling block to Gideon and his house. Midian, was straightened before the Israelites, and they did not lift their head anymore, and the land had rest forty years in the days of Gideon. Jerubbaal the son of Joash went and sat in his house. Gideon had seventy sons begotten of his body, for he had many wives. His concubine in Shechem carried him a son and gave him the name Abimelech.

Gideon son of Joash died in his city, and he was buried in the sepulcher of Joash his father in Ephrath of Abi-Esdri. It happened when Gideon was dead, that the Israelites turned, and went whoring after Ba'als, and made for themselves a covenant with Ba'al that he should be their god. The Israelites did not remember the Lord God who had delivered them out of the hand of all that attacked them. They did not deal mercifully with the house of Jerubbaal (this is Gideon), according to all the good which he did for Israel.

Judges: Chapter 8 Notes

1 Codex Vaticanus: allophylôn (ᴀᴧᴧoϕʏᴧɷN). Translation: foreigners (or aliens, gentiles)

• Codex Alexandrinus: huiôn anatolôn (ʏιɷNᴀNᴀᴛoᴧɷN). Translation: sons of the easterners

• Aleppo Codex: bny qdm (בני קדם). Translation: sons of the east (or easterners)

• Leningrad Codex: venei-kedem (בְנֵי־קֶדֶם). Translation: sons of the east (or easterners)

• Targum Jerusalem: benei madincha (בְּנֵי מַדִנְחָא). Translation: sons of east (or Medina)

As the sons of the east in this story are the Neshites, that name is used in the translation.

2 Codex Vaticanus: parataxeôs Ares (ᴨᴀᴩᴀᴛᴀᴤᴇɷᴄᴀᴩᴇᴄ). Translation: phalanx (or side by side) of Ares

• Codex Alexandrinus: anabaseôs Ares (ᴀNᴀʙᴀᴄᴇɷᴄᴀᴩᴇᴄ). Translation: ascent of Ares

• Aleppo Codex: mlmôlh hḥrs (מלמעלה החרס). Translation: from above the destruction (or demolished, destroyed)

• Leningrad Codex: milma'aleh heChares (מִלְמַעֲלֵה הֶחָרֶס). Translation: from above the Chares

• Targum Jerusalem: me'al shimsha (מֵעַל שִׁמְשָׁא). Translation: upper (or fraudulent) sun (or servant, minister)

The Greeks transliterated Ḥrs as Ares, however, the Semitic term meant variations of 'destruction.' The Hebrew and Aramaic term also referred to pottery, clay, or ceramic, as did the cuneiform word ḥarši (⊨⧧) used in Nesite. In this case, the Greek translations and Masoretic interpretation seem consistent, as each of them interpreted the term as a proper name, suggesting a town named Heres, or if the Codex Alexandrinus is correct: Ascent of Heres. It is possible that Heres was the name of a god of destruction worshiped in Canaan, in which case it may have been the origin of the Greek Ares, whose origin is unclear.

As the sources do not agree on the word before Ares/Heres, the term 'Ascent of' is used from the Codex Alexandrinus, as that does seem consistent with the naming conventions of Canaanite towns.

3 Codex Vaticanus: ôs su ôs autoi eis omoiôma uiou basileôs (ⲱⲥ ⲥⲩ ⲱⲥ ⲁⲩⲧⲟⲓ ⲉⲓⲥ ⲟⲙⲟⲓⲱⲙⲁ ⲩⲓⲟⲩ ⲃⲁⲥⲓⲗⲉⲱⲥ). Translation: like you like himself (or he, she, it) into effigy son (or child) king (or chief, master lord)

• Codex Alexandrinus: ôsi sy omoeos soe, omoeos autôn, ôs idos morphê uiôn basileôn (ⲱⲥⲉⲓ ⲥⲩ ⲟⲙⲟⲓⲟⲥ ⲥⲟⲓ ⲟⲙⲟⲓⲟⲥ ⲁⲩⲧⲱⲛ ⲱⲥ ⲉⲓⲇⲟⲥ ⲙⲟⲣⲫⲏ ⲩⲓⲱⲛ ⲃⲁⲥⲓⲗⲉⲱⲛ). Translation: just as you resembling (or equal to) you resembling (or equal to) himself (or he, she, it), like the appearance (or kind, species, image) form (or appearance, kind, type) son (or child) king (or chief, master lord)

• Aleppo Codex: kmůk kmůhm åhd ktår bny hmlk (כמוך כמוהם אחד כתאר בני המלך). Translation: as like one of like the title (or rank, appearance) of the sons (or children, boys) of the king

• Leningrad Codex: kamovcha chemovhem echad keto'ar benei hammelech (כְּמוֹךָ כְּמוֹהֶם אֶחָד כְּתֹאַר בְּנֵי הַמֶּלֶךְ). Translation: as like one of like the title (or rank, appearance) of the sons (or children, boys) of the king

• Targum Jerusalem: me'al shimsha (מֵעַל שִׁמְשָׁא). Translation: upper (or fraudulent) sun (or servant, minister)

Judges: Chapter 9

Abimelech the son of Jerubbaal went to Shechem to his mother's brothers, and he said to them and all the families of the house of his mother's father, "Speak, I beg you, in the ears of all the men of Shechem, and say, 'Which is better for you? That seventy men, even all the sons of Jerubbaal, should reign over you, or that one man should reign over you? And remember that I am your bone and your flesh."

His mother's brothers spoke about him to all the men of Shechem, and their hearts turned towards Abimelech, and they said, "He is our brother. They gave him seventy pieces of silver out of the Temple of the Lord of the Covenant,[1] and Abimelech hired vain and cowardly men, and they followed him. He went to the house of his father in Ephrath and executed his brothers, the sons of Jerubbaal, seventy men on one stone. Jotham the youngest son of Jerubbaal was not executed, as he hid. All the men of Shechem and all the House of Millo were gathered together, and they made Abimelech king by the Oak of Sedition, which was at Shechem.

It was reported to Jotham, and he went and stood on the top of Mount Gerizim, and shouted to them, "Hear me, you men of Shechem, and God will hear you. The trees went out once on a time to anoint a king over them, and they said to the olive, 'Reign over us.' But the olive replied to them, 'Will I leave my fatness, with which men will glorify God, and go to be promoted over the trees?' The trees said to the fig tree, 'Come, reign over us.' But the fig tree replied to them, 'Will I leave my sweetness and my good fruits, and go to be promoted over the trees?' The trees said to the vine, 'Come, reign over us.' The vine replied to them, 'Will I leave my wine that gladdens God and men, and go to be promoted over the trees?' Then all the trees said to the bramble, 'Come, and reign over us.' The bramble replied to the trees, 'If you in truth anoint me to reign over you, come, stand under my shadow, and if not, let fire come out from me and devour the cedars of Lebanon.'"

"Now, if you have done it in truth and integrity, and have made Abimelech king. If you have worked well with Jerubbaal, and with his house. If you have done to him according to the reward of his hand, as my father fought for you, and put his life in jeopardy, and delivered you out of the hand of Midian, and you are risen up this day against the house of my father, and have slain his sons, being seventy men, on one stone, and have made Abimelech the son of his slave-woman king over the men of Shechem, because he is your brother. If then you have done truly and faithfully with Jerubbaal, and with his house today, rejoice in Abimelech, and let him also rejoice over you. But, if not, let fire come out from Abimelech, and devour the men of Shechem, and the House of Millo, and let fire come out from the men of Shechem and the House of Millo, and devour Abimelech."

Jotham fled, and ran away and went as far as Beer, and lived there, out of the way of his brother Abimelech. Abimelech reigned over Israel for three years. God sent an evil spirit between Abimelech and the men of Shechem, and the men of Shechem dealt treacherously with the house of Abimelech, to bring the injury done to the seventy sons of Jerubbaal, and to lay their blood on their brother Abimelech, who killed them, and on the men of Shechem because they strengthened his hands to kill his brothers. The men of Shechem set men to lay in wait against him on the top of the mountains and robbed everyone who passed by them on the way, and it was reported to King Abimelech. Gaal the son of Jabal came, and his brothers, and passed by Shechem, and the men of Shechem trusted in him. They went out into the field, and gathered their grapes, and crushed them, and had a part, and they brought the grapes into the house of their god, and ate and drank, and cursed Abimelech.

Gaal the son of Jabal asked, "Who is Abimelech, and who is the son of Shechem, that we should serve him? Is he not the son of Jerubbaal, and is not Zebul his steward, his servant with the son of Hamor the father of Shechem? Why should we serve him? If only these people were under my hand! I would then remove Abimelech, and I would say to him, 'Multiply your army, and come out.'"

Zebul the ruler of the city heard the words of Gaal the son of Jabal, and he was very angry. He sent messengers to Abimelech secretly, saying, "Look, Gaal the son of Jabal and his brothers have come to Shechem, and they have besieged the city against you. Now rise by night, you and the people with you, and lay wait in the field. It will come to pass in the morning at sunrise, you will rise early and approach the city, and he and the people with him will come out against you, and you will do to him according to your power."

Abimelech and all the people with him rose up by night and formed an ambuscade against Shechem in four companies. Gaal the son of Jabal went out and stood by the door of the gate of the city, and Abimelech and the people with him rose up from the ambuscade. Gaal the son of Jabal saw the people, and said to Zebul, "Look, people come down from the top of the mountain."

Zebul replied to him, "You see the shadow of the mountain as men."

Gaal continued and said, "Look, people come down from the west, from the area bordering the middle of the land, and another company comes by the road to the Oak of Visions."[2]

Zebul asked him, "Where is your mouth as you said, 'Who is Abimelech that we should serve him?' Are not these the people you despised? Go out now, and set the battle formation against him."

Gaal went out before the men of Shechem and set the battle formation against Abimelech. Abimelech pursued him, and he fled from before him, and many fell slain as far as the door of the gate. Abimelech entered into Arumah, and Zebul drove out Gaal and his brothers so that they should not live in Shechem. On the second day, people went out into their field, and one brought word to Abimelech. He took the people, and divided them into three companies, and formed an ambush in the field, and he looked, and the people went out of the city, and he rose up against them and struck them.

Abimelech and the chiefs of companies that were with him rushed forward and stood by the door of the gate of the city, and the two other companies rushed forward on all that were in the field and slaughtered them. Abimelech fought against the city all that day, and captured the city, and killed the people that were in it, and destroyed the city, and sowed it with salt.

All the men of the tower of Shechem heard and came to the gathering at the fortified Temple of the Lord of the Covenant.[3] It was reported to Abimelech, that all the men of the tower of Shechem were gathered together. Abimelech went up to Mount Zalmon, and all the people that were with him, and Abimelech took an ax in his hand, and cut down a branch of a tree, and took it, and laid it on his shoulders. He said to the people that were with him, "Follow my example, quickly,"

They cut down branches, each man, and followed Abimelech, and laid them against the place of gathering, and burnt the place of gathering with fire, and they died, all the men of the tower of Shechem, about a thousand men and women. Abimelech went out of the fortified temple of the covenant, and camped in Tubas[4] and captured it. There was a fortified tower in the middle of the city, where all the men and the women of the city fled and shut the door and went up on the roof of the tower. Abimelech approached the tower and besieged it.

When Abimelech approached the door of the tower to burn it with fire, a woman threw a piece of a millstone on his head and broke his skull. He cried out quickly to the young man, his armor-bearer, saying, "Draw your sword and kill me, so they should never say, 'A woman killed him,'" and the young man stabbed him through, and he died. The men of Israel saw that Abimelech was dead, and they went each to his place. So God repaid the wickedness of Abimelech, which he worked against his father, in slaying his seventy brothers. All the wickedness of the men of Shechem, God repaid on their head and also the curse of Jotham, the son of Jerubbaal.

Judges: Chapter 9 Notes

1 Codex Vaticanus: oecou Baalberith (ΟΙΚΟΥΒΑΑΛΒΕΡΙΘ). Translation: house of Ba'al-Berith

• Codex Alexandrinus: oecou Ba'al diathêcês (ΟΙΚΟΥΒΑΑΛΔΙΑΘΗΚΗC). Translation: house of Ba'al of the testament

• Aleppo Codex: byt bôl bryt (בית בעל ברית). Translation: Temple of the Lord of the Covenant

• Leningrad Codex: beit ba'al berit (בֵּית בַּעַל בְּרִית). Translation: Temple of the Lord of the Covenant

• Targum Jerusalem: beit ba'eil keyam (בֵּית בָּעֵיל קְיָם). Translation: Temple of the Lord of establishment

As Ba'al translates as 'Lord,' and berith translates as 'covenant' or 'testament,' the translation 'Temple of the Lord of the Covenant' is used.

2 Codex Vaticanus: êlônmaônenim (ΗΛΩΝΜΑΩΝΕΝΙΜ)

• Codex Alexandrinus: dryos apoblepontôn (ΔΡΥΟCΑΠΟΒΛΕΠΟΝΤΩΝ). Translation: oak of visions

• Aleppo Codex: âlûn môûnnym (אלון מעונים). Translation: oak of clouds (or diviners)

• Leningrad Codex: elovn me'ovnnim (אֵלוֹן מְעוֹנְנִים). Translation: oak of clouds (or diviners)

• Targum Jerusalem: meishar me'onenaya (מֵישַׁר מְעוֹנְנַיָא). Translation: straight from Onnaya

The Greeks transliterated the words for 'oak of diviners' as ηλωνμαωνενιμ at the Library of Alexander, and later translated is as δρυος αποβλεποντων in the early Christian Era. While the term was a proper name, the name also had a meaning, and therefore this translation uses the later translation found in the Codex Alexandrinus. It is possible that this oak was one of the Asherah trees that were later banned by King Josiah in circa 625 BC.

3 Codex Vaticanus: syneleusin Baethêlberith (ϹΥΝΕΛΕΥϹΙΝΒΑΙΘΗΛΑΒΕΡΙΘ). Translation: meeting place (or coming together) Baethêlberith

• Codex Alexandrinus: to ochyrôma oecou tou Ba'al diathêcês (ΤΟΟΧΥΡѠΜΑΟΙΚΟΥ ΤΟΥΒΑΑΛΔΙΑΘΗΚΗϹ). Translation: the fortified house (or temple) the Ba'al covenant

• Aleppo Codex: sryḥ byt âl bryt (צריח בית אל ברית). Translation: fortified house (or temple) god covenant

• Leningrad Codex: tzeriach veit El berit (צְרִיחַ בֵּית אֵל בְּרִית). Translation: fortified temple god covenant

• Targum Jerusalem: veit El lemigzar keyam (בֵּית אֵל לְמִגְזַר קְיָם). Translation: temple god of the separation of establishment

The Codex Vaticanus and Masoretic Text are phonetically similar here, however, the 5th century AD Codex Alexandrinus has a significant deviation. The earlier Greek translation from the Library of Alexandria appears to have transliterated the term preserved in the Masoretic Text as byt âl bryt (בית אל ברית) as Baethêlberith (Βαιθηλβεριθ), indicating it was viewed as a proper name. The later Codex Alexandrinus translation, from the 5th century AD, which was based on the Hebrew translation in circulation at the time, refers to the Ba'al of the Covenant instead of the god of the Covenant. As the Greeks could not have transliterated a word that was not in the Hebrew text, the term must have been present at the time, however, the earlier Vaticanus Codex supports the text found in the Masoretic Text as having also been in the Aramaic version of Judges that the Greeks translated in the 3rd century BC.

It isn't clear where the version of the verse preserved in the Codex Alexandrinus came from, however, must have been Aramaic, suggesting the verse was edited to change the 'Temple of the God of the Covenant' to a temple of some ba'al. As this temple was in Shechem, it was likely part of the Hasmonean anti-Samaritan propaganda between 113 and 69 BC. The fact that the Temple of the God of the Covenant already existed in Shechem before the time of Solomon supports the Samaritan claim that

Solomon's Temple was not the original temple of their God, as Shechem was the ancient capital of Samaria.

4 Codex Vaticanus: Thêbês (ⲐⲎⲂⲎⲤ)

- Codex Alexandrinus: Thebes (ⲐⲈⲂⲈⲤ)

- Aleppo Codex: Tbs (תבץ)

- Leningrad Codex: Tevetz (תֵּבֵץ)

- Targum Jerusalem: Tevetz (תֵּבֵץ)

This is believed by some to be a reference to the city of Tubas (طوباس) in the northern area of the modern Palestinian West Bank, which is near Mount Gerizim, and so the name Tubas is used in this translation.

Judges: Chapter 10

After Abimelech, Tola the son of Puah rose up to save Israel, being the son of his father's brother, an Issacharite, and he lived in Samaria[1] in the mountains of Ephraim. He judged Israel twenty-three years, and died, and was buried in Samaria. After him arose Jair of Gilead, and he judged Israel twenty-two years. He had thirty-two sons riding on thirty-two colts, and they had thirty-two cities, and they called them Jair's towns until this day in the land of Gilead. Jair died and was buried in Ramnon.[2] The Israelites did evil again in the sight of the Lord and served the Lords and Ashteroths, the gods of Arameans, Sidonians, Moabites, Ammonites, and Pelesets, and they forgot the Lord and did not serve him. The Lord was very angry with Israel and sold them into the hands of the Pelesets and the hands of the Ammonites. They afflicted and bruised all the Israelites beyond Jordan in the land of the Amorites in Gilead at that time and for eighteen years. The Ammonites crossed the Jordan to attack Judah, Benjamin, and Ephraim, and the Israelites were greatly afflicted. The Israelites cried to the Lord, "We have sinned against you because we have forgotten God and served the Lords."

The Lord said to the Israelites, "Didn't I save you from Egypt and the Amorites, and from the sons of Ammon (and Moab),[3] and from the Pelesets, and from the Sidonians, Amalekites, and Midianites[4] who afflicted you? And you cried to me, and I saved you out of their hands? Yet you forgot me and served other gods, therefore I will not save you anymore. Go, and pray to the gods who you have chosen for yourselves, and let them save you in the time of your affliction."

The Israelites said to the Lord, "We have sinned. Do to us whatever is good in your eyes, but save us this day."

They put away the foreign gods from among them and served only the Lord, and his mind was pained for the trouble of Israel. The Ammonites went up and camped in Gilead, and the Israelites were gathered together and camped on the hill. The people and the princes of Gilead said each man to his neighbor, "Who is he that will begin to fight against the Ammonites? He will be the head over all that live in Gilead."

Judges: Chapter 10 Notes

1 Codex Vaticanus: Samir (cΑΜιρ)

• Codex Alexandrinus: Samaria (cΑΜΑρειΑ)

- Aleppo Codex: Šmyr (שמיר). Translation: dill, emery-stone, brier, flint, thistle, adamant, fennel, batch, aggregate, bribe

- Leningrad Codex: Shamir (שָׁמִיר). Translation: dill, emery-stone, brier, flint, thistle, adamant, fennel, batch, aggregate, bribe

- Targum Jerusalem: Shamir (שָׁמִי). Translation: dill, emery-stone, brier, flint, thistle, adamant, fennel, batch, aggregate, bribe

Lucian's version of the Septuagint deviates from both the Codex Vaticanus and Masoretic Text at this point, however, it is not clear if he had a Hebrew or Aramaic copy of Judges which included the word Samaria (שומרון), or simply interpreted Šmyr (שמיר) as Samaria. The term may be a relic of the Akkadian version of Judges, as the land was known as ᴷᵘʳSamerina (𒆳𒊮𒈨𒊑𒈾) in Cuneiform, meaning 'land Samerina.' In any event, Shamir does appear to be a reference to the land that would later be called Samaria, and therefore the Codex Alexandrinus is followed.

2 Codex Vaticanus: Ramnôn (ΡΑΜΝωΝ)

- Codex Alexandrinus: Rammô (ΡΑΜΜω)

- Aleppo Codex: Qmůn (קמון)

- Leningrad Codex: Kamovn (קָמֹון)

- Targum Jerusalem: Kamovn (קמֹון)

This location is unknown today, however, would have been in northwest Jordan. As both versions of the Septuagint generally agree, the Greek name is retained.

3 Codex Vaticanus: cai apo uiôn Ammôn (ΚΑΙΑΠΟΥΙωΝΑΜΜωΝ). Translation: and from sons of Ammon

- Codex Alexandrinus: cae oe uioe Ammôn cae Môab (ΚΑΙΟΙΥΙΟΙΑΜΜωΝΚΑΙ ΜωΑΒ). Translation: and of the sons of Ammon and Moab

- Aleppo Codex: ůmn bny Ômůn (ומן בני עמון). Translation: and from the sons of Ammon

- Leningrad Codex: umin-benei Ammovn (וּמִן־בְּנֵי עַמֹּון). Translation: and from the sons of Ammon

- Targum Jerusalem: umin emora'ah umin benei Amon (וּמִן אֱמֹורָאָה וּמִן בְּנֵי עַמֹון). Translation: and from the speakers and the sons of Ammon

As Moab is only mentioned in the Codex Alexandrinus, is may be a later scribal note, and is therefore placed in parentheses. It is unclear if it was the source of the Targum Jerusalem's 'speakers' as the words are similar. It is possible that the term Moabite was mistranslated from the term 'speaker' in the targums of the era.

4 Codex Vaticanus: Sidôniôn cae Amalêc cae Madiam (ϹΙΔѠΝΙѠΝΚΑΙΑΜΑΛΗΚΚΑΙ ΜΑΔΙΑΜ). Translation: Sidonians and Amalakites and Midianites

- Codex Alexandrinus: Sidônioe cae Madiam cae Amalêc (ϹΙΔѠΝΙΟΙΚΑΙΜΑΔΙΑΜΚΑΙ ΑΜΑΛΗΚ). Translation: Sidonians and Madianites and Amakites

- Aleppo Codex: sydǔnym ûômlq ûmôûn (צידונים ועמלק ומעון). Translation: Sidonians and Amalakite and abode (or dwelling)

- Leningrad Codex: Tzidovnim va'Amalek uma'ovn (צִידוֹנִים וַעֲמָלֵק וּמָעוֹן). Translation: Sidonians and Amalakites and abode (or dwelling)

- Targum Jerusalem: Tzidona'ei va'Amalka'ei ve'enashei (צִידוֹנָאֵי וַעֲמַלְקָאֵי וֶאֱנָשֵׁי). Translation: Sidonians and Amalakites and people

The Hebrew term ma'ovn (מָעוֹן) in the Masoretic Text is not the same as the name Midian (Μαδιαμ) in the Septuagint, however, is likely a transcription error from Midyan (מִדְיָן), as it only appears once in Masoretic Judges.

Judges: Chapter 11

Jephthah the Gileadite was a mighty man, but he was the son of a prostitute who carried Jephthah for Gilead. The wife of Gilead carried his sons, and the sons of his wife grew up, and they drove out Jephthah, and said to him, "You will not inherit from the house of our father as you are the son of a concubine!"

Jephthah fled from the face of his brothers and lived in the land of Tob, and vain men gathered around Jephthah and went out with him. It happened when the Ammonites prepared to fight with Israel, that the elders of Gilead went to fetch Jephthah from the land of Tob.[1]

They said to Jephthah, "Come, and be our leader, and we will fight with the Ammonites."

Jephthah said to the elders of Gilead, "Did you not hate me, and drive me out of my father's house, and banish me from you? And now you have come to me when you need me?"

The elders of Gilead said to Jephthah, "We have now turned to you that you should go with us and fight against the Ammonites, and be our head over all the inhabitants of Gilead."

Jephthah said to the elders of Gilead, "If you turn back to me to fight with the Ammonites and the Lord should deliver them before me then will I be your leader."

The elders of Gilead said to Jephthah, "The Lord be a witness between us if we do not do according to your word."

Jephthah went with the elders of Gilead, and the people made him head and ruler over them, and Jephthah spoke before the Lord in Mizpeh. Jephthah sent messengers to the king of Ammon, saying, "What have I to do with you, that you have come against me to fight in my land?"

The king of Ammon said to the messengers of Jephthah, "Israel took my land when he went up out of Egypt, from Arnon to Jabbok, and to the Jordan, now then, return it peaceably and I will leave."

Jephthah again sent messengers to the king of Ammon, who said to him, "Jephthah says, 'Israel did not take the land of Moab, or the land of Ammon, in their going up out of Egypt, Israel went in the wilderness as far as the Papyrus

Sea[2] and came to Kadesh. Israel also sent to the king of Moab, and he did not consent, and Israel stayed in Kadesh. They journeyed in the wilderness and circumnavigated the land of Edom and the land of Moab. They traveled to the east of the land of Moab, and camped in the country beyond Arnon, and did not enter into the borders of Moab, as Arnon is the border of Moab. Israel sent messengers to Sihon king of the Amorites and the king of Heshbon, and Israel said to him, 'Let us pass, we beg you, through your land to our place.' Sihon did not trust Israel to pass by his borders, and Sihon gathered all his people, and they camped at Jahaz, and he set the battle formation against Israel."

"Lord the god of Israel delivered Sihon and all his people into the hand of Israel, and they slaughtered him, and Israel inherited all the land of the Amorites who lived in that land, from Arnon and to Jabbok, and from the wilderness to the Jordan. Now Lord the god of Israel has removed the Amorites from before his people Israel, and will you inherit his land? Won't you inherit the possessions which Chemosh your god will cause you to inherit? Won't we inherit the land of all those who Lord the god has removed from before you? Now, are you any better than Balak son of Zippor, king of Moab? Did he not fight with Israel and make war with them when Israel lived in Heshbon and in its borders, and in the land of Aroer and in its borders, and in all the cities by the Jordan for three hundred years? And did you recover them at that time? Now I have not sinned against you, but you wrong me in preparing war against me. Now decide, Lord Judge,[3] today between the Israelites and the Ammonites."

But the king of Ammon did not listen to the words of Jephthah, which he sent to him. The spirit of the Lord came on Jephthah and he passed through Gilead and Manasseh and passed by the watch-tower of Gilead to the other side of the Ammonites. Jephthah vowed a vow to the Lord, saying, "If you will indeed deliver the Ammonites into my hand, then it will come to pass that whoever will first come out of the door of my house to meet me when I return in peace from the Ammonites, he will be the Lord's, and I will offer him up for a whole burnt offering."

Jephthah advanced to meet the Ammonites to fight against them, and the Lord delivered them into his hand. He slaughtered them from Aroer all the way to Arnon,[4] in twenty cities, and as far as Abel's vineyard[5] with massive great destruction. The Ammonites were straightened before the Israelites, and Jephthah returned to his house in Mizpeh and saw his daughter come out to meet him dancing with tambourines. She was his only child, he had no other son or daughter. When he saw her, he tore his clothes, and said, "Oh, oh, my daughter! You have indeed troubled me, and you are the cause of my trouble! I have vowed against you to the Lord, and I will not be able to return from it!"

She said to him, "Father, have you vowed to the Lord? Do to me accordingly as the words of your mouth, in that the Lord has worked vengeance for you on your enemies of the Ammonites. Let my father now do this thing. Leave me alone for two months, and I will go up and down in the mountains, and I will mourn my virginity with my friends."

He said, "Go," and he sent her away for two months. She went with her friends, and mourned her virginity in the mountains. It happened at the end of the two months that she returned to her father, and he performed her his vow which he vowed, and she had known no man. It was an ordinance in Israel, that the daughters of Israel went from year to year to mourn the daughter of Jephthah the Gileadite for four days in a year.

Judges: Chapter 11 Notes

1 Codex Vaticanus: Tôb (ΤѠB)

- Aleppo Codex: Tŭb (טוּב)

- Leningrad Codex: Tovv (טֽוֹב)

- Targum Jerusalem: tava (טָבָא). Translation: rumor

The town of Tob is believed to have been in Amman southeast of the Sea of Galilee. It is generally accepted that it is the town of Tubu (𒌅𒁀) mentioned in the Amarna Letter EA205 from circa 1350 BC.

2 Codex Vaticanus: thalassês Siph (ΘΑΛΑϹϹΗϹϹιφ). Translation: Siph Sea

- Codex Alexandrinus: thalassês erythras (ΘΑΛΑϹϹΗϹΕΡΥΘΡΑϹ). Translation: Erythrean Sea

- Aleppo Codex: ym sŭp (יַּם סוּף). Translation: Papyrus (or reed) Sea

- Leningrad Codex: yam-Suf (יַם־סֽוּף). Translation: Papyrus (or reed) Sea

- Targum Jerusalem: yama deSuf (יַמָּא דְסוּף). Translation: sea of papyrus (or reeds)

The older Codex Vaticanus maintains the Greek transliteration of the name the Suf (סוּף) Sea as Siph (Σιφ) Sea, while the later Codex Alexandrinus uses the more common Greek translation of Erythrean ('Ερυθρᾶσ) Sea. The confirms that the Aramaic text the Greeks translated included the name Swf Sea. Both the Aramaic sůf (סוף) and Phoenician term sůf (𐤒𐤅𐤐), meaning papyrus plants, were adopted from the Egyptian term tjůfi (⸗𓇋𓆱𓈘), which referred to papyrus, papyrus plants, and papyrus marshes. The Egyptian term continued to be used into the Classical era as the Coptic words čoouf (ϫⲟⲟⲩϥ), conf (ϭⲟⲛϥ), and comf (ϭⲟⲙϥ), all meaning papyrus. Conversely, the Egyptian name of the Red Sea was the Sea of Heh (𓎛), meaning 'very large sea' from the Middle Kingdom era onward, however, it is believed to have originally been named after the ancient Egyptian frog god Heh (𓎛𓆓). As the Greek translation of Erythrean Sea is anachronistic, the translation of Papyrus Sea is imported from the Masoretic Text.

3 Codex Vaticanus: crinae c̄s̄ crinôn (ΚΡΙΝΑΙΚ̄C̄ΚΡΙΝШΝ). Translation: decide Lord Judge

• Codex Alexandrinus: crinae cyrios o crinôn (ΚΡΙΝΑΙΚΥΡΙΟCΟΚΡΙΝШΝ). Translation: decide lord the judge

• Aleppo Codex: yšpt Yhůh hšpt (יִשְׁפֹּט יהוה השפט). Translation: will decide Yhůh the judge

• Leningrad Codex: yishpot Yehvah hashofet (יִשְׁפֹּט יְהוָה הַשֹּׁפֵט). Translation: will decide Yehvah the judge

• Targum Jerusalem: yedin yeyah da'avad dina (יְדִין יְיָ דְּעָבֵד דִּינָא). Translation: powers of Yhů the slave (or servant) of law (or judgment)

As Shofet does not appear to be the name of a Canaanite god, in the Septuagint's version of Judges Jephthah is recognizing the King of Amman as a Lord Judge, implying the King of Amman is one of Egypt's local magistrates under Ramesses II and Merneptah. As Amman was one of the few Canaanite cities not listed as being in revolt during the reign of Merneptah, while Israel was listed as being in revolt, it seems this story of Jephthah's revolt against Amman was the Israelite revolt listed in Egyptian records.

4 Codex Vaticanus: Arnôn (ΑΡΝШΝ).

• Codex Alexandrinus: Semôith (ⲥⲉⲙⲱⲓⲑ)

• Aleppo Codex: Mnyt (מנית)

• Leningrad Codex: Minnit (מִנִּית)

• Targum Jerusalem: Minit (מְנִית)

As none of the sources agree, the oldest source-text, the Codex Vaticanus' Arnon is used in this translation. The Arnon stream is generally accepted as being the Wadi Mujib river canyon in Jordan, approximately 90 km (56 miles) south of Amman.

5 Codex Vaticanus: Ebelcharmin (ЄΒЄλΧλⲢⲘⲓⲚ).

• Codex Alexandrinus: Abel ampelônô (ΑΒЄλλΜⲠЄλⲱⲚⲱ). Translation: Abel's vineyard

• Aleppo Codex: Åbl krmym (**אבל כרמים**). Translation: Abel's vineyard

• Leningrad Codex: Avel keramim (אָבֵל כְּרָמִים). Translation: Abel's vineyard

• Targum Jerusalem: yshar keramaya (יְשַׁר כְּרָמַיָּא). Translation: directly to (or even) vineyard

As the Codex Vaticanus includes a transliteration of the name found in the Masoretic Text, and the Codex Alexandrinus includes a translation of the name found in the Masoretic Text, the Masoretic name is imported.

Judges: Chapter 12

The Ephraimites assembled and went to the north, and said to Jephthah, "Why did you go and fight Amman, and did not call us to go with you? We will burn your house!"

Jephthah answered them, "I and my people and Amman were engaged in war, and I called for you, and you did not save me out of their hand. I saw that you were no ally, and I took my life in my own hand and invaded Amman, and the Lord delivered them into my hand. Why have you come up against me today to fight with me?" Jephthah gathered all the men of Gilead and fought with Ephraim, and the men of Gilead slaughtered Ephraim, because they that escaped of Ephraim said, "You are of Gilead among Ephraim and among Manasseh."

Gilead took the fords of the Jordan near Ephraim, and they who escaped among the Ephraimites said to them, "Let us go across," and the men of Gilead asked, "Are you an Ephraimite?"

He answered, "No."

Then they said to him, "Now say, 'stalk of grain,'"[1] and he did not pronounce it right, so they captured him and killed him at the fords of the Jordan. Forty-two thousand Ephraimites died there at that time. Jephthah judged Israel six years, and Jephthah the Gileadite died and was buried in his city in Gilead.

After him, Ibzan of the Temple of Lehem[2] judged Israel. He had thirty sons, and thirty daughters, who he sent out, and he brought in thirty daughters for his sons from outside, and he judged Israel seven years. Ibzan died and was buried at the Temple of Lehem. After him, Elon of Zebulun judged Israel for ten years. Elon of Zebulun died and was buried in Aijalon in the land of Zebulun.

After him, Abdon the son of Hillel, a Per-Atenite, judged Israel. He had forty sons, and thirty grandsons, that rode on seventy colts, and he judged Israel eight years. Abdon the son of Hillel, the Per-Atenite, died and was buried in Per-Aten[3] in the land of Ephraim in the mountains of Amalek.

Judges: Chapter 12 Notes

1 Codex Vaticanus: stachys (ⲤⲦⲀⲬⲨⲤ). Translation: stalk of grain (or progeny)

• Codex Alexandrinus: synthêma (ⲤⲨⲚⲐⲎⲘⲀ). Translation: anything agreed upon

- Aleppo Codex: šblt (שבלת). Translation: stalk of grain

- Leningrad Codex: shibbolet (שִׁבֹּ֫לֶת). Translation: stalk of grain

- Targum Jerusalem: shubbalta (שׁוּבַּלְתָּא). Translation: stalk of grain (or branch of river)

The spelling of šblt (שבלת) in the Masoretic Text is not the Hebrew spelling of šybŭlt (שיבולת), but the older Canaanite spelling, recorded as šblt (⟨𐎌𐎁𐎍𐎚—⟩) in Ugaritic Canaanite, and šblt (𐤔𐤁𐤋𐤕) in Phoenician Canaanite. This older Canaanite spelling developed into the Hebrew spelling during the Persian era, under the influence of Imperial Aramaic. The Aramaic spelling found in the Targum Jerusalem is virtually identical to the older Akkadian cuneiform term šubulta (𒂄𒌋𒁻𒋫), indicating that the division among the Israelites was already between those speaking Canaanite versus Aramaic. Arameans appeared in Mesopotamian records centuries earlier than the Habirus, and the two cultures were generally described as inhabiting the same regions, although the Arameans were more urban, and the Habirus were more nomadic.

2 Codex Vaticanus: Baethleem (ΒΑΙΘΛΕΕΜ)

- Aleppo Codex: byt lhm (בית לחם). Translation: house (or temple) of Lehem (or grain)

- Leningrad Codex: beit Lachem (בֵּית לֶחֶם). Translation: house (or temple) of Lehem (or grain)

- Targum Jerusalem: beit Lechem (בֵּית לֶחֶם). Translation: house (or temple) of Lehem (or grain)

Lehem was an ancient Canaanite god of grain, rebirth, and life, similar in nature to the Egyptian god Osiris, and Greek god Dionysus. Lehem was also the word meaning 'grain,' meaning the name could be interpreted as anything from the 'Temple of Lehem' to the 'grain silo,' however, the ancient Samaritan city of Bethlehem is being referenced, which was named after the Temple of Lehem, and so the name is translated directly from the Masoretic text.

3 Codex Vaticanus: Pharathôm (ΦΑΡΑΘΩΜ).

- Codex Alexandrinus: Phraathôn (ΦΡΑΑΘΩΝ)

- Aleppo Codex: prôtŭn (פרעתון)

- Leningrad Codex: Fir'atovn (פִּרְעָתוֹן)

- Targum Jerusalem: Fir'atovn (פִּרְעָתוֹן)

The Hebrew name is a translation of an Egyptian name, Per-Aten. It is unknown where the town of Per-Aten (or Per-Atum) in the land of Ephraim was located, however, it seems evident that it started as an Egyptian colony during the New Kingdom era. As it was named Per-Aten (𓉐𓏤𓇋𓏏𓈖𓇳) the foundation of the colony would have almost certainly taken place during the Amarna Period, between 1353-1336 BC. During that era, Ephraim was ruled by the Judges Ehud and Shamgar, and the land was described as being at peace until the end of the era.

Judges: Chapter 13

The Israelites again committed iniquity before the Lord, and the Lord delivered them into the hands of the Pelesets for forty years. There was a man of Zorah, of the family of the Danites whose name was Manoah, and his wife was barren and did not become pregnant.

The messenger of the lord appeared to the woman, and said to her, "Look, you are barren and have not carried, yet you will conceive a son. Now be very cautious, and drink no wine or strong drink, and eat nothing unclean, as you are with child, and will give birth to a son. No iron must touch his head, for the child will be a Nazarite to God from the womb, and he will begin to save Israel from the hand of the Pelesets."

The woman went in, and told her husband, "A man of God came to me, and he looked like a messenger of God, very dreadful, and I did not ask him from where he was, and he did not tell me his name. He said to me, 'Look, you are with child and will give birth to a son, and now drink no wine or strong drink, and eat nothing unclean, for the child will be holy to God from the womb until the day of his death."

Manoah prayed to the Lord, "If you, Lord, sent to me a man of God, let him now come to us once more, and teach us what we will do to the child about to be born."

The Lord heard the voice of Manoah, and the messenger of God came again to the woman, as she sat in the field, and Manoah her husband was not with her. The woman rushed, and ran to bring word to her husband, and said to him, "Look the man who came to me the other day has appeared to me."

Manoah arose and followed his wife, and came to the man, and said to him, "Are you the man that spoke to the woman?"

The messenger answered, "I am."

Manoah said, "Now your word will come to pass. How will we judge the child and our dealings with him?"

The messenger of the lord said to Manoah, "Of all things concerning which I spoke to the woman, she will beware. She will eat nothing that comes of the vine yielding wine, and let her not drink wine or strong liquor, and let her not eat anything unclean. All the things that I have ordered her she will observe."

Manoah said to the messenger of the lord, "Let us keep you here, and prepare for you a kid of the goats."

The messenger of the lord replied to Manoah, "If you should detain me, I will not eat of your bread, and if you would offer a whole burnt offering, to the Lord you will offer it."

Manoah did not know that he was the messenger of the lord. Manoah said to the messenger of the lord, "What is your name, that when your word will come to pass, we may glorify you?"

The messenger of the lord said to him, "Why do you ask my name when it is wonderful?"

Manoah took a kid of the goats and its meat offering and offered it on the rock to the Lord, and the messenger worked a distinct work, and Manoah and his wife were looking on. It happened when the flame went up above the altar towards the sky, that the messenger of the lord went up in the flame, and Manoah and his wife were looking, and they fell on their face to the earth. The messenger did not appear again to Manoah or his wife. Then Manoah knew that this was the messenger of the lord. Manoah said to his wife, "We will certainly die because we have seen God."

But his wife said to him, "If the Lord wanted to kill us, he would not have received from our hand a whole burnt offering and a meat offering. He would not have shown us all these things, and he would have made us hear all these things."

The woman gave birth to a son, and she called his name Samson, and the child grew, and the Lord blessed him. The spirit of the Lord began to go out with him in the camp of Dan and between Zorah and Esthaol.

Judges: Chapter 14

Samson went down to Timnah and saw a woman in Timnah from the daughters of the Pelesets. He returned and told his father and his mother, and said, "I have seen a woman in Timnah of the daughters of the Pelesets, and now procure her for me as a wife."

His father and his mother replied to him, "Are there no daughters of your brothers, and is there not a woman of all my people, that you go to take a wife instead of from the uncircumcised Pelesets?"

Samson said to his father, "Take her for me, as she is good-looking."

His father and his mother did not know that it was of the Lord. That he wanted to take revenge on the Pelesets. At that time the Pelesets lorded over Israel. Samson and his father and mother went down to Timnah, and he came to the vineyard of Timnah. A young lion roared in meeting him. The spirit of the Lord came powerfully over him, and he crushed him as he would have killed a kid of the goats, barehanded. He did not tell his father and his mother what he had done.

They went down and spoke to the woman, and she was beautiful in the eyes of Samson. After some time he returned to take her, and he turned aside to see the carcass of the lion, and in the mouth of the lion was a hive of bees with honey. He collected some and ate some, and he took some to his father and mother and gave it to them, and they also ate, but he did not tell them that he took the honey out of the mouth of the lion. His father went down to the woman, and Samson made a banquet there for seven days, as the young men used to. When they saw him they took thirty guests and joined him.

Samson said to them, "I propound a riddle for you. If you will answer it for me, and solve it within the seven days of the feast, I will give you thirty sheets and thirty changes of clothing. If you can't answer it for me, you will give me thirty sheets and thirty changes of clothing."

They answered him, "Propound your riddle, and we will hear it."

He said to them, "Meat came out of the eater, and sweetness out of the strong."

They could not answer the riddle for three days. On the fourth day, they said to the wife of Samson, "Deceive now your husband and let him tell you the riddle, in case we burn you and your father's house with fire. Did you invite us to do violence?"

Samson's wife wept in front of him, and said, "You hate me, and don't love me! The riddle which you have propounded to my people, you have not told me."

Samson said to her, "If I have not told it to my father and my mother, will I tell it to you?"

She wept in front of him seven days, during which their banquet lasted, and on the seventh day, he told her because she troubled him, and she told it to her people. The men of the city said to him on the seventh day, before sunrise, "What is sweeter than honey, and what is stronger than a lion?"

Samson said to them, "If you had not plowed with my heifer, you would not have known my riddle."

The Spirit of the Lord came on him powerfully, and he went down to Ashkelon, and murdered thirty of the men that lived there, and took their clothes, and gave the changes of clothing to those that answered the riddle. Samson was very angry and went back to the house of his father. The wife of Samson was given to one of his friends that he was close with.

Judges: Chapter 15

In the days of wheat harvest, Samson visited his wife with a kid, and said, "I will go to my wife to the bed-chamber, but her father did not allow him to go."

Her father said, "I said that you did certainly hate her, and I gave her to one of your friends. Is not her younger sister better than she? Let her be for you instead of her."

Samson said to them, "For once am I blameless among the Pelesets, even though I cause problems among them."

Samson went and caught three hundred foxes, and took torches, and turned tail to tail, and put a torch between two tails, and fastened it. He set fire to the torches and sent the foxes into the grain of the Pelesets, and everything was burnt from the threshing floor to the standing grain, including the vineyard and olives.

The Pelesets inquired, "Who has done these things?"

They answered, "Samson the son-in-law of the Timnahite, because he has taken his wife, and given her to one of his friends.

The Pelesets went up and burnt her and her father's house with fire. Samson said to them, "Though you may have dealt so with her, verily I will be avenged against you, and afterward I will stop."

He knocked them down, and ran down and hid in a cave of the rock Etam. The Pelesets went up, and camped in Judah, and spread themselves abroad in Lehi. The men of Judah asked, "Why have you come up against us?"

The Pelesets answered, "We have come up to catch Samson, and to do to him as he has done to us."

The three thousand men of Judah went down to the cave in the rock Etam, and they said to Samson, "Don't you know that the Pelesets rule over us? What is this that you have done to us?"

Samson answered to them, "As they did to me, so have I done to them."

They said to him, "We have come down to catch you and deliver you into the hand of the Pelesets."

Samson replied to them, "Swear to me that you will not kill me yourselves."

They answered him, "No, we will only tie you tight, and deliver you into their hand, and will not kill you," and they tied him with two new ropes, and brought him from that rock.

They came to Lehi, and the Pelesets shouted, and ran to meet him, and the Spirit of the Lord came mightily on him, and the ropes that were on his arms became as kindling which is burnt with fire, and his bonds were consumed from off his hands. He found the jaw-bone of a donkey that had been thrown away, and he took it in his hand and killed a thousand men with it.

Samson said, "With the jaw-bone of a donkey I have completely destroyed them, for with the jaw-bone of a donkey I have slaughtered a thousand men!"

When he stopped speaking, then he threw the jaw-bone from his hand, and he called that place Raising-the-Jaw-Bone. He was very thirsty, and wept before the Lord, and said, "You were willing to grant this great deliverance by the hand of your servant, but now I will die from thirst, and fall into the hand of the uncircumcised?" He was very thirsty, and wept before the Lord, and said, "You were willing to grant this great deliverance by the hand of your servant, but now will I die from thirst, and fall into the hand of the uncircumcised?"

God broke open a hollow place in the jaw, and there came out water, and he drank, and his spirit returned and he revived. Therefore the name of the fountain was called The Well of the Invoker, which is in Lehi until this day. He judged Israel in the days of the Pelesets twenty years.

Judges: Chapter 16

Samson went to Gaza, and visited a prostitute there, and went into her. It was reported to the Gazites, saying, "Samson has come here," and they surrounded him and laid wait for him all night at the gate of the city, and they were quiet all the night, saying, "Let's wait until the dawn, and we'll kill him."

Samson slept until midnight, and rose up at midnight, and took hold of the doors of the gate of the city with the two posts, and lifted them up with the bar, and laid them on his shoulders, and he went up to the top of the mountain that is before Hebron and laid them there. After this, he loved a woman in Sorek, and her name was Delilah. The princes of the Pelesets came up to her, and said to her, "Seduce him, and see where his great strength comes from, and how we will prevail against him, and bind him to humble him, and we will give you each eleven hundred pieces of silver."

Delilah said to Samson, "Tell me, I beg you, what is your great strength, and how will you be bound that you may be humbled?

Samson said to her, "If they tie me with seven moist cords that have not been stretched, then I will be as weak as one of the ordinary men."

The princes of the Pelesets brought her seven moist cords that had not been stretched, and she tied him with them. The men were hiding in her chamber, and she said to him, "The Pelesets are on you, Samson!"

He broke the cords like anyone would break a thread when it has touched the fire, and his strength was unknown. Delilah said to Samson, "Look, you have cheated me, and told me lies. Now then tell me how you will be tied."

He said to her, "If they should tie me fast with new ropes with which work has not been done, then will I be as weak as another man."

Delilah took new ropes and tied him with them, and the men that were hiding, came out of the chamber, and she said, "The Pelesets are on you, Samson,' and he broke them off his arms like a thread."

Delilah said to Samson, "Look, you have deceived me, and told me lies. Tell me, I demand of you, how you may be tied."

He said to her, "If you should braid the seven locks of my head with a braid, and should fasten them with the pin into the wall, then I will be weak as another man."

When he was asleep, Delilah took the seven locks of his head, and braided them into a braid, and fastened them with the pin into the wall, and she shouted, "The Pelesets are on you, Samson!"

He awoke out of his sleep and pulled the pin of the braid out of the wall. Delilah said to Samson, "How can you say, 'I love you,' when your heart is not with me? This third time you have deceived me, and have not told me where your great strength is."

She hurt him with her words and chastised him so much that his spirit failed almost to death. Then he told her all his heart, and said to her, "A razor has not come on my head, because I have been a holy one of God from my mother's womb. If then I should be shaven, my strength will leave from me, and I will be weak, and I will be like all other men."

Delilah saw that he told her all his heart, and she sent and called the princes of the Pelesets, saying, "Come up one more time, as he has told me all his heart."

The chiefs of the Pelesets went up to her and brought the money in their hands. Delilah made Samson sleep on her knees, and she called a man, and he shaved the seven locks of his head, and she began to humble him, and his strength departed from him. Delilah yelled, "The Pelesets are on you Samson!"

He woke out of his sleep and said, "I will go out as I did before, and shake myself," and he did not know that the Lord was departed from him. The Pelesets took him, and cut out his eyes, and brought him down to Gaza, and bound him with brass shackles, and he ground grain in the prison-house. The hair of his head began to grow as before it was shaven.

The chiefs of the Pelesets met to offer a great sacrifice to their god Dagon, and to celebrate, and they said, "God has given into our hand our enemy Samson." The people saw him, and sang praises to their god, "Our god," they said, "has delivered into our hand our enemy, who destroyed our land, and who murdered many of us."

When their heart was happy, they said, "Call Samson out of the prison-house, and let him play before us," and they called Samson out of the prison-house, and he played before them. They slapped him with the palms of their hands and tied him between the pillars.

Samson said to the young man that guided him, "Allow me to feel the pillars on which the house rests, so I can lean on them."

The house was full of men and women and all the chiefs of the Pelesets were there, and on the roof were about three thousand men and women looking at the sports of Samson. Samson wept before the Lord, and said, "Lord, my lord! Remember me, I beg you, and strengthen me, God, just this once, and I will repay the Pelesets for my eyes."

Samson took hold of the two pillars which supported the house, and leaned on them, and laid hold of one with his right hand, and the other with his left. Samson yelled, "Let me die with the Pelesets!" and he put his back into it, and the house fell on the princes, and on all the people that were in it. The dead who Samson killed in his suicide was more than those he murdered during his life. His brothers and his father's house went down, and they took him, and they went up and buried him between Zorah and Esthaol in the sepulcher of his father Manoah, and he judged Israel twenty years.

Judges: Chapter 17

There was a man from the mountains of Ephraim, and his name was Micah. He said to his mother, "The eleven hundred pieces of silver which you took of yourself, and about which you cursed me, and spoke in my ears, look, the silver is with me. I took it."

His mother said, "Blessed be my son of the Lord."

He restored the eleven hundred pieces of silver to his mother, and his mother said, I had wholly consecrated the money to the Lord out of my hand for my son, to make a graven and a molten image, and now I will restore it to you. But he returned the silver to his mother, and his mother took two hundred pieces of silver and gave them to a silversmith, and he made from it a molten idol, and it was in the house of Micah. The house of Micah was for him, a Temple of God, and he made a vest and teraphim, and he consecrated one of his sons, and he became to him a priest.

In those days there was no king in Israel, and every man did that which was right in his own eyes. There was a young man in the House of Lehem of the tribe of Judah, and he was a Levite, and he was traveling there. The man departed from House of Lehem in a town of Judah to stay in whatever place he might find, and he came as far as Mount Ephraim and stopped at the house of Micah. Micah asked him, "From where have you come?"

He answered him, "I am a Levite from the Temple of Lehem in Judah, and I go to stay in any place I may find."

Micah offered him, "Live with me and be for me a father and a priest, and I will give you ten pieces of silver each year, and a change of clothing, and your living."

The Levite began to live with the man, and the young man was to him as one of his sons. Micah consecrated the Levite, and he became for him a priest, and he was in the house of Micah. Micah said, "Now I know that the Lord will do good for me because a Levite has become my priest."

Judges: Chapter 18

In those days there was no king in Israel, the tribe of Dan wanted for itself an inheritance to inhabit because no inheritance had fallen to it until that day among the tribes of Israel. The sons of Dan sent from their families five men of valor, from Zorah and Esthaol, to spy out the land and to search it. They said to them, "Go and search out the land."

They came as far as the mountains of Ephraim to the house of Micah and they lodged there, in the house of Micah, and they recognized the voice of the young man the Levite, and turned in there, and asked him, "Who brought you in here? And what are you doing in this place? And what have you here?"

He answered them, "Micah hired me, and I became his priest."

They said to him, "Inquire of God, now, whether the path in which we are going will be prosperous."

The priest answered them, "Go in peace. Your way in which you go is before the Lord."

The five men traveled on, and arrived at Laish and saw the people in it living peacefully, and at ease like the Sidonians. There was no one perverting or shaming anything in the land, and no heir extorting their wealth, yet they were far from the Sidonians, and they had no trade with anyone. The five men went to their brothers, to Zorah and Esthaol, and asked their brothers, "Why do you sit here idle?"

They said, "Get up, and let us go up against them, for we have seen the land, and, saw it is very good. Yet you are idle. Don't delay leaving. Enter in and seize the land. When you will go, you will come to a peaceful people, and the land is extensive, but God has given it into your hand. A place where nothing is lacking that the earth provides. They departed there from the families of Dan, from Zorah and Esthaol, six hundred men, equipped with weapons of war. They went up and camped in the village of Ye'arim in Judah. (Therefore that place was called the Camp of Dan, until this day. Look, it is near the village of Ye'arim.)

They went on from there to the mountains of Ephraim and came to the house of Micah. The five men who went to spy out the land of Laish answered, and said to their brothers, "You know that there is in this place, a vest and teraphim, and a molten idol, and now consider what you will do."

They turned aside there, and went into the house of the young man, the Levite, into the Temple of Micah, and asked him how he was. The six hundred Danites who were equipped with their weapons of war stood by the door of the gate. The five men who went to spy out the land went up and entered into the Temple of Micah, and the priest stood. They took the idol, and the vest and teraphim, and the priest asked them, "What are you doing?"

They answered him, "Be silent, lay your hand on your mouth, and come with us, and be for us a father and a priest. Is it better for you to be the priest of the house of one man, or to be the priest of a tribe and house for a family of Israel?"

The heart of the priest was glad, and he took the vest, and teraphim, and molten idol, and went among the people. So they turned and departed, and put their children and their property and their baggage before them. They went some distance from the Temple of Micah, and Micah, and the men in the houses near Micah's Temple, called out, and chased after Dan. Dan turned around, and asked Micah, "What is the matter with you that you have called out?"

Micah said, "You have taken my molten idol which I made, and my priest is gone, and what have I remaining? Yet you ask me, 'Why do you call out?'"

The children of Dan said to him, don't let your voice be heard by us, in case angry men attack you, and take away your life, and the lives of your house. The children of Dan went their way, and Micah saw that they were stronger than he was, and he returned to his house. The children of Dan took what Micah had made, and the priest that he had, and they came to Laish, to a quiet and peaceful people, and they slaughtered them with the edge of the sword and burnt the city with fire. There were no survivors, because the city was far from the Sidonians, and they had no trade with other men. It was in the valley of the house of Ereo, that they built the city, and lived in it. They called the name of the city Dan, after the name of Dan their fore-father, who was born to Israel.

(The name of the town had been Hall of the Lion[1] before.)

The children of Dan set up the molten idol for themselves, and Jonathan son of Gershom son of Manasseh, he and his sons were priests to the tribe of Dan until the time the nation was taken away captive. They set up for themselves the molten idol which Micah made, all the days that the Temple of God was in Shiloh. It was so in those days that there was no king in Israel.

Judges: Chapter 18 Notes

1 Codex Vaticanus: Oylamaes (ΟΥΛΑΜΑΙϹ)

- Codex Alexandrinus: an Laes (ΗΝΛΑΙϹ). Translation: it was Laes

- Aleppo Codex: aŭlm lyš (אולם ליש). Translation: but (or Hall of) or lion (or wealth)

- Leningrad Codex: ulam layish (אוּלָם לְיִשׁ). Translation: but (or Hall of) lion (or wealth)

- Targum Jerusalem: veram layish (בְּרַם לְיִשׁ). Translation: besides lion (or Leo)

The translators at the library of Alexandria, or the earlier translators of the Aramaic version they worked from interpreted the name differently from the Hebrew translators. The term aŭlm (אולם) can be interpreted as 'but,' as the Hebrew translators rendered it, or as 'hall,' or 'salon' as the early Aramaic translators interpreted it. As the Greeks considered it part of the name they transliterated it, meaning they interpreted the Aramaic text as reading 'Hall of Aes.' Either they missed the L (Λ / ל) at the beginning of the name Lysh, or it had been dropped in the Aramaic translation. Reading aŭlm lyš (אולם ליש) the way it was read at the Library of Alexandria renders the old name of the town as 'Hall of the Lion' using the unusual but documented translation of lyš (ליש) as 'lion,' or 'Hall that's there,' using the more common interpretation of lyš (ליש). The term lyš does not appear to have had meant 'lion' in early Aramaic, and was probably interpreted as 'the aesh' by the Aramaic translator, who also interpreted Aesh as a proper name, resulting in the translation of 'Hall of Aesh' instead of 'Hall of the Aesh.' As Hall of the Lion is probably the origin of the name, however, that name is imported from the Aleppo Codex.

Judges: Chapter 19

A Levite was traveling along the sides of Mount Ephraim, and he took for himself a concubine from the House of Lehem in Judah. His concubine left him and traveled from him to the house of her father, in the House of Lehem in Judah, and she was there four months. Her husband rose up and went after her, to speak kindly to her, and to restore her to himself. He had a young man with him, and a pair of donkeys. She brought him into the house of her father, and the father of the woman saw him and was very pleased to meet him. His father-in-law, the father of the woman, detained him, and he stayed with him for three days, and they ate and drank, and lodged there. It happened on the fourth day, that they rose early, and he stood up to leave, and the father of the woman said to his son-in-law, "Strengthen your heart with a morsel of bread, and afterward you will go."

They two sat down together and ate and drank, and the father of the woman said to her husband, "Wait now the night, and let your heart be happy."

The man rose to leave, but his father-in-law detained him, and he stayed and lodged there. He rose early in the morning on the fifth day to leave, and the father of the woman said, "Strengthen your heart, and equip yourself as a soldier until the evening, and the two ate."

The man rose up to leave, he and his concubine, and his young man, but his father-in-law the father of the woman said to him, "Look now, it's late in the day, almost evening, stay here and let your heart rejoice, and you will rise early tomorrow for your journey and you will leave to your home."

But the man would not lodge there, he rose and departed, and came to the area opposite Jebus, (this is Jerusalem,) and there was with him a pair of donkeys saddled, and his concubine was with him. They came as far as Jebus, and the day had advanced, and the young man said to his master, "Come, I beg you, and let us turn aside into this city of the Jebusites, and let us lodge in it."

His master said to him, "We will not turn aside into a strange city, where there are none one of the Israelites. We will pass on as far as Gibeah." He said to his young man, "Come, and let's approach one of the places, and we will lodge in Gibeah or Ramah."

They continued and went on, and the sun set on them near Gibeah, which is in Benjamin. They turned aside there to go into a lodge in Gibeah, and they went in and sat down in the street of the city, and no one took them into a house to lodge. An old man came out of the field from his work in the evening, and the man was from Mount Ephraim, and he stayed in Gibeah, and the men of the place were Benjaminites. He lifted his eyes and saw a traveler in the street of the city, and the old man said to him, "To what place go you, and from where come you?"

He answered him, "We are passing by from House of Lehem in Judah to the sides of Mount Ephraim. I am from there, and I went as far as House of Lehem in Judah, and I am going home, and there is no man to take me into his house. Yet is there straw and food for our donkeys, and bread and wine for me and my handmaid and the young man with your servants, there is no lack of anything."

The old man said, "Peace be to you, only do by no means lodge in the street." He brought him into his house and made room for his donkeys, and they washed their feet and ate and drank.

They were comforting their heart, when look, the lawless men of the city surrounded the house and knocked at the door. They spoke to the old man, the owner of the house, saying, "Bring out the man who came into your house, that we may rape him."

The master of the house came out to them, and said, "No, brothers, do not do wrong, I beg you. After this man has come into my house, do not do this foolish - ness. Look my daughter a virgin, and the man's concubine, I will bring them out, and humble you them, and do to them that which is good in your eyes, but to this man do not this folly."

But the men would not consent to listen to him, so the man grabbed hold of his concubine, and threw her out to them, and they raped her, and abused her all night until the morning, and let her go when the morning dawned. The woman came back in the early morning and fell at the door of the house where her husband was until it was light. Her husband rose up in the morning, and opened the doors of the house, and went out to go on his journey, and look, the woman his concubine had fallen by the doors of the house, and her hands were on the threshold. He said to her, "Rise, and let us go."

She did not answer, as she was dead. He took her on his donkey and went to his place. He took his sword, and laid hold of his concubine, and divided her into twelve parts, and sent them to every coast of Israel. It was so, that everyone who saw it said, "Such a day as this has not happened nor has been seen from the day of the going up of the Israelites out of the land of Egypt until this day. Take counsel concerning it, and speak."

Judges: Chapter 20

All the Israelites went out, and all the congregation was gathered as one man, from Dan to Beersheba, and in the land of Gilead, to the Lord at Mizpeh. All the tribes of Israel stood before the Lord in the assembly of the people of God, four hundred thousand men who drew a sword. The Benjaminites heard that the Israelites had gone up to Mizpeh, and the Israelites came and said, "Tell us, where did this wickedness take place?"

The Levite, the husband of the woman that was slain, answered and said, "I and my concubine went into Gibeah in Benjamin to lodge. The men of Gibeah rose against me and surrounded the house at night against me. They wished to kill me, and they abused my concubine, and she is dead. I took hold of my concubine, and cut her into pieces, and sent the parts to every border of the inheritance of the Israelites, as they have worked immorally and an abomination in Israel. Look, all you are Israelites. Consider and take counsel here among yourselves."

All the people rose up as one man, saying, "Not one of us will return to his tent, and not one of us will return to his house. Now this is what will be done in Gibeah, we will go up against it by lot. Moreover, we will take ten men for a hundred for all the tribes of Israel, and a hundred for a thousand, and a thousand for ten thousand, to take provisions, for them to come to Gibeah of Benjamin, to do to it according to all the abomination, which they worked in Israel."

All the men of Israel were gathered to the city as one man. The tribes of Israel sent men through the whole tribe of Benjamin, saying, "What is this wickedness that has been worked among you? Now then give up the lawless men that are in Gibeah, and we will put them to death, and purge out wickedness from Israel, but the Benjaminites did not agree to listen to the voice of their brothers the Israelites. The Benjaminites were gathered from their cities to Gibeah, to go out to fight with the Israelites. The Benjaminites from their cities were numbered on that day, twenty-three thousand, every man drawing a sword, besides the inhabitants of Gibeah, who numbered seven hundred chosen men of all the people able to use both hands alike.

All these, could sling stones at a rabbit, and not miss. The men of Israel, other than Benjamin, numbered four hundred thousand men that drew a sword, all these were men of war. They rose and went up to the Temple of El, and asked God, "Who will lead us to fight with the Benjaminites?"

The Lord said, "Judah will go up first as a leader."

The Israelites rose up in the morning and camped near Gibeah. They went out, all the men of Israel, to fight with Benjamin, and engaged with them at Gibeah. The Benjaminites went out from Gibeah, and they destroyed in Israel on that day twenty-two thousand men. The men of Israel strengthened themselves and again engaged in battle in the place where they had engaged on the first day. The Israelites went up, and cried out to the Lord until evening, and inquired of the Lord, saying, "Will we enter battle again with our brothers the Benjaminites?"

The Lord said, "Go up against them."

The Israelites advanced against the Benjaminites on the second day. The Benjaminites went out to meet them from Gibeah on the second day and destroyed another eighteen thousand of the Israelites of those who drew a sword. The Israelites and all the people got up, and went to the Temple of El, and they wept and sat there, before the Lord. They fasted on that day until evening, and offered whole burnt offerings and perfect sacrifices to the Lord, for the box of Lord the god was there in those days. Phinehas the son of Eleazar the son of Aaron stood before it in those days, and the Israelites inquired of the Lord, "Will we again go out to fight with our brothers, the Benjaminites?"

The Lord answered, "Go up, tomorrow and I will give them into your hands."

The Israelites set an ambush near Gibeah, and the Israelites went up against the Benjaminites on the third day and formed up against Gibeah as before. The Benjaminites went out to meet the people, and were all drawn out of the city, and began to attack and kill the people as before in the roads, which go up to the Temple of El, and each from Gibeah was outnumbered by about thirty men of Israel. The Benjaminites said, "They'll fall before us like before."

The Israelites said, "Let us flee, and draw them out from the city into the roads," and they did so. All the men rose up out of their places and engaged in Ba'al Tamar,[1] and those laying in wait of Israel advanced from their place, the cave of Geba.[2] There came against Gibeah ten thousand men were chosen out of all of Israel, and the fight was severe, and they did not know that evil was coming on them. The Lord slaughtered Benjamin before the Israelites, and the Israelites destroyed 25,100 Benjaminites on that day, all those that drew a sword. The Benjaminites saw that they were slaughtered.

The men of Israel gave place to Benjamin because they trusted in the ambuscade which they had prepared against Gibeah. When they retreated, then the layers in wait rose up, and they moved towards Gibeah, and the whole ambush came out, and they struck the city with the edge of the sword. The Israelites had a signal of battle with the layers in wait, that they should send up a signal of smoke from the city. The Israelites saw that the layers in wait had seized Gibeah, and they stood in battle formation, and Benjamin began to kill the wounded ones among the men of Israel, about thirty men, as they said, "Certainly they will fall again before us, as in the first battle."

The signal went up increasingly over the city as a pillar of smoke, and Benjamin looked behind him and saw the destruction of the city rose to the sky. The men of Israel turned back, and the men of Benjamin rushed because they saw that evil had come on them. They ran to the wilderness from before the Israelites and fled, but the battle caught up to them, and they from the cities and destroyed them in the middle of them. They cut down Benjamin, and put an end to them, stopping and trampling them[3] until they came near Gibeah on the east. There fell from Benjamin eighteen thousand men, all these were men of might.

The rest turned and fled to the wilderness to the rock of Rimmon, and the Israelites picked off another five thousand men, and the Israelites chased after them as far as Gedan, and they slaughtered another two thousand of them. All that fell of Benjamin were twenty-five thousand men that drew a sword on that day, all these were men of might. The rest turned and fled to the wilderness to the rock of Rimmon, only six hundred men, and they stayed four months in the rock of Rimmon. The Israelites returned to the Benjaminites and slaughtered them with the edge of the sword from the city of Methla,[4] including the livestock and everything that was found in all the cities, and they burnt with fire the cities they found.

Judges: Chapter 20 Notes

1 Codex Vaticanus: Baalthamar (ΒΑΑΛΘΑΜΑρ)

• Aleppo Codex: bôl tmr (**בעל תמר**)

• Leningrad Codex: ba'al Tamar (בַּעַל תָּמָר)

• Targum Jerusalem: Yericho (יְרִיחוֹ). Translation: Jericho

Eusebius reported the existence of a Beth-Tamar in Roman Judea as late as the 4th century AD, however, nothing is known about Ba'al Tamar or Beth-Tamar today. Apparently, nothing was known about is when the Targum Jerusalem was translated as well, as the translator substituted Jericho.

2 Codex Vaticanus: Maaragabe (ΜΑΑΡΑΓΑΒΕ)

• Codex Alexandrinus: dysmôn tês Gabaa (ΔΥϹΜΩΝΤΗϹΓΑΒΑΑ). Translation: setting the Gabaa

• Aleppo Codex: môrh gbô (מערה גבע). Translation: cave Geba

• Leningrad Codex: ma'areh-Gava (מַעֲרֵה־גָבַע). Translation: cave of Gava

• Targum Jerusalem: meishar Giv'ata (מֵישַׁר גִבְעָתָא). Translation: strength (or flat) of Givata

As the Codex Vaticanus includes a transliteration of the term found in the Masoretic Text, that term is imported into this translation as 'cave of Geba.'

3 Codex Vaticanus: cae ediôxan auton apo Noua cata poda autou (ΚΑΙ ΕΔΙΩΞΑΝ ΑΥΤΟΝΑΠΟΝΟΥΑΚΑΤΑΠΟΔΑΑΥΤΟΥ). Translation: and chased them from Noua and against them

• Codex Alexandrinus: catapausae auton catapausin cae catepatêsan auton (ΚΑΤΑΠΑΥϹΑΙΑΥΤΟΝΚΑΤΑΠΑΥϹΙΝΚΑΙΚΑΤΕΠΑΤΗϹΑΝΑΥΤΟΝ). Translation: put an end to them stopped and trampled them

• Aleppo Codex: hrdyphû mnûhh hdrykhû (הרדיפהו מנוחה הדריכהו). Translation: persecuted them easily guided (or directed, commanded)

• Leningrad Codex: hirdifuhu menuchah hidrichuhu (הִרְדִיפֻהוּ מְנוּחָה הִדְרִיכֻהוּ). Translation: persecuted them easily guided (or directed, commanded)

• Targum Jerusalem: redafunun mibbeit neyachahon teradunun (רְדָפוּנוּן מִבֵּית נְיָחֲהוֹן טְרָדוּנוּן). Translation: chased them away from inside their inheritance

The translation in the Codex Vaticanus appears to have an error, which was fixed in the Codex Alexandrinus. The Greek translators appear to have mistranslated menuchah (מְנוּחָה), meaning 'easily,' as 'from Noua' (from Noua), therefore the Codex Alexandrius is followed here.

4 Codex Vaticanus: Methla (ⲘⲉⲐⲗⲁ)

- Codex Alexandrinus: hexês (ⲉⲌⲎⲥ). Translation: following

- Aleppo Codex: mtm (מתם). Translation: men

- Leningrad Codex: metom (מְתֹם). Translation: men

- Targum Jerusalem: mikirveihon (מִקִרְוֵיהוֹן). Translation: original wealth

As all three sources have a different term here, the Codex Vaticanus is followed as it is the oldest.

Judges: Chapter 21

The Israelites swore in Mizpeh, "None of us will give his daughter to a Benjamin as a wife."

The people came to the Temple of El, and sat there until evening before God, and they lifted their voice and cried with a great voice, and said, "Lord the god of Israel! Has this come to pass, That today one tribe should be missing from Israel?"

In the morning the people rose up early, and built an altar, and offered up whole burnt offerings and peace offerings. The Israelites said, "Who of all the tribes of Israel, did not go up in the congregation to the Lord?" as there was a great oath concerning those who did not go up to the Lord in Mizpeh, saying, "He will certainly be put to death."

The Israelites relented towards Benjamin their brothers, and said, "Today one tribe is cut off from Israel. What will we do for wives for the rest that remain? We have sworn by the Lord, not to give them of our daughters as wives."

They asked, "Which man is there of the tribes of Israel, who did not go up to the Lord in Mizpeh?"

No man came to the camp from Jabin Gilead to the assembly. The people were counted, and there was not a man there from the inhabitants of Jabin Gilead. The congregation sent twelve thousand of the strongest men, and they ordered, "Go and slaughter the inhabitants of Jabin Gilead with the edge of the sword. Do this to every male, and you will murder every woman that has laid with a man, but the virgins you will keep alive," and they did so.

They found among the inhabitants of Jabin Gilead four hundred young virgins, who had not known a man by lying with him, and they brought them to Shiloh in the land of Canaan. All the congregation sent and spoke to the Benjaminites in the rock Rimmon, and invited them to make peace. Benjamin returned to the Israelites at that time, and the Israelites gave them the women who they had not murdered from the daughters of Jabin Gilead, and they were content. The people repented for Benjamin because the Lord had made a breach in the tribes of Israel.

The elders of the congregation said, "What will we do for wives for those who remain? For the women of Benjamin have been slaughtered."

They said, "There must be an inheritance for them that escaped of Benjamin, or a tribe will be destroyed out of Israel. We will not be able to give them wives from our daughters, because we swore among the Israelites, saying, 'Cursed is he that gives a wife to Benjamin.'"

They said, "Look! Now there is a feast of the Lord from year to year in Shiloh, which is to the north of Bethel, eastward on the road that goes up from Bethel to Shechem, and from the south of Libnah."

They ordered the Benjaminites, saying, "Go and lie in wait in the vineyards, and you will see, and if the daughters of the inhabitants of Shiloh come out to dance in dances, then you will go out of the vineyards and kidnap for yourselves every man a wife of the daughters of Shiloh, and return to the land of Benjamin. When their fathers or their brothers come to dispute with us, then we will say to them, 'Grant them freely to us, for we have not taken each man his wife in battle. Because you did not give to them at the time, you transgressed.'"

The Benjaminites did so, and they took wives according to their number from the dancers who they kidnapped and they went and returned to their inheritance, and built the cities, and lived in them. The Israelites went home at that time every man to his tribe and his families, and they went every man to his inheritance.

In those days there was no king in Israel, every man did that which was right in his own sight.

Ruth: Chapter 1

In the time when the judges ruled, there was a famine in the land, and a man went from the House of Lehem[1] in Judah[2] to stay in the land of Moab[3] with his wife and his two sons. The man's name was Abimelech,[4] and his wife's name Naomi, and the names of his two sons Mahlon and Chilion, Ephrathites[5] from the House of Lahem in Judah who also traveled to the land of Moab and remained there. Abimelech the husband of Naomi died, and she was left with her two sons. They took for themselves as wives, Moabite women. The name of the one was Orpah, and the name of the second Ruth. They lived there for about ten years. Both Mahlon and Chilion also died, and the woman was left without her husband and her two sons.

She rose up with her two daughters-in-law, and they left out of the land of Moab, for she heard in the country of Moab that the Lord[6] had visited his people to give them bread. She left the place where she was, and her two daughters-in-law with her, and they traveled by road to return to the land of Judah. Naomi said to her daughters-in-law, "Return now, return each to the house of her mother. The Lord deal mercifully with you, as you have dealt with the dead, and with me. The Lord grant you that you may find rest, each of you in the house of her husband," and she kissed them.

They lifted their voice and wept. They said to her, "We will return with you to your people."

Naomi said, "Return now, my daughters. Why do you go with me? Have I more sons in my womb to be your husbands? Turn now, my daughters, for I am too old to be married. As I said, 'Suppose I were married and should carry sons, would you wait for them until they should be grown? Or would you refrain from being married for their sake?' No, my daughters, I am sad for you, that the hand of the Lord has gone out against me."

They lifted their voice and wept again, and Orpah kissed her mother-in-law and returned to her people, but Ruth continued to follow her. Naomi said to Ruth, "Look, your sister-in-law has returned to her people and to her gods, now turn also and follow after your sister-in-law."

Ruth replied, "Don't ask me to leave you, or to turn from following you. Wherever you go, I will go, and wherever you lodge, I will lodge. Your people will be my people, and your god will be my god. Wherever you die, I will die, and there I will be buried. The Lord do so for me, and more also, if I leave you. Only death will divide me and you."

Naomi, seeing that she was determined to go with her, stopped speaking to her about it. They both traveled until they came to the Temple of Lahem, and it came to pass, when they arrived at the Temple of Lahem, that all the city rang with them, and they asked, "Is this Naomi?"

She said to them, "No, do not call me Naomi. Call me Bitter, as Shaddayin[7] has dealt very bitterly with me. I went out full, and the Lord has brought me back empty. Why do you call me Naomi, when the Lord has humbled me and Shaddayin has afflicted me?"

So Naomi and Ruth the Moabitess, her daughter-in-law, returned from the country of Moab, and they arrived at the Temple of Lahem at the beginning of barley harvest.

Ruth: Chapter 1 Notes

1 Codex Vaticanus: Baethleem (ΒΑΙΘΛΕΕΜ)

• Codex Alexandrinus: Bêthleem (ΒΗΘΛΕΕΜ)

• Septuagint ms. 376: Bithleem (βιθλϭϭμ)

• Septuagint ms. 131: Bêthlaeem (βℓθλΔιϭμ)

• Aleppo Codex: byt lhm (**בית לחם**). Translation: house (or temple, abode) of Lehem (or bread)

• Leningrad Codex: beit Lechem (בֵּית לֶחֶם). Translation: house (or temple, abode) of Lehem (or bread)

• Vetus Latina: Bethlem

• Targum on Ruth: beit Lechem (בֵּית לֶחֶם). Translation: house (or temple, abode) of Lehem (or bread)

2 Codex Vaticanus: Iouda (ΙΟΥΔΑ). Translation: Judah

• Septuagint ms. 119: Ioudaeas (ιουΔΔϕΔc). Translation: Judea

• Aleppo Codex: Yhůdh (**יהודה**). Translation: Judah

- Leningrad Codex: Yehudah (יְהוּדָֽה). Translation: Judah

- Targum on Ruth: Yehudah (יְהוּדָה). Translation: Judah

Judah was an iron age kingdom in southern modern Israel and the Palestinian West Bank between approximately 930 and 586 BC, which indicates the story was likely written during this era. The time period mentioned when the judges ruled, dates the story to earlier. Based on the later reference to Naomi being the mother of Obed, the grandfather of King David, the story is set around 1100 BC.

3 Codex Vaticanus: Môab (ΜѠΔΒ). Translation: Moab

- Aleppo Codex: Mŭåb (מואב). Translation: Moab

- Leningrad Codex: Mo'av (מוֹאָב). Translation: Moab

- Targum on Ruth: Mo'av (מוֹאָב). Translation: Moab

Moab was a kingdom in modern Jordan, on the east shore of the Dead Sea from sometime before King Ramesses II of Egypt, who recorded them as a country he conquered during his third Syrian campaign in 1291 BC.

4 Codex Vaticanus: Abimelech (ΑΒΕΙΜΕΛΕΧ)

- Codex Alexandrinus: Alimelec (ΑΛΙΜΕΛΕΚ)

- Codex Basiliano-Vaticanus: Elimelech (ΕΛΙΜΕΛΕΧ)

- Septuagint ms. 241: Alimelech (Αλιμϵλϵχ)

- Septuagint ms. 243: Ailimelech (Αιλιμϵλϵχ)

- Aleppo Codex: Ålymlk (אלימלך)

- Leningrad Codex: Elimelech (אֱלִימֶ֣לֶךְ)

- Targum on Ruth: Elimelech (אֱלִימֶלֶךְ)

This name does not survive in this verse among the Dead Sea Scrolls, however, has survived in later verses.

- Dead Sea Scroll 4QRuthᵃ: ålymlk (אלימלך)

There is no obvious reason the Hasmoneans would have changed the name of Abimelech to Elimelech, unless it was to disassociate King David's house from circa 1000 BC, from the earlier house of King Abimelech, the first King of Israel, circa 1267 to 1264 BC. These two Abimelechs cannot be the same person, as their stories have nothing in common, and they lived a century apart, nevertheless, the names are different in the Septuagint's version of Ruth, translated circa 225 BC and the oldest pre-Masoretic version of Ruth, the Dead Sea Scroll 4QRuthª, dates to the Hasmonean Dynasty (140-37 BC). It is possible that the Hasmoneans did not change the name and there were two versions of the texts in circulation before the Greeks translated the text, or, that the Greeks mistranslated the name.

5 LXX 236: Ephraam (Ε$ραλμ)

- LXX 29: Ephrathaeoe (Ε$ραθλιοι)

- LXX 54: Ephranthaeoe (Ε$ρανθλιοι)

- Aleppo Codex: Åfrtym (אפרתים)

- Leningrad Codex: Efratim (אֶפְרָתִים)

- Targum on Ruth: Efratin rabbanin (אֶפְרָתִין רַבְּנִין). Translation: Ephramite nobles

- Dead Sea Scroll 4QRuthª: Åfrtym (אגרתים)

- Vetus Latina: euphratei

Ephratha (ΕΦΡΑΘΑ) / Efratah (אֶפְרָתָה) was listed as the former name of Bethlehem in the Torah. The name appears to be the Egyptian name, r-pr-t ( ), which translates as 'temple of bread, a direct translation of the Canaanite name byt lhm (𐤁𐤉𐤕 𐤋𐤇𐤌). The same region is later known as the land of Ephriam (אֶפְרַיִם) during the early iron age, and part of the Kingdom of Samaria until it was conquered by Assyrian war in 723 BC. While LXX 236 reads Ephriam, the rest of the sources support the reading or Ephrathiam, indicating that these were the remnants of the Egyptized Bethlehemites that would have still been present in the region in the era the book is set in. This suggests the book of Ruth dates back to the early iron age.

6 Greek: c̄s (κͨ). Translation: lord

- Dead Sea Scroll 4QRuthª: Yhůh (יהוה).

- Aleppo Codex: Yhůh (יהוה)

- Leningrad Codex: Yehvah (יְהוָה)

- Targum on Ruth: yeyah (??). Translation: Yhů

The Septuagint's version of the Ruth was translated before 200 BC, as it was carried south by the Beta Israel community, who left Egypt for Kush (modern Sudan) during the Jewish Rebellion against the Ptolemys in 200 BC. This means it predates the Hasmonean redaction and contains the term Lord (Κύριος) instead of Iaw (Ιαω).

There are no surviving early fragments of the Septuagint's Ruth that include the name, suggesting the word in the Aramaic version of Exodus was Adonai, which meant 'lord' and was also the name of a god in the Canaanite religion, especially in the region around Baalbek, in modern Lebanon. Like the Samaritan Yhů, Adonay was the son of Asherah, suggesting that the Aramaic term in the text the Greek translation was made from used the name Adonay.

The Aramaic sections of Masoretic Daniel that were not translated into Hebrew maintain the term adonai ha'elohim (אֲדֹנָי הָאֱלֹהִים), meaning the 'Lord the gods' where the Septuagint has 'Lord the god' (Κύριον τὸν θεὸν), however, the Hebrew sections have Yehvah elohim (יְהוָה אֱלֹהִים) where the Septuagint has 'Lord the god,' suggesting the Greek more accurately reflects the Aramaic source texts than the Hebrew translation. According to Sanhedrin (103b) tractate in the Talmud, King Manasseh was blamed for removing the name, however, as his grandson Josiah 'restored' the Torah circa 625 BC, one would expect that he would have restored the name as well, if it had have been in Exodus to begin with. Furthermore, the early Torah appears to have already been translated into Aramaic during the era of Manasseh's father king Hezekiah, suggesting that he removed the name during his religious reforms.

As the original translation of Ruth does not appear to have included the name, the term 'Lord' is used in this translation. Lord (Ba'al and Adon) were commonly used in ancient Canaan as titles of the various Canaanite gods, and early Israelites appear to have used the terms the same way themselves. In this context, the Lord in question is Lord Lehem, the Canaanite god of fertility, grains, and rebirth. The limited amount of information that survives about him, suggests he was similar to Osiris and Dionysus, meaning he would have been a precursor to Lord Sabaoth.

---

7 Greek: icanos (ΙΚΑΝΟΣ). Translations: capable (or able, competent, skillful, fit, potent, efficient, apt, shifty)

• LXX 29: ischyros (ισχυβος). Translations: strong (or powerful, mighty)

• Aleppo Codex: šdy (שׁדי). Translation: demons (or phantoms, demonic, ghoulish, devilish)

• Leningrad Codex: Shaddai (שַׁדְּי). Translation: (or demons, phantoms, demonic, ghoulish, devilish)

• Targum on Ruth: Shaddai (שַׁדַּי). Translation: (or powerful)

• Vetus Latina: deus. Translation: god

In the Septuagint, the term El Shaddai was directly transliterated as theos Saddai (θεος Σαδδαι) once in Ezekiel, and therefore the term must have been in the Aramaic texts the Greeks used to translate Ezekiel, however, in the other books of the Septuagint, the term 'almighty' (παντοκρατορος) appears where the Masoretic Texts have Shaddai. Šdyn (𐤔𐤃𐤉𐤍), generally anglicized as Shaddayin, was a Moabite god in the 800s BC, as evidenced by the Deir Alla Inscription (or KAI 312), which was found during an excavation at Deir 'Alla, Jordan, and described Balaam as the prophet of the Elohin and Shaddayin, believed to be Moabite translations of 'Elohim' and 'Shaddai.'

In the Book of Ruth, Shaddai is placed in opposition to the Lord God of Israel, which implies the name was left in the Judahite version of Ruth after the Hasmonean redaction as it was viewed as a reference to the Moabite god, who 'dealt very bitterly' with Naomi when she was in Moab. The Greek and Hebrew translations often differ in regards to the name or title Shaddai, suggesting that the Aramaic and Canaanite (Judahite or Samaritan) source texts they worked from differed in regards to this word. The term was omitted throughout Cosmic Genesis, suggesting that when the word was first encountered the Greeks did not know how to interpret it. It is equally possible that it was the Aramaic translator who had omitted it, however, it was almost certainly in the Canaanite version the translator worked from, as it is used consistently in the rest of Genesis, and is mentioned again when Moses god's name Ān is introduced in the Septuagint's Exodus. The cause of the confusion over the term Shaddai, is likely due to the difference between the meaning of the word in Canaanite versus Aramaic.

In Akkadian cuneiform, which was adopted as the written script by many cultures, the term was ^{deity}Šēdu (𒀭𒆳), however, it referred to a 'protective spirit' or 'lesser god.' In the later Aramaic language, the word became šydå (𐡔𐡉𐡃𐡀), meaning 'demon' in the classical sense, as a type of muse or nymph. Whereas in Canaanite, šd (𐤔𐤃) took on a different meaning, generally interpreted as 'powerful' by the Early Classical Era, which is likely where the Greeks ultimately derived the term 'omnipotent' (παντοκράτορος), which was used later in the Septuagint where the Masoretic Text generally uses the term Shaddai.

This alternate interpretation of the šd (𐤔𐤃) in Canaanite is likely due to the Egyptian New Kingdom era rule over Canaan, when Shed (𓈙𓂧𓀭, transliteration: šd), was worshiped in the region. Shed, who was often referred to as 'the savior,' was virtually identical to the earlier Canaanite god Resheph who was largely suppressed after the fall of the Hyksos dynasty. In the Masoretic Book of Job, Eliphaz referred to humanity as the 'sons of Resheph' (בני-רשף) instead of the 'sons of Adam,' and then refers god as šdy (שדי).

This usage is consistent throughout Masoretic Job, indicating that at some point the name Resheph was updated to Shaddai, likely during the New Kingdom era, when Resheph worship was suppressed due to his associated with the earlier Hyksos dynasty. During the early New Kingdoms era, holy texts about Resheph would have been updated to Shed (𐤔𐤃𐤉), which would have been transliterated into Canaanite using the Akkadian Cuneiform script in the late New Kingdom era as ^{deity}Šēdu (𒀭𒂊), before being translated into Canaanite using the Phoenician script in the early iron age as šdy (𐤔𐤃𐤉), resulting in the confusing 'god of demons' (𐤔𐤃𐤉) in Aramaic. In this particular verse, 'capable' (ικανος) appears to be a translation of a word similar to šdy (שׁדי), but not actually šdy, or 'omnipotent' (παντοκράτορος) would have been used, as in other books of the Septuagint, and therefore the Moabite version of the name, Shaddayin, is used in this translation.

Ruth: Chapter 2

Naomi had a friend, an acquaintance of her husband, and the man was a mighty man of the families of Abimelech. His name was Boaz. Ruth the Moabitess said to Naomi, "Let me go now to the field, and I will glean from the ears behind whichever man will let me."

She replied to her, "Go, daughter."

She went and gleaned in the field behind the reapers and she happened by chance to come on a portion of the land of Boaz of the families of Abimelech, and Boaz came from the Temple of Lahem and said to the reapers, "The Lord be with you."

They said to him, "The Lord bless you."

Boaz asked his servant who was in charge of the reapers, "Whose is this girl?"

His servant who was in charge of the reapers answered and said, "It is the Moabite girl who returned with Naomi out of the land of Moab. She asked, 'I beg you, let me glean and gather among the sheaves after the reapers,' and she came and worked from morning until evening, and did not rest even a little in the field."

Boaz said to Ruth, "Have you not heard, my daughter? Don't go to glean in another field and don't leave here. Stay close with my girls, and watch the field where my men reap, and go after them. Look, I have ordered the young men not to touch you, and when you thirst, then you may go to the vessels, and drink of that which the young men will have drawn."

She fell on her face, and did reverence to the ground, and said to him, "How is it that I have found grace in your eyes, that you should take notice of me, when I am a foreigner?"

Boaz answered her, "It has been told to me how you have dealt with your mother-in-law after the death of your husband, and how you left your father and your mother, and the land of your birth, and came to a people who you did not know before. The Lord repay your work, may a full reward be given you of the Lord God of Israel, to whom you have come to trust under his wings."

She said, "Let me find grace in your sight, my lord, because you have comforted me, and because you have spoken kindly to your handmaid, and look, I will be one of your servants."

Boaz said to her, "Now it is time to eat. Come here, and you will eat of the bread, and you will dip your food in the vinegar."

Ruth sat by the side of the reapers, and Boaz handed her a meal and she ate until she was satisfied and left. She rose up to glean and Boaz ordered his young men, "Let her even among the sheaves, and do not reproach her. You, carry it for her and drop for her some of that which is piled up. Let her eat and glean, and don't rebuke her."

So she gleaned in the field until evening and beat out all that she had gleaned, and it was about a bushel of barley. She picked it up and went into the city. Her mother-in-law saw what she had gleaned, and Ruth brought out and gave her the food which she had left after she had been satisfied. Her mother-in-law said to her, "Where have you gleaned today, and where have you worked? Blessed be he that took notice of you."

Ruth told her mother-in-law where she had worked, and said, "The name of the man with who I worked today is Boaz."

Naomi said to her daughter-in-law, "Blessed is he by the Lord because he has not failed in his mercy with the living and with the dead. The man is a close relative to us, he is one of our relations."

Ruth said to her mother-in-law, "Yes, he also told me, 'Keep close to my girls, until the men will have finished all my reaping.'"

Naomi said to Ruth her daughter-in-law, 'It is well, daughter, that you went out with his girls, so they will not meet you in another field."

Ruth joined herself to the girls of Boaz to glean until they had finished the barley harvest and the wheat harvest.

Ruth: Chapter 3

She lodged with her mother-in-law, and Naomi her mother-in-law said to her, "My daughter, should I not seek rest for you, that it may be well with you? Now is not Boaz our relative, with whose girls you were? Look, he winnows barley this night on the floor. Wash and anoint yourself, and get dressed and go up to the threshing floor. Do not show yourself to the man until he has done eating and drinking. It will come to pass when he lies down, that you will watch the place where he lies down, and will come and lift up the covering of his feet, and will lie down. He will tell you what to do."

Ruth said to her, "I will do all that you say, She went down to the threshing floor, and did according to all that her mother-in-law told her. Boaz ate and drank, and his heart was glad, and he came to lie down by the side of the heap of grain, and she sneaked to him and lifted the covering off his feet. It was past midnight and the man was amazed, and troubled, and saw a woman laying at his feet."

He asked, "Who are you?"

She answered, "I am your handmaid Ruth, spread your skirt over your handmaid, for you are a near relative."

Boaz said, "Blessed are you by the Lord God,[1] my daughter, for you have made your latter kindness greater than the former, in that you don't chase after young men, whether they are poor or rich. Now don't be afraid, my daughter, whatever you will say I will do to you, for all the tribe of my people know that you are a virtuous woman. Now I am truly related to you, nevertheless, there is a relative nearer than I. Lodge here for the night, and it will be in the morning, if he will do the duty of a relative to you, well let him do it, but if he will not do the duty of a relative to you, I will do the relative's duty to you, as the Lord lives. Lie down until the morning."

She lay at his feet until the morning, and she rose up before the sun rose, and Boaz said, "Let it not be known that a woman came into the floor."

He said to her, "Bring the apron that is on you," and she held it, and he measured six measures of barley and put them on her, and she went into the city. Ruth went to her mother-in-law, and she said to her, "My daughter!" and Ruth told her all that the man had done to her.

She said to her, "He gave me these six measures of barley, as he said to me, 'Don't go empty to your mother-in-law.'"

She replied, "Sit still, my daughter, until you will know how the matter will fall out. The man will not rest today until the matter is accomplished.

Ruth: Chapter 3 Notes

1 Codex Vaticanus: c̅ô̅ t̅h̅ô̅ (κ̅ω̅θ̅ω̅). Translation: Lord God

- Codex Alexandrinus: cyriô (κυριω). Translation: Lord
- LXX 106: Cyriô tô theô (κυριω τω θεω). Translation: Lord the god
- LXX 29: Theô (θεω). Translations: God
- Aleppo Codex: Yhůh (יהוה)
- Leningrad Codex: Yhvah (יְהוָה)
- Targum on Ruth: yeyah (יְיָ). Translation: Yhů

The Septuagint's version of the Ruth was translated circa 225 BC, before the Hasmonean redaction, and contains the term Lord God (Κυριω Θεω) instead of the name Yhvah / Yhů. The Aramaic sections of Masoretic Daniel that were not translated into Hebrew maintain the term adonai ha'elohim (אֲדֹנָ֗י הָאֱלֹהִ֛ים), meaning the 'Lord the gods' where the Septuagint has 'Lord the god' (Κύριον τὸν θεὸν), however, the Hebrew sections have Yehvah elohim (יְהוָ֥ה אֱלֹהִ֖ים) where the Septuagint has 'Lord the god,' suggesting the Greek more accurately reflects the Aramaic source texts than the Hebrew translation.

According to the Sanhedrin (103b) tractate in the Talmud, King Manasseh was blamed for removing the name, however, as his grandson Josiah 'restored' the Torah circa 625 BC, one would expect that he would have restored the name as well, if it had have been in Exodus to begin with. Furthermore, the early Torah appears to have already been translated into Aramaic during the era of Manasseh's father king Hezekiah, suggesting that he removed the name during his religious reforms.

As the original text of Ruth was almost certainly written in Phoenician (Paleo-Hebrew), the original term was probably Ådn Ålm (𐤀𐤃𐤍 𐤀𐤋𐤌). Ådn Ålm was a Canaanite epithet for El, found in the Ugaritic Texts from the 1300s BC. In the polytheistic Canaanite religion, the term translates as 'Father of the gods' as El was the father of the 70 Elohim (gods) and creator of the world in the Canaanite religion. The term 'father of the gods' subsequently became Lord God in the Aramaic translation made in the Babylonian or Persian era, before being replaced by Yehvah in the Hasmonean dynasty. According to several ancient Hebrew scriptures, El had a major temple in Shiloh, the capital of ancient Samaria, which Jacob built in the Book of Genesis. El is also mentioned in later books of the Septuagint and appears to have been one of the main gods worshiped by the ancient Israelites, as well as other Canaanites. As Κυριω Θεω translates directly as Lord God, that term is used in this translation.

Ruth: Chapter 4

Boaz went up to the gate and sat there, and watched until the relative passed by, of whom Boaz had spoken. Boaz said to him, "Turn aside, and sit here," and he turned aside and sat down. Boaz called ten men of the elders of the city, and said, "Sit here," and they sat down.

Boaz said to the relative, "The matter regards the portion of the field which was our brother Abimelech's which was given to Naomi when she returned out of the land of Moab. I said, 'I will inform you. Buy it before those who sit, and before the elders of my people. If you will redeem it, redeem it, but if you will not redeem it, tell me, and I will know, for there is no one beside you to do the duty of a relative, and I am next after you."

He replied, "I am here, and I will redeem it."

Boaz said, "In the day of your buying the field of the hand of Naomi and of Ruth the Moabitess the wife of the deceased, you must also buy her, to raise up the name of the dead on his inheritance."

The relative said, "Will I not be able to redeem it for myself, in case I damage my own inheritance? You redeem my right for yourself, as I will not be able to redeem it."

This was the ordinance in Israel for redemption in former times, and for a bargain, to confirm every word, a man removed his shoe and gave it to his neighbor that redeemed his right. This was a testimony in Israel. The relative said to Boaz, "Buy my right for yourself, and he took off his shoe and gave it to him."

Boaz said to the elders and to all the people, "You are this day witnesses, that I have bought all that was Abimelech's, and all that belonged to Chilion and Mahlon, of the hand of Naomi. Moreover, I have bought for myself as wife Ruth the Moabitess, the wife of Mahlon, to raise up the name of the dead on his inheritance, so the name of the dead will not be destroyed from among his brothers, and from the tribe of his people. You are on this day witnesses."

All the people who were in the gate said, "We are witnesses," and the elders said, "The Lord make your wife who goes into your house, as Rachel and as Leah, who both together built the house of Israel, and worked mightily in Ephrath, and there will be a name for you in the Temple of Lahem. Let your house be as the house of Pharez, who Tamar carried for Judah, of the seed which the Lord will give you of this handmaid. Boaz took Ruth, and she became his wife, and he went into her, and the Lord gave her conception, and she carried a son.

The woman said to Naomi, "Blessed is the Lord, who has not allowed a redeemer to fail you this day, even to make your name famous in Israel. He will be for you a restorer of your mind, and one to cherish your old age. For your daughter-in-law which has loved you, who is better to you than seven sons, has born him."

Naomi took the child and laid it on her chest, and became a nurse to it. The neighbors gave it a name, saying, "A son has been born to Naomi," and they called his name Obed. This is the father of Jesse the father of David.

These are the generations of Pharez:

Pharez fathered Hezron,

Hezron fathered Ram,

Ram fathered Amminadab,

Amminadab fathered Nahshon,

Nahshon fathered Salmon,

Salmon fathered Boaz,

Boaz fathered Obed.

Obed fathered Jesse,

and Jesse fathered David.

Maps

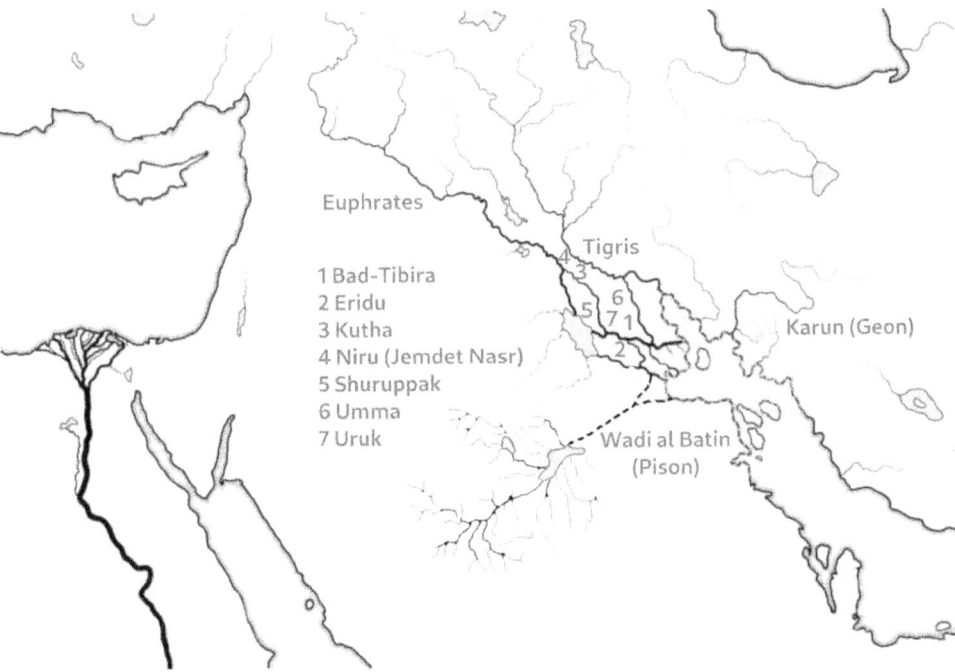

A map of Sumer between 6500 and 2900 BC.

Euphrates

Tigris

1 Bad-Tibira
2 Eridu
3 Kutha
4 Niru (Jemdet Nasr)
5 Shuruppak
6 Umma
7 Uruk

Karun (Geon)

Wadi al Batin
(Pison)

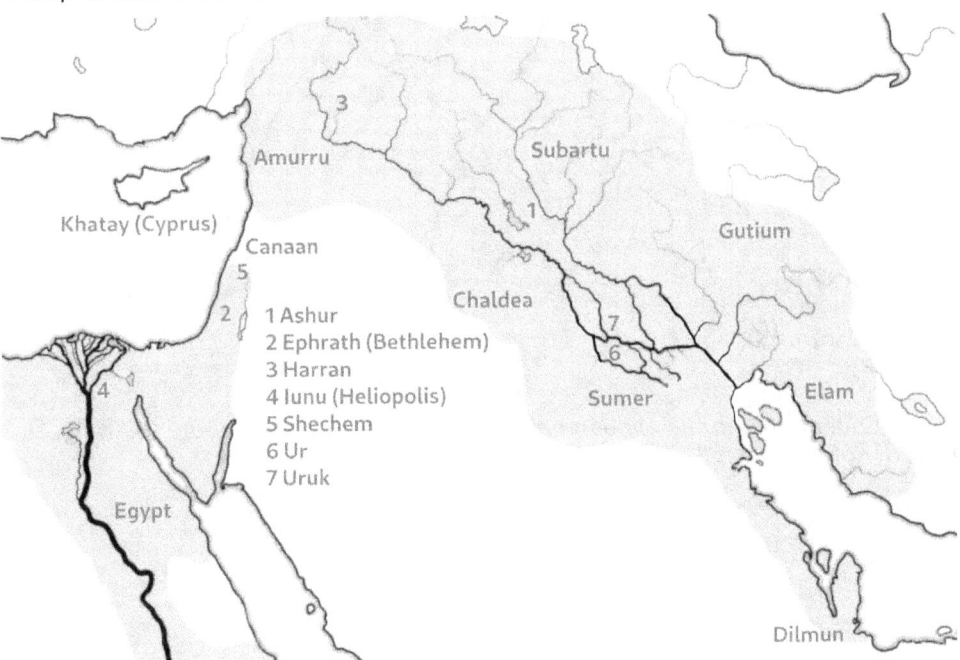

Map of the Neo-Sumerian Empire (Ur III) and Egypt circa 2000 BC.

Amurru

Subartu

Khatay (Cyprus)

Canaan

Gutium

Chaldea

1 Ashur
2 Ephrath (Bethlehem)
3 Harran
4 Iunu (Heliopolis)
5 Shechem
6 Ur
7 Uruk

Sumer

Elam

Egypt

Dilmun

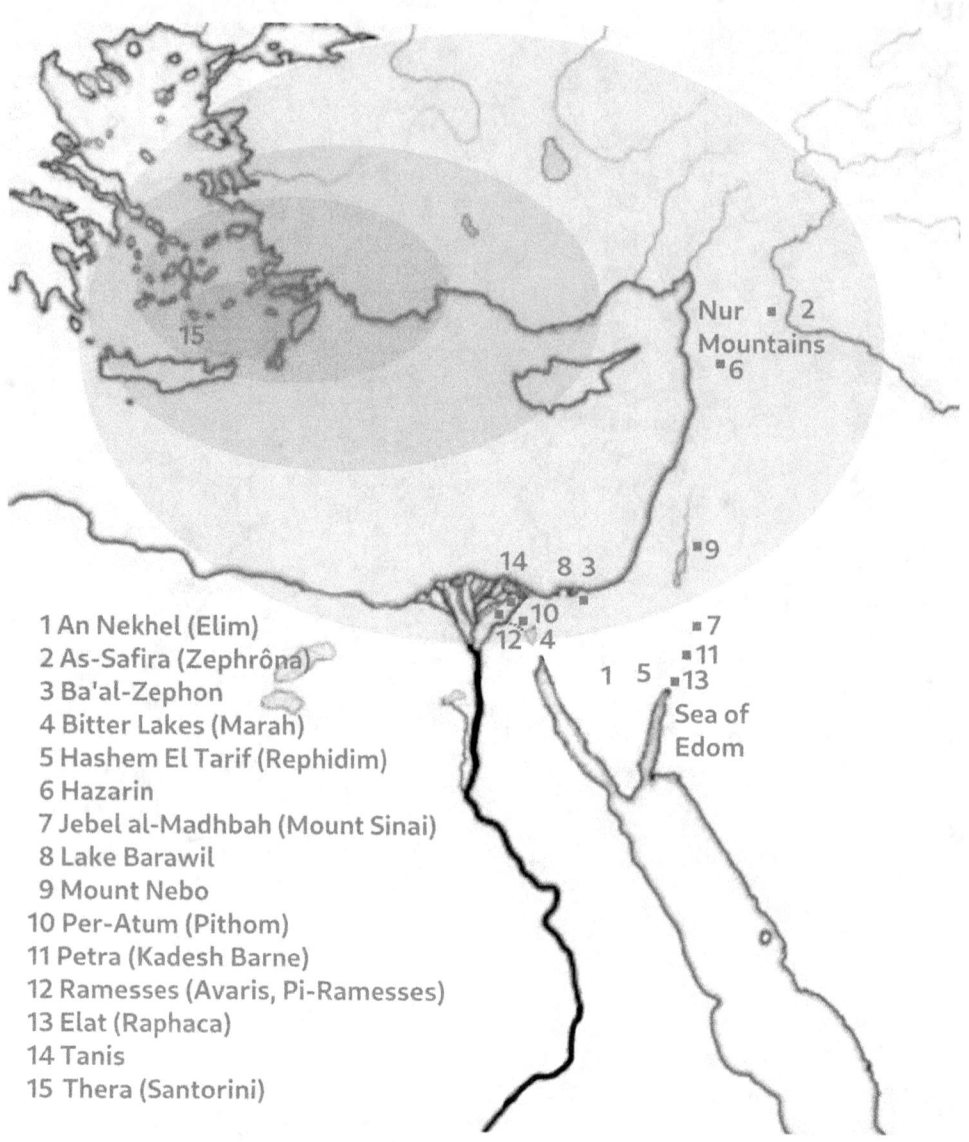

1 An Nekhel (Elim)
2 As-Safira (Zephrôna)
3 Ba'al-Zephon
4 Bitter Lakes (Marah)
5 Hashem El Tarif (Rephidim)
6 Hazarin
7 Jebel al-Madhbah (Mount Sinai)
8 Lake Barawil
9 Mount Nebo
10 Per-Atum (Pithom)
11 Petra (Kadesh Barne)
12 Ramesses (Avaris, Pi-Ramesses)
13 Elat (Raphaca)
14 Tanis
15 Thera (Santorini)

Egypt and Canaan during the Minoan Eruption. The gray regions denote the range and severity of the ash fall.

Septuagint Manuscripts

The following is a list of the Septuagint manuscripts referenced in the notes for this book.

LXX A (Codex Alexandrinus) is dated to the 5th century. It is currently located at the British Library (Royal 1 D. VIII) in London.

LXX B (Codex Vaticanus) is dated to the 4th century. It is currently located at the Vatican Library (Gr. 1209) in Vatican City.

LXX D (Cotton Genesis) is dated to the 4th through 6th centuries. It is currently located at the British Library (Otto B VI) in London.

LXX F (Codex Ambrosiano A 147) is dated to the 5th century. It is currently located at the Ambrosian Library (A. 147 inf.) in Milan.

LXX G (Codex Colberto-Sarravianus) is dated to the 4th or 5th century. Sections are currently located at the University Library (Voss. Graec. in qu. 8) in Leiden, National Library of France (Coisl. Gr. 17) in Paris, and the National Library of Russia (Gr. 3) in St. Petersburg.

LXX L (Vienna Genesis) is dated to the 5th or 6th century. It is currently located at the Austrian National Library (Theol. Gr. 31) in Vienna.

LXX V (Codex Venetus) is dated to the 8th century. It is currently located at the Marciana Library (Gr. 1) in Venice.

LXX W^{I} (Codex Freer Greek MS. V) is dated to the 5th century. It is currently located at the Smithsonian Freer Gallery of Art (Inv. Nr. 06.292) in Washington.

LXX 14 is dated to the 11th century. It is currently located at the Vatican Library (Vat. Palat. Gr. 203) in Vatican City.

LXX 15 is dated to the 10th century. It is currently located at the National Library of France (Coisl. Gr. 2) in Paris.

LXX 16 is dated to the 11th century. It is currently located at the Laurentian Library (v. 38) in Florence.

LXX 17 is dated to the 10th century. It is currently located at the State Historical Museum (Gr. 385) in Moscow.

LXX 18 is dated to the 11th century. It is currently located at the Laurentian Library (Pal. 242) in Florence.

LXX 19 is dated to the 12th century. It is currently located at the Chigi Palace (R. VI. 38) in Rome.

LXX 25 is dated to the 11th century. It is currently located at the Bavarian State Library (Gr. 9) in Munich.

LXX 28 is dated to the 10th or 11th centuries. It is currently located at the Vatican Library (Vat. gr. 2122) in Vatican City.

LXX 29 is dated to the 14th century. It is currently located at the Marciana Library (Gr. 2) in Venice.

LXX 30 is dated to the 11th or 12th centuries. It is currently located at the Casanatense Library (1444) in Rome.

LXX 31 is dated to the 15th century. It is currently located at the Austrian National Library (Theol. Gr. 7) in Vienna.

LXX 44 is dated to the 15th century. It is currently located at the Stadtbibliothek (A 1) in Zittau.

LXX 46 is dated to the 15th century. It is currently located at the National Library of France (Coisl. Gr. 4) in Paris.

LXX 52 is dated to the 14th century. It is currently located at the Laurentian Library (Acquisti 44) in Florence.

LXX 53 is dated to 1439. It is currently located at the National Library of France (Gr. 17 A) in Paris.

LXX 54 is dated to the 13th or 14th century. It is currently located at the National Library of France (Gr. 5) in Paris.

LXX 55 is dated to the 10th century. It is currently located at the Vatican Library (Regin. Gr. 1) in Vatican City.

LXX 56 is dated to 1093. It is currently located at the National Library of France (Gr. 3) in Paris.

LXX 57 is dated to the 11th century. It is currently located at the Vatican Library (Gr. 747) in Vatican City.

LXX 58 is dated to the 11th century. It is currently located at the Vatican Library (Regin. gr. 10) in Vatican City.

LXX 59 is dated to the 15th century. It is currently located at the University Library (BE 7b. 10) in Glasgow.

LXX 64 is dated to the 10th century. It is currently located at the National Library of France (Gr. 2) in Paris.

LXX 68 is dated to the 15th century. It is currently located at the Biblioteca Marciana (Gr. 5) in Venice.

LXX 71 is dated to the 13th century. It is currently located at the National Library of France (Coisl. Gr. 1) in Paris.

LXX 72 is dated to the 13th century. It is currently located at the Bodleian Library (Canonic. Gr. 35) in Oxford.

LXX 73 is dated to the 11th and 12th century. It is currently located at the Vatican Library (Vat. gr. 746) in Vatican City.

LXX 74 is dated to the 13th century. It is currently located at the Laurentian Library (S. Marco 700) in Florence.

LXX 75 is dated to 1125. It is currently located at University College (52) in Oxford.

LXX 76 is dated to the 13th century. It is currently located at National Library of France (Coisl. Gr. 4) in Paris.

LXX 77 is dated to the 13th or 14th centuries. It is currently located at the Vatican Library (Gr. 748) in Vatican City.

LXX 78 is dated to the 12th century. It is currently located at the Vatican Library (Gr. 383) in Vatican City.

LXX 79 is dated to the 12th or 13th centuries. It is currently located at the Vatican Library (Gr. 1668) in Vatican City.

LXX 82 is dated to the 12th century. It is currently located at the National Library of France (Coisl. Gr. 3) in Paris.

LXX 83 is dated to the 16th century. It is currently located at the Archivo da Torre do Tombo (540. 669. 668. 671. 670.) in Lisbon.

LXX 84 is dated to the 10th or 11th centuries. It is currently located at the Vatican Library (Gr. 1901) in Vatican City.

LXX 106 is dated to the 14th century. It is currently located at the Biblioteca Comunale Ariostea (187 I-III) in Ferrara.

LXX 107 is dated to 1334. It is currently located at the Biblioteca Comunale Ariostea (188 I) in Ferrara.

LXX 108 is dated to the 13th century. It is currently located at the Vatican Library (Gr. 330) in Vatican City.

LXX 118 is dated to the 11th or 12th century. It is currently located at the National Library of France (Gr. 6) in Paris.

LXX 119 is dated to the 10th century. It is currently located at the National Library of France (Gr. 7) in Paris.

LXX 120 is dated to the 12th or 13th centuries. It is currently located at the Biblioteca Marciana (Gr. 23) in Venice.

LXX 121 is dated to the 10th century. It is currently located at the Biblioteca Marciana (Gr. 3) in Venice.

LXX 122 is dated to the 15th century. It is currently located at the Biblioteca Marciana (Gr. 6) in Venice.

LXX 125 is dated to the 14th century. It is currently located at the State Historical Museum (Gr. 30) in Moscow.

LXX 126 is dated to the 1475. It is currently located at the State Historical Museum (Gr. 19) in Moscow.

LXX 127 is dated to the 10th century. It is currently located at the State Historical Museum (Gr. 31) in Moscow.

LXX 128 is dated to the 11th century. It is currently located at the Vatican Library (Gr. 1657) in Vatican City.

LXX 129 is dated to the 11th or 12th centuries. It is currently located at the Vatican Library (Gr. 1252) in Vatican City.

LXX 130 is dated to the 12th or 13th centuries. It is currently located at the Austrian National Library (Theol. Gr. 23) in Vienna.

LXX 131 is dated to the 10th century. It is currently located at the Austrian National Library (Theol. Gr. 57) in Vienna.

LXX 134 is dated to the 11th centuries. It is currently located at the Biblioteca Marciana (Plut. 5.1) in Venice.

LXX 135 is dated to the 10th centuries. It is currently located at the University Library (A. N. III. 13) in Basel.

LXX 241 is dated to the 17th century. It is currently located at the British Museum (Harley MS 7522 A) in London.

LXX 246 is dated to 1195 AD. It is currently located at the Vatican Library (Gr. 1238) in Vatican City

LXX 313 is dated to the 11th century. It is currently located at the National Library of Greece (43) in Athens.

LXX 314 is dated to the 13th century. It is currently located at the National Library of Greece (44) in Athens.

LXX 318 is dated to the 10th or 11th centuries. It is currently located at the Vatopedi (598) on Mount Athos.

LXX 319 is dated to 1021. It is currently located at the Vatopedi (600) on Mount Athos.

LXX 320 is dated to the 12th century. It is currently located at the Vatopedi (602) on Mount Athos.

LXX 321 is dated to the 14th century. It is currently located at the Vatopedi (603) on Mount Athos.

LXX 343 is dated to the 11th century. It is currently located at the Great Lavra (352) on Mount Athos.

LXX 344 is dated to the 10th century. Sections are currently located at the Pantokratoros Monastery (24) on Mount Athos, and the Patriarchal Library (Τάφου 510 β) in Jerusalem.

LXX 346 is dated to 1326. It is currently located at the Protaton (53) on Mount Athos.

LXX 370 is dated to the 11th through 14th centuries. It is currently located at the Vatican Library (Chis. R VIII 61) in Vatican City.

LXX 376 is dated to the 15th century. It is currently located at the Royal Library (Y (Griech.)-II-5) in El Escorial.

LXX 381 is dated to the 11th century. It is currently located at the Royal Library (Ω-1-13) in El Escorial.

LXX 392 is dated to the 10th century. It is currently located at the Abbey of Saint Mary of Grottaferrata (A. γ. I) in Grottaferrata.

LXX 400 is dated to the 11th century. It is currently located at the National Library of Greece (Μετ. Τάφου, 224) in Athens.

LXX 407 is dated to the 9th century. It is currently located at the Patriarchal Library (Τάφου 2) in Jerusalem.

LXX 408 is dated to the 12th or 13th centuries. It is currently located at the Patriarchal Library (Τάφου 3) in Jerusalem.

LXX 413 is dated to the 13th century. It is currently located at the Library of the Topkapı Palace (8) in Istanbul.

LXX 414 is dated to the 14th century. It is currently located at the University Library (Voss. Graec. in fol. 13) in Leiden.

LXX 416 is dated to the 14th century. It is currently located at the University Library (Gr. 16, Bl 150-253) in Leipzig.

LXX 417 is dated to 1103. It is currently located at the Archiepiscopal. Library (1214) in London.

LXX 422 is dated to the 12th century. It is currently located at the British Library (Add. 35123) in London.

LXX 426 is dated to the 11th century. It is currently located at the British Library (Add. 39585) in London.

LXX 458 is dated to the 12th century. It is currently located at the University Library (62) in Messina.

LXX 500 is dated to the 11th or 12th centuries. It is currently located at the Austrian National Library (Suppl. Gr. 176) in Vienna.

LXX 509 is dated to the 9th or 10th centuries. Sections are currently located at the Bodleian Library (Auct. T. inf. 2. 1) in Oxford, University Library (Add. 1879. 7) in Cambridge, British Library (Add. 20002) in London, and the National Library of Russia (Gr. 62) in St. Petersburg.

LXX 527 is dated to the 14th century. It is currently located at the Bibliothèque de l'Arsenal (Gr. 8415) in Paris.

LXX 528 is dated to 1264. It is currently located at the National Library of France (Coisl. Gr. 5) in Paris.

LXX 529 is dated to the 13th century. It is currently located at the National Library of France (Coisl. Gr. 6) in Paris.

LXX 537 is dated to the 13th century. It is currently located at the National Library of France (Coisl. Gr. 184) in Paris.

LXX 550 is dated to the 12th century. It is currently located at the National Library of France (Gr. 128) in Paris.

LXX 551 is dated to the 13th century. It is currently located at the National Library of France (Gr. 129) in Paris.

LXX 569 is dated to the 13th century. It is currently located at the National Library of France (Gr. 161) in Paris.

LXX 610 is dated to the 14th century. It is currently located at the National Library of France (Suppl. gr. 609) in Paris.

LXX 615 is dated to the 11th century. It is currently located at the Pelekete monastery (216) on Patmos Island.

LXX 616 is dated to the 11th century. It is currently located at the Pelekete monastery (217) on Patmos Island.

LXX 618 is dated to the 13th century. It is currently located at the Pelekete monastery (410) on Patmos Island.

LXX 619 is dated to the 15th century. It is currently located at the Pelekete monastery (411) on Patmos Island.

LXX 624 is dated to the 5th or 6th centuries. It is currently located at the National Library of Russia (Gr. 5) in St. Petersburg.

LXX 630 is dated to the 10th century. It is currently located at the National Library of Russia (Gr. 673) in St. Petersburg.

LXX 646 is dated to the 12th century. It is currently located at the Vatican Library (Barber. gr. 474) in Vatican City.

LXX 664 is dated to the 14th century. It is currently located at the Vatican Library (Pii. II. gr. 20) in Vatican City.

LXX 669 is dated to the 14th century. It is currently located at the Vatican Library (Vat. gr. 332) in Vatican City.

LXX 707 is dated to the 10th or 11th centuries. Sections are currently located at Saint Catherine's Monastery (Codex Gr. 1) in the Sinai, and the National Library of Russia (Gr. 260) in St. Petersburg.

LXX 730 is dated to the 10th century. It is currently located at the Biblioteca Marciana (Gr. 15) in Venice.

LXX 739 is dated to the 10th century. It is currently located at the Biblioteca Marciana (Gr. 534) in Venice.

LXX 761 is dated to the 13th century. It is currently located at the Zentralbibliothek (C 11) in Zürich.

LXX 767 is dated to the 13th or 14th centuries. It is currently located at the Great Lavra (603) on Mount Athos.

LXX 799 is dated to 1280. It is currently located at the National Library of Greece (2491) in Athens.

LXX 802 (4QpapLXXLev^{b}) is dated to the 1st century BC. It is currently located at the Rockefeller Museum (4Q120) in Jerusalem. This document is also known as DSS 4Q120.

LXX 803 (4QLXXNum) is dated to the 1st century BC. It is currently located at the Rockefeller Museum (4Q121) in Jerusalem. This document is also known as DSS 4Q121.

LXX 814 (Yale Genesis) is dated to the 1st through 3rd centuries. It is currently located at Yale University (P. CtYBR Inv. 419) in New Haven.

LXX 833 is dated to the 8th or 9th centuries. It is currently located at the University Library (S. Salv. 140+126) in Messina.

LXX 847 (Papyrus Fouad 266) is dated to the late 2nd or early 1st century BC. It is currently located at the Sociandé Royale de Papyrologie (Gr. P. 458) on Cairo. It is a fragment of the Papyrus Fouad 266; all three known pieces are cataloged and on display together.

LXX 848 (Papyrus Fouad 266) is dated to the late 2nd or early 1st century BC. It is currently located at the Sociandé Royale de Papyrologie (Gr. P. 458) on Cairo. It is a fragment of the Papyrus Fouad 266; all three known pieces are cataloged and on display together.

LXX 903 is dated to the 3rd or 4th centuries. It is currently located at the Ägyptisches Museum (P. 9778) in Berlin.

LXX 907 (Papyrus Oxyrhynchus 1007) is dated to the 3rd century. It is currently located at the British Library (Inv. 2047) in London.

LXX 911 (Berlin Genesis) is dated to the 3rd century. It is currently located at the Institute of Archaeology at the University of Warsaw (P. Berlin G 2a-17b, u 46-61) in Warsaw.

LXX 912 (Papyrus 12) is dated to the 3rd century. It is currently located at the Morgan Library & Museum (Pap. Gr. 3; P. Amherst 3b) in New York.

LXX 920 is dated to the late 4th century BC. It is currently located at the John Rylands Library (P. Gr. 1) on Manchester.

LXX 942 (Papyrus Fouad 266) is dated to the late 2nd or early 1st century BC. It is currently located at the Sociandé Royale de Papyrologie (Gr. P. 458) on Cairo. It is a fragment of the Papyrus Fouad 266; all three known pieces are cataloged and on display together.

LXX 961 is dated to the 4th century. It is currently located at the Chester Beatty Library (P. Ch. Beatty IV) in Dublin.

LXX 963 is dated to the 2nd century. Sections are currently located at the Chester Beatty Library (P. Ch. Beatty VI) in Dublin, and the University of Michigan (P. Mich. Inv. 5554) in Ann Arbor.

Alternative Translations

The following is a list of alternative translations that were used for comparative analysis. Both the Peshitta and Coptic translations are believed to have been heavily based on the Septuagint, although do inherit relics of older Imperial Aramaic translations, or imports from the Hebrew translation.

The Aleppo Codex is dated to circa 920 AD. For centuries it was housed at the Central Synagogue of Aleppo, from which its name is derived. It was the oldest known complete copy of the Hebrew scriptures used within Judaism until 1947, when it was seized and divided among Jewish families during anti-Jewish riots in Aleppo. The sections that have resurfaced are currently at the Israel Museum in Jerusalem. Approximately 40% is still missing.

The Leningrad Codex is dated to 1008 (or 1009) AD. It is currently located at the National Library of Russia (Firkovich B 19 A) in St. Petersburg. The Leningrad Codex is the oldest complete copy of the Hebrew scriptures used within Judaism.

Peshitta: The Syriac translation of the Christian bible. The Old Testament was translated from older Aramaic and Hebrew sources during the late-2nd century AD.

Peshitta manuscript 5b1 is dated to the 5th century. It is currently located at the British Library (Add. 14,425) in London.

Peshitta manuscript 7a1 is dated to the 6th or 7th centuries. It is currently located at the Ambrosian Library (B. 21 Inf.) in Milan.

The Targum Onkelos is generally accepted as having been compiled by Aquila (Onkelos) of Sinope between 100 and 120 AD, although the surviving copies are all in Babylonian Aramaic, and the text appears to have been updated linguistically in Babylon in the 4th or 5th centuries AD. Some scholars believe Aquila was reworking a now lost, older Judean-Aramaic targum from the 1st century. The Megillah (3a) tractate of the Babylonian Torah claims that the Onkelos Targum is a restoration of a version of the Torah in use before the time of Ezra the scribe in the 4th century BC. While the idea that Aquila and Onkelos were the same person, the Talmuds mention both of them doing the same thing, creating a targum in the same era, but do not confirm they are the same person. Therefore, the Onkelos is sometimes viewed as being a continuation of an older Babylonian Aramaic translation from the Neo-Babylonian, Persian, or Greek eras.

The Fragment Targums are a collection of fragments from one or more targums that were written in Judean-Aramaic, and surfaced in Italy during the medieval era. They contain a number of heretical concepts, such as Judean-polytheism, suggesting some are a relic of a polytheist Israelite sect from before the Maccabean Revolt. They have also labeled as the Jerusalem Targum, or Jerusalem Targum II in older literature due to the dialect.

Targum Jerusalem has historically been misidentified as the Targum Jonathan, and is commonly called the Targum Pseudo-Jonathan in academic literature. Its oldest name is the Targum Jerusalem, which is used here. It is written in Palestinian-Aramaic, and generally dated to sometime between the 4th and 11th centuries. Some scholars believe it originated in the 4th century, and was modified after the Islamic conquest of Palestine, as it includes some Arabic names generally found in Islamic sources. It existed before the crusades, as it was documented at the time.

The Targum on Ruth was published in the 1516 edition of the Mikraot Gedolot, a Hebrew language translation and commentary on the Hebrew Bible, that included Aramaic targums on the various books. The origin of the Targum on Ruth is unknown, however, it is accepted as being composed earlier than 600 AD.

Bohairic manuscripts are translations of the Septuagint into Bohairic (also known as Memphitic), one of the six dialects of Coptic, the classical era form of the Egyptian language. These dialects were written slightly differently, and therefore words transliterated into Coptic retain slightly different pronunciations, reflecting the different source texts used. Bohairic originated in the western Nile Delta of northern Egypt. The earliest Bohairic manuscripts date to the 4th century, however, the majority of texts come from the 9th century or later. Bohairic is the dialect used today as the liturgical language of the Coptic Orthodox Church, although Sahidic was used before the 11th century. Translations of the Septuagint were made into at least five of the Coptic dialects, however, complete copies only survive in Bohairic and Sahidic.

Bohairic manuscript Vatican Coptic 1, is dated to the 9th century. It is currently located at the Vatican Library (Copto 1) in Vatican City.

Bohairic manuscript BnF Coptic 1 is dated to 1356 to 1359. It is currently located at the National Library of France (1675: 520).

Sahidic manuscripts are translations of the Septuagint into Sahidic (also known as Thebaic), one of the six dialects of Coptic, the classical era form of the Egyptian language. Sahidic was the dominant form of Coptic used before the 11th century, and is believed to have originated in the region around Hermopolis, at the boundary between Upper and Lower Egypt. Translations of the Septuagint into Sahidic are known to have existed by the 4th century, however, early non-dialect specific translations are generally accepted as having been made as early as the 1st century AD, with some scholars suggesting the 1st century BC. The early non-dialect specific forms of Coptic are generally grouped with Sahidic, as Sahidic did not have a standardized spelling until the 6th century.

Sa 17 is a Sahidic manuscript at the British Library (Or. 7594) which is dated to the 4th century. It occasionally differs from the other manuscripts in the transliterations of names.

ALTERNATIVE TRANSLATIONS

The Armenian bible was translated from the Septuagint in the 5th century, replacing the older Armenian bible that had been translated from Aramaic texts, however, includes some of the older names.

The Vetus Latina are the old Latin translations of the Septuagint and other Israelite texts that predate Jerome's Latin Orthodox Bible in the 5th century. Some of the texts appear to have been translated directly from Aramaic or Hebrew source texts, however, most appear to have been translations from the Greek translations.

The Codex Gothicus Legionensis (VL 91) is a 10th century Vulgate manuscript currently located at the Basilica of San Isidoro, in León.

The Codex Lugdunensis (VL 100) is composed of two manuscripts: 403 and 1964 which are dated to between 550 and 600 AD. They are currently located at the Bibliothèque de la Ville in Lyon.

The Munich Palimpsest (VL 104) is dated to circa 650 AD. It is currently located at the Bavarian State Library in Munich.

The original Vulgate was the Latin translation created by Jerome in the 5th century. Jerome's translation used both the Greek and Hebrew text for sources. It was used along side the Vetus Latina texts in Latin speaking regions until the Roman Catholic church adopted a formal form of it in 1590 known as the Sixtine Vulgate.

Dead Sea Scrolls

The following is a list of the Dead Sea Scrolls mentioned in the notes for this book. Most are held by the Israel Museum in Jerusalem.

DSS 1Q1 (1QGen) is dated to the Herodian Dynasty in Judea (37 BC to 6 AD)

DSS 1Q2 (1QExod^a) is dated to the Roman rule of Judea (6 to 390 AD).

DSS 1Q3 (1QpaleoLev) is dated to the Roman rule of Judea and Palestine (6 to 390 AD).

DSS 1Q4 (1QDeut^a) is dated to the Roman era in Judea and Palestine (6 to 390 AD).

DSS 1Q5 (1QDeut^b) is dated to the Roman era in Judea and Palestine (6 to 390 AD).

DSS 2Q2 (2QExod^a) is dated to the Herodian Dynasty in Judea (37 BC to 6 AD).

DSS 2Q3 (2QExod^b) is dated to the Herodian Dynasty in Judea (37 BC to 6 AD).

DSS 2Q6 (2QNum^a) is dated to the Herodian Dynasty in Judea (37 BC to 6 AD).

DSS 2Q7 (2QNum^b) is dated to the Herodian Dynasty in Judea (37 BC to 6 AD).

DSS 4Q1 (4QGen-Exod^a) is dated to the Hasmonean Dynasty in Judea (140 to 37 BC).

DSS 4Q2 (4QGen^b) is dated to the Roman era in Judea and Palestine (6 to 390 AD).

DSS 4Q4 (4QGen^d) is dated to the Hasmonean Dynasty in Judea (140 to 37 BC)

DSS 4Q5 (4QGen^e) is dated to the Herodian Dynasty in Judea (37 BC to 6 AD)

DSS 4Q6 (4QGen^f) is dated to the Hasmonean Dynasty in Judea (140 to 37 BC)

DSS 4Q7 (4QGen^g) is dated to the Hasmonean Dynasty in Judea (140 to 37 BC).

DSS 4Q9 (4QGen^j) is dated to the Hasmonean Dynasty in Judea (140 to 37 BC)

DSS 4Q11 (4QpaleoGen-Exod^l) is dated to the Hasmonean Dynasty in Judea (140 to 37 BC)

DSS 4Q13 (4QExod^b) is dated to the Herodian Dynasty in Judea (37 BC to 6 AD).

DSS 4Q14 (4QExod^c) is dated to the Herodian Dynasty in Judea (37 BC to 6 AD).

DSS 4Q17 (4QGen-Lev^f) is dated to the Maccabean Revolt in Judea (165-140 BC).

DSS 4Q22 (4QpaleoExod^m) is dated to the Hasmonean Dynasty in Judea (140 to 37 BC).

DSS 4Q23 (4QLev-Num^a) is dated to the Hasmonean Dynasty in Judea (140 to 37 BC).

DSS 4Q24 (4QLev^b) is dated to the Hasmonean Dynasty in Judea (140 to 37 BC).

DSS 4Q25 (4QLev^c) is dated to the Roman rule of Judea and Palestine (6 to 390 AD).

DSS 4Q26 (4QLev^d) is dated to the Roman rule of Judea and Palestine (6 to 390 AD).

DSS 4Q26a (4QLev^e) is dated to the Roman rule of Judea and Palestine (6 to 390 AD).

DSS 4Q27 (4QNum^b) is dated to the Herodian Dynasty in Judea (37 BC to 6 AD).

DSS 4Q28 (4QDeut^a) is dated to the Maccabees Revolt in Judea (165 to 140 BC).

DSS 4Q29 (4QDeut^b) is dated to the early Hasmonean dynasty of Judea (140 to 100 BC).

DSS 4Q30 (4QDeut^c) is dated to the early Hasmonean dynasty of Judea (140 to 100 BC).

DSS 4Q31 (4QDeut^d) is dated to the middle Hasmonean dynasty of Judea (100 to 50 BC).

DSS 4Q32 (4QDeut^e) is dated to the late Hasmonean dynasty of Judea (50 to 40 BC).

DSS 4Q33 (4QDeut^f) is dated to the late Hasmonean dynasty of Judea, circa 50 BC.

DSS 4Q34 (4QDeut^g) is dated to the late Herodian dynasty of Judea, or the early Roman rule of Judea (1 to 25 AD).

DSS 4Q35 (4QDeut^h) is dated to approximately the transition from the Hasmonean to Herodian dynasties of Judea, circa 37 BC.

DSS 4Q36 (4QDeut^i) is dated to the middle Hasmonean dynasty of Judea (100 to 50 BC).

DSS 4Q37 (4QDeut^j) is dated to the Roman rule of Judea, circa 50 AD.

DSS 4Q38 (4QDeut^{k1}) is dated to the Herodian dynasty in Judea (37 BC to 6 AD).

DSS 4Q38a (4QDeut^{k2}) is dated to the Herodian dynasty in Judea (37 BC to 6 AD).

DSS 4Q39 (4QDeut^l) is dated to the late Hasmonean dynasty of Judea, circa 50 BC.

DSS 4Q40 (4QDeut^m) is dated to approximately the transition from the Hasmonean to Herodian dynasties of Judea, circa 37 BC.

DSS 4Q41 (4QDeut^n) is dated to the Herodian dynasty in Judea (37 BC to 6 AD).

DSS 4Q42 (4QDeut^o) is dated to the late Hasmonean dynasty of Judea (75 to 37 BC).

DSS 4Q43 (4QDeut^p) is dated to the late Hasmonean dynasty of Judea (75 to 37 BC).

DSS 4Q44 (4QDeut^q) is dated to approximately the transition from the Hasmonean to Herodian dynasties of Judea, circa 37 BC.

DSS 4Q45 (4QpaleoDeut^r) is dated to the late Hasmonean dynasty of Judea (100 to 37 BC).

DSS 4Q47 (4QJosh^a) is dated to the Herodian Dynasty in Judea (37 BC to 6 AD).

DSS 4Q48 (4QJosh^b) is dated to the Herodian Dynasty in Judea (37 BC to 6 AD).

DSS 4Q49 (4QJudg^a) is dated to the Hasmonean Dynasty in Judea (140 to 37 BC).

DSS 4Q50 (4QJudg^b) is dated to the Hasmonean Dynasty in Judea (140 to 37 BC).

DSS 4Q104 (4QRuth^a) is dated to the Hasmonean Dynasty in Judea (140 to 37 BC).

DSS 4Q120 (4QpapLXXLev^b) is dated to the Hasmonean Dynasty in Judea (140 to 37 BC). This document is also known as LXX 802.

DSS 4Q121 (4QLXXNum) is dated to the Hasmonean Dynasty in Judea (140 to 37 BC). This document is also known as LXX 803.

DSS 5Q1 (5QDeut) is dated to the Maccabees Revolt in Judea (165 to 140 BC).

DSS 6Q2 (6QpaleoLev) is dated to the Greek rule of Judea (330 to 140 AD).

DSS 11Q1 (11QpaleoLev^a) is dated to the Herodian Dynasty in Judea (37 BC to 6 AD).

DSS 11Q2 (11QLev^b) is dated to the Herodian Dynasty in Judea (37 BC to 6 AD).

DSS Mas1a (MasLev^a) is dated to the Roman rule of Judea and Palestine (6 to 390 AD).

DSS Mas1b (MasLev^b) is dated to the Roman rule of Judea and Palestine (6 to 390 AD).

DSS Mur1 is dated to the Roman era in Judea and Palestine (6 to 390 AD).

Ketef Hinnom Scrolls

The Ketef Hinnom scrolls are two very damaged Judahite or Samaritan silver scrolls discovered during an archaeological dig into a Persian era pile of refuse in the Hinnom valley near Jerusalem. The first (KH1) contains a prayer or hymn that bears similarity to several verses from various books of the Tanakh (Old Testament), however, doesn't actually match any.

The second (KH2) is very similar to a verse from Numbers chapter 6 which is generally reconstructed as: "-hbrw. May be blessed he by Yhǔ[h], the warrior and the rebuker of [E]vil, may bless you, Yhǔh keep you. May shine, Yh[w]h, his face [on] you and grant you p[ea]ce."

They are generally considered to be magical amulets created sometime between the 7th and 4th centuries BC. It is unclear if it was a paraphrase of this verse in Numbers, or simply a similar phase, however, if it was a paraphrase from Numbers, it would mean the text of Numbers was different at the time, as Yhǔh is not referred to as 'the warrior,' in Numbers. They are currently on display in the Israel Museum in Jerusalem.

Shapira Scrolls

The Shapira scrolls, also known as the Shapira manuscript or Moabite Deuteronomy, are a collection of leather strips supposedly discovered in the Arnon valley of modern Jordan in the 1860s. While they were initially accepted as authentic by the Jewish antiquities dealer Moses Shapira, they were later discredited as forgeries by both German and British biblical scholars. Since the discovery of the Dead Sea scrolls in the 1940s, there have been several scholars who have called into question the claims that the scrolls were a forgery, however, their whereabouts is unknown, and therefore no modern analysis of the leather scrolls is possible.

Several reasons were given for the initial claims that the scrolls were a forgery, including the script, language, and content. The script is a form of Phoenician, similar to the Moabite script of the 800s BC, however, the language includes Imperial Aramaic terms not used until the Persian era, several centuries later. The content is not a match for any surviving translation of Deuteronomy, however, does include many parallel statements. Some of the statements are somewhat heretical, however, do seem similar to the beliefs of the Hasidian sect of Judahites reported to have been living in the region under Greek rule between 330 and 240 BC.

Moses Shapira had previously been involved in discovery and authentication of both authentic and fraudulent artifacts for the museums and universities of Europe, including 1700 fake Moabite artifacts that the Berlin museum bought. After German and British scholars reported the scrolls were a forgery, Shapira fled to Holland, where he continued to claim the scrolls were authentic until killing himself several weeks later. The leather strips were subsequently sold at Sothby's a couple of years later, before disappearing.

While the leather was reported to have looked very old, the idea that it could be thousands of years old was dismissed until the discovery of the Dead Sea scrolls in a similar climate in the 1940s. The scrolls are included in this analysis, however, it is not clear that the scrolls weren't forged in the 1860s. If the manuscript was not forged in the 1860s, it was probably the remains of a Torah used by either the Hasidian or Tobian Judahite sects during the Greek era, both of which were reported to have been living in the region.

Also Available

Also Available

ENOCH AND METATRON SERIES:

- Books of Enoch Collection

- Books of Enoch and Metatron Collection

- Books of Metatron Collection

- Secrets of Enoch

OTHER TRANSLATIONS:

- Apocalypses of Ezra

- Arabic Maccabees

- Hebrew Maccabees

- Life of Adam and Eve

- Memories of the New Kingdom

- Septuagint's Esther and the Vetus Latina Esther

- Septuagint's Ezekiel and the Ba'al Cycle

- Septuagint's Proverbs and the Wisdom of Amenemope

- Septuagint's Solomon and the Testament of Solomon

- Testaments of the Patriarchs Collection

- The Amarna Letters

- Tobit and Ahikar

- Ugaritic Texts: Ba'al Cycle

- Words of Ahikar

www.ingramcontent.com/pod-product-compliance
Lightning Source LLC
Chambersburg PA
CBHW081003140626
46546CB00019B/3182